Twentieth-Century
Literary Criticism

Guide to Gale Literary Criticism Series

For criticism on	Consult these Gale series
Authors now living or who died after December 31, 1959	*CONTEMPORARY LITERARY CRITICISM (CLC)*
Authors who died between 1900 and 1959	*TWENTIETH-CENTURY LITERARY CRITICISM (TCLC)*
Authors who died between 1800 and 1899	*NINETEENTH-CENTURY LITERATURE CRITICISM (NCLC)*
Authors who died between 1400 and 1799	*LITERATURE CRITICISM FROM 1400 TO 1800 (LC)* *SHAKESPEAREAN CRITICISM (SC)*
Authors who died before 1400	*CLASSICAL AND MEDIEVAL LITERATURE CRITICISM (CMLC)*
Authors of books for children and young adults	*CHILDREN'S LITERATURE REVIEW (CLR)*
Dramatists	*DRAMA CRITICISM (DC)*
Poets	*POETRY CRITICISM (PC)*
Short story writers	*SHORT STORY CRITICISM (SSC)*
Black writers of the past two hundred years	*BLACK LITERATURE CRITICISM (BLC)*
Hispanic writers of the late nineteenth and twentieth centuries	*HISPANIC LITERATURE CRITICISM (HLC)*
Native North American writers and orators of the eighteenth, nineteenth, and twentieth centuries	*NATIVE NORTH AMERICAN LITERATURE (NNAL)*
Major authors from the Renaissance to the present	*WORLD LITERATURE CRITICISM, 1500 TO THE PRESENT (WLC)*

ISSN 0276-8178

Volume 93

Twentieth-Century Literary Criticism

**Criticism of the
Works of Novelists, Poets, Playwrights,
Short Story Writers, and Other Creative Writers
Who Lived between 1900 and 1999,
from the First Published Critical
Appraisals to Current Evaluations**

Jennifer Baise
Editor

Thomas Ligotti
Associate Editor

GALE GROUP

*Detroit
New York
San Francisco
London
Boston
Woodbridge, CT*

STAFF

Jennifer Baise, *Editor*

Thomas Ligotti, *Associate Editor*

Maria Franklin, *Permissions Manager*
Kimberly F. Smilay, *Permissions Specialist*
Kelly A. Quin, *Permissions Associates*
Sandy Gore, *Permissions Assistant*

Victoria B. Cariappa, *Research Manager*
Andrew Guy Malonis, Barbara McNeil, Gary J. Oudersluys, Maureen Richards,
Cheryl L. Warnock, *Research Specialists*
Patricia T. Ballard, Tamara C. Nott, Tracie A. Richardson, *Research Associates*
Phyllis Blackman, Timothy Lehnerer, *Research Assistant*

Mary Beth Trimper, *Production Director*
Stacy Melson, *Buyer*

Michael Logusz, *Graphic Artist*
Randy Bassett, *Image Database Supervisor*
Robert Duncan, *Imaging Specialists*
Pamela Reed, *Imaging Coordinator*

Library of Congress Catalog Card Number 76-46132
ISBN 0-7876-2750-X
ISSN 0276-8178

Printed in the United States of America
10 9 8 7 6 5 4 3 2 1

Contents

Preface   vii

Acknowledgments   xi

Preface

Since its inception more than fifteen years ago, *Twentieth-Century Literary Criticism* has been purchased and used by nearly 10,000 school, public, and college or university libraries. *TCLC* has covered more than 500 authors, representing 58 nationalities, and over 25,000 titles. No other reference source has surveyed the critical response to twentieth-century authors and literature as thoroughly as *TCLC*. In the words of one reviewer, "there is nothing comparable available." *TCLC* "is a gold mine of information—dates, pseudonyms, biographical information, and criticism from books and periodicals—which many libraries would have difficulty assembling on their own."

Scope of the Series

TCLC is designed to serve as an introduction to authors who died between 1900 and 1960 and to the most significant interpretations of these author's works. The great poets, novelists, short story writers, playwrights, and philosophers of this period are frequently studied in high school and college literature courses. In organizing and reprinting the vast amount of critical material written on these authors, *TCLC* helps students develop valuable insight into literary history, promotes a better understanding of the texts, and sparks ideas for papers and assignments. Each entry in *TCLC* presents a comprehensive survey of an author's career or an individual work of literature and provides the user with a multiplicity of interpretations and assessments. Such variety allows students to pursue their own interests; furthermore, it fosters an awareness that literature is dynamic and responsive to many different opinions.

Every fourth volume of *TCLC* is devoted to literary topics. These topic entries widen the focus of the series from individual authors to such broader subjects as literary movements, prominent themes in twentieth-century literature, literary reaction to political and historical events, significant eras in literary history, prominent literary anniversaries, and the literatures of cultures that are often overlooked by English-speaking readers.

TCLC is designed as a companion series to Gale's *Contemporary Literary Criticism,* which reprints commentary on authors now living or who have died since 1960. Because of the different periods under consideration, there is no duplication of material between *CLC* and *TCLC*. For additional information about *CLC* and Gale's other criticism titles, users should consult the Guide to Gale Literary Criticism Series preceding the title page in this volume.

Coverage

Each volume of *TCLC* is carefully compiled to present:

- criticism of authors, or literary topics, representing a variety of genres and nationalities

- both major and lesser-known writers and literary works of the period

- 6-12 authors or 3-6 topics per volume

- individual entries that survey critical response to each author's work or each topic in literary history, including early criticism to reflect initial reactions; later criticism to represent any rise or decline in reputation; and current retrospective analyses.

Organization of This Book

An author entry consists of the following elements: author heading, biographical and critical introduction, list of principal works, reprints of criticism (each preceded by an annotation and a bibliographic citation), and a bibliography of further reading.

- The **Author Heading** consists of the name under which the author most commonly wrote, followed by birth and death dates. If an author wrote consistently under a pseudonym, the pseudonym will be listed in the author heading and the real name given in parentheses on the first line of the biographical and critical introduction. Also located at the beginning of the introduction to the author entry are any name variations under which an author wrote, including transliterated forms for authors whose languages use nonroman alphabets.

- The **Biographical and Critical Introduction** outlines the author's life and career, as well as the critical issues surrounding his or her work. References to past volumes of *TCLC* are provided at the beginning of the introduction. Additional sources of information in other biographical and critical reference series published by Gale, including *Short Story Criticism, Children's Literature Review, Contemporary Authors, Dictionary of Literary Biography,* and *Something about the Author,* are listed in a box at the end of the entry.

- Some *TCLC* entries include **Portraits** of the author. Entries also may contain reproductions of materials pertinent to an author's career, including manuscript pages, title pages, dust jackets, letters, and drawings, as well as photographs of important people, places, and events in an author's life.

- The **List of Principal Works** is chronological by date of first book publication and identifies the genre of each work. In the case of foreign authors with both foreign-language publications and English translations, the title and date of the first English-language edition are given in brackets. Unless otherwise indicated, dramas are dated by first performance, not first publication.

- Critical essays are prefaced by **Annotations** providing the reader with information about both the critic and the criticism that follows. Included are the critic's reputation, individual approach to literary criticism, and particular expertise in an author's works. Also noted are the relative importance of a work of criticism, the scope of the essay, and the growth of critical controversy or changes in critical trends regarding an author. In some cases, these annotations cross-reference essays by critics who discuss each other's commentary.

- A complete **Bibliographic Citation** designed to facilitate location of the original essay or book precedes each piece of criticism.

- Criticism is arranged chronologically in each author entry to provide a perspective on changes in critical evaluation over the years. All titles of works by the author featured in the entry are printed in boldface type to enable the user to easily locate discussion of particular works. Also for purposes of easier identification, the critic's name and the publication date of the essay are given at the beginning of each piece of criticism. Unsigned criticism is preceded by the title of the journal in which it appeared. Some of the essays in *TCLC* also contain translated material. Unless otherwise noted, translations in brackets are by the editors; translations in parentheses or continuous with the text are by the critic. Publication information (such as footnotes or page and line references to specific editions of works) have been deleted at the editor's discretion to provide smoother reading of the text.

- An annotated list of **Further Reading** appearing at the end of each author entry suggests secondary sources on the author. In some cases it includes essays for which the editors could not obtain reprint rights.

Cumulative Indexes

- Each volume of *TCLC* contains a cumulative **Author Index** listing all authors who have appeared in Gale's Literary Criticism Series, along with cross references to such biographical series as *Contemporary Authors* and *Dictionary of Literary Biography.* For readers' convenience, a complete list of Gale titles included appears on the first page of the author index. Useful for locating authors within the various series, this index is particularly valuable for those authors who are identified by a certain period but who, because of their death dates, are placed in another, or for those authors whose careers span two periods. For example, F. Scott Fitzgerald is found in *TCLC,* yet a writer often associated with him, Ernest Hemingway, is found in *CLC.*

- Each *TCLC* volume includes a cumulative **Nationality Index** which lists all authors who have appeared in *TCLC* volumes, arranged alphabetically under their respective nationalities, as well as Topics volume entries devoted to particular national literatures.

- Each new volume in Gale's Literary Criticism Series includes a cumulative **Topic Index**, which lists all literary topics treated in *NCLC, TCLC, LC 1400-1800,* and the *CLC* yearbook.

- Each new volume of *TCLC,* with the exception of the Topics volumes, includes a **Title Index** listing the titles of all literary works discussed in the volume. In response to numerous suggestions from librarians, Gale has also produced a **Special Paperbound Edition** of the *TCLC* title index. This annual cumulation lists all titles discussed in the series since its inception and is issued with the first volume of *TCLC* published each year. Additional copies of the index are available on request. Librarians and patrons will welcome this separate index; it saves shelf space, is easy to use, and is recyclable upon receipt of the following year's cumulation. Titles discussed in the Topics volume entries are not included *TCLC* cumulative index.

Citing Twentieth-Century Literary Criticism

When writing papers, students who quote directly from any volume in Gale's literary Criticism Series may use the following general forms to footnote reprinted criticism. The first example pertains to materials drawn from periodicals, the second to material reprinted from books.

[1]William H. Slavick, "Going to School to DuBose Heyward," *The Harlem Renaissance Reexamined,* (AMS Press, 1987); reprinted in *Twentieth-Century Literary Criticism,* Vol. 59, ed. Jennifer Gariepy (Detroit: Gale Research, 1995), pp. 94-105.

[2]George Orwell, "Reflections on Gandhi," *Partisan Review,* 6 (Winter 1949), pp. 85-92; reprinted in *Twentieth-Century Literary Criticism,* Vol. 59, ed. Jennifer Gariepy (Detroit: Gale Research, 1995), pp. 40-3.

Suggestions Are Welcome

In response to suggestions, several features have been added to *TCLC* since the series began, including annotations to critical essays, a cumulative index to authors in all Gale literary criticism series, entries devoted to criticism on a single work by a major author, more extensive illustrations, and a title index listing all literary works discussed in the series since its inception.

Readers who wish to suggest authors or topics to appear in future volumes, or who have other suggestions, are cordially invited to write the editors.

Acknowledgments

The editors wish to thank the copyright holders of the criticism included in this volume and the permissions managers of many book and magazine publishing companies for assisting us in securing reproduction rights. We are also grateful to the staffs of the Detroit Public Library, the Library of Congress, the University of Detroit Mercy Library, Wayne State University Purdy/Kresge Library Complex, and the University of Michigan Libraries for making their resources available to us. Following is a list of the copyright holders who have granted us permission to reproduce material in this volume of *TCLC*. Every effort has been made to trace copyright, but if omissions have been made, please let us know.

PHOTOGRAPHS AND ILLUSTRATIONS APPEARING IN *TCLC*, VOLUME 93, WERE RECEIVED FROM THE FOLLOWING SOURCES:

D. H. Lawrence

1885-1930

(Full name David Herbert Lawrence. Also wrote under the pseudonym Lawrence H. Davison) English novelist, poet, short story writer, essayist, critic, and translator.

The following entry presents criticism of Lawrence's poetry. For information on Lawrence's complete career, see TCLC, Volume 9.

INTRODUCTION

Highly acclaimed as a forerunner in adapting psychological themes for literary purposes in such novels as *Sons and Lovers*, *The Rainbow*, *Women in Love*, and *Lady Chatterley's Lover*, Lawrence's status as a poet is among the most heatedly disputed topics of twentieth-century literature. Much of the debate stems from the perception that Lawrence published a large quantity of poetry that is often considered very uneven in quality. Although many of his detractors concede that Lawrence wrote several classic poems, they claim that these works are the exceptions rather than the rule when compared to the bulk of poems Lawrence published. Many of his defenders, however, claim that Lawrence's body of poetry constitutes one unified work in which no one piece can be isolated from the whole, and that Lawrence's occasional lapses of poetic technique are minor when weighed against his thematic concerns and the instantaneous nature of his poems. His poetic work is often described as visionary, prophetic, and Romantic in intent. Furthermore, Lawrence insisted that his work be read as an autobiography as well as a manifesto for the Utopia he envisioned, a "new heaven and earth" that rejected Victorian prudishness and rampant industrialization in favor of a more primitive "blood-wisdom" and sexual freedom. Despite disagreements over his rank among twentieth-century poets, Lawrence's influence is noted in the works of such writers as Galway Kinnell, Denise Levertov, Karl Shapiro, Ted Hughes, Adrienne Rich, and Robert Bly.

Biographical Information

The fourth child of an illiterate coal miner and his wife, a former school teacher, Lawrence was raised in the colliery town of Eastwood, Nottinghamshire. Temperamentally alienated from his environment, he grew to hate the debilitating mine work that he blamed for his father's debased condition. Lawrence won a scholarship to the local grammar school and later to Nottingham University College. He taught school at Coyden for three years, during which time Ford Madox Ford published some of Lawrence's poems in the *English Review*. The onset of tuberculosis forced Lawrence to resign from teaching in 1911, and that same year he published his first novel,

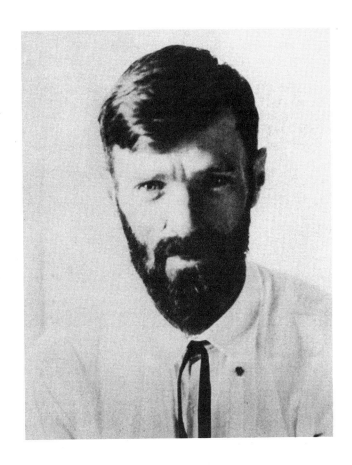

The White Peacock, which received positive critical reviews. When he was twenty-seven, Lawrence eloped with Frieda von Richtofen Weekly, the wife of one of his college professors. The couple's erotic and emotional life during their first years together is chronicled in *Look! We Have Come Through!* After their marriage, the Lawrences lived briefly in Germany, Austria, Italy, Sicily, England, France, Australia, Mexico, and in the southwestern United States, where Lawrence hoped to establish a Utopian community. These locales provided the settings of many of his novels written during the 1920s, and also inspired his books of travel sketches. In 1930, Lawrence entered a sanitorium in Vence, France, in an attempt to cure the tuberculosis that afflicted him throughout his adult life. He died soon after.

Major Works

Like his fiction, most of Lawrence's poetry is intensely personal. His earliest poetry, which he began writing in his twenties, adhered to traditional poetic forms and is seldom as highly regarded as his later free-verse works.

His first four volumes—*Love Poems and Others, Amores, New Poems*, and *Bay*—display Lawrence's adherence to traditional rhyme schemes. Poems from these volumes were placed by Lawrence in the "Rhyming Poems" section of *The Collected Poems of D. H. Lawrence*. These poems are often compared to the poetry of Thomas Hardy, who was an acknowledged influence on Lawrence, in their reliance on regional dialects and subject matter. *Look! We Have Come Through!* marks a departure in Lawrence's poetics from closed forms to free verse forms that display Lawrence's affinity for the work of American poet Walt Whitman. *Birds, Beasts, and Flowers* features celebratory and mystical poems about flora and fauna, including his most famous poem, "Snake," and the frequently anthologized and discussed "Medlars and Sorb Apples." He followed this work with *Pansies* and *Nettles*, two works noted for their acerbity and use of doggerel. Critics note that the poems in the posthumously published *Last Poems* are preoccupied with death, including the frequently anthologized "Bavarian Gentians" and "The Ship of Death."

Love among the Haystacks (short stories) 1930
Nettles (poetry) 1930
The Virgin and the Gipsy (novel) 1930
Etruscan Places (essay) 1932
Last Poems (poetry) 1932
The Lovely Lady (short stories) 1933
The Ship of Death (poetry) 1933
A Modern Lover (short stories) 1934
The Spirit of the Place (essays) 1935
Phoenix (essays and criticism) 1936
Fire (poetry) 1940
The First Lady Chatterley (novel) 1944
The Complete Short Stories of D. H. Lawrence, 3 vols. (short stories) 1955
The Collected Letters of D. H. Lawrence, 2 vols. (letters) 1962
The Complete Poems of D. H. Lawrence, 2 vols. (poetry) 1964
The Complete Plays of D. H. Lawrence (drama) 1966
Phoenix II (essays and criticism) 1968
John Thomas and Lady Jane (novel) 1972

PRINCIPAL WORKS

The White Peacock (novel) 1911
The Trespasser (novel) 1912
Love Poems and Others (poetry) 1913
The Prussian Officer (short stories) 1914
The Rainbow (novel) 1915
Amores (poetry) 1916
Twilight in Italy (essays) 1916
Look! We Have Come Through! (poetry) 1917
New Poems (poetry) 1918
Bay (poetry) 1919
The Lost Girl (novel) 1920
Women in Love (novel) 1920
Psychoanalysis and the Unconscious (essay) 1921
Sea and Sardinia (essays) 1921
Tortoises (poetry) 1921
Aaron's Rod (novel) 1922
England, My England (short stories) 1922
Fantasia of the Unconscious (essay) 1922
Movements in European History [as Lawrence H. Davison] (essays) 1922
Birds, Beasts and Flowers (poetry) 1923
Kangaroo (novel) 1923
Studies in Classic American Literature (essays) 1923
Reflections on the Death of a Porcupine (essays) 1925
The Plumed Serpent (novel) 1926
Mornings in Mexico (essays) 1927
The Collected Poems of D. H. Lawrence, 2 vols. (poetry) 1928
Lady Chatterley's Lover (novel) 1928
The Woman Who Rode Away (short stories) 1928
Pansies (poetry) 1929
The Escaped Cock (novella) 1930; also published as *The Man Who Died*, 1931

CRITICISM

Ezra Pound (essay date 1913)

SOURCE: A review of *Love Poems and Others*, in *Poetry*, Vol. 2, No. 4, July, 1913, pp. 149-51.

[*In the following review of* Love Poems and Others, *Pound concludes that Lawrence poetry succeeds in realistically detailing everyday lives whereas the poetry of John Masefield does not.*]

The *Love Poems,* if by that Mr. Lawrence means the middling-sensual erotic verses in [*Love Poems and Others,*] are a sort of pre-raphaelitish slush, disgusting or very nearly so. The attempts to produce the typical Laurentine line have brought forth:

> I touched her and she shivered like a dead snake.

which was improved by an even readier parodist, to

> I touched her and she came off in scales.

Jesting aside, when Mr. Lawrence ceases to discuss his own disagreeable sensations, when he writes low-life narrative, as he does in **"Whether or Not"** and in **"Violets,"** there is no English poet under forty who can get within shot of him. That Masefield should be having a boom seems, as one takes count of these poems, frankly ridiculous.

It is no more possible to quote from them as illustration than it would be to illustrate a Rembrandt by cutting off two inches of canvas. The first is in mood-ridden *chiaroscuro,* the characters being a policeman, his sweetheart, his mother, and a widow who has taken advantage of his excitement and by whom he has had a child. It is sullen and heavy, and as ugly as such a tale must be.

> Yi, tha'rt a man, tha'rt a fine big man, but never a
> baby had eyes
> As sulky an' ormin as thine,
>
> I damn well shanna marry 'er,
>   So chew at it no more,
> Or I'll chuck the flamin' lot of you—
>   You needn't have swore.

So much for the tonality. Kipling has never done it as well in verse, though he gets something like the same range in his prose of *Bedelia Harrodsfoot.* The comparison with Masefield is, as I have said, ridiculous. It is what Masefield would like to do and can not.

"Violets" presents two girls and another at the funeral of a young fellow who has died among

> Pals worse n'r any name as you could call.
>
> Ah know tha liked 'im better nor me. But let
> Me tell thee about this lass. When you had gone
> Ah stopped behind on t' pad i' th' drippin' wet
> An' watched what 'er 'ad on.

If this book does not receive the Polignac prize a year from this November, there will be due cause for scandal.

Mr. Lawrence was "discovered" by Ford Madox Hueffer during the latter's editorship of the *English Review,* about four years ago. Some of his verses appeared then, and he has since made a notable reputation by his prose works, **The White Peacock** and **The Trespasser.**

His prose training stands him in good stead in these poems. The characters are real. They are not stock figures of "the poor," done from the outside and provided with *cliché* emotions.

> I expect you know who I am, Mrs. Naylor!
>   —Who yer are? yis, you're Lizzie Stainwright.
> An appen you might guess what I've come for?
>   —'Appen I mightn't, 'appen I might.

Mr. Lawrence has attempted realism and attained it. He has brought contemporary verse up to the level of contemporary prose, and that is no mean achievement. These two poems at least are great art.

John Gould Fletcher (essay date 1918)

SOURCE: A review of *Look! We Have Come Through,* in *Poetry,* Vol. XII, No. V, August, 1918, pp. 269-74.

[*In the following review of* Look! We Have Come Through! *Fletcher praises Lawrence's poetry as uncompromising and original, and finds similarities with the poetry of Walt Whitman.*]

D. H. Lawrence has recently published [**Look! We Have Come Through!**] a third volume of poetry to stand beside his **Love Poems** and **Amores.** This event has, so far as I am aware, passed almost without notice in the English press. The reviewers of the English press know perfectly well that Mr. Lawrence is supposed to be a dangerous man, writing too frankly on certain subjects which are politely considered taboo in good society, and therefore they do their best to prevent Mr. Lawrence from writing at all, by tacitly ignoring him. If they are driven to the admission, these selfsame reviewers are obliged grudgingly to acknowledge that Mr. Lawrence is one of the most interesting of modern writers. Such are the conditions which a modern writer with something new to say is obliged to accept in England to-day. The press can make a great to-do about the innocuous, blameless and essentially minor poetry of Edward Thomas (to take but one example); they politely refuse to discuss the questionable, but essentially major effort of a D. H. Lawrence. Is it any wonder that such an attitude drives a man to sheer fanaticism?

For a fine, intolerant fanatic D. H. Lawrence undoubtedly is. That is his value for our present day, so rich in half-measures and compromises. Lawrence does not compromise. In this last collection of poetry he gives us works which are not good poetry, which are scarcely readable prose. He includes them because they are necessary to the complete understanding of his thought and gospel. We, if we are wise, will read them for the same reason. For Lawrence is an original thinker, and his message to our present day is a valuable message.

Briefly, the message is this: that everything which we call spiritual is born and comes to flower out of certain physical needs and reactions, of which the most patent is the reaction of sex, through which life is maintained on this planet. Lawrence therefore stands in sharp contrast to the Christian dogma of the middle ages, and to those writers of the present day who still maintain an attitude of respect to the Christian view, which is that we are each endowed with an immortal soul, at strife with our physical needs, which can only be purged by death. Lawrence, like a recent French writer, "does not desire to spit out the forbidden fruit, and recreate the Eden of the refusal of life." He is frankly pagan. To him, the flesh is the soil in which the spirit blossoms, and the only immortality possible is the setting free of the blossoming spirit from the satiated flesh. When this is accomplished, then the spirit becomes free, perfect, unique, a habitant of paradise on earth. This is the doctrine of which he is the zealot, the intolerant apostle.

The specific value of this idea need not concern us very greatly. The question is, rather, of its poetical value; and there is no doubt that it is a system of philosophy which is essentially poetical. Poetry is at once highly objective and highly subjective. It is objective in so far as it deals with words, which are in a strong sense objects, and with the external world, in its objective aspects. It is subjective, because it also states the poet's subjective reactions to words and to all external phenomena. Lawrence is one of the few poets in England to-day who keeps this dual role of poetry well in mind; and that is why his poetry, though it may often be badly written, is never without energy and a sense of power.

The reason for his failings as a poet must be sought elsewhere than in his attitude to life. We can only understand why he fails if we understand the conditions under which he is forced to write. With a reasonable degree of independence, a public neither openly hostile nor totally indifferent, an intellectual *milieu* capable of finer life and better understanding, Lawrence would become nothing but an artist. He has none of these things; and so he is forced, by destiny itself, to become the thing he probably began by loathing, a propagandist, a preacher, an evangelist.

This brings him into close connection with Walt Whitman, who similarly spent his life in preaching with puritanical fervor a most unpuritan gospel. Indeed, if one examines closely Lawrence's latest technique as shown here in such poems as **"Manifesto"** and **"New Heaven and Earth,"** one is surprised to see how close this comes in many respects to that of the earlier Whitman, the Whitman of "The Song of Myself." For example, note the selfsame use of long, rolling, orchestral rhythm in the two following passages:

> When I gathered flowers, I knew it was myself
>   plucking my own flowering,
> When I went in a train, I knew it was myself
>   travelling by my own invention,
> When I heard the cannon of the war, I listened
>   with my own ears to my own destruction.
> When I saw the torn dead, I knew it was my own
>   torn dead body.
> It was all me, I had done it all in my own flesh.

> Every kind for itself and its own, for me, mine,
>   male and female,
> For me those that have been boys and that love
>   women,
> For me the man that is proud and feels how it
>   stings to be slighted,
> For me the sweet-heart and the old maid, for me
>   mothers and the mothers of mothers,
> For me lips that have smiled, eyes that have shed
>   tears,
> For me children and the begetters of children.

The difference is (and this too is curiously brought out in the technique) that Lawrence is more delicate, more sensitive, more personal. He deliberately narrows his range, to embrace only life and his own life in particular. Unlike Whitman, he has a horror of the infinite, and I am sure that he could never bring himself to "utter the word Democracy, the word en-masse." He is an aristocrat, an individualist, and indeed, he has only a horror of the collective mass of mankind, which he sees (and in this case, he sees more clearly than Whitman) to have been always conservative, conventional, timid, and persecutors of genius. In fact, the only similarity is, that both he and

Whitman are preachers of new gospels, and therefore are obliged to adopt a similar tone of oratory in their work.

For this reason, Lawrence in his best poetry is unquotable, as is the case with all poets who depend rather on the extension of emotion, than on its minute concentration. But now and again he produces something that seems to transform all the poetry now written in English into mere prettiness and feebleness, so strong is the power with which his imagination pierces its subject. Such a poem, for example, is the one called **"The Sea."** I have space for only its last magnificent stanza:

> You who take the moon as in a sieve, and sift
> Her flake by flake and spread her meaning out;
> You who roll the stars like jewels in your palm,
> So that they seem to utter themselves aloud;
> You who steep from out the days their color,
> Reveal the universal tint that dyes
> Their web; who shadow the sun's great gestures
>   and expressions
> So that he seems a stranger in his passing;
> Who voice the dumb night fittingly;
> Sea, you shadow of all things, now mock us to
>   death with your
>   shadowing.

The man who wrote this, and many other passages in this volume, has at last arrived at his maturity—the maturity of the creative artist who is able to grasp a subject through its external aspect and internal meaning simultaneously, and to express both aspects in conjunction, before, the subject is laid aside.

Conrad Aiken (essay date 1919)

SOURCE: "The Melodic Line: D. H. Lawrence," in *Scepticisms: Notes on Contemporary Poetry*, Alfred A. Knopf, 1919, pp. 91-104.

[*In the following essay on Lawrence's* Look! We Have Come Through! *Aiken argues that the poem reads more like a novel, and that Lawrence's grasp of poetic techniques are limited.*]

It has been said that all the arts are constantly attempting, within their respective spheres, to attain to something of the quality of music, to assume, whether in pigment, or pencil, or marble, or prose, something of its speed and flash, emotional completeness, and well-harmonied resonance; but of no other single art is that so characteristically or persistently true as it is of poetry. Poetry is indeed in this regard two-natured: it strikes us, when it is at its best, quite as sharply through our sense of the musically beautiful as through whatever implications it has to carry of thought or feeling: it plays on us alternately or simultaneously through sound as well as through sense. The writers of free verse have demonstrated, to be sure, that a poetry sufficiently effective may be written in almost entire disregard of the values of pure rhythm. The poetry of "H.D." is perhaps the clearest example of this. Severe concentration upon a damascene sharpness of sense-impression, a stripping of images to the white clear kernel, both of which matters can be more meticulously attended to if there are no bafflements of rhythm or rhyme-pattern to be contended with, have, to a considerable extent, a substitutional value. Such a poetry attains a vitreous lucidity which has its own odd heatless charm. But a part of its charm lies in its very act of departure from a norm which, like a background or undertone, is forever present for it in our minds; we like it in a sense because of its unique perversity as a variation on this more familiar order of rhythmic and harmonic suspensions and resolutions; we like it in short for its novelty; and it eventually leaves us unsatisfied, because this more familiar order is based on a musical hunger which is as profound and permanent as it is universal.

When we read a poem we are aware of this musical characteristic, or analogy, in several ways. The poem as a whole in this regard will satisfy us or not in accordance with the presence, or partial presence, or absence, of what we might term musical unity. The "Ode to a Nightingale" is an example of perfect musical unity; the "Ode to Autumn" is an example of partial musical unity,—partial because the resolution comes too soon, the rate of curve is too abruptly altered; many of the poems by contemporary writers of free verse—Fletcher, or Aldington, or "H.D."—illustrate what we mean by lack of musical unity or integration, except on the secondary plane, the plane of what we·might call orotundity; and the most complete lack of all may be found in the vast majority of Whitman's poems. This particular sort of musical quality in poetry is, however, so nearly identifiable with the architectural as to be hardly separable from it. It is usually in the briefer movements of a poem that musical charm is most keenly felt. And this sort of brief and intensely· satisfactory musical movement we might well describe as something closely analogous to what is called in musical compositions the melodic line.

By melodic line we shall not mean to limit ourselves to one line of verse merely. Our melodic line may be, indeed, one line of verse, or half a line, or a group of lines, or half a page. What we have in mind is that sort of brief movement when, for whatever psychological reason, there is suddenly a fusion of all the many qualities, which may by themselves constitute charm, into one indivisible magic. Is it possible for this psychological change to take place without entailing an immediate heightening of rhythmic effect? Possible, perhaps, but extremely unlikely. In a free verse poem we shall expect to see at such moments a very much closer approximation to the rhythm of metrical verse; in a metrical poem we shall expect to see a subtilization of metrical effects, a richer or finer employment of vowel and consonantal changes to that end. Isolate such a passage in a free verse poem or metrical poem and it will be seen how true this is. The change is immediately perceptible, like the change from a voice talking to a voice singing. The change is as profound in time as it is in tone, yet it is one which escapes any but the most superficial analysis. All we can say of

it is that it at once alters the character of the verse we are reading from that sort which pleases and is forgotten, pleases without disturbing, to that sort which strikes into the subconscious, gleams, and is automatically remembered. In the midst of the rich semi-prose recitative of Fletcher's White Symphony, for example, a recitative which charms and entices but does not quite enchant, or take one's memory, one comes to the following passage:

> Autumn! Golden fountains,
> And the winds neighing
> Amid the monotonous hills;
> Desolation of the old gods,
> Rain that lifts and rain that moves away;
> In the green-black torrent
> Scarlet leaves.

It is an interlude of song and one remembers it. Is this due to an intensification of rhythm? Partly, no doubt, but not altogether. The emotional heightening is just as clear, and the unity of impression is pronounced; it is a fusion of all these qualities, and it is impossible to say which is the primum mobile. As objective psychologists all we can conclude is that in what is conspicuously a magical passage in this poem there is a conspicuous increase in the persuasiveness of rhythm.

This is equally true of metrical poetry. It is these passages of iridescent fusion that we recall from among the many thousands of lines we have read. One has but to summon up from one's memory the odds and ends of poems which willy nilly one remembers, precious fragments cherished by the jackdaw of the subconscious:

> A savage spot as holy and enchanted
> As e'er beneath a waning moon was haunted
> By woman wailing for her demon-lover.

> I have seen them riding seaward on the waves
> Combing the white hair of the waves blown back
> When the wind blows the water white and black.

> Beauty is momentary in the mind,—
> The fitful tracing of a portal:
> But in the flesh it is immortal.

> And shook a most divine dance from their feet,
> That twinkled starlike, moved as swift, and fine,
> And beat the air so thin, they made it shine.

> Part of a moon was falling down the west
> Dragging the whole sky with it to the hills.
> Its light poured softly in her lap. She saw
> And spread her apron to it. She put out her hand
> Among the harp-like morning-glory strings,
> Taut with the dew from garden-bed to eaves,
> As if she played unheard the tenderness
> That wrought on him. . . .

> Awakening up, he took her hollow lute,—
> Tumultuous,—and in chords that tenderest be,

> He played an ancient ditty long since mute,
> In Provence called, "La Belle Dame Sans Merci."

Ay, Mother, Mother,
What is this Man, thy darling kissed and cuffed,
Thou lustingly engenders't,
To sweat, and make his brag, and rot,
Crowned with all honours and all shamefulness?
He dogs the secret footsteps of the heavens,
Sifts in his hands the stars, weighs them as gold-
    dust,
And yet is he successive unto nothing,
But patrimony of a little mould,
And entail of four planks.

And suddenly there's no meaning in our kiss,
And your lit upward face grows, where we lie,
Lonelier and dreadfuller than sunlight is,
And dumb and mad and eyeless like the sky.

All of these excerpts, mangled as they are by being hewed from their contexts, have in a noticeable degree the quality of the "melodic line." They are the moments for which, indeed, we read poetry; just as when in listening to a modern music however complex and dissonantal, it is after all the occasionally-arising brief cry of lyricism which thrills and dissolves us. When the subconscious speaks, the subconscious answers.

It is because in a good deal of contemporary poetry the importance of the melodic line is forgotten that this brief survey has been made. In our preoccupations with the many technical quarrels, and quarrels as to aesthetic purpose, which have latterly embroiled our poets, we have, I think, a little lost sight of the fact that poetry to be poetry must after all rise above a mere efficiency of charmingness, or efficiency of accuracy, to this sort of piercing perfection of beauty or truth, phrased in a piercing perfection of music. It is a wholesome thing for us to study the uses of dissonance and irregularity; we add in that way, whether sensuously or psychologically, many new tones; but there is danger that the habit will grow upon us, that we will forget the reasons for our adoption of these qualities and use them *passim* and without intelligence, or, as critics, confer a too arbitrary value upon them.

The poetry of Mr. D. H. Lawrence is a case very much in point. His temperament is modern to a degree: morbidly self-conscious, sex-crucified, an affair of stretched and twanging nerves. He belongs, of course, to the psychological wing of modern poetry. Although we first met him as an Imagist, it is rather with T. S. Eliot, or Masters, or the much gentler Robinson, all of whom are in a sense lineal descendants of the Meredith of "Modern Love," that he belongs. But he does not much resemble any of these. His range is extremely narrow,—it is nearly always erotic, febrile and sultry at the lower end, plangently philosophic at the upper. Within this range he is astonishingly various. No mood is too slight to be seized upon, to be thrust under his myopic lens. Here, in fact, we touch his cardinal weakness: for if as a novelist he often writes like a poet, as a poet he far too often writes like a novelist. One observes that he knows this himself—he asks the reader of ***Look! We Have Come Through!*** to consider it not as a collection of short poems, but as a sort of novel in verse. No great rearrangement, perhaps, would have been necessary to do the same thing for ***New Poems*** or ***Amores,*** though perhaps not so cogently. More than most poets he makes of his poetry a sequential, though somewhat disjointed, autobiography. And more than almost any poet one can think of, who compares with him for richness of temperament, he is unselective in doing so, both as to material and method.

He is, indeed, as striking an example as one could find of the poet who, while appearing to be capable of what we have called the melodic line, none the less seems to be unaware of the value and importance of it, and gives it to us at random, brokenly, half blindly, or intermingled with splintered fragments of obscure sensation and extraneous detail dragged in to fill out a line. A provoking poet! and a fatiguing one: a poet of the dæmonic type, a man possessed, who is swept helplessly struggling and lashing down the black torrent of his thought; alternately frenzied and resigned. "A poet," says Santayana, "who merely swam out into the sea of sensibility, and tried to picture all possible things . . . would bring materials only to the workshop of art; he would not be an artist." What Santayana had in mind was a poet who undertook this with a deliberateness—but the effect in the case of Mr. Lawrence is much the same. He is seldom wholly an artist, even when his medium is most under control. It is when he is at his coolest, often,—when he tries rhyme-pattern or rhythm-pattern or colour-pattern in an attempt at the sort of icy kaleidoscopics at which Miss Lowell is adept,—that he is most tortuously and harshly and artificially and altogether unreadably at his worst. Is he obsessed with dissonance and oddity? It would seem so. His rhymes are cruel, sometimes, to the verge of murder.

Yet, if he is not wholly an artist, he is certainly, in at least a fragmentary sense, a brilliant poet. Even that is hardly fair enough: the two more recent volumes contain more than a handful of uniquely captivating poems. They have a curious quality,—tawny, stark, bitter, harshly coloured, salt to the taste. The sadistic element in them is strong. It is usually in the love poems that he is best: in these he is closest to giving us the melodic line that comes out clear and singing. Closest indeed; but the perfect achievement is seldom. The fusion is not complete. The rhythms do not altogether free themselves, one feels that they are weighted; the impressions are impetuously crowded and huddled; and as concerns the commanding of words Mr. Lawrence is a captain of more force than tact: he is obeyed, but sullenly. Part of this is due, no doubt, to Mr. Lawrence's venturings among moods and sensations which no poet has hitherto attempted, moods secret and obscure, shadowy and suspicious. This is to his credit, and greatly to the credit of poetry. He is among the most original poets of our time, original, that is, as regards sensibility; he has given us sombre and macabre tones, and tones of a cold and sinister clarity, or of a steely passion, which we have not had before. His nerves are raw, his reactions are idiosyncratic: what is clear enough to him has sometimes an unhealthily mottled look to us,—esuriently etched, none the less. But a great deal of the time he over-reaches: he makes frequently the mistake of, precisely, trying too hard. What cannot be captured, in this regard, it is no use killing. Brutality is no substitute for magic. One must take one's mood alive and singing, or not at all.

It is this factor which in the poetry of Mr. Lawrence most persistently operates to prevent the attainment of the perfect melodic line. Again and again he gives us a sort of jagged and spangled flame; but the mood does not sing quite with the naturalness or ease one would hope for, it has the air of being dazed by violence, or even seems, in the very act of singing, to bleed a little. It is a trifle too easy to say of a poet of whom this is true that the fault may be due to an obtrusion of the intellect among the emotions. Such terms do not define, are scarcely separable. Perhaps it would more closely indicate the difficulty to say that Mr. Lawrence is not only, as all poets are, a curious blending of the psycho-analyst and patient, but that he endeavours to carry on both rôles at once, to speak with both voices simultaneously. The soliloquy of the patient—the lyricism of the subconscious—is for ever being broken in upon by the too eager inquisitions of the analyst. If Mr. Lawrence could make up his mind to yield the floor unreservedly to either, he would be on the one hand a clearer and more magical poet, on the other hand a more dependable realist.

One wonders, in the upshot, whether the theme of ***Look! We have Come Through!*** had better not have been treated in prose. The story, such as it is, emerges, it is true, and with many deliciously clear moments, some of them lyric and piercing; but with a good deal that remains in question. It is the poet writing very much as a novelist, and all too often forgetting that the passage from the novel to the poem is among other things a passage from the cumulative to the selective. Sensations and impressions may be hewed and hauled in prose; but in poetry it is rather the sort of mood which, like a bird, flies out of the tree as soon as the ax rings against it, that one must look for. Mr. Lawrence has, of this sort, his birds, but he appears to pay little heed to them; he goes on chopping. And one has, even so, such a delight in him that not for worlds would one intervene.

Arthur Waugh (essay date 1919)

SOURCE: "Mr. D. H. Lawrence," in *Tradition and Change: Studies in Contemporary Literature*, Books for Libraries Press, 1919, pp. 131-7.

[*In the following essay, Waugh assesses Lawrence's poetry as lacking in unifying ideas and the poetic skills necessary to espouse them.*]

The modern conception of poetry is so astonishingly different from the conception, for example, of the last generation before our own, that it is worth while to take stock of the situation now and again, and to try to get some clear notion of the direction in which we are drifting.

Changes there must be, of course; and the critic who withstands change for its own sake is self-condemned already. But in the realm of the arts there are certain fixed principles which have survived all the vagaries of fashion; and work which has defied those principles has never lasted. Novelty and audacity attract their momentary public; but novelty is soon stale, and audacity has an awkward way of petering out into impertinence. It is a good thing to overhaul our equipment from time to time, and to refer it by comparison to those irrefutable truths upon which all sincere art must be grounded.

Some such comparison seems to be particularly invited in the case of the poetry of Mr. D. H. Lawrence. It would appear that the newest school of criticism is in no sort of doubt about the quality of his performance; he can point to a glittering consensus of eulogy from the Press; and he has been admitted into that privileged circle of Georgian Poetry which issues crowned with the imprimatur of the Poetry Bookshop. And yet, surely, even those who are most completely dazzled by the novelty of his work must admit that Mr. Lawrence's verse is of a kind which, before the coming of the most recent impressionist movement in letters, not gods, nor men, nor booksellers have ever recognised under the name of poetry. Much controversy, of course, has raged from time immemorial around the limits of the poet's art; and (to go no further back than our own time), since the experiments of Robert Browning were recognised at their true value, the boundaries of poetry have been perpetually enlarged. But two essentials have hitherto been required inexorably of the poet: it has been demanded of him that his work should be dominated by an idea, and that the idea should be expressed in terms of technical beauty. Without an animating idea a poem drifts away into a mist of words; without beauty, alike of vision and of melody, the form of the expression degenerates into mere rhetoric. All the great poetry in all languages will be found to base its claim upon these two qualities: it has survived by virtue of the ideas that it expresses, and by the perfect beauty of the expression in which those ideas are embodied and translated into words.

Mr. Lawrence, on the contrary, is a typical representative of a literary movement which deliberately eschews these qualities. He is concerned not with ideas but with moods, while the object of his art is to express those moods with as much vivid actuality as he can cram into metrical form, without regard for the restraints or responsibilities of prosody or technique. If the metre will hold the bubbling mood within its cup, all well and good; but if the mood runs over the metre's brim—never mind, let it go; the one thing needful is to keep the realism of the passionate moment intact. So you write like this, and impressionism is held justified of its effect:

> Into a deep pond, an old sheep-dip,
> Dark, overgrown with willows, cool, with the
>   brook ebbing through so slow,
> Naked on the steep, soft lip
> Of the bank I stand watching my own white
>   shadow quivering to and fro.

What if the gorse flowers shrivelled and kissing
     were lost?
Without the pulsing waters, where were the mari-
     golds and the songs of the brook?
If my veins and my breasts with love embossed
Withered, my insolent soul would be gone like
     flowers that the hot wind took.

And you make no trouble about a clash of discordant
consonants:

Though her kiss betrays to me this, this only
Consolation, that in her lips her blood at climax
     clips
Two wild, dumb paws in anguish on the lonely
Fruit of my heart, ere down, rebuked, it slips.

And if a Cockney rhyme falls easily into its place, you
leave that standing also:

Over the nearness of Norwood Hill, through the
     mellow veil
Of the afternoon glows to me the old romance of
     David and Dora,
With the old, sweet, soothing tears, and laughter
     that shakes the sail
Of the ship of the souls over seas where dreamed
     dreams lure the unoceaned explorer.

It was not so that they sang in the golden days, when
Plancus was consul; but Plancus himself, no doubt, is out
of date to-day, and the new impressionism aims rather at
violent effect than at charmed and charming minstrelsy.
Mr. Lawrence is only too wisely aware that his audacities
will shock convention, and forestalls the criticism in a
pungent quatrain:

Ah, my darling, when over the purple horizon
     shall loom
The shrouded mother of a new idea, men hide
     their faces,
Cry out, and fend her off, as she seeks her
     procreant groom,
Wounding themselves against her, denying her
     fecund embraces.

Let us, then, at any rate not hide our faces; but do our
best to follow the "shrouded mother" to the secret nup-
tials of mood and expression. It is not always an easy
path, for the poet's method (as perhaps our quotations
have already suggested) is congenitally obscure and
murky. Nevertheless, by degrees a certain recognisable
scheme appears to emerge from the tangle of Mr.
Lawrence's over-heated phrase-making, and that scheme
is evidently deliberate and purposeful.

The principle of Mr. Lawrence's poetry, then (as it seems
to one sincere, if somewhat uninitiated reader), is the
exposition in high light of a momentary mood, preferably
sensuous, expressed in glowing terms of an elaborately-
wrought symbolism of the senses. As the nature-poets of
the nineteenth century represented the heaven and earth
as sharing in the emotions of humanity, and so set their
pictures in a harmonious environment of storm and sunlight;

so Mr. Lawrence, allowing his imagination freer rein, conceives the whole natural world as a passionate allegory of
human desire, human satisfaction, and human satiety.
This world of emotion is physical, not spiritual. The very
flowers, in a riot of suggestion, tempt the lover to the gratification of his desire; the roving bee is a profligate rav-
isher of innocence. The earth is full of hidden imagery,
and its apparent peace is tortured by secret sensuality:

You amid the bog-end's yellow incantation,
You sitting in the cowslips of the meadow above,
Me, your shadow on the bog-flame, flowery may-
     blobs,
Me full length in the cowslips, muttering you love;
You, your soul like a lady-smock, lost,
     evanescent,
You with your face all rich, like the sheen of a dove.

And again:

Ah, love, with your rich, warm face aglow,
What sudden expectation opens you
So wide as you watch the catkins blow
     Their dust from the birch on the blue
Lift of the pulsing wind—ah, tell me you know

Ah, surely! Ah, sure from the golden sun
A quickening, masculine gleam floats in to all
Us creatures, people and flowers undone,
     Lying open under his thrall,
As he begets the year in us. What then, would you
     shun?

The entire firmament is summoned to assist the lover in
his wooing; and virgin youth is displayed as a tossing
torrent of "urgent, passionate waves," where "docile, flu-
ent arms" knot themselves "with wild strength to clasp"
the imagined nymph; where the body is all a "wild
strange tyranny," and the eyes reassert themselves with
difficulty in "relentless nodality." It will be conceived
that this riotous symbolism can soon become uncom-
monly sultry; indeed, if there is a more suggestive poem
in the English language than **"Snapdragon,"** we should
be sorry to be set the task of unravelling its allegory.

Well, what are we to make of it all? For Mr. Lawrence
is clearly not a writer to be dismissed in a flash of quotation. He has caught the ear of critics who demand respect. He has an overwrought, perverted, but very powerful imagination. You may not like him, but you cannot
deny that he cuts into your perception. His lack of taste
may revolt you, but he hits his mark. He is not negligible,
though you may confess that there are times when his
fancy seems little less than disgusting. He can write, undoubtedly: but does he write poetry? If so, it is certainly
a sort of poetry that runs upon entirely different lines
from all the proved traditions of the past. Technically, it
is at intervals only a little less inchoate than Walt
Whitman, and in expression it is invariably much more
nebulous. The poet indulges his symbolism until it becomes his master; his fecund fancy overwhelms him, like
the serpents of Laocoön. He is perpetually struggling
with his own wilful and contorted metaphors. Almost

every verse that he writes requires to be read more than once, before its meaning takes definite shape in the mind; and by dropping the connecting links of his thought, in a sort of post-Browningesque obliquity, he is apt to render confusion doubly confounded. Worst of all, he does outrageous violence to Nature by dragging her beauties into a sort of guilty condonation of the excesses of his imagination; he is not ashamed to ravish the goddess Flora in sudden spasms of a tortured imagery. What Mr. Lawrence's art stands most desperately in need of is a shower-bath of vital ideas. At present his fancy is half asleep upon a fætid hot-bed of moods. It is a vigorous, masculine fancy, but it seems to have got into bad company, and to have been left deserted on a midden. Perhaps some vivifying, ennobling, human experience will yet help it to save its soul alive.

Richard Aldington (essay date 1926)

SOURCE: "D. H. Lawrence as Poet," in *The Saturday Review of Literature*, New York, Vol. 11, No. 40, May 1, 1926, pp. 749-50.

[*In the following overview of Lawrence's poetry, including* Birds, Beasts, and Flowers, *Aldington attempts to cast aside the poet's ideology and sexual subject matter in order to isolate the poetry he writes, which Aldington believes to be representative of its author's genius.*]

If a difficult problem were being set for what Mr. Bennett calls the "young aspirant" in criticism, there could scarcely be found a better topic than Mr. D. H. Lawrence. He is not the sort of man who becomes master of Balliol or an Oracle to thoughtful, cautious *rentiers*. His personality is abrupt, independent, and unreliable. His writings are full of faults and also of possible qualities. You can dislike him irrelevantly, because you have the Anglo-Saxon complex about sexual matters or because you share the pedant's follies about correctness and "models" or because you hate a man with a red beard. You may like him equally irrelevantly, because you share his lust for metaphysics, or because you think he has a working hypothesis of Love and Hate, or because he was stupidly persecuted during the war. But the point I wish to make about Mr. Lawrence's work in general, and his poetry in particular, is simply this; he is a great artist in words. And he is an artist almost unconsciously, certainly without troubling about it. To me it is a matter of indifference whether Mr. Lawrence's philosophical and psychological notions are accurate and original or not. (Who wants to argue Dante's theology or Tasso's history?) What I seek in poetry is poetry. In some of Mr. Lawrence's free verse I seem to find it.

Like many writers of wayward and independent genius, Mr. Lawrence has been more influenced by contemporaries—often far less gifted—than he or his professed admirers would admit. Take his three salient books of poetry, **Amores, Look, We Have Come Through,** and **Birds, Beasts, and Flowers.** The first is not a little Georgian; the second shows the influence of the Imagists; the

third of the modern Americans. A tendency to redundant and merely decorative language in the first book is purged away in the next, which shows a tight discipline, and this is abandoned in turn for a reckless liberty and colloquialism in the last. But, in a larger sense, these are mere accidents of form, and are more interesting to other poets than to the public. The permanent interest of Mr. Lawrence's poetry lies in his essentially poetical way of seeing and feeling. That poetic mind is startlingly present in his novels. Even the preface to the "M. M." book contains that marvellous evocation of the Italian hill monastery; even the *Dial* articles gave us the vivid and penetrating dance of the Indians. These things live in one's mind with a special vitality of impression given us only by great poetry. And the wonderful thing is that this is given us, not by some long dead and consecrated master, but by a living man who has passed through the same great events as ourselves, whose work, therefore, has a peculiar poignancy and meaning for us, such as it will never have for the future which can only make up in reverence for prestige what we gain from intimacy and sympathy.

In judging poetry, remember Schlegel's "Internal excellence is alone decisive," and "there is no monopoly of poetry for particular ages and nations." What is it one admires in Mr. Lawrence's poetry? It seems to me he is one of the small number of men who think, feel, and live for themselves, a man intensely alert to the life of the senses and the mind, whose great purpose and pleasure are the explanation of himself and the universe. Add to this the talent for conveying these discoveries in poetic symbols. Mr. Lawrence lives poetically. I don't mean that he dresses a part or is languishing or literary or any of the stock libels of the ignorant; I mean that he apprehends the world directly by images. How useless is the discussion about Mr. Lawrence's "attitudes," and whether he has taken the wrong or the right philosophical path! *D'abord il faut être poète.* And a poet is the antithesis of the English gentleman, educated or the reverse. In our society, and in all over-organized societies, poetry either droops heavily and wearily or dances and giggles politely, or the poet becomes an outcast. Even Voltaire was an outcast in an unpoetical society. For it is the glory of a poet like Mr. Lawrence that he does not accept a ready-made existence, that he scorns futile social laws, amusements, behavior, all herd-suggestions, and tastes the dangerous voluptuousness of living.

Take Mr. Lawrence's poems and observe how absolutely free his mind and body are; his revolt against stale, tame lives is perhaps too vehement and scornful, but how comprehensible! See the pallid senses, the cautious, confined spiritual and mental life of our tame intellectuals and *arrivistes,* and then observe the sensual richness, the emotional variety, of Mr. Lawrence. "Better to see straight on a pound a week, than squint on a million," said Mr. G. B. Shaw; and better, how much better, to starve and suffer and endure pangs of intolerable pleasure and bitter disappointment and ecstasies for the love of beauty with Lawrence, an outcast, a wanderer, than to live in the dull monotony of comfort. "The world's good word, the Institute!" All that a man like Lawrence asks of the world is to be left alone; it is all the world can do for him.

Now that ecstasy for life and beauty blows through Mr. Lawrence, as he says, "like a fine wind," and he has an almost mystic sense of loyalty to his talent:

> If only I let it bear me, carry me, if only it carry me!
> If only I am sensitive, subtle, oh, delicate, a
>   winged gift!
> If only, most lovely of all, I yield myself and am
>   borrowed
> By the fine, fine wind that takes its course through
>   the chaos of the world
> Like a fine, an exquisite chisel, a wedge-blade
>   inserted;
> If only I am keen and hard like the sheer tip of a
>   wedge
> Driven by invisible blows,
> The rock shall split, we shall come at the wonder,
>   we shall find the Hesperides.
> Oh, for the wonder that bubbles into my soul,
> I would be a good fountain, a good well-head,
> Would blur no whisper, spoil no expression.

"Sensitive, subtle, delicate," these Mr. Lawrence is indeed in his poetry, though he has other and uglier moods, the worst of which is the poetical equivalent to that little mocking titter of his—a useful thing, though, to keep him hard and unsentimental. Perhaps that sense of mockery has been as valuable as his fearlessness in exploring and expressing a whole country of emotions into which nearly all contemporary English poets are afraid to penetrate. They are eaten up with the disease of self-love and respectability. Mr. Lawrence is a poet as untramelled as an Elizabethan. To me he seems one of the last authentic voices of the great but decaying English people. Angry revolt against the grey, servile, querulous, futile, base personalities of the world, stabs Mr. Lawrence to almost hysterical denunciation:

> I long to see its chock-full crowdedness
> And glutted squirming populousness on fire
> Like a field of filthy weeds
> Burnt back to ash
> And then to see the new, real souls spring up.

I do not think that Mr. Lawrence is at his best in such passages, but they have a sinister significance for those who understand the meaning of poetry in human life. It should be sinister, at least for modern society to know that its best poets despair of it utterly, as they do. Life, said Marcus Aurelius, may be lived well even in a palace; but in a ruthless, mechanistic commercialism—? If the poetry of D. H. Lawrence is largely a revolt, it is a revolt against a non-human scale of values.

R. P. Blackmur (essay date 1935)

SOURCE: "D. H. Lawrence and Expressive Form," in *Language as Gesture: Essays in Poetry,* Harcourt, Brace and Company, 1935, pp. 286-300.

[*In the following essay, Blackmur argues that Lawrence's poetry is too often marred by the author's unchecked inclusion of biographical detail and personal feelings.*]

As a poet, and only to a less degree as a novelist, Lawrence belongs to that great race of English writers whose work totters precisely where it towers, collapses exactly in its strength: work written out of a tortured Protestant sensibility and upon the foundation of an incomplete, uncomposed mind: a mind without defenses against the material with which it builds and therefore at every point of stress horribly succumbing to it. Webster, Swift, Blake, and Coleridge—perhaps Donne, Sterne, and Shelley, and on a lesser plane Marston, Thompson (of the Dreadful Night), and Beddoes—these exemplify, in their different ways, the deracinated, unsupported imagination, the mind for which, since it lacked rational structure sufficient to its burdens, experience was too much. Their magnitude was inviolate, and we must take account of it not only for its own sake but also to escape its fate; it is the magnitude of ruins—and the ruins for the most part of an intended life rather than an achieved art.

Such judgment—such prediction of the terms of appreciation—may seem heavy and the operation of willful prejudice (like that of our dying Humanism), but only if the reader refuses to keep in mind that of which he can say more. Criticism, the effort of appreciation, should be focused upon its particular objects, not limited to them. Shakespeare, Dante, and Milton, for example, remain monuments (not ruins) of the imagination precisely in what is here a relevant aspect. Their work, whatever the labors of exegesis, remains approximately complete in itself. The work of Shakespeare, even the Sonnets, is not for us an elongation of the poet's self, but is independent of it because it has a rational structure which controls, orders, and composes in external or objective form the material of which it is made; and for that effect it is dependent only upon the craft and conventions of the art of poetry and upon the limits of language. We criticize adversely such work where it fails of objective form or lacks unarticulated composition, as in the Sonnets or *Hamlet.* We criticize *Lycidas* because the purpose of the digressions is not articulated and so there is injury to the composition—the growing together into an independent entity—of the poem. And this is the right meat for criticism; this is the kind of complaint to which poetry is of its own being subject; the original sin of which no major work is entirely free.

This essay proposes to outline an attack upon Lawrence as a poet on the grounds just laid out: that the strength of his peculiar insight lacks the protection and support of a rational imagination, and that it fails to its own disadvantage to employ the formal devices of the art in which it is couched. Thus the attack will be technical. No objections will be offered to the view of life involved—which is no more confused than Dostoevski's, and no less a mirror than Shakespeare's; only admiration for its vigor, regret that it did not, and argument that in the technical circumstances it could not, succeed. For it should be remembered that the structure of the imagination no less than the sequence of rhyme is in an important sense a technical matter.

Perhaps our whole charge may be laid on the pretension, found in the Preface to the **Collected Poems,** that the radical imperfection of poetry is a fundamental virtue. That is not how Lawrence frames it; he says merely that certain of his early poems failed "because the poem started out to be something it didn't quite achieve, because the young man interfered with his demon"; which seems harmless enough until we read that he regards many of his poems as a fragmentary biography, asks us to remember in reading them the time and circumstance of his life, and expresses the wish that in reading the Sonnets we knew more about Shakespeare's self and circumstance. After consideration, I take the young man in the quotation to be just what Lawrence thought he was not, the poet as craftsman, and the demon was exactly that outburst of personal feeling which needed the discipline of craft to become a poem. As for Shakespeare's Sonnets, if we did know more about Shakespeare's self, we should only know a little more clearly where he failed as a poet; the Sonnets themselves would be not a whit improved. A statement of which—since there is always a necessary baggage of historical and intellectual background—I wish to assert only the comparative or provisional truth.

However wrong Lawrence was about the young man, the demon, and Shakespeare's self, the point here is that his remarks explain why there is so little to say about his important poems as poetry, and they characterize the seed of personal strength, which, nourished exclusively, became his weakness, and ultimately brought about his disintegration and collapse as a poet. Lawrence was the extreme victim of the plague afflicting the poetry of the last hundred and fifty years—the plague of expressive form.

You cannot talk about the art of his poetry because it exists only at the minimum level of self-expression, as in the later, more important poems, or because, as in the earlier accentual rhymed pieces written while he was getting under way, its art is mostly attested by its badness. The ordering of words in component rhythms, the array of rhymes for prediction, contrast, transition and suspense, the delay of ornament, the anticipation of the exactly situated dramatic trope, the development of image and observation to an inevitable end—the devices which make a poem cohere, move, and shine apart—these are mostly not here, or are present badly and at fault. This absence of the advantages of craft is not particularly due to the inability to use them, but to a lack of interest. Lawrence hardly ever, after the first, saw the use of anything that did not immediately devour his interest, whether in life or in art. (Poetry, it may be remarked, is never an immediate art but always of implication.)

And he had besides, to control his interests, a special blinding light of his own, and it was only what this light struck or glared on that captured his interest, and

compelled, by a kind of automatism, the writing hand. If a good deal else got in as well, it was not from concession or tactical motives, but by accident and willy-nilly, or because Lawrence was deceived and thought his demon illuminated him when not present at all. This is the presumptive explanation of the long reaches of dead-level writing. When you depend entirely upon the demon of inspiration, the inner voice, the inner light, you deprive yourself of any external criterion to show whether the demon is working or not. Because he is yours and you willfully depend on him, he will seem to be operating with equal intensity at every level of imagination. That is the fallacy of the faith in expressive form—the faith some aspects of which we have been discussing, that if a thing is only intensely enough felt its mere expression in words will give it satisfactory form, the dogma, in short, that once material becomes words it is its own best form. By this stultifying fallacy you cannot ever know whether your work succeeds or fails as integral poetry, can know only and always that what you have said symbolizes and substitutes for your experience to you, whatever it substitutes for in the minds of your readers. That Lawrence was aware of this fallacy, only thinking it a virtue, is I think evident; he would not otherwise have pled with his readers to put themselves in his place, to imagine themselves as suffering his experience, while reading the long section of his poems called **"Look! We Have Come Through!"**; which is a plea, really, for the reader to do the work the poet failed to do, to complete the poems of which he gave only the expressive outlines.

There is a further vitiating influence of Lawrence's dogma as he seems to hold it, whether you take it as the demon of enthusiastic inspiration or the reliance on expressive form; it tends, on the least let-up of particularized intensity, to the lowest order of the very formalism which it was meant to escape: the formalism of empty verbiage, of rodomontade, masquerading as mystical or philosophical poetry. If you become content, even tormentedly, with self-expression, the process of education no less than that of taste ceases, and anything may come to stand, and interchangeably, for anything else. On the one hand the bare indicative statement of experience seems equivalent to insight into it, and on the other the use of such labels as Good or Evil, however accidentally come by, seems to have the force of the rooted concepts which they may, when achieved by long labor or genuine insight, actually possess. Thus a dog's dying howl may be made to express in itself the whole tragedy of life, which it indeed may or may not do, depending on the reach of the imagination, of represented experience, you bring to bear on it. In Lawrence's later poems, where he is most ambitious, there is more of this empty formalism, unknown to him, than in any poet of similar potential magnitude. Whatever happened in his own mind, what transpires in the poems is the statement without the insight, the label without the seizable implied presence of the imaginative reach. The pity is that had Lawrence matured an external form to anywhere near the degree that he intensified his private apprehension, that form would have persuaded us of the active presence of the insight and the imagination which we can now only take on trust or *ipse dixit.*

These radical defects in Lawrence's equipment and in his attitude toward his work, may be perhaps exhibited in certain of the early poems when he had not deliberately freed himself from those devices of form which, had he mastered them, might have saved him. He began writing in the ordinary way, using to express or discover his own impulses the contemporary models that most affected him. The freshness of his personal life, the process of personal awakening (since he had something to awaken) provided, by rule, a copious subject matter; and the freshness, to him, of other men's conventions amply supplied him and even, again by rule, sometimes overwhelmed him with forms. Occasionally, still in the natural course of a poet's progress, there was in his work a material as well as a formal influence, but rather less frequently than in most poets. For instance, **"Lightning"** and **"Turned Down"** are so strongly under the influence of the Hardy of *Time's Laughingstocks* and *Satires of Circumstances,* that there was very little room for Lawrence himself in the poems; Hardy's sensibility as well as Hardy's form crowded him out. By apparent paradox, the value of the poems to Lawrence was personal; as renderings of Hardy they add nothing. Where the influence was less apparent, it was more genuine because more digested, and far more successful, as, for example, in the two quatrains called **"Gipsy."** Hardy was the only then practicing poet who was in the hard-earned habit of composing so much implication in so brief a space and upon the nub of a special circumstance. It was from Hardy that Lawrence learned his lesson. (The nub of circumstance is of course the gypsy's traditional aversion to entering a house.)

> I, the man with the red scarf,
>   Will give thee what I have, this last week's
>   earnings.
> Take them and buy thee a silver ring
>   And wed me, to ease my yearnings.
>
> For the rest, when thou art wedded
>   I'll wet my brow for thee
> With sweat, I'll enter a house for thy sake,
>   Thou shalt shut doors on me.

Thus houses and doors become "really" houses and doors. The poem is for that quality worth keeping in the early Lawrence canon; but its importance here is in the technical faults—by which I mean its radical and unnecessary variations from the norm of its model. It represents, I think (subject to correction), about as far as Lawrence ever went in the direction of strict accentual syllabic form; which is not very far. Hardy would have been ashamed of the uneven, lop-sided metrical architecture and would never have been guilty (whatever faults he had of his own) of the disturbing inner rhyme in the second quatrain. Lawrence was either ignorant or not interested in these matters; at any rate he failed to recognize the access of being which results from a perfected strict form. He preferred, in this poem, to depend on the best economical statement of his subject with the least imposition of external form, strict or not. This is an example of the fallacy of expressive form; because, granted that he used a set form at all, it is his substance, what he had to say and was really interested in, that suffers through his failure to complete the form. If the reader compares this poem with say Blake's "To the Muses," which is not a very strict poem in itself, the formal advantage will be plain.

A more important poem, a poem which measurably captured more of Lawrence's sensibility, and as it happens more of ours, will illustrate the point, at least by cumulation, more clearly. Take the first poem preserved in the collected edition, **"The Wild Common."** We have here, for Lawrence says that it was a good deal rewritten, the advantage of an early and a late poem at once. It is, substantially, in its present form, one of the finest of all Lawrence's poems. It presents the pastoral scene suggested by the title, proceeds to describe a naked man (the narrator) watching his white shadow quivering in a sheep-dip; either actually or imaginatively the man enters the water and the shadow is resolved with the substance and is identified; the poem ends with the affirmation, confirmed by singing larks and a lobbing rabbit, that "all that is good, all that is God takes substance!" The feeling is deep and particularized and the emotion is adequate to the material presented. The point here is that in gaining his ends Lawrence used an extraordinary combination of inconsistent modes and means. I ask only, for the sake of the argument, that the reader look at the poem with the same attention to craft as is customary (and is indeed the common proof of appreciation) in the examination of a drawing or a fugue: that he look and read *as if* he had a trained mind. Take the matter of rhymes. Whether by weakness of sound, weakness of syntactical position, lack of metrical propulsion or, as the case is, restraint, superfluity with regard to sense, or the use of mere homonym for true rhyme—the rhyme words not only fail as good rhymes but because of the distortions they bring about injure the substance and disfigure the outline of the poem. (In other poems such as **"Discord in Childhood"** the exigencies of rhyme misunderstood dictate actually inconsistent images and tropes.) That is a formal defect; there are also faults in the combinations of the modes of language. In this same poem, without dramatic change to warrant the variation, there are examples of fake "poetic" language, explicit direct presentation, the vague attribute and the precise attribute, colloquial language, and plain empty verbiage. It is as if in one drawing you found employed to the disadvantage of each the modes of outline and inner marking, chiaroscuro, and total visual effect.

Another poem, **"Love on a Farm,"** has the special power of a dramatic fiction; it employs, dramatically, a violent but credible humanitarianism to force the feeling of death into the emotion of love. But it would have been better expanded and proved in prose. There is nothing in the poem to praise as poetry between the image of the intention and the shock of the result. Lawrence simply did not care in his verse—and, after *Sons and Lovers,* in many reaches of his more characteristic prose—for anything beyond the immediate blueprint expression of what he had in mind. The consequence is this. Since he willfully rejected as much as he could of the great mass of expressive devices which make up the craft of poetry, the success of his poems depends, not so much on his bare statements, as upon the constant function of communication which cannot be expunged from the language.

Only the articulate can be inarticulately expressed, even under the dogma of expressive form, and Lawrence was, within the limits of his obsessive interests, one of the most powerfully articulate minds of the last generation. Since he used language straightforwardly to the point of sloppiness, without ever willfully violating the communicative residue of his words, so much of his intention is available to the reader as is possible in work that has not been submitted to the completing persuasiveness of a genuine form. That much is a great deal; its capacity is the limit of greatness in the human personality. Being human, Lawrence could not escape in his least breath the burden of human experience, and, using language in which to express himself *for* himself, could not help often finding the existing, readily apprehensible word-forms the only suitable ones. That is a discipline by implication upon the soul of which the purest Protestant, as Lawrence was, cannot be free: the individual can contribute only infinitesimally even to his own idea of himself. In addressing even his most private thoughts he addresses a stranger and must needs find a common tongue between them. Thus Lawrence at his most personal, where he burrowed with most savage rapacity into himself, stood the best chance of terminating his passion in common experience. The language required, the objects of analogy and the tropes of identification, necessarily tended to the commonplace. This is at least negatively true of Lawrence's later, prophetic poems (as it is true on a level of greater magnitude in the prophetic poems of Blake); the fundamental declarations of insight, what Lawrence was after, in the *Tortoise* poems, could not help appearing in language commonplace for everything except its intensity. Here again it may be insisted, since such insistence is the object of this essay, that had Lawrence secured the same intensity in the process of his form as came naturally to him in seizing his subject, the poems would have escaped the inherent weakness of the commonplace (the loss of identity in the reader's mind) in the strength of separate being.

Before proceeding, as we have lastly to do, to measure and provisionally characterize the driving power in Lawrence's most important work, let us first examine, with a special object, one of the less important but uniquely successful poems. This is the poem called **"Corot."** It is written at the second remove from the experience involved. Not so much does it deal with a particular picture by Corot, or even with the general landscape vision of Corot, as it attempts a thinking back, by Lawrence, through Corot, into landscape itself as a major mode of insight. Corot—the accumulation of impressions, attitudes, and formal knowledge with which Corot

furnishes the attentive mind—is the medium through which the poem transpires. It is perhaps the only poem of its kind Lawrence wrote; a poem with a deliberately apprehended external scaffolding. We know that most poems about pictures, and most illustrations of literature, stultify themselves by keeping to the terms of the art they re-represent—or else come to mere minor acts of appreciation—come, in short, in either case, pretty much to nothing. Something very different took place here. By finding his material at a second remove—the remove of Corot past the remove of language—Lawrence provided himself, for once, with a principle of objective form; which in the fact of this poem composed his material better than he was ever able to compose in terms of mere direct apprehension however intense. Despite the cloudy words—we have the word "dim" used imprecisely three times in thirty-six lines—despite the large words and phrases such as Life and Time, goal, purpose, and mighty direction—and despite the inconsistent meters, Lawrence nevertheless was able to obtain merely because of the constant presence of an external reference ("Corot"), a unity of effect and independence of being elsewhere absent in his work. That the poem may have been as personal for Lawrence as anything he ever wrote makes no difference; for the reader the terms of conception are objective, and the poem could thus not help standing by itself.

The poem is small, its value merely illustrative, and if it is remembered at all it will be so only in the general context of Lawrence; but I have emphasized the principle of its compositional success because it is on similar principles that most great poetry has been composed; or at least—a more prudent statement—similar principles may be extracted from most of the poetry we greatly value: the principle that the reality of language, which is a formal medium of knowledge, is superior and anterior to the reality of the uses to which it is put, and the operative principle, that the chaos of private experience cannot be known or understood until it is projected and ordered in a form external to the consciousness that entertained it in flux. Of the many ways in which these principles may be embodied, Lawrence's poetry enjoys the advantage of but few, and those few by accident, as in **"Corot,"** or because he could not help it, as in the constant reliance on the communicative function of language mentioned above. But he worked in the poverty of apparent riches and felt no need. There was a quality in his apprehension of the experience that obsessed him that in itself sufficed to carry over the reality of his experience in the words of his report—always for him and sometimes for the reader. This I think, for lack of a better word, may be called the quality of hysteria.

Hysteria comes from the Greek word for womb, and, formerly limited to women, was the name given to extraordinary, disproportionate reactions to the shock of experience. In hysteria the sense of reality is not annulled, resort is not to fancy or unrelated illusion; the sense of reality is rather heightened and distorted to a terrifying and discomposing intensity. The derangement of the patient is merely the expression, through a shocked nervous system, of the afflicting reality. But hysteria is not limited in its expressive modes to convulsions and shrieking. We have hysterias which express themselves in blindness, deafness, paralysis, and even secondary syphilis (lacking of course the appropriate bacteria). Some forms of romantic love may be called habit-hysterias of a comparatively benign character. In all these modes what is expressed has an apparent overwhelming reality. The blind man is really blind, the deaf deaf, and the paralytic cannot move—while hysteria lasts.

Now I do not wish to introduce Lawrence as a clinical example of hysteria; it would be inappropriate and unnecessary to any purpose of literary criticism; but I think it can be provisionally put that the reality in his verse, and in his later prose (from *The Rainbow* to *Mornings in Mexico* if not in *Lady Chatterley's Lover*) is predominantly of the hysterical order. Hysteria is certainly one of the resources of art—as it represents an extreme of consciousness; and it is arguable that much art is hysteria controlled—that is, restored to proportion by seizure in objective form. And the reader should remember that in a life so difficult to keep balanced, plastic, and rational, the leaning toward the expressive freedom of hysteria may often be intractable. The pretense or fact of hysteria is an ordinary mode of emotional expression. The reality of what is expressed is intense and undeniable, and is the surest approach to the absolute. But what is expressed in hysteria can never be wholly understood until the original reality is regained either by analysis or the imposition of limits. Otherwise, and in art, the hysteria is heresy and escapes the object which created it. That is how I think Lawrence worked; he submitted the obsessions of his experience to the heightening fire of hysteria and put down the annealed product just as it came. His special habit of hysteria is only a better name for the demon, the divinity, referred to in the Preface to the *Collected Poems;* and there is no reason to suppose that Lawrence would himself reject the identification. The reality persists, and is persuasive to those who catch the clue and accept the invitation by its very enormity.

Certainly it is in terms of some such notion that we must explain Lawrence's increasing disregard of the control of rationally conceived form and his incipient indifference, in the very last poems, to the denotative functions of language. So also we may explain the extraordinary but occasional and fragmentary success of his poetry as expression: by the enormity of the reality exposed. As it happens, Lawrence's obsessions ran to sex, death, the isolation of the personality, and the attempt at mystical fusion. Had he run rather to claustrophobia, fetish-worship, or some of the more obscure forms of human cowardice, his method of expression would have been less satisfactory: since it would not have commanded the incipient hysteria of sympathy. The normal subject matter, in the sense of a sturdy preoccupation with ordinary interests, kept his enormity of expression essentially accessible in most of his poems, although there are some places, for example in **"The Ship of Death"** or **"Sicilian Cyclamens,"** where the hysteric mode carries the pathetic fallacy and the confusion of symbols beyond any resolution.

But normal subject matter was not the only saving qualification; there is in the best poems a kind of furious underlying honesty of observation—the very irreducible surd that makes the hysteria an affair of genius not of insanity. One aspect of this honesty is perhaps most clearly seen in the poem called **"She Said as Well to Me,"** which I think marks the climax of the long series called **"Look! We Have Come Through!"** There Lawrence manages to present, for all the faults of the work he did not do, and merely by the intensified honesty of the observation, the utter dignity of the singleness and isolation of the individual. Later in **"Medlars and Sorb Apples,"** the hysteria is increased and the observation becomes vision, and leaves, perhaps, the confines of poetry.

> Orphic farewell, and farewell, and farewell
> And the *ego sum* of Dionysos
> The *sono io* of perfect drunkenness
> Intoxication of final loneliness.

It became, in fact, ritual frenzy; a matter to which we shall return. But first let us examine the eighteen pages of the poems about tortoises. Here we have the honesty working the other way round. In **"She Said as Well to Me"** and in all the poems of *Look! We Have Come Through!* which make up Lawrence's testament of personal love, the movement is from the individual outward: it is the report or declaration, made unequivocally, of an enormously heightened sense of self. The self, the individual, is the radial point of sensibility. The six tortoise poems (which I take as the type of all the later poems) have as their motive the effort to seize on the plane of self-intoxication the sense of the outer world. The exhilarated knowledge of the self is still the aim, but here the self is the focal, not the radial, point of sensibility. The bias, the predicting twist of the mind, is no longer individual love, but the sexual, emergent character of all life; and in terms of that bias, which is the controlling principle, the seed of reality, in the hysteria of expression, Lawrence brings every notation and association, every symbolic suggestion he can find, to bear upon the shrieking plasm of the self. I quote the concluding lines of **"Tortoise Shout."**

> The cross,
> The wheel on which our silence first is broken,
> Sex, which breaks up our integrity, our single
>   inviolability, our deep silence,
> Tearing a cry from us.
>
> Sex, which breaks us into voice, sets us calling
>   across the deeps, calling, calling for the
>   complement,
> Singing and calling, and singing again, being
>   answered, having found.
>
> Torn, to become whole again, after long seeking
>   what is lost,
> The same cry from the tortoise as from Christ, the
>   Osiris-cry of abandonment,

That which is whole, torn asunder,
That which is in part, finding its whole again
    throughout the universe.[1]

Here again the burden of honesty is translated or lost in the condition of ritual, of formal or declarative prayer and mystical identification; which is indeed a natural end for emotions of which the sustaining medium is hysteria. To enforce the point, let us take **"Fish"** (the poems of the four Evangelistic Beasts would do as well), which represented for Lawrence, in the different fish he observes, the absolute, untouchable, unknowable life, "born before God was love, or life knew loving," "who lies with the waters of his silent passion, womb-element," and of whom he can write, finally:

    In the beginning
    Jesus was called The Fish . . .
    And in the end.

Per omnia saecula saeculorum. The Fish and likewise the Tortoise are acts of ceremonial adoration, in which the reader, if he is sympathetic, because of the intensity of the act, cannot help sharing. Lawrence was by consequence of the type of his insight and the kind of experience that excited him, a religious poet. His poetry is an attempt to declare and rehearse symbolically his pious recognition of the substance of life. The love of God for him was in the declaration of life in the flux of sex. Only with Lawrence the piety was tortured—the torture of incomplete affirmation. The great mystics saw no more profoundly than Lawrence through the disorder of life to their ultimate vision, but they saw within the terms of an orderly insight. In them, reason was stretched to include disorder and achieved mystery. In Lawrence, the reader is left to supply the reason and the form; for Lawrence only expresses the substance.

The affirmation to which the more important poems of Lawrence mount suffers from incompleteness for the same reasons that the lesser poems examined in the first part of this essay suffered. On the one hand he rejected the advantage of objective form for the immediate freedom of expressive form, and on the other hand he preferred the inspiration of immediate experience to the discipline of a rationally constructed imagination. He had a powerful sensibility and a profound experience, and he had the genius of insight and unequivocal honesty: he was in contact with the disorder of life. In his novels and tales the labor of creating and opposing characters, the exigencies of narrative, all the detail of execution, combined to make his works independent, controlled entities to a great extent. But in his poetry, the very intensity of his self-expression overwhelmed all other considerations, and the disorder alone prevailed.

The point at issue, and the pity of it, can be put briefly. Lawrence the poet was no more hysterical in his expressive mode than the painter Van Gogh. But where Van Gogh developed enough art to control his expression objectively, and so left us great paintings, Lawrence developed as little art as possible, and left us the ruins of

great intentions; ruins which we may admire and contemplate, but as they are ruins of a life merely, cannot restore as poetry. Art was too long for Lawrence; life too close.

NOTES

[1] May I suggest that the reader compare this passage from Lawrence with the following lines from T. S. Eliot's *Ash Wednesday* as a restorative to the sense of *controlled* hysteria. The two poems have nearly the same theme.

Lady of silences	The greater torment
Calm and distressed	Of love satisfied
Torn and most whole	End of the endless
Rose of memory	Journey to no end
Rose of forgetfulness	Conclusion of all that
Exhausted and life-giving	Is inconclusible
	Speech without word and
Worried reposeful	Word of no speech
The single Rose	Grace to the Mother
Is now the Garden	For the Garden
Where all loves end	Where all love ends.
Terminate torment	
Of love unsatisfied	

Kenneth Rexroth (essay date 1947)

SOURCE: An introduction to *D. H. Lawrence: Selected Poems,* New Directions, 1947, pp. 1-23.

[*In the following introduction to Lawrence's* Selected Poems, *Rexroth believes that, rather than being a major poet like Thomas Hardy, Lawrence was a minor prophet like William Blake and William Butler Yeats.*]

At the very beginning Lawrence belonged to a different order of being from the literary writers of his day. In 1912 he said: "I worship Christ, I worship Jehovah, I worship Pan, I worship Aphrodite. But I do not worship hands nailed and running with blood upon a cross, nor licentiousness, nor lust. I want them all, all the gods. They are all God. But I must serve in real love. If I take my whole passionate, spiritual and physical love to the woman who in turn loves me, that is how I serve God. And my hymn and my game of joy is my work. All of which I read in . . ."

Do you know what he read all that in? It makes you wince. He thought he found that in *Gregorian Poetry, 1911-1912!* In Lascelles Abercrombie, Wilfred Gibson, John Drinkwater, Rupert Brooke, John Masefield, Walter de la Mare, Gordon Bottomley! What a good man Lawrence must have been. It is easy to understand how painful it was for him to learn what evil really was. It is easy to understand why the learning killed him, slowly and terribly. But he never gave up. He was always hunting for comradeship—in the most unlikely places—Michael Arlen, Peter Warlock, Murry, Mabel Dodge. He never stopped trusting people and hoping. And he went on writing exactly the gospel he announced in 1912, right to the end.

Lawrence thought he was a Georgian, at first. There are people who will tell you that his early poetry was typical Georgian countryside poetry—*Musings in the Hedgerows,* by the Well Dressed Dormouse. It is true that early poems like **"The Wild Common," "Cherry Robbers,"** and the others, bear a certain resemblance to the best Georgian verse. They are rhymed verse in the English language on "subjects taken from nature." Some of the Georgians had a favorite literary convention. They were anti-literary. Lawrence was the real thing. His "hard" rhymes, for instance, "quick-kick, rushes-pushes, sheep dip-soft lip, gudgeon-run on." I don't imagine that when Lawrence came to "soft lip" he remembered that bees had always sipped at soft lips and that, as a representative of a new tendency it was up to him to do something about it. I think his mind just moved in regions not covered by the standard associations of standard British rhyme patterns. At the end of his life he was still talking about the old sheep dip, with its steep soft lip of turf, in the village where he was born. Why, once he even rhymed wind and thinned, in the most unaware manner imaginable. That is something that, to the best of my knowledge, has never been done before or since in the British Isles.

The hard metric, contorted and distorted, and generally banged around, doesn't sound made up, either. Compulsion neurotics like Hopkins and querulous old gentlemen like Bridges made quite an art of metrical eccentricity. You turned an iamb into a trochee here, and an anapest into a hard spondee there, and pretty soon you got something that sounded difficult and tortured and intense. I think Lawrence was simply very sensitive to quantity and to the cadenced pulses of verse. In the back of his head was a stock of sundry standard English verse patterns. He started humming a poem, hu hu hum, hum hum, hu hu hum hu, adjusted it as best might be to the remembered accentual patterns, and let it go at that. I don't think he was unconscious of the new qualities which emerged, but I don't think he went about it deliberately, either.

This verse is supposed to be like Hardy's. It is. But there is always something a little synthetic about Hardy's rugged verse. The smooth ones seem more natural, somehow. The full dress, Matthew Arnold sort of sonnet to Leslie Stephen is probably Hardy's best poem. It is a very great poem, but Arnold learned the trick of talking like a highly idealized Anglican archbishop and passed it on to Hardy. That is something nobody could imagine Lawrence ever learning, he just wasn't that kind of an animal.

Hardy could say to himself: "To-day I am going to be a Wiltshire yeoman, sitting on a fallen rock at Stonehenge, writing a poem to my girl on a piece of wrapping paper with the gnawed stub of a pencil," and he could make it very convincing. But Lawrence really was the educated son of a coal miner, sitting under a tree that had once been part of Sherwood Forest, in a village that was rapidly becoming part of a world-wide, disemboweled hell, writing hard, painful poems, to girls who carefully had been taught the art of unlove. It was all real. Love really

was a mystery at the navel of the earth, like Stonehenge. The miner really was in contact with a monstrous, seething mystery, the black sun in the earth. There is a vatic quality in Lawrence that is only in Hardy rarely, in a few poems, and in great myths like *Two on a Tower.*

Something breaks out of the Pre-Raphaelite landscape of **"Cherry Robbers."** That poem isn't like a Victorian imitation of medieval illumination at all. It is more like one of those crude Coptic illuminations, with the Christian content just a faint glaze over the black, bloody "babylonian turbulence" of the Gnostic mystery. I don't know the date of the **"Hymn to Priapus,"** it seems to lie somewhere between his mother's death and his flight with Frieda, but it is one of the Hardy kind of poems, and it is one of Lawrence's best. It resembles Hardy's "Night of the Dance.' But there is a difference. Hardy is so anxious to be common that he just avoids being commonplace. Lawrence *is* common, he doesn't have to try. He is coming home from a party, through the winter fields, thinking of his dead mother, of the girl he has just had in the barn, of his troubled love life, and suddenly Orion leans down out of the black heaven and touches him on the thigh, and the hair of his head stands up.

Hardy was a major poet. Lawrence was a minor prophet. Like Blake and Yeats, his is the greater tradition. If Hardy ever had a girl in the hay, tipsy on cider, on the night of Boxing Day, he kept quiet about it. He may have thought that it had something to do with "the stream of his life in the darkness deathward set," but he never let on, except indirectly.

Good as they are, there is an incompleteness about the early poems. They are the best poetry written in England at that time, but they are poems of hunger and frustration. Lawrence was looking for completion. He found it later, of course, in Frieda, but he hadn't found it then. The girl he called Miriam wrote a decent, conscientious contribution to his biography. She makes it only too obvious that what he was looking for was not to be found in her. And so the Miriam poems are tortured, and defeated, and lost, as though Lawrence didn't know where he was, which was literally true.

Between Miriam and Frieda lies a body of even more intense and troubled poems. Those to his mother, the dialect poems, and the poems to Helen are in this group. The 'mother' poems are amongst his best. They are invaluable as direct perspectives on an extraordinary experience.

From one point of view Lawrence is the last of a special tradition that begins with St. Augustine and passes through Pascal and Baudelaire amongst others, to end finally in himself. There is no convincing evidence for Freud's theory that the Oedipus Complex dates back to some extremely ancient crime in the history of primitive man. There is ample evidence that Western European civilization is specifically the culture of the Oedipus Complex. Before Augustine there was nothing really like it. There were forerunners and prototypes and intimations, but there wasn't the real thing. The *Confessions* introduce a new sickness of the human mind, the most horrible pandemic and the most lethal ever to afflict man. Augustine did what silly literary boys in our day boast of doing. He invented a new derangement. If you make an intense effort to clear your mind and then read Baudelaire and Catullus together, the contrast, the new thing in Baudelaire, makes you shudder. Baudelaire is struggling in a losing battle with a ghost more powerful than armies, more relentless than death. I think it is this demon which has provided the new thing in Western Man, the insane dynamic which has driven him across the earth to burn and slaughter, loot and rape.

I believe Lawrence laid that ghost, exorcised that demon, once for all, by an act of absolute spiritual transvaluation. **"Piano," "Silence," "The Bride",** and the other poems of that period, should be read with the tenth chapter of the ninth book of the *Confessions*. It is the beginning and the end. Augustine was a saint. There are acts of salvation by which man can raise himself to heaven, but, say the Japanese, a devil is substituted in his place. Lawrence drove out the devil, and the man stepped back. Or, as the Hindus say, with an act of absolute devotion from the worshipper, the goddess changes her aspect from maleficent to benign.

It is not only that Lawrence opened the gates of personal salvation for himself in the 'mother' poems. He did it in a special way, in the only way possible, by an intense realization of total reality, and by the assumption of total responsibility for the reality and for the realization. Other people have tried parts of this process, but only the whole thing works. This shows itself in these poems, in their very technique. There, for the first time, he is in full possession of his faculties. He proceeds only on the basis of the completely real, the completely motivated, step by step along the ladder of Blake's "minute particulars." Ivor Richards' *Practical Criticism* contains a symposium of his students on Lawrence's **"Piano"**. It makes one of the best introductions to Lawrence's poetry ever written. And one of the qualities of his verse that is revealed there most clearly is the uncanny, "surreal" accuracy of perception and evaluation. Objectivism is a hollow word beside this complete precision and purposiveness.

From this time on Lawrence never lost contact with the important thing, the totality in the particular, the responsibility of vision. Harrassed by sickness and betrayal, he may have faltered in fulfilling that most difficult of all the injunctions of Christ, to suffer fools gladly. He may have got out of contact with certain kinds of men at certain times. He may have become cross and irritable and sick. But he never lost sight of what really mattered: the blue vein arching over the naked foot, the voices of the fathers singing at the charivari, blending in the winter night, Lady Chatterley putting flowers in Mellers' hair.

The 'Helen' poems are strange. (See **"A Winter's Tale,"** **"Return; Kisses in the Train;" "Under the Oak,"** **"Passing Visit To Helen," "Release;" "Seven Seals,"** 8).

They all have a weird, dark atmosphere shot through with spurts of flame, a setting which remained a basic symbolic situation with Lawrence. It is the atmosphere of the pre-War I novel, young troubled-love in gaslit London—draughty, dark, and flaring, and full of mysterious movement. Probably the girl's name was not Helen. Lawrence thought of her as dim, larger than life, a demigoddess, moving through the smoke of a burning city. For certain Gnostics Helen was the name of the incarnate "female principle," the power of the will, the sheath of the sword, the sacred whore who taught men love. Helen seems to have been the midwife of Lawrence's manhood. At the end, something like her returns in the Persephone of **"Bavarian Gentians."** Re-birth. No one leaves adolescence cleanly without a foretaste of death.

Ezra Pound said that the dialect poems were the best thing Lawrence ever wrote. This is just frivolous eccentricity. But they are fine poems, and in them another figure of the myth is carefully drawn. They are poems about Lawrence's father, the coal miner who emerges nightly from the earth with the foliage of the carboniferous jungles on his white body. Lawrence's little dark men, his Gypsies, and Indians, and Hungarians, and Mexicans, and all the rest, are not dark by race, but dark with coal dust. The shadow of forests immeasurably older than man has stained their skins. Augustine was never at peace until he found his father again in the pure mental absolute of Plotinus. Lawrence found his father again in the real man, whose feet went down into the earth. In certain poems where he speaks as a fictional woman, the erotic intensity is embarrassing to those of us who still live in the twilight of the Oedipus Complex. What had been evil in the father image becomes a virtue, the source of the will; deep behind the mother image lies the germ of action, the motile flagellate travelling up the dark hot tube seeking immortality.

The boy watching the miners rise and descend in the yawning maw of the earth in Nottinghamshire grows into the man of forty watching the Indians pass in and out of a lodge where and old man is interminably chanting—there is a sense of strangeness, but no estrangement. There is no effort to violate the mystery of paternity because it is known in the blood. Lawrence knew by a sort of sensual perception that every cell of his body bore the marks of the striped Joseph's coat of the paternal sperm.

All this world of the early poems, and of the novels, *The White Peacock, The Trespasser,* the first draft of *Sons and Lovers,* is an unborn world, a cave, a womb, obscure and confused. The figures have a mythic vagueness about them. The sensual reality seems to be always struggling beneath an inhibiting surface of flesh, struggling to escape into another realm of meaning. So many of the images are drawn from birth, escape, confinement, struggle. Critics have found much of their Freudianism in the work of this period. Had they been better read they would have found Jung above all else, and certainly Rank. Lawrence had yet to read Freud or Jung and may never have heard of Rank.

Some shockingly ill-informed things have been written about Lawrence's relation to psychoanalysis. In the first place, he was not a Freudian. He seems to have read little Freud, not to have understood him any too well, and to have disliked him heartily. In the winter of 1918-1919 he read Jung, apparently for the first time, in English. Presumably this was *The Psychology of the Unconscious.* Jung was very much in the air in those days, as he is again. There was probably a great deal of amateur talk about his ideas amongst Lawrence's friends. But Lawrence does not seem to have had much more to go on, and *The Psychology of the Unconscious* is only the beginning of the system later elaborated by Jung. Nor did he ever become intimate with any of his students. Later Mabel Dodge tried to bring them together by correspondence. The story goes that Jung ignored her letters because they were written in pencil. So much for that.

Lawrence wrote quite a bit on psychoanalysis. There are the two books, *Psychoanalysis and the Unconscious,* a somewhat sketchy popularization of some of Jung's basic concepts, and *Fantasia of the Unconscious,* of which, more in a moment. And then there are the reviews of Trigant Burrow's book, and miscellaneous remarks scattered through correspondence and reviews. This is all of the greatest importance to the understanding of Lawrence.

Fantasia of the Unconscious is an extraordinary book. It is foully written, unquestionably Lawrence's worst writing, but it is certainly a landmark in the history of psychoanalysis. It is an attempt to combine the empirical neurology of Kundalini Yoga with his own interpretation of Jung's psychology and with a theory of sexuality which may be either his own or derived from popular, occultist expositions of certain Gnostic sects and rumors of the practices of Shakti-Yoga. When it appeared, it must have seemed like pure fantasy of the Lost Atlantis variety. Jung's *Secret of the Golden Flower,* and his studies of "spiritual alchemy" lay in the future. The "psychology of the autonomic system" was unheard of. It is all there, in Lawrence's inspired guesses. The white race is going mad, but it is the autonomic nervous system which is out of kilter; what goes on in the head is secondary—and the autonomic nervous system is, as a whole, the organ of communion.

To return to the poems. There is an hallucinatory quality in the images of the poems which precede Frieda which it is interesting to compare with the induced hallucination of H.D. The conflict in H.D. is hidden in herself. It is still there to this day, although her latest prose work has been the journal of a Freudian analysis. Her images are purified of conflict, then the intensity which has been distilled from the sublimation of conflict is applied from the outside. ("Your poetry is not pure, eternal, sublimated," she told Lawrence). What results is a puzzling hallucination of fact, a contentless mood which seems to reflect something tremendously important but whose mystery always retreats before analysis.

Lawrence's early poems are poems of conflict. The images are always polarized. Antagonisms struggle through the texture. But the struggle is real. The antagonisms are struggling towards the light. The conflict yields to insight, if not to analysis. It is like the propadeutic symbolism of the dream, as contrasted to the trackless labyrinths of falsification which form the patterns of most waking lives. The hallucination is real, the vision of the interior, personal oracle. Its utterance has meaning, more meaning than ordinary waking reality because the subjective is seen in the objective, emerging from it, the dream from the reality—not dislocated or applied from outside the context.

The poems of *Look We Have Come Through* fall into three groups. First there are the structurally more conventional pieces like "Moonrise," which sounds a little like Masefield's sonnets though it is incomparably finer, and the **"Hymn to Priapus,"** and the others—they are all probably earlier and have already been discussed. Second, there are the poems of the Rhine Journey, **"December Night," "New Year's Eve," "Coming Awake," "History;"** erotic epigrams, intense as Meleager, more wise than Paul the Silentiary. Lawrence was still a young man, and had many great poems to write—but put these beside the few poets who have survived from that day, Sturge Moore, Monro, De La Mare, they look like pygmies. Only Yeats stands up against Lawrence. And last, there are the Whitmanic free verse manifestoes, "explaining" marriage to a people who had forgotten what it was.

With Frieda the sleeper wakes, the man walks free, the "child" of the alchemists is born. Reality is totally valued, and passes beyond the possibility of hallucination. The clarity of purposively realized objectivity is the most supernatural of all visions. Bad poetry always suffers from the same defects: synthetic hallucination and artifice. Invention is not poetry. Invention is defense, the projection of psuedopods out of the ego to ward off the 'other.' Poetry is vision, the pure act of sensual communion and contemplation.

That is why the poems of Lawrence and Frieda on their Rhine Journey are such great poetry. That is why they are also the greatest imagist poems ever written. Reality streams through the body of Frieda, through everything she touches, every place she steps, valued absolutely, totally, beyond time and place, in the minute particular. The swinging of her breasts as she stoops in the bath, the roses, the deer, the harvesters, the hissing of the glacier water in the steep river—everything stands out lit by a light not of this earth and at the same time completely of this earth, the light of the Holy Sacrament of Marriage, whose source is the wedded body of the bride.

The accuracy of Lawrence's observation haunts the mind permanently. I have never stood beside a glacier river, at just that relative elevation, and just that pitch, with just that depth of swift water moving over a cobbled bed, without hearing again the specific hiss of Lawrence's Isar. These poems may not be sublimated (whatever Y.M.C.A. evasion that may refer to) but they are certainly pure and eternal.

Again, it is fruitful to compare the Rhine Journey poems with the only other poems of our time which resemble them much, Ford Madox Ford's *Buckshee*. Ford was writing about something very akin to what Lawrence was, about an aspect of marriage. But he was writing about its impossibility, about how life had bled away its possibility from both him and his girl, and how they had taken, in middle age and in the long Mediterranean drouth, the next best thing—intense erotic friendship. And about how, every once in a while, marriage comes and looks in at the window. The contrast with Lawrence and Frieda, sinking into the twilight in the fuming marsh by the Isar, "where the snake disposes," is pathetic past words.

Ford's *L'Oubli—Temps de Secheresse* and Lawrence's **"River Roses"** and **"Quite Forsaken"** are things of a kind and the best of their kind, but like the north and south poles, there is all the difference in the world between them. There is more communion in Frieda's temporary absence than in the closest possible kiss "under the catalpa tree, where the strange birds, driven north by the drouth, cry with their human voices." "Singular birds, with their portentuous, singular flight and human voices" says Ford. This is the Persephone of **"Bavarian Gentians"** and the Orphic birds which flutter around the dying who are withdrawing themselves, corpuscle by corpuscle, from communion. Lawrence would come there one day, with the dark blue flowers on the medicine table and Frieda sleeping in a chair beside him, but he was on the other side of the universe then—the early summer of 1912, in the Isartal, the snow leaving the mountains.

After the Rhine Journey come the poems of struggle for a living adjustment. The ceremonial glory of the sacrament passes from the forefront of consciousness and the period of adjustment to the background of life begins. Every detail of life must be transformed by marriage. This means creative conflict on the most important level.

Sacramental communion is bound by time. Mass does not last forever. Eventually the communicant must leave the altar and digest the wafer, the Body and Blood must enter his own flesh as it moves through the world and struggles with the devil. The problem lies in the sympathetic nervous system, says Lawrence. And it is not easy for two members of a deranged race, in the Twentieth Century, to learn again how to make those webs mesh as they should.

Some of these poems are, in a sense, Frieda's—records of her own interior conquest. It is amazing how much they accomplished, these two. Today, revisiting this battlefield between love and hate that is so carefully mapped in certain of the poems, it is like Gettysburg, a sleepy, pastoral landscape dotted with monuments and graves. Only maimed women and frightened men are Suffragettes anymore. Hedda Gabbler is dead, or lurking in the suburbs. We should be grateful to Frieda. It was she who gave the dragon its death blow, and the Animus no longer prowls the polls and bedrooms, seeking whom it may devour.

The Whitmanic poems seem to owe a good deal to *Children of Adam and Calamus*. They look like Whitman on the page. But if read aloud with any sort of ear, they don't sound much like him. Whitman flourished in the oratorical context of Nineteenth Century America. He isn't rhetorical in the invidious sense, that is, there is nothing covert or coercive about him. He says what he means, but he says it in the language of that lost art of elocution so popular in his day. There is little of this in Lawrence. At this period his long-lined free verse is derived almost entirely from the poetry of the Bible, the Psalms, the song of Deborah, the song of Hezekiah, of Moses, the Benedicite, the Magnificat, the Nunc Dimitus. All the devices of Hebrew poetry are there, and in addition, the peculiar, very civilized, self-conscious "sympathetic" poetry of St. Luke—those poems which have made his the "women's Gospel," and which all good Englishmen must learn in childhood as part of the Morning and Evening Prayer of the Church.

In the volume ***Look We Have Come Through*** Lawrence was just beginning to learn to write free verse. I don't think some of the poems are completely successful. They are diffuse and long winded. He tries to say too much, and all at the same pitch of intensity; there are no crises, no points of reference. On the whole the most successful is **"New Heaven and Earth"**. It may not be a perfect object of art but it is a profound exhortation.

Beyond Holy Matrimony lies the newly valued world of birds, beasts, and flowers—a sacramentalized, objective world. "Look, we have come through"—to a transformed world, with a glory around it everywhere like ground lightning. The poems of ***Birds Beasts, and Flowers*** have the same supernatural luster that shines through the figures of men and animals and things, busy being part of a new redeemed world, as they are found carved around the mandala of the Blessed Virgin above some cathedral door or on some rose window.

Birds, Beasts, and Flowers is the mature Lawrence, in complete control of his medium, or completely controlled by his demon. He never has any trouble. He can say exactly what he wants to say. Except for the death poems, he would never write better. (And too, after this, he would never be well again.) He seems to have lived in a state of total realization—the will and its power, positive and negative, at maximum charge, and all the universe streaming between them glowing and transformed. The work of art grows in that electric field, is a "function" of it. It is the act of devotion in the worshipper that forces the god to occupy the statue. It is the act of devotion in the sculptor that forces the god to occupy the stone which the artist then pares to his invisible limbs, tailors like cloth. It is never theology in the first; it is never aesthetics or any teachable craft in the second. The craft is the vision and the vision is the craft.

Good cadenced verse is the most difficult of all to write. Any falsity, any pose, any corruption, any ineptitude, any vulgarity, shows up immediately. In this it is like abstract painting. A painting by Mondrian may look impersonal enough to be reduced to code and sent by telegraph. Maybe. But it offers no refuge, no garment, no mask, no ambush, for the person. The painter must stand there, naked, as Adam under the eye of God. Only very great or very trivial personalities dare expose themselves so.

Think of a few typical writers of cadenced verse, Whitman, Sandburg, Wallace Gould, F. M. Ford, F. S. Flint, Aldington, Lola Ridge, and James Oppenheim. (H.D.'s verse is primarily a counterpointing of accentual and quantitative rhythms in patterns of Greek derivation. Pound's verse is Latin in reference, and usually quantitative.) How the faults stand out! Every little weakness is revealed with glaring cruelty. Whitman's tiresome posturing, Sandburg's mawkishness, Aldington's erotic sentimentality, the over-reaching ambition of Lola Ridge and Oppenheim—what a lot of sore thumbs standing out! Yet in many ways these are good poets, and Whitman is a very great one.

Gould, Flint and Ford were never dishonest, never over-reached themselves, did their best to say what they meant and no more, never bargained with art. "The sentimentalist," said Daedalus, "is he who would enjoy, without incurring the immense debtorship for a thing done." They are not prophets, but they are good poets because they rendered a strict accounting with their own souls.

Sentimentality is spiritual realization on the installment plan. Socially viable patterns, like conventional verse, are a sort of underwriting or amortization of the weaknesses of the individual. This is the kernel of sense in the hollow snobbery of Valéry. The sonnet or quatrain are like the national debt, devices for postponing the day of reckoning indefinitely. All artistic conventions are a method of spiritual deficit-financing. If they were abandoned, the entire credit structure of Poets, Ltd. would be thrown into hopeless confusion. It is just as well that the professors have led the young, in my lifetime, away from free verse to something that can be taught. No one could be taught to be Lawrence, but in a world where the led lead the leaders, those who might pretend to do so are sure to be confidence men.

Lawrence's free verse in *Birds, Beasts, and Flowers* is amongst the small best ever written. It can be analysed, but the paradigms produced by the analysis are worthless. It cannot be explained away, demonstrated in a mathematical sense. Neither, certainly, can any other great poetry; but at least a convincing illusion can be created, and the young can be provided with something to practice. A poem like **"Bat"** or the **"Lion of St. Mark,"** moves with a stately, gripping sonority through the most complex symphonic evolutions. The music is a pattern of vibration caught from the resonant tone of Lawrence himself. The concerto is not on the page, little spots with flags and tails on a stave, but the living thing, evolving from the flesh of the virtuoso. It is like Gregorian chant or Hindu music, one thing when sung at Solesmes, or in the ruins of Konarak, another when

"rendered" by the Progressive Choral Group or at a concert of the Vedanta Society of Los Angeles.

Again, the faults of *Birds, Beasts, and Flowers* are the excess of virtue. Like anyone who knows he has something intensely important to say, Lawrence found it hard to keep from being long winded. I think a good deal of his over-expansiveness and repetition is due to his methods of composition.

Some poets meditate in stillness and inactivity, as far away as possible from the creative act. We know that Baudelaire and T. S. Eliot, by their own testimony, spent long periods of time quiescent, inert as artists, turning over and over the substance of vision within themselves. Sometimes, as in Baudelaire, this process is extremely painful, a true desert of the soul. Months went by in which the paper and pen were red hot, it was impossible for him to read, his whole personality seemed engulfed in a burning neurasthenia. And then there would come a period of peace, and slowly growing exhaltation, and finally the creative act, almost sonambulistic in its completion. Actual composition by this sort of personality tends to be rare, and usually as perfect as talent permits.

Lawrence meditated pen in hand. His contemplation was always active, flowing out in a continuous stream of creativity which he seemed to have been able to open practically every day. He seldom reversed himself, seldom went back to re-work the same manuscript. Instead, he would lay aside a work that dissatisfied him and re-write it all from the beginning. In his poetry he would move about a theme, enveloping it in constantly growing spheres of significance. It is the old antithesis: centrifugal versus centripetal, Parmenides versus Heraclitus. He kept several manuscript books of his verse and whenever he wanted to publish a collection he would go through them and pick out a poem here and there, the ones he considered had best handled their themes. Behind each poem was usually a group of others devoted to the same material. His selection was always personal, and sometimes it was not very "artistic." *Nettles,* for instance, is a selection of what are, by any standard, the poorer poems of the collections of epigrams printed in *Last Poems.*

There are those who think these epigrams, the ones in *Pansies,* and those in *Last Poems,* aren't art. This opinion is the product of a singular provincialism. It is true that, due to the reasons just mentioned, they aren't all successful, but they belong to a tradition, are members of a species, which has produced some of the greatest poetry. Epigram or maxim, Martial or La Rochefoucauld, the foundations of this tradition are far more stable than those of the neo-metaphysical poetry produced, with seven ambiguities carefully inserted in every line, by unhappy dons between the wars.

Any bright young man can be taught to be artful. It is impossible to teach taste, but you can teach most anybody caution. It is always the lesser artists who are artful, they must learn their trade by rote. They must be careful never to make a false step, never to speak out of a carefully synthesized character. The greatest poetry is nobly dishevelled. At least, it never shows the scars of taking care. "Would he had blotted a thousand lines," said Ben Jonson of Shakespeare. Which thousand? Lawrence was always mislaying those manuscript books of poetry and writing around the world for them, just as Cézanne left his paintings in the fields. Not for any stupid reason—that they were not Perfect Works of Art—but simply because he forgot.

Eliot, (who does not write that way), writing of Pound's epigrams, points out that the major poet, unlike the minor, is always writing about everything imaginable, and so, is in good form for the great poem when it comes. Practice makes perfect, and those who wait for the perfect poem before putting pen to paper may wait mute forever. I suppose it is the absolutism which has swept over popular taste in the wake of Cubism which has encouraged the ignorant to expect a canzone of Dante's in each issue of their favorite little magazine, a School of Athens in every WPA mural. This is just greediness, like children who want it to be Christmas every day. And it produces an empty, pretentious, greedy art. Meanwhile, Pound's *Les Millwin,* and Lawrence's **"Willy Wet-Legs"** quietly preëmpt immortality, a state of being only rarely grandiose.

As far as I know the poems in the novel **The Plumed Serpent** (see pages 122-130) have never been printed separately. This book is one of the most important (he thought it the most important) Lawrence ever wrote. It has brought forth all sorts of pointless debate. People are always saying: "Well, I have lived in Mexico for years and it *simply* isn't like that." Lawrence was not an idiot. He knew it wasn't. And in the first chapter he gave a very accurate and pitiful picture of the 'real' Mexico, sterile, subcolonial, brutal, with the old gods gone, and the church gone, and the revolution a swindle, and nothing left but a squalid imitation of Ashtabula, Ohio. And he knew the other side too, the pasty frigid nymphomaniacs, the deranged women of Europe and America, who consider themselves disciples of Lawrence and prowl the earth seeking Dark Gods to take to bed. He wrote a story which should have destroyed them forever—**"None of That."** It should be read with **The Plumed Serpent.**

Every year there is less, but in Lawrence's day there was still something, of the primeval Mexico—at the great feast in Oaxaca, in the life of the peasants in the remote villages, in the Indian communities in the back country. Lawrence did not make any very definite contact with the ancient Mexico but he could see and sense it, and he was fresh from a much less-touched primitive world—that of the Navaho and Pueblo Indians of the Southwest. His materials were not as abundant as they might have been but they were enough to build a book of ritual, of the possible that would never be, of potentialities that would never emerge. It is a book of ceremonial prophecy, but prophecy uttered in the foreknowledge it would never be fulfilled.

The re-awakening of mystery, the revival of the old Aztec religion, the political "Indianism"—even if it all came

true, one knows it would be a fraud, a politician's device, as Indianism is in Latin America today. Lawrence knew that, of course, and so the book is dogged with tragedy. One constantly expects the characters to go out in a blazing Götterdämmerung in some dispute with the police, like a gangster movie. They don't, but maybe it would have been better if they had, for eventually they tire; they seem to become secretly aware that all this gorgeous parading around in primitive millinery, this Mystery, and Fire, and Blood, and Darkness, has been thought up. There is something Western European, British Museum, about it. The protagonist, Kate, submits to her lover's insistent Mystery, but rather out of ennui and loathing of Europe than out of any conviction, and one feels that the book could have no sequel, or only a sequel of disintegration, like **Women in Love.**

Still, in the middle of the book, before the fervor dies out, Lawrence wrote as nearly as he could what be believed should be. If the religion of Cipriano and Ramon is taken as an otherworldly system of values, it is profound and true, and, due to the freshness of its symbols, tremendously exciting. Also, it differs very little from any other religion that has maintained its contacts with its sources. Ramon and Cipriano short-circuit themselves where Christianity was short-circuited by Constantine, in the desire to have both worlds, to found a political religion—a Church. That, if any, is the "message" of the book.

The mystery survives in the poems, just as the sacraments survived Constantine. They are not the greatest poems Lawrence ever wrote, but they are amongst the most explicit. This is Lawrence's religion. Wherever he found it he is now in complete possession of a kind of orthodoxy, the orthodoxy of the heterodox—the symbolic world of the Gnostics, the Occultists, Tantrism, Jung. In a sense they are failures, these poems, in the way that the Indian songs published by the United States Bureau of Ethnology are not failures. But, again, that is the message of the book. Finally you discover that you cannot make up paganism. What you make up is a cult. There is nothing primitive about Gnosticism, anymore than there is anything primitive about Theosophy. It is the creation of over-civilized Hellenistic intellectuals. Tantrism too grew up in India, in Buddhism and Hinduism, when civilization was exhausting itself. Jung comes, with Lawrence, at the end of the career of Western European Man. Lawrence, after all, was a contemporary of Niels Bohr and Picasso. And so his poems are mystical poems—and the Aztecs were not mystics, they were just Aztecs. This doesn't invalidate the poems. They have very little to do with ancient or modern Mexico but they do express, very well, the personal religion of D. H. Lawrence. They may be full of "occult lore," but behind the machinery is an intense, direct, personal, mystical apprehension of reality.

In the last hours Lawrence seems to have lived in a state of suspended animation, removed from the earth, floating, transfigured by the onset of death. Poems like **"Andraitix, Pomegranate Flowers"** have an abstracted, disinterested intensity, as though they were written by a being from another planet. Others are short mystical apothegms. There is no millinery anymore, no occultism, they differ only in their modern idiom from any and all of the great mystics. And finally there are the two death poems, **"Bavarian Gentians,"** and **"The Ship of Death"**. Each was written over several times. There exists a variant which can be taken as a final, or pre-final, version of **"Bavarian Gentians,"** but both are clusters of poems rather than finished products.

"The Ship of Death" material alone would make a small book of meditations, a contemporary *Holy Dying*. It is curious to think that once such a book would have been a favorite gift for the hopelessly ill. Today people die in hospitals, badgered by nurses, stupefied with barbiturates. This is not an age in which a "good death" is a desired end of life.

All men have to die, and one would think a sane man would want to take that fact into account, at least a little. But our whole civilization is a conspiracy to pretend that it isn't going to happen—and this, in an age when death has become more horrible, more senseless, less at the will of the individual than ever before. Modern man is terribly afraid of sex, of pain of evil, of death. Today childbirth, the ultimate orgiastic experience, has been reduced to a meaningless dream; dentists insist on injecting novocaine before they clean your teeth, the agonies of life have retreated to the source of life. Men and women torture each other to death in the bedroom, just as the dying dinosaurs gnawed each other as they copulated in the chilling marshes. Anything but the facts of life. Today you can take a doctor's degree in medicine or engineering and never learn how to have intercourse with a woman or repair a car. Human self-alienation, Marx called it. He said that was all that was really wrong with capitalism. "Let us live and lie reclined" in a jet-propelled, streamlined, air-cooled, lucite incubator. When we show signs of waking, another cocktail instead of the Wine of God. When we try to break out, flagellation instead of Holy Matrimony, psychoanalysis instead of Penance. When the machinery runs down, morphine for Extreme Unction.

In a world where death had become a nasty, pervasive secret like defecation or masturbation, Lawrence re-instated it in all its grandeur—the oldest and most powerful of the gods. **"The Ship of Death"** poems have an exhaltation, a nobility, a steadiness, an insouciance, which is not only not of this time but which is rare in any time. It doesn't matter who: Jeremy Taylor, the Orphic Hymns, the ancient Egyptians—nobody said it better. And there is one aspect of the **"Ship of Death"** which is unique. Lawrence did not try to mislead himself with false promises, imaginary guarantees. Death is the absolute, unbreakable mystery. Communion and oblivion, sex and death, the mystery can be revealed—but it can be revealed only as totally inexplicable. Lawrence never succumbed to the temptation to try to do more. He succeeded in what he did do.

Charles I. Glicksberg (essay date 1948)

SOURCE: "The Poetry of D. H. Lawrence," in *The New Mexico Quarterly Review,* Vol. 14, March 13, 1948, pp. 289-303.

[*In the following essay, Glicksberg examines Lawrence's poetry to support his thesis that Lawrence was engaged in creating his own religion that eschewed science and materialism.*]

There is no contradiction in the fact that Lawrence's ideas on human nature and society are muddled while his poetry is flame-like, instinct with beauty organically felt and sensuously communicated. When he trusted his feelings he was on firm ground; when his powerful sensibility ruled him he could not go wrong. Each impression leaped forth like a radiant beam of sunlight; form and substance fused in a lyrical moment of incandescent, imaginative perception. His poems are vascular, charged with a living bloodstream. They could no more be composed according to rule than a flower can be prepared synthetically in a crucible. The art seems as instinctive as breathing, as natural as the beating of the heart.

Unfortunately, there was a raging conflict within him between heart and head, mind and body, thalamus and cortex, instinct and intelligence. In an intensely personal writer like Lawrence, this conflict was bound to make itself felt and inhibit the disciplined mastery of his material. His great strength was also his weakness. In his tirades against the desiccated intellect and the Dead Sea fruits of consciousness, in his embittered, chuckle-headed fight against science and industrialism, he was guilty of childish petulance—the eccentric individualism of one who found it hard to remain a poet in an uncongenial and oppressive environment. The world of the twentieth century did not suit him in the least: the regimentation of life, the hideously ugly, prison-like factories, the terrible gregariousness and mechanization of people in large cities, the crippling loss of spontaneity; therefore he vented his rage and spleen. He would throw this rotten civilization on the rubbish heap and start anew. Salvation lay in returning to the innocence and instinctive joyousness of primitive man who felt an organic connection with earth and sun. Science was the great enemy to be destroyed, since it prevented the flowering of this organic consciousness.

Lawrence's individuality is unmistakably present in his first four volumes of poetry, *Love Poems and Others, Amores, New Poems,* and *Bays,* though as he matures, his poetic work betrays a steady growth in expressive power and in command of imagery and rhythm. These early poems, like his later productions, are intensely personal, revelatory of the conflicts through which Lawrence was passing at the time. He strips himself naked as he reveals the tumult of his passion, his fierce struggle for independence, but the conflict is not resolved. The lyric, **"Monologue of a Mother,"** which thematically is not unlike the problem elaborated in *Sons* *and Lovers,* is nakedly subjective in tone and content. Lawrence understands imaginatively what a mother must feel whose son has grown a stranger to her, now that he has broken out of the maternal cage, and he records with painful honesty what must have gone on in the mind and heart of his mother:

> I must look away from him, for my faded eyes
> Like a cringing dog at his heels offend him now,
> Like a toothless hound pursuing him with my will;
> Till he chafes at my crouching persistence, and a
>   sharp spark flies
>
> In my soul from under sudden frown of his brow
> As he blenches and turns away, and my heart
>   stands still.

Here an emotional involvement, though poignantly rendered, has not been transmuted into the universal. As Lawrence admits in a note, many of his poems are so personal that despite their fragmentariness they constitute the story of his inner life, though a number of them are obviously imaginative in content and therefore timeless. Through the itinerary of his lyrics we are enabled to follow Lawrence as he leaves Nottingham and goes off to teach school in the fringes of South London—his feeling of loneliness and distress, his attachment to Helen, his experiences while in London, the death of his mother, his reactions to World War I, his leaving England, his aspirations and loves. Some of these poems had to be rewritten a good deal, since at the time he was still afraid of his demon. "A young man," he says, "is afraid of his demon and puts his hand over the demon's mouth sometimes and speaks for him. And the things the young man says are very rarely poetry."

Even in the early poems there is the same sensuous awareness, the same amazing descriptive power as in his later work, but not yet fully mastered, integrated with the whole man. He is still experimenting, searching within for his real self, groping for poignant directness and inevitability of expression. But the lyrical gift, plangent and earth-nurtured, is abundantly present. Though there is a lingering trace of youthful sentimentality and uncurbed wonder, the freedom with which the verse forms are handled shows that the creative demon is breaking out of harness. Lawrence recalls with anguish memories of violent quarrels between his parents, as in **"Discord in Childhood,"** with its sustained mood and image serving as objective correlative of the emotion communicated:

> Outside the house an ash-tree hung its terrible whips,
> And at night when the wind rose, the lash of the tree
> Shrieked and slashed the wind, as a ship's
> Weird rigging in a storm shrieks hideously.
>
> Within the house two voices arose, a slender lash
> Whistling she-delirious rage, and the dreadful sound
> Of a male thong booming and bruising, until it has
>   drowned
> The other voice in silence of blood, 'neath the
>   noise of the ash.

In addition to these recollections of cruelty and pain, there are lyrics dealing with lovers' quarrels, misunderstandings, the wisdom that the body of woman communicates. There is, above all, the internal conflict between virginity and animal passion, the passion insurgent, not to be resisted, flaring up from the abysmal depths. Also of interest are his vibrant lyrics about his experiences as a teacher and his poems grappling with the baffling mystery of death, the end of consciousness as well as the bewilderment and pain of life. **"The Best of School"** gives us this vivid picture:

> The blinds are drawn because of the sun,
> And the boys and the room in a colourless gloom
> Of underwater float: bright ripples run
> Across the walls as the blinds are blown
> To let the sunlight in; and I,
> As I sit on the shores of the class, alone,
> Watch the boys in their summer blouses
> As they write, their round heads busily bowed:
> And one after another rouses
> Its face to look at me,
> To ponder very quietly,
> As seeing, he does not see.

And in **"Piccadilly Circus at Night,"** a poem concerned with street-walkers, we get this quatrain:

> All the birds are folded in a silent ball of sleep,
>   All the flowers are faded from the asphalt isle
>   in the sea.
> Only we hard-faced creatures go round and round,
>   and keep
>   The shores of this innermost ocean alive and
>   illusory.

Chiefly, these are lyrics of awareness and awakening, without intellectual conclusions—the quick of experience transmuted into singing words and shining images.

What is striking even in his early poetry is the impress of a powerful personality, eager for freedom, for the challenge of a larger life, for fulfillment. It is still groping for a sense of direction, waiting to be born in its own image, but the power and passion is there. The love poems are filled with the lacerating complexity of passion which Lawrence described in *The Rainbow, Women in Love,* and *Aaron's Rod*—the barbed hatred, the fierce anger, the dialectical play of attraction and repulsion. Each lyric is a kindling spark, the lines flowing with compelling naturalness, born as they are of the fire and heat of the moment. Lawrence knows that "The world within worlds is a womb," from which everything issues, the creative flame suffusing mortal flesh, giving and taking the incarnate seed of life—life which is eternal creation. The truth of love cannot be faked. In the root of his being, in the nether darkness of his soul, he can tell when he is not meant for a woman nor she for him. All this cannot be analyzed or known; it simply *is.* In **"These Clever Women,"** he strikes the note that was later to become so obsessive: his distrust and detestation of those women who reason and dissect, ask probing questions, talk without end, when the true answer lies in intuitive surrender of body, the sensual response to the elemental mating call.

In *Look! We Have Come Through!* (the story of his love for Frieda, the woman who helped to free him from his mother, and his struggle to hold her love), Lawrence at last finds himself, hailing his deliverance from the cell of the old isolated self. Love is fruition and fulfillment. No more is needed, and yet—a characteristic Laurentian theme—how they suffer in spite of this! The fundamental conflict springs from Frieda's attachment to her children by a former marriage; motherhood is a spear of separation. In **"Both Sides of the Medal,"** Lawrence gives expression to the cruel, inescapable polarity of love. Finally they come through, achieve communion of body and spirit, the sacramental oneness. Hate and love are fused in a new consummating synthesis. There is the intimately revealing **"Song of a Man Who Has Come Through,"** with its jubilant first lines:

> Not I, but the wind that blows through me!
> A fine wind is blowing the new direction of Time.

Touching the body of the woman he loves, he touches the unknown, that which is not the eternal, oppressive I, and this is a "mystery beyond knowledge or endurance." This is the heaven that men seek—to cease to know, to surpass the self.

Few poets have stated with such piercing insight and vehemence the sickness that preoccupation with subjectivity breeds, the taint and blight of a self that pervades all and identifies itself with all: fields, flowers, government, nations, war, destructiveness, death. This hypertrophied ego was a horror, and Lawrence could not bear it. Then came the resurrection: out of his own ashes consumed in the fire of love rose the new and splendid phoenix. Now he can experience a new incarnation, transcend the sickly, fearful self. It was the flesh of his wife that carried him over to the new world of freedom. It is woman who has given him courage, strength, life, peace.

Freedom for man is bound up with freedom from the ego-bound soul rooted in mental consciousness. Men must sink their roots into the earth again. Beneath the superficial layers of the self slumbers a great desire for elemental passions, for all of life and experience. Over and over again Lawrence preaches the same impassioned theme: the need for transcending the limitations of the ego, for escaping from the cage of the self and experiencing the freshets of a new life. This repudiation of a restrictive, life-denying individualism (which he personally never achieved) is bound up with his attack on our artificial, commercialized civilization. The root of our present evil, as he sees it, is that we buy and sell, that we assume everything—including human beings—can be bought and sold on the market. What we want, he cries out, is a communion based not on wages or profits but on a religion of life.

This is the leitmotif that runs through his poetry. In **"Money Madness"** he charges that money is our collective madness, our doom. Therefore he would excise this perverted instinct from the brain and the blood. Society, he insists, must be established upon a different principle: "the courage of mutual trust," "the modesty of simple living," with house and food and animal comfort free to all. The only thing worth fighting for is the oneness of the self, inward peace, and that battle never ends.

Lawrence derives his patent of nobility, his true golden income, from the sun, from the core of the atom. His intuitive perceptions reach beyond conceptual limits. This earth-nurtured consciousness is poles removed from the sickly cerebral emotions people pretend to have in their minds. It is because people accept lies that they become emotionally stunted, incapable of distilling the precious essence of experience. Even if one feels nothing but frankly acknowledges his nothingness, there is still hope for him if he allows the potentialities to grow within him. These periods of lying fallow are creative pauses in which immense evolutionary changes are taking place. Like a modern Jeremiah, Lawrence warns us of the impending doom: how the house of civilization will come toppling down.

> At the core of space the final knell
> of our era has struck, and it chimes
> in terrible rippling circles between the stars.

There is no averting this cataclysmic doom. The flesh must be resurrected in the new day which will mark the passing of the flesh-trammeled, ego-enslaved selves. The poem, **"Nemesis,"** sums up his philosophy and his faith:

> The Nemesis that awaits our civilization
> is social insanity
> which in the end is always homicidal.
>
> Sanity means the wholeness of the consciousness.
> And our society is only part conscious, like an idiot.
>
> If we do not rapidly open all the doors of
>   consciousness
> and freshen the putrid little space in which we are
>   cribbed
> the sky-blue walls of our unventilated heaven
> will be bright red with blood.

Lawrence sees the hopelessness of the situation, the slavery of the industrialized masses, millions of his fellow-men crushed by the iron of the machine. Modern man is the machine incarnate. But Lawrence hopes for amelioration once men are filled with disillusion and abandon the drugged dream of brotherhood and humanitarian progress. Then the individual, alone with himself, no longer acknowledges the power of masses and classes, which are spawned by the machine. This enslavement to the machine breeds not the greatness of love but a grinding, nihilistic hate, a democracy of festering hate. Only the pristine men, looking straight into the eyes of the unknown gods, can save these twentieth-century robots from disintegrating.

"Democracy Is Service," sets forth Lawrence's conception of democracy; it is not the service of the mob, but the mob worshiping those few whose faces gleam with godliness. That is, man must not look to man for inspiration and guidance, only to the gods.

> Democracy is service, but not the service of demos.
> Democracy is demos serving life
> and demos serves life as it gleams on the face of
>   the few,
> and the few look into the eyes of the gods, and
>   serve the sheer gods.

Though the gods are nameless they are everywhere, and the experience of them is real. If one worships these gods—the born leaders of the earth, the natural aristocrats of the spirit—he does away with false Whitmanesque sympathy and false, indiscriminate humanitarian love. Truth is to be felt in all the senses, otherwise it does not exist. The injunction to love our neighbors is a great lie. Love cannot be coerced. It is when the blood is kindled that one is most alive; then the god flows through the veins: one acts instinctively, in tune with the primal energy of the cosmos.

Hence, a plague on both the revolutionary and the bourgeoisie. The only way to settle the question of property is to ignore it. The lovers of life, united by their indifference to property and money, must band together and open their consciousness to the deep, mysterious tides of life from which they are now cut off. Lawrence asserts that man must cease to know himself mentally, must give up knowledge and surrender to touch, the mystery of wonder. Thought is not a dialectical play of ideas but "the welling up of unknown life into consciousness." As he declares in **"Terra Incognita,"**

> There are vast realms of consciousness still
>   undreamed of
> vast ranges of experience, like the humming of
>   unseen harps,
> we know nothing of, within us.
>
> Oh when man escaped from the barbed-wire
>   entanglement
> of his own ideas and his own mechanical devices
> there is a marvellous rich world of contact and
>   sheer fluid beauty
> and fearless face-to-face awareness of now-naked
>   life.

The volume *Pansies* expresses intense disgust as well as a throbbing sensibility. If he hates the mercenary human animal, he has a plasmic awareness of the instinctive rightness of animals who trust their native impulses. Each of these poems is not only a pulse of thought but a vivid, self-sustaining image. Subject and object are brought together in flame-like oneness. In **"Wealth"** he declares:

> Peace I have from the core of the atom, from the
>   core of space,
> and grace, if I don't lose it, from the same place.
> and I look shabby, yet my roots go beyond my
>   knowing,
> deep beyond the world of man,

> And where my little leaves flutter highest
> there are no people, nor will ever be.

Beholding the new moon, a wave bursting on a rock, Lawrence becomes that white sibilant spray, quivers with its orgiastic rage, its beauty of violent frustration, and is diffused with the pearl-like pallor of moonlight. The secret of life is still touch, and it is the measure of our decadence today that we cannot bear touch, that we have become cerebrated, cut off from the primal sources of life. Touch comes slowly, especially when the mind is asleep and the blood can express its instinctive sympathy and longing. Touch is of the blood. It is best to leave sex strictly alone so that it may function spontaneously. "For while we have sex in our mind, we truly have none in our body."

There is a striking pattern of consistency in this preachment: an emergent philosophy of the unconscious, a religion of the instincts. Lawrence's feelings about sex are closely tied up with his views on consciousness, his opposition to the domination of the tainted, egocentric, possessive mind. The absolutism of human consciousness, the triumph of the cerebrated ego, must be ended once for all. Passionately Lawrence exalts intuitive knowing, the knowledge of the self and its mortality that the mind can never fathom, for it has only one mode of knowing. It sees in daylight but it is blind in the infinite dark; whereas the blood, forever dark, is at home in darkness. It knows "religiously," instinctively. "Only that exists which exists dynamically and unmentalised in my blood." Lawrence revises the philosophical epigram of Descartes to read: Man is; he does not think he is. What man needs is to re-establish communion with the dark gods, to yield to the influence of the moon, to release the dark ocean within him and its sea-beats of brightness and anger. Man must dive down and be lost—and thus be saved—in the fathomlessly deep currents of the creative unconscious.

When Lawrence, in *Apocalypse,* as in his poetry, writes of establishing communion with the primitive gods, getting in vital touch with the cosmos, letting the sun and moon have their way with him, the reader who depends primarily on conceptual understanding must think him utterly mad. This is precious mystical nonsense parading as lyrical inspiration, but not so! The lyrical genius of the man confounds us, overcomes temporarily the resistance of our discursive skeptical intelligence. His poetry, in *Birds, Beasts and Flowers,* betrays a quivering, clairvoyant sensibility able sensuously to project itself into the life of bird and beast and flower. It is even more passionately sensuous than the God-haunted, sense-intoxicated lyrics of Gerard Manley Hopkins. For Lawrence's poetry expresses more than an act of imaginative insight or mystical intuition. It is literal identification so that one catches the terrifying, non-rational sense of participating in the persistent sensual hunger of the male tortoise and his act of screaming coition; one flashes with the hummingbird and mocks with the blue jay. Like a Van Gogh, he is able to evoke the iridescent, palpable reality of fruits and flowers; he communicates not only their surface contours and brilliant colors but also their interior dynamism, the universal plasmic life that throbs in them. With a few sharp strokes he etches an object and then goes further to suggest its mysterious essence: pomegranates "like bright green stone," "barbed with a crown," actually growing; the heart of a peach: velvety, voluptuous, heavy, indented, "the lovely, bivalve roundness," "the ripple down the sphere." Or his rhapsodic evocation in **"Medlars and Sorb-Apples"**:

> Wineskins of brown morbidity
> Animal excrementa:
> What is it that reminds us of white gods?

This is the extraordinary power he possesses of bringing to pass before us the mystery of transubstantiation in nature, the sensuous particularity of an experience, the felt reality of the fruit-world in all its exquisite tactile and visual actuality. Each fruit is there before us, seemingly more real than any painting, more tempting to the imagination than the fruit itself. Figs and grapes and apples are dangled dazzlingly, appetitizing, before our vision. As he beholds the cluster of grapes, Lawrence's imagination slips across the frontier of time, returns to the primordial beginning of things when communion was naked and palpable and inexpressible. Though we have grown more democratic and more enlightened, we have lost, according to Lawrence, what is infinitely more precious: the ecstacy of immediate vision, the innocence of primitive perception. Lawrence sinks himself down into the earth where trees have their roots, feels the sap striving upward, the miracle of creation and renewal. He becomes the cypress or purple anemone or almond blossom he describes. With what sensuous intensity he paints this picture:

> Dawn-rose
> Sub-delighted, stone-engendered
> Cyclamens, young cyclamens
> Arching
> Walking, pricking their ears
> Like delicate very-young greyhound bitches
> Half-yawning at the open, inexperienced
> Vista of day,
> Folding back their soundless petalled ears.

In **Birds, Beasts and Flowers** the senses quiveringly respond to something other than human life, yet powerfully alive. He tells how he once caught "a gold-and-greenish, lucent fish" and unhooked its "groping, watery-horny mouth," looked into its "red-gold, water-precious, mirror-flat bright eyes," and felt the beat of its "mucous, leaping life-throb." We are amazed at his gift of projecting himself into the skin of a fish whose life is "a sluice of sensation along your sides." He partakes of its watery life, its goggling gaze, its sensations, its mindless fear.

Lawrence's poetry represents the triumph of the mythical, intuitive thinking that he makes so much of in practically all of his writing, and it is clear that he spoke from deep, vital sources of experience within him. Certainly he gave expression to a lyrical strain which is not to be found in

contemporary poetry with its post-Eliotic "dissociation" of ideas, its allusiveness, its deliberate richness of ambiguity, its pastiche of erudition, its intellectual toughness and sophisticated complexity. Lawrence scorned all that. He was not defining and formulating conceptual categories, fitting the contents of sensory experience within some antecedent order of cognition. He is thinking mythically, reveling in the immediate data of sensation and feeling, without seeking to impose uniformities: the kind of primitivistic, pre-logical thinking Cassirer describes in *Language and Myth.*

In **Last Poems,** Lawrence comes to grips with ultimate problems, the mystery of death, the meaning of the gods. Refusing to believe in the philosophy of pure spirit, he declares that first comes the sensual body, the body of the flesh and its instincts. The divine urge of creation is not to be identified with a Mind. It is the body that shapes beauty. Even God is but a great urge seeking incarnation in the body, whether it be the body of a woman or flower or animal. There is no god, Lawrence calls out in an ecstasy of discovery,

> apart from poppies and the flying fish,
> men singing songs, and women brushing their hair
>   in the sun

Hence man should be at one with the living God, instead of prostituting himself to knowledge and suffering the endless torture of unattainable self-analysis. In **"Mystic,"** Lawrence formulates his credo and in **"Anaxagoras"** he takes his fling at the stupidity of the scientists with their principles and laws and their apprehension of a dead reality. Such science is the product of mental conceit, a species of mystification. Snow is white, pure white, and not what science says it is. The self-centered will is the root of all evil. Lawrence has a perfect horror of mechanical men, soulless automatons. Science and mechanics and education and all abstractions, these constitute the essence of the evil he abhorred and repudiated.

Pansies is the anguished cry of Samson among the Philistines, only he is not blinded nor yet shorn of his strength. The whole man is implicit in this volume. The hate cuts clean like a knife. Lawrence is determined not to be deceived nor to deceive others. A recurrent theme in his poetry is the perception that death has overtaken Western civilization. The wealthy, the self-absorbed, the robots are slated for extinction; nothing can save them, but after them will rise a cleaner life. Mankind must now pay the price for having lost touch with the cosmos, the primitive gods, the primal realities. The long night of time is upon us. Coupled with this is his remarkable awareness of the primordial influence of sun and moon, sky and earth, on the tides of the soul. Lawrence maintains creative touch with the earth and its creatures and its subterranean fountains of energy.

In one sense, **Pansies** constitutes a unique experiment in poetic composition, since it brings to a head one of the important issues in contemporary criticism: the relation between thought and feeling. Though Lawrence repudiates the sterile, mechanical intellect, in these poems he is plainly the man thinking as well as feeling, even though his thoughts are directed to the task of annihilating thought. Yet there is a distinctive difference. What these poems aim to do is to fuse thought and feeling, to incarnate a pulse of real thought, brief, compact, poignant. There is no attempt at formal elaboration, no offer of convincing proof. "That," Lawrence seems to say, "is how I think and feel, what I believe at this moment of time." *Pansies* is therefore not so much an intellectual autobiography as a confession of intense moments and moods, visions and perceptions, aversions and ecstasies, which are unified not by a strategy of conceptual coherence but by the lambent personality of the poet. In his Foreword, Lawrence tells us that he wishes them to be taken as "casual thoughts that are true while they are true and irrelevant when the mood and circumstances change." In short, the principle of consistency does not apply. There can be no objections to contradictions that emerge in Lawrence's lyrics, because change and contradictions are the very heart of the process of growth.

Though there are instances of intellectual contradiction, fundamentally these "pansies" articulate a fairly coherent *Weltanschauung*. To appreciate them at their full value, one must know Lawrence's letters and fiction and essays. He has not changed. He is giving an almost word for word restatement of his basic beliefs, his antipathies and attachments. The list of what he hates is long indeed. He hates the bourgeoisie and the Bolsheviks, industrialism, our mechanized civilization, the worship of money and the bitch goddess Success, the infernal desire for superiority and self-assertion, the blather about masses and classes, the empty talk about economic revolutions, the futility of the life of the poor and the deadness of the elite, the ennui that proliferates like cancer cells through the body of modern society, the ridiculous twaddle about equality and democracy. About these things he writes with inflamed earnestness, crying out hoarsely against the indecency and tragic waste of such a life.

But when he seeks to convey his own personal religion he becomes mystical, inspired but rhapsodically vague. He adumbrates a philosophy of touch, the need for vital contacts, and he has much to say about recovering the energy of the sun, each man being the focal source of solar energy. Each man must emancipate the god within him and worship no other gods, but those who have caught no such gleam must live by the gleam reflected in the faces of those who have experienced this vision in all its radiant fullness. That is "true democracy": the leadership of those who are called and chosen and the service of those who are born to serve. That is the "revolution" he would inaugurate, the freedom he would establish in England and throughout the world. What we need is to be much alone. Those who are gods discover that loneliness is a creative experience, a period of renewal.

Lawrence is not only a man of intense feeling, he is also a man of shifting moods. He is carried away by what he

happens to feel at the moment. Precisely for that reason is he not to be taken too seriously as a thinker? It is curious that one who raves so furiously against mental consciousness and the diseased tendency to indulge in intellectual analysis, should expend so much energy in emotionalized arguments. True, the debate is not conducted according to rules of logic and evidence. What we get is a magnesium flare of temper, a flaming negation, affirmation by contrariety. As soon as something irritates him, he is off on a crusade. A preacher in verse, he is almost fanatical in his hatred of fanaticism; he is frenzied in his condemnation of puritanism, money, ideal women, machinery, and America. This is the one tune he knows, and he plays it with virtuosity and passion.

For example, Lawrence wages guerilla warfare against science, the analytical and the mechanical. Though the chemist breaks up water into hydrogen and oxygen, he fails to know the force which binds the two energies; he is blind to the third thing that makes it water. This is obviously neither profound nor particularly original, but the lyrical energy of conviction with which it is enunciated helps to fix it in our memory. In the heart of the atom—in space and earth and water—there is sanity to be found. Contrasted with this is the irrationality and evil of contemporary society, the horribly abnormal life of contemporary civilization. The mania of owning things together with the fearful blight of poverty is threatening to destroy the world. Hence if a revolution is to be carried out, it should not be under the auspices of the priests of Communism with their talk of equality and fraternity, nor in the name of money and materialism. In the name of life and for the sake of life should the revolution be consummated. That is the banner under which he would gladly fight.

In actual life, however, Lawrence's beliefs cannot be applied, cannot be lived. It is not possible to scrap machinery altogether and revert to a stage of Arcadian simplicity and Adamic innocence. No one in his right senses would actually carry the Laurentian opposition to science to a point where he would forego the use of all medical aid. Yet Lawrence is not in the least put out by such contradictions as he fulminates against the plague of science. For by fighting it he succeeds in preserving his integrity as an artist, his creative health and wholeness. And it is this which makes him so significant and representative a figure for our age. His lyrical protests bring to a head the dominant conflicts of our culture. He forces us to re-examine our implicit assumptions, our whole system of traditional values. He smashes the scientific philosophy of survival and adaptations to bits in order to make possible a more creative affirmation of life.

That is the whole of Lawrence: the alternation between absolute loneliness and the need for companionship, alienation and the fulfillment of his societal instincts, the polarity of love and hate. The truth was that most people with their Narcissus-like glorification of life, each one absorbed in ego-idolatry, repelled him. He tried to escape from it all into the fastness of the heart, the nameless, the unknown. The kind of democracy he looked forward to is not a democracy of ideas or ideals but a democracy of touch, the mystery of touch that transcends mind and spirit. This is the sovereign remedy against the cruelty and impersonality of the machine, the curse of cosmopolis, the centralizing drift of industrialism. Each one will then recoil into separateness, intensely alive and individual. When we have surrendered the possessive ego and the assertive will, we shall not need to be saved for we shall no longer feel lost. Once we realize that the Holy Ghost is the deepest part of consciousness, the understanding is born that we are dependent for the tides of our life on the creative beyond.

With such a mystical creed as his touchstone of value, it is not surprising that Lawrence held originality to be the sacred and supreme principle of poetic composition. He divided poetry into two categories: the poetry of the past, formalized, known, completed, dead; and the poetry of the future, throbbing with undiscovered potentialities. The poetry of the immediate present, Lawrence contended, must lack exquisite finish, consummate grace, classic perfection of form. It must be quick with the pulsations of immediacy, alive with the essence of creative change, emergent, Adamic, new. He wished to explore the quality of experience in all its concrete actual radiance, the incandescence of the mystical Now. Such poetry, he maintained in the preface to the American edition of **New Poems,** manages to suggest the protean, fluid, mobile, incalculable quality of life itself. Only thus can the strait-jacket of habit and precedent be thrown off, inspiration pouring out spontaneously like flame, without artificial elegance or prescribed form. In his terror of chaos man builds walls and roofs and shuts himself within a formula until he begins to stifle for want of air and space and can no longer break through to the light of the sun. The poets can help us in this essential work of liberation by throwing off the fetters of convention and reaching back to chaos. Better than the starvation-diet of outworn thought-forms is the imaginative experience, taking the whole soul and body captive, even if this means the repudiation of reason.

"The quick of the universe is the *pulsating, carnal self,* mysterious and palpable," Lawrence declared. But his jeremiads against modern mechanical civilization are rendered absurd and ineffectual by his inner knowledge that he can make no headway against it. He is shouting furiously against the wind, and his mad, impassioned words are hurled back with terrific force in his teeth. Since he cannot make his peace with the insane present, he begins to idealize the mythical past and reconstructs a primitive utopia, a golden age of the remote past. He has thrown up the sponge; he reveals our evils, our follies and waste and tragic conflicts, but he has no solution—none except a precipitate retreat to solar-plexus feelings, instinctive savagery. He is waging a losing battle all the time and that adds a touch of feverish futility to his utterances. Modern man cannot hope to recapture the virtues of primitivism, he cannot again worship the primal mysteries of sex and blood, not even if psychologists like Jung

recommend such reversions to archetypal patterns of experience. If we read Lawrence's pulse-like lyrics with suspended judgment, without intruding serious matters of belief, he is irresistible, overwhelming, but as soon as we begin to reflect, his power over us wanes and the defeatism of his cause becomes apparent.

Fortunately, the value of poetry is not judged by the validity of the logic or philosophy that can be abstracted from it. The lyrical heritage Lawrence left behind him has many precious qualities which can invigorate and fructify modern poetry. It is vital, passionate, intensely alive and affirmative. It expresses a self-contained, integrated personality. It is not afraid to be poignantly sensual, naked in its confession of man's response to earth and moon and sun. It gives voice to man feeling, man experiencing, man joyous, man liberated from the prison of selfhood, resurrected, quick to enjoy the beauty and miracle of life on earth. Experimental in form and original in content, it has, despite its aberrations, much to give that modern poetry, intellectualized and introverted, is urgently in need of.

W. H. Auden (essay date 1948)

SOURCE: "D. H. Lawrence," in *The Dyer's Hand and Other Essays,* Random House, 1948, pp. 277-95.

[*In the following essay, Auden echoes Richard Aldington's assessment that readers should not read Lawrence to reinforce ideologies—which are better expressed elsewhere by other writers—and that his genius lay in his ability to articulate humankind's aggressive and hateful natures.*]

> *If men were as much men as lizards are lizards,*
> *They'd be worth looking at.*

The artist, the man who makes, is less important to mankind, for good or evil, than the apostle, the man with a message. Without a religion, a philosophy, a code of behavior, call it what you will, men cannot live at all; what they believe may be absurd or revolting, but they have to believe something. On the other hand, however much the arts may mean to us, it is possible to imagine our lives without them.

As a human being, every artist holds some set of beliefs or other but, as a rule, these are not of his own invention; his public knows this and judges his work without reference to them. We read Dante for his poetry not for his theology because we have already met the theology elsewhere.

There are a few writers, however, like Blake and D. H. Lawrence, who are both artists and apostles and this makes a just estimation of their work difficult to arrive at. Readers who find something of value in their message will attach unique importance to their writings because they cannot find it anywhere else. But this importance may be short-lived; once I have learned his message, I cease to be interested in a messenger and, should I later come to think his message false or misleading, I shall remember him with resentment and distaste. Even if I try to ignore the message and read him again as if he were only an artist, I shall probably feel disappointed because I cannot recapture the excitement I felt when I first read him.

When I first read Lawrence in the late Twenties, it was his message which made the greatest impression on me, so that it was his "think" books like *Fantasia on the Unconscious* rather than his fiction which I read most avidly. As for his poetry, when I first tried to read it, I did not like it; despite my admiration for him, it offended my notions of what poetry should be. Today my notions of what poetry should be are still, in all essentials, what they were then and hostile to his, yet there are a number of his poems which I have come to admire enormously. When a poet who holds views about the nature of poetry which we believe to be false writes a poem we like, we are apt to think: "This time he has forgotten his theory and is writing according to ours." But what fascinates me about the poems of Lawrence's which I like is that I must admit he could never have written them had he held the kind of views about poetry of which I approve.

Man is a history-making creature who can neither repeat his past nor leave it behind; at every moment he adds to and thereby modifies everything that had previously happened to him. Hence the difficulty of finding a single image which can stand as an adequate symbol for man's kind of existence. If we think of his ever-open future, then the natural image is of a single pilgrim walking along an unending road into hitherto unexplored country; if we think of his never-forgettable past, then the natural image is of a great crowded city, built in every style of architecture, in which the dead are as active citizens as the living. The only feature common to both images is that both are purposive; a road goes in a certain direction, a city is built to endure and be a home. The animals, who live in the present, have neither cities nor roads and do not miss them; they are at home in the wilderness and at most, if they are social, set up camps for a single generation. But man requires both; the image of a city with no roads leading away from it suggests a prison, the image of a road that starts from nowhere in particular, an animal spoor.

Every man is both a citizen and a pilgrim, but most men are predominantly one or the other and in Lawrence the pilgrim almost obliterated the citizen. It is only natural, therefore, that he should have admired Whitman so much, both for his matter and his manner.

> Whitman's essential message was the Open Road. The leaving of the soul free unto herself, the leaving of his fate to her and to the loom of the open road. . . . The true democracy . . . where all journey down the open road. And where a soul is known at once in its going. Not by its clothes or appearance. Not by its family name. Not even by its reputation. Not by works at all. The soul passing unenhanced, passing on foot, and being no more than itself.

In his introduction to *New Poems,* Lawrence tries to explain the difference between traditional verse and the free verse which Whitman was the first to write.

> The poetry of the beginning and the poetry of the end must have that exquisite finality, perfection which belongs to all that is far off. It is in the realm of all that is perfect . . . the finality and perfection are conveyed in exquisite form: the perfect symmetry, the rhythm which returns upon itself like a dance where the hands link and loosen and link for the supreme moment of the end . . . But there is another kind of poetry, the poetry of that which is at hand: the immediate present. . . . Life, the ever present, knows no finality, no finished crystallisation. . . . It is obvious that the poetry of the instant present cannot have the same body or the same motions as the poetry of the before and after. It can never submit to the same conditions, it is never finished. . . . Much has been written about free verse. But all that can be said, first and last, is that free verse is, or should be, direct utterance from the instant whole man. It is the soul and body surging at once, nothing left out. . . . It has no finish. It has no satisfying stability. It does not want to get anywhere. It just takes place.

It would be easy to make fun of this passage, to ask Lawrence, for example, to tell us exactly how long an instant is, or how it would be physically possible for the poet to express it in writing before it had become past. But it is obvious that Lawrence is struggling to say something which he believes to be important. Very few statements which poets make about poetry, even when they appear to be quite lucid, are understandable except in their polemic context. To understand them, we need to know what they are directed against, what the poet who made them considered the principal enemies of genuine poetry.

In Lawrence's case, one enemy was the conventional response, the laziness or fear which makes people prefer second-hand experience to the shock of looking and listening for themselves.

> Man fixes some wonderful erection of his own between himself and the wild chaos, and gradually goes bleached and stifled under his parasol. Then comes a poet, enemy of convention, and makes a slit in the umbrella; and lo! the glimpse of chaos is a vision, a window to the sun. But after a while, getting used to the vision, and not liking the genuine draft from chaos, commonplace man daubs a simulacrum of the window that opens into chaos and patches the umbrella with the painted patch of the simulacrum. That is, he gets used to the vision; it is part of his house decoration.

Lawrence's justified dislike of the conventional response leads him into a false identification of the genuine with the novel. The image of the slit in the umbrella is misleading because what you can see through it will always be the same. But a genuine work of art is one in which every generation finds something new. A genuine work of art remains an example of what being genuine means, so that it can stimulate later artists to be genuine in their turn. Stimulate, not compel; if a playwright in the twentieth century chooses to write a play in a pastiche of Shakespearian blank verse, the fault is his, not Shakespeare's. Those who are afraid of firsthand experience would find means of avoiding it if all the art of the past were destroyed.

However, theory aside. Lawrence did care passionately about genuineness of feeling. He wrote little criticism about other poets who were his contemporaries, but, when he did, he was quick to pounce on any phoniness of emotion. About Ralph Hodgson's lines

> The sky was lit,
> The sky was stars all over it,
> I stood, I knew not why

he writes, "No one should say *I knew not why* any more. It is as meaningless as *Yours truly* at the end of a letter," and, after quoting an American poetess

> Why do I think of stairways
> With a rush of hurt surprise?

he remarks, "Heaven knows, my dear, unless you once fell down." Whatever faults his own poetry may have, it never puts on an act. Even when Lawrence talks nonsense, as when he asserts that the moon is made of phosphorous or radium, one is convinced that it is nonsense in which he sincerely believed. This is more than can be said of some poets much greater than he. When Yeats assures me, in a stanza of the utmost magnificence, that after death he wants to become a mechanical bird, I feel that he is telling what my nanny would have called "A story."

The second object of Lawrence's polemic was a doctrine which first became popular in France during the second half of the nineteenth century, the belief that Art is the true religion, that life has no value except as material for a beautiful artistic structure and that, therefore, the artist is the only authentic human being—the rest, rich and poor alike, are canaille. Works of art are the only cities; life itself is a jungle. Lawrence's feelings about this creed were so strong that whenever he detects its influence, as he does in Proust and Joyce, he refuses their work any merit whatsoever. A juster and more temperate statement of his objection has been made by Dr. Auerbach:

> When we compare Stendhal's or even Balzac's world with the world of Flaubert or the two Goncourts, the latter seems strangely narrow and petty despite its wealth of impressions. Documents of the kind represented by Flaubert's correspondence and the Goncourt diary are indeed admirable in the purity and incorruptibility of their artistic ethics, the wealth of impressions elaborated in them, and their refinement of sensory culture. At the same time, however, we sense something narrow, something oppressively close in their books. They are full of

reality and intellect, but poor in humor and inner poise. The purely literary, even on the highest level of artistic acumen, limits the power of judgment, reduces the wealth of life, and at times distorts the outlook upon the world of phenomena. And while the writers contemptuously avert their attention from the political and economic bustle, consistently value life only as literary subject matter, and remain arrogantly and bitterly aloof from its great practical problems, in order to achieve aesthetic isolation for their work, often at great and daily expense of effort, the practical world nevertheless besets them in a thousand petty ways.

> Sometimes there are financial worries, and almost always there is nervous hypotension and a morbid concern with health. . . . What finally emerges, despite all their intellectual and artistic incorruptibility, is a strangely petty impression; that of an upper bourgeois egocentrically concerned over his aesthetic comfort, plagued by a thousand small vexations, nervous, obsessed by a mania—only in this case the mania is called "Literature." *(Mimesis.)*

In rejecting the doctrine that life has no value except as raw material for art, Lawrence fell into another error, that of identifying art with life, making with action.

> I offer a bunch of pansies, not a wreath of immortelles. I don't want everlasting flowers and I don't want to offer them to anybody else. A flower passes, and that perhaps is the best of it. . . . Don't nail the pansy down. You won't keep it any better if you do.

Here Lawrence draws a false analogy between the process of artistic creation and the organic growth of living creatures. "Nature hath no goal though she hath law." Organic growth is a cyclical process; it is just as true to say that the oak is a potential acorn as it is to say the acorn is a potential oak. But the process of writing a poem, of making any art object, is not cyclical but a motion in one direction towards a definite end. As Socrates says in Valéry's dialogue *Eupalinos:*

> The tree does not construct its branches and leaves; nor the cock his beak and feathers. But the tree and all its parts, or the cock and all his, are constructed by the principles themselves, which do not exist apart from the constructing. . . . But, in the objects made by man, the principles are separate from the construction, and are, as it were, imposed by a tyrant from without upon the material, to which he imparts them by acts. . . . If a man waves his arm, we distinguish this arm from his gesture, and we conceive between gesture and arm a purely possible relation. But from the point of view of nature, this gesture of the arm and the arm itself cannot be separated.

An artist who ignores this difference between natural growth and human construction will produce the exact opposite of what he intends. He hopes to produce something which will seem as natural as a flower, but the qualities of the natural are exactly what his product will lack. A natural object never appears unfinished; if it is an inorganic object like a stone, it is what it has to be, if an organic object like a flower, what it has to be at this moment. But a similar effect—of being what it has to be—can only be achieved in a work of art by much thought, labor and care. The gesture of a ballet dancer, for example, only looks natural when, through long practice, its execution has become "second nature" to him. That perfect incarnation of life in substance, word in flesh, which in nature is immediate, has in art to be achieved and, in fact, can never be perfectly achieved. In many of Lawrence's poems, the spirit has failed to make itself a fit body to live in, a curious defect in the work of a writer who was so conscious of the value and significance of the body. In his essay on Thomas Hardy, Lawrence made some acute observations about this very problem. Speaking of the antimony between Law and Love, the Flesh and the Spirit, he says

> The principle of the Law is found strongest in Woman, the principle of Love in Man. In every creature, the mobility, the law of change is found exemplified in the male, the stability, the conservatism in the female.

> The very adherence of rhyme and regular rhythm is a concession to the Law, a concession to the body, to the being and requirements of the body. They are an admission of the living positive inertia which is the other half of life, other than the pure will to motion.

This division of Lawrence's is a variant on the division between the City and the Open Road. To the mind of the pilgrim, his journey is a succession of ever-new sights and sounds, but to his heart and legs, it is a rhythmical repetition—tic-toc, left-right—even the poetry of the Open Road must pay that much homage to the City. By his own admission and definition Lawrence's defect as an artist was an exaggerated maleness.

Reading Lawrence's early poems, one is continually struck by the originality of the sensibility and the conventionality of the expressive means. For most immature poets, their chief problem is to learn to forget what they have been taught poets are supposed to feel; too often, as Lawrence says, the young man is afraid of his demon, puts his hand over the demon's mouth and speaks for him. On the other hand, an immature poet, if he has real talent, usually begins to exhibit quite early a distinctive style of his own; however obvious the influence of some older writer may be, there is something original in his manner or, at least, great technical competence. In Lawrence's case, this was not so; he learned quite soon to let his demon speak, but it took him a long time to find the appropriate style for him to speak in. All too often in his early poems, even the best ones, he is content to versify his thoughts; there is no essential relation between what he is saying and the formal structure he imposes upon it.

> Being nothing, I bear the brunt
> Of the nightly heavens overhead, like an immense
>   open eye

> With a cat's distended pupil, that sparkles with
>   little stars
> And with thoughts that flash and crackle in far-off
>   malignancy
> So distant, they cannot touch me, whom nothing
>   mars.

A mere poetaster with nothing to say, would have done something about *whom nothing mars.*

It is interesting to notice that the early poems in which he seems technically most at ease and the form most natural, are those he wrote in dialect.

> I wish tha hadna done it, Tim,
>   I do, an' that I do,
> For whenever I look thee i'th' face, I s'll see
>   Her face too.

> I wish I could wash er off'n thee;
>   'Appen I can, If I try.

> But tha'll ha'e ter promise ter be true ter me
>   Till I die.

This sounds like a living woman talking, whereas no woman on earth ever talked like this:

> How did you love him, you who only roused
> His mind until it burnt his heart away!
> 'Twas you who killed him, when you both
>   caroused
> In words and things well said. But the other way
> He never loved you, never with desire
> Touched you to fire.

I suspect that Lawrence's difficulties with formal verse had their origin in his linguistic experiences as a child.

> My father was a working man
>   and a collier was he,
> At six in the morning they turned him down
>   and they turned him up for tea.

> My mother was a superior soul
>   a superior soul was she,
> cut out to play a superior role
>   in the god-damn bourgeoisie.

> We children were the in-betweens,
>   Little non-descripts were we,
> In doors we called each other *you*
>   outside it was *tha* and *thee.*

In formal poetry, the role played by the language itself is so great that it demands of the poet that he be as intimate with it as with his own flesh and blood and love it with a single-minded passion. A child who has associated standard English with Mother and dialect with Father has ambivalent feelings about both which can hardly fail to cause trouble for him in later life if he should try to write formal poetry. Not that it would have been possible for Lawrence to become a dialect poet like Burns or William Barnes, both of whom lived before public education had made dialect quaint. The language of Burns was a national not a parochial speech, and the peculiar charm of Barnes' poetry is its combination of the simplest emotions with an extremely sophisticated formal technique: Lawrence could never have limited himself to the thoughts and feelings of a Nottinghamshire mining village, and he had neither the taste nor the talent of Barnes for what he scornfully called word games.

Most of Lawrence's finest poems are to be found in the volume **Birds, Beasts, and Flowers,** begun in Tuscany when he was thirty-five and finished three years later in New Mexico. All of them are written in free verse.

The difference between formal and free verse may be likened to the difference between carving and modeling; the formal poet, that is to say, thinks of the poem he is writing as something already latent in the language which he has to reveal, while the free verse poet thinks of language as a plastic passive medium upon which he imposes his artistic conception. One might also say that, in their attitude towards art, the formal verse writer is a catholic, the free verse writer a protestant. And Lawrence was, in every respect, very protestant indeed. As he himself acknowledged, it was through Whitman that he found himself as a poet, found the right idiom of poetic speech for his demon.

On no other English poet, so far as I know, has Whitman had a beneficial influence; he could on Lawrence because, despite certain superficial resemblances, their sensibilities were utterly different. Whitman quite consciously set out to be the Epic Bard of America and created a poetic *persona* for the purpose. He keeps using the first person singular and even his own name, but these stand for a *persona,* not an actual human being, even when he appears to be talking about the most intimate experiences. When he sounds ridiculous, it is usually because the image of an individual obtrudes itself comically upon what is meant to be a statement about a collective experience. *I am large. I contain multitudes* is absurd if one thinks of Whitman himself or any individual; of a corporate person like General Motors it makes perfectly good sense. The more we learn about Whitman the man, the less like his *persona* he looks. On the other hand it is doubtful if a writer ever existed who had less of an artistic *persona* than Lawrence; from his letters and the reminiscences of his friends, it would seem that he wrote for publication in exactly the same way as he spoke in private. (I must confess that I find Lawrence's love poems embarrassing because of their lack of reticence; they make me feel a Peeping Tom.) Then, Whitman looks at life extensively rather than intensively. No detail is dwelt upon for long; it is snapshotted and added as one more item to the vast American catalogue. But Lawrence in his best poems is always concerned intensively with a single subject, a bat, a tortoise, a fig tree, which he broods on until he has exhausted its possibilities.

A sufficient number of years have passed for us to have gotten over both the first overwhelming impact of

Lawrence's genius and the subsequent violent reaction when we realized that there were silly and nasty sides to his nature. We can be grateful to him for what he can do for us, without claiming that he can do everything or condemning him because he cannot. As an analyst and portrayer of the forces of hatred and aggression which exist in all human beings and, from time to time, manifest themselves in nearly all human relationships, Lawrence is, probably, the greatest master who ever lived. But that was absolutely all that we knew and understood about human beings; about human affection and human charity, for example, he knew absolutely nothing. The truth is that he detested nearly all human beings if he had to be in close contact with them; his ideas of what a human relationship, between man and man or man and woman, ought to be are pure daydreams because they are not based upon any experience of actual relationships which might be improved or corrected. Whenever, in his novels and short stories, he introduces a character whom he expects the reader to admire, he or she is always an unmitigated humorless bore, but the more he dislikes his characters the more interesting he makes them. And, in his heart of hearts, Lawrence knew this himself. There is a sad passage in **An Autobiographical Sketch:**

> Why is there so little contact between myself and the people I know? The answer, as far as I can see, has something to do with class. As a man from the working class, I feel that the middle class cut off some of my vital vibration when I am with them. I admit them charming and good people often enough, but they just stop some part of me from working.
>
> Then, why don't I live with my own people? Because their vibration is limited in another direction. The working class is narrow in outlook, in prejudice, and narrow in intelligence. This again makes a prison. Yet I find, here in Italy, for example, that I live in a certain contact with the peasants who work the land of this villa. I am not intimate with them, hardly speak to them save to say good-day. And they are not working for me. I am not their padrone. I don't want to live with them in their cottages; that would be a sort of prison. I don't idealise them. I don't expect them to make any millennium here on earth, neither now nor in the future. But I want them to be there, about the place, their lives going along with mine.

For the word *peasants,* one might substitute the words *birds, beasts and flowers.* Lawrence possessed a great capacity for affection and charity, but he could only direct it towards non-human life or peasants whose lives were so uninvolved with his that, so far as he was concerned, they might just as well have been nonhuman. Whenever, in his writings, he forgets about men and women with proper names and describes the anonymous life of stones, waters, forests, animals, flowers, chance traveling companions or passers-by, his bad temper and his dogmatism immediately vanish and he becomes the most enchanting companion imaginable, tender, intelligent, funny and, above all, happy. But the moment any living thing, even a dog, makes demands on him, the rage and preaching return. His poem about **"Bibbles,"** "the walt whitmanesque love-bitch who loved just everybody," is the best poem about a dog ever written, but it makes it clear that Lawrence was no person to be entrusted with the care of a dog.

> All right, my little bitch.
> You learn loyalty rather than loving,
> And I'll protect you.

To which Bibbles might, surely, with justice retort: "O for Chris-sake, mister, go get yourself an Alsatian and leave me alone, can't you."

The poems in *Birds, Beasts, and Flowers* are among Lawrence's longest. He was not a concise writer and he needs room to make his effect. In his poetry he manages to make a virtue out of what in his prose is often a vice, a tendency to verbal repetition. The recurrence of identical or slightly varied phrases helps to give his free verse a structure; the phrases themselves are not particularly striking, but this is as it should be, for their function is to act as stitches.

Like the romantics, Lawrence's starting point in these poems is a personal encounter between himself and some animal or flower but, unlike the romantics, he never confuses the feelings they arouse in him with what he sees and hears and knows about them.

Thus, he accuses Keats, very justly, I think, of being so preoccupied with his own feelings that he cannot really listen to the nightingale. *Thy plaintive anthem fades* deserves Lawrence's comment: *It never was a plaintive anthem—it was Caruso at his jauntiest.*

Lawrence never forgets—indeed this is what he likes most about them—that a plant or an animal has its own kind of existence which is unlike and uncomprehending of man's.

> It is no use my saying to him in an emotional voice:
> 'This is your Mother, she laid you when you were
>   an egg.'
> He does not even trouble to answer: 'Woman,
>   what have I to do with thee?'
> He wearily looks the other way,
> And she even more wearily looks another way still.
>   (**"Tortoise Family Connections."**)

> But watching closer
> That motionless deadly motion,
> That unnatural barrel body, that long ghoul nose . . .
> I left off hailing him.
> I had made a mistake, I didn't know him,
> This grey, monotonous soul in the water,
> This intense individual in shadow,
> Fish-alive.
> I didn't know his God.
>   (**"Fish."**)

When discussing people or ideas, Lawrence is often turgid and obscure, but when, as in these poems, he is contemplating some object with love, the lucidity of his language matches the intensity of his vision, and he can make the reader *see* what he is saying as very few writers can.

> Queer, with your thin wings and your streaming
>   legs,
> How you sail like a heron, or a dull clot of air.
>   (**"The Mosquito."**)

> Her little loose hands, and sloping Victorian
>   shoulders
>   (**"Kangaroo."**)

> There she is, perched on her manger, looking over
>   the boards into the day
> Like a belle at her window.
> And immediately she sees me she blinks, stares,
>   doesn't know me, turns her head and ignores
>   me vulgarly with a wooden blank on her face.
> What do I care for her, the ugly female, standing
>   up there with her long tangled sides like an old
>   rug thrown over a fence.
> But she puts her nose down shrewdly enough
>   when the knot is untied,
> And jumps staccato to earth, a sharp, dry jump,
>   still ignoring me,
> Pretending to look around the stall
> *Come on, you crapa! I'm not your servant.*
> She turns her head away with an obtuse female
>   sort of deafness, bête.
> And then invariably she crouches her rear and
>   makes water.
> That being her way of answer, if I speak to her.—
>   Self-conscious!
> *Le bestie non parlano, poverine! . . .*

> Queer it is, suddenly, in the garden
> To catch sight of her standing like some huge
>   ghoulish grey bird in the air, on the bough of
>   the leaning almond-tree,
> Straight as a board on the bough, looking down
>   like some hairy horrid God the Father in a
>   William Blake imagination.
> *Come, down, Crapa, out of that almond tree!*
>   (**"She-Goat."**)

In passages like these, Lawrence's writing is so transparent that one forgets him entirely and simply sees what he saw.

Birds, Beasts, and Flowers is the peak of Lawrence's achievement as a poet. There are a number of fine things in the later volumes, but a great deal that is tedious, both in subject matter and form. A writer's doctrines are not the business of a literary critic except in so far as they touch upon questions which concern the art of writing; if a writer makes statements about nonliterary matters, it is not for the literary critic to ask whether they are true or false but he may legitimately question the writer's authority to make them.

The Flauberts and the Goncourts considered social and political questions beneath them; to his credit, Lawrence knew that there are many questions that are more important than Art with an *A,* but it is one thing to know this and another to believe one is in a position to answer them.

In the modern world, a man who earns his living by writing novels and poems is a self-employed worker whose customers are not his neighbors, and this makes him a social oddity. He may work extremely hard, but his manner of life is something between that of a *rentier* and a gypsy, he can live where he likes and know only the people he chooses to know. He has no firsthand knowledge of all those involuntary relationships created by social, economic and political necessity. Very few artists can be *engagé* because life does not engage them: for better or worse, they do not quite belong to the City. And Lawrence, who was self-employed after the age of twenty-six, belonged to it less than most. Some writers have spent their lives in the same place and social milieu; Lawrence kept constantly moving from one place and one country to another. Some have been extroverts who entered fully into whatever society happened to be available; Lawrence's nature made him avoid human contacts as much as possible. Most writers have at least had the experience of parenthood and its responsibilities; this experience was denied Lawrence. It was inevitable, therefore, that when he tried to lay down the law about social and political matters, money, machinery, etc., he could only be negative and moralistic because, since his youth, he had had no firsthand experiences upon which concrete and positive suggestions could have been based. Furthermore, if, like Lawrence, the only aspects of human beings which you care for and value are states of being, timeless moments of passionate intensity, then social and political life, which are essentially historical—without a past and a future, human society is inconceivable—must be, for you, the worthless aspects of human life. You cannot honestly say, "This kind of society is preferable to that," because, for you, society is wholly given over to Satan.

The other defect in many of the later poems is a formal one. It is noticeable that the best are either of some length or rhymed; the short ones in free verse very rarely come off. A poem which contains a number of ideas and feelings can be organized in many different ways, but a poem which makes a single point and is made up of no more than one or two sentences can only be organized verbally; an epigram or an aphorism must be written either in prose or in some strictly measured verse; written in free verse, it will sound like prose arbitrarily chopped up.

> It has always seemed to me that a real thought, not an argument can only exist in verse, or in some poetic form. There is a didactic element about prose thoughts which makes them repellent, slightly bullying, "He who hath wife and children hath given hostages to fortune." There is a point well put: but immediately it irritates by its assertiveness. If it were put into poetry, it would not nag at us so practically. We don't want to be nagged at.
>
> (Preface to *Pansies*)

Though I personally love good prose aphorisms, I can see what Lawrence means. If one compares

> *Plus ça change, plus c'est la même chose*

with

> The accursed power that stands on Privilege
> And goes with Women and Champagne and
> 　　Bridge
> Broke, and Democracy resumed her reign
> That goes with Bridge and Women and
> 　　Champagne

the first does seem a bit smug and a bit abstract, while, in the second, the language dances and is happy.

> The bourgeois produced the Bolshevist inevitably
> As every half-truth at length produces the
> 　　contradiction of itself
> In the opposite half-truth

has the worst of both worlds; it lacks the conciseness of the prose and the jollity of the rhymed verse.

The most interesting verses in the last poems of Lawrence belong to a literary genre he had not attempted before, satirical doggerel.

If formal verse can be likened to carving, free verse to modeling, then one might say that doggerel verse is like *objets trouvés*—the piece of driftwood that looks like a witch, the stone that has a profile. The writer of doggerel, as it were, takes any old words, rhythms and rhymes that come into his head, gives them a good shake and then throws them onto the page like dice where, lo and behold, contrary to all probability they make sense, not by law but by chance. Since the words appear to have no will of their own, but to be the puppets of chance, so will the things or persons to which they refer; hence the value of doggerel for a certain kind of satire.

It is a different kind of satire from that written by Dryden and Pope. Their kind presupposes a universe, a city, governed by, or owing allegiance to, certain eternal laws of reason and morality; the purpose of their satire is to demonstrate that the individual or institution they are attacking violates these laws. Consequently, the stricter in form their verse, the more artful their technique, the more effective it is. Satirical doggerel, on the other hand, presupposes no fixed laws. It is the weapon of the outsider, the anarchist rebel, who refuses to accept conventional laws and pieties as binding or worthy of respect. Hence its childish technique, for the child represents the naïve and personal, as yet uncorrupted by education and convention. Satire of the Pope kind says: "The Emperor is wearing a celluloid collar. That simply isn't done." Satiric doggerel cries: "The Emperor is naked."

At this kind of satiric doggerel, Lawrence turned out to be a master.

And Mr. Meade, that old old lily,
Said: "Gross, coarse, hideous!" and I, like a silly

Thought he meant the faces of the police court
  officials
And how right he was, so I signed my initials.

But Tolstoi was a traitor
To the Russia that needed him most,
The great bewildered Russia
So worried by the Holy Ghost;
He shifted his job onto the peasants
And landed them all on toast.

Parnassus has many mansions.

George G. Williams (essay date 1951)

SOURCE: "D. H. Lawrence's Philosophy as Expressed in His Poetry," in *The Rice Institute Pamphlet,* Vol. XXXVIII, No. 2, July, 1951, pp. 73-94.

[*In the following essay, Williams proposes that the body of Lawrence's poetical works must be read in order to give a full understanding of the author's philosophical and sociological intent.*]

I. A NEGLECTED POETRY

Books by D. H. Lawrence would fill a good-sized shelf, and books about him would fill an even larger shelf. Ten years after his death an editorial writer in the *Saturday Review of Literature* said that he has been the subject of "more books than any other writer since Byron";[1] and now, twenty years after his death, the same magazine remarks that "Lawrence's reputation is on the upswing . . . and in many countries he has 'become a standard author'."[2] A steady trickle of essays about him continues to appear in the popular as well as the learned journals of America, England, and the Continent, and anthologies and new printings of his work continue to issue from the presses.

Most curiously, however, very little of all that has been written about him deals with his poetry. A few reviews of poetical volumes as they appeared, a few perfunctory comments in the midst of general discussions, a few introductory paragraphs in anthologies—and that is the limit of attention that criticism has accorded Lawrence's poetry. Yet he wrote 10 volumes of poetry; his *Collected Poems* and his *Last Poems* fill over 800 pages; the refrain of most writers about his prose is that he is "a poet even in his novels"; and poets (like W. H. Auden, C. Day Lewis, Humbert Wolfe, Stephen Spender, Ford Madox Ford, Louise Bogan, and Horace Gregory[3]) have been his most consistent defenders.

Professor William York Tindall, who has written the most elaborate study[4] of Lawrence's thought that has yet been published, virtually ignores the poetry. "Since the evidence in verse is meager," he says, "and no more than

parallel to that of the prose, I have confined my remarks to the prose, citing poetical evidence in the notes."[8] He must consider the evidence in the poems meager indeed, for only 7 of the 400 notes in his volume refer to poems by Lawrence.

Tindall's book has a special importance because it is the only long and scholarly treatment in English of Lawrence the Thinker as opposed to Lawrence the Personality. In a way, therefore, the present paper, by dealing with Lawrence's poems exclusively, is an attempt to supplement Tindall's book. It explores an area that Tindall neglected and that no one else has seriously studied. In a way, too, this paper may end by becoming a slight antidote to Tindall. For, as David Garnett says, Lawrence "is one of the easiest of great writers to get hold of by the wrong end"[6]—and Tindall, for all his scholarship, seems to have done just that. Frieda Lawrence said of Tindall that he had "no enthusiasm, no sympathy for his subject. Lawrence is to him a bad writer, a bad thinker; and he thoroughly dislikes Lawrence as a man."[7]

Perhaps Tindall made the initial error of trying to evaluate Lawrence as a systematic rationalist, instead of realizing that Lawrence can never be understood (any more than Blake can be understood) unless he is viewed as a poet. But Lawrence's poetry discourages philosophical analysis—just because it *is* poetry and not philosophy. The difficulty is made even worse by the fact that not one of his poems really develops any considerable part of his thought—as, for example, the "Ode on a Grecian Urn" and "Tintern Abbey" develop certain aspects of each author's thought. Each of Lawrence's poems is like a highly colored fragment of some unassembled whole. To put the fragments together, to construct from them the complete philosophical mosaic, is not an easy task. At any rate, it is one that students of Lawrence have shunned heretofore.

How early Lawrence formulated the essential elements of his thought cannot be told from his poetry. Comparison of the early poems—that is, up to about 1917—with the prose of the same period shows that the prose considerably antedates the poetry in expressing anything like a philosophy. As a matter of fact, some of the letters (as edited and published by Aldous Huxley in 1932) show that Lawrence had adopted his basic ideas as early as 1913, at least. But not until five or six years later does his poetry become a vehicle for constant expression of his ideas. For this very reason, his poems, largely concerned as they are with philosophical ideas only after those ideas have matured and fixed themselves in Lawrence's mind, are a better source, in some ways, for study of Lawrence's thought than are his prose works.

II. RELIGION AND METAPHYSICS

Lawrence was born in 1885 and died in 1930. During his lifetime the culture of western Europe underwent developments and received shocks hardly paralleled since the late fifteenth and early sixteenth centuries.

The Darwinian theory of evolution, with its inevitable undermining of old Christian orthodoxy, finally prevailed in the minds of informed and intelligent men; the industrialization and mechanization of society at last triumphed unmistakably; socialism became a force to be reckoned with; Freudian psychology discovered a whole vast continent of mind that had formerly been unsuspected; the First World War came at a time when many thinking people had convinced themselves that wars were no longer conceivable among civilized peoples; and the bolshevists succeeded in setting up a stable government in Russia. Every one of these forces and events had its effect upon Lawrence; and his complex and manifold reactions to them constitute the body of his thought.

Though it seems impossible to define precisely the stages of Lawrence's poetic development, his earliest work suggested the poetry of the 1890's, and from there he passed on to a kind of rugged Georgianism (he was represented in *Georgian Poetry*); then to imagism; then to certain passionate, fiercely autobiographical poems that brought him up to about 1920; and then to ten years of intensely poetic *matter* expressed in a loose Whitmanesque *manner* that has the ease and naturalness of good conversation, and the quick, sharp brilliance of genius.

Brought up by a strictly orthodox Methodist mother, he could write, long after he had ceased believing in Christ as anything more than "one of Nature's phenomena,"[8]

> The Cross, the Cross
> Goes deeper than we know.[9]

And he always maintained that he was "a profoundly religious man," and that "One has to be so terribly religious to be an artist."[10] But his religion was far from being formal and orthodox; it was essentially mystical, in the same way that Shelley's, Emerson's, Francis Thompson's, Yeats', A. E.'s, and even Wordsworth's religions were mystical. Apparently Tindall (in the first chapter of his book) had no real understanding of the nature of mysticism, expected Lawrence to be quite logical in his religion, and would not have comprehended such lines as these by Lawrence:

> But to something unseen, unknown, creative
> from which I feel I am derivative
> I feel absolute reverence. Say no more![11]

There is no logic in such lines, or in the following:

> Forever nameless
> Forever unknown
> Forever unconceived
> Forever unrepresented
> Yet forever felt in the soul.[12]

Lawrence's religion was real enough. But it was not Christian. His objection to modern Christianity was that it knows only "the useful Godhead of Providence"; it has lost the "Creative Godhead"[13] which is "the centre of all things."[14]

Lawrence would certainly emphasize "*all* things"—not merely those things which orthodox Christianity would label "good." Lawrence's Creative Godhead is the Life Force of the universe. It manifests itself in every innate and irresistible impulse (or urge, or growth, or instinct, or longing) that dwells within, or finds expression in, material beauty strong, primitive, and unspoiled.[15] Spirit and matter are not two things; they are one—or rather, spirit has no existence until the vague demiurge of the universe expresses itself in a material form that is both spirit and body:

> There is no god
> apart from poppies and flying fish,
> men singing songs, and women brushing their hair
>   in the sun.
> The lovely things are god that has come to pass,
>   like Jesus came.[16]

Far from being an anti-materialist (as Tindall tries to prove in the second chapter of his book) Lawrence is primarily and absolutely a materialist in the strict, literal sense of that word. The central value in his system is the material, concrete, sensuously experienced substance of the universe. But like Wordsworth, like many other mystics who can perceive the divine One manifesting itself in the various All, Lawrence may perceive a spirit interfusing or being all material things.[17] Nevertheless, the material things are the essential reality, and the divine spirit has reality only in them:

> They say that reality exists only in the spirit
> that corporal existence is a kind of death
> that pure being is bodiless
> that the idea of the form precedes the form
>   substantial.
> But what nonsense it is.[18]

Nothing is more characteristic of Lawrence (in both his poetry and his prose) than this reverence for material things that spring directly from the Life Urge—that is, for every aspect of nature: the gentle and the strong, the beautiful and the ugly, the highly developed and the degenerate, the symmetrical and the grotesque, the inspiring and sometimes even the disgusting. All these aspects of nature fill the volume of poems called ***Birds, Beasts and Flowers*** (1923), and they appear again and again in all the other volumes.

He reveres nature because nature is one with, and springs from, God; and "God is a great urge, wonderful, mysterious, magnificent."[19] God is not a *mind;*[20] God is creative force.[21] God is "nameless and imageless";[22] God is the *living* God, the God of Life, the Force that creates life: God is Life.[23] "Lawrence's principal message was one of life."[24]

To Lawrence, even death is life. For evil men (that is, for egotistical, self-sufficient men who have never had any communion with the Life Force) death is a torture-chamber wherein "their hardened souls are washed with fire . . . till they are softened back to life-stuff again";[25] and for good men (those who have lived in knowledge and reverence of the Life Force) death is an "unfolding . . . to something flowery and fulfilled." In life

> Men prevent one another from being men
> but in the great spaces of death
> the winds of the afterwards kiss us into blossom
> of mankind.[26]

"At the core of everything" lies "dark oblivion," the ultimate reality and the ultimate blessing;[27] but out of this oblivion rises procreation;[28] and out of it the soul, having died, rises like a mist into a more lovely life.[29]

It is his pantheistic, mystical, unswerving, and wholly sincere worship of life and the Life Force that lies at the root of all Lawrence's thinking. Illogical it may be, impracticable it certainly is, and shocking in some of its ramifications it has been; but it is not the pure nonsense that some critics have thought it.

III. ROMANTIC PRIMITIVISM

Horace Gregory calls Lawrence "a great English poet in the Romantic tradition," and goes on to say, "Like most Romantic poets, Lawrence had a strong nostalgia for the past—not for the immediate past, or the Hellenic-Christian culture that had historical reference to his own civilization . . . his was a biological past: 'the blood, the flesh' of man, of animals, of flowers. A union with this life force, this dark, unseen flow . . . was a means of justifying human life and breaking down walls of human isolation."[30]

This is a very discerning analysis that connects Lawrence with his proper literary tradition. A respecter of all that is elemental and primal in human life, Lawrence would undoubtedly have cried a hearty "Amen!" to Burns'

> Gie me ae spark o' Nature's fire!
> That's a' the learning I desire.

And he would have approved equally of Wordsworth's

> One impulse from a vernal wood
> Can teach you more of man,
> Of moral evil and of good,
> Than all the sages can.

Yet many critics (including Tindall) have attacked Lawrence quite bitterly for his distrust of scientific logic and intellect, and his reliance on the innate, instinctive impulses of man. The point is that Lawrence, in his reverence for all things in nature, all things created by the Life Force, reveres the elemental nature of man. He thinks that man is—by nature, because he is a part of nature—a creature who rests naturally in "the hands of the living God."[31]

Like the earlier Romantics, he would have liked to believe that simple and primitive men are closer to the living God than are men "corrupted by civilization." Any

conviction he may have had on this subject, however, is reserved almost entirely for his prose. In a few of his earlier poems[32] there appears some vague feeling that simple working-men help bring our age into closer communion with the Life Force; and in a later poem called **"Amo Sacrum Vulgus"** he sings (almost like Carl Sandburg) the joyous refrain, "The people, the people, the people!"[33] Nevertheless, in far the greater part of his poetry he escapes those Romantic fallacies of the Noble Savage, the Child of Nature, and the Common Man that the eighteenth and early nineteenth centuries fell into. The retreat toward the Life Force, he realizes, must carry farther than simplicity or savagery. Plants and animals (unconscious, not self-conscious, not egotistical, without will) live closer to the center of the Life Force than even simple men or savages. Plants and animals, therefore, interest him, or even inspire him, as much as do elemental people, or people who live according to their elemental impulses.

But those critics of Lawrence (and they seem to be in the majority) who think that he advocates humanity's descending to the level of plants and animals, and abandoning thought, intellect, and nobility, do not understand him. He would not have a tortoise try to be an elephant, nor would he have a man try to be anything but a man. Intellect is a human trait, and Lawrence would have human beings use their intellect:

> Thought, I love thought.
> But not the jaggling and twisting of already
>   existent ideas . . .
> Thought is the welling up of unknown life into the
>   consciousness
> Thought is the testing of statements on the
>   touchstone of conscience
> Thought is gazing on the face of life, and reading
>   what can be read,
> Thought is pondering over experience and coming
>   to conclusion . . .
> Thought is man in his wholeness wholly
>   attending.[34]

It would be difficult to find a more intelligent, a more cleanly intellectual definition of thought than this. Lawrence did not wish men to be animals:

> Oh, sacrifice not that which is noble and generous
>   and spontaneous in humanity
> but that which is mean and base and squalid and
>   degenerate.[35]

An unregenerate optimist concerning the deep nature of man, he wished merely that man would be as godlike as he is capable of being:

> Now let me be myself,
> now let me be myself and flicker forth
> now let me be myself, in the being, one of the gods.[36]

Diana Trilling was quite right when she said, a few years ago, that Lawrence believed "Our trouble is not that we know too much but that we do not know enough."[37]

IV. GOOD AND EVIL IN INDIVIDUAL AND IN SOCIETY

Both Lawrence and his readers have suffered because Lawrence found no developed terminology to express his meanings. Lacking a language, he could never quite clarify what he meant by the elemental Life Force, or by that portion of it which is contained in all life. Sometimes he called this latter "blood." Nor could he easily explain what he meant by an individual's recovering, or rediscovering, the elemental force within himself. He usually called the process "getting in touch";[38] later in life, he was likely to call it being "in the hands of God."[39]

Lawrence's entire religion, all of his ethics, all of his mental endeavor, all of his message for his time consists in striving to be, and in urging others to be, "in touch." "We don't exist unless we are deeply and sensually in touch."[40] To Lawrence, being "in touch" is as "the knowledge of God" to a Christian saint. It is living in the house of God

> Like a cat asleep on a chair
> at peace, in peace
> and at one with the master of the house . . .
> feeling the presence of the living God
> like a great reassurance
> a deep calm in the heart.[41]

It is living life deeply, experiencing life intensely, understanding life with the entire personality, missing nothing of life, adjusting all the elements of mind and heart and body to one another, drinking life to the lees:

> And life is for delight and bliss
> and dread, and the dark, rolling ominousness of
>   doom
> and the bright dawning of delight again.[42]

> Life is for kissing and for horrid strife.
> Life is for angels and the Sunderers
> Life is for the daimons and the demons
> those that put honey on your lips and those that
>   put salt.[43]

But Lawrence feels that only a few people are "in touch," that our entire civilization is out of touch; somewhere, long ago, man took the wrong turning and wandered away from God, "out of touch," and has been wandering farther ever since. A hundred evils that have developed in man and in his society are still preventing men from coming "in touch." Lawrence attacks these evils in a very large number of his later poems; and it is these attacks, more than anything else he has written, that have caused him to be frequently misunderstood, disliked, and accused of being immoral.

Like other mystics, he distrusts the final authority of mind. "The mind is touchless."[44] Nowhere in his poetry, however, is Lawrence guilty of what he has been accused of—waging "a crusade against mind,"[45] of "hating the world of mind."[46] What he actually believes is what all mystics and all romantics have always believed: that the mind with its knowledge is inadequate to discover the ultimate truth, to achieve the final salvation. Burns said the same thing in his remarks on schools and learning in the "Epistle to John Lapraik"—and Lawrence:

> All that we know is nothing, we are merely
>   crammed wastepaper baskets
> Unless we are in touch with that which laughs at
>   all our knowing.[47]

The title of another of his poems is **"Man Is More than Homo Sapiens."** He does not wish to abandon mind and knowledge, but to use them for high purposes that are beyond mind and knowledge:

> You must fuse mind and wit with all the senses
> before you can feel truth.[48]

And truth "alone satisfies in the end."[49] Perhaps the generally circulated idea that Lawrence crusades against mind comes from the fact that (like the Christian who believes that the sinner must become as a little child again before he can be saved) Lawrence demands the casting-off of egotism and self-sufficiency, the regeneration in elemental oblivion, a completely new start, before man can really be "in touch" with God.[50]

Lawrence has been accused of rejecting science; and he does reject the science that merely classifies and categorizes individual things without comprehending their individuality.[51] On the other hand, he accepts biology—the dominant science of his day—with its central theory of evolution. Nor can one understand Lawrence without understanding the theory of evolution; his poetry is full of it.

> The history of the cosmos
> is the history of the struggle of becoming.[52]

All the sensuous world, God himself, was evolved through struggle from "the dim flux of unformed life"; God himself is still evolving; and man evolves with God.[53]

The failure of contemporary intellect, Lawrence believes, is not that it knows too much, but that it has settled into "the rigidity of fixed ideas."[54] It no longer actually feels or believes what it worships as truth; it is the perpetual and universal victim of its own lies, self-deceit, and hypocrisy. "What has killed mankind . . . is lies."[55] Lies about loving our neighbor, lies about loving our husband or wife, lies in our laughter, lies in our talk, lies in our singing, lies in our moralizing, lies in our faithfulness to the truth of yesterday that has become the untruth of today. The world is caught in a web of lies. Valuing truth as he does, Lawrence sneers at, snarls at, or rails at conventional men for what he considers their inward rottenness of spirit and their outward sanctimoniousness of behavior—for their pride in sin, their worship of property, their crowd-thinking, their insensitiveness to beauty, their bigotry, their self-satisfaction, their vapid pleasures, their desire to hurt all that is not like themselves, their bland hypocrisy, their pretentiousness, their cowardice in the face of both mystery and truth, their love of the ugly and the unimportant.[56] Modern men are "tarnished with centuries of conventionality,"[57] which makes them "go counter to their own deepest consciousness."[58]

All these lies are a symptom of that mortal disease, that "pure evil," of man not "in touch"—of man who has separated himself from the sensual Life Force, and is living as a self-important, self-reliant, self-centered ego—a "self-apart-from-God." Again language fails Lawrence here, and he has difficulty defining this "obscene ego" that has lost touch with all the beautiful, vital, sensual, elemental, instinctive, creative force of the universe, and is living separately within a pattern of ready-made customs. Lawrence speaks of this sort of man as having "absolute self-awareness," "absolute freedom," "self-consciousness"—as being "self-willed," "self-motived," "self-centered." To be thus separate from God, living in a world made not by God but by man, is the ultimate evil.[59]

And this world that egoistic man has created and lives in—what is it like? For one thing, it is a machine world—and Lawrence hates machines with a living passion. They are bloodless, having no possible connection with the elemental Life Force; they, and the making of them, are about to "reduce the world to grey ash"; they destroy natural beauty; they enslave the bodies and stupefy the minds of those that work for them; they become models on which men pattern their own machine lives[60]—these are some of the reasons why Lawrence hates machines.

For another thing, this world of men-apart-from-God is a world in which crowds, mobs, and masses have replaced the separateness and the individuality which every creature must preserve if he is to be "in touch" with God. The breath of the crowd defiles and salvation is to be found only in "pure aloneness."[61] Yet the "great word of our civilization" is *en masse,* and the irresistible tendency of the time is toward centralization.[62]

Finally, people themselves, corrupted by the machines (radio, cinema, automobile, factory, and daily newspaper) have lost all "touch" with God, and have become repulsive. By endless repetition they have sanctified ancient mistakes;[63] they resent the different and the superior;[64] they are robots governed by robots;[65] they have become identical with the machines that they serve[66]—machine people destroying the earth's natural beauty,[67] hating one another and making revolutions and wars,[68] fighting over property.[69] Regarding them as the Yahoos of the modern world, Lawrence does not pretend either to value or to love most of his fellow men:

> You tell me every man has a soul to save?
> I tell you, not one man in a thousand has even a
>   soul to lose.[70]

Here Lawrence comes to the only real antinomy in his system. Some of his poems are more passionately sympathetic with working-people caught in the industrial vortex than are any other English poems since Shelley.[71] Yet he sees that all these people, once they are hooked and caught by the machines, are lost; they are so much divine material wasted and made worthless. Therefore, he sometimes feels no respect for them, feels no Christian obligation toward them. "Most men don't matter at all"; they "are not my fellow-men, and I repudiate them as such."[72] This is a bitter and cruel attitude, and it is not consistent with the other poems about working people.

This may be a good place to say something about Lawrence's political beliefs. They have often been called fascist. He wants each individual to be "in touch" with God; and he is Protestant enough to think that getting "in touch" is an individual affair.[73] When each man is "in touch"; when each man reveres earth, beauty, and love; when each man is passionately and holily alive; when each man, by being "in touch" with God, is "in touch" with all creation, which *is* God—there will be no disrespect for any created being, no urge toward centralizing,[74] no "obsession of oneness."[75] Therefore, there will be no war, no "universalism and cosmopolitanism," but only "a democracy of men, a democracy of touch."[76] He is impatient with both the "hard-boiled conservatives" and the "soft-boiled liberals";[77] and he loathes both the bourgeois and the bolshevist[78] though he confesses that, if he had to choose between them, he would choose the bourgeois because the bourgeois would interfere with him less.[79] In short, therefore, his ideal state would be one of virtually complete individualism in which all men, being "in touch," would have as little government as possible. This is hardly fascism.

On the other hand, Lawrence is realist enough to see that a vast number of robot-men now living can never succeed in getting "in touch";[80] they will remain forever robot-men—and utopia is, accordingly, impossible. Nevertheless, there remain two worthwhile classes of people: those few "who look into the eyes of the gods," and "those who look into the eyes of the few."[81] But all men must learn to obey, "not a boss, but the gleam of life" on the face of those men who have looked into the eyes of the gods.[82] This is not fascism, either. It is more like Plato's Republic; and the leaders are not "bosses" but heroes of mind and spirit—like Jesus, or Plato himself, or Shakespeare—whose eyes have seen God, and from whom lesser men may catch some of the divine gleam. It has been unfortunate for Lawrence that this visionary political scheme of his has been mistaken for fascism. Even Karl Shapiro has mistaken it, and has been one of the few poets who have written unfavorably about Lawrence.[83]

Lawrence's entire political philosophy is one of individualism—an impracticable and impossible individualism. He himself desires only to be left alone to discover God and beauty for himself, and his highest hope for other men is that they may have the same desire. Political revolutions are not the answer; revolutions are the work of robots.[84] Men really alive and "in touch" don't bother about such matters.

VI. LOVE

Lawrence is, of course, best, if not most favorably, known as a writer on sex. His most widely read novels revolve about the problem, and a very large portion of his poetry (up to about 1920) deals with it. Reasons why Lawrence was attracted to sex are several. First, he was wise enough to perceive, before the fact was generally admitted in England, that sex is extremely important in man's psychology; next, he saw that the dishonest conventionalities and hypocritical evasions which, he believed, characterize modern civilization were most glaringly apparent in relation to sex; third, the concept of sex is intimately associated with the generative and creative Life Force that lies at the center of Lawrence's philosophy; and finally, Lawrence began writing at just that period when Freudian psychology was being introduced into England, and he was immensely stimulated by it. The Freudian concept of the Unconscious out of which human personality springs was exactly in line with Lawrence's own concept of being "in touch" with the deeper, more elemental portions of the personality. It should be noted, however, that Lawrence, in his prose works if not in his poetry, rejected Freud's interpretation of the Unconscious as being "Nothing but a huge slimy serpent of sex, and heaps of excrement, and a myriad repulsive little horrors."[85] Lawrence's own Unconscious is very different.

The chief problem of modern man, and of Lawrence as an individual, is to break from under the all but impenetrable and immovable pyramid of tradition, egoism, falsity, and misunderstanding under which modern love and sex are buried, and to come "in touch" with the Life Force as healthily and normally as an animal, and as quietly and beautifully as a flower. We must learn to satisfy the sex instinct "with pure, real satisfaction, or perish, there is no alternative."[86] He studies the problem, probes it, speculates about it, and through much of his career writes about it. He approaches it from every possible angle. With him love is, in turn, sadism, masochism, autoeroticism, nympholepsy, the Oedipus complex, heterosexuality, and every other noun in psychoanalytic jargon.[87] It is terror, an unbearable desire, a renunciation, an abandonment, a hatred, a comfort, a delight, a wisdom, a frustration, an anguish, a jealousy, a humiliation, a pride.[88]

The philosophy of love that he finally evolves is poles removed from the animalism that many of his critics have tried to find in him. In his philosophy, love is not an emotion which unifies two people and makes them mutually absorb each other. Such love is disease and death. Rather, says the poet, when a man and a woman have learned to love each other perfectly, there comes into being the kind of individual who is "in touch" with God, and who is Lawrence's ideal.

> Then, we shall be two and distinct, we shall have
>   each our separate being,
> And that will be pure existence, real liberty.

> Till then, we are confused, a mixture, unresolved,
>   unextricated one from the other.
> It is in pure, unutterable resolvedness, that one is
>   free,
> Not in mixing, merging, not in similarity.[89]

This philosophy of love (not very different from Browning's, by the way) makes a consistent pattern with the rest of Lawrence's essentially individualistic philosophy. In it the satisfaction of the mere primary sex urge is only one of the many ways in which complex human nature achieves "real liberty." Mr. Louis Untermeyer was as wrong as it was possible for a critic to be when he wrote that Lawrence's "gamut has never extended beyond sex."[90]

VII. INDEBTEDNESS AND ORIGINALITY

The sources of Lawrence's philosophical system are many. Yet, like Shakespeare, he never takes from other writers without adding something of his own, and becoming a unique original.

The mystical element in his philosophy is derived from a long European tradition in religion and in literature. But the passionate materialism that Lawrence develops from his mystical faith is new.

From orthodox Christianity itself Lawrence borrows the idea of escaping from worldly vanity, returning to God, and undergoing a spiritual rebirth. But in Lawrence's thought this process of regeneration is conceived in terms that are completely unorthodox.

His concept of the Life Force is derived from a great deal of biological thinking in the previous century, as well as from Bergson and his *élan vital* in the present century. But Lawrence fuses this concept with the Romanticists' adoration of nature as a proto-divinity in an alliance quite new to modern thought.

His advocacy of return to the elemental in man is a continuation of the Romantic tradition. But it is an extension as well as a continuation: it would return to an elementalness more profound, more biological, than any that the Romanticists advocated.

His ideal of being "in touch" with the divine is related to a great many reforming ideals of a great many reformers in the history of human thought. But in Lawrence it encompasses not merely some selected "good" traits of human nature, but the whole man—body, mind, and spirit—flesh, knowledge, and intuition—the material world, human intellect, and religion.

Criticisms of the hypocrisy and folly of society are as old as society itself, and a good many of the suggested cures have involved a "return to nature." But very few of the advocates of a "return to nature" have been so courageous as Lawrence in dealing with society's very first and most essential relationship (without which there would be no society)—the relationship of men and women.

It is true that most of Lawrence's answers to the social problems of his time and ours are as impracticable as the answers that most other social philosophers have given. Society cannot and will not need Lawrence. Indeed, Lawrence never thought it would. His answers are those of an individualist writing for individuals. And any individual can find in Lawrence's poetry a philosophical system that is original, consistent, complex, and stimulating.

NOTES

In the following notes Lawrence's *Collected Poems* (Martin Secker, London, 1933) will be referred to by the Roman numeral "I." The *Last Poems* (edited by Richard Aldington and Giuseppe Orioli, The Viking Press, New York, 1933) will be referred to by the Roman numeral "II."

[1] *Saturday Review of Literature,* XXI, 8 (March 2, 1940).

[2] "Poet to Vagabond to Legend," by Harry Thornton Moore, *Saturday Review of Literature,* XXXIII, 20 (April 29, 1950).

[3] Auden: *Nation,* CLXIV, 482 (April 26, 1947).

Lewis: "A Hope for Poetry," *Collected Poems* (1935).

Wolfe: *Nineteenth Century,* CVII, 568 (April, 1930).

Spender: "Notes on D. H. Lawrence," *The Destructive Element* (1935).

Ford: *American Mercury* XXXVIII, 167 (June, 1936).

Bogan: *Nation,* CXLIX (October 7, 1939).

Gregory: *New Republic,* LXXIII, 133 (December 14, 1932).

[4] *D. H. Lawrence and Susan His Cow* (Columbia University Press, New York, 1939).

[5] Note 2, ix.

[6] In "A Whole History of Genius," *Saturday Review of Literature,* IX, 141 (October 1, 1932).

[7] In "A Small View of D. H. Lawrence," *Virginia Quarterly Review,* XVI, 127 (Winter, 1940).

[8] I, 417.

[9] I, 452.

[10] *Letters of D. H. Lawrence* (edited by Aldous Huxley, Wm. Heinemann, London), p. 109.

[11] II, 149.

[12] II, 150.

[13] II, 105.

[14] II, 106.

[15] II, 151, 214, 215.

[16] II, 11.

[17] II, 214, 215, 216.

[18] II, 7. See also II, 8, 9, 10, 12, 13.

[19] II, 8.

[20] II, 7, 9.

[21] II, 11.

[22] II, 213.

[23] II, 7, 8, 10, 11, 26, 27, 28, 29.

[24] "The Status of D. H. Lawrence," by Henry Thornton Moore, *New Republic,* XCVII, 210 (December 21, 1938).

[25] II, 251.

[26] II, 286.

[27] II, 69.

[28] II, 306.

[29] II, 60-61.

[30] In "D. H. Lawrence: The Phoenix and the Grove," *New Republic,* LXXIII, 133 (December 14, 1932).

[31] II, 26, 27, 28.

[32] I, 72, 73, 225.

[33] II, 159.

[34] II, 278.

[35] II, 289.

[36] II, 280.

[37] In "Lawrence: Creator and Dissenter," *Saturday Review of Literature,* XXIX, 17 (December 7, 1946).

[38] For example, II, 111, 113, 114, 115, etc.

[39] For example, II, 26, 28, 29, etc.

[40] II, 119.

[41] II, 27.

[42] II, 41.

[43] II, 43.

[44] II, 111.

[45] Tindall, p. 48.

[46] Tindall, p. 57.

[47] II, 120.

[48] II, 221.

[49] II, 222.

[50] II, 115-18.

[51] II, 55, 141.

[52] II, 296.

[53] II, 297.

[54] II, 266.

[55] II, 224, 225, 228, 229, 238, 241, 242, 247, 248.

[56] II, 100, 123, 134, 135, 143, 155, 157, 163, 173, 174, 241, 251, 266, 270, 288.

[57] II, 123.

[58] II, 144.

[59] II, 47, 48, 50, 90, 91, 92, 93, 132, 203, 208, 280.

[60] II, 47, 48, 55, 154, 167, 168, 170, 172, 187, 190, 191, 192, 194, 195, 196.

[61] II, 98, 100, 106-08, 115, 143, 158, 176.

[62] II, 143.

[63] II, 142.

[64] II, 159.

[65] II, 180.

[66] II, 191.

[67] II, 186-88.

[68] II, 204, 205, 207.

[69] II, 253-55, 258-61.

[70] II, 185.

[71] II, 165, 167, 168, 170, 172.

[72] II, 183, 184, 197-99, 219.

[73] II, 132.

[74] II, 112.

[75] II, 113.

[76] II, 110.

[77] II, 257.

[78] II, 254-63.

[79] II, 256.

[80] II, 131.

[81] II, 209.

[82] II, 209-13.

[83] "D. H. L.," *Harper's,* CLXXXVI, 463 (April, 1943).

[84] II, 204.

[85] Quoted by a correspondent in *Saturday Review of Literature,* VI, 1130 (June 14, 1930).

[86] I, 334. See also I, 66, 96, 276, 279, 317, 452, 463, 499.

[87] I, 14, 16, 133, 152, 174, 260, 300, 303, 318, 323; I, 23, 66; I, 9, 18, 325; I, 15, 44, 146, 177; I, 31, 116 ff., 426.

[88] I, 54, 278; I, 160, 161, 315; I, 31, 56, 158; I, 108, 136, 358; I, 287; I, 11; I, 144, 148, 156, 270, 298, 299, 302, 306, 308, 310, 318; I, 16, 19; I, 91, 93, 98, 112, 121, 143, 145, 150, 173, 192, 251; I, 250, 275; I, 253; I, 264; I, 287.

[89] I, 337.

[90] *Saturday Review of Literature,* VI, 17 (August 3, 1929).

Phyllis Bartlett (essay date 1951)

SOURCE: "Lawrence's Collected Poems: The Demon Takes Over," in *PMLA,* Vol. 66, 1951, pp. 583-93.

[*In the following essay, Bartlett examines the nature and breadth of Lawrence's revisions of his earlier poems for the 1928* Collected Poems.]

It is well known that D. H. Lawrence was an unsparing rewriter of his fiction, and the tradition persists that "he could never revise, he could only rewrite." Yet, although he rewrote a number of poems, as he did his short stories and novels, he revised many more—nearly all of them, in fact, either before or after publication. His most concentrated period of activity as a poetic reviser was the winter of 1927-28, when he collected his poems for the publisher Martin Secker, and he remarked at this time that he felt "like an autumn morning, a perfect maze of gossamer of rhythms and rhymes and loose lines floating in the air." No wonder he felt this way, for he had been altering rhythms, rhymes, single words, and punctuation in addition to rewriting whole stanzas and sometimes whole poems. In a few weeks he altered the face of his early poems as drastically as the arch-revisers Wordsworth and Tennyson altered theirs in the course of many years.

The poems that may be considered "early" are those that he wrote before he left England with Frieda in 1912. They had made up the volume *Love Poems and Others* (1913), most of the volume *Amores* (1916), and had been rifled more sparingly for *New Poems* (1918). When the time came for a collected edition, it was the product of this early vintage that left him most dissatisfied, although he found a number of changes to make in *Birds, Beasts and Flowers,* poems written 1920-23. The poems of his marriage, *Look! We Have Come Through* (1917), were left untouched.[1]

By the middle of March 1928, at Scandicci, Florence, Lawrence was correcting proofs for the *Collected Poems,* and in May he dated his prefatory Note from the same place. That Note also exists in a longer, more personal version that appeared among his posthumously published papers in *Phoenix,* and the two versions explain why he had undertaken his great labor of revision. He did not dwell on the small faults which he evidently had found in abundance—the misuse of prepositions and grammatical constructions, the inaccuracy of much of his diction—but emphasized the two motivations that lay behind his most complete rewritings. In the printed Note he stated his case thus:

> Some of the earliest poems, like **"The Wild Common"** and **"Virgin Youth,"** are a good deal rewritten. They were struggling to say something which it takes a man twenty years to be able to say. Some of the fictional poems are changed, to make the "fiction" more complete. A young man is afraid of his demon and puts his hand over the demon's mouth sometimes and speaks for him. And the things the young man says are very rarely poetry. So I have tried to let the demon say his say, and to remove the passages where the young man intruded. So that, in the first volume, many poems are changed, some entirely rewritten, recast. But usually this is only because the poem started out to be something which it didn't quite achieve, because the young man interfered with his demon.

In what ways did the demon of Lawrence's mature years take over from the young man; and in what ways did Lawrence, the seasoned writer of stories and novels, make the fiction of his fictional poems more complete?

For one thing, as any reader of the different versions of *Lady Chatterley's Lover* would expect, the demon had been completely released from the young man's inhibitions where the expression of sexual experience was concerned. This is evident in the rewriting of **"Virgin Youth"** to which Lawrence himself called attention. He expanded the poem from twenty-two to sixty-two lines, and a virginal phallic experience is shown for just what it was instead of being hinted at murkily. Moreover, in some of the later poems to Miriam (the girl of *Sons and Lovers,* in real life Jessie Chambers), as he pointed out in the unpublished version of his prefatory note, "the hand of the commonplace youth had been laid on the mouth of the demon," so that he altered them not for technique but "to say the real say." **"Scent of Irises"** and **"Last Words to Miriam"** are illustrative. **"Scent of Irises"**[2] tells of a gulf between lovers that is now "half grown over." It was the result of an experience in a "buttercup bog-end" and the revised version makes clear, as the first did not, that the woman was "taken" and that the gulf was the result of their "bodies' clash." **"Last Words to Miriam"** (*Amores,* 42; *C.P.,* I, 133) was more considerably rewritten, the present third stanza being added "to say the real say":

> Body to body I could not
>   Love you, although I would.
> We kissed, we kissed though we should not.
> You yielded, we threw the last cast,
>   And it was no good.

This, then, was why he failed, as he said in both versions, to give her the last "Fine torture" she deserved. In removing the young man's hand from the demon's mouth Lawrence revealed what he meant by the torture; and in the light of this revelation the concluding lines of the poem, where at first, rather vapidly, her face had been hardening, "Warping the perfect image of God, / And darkening my eternal fame," are brought back to the point:

> I should have been cruel enough to bring
>   You through the flame.

Two more poems from *Amores,* **"A Spiritual Woman"** (*Amores,* 106; *C.P.,* I, 145, retitled **"These Clever Women"**) and **"Liaison"** (*Amores,* 88; *C.P.,* I, 137, retitled **"The Yew-Tree on the Downs"**) were considerably changed for the same purpose, the last stanza of **"A Spiritual Woman"** being rewritten and the sixth and seventh of **"Liaison."** In both, the demon now says flatly what Lawrence undoubtedly remembered he had felt at the time: that he wanted the woman to accept him completely as a lover. Having been thus outspoken in his revision of the early poems of personal, sexual experience, Lawrence occasionally retouched the impersonal poems in the same way. Thus two lines added and a few changed in **"Fig"** (from *Birds, Beasts and Flowers*[3]) make even more specific the already heavily underscored comparison of the fig with the human female organ. It is in the realms of plain talk about sex needs and of sexual symbolism that the demon is most obviously released.

Lawrence's other gestures of freedom are more subtle and therefore more interesting. **"The Wild Common"** (*Amores,* 4; *C.P.,* I, 9), for instance, probably the earliest written of Lawrence's published poems, and the one to whose revision—along with **"Virgin Youth"**—he called particular attention in his prefatory Note, was written entirely anew from the fifth stanza to the end. The image of the boy standing on the bank of the old sheep-dip looking at his shadow on the water must have stirred his memory deeply, and it was the concept of substance versus shadow that took hold of him. Evidently he felt a falseness in the woman-imagery which he had first used, the confusing dual comparison both of his soul and of the water to a woman, and he remembered instead the joyous spring scene and how fine it was to be alive in the midst of it—to be substance, not shadow. This theme took hold of him and lifted the poem into one of celebration:

> But how splendid it is to be substance, here!
> My shadow is neither here nor there; but I, I am
>   royally here!

" . . . all that is God takes substance!" The mature Lawrence doctrine was read back into a youthful experience that seemed so well to fit it.

Comparably, one of the images in **"Nascent"** attracted him more than others and started him to recompose. This poem had been in the little sheaf of verses that Miriam sent to Ford Madox Hueffer, who printed them in the *English Review* of November 1909. It was considerably revised for inclusion in *Amores,* and was not only revised but doubled in length for **Collected Poems.** Even the verse form was changed. The poem as it appeared in the *English Review* (III, 562) was written in free verse, but when revising it for *Amores* (p. 26) Lawrence plucked a rhymed quatrain from the end of the poem that preceded it, **"Dreams Old,"** and used these lines as the opening of **"Dreams Nascent."** After that start he added other rhymes here and there in the poem,[4] so that he had before him a strange mixture of rhymed and unrhymed verse when he embarked on the revision of the poem in 1928 (*C.P.,* I, 225). He decided in favor of the rhymed quatrains throughout, thus making the poem more consonant with his other early verses.[5] The schoolroom and schoolboys were read out of it entirely, and he concentrated his imagery on the railway men who at first had been mentioned cursorily as breaking the surface of his day dreams as he noticed them, through the schoolroom window, moving along the track. In the new poem they become the central symbol, as they walk with axe and pick-axe, "alive, and with something to do." They are made into Whitmanesque figures who are invited to "break this prison, this house of yesterday," to break the walls of possession and release us from a filthy dream. It is as if his intervening discovery of Whitman had reshaped his memory. He implicitly acknowledged **"Nascent"** as a completely new poem by separating it from those written at the same time and putting it near the end of his first volume of **Collected Poems,** in which the poems were arranged somewhat in order of composition.

"Discipline" was another of the poems that launched his literary career in the *English Review* and that he rewrote for **Collected Poems.** There are really three poems of that name: the one in the *English Review* which has six stanzas, the one in *Amores* which has nine, and the one in **Collected Poems** which has fourteen. The first two stanzas, with slight verbal revisions, are the only constant throughout. As in **"The Wild Common"** he let the original scene stand. Here it is a classroom on a stormy day where the poet-teacher sees the schoolboys as woven in the "dark net" of his discipline. The essential situation is that he has come to these boys with forbearance, pity, and love, but they have turned on him. In each of the three poems he has something different to say about this situation. In the first (*Eng. Rev.,* III, 564) he is rather gnomic, so much so that he could afford to save one of the discarded stanzas and publish it later as **"The Prophet."** Terribly upset by the boys' rejection of him, he concludes:

> The flower of forgiveness is plucked from off the
>   offender's plot
> To wither on the bosom of the merciful:—so many
>   seeds the less,
> So much more room for riot! The great God
>   spareth not,
> He waters our face with tears, our young fruits
>   fills with bitterness.

Very confusing. In the second poem (*Amores,* 34) he is pathetic and concludes that fundamentally in his heart he has nothing to do with the boys but only with his one true love (almost surely Miriam), whom he asks to comfort him. In the third (*C.P.,* I, 102), where the grown-up demon speaks, he is philosophic. Perhaps the boys were right in rejecting his love,

> for the young are busy deep down at the
>   roots,
> And love would only weaken their under-earth
>   grip, make shallow
> Their hold on reality, enfeeble their rising shoots
> With too much tincture of me, instead of the
>   dark's deep fallow.

There is a depth below love where the fight for being must be fought by the young, and the old must never win over them. The poet-teacher for the moment is broken, but he has a knowledge of roots and in the future will love only when his love is wanted; then his blossoms will live. This third poem is scarcely what Lawrence would have said as a young man had he been able to say it; it is what twenty years later he found he would have liked to have wanted to say.[6]

"Weeknight Service" is another poem which he revised chiefly because he found that the tone was wrong. The poem is about church-bells ringing for service and, in essence, how cheap they sound against the greatness and patience of a beautiful night. But he had chosen many of his words poorly, so that the effect was blurred by a vocabulary that seemed to reveal a sort of sneaking affection for the bells. This is what either the artist or the demon saw and remedied. The first and last stanzas of the poem may be quoted as fair specimens of the verbal improvements Lawrence made throughout his early poetry in 1928, when he was content to revise rather than rewrite. The words in italics (*Amores,* 18) are the ones replaced in the version made for Collected *Poems* (I, 42) and his revisions are written above them. The poem opens:

The five old bells
           stridently
Are hurrying and *eagerly* calling,
  Insisting
Imploring, protesting
    are right
They *know,* but clamorously falling
        confusion, without
Into gabbling *incoherence, never* resting,
      shouts of an orator endlessly
Like spattering *showers from a bursten sky-rocket*
   dropping
From the tower on the town, but
In splashes of sound, endlessly, never stopping.

There were overtones of sympathy in the "eagerly" and the "imploring" which were not wanted, and the "splashes of sound" from the "bursten sky-rocket" have bright, holiday associations, unlike the shouts of orators. The rhythm is improved in the fifth line. The second stanza required less correction. It describes the moon caught up high "In the net of the night's balloon," smiling at nothing unless it is the little star that makes jests at the bells' "insanity," revised to the more shocking word "obscenity." In the third stanza the Night is said to be indifferent to the reason "Why the old church bellows and brags" (the "bellows" having replaced "sobs," which again suggested pity for the church), though "The noise distresses her ears"—an improvement over "The light distresses her eyes," which was silly since the light must have been moonlight and had nothing to do with the noise from the bells. Finally:

The wise old trees

Drop their leaves with a faint, sharp hiss of
  contempt,
[Deleted]
While a car at the end of the street goes by with a
  laugh;

As by degrees
    damned   we are
The *poor* bells cease, and *the Night is* exempt,
And the stars can chaff
    cool high   droning
The *ironic* moon at their ease, while the *dim old*
  church
              wailing, and last ghosts that
  lurch
Is peopled with shadows and *sounds and ghosts*
  that lurch
Towards
In its cenotaph.

Here are the final strokes that eliminate any suggestion of sentiment for the church. The poem, like any number of others, makes its point far more sharply after its alteration.

In other poems it was not the tone so much as the meaning that needed clarification. It was sometimes necessary to add only a single word, as in the little poem **"Anxiety"** (*Amores,* 57; *C.P.,* I, 115, retitled **"Endless Anxiety"**), where the poet is apprehensive about the arrival of a bicycle and introduced the new reading "Telegram bicycle" to make clear that it was a telegram telling of his mother's death that he fears. The identity of the speaker in the poem **"Epilogue"** (*Amores,* 31; *C.P.,* I, 100, retitled **"Forecast"**) is entirely vague, but by adding five lines and considerably revising others Lawrence revealed it as a woman addressing her man. Part of the confusion in the early version was that the coming of a "June-hot," tiger-lily woman was forecast, whereas the poem was called **"Epilogue"** but did not say any last words. The heart of the lover was only told that it would thirst for daffodils when they were dead. In the revised version the daffodils are explicitly associated with the woman who speaks the piece, now properly called **"Forecast."** A misty poem, **"Discord in Childhood"** (*Amores,* 9; *C.P.,* I, 13), was immediately illuminated by the simple device of naming the sexes of the two voices which the child heard quarreling in a house: in the revised version one was said to whistle with a "she-delirious rage," the other to be a "male thong" booming. The situation springs to life. Such clarifications were obvious needs that any reader might have pointed out to Lawrence.

Lawrence's demon was never especially motivated by consistency, but it did become aware of the young poet's allusions to God and occasionally took them over. In 1924 Lawrence had published in the *Adelphi* an article **"On Being Religious,"** in which he said that no man can define God, "And a word nobody can define isn't a word at all. It's just a noise and a shape, like pop! or Ra or Om." The young Lawrence doubtless had never thought of this point, but the older Lawrence having thought of it was fretted by his early, easy allusions to the Deity. Many of them went out, as in the lines from **"Last Words to Miriam"** already quoted. He no longer cared to write in his own person about "the image of God," when he had no idea what the pattern might be. On the other hand, the wife in **"Wedding Morn"** (*C.P.,* I, 50) might still be allowed to wonder "which image of God" her "man is made toward" because she would think in these terms. Also it was all right for the poet himself in **"The Wild Common"** to say "all that is God takes substance," because this is one point he could be sure of. In **"Corot"**[7] the word "God" is replaced throughout by **"Life"** or **"Time,"** a shift that necessitated a good many verbal changes and one change of rhyme. To eliminate "God" from the poem **"Michael Angelo"** meant that he had to rewrite the poem. In its early version (*Love Poems,* xli) God was the maker and life-giver throughout and He was capitalized. Since the older Lawrence could no longer accept this concept, the rewritten poem (*C.P.,* I, 68) is framed in questions: "Who" was the moulder and the life-giver, etc.? An added stanza says that the question "Who?" will never be answered.

These, then, are some of the ways in which Lawrence, at forty-two, allowed his demon to push away the hand that the youthful poet had sometimes clapped over his mouth. The mature poet also spoke out more boldly in some of the fictional poems which he said he had changed "to make the 'fiction' more complete." **"Whether or Not,"** **"The Drained Cup," "Violets,"** and **"Two Wives"** are good examples of this operation, the narrative interest in all four of these poems being strengthened chiefly by new conclusions.

In his unpublished preface to *Collected Poems* Lawrence remarked, "I remember Garnett disliked the old ending to **'Whether or Not.'** Now I see he was right, it was the voice of the commonplace me, not the demon. So I have altered it." This is a dialect poem, all conversation, about the girl Liz whose policeman fiancé has begot a child on his widow landlady because Liz, while exciting him, was righteous whereas the widow was generous. By adding the eleventh section Lawrence changed the outcome of the story entirely. At first it had seemed that Liz, by being given the last words, would have her way: her policeman was to pay off the widow and come contritely back to her (*Love Poems,* xliv). When Lawrence revised the poem he made Tim show some spunk and brought a nasty jolt to Liz (*C.P.,* I, 80). The new section gave the policeman the last words which he uses to tell his girl flatly:

> Tha *art* so sure tha'rt right, Liz!
>   That damned sure!
> But 'ark thee 'ere, that widder woman
>   's less graspin', if 'er's poor.

As for himself, he intends to get away from the place and not marry either of them. The reader feels completely satisfied that Liz had it coming to her.

"The Drained Cup" is truly a new poem in its final version, for, after revising the first five stanzas, Lawrence entirely rewrote the rest of the poem. He made a change in the characterizations as well as in the ending of this dramatic monologue. The speaker is a tough-minded, vigorous woman, who is sending her man on his way to marry another. He has been snowed in with her for a week which they have spent in lovemaking. In the first version (*Love Poems,* lvi) she warns him about all the hazards of the road home, then shows him his face in a mirror to reveal to him how worn-out he is; she can part with him because he has said good-by so thoroughly. He is shown only as exhausted and scared. In the rewritten poem (*C.P.,* I, 174), instead of making him look at himself in a real mirror, she tells him in unsparing, analytical language just what he is like. He emerges as the kind of man who *must* be drained in love. He is welcome to marry a nice, fresh "little wench" because he won't have any peace until he has tried such a one, but she won't satisfy him and he'll be back. Even the kind of girl he is going to marry is thus established, whereas in the early version she had merely been referred to as "grander" and better for marrying. The speaker, although she has not changed

nature, shows more thoroughly how well she understands and loves the needs of men.

There is more punch too in the revised version of the short dialect poem **"Violets."** The fourth stanza is effectively rewritten and a concluding tenth stanza is added that underscores the point of the poem (*C.P.,* I, 52). One sister is addressing another about the funeral of a man who presumably was their brother. The sister who is being addressed levels the charge that the man had come to his end by drink and "carrying's on," bad habits induced by his having got in with her sister's lot of friends. But the speaker wants only to tell how she is touched by the warmth of an unknown girl who, after the mourners had left the grave, slipped a bunch of violets out of her bosom and dropped them in. The first version (*Love Poems,* xlii) had described the gesture without comment, but the added stanza thrusts at the puritanical sister:

> But I thowt ter mysen, as that wor th' only bit
> O' warmth as 'e got down theer; th' rest wor stone
>   cold.
> From that bit of a wench's bosom; 'e'd be glad of it,
> Gladder nor of thy lilies, if tha maun be told.

As in **"Whether or Not,"** Lawrence so revised **"Two Wives"** as to make a different speaker end the poem.[8] In six added stanzas the wedded wife was allowed to have her say and speak the last words in answer to the strange "bride" who had entered the death-chamber of the man they both loved. Fundamentally Lawrence would have had no use for the intruder who was the kind of woman he had castigated in **"A Spiritual Woman"** (or **"These Clever Women"**), and it was right that the crushed wife should revive sufficiently to flare up at her and tell her to get out. The wedded wife loved her man for his substance, his "mortality." It was the real thing. It was not just words or the spiritual woman's claim on an "eternity" of love.

While speaking in the unpublished preface of what he called his "imaginative or fictional" poems, Lawrence was inconsistent in his statements about the demon's relation to them. He admitted, as already seen, that the end of **"Whether or Not"** was weak because the commonplace man, not the demon, had spoken, and he amended the poem accordingly, thus implying that it should have been the demon's work in the first place. But in another context he said that the form of these fictional poems can be played with, unlike the form of those over which the demon had control, and called attention specifically to **"Love on the Farm"** and **"Wedding Morn"** as poems he had changed "to get them into better form, and take out the dead bits." By "form" he meant verbal improvements, such as he had made in most of his poems, and neither the fictional **"Love on the Farm"** (formerly titled **"Cruelty and Love"**) nor **"Wedding Morn"** is altered more than the personal **"Weeknight Service,"** which I have used as a typical example of his revising. But it would be foolish to expect strict logic of Lawrence when he was making the uncongenial effort of ascribing limits to his demon's domain.

It is only surprising that he ever stirred himself to frame a theory of poetry as he did in a preface for the New York edition of *New Poems* (1920), adding that it should have accompanied *Look! We Have Come Through.* Eight years later this theory partially underlay the selection of poems which he chose to revise. In the preface he had said that "Poetry is, as a rule, either the voice of the far future, exquisite and ethereal, or it is the voice of the past, rich, magnificent." The Greeks heard both of these voices in Homer's epics and Englishmen heard them in the lyrics of Shelley and Keats. "But there is another kind of poetry: the poetry of that which is at hand: the immediate present," and of this poetry Whitman's is the best. "The clue to all his utterance lies in the sheer appreciation of the instant moment, life surging itself into utterance at its very well-head. . . . The quick of the universe is the *pulsating, carnal self,* mysterious and palpable," and Whitman brings us so near this quick that we fear him. The mark of the immediate present, Lawrence insisted, is that in it "there is no perfection, no consummation, nothing finished. "Life, the ever-present, knows no finality, no finished crystallisation. Free verse *is* the instant, the quick, because its utterance "just takes place." True to this belief, Lawrence did not touch the free verse poems of *Look! We Have Come Through*—but then neither did he the rhymed poems in the same volume. Unrhymed or rhymed, these poems must have seemed to him closest to Whitman's achievement in touching the quick. (Had he wanted to revise them, however, he would have had ample precedent in Whitman himself.)

Most of the early poems, on the other hand, were not written in free verse and these are the ones he amended so liberally. In these unsatisfactory poems Lawrence must have found an immediate present, though cast in forms that had not instantly apprehended it. He recognized his demon lurking in them somewhere. And since, according to the unpublished preface to *Collected Poems,* for the demon "the past is not past. The wild common, the gorse, the virgin youth are here and now. The same: the same me, the same one experience," Lawrence felt right about trying to give "more complete expression" to the present-past. By this argument he vindicated, as most poets have not chosen to do, the refurbishing of his immature utterances. And though his critical language was that of an inspired poet, he operated as an artist—to the immense improvement both of his personal and impersonal poems.

NOTES

[1] Except that "The Song of a Man Who is Loved," which the publisher of *Look! We Have Come Through* had omitted, was restored in *Collected Poems.* See Richard Aldington, *D. H. Lawrence, Portrait of a Genius But . . .* (New York, 1950), p. 163, for the original text.

[2] *Amores* (London, 1925), p. 38; *Collected Poems,* 2 vols. (London, 1928), I, 98 (this work hereafter referred to as *C.P.*).

[3] (New York, 1923), p. 5; *C.P.,* II, 129 retitled "Figs."

[4] There had been two rhymes in stave vii of the version in the *English Review.*

[5] Comparably, he turned the 13-line sketch, "Baby-Movements: 1. Running Barefoot" (*Eng. Rev.*, III, 565), into a sonnet with Shakespearian rhyme scheme: "Baby Running Barefoot" (*C.P.,* I, 59).

[6] Richard Aldington, in *D. H. Lawrence, Portrait of a Genius But . . .* (p. 77), used the final version of this poem to make a point about Lawrence's attitude to his pupils, and perhaps Jessie Chambers, at the time the poem was first written. But the thesis of this paper indicates that future students of Lawrence who are using the poems as biographical material should always quote the version that appeared nearest the time under discussion, not neglecting magazine versions, which furnish many surprises.

[7] *Love Poems and Others* (London, 1913), p. xxxiii; *C.P.,* I, 66.

[8] *New Poems* (New York, 1920), p. 65; *C.P.,* I, 198.

William J. Fisher (essay date 1956)

SOURCE: "Peace and Passivity: The Poetry of D. H. Lawrence," in *The South Atlantic Quarterly,* Vol. 55, 1956, pp. 337-48.

[*In the following essay, Fisher examines what he believes is the paradoxical nature of Lawrence's poetry.*]

To read the poems of D. H. Lawrence after knowing his novels and other prose is to confront the paradox of the romantic. The rebellious individualism which distinguishes Lawrence's fiction is inverted in the poetry into a continuing desire to be merged, to be soothed into some harmonious and self-obliterating whole. In contrast with the turbulent fiction, Lawrence's poetry is generally temperate, expressing a craving for an "oblivion," for an "utter sleep," or for some other quiescent oneness. The passive conception and the passive image prevail: the poet yearns to be taken, touched, folded, enclosed; to be eased into darkness; to be immersed softly and unconsciously.

Throughout his life and his writings, Lawrence re-enacted the perennial tragedy of romanticism: proclaiming rebellion ("Certainly with this world I am at war"), he longed for peace and security; demanding liberation in behalf of life, he perpetually sought escape from it to deathlike states; urging an unrestrained self-assertion, if not self-indulgence, he kept trying to effect a merging, a self-obliteration. The poetry reflects most clearly and consistently this latter passive side and thereby escapes the dilemma of an unresolved dualism.

The "phallic quest" of the novels was seldom convincing. There was generally an element of "passivity" in the make-up of the dark, goaty heroes. Lawrence tried to free them from the natural demands of their role by enveloping them in his religion of the blood, his idea that true sexuality exists only in the precivilized unconscious, in the dark oblivious depths, independent of will and personality. The result was that these strangely ambivalent characters usually alternated between the desire to be assimilated and the need to triumph over the female. Birkin of *Women in Love* is a typical Lawrencean hero. By turns, he is a noble idealist, a pouting adolescent, a flaming lover, a finicky hermit, and a tedious pseudo-philosopher. In one scene he retreats from the advances of the overcivilized Hermione to the consolation of a dewy hillside, where he strips off his clothes and loses himself in herbaceous intercourse. Saturated with the touch of flowers and shrubs, he discovers that "to lie down, and roll in the sticky, cool hyacinths" is "more delicate and more beautiful than the touch of any woman. . . . How fulfilled he was, how happy!" He knew now "where he belonged." But Birkin is the main personage of a novel, and he must stir himself, must arise and return to the world of human beings, where he has his virile role to perform. The novel bloats and blurs under the strain.

Yet Lawrence was able to use an almost identical episode as the core experience of a poem without running the same risks or committing the same excesses, and without violating the integrity of his conception. **"The Wild Common"** describes a youth exulting in his discovery of nature, finding in air, earth, and water the elements of an exuberant love. Like Birkin, the "naked lad" takes a passive part, yielding himself into a happy harmony as air and water embrace him and take him into themselves. But by contrast with the novel, the lyric is self-sufficient in its containment of the joyful moment; there is no need in a poem to disturb the equilibrium:

> Over my skin in the sunshine, the warm, clinging air
> Flushed with the songs of seven larks singing at
>   once, goes kissing me glad.
> You are here! You are here! We have found you!
>   Everywhere
> We sought you substantial, you touchstone of
>   caresses, you naked lad!
> Oh, but the water loves me and folds me,
> Plays with me, sways me, lifts me and sinks me,
>   murmurs: oh marvellous stuff!
> No longer shadow!—and it holds me
> Close, and it rolls me, enfolds me, touches me, as
>   if never it could touch me enough.

Thus it was in his poems that Lawrence gave in to the passivity and allowed it to govern his literary design. The poems disclose forthrightly the yearning for an "immersion," which is immanent both as temper and as subject. The poet can symbolize undisguised goals: a Lethe in which human activity is suspended; a selfless self wholly free from demands; a sanctuary of darkness, silence, warmth, comfort.

In landscapes and other natural surroundings, Lawrence found an ideal way of making things harmonize and of relieving the aching consciousness. Communion with the inanimate was satisfying because it demanded no response. Through identification with the physical world, the poet can experience an untroubled awareness:

> So now I know the valley
>   Fleshed all like me
> With feelings that change and quiver
> And clash, and yet seem to tally,
> Like all the clash of a river
>   Moves on to sea.
>
>   **("Renascence")**

Frequently the soothing power of nature restores a disturbed peace, as in **"First Morning."** The night had been a failure, the poet laments; "I could not be free." Yet—

> Now in the morning
> As we sit in the sunshine on the seat by the little
>   shrine
> And look at the mountain-walls,
> Walls of blue shadow
> And see so near at our feet in the meadow
> Myriads of dandelion pappus
> Bubbles ravelled in the dark green grass
> Held still beneath the sunshine—
> It is enough, you are near—
> The mountains are balanced,
> The dandelion seeds stay half-submerged in the
>   grass.

Sometimes in his merging and submerging the poet identifies himself with specific natural elements or animals, so that he becomes one with the nonvolitive: with sea, wind, trees. "I am the sea, I am the sea!" is the ardent cry of one poem; while another contemplates a more serene absorption:

> Imitate the magnificent trees
> That speak no word of their rapture, but only
> Breathe largely the luminous breeze.

The poet especially envies the fish, because "so little matters" to it; it is free from the awful demands of consciousness, living "utterly without misgiving" in its watery suspension: "To be a fish!" It is equally satisfying for the poet to yield his will to an outside force, abdicating all need to act, in deference to "my best/Soul's naked lightning, which should sure attest/God stepping through our loins in one bright stride"; or simply to disclaim his own volition: "Not I, not I, but the wind that blows through me."

The quintessence of Lawrence's feelings toward nature as expressed in his verse is contained in a single four-stanza poem titled **"Nonentity":**

> The stars that open and shut
> Fall on my shallow breast
> Like stars on a pool.
>
> The soft wind, blowing cool,
> Laps little crest after crest
> Of ripples across my breast.

And dark grass under my feet
Seems to dabble in me
Like grass in a brook.

Oh, and it is sweet
To be all these things, not to be
Any more myself.

Ironically, the author of this paean to **"Nonentity"** later ridiculed Walt Whitman for being one of the "great mergers" and for trying to achieve an "identity," an "Allness," with everything. "There can't be much left of *you* when you've cooked the awful pudding of Identity," Lawrence declared, neglecting to say what might be left of you when you've cooked the pudding of Nonentity. And though he celebrated Whitman's genius and acknowledged a debt to the poet of the Open Road, Lawrence protested that too often "Whitman becomes in his own person the whole world, the whole universe, the whole eternity of time."

Compounding the irony, Lawrence elsewhere used the same objection to decry the kind of "love" which becomes (as in Poe) a "glowing unison with all the universe." Yet Lawrence himself was as great a Merger in his poems of love as in his nature poetry. Sometimes, indeed, he combined the two themes: The poet-lover and his beloved know bliss when they can diffuse into a setting of pastoral harmony, misery when they and nature cannot coalesce.

In one of his first love lyrics, Lawrence wrote of a wish to "lie quite still, till the green/Sky ceased to quiver, and lost its active sheen./

I should like to drop
On the hay, with my head on her knee,
And lie dead still, while she
Breathed quiet above me; and the crop
Of stars grew silently.

I should like to lie still
As if I was dead; but feeling
Her hand go stealing
Over my face and my head, until
This ache was shed.

The image expresses the desire for an experience that is unconscious, yet conscious and feeling too; to be free of demands and responsibilities, of pain and struggle, to merge with something warm and comforting in suspended, isolated darkness: that is the recurring prospect of the love poems. Instead of the drive for conquest and exaggerated sexual triumph which we find in the novels, the poetry expresses a desire for nirvana and a sexual yielding.

This love which the poet craves is invoked repeatedly in the mother poems:

Then I longed for you with your mantle of love
    to fold
Me over, and drive from out my body the deep
Cold that had sunk to my soul, and there kept hold.

And years later, in the poems celebrating his relationship with Frieda, Lawrence was still writing of the love-impulse this way:

So I hope I shall spend eternity
With my face down buried between her breasts;
And my still heart full of security
And my still hands full of her breasts.

Elsewhere, the poet wishes to blend with the beloved in a fluid harmony, "liquid" frequently becoming the medium of total immersion:

Ah, drink me up
That I may be
Within your cup
Like a mystery,
Like wine that is still
In ecstasy.

Glimmering still
In ecstasy
Commingled wines
Of you and me
In one fulfill
The mystery.

And in a common variation of the pattern, the lovers figuratively melt into a flame, "a bonfire of oneness."

The merge-wish appears in still other love poems as a desire to *be* the beloved, to assume the passive role of the woman. "But how lovely to be you!" is the cry in **"Wedlock."** In **"Wedding Morn,"** the man yields himself to the overpowering love of the woman: "carelessly," "unconsciously," "helplessly," he is "at last laid low" by her. The woman speaks the piece, for the man in his fulfillment sleeps "satiate/with a sunk, unconscious head." In other narrative poems in which the narrator is a woman, the focus is on her experience as she submits to the male's advances. Thus, the final stanza of **"Love on the Farm"** is a direct evocation of sexual passivity:

And down his mouth comes to my mouth! and down
His bright dark eyes come over me, like a hood
Upon my mind! his lips meet mine, and a flood
Of sweet fire sweeps across me, so I drown
Against him, die, and find death good.

"The effect is startling . . . ," as S. W. Powell has stated. "For one feels that [the poet] is not merely impersonating the woman: he *is* the woman, and Lawrence the man is deleted."

While the poet craves inactive love, he fears the love which makes demands, which insists on a participation or action. From this love, the poet longs to be free. He hates "the burden of self-accomplishment:/The charge of fulfillment!" and he seeks escape. In **"End of Another Home Holiday,"** a mother-poem contemporaneous with the early love lyrics to Miriam, Love is described as "the great Asker," "the beggar-woman," and is contrasted throughout the poem with the animals and the natural elements, for the latter are happy and peaceful in undisturbed isolation:

> The sun and the rain do not ask the secret
> Of the time when the grain struggles down in the
>   dark. . . .
> The moon sets forth o'nights
> To walk the lonely, dusky heights
> Serenely, with steps unswerving;
> Pursued by no sight of bereavement
> No tears of love unnerving
> Her constant tread.

The heifer seeks a "loneliness"; the grain buries itself in the earth, "to hide."

> Nay, even the slumberous egg, as it labours under
>   the shell
>   Patiently to divide and self-divide,
> Asks to be hidden, and wishes nothing to tell.
> But when I draw the scanty cloak of silence over
>   my eyes
> Piteous love comes peering under the hood. . . .
> With a hoarse, insistent request that falls
>   Unweariedly, unweariedly,
>   Asking something more of me,
>   Yet more of me.

The emotional balance of the poem is thus established between the tired wretchedness of the poet, who is crying in plaintive protest against the beggar-woman, and the peacefulness of nature, which is allowed to go its way unmolested. In his desire for silent serenity, the poet likens himself to nature; it is only "love" which disturbs him, as if a hound were intruding on a sleeping calf.

Lawrence's poems on tortoises reiterate this theme. The poet sympathizes with the male tortoise, the "poor darling" who is the smaller and more delicate of the species, who has to suffer in humiliation the sex demands of the laconic and insensitive female hulk. He is "doomed," "divided into passionate duality,"

> . . . now broken into desirous fragmentariness
> Doomed to make an intolerable fool of himself
> In his effort toward completion again.

Meanwhile, the baby tortoise enjoys the perfect freedom of "isolation"; one must envy this creature who thrives alone, untouched by demands of any kind.

> To be a tortoise!
> Think of it, in a garden of inert clods
> A brisk, brindled little tortoise, all to himself—
> Adam!
>
>   . . . . .
>
> Moving and being himself,
> Slow, and unquestioned.

And one must grieve that the baby will some day face an adult sex responsibility. For this is the deadly fate of the male:

> Grim, gruesome gallantry, to which he is doomed,
> Dragged out of an eternity of silent isolation,
> And doomed to partiality, partial being,
> Ache, and want of being,
> Want,
> Self-exposure, hard humiliation, need to add
>   himself to her.
>
>   . . . . .
>
> And the still more awful need to persist, to follow,
>   follow, continue,
> Driven, after aeons of pristine, fore-god-like
>   singleness and oneness,
> At the end of some mysterious red-hot iron,
> Driven away from himself into her tracks. . . .

The consistency in Lawrence's poems of love resides in the poet's yearning for harmony and inactivity. Whether the immediate objective is to merge or to isolate, whether the wish is to be free of a discordant demand or to be folded over in an oblivion, the goal is a passive oneness. There must be no infringement on the poet's "freedom"; there must be no need for action or response. When others come too close, he retreats. Explicitly, **"Excursion Train"** at once acknowledges the anguish of demanding love and cherishes the peacefulness of an undemanding envelopment:

> You hurt my heart-beat's privacy;
> I wish I could put you away from me;
> I suffocate in this intimacy
>   In which I half love you. . . .
> Though surely my soul's best dream is still
> That a new night pouring down shall swill
> Us away in an utter sleep.

We know that in his personal life Lawrence ran into constant conflict with other people. All his life he searched for some "sweet home" of peace, purity, and brotherhood. His plans for a brotherly utopia filled dozens of letters and occupied much fervent conversation, but the dream never approached realization, principally because of Lawrence's perfectionism, his dissatisfaction with each person and place as it became here and now. ("I sort of wish I could go to the moon.") The way in which Lawrence projected into his novels an inadequate resolution of this dilemma is typified by *The Plumed Serpent,* where he contrasts the real, modern Mexico which disgusted him with an ideal reprimitivized culture of his own incredible design. In his poems, he was writing more credibly, without ambivalence:

> I like people quite well
> at a little distance.
> I like to see them passing and passing
> and going their own way,
> especially if I see their aloneness alive in them.
>
> Yet I don't want them to come near.
> If they will only leave me alone
> I can still have the illusion that there is
>   room enough in the world.

This way, in the vicinity of people yet undefiled by them, the poet retains the integrity of his quiescence. Otherwise, the discordant world must be shunned. In a verse about misunderstood adolescence, the young Lawrence wrote that he was glad to be "remote":

> I sit absolved, assured I am better off
> 　Beyond a world I never want to join.

In the poems of his maturity, the world is still oppressive and threatening:

> . . . . Ah, if only
> There were no teeming
> Swarms of mankind in the world, and we were
> 　less lonely.

For aloneness can become intolerable too. The harmony can be spoiled by the discord of one's self and its awareness. Knowing per se, the consciousness of existence, can be too active. Whereupon the poet cries out against the demands of his own being:

> And oh—
> 　That the man I am
> 　Might cease to be.

For, although Lawrence insisted in his mystical psychology on "the deep, rich aloneness" by which a man should "possess his own soul in strength within him, deep and alone," he never portrayed self-sufficiency with conviction. His novels fracture on characters who aggressively declare their independence, yet who unwittingly reveal their dependencies. The poems not only acknowledge the dependencies, but focus especially upon them.

When Lawrence called Whitman "fearfully mistaken" for trying to merge with the whole world, he granted the need for some intimacy, but claimed that Whitman had gone so far in embracing the "All" that he had led himself straight to **"Death."** Though each organism, including man, is intrinsically "isolate and single," Lawrence explained, it must be continually "vivified" through "contact with other matter." The "blood systems" of man and woman should meet and "almost fuse." But, Lawrence emphasized, they must maintain that final thin barrier. Merging would mean some form of Death. And so, Lawrence charged, apparently unaware of the irony, Whitman the self-styled poet of Life had betrayed his own cause: "Love, and Merging, brought Whitman to the edge of Death! Death! Death!"

> This is strange from the exultant Walt.
> Death!
> Death is now his chant! Death!
> Merging! And Death! Which is the final merge.
> The great merge into the womb. Woman.
> And after that, the merge of comrades: man-for-man love.
> And almost immediately with this, death, the final merge of death.

> There you have the progression of merging. For the great mergers, woman at last becomes inadequate.

For those who love to extremes, Woman is inadequate for the last merging. So the next step is the merging of the man-for-man Love. And this is on the brink of death. It slides over into death.

Lawrence's description of Whitman's "progression" could, of course, stand as a tracing of the cycle in his own works. For death, a subject which hovers about a good deal of Lawrence's poetry, predominates in the *Last Poems*. Images of darkness and oblivion and the silence of waters convey the theme. Praising these poems as among Lawrence's best, Kenneth Rexroth has written, "In the last hours Lawrence seems to have lived in a state of suspended animation, removed from the earth, floating." But whereas Rexroth attributes this state exclusively to the fact that Lawrence was "transfigured by the immediacy of death," these poems actually carry through to their logical conclusion the moods, attitudes, and themes of Lawrence's whole previous body of poetry. Early in his career, Lawrence had written:

> I wish the church had covered me up with the rest
> In the home-place. Why is it she should exclude
> Me so distinctly from sleeping the sleep I'd love
> 　best?

And he had often used such images as this one:

> Not sleep, which is grey with dreams,
> nor death, which quivers with birth,
> but heavy, sealing darkness, silence, all
> 　immovable. . . .

Compare these earlier poems with a typical "last" poem, **"The End, The Beginning"**:

> And if there were not an absolute, utter forgetting
> and a ceasing to know, a perfect ceasing to know
> and a silent, sheer cessation of all awareness
> how terrible life would be!
> how terrible it would be to think and know, to
> 　have consciousness!
> But dipped, once dipped in dark oblivion
> the soul has peace, inward and lovely peace.

If there is any change, the quiescence has become an immediate, felt reality rather than a yearning. "The waters of oblivion" are at hand without the seeking for them that had marked many of the earlier poems. Where the younger poet had written, "You know how it rests/One to be quenched, to be given up, to be gone in the dark;/To be blown out, to let night douse the spark," the later poet is at peace for the most part. In one version of **"The Ship of Death,"** written during his last days, Lawrence carries through a figure of the "little soul" rowing over the seas on its "longest journey, towards the greatest goal"—"the womb of silence in the living night." And in the same final period, he wrote **"The Breath of Life,"** quoted here in its entirety:

> The breath of life is in the sharp winds of change
> Mingled with the breath of destruction.
> But if you want to breathe deep, sumptuous life,
> Breathe all alone, in silence, in the dark
> and see nothing.

It would be oversimplification to label the impulse a "death wish." For the ideal is still what Lawrence calls "an oblivion of uttermost living." One is "not quite dead"—or more than dead. The poet seeks to be acted upon so that his state of perfect harmony will be perpetuated in sensate consciousness. He shall have only to *be* in the most quiescent sense as he is lulled softly within the darkness. Life is "a cat asleep on a chair, at peace," and the end for which the poet prepares is a goal he has sought all his life: "a long, long journey . . . to the sweet home of pure oblivion."

NOTES

* All quotations from Lawrence's poems are from the two-volume *Collected Poems* (1928) and the *Last Poems* (1933) edited by Richard Aldington.

Adrienne Rich (essay date 1965)

SOURCE: "Comment: Reflections on Lawrence," in *Poetry*, Vol. 106, 1965, pp. 218-25.

[*In the following review of* The Complete Poems of D.H. Lawrence, *Rich assesses Lawrence as a major poet, finding evidence that Lawrence deliberately reduced many poems to doggerel for effect, and arguing that Lawrence is the English language's best love poet since William Shakespeare.*]

"Thought," he says in **More Pansies,** "is a man in his wholeness wholly attending." Have his readers wholly attended to him? "But, my dear God, when I see all the understanding and suffering and the pure intelligence necessary for the simple perceiving of poetry, then I know it is an almost hopeless business to publish the stuff at all," he wrote to Harriet Monroe. It seems scarcely possible that the old charges of hysteria, anti-craftsmanship, can still be leveled, that his own references to "the demon" (in the Preface to the **Collected Poems,** 1928) can still be misread. ("From the first, I was a little afraid of my real poems—not my 'compositions' but the poems that had the ghost in them. . . . Now I know my demon better, and after bitter years, respect him more than my other, milder and nicer self.") Organic form, about which we still understand so little, for which the textbooks have yet to be written, we perhaps now know better than to equate with formlessness. That Lawrence was capable of writing formless poems (some of them in traditional patterns, e.g. the early, curiously perfunctory **Sigh No More**) cannot be denied, any more than it can be denied of Whitman or Emily Dickinson. What is clearly visible in the early poetry is the process, the struggle, of choice, the wresting out of other identities into his own, the growing knowledge that Hardy, Whitman, though natural affinities, can provide no final solutions: he must create his own forms.

Reading the essay on **"Poetry of the Present"** (here published as a preface to the **Unrhymed Poems**): could anything be clearer, more conscious of its purpose? It works organically, like a poem: very rarely a piece of criticism can do this, demonstrate in its own movement and texture the possibilities of which it speaks. Lawrence draws his distinction between poetry which is "the voice of the far future or of the past, and the poetry of the quick, pulsing, immediate. The former must have that exquisite finality, perfection which belongs to all that is far off. . . . This completeness, this consummateness . . . are conveyed in exquisite form: the perfect symmetry, the rhythm which returns upon itself like a dance where the hands link and loosen and link for the supreme moment of the end." The "rare new poetry" of the flux and flight of the immediate present "cannot have the same body or the same motion as the poetry of the before and after. . . . There is no static perfection, none of that finality which we find so satisfying because we are so frightened." There follows an enlightening passage on the metrics of free verse. Lawrence never argues that the poetry of the present moment is or should be the unique, the only true poetry; he is never programmatic. This essay in fact prepares the awareness for poems to come, breaking down certain mental blockades or ways of taking a poem. But when you finish reading the essay, this has been done to you not by reasoned manifesto but by a process of almost physical exposure to the quality of the thing itself. The intelligence working in it is far from being purely ecstatic; but it is the intelligence of the artist, not of the literary analyst. It is an essay of large importance for the poet, for the literary historian, for the reader of Lawrence, for the reader of existing poetry of all kinds.

Let it be said clearly: Lawrence is a major poet, and the present collection fully reveals the quantity as well as the quality of his best poems. And the organic shape and movement of these poems has nothing mindless and happenstance about it: he knows what he is doing with line-length, with diction, with pause, repetition, termination.

Love, hate, the self. How repeatedly, in Lawrence, the longing for escape appears, escape of the kind Eliot meant when he said, "But of course, only those who have personality and emotions know what it is to want to escape from those things." Remarkable men, who see the nature of experience in almost mutually exclusive ways, have also their moments of consanguinity. Lawrence is forever searching for an inward zone of apartness. To be as private as an animal!

> You would think twice before you touched a weasel
> on a fence
> as it lifts its straight white throat.
> Your hand would not be so flig and easy.
> Nor the adder we saw asleep with her head on her
> shoulder,
> curled up in the sunshine like a princess;
> when she lifted her head in delicate, startled wonder
> you did not stretch forward to caress her . . .
>   (**"She Said as Well to Me"**)

To exist in one's uniqueness, and still in profound relation to another—

I want her to touch me at last, ah, on the root and
    quick of my darkness
and perish on me as I have perished on her.

. . . . .

When she has put her hand on my secret, darkest
    sources, the darkest outgoings,
when it has struck home to her, like a death, "this
    is *him!*"
she has no part in it, no part whatever,
it is the terrible *other,*

. . . . .

then I shall be glad, I shall not be confused with
    her,
I shall be cleared, distinct, single as if burnished
    in silver,

. . . . .

one clear, burnished, isolated being, unique,
and she also, pure, isolated, complete,
two of us, unutterably distinguished, and in
    unutterable conjunction.

                          ("Manifesto")

Love, the word itself, being today an emotional pantry
even more than when Lawrence wrote, it's easy to read
hate as the final destination of Lawrence's journey beyond love; to diagnose his "problem" even more crudely
as fear of women, as embryonic Fascism, as egomania.
But Lawrence knew the shallowness of pure ego-satisfac-
tion for what it was: see for example the ironic little
portraits in **"True Love at Last"** or **"Ultimate Reality"**
or **"Intimates"** (all in *More Pansies*). And he knew the
frenetic sterility of the soul that, like the little black dog
in New Mexico, is "Such a waggle of love you can hardly
distinguish one human from another." The naked irrita-
bility, and revulsion, that Lawrence felt in the face of
many human contacts was the price he paid, and that we
pay in suffering much of it through his poems, for his
enormous sense of the possibilities inherent in human
contacts and human separateness. At times it is paid brilliantly, in poems like **"Frost Flowers;"** elsewhere it simply devours the poem. Yet everywhere is evidence that he
found man sacred in design even if degraded in execution. And nature, which he never sentimentalized, was
always sacred to him. He was able to fuse them—the
natural world and the possible nature of man—in poems
which purify as they redefine love and sex in both their
spasmodic and timeless modes:

Go deeper than love, for the soul has greater depths;
love is like the grass, but the soul is deep wild rock
molten, yet dense and permanent.

Go down to your deep old heart, woman, and lose
    sight of yourself,
And lose sight of me, the me whom you
    turbulently loved.
Let us lose sight of ourselves, and break the
    mirrors.

But say, in the dark wild metal of your heart
is there a gem, which came into being between us?
is there a sapphire of mutual trust, a blue spark?
Is there a ruby of fused being, mine and yours, an
    inward glint?
    ("Know Deeply, Know Thyself More Deeply")

And one style Lawrence never had, as poet or in life. His
pride, his intolerance, stand invincibly opposed to the
posture of the loving fool, the ironic self-depreciation of
God's poor slob. There is something cleanly arrogant in
Lawrence's bitterness, the astringency of a drop of pure
alcohol. His vituperation is nearly always aimed at some
form of self-indulgence, of narcissism, of emotional neurasthenia. He would have been ill at home in a society
where people not only eat the ones they love but do so
out of simplistic moral motives.

Pansies; More Pansies. The ones that get most often
quoted and anthologized are the anti-bourgeois squibs,
the outbursts against mass society, the machine, censorship. Lawrence himself fosters, in his prefaces, the notion
that we have to do here with "a little bunch of fragments"; "casual thoughts". And in fact, while some of
these crackle and sting with nervous wit, others are deliberate doggerel, Lawrence rhyming and fuming aloud. But
a large number are poems, part of Lawrence's central
achievement: e.g., the short series on **"Touch,"** the poem
"Know Deeply" quoted in part above, and the one just
preceding it, **"Fidelity."** And some of the religious poetry:

Who is it that softly touches the sides of my breast
and touches me over the heart
so that my heart beats soothed, soothed, soothed
    and at peace?

Who is it smooths the bed-sheets like the cool
smooth ocean where the fishes rest on edge
in their own dream?

Who is it that clasps and kneads my naked feet,
   till they unfold,
till all is well, till all is utterly well? the lotus-
    lilies of the feet!

I tell you, it is no woman, it is no man, for I am
    alone.
                ("There Are No Gods")

How many little anthologies could be put together out of
the two *Pansies* volumes alone! anthologies compiled to
prove almost anything for or against Lawrence. And of
course, they would all be misleading. Because the total
impression in the **Collected Poems** is the refusal to
belong, to become anyone's pet D.H.L. or straw man.
After all the memoirs, the letters, the photographs on
sunny terraces, the *romans à cléf* by other hands, the
toilsome efforts to come to terms with him posthumously by those who knew him, the fact remains that we
have long had an imperfect notion of Lawrence and a
poorly balanced vision of his ideas. The use of the
phrase "Lawrentian" to indicate a kind of primitivism; the
odd assumption that Lawrence was attracted by political

power or could have stomached any process of mob-manipulation; the belief that sexual union was for him a cure-all or an exclusive source of truth—these and other equally blurred gropings for a formula are gainsaid in the experience of the poetry in full.

> Oh leave off saying I want you to be savages.
> Tell me, is the gentian savage, at the top of its
>   coarse stem?
> Oh what in you can answer to this blueness?

Look! We Have Come Through! This sequence has more diversity of tone, intention, accent than any unified sequence of love poems since Shakespeare. In a literal sense the man and woman of *Look!* . . . are a microcosm, a world in which nearly everything happens. It is Lawrence's functional honesty that produces this variety, his rejection of the blandishments of false consistency, of turning a good face to the world. Compare **"She Looks Back,"** a poem bitter at the division in the woman's soul, her longing for her children, with **"Meeting among the Mountains,"** in which the face of a bullock-cart driver encountered "among the averted flowers" near a wayside crucifix seems to recall the woman's suffering husband. Neither poem is a vindication, nowhere in this series do we smell the odor of self-pity, or the lust to charm or wheedle. And, blisteringly close as these poems are to actual events, conversations, sufferings, you can feel the quality of the mind that could render its and another's anguish so precisely even while it was gradually inventing the texture and dimensions of the later great poetry concerned with love: **"She Said as Well to Me"**, **"Manifesto,"** **"Know Deeply, Deeper Than Love,"** etc. If the poems are rooted in personal history they are also rooted in the development of a mind, for this hero of the instinctual was one of the most intelligent men of any time, who knew that "The profoundest of all sensualities / is the sense of truth"; and that "All vital truth contains the memory of that for which it is not true."

Language. More than any other poet-novelist's, Lawrence's fiction and his poems breathe in the same language. It appears at first startlingly simple, direct, almost *naïf* at moments, with its abrupt entrances and exits, its declarative sentences, its repetitions, with infinitesimal variations, of a word or a phrase. The directness and repetition are related to the English of the King James Version, more than to Imagist or Georgian poetry, as the editor of this edition rightly notes. But Lawrence's use of repetition is more than incantation. It has to do with his passionate grasp upon the physical world, as total as any in our language. With delicate, deliberate touch he palpates the physical shell or skin of reality until it seems to relax and fall open:

> Fig-trees, weird fig-trees
> Made of thick smooth silver,
> Made of sweet, untarnished silver in the sea-
>   southern air—
> I say untarnished, but I mean opaque—
> Thick, smooth-fleshed silver, dull only as human
>   limbs are dull

> With the life-lustre,
> Nude with the dim light of full, healthy life
> That is always half-dark,
> And suave like passion-flower petals,
> Like passion-flowers,
> With the half-secret gleam of a passion-flower
>   hanging from the rock,
> Great, complicated, nude fig-tree, stemless flower-
>   mesh,
> Flowerily naked in flesh, and giving off hues of life.

He was able to redeem the old words of richness, plenitude, light, and darkness in their primalness, through his insistence on keeping close to the power of the object, seeing it from every side (those suave, lustrous fig-trees become concretely absurd and admirable as the poem moves on, ending as the "equality-puzzle", the ego-mystery ironically perceived). To do this for language it is not enough to be "intoxicated with words"; one has to be intoxicated with things in their natures, their detail, their physical essences. And Lawrence was. If in **"Bavarian Gentians"** the words "dark", "blue", and "darkness' become key-notes to an hypnotic chant of passage, it is first of all because the living flower in its precise, physical truth hypnotizes Lawrence:

> ribbed and torch-like, with their blaze of darkness
>   spread blue
> down flattening into points, flattened under the
>   sweep of white day,
> torch-flower of the blue-smoking darkness,
>   Pluto's dark-blue daze . . .

And as with language, so with the world: it was in a very real sense sacramentally that Lawrence saw what he saw. The poems that fail seem to be the ones where he failed to attach his vision to anything which could be thus seen; where all that is observable is his disgust and disappointment at loss of possibility, loss of potency. The language becomes thin, vituperative, loose as a torn sail flapping in a squall; the language of a man whose nerves are worn out.

> O cease to listen to the living dead.
> They are only greedy for your life!
> O cease to labour for the gold-toothed dead.
> they are so greedy, yet so helpless if not worked for.
>
>   . . . . .
>
> Don't ever be kind to the dead
> it is pandering to corpses,
> the repulsive, living fat dead.

In studying the complete work of a major poet, there is always a group of poems to which we revert over and over, not only for their individual force and beauty, but because through them we come to trust the entire *oeuvre,* to give a hearing to other poems less immediately attractive or accessible to us. It is as if we watched a man in certain situations and said: "There, the man who could do this, or that, is one to whom I can give credence in whatever he does; such a man has value for me even where I do not understand him or feel sympathy for his ideas."

For me, a list of such poems by Lawrence would include, of the earlier poems, **"End of Another Home Holiday,"** **"The Collier's Wife," "Bei Hennef," "In the Dark,"** **"Mutilation," "Sinners," "She Said as Well to Me",** **"Frost Flowers;"** most of *"Birds, Beasts and Flowers,"* but especially **"Bare Almond-Trees," "Bare Fig-Trees,"** **"Sicilian Cyclamens," "The Mosquito," "Man and Bat,"** **"Peach," "Snake," "Baby Tortoise."** It would also include **"The Man of Tyre," "There Are No Gods,"** **"Know Deeply, Know Thyself More Deeply," "Swan,"** **"Elemental,"** and the two late poems, **"Bavarian Gentians"** and **"The Ship of Death."** The last two poems alone, it seems to me, must persuade anyone that this poet's entire work bears listening to, that the full dimensions are worth having. The present edition should have influence and significance far beyond a specialized audience.

Michael Kirkham (essay date 1972)

SOURCE: "D. H. Lawrence's Last Poems," in *The D. H. Lawrence Review*, Vol. 5, No. 2, Summer, 1972, pp. 97-120.

[*In the following essay, Kirkham examines Lawrence's* Last Poems *as a poetic sequence with consistent themes and execution.*]

This essay falls into three parts. In the first part I suggest that *Last Poems* is best read as a single work, forming a loosely connected sequence of thought. I see Lawrence performing an act of spiritual preparation, the directing purpose of which is to construct a state of mind that will steady him in the face of death. In the second part I discuss the central themes of the sequence. I try to show that, though much of the thought expressed here is inherited from his previous work, a number of poems, in meeting the challenge of the fact of death to a doctrine centered on physical existence, reveal a startling change of attitude. In my final section, through a close analysis of two or three poems, I illustrate Lawrence's poetic embodiment of his themes. I am concerned to gain recognition for Lawrence's mastery of his poetic medium, and to draw attention to the prominent part played by tones of voice, superbly controlled, in the formal organization of his poetry. The order in which the *Last Poems* are printed, following in this the MS book, is probably the order in which they were written. And in that order they form a loosely connected sequence of thought. If they were, as Aldington suggests, a kind of diary, they were so only in the sense that this thought-sequence was unplanned. The continuity from one poem to the next exhibits the natural exploratory movement of the poet's mind as, in a mood of summation and self-preparation, he checks the pulse of his intuitions about the death approaching and tests his developed convictions about life against a retrospective view of it from its conclusion. Certain poems—**"Butterfly," "Invocation to the Moon,"** **"The Man of Tyre," "Shadows"**—are exceptionally fine in themselves, but even they are enlarged by the place they occupy in the full progression: to know them within the total movement of thought and feeling is also to be aware of an urgent impulsion in one direction, which is part of the experience of each poem but is not perhaps evident in the poem when separated from its context. For the reviewing, modifying, and re-stating of his beliefs undertaken by Lawrence in *Last Poems* is directed by a single need or purpose: to set his house in order, to prepare his soul for "the longest journey," the death-voyage. To make this claim convincing, I must first indicate the nature of the themes treated successively in these poems and draw attention to the thread of connection joining them together.

The first four poems invoke and celebrate the prehistoric civilizations of Greece, Minoan Crete and Etruria for their knowledge, now lost, of fulfilment in the flesh.[1] The following eight poems, ending with **"The Man of Tyre,"** play variations on the theme that "corporal existence" is the primary reality: "God is the great urge that has not yet found a body/but urges towards incarnation with the great creative urge" (689-693). Even in the sea, Lawrence then tells us, in "the waters of the beginning and the end," cold and loveless whales and dolphins express the "sheer delight" of sensual life (693-695). The next two poems introduce the death theme. In **"Invocation to the Moon"** death, or dying, is greeted tenderly as the "garmentless beauty" who will, in a sense that I shall discuss later, restore to him his "lost limbs" and make him again "a healed, whole man." The link between this and the preceding poems is their common affirmation of physical life: death is invoked as a lover. In **"Butterfly"** we first hear the sombre accents that will dominate **"The Ship of Death"**: "Already it is October, and the wind blows strong to the sea." Both poems—the first explicitly and the second by implication—are invitations to death (695-696). They are followed by **"Bavarian Gentians"** and three poems which express the paradox of death as life in its essence: death as a living darkness, as the bridegroom, as the silence of God (697-699). The paradox is opened out then in a group of poems which depend on the equation of God with physical process; "to be at one with the living God" means to be at one with the living universe. The only blasphemy is to set ourselves apart from the natural process of life in mental self-contemplation (699-701). Having said this much Lawrence is able to give an almost light-hearted assent to death, in **"Return of Returns"** (702). In another four poems he distinguishes the living universe of his experience, with man as part of it, from the world of dead matter of scientific conception, in which the moon is no more than "a dead orb wheeled once a month round the park" (702-705). A longer series follows that presents life as a polarity of contraries—delight and dread, living and dying, creation and destruction. When the time comes the "angels of the Kiss" give way to "the Sunderers," whose "sharp black wings/and the shudder of electric anger" remembers the death-horrid bats of the *Birds, Beasts and Flowers* poem; the bright and dark angels are also complementary after the manner of the swallows and the bats in the earlier poem (705-710). "But evil is a third thing." Evil is the egocentric after the manner of the swallows and the bats in the earlier poem (705-710). "But evil is a third thing." Evil is the egocentric will which, machine-like, aims at independence from organic life; it is a denial of mortality, which means both life and death (710-716). This brings us to **"The Ship of Death"** and its tail-piece **"Difficult Death,"** which speak of man's need to be prepared for death and describe the death-journey and a possible resurrection (716-721). The next four poems develop the idea of preparation. Those who find peace in death have first been fulfilled in life and are "wrapped in the dark-red mantle of warm memories" (721-723). The sequence concludes with something like a coda. The motifs of oblivion and polarity recur in poems of quiet resignation and final assent, which celebrate the cosmic rhythm of waking and sleeping, death and renewal—most fully and movingly in one of Lawrence's finest poems, **"Shadows."**

Also holding these poems together are certain images repeated, many of them transmuted memories of Burnet's *Early Greek Philosophy*, Murray's *Five Stages of Greek Religion,* and possibly Jane Harrison's *Prologomena to the Study of Greek Religion,* some reminiscent of Dante's *Inferno.* Nearer the thought-centre of the sequence is Lawrence's experience of the Etruscan tombs. He had visited them in 1927, and in a series of articles, posthumously collected in *Etruscan Places,* described the wall-paintings and speculated on their symbolic meaning and inferred from them the religious beliefs of the Etruscans. These, he concluded, were centered on the fulfilment of physical life. "To the Etruscan all was alive; the whole universe lived; and the business of man was himself to live amid it all."[2] "The Etruscan religion is concerned with all those physical and creative powers and forces which go to the building up and destroying of the soul: the soul, the personality, being that which gradually is produced out of chaos, like a flower, only to disappear again into chaos, or the underworld."[3] "To the peoples of the great natural religions the after-life was a continuing of the wonder-journey of life."[4] The direct connection between this line of thought and the poems is obvious. Some of the poems' imagery originates in the paintings; the men daubed scarlet to represent the holiness of the body, the dolphins "with the nose-dive of sheer delight" (**"They Say the Sea is Loveless"**), the ship of death itself "continuing the wonder-journey of life," the little utensils that the dead take with them. After emerging from the painted tombs of Tarquinia, he notes: "The upper air seems pallid and bodiless, as we emerge once more, white with the light of the sea and the coming evening."[5] The pallid and bodiless air, the sea and the evening: these are recurrent images in *Last Poems,* denoting the coming end of life. A contrast is implied with the vitality of the paintings. But Lawrence's mind was most deeply marked by another aspect of his experiences in Tuscany. His book describes not only the contents of the tombs but also his impressions of the places and people of modern Italy that he encountered during his visits. The repeated descent out of the pale, desultory life of modern Tuscany into the darkness of the tombs to

discover these gay, winsome, archaic testimonies to a belief in natural life suggested to Lawrence a reversal of roles, death folding in its darkness the withheld central secret of life, and was the model for a movement of feeling reenacted in some of the poems.

There are two other notable presences in *Last Poems, Hamlet* and a Protestant Christianity. Lawrence's mind always carried a miscellaneous stock of usable quotations from his reading, and often one is the starting-point for a "pansy." But, still, there are reasons to assume a less casual connection between this sequence and the references, direct and indirect, to *Hamlet.* For the Shakespeare recalled is the poet much possessed by death; three of his allusions are to the "To be or not to be" soliloquy. In **"The Ship of Death,"** with a characteristic note of pert challenge, he quotes directly in order, by questioning his text, to further the poem's argument: "And can a man his own quietus make/with a bare bodkin?" Lawrence denies that he can, and then pointedly substitutes "quiet" for the hieratic solemnities of "quietus": "O let us talk of quiet that we know." And this attitude is representative. Hamlet is here set up as spokesman for those traditional (and I do not mean entirely Christian) approaches to the theme of death whose authority Lawrence all along is calling in question. The celebration of death in **"Sleep and Waking"** as a "dreamless sleep" from which there is "waking new" is also perhaps meant as a contradiction of Hamlet's fears— "For in that sleep of death what dreams may come . . . ?" Even the image of death as a journey, though common enough and in its details related here to the Etruscan tomb-paintings, in Lawrence's use exactly reverses the spirit in which Hamlet contemplates "The undiscovered country from whose bourn/No traveller returns." But the most interesting parallel occurs in **"Beware the Unhappy Dead!":**

> Beware the unhappy dead thrust out of life
> unready, unprepared, unwilling, unable
> to continue on the longest journey.

This as it were freely translates into a secular vocabulary—and another context of belief—the Ghost's plaint:

> Cut off even in the blossoms of my sin,
> Unhousel'd, disappointed, unaneled,
> No reckoning made, but sent to my account
> With all my imperfections on my head.
>
> (I, v)

The effect of this is less simple. In a characteristic manner Lawrence is working within traditional forms of thought and feeling the doctrinal core of which he has disowned, and is adapting them to a related but different content. An example already cited is his use of the biblical "the living God." The second of these lines derives both emotional resonance and a conceptual precision from its oblique reference to, so to speak, theological technicality. Unable to touch the capital he can yet employ the accrued interest—although, as I shall be arguing, not without some ambiguity. He echoes biblical rhythms, especially the psalmic structure of repetition with varia-

It is most illuminating to regard these poems as comprising an act of spiritual preparation. The thought-movement of the sequence, I have suggested, bears out this view of them: its directing purpose being to give final order to the poet's beliefs and set them moving towards one goal, the construction of a state of mind that will steady him in the face of death, "survive" death in that sense. This, the state of mind, which is better described as a state of feeling, is the ship that is meant to carry him on his last journey; the fragments of myth and philosophy all subserve this end. Doctrinally there is nothing specifically Christian about this act; yet, as we have seen in the lines quoted from the Ghost's speech, the Christian paradigm was present to him. For the diction and rhythms of such poems as **"Silence"** and **"Shadows"** Lawrence has drawn heavily on the Old and New Testaments. It seems that to plot his mental position he needed—and this is true for much of his writing life—to take his bearings from the, in many ways, antithetical Christian ordering of experience. The recasting towards the end of his life of the story of Jesus in *The Man Who Died* spells out what was already evident in his previous work: that the sequence of death and rebirth, a pattern to which life was made to conform in so much of his writing, took that shape principally from the Christian myth, the religion of his youth proving to be the most potent source for his symbolism. Much of the imagery in *Last Poems* is pagan and some of the feeling, but—in **"Shadows,"** for example—the seeing life as a recurrence of spiritual devastations and renewals, the quality of "sweetness" in the voice which announces the poet's relinquishment of life, statements like "my soul may find her peace," "I have been dipped again in God," "I am walking still with God," "my wrists seem broken and my heart seems dead": these are the experiential patterns, the quality of feeling, the words and images, of Christian faith.

II

The beliefs that Lawrence chooses to prepare his soul for death derive from attitudes to life some of which were expounded or dramatized in Lawrence's earlier work. Firstly, he cannot imagine a "happy" death without the previous fulfilment of the body and the body's emotions; bodily contentment wraps the soul in a "dark-red mantle of warm memories." The "unhappy dead" are those without the "warm memories" of such fulfilment; they therefore haunt the "marginal stretches of our existence" with a "cold ghostly rage." For the dying need the consciousness of "warm love from still-living hearts": as in life fulfilment depended not only upon their own emotional generosity but also on the reciprocal tenderness of friends and lovers, so the "still-loving" friends and lovers must "with their hearts/ speak with them and give them peace and do them honour"; their past failure in this duty is the accusation implied in the last lines of **"Beware the Unhappy Dead!"**:

> Perhaps even now you are suffering from the
>   havoc they make
> unknown within your breast and your deadened
>   loins.

Secondly, since God is the apotheosis, or the "flower," of physical process, death is its consummation. Certain Christian metaphors—"the body of God," "the living God"—are literalized. "God is the great urge that has not yet found a body/but urges towards incarnation, with the great creative urge" (p. 691). "It is not easy," begins "Abysmal Immortality," "to fall out of the hands of the living God:/they are so large, and they cradle so much of a man"—it is not easy except, as this poem goes on to say, by the mind's turning upon itself in self-contemplation: this is man's fall out of the community of nature into "himself alone." Acceptance of death is, then, ultimate acceptance of the physical universe. Since the universe has given you life, religious gratitude is willingly to render back your fulfilled self to this universe. "To be able to forget is to be able to yield/to God who dwells in deep oblivion" (p. 725).

But with this word "oblivion" Lawrence tries repeatedly to turn the act of willing self-surrender, to nothingness, into a positive accomplishment, of something, a tribute to a larger *reality* than that of self alone.

Death is not so easily accepted. In his previous work both death and resurrection were metaphors for the disintegration and reconstitution of the personality. Whether he wrote of sickness or health he rarely drew a line of demarcation between the physical and the psychical. The illnesses of, say, Birkin and Aaron were symptomatic of disturbances in "the deep emotional self." These in turn were held to intimate, however indirectly, a soul-sickness in the collective consciousness of modern man. And these metaphors also dominate *Last Poems*. The interdependence of the three meanings of "sickness" is the theme of one of the later 'pansies,' **"Healing"**:

> I am not a mechanism, an assembly of various
>   sections.
> And it is not because the mechanism is working
>   wrongly, that I am ill.
> I am ill because of wounds to the soul, to the deep
>   emotional self
> and the wounds to the soul take a long, long time,
>   only time can help
> and patience, and a certain difficult repentance
> long, difficult repentance, realisation of life's
>   mistake, and the freeing oneself
> from the endless repetition of the mistake
> which mankind at large has chosen to sanctify.
>   (p. 620)

The poem states one thought-premise on which the *Last Poems* are founded. It explains the naturalness for Lawrence of that movement from the first poems which nostalgically evoke the consciousness of the prehistoric Mediterranean races—the historical death of their civilization, the imagined revival of that consciousness—to the poems focussed on personal death and imagined resurrection. There is here grandeur of mental sweep but there is also, now, a central equivocation. With the appearance of literal death, physical extinction, as part of his theme, Lawrence needed to revise his metaphors. He did not, presumably, because he could not match the (for the most part) unwavering acknowledgement of his approaching death with an equal certainty of a literal survival of personality. But at least as early as the fifteenth poem in the sequence, **"Invocation to the Moon,"** whatever else he has in mind Lawrence is thinking of the body's death and of his own death in particular, and "time" at least will not heal *that* wound. "Patience" and the short time left to him may be all he needs to make his "difficult repentance," to cleanse and compose his spirit—and doubtless this is often what the metaphors of renewal and reawakening signify. Indeed it seems to be part of what is meant in most cases: almost the last words of **"The Ship of Death"** are "Swings the heart renewed with peace." But the phrase following, "even of oblivion," gives the experience another context.

Holding the doctrine that being incarnate is the primary reality, Lawrence must, and does, in these poems as in others insist, after the body's death, upon the body's return to life. It is the body that at the end of its journey, in **"The Ship of Death,"** "like a worn sea-shell/emerges strange and lovely." Although in these moving two last sections of the poem Lawrence is apparently aware that he is creating more an image of desire than of faith ("Is it illusion? or does the pallor fume/a little higher?"), and gives to his lines a tentative air and a wistfulness, yet his imagination, associating itself with some of the traditional meanings of the Noah story—"the fragile ship of courage, the ark of faith" . . ."And the little ship wings home . . . /and the frail soul steps out, into her house again"—expresses itself in terms of the Christian belief in the resurrection of the body. A third possible meaning, one to add to spiritual renewal and survival after death—and perhaps most in consonance with the implications of **"Healing"**—is the mortal body's recovery of health. It is hard to decide whether Lawrence has this in mind or an immortal life in the last lines of **"Difficult Death"**:

> It is not easy to die, O it is not easy
> to die the death.
>
> For death comes when he will
> not when we will him.
>
> And we can be dying, dying, dying
> and longing utterly to die
> yet death will not come.
>
> So build your ship of death, and let the soul drift
> to dark oblivion.
> Maybe life is still our portion
> after the bitter passage of oblivion.
>
> (p. 721)

Frequently all three possibilities can be entertained at the same time. While the hovering between several meanings is managed with great delicacy, the uncertainty which dictated this procedure undoubtedly makes these poems fall short of a more substantial achievement—of, for example, the clarity and complexity of insight manifested by such poems, in the *Birds, Beasts and Flowers* collection,

as **"Bare Almond Trees," "Almond Blossom," "Sicilian Cyclamens," "Fish," "The Ass," "Kangaroo,"** or the Tortoise sequences. And I attribute this diminution of Lawrence's achievement in *Last Poems,* in part, to his failure to define for himself his relationship to the Christian tradition. The poems would not have been so good as they are without the Christian presences, to which I have drawn attention, but that they are not better, that many of them remain ambiguous at the core, comes of the poet's inability quite to divorce the emotional power of the metaphors and symbols used in them from the literal beliefs of Christianity which generate that power.

As we have seen, in the lines quoted, in a previous paragraph from the conclusion of **"The Ship of Death,"** "oblivion" is made a precondition of "the heart renewed with peace"—itself a reminder of that phrase in the fourth section of the poem, "a strong heart at peace": through "oblivion," says Lawrence, is to be found strength of heart, and "peace" is the peace not of resignation but of the soul's final composure. And, it is true, in **"The Houseless Dead"** he distinguishes the "non-existence" of the unfulfilled from the properly completed existence of those who have been "delivered" into "far Oblivion." But, though "oblivion" is nearer the literal truth of death than "sleep," it does permit (barely) entertainment, in the suggestion of consciousness suspended, of the idea of a return to consciousness—bringing another life, unburdened with memory of the old. The word harbours the poet's desire to leave the possibility open but confesses his inability to turn it for himself into a certainty or to make substantial the notion of new life.

These two beliefs—that a happy death entails the previous fulfilment of the body, and that death is the consummation not the enemy of life—follow naturally from, and complement, convictions familiar to us from earlier work of Lawrence. But a third makes, I think, its first appearance here—an invention to meet the challenge to a doctrine centred on physical existence of the fact of death. For a number of these poems have no need to equivocate uncertainty as to whether, when mortality is added to the account, healing and liberation of the soul includes resurrection of the body. Death is transcended in these poems by the spirit alone, but at the same time without, for Lawrence, any fundamental change in values: a sick man, his direct enjoyment of the life of the body cruelly diminished, he maintains faithfulness to physical, and specifically sexual, experience through an act of memory and imagination. That is, imagination distills from memory of the body's phases an essence of unchanging loveliness which is the divinity of life. For a symbol of this state of resurrection into a loving retrospective affirmation of physical existence Lawrence has chosen the moon, whose light, so to speak, "remembers" the sun, to define the relation of his present attitudes to those focussed in his previous writing by the symbol of the sun. The sun of male sexuality, for Lawrence, is now past, as is the sexual hospitality to him of woman. He writes in **"Invocation to the Moon,"** his principal metaphor taken from the "houses" of astrology:

Far and forgotten is the Villa of Venus the
    glowing
and behind me now in the gulfs of space lies the
    golden house of the sun.

(p. 695)

This is wistful but not forlorn. In the poem that concludes
More Pansies, **"Prayer,"** the glory of physical life is
willingly surrendered for the grace of what is represented
by the moon:

Give me the moon at my feet
Put my feet upon the crescent, like a Lord!
O let my ankles be bathed in moonlight, that I
    may go
sure and moon-shod, cool and bright-footed
towards my goal.

For the sun is hostile, now
his face is like the red lion.

(p. 684)

This new state of being—its coolness—is presented not
as a limitation: it is associated with delicacy and sureness
of spiritual illumination—offered as a lovelier vehicle for
the soul in the last stages of its journey. But what, then,
is this moon-state? All we know from **"Prayer"** is that it
is the medium of the poet's release from a sick body. At
first, in **"Invocation to the Moon,"** as the poet bids farewell to the "houses" of the flesh, with tender gratitude
but without regret, and is kissed in turn by the four
lords—Mars, Mercury, Saturn and Jupiter—and the lady
Venus who dwell in them, with lastly "one warm kiss of
the lion with golden paws," it seems that the "glistening
garmentless beauty" of the moon invited by him to fill
their place can only be death itself. But no:

Now, lady of the Moon, now open the gate of your
    silvery house
and let me come past the silver bells of your
    flowers, and the cockleshells
into your house, garmentless lady of the last great
    gift:
who will give me back my lost limbs
and my lost white fearless breast
and set me again on moon-remembering feet
a healed, whole man, O Moon!

(p. 696)

The last house, it emerges, is the house of memory redeemed by tenderness of imagination, a gift to those who
are ready for death, a gift to the poet in return for his
acquiescence in the loss of his physical powers and be-
quest of his body back to the universe. The assurance—
"sure and moon-shod"—prayed for in **"Prayer"** is, it is
evident from comparison with this poem, at the bestowal
of memory alone; further, Lawrence is clear in this poem
at least that a cure exists for "wounds to the soul" but not
to the body, and the "healing" envisaged is unambiguously the recovery of an image of health, not the body's
actual return to health. In a curious way characteristic of
many of these poems these lines suggest both a physical
and non-physical reality. The "lady of the Moon" is
"garmentless" and her gift seems to be to the poet's body,

and yet she is serenaded with echoes of nursery rhyme
innocence, invoked as the Mary whose garden grew with
silver bells and cockle shells, and not without a suggestion of the Virgin Mary, Mother of Heaven. The role of
memory in this group of poems is to put forward for homage
a sexuality perfected in the mind. This seems to me, when
set in context with the rest of Lawrence's thought, in
which formerly there was no room for ideal sexuality, the
reversal of a central tenet (one proclaimed, too, with no
less vehemence elsewhere in this sequence)—at the very
least a modification that reveals the earnestness of his
struggle to reconcile a faith established on a belief in the
sacredness of the body with the facts of dying.

The scope of the reality given a reflected and refined
existence in the poet's mind extends beyond that embraced by his personal life, takes in the total reality of
those cultures, the Minoan and the Etruscan, which, in
Lawrence's opinion, gave pride of place to physical life.
When in the first four poems of the sequence he hails the
"return" of life as they lived it, he means the return of
their particular consciousness of life, life as they felt it,
to our memories and imaginations as to his. And—in, for
example, **"The Argonauts"**—he employs the same images to express his sense of this collective life as to express a sense of his own:

They are not dead, they are not dead!
Now that the sun, like a lion, licks his paws
and goes slowly down the hill:
now that the moon, who remembers, and only cares
that we should be lovely in the flesh, with bright,
    crescent feet,
pauses near the crest of the hill, climbing slowly,
    like a queen
looking down on the lion as he retreats—

(p. 687)

"They are not dead" in that they live again in the mind of
the poet, or whoever so wishes; "lost" peoples—the next
poem, **"Middle of the World,"** speaks nostalgically of
"the music of lost languages"—are restored, as are "lost
limbs," by the imagination, and the life of physical
fulfilment glorified by them, as by Lawrence, finds transfiguration in the light shed by "the moon, who remembers." The physical loveliness evoked here lives away
from the sun's heat, the lion of the flesh has had his meal
and licks his paws reminiscently. **"Middle of the World"**
is more explicit:

And now that the moon who gives men glistening
    bodies
is in her exaltation, and can look down on the sun
I see descending from the ships at dawn
slim naked men from Cnossos, smiling the archaic
    smile
of those that will without fail come back again . . .

(p. 688)

Flesh is made to "glisten" by the action of the loving
imagination; we have met the word in **"Invocation to the
Moon,"** and it turns up again in **"For the Heroes are
Dipped in Scarlet."**

There is a puzzling quality in **"The Man of Tyre"**—an atmosphere out of keeping with the apparent intention of the poem, a glorification of the flesh—that opens to the understanding most readily when related to these poems celebrating the action of memory and imagination symbolized by moonlight. The poem introduces us, in accents of sympathetic amusement to the earnest, timorous man of antiquity named in the title, who because he was a Greek was pondering (in a formula that echoes a semi-nonsense song) "that God is one and all alone and ever more shall be so." It proceeds to a description of the occasion which convinced him of his error. On this occasion he saw a woman going out into the sea, washing herself and wading slowly back to the shore, revealing at last "the dim notch of black maidenhair like an indicator,/ giving a message to the man":

> So in the cane-brake he clasped his hands in
>   delight
> that could only be god-given, and murmured:
> Lo! God is one god! But here in the twilight
> godly and lovely comes Aphrodite out of the sea
> towards me!
>
>   (p. 693)

Without a doubt this is the divinity of bodily life, Aphrodite, the naked Venus whose house in **"Invocation to the Moon"** is said to be "far and forgotten"; but, nevertheless, is the message of the poem precisely the "message" received by the man from sight of the woman's "notch of black maidenhair"? Does not her loveliness in fact have something in common with that of "the lady of the Moon"? She is not, at least, "Venus the glowing," for the episode takes place in evening twilight and except for "the pale green sea" the scene lacks colour and is depicted in tones of white and black and a twilight shadowy merging of these: she "spread white washing on the gravel banked above the bay," and returning from the sea "with her back to the evening sky" she was "lovely with the dark hair piled up,"

> and the shoulders pallid with light from the silent
>   sky behind
> both breasts dim and mysterious, with the
>   glamorous kindness of twilight between them
> and the dim notch of black maidenhair. . . .
>
>   (p. 693)

Though the "message to the man" concerns sexual reality, the man's joyous attitude remains, surely, that of a spectator, a non-participant. The poet is amused by his ingenuous childlike delight, but, even more, sympathetic to the purity and innocence of his emotion: we feel that the poet's position too, in this epiphany, is "in the cane-brake."

The real woman, who is first pictured washing clothes, as she advances towards the man—and the poet—loses some of her common reality to become the divinity of male imagination. We must give full weight to the visual setting. Only "here in the twilight" is she "godly and lovely"; the twilight of evening is not yet moonlight but its dim pallor has the same effect of draining colour from—of dematerializing—the scene; it sheds a (more than natural) glamour and mystery over the natural form of the woman; movement has the dream-slowness of something being contemplated. And we cannot ignore, in the context given by the sequence as a whole, the time of day. It is, with point, evening: the woman as she wades out to sea moves westward, towards night, away from the man, and in her transformation into goddess returns, still, "with her back to the evening sky," suffused in "the glamorous kindness of twilight"—as it were an unexpected gift from the "silent sky" that prefigures death. In **"They Say the Sea is Loveless"** and **"Whales Weep Not,"** two poems that immediately follow **"The Man of Tyre,"** the sea symbolizes basic reality and the source of life, the general carbon (to borrow a metaphor used by him in another context) of which individual diamond is composed, and Lawrence's theme is that this core of reality is not a "loveless" indifference but sexual delight. The sea's part in **"The Man of Tyre"** is firstly to represent the source and end of life: from which life emerges and to which it returns. But the order is here reversed: what is being hinted is that death in some sense entails a rebirth. The sea waits to receive the woman, physical loveliness rendered back to the cosmos, and so she has "waded to the pale green sea of evening"; but, "glamourized" by the pale light of evening, of death forseen, she is given back, reborn, to the tenderness of the poet's memory. That the core of reality is sexual is here an implication, as it is the explicit burden of the following two poems. The twilight of evening is kind, and even the pressing knowledge of death cannot destroy the lovingness of the poet's imagination.

III

The knowledge of his approaching death, astonishingly, restored to Lawrence a sense of common humanity, the failure of which he had lamented in his letter to Trigant Burrow and in *An Autobiographical Sketch.* To give closer attention to this increased sense of common humanity, let us return to **"The Man of Tyre."** Consider how much of its distinction lies in the tonal quality of the poem, and how this reflects, in its balance of attitudes towards the Greek, sympathetic if discriminative engagement with his personality. At this point quotation of the complete poem will be useful:

> The man of Tyre went down to the sea
> pondering, for he was Greek, that God is one and
>   all alone and ever more shall be so.
> And a woman who had been washing clothes in
>   the pool of rock
> where a stream came down to the gravel of the sea
>   and sank in.
> who had spread white washing on the gravel
>   banked above the bay,
> who had lain her shift on the shore, on the shingle
>   slope,
> who had waded to the pale green sea of evening,
>   out to a shoal,
> pouring sea-water over herself
> now turned, and came slowly back, with her back
>   to the evening sky.

Oh lovely, lovely with the dark hair piled up, as
   she went deeper, deeper down the channel,
   then rose shallower, shallower,
with the full thighs slowly lifting of the wader
   wading shorewards
and the shoulders pallid with light from the silent
   sky behind
both breasts dim and mysterious, with the
   glamorous kindness of twilight between them
and the dim notch of black maidenhair like an
   indicator,
giving a message to the man—

So in the cane-brake he clasped his hands in
   delight
that could only be god-given, and murmured:
Lo! God is one god! But here in the twilight
godly and lovely comes Aphrodite out of the sea
   towards me!

                  (pp. 692-693)

The poem is framed, in the opening and closing stanzas, by the description of the man. Certainly, between the first and last lines the warmth of feeling for him has grown, or grown more conspicuous; but it is already there, if covertly, in the first two lines. (I am concerned to show not only that, but generally Lawrence's mastery of his medium here.) At first we hear most clearly the irony in the poet's voice. There is a hint of tacit mockery already in the transition from the first to the second line, where after the brisk neutrality (deceptively nonchalant, as we realize afterwards) the hushed pause followed by the slow rumination of the word "pondering" mimics irreverently the self-conscious solemnity of this kind of thinking; "for he was a Greek," adding a poker-faced respectfulness, makes the hint heavier; and through the rest of the line is released the full force of the poet's amusement. In this last part Lawrence is quoting for ironic effect from a semi-nonsense counting song—"I'll sing you one-o . . . What is your one-o? One is one and all alone and ever more shall be so." The metronomic regularity and rapid patter of the rhythm stuns all serious meaning out of the words (an effect intensified by the tune), and the discrepancy between this quality of mechanical childlike recitation and the portentous implications of "pondering" gives the critical insight that earns for the poet his right to the tone adopted. And yet the tone is critical of the attitude rather than of the man. The earnest Greek, it is intimated, has the simplicity, the gravity, the innocence of a child. He has, too, another kind of simplicity, more difficult to describe: he belongs for Lawrence, as his title "man of Tyre" and the psalmist's phrase "down to the sea" reveal, to the simple, semi-legendary worlds of, say, the Old Testament or Homer, which guarantee him, for Lawrence, a certain immunity from satire, a certain indulgence. The verse movement, too, is buoyant, light and darting in its changes of tempo, and the attitude expressed by it is that of gay irreverence for play-acting solemnities founded on a childlike thinness of experience. The man is enjoyed not dismissed, and the poet can even, in the third stanza, allow himself to speak partly for him: "Oh lovely, lovely. . . ." We hear both the voice of the poet, enraptured, and of the Greek, whose rapture the poet views

with kindly detachment. The stanza has the delicate poise of one who is at once entranced and conscious of being entranced, who can place his emotion in the quotation marks of a self-awareness (as though the poet were in this character seeing himself at a distance). We return to description of him in the last stanza. The line division is again used subtly, here to balance on either side of it the two contrasting halves of what now appears as a single attitude: on the one hand amusement with no touch of mockery at the dainty gesture of appreciation—"he clasped his hands in delight"—on the other, in the further explanation—"delight/that could only be god-given"—fellow-feeling. And the fulcrum of balance is the word "delight," which we are made to read in two ways—first as the fitting name for an immature but innocent emotion, then as the word to contain the full measure of the emotion held by Lawrence to be appropriate to the scene's revelation. The sympathy in the irony expresses a tolerance of limitation not usual in his previous work. One qualification of this estimate of the poem must be made: that this tolerance, coming out of an increased sense of common humanity, is reserved for a person whom Lawrence could encounter only in imagination, not in reality. His feelings flow in fellowship only with the "lost" peoples.

This seems to me, by any standards, poetry, and good poetry in all aspects of performance. I have claimed for **Last Poems** rhythmic and formal subtlety, a fine control by Lawrence of his medium, and already I have begun to illustrate this subtlety and control. I shall attempt to make good my claim by further examination of **"The Man of Tyre."** In the second stanza, lines 3 to 9, form can be discussed almost entirely in terms of movement and syntax. In lines 3 to 7 a sequence of actions is described, each action separate and therefore separated (given a line to itself) from the others, each line, roughly speaking, equal in weight, speed and time-length. This parallel relationship between independent, though serial, actions is, however, counter-balanced by the strongly marked syntactic repetition and the rhythmic resemblance between each line, which causes the separate movements of each line to fuse in the reader's mind into one continuous movement, not only by focussing his attention on the actions as one sequence but by expressing a contemplation of the sequences keyed to one emotional note. That is to say, the mood is one of ritual celebration in which nevertheless distinction between details of the action celebrated is not lost. In most of these poems variation of line-length is *used* sensitively and with precise effect. Here the short line comes at a moment of pause between the actions leading up to and including the entry into the water and the return described in line 9, the last of this stanza. Not only is it a division and bridge between the woman's going and coming back, but, with the preceding five lines in their movement suggesting the steady ebb of the tide, and the last of the five (with its length of vowels, assonances, and the pause after "evening") suggesting the slowing-down of that movement, the short lines so interrupt the movement as to give a sense of the sea's resting a moment on the turn of the tide, and the last line begins the flow back, which is continued in the next stanza. Nor is this idle mimicry; the structure of the verse-movement supports and enhances the symbolic implications of the woman's wading out into and back from the sea: the sea (of life) like the woman (of sexual life) ebbs away and then is given back—an ebbing away and flowing back of life is being enacted.

The movement in the third section has another, more immediate function than to represent the flow of the tide. The long lines enact the speaker's entrancement in his vision. The first, very long line, for example, is a prolonged exhalation (one says it in one breath) of rapture. The third and fourth lines begin to dissipate the drugged oppression weighing down and slowing down the first lines by spreading out the stresses and quickening the tempo a little. Then in lines 5 and 6, which get progressively shorter, the consonants are hard and the movement is sharp and uneven, as the sense of the words has become *un*glamorous and the tone matter-of-fact. The speaker, as it were,—and the reader with him—emerges from trance once again into full waking consciousness.

This is a sensitive, precisely gauged *use* of verse, whether or not it is called "free verse." I shall not attempt a definition of free verse, not even of the kind practised by Lawrence, which itself varies considerably. However we assess the usefulness of this form, in the case of Lawrence the poems ordinarily referred to as written in free verse are conspicuous for the prominent part is played by tones of voice in the patterning of individual lines and the total organization of poems. (A simple, well-known example of their active part in the total organization of a poem is the alternation of the two voices, one of them italicized, in **"Snake."**) *Last Poems* exhibits Lawrence's usual flexibility of tone. Perhaps its tonal range is less than that commanded by ***Birds, Beasts and Flowers,*** which expresses the engagement of the full complexity of Lawrence's personality with his subject-matter. But as I have noted, it introduces a new attitude, reflected in movement and tone, of fellowship with humanity, a new sense of community in the human condition, and in weighing the human value of these poems I set this expansion of personality against the reduced complexity of response. I want to draw attention now to one more quality of the poet's voice, not new in Lawrence but more noticeable in his latest work, both inverse and prose: I hear it as much in the first paragraph of *Lady Chatterley's Lover* as in the opening lines of **"For the Heroes are Dipped in Scarlet":**

> Before Plato told the great lie of ideals
> men slimly went like fishes, and didn't care.
>
> They had long hair like Samson,
> and clean as arrows they sped at the mark
> when the bow-cord twanged.
>
> (p. 688)

What this shows is an athletic quality—a spareness and energy of statement which is expressive of thought purged of inessentials. In this kind of verse, I think it is true to say, the ear is attuned more to voice-pitch and tempo than to rhythm; each line seems to be a distinct gesture of the voice; the whole line is more important than the word or phrase.

The range of expression stretches, roughly speaking, from the hypnotic voice and the coiled rhythmic, verbal and syntactic patterns of **"Bavarian Gentians"** (an impressive poem but, surely, over-rated, limited precisely by this specialization in one mode) to the whip-crack energy of the lines just quoted from **"For the Heroes are Dipped in Scarlet."** Towards the one end, occupied by **"Bavarian Gentians,"** lies **"The Man of Tyre";** nearer the other end is the first poem of the sequence, **"The Greeks are Coming!"** Here are the first seven of its eleven lines:

> Little islands out at sea, on the horizon
> keep suddenly showing a whiteness, a flash and a
>   furl, a hail
> of something coming, ships a-sail from over the
>   rim of the sea.
>
> And every time, it is ships, it is ships,
> it is ships of Cnossos coming, out of the morning
>   end of the sea,
> it is Aegean ships, and men with archaic pointed
>   beards
> coming out of the eastern end.
>
> (p. 687)

It is easy to overlook the precision of effect in this kind of verse. The poem makes an emotional gesture, a gesture of excitement and welcome: hence the staccato movement—constituted of frequent pauses, little bursts of syllables, sprints from one accent to the next—and the repetition of those words which focus the emotion, "ships," "coming," "out." The method of progression, as it were, taking one step back before making a longer leap forward, enacts an augmentation and a growing specification of emotion: from "something" to "ships a-sail" to "ships of Cnossos" to "Aegean ships"; from "coming . . . over the rim of the sea" to "coming, out of the morning end of the sea" to "coming out of the eastern end." "Method of progression" is a somewhat misleading phrase: the poem's emotion does not so much change and develop as reveal, progressively, more and more of itself, and the repetition, with the slight variation, of a basic syntactic form making, in outline, the same statement is the formal expression of this process. First there is the movement from "islands out at *sea*" to "*something* coming." The order is reversed in the last phrase of the first stanza, which moves from "ships" to "sea," and this arrangement of basically the same statement is twice repeated in the next stanza. Now we must notice that the gesture made by the voice has two elements: not only is the tone one of excitement and welcome but, moderating this, one of contentment. The excitement climbs, progressively disclosing itself, but then rounds to a close. This arc of feeling described by the voice in the first stanza, is also the pattern of the second. In the second stanza it is reflected in the shape of the lines, the expansion and reduction. The means are different in the first stanza, but the effect is the same: the rhyme of "hail" with "a-sail" at the mid-point of the third line detaches the last phrase from the rest of the line and relaxes the voice into a falling, slowing-down tone of one about-to-conclude. The movement of voice reflected in this structure presents us with a dual mood—anticipation of something coming, acknowledgement of something that has come. The emotion unfolds gradually, until it is fully open: until the promise in the vision of the early Greek ships has become confident possession of the Greek way of consciousness.

I have been illustrating in poems differing widely in manner and structure Lawrence's original and controlled handling of free verse. There is a neater way of demonstrating his mastery of expressive rhythm. **"Lord's Prayer"** is a revision, and a doctrinal reversal, of the Christian prayer as it is worded in the Anglican *Book of Common Prayer*. At the same time its rhythms are both a reminiscence of, and a calculated deviation from, the rhythms of the original. It opens with a direct quotation:

> For thine is the kingdom
> the power, and the glory—
>
>   (p. 704)

The line-division at "kingdom"—a voice-pause indicated in the Prayer Book by the capitalization of "The" in the next phrase—renders faithfully the clipped, resolute utterance of the whole prayer, conveys the restraint of appeal dictated by an attitude of respectful submission to omnipotence. Beginning again with quotation, the second stanza, however, diverges sharply from the original:

> Hallowed be thy name, then
> Thou who art nameless—
>
>   (p. 704)

The second line, with "nameless" contradicting "name," challenges, for reasons not yet made clear, the Christian concept of deity. Lawrence's poem counters the unquestioning obedience assumed in the prayer with an insistence that acknowledgement of God's power by man requires from God an equal gift to each man of his own kingdom, power and glory. And the form of the poem (rhythm, length of line, tone) dramatizes this confrontation. Already the attachment of the pert "then" to the awed and deferential "Hallowed be thy name" has introduced a subversive note, conceding rather than glorifying God's omnipotence, taking away from the line's movement the suggestion of self-denying staunchness. The gradual unloosing of the poem's versification from the tight rhythmic bonds of the Christian prayer proceeds now, in three distinguishable stages. At first, in the next two stanzas, a measure of the original impersonal formality is retained despite the pressing-forward of personal feeling into the lines. Here is the third stanza:

> Give me, Oh give me
> besides my daily bread
> my kingdom, my power, and my glory.
>
>   (p. 704)

In the (mostly) longer lines of stanzas five, six, and seven emotion flows naturally, free from impediments; for example, take the development from the fourth to the fifth stanza:

> All things that turn to thee
> have their kingdom, their power, and their glory
>
> like the kingdom of the nightingale at twilight
> whose power and glory I have often heard and
>   felt.
>
>   (p. 704)

And the last stanza is furthest of all from the imposed discipline of communal prayer:

> And I, a naked man, calling
> calling to thee for my mana,
> my kingdom, my power, and my glory.
>
>   (p. 704)

It is unashamedly insistent in its direct personal appeal. The poem exemplifies the organic relationship of Lawrence's technique to his theme. With great sensitivity, by counterpointing his own rhythms with those of the Prayer Book, he has defined the nature of his quarrel with Christian submission.

NOTES

[1] *The Complete Poems of D. H. Lawrence*, eds. F. Warren Roberts and Vivian de Sola Pinto (New York: Viking, [1971]), pp. 687-689. Further references to *Last Poems* will be cited from this edition with page numbers in the text.

[2] *Mornings in Mexico and Etruscan Places* (London: Heinemann, [1956]), p. 49.

[3] *Ibid.*, p. 67.

[4] *Ibid.*, p. 76.

[5] *Ibid.*, p. 47.

Evelyn Shakir (essay date 1975)

SOURCE: "'Secret Sin': Lawrence's Early Verse," in *The D. H. Lawrence Review*, Vol. 8, No. 2, Summer, 1975, pp. 155-75.

[*In the following essay, Shakir examines Lawrence's early poems for evidence of his sexual preoccupations.*]

Throughout his career as a writer, Lawrence's attitude toward literature was remarkably ambivalent. "Art-speech is the only truth," he declared (*SCAL* 2).[1] Yet his mistrust of art was profound. He knew how easily it could degenerate into pretty artifice or aesthetic exercise and so seduce the artist into a lie. But when literature spoke truth, it was perhaps most dangerous and the artist finally most guilty. An examination of Lawrence's early verse, together with his later comments on it, helps explain his misgivings.

In 1928, Lawrence wrote an essay (originally intended as a foreword to his *Collected Poems*) in which he recalled his early efforts at writing verse.

> . . . I remember . . . half-furtive moments when I would absorbedly scribble at verse for an hour or so, and then run away from the act and the production as if it were secret sin. It seems to me that "knowing oneself" was a sin and a vice for innumerable centuries, before it became a virtue. It seems to me, that it is still a sin and vice, when it comes to new knowledge.—In those early days— for I was very green and unsophisticated at twenty— I used to feel myself at times haunted by something, and a little guilty about it, as if it were an abnormality. Then the haunting would get the better of me, and the ghost would suddenly appear, in the shape of a usually rather incoherent poem. Nearly always I shunned the apparition once it had appeared. From the first, I was a little afraid of my real poems—not my "compositions," but the poems that had the ghost in them. They seemed to me to come from somewhere, I didn't quite know where, out of a me whom I didn't know and didn't want to know, and to say things I would much rather not have said: for choice.

A few sentences later, Lawrence confessed,

> To this day, I still have the uneasy haunted feeling, and would rather not write most of the things I do write—including this note. Only now I know my demon better, and, after bitter years, respect him more than my other, milder and nicer self.

> (*CP* 849-50)

To Lawrence, then, writing poetry seemed like engaging in a furtive quest for self-knowledge, a process at once "guilty" and "abnormal." Such language suggests a secret act more sexual than literary. Specifically, it suggests that most common and highly-charged adolescent secret, masturbation. The association is not so far-fetched: the conscious exploration of one's feelings might be interpreted as a kind of narcissistic self-manipulation. At any rate— and this is the important fact—Lawrence saw the analogy. In **"Introduction to These Paintings,"** an essay also written in 1928, he bitterly referred to his age as "the great day of the masturbating consciousness when the mind prostitutes the sensitive responsive body, and just forces the reactions" (*P* 575). Six years earlier, in *Fantasia of the Unconscious*, Lawrence had already discerned an identity between the urge toward self-examination and masturbation.

> And so you get first and foremost, self-consciousness, an intense consciousness in the upper self of the lower self. This is the first disaster. Then you get the upper body exploiting the lower body. You get

the hands exploiting the sensual body, in feeling, fingering, and in masturbation.

> (*FU* 155)

Lawrence specifies that in writing verse, not only the "act," but the "production" as well seemed evil. The production was evil apparently because of what he discovered, "a me I didn't know and didn't want to know," a self who was not "mild," not "loveable," not "nice," who was then, by implication, aggressive, hateful (and perhaps terrifying), and certainly sexual. Many years later, in decrying the "unaccountable and disastrous fear of sex" that torments the modern Englishman, Lawrence brought his own early experience to bear in his essay **"The State of Funk":**

> I know when I was a lad of eighteen [Lawrence wrote his first poems, he said, at nineteen], I used to remember with shame and rage in the morning the sexual thoughts and desires I had had the night before. Shame, and rage, and terror lest anybody else should have to know. And I *hated* the self that I had been, the night before.

> (*P II* 568)

The "sexual thoughts and desires" accompanying masturbation must have provoked in Lawrence more anxiety than the act itself. His habitual denunciation of "sex-in-the-head" probably reflects, in great part, the revulsion he felt at these masturbatory fantasies, just as his romantic portrayal of himself as poet possessed suggests a need to deny responsibility for his own wishes. The demon forces him to write things he would "rather not write." Certainly the allegorical projection of two selves, demon and mild young man, is a way of distancing both from a real self who remains the "I."

But though such guilty imaginings can be disguised or disowned, they must sometimes be acknowledged as faithful expressions of one's wishes. Fantasy can be, after all, not merely an escape from reality, but, like art, a way of tapping the reality of what Lawrence called one's "deep, real feelings." The point then is not that Lawrence's writing of poetry is a sublimated form of masturbation but that it is associated in his mind with secret feelings, secret fantasies, of which he need not always be aware, and that this association taints the activity and makes it somehow forbidden and forbidding.

As we would expect, Lawrence's early verse (later collected under the title *Rhyming Poems*) abounds with "guilty" fantasy and "criminal" desire. The clause "I wish" echoes in poem after poem, along with such variations as "I would like to," "If I could have," "If only you had," "If she would." Poems like **"Last Words to Miriam"** and **"Reminder"** confirm the assumption that Lawrence's fantasies, the more conscious ones at least, were mostly concerned with sexual fulfillment and release, usually presented in highly romanticized terms—"the moon/ Never magnolia-like unfurled/Her white, her lamp-like shape" (**"Reminder,"** ll. 28-29, *CP* 103).

But the "rhyming" poems betray fantasy less "innocent" than that suggested by such conventional romantic posture. **"Discord in Childhood"** (*CP* 36), a poem which Lawrence described as a fragment with the demon "fuming" in it, is of central importance in understanding Lawrence's sexual preoccupations and the anxieties they aroused. In a letter written when his mother was near death, Lawrence characterized the marriage of his parents as "one carnal, bloody fight" (*CL* 69). Only **"Discord in Childhood"** bears direct witness to this terrifying home life.

> Outside the house an ash-tree hung its terrible whips,
> And at night when the wind rose, the lash of the tree
> Shrieked and slashed the wind, as a ship's
> Weird rigging in a story shrieks hideously.
>
> Within the house two voices arose, a slender lash
> Whistling she-delirious rage, and the dreadful sound
> Of a male thong booming and bruising, until it
>   had drowned
> The other voice in a silence of blood, 'neath the
>   noise of the ash.

CP 36)

This violent relationship between mother and father, which to a child could only be "dreadful," became for Lawrence the archetypal pattern of male-female relationships. The archetype appears in several of the "rhyming poems." It is hinted at, for instance, in the early version of **"The Wild Common"** (*CP* 894-95) with its strange bit of psychomachia in which the speaker's soul, suddenly realizing her absolute dependence on his body, "like a passionate woman turns,/Filled with remorseful terror to the man [i.e., the body] she scorned" (ll. 21-22).

But **"Love on the Farm"** (*CP* 42-43), originally titled **"Cruelty in Love,"** most clearly reveals the sado-masochistic nature of Lawrence's sexual fantasies, further liberated by the use of fiction. In this poem, a woman watches her husband move toward the farmhouse in which she waits. As he moves across the fields and through the barn, his "ominous tread" arouses terror in water hen and swallow. A rabbit spurts to flee, only to be caught by a "fine wire" around its neck, and "soon in his large, hard hands she dies." The wife too knows the terror of a helpless creature as her husband enters the room with a "smile like triumph" and the "uplifted sword/Of his hand against my bosom!" (ll. 52, 54-55). She is the rabbit "caught in a snare!" (l. 59). His mouth is at her throat like "a stoat/Who sniffs with joy before he drinks the blood" (ll. 62-63). He kisses her mouth, and "so I drown/Against him, die, and find death good" (ll. 67-68).

Lawrence must have learned early on to associate sexuality and brutality, to find erotic excitement in the very violence he had witnessed and suffered. His was no mild demon. And he must have learned as well to identify male and female according to the role each played, tyrant or victim.

In **"Love on the Farm,"** Lawrence adopts the perspective of the woman who submits with a voluptuous thrill to male domination and who can experience sexual satisfaction only insofar as she perceives herself as helpless. The portrait of her husband has, after all, no objective validity. It is her own deliberately fashioned, titillating fantasy. It is also Lawrence's fantasy, and bespeaks his own desire to play the female. In **"Snap-Dragon"** (*CP* 122-26), on the other hand, Lawrence assumes the role of the masterful male who finds excitement in imposing his will on the female.

> I pressed the wretched, throttled flower between
> My fingers, till its head lay back, its fangs
> Poised at her. Like a weapon my hand was white
>   and keen,
> And I held the choked flower-serpent in its pangs
> Of mordant anguish, till she ceased to laugh.
> Until her pride's flag, smitten, cleaved down to
>   the staff.

(ll. 87-92)

. . . . .

> Then I laughed in the dark of my heart, I did exult
> Like a sudden chuckling of music. I bade her eyes
> Meet mine, I opened her helpless eyes to consult
> Their fear, their shame, their joy that underlies
> Defeat in such a battle. . . .

(ll. 99-103)

Clearly in playing such a role, Lawrence is identifying with his father, partly in an attempt to assert his own masculinity, and partly in an attempt to deny his weakness and vulnerability. He flaunts his fangs, and guards against the danger of castration by inflicting a castration of his own—"her pride's flag, smitten, cleaved down to the staff"[2] (l. 92). But the sudden note of bravado on which the poem ends reveals Lawrence's sense of guilt and the punishment he anticipates:

> And I do not care, though the large hands of
>   revenge
> Shall get my throat at last, shall get it soon,
> If the joy that they are lifted to avenge
> Have risen red on my night as a harvest moon.[3]

(ll. 110-113)

As everyone now recognizes, Lawrence's adolescent "shame and rage" were intensified by his peculiar family situation, and his "terror lest anybody else should have to know" the sexual thoughts and desires of the night before is in large part a terror lest his father intuit his guilty secrets. "The large hands of revenge" belong to Mr. Lawrence.

Freud's Oedipus complex aside, it is undeniable that Lawrence was bound to his mother by exceptionally strong emotional ties and saw himself, rather than his father, as her true mate. His desire for "incestuous" intimacy with his mother is most obvious in those poems that are responses to her illness and death. The bereaved son pledges his troth forever to his "darling" who "sleeps like a bride" on her bier. With his mother actually dead, fantasy is given free play as Lawrence denies her marriage to his father and she becomes, as the title of one poem suggests, "the virgin mother." But Lawrence's half-conscious desire to assert his claim on his mother and to supplant the father he hated was dangerous. Lawrence must have retained a child's terror of this man who seemed so powerful and so capable of violent revenge. In **"Cherry Robbers"** (*CP* 36), the would-be lover is identified with the "robberling" birds who have been feasting on the forbidden fruit of the cherry orchard. Sexual desire is seen as thievery, and the dead birds, "stained with red dye," lie as tokens of the danger inherent in such crime.

Denial is the other side of the coin of fantasy. A striking feature of the *Rhyming Poems* is the almost total suppression of any reference to Lawrence's father or to the ugliness and violence of Lawrence's home life. **"Discord in Childhood"** is one exception. **"The Collier's Wife"** (*CP* 46) is another. This little drama in dialect between mother and son tells again the story of the father injured in the pits. Behind Lawrence's preoccupation with this story lay the wish that his father would die: "'Lord, let my father die," he [Paul Morel] prayed very often. 'Let him not be killed at pit,' he prayed when, after tea, the father did not come home from work" (*SL* 60). Like Paul Morel, Lawrence must have feared the efficacy of his angry wishes.

Lawrence's attempt to deny his father is finally, futile. Though Mr. Lawrence is never mentioned in the verse, his violent presence is frequently felt, and though his embodiments are various—"large hands of revenge," "a male thong booming and bruising," the anonymous assassin of the robberling birds, the husband who "sniffs with joy before he drinks the blood"—they are all such as to strike terror into the guilty heart of a child.

Little wonder then that Lawrence was afraid of his "real poems" and fled from them as if from secret sin. He plays Oedipus with almost embarrassing obviousness. His classic desires to kill his father and marry his mother emerge clearly in the verse, as does his own infatuation with the violent and cruel. And just as Lawrence feared that a father-god would reach out of the sky to punish him for his wicked wishes, so too, at a less conscious level, he must have feared punishment for writing verse that expressed and thus, in a sense, fulfilled these very wishes. Lawrence "ran away from the act and the production" not only to avoid recognizing the demon within but also, and more importantly perhaps, to escape a violent chastisement. He fled in terror of castration, or, rather, whatever sense of personal victimization that term represents.

Unfortunately, the Oedipal formula, neat as it is, does not completely account for Lawrence's ambivalence toward the act of poetry nor for his demon. The fear of castration, which seems to be the single most powerful motive in his flight from verse, probably has its roots in a struggle even more primitive than the Oedipal. In psychoanalytic theory, an anxious fixation on the genitals seems to be symbolically linked, at least in retrospect, with the

child's earliest experience of loss, the loss of intimate union with his mother. As he falls from this paradisal state into a world of new demands and denials, he becomes enraged at his mother, the agent of demands and denials. But rage at the mother, like rage at the father, brings with it the fear of retaliation; others may do to the child what he would like to do to them. Once again, bodily injury is the threat, especially to one's most valued and vulnerable parts.

Still, there is a felt need for self-assertion, and self-assertion necessitates differentiating oneself from the mother. The boy's genitals most accurately and economically symbolize that differentiation. Submission to the mother then would imply a kind of symbolic castration, even as identification with her means identifying with a "castrated" being. Thus both defiance and obedience, hate and love, carry the same danger.

The child's struggle to come to terms with this early frustration provides the prototype of all subsequent human struggles between the desire for dependency and nurturance, on the one hand, and aggressive self-assertion on the other. In Lawrence's case, as he was the first to recognize, this conflict was especially acute, and *Rhyming Poems,* like much of his later work, reflects two mutually exclusive desires: to be reunited with his mother and to escape and destroy her. The first is the "unmanly" wish to enjoy a passive and child-like role. In the early verse, Lawrence repeatedly voices the desire to be acted upon, to be passive, to be "drunk up," or simply to be fondled and find rest in the lap or at the breast of a maternal figure. But in one of the most moving poems of the volume, he characterizes his mother's love as a "beggar-woman," always "asking something more of me,/Yet more of me" (**"End of Another Home Holiday,"** ll. 62-63, *CP* 64). And the urge, so apparent in Lawrence's writing, toward the cruel imposition of the male will suggests Lawrence's primitive rage at maternal deprivation. It suggests as well, of course, the need to master lest one be mastered, a fear that itself suggests a desire to be mastered.

Mrs. Lawrence's final illness and death made the issue of separation from the mother once again immediate. The poems on her death are often undisguised outpourings of passionate love. Yet even in these poems, charged though they are with the pain of loss, the word "free" recurs with insistent frequency. Lawrence waits

> . . . to get
> The news that she is free;
> But [is] ever fixed, as yet,
> To the lode of her agony.

> (**"Suspense,"** ll. 10-13, *CP* 99)

Her release implies his own. But the angry desire to be rid of his mother is one more guilty wish betrayed by the verse, which, on that account, becomes all the more suspect, especially since that wish is in the process of being fulfilled.

Several early poems, which Lawrence revised just a few years later, show in their re-working his continuing struggle to come to terms with contradictory feelings toward his mother, and they suggest as well, how those feelings inhibited Lawrence's sexuality. In an early un-published version of **"Brother and Sister,"** for instance, a poem written after his mother's death, Lawrence assures his sister that "still plies the love of our mother for us, straining our way" (**"To Lettice, My Sister,"** l. 33, *CP* 941). Thus he denies her death and clings in fantasy to a child-like state of dependence, but in the later version, published in *Amores,* he confronts the fact of her death and urges his sister to "rise and leave her now, she will never know" (l. 30, *CP* 132). This realization is sad—the mother no longer looks over her children—but liberating as well—she cannot be hurt by their pursuit of life and other loves.

The revised version of **"Piano"** provides another example of dramatic reversal of statement. In the earlier version, never published by Lawrence, the music of the sensuous woman at the piano drowns out the memory of his mother's song (*CP* 943). In the revised version, first published in *New Poems,* Lawrence admits his mother's triumph and its crippling effect on his sexuality. His "manhood" is "cast down," as he weeps "like a child for the past" (ll. 11-12, *CP* 148). **"Piano"** reminds us that Lawrence's "unmanning" is not an affliction visited from without but the product of his own burdened and burdening fantasy.

In revising **"Honeymoon"** (*CP* 933-34), Lawrence arrived at a similar insight. In the early version, Lawrence's conflicting feelings toward his mother, and by extension toward all women, are present but unacknowledged. Tortured by his lover's apparent indifference, the speaker wonders, "can the night go by . . . without once your turning/Your face toward my agony?" (l. 1, ll. 6-7), and in his agony, he longs to be touched, stripped naked, taken. Yet his own failure to act or speak is obvious. In the version entitled **"Excursion Train"** published in *Amores* two years later, the speaker admits his share of responsibility for the emotional impasse.

> You hurt my heart-beat's privacy;
> I wish I could put you away from me;
> I suffocate in this intimacy
>   In which I half love you.

(ll. 15-18, *CP* 116)

He still longs to be taken—"I ache most earnestly for your touch" (l. 33)—but he acknowledges, too, the fear of powerful intrusion, a fear that turns any woman he loves into a potential enemy, thus paralyzing his initiative and his sexuality and making real the "castration" he had hoped to avert.

> . . . closely bitten in to me
> Is this armour of stiff reluctance
>
>   . . . . .

> . . . I cannot move, however much
> I would be your lover.

(ll. 26-27, ll. 34-35)

The poem **"Forecast"** (*CP* 91) best sums up Lawrence's horror of maternal suffocation as it describes a woman whose breasts

> . . . will keep the night at bay,
> Leaning in your room like two tiger-lilies, curving
> Their pale-gold petals back with steady will,
> Killing the blue dusk with harsh scent, unnerving
> Your body with their nipple-thrust, until
> You thirst for coolness with a husky thirst.

(ll. 5-10)

Everywhere in the *Rhyming Poems* is evidence of Lawrence's desire to escape the bonds not only of mother-love, but also of chastity, the ego, conscience, school, even verse form (although his rage at limitations, external and internal, is not yet fully articulated), and all these desires can be seen as reflections of the urge to assert one's own will and individuality, to make the archetypal escape from the womb. On the other hand, one might well argue that all these bonds are simply symbolic of adulthood and its responsibilities and the desire to burst them asunder is the desire to return to an infantile condition which was amoral and sensually satisfying, a state of union with the mother before there was a sense of the self differentiated from the world, a time when one knew only the pleasures and gratifications of love and none of its demands. In short, the conflict posited has a way of reducing itself to an identity.

A similar paradox underlies the child's fear of castration. The boy's genitals distinguish him from his mother and thus become a token of his independence and "manhood." Their loss would be tantamount to loss of the self, a kind of death. At the same time, the penis is the instrument for reunion with the female. Its loss would mean final isolation, and abandonment to the impoverished and lonely state of selfhood, a death of a different sort.

In either case, the fear of castration remains the fear of being "reduced" to a woman, or, more to the point perhaps, being revealed as one.[4] One recalls, however, that it is not just the production, the fantasy embodied in the verse, that is guilty but the act as well. The sense of abnormality Lawrence describes in recounting his first attempts at writing verse was probably caused in part by an association between the act of poetry and effeminacy. He showed his first poems to Miriam, not her farmboy brother, and later commented that "any young lady" might have written them. Then, too, as poet, Lawrence was clearly his mother's son. His father, he knew, would only scoff at or be bewildered by his work. Finally, if writing poetry was, for Lawrence, analogous in some respects to masturbation, it might be as "unmanly" as he believed masturbation to be.[5]

Late in his career, Lawrence wrote an essay in which he described the nightingale's song as "a male sound, a most intensely and undilutedly male sound." But Keats, wrote Lawrence, had projected his own sadness onto the nightingale's song. He should have had better things to do with his midnights than "cease . . . with or without pain." Poor Fanny, one "understands why she wasn't having any. Much good such a midnight would have been to *her!*" (*P* 40, 44). The mockery of Keats suggests Lawrence's own anxieties: he prefers to identify his verse with the male song of the nightingale.

In the deleted "**Prologue to *Women in Love,*"** Lawrence discusses the homosexuality of Birkin, who is clearly a surrogate for Lawrence himself.

> This was the one and only secret he kept to himself, the secret of his passionate and sudden spasmodic affinity for men he saw. He kept this secret even from himself. He knew what he felt, but he always kept the knowledge at bay. His a priori were: "I *should not* feel like this," and "It is the ultimate mark of my own deficiency, that I feel like this."
>
> Therefore, though he admitted everything, he never really faced the question.

(*P II* 107)

From the beginning, an impulse toward homosexuality and a sense of his own masculine "deficiency" were potentially Lawrence's most sinful, most terrifying secrets of all.

In order for Lawrence to continue to write poetry, perhaps to write at all, he must quiet the anxieties aroused in the process. And they are many. But they all center on his need to establish a "masculine" identity. He will ward off the danger of parental castration by denying his Oedipal fantasies. He will ward off the danger of maternal castration by insisting on his self-sufficiency and justifying his own will toward domination. Both efforts require the reversal of early loyalties. He must repudiate the mother and identify with the father. Increasingly, in verse and fiction, Lawrence angrily denounces the "spiritual" woman, a caricature of his mother, and celebrates the sensual, non-intellectual man, an idealized version of his coal-miner father. His manner alters as well, as he turns away from the flaccid romanticism of much of the *Rhyming Poems* to cultivate a more vigorous, aggressive, sometimes sardonic style. The suspect urge toward introspection and self-exploration, which lay at the heart of his verse, is re-formulated as a "mining" of the psychic underworld, and Mr. Lawrence, a miner of a different sort and apparently the least introspective of men, is eventually associated with the demonic forces of the unconscious that inspire Lawrence's verse. As his father's son, neither "mild," nor "lovable," nor "nice," Lawrence asserts his masculinity and denies his castration. As a result, it becomes possible for him to examine and, ostensibly at least, to accept elements in his own nature that he had earlier to repress. It becomes possible for him to write.[6]

II

The conflicts revealed in Lawrence's early verse are seen again with special clarity in *Pansies,* a late volume which represents a regression of sorts. Lawrence wrote *Pansies* about three years before his death, at a time when he was already ill and sexually impotent. The loss of sexual capacity, frightening both in itself and as a harbinger of the ultimate loss of life, apparently reactivated once again his infantile anxieties. The earliest separation from the mother had been only type and precursor of the inevitable final separation. The implication of selfhood had always been death. In *Pansies,* Lawrence makes a last desperate effort to avert final disaster. His celebration of the phallic reaches suspicious heights as he attempts to deny the appeal of earlier, non-phallic, and therefore potentially "perverse" pleasures. Nevertheless, his desire for maternal nurturance is probably intensified by his illness. It finds clear expression in **"Bowls,"** a short poem which reveals, too, Lawrence's grief at the loss of sexual vigor.

> Take away all this crystal and silver
> and give me soft-skinned wood
> that lives erect through long nights, physically
> to put to my lips.

(*CP* 427)

But, under threatening circumstances, Lawrence is less able than in his youth to acknowledge the need for "one warm, sweet room" and "a woman who loved me to rest me" (*L* 81-82).

Most obvious in the verse is Lawrence's need to ally himself once more with the "masculine." His sympathies are engaged by the coal-miners striking for higher wages, and he writes verse urging the working class, with whom he now chooses to identify himself, to rebel.

> . . . . if you amount to a hill o' beans
> start in and bust it all;
> money, hypocrisy, greed, machines
> that have ground you so small.

(**"Fight! O My Young Men,"** ll. 25-28, *CP* 457)

While thus associating himself with his father's world, he heaps scorn on "Willy Wet-Leg," the effete, obviously incapacitated, upperclass male and abjures all sexual relationship with the "spiritual" woman of whom his mother is his personal archetype.

> To proceed from mental intimacy
> to physical is just messy,
> and really, a nasty violation,
> and the ruin of any decent relation
> between us.

(**"Let Us Talk, Let Us Laugh,"** ll. 15-19, *CP* 470)

At this point in his life, when Lawrence is faced with actual loss of physical, and specifically sexual vitality, he reacts by denying with new vigor his various fantasies of union with his mother and racing headlong to join his father's forces. And though he does not stop writing poetry, the verse produced is of a peculiar kind, which some have claimed is hardly poetry at all. What concerns us here is not only the turning away from lyricism and the increased reliance on colloquialism and slang (his father's language) but also the rigid, almost mathematical structuring of the verse, suggesting as it does an obsessive need to control and order. Repression is diligently at work defending Lawrence against conscious awareness of his true fears and deep angers, although these feelings are nevertheless revealed in the verse. Its "biting" words and "dirty" words, suggesting infantile modes of expressing rage, betray the intensity of Lawrence's frustration and despair. And when he wishes, "like Tiberius," that "the multitude had only one head," so that he could "lop it off," that very multitude he has been celebrating throughout the volume, one glimpses his concealed fury at his father and the desire for appropriate revenge.

III

At the same time that Lawrence was working on *Pansies,* he was also revising his early verse in preparation for the publication of his *Collected Poems* (1928). And, of course, he was writing, too, the foreword originally intended for that volume, the essay in which he revealed the association in his mind between verse and secret sin. Even a cursory examination of Lawrence's revisions tends to confirm the state of mind suggested by *Pansies.* Lawrence wants to deny the "commonplace youth," that part of himself associated with the gentler virtues of spirit and mind, but also with moral inhibition, passivity, and effeminacy, and to vindicate his demon, that aggressively masculine self. The foreword to the *Collected Poems* is itself the most explicit expression of that desperate effort at vindication.

Of all the revised poems, **"Virgin Youth"** seems of particular importance given Lawrence's obsession with his genital apparatus. In rewriting this poem, Lawrence eliminated the languishing tenderness originally expressed toward his "beautiful, lonely body/Tired and unsatisfied" (ll. 21-22, *CP* 896). But the exaggerated celebration of the masculine that he introduces in the revised version suggests merely a narcissism of a different sort. The phallus becomes a god: "Thou dark one, thou proud curved beauty! I/Would worship thee" (ll. 55-56, p. 40). Although the revised poem is often wittier than the original, the solemnity of dogma distorts the whole, and we are left with the uncomfortable feeling that Lawrence has no notion how ludicrous is his plea, "Dark, ruddy pillar, forgive me!" (l. 47), that there is not, unfortunately, a trace of irony in his conclusion, "Thy tower impinges/On nothingness. Pardon me!" (ll. 61-62).

In this poem, the "real say" seems the imposition of doctrine, the holiness of the phallus' affections. In **"Virgin Youth,"** as in some other revised poems, we have not so much a falsehood giving way to a truth, as an attitude

apparently truly experienced in youth yielding to a later conviction. Lawrence seems to be saying, "This is the way I should have felt," and to deny his youth its say. He is trying to rehabilitate his younger self by transforming him into a more virile figure.[7]

The attempt involves revision of both subject matter and style, best exemplified perhaps in the reworking of **"Yesternight"** (*CP* 919-20). In this poem (first published in 1910 as a section of **"Night Songs"**), workers tell of leaving their office at the end of the day and going out into a soft, flower-like night to which they flower open in response. Dream-like reverie permeates the verse and the characters of the men. Romanticism is rampant: the men are flowers; the street lamps, censers; the river lamps, full-blown roses; and the moon, a reddening lantern. The ebb of evening whispers of the full swell of life the men have missed, and the night offers only a kind of oblivion as consolation for their loss. They have "eaten the narcotics of night," and "forgotten the sunny apples of the day" that they had "craved to eat" (l. 26).

The revised (1928) version, **"Clerks"** (part of **"Hyde Park at Night, Before the War,"** p. 70) is less languid. The contrast between the drab daytime world and the fantasy life of night is more boldly delineated. The "chambered weariness" of each man's soul has become a "chambered wilderness" from which a "spirit" wanders abroad on its explicitly sexual enterprise. No longer are the men defeated and weak. Their vitality has simply been held in abeyance during the day. Now the men are associated not with perfumed flowers, but with elephants (their phallic significance is unmistakable) who "scream aloud/For joy of the night when masters are/Asleep and a dream" (ll. 10-12). The primal animal is liberated, and while the ego sleeps, the dreams of the unconscious are given full sway.

The most dramatic changes in the verse, however, are those in which the sense is even more drastically altered. **"Whether or Not"** (*CP* 921-28), **"The Drained Cup"** (*CP* 137-40), and **"Two Wives"** (*CP* 154-58) are all stories of romantic triangles involving a man and two women, one the bride of his spirit, the other the bride of his flesh. In each poem, as first published, the claims of the spirit are finally acceded to while the sensual is, at best, relegated to a position of secondary value, and, at worst, associated with the demonic. In revising these poems "to say the real say," Lawrence in each case overturned the triumph of the spiritual bride, thus vindicating the desires of the flesh. Other changes also reveal his increased antagonism toward the "spiritual" woman whom he had tended at first to treat more tenderly. Now she becomes the victim of his ironic comment, often introduced at the end of the poem:

> It is well
> Since I am here for so short a spell
> Not to interrupt her? Why should I
> Break in by making any reply!

> (**"Passing Visit to Helen,"** ll. 46-49, *CP* 152)

In general, Lawrence's revisions confirm the movement toward the "nightingale's song." He attempts to shed what he once, in a different context, called "all my pathetic sadness and softness," and, more specifically, to free his work of archaic, stilted, or romantic diction. His language becomes more colloquial and spirited, approximating the speaking voice, while an expanded use of direct address and dialogue heightens the dramatic element. The imagery becomes more coherent, less diffuse. There is a toughening of attitude, a greater aggressiveness and variety of tone, including a bracing dash of mockery.

But while most of Lawrence's revisions reflect his insistence on the "male song," others seem to contradict this motive. **"Kisses in the Train"** and **"Last Words to Miriam,"** the poems in question, anticipate the spirit of reconciliation that informs Lawrence's **Last Poems.**

The early version of **"Kisses in the Train"** describes the quiet at the center of a storm of passion:

> But firm at the centre
>   My heart was found;
> Her own to my perfect heart-beat bound.

>   (***Love Poems*** version)

In the ***Love Poems*** version, the woman's heart sets the pace:

> My own to her perfect
>   Heartbeat bound.

>   (ll. 33-34, ***CP*** 121)

The change allows Lawrence both to assume and to admit his dependent role, analogous to that of the foetus in the womb or the baby at its mother's breast. The enemy whose power he had had to deny is becoming the friend whose strength nourishes and protects. The "good" mother is replacing the "devouring" mother.

In **"Last Words to Miriam"** (an ironic title for a poem so much revised), there is a similar but more extended reversal. In the earliest manuscript version (***CP*** 930) and in the text published in ***Amores*** (*CP* 931-32), it is Lawrence who has awakened Miriam, has created her as his creature. Her love was "dark and thorough," but

> Mine was the love of the sun for a flower
>   He creates with his shine.
> I was diligent to explore you,
>   Blossom you stalk by stalk,
> Till my fire of creation bore you
>   Shrivelling down. . . .

>   (***Amores*** version, ll. 4-9, ***CP*** 931)

Through a reversal of roles in the 1928 edition, Lawrence reinterprets their relationship and acknowledges his debt to Miriam.

> Mine was the love of a growing flower
>   For the sunshine.

> You had the power to explore me,
>   Blossom me stalk by stalk;
> You woke my spirit, you bore me
>   To consciousness . . .

>   (ll. 4-9, ***CP*** 111)

Perhaps the willingness to relinquish fantasies of narcissistic omnipotence helped prepare the way for Lawrence's final confrontation with death, and for the masterful ***Last Poems,*** which issued from that confrontation. What Lawrence had feared most was castration, a deficiency that would render him impotent to act. But it was his own fantasies and fears that threatened to paralyze his capacity for action—whether the act of love or the act of poetry. Whenever, as in some of the ***Pansies,*** self-justification became his primary motive, the result was dogma, diatribe, and something less than poetry. But in accepting the human limitations on his power, Lawrence could be less afraid of the consequences of his anger, and for that very reason, or for others, was no longer so afraid of a violent retaliation.

At the end of his life, Lawrence does not necessarily deny the bitter self-knowledge he has arrived at; he seems rather to assume and then transcend it. The result is magnificent poetry. In the ***Last Poems,*** individual power is sacrificed for the sake of security in community. Lawrence becomes again like a little child and somehow—one does not know how—earns to trust in idealized parent-gods, gentle and beautiful, and in their forgiveness.

From the beginning of his career as a poet, Lawrence was committed to the search for truth, by which he seems to have meant primarily truth about the self. Art was the "medium through which men express their deep, real feelings," and poetry was the act of knowing oneself. Lawrence's earliest poems make abundantly clear the powerful desires and fears that will continue to provide the emotional impetus behind his later verse, and which, in the years that follow, he will explore with increasing frankness and self-awareness. According to Lawrence, writing poetry is the attempt not only to know but also to heal oneself. The artist, he said, creates "to get at the meaning of his own soul's anguish," "to see himself emerge," so that he can "understand his own suffering" and "go on further, leaving it" (**"Christs in the Tirol,"** *P* p. 83). But the guilty discoveries made in the process are sufficient to create considerable anxiety. Here is the root of Lawrence's suspicion of literature, and, since his "unmanning" fantasies are perhaps the most threatening, here too is the source of his struggle, almost lifelong, to achieve a "masculine" art.

NOTES

[1] Lawrence's works are cited parenthetically in my text by abbreviated title, page number, and poetic line number in the following editions:

A Amores (New York: B. W. Heubsche, 1916).

CL The Collected Letters of D. H. Lawrence, ed. Harry T. Moore (New York: Viking Press, 1962).

CP The Complete Poems of D. H. Lawrence, ed. Vivian de Sola Pinto and Warren Roberts (New York: Viking Press, 1971).

FU Fantasia of the Unconscious, in *Psychoanalysis and the Unconscious* and *Fantasia of the Unconscious* (New York: Viking Press, Compass Book, 1960).

P Phoenix: The Posthumous Papers of D. H. Lawrence, ed. Edward D. McDonald (1936; rpt. New York: Viking Press, 1964).

P II Phoenix II: Uncollected, Unpublished and Other Prose Works by D. H. Lawrence, ed. Warren Roberts and Harry T. Moore (New York: Viking Press, 1967).

SL Sons and Lovers (New York: Viking Press, Compass Book, 1960.

SCAL Studies in Classic American Literature (New York: Viking Press, 1961.

[2] "If sexual pleasure is disturbed by anxiety, it is comprehensible that an 'identification with the aggressor' . . . can be a relief. It is able to person is able to do to others what he fears may be done to him, he no longer has to be afraid. Thus anything that tends to increase the subject's power or prestige can be used as a reassurance against anxieties. *What might happen to the subject passively is done actively by him, in anticipation of attack, to others.*"—Otto Fenichel, *The Psychoanalytic Theory of Neurosis* (New York: W. W. Norton, 1945), p. 354.

[3] Daniel Weiss, who has written the most thorough psychoanalytic study of Lawrence's work, notes in the fiction the recurrence of "sadistic beating and retaliation by strangling."—*Oedipus in Nottingham: D. H. Lawrence* (Seattle: University of Washington Press, 1962), p. 91.

[4] The fear of castration, although it no doubt has its roots in a literal fear, makes most sense when understood symbolically. It is the fear that one will be or already has been, in some absolutely essential sense, mutilated and thus rendered impotent to act, sexually or otherwise, as a whole "man" ought. But according to primitive reasoning, a mutilated man is a woman. Thus, for instance, a father who is perceived by his son as overwhelmingly powerful and dangerous has already done violence to that child's sense of himself and created in him a nagging anxiety that he is a woman.

[5] If Lawrence had a son, he would tell him, "leave yourself alone. . . . Don't you go creeping off by yourself and doing things on the sly. . . . Remember that I want you to leave yourself alone. I know what it is, I tell you. I've been through it all myself. . . . And the only thing I want of you is to be manly. Try and be manly, and quiet in yourself."—*FU* 146-47.

[6] David Cavitch's psychoanalytic reading of Lawrence in *D. H. Lawrence and the New World* (New York: Oxford University Press, 1969) is often similar to my own. Cavitch recognizes, for instance, an "unsatisfied need for masculine identification" (p. 30) and an "excessive fear of man's aggression" (p. 128) as important sources of Lawrence's chronic anxiety. And Cavitch points out, as I do, that in Lawrence's willingness to rationalize or glorify . . . viciousness and brutality in male sexual activity" (p. 150), he "idealizes the very notion of manhood that makes masculinity frightening to him" (p. 168).

[7] Emile Delavenay suggests, as I do, that Lawrence's revisions often seem intended to disguise rather than to expose his early feelings. But Delavenay ascribes a somewhat different motive. He asserts that Lawrence "mutilated" his early poems because by 1928, he was "much more alive to the possible clinical interpretation of his adolescent symptoms."—"D. H. Lawrence and Sacher-Masoch," *DHLR*, 6 (Summer 1973), 143.

Del Ivan Janik (essay date 1975)

SOURCE: Del Ivan Janik, "D. H. Lawrence's 'Future Religion': The Unity of Last Poems," in *Texas Studies in Literature and Language*, Vol. XLV, No. 4, Winter, 1975, pp. 739-54.

[*In the following essay, Janik explicates Lawrence's posthumously published poems "Bavarian Gentians" and "The Ship of Death" among others to support claims that Lawrence is among the major poets of the twentieth century.*]

Several of the poems that D. H. Lawrence wrote in the last months of his life are considered to be among his finest, and among the finest English poems of the century; but it has not been observed that the posthumously published notebook that includes **"Bavarian Gentians"** and **"The Ship of Death"** is a unified and cohesively organized work that extends Lawrence's most fundamental religious perceptions into one of his major literary accomplishments. In his introduction to Lawrence's ***Last Poems,*** first published by Giuseppe Orioli in 1932, Richard Aldington lamented the fact that the poet had not lived to complete his work: "He was too weary, he could not find the strength to build his ship of death and at the same time to build the full whole song of it."[1] But whether or not the sequence of sixty-seven poems that begins with **"The Greeks Are Coming!"** and ends with **"Phoenix"** represents Lawrence's final intention, it stands as a coherent and important work. As Tom Marshall has implied and Elizabeth Cipolla and Michael Kirkham have stated, ***Last Poems*** can and should be read as if it were a single long poem.[2] It is a poem that expresses Lawrence's fervent and very personal religious understanding of life as a preparation for death and ultimate rebirth. ***Last Poems*** asserts the primary importance of each individual's relationship with the world of experience, so that in the ems asserts the primary importance of each individual's relationship with the world of experience, so that in the context of Lawrence's whole career it strongly qualifies the collectivistic emphasis of *Apocalypse,* Lawrence's other late religious statement.[3]

It could be maintained that in a loose sense all of Lawrence's mature poetry is religious, but *Last Poems* differs from *Look! We Have Come Through!, Birds, Beasts and Flowers,* and the bulk of *Pansies* in that it expresses Lawrence's beliefs in explicitly religious terms, in a sacramental and mythological framework. The sequence deals with the areas of experience that have always been the province of religion: the conduct of life, the nature of evil, the identity of God or the gods, the problem of death and life after death. In *Last Poems* Lawrence gave poetic life to the "Future Religion" that he had outlined in one of his *Pansies.*

> The future of religion is in the mystery of touch.
> The mind is touchless, so is the will, so is the spirit.
> First comes the death, then the pure aloneness,
>   which is permanent
> then the resurrection into touch.

(II, 611)

It is this basic pattern that informs the volume of *Last Poems,* giving it structural and thematic coherence. The opening sequence of some twenty poems deals with the "mystery of touch," exploring the varied possibilities of the world of the senses. The poems from **"The Hands of God"** to **"Departure"** evoke the emptiness and horror of a life without touch, a life dominated by the mind and the will. Finally, the sequence that begins with **"The Ship of Death"** offers Lawrence's vision of the journey of death, oblivion, and bodily resurrection—a vision that was intensely personal yet was drawn from the distant reaches of human memory.

The personal quality of *Last Poems* is made clear at once by its setting: the Mediterranean as it existed for Lawrence's consciousness as he sat beside its waters at Bandol in the autumn of 1929.[4] The modern Mediterranean was there, with its sunbathers and ocean liners, but for Lawrence the ancient sea of the Argonauts and the Etruscans was also present, just as physically and just as convincingly. The thematic structure of *Last Poems* is analogous to that of symphonic music. Themes, images, and verbal motifs are stated and developed through a series of poems; new themes are introduced and developed in turn, and earlier ones are recapitulated and juxtaposed. The volume begins with a vision of the return of the ancient Greek gods and heroes to the modern Mediterranean. Subsequent poems turn to Judeo-Christian imagery, but **"Maximus," "The Man of Tyre," "They Say the Sea is Loveless,"** and **"Bavarian Gentians"** return to classical themes; all of these poems express and affirm the importance of the senses—"the mystery of touch." The fall of Lucifer sets the tone for the second sequence of poems, which is antithetical to the first. Here Lawrence juxtaposes Judeo-Christian formulations with

observations about the modern "touchless" world and more poems that draw on the Greek heritage—this time the pre-Socratic philosophers. The concluding **"Ship of Death"** sequence is founded on Lawrence's understanding of the customs of ancient Egypt and Etruria, expressing through them Lawrence's vision of death, oblivion, and the "resurrection into touch."

The civilizations of the ancient world assert their presence in *Last Poems* not only in the subject matter but also in the form of the poetry, which reflects their modes of consciousness as Lawrence understood them. Mark Spilka has recognized the connection between the primitive concept of *theos* or *mana* and Lawrence's manner of writing, in prose as well as verse.[5] For Lawrence as for the ancient peoples of the Mediterranean, spiritual value is immanent in the things of the world, and meaning is not fixed or static but rather shifts constantly among the things that pass through an individual consciousness; this is why the immediacy of touch—intuitive understanding—is so important to Lawrence. As Spilka points out, the fluidity and apparent "carelessness" of Lawrence's writing is really a function of his adherence to a different concept of meaning and value than that which governs most modern literature. For Lawrence poetry is not a means of discovering a pre-existent or ideal Truth, but a way of recording the passing physical truths that present themselves to an alert consciousness.

Lawrence enunciated the attitudes that underlie the overall structure of *Last Poems* in his description in *Apocalypse* of the old, sensual "cult-lore" that preceded the more intellectual "culture" of the Hellenic Greeks.

> We have not the faintest conception of the vast range that was covered by the ancient sense-consciousness. We have lost almost entirely the great and intricately developed sense-awareness, and sense-knowledge, of the ancients. It was a great depth of knowledge based not on words but on images. The abstraction was not into generalisations or into qualities, but into symbols. And the connection was not logical but emotional. The word "therefore" did not exist. Images or symbols succeeded one another in a procession of instinctive and arbitrary physical connection—some of the psalms give us examples—and they "get nowhere" because there was nowhere to get to, the desire was to achieve a consummation of a certain state of consciousness, to fulfill a certain state of feeling-awareness.[6]

Similarly, the goal of *Last Poems* is a state of awareness rather than a state of conviction, for the "Future Religion" that Lawrence imagined was basically a process, a way of living, rather than a set of beliefs. The volume moves toward the evocation of that state not through logical connections but through a succession of images, symbols, and contrasting rhythms.

As the critical response to **"Bavarian Gentians"** and **"The Ship of Death"** has demonstrated, the individual poems in the volume can be appreciated independently. But of each poem are defined only vaguely. For example, the first four pieces in *Last Poems* are separate and distinct in subject and expression, yet together they form a unit and, in turn, part of a larger cycle of some twenty poems. These patterns of interconnection are not solely thematic; *Last Poems* is given coherence and also variety through a broad formal structure that results from the placement of poems of varied length, diction, and rhythm. More carefully than in any of his earlier poetic works, Lawrence here took advantage of the flexibility of his free-verse medium to create a controlled pattern of emotional peaks, valleys, and plains that underscores the volume's thematic structure. The prosaic flatness of poems like **"In the Cities"** and **"The Evil World-Soul"** emphasizes the odiousness of the touchless, will-dominated existence they describe,[7] and contrasts with the lyric intensity of **"For the Heroes Are Dipped in Scarlet," "Whales Weep Not,"** and **"The Ship of Death."** *Last Poems* has a complexity and at the same time a unity of expression that exceeds anything that Lawrence had accomplished in earlier volumes of poetry.

As I have indicated, the thematic and formal patterns of *Last Poems* follow the outlines of Lawrence's earlier poem, **"Future Religion,"** presenting a way of life, a warning, and finally a new sacrament of death, oblivion, and rebirth. The first cycle or sequence of poems, the poems that explore the "mystery of touch," establishes the physical and emotional setting for the volume as a whole. The first, **"The Greeks Are Coming!,"** is a poem of rebirth and return: the return of the gods and heroes of the Homeric age; yet it is also a poem of the present, in which graceless ocean liners cross the Mediterranean distances once traversed by the Argonauts.

> And every time it is ships, it is ships,
> It is ships of Cnossos coming, out of the morning
>   end of the sea,
> It is Aegean ships, and men with archaic, pointed
>   beards
> coming out of the eastern end.
>
> But it is far-off foam.
> And an ocean liner, going east, like a small beetle
>   walking the edge
> is leaving a long thread of dark smoke
> like a bad smell.

(II, 687)

This is poetry of the "immediate, instant moment,"[8] reflecting Lawrence's unstudied response to his changing perceptions of the scene before him. But the apparently spontaneous flow of words is given poetic coherence through the repetition of words and phrases whose significance is amplified as the poem—and the poetic sequence—progresses. In **"The Argonauts,"** the second poem, the waning of day gives the ancient ships new reality, and the poet's excitement mounts in the third poem as the heroes actually assert their physical presence. In **"For the Heroes are Dipped in Scarlet"** he plainly states the theme that had been developed symbolically in the first three poems.

> Before Plato told the great lie of ideals
> men slimly went like fishes, and didn't care.

(II, 688)

Before Plato told men that they were nothing and that reality was somewhere outside and beyond them, they simply lived and laughed and fought and danced and were beautiful, like these bearded warriors whose being is so vital and whose *mana* is so strong that they are still present in the flesh. They are painted red in affirmation of the power of the blood pulsing in their bodies. The poem rises from the quiet assertions of the opening stanzas to a series of excited exclamations that brings the opening sequence of four poems to an end.

> So now they come back! Hark!
> Hark! the low and shattering laughter of bearded
>   men
> with slim waists of warriors, and the long feet
> of moon-lit dancers.
>
> Oh, and their faces scarlet, like the dolphin's blood!
> Lo! the loveliest is red all over, rippling
>   vermillion
> as he ripples upwards!
> Laughing in his black beard!
>
> They are dancing! they return, as they went, dancing!
> For the thing that is done without the glowing as
>   of God, vermillion,
> were best not done at all.
> How glistening red they are!

(II, 689)

"Demiurge," the poem that follows, provides a direct contrast to the initial sequence, and thus establishes the volume's overall rhythm. The agitated exclamations and vivid symbols are gone. **"Demiurge"** and the poems it introduces are further refutations of the "lie of ideals," but their movement is logical rather than imagistic, and their language is more abstract.

> They say that reality exists only in the spirit
> that corporal existence is a kind of death
> that pure being is bodiless
> that the idea of the form precedes the form
>   substantial.
>
> But what nonsense it is!
> as if any mind could have imagined a lobster
> dozing in the under-deeps, then reaching out a
>   savage and iron claw.
>
> Even the mind of God can only imagine
> those things that have become themselves:
> Bodies and presences, here and now, creatures
>   with a foot-hold in creation
> even if it is only a lobster on tip-toe.

(II, 689)

The succeeding poems also develop the thought and its implications in generally Christian frames of reference, but in varying tones: humorously as in **"Red Geranium and Godly Mignonette,"** or assertively as in **"The Body of God."** Together, they provide a release from the intensity of the opening sequence, and they contrast with the even greater intensity of the next group of poems, which includes **"The Man of Tyre," "Whales Weep Not,"** and **"Bavarian Gentians."**

These later poems return the focus of the volume to the sea and to the civilization of the ancient Greeks; they also create a second peak of lyric expression, linking them with the opening sequence and, later, with **"The Ship of Death."** But within the larger emotional rhythm of *Last Poems* there are subtler movements, and these poems cannot be considered a unit in the same sense as the group of four that opens the volume. **"The Body of God"** prepares for them thematically by stating that God has many manifestations: "men singing songs, and women brushing their hair in the sun"; and the poem **"Maximus,"** in the calm, ordinary diction of **"Demiurge,"** gives an account of one such manifestation: the god Hermes, warming himself at the poet's hearth.

"The Man of Tyre" also deals with the nature of God, in a scene that parallels Stephen Dedalus' vision in section IV of Joyce's *A Portrait of the Artist.* There is no need to emulate Michael Kirkham's exegesis of the poem in a recent essay,[9] but it should be recognized that the poem is central to Lawrence's exposition of the spiritual significance of physical presences. The man of Tyre walks along the shore pondering the unity of God when he suddenly sees a woman bathing naked in the sea.

> Oh lovely, lovely with the dark hair piled up, as
>   she went deeper, deeper down the channel,
>   then rose shallower, shallower
> With the full thighs slowly lifting of the wader
>   wading shorewards
> and the shoulders pallid with light from the silent
>   sky behind
> both breasts dim and mysterious, with the
>   glamorous kindness of twilight between them
> and the dim notch of black maidenhair like an
>   indicator,
> giving a message to the man—
>
> So in the cane-break he clasped his hands in delight
> that could only be god-given, and murmured:
> Lo! God is one god! But here in the twilight
> godly and lovely comes Aphrodite out of the sea
> towards me!

(II, 693)

The specificity and physicality of this description, as well as its carefully controlled formal structure, contrast sharply with the loose, conversational movement of the poems that precede it. The poet follows every movement as the woman goes "deeper, deeper" into the channel and then "shallower, shallower" to reveal her full godlike beauty to the watcher. The poem exemplifies the delicate balance in Lawrence's diction which lends a quality of spiritual immanence to what is also sensuously physical.

The description focuses on the woman's sexuality: her "full things" and the "glamorous kindness of twilight" between her breasts; but the vague adjectives—"pallid," "dim," "mysterious"—give her an ethereal quality and invest her with another kind of mystery.

This balance and interpenetration between the spiritual and the physical in Lawrence's sacramental vision of earthly experience receives further expression in **"Whales Weep Not,"** where the mating of the great mammals is described as the movement of "archangels of bliss."

> And they rock, and they rock, through the sensual
>   ageless ages
> on the depths of the seven seas,
> and through the salt they reel with drunk delight
> and in the tropics tremble they with love
> and roll with massive, strong desire, like gods.

(II, 694)

The sensuality of **"The Man of Tyre"** and the rhythmic drive of **"For the Heroes Are Dipped in Scarlet"** are both exceeded in this poem as strongly stressed syllables are crowded one upon another in an evocation of the silent thunder of the mating whales.

> And over the bridge of the whale's strong phallus,
>   linking the wonder of whales
> and burning archangels under the sea keep
>   passing, back and forth,
> keep passing archangels of bliss
> from him to her, from her to him, great Cherubim
> that wait on whales in mid-ocean, suspended in
>   the waves out of the sea
> great heaven of whales in the waters, old
>   hierarchies.

(II, 694)

This is the climax of the volume's first section, an ultimate manifestation of the wonder and mystery of the world of touch. The poem calls the whole of Lawrence's earlier volume *Birds, Beasts and Flowers* retrospectively into this new context. The hot-blooded, mountainous whales are living manifestations of God; they have a unique and wonderful *mana*—and so by implication do, in their smaller ways, the fishes and tortoises and mountain lions and almond trees of the earlier volume. This is one of the sudden changes in levels of awareness that Lawrence associated with the ancient "cult-lore" he described in *Apocalypse:* "To appreciate the pagan manner of thought we have to drop our own manner of on-and-on-and-on, from a start to a finish, and allow the mind to move in cycles, or to flit here and there over a cluster of images. . . . One cycle finished, we can drop or rise to another level, and be in a new world at once."[10] Here, Lawrence shifts from the world of the Mediterranean gods and heroes to the "great heaven of whales in the waters," and through them back to the world of *Birds, Beasts and Flowers,* where every living thing is suddenly revealed as a god, a *theos,* in itself.

"Whales Weep Not" is followed by two more poems that present *theoi* in the manner of *Birds, Beasts and Flowers;* but **"Butterfly"** also reasserts the physical setting of the volume at a villa by the Mediterranean, and **"Bavarian Gentians"** introduces the theme that will dominate the final section of *Last Poems.* This is the first of the poems that deals directly with death and the preparation for it. The death imagined here follows the pattern of Persephone's descent into the underworld, a place which has a dark beauty that mirrors the daylight beauty of the world under the sky.

> Reach me a gentian, give me a torch!
> let me guide myself with the blue, forked torch of
>   this flower,
> down the dark and darker stairs, where blue is
>   darkened on blueness
> even where Persephone goes, just now, from the
>   frosted September
> to the sightless realm where darkness is awake
>   upon the dark
> and Persephone herself is but a voice
> of a darkness invisible enfolded in the deeper dark
> of the arms Plutonic, and pierced with the passion
>   of dense gloom,
> among the splendour of torches of darkness,
>   shedding darkness on the lost bride and her
>   groom.

(II, 697)

As the poet imagines himself descending deeper, the repetitions of the words "blue" and "blueness," "dark" and "darkness" multiply until there is little else, perhaps prefiguring the "oblivion" of the volume's final sequence. But at the same time **"Bavarian Gentians"** also brings the poems about the varieties of sensual experience to an appropriate close. The underworld is dim and gloomy, but it is still a world of the senses whose darkness has a certain splendor. Seasonal myths like that of Persephone imply an eventual rebirth, a resurrection in the flesh. This aspect of the pattern of Lawrence's **"Future Religion"** does not figure directly in **"Bavarian Gentians,"** but the unspoken implication helps to prepare for the affirmations of the **"Ship of Death"** sequence.

More immediately, however, the myth of Persephone suggests another descent: the fall of Lucifer, with whose story the second major cycle of poems begins. In more than thirty poems Lawrence explores the "touchless" life of mind and will, the negative inversion of the life of the senses. Lucifer's sin—and the sin of any man who "falls from the hands of God"—is willful self-knowledge; and hell is "the turning-down plunge of writhing of self-knowledge, self-analysis / which goes further and further, yet never finds an end" (II, 701). As these lines suggest, these poems are abstract rather than imagistic, expository rather than symbolic; and that fact is itself symbolic in the larger scheme of *Last Poems.* A dry, intellectual mode of expression becomes dominant over a long series of poems: from the plight of Lucifer, Lawrence turns to the errors of the early Greek philosophers who denied the primacy of the senses, and then to

the manifestations of "touchless" evil in the modern world. These poems are abstract and argumentative; Richard Aldington has called these meditations on evil "a series of scoldings, which are little better than Pansies," the casual satirical verses that Lawrence had published in 1928.[11] Aldington failed to recognize, however, that these admittedly angry and often prosaic verses form an integral part of the thematic and formal movement of *Last Poems.* They are anticipated in the ugly modern steamship of **"The Greeks Are Coming!"** and they lead directly to the climactic poem, **"The Ship of Death."** In terms of the volume's poetic texture, their verbal and rhythmic flatness sets off the lyricism of the poems that precede them and of the **"Ship of Death"** cycle that follows.

Evil, as Lawrence understands it, is the inevitable outcome of the dominance of mind. Man becomes evil when, insisting on the superiority of the mind over the body, he releases his ego from the constraints and checks offered by the rest of the physical world. He becomes a human machine recklessly proceeding toward his own willed ends, and becomes finally the servant of machines.

> When the mind makes a wheel which turns on the
>   hub of the ego
> and the will, the living dynamo, gives the motion
>   and the speed
> and the wheel of the conscious self spins on in
>   absolution, absolute
> absolute, absolved from the sun and the earth and
>   the moon,
> absolute consciousness, absolved from strife and
>   kisses
> absolute self-awareness, absolved from the
>   meddling of creation
> absolute freedom, absolved from the great
>   necessities of being
> then we see evil, pure evil
> and we see it only in man
> and in his machines.

(II, 712)

The last several of these poems are progressively fragmented; there is no pretense of sustained thought, but merely a rush to express each angry observation. In **"Departure"** the poet catalogues the modern manifestations of evil, always returning to the word itself to build up a verbal tension that finds sudden release in **"The Ship of Death."**

> All forms of abstraction are evil:
> finance is a great evil abstraction
> science has now become an evil abstraction
> education is an evil abstraction.
> Jazz and film and wireless
> are all evil abstractions from life.
> Evil is upon us and has got hold of us.
> Men must depart from it, or all is lost.
> We must make an isle impregnable
> against evil.

(II, 716)

"Departure" ends with a challenge: evil, mechanical abstraction has conquered the modern world, and the only hope is that individuals may turn away from evil and somehow "make an isle impregnable" against it.

Lawrence's response to this challenge comes in **"The Ship of Death"** and the shorter poems that accompany it. In them he develops the pattern of death and rebirth that he had stated in **"Future Religion"**: first comes death, then the aloneness of oblivion, and finally the resurrection into touch. **"The Ship of Death"** brings another of the changes in mode and shifts in levels of awareness that characterize *Last Poems*. The invective against abstraction and absolutism is suddenly shut off, as if the poet had closed a door on a room full of noise. The poem does not plunge into the world of the senses like **"For the Heroes Are Dipped in Scarlet"** and **"Whales Weep Not"**; it begins quietly and cautiously, proceeding through neatly divided sections with surprising rhythmic regularity. This is still free verse, but it has an iambic core that helps to create a mood of calm determination. Unlike the poems of the volume's second major cycle, **"The Ship of Death"** is not abstract. It has the same physical immediacy, the same sense of a consciousness reacting directly to experience, that can be found in *Birds, Beasts and Flowers* and in poems like **"The Man of Tyre"**; but this world of experience is a very different one, and this consciousness proceeds in it with more deliberation.

I

Now it is autumn and the falling fruit
and the long journey towards oblivion.

The apples falling like great drops of dew
to bruise themselves an exit from themselves.

And it is time to go, to bid farewell
to one's own self, and find an exit
from the fallen self.

II

Have you built your ship of death, O have you?
O build your ship of death, for you will need it.

The grim frost is at hand, when the apples will fall
thick, almost thundrous, on the hardened earth.
And death is on the air like a smell of ashes!
Ah! can't you smell it?

(II, 716-17)

Although Lawrence knew when he wrote this that he was fatally ill, the poem's autumnal imagery gives it a more than merely personal significance. The ancient seasonal myths are suggested indirectly (that of Persephone having figured in **"Bavarian Gentians"**), and with them a hint of the bodily rebirth that will follow death. But this is not a "mythological" poem that solves the problem of the preparation for death for a whole civilization on a symbolic level. It is an invitation to introspection and self-questioning: how can we, in the face of the

fact of death, attain "the deep and lovely quiet / of a strong heart at peace"?

Lawrence's answer is put in terms of a ritual suggested by the funerary practices of the ancient Etruscans. Death is seen as a lonely journey for which each man must build a suitable vessel to sustain him.

Now launch the small ship, now as the body dies
and life departs, launch out, the fragile soul
in the fragile ship of courage, the ark of faith
with its store of food and little cooking pans
and change of clothes . . .

(II, 719)

The ship of the soul is patterned after the little bronze arks that Lawrence saw in the Etruscan tombs at Cerveteri. He explained in *Etruscan Places* why the Etruscans provided for the physical well-being of their dead: death was more a place than a state of being (or not-being); its boundary with life was not marked by distinctions of flesh and spirit.

And death, to the Etruscan, was a pleasant continuance of life, with jewels and wine and flutes playing for the dance. It was neither an ecstasy of bliss, a heaven, nor a purgatory of torment. It was just a natural continuance of the fullness of life. Everything was in terms of life, of living.[12]

In Lawrence's poem "the body dies," but the state of the soul after death is never explained, because explanation would be more falsification and dishonesty. Instead, the journey of death is imagined as a real journey, with all the fear and doubt and wonder that would attend a lone mariner on the open sea.

There is no port, there is nowhere to go
only the deepening blackness darkening still
blacker upon the soundless, ungurgling flood
darkness at one with darkness, up and down
and sideways utterly dark, so there is no direction
    any more.
and the little ship is there; yet she is gone.
She is not seen, for there is nothing to see her by.
She is gone! gone! and yet
somewhere she is there.
Nowhere!

VIII

And everything is gone, the body is gone
completely under, gone, entirely gone.
The upper darkness is heavy as the lower,
between them the little ship
is gone
she is gone.
It is the end, it is oblivion.

(II, 719)

What "oblivion" means is not yet clear, nor does it become clear in this one poem. **"The Ship of Death"** is not an appeal to the rational consciousness; it is an account of a religious experience—"an experience deep down in the senses, inexplicable and inscrutable."[13] It is the sensual detail of Lawrence's description of a dawn at sea, in the poem's final stanzas, that creates an atmosphere of intuitive acceptance for his assertion that the journey of death ends in the resurrection of the body.

> Wait, wait, the little ship
> drifting, beneath the deathly ashy grey
> of a flood-dawn.
>
> Wait, wait! even so, a flush of yellow
> and strangely, O chilled wan soul, a flush of rose.
>
> A flush of rose, and the whole thing starts again.

> (II, 720)

Richard Aldington has expressed regret that the final sequence of *Last Poems* was not integrated into a longer version of "**The Ship of Death**": "As the first draft shows, Lawrence probably meant to make this one long poem, and if this could have been done it would have been his greatest achievement as a poet."[14] As Elizabeth Cipolla has observed,[15] Aldington failed to consider that throughout his poetic career, and certainly in *Last Poems,* Lawrence wrote in extended poetic sequences rather than in sharply delimited individual poems. Each titled poem is an extension of or a commentary upon the others around it, creating a larger unit that reflects the changes of thought and feeling that a man undergoes over a period of time. Furthermore, in the context of *Last Poems,* even an extended version of "**The Ship of Death**" would have been too short, and perhaps too tentative, to balance and resolve the long cycle of negative poems that precedes it. The first draft of "**The Ship of Death**" which Aldington found in another manuscript probably represents a limited, early attempt at expression, while the long sequence from "**The Ship of Death**" to "**Phoenix**" is a more finished and, at least in Lawrence's estimation, a superior work.[16] The shorter poems that follow it explain some of the implications of the journey of "**The Ship of Death**," and they extend and clarify its symbolic significance. In his own characteristic way Lawrence did write the single long poem that Aldington looked for.

These poems underscore the importance of a conscious preparation for death; living men must learn to see death in proper perspective, as the necessary complement to the fulness of life.

> Sing then the song of death, and the longest journey
> and what the soul takes with him, and what he
>   leaves behind,
> and how he enters fold after fold of deepening
>   darkness
> for the cosmos even in death is like a dark
>   whorled shell
> whose whorls fold round to the core of soundless
>   silence and pivotal oblivion
> where the soul comes at last, and has utter peace.
>
> Sing then the core of dark and absolute
> oblivion where the soul at last is lost

> in utter peace.
> Sing the song of death, O sing it!

> (II, 724)

The "oblivion" that Lawrence describes is more than mere insensateness; it is the "pure aloneness" of the poem "**Future Religion**," the death of the ego that must precede the resurrection of the body. Oblivion is not the renunciation of experience but the fulfillment of a life lived in sensual awareness. Only abstract, mechanical knowledge, the kind of touchless self-knowledge that Lawrence rejects in the poems that precede "**The Ship of Death**," is cast out. Rather than nothingness, oblivion means the renunciation of the personal, self-knowing ego in an opening of the personality to spontaneity and change.

In Lawrence's "**Future Religion**" the rebirth from oblivion may come after actual, physical death; but "**Shadows**," one of the last poems in the volume, affirms that the building of the ship of death is also a preparation for life. The "resurrection into touch" can come in the midst of a man's life if he is willing to cease from static knowledge and enter into the universal pattern of vital change.

> And if, as autumn deepens and darkens
> I feel the pain of falling leaves, and stems that
>   break in storms,
> and trouble and dissolution and distress
> and then the softness of deep shadows folding,
>   folding
> around my soul and spirit, around my lips
> so sweet, like a swoon, or more like the drowse of
>   a low, sad song
> singing darker than the nightingale, on, on to the
>   solstice
> and the silence of short days, the silence of the
>   year, the shadow,
> then I shall know that my life is moving still
> with the dark earth, and drenched
> with the deep oblivion of the earth's lapse and
>   renewal.

> (II, 727)

Thus oblivion means a willingness to be blotted out as a fixed personality again and again in the continuing movement of the universe, and to be made anew by the contingencies of the living world. "**Phoenix**," the final poem in the sequence of *Last Poems,* is a challenge to face this kind of oblivion and rebirth.

> Are you willing to be sponged out, erased,
>   cancelled, made nothing?
> Are you willing to be made nothing?
> dipped into oblivion?
>
> If not, you will never really change.
>
> The phoenix renews her youth
> only when she is burnt, burnt alive, burnt down
> to hot and flocculent ash.
> Then the small stirring of a new small bub in the nest
> with strands of down like floating ash

Shows that she is renewing her youth like the
   eagle,
immortal bird.

(II, 728)

Like almost all of Lawrence's works, his **Last Poems** ends with a beginning. Admittedly, the sequence of poems from **"The Greeks Are Coming!"** to **"Phoenix"** is in more than one sense a culmination. It is a mature statement of religious belief, for it presents a summation in symbolic form of Lawrence's approach to life. It exhibits a subtle, confident handling of the free-verse techniques that Lawrence had developed in earlier volumes of poetry. In spite of the fact that it is only a manuscript, never prepared for publication by its author, it is a complex and unified work that embodies Lawrence's spontaneous approach to the world of experience. Yet **Last Poems** is not a completion; there is no ultimate answer for Lawrence, but only a series of explorations, celebrations, warnings, and challenges. The highest and most deserved praise of Lawrence's **Last Poems** is that it is in no sense fixed or complete; like the **"Future Religion"** that Lawrence imagined, it is spontaneous, open-ended, and vital.

NOTES

[1] *The Complete Poems of D. H. Lawrence,* ed. Vivian de Sola Pinto and F. Warren Roberts (London: Heinemann, 1967), II, 598. Volume and page references in the text are to this edition.

[2] Tom Marshall, *The Psychic Mariner: A Reading of the Poems of D. H. Lawrence* (New York: Viking, 1970), pp. 195-225; Elizabeth Cipolla, "*The Last Poems* of D. H. Lawrence," *D. H. Lawrence Review,* 2 (Summer, 1969), 111; Michael Kirkham, "D. H. Lawrence's *Last Poems,*" *D. H. Lawrence Review,* 5 (Summer, 1972), 97-120. Cipolla observes that "the poems show Lawrence's thoughts gradually turning from life to depth." As I hope to demonstrate, the structure of *Last Poems* is in fact more complex.

[3] D. H. Lawrence, *Apocalypse* (Florence: G. Orioli, 1931). For a discussion of the development towards communalism in Lawrence's writings, see Baruch Hochman, *Another Ego* (Columbia, S.C.: Univ. of South Carolina Press, 1970).

[4] See Lawrence's letter to Else Jaffe, 4 October 1929, *The Collected Letters of D. H. Lawrence,* ed. Harry T. Moore (London: Heinemann, 1962), II, 1206.

[5] Mark Spilka, "Was D. H. Lawrence a Symbolist?" *Accent,* 15, No. 1 (Winter, 1955), 50-51.

[6] *Apocalypse,* pp. 133-34.

[7] Kirkham (p. 101) observes that in these poems "Lawrence is working within traditional forms of thought and feeling the doctrinal core of which he had disowned." See Lawrence's 1918 essay, "Poetry of the Present" in *Complete Poems,* I, 181 ff.

[8] "Poetry of the Present," *Complete Poems,* I, 181.

[9] Kirkham, pp. 110-16.

[10] *Apocalypse,* pp. 133-34.

[11] *Complete Poems,* II, 597.

[12] D. H. Lawrence, *Etruscan Places* (London: Martin Secker, 1932), p. 28.

[13] D. H. Lawrence, "New Mexico" (1931), in *Phoenix: The Posthumous Papers of D. H. Lawrence,* ed. Edward McDonald (London: Heinemann, 1936), p. 144.

[14] *Complete Poems,* II, 598.

[15] Cipolla, p. 111.

[16] For descriptions of these manuscripts, see Aldington's introduction to *Last Poems,* in *Complete Poems,* II, 597.

John W. Presley (essay date 1979)

SOURCE: "D. H. Lawrence and the Resources of Poetry," in *Language and Style,* Vol. XII, No. 1, Winter, 1979, pp. 3-12.

[*In the following essay, Presley examines Lawrence's deployment of free verse and its relationship to the themes of his poetry.*]

The poetry of D. H. Lawrence presents an interesting problem for stylistic investigation. Nearly all critics agree that Lawrence evolved a new form; that, from a mediocre Georgian lyricist, he became a sometimes excellent free-verse lyricist. Though his mature work has been widely influential, especially in America, his poetry is often treated as an adjunct to the novels, and has received little detailed examination.

Lawrence has always been respected by his fellow poets, even when they disagree with him. Though Pound referred to the early work as "a sort of pre-raphaelitish slush, disgusting or very nearly so,"[1] he praised the dialect poems and, in a letter to Harriet Monroe, admitted, "I think he learned the proper treatment of modern subjects before I did."[2] Eliot, though disliking the poems themselves, wrote admiringly of Lawrence's advice to Catherine Carswell, which was that "the essence of poetry . . . is a stark directness, without a shadow of a lie, or a shadow of deflection anywhere. Everything can go, but this stark, bare, rocky directness of statement, this alone makes poetry, today."[3] Eliot recognized a similarity of aims.

> This speaks to me of that at which I have long aimed, in writing poetry; to write poetry which should be essentially poetry, with nothing poetic about it, poetry standing naked in its bare bones,

or poetry so transparent that we should not see the poetry, but that which we are meant to see through the poetry, poetry so transparent that in reading it we are intent on what the poem *points at,* and not on the poetry, this seems to me the thing to try for. To get *beyond poetry,* as Beethoven, in his later works, strove to get *beyond music.* We never succeed, perhaps, but Lawrence's words mean this to me. . . . [4]

Eliot's quarrel with Lawrence's subject matter, however, left only W. H. Auden's *The Dyer's Hand* praising Lawrence for having achieved this transparency.

Contemporary poets have been more wholehearted in their approval of Lawrence, since many contemporaries trace their forms back to Lawrence's later work. Kenneth Rexroth claims that Lawrence's **Look! We Have Come Through!** contains "the greatest imagist poems ever written," praising Lawrence for his "uncanny, 'surreal' accuracy of perception and evaluation."[5] The poets Stephen Berg and Robert Mezey maintain that "nothing much new has happened in English poetry since Lawrence laid down his pen and died." In the same collection, Robert Lowell ranks Lawrence's free verse with the Bible, Whitman, Pound, and Williams.[6]

Lawrence's critics are mainly apologetic in tone; Graham Hough, whose *Dark Sun* contains a chapter on the poetry, allows the poems to "assume the status of a running commentary to the course of development outlined in the novels" (New York: Macmillan, 1957, p. 191). The most easily available book-length treatment is Tom Marshall's *The Psychic Mariner* (New York: Viking, 1970), in which the poems are treated as indicative of Lawrence's psychic development, with little attention to the language of the poems. Indeed, nearly all criticism of Lawrence's poetry has tended to focus on *what* he was saying, rather than how he said it, discussing his poetic method in terms of delicacy, wit, irony, and vision, clearing up obscurities of imagery and emphasizing the perception of the poet.

This approach to Lawrence was made necessary by the devastating effect of "D. H. Lawrence and Expressive Form," an essay by R. P. Blackmur.[7] Subsequent critics have found themselves in the shadow of this essay, in which Blackmur attacks the forms of poetry Lawrence used. The forms, Blackmur says, are evidence that Lawrence had fallen victim to the fallacy of expressive form, which holds that merely to verbalize an idea is to give it sufficient artistic form. This, according to Blackmur, leaves the critic without a real standard of judgment, and, by giving up regular meter, regular line length, and rhyme, the poet impoverishes his mode of expression.

> . . . the strength of his peculiar insight lacks the protection and support of a rational imagination, and . . . it fails to its own disadvantage to employ the formal devices of the art in which it is couched. (p. 287)

The bias is obvious: the critic is taking the poet on the critic's terms. Whatever Lawrence's reasons for relinquish-

ing certain of his poetic resources, the interest of the critic should be in evaluating what Lawrence does with the resources he does use, such as phonology, syntax, line ending, and rhythm. The question of expressive form can be largely discounted in a linguistic examination of the poems, especially since there exists manuscript evidence of Lawrence's extensive revisions and the testimony of Frieda Lawrence that her husband labored long and hard over his poetry. Blackmur's conviction that Lawrence believed in "expressive form" arises from a misunderstanding of Lawrence's ironic use of the term "craftsman" and his metaphoric tendency in his essays on poetry. "Poetry of the instant" does not necessarily mean poetry *created* in an instant; rather, Lawrence is contrasting the form he attempts to create with the geometric perfection of older forms which implies a distance in time from the subject of the "perfect" verse.

The important question raised by Lawrence's use of free verse is the nature of poetic language: How many things can be subtracted from poetic form and still leave a remainder to be called poetry? Jan Mukařovský's essay "Standard Language and Poetic Language" suggests that poetry, the act of arranging an utterance into lines different from prose paragraphs, "foregrounds" its language; poetic language calls attention to itself *as language.* "Mukařovský characterized poetic (that is, literary) language as an aesthetically purposeful distortion of standard language."[8] The opposite of foregrounding is automatization, the use of devices which once foregrounded language but grew to be habitual. Lawrence foregoes the rhyme and meter which were automatized in his day, but his language still is foregrounded. The language of Lawrence's poetry is distorted, if simply by being titled and broken into lines and stanzas rather than paragraphs. Lawrence's worth as a poet depends upon whether or not the distortion of the language of his poetry is "aesthetically purposeful." The traditional devices that reinforce meaning—rhyme, meter, regular stanza form—Lawrence chooses not to employ, so that his poetry will not give the impression of a geometric perfection and temporal distance. This creates a free verse which is "transparent," pointing at the object or event described, but the language still announces itself; it is poetic language, and there are still resources left for the poet to manipulate so that meaning may be reinforced.

A quick survey of Lawrence's poetry, before attending closely to a particular poem, will show the shift in style and illustrate the development of specific techniques. The best known of the early poems, **"The Wild Common,"** easily characterizes this period, and shows Lawrence struggling with an inadequate medium. His nature is not a Georgian nature, and the automatized conventions of Georgian verse do little to reinforce meaning.

> Much of the verse of this period is formally indistinguishable from prose except for the intervention of the rhyme; and since there is hardly any discernible verse rhythm the lines have no existence as separate units, the rhymes mark nothing and seem curiously irrelevant. (Hough, p. 194)

Georgian rhyme schemes begin to reinforce meaning in **"Lightning,"** a five-stanza poem with a simple ABCCBA rhyme scheme in all but one stanza. The chiasmus of the rhyme reflects the emotional progress of the persona: at first he is drawn by the girl he holds, but a lightning flash shows the grudging resignation of her face and the speaker is suddenly repelled. The point at which the emotions reverse comes exactly in the center of the central verse:

> I leaned in the darkness to find her lips
> And claim her utterly in a kiss,
> When the lightning flew across her face
> And I saw her for the flaring space
> Of a second, like snow that slips
> From a roof, inert with death, weeping "Not
> this! Not this!"[9]

This stanza also marks the only change in the rhyme scheme, which here becomes ABCCAB, possibly reflecting the emotional disequilibrium of the speaker. The language also suddenly becomes more figurative after the central lines; the first simile of the poem appears, and simile and metaphor cascade through the two final stanzas.

In **"Medlars and Sorb-Apples"** Lawrence discards the conventions he finds oppressive and disjoints the syntax, leaving dangling nominal phrases after the colloquial, syntactically complete opening lines. Polyptoton, the repetition of a word with varying inflections, abounds, even in the opening lines:

> I love you, rotten,
> Delicious rottenness.
>
> (p. 280)

The phonology serves to unify the syntactic and rhythmic disparity of the poem, with echoes, internal rhymes, assonance and alliteration: "flux . . . sucked . . . rambling sky dropped grape . . . smack of preciosity/Soon in the pussy-foot west . . . so brown and soft and coming suave . . . spasm . . . orgasm" (Marshall, p. 124). But this unity of phonology is in great contrast to the much altered syntax:

> A kiss, and a spasm of farewell, a moment's
> orgasm of rupture,
> Then along the damp road alone, till the next
> turning.
> And there, a new partner, a new parting, a new
> unfusing into twain
> A new gasp of further isolation,
> A new intoxication of loneliness, among decaying,
> frost-cold leaves.
>
> (pp. 280-81)

Here, Lawrence uses no finite verbs to indicate movement or temporal succession; only the sequence markers *and, then,* and *till.* It has been suggested that the atactic nature of the poetry reflects Lawrence's vision—"rapid intuitive glimpses" (Hough, p. 206)—but here the syntax seems disjointed more for the sake of subtlety of argument. Lawrence is attempting to prove that the "morbid" flavor of medlars is emblematic of the dark gods, of Orpheus and Dionysos in the underworld, and the absence

of verbs allows absence of substantives, thus generalizing the journey. This could now be the travels of Orpheus, Dionysos, a sorb-apple, or the soul after death. Proof that Lawrence has been using his vagueness as argument comes two stanzas later:

> So, in the strange retorts of medlars
> and sorb-apples
> the distilled essence of hell.
>
> (p. 281)

So implies that what follows is a consequence of what has preceded, but this is not really the case here; the disjointed syntax has been a rhetorical trick: we concede to an argument that really has not occurred. The tightly knit phonological effects may help lull the reader into following the argument, but syntax and phonology do not work together to reinforce a meaning; rather, they help cover the vagueness of association. The poem is important, however, in that it shows Lawrence making original use of his resources.

The syntax of the last stanzas of a sister-poem, **"Almond Blossom,"** is more successful. The first part of the poem is a celebration of the obstinacy of the almond, blossoming in the snow; Lawrence, in long Whitmanesque lines, compares the almond first to iron, then to the history of the race, finally to the race's sufferings as particularized in Christ. Finally the poem ends with an apostrophe to the almond blossom which modulates into description:

> Oh, honey-bodied beautiful one
> Come forth from iron,
> Red your heart is.
> Fragile-tender, fragile-tender life-body,
> More fearless than iron all the time
> And so much prouder, so disdainful of
> reluctances.
>
> (p. 306)

This stanza, like those that follow, is composed of appositive after appositive, all repetitive variations of particular adjectives. The effect is that the syntax approximates the unfolding blossom (note that the inversion above places the heart-color of the blossom in the heart of the sentence); attribute after attribute is unfolded like the petals of the blossom. The phonological effects depend upon the repetition of key adjectives, and occasionally the effects are spectacular.

> In the distance, like hoar-frost, like silvery
> ghosts communing on a green hill,
> Hoar-frost-like and mysterious.
>
> (p. 306)

Inside the unfolding syntax and the multiplying similes, the phonological chiasmus of "hoar-frost" and "like," with its subtle syntactic alteration, is mimetic of the blossom's heart, "red at the core," unfolding even while the outer petals are still moving.

The pattern is repeated to the end of the poem, with slight variations. Intermittent repetition occurs in:

Unpromised,
No bounds being set.
Flaked out and come unpromised . . .

Another complex chiasmus occurs in this stanza:

Knots of pink, fish-silvery
In heaven, in blue, blue heaven,
Soundless, bliss-full, wide-rayed,
  honey-bodied,
Red at the core,
Red at the core,
Knotted in heaven upon the fine light.

(p. 307)

Here the chiasmus is between ideas; the syntax changes. Expressed schematically as ABBA, item B (the heart of the blossom) is syntactically the same in its two repetitions, but Item A, the comparison of the blossoms to heaven-knots, appears once as a noun phrase and once as a participial phrase. In addition, more attributes are unfolded with the compound adjectives between the first appearance of A and B. Thus Lawrence plays with the basic device of mimetic syntax like a composer with a four-note theme, subtly altering it in each instance. He closes the poem with a polyptoton, a play on one of his characteristic combination adjectives.

And red at the core with the
  last sore-heartedness,
Sore-hearted-looking.

(p. 307)

The ability to use syntax, line length, and rhythm to *force* his language to be transparent to its referent becomes Lawrence's strongest resource. **"Snake,"** his best known poem, is famous for just this effect.

In **"Snake"** . . . no one sensitive to the rhythms of English speech can fail to observe the lovely fluidity of movement (like that of the snake itself) . . . the rhythm trembles on the verge of regular iambic for a line or two, then lapses into a loose conversational run. (Hough, p. 207)

Both the rhythms and the insistent sibilants have been often noted, but the less-noticed syntax also adds to the poem's meaning. The opening lines are mimetic:

A snake came to my water-trough
On a hot, hot, day, and I in pyjamas for the heat,
To drink there.

(p. 349)

In one sense, the syntax helps diminish the importance of the persona; the phrase "and I in pyjamas for the heat" contains no finite verb and thus cannot be syntactically related to "To drink there," and the *and* reduces the human to the equal of the adverbial; in effect, the persona becomes a modifier, part of the environment. This idea is repeated in

Someone was before me at my water-trough,
And I, like a second comer, waiting.

(p. 349)

Here again, the human receives second-class treatment; the absence of a finite verb allows the static participle to change the human into a fact, a passive bit of environment, while the snake acts through a full verb.

In another sense, the first two lines of the poem are mimetic; since the infinitive phrase is separated from the word it modifies by three other phrases, three comma pauses, and two line-end pauses, the tendency is to relate it to the nearer subject, the human. Since this is logically possible, the referential mechanisms of the syntax are actually coiled upon themselves. In fact, if Lawrence had not used a similar image to describe "poetry of the past," one would be tempted to say the sentence "has its tail in its mouth."

Similar effects are achieved, at least momentarily, in another ***Birds Beasts and Flowers*** piece, **"Fish."** In this poem, while the persona, speaking in long lines of varied rhythm, maintains that the life of a fish cannot be understood or appreciated by man, the poet uses short choppy lines and rhythms to express the fish's "wave-bound being" (Marshall, pp. 138-40). Syntax and phonology are also employed here to mimic the movements of the fish, and the sounds and movements of water:

Whether the waters rise and cover the earth.

(p. 334)

The phonology of this line reflects the action described: the movement inside "waters rise" is an upward movement, from a low back vowel to a high front vowel with a high off-glide. The flatness of a world covered with water is reflected in "cover the earth," with its monotonous reduced vowels.

A lexical chiasmus prepares the reader for the more spectacular effects to follow:

Aqueous, subaqueous,
Submerged
And wave-thrilled.

(p. 334)

The movement from surface to sub-surface and back again, with the quick motion of the short lines, mimics the fish's movements in the sea. A syntactic chiasmus further develops this theme:

As the waters roll
Roll you.

(p. 335)

The movement from the doubled verb in opposite directions mimics the effects of a wave upon a fish. Furthermore, the reversal in the second line seems to place the fish in a passive position, accepting his oneness with the water, an idea that is developed in the phonological repetitions:

The waters wash,
You wash in oneness
And never emerge.

(p. 335)

Phonology also mimics the fish's life in

> Your life a sluice of sensation along your
>   sides,
> A flush at the flails of your fins down the
>   whorl of your tail
> And water wetly on fire in the grates of your
>   gills.

(p. 335)

The fricatives and sibilants of the first line echo the sound of water rushing along the fish's scales; in the second line, the repetition of the initial consonant cluster combines with another fricative to mimic the swishing movements of the fish's tail. The repetition of liquids, fricatives, and on-glides throughout the poem give a wet atmosphere. "Whorl" is an interesting word in this stanza; spelled as it is here, it is onomatopoetic in a strange way. The points of sound production move in a whorl when the word is pronounced, from the front of the mouth to the rear of the palate, back to the front for the alveolar closure.

One of the most successful uses of the compound is

> You and the naked element,
> Sway-wave.

(p. 335)

The syntax is ambiguous, allowing the compound "sway-wave" to be either verb or modifier; either way, it perfectly reflects the fish's movement (the syntactic ambiguity may be an advantage). The short line with two stresses gives the impression of quick movement, combining the "wave" of water with the "sway" of the fish in a reciprocal relationship. The phonology, clustered around the same vowel-glide combination, is a miniature of the whole poem's phonology, combining swishing sibilants and fricatives with watery glides.

Another resource of poetic language Lawrence manipulates is the tension between line length and syntax; this is illustrated in the first stanzas of **"The Elephant Is Slow to Mate,"** a poem whose lingering, halting pace points to the patience of the elephants.

> The elephant, the huge old beast,
>   is slow to mate;
> he finds a female, they show no haste,
>   they wait
>
> for the sympathy in their vast shy hearts
>   slowly, slowly to rouse
> as they loiter along the river-beds
>   and drink and browse
>
> and dash in panic through the brake
>   of forest with the herd . . .

(p. 465)

The last line of each stanza creates an odd rhythmic effect. The rhyme word of each line rhymes perfectly with the rhyme of the complementary line, creating a sense of finality which is abetted by the fact that each of the rhyme words receives a strong accent. A tension is set up with this finality since each final line seems syntactically complete, but after a stanza-end pause the reader learns that the line is yet to be completed.

This tension is necessary for the success of **"Bombardment,"** a short Imagist piece and one of Lawrence's most successful poems. The poem is free of Whitman's influence, and Lawrence uses all the resources surveyed thus far:

> The town has opened to the sun.
> Like a flat red lily with a million petals
> She unfolds, she comes undone.
> A sharp sky brushes upon
> The myriad glittering chimney-tips
> As she gently exhales to the sun.
>
> Hurrying creatures run
> Down the labyrinth of the sinister flower.
> What is it they shun?
>
> A dark bird falls from the sun.
> It curves in a rush to the heart of the vast
> Flower: the day has begun.

(p. 166)

Nearly all the techniques discovered in the brilliant moments of Lawrence's other poems are combined here to make this poem very nearly perfect. The tone is colloquial, conversational; there are no emotional exclamations, yet the language of everyday speech is combined with the resources of poetic language to make this poem, more than any other of Lawrence's except **"Snake,"** transparent to the thing described.

In the first stanza, chiming sounds help unify the lines; the metaphor of town and flower is announced flatly in the first line, and Lawrence demonstrates again a favorite effect, approximating the opening of a blossom by repetitive, balanced syntax. The line "like a flat red lily with a million petals" divides with a syntactic juncture between the two phrases and precisely in the center of the line. The repetition "she unfolds, she comes undone" emphasizes the slow continuity of the movement and the nasals slow the line, as do the heavy accents upon the low central vowels—all producing a line monotonously flat and doubled, as line 2 described the "flower" itself.

The phonology of stanza two is mimetic. The alliteration of "sharp sky brushes" uses fricatives and the consonant cluster /sk/ to produce the sound of brushing against all the high front vowels of "the myriad glittering chimney-tips." The "dying fall" of the town's breath "as she gently exhales to the sun" is produced by the vowel movement within the line, from the high front vowel of *she* to the mid front of *ex-* to the low central vowel of *sun*. The same pattern occurs throughout stanza three with the high front vowels of "hurrying creatures" moving to low central in "run," with a similar pattern in "sinister flower." All the movement in the poem is downward or flattening out, and the poem seems to be dominated by low, reduced, or low back vowels.

The slow pace of the poem continues until line 11. The slowed pace comes from the lack of tension between line endings and syntax, since seven of the twelve lines are end-stopped, syntactically complete. Eight of the twelve lines end on a heavily stressed syllable with a terminal nasal, a continuant. Three of the other lines end in other continuants: liquids or fricatives. Only one line ends with a phonological stop, a sound which cannot be continued indefinitely; the line is

> It curves in a rush to the heart of the vast . . .
>
> (p. 166)

With this line, Lawrence speeds up the rhythm of the poem, matching the swoop of the dark "bird" falling from the sun. The heavy stresses and irregular rhythms are suddenly changed; only "curves" receives a heavy stress, forming an iambic foot. The rest of the line is composed of extremely fast anapests with light stresses on the third syllable in each. The only stop in a terminal position also marks the most extreme enjambment in the poem; the other lines which are not end-stopped are stopped at syntactic junctures between phrases, but this line ending separates a noun and its modifier. The effect speeds up the rhythm even more, forcing a quick movement to "flower." Here, however, as the bird's quick flight would end, so does the fast rhythm end. The "flat" low and reduced vowels of "flower" are stopped short by the colon, marking the only major syntactic juncture to occur within a line in **"Bombardment,"** and this is a juncture preceded by an unstressed syllable, making any performance of the juncture sound even longer than a juncture preceded by a stress. The line continues, anticlimactically, to end in another heavily stressed nasal.

In this poem, a short *tour de force*, Lawrence achieves an intensity of effect often missing from his longer poems, but **"Bombardment"** illustrates the characteristic uses he makes of language. Lawrence was "a major poet groping his way towards the discovery of a new kind of poetic art"[10] and, like Wordsworth, he wrote "a good deal of bad poetry," but in some Lawrence poems he did discover and use his new kind of poetic art. In poems like **"Bombardment,"** some of *Pansies,* such as **"November by the Sea,"** and in the *Last Poems* Lawrence uses the resources of poetry—those left after ridding himself of automatized conventions—to support his meanings. What is left is bare language, with the resources of everyday language aesthetically and purposefully distorted to make the language, by calling attention to itself, actually become transparent to its referent.

NOTES

[1] Ezra Pound, *Literary Essays of Ezra Pound,* ed. T. S. Eliot (New York: New Directions, 1968), p. 387.

[2] Ezra Pound, *The Letters of Ezra Pound 1907-1941,* ed. D. D. Paige (New York: Harcourt, Brace, 1950), pp. 52-53.

[3] D. H. Lawrence, *Collected Letters,* ed. Harry T. Moore (New York: Viking, 1962), p. 413.

[4] F. O. Matthiessen, *The Achievement of T. S. Eliot* (London: Oxford, 1958), 3rd ed., pp. 89-90.

[5] Kenneth Rexroth, "Introduction," in *D. H. Lawrence, Selected Poems,* ed. Kenneth Rexroth (New York: Viking, 1959), pp. 1-23.

[6] Stephen Berg and Robert Mezey, ed., *Naked Poetry* (New York: Bobbs-Merrill, 1969), pp. xii, 124.

[7] In *Language as Gesture* (New York: Harcourt, Brace, 1935).

[8] Donald C. Freeman, "Linguistic Approaches to Literature," in *Linguistics and Literary Style,* ed. Donald C. Freeman (New York: Holt, Rinehart and Winston, 1970), pp. 6-8. The Mukařovský essay appears on pp. 40-56.

[9] D. H. Lawrence, *Complete Poems,* ed. Vivian de Sola Pinto and Warren Roberts (New York: Viking, 1971), rev. ed., p. 62. All references to Lawrence's poetry are to this edition.

[10] Pinto, "Introduction" to *Complete Poems,* p. 21.

George Y. Trail (essay date 1979)

SOURCE: "The Psychological Dynamics of D. H. Lawrences's 'Snake'," in *American Imago,* Vol. 36, No. 4, Winter, 1979, pp. 345-56.

[In the following essay, Trail employs Freudian psychology to explicate Lawrence's poem "The Snake."]

"Snake" is D. H. Lawrence's best known poem. It is not only the most anthologized (and hence the most taught) but also the most analyzed. A glance at the poem itself provides some immediate, if only surface, explanations:

The poem has a narrative line. A man, on a hot noon in Italy, comes to fill his water pitcher from a trough and finds a snake there. For an interval, in spite of the "voice" of his education which tells him the snake is dangerous and should be killed, he is fascinated and feels honored by the snake's presence. However, as the snake turns to leave the speaker is overcome with horror and throws a log at it. He immediately regrets the act, curses the voice of his education, and, after comparing the snake to Coleridge's famous albatross, wishes for its return, realizing that he has a "pettiness" to expiate.

Since the "voice" of the poet's "education" is declared "accursed" at the end of the poem, and is detested, it allows us to deprecate authority and celebrate the "natural" response which authority is traditionally seen as stifling. Yet since we have all obeyed, at one time or another, our education to our regret, the poem lets us off the hook by its statement that what we have to expiate is only a "pettiness."

And finally, since many modern readers will regard snakes as phallic, it gives the reader the thrill of approving the sexual, the "uninhibited," with no risk attached. Teachers of literature and makers of anthologies can justify including the poem in their respective courses and books as a way to introduce Lawrence, the "prophet of sexuality," precisely because the sexuality of the poem is symbolic rather than overt. Lawrence, the writer of *Lady Chatterley's Lover* can here be shown as a poet of high skill and intensely serious moral purpose.

Academic criticism of the poem most often sees **"Snake,"** in the context of the volume *Birds, Beasts and Flowers* where Lawrence first collected it, as a striking example of the poet's acknowledgement of the unknowable "otherness" of the animal and vegetable world. The speaker evokes his humility in the face of the multiplicity of the creation. But, surprisingly, there has been no psychoanalytic analysis of the poem. One of Lawrence's best critics, Keith Sagar, has come the closest. I quote Sagar at length (with the caution to note his practically knee-jerk use of the word "reduce").

> . . . the snake comes to serve as an analogue for the poet's own manhood, his real "I" as opposed to "voices in me," or, to reduce it to Freudian terms, the ego which seeks to mediate between the id (the spontaneous, instinctive self) and the universe. As the snake issues clear from the burning bowels of the earth, so the man must meet him with a response (gladness and humility) which issues cleanly from his own bowels without the intervention of the super-ego (the voices of his education). . . . The "fissure" above the water-through (which itself suggests fertility), the dark door of the secret earth . . . combines with the phallic snake in a sexual metaphor. When the voices of education have done their work it becomes, we notice, a "horrid black hole." The poet's violent, almost hysterical response to the snake's putting his head into the hole is a symptom of that horror of the sex act which Lawrence saw to be at the root of our nullity and neurosis.[1]

Sagar has done the greatest amount of contextual work on Lawrence, and of all his critics has come, I think, closest to the mark. But in his desire to make the poem "doctrinal," to make it an extension and a clarification of Lawrence's developing conscious philosophy, I suggest that he misreads the poem. In putting it in the context of Lawrence's declared position, he has still not provided enough context in the light of the complexity of the text itself.

"Snake" was first published in the *Dial* in July of 1921. We can say from both internal and external evidence that it was almost certainly written in the same month a year earlier, in July of 1920. In December of 1919 Lawrence began his first literary attack on Freud, the book of amateur psychoanalytic theory published in early May of 1921 as *Psychoanalysis and the Unconscious*. The critical reception of Lawrence's venture was varied, but it was not warm. Undaunted, Lawrence began another attack

in May of 1921, clearly in response to the reviews, which was published in 1922. He begins the book with a personal defense and titles it aggressively *The Fantasia of the Unconscious.*

Three differing but satisfactory discussions of Lawrence's theories are extant so I will give no extended account of them here.[2] What can summarily be said is that Lawrence found the unconscious, which he associated directly with the id, "pristine." Freud, he reports, found in the unconscious only a "huge slimy serpent of sex, and heaps of excrement. . . . "[3] However, when Lawrence began his second book in reply to Freud, he found that he and Freud were being shelled in the same boat. Lawrence, attacking Freud in 1919, found in 1921 that he had to scramble to defend the unconscious, the area, if not the concept in which he and Freud agreed. The enemy, to some extent, was now an ally. "Snake," however, emerges from the period six months after *Psychoanalysis and the Unconscious* was completed, and eleven months before its earliest reviews. Lawrence had not as yet acknowledged Freud as even a begrudged ally.

It is in this context, then, that I propose an interpretation of **"Snake"** which is finally more in accord with the text itself. I propose that **"Snake"** begins as a deliberate, even careful repudiation of Freudian theory, particularly as it concerns the Oedipus complex, and then breaks down under the pressures of a severe confrontation with castration anxieties. Far from being a moral triumph, the concluding third of the poem presents us with confusion, recognition, and compensatory (excuse making) activity, the purpose of which is to relieve the anxiety and guilt felt at the compulsive behavior exhibited in the second part of the poem. While I will quote extensively from the text, it will be helpful to the reader to have a copy of the poem. What I refer to as part I comprises lines 1-40, part 2, lines 41-57, and part 3, lines 58-74.

The poem begins after the discovery of the snake, and shifts immediately back to the present of the experience. The vacillation between present and past tense continues throughout sections one and two. Section three is past tense throughout.

The first two stanzas read:

> A snake came to my water-trough
> On a hot, hot day, and I in pyjamas for the heat,
> To drink there.
> In the deep, strange-scented shade of the great
>   dark carob-tree
> I came down the steps with my pitcher
> And I must wait, must stand and wait, for there he
>   was at the trough before me.[4]

Line 63 of the poem identifies the time of the action of the poem more closely as "intense still noon. . . . " It is day, but Lawrence is in his pajamas, and further, in the "deep strange-scented shade of the great dark carob-tree. . . . " The snake reaches down, in line 7 "in the gloom." Line 63 provides another odd insistence on the day/dark contrast.

The snake has disappeared "Into the black hole, the earth lipped fissure in the wall front,/At which, in the intense still noon I stared with fascination." The effect is that the blackness of the hole is accentuated by the brilliance of the sunlight; yet the poem has earlier told us that the arena of the snake's action is in "gloom." This contradiction, however, only appears in the third section of the poem. The fissure which becomes "black" and horrible in the third section, shows only in the first section "a fissure in the earth-wall in the gloom."

The repetition in line two, "On a *hot, hot* day, and I in my pyjamas for the *heat* [italics mine]," is unnecessary. The poet needs to convince us, or himself (or both) that the pajamas and the journey to the water trough were appropriate. He finds, at the end of his journey "down the stairs," that "there he was at the trough before me." The line can be read as meaning "in front" of me. But the poem will not allow only this reading. Lines 14 and 15, a stanza to themselves, insist:

> Someone was before me at my water-trough,
> And I, like a second comer, waiting.

The tense shifting I referred to earlier can account for part of the control evidenced in the section, but we are apparently presented with a symbolic rendition of the primal scene. The poet, in his pajamas, with the excuse of heat, and his pitcher in his hand to demonstrate his sincerity, moves down-stairs in the dark to the source of solace and nurture, here a "trough," and finds that "he" occupies the speaker's place in a dark area that smells "strange."

What is missing, however, is the sense of violence, noise, motion, and fear which we expect to be associated with such traumatic occurrence. Is this in fact the primal scene? Yet, how otherwise are we to account for the insistent details?

After the third stanza cited earlier, and the fifth, which elaborate the speaker's fascinated watching of the drinking snake, the poem resumes with:

> The voice of my education said to me
> He must be killed.
> For in Sicily the black, black snakes are innocent,
> 　　the gold are venomous.
> And voices in me said, If you were a man
> You would take a stick and break him now, and
> 　　finish him off.

Here, then, is the violence we looked for earlier, but its source, we are told, is not in the "self," but in the voice, which becomes, almost immediately, "voices" accusing the poet of being less than a man. The speaker, however, is not alarmed. He is, he reports, pleased.

> But must I confess how I liked him,
> How glad I was he had come like a guest in quiet,
> 　　to drink at my water-trough
> And depart peaceful, pacified, and thankless,
> Into the burning bowels of this earth?

> Was it cowardice, that I dared not kill him?
> Was it perversity, that I longed to talk to him?
> Was it humility, to feel so honoured?
> I felt so honoured.

The "must I," rather than the anticipated "I must" provides the answer. It is part of the first of four questions, on the surface asked by the speaker of himself, but on closer examination, clearly asked by the speaker of the reader. The point is somewhat difficult to make because of a difference between British and American English. A native American might write, and, less probably, might say "I must." He is much more likely to say "I have to." Were he to say "must I," he would be accused of affectation. In British English, the construction carries very nearly the American sense of "is this really necessary," and I propose that it is precisely in this sense that Lawrence uses the otherwise unnecessary inversion. It is *not* really necessary. The calm in the poem demonstrates that it is not really necessary. This, and the following three questions are rhetorical. The speaker asserts by implication that he is *not* humble, is *not* a coward, and is no pervert. The next two stanzas provide ample substantiation.

And yet those voices:

> *If you were not afraid, you would kill him!*

> And truly I was afraid, I was most afraid.
> But even so, honoured still more
> That he should seek my hospitality
> From out the dark door of the secret earth.

The language slips into Biblical "I was afraid, I was most afraid. . . . " But the intent here is not to establish the sacredness of the moment; rather it is to show that this is no crass fear; this is the fear which is to be identified with respect and awe in the sense that Job is reported to "fear God and eschew all evil." The situation which is supposed to be *terrifying* is, rather, awe producing. While the speaker feels no humility, he is honored. He stands in awe before his god, but his knees do not knock. Much of what is meant can be seen by comparing, say, the phrase "the awful presence of the Lord" with a statement like "it was awful" in contemporary vernacular.

All of the components, then, of the primal scene are here, but they are changed, the predicted responses, the "normal" responses are denied; they are, in fact, transmuted. The super-ego "voice of my education" is denied, is conquered. In the most basic terms, the ego is represented as having triumphed over the super-ego in the service of the id. There is no real struggle. There is even a kind of coyness in the "But I must confess how I liked him. . . . " Lawrence is saying, from one perspective: I have looked in the face of the god, despite prohibitions, and I have lived and was honored. If then we consider the strength of Lawrence's animus against Freud—it must have rankled him considerably to have been told repeatedly that a book which was as difficult and costly for him to write as **Sons and Lovers** was "Freudian"—then I suggest that we don't have to look very far to find the identity of the first "voice" that Lawrence refers to as the voice of education, nor is it difficult to understand how that voice becomes "voices" a few lines later. Lawrence's quarrel with Freud was based, as I stated, on his notion that the unconscious was pristine while as he saw it, Freud found there "the slimy serpent of sex, and heaps of excrement." Lawrence has here looked on the face of the serpent and found him likeable, even well mannered, a "guest." Further, he has looked on the serpent in the most threatening of circumstances, when its position denies him his rightful place beside the access to his source of comfort and nurture. Lawrence felt, that Freud was thus answered.

But the poem continues.

> He drank enough
> And lifted his head, dreamily, as one who has
>   drunken,
> And flickered his tongue like a forked night on the
>   air, so black,
> Seeming to lick his lips,
> And looked around like a god, unseeing, into the air,
> And slowly, very slowly, as if thrice a dream,
> Proceeded to draw his slow length curving round
> And climb again the broken bank of my wall-face.
> And as he put his head into that dreadful hole,
> And as he slowly drew up, snake-easing his
>   shoulders, and entered farther,
> A sort of horror, a sort of protest against his
>   withdrawing into that horrid black hole,
> Deliberately going into the blackness, and slowly
>   drawing himself after,
> Overcame me now his back was turned.

If we identify the trough as the mother, what are we to do with the hole in the wall face? I suggest that what Lawrence has done, and that his ability to do so makes possible the control in the first part of the poem, is to split the function of the mother into two aspects, the nurturing and the sexual. The water-trough represents her as comforter and nurturer, in which aspect Lawrence, one of several children, is capable of sharing her. The mother's other aspect is that of creator and destroyer. Hers is the "dark door of the secret earth" from which the snake issued. Hers are also the "Burning bowels of this earth . . ." into which he will return. If we look back now at the fifth stanza of the poem we see the power attributed to this figure. Lawrence tells us that the snake is "earth-brown, earth-golden from the burning bowels of the earth/On the day of Sicilian July, with Etna smoking." Why should the bowels of the earth be burning unless Lawrence conceives them as the source of the volcano? Further, this is a volcano with which Lawrence has very particular associations.

In *Sea and Sardinia,* a travel book composed between February and March of 1921 (seven months later than **"Snake"**), Lawrence writes about the mountain:

> Ach, horror! How many men, how many races, has
> Etna put to flight? It was she who broke the quick
> of the Greek soul. And after the Greeks, she gave
> the Romans, the Normans, the Arabs, the Spaniards,

the French, the Italians, even the English, she gave them all their inspired hour and broke their souls. Perhaps it is she one must flee from. At any rate, one must go: and at once.[5]

Etna is again, both life giver ("Gave them all their inspired hour") and life denier ("broke their souls"). We cannot help but note here the similar usage of "break" in the 26th line of **"Snake,"** "If you were a man/You would take a stick and break him now, and finish him off." The snake, as the poet thinks back after its departure, "seemed to me again like a king,/Like a king in exile, uncrowned in the underworld,/Now due to be crowned again." The operative part of the statement is "uncrowned in the underworld," which implies that the snake has power only when he has left the underworld, the "burning bowels of *this* earth [emphasis added]." It is "this" earth in the second part of the poem, while it was "the" earth in line 20 and "the secret earth" in line 39. The vision has been particularized. The aspect of mother as nurturer has been separated from her aspect as castrator, as "uncrowner."

The snake, for his part, is represented in strangely contradictory language as both willing victim and as bewitched. When he turns to reenter the wall face, Lawrence tells us that he "lifted his head dreamily, as one who has drunken" and moved "slowly, very slowly, as if thrice a dream. . . ." Yet, his entry into the wall face is described very differently. He "put his head into that dreadful hole,/ . . . he slowly drew up, snake-easing his shoulders, and entered farther, . . . / Deliberately going into the blackness, and slowly drawing himself after. . . . " A possible explanation is that Lawrence wishes to convey that the deliberateness of the snake's actions are to be accounted for by his being "a dream," that he moves not "quickly," but as one controlled, in the sense of deliberate meaning slow, unhurried, and steady, rather than in the sense characterized by or resulting from careful and thorough consideration (as in "Let us move with all deliberate speed"). But if this explanation is correct, we encounter further difficulty in the following two stanzas.

> I looked round, I put down my pitcher,
> I picked up a clumsy log
> And threw it at the water-trough with a clatter.
>
> I think it did not hit him,
> But suddenly that part of him that was left behind
>   convulsed in undignified haste,
> Writhed like lightning, and was gone
> Into the black hole, the earth lipped fissure in the
>   wall front,
> At which, in the intense still noon, I stared with
>   fascination.

Why, if disturbed by the thrown "log," and hence presumably awakened from his spell, would the snake continue to enter the wall face? Why does it lose its dignity at the moment it is awakened? It is at this point in the poem, I suggest, that Lawrence's reply to Freud begins to break down. Having separated the mother figure into two aspects, the poet finds that he cannot cope with the implications of the second. The snake, bewitched or deliberately, is committing himself to the female in a way that Lawrence can only view with "A sort of horror, a sort of protest. . . ." The articulate and controlled poet who had no difficulty with the voice of his education has uncontrollable difficulty dealing with the snake entering "that dreadful hole," "that horrid black hole. . . ." The convulsion of the snake, the "undignified haste," are equally apt if they are applied to the behavior of the speaker himself. If the snake has been "other" earlier in the poem, here the poet is painfully identifying with it. He throws the "log" to prevent the snake from leaving, to keep it from entering the fissure in the wall. Nothing that the voices of his education could have told him will account for this action. The voices of his education tell him to kill the snake, or at least to drive it off. Yet it is clear, if we look at the passages carefully that what the poet protests is not the snake, but the snake entering the fissure. For all the confusion in the section, the language is clear on this point. "And as he put his head into that dreadful hole, / And as he slowly drew up . . . and entered farther, / A sort of horror, a sort of protest *against his withdrawing into that horrid black hole/ / . . . / Over-came me . . . [my italics]."

Whatever the voice of his education has taught the poet, it has not taught him to be horrified at the departure of a snake, nor has it taught him to "protest" such a departure. The speaker's actions cannot be called "educated" in any sense; they are instead manifestations of a violent psychological reaction to a symbolically perceived castration. Just how violent this reaction has been is attested to by the poet's attempt to deny it. He concludes the poem with these four stanzas.

> And immediately I regretted it
> I thought how paltry, how vulgar, what a mean act!
> I despised myself and the voices of my accursed
>   human education.
>
> And I thought of the albatross,
> And I wished he would come back, my snake.
>
> For he seemed to me again like a king,
> Like a king in exile, uncrowned in the
>   underworld,
> Now due to be crowned again.
>
> And so, I missed my chance with one of the lords
> Of life.
> And I have something to expiate:
> A pettiness.

Surely, this is an odd collection of words to describe such an act. How is the act "paltry," "mean," "vulgar," or petty? The words have one consistency, they can all be used to describe the acts of a peasant, and it seems possible that Lawrence intended them to reinforce the concept of the snake as a king. The act is thus not so much a crime as it is a failure to recognize royalty and give it its due. In this case, the "I despised myself" is a becoming attitude. The poet is saying; I will not lay the entire blame for my act on the "voices of my accursed human education," I will accept personal blame for having given

in to them. They ought not to have been strong enough to have so influenced my action, so while they are in part culpable, I will not deny my own doltishness in not remaining responsive to the real order of the natural world. If this is in fact Lawrence's intention, then it is clear that aesthetically the strategy fails. A peasant, after all, is precisely uneducated. It is the paltry, mean, vulgar, peasant who would be closest to the rhythms of "natural" life. It is the peasant who would be most susceptible to the kind of priapic worship that Lawrence would seem to be advocating. It is the peasant who recognizes the king.

But whatever the motivation for the particular choice of words, the effect is that Lawrence is saying "How could I have been so insensitive as to commit this inconsequential, common, small, ordinary, act?" One does not raise one's hand against a king, but if one does, one hardly justifies it by calling it a pettiness. Whatever his strategy for doing so, Lawrence's choice of words shows a serious divigation of purpose from his apparent initial intention. The poem which has set itself up as a lesson in natural religion a la Wordsworth and Coleridge has become complicated beyond any boundaries that their systems will allow. Indeed, I find no "system" per se that the poem, taken in its entirety, will support. I do not particularly doubt that Sagar's explanation is in accord with Lawrence's intention, or even that Lawrence may have felt that what Sagar suggests is what the poem says, but I think in the face of its inconsistency, we must seek the unity of the poem in its psychology rather than its doctrine. If we are willing to accept this, then we can see that the poem's aesthetic inconsistency is to be accounted for by Lawrence's psychological inability to face the symbolic import of his own act. Having mocked Freud by the mechanism of dividing the mother into two aspects, Lawrence reacts compulsively and in horror to the castrating aspect as a result of his identification with the snake. To distance himself from recognizing this identification, he then casts himself as the snake's inferior, using demeaning terminology in reference to himself and simultaneously strengthening and recalling his earlier recognition of the snake as a god by calling him now "one of the lords / Of life."

The strategy, unsuccessful in terms of the aesthetic consistency of the poem, reveals to us the profundity of the poet's anxiety. That the poem could be written at all testifies to the success of the strategy psychologically. The greatness of Lawrence's **"Snake"** lies not in its expression of Lawrentian "doctrine," but in the courage it demonstrates in presenting a traumatic incident with utter fidelity to its psychological dynamics.

NOTES

[1] Keith Sagar, *The Art of D. H. Lawrence*, (Cambridge: Cambridge University Press, 1966), pp. 124-125.

[2] See: Frederick J. Hoffman, "Lawrence's Quarrel with Freud," *Freudianism and the Literary Mind* (Baton Rouge: Louisiana State University Press, 1957); Claudia C. Morrison, *Freud and the Critic: The Early Use of*

Depth Psychology in Literature Criticism (Chapel Hill: University of North Carolina Press, 1968), pp. 203-210; James C. Cowan, *D. H. Lawrence's American Journey: A Study in Literature and Myth* (Cleveland and London: Case Western Reserve University Press, 1970), pp. 15-24.

[3] D. H. Lawrence, *Psychoanalysis and the Unconscious* (New York: Thomas Seltzer, 1921), p. 15.

[4] All quotations from "Snake" are from *The Complete Poems of D. H. Lawrence*, eds. Vivian de Sola Pinto and F. Warren Roberts (New York: Viking Press, 1971).

[5] D. H. Lawrence, *Sea and Sardinia* (New York: Thomas Seltzer, 1921), pp. 2-3.

Ross C. Murfin (essay date 1980)

SOURCE: "Hymn to Priapus: Lawrence's Poetry of Difference," in *Criticism*, Vol. XXII, No. 3, Summer, 1980, pp. 214-29.

[*In the following essay, Murfin finds similarities and differences between Lawrence's "Hymn to Priapus" and works by Charles Algernon Swinburne and Thomas Hardy.*]

The speaker of the **"Hymn to Priapus,"** like the speakers in all the other lyrics in D. H. Lawrence's volume of poems entitled ***Look! We Have Come Through!,*** may be taken to be Lawrence himself. He tells us he "danced at a Christmas party/Under the mistletoe"

> Along with a ripe, slack country lass
> Jostling to and fro.

At the dance or, more likely, after the dance, the country lass "slipped through" the speaker's "arms on the threshing floor," where he found her "Sweet as an armful of wheat." As if words like "armful" and images of "threshing" a "ripe . . . country" woman on the "floor" were not explicit enough to convince us of what has transpired, Lawrence plays blasphemously with Christ's words at the Last Supper. She "was broken, was broken/For me, and ah, it was sweet," Lawrence says, making absolutely clear the fact that "this is [her] body" that the "big, soft country lass" has broken for the remission of his appetites.

Lawrence leaves the barn (as well as the woman) behind, and as he goes home through a silent country landscape he feels "Fulfilled" but also "alone." Part of that feeling of loneliness seems to stem from guilt and even a feeling that some sin has transpired, a fact suggested rather obviously through the presence of words like "commission," somewhat more subtly and potently through the speaker's representation of the constellation Orion as a father figure. He sees "the great Orion standing/Looking down," the "witness" of his "first beloved/Love-making" (which in Lawrence, after Freud, could refer to a child's Oedipal affair). Orion

> Now sees . . . this as well,
> This last commission.
> Nor do I get any look
> Of admonition.
> He can add the reckoning up
> I suppose, between now and then,
> Having walked himself in the thorny, difficult
> Ways of men.

Having partaken of the sensual fulfillments offered by a rustic woman and wondered if his father would have words of "admonition," the speaker lapses in the later stanzas of the poem into thoughts of his mother, that sweeter, better love who now

> . . . lies underground
> With her face upturned to mine,
> And her mouth unclosed in the long last kiss
> That ended her life and mine.[1]

"She fares in the stark immortal/Fields of death," Lawrence bitterly complains, and "I in these goodly, frozen/Fields. . . ."[2] She is a Proserpine, Lawrence implies, only she is a Proserpine lost forever to Plutonian darkness. He, the "frozen" inhabitant of sterile "fields," is powerless to bring her to light or love again.

This love for that which Lawrence is powerless to bring back, in turn, breeds a powerful, secondary form of impotence. Any man who spends his time after lovemaking thinking morbid thoughts of his unforgettable mother has clearly not been "fulfilled" by his sexual experience as an adult, no matter what he may claim to the contrary. The impossible love for the mother, as symbolized by the deathbed kiss, seems to have rendered the poet incapable, for a while at least, of enjoying his own loves in his own time. It has, indeed, turned the course of his life against life itself:

> Something in me remembers
> And will not forget.
> The stream of my life in the darkness
> Deathward set.

I take this stanza to refer, in part, to the returning memory of that "long last kiss/That ended her life and mine." If we suspect, however, that the reference is also to the moment of the poet's own conception, the sexual act between father and mother that brought him into being, the import of the stanza is little changed. For to be so burdened by the past that coitus triggers "memories" of one's own conception is to be a man always driven by reality back into the womb and into the world of the deep, parental past, now quiet like Orion in the blackness of the heavens, now peaceful and still in the "stark immortal fields of death" that stretch beyond the reach of our "frozen/Fields."

One thing is sure. The poem, whatever else it may be, doesn't seem much of a **"Hymn to Priapus."** The poem hardly can be said to celebrate the sexual relationship abandoned after only three stanzas, and however much Lawrence might hold to a neo-Freudian view of the family, we can hardly suppose that "Priapus" is a figure for the relationship which the poem seems more interested in and certainly talks in more "hymnal" language about, the love between mother and son. Where, then, is Lawrence taking us? What has he written a poem about?

It is only when we consider the fact that the poem associates the mother figure with an immortal, controlling influence over the life of the son, when we realize that the imagery of the poem ("underground," "fields of death") associates the mother with the goddess Proserpine, when we recall that Swinburne, whom Lawrence once called our greatest poet,"[3] wrote not a **"Hymn to Priapus"** but a "Hymn to Proserpine," and when we remember that the elder poet's hymn treated the subject of two kinds of love, one current but dead—it is only then that we begin to realize what we are encountering in the **"Hymn to Priapus."** This is a poem that becomes compelling only when we see it interplaying with other poems. Through his title, Lawrence might lead us to expect a poem that is a paean to a simple and primal urge. After we have studied the lines following, however, we take the title as an illustrative admission. **The "Hymn to Priapus"** is a revisionary "Hymn to Proserpine" that half develops and half covers over the traces of a Victorian original. That is the work, Lawrence makes us realize, that has first to be done before any convincing hymns to sexual being can be sung.

In Swinburne's powerful poem, the speaker, upon the proclamation in Rome of the Christian faith, weeps for the passing of the old, Olympian order (whose gods, once "fair," are now "broken"). He also decries the elevation of a new, pale, son of man who is now "crowned in the city" but whose "days are bare" and "device is barren" to a man raised a passionate devotee of those older, more majestic deities who were "more than the day or the morrow, the seasons that laugh or that weep." The speaker especially laments the passing of Proserpine,

> our mother, a blossom of flowering seas,
> Clothed round with the world's desire as with
>   raiment, and fair as the foam,
> And fleeter than kindled fire, and a goddess and
>   Mother of Rome.

Who or what has replaced this "mother" of "desire" in the new scheme of things? A mere girl, Mary, a mere "maiden men sing as a goddess" and have "crowned . . . where another was queen."

In despair, with no object worth desire or devotion in the present and no viable goddess of love left over from the previous epoch, the speaker admits that his life, nurtured in a time and in a view of things now forever past, is now meaningless. "I am sick of singing" and "fain" only "to rest," the Swinburnian speaker sighs (for Swinburne, too, was raised on faiths which were, in his lifetime, "dethroned and deceased, cast forth, wiped out in a day"). He longs only for "sleep"; he would "look to the end," the time in which he will forever join the "hidden head" of Proserpine in "death." "I will go,"

he says, "as I came," to "abide" in the "earth" with "my mother." In a companion poem, entitled "The Garden of Proserpine," Swinburne associates this death and this mother with "Pale beds of blowing rushes/Where no leaf blooms or blushes," and he ends his prayer in the garden on a note of thanks

> That no life lives for ever;
> That dead men rise up never;
> That even the weariest river
> Winds somewhere to the sea.

Swinburne's Proserpine poems would seem to be important sources of Lawrence's images, themes, and larger poetic structures in the **"Hymn to Priapus."** The elder poet's characterization of life as a weary flow from origins to the finality of death informs both Lawrence's memory of that "stream of [his] life in the darkness . . . set" and his lament, which may ultimately be an anxious hope, that his parents will "rise up never," will never return to repossess him, to offer "admonition," to "add the reckoning up." The dead mother who is also a lover and a deity, who "fares in the stark immortal/Fields of death" with her "underground . . . face upturned" to her son's, clearly descends from Swinburne's Proserpine, at once a mother and goddess of desire whose "head" is now "hidden" in death, in a "Pale" garden where "no leaf blooms or blushes." Lawrence's poem, like Swinburne's, is founded upon a structure of diametrical opposition: there are two women representing two kinds of love, one available but unmeaningful, the other, maternal one "Clothed round with . . . desire" but out of present reach. The speakers of both poems, caught between an unrecallable past and an unfulfilling present, live in memory. Each of them, consequently, tends to see life as a flow from origins towards death.

There are still more parallels to be drawn. In Swinburne's hymn, "love is sweet for a day" but soon "grows bitter"; Lawrence says of his bliss on the "threshing floor," "Ah, it was sweet," but soon he thinks of his "first beloved/ Lovemaking" and remembers that it soon became a "bitter-sweet/Heart-aching." Lawrence completes the symbolism Swinburne began by associating his minimally loved country lass with wheat (she's an "armful of wheat") and even with the "bread" of Christ's body ("was broken/For me"). (Swinburne had associated his most dearly loved mother with "green grapes" in order to contrast her with Christ, from whose blood the "Sweet . . . wine" of mercy and sacrifice is made.) The important thing for the reader to be aware of, however, is not the number of echoes, parallels, and debts but, rather, the reason for their existence. Lawrence intends to discuss, poetically, the situation of being torn between two sensibilities, two visions of things (***Look! We Have Come Through,*** as its title indicates, is a volume about the arduous struggle for emergence, spiritual and aesthetic). Swinburne, in his Proserpine poems, gave him a poetic system with which to do so. Through appropriation of Swinburne's poetic structure Lawrence can make the following claim through an unstated but powerful analogy: mere sexual experience with a "ripe" country lass at a

"Christmas dance" is, for him, for the moment, as pale, grey, empty—even barren—as the living cult of the Galilean, Christ, was to the speaker of Swinburne's hymn, raised in adoration of a beautiful old goddess whose time has passed, nurtured in a world that now lies dead and buried.

Swinburne thus provides Lawrence with a poetic model for talking about his own inability to emerge fully from adolescence into adulthood, from an old sensibility into a new one. Swinburne is not, however, the only Victorian to inform Lawrence's **"Hymn."** Indeed, Thomas Hardy's very different kind of poetry, which in many ways proves the more challenging source of inspiration for Lawrence, must be faced off against or even married to the Swinburnian strain of Victorian lyric if Lawrence is to come through, if he is to generate the much-needed new *ethos.*

The scene (and the earthy, erotic world of being it represents) that Lawrence suddenly drops in stanza five of the **"Hymn to Priapus"** and thus leaves curiously unfulfilled and incomplete is one that can be found energetically set forth in *Tess of the d'Urbervilles.* In that novel, Hardy describes a barn dance attended by villagers and farmhands of the Trantridge region:

> Through this floating fusty *debris* of peat and hay, mixed with the perspirations and warmth of the dancers, and forming together a sort of vegeto-human pollen, the muted fiddles feebly pushed their notes, in marked contrast to the spirit with which the measure was trodden out. They coughed as they danced, and laughed as they coughed. Of the rushing couples there could barely be discerned more than the high lights—the indistinctness shaping them to satyrs chasing nymphs—a multiplicity of Pans whirling a multiplicity of Syrinxes; Lotis attempting to elude Priapus, and always failing.[4]

The passage from *Tess,* certainly, is enough to suggest that Hardy was the first-comer to the world of the barn and to its sensual, country Lotises, that Lawrence is thus a son with a juvenile passion for something that isn't his. If Hardy is the "Priapus" that never "fails" in his rustic relations, a procreative force in a primeval world, then Lawrence, as a second-generation barnyard guest, proves to be something of an Oedipal "dancer." The "country lass" and the dead mother are thus, in a horrible sense, psychologically inseparable, a fact which may suggest that Lawrence suspects here, even more fearfully than in later works that all his attempts at new creation begin in incest, that the words and things out of which he would attempt to bring or make something original are always his own parents.

The passage from *Tess,* however, is not the most convincing, let alone the exclusive, evidence of Hardy's most powerful precedence. In the process of examining all the Swinburnian images, myths, and diametrical patterns present in Lawrence's poem, we may have felt that the **"Hymn to Priapus"** doesn't look or sound or feel very much like Swinburne. Take a stanza like

> Something in me remembers
> And will not forget.
> The stream of my life in darkness
> Deathward set!

This sounds somewhat less like Swinburne's

> Thou art more than the day or the morrow, the
>   seasons that laugh or that weep;
> For these give joy and sorrow; but thou,
>   Proserpine, sleep

than like one "Ditty" by Thomas Hardy—

> Upon that fabric fair
>   "Here is she!"
> Seems written everywhere
>   Unto me!

or another:

> And we were left alone
> As Love's own pair;
> Yet never the love-light shown
> Between us there!
>
> . . . . .
>
> Face unto face, then, say,
> Eyes my own meeting,
> Is your heart far away,
> Or with mine beating?
>
> . . . . .
>
> Yet, Dear, though one may sigh,
> Raking up leaves,
> New leaves will dance on high—
> Earth never grieves![5]

On closer inspection, we find that what Lawrence has in fact done is to compromise the very regular, anapestic hexameter couplets of Swinburne's "Hymn to Proserpine" with Hardy's looser stanza form. If we rewrite the following ABAB quatrain from Lawrence's **"Hymn to Priapus,"**

> He can add the reckoning up
> I suppose, between now and then,
> Having walked himself in the thorny, difficult
> Ways of men,

in the form of a rhyming couplet, the secondary presence of Swinburne begins to be noticeable:

> He can add the reckoning up I suppose, between
>   now and then,
> Having walked himself in the thorny, difficult
>   ways of men,

Swinburne's presence, nonetheless, remains secondary, not just because it is only felt when Lawrence's lines are so altered but also because it is the meaning and implications of Hardy's art—not his rhythms—that preoccupy the later poet in the **"Hymn to Priapus."** One of Hardy's *Wessex Poems* that Lawrence no doubt knew well, "The Dance at the Phoenix," tells the tale of a woman whose girlhood "had hardly been/A life of modesty"; by sixteen she had known half the "troopers of/The King's-Own Cavalry." At age sixty, lying in bed next to the sleeping husband to whom she has always been faithful, she hears some soldiers making merry at "The Phoenix Inn." "'Alas for chastened thoughts!'" she says, and soon she has left the house, her "springtide blood" aflow. Hardy describes her ensuing night of "unchastening," her re-entry into the life of her youth (like a Lawrentian Phoenix rising from its ashes even as it dies), through the metaphor of "dancing." She "soared and swooped" until the

> chime went four,
> When Jenny, bosom-beating, rose
> To seek her silent door.

Because such moments of ecstasy have no place in what we deem mature life, because the social repercussions that will inevitably follow such a night's revelry would end the old woman's life as she has come to know it, morning finds Jenny dead.

Hardy published a number of other poems about "dancing," most of them in the same volume, *Time's Laughingstocks,* in 1909 (the year of Swinburne's death and three years before Lawrence composed his **"Hymn"**). "The Night of the Dance" describes a man's anticipation of festivities to come in an old "thatch" barn where "sparrows flit" and "owls . . . whoo from the gable[s]." He seems to sense that "Sweet scenes are impending here" (Lawrence will later say "Ah, it was sweet!") and "That She will return" his vows tonight in "Love's low tongue." As the speaker thinks these amorous thoughts and awaits the anticipated hour, it would seem, he thinks, that "The cold moon . . . centers its gaze on me." Like the "star" that "witness[es]" Lawrence's doings and thoughts,

> The stars, like eyes in reveries,
> Their westering as for a while forborne,
> Quiz downward curiously.

"After the Club Dance," another and perhaps the most important influence on the **"Hymn to Priapus"** that can be found in Hardy's 1909 volume, is the narrative of a woman walking home alone from a rural dance. There she, like the "soft country lass" of Lawrence's poem, has "been broken" for some fellow. And he, it now seems, blames her for allowing him the pleasure he himself sought:

> Black'on frowns east on Maidon
> And westward to the sea,
> But on neither is his frown laden
> With scorn, as his frown on me!
>
> At dawn my heart grew heavy,
> I could not sip the wine,
> I left the jocund bevy
> And that young man o'mine.

> The roadside elms pass by me—
> Why do I sink with shame
> When the birds a-perch there eye me?
> They too have done the same!

The poet delivers his ironic commentary indirectly through the confused mind of the girl. She is an "innocent" in the way that Tess Durbeyfield is, for Hardy, "A Pure Woman." She knows—or *thinks* she knows—her indulgences to be perfectly natural. What is more, she knows her "young man" has "done the same" as she. She cannot understand why pleasure should turn to "scorn" and why her spirits, recently high, should now have to "sink with shame." Whether or not the last, exclamatory line of the poem is a triumph for the speaker is not clear. But the poet's triumph is: Hardy's ironic structure celebrates natural energies and scorns those perverse laws of society which would always identify as corrupt their manifestation.

Thus, although several poems by Hardy together with Swinburne's Proserpine poems can be seen providing some of the poetic building blocks of Lawrence's **"Hymn,"** Hardy is far more to the poem than a way of expressing, analyzing, and coming to terms with life, an artistic problem, or both. He is, rather, the reason why terms need to be come to. In generating a sensibility, a world-view, he generated the crisis Lawrence's poem depicts, responds to, and in a sense *is.* That sensibility—an appreciation for the sensual, for the quick throb of the physical in everything—is one that Lawrence is greatly compelled by: this much we know from his criticism of Shelley, who, according to Lawrence was primarily a bloodless, bodiless abstraction.[6] What we see in the **"Hymn to Priapus,"** however, is that Lawrence fears that he, himself, may be something of an old-fashioned, asensual abstraction. How, then, is Lawrence to continue the work that Hardy began? How is *he* to develop Hardy?

Hardy's poem about the old woman who thrills to "The Dance at the Phoenix," like Lawrence's **"Hymn to Priapus,"** relates the dances of sex and death. But where Lawrence's poem is threatened by morbidity, Hardy's is witty and satiric. The "death" of Jenny, after all, cleverly signifies on the one hand a renewed, orgasmic intensity of life and, on the other, the killing guilt which society instills. Hardy's Jenny, like the speaker of Lawrence's poem, might seem to want to revivify a dead past, but the important difference is this: whereas Jenny's search for a dead past becomes an intensely living present, Lawrence's plunges him into gloomy thoughts of a love lost to time. The treatment of incest in Lawrence's poem is reminiscent of Hardy's somewhat quieter exploration, and again the predecessor manages a brighter tone. At "The Dance at the Phoenix," young men dance in high spirits and reckless abandon with a woman their "fathers" once "knew," a woman old enough to be their mother. At Lawrence's Christmas dance, the poet's subliminal recognition that his dance follows the same steps that his father's did (whether or not one accepts the suggestion that Lawrence has been the guest of a barn and a girl to whom Hardy was the original "Priapus") causes him to drown his poem in guilt and self-consciousness unknown to Hardy's more ebullient ballad.

Or take "The Night of the Dance." Hardy's ballad is excited, optimistic, poetic foreplay to the "sweet scene" to come, the dance in which "She will return" the speaker's love in "Love's low tongue." (Even the "gaz[ing]" moon and "quiz[zing]" stars reflect the protagonist's present "curious[ity]," not doubts or questions about the past or the future). Lawrence, by positioning a poem seven or eight hours in time after the setting of the poem Hardy had published some three years earlier, opts for a post-climatic scenario that betrays his lack of optimism, his mixed feelings, about both the sensual dance and the sensual poetry he would enjoy.

In the **"Hymn to Priapus,"** then, Lawrence would seem at once to repress and indulge a fear. The fear is that rather than proving his own poetic viability by recalling and developing poetic history, he takes one step forward only to fall two steps back to the position of Swinburne, whose "new words" were responsible for pointing Hardy (by Hardy's own admission) on the way of his own poetic quest.[7] Is the fear, however, fully justified? It seems so only if we compare Lawrence's **"Hymn"** to Hardy's poems about dancing. If we compare it to any of the number of poems about dead or dying mothers that Hardy had published in the dozen years before Lawrence began writing the **"Hymn to Priapus,"** however, a very different answer emerges.

Writing some fifty years after Wordsworth's *Prelude* had made the mother into a symbol of a vastly meaningful and morally nourishing world, Hardy gives voice to a mother who regrets that man ever dreamed of a Nature so vastly meaningful and beneficent.[8] He gives voice to a Nature, in other words, which regrets that she was ever conceived as a mother who could speak to, irradiate, exalt man and his moral sense. She deplores the fact that for years man insisted on seeing her "sun as a Sanct-shape," her "moon as the Night-queen," her "stars as august and sublime." His "mountings of mindsight," the "range of his vision," now reach so high that, the sad-dened mother laments, man only "finds blemish / Through-out my domain." So, she declares,

> Let me grow, then, but mildews and mandrakes,
>   And slimy distortions,
> Let nevermore things good and lovely
>   To me appertain.

Hardy's poem, entitled "The Mother Mourns," describes a fictional mother dying, a man-projected mother who was thought to reflect man's highest hopes and most fanciful dreams, a "Nature" who was once for more than just some "country lass" to be "broken" for man but who is now as carelessly used as she once was revered and exalted. ("My species are dwindling," Hardy's mother protests before she lapses into silence; "my forests are barren," my "leopardine beauties are rarer / My tusky ones vanish.")

In coming to a Hardy piece like "The Mother Mourns" from a poem such as the **"Hymn to Priapus,"** we sud-denly become dissatisfied enough with the literary anxi-ety that permeates one level of Lawrence's work to look beyond it and discover a deeper level of significance. Anyone, after Lawrence, who considers carefully the Hardyan "Mother," whether specifically in this particular poem or generally in any one of the elder author's many lyrics treating once-worshiped deities or ideals, can't help feeling it an oversimplification to state that Hardy's attitude towards the mothering past is that it is mordant and that we are well-rid of it and its fictions. The more we look at a lyric like "The Mother Mourns" the more we decide that its sensibility is more deeply ambivalent than Lawrence's own. After all, Lawrence speaks in his own voice and admits, though he laments, the passing of a maternal sensibility. But doesn't Hardy, by letting his "Mother" deliver her own lament and sing her own swan song, put himself in a terribly compromised position? Although he admits that his mother may speak no di-vine messages, he will not give up on the idea that she may still speak to man. Although he lets his mother con-fess that man's mind far eclipses nature's dumb indiffer-ence, he also gives her the tone of a miffed deity critical of man, an insulted goddess who will write on the tablets of an inspired poet.

Lawrence, by remembering Thomas Hardy and protest-ing, implicitly, his own insufficiency in a work like the **"Hymn to Priapus,"** sends us into the texts of the pre-cursor with a particular point of view that allows or causes us to see them in a new light. Thinking of Lawrence's own predicament, we are led to realize that his forerunner's lyrics turn from and yet, in the last analysis, sneak back towards an old romantic sensibility considerably more quickly (if considerably less obvi-ously) than do Lawrence's own. The "anxiety" of a poem such as the **"Hymn to Priapus"** thus unmakes itself by positing the Hardyan source. As it does so it propels us into a whole new awareness of Thomas Hardy's world-view, Lawrence's interreactions with it, and the nature of the emerging—and emergent—results.

I have spoken of Hardy's "Mother" poems as if they were the point at which Lawrence jolts us into a critical re-assessment of Hardy's sensibility. My choice is, of course, arbitrary. Another reader might first experience a revisionary recollection during contemplation of some of the images and terms that are absent in Lawrence's poem but that are to be found in Hardy's description of the barnyard dance in *Tess*, namely, *débris*, vegeto-human, trodden, coughing, indistinctness, and failing. Still an-other might become aware of *these* images after first being made aware, by the authorial-philosophical per-spective of the **"Hymn to Priapus,"** of the total absence of such a viewpoint in "After the Club Dance," the poem in which a young girl asks why she should feel guilty for having indulged in an activity that all Nature takes de-light in. Does Hardy's artistic decision to present no more than a young girl's half-guilty questions derive from his own strong convictions of her innocence? Or does his reluctance to speak a line in his own voice grow out of a simultaneous willingness and inability fully to leave behind the punitive values of the age that bore him?

The significant fact about Lawrence's poem, then, has little to do with whether the doubts it may raise about Hardy stem primarily from its differences with one old "dancing" passage or another. It has little to do with whether the view Lawrence affords us of Hardy's living Romantic "Mother" causes, is caused by, or is simultaneous with the questions we may find ourselves raising about the depths of Hardy's earthly sensuality. The important revelation made by the **"Hymn to Priapus,"** rather, is that its author's failure to extend the path Hardy began to cut is not due to any lack of artistic power or modern spirit. The most profound cause of Lawrence's retreat from the Hardyan sensibility (and the attitude towards the sexual partner it might entail), rather, is the critical assessment of that sensibility by the more modern poet's central self, the poet's act of understanding that although in Hardy there are developable elements of a modern sensibility, the Hardyan sensibility as it stands is not the way of the future. Lawrence has sensed that to make sexual encounter into a more simple, natural indulgence than it has been, or to imply that but for Christian society and its muddle-headed ideas the Tess Durbeyfields of the world should have no serious misgivings about what happens in barns or under the darkness of the primeval trees, may be to bring more Priapan enjoyment into a Victorian world but it is *not* to offer a new world-view. To intimate that the coming together of a man and a woman is analogous to a madcap dance at the Phoenix or a tying up of the garter before "jog[ging] on again" down "Crimmercrock lane" (which is what Hardy makes it in a poem called "The Dark-Eyed Gentleman"), even to suggest that it is or should be "the same" as what "the birds a-perch" in the "roadside elms . . . have" so often "done," is not to revise drastically the prevailing education. It is, rather, to offer but another version of the old, old story which holds that the earthy, sensual life is not a thing to be valued or prized. Far from being the locus of divine mystery, it is, quite the contrary, just about as common as it can be. Lawrence walks away from his casual sexual encounter with a Hardyan subject to return, in thought, to an absent mother. He does so not because the encounter was sexual but, rather, because it was casual. Put another way, the poet ends up in a dark no-man's-land that is outside two realms—the realm of the barn and the realm of the dead—because something in him has managed to make a connection between the two. Speaking of the "anxious" level of the **"Hymn to Priapus,"** I said that Lawrence connects the living lass with the dead mother because if his fear as a poet that, in the words of Hardy's "Dance at the Phoenix," the world in which he "dances" is a world his "father knew." At the deeper level of discourse the same connection is inevitably made, but its meaning is different. Lawrence mentally connects the two women because something in him senses that the image of a discardable reality is the look that old ideals project from just beyond the grave.

In his *Study of Thomas Hardy,* Lawrence suggests that Hardy began the development of a wonderful, residual, primitive strain of sensuality that existed in Shelley but that Shelley repressed almost out of his poems. Speaking of Shelley's poem "To a Skylark," Lawrence says that although "Shelley wishes to say" that "the skylark is pure, untrammeled spirit," the line "Bird thou never wert," together with the very regular metrics and rhyme scheme of the poem, suggest that the romantic predecessor knows "that the skylark *is* in fact a bird" and that birds *are,* in fact, "concrete, momentary thing[s]."[9] If we think of Hardy's poem entitled "Shelley's Skylark," a lyric in which the recycled organic remains of the bird that Shelley never even saw is pictured "throb[bing] in the myrtle green," we can hear that primitive strain in Hardy that Hardy had heard in Shelley and amplified. That strain, in turn, is recombined by Lawrence with the strain of spirituality that had stood opposed, in Shelley, to the world of earthly sensuality and that Hardy had sought to reject for reasons of its opposition. Beginning with the basic rhetorical model of Swinburne's "Hymn to Proserpine," which allows the poet to position himself between half-tenable philosophies (the Christianity available is far less attractive than the Hellenism that is not), Lawrence emerges from the Victorian's situation of self-division with what he hopes will be a new poetics of living. Starting with an almost indeterminate act of self-criticism, he ends up recalling from destructive eminence two dreams that amount to what Hardy might call "twin halves of one . . . august event"—Shelley's spiritual love and Hardy's demystified (or casual) sex.[10] What he will be left with, when the work is complete, is a new creation presided over by a new, quasi-Greek, Sex-God or Priapus.

The arrival at this level of understanding allows us to make sense both of the conclusion and the title of Lawrence's poem. When it is seen solely as the work of a poet obsessed with influence anxiety, the **"Hymn to Priapus"** makes us wonder just how it is that "Desire comes up, and contentment," makes us wholly unsatisfied by the answer Lawrence provides to the last question he poses:

> How is it I grin then, and chuckle
> Over despair?
>
> Grief, grief, I suppose and sufficient
> Grief makes us free
> To be faithless and faithful together
> As we have to be.

As the statement of a poet, however, who by having been "faithless and faithful together" to the several influences of his past is emerging from a double sense of dissatisfaction into a unified sense of contentment-in-liberty, the last stanza makes sense enough. And whereas the penultimate stanza is still self-conscious and introspective in the way that all the previous ones have been ("how much do I care?/How do I grin . . . ?"), the final quatrain has a steady, relaxed, matured, conversational tone ("Grief, grief, I suppose . . . makes us free"). The change in sound may not imply that an interlocutor has come on the scene, but it does seem to suggest that the speaker now might be ready for one.

NOTES

[1] It is not necessary to have read biographies of Lawrence to know that the dead beloved is the writer's mother. *Look! We Have Come Through!*—the volume in which the "Hymn to Priapus" appears—contains at least four poems that seek to be, in the words of one title, "Everlasting Flowers for a Dead Mother."

[2] My ellipsis stands in place of the word "beneath." I have not quoted the word in my text because although its presence would in no way damage my argument, it seems a wholly diversionary word the logic (or creative illogic) of which I am not sure I can explain. Why would Lawrence say that he is "beneath" his "underground" love? He cannot be accused of having sacrificed sense for a rhyming word, since "beneath" and "death" form only an eye rhyme anyway. Perhaps "beneath" is intended as a figurative, valuative word. (The mother, although dead, still reigns over her son). Or the poet may intend to recall the downward-looking, male Orion in such a way as to make clear the status of both images as symbols of the parental past and yet confuse corpse and constellation just enough to keep either or both of them from being read too autobiographically.

[3] Harry T. Moore, *The Collected Letters of D. H. Lawrence* (New York: Viking, 1962), p. 474.

[4] Thomas Hardy, *Tess of the d'Urbervilles,* Chapter 10.

[5] The four Hardy poems from which I quote are: "Ditty," "At an Inn," "Between Us Now," and "Autumn in King Hintock's Park."

[6] D. H. Lawrence, *Study of Thomas Hardy,* collected in *Phoenix: The Posthumous Papers of D. H. Lawrence,* ed. Edward McDonald (New York: Viking, 1946), p. 459.

[7] Thomas Hardy, in his elegy entitled "A Singer Asleep," refers to Swinburne's *Poems and Ballads* as "New words, in classic guise." Hardy's various testimonies to Swinburne's influence can be found in my study of *Swinburne, Hardy, Lawrence, and the Burden of Belief,* (Chicago: University of Chicago Press, 1978).

[8] William Wordsworth, *The Prelude,* Book II, 11. 233-41.

[9] D. H. Lawrence, *Study of Thomas Hardy, op. cit.,* p. 459.

[10] Thomas Hardy, "The Convergence of the Twain," 1. 30.

Sandra M. Gilbert (essay date 1980)

SOURCE: "D. H. Lawrence's Uncommon Prayers," in *D. H. Lawrence: The Man Who Lived,* edited by Robert B. Partlow, Jr., and Harry T. Moore, Southern Illinois University Press, 1980, pp. 73-93.

[*In the following essay, Gilbert agrees with T. S. Eliot's assessment of Lawrence as a hater of orthodoxy, but disagrees with Eliot when he negatively evaluates Lawrence's moral canon.*]

. . . we've got the world inside out. The true living world of fire is dark, throbbing, darker than blood. Our luminous world that we go by is only the reverse of this.

—Count Johann Dionys Psanek, in "The Ladybird"

Who gave us flowers?
Heaven? The white God?

Nonsense!
Up out of hell,
From Hades;
Infernal Dis!

—"Purple Anemones"

I

As the title of this essay implies, I have lately been rereading T. S. Eliot's *After Strange Gods,* and as I'm sure many people will agree, almost the only experience stranger than reading *After Strange Gods* is rereading it. Indeed, most of its readers will no doubt also agree that this frankly sermonizing work of literary criticism, which was first incarnated in 1933 as a series of lectures at the University of Virginia, is not just strange, it is quite distressing. Here, after all, is the "primer of modern heresy" in which, as Nazi Germany grew more powerful, Eliot declared that populations "should be homogeneous" both in race and in religion, adding infamously that "reasons of race and religion combine to make any large number of free-thinking Jews undesirable" and that "a spirit of excessive tolerance is to be deprecated."[1]

Almost as disturbing as statements like these, moreover, was (and is) the tone in which modernist poetry's elder statesman made them. Ostensibly benevolent and cautionary, it barely concealed a sneer of social snobbery so irritating that I can still remember my anger when I first read that "nothing could be much drearier (so far as one can judge from his own account) than the vague hymn-singing pietism which seems to have consoled the miseries of Lawrence's mother, and which does not seem to have provided her with any firm principles by which to scrutinize the conduct of her sons."[2] Because I was naturally sympathetic to Lawrence, I felt—as I recall—like some underservant in the Palace of Art who has suddenly gotten a grotesquely unjust slap from a very uppity butler. My cheeks burned, my head ached.

And yet my speculations here are going to begin with the idea that a good deal of what Eliot said about Lawrence in *After Strange Gods* was essentially accurate, accurate not in its moral evaluation of Lawrence's work but in its perception of the radical, heretical (and, indeed, blasphemous) mythology that is at the center of almost everything Lawrence wrote and that specifically energizes most of his finest poetry. I am going to argue, in other words, that Eliot was quite right to think that what he called "the daemonic powers" had found an instrument in Lawrence, and right to perceive that Lawrence hated "orthodoxy" (whereas Joyce, as Eliot also saw, was a model of "ethical orthodoxy"). In fact, from his own perspective, Eliot was quite correct to suggest that, like Thomas Hardy, Lawrence introduces us into "a world of pure evil."[3] For, as the Anglican/American poet understood, the tradition in which Lawrence increasingly worked, and worked with increasing consciousness, was that revisionary Blakeian tradition which wants to turn the world upside down, wants, in Eliot's words, to introduce "the diabolic into modern literature."[4]

A number of critics have, of course, noted that Lawrence was, as Eugene Goodheart puts it, a "tablet-breaker" who assumed "at various times the roles of nihilist, mystic, *diabolist,* and obscurantist" [italics mine].[5] Since I am particularly concerned here with his poetry, however, I want to stress my belief that, paradoxically, it was just Lawrence's introduction of the so-called "diabolic" into poetry that ultimately redeemed this poet-novelist's sometimes problematic work in verse. Seven or eight years ago, I wrote that I concurred whole-heartedly in Wright Morris's assertion that "in this world—the one in which we must live—the strange gods of D. H. Lawrence appear to be less strange than those of Mr. Eliot."[6] Interestingly, there were several book reviewers who took me to task even for agreeing with Morris, suggesting that the roots of Eliotian orthodoxy clutch deep indeed, even among the "stony rubbish" of academia in the seventies. What now interests me most about my interest in Morris's remark, though, is how tentative it then was, how hard I worked to prove that Lawrence's strange gods were really as comfortable and familiar as so many priestly grandpas, and that, indeed, they were not very different from the gods of Eliot, or Herbert, or Donne. I knew, I think, that Lawrence was an apparently irreligious religious poet, but I don't think I understood just how uncommon his book of uncommon prayers was.

What I did not know, however—or perhaps, more accurately, what I was not yet prepared to admit to myself— is a secret truth on which Lawrence's extraordinarily odd, elusive, glimmering, and yet powerful reputation as a poet has been based. For years, in fact, *poets* have read and revered Lawrence because his poems are uncommon prayers, prayers blasphemously addressed to gods whom Eliot would define as devils, prayers empowered by that demonic energy, that other-self-within-the-self, which the Spanish call the *Duende.* As Karl Shapiro wrote some twenty years ago, Lawrence is "declassed" but he "enjoys a kind of underground popularity among writers, even though he is outside the pale of the Tradition."[7] I would say, however, that Lawrence's popularity among writers has grown—and indeed, lately it has blossomed—precisely *because* he is outside what so many writers have perceived as the impregnable tradition of Eliotian orthodoxy,

a fortress into which it has often seemed no Individual Talent could ever penetrate. Poets love Lawrence, in other words, because he is an underground poet—both an outsider-poet and a poet of the underground or, more exactly, the underworld. They love him because he is a diabolical poet, a Blakeian prophet of hell.

Thus Shapiro wrote admiringly of Lawrence's "leap" into "aboriginal darkness" and of Lawrence's quest for "the aboriginal, the pure energy of the soul,"[8] and William Carlos Williams, who so famously thought that Eliot set poetry back half a century, obsessively eulogized Lawrence (whom he considered "so English / he had thereby raised himself / to an unenglish greatness") with a re-vision of the Lawrentian serpent, triumphantly returning to an underwater underground world:

> Slowly the serpent leans
> to drink by the tinkling water
> the forked tongue alert.
> Then fold after fold,
> glassy strength, passing
> a given point,
> as by desire drawn
> forward bodily, he glides
> smoothly in
> ("An Elegy for D. H. Lawrence").[9]

Williams, of course, was a writer whose commitment to what we might call the "hellish" or diabolic tradition in modern letters evolved almost simultaneously with Lawrence's, for in 1920 the American doctor published a revolutionary book of "improvisations" (or prose poems) entitled *Kora in Hell,* one of which might serve as a motto for the whole group of Lawrentian poets I am thinking of: *"Seeing a light in an upper window the poet by means of the power he has enters the room and of what he sees there brews himself a sleep potion."*[10]

Williams's sense that the poet is *below* the phenomenal windows of light, together with the conviction that he has magical power to enter that room of experience and there to create a diabolical brew of unconsciousness or darkness—together these constitute crucial ideas that characterize the underground poetic tradition I am trying to define here. More recent writers in this tradition would include such diverse figures as Denise Levertov, Gary Snyder, Joyce Carol Oates, Adrienne Rich, Ted Hughes, Robert Bly; and that is a minimal catalogue which nevertheless includes many of the most powerful poets writing today in English. (Moreover, if I leave out such charismatic recent artists as Sylvia Plath and Robert Lowell, that is not because I think them un-Lawrentian but because their approach to the diabolical seems to me to revise what is already revisionary even in Lawrence and his obvious disciples.)

Denise Levertov, for instance, is perhaps most frequently described as an admirer of Williams. But although her interest in organic form and specifically in the American grain of Williams's poetry would in any case bring her close to Lawrence, she has herself acknowledged a more direct connection, for she defines Lawrence as one of the major figures who was "of great importance to me as a writer, not only as a reader."[11] (And she specifically notes that Eliot did *not* have such importance for her.) Elsewhere, moreover, this woman whose "Song for Ishtar" is only one of a number of verses dedicated to what Eliot would have called strange gods, clarifies her sense of Lawrence's special significance. Explaining "the *kind* of knowledge from which [she believes] myth in poetry can grow," she quotes in full his wonderful "There are No Gods," one of a series of late "pansies" that meditate upon the demonic *élan vital* Lawrence thought darkly godly and Eliot considered diabolical.[12]

Like Levertov, Gary Snyder feels a special, radically theological but "post-Christian" commitment both to the poetry of the sacred and to the sacred-as-poetry. Moreover, because he is so passionate a student of comparative anthropology, both his poems and the essays he has collected in *Earth House Hold* are written in Lawrentian praise of "the most archaic values on earth." Particularly in his thoughtful piece on "Poetry and the Primitive" he explores the ancient connection between poetry and the demonic that is central to the underground poetic tradition of which Lawrence is an unsaintly patron. Consider, for instance, the Lawrentian implications of Snyder's remark that the "primitive ritual dramas, which acknowledged all the sides of human nature, including the destructive, demonic, and ambivalent, were liberating and harmonizing."[13]

Different as they are in other ways, such major contemporary writers as Joyce Carol Oates, Robert Bly, and Ted Hughes would clearly agree with that statement of Snyder's. Oates, who has written a perceptive study of Lawrence's poetry, notes that "the critic who expects to open Lawrence's poems and read poems by T. S. Eliot . . . is bound to be disappointed" and her realization that "Lawrence loves the true marriage of heaven and hell, illusory opposites" shows that she knows just exactly why the Eliotian reader will be disappointed in Lawrence's uncommon prayers.[14] Similarly, Robert Bly has written of the Norwegian poet Harry Martinson that "everything [in his work] feels alive, resilient, fragrant, like seaweed under water . . . a little like Lawrence in **'Bavarian Gentians,'**"[15] and in a comment on Neruda's poetry he describes Neruda, perhaps his greatest master, in the same way that I would myself now describe Lawrence, as "a new kind of creature moving about under the surface of everything. Moving under the earth, he knows everything from the bottom up (*which is the right way to learn the nature of a thing*) and therefore is never at a loss for its name" [italics mine].[16] Such statements are mottos of underground poetry notably similar to the "improvisation" I quoted from *Kora in Hell,* and they come quite inevitably from a writer whose meditation upon "A Bird's Nest Made of White Reed Fiber" ends in a vision of an "ecstatic and black" rebirth in the other world, a vision exactly comparable to the one Lawrence has in **"Medlars and Sorb Apples."**

With the problematic exception of Denise Levertov, Ted Hughes is the only one of Lawrence's countrymen whom I feel qualified to include in this tradition, but he is perhaps the most obvious heir of Lawrence's diabolical vision. Bleaker than the hymn-sequences in **The Plumed Serpent,** Hughes's *Crow* cycle nevertheless picks up where Lawrence's Aztec imitations left off, and *Gaudete,* Hughes's latest book, not only chronicles the demonic career of a "changling" clergyman, it is prefixed by an epigraph from Heraclitus which asserts, diabolically enough, that "Hades and Dionysos are one."[17] Yet none of this underground thought should come as a surprise if it is seen in the context of other Lawrentian works by a poet whose career began with a hellish but sacramental vision of "pike so immense and old / That past nightfall I . . . silently cast and fished / With the hair frozen on my head" for the "dream / Darkness beneath night's darkness had freed, / That rose slowly towards me, watching."[18]

Interestingly, even Adrienne Rich, who is probably now best known as a feminist poet, has acknowledged an early debt to Lawrence, pointing out that "women can find something for themselves in the poetry of men like Shelley and Lawrence because, while these poets are sexist, their imaginations act from their 'feminine,' intuitive nature."[19] In fact, despite her comment about Lawrence's "sexism," it seems to me that what Rich is defining here is the crucial place the author of **Birds, Beasts and Flowers** occupies in a tradition of radically revisionary underground poetry that has been of major importance not only in the lives and works of the best contemporary poets in English but also in the lives and thoughts of most contemporary feminists. Indeed, if I had more space here, I'd probably want to argue that the central tenets of this Lawrentian underground tradition are most likely underworld visions that have helped recent American and British poets to appreciate those European and South American writers, like Neruda, Rilke, Vallejo, Martinson, Tranströmer, and Lorca, who are their most powerful non-English influences. It is no coincidence that Lorca, for instance, shared with Lawrence a deep admiration for the strange gods of Walt Whitman, that demonically energetic writer whom, as Shapiro reminded us, Lawrence called the "first white aboriginal." In fact, Lorca ended his famous "Ode to Walt Whitman" with lines that also summarize Lawrence's underground vision:

> I want the strong air of the most profound night
> to remove flowers and words from the arch where
>   you sleep,
> and a black boy to announce to the gold-minded
>   whites
> the arrival of the reign of the ear of corn.[20]

II

I think it is not only interesting but very significant that all these passionate devotees of Lawrence's strange gods are poets (including Oates). Though I am not especially expert in contemporary fiction, I doubt that I could make much of a case for Lawrentian diabolism among recent novelists in England and America. Lawrence's strange gods have been of greatest importance to poets, which is

I think it is not only interesting but very significant that all these passionate devotees of Lawrence's strange gods are poets (including Oates). Though I am not especially expert in contemporary fiction, I doubt that I could make much of a case for Lawrentian diabolism among recent novelists in England and America. Lawrence's strange gods have been of greatest importance to poets, which is perhaps why they were most violently attacked by a preacher who began his theological career as a poet named T. S. Eliot. Lawrence himself, moreover, seems to me to have expressed his own devotion to these strange gods in uncommon prayers most often disguised as lyric poems. Indeed, I suspect that Lawrence's poet-disciples may have consciously or unconsciously perceived that not only such obviously prayerful works as those collected in *Last Poems* but even the apparently "realistic" nature poems in *Birds, Beasts and Flowers* originated in anti-Christian vision such as those I have been describing here. At this point, therefore, I would like to pause and consider in greater detail the possibility that *Birds, Beasts and Flowers* may not only be energized but organized by a subversive narrative structure.[21]

Of course, *Look! We Have Come Through!*, Lawrence's third book of poetry, has long been read as a narrative sequence or "verse novel." Lawrence himself provided the work with an official "Argument" and insisted that "these poems should not be considered separately. . . . They are intended as an essential story, or history, or confession, unfolding one from the other in organic development." But in any case it is easy enough to see the dramatic and narrative coherence of a group of confessional poems chronicling "the conflict of love and hate [that] goes on between [a] man and [a] woman, and between these two and the world around them, till . . . they transcend into some condition of blessedness."[22]

On first consideration, however, readers would not tend to perceive the same narrative coherence in *Birds, Beasts and Flowers,* the great collection whose tone and technique *Look!* both foreshadowed and created. With Kenneth Rexroth and Tom Marshall, most would see this volume not as a narrative sequence but as a philosophical "exploration" of the "newly valued world of birds, beasts, and flowers—a sacramentalized, objective world" to which the poet has been mystically wedded by the ritual of holy matrimony recorded in *Look!*[23] I myself have described the poems \in *Birds, Beasts and Flowers,* as essays of discovery, processes of definition, with Lawrence a metaphysical or metaphorical Linnaeus cataloguing the varieties of otherness in nature.[24]

I want to argue here, however, that as a collection *Birds, Beasts and Flowers* is consciously or unconsciously organized and unified by a submerged narrative structure which gives it exactly the dramatic coherence Lawrence sought in *Look!* Further, I want to suggest that this narrative structure is not only submerged but subversive, for it seems to me to depend on a revisionary synthesis of a group of those myths of darkness to which

so many poets have recently been drawn and which were to become increasingly important to Lawrence: the story of Persephone and Dis (or Pluto), the story of Orpheus and Eurydice, the stories of Osiris and Dionysus, the story of Samson, and last but not least the story of the fall of Lucifer, and the subsequent falls or failures of all humanity.

As we might expect, Lawrence does not "tell" these stories in received, official ways; at every point his perspective on them is that of the illegitimate, dangerous, Blakeian outsider he felt he had become in his postwar flight from England. Thus Persphone's marriage to Dis/Pluto is the best thing that ever happened to her (and Lawrence enacts in turn her part and the part of her dark lover); Orpheus's separation from Eurydice and journey down the "winding, leaf-clogged silent lanes of hell" (*CP*, p. 281) is lucky and full of wonder; Samson is not, as Milton thought, imprisoned by his blindness in the dungeon of himself but rather freed from ordinary vision to perceive that "the dome of high ideal heaven" (*CP*, p. 287) is his prison; and Lucifer, the Son of the morning, whom Milton called Satan and Blake called Los, is not a slimy lord of evil but a lord of life, "a king in exile . . . Now due to be crowned again" (*CP*, p. 351).

With Kenneth Rexroth, then, I believe that the poems of *Birds, Beasts and Flowers* do not have a "supernatural luster." But where Rexroth thought this luster the light "that shines through the figures of men and animals and things . . . as they are found carved around the mandala of the Blessed Virgin above some cathedral door or some rose window,"[25] I would say it is exactly the opposite. For, as my Blake reference was meant to imply, the subversive narrative of *Birds, Beasts and Flowers* is not a celebration of the radiant Christian sacrament of holy matrimony but a version of Blake's sardonic *Marriage of Heaven and Hell,* a botanist's or zoologist's Black Mass in which at one point Lawrence, speaking as St. Matthew (whom he defines as representative man) insists that since he has already "mounted up on the wings of the morning," he must now dredge "down to the zenith's reversal" (*CP*, p. 323). Rather than being a metaphysical Linnaeus, in other words, Lawrence is here a Satanic Darwin, journeying in thought to the black center of the earth to trace an evolutionary history we citizens of the "pussyfoot west" (*CP*, p. 280) have forgotten. In the radically revisionary etiology he uncovers, the sacred energy of life comes "Flying not down from heaven, but storming up . . . from the dense underearth. . . . Setting supreme annunciation to the world" (*CP*, p. 304). And of course, therefore, the annunciation he imagines is an upside down (or perhaps downside up) event, not the airy visitation about which poets from Dante to Yeats have written, but a fierce kiss of darkness, even, at times, a kiss of death.

Finally, then, I want to argue that in its sophisticated and subversive engagement with Christian mythology and its consequent espousal of an alternative religion which grows from a variety of irreligious experiences, *Birds, Beasts and Flowers* is, as much as *Aaron's Rod, The*

Lost Girl, and *Kangaroo,* a fictional link between Lawrence's great middle-period novels of society— *Sons and Lovers, The Rainbow, Women in Love*— and such late, openly revisionary mythologies and romances as *The Plumed Serpent,* "The Woman Who Rode Away," "Sun," *Lady Chatterley's Lover,* and *The Escaped Cock.* We might even speculate, indeed, that because *Birds, Beasts and Flowers* is a more successful and coherent work than any of the so-called "problem" novels I have mentioned, it is a far more significant bridge than they are between this author's very different middle and late periods.

Did Lawrence actually intend *Birds, Beasts and Flowers* to have the narrative and allusive coherence I am suggesting it has? I think that is hard to say. Because he was also a novelist, this poet did frequently and inevitably shape literary materials into stories. As a critic/essayist, moreover, he was highly conscious of his own revisionary impulses. The title he gave this collection, for instance, has been drawn from stanza two of S. Baring-Gould's "Evening Hymn": "Now the darkness gathers, / Stars begin to peep. / Birds and beasts and flowers, / Soon will be asleep."[26] But, given the anti-Christian cast of Lawrence's thought in this period, it is hard to imagine that he didn't use Baring-Gould's phrase with some conscious irony, and hard to imagine, too, that he did not think of even the gathering "darkness" with a very different reverence from that of the Reverend Mr. Baring-Gould. In addition, although Lawrence did not provide *Birds, Beasts and Flowers* with an "Argument"—that is, a plot summary—like the one he wrote for *Look!,* it is clear that he organized the book very carefully, beginning with "Fruits" and moving through "Trees," "Flowers," "Evangelical Beasts," "Creatures," "Reptiles," "Birds," and "Animals" to "Ghosts." Some explanation of why he did this seems to me to begin to emerge when we consider that this modern *Marriage of Heaven and Hell* opens with a quarrelsome poem about eating a pomegranate, has at its center an emotionally charged but unsatisfactory confrontation with a serpent, and, after a baptismal encounter between the poet/narrator (who renames himself "Red Wolf") and a dark figure he dubs "Harry" or "Old Nick," ends with the speaker's accession to what we must call shamanistic powers, his summoning up of the spirits of the dead, and his expression of interest in a kind of anti-religious colony in the New World.

I am suggesting, in short, that the processes of discovery in *Birds, Beasts and Flowers* are held together by the covert story of a trip underground, a voyage of death and resurrection exactly like the ones that Lawrence would describe in *The Escaped Cock* or "The Ship of Death." But in the *Birds, Beasts and Flowers* narrative, perhaps more than anywhere else, this Blakeian poet makes it quite clear that in his version of the night sea-journey the protagonist does not, like Beowulf, go down into the mere to slay the forces of darkness but rather to be strengthened and even transformed by them; his fall is fortunate not because it will enable him, like Milton's Adam, to rise again by his own efforts, but because it is

a fall into a hell that he knows is really a darkly radiant heaven, and he may be lucky enough to fall even further, deeper, into the center of all energy; finally, when he comes back from his trip into the demonic darkness behind appearances, he is not, like Hawthorne's Goodman Brown, horrified by what he has learned, but ennobled, even blessed.

All this may seem quite mystical, but I think my reading (if not my rhetoric) is fairly quickly justified by "Fruits," the opening section of the book. This section contains (in order of their appearance) the poems called "Pomegranate," "Peach," "Medlars and Sorb Apples," "Figs," "Grapes," "The Revolutionary," "The Evening Land," and "Peace." It is followed by "Trees" and "Flowers." In 1930 Lawrence prefaced the section with an epigraph (from Burnet's *Early Greek Philosophy*) declaring that "fruits are all of them female, in them lies the seed. And so when they break and show the seed, then we look into the womb and see its secrets. So it is that the pomegranate is the apple of love to the Arab, and the fig has been a catch-word for the female fissure for ages . . . the apple of Eden, even, was Eve's fruit . . ." (*CP,* p. 277) and so on.

If we put all this information together, our first thought might be that "Fruits" simply begins the collection because the book is organized like a great chain of being, from the least animate, the least developed life-forms (the fruit, the pit, the seed) to the most intensely alive, the subtlest, the most complex (human beings and their ghosts). And to some extent this is true. But we might quibble over which came first, the fruit or the tree. And more important, we must ask why poems which are neither about fruits nor seeds—poems like "The Revolutionary," "The Evening Land," and "Peace"—are included in this section. (A related question would be: why have the "Evangelical Beasts" been placed between "Flowers" and "Creatures"?) If, as seems reasonable, we see the placement and organization of "Fruits" as somehow paradigmatic for the volume as a whole, then we must conclude that this section has a narrative and emotional as well as a logical or categorizing function; it both tells a story and begins a story. And I believe the tale it tells is an archetypal story about eating fruit and being changed by the magical properties of fruit.

I am sure the fruit-eater here is Lawrence himself, so I will not refer to him as a *persona* but compromise and call him the poet/narrator. This poet/narrator dramatically defines and describes himself in the very first lines of the book:

> You tell me I am wrong.
> Who are you, who is anybody, to tell me I am
>   wrong?
> I am not wrong.

The "you" here is of course us, the audience, the bystanders, the *hypocrite lecteurs* who watch but do not—cannot—participate in the poet/narrator's ceremonial meal. Since he is writing in English, we are also obviously English-speaking. Thus we represent or at least we are surface of the phenomenal world," a fissure, a rupture, through which glow the beginnings and the ends of things. But what he sees implies also what he does and what he will eat. The timid and genteel reader, refusing to see the dangerous, suggestively sexual fissure, insists upon looking only "on the plain side" of life. But from that side there is no nourishment, and on that side there is no entrance into the mysteriously flaming realm behind the setting sun, whose fissure in the darkness of the sky beckons like a doorway into paradoxical possibilities. When he cracks open the pomegranate, therefore, we have to assume that this defiant speaker begins the revolutionary process of eating *and* entering the fruit—that is, eating and being eaten by it. In a sense, in this poem he is planting the seed of his whole book within himself, and this poem/seed is the kernel of transformation.

It seems fairly clear that the poet/narrator here eats the "glittering compact drops of dawn" that are the pomegranate's seeds with considerable equanimity. "For my part, I prefer my heart to be broken," he assures us. "It is so lovely, dawn-kaleidoscopic within the crack." But as Lawrence's imagery of heartbreak suggests, the ceremonial fruit meal is traditionally a dangerous one. In countless folk narratives fearful metamorphoses begin with the ingestion of some alien substance, and Judeo-Christian mythology itself, of course, starts with such a meal of poison fruit: when Eve ate the apple she "ate" death and, as Milton puts it, even "Earth felt the wound" and all Nature sighed.[28] Similarly, nineteenth-century poets like Keats (in "La Belle Dame") or Christina Rossetti (in "Goblin Market") tell stories of transformation and self-confrontation which begin with the eating of strange fruits or roots, and Lawrence's poem certainly depends at least in part on our grasp of the tradition in which all these tales of eating participate. But most particularly, Lawrence's poem alludes to the myth of Persephone, the queen of the underworld and the daughter of the earth goddess, who was irrevocably committed to her half-time life in hell—that is, to her traveling back and forth between the upper and lower worlds—when she ate a few pomegranate seeds.

That Lawrence chose to begin his account of a journey through the alien kingdom of *Birds, Beasts and Flowers* not with Eve's fall but with Persephone's seems to me significant in several ways. First, and most obviously, it emphasizes the deliberately anti-Christian nature of the cosmology he is outlining. Second (and perhaps more important), it establishes the essentially amoral or at least morally unconventional tone of this collection. For where Eve's fall (especially as Milton presents it) was a moral one, Persephone's was mystical, or anyway mysterious. Eve wickedly ate the apple because she was angry, but Persephone only ate the pomegranate seeds because she was hungry. In other words, although Eve deserved punishment—falling;—Persephone did not deserve to "fall"; she simply fell, through the neutrality and energy of natural appetite, thereby both entering and creating the seasonal cycle of life and death that constitutes the essence of natural process. Because Eve's fall

was a moral event, it follows, too, that the world it created is, as we know, a sadly material and ruined landscape from which the divine spirit has irrevocably withdrawn itself. But—and this is crucial to Lawrence's revision of the myth of the fall—since Persephone's fall was morally neutral, the world it brought about (especially as Lawrence sees it) is a radiant realm the goddess herself still visits: she withdraws and returns, withdraws and returns, in a divine Heraclitean flux that helps us understand why the poet used so many quotations from Burnet's *Early Greek Philosophy* as epigraphs for this volume.

Moreover, to the extent that Lawrence wants to celebrate the natural world he must celebrate not only Persephone, the traveler back and forth, but also her demonic mate, the god of darkness who first entangled her in this seasonal process. Particularly in celebrating this god of darkness, however, he is revising the myth of the fall to say: *no, it was not really a fall, it was a downward journey.* If it has not already been made clear, his revisionary awareness is definitively revealed both in **"Peach"** and **"Medlars and Sorb Apples,"** the two poems that follow **"Pomegranate."** Defending the fruit's "groove," its "suggestion of incision," **"Peach"** continues the defiant dialogue with a *hypocrite lecteur* audience that **"Pomegranate"** began. At the same time, though, through a passage that wittily parodies Blake's "Tyger," Lawrence implies that the transition from **"Pomegranate"** to **"Peach"** is a necessary fall or downward journey from innocence to Experience, a journey from the virginal dawn-country of Beulah to the riper realm of Generation. "Why so velvety, why so voluptuous heavy?" he asks. "Why hanging with such inordinate weight? / Why so indented?" And though (like Blake before him) he does not answer these questions, he does playfully offer the reader a peach stone to throw at him, showing that he at least *has* eaten the fruit.

In **"Medlars and Sorb Apples"** it becomes even plainer that in eating the fruit the poet/narrator has not only eaten Nature but has himself entered Nature through cracks and grooves in the "bivalve roundness" of the seasonal world. Having "eaten death," however, he does not despair like Eve, but instead exclaims that "Wonderful are the hellish experiences:" and embarks upon his crucial journey down the "winding, leaf-clogged, silent lanes of hell." And though Lawrence describes this trip as Orphic or Dionysiac, it is also Persephone's journey, a journey that begins with a kiss of death—"a kiss and a spasm of farewell"—in the "flux of autumn," "a journey that is given sacramental savour by the rambling, sky-dropped grape" and a journey that ends with the soul entering Pluto's realm "naked-footed . . . Ever more exquisite, distilled in separation." Along with Persephone, Orpheus, Dionysus, and all other mortal beings, the poet/narrator gropes downward into the "intoxication of final loneliness." As if to show that you are what you eat, he himself has become a seed falling through the dead walls of the fruit into the labyrinthine ways of an underworld where he must re-create his own energies.

Approached by winding lanes and "orgasm[s] of rupture," this dark central hell is not, of course, so much a tomb as it is a womb; as Lawrence's epigraph noted, "fruits are all of them female" so that entering the labyrinth of nature "we look into the womb and see its secrets." **"Figs,"** therefore, quite appropriately follows the journey-imagery of **"Medlars and Sorb Apples"** with a meditation upon the place that is the Journey's goal, or one of its goals. For years, I must confess, I have been troubled by what has seemed to be the anti-feminism of this poem, and I am still disturbed by Lawrence's comparison of a "bursten fig" to a "prostitute . . . making a show of her secret," and by his editorial insistence that "women the world over" who burst "into self-assertion" are like "bursten figs [which] won't keep." Nevertheless, it is easier to understand and at least partly justify **"Figs"** when we consider its position in the submerged narrative that structures *Birds, Beasts and Flowers.* Having begun his journey into the center of nature, the poet/narrator becomes ever more certain that the natural world is divinely emblematic. "The fig, the horseshoe, the squash-blossom. / Symbols," he says, as if murmuring this hard-won information to himself. And the fig, as he sees it, symbolizes not only female creative energy but the mystical darkness or secrecy in which female energy generates and regenerates life.

In a real sense, then, the magical interior of the. fig, "where everything happens invisible, flowering, fertilisation, and fruiting / In the inwardness of your you," is analogous to the secret central chamber of hell where Persephone lies with Dis in what Lawrence was later to call "the marriage of the living dark" (*CP,* p. 960), that continually restores life. But to shed any light in this room other than the paradoxical light of "torches of darkness" (*CP,* p. 697) would be (as in the tale of Cupid and Psyche) like bringing to consciousness what must be done intuitively. In folk tale after folk tale we learn, after all, that *to tell the secret is to lose the power,* and indeed, in *Birds, Beasts and Flowers* this notion links **"Figs"** to the forthcoming story of Samson, who lost his (male) power by kissing and telling. It explains, too, why the stone in **"Peach"** is "wrinkled with secrets and hard with the intention to keep them," and why the poet/narrator only half-ironically invites his hostile reader to throw a peach stone at *him,* the speaker. Self-enclosed, dense with the power of secrecy, the peach pit is yet another talisman of transformation by which one may pass from here to there, from this foolishly assertive upper world to the magic shadows below.

Lawrence elaborates even further in **"Grapes"** on the virtues of secrecy and the disadvantages of what he calls "the universe of the unfolded rose, / The explicit / the candid revelation." His attack upon the "rose of all roses, rose of all the world" which has begun to "simper supreme" in western culture is an attack upon both Yeats and Plato (or neo-Plato), for the heavenly beauty that Yeats defined in his rose poems[29] as not only eternal but emblematic of eternity was clearly a Platonic ideal; abstract, brilliant, disembodied, existing to be seen and not touched, a symbol of the mind willfully yearning to separate itself from nature rather than the body reincarnating itself in nature. Lawrence's journey, however, continues to be a trip into an antediluvian and anti-Platonic Hades—a fleshly cave—that he defines as the true Eden, the primordial place of origin we must re-remember. In this "dusky, dowerless, tendrilled world" the vine bears an *invisible* rose whose blue-black sacred grapes hang "globed in Egyptian darkness." And modern westerners, the prissy readers who were the "you" of **"Pomegranate"** and **"Peach,"** fear re-remembrance of such a dangerously invisible kingdom, fear substituting Pluto for Plato. Indeed, the poet/narrator sometimes seems himself to feel such fear, for despite his obvious scorn of his contemporaries, he speaks throughout this poem as "we" (rather than "I" versus "you"). "We must cross the frontiers, though we will not," he notes, adding with grim determination that we must "take the fern-seed in our lips, / Close the eyes, and go / Down the tendrilled avenues of wine and the otherworld." Here, blind, fallen from our daylight lives, intoxicated with loneliness, shrouded in secrecy, we must seek our own lost powers.

Since both the horror and the necessity of blindness are almost insurmountable obstacles to the fall or downward journey that is the subject of the *Birds, Beasts and Flowers* narrative, it seems inevitable that the poet/narrator should pause here to consider the implications of blindness for one famously sightless hero, Samson. Not surprisingly, however, Lawrence drastically revises the story that is told in the Bible and in Milton's *Samson Agonistes,* and there are enough allusions to the latter source for us to be certain that just as he was attacking Yeats in **"Grapes,"** he is here severely criticizing Milton. To begin with, as I noted earlier, Lawrence's Samson does not mourn his blindness, the way Milton's does. Rather, he vaunts it, as if having rashly told one secret he has luckily learned another. Captive and defeated, Milton's agonized hero complains that he has been "exiled from light" to "a living death . . . Myself my sepulcher, a moving grave."[30] But Lawrence's Samson makes plot necessities' into mystical virtues.

Because he is an exile, this revisionary hero is a revolutionary, setting himself sardonically against the "pale-face authority" of those pillars of society who hold up "the high and super-gothic heavens." Because he is blind, he need not "yearn" or "aspire," for "what is daylight to me that I should look skyward?" Because he is imprisoned in the "living grave" of his own body, he experiences things as Pluto and Persephone must in their hot black chamber—intuitively, receptively: "To me, the earth rolls ponderously, superbly . . . To me, men's footfalls fall with a dull, soft rumble . . . To me, men are palpable, invisible nearnesses in the dark." Most important, perhaps, where Milton's warrior defines the labor to which he had been condemned as the ultimate sign of degradation—for is he not "eyeless in Gaza, at the Mill with *slaves?*"[31]—Lawrence's revolutionary seems actually to take pride in his work: "Am I not blind at the round-turning mill? / Then why should I fear their pale faces? / Or love the effulgence of their holy light?" We might almost speculate, in fact, that for Lawrence the "round-turning mill" is a kind of generator, an energy source that gives his hero the power to make the skies of piety come tumbling down. And unlike the Bible's and Milton's Samson, Lawrence's will certainly survive: "My head," he says, "is thick enough to stand it, the smash."

Indeed, not only will Lawrence's revolutionary survive, he will be "Lord of the dark and moving hosts / Before I die." As such a lord, however, this blind and blinding hero begins to seem like someone other or larger than simply the Samson of Biblical or Miltonic legend. Lawrence has in any case been careful only to refer to him as "the revolutionary," never specifically naming him Samson. Now we begin to see why, for this speaker does seem to have a multiple identity. Blind and vengeful, he is Samson. But potent with dark energy, mysteriously regal, he is also Lucifer (who was exiled in darkness but lived to create an alternative kingdom), Osiris (who was torn apart in defeat but reconstituted as the ruler of the underworld), and Dis/Pluto (who has been defined as the Lord of the Dead but whose marriage with Persephone sustains the "moving hosts" of the living).

Lawrence has been suggesting, then, that at the center of things, when one has embarked upon the journey into darkness, tombs become wombs, hell becomes an experience more ecstatic than heaven, and night implies fiercer energies than day. His exploration of such mystical paradoxes neatly links **"The Revolutionary"** with its successor, **"The Evening Land,"** for although the latter work seems at first like just another one of this poet's characteristically apocalyptic polemics on the subject of America, much of its imagery extends and elaborates upon the story of the Black Mass voyage that *Birds, Beasts and Flowers* is covertly narrating. As most Lawrence critics have noted, at this point in his career—before he had literally left the old world for the new—Lawrence's America was as mythic a realm as Shakespeare's or Blake's. The poet/narrator of *Birds, Beasts and Flowers* is quite willing to confess this. "Oh, America / The sun sets in you. / Are you the grave of our day?" he asks, then devotes the rest of the poem to an analysis of his own anxiety about the "death" America promises. Is it what Lawrence's own revolutionary lord would define as a real death, the death that permeates the long ash-gray coffin of England, the "winding sheet of . . . boundless love / Like a poison gas?" Or is it a death that implies Osiris-like rebirth? America has an "elvishness," he declares, that "carries me beyond . . . what we call human, / Carries me where I want to be carried." Perhaps then, he implies, America as the "evening land" is a way station on the downward, night sea-journey that began when the Persephone-like speaker of **"Pomegranate"** ate a few "glittering compact drops of dawn." If so, the real goal is still ahead; it is the raging central core the poet/speaker sees in a kind of dream-vision that ends this section.

Perversely entitled **"Peace,"** this concluding poem is about the volcanic apocalypse that would occur if the Satanic/Plutonic energy Lawrence seeks should suddenly surface, unbidden, as "Brilliant, intolerable lava," engulfing "forests, cities, bridges," all the historical monuments of "pale-face authority." Would it be **"Peace"**? Would the traveler's urge to journey toward a blinding center finally be satisfied? Or would the "dark and nude vast heaven" of that prehistory we pious readers have labeled Satanic be fearsome and intolerable? Looking forward to the dramatic climaxes of this collection's underground narrative—the unsuccessful meeting with the snake in Sicily and the successful encounter with "Old Nick" in America—Lawrence's wonderful image of lava "walking like a royal snake down the mountain towards the sea" gives us an obvious clue to the hellish consummation he undevoutly wishes. But although the poet/narrator has here a definitive vision of the energy roaring behind the fissure in the pomegranate, we are still left wondering, as the section concludes, whether he himself will have the energy to take us further into the heart of darkness.

III

Those who have read all the way to the end of *Birds, Beasts and Flowers* will know, of course, that Lawrence as poet/narrator does seem, symbolically speaking, to reach his journey's goal, the promised end of a penetration into the invisible fire behind the visible world. Or rather, more accurately, his journey ends in a series of increasingly intense meetings with hell on earth, for more often than not in these poems the underworld sends emissaries out or up to the poet and his world. Thus almost all the poems in **"Trees"** are wondering re-examinations of demonic plants that grow like trunks of darkness out of what might be called the buried life. Just as the cracking open of a pomegranate appropriately began the **"Fruits"** section, a meditation upon cypresses—in fact, an attempt at dialogue with them—significantly begins this section. Associated with Tuscany and the lost, supposedly "evil" Etruscans (whose reputations Lawrence wishes to rescue), the cypress is also traditionally the death tree, dark, immortal, hovering like a black flame over the tombs of "the silenced races and all their abominations" as if it rose straight from the breast of hell. In this poem, therefore, Lawrence for the first time becomes openly shamanistic, summoning ghosts while repudiating the rational, pale-face optimism of Darwin: "They say the fit survive, / But I invoke the spirits of the lost." By the end of this section, moreover, his invocations no longer need the solidity of trees to focus them; they are addressed directly to larger forces—to the "Sun of black void heat" (*CP,* p. 301) and the "red thing . . . blood-dark" for which we have no word but "moon" (*CP,* p. 302).

Similarly, in **"Flowers"** more messengers from the underground kingdom appear in the country of daylight to declare esoteric meanings to the poet/narrator. Almond blossom storms up from the center of things to set "supreme annuciation to the world." Purple anemones rise like hell on earth, "little hells of colour, caves of darkness" in pursuit of a lost Persephone. Sicilian cyclamens whisper "witchcraft / Like women at a well, the dawn-fountain."

Royal hibiscus, worn by a pagan Eve "Before she humbled herself, and knocked her knees with dirt," offers an "exquisite assertion . . . Risen from the roots," and furious salvia flower, red as an "extinct race" of "red angry men," flickers like "living wrath / Upon the smouldering air" with a "throat of brimstone-molten angry gold." It is no wonder that, having confronted and contemplated so many emissaries of hell, Lawrence feels he must pause in the next section to attempt an even more direct re-examination of the Christian Bible, and specifically of the New Testament's Evangelistic Beasts.

As I commented earlier, his Matthew is a traveler back and forth exactly like his Persephone. Since Lawrence is subversively revising Christian mythology, however, he inevitably emphasizes the necessity of the downward plunge rather than the joys of the upward flight. Thus many of Matthew's self-defining statements could act as Blakeian epigraphs for the book as a whole: "Put me down again on the earth, Jesus, on the brown soil / Where flowers sprout in the acrid humus, and fade into humus again," or "At evening I must leave off my wings of the spirit . . . And I must resume my nakedness like a fish, sinking down the dark reversion of night / Like a fish seeking the bottom, Jesus," or "Remember, Saviour / That my heart . . . Throws still the dark blood back and forth / In the avenues where the bat hangs sleeping, upside-down / And to me undeniable."

Upside-down: as so often, Lawrence is his own best exegete, for the remaining three Evangelical Beasts present images of Mark, Luke, and John that are as upside-down as any bat. The poet-narrator's bat-vision of a "reversed zenith," creates, for instance, a Blakeian parable of the fall of the lion of the spirit from a savage king of the beasts of an ignominious servant of the redcross Lamb, a Urizenic sheepdog with a bourgeois Victorian family. Similarly, Lawrence's upside-down consciousness leads him to argue that "Luke, the Bull, the father of substance," has been sadly bewitched by the Lamb, while in the most inevitable yet sardonic joke of all the phoenix-like Eagle of St. John, once the symbol of pure intellect, has become merely "the badge of an insurance company," the emblem of profit-and-loss capitalism. Serving as a kind of bridge between Lawrence's confrontations with the apparently inanimate vegetable kingdom and the journey his poet/narrator must now take through the animal world, these subversive redefinitions of Biblical symbols prepare us, finally, for even more outrageous reappraisals to come: the snake who is poisonous but lordly, the ass who was foolish *because* he carried Jesus into Jerusalem, the demonic turkeycock who should replace the ethereal peacock, the mountain lion who is more valuable than a million people, the bulldog who ought to "learn" pagan loyalty rather than Christian loving, and the tortoise whose inchoate orgasmic scream is a kind of anti-Platonic paradigm for human speech.

As the creatures the poet/narrator encounters grow more complex, more neural, more autonomous, it becomes increasingly clear that now, besides being talismans of Hades, they are totemic familiars, spiritual guides and judges; besides representing the underworld, they incarnate its grave ruler. Paradoxically, in other words, the "higher" Lawrence's quest takes him on the evolutionary scale, the closer he comes to a significant dialogue with the "lower" kingdom. But the obstacles to true communion are of course very great. Like the space traveler that in a sense he is, this poet/narrator must catch at obscure hints and decipher mysterious signs as if he were a linguist decoding an extragalactic language on the basis of only a few fragmentary clues. The Christian humanist assumptions that he cannot escape, moreover, cause attempts at dialogue to break down on several occasions—in **"The Mosquito,"** in **"Man and Bat,"** and in **"Fish,"** for example, and most famously in **"Snake."** By the end of **"Reptiles,"** however, in **"Tortoise Shout,"** the poet/narrator has heard what we might define as the primal scream of hell, the "strange faint coition yell / Of the male tortoise at extremity / Torn from under the very edge of the farthest far-off horizon of life," and he has grasped the deep metaphysical connection between this cry, "the first elements of foreign speech / On wild dark lips," and the "Osiris-cry of abandonment" uttered *in extremis* by Christ, whose crucifixion plunged him from the upper air into the shadowy underworld of the Egyptian god.

It is significant, I think, that after **"Tortoise Shout"** Lawrence as poet/narrator begins to engage in far more vigorous dialogue with the beings he encounters, translating the ass's speech, for instance, and himself admonishing the he-goat ("Fight, old Satan, with a selfish will") and the elephants ("Serve, vast mountainous blood"). Finally, at the edge of a canyon—a fissure in the earth not unlike the crack in the pomegranate—in "the heart of the west," in the symbolic shadow of a subversively "black crucifix like a dead tree spreading wings," this phenomenal traveler has his visionary encounter with the shrouded, demonic Indian who calls himself "Old Harry" or "Old Nick." "Across the pueblo river"—a stream as mystically significant, in this context, as Styx or Lethe— "That dark old demon and I / . . . say a few words to each other," Lawrence tells us. But the few words they say are important indeed: "Where's your God, you white one? / Where's your white God?" the Indian/demon asks, and the poet/narrator confesses that "He fell to dust as the twilight fell, / Was fume as I trod / The last step out of the east." At this, albeit reluctantly, the dark interlocutor renames him "Red Wolf," and metaphorically speaking Lawrence does *become* a red wolf, symbolically entering the realm of ***Birds, Beasts and Flowers*** that has grown increasingly less alien throughout his narrative. For when the "dark old father" protests fastidiously that *"We take no hungry stray from the pale-face,"* the poet declares "Father, you are not asked. / I am come. I am here. / The red-dawn-wolf / Sniffs round your place."

As I began by arguing, this transformation is the principal denouement of Lawrence's narrative. Like the protagonist of ***Look!,*** the poet/narrator has here entered into some "condition of blessedness," although its characteristics are subversive indeed. Nor do they always seem like blessings, even after Lawrence's Blakeian redefinitions. We are told in **"Men in New Mexico,"** for example, that in this new world there is "a dark membrane over the will, holding a man down / Even when the mind has flickered awake." This black membrane is perhaps the weight of blind Samson's "dark and nude vast heavens," finally experienced firsthand; this is perhaps what it means, not just to imagine Osiris but to become Osiris, if only for a moment.

Still, despite its dangers, a demonic blessedness does now permeate everything, and Lawrence says he wants it to. Not only has the poet/narrator himself become a beast, a red wolf, in **"Autumn at Taos"** the whole landscape becomes animal and magical: the pines are bear fur, the desert a wolf pelt, the aspens, significantly, the "glistening-feathered legs of the hawk of Horus," legs of the divine son of Osiris who was conceived through a downside-up annunciation from the kingdom of the dead. In **"Spirits Summoned West,"** moreover, Lawrence's poet/narrator asks others from that kingdom to forget their old rational/social functions as "wives and mothers" and join him in this new world as newly powerful virgins, Persephones to his Dis. Then, as if wondering how long a new world can *stay* new, in **"The American Eagle,"** he adds a last ironic question about his own vision of a new hell and a new earth: can the eagle of the Rockies, the demonic "bird of men that are masters," sustain its attack upon the redcross Lamb, or will the emblematic American bird itself be tamed by the "dove of Liberty," and become a mere goose laying an "addled golden egg"?

IV

As this last poem suggests, and as most students of Lawrence will suspect anyway, America both as myth and as reality is crucial to the metamorphic journey *Birds, Beasts and Flowers* describes. Indeed, some readers may object that the narrative I have defined so far is simply an account of this writer's famous emigration from the old world to the new one, a trip which accompanied and inspired his composition of this cycle of poems. For my purpose here, however, what is most significant about this journey—at least as the poet/narrator of *Birds, Beasts and Flowers* presents it—is the paradoxical direction in which it was taken. "I'm a pale face like a homeless dog / That has followed the sun from the dawn through the east," Lawrence writes in **"Red Wolf,"** "Trotting east and east and east till the sun himself went home, / And left me homeless here in the dark at your door." And of course that is simply true. Lawrence and Frieda went east from England to Italy, then east from Italy to Ceylon, Australia, San Francisco, and Taos. Both in reality and in these poems, in other words, Lawrence went west paradoxically, by going east. He did not take the conventional "westward ho" journey that rational "empire" supposedly ought to take in western culture, nor did he ride consciously, wearily westward like Donne riding toward death.[32] Thus he seems really to have confirmed his own subversive desire for a downside-up annunciation by going east to get west, entering the dawn fissure of the pomegranate to reach the evening land of America.

Prepared as he was for transformation, every place Lawrence touched upon in the course of his actual journey was, as we know, radiant with a "symbolic meaning." England, pious and rational, was the Urizenic heaven from which he had fallen—or exiled himself—like a new Lucifer. In the garden of his childhood, he obviously felt, Blakeian priests in black gowns were walking their rounds and binding with briars his joys and desires. Italy, closer to the pagan world yet ruined by history, must have seemed to be a kind of purgatorial *paysage moralisé,* offering him the talismanic pomegranate through whose crack he could enter like Persephone into the roaring energy behind appearances. Even the southward journey *within* Italy may have seemed symbolic, for in a sense the Lawrences traveled backwards in time, from Renaissance Tuscany to pagan Sicily, and, going south, they journeyed from the calm vineyards around Florence to the quaking slopes of Aetna, from common ground to royal lava. Finally, like his own Persephone, Lawrence went west by going east; he reached the country he defined as the evening land of death—and rebirth—by entering the morning and groping his way to the darkness behind the light, the numinous behind the luminous. As he traveled, moreover, he passed (both literally and figuratively) through a cycle of seasons—fall, winter, spring/summer, fall—and these help structure his narrative almost as much as its paradoxical geography.

Did Lawrence do any of this consciously, intentionally— that is, did he travel east-west for mystical as well as practical reasons? Or was the conjunction of real voyaging and fantasy voyage merely a coincidence? Given Lawrence's Romantic tendency to mythologize himself, his habit of divining meanings by reading the entrails of his own experience, I think we have to assume that he did perceive a message both in his poems and in his east-west passage, and that perhaps intuitively, perhaps intellectually, he arranged his poems so as to present this message as dramatically as possible. He may have understood, too, that the journey his poems described was a voyage of literary as well as spiritual metamorphosis, a journey from one genre into another. For, depending as they do on folk tales, myths, and revisionary encounters with the invisible powers that manifest themselves in the visible, Lawrence's poetic notes from underground not only linked two stages in his career, they actually played a crucial part in his transformation from the romantic yet realistic novelist of *Women in Love* and *Aaron's Rod* to the mythic romancer of *The Plumed Serpent, The Escaped Cock,* **"The Woman Who Rode Away,"** and *Last Poems.*

As he traveled away from England, I believe, Lawrence traveled continually away from the traditional novel and increasingly toward the fabulist mode in which he was to be one of our century's major pioneers. And though this will sound like yet another paradox, I would speculate that it was important to this poet-novelist's novelistic evolution that the narrative of *Birds, Beasts and Flowers* was submerged in poetry. Liberating him temporarily from the exigencies of all plot except those mythic paradigms which seemed to him to be implicit in his own voyage, the composition of this poem sequence prepared him not only for such a generic experiment as *The Plumed Serpent* but also for the revisionary mythmaking of *The Escaped Cock* and other late tales. Ultimately, by going east toward the primitive dawn-sources of all culture, toward the poetry at the heart of prose, Lawrence had gone further west, deeper into what we call modernism. In a sense, then, the poems of *Birds, Beasts and Flowers* not only tell the story of his transformation, they *are* the story.

V

Of course, as most of the contemporary Lawrentian poets mentioned earlier would understand, this story is one that continues throughout the rest of Lawrence's life-and-poetry, for, like a subversive form of the plot that organizes all Christian liturgy, it is a tale of the cyclical mysteries of transformation that must be re-enacted time and time again. Certainly, although most of the meditative verses in *Last Poems* are more overtly religious than the *Birds, Beasts and Flowers* works, they are just as diabolically unorthodox. Indeed, like the *Birds, Beasts and Flowers* poems, they frequently present downside-up versions of Christian myths. Thus, where the central Christian transformation is from flesh to spirit, the crucial Lawrentian transformation, throughout both *Last Poems* and the late stories, is from spirit to flesh, as if Lawrence were now actually writing the uncommon prayers he wants spoken as part of the Black Mass he imagined in *Birds, Beasts and Flowers.* Even the newly fleshly Jesus of *The Escaped Cock* seems rather Satanic, with his black pointed beard and "dusky skin" that has a "silvery glisten,"[33] so that it is quite appropriate for the priestess of Isis to identify him with Osiris, another demonic power of the lower depths. (In *Apocalypse,* moreover, Lawrence actually does conflate Christ with the "Lord of the Underworld [and with] Hermes, the guide of souls through the death-world, over the hellish stream. . . . "[34]

It is not surprising, then, that *More Pansies* includes a cheeky little anti-sermon called **"The Church,"** in which Lawrence sketches a few theological pointers for his heretical new Church of spirit-turned-flesh:

> If I was a member of the Church of Rome
> I should advocate reform:
> the marriage of priests
> the priests to wear rose-colour or magenta in the
>   streets
> to teach the Resurrection in the flesh
> to start the year on Easter Sunday
> to add the mystery of Joy-in-Resurrection to the
>   Mass
> to inculcate the new conception of the Risen Man
>   (*CP,* p. 609).

Yet another late *Pansy,* simply entitled **"Lucifer,"**, is even more specific about the poet's allegiance to the Blakeian angel whose fall, according to Lawrence, paradoxically intensified his brightness:

> Angels are bright still, though the brightest fell.
> But tell me, tell me, how do you know

that he lost any of his brightness in falling?
He only fell out of your ken, you orthodox angels,
you dull angels, tarnished with centuries of
    conventionality
                          (*CP*, p. 614).

Finally, in a revision of this poem that was included in the *Last Poems* notebooks, Lawrence revealed himself, in a kind of Satanic epiphany, as the diabolist that I believe he always was:

> Angels are bright still, though the brightest fell.
> But tell me, tell me, how do you know
> he lost any of his brightness in the falling?
> In the dark-blue depths, under layers and layers of
>   darkness,
> I see him more like a ruby, a gleam from within
> of his own magnificence
> coming like the ruby in the invisible dark,
>   glowing
> with his own annunciation, towards us
>   (*CP*, p. 697).

"Glowing with his *own* annunciation": proud as any devil, this Lucifer is clearly a demonically self-made god, and thus it is the "magnificence" of his fallen flesh that magically hushes and darkens even the brightest noon in which Lawrence finds himself. Similarly, his emissaries, the pomegranate flowers of Andraitx that Lawrence describes in yet another late poem, mysteriously make "noon . . . suddenly dark . . . lustrous . . . silent and dark." At the same time, testifying to the sacred erotic power of the god, the poet notices that in this anti-Miltonic darkness at noon "from out the foliage of the secret loins / red flamelets here and there reveal / a man, a woman there" (*CP,* pp. 605-6).

Significantly, the holy Lucifer to whom Lawrence alludes in all these poems is the same subversive god that Denise Levertov describes in a 1966 poem called "Eros,"[35] for as she says,

> simply he is
> the temple of himself,
>
> hair and hide
> a sacrifice of blood and flowers
> on his altar
>
> if any worshipper
> kneel or not.

In the end, Levertov's revision of Lawrence's re-vision of Lucifer suggests that, though Lawrence himself may once have fallen out of the ken of orthodox literary critics, though he would never be praised at Mr. Eliot's Sunday Morning Service, he still hangs gleaming, like the demonic Morning Star he loved, on the horizon of contemporary verse. Insisting that "the only Riches" are the self-created "Great Souls,"[36] he hymns a world without Established Churches, a world with only the flickering of sacred pomegranate seeds in the shadows behind the crack of dawn.

NOTES

[1] T. S. Eliot, *After Strange Gods: A Primer of Modern Heresy* (London: Faber and Faber, 1934), p. 20.

[2] Ibid., p. 39.

[3] Ibid., p. 58.

[4] Ibid., p. 56.

[5] Eugene Goodheart, *The Utopian Vision of D. H. Lawrence* (Chicago: University of Chicago Press, 1963), pp. 5-7. For other useful discussions of Lawrentian "diabolism," see also George H. Ford, *Double Measure: A Study of the Novels and Stories of D. H. Lawrence* (New York: Holt, 1965), and James C. Cowan, *D. H. Lawrence's American Journey: A Study in Literature and Myth* (Cleveland: Case Western Reserve University Press, 1970).

[6] See my *Acts of Attention: The Poems of D. H. Lawrence* (Ithaca, N. Y.: Cornell University Press, 1973), pp. 316-17.

[7] Karl Shapiro, "The First White Aboriginal," reprinted in *The Poetry Wreck, Selected Essays: 1950-1970* (New York: Random House, 1975), p. 160.

[8] Ibid., p. 156.

[9] William Carlos Williams, *Selected Poems* (New York: New Directions, 1963), pp. 95-99.

[10] William Carlos Williams, *Kora in Hell: Improvisations* (San Francisco: City Lights Books, 1967), p. 55.

[11] Denise Levertov, *The Poet in the World* (New York: New Directions, 1973), p. 178.

[12] Ibid., p. 85.

[13] Gary Snyder, *Earth House Hold* (New York: New Directions, 1969), p. 122.

[14] Joyce Carol Oates, *New Heaven, New Earth: The Visionary Experience in Literature* (New York: Fawcett, 1974), pp. 50, 52. ("The Hostile Sun," Oates's study of Lawrence's poetry, was also published separately by Black Sparrow Press, Santa Barbara, California, in 1973.)

[15] Robert Bly, ed. and trans., *Friends, You Drank Some Darkness, Three Swedish Poets: Martinson, Ekelof, and Transtromer* (Boston: Seventies Press / Beacon Press, 1975), p. 3.

[16] Robert Bly, ed., *Neruda and Vallejo: Selected Poems* (Boston: Seventies Press / Beacon Press, 1971), pp. 14-15.

[17] Ted Hughes, *Gaudete* (New York: Harper & Row, 1977), p. 8.

[18] Ted Hughes, "Pike," in *Selected Poems: 1957-1967* (New York: Harper & Row, 1972), p. 51.

[19] Adrienne Rich, "Three Conversations" (with Barbara Gelpi), in *Adrienne Rich's Poetry,* ed. Barbara Charlesworth Gelpi and Albert Gelpi (New York: Norton, 1975), p. 112.

[20] Stephen Spender and J. L. Gili, trans., and Francisco Garcia Lorca and Donald M. Allen, eds., *The Selected Poems of Federico Garcia Lorca* (New York: New Directions, 1955), p. 135.

[21] Portions of the discussion below were originally delivered at the 1978 Modern Language Association Conference in New York as a paper entitled "Hell on Earth: *Birds, Beasts and Flowers* as Subversive Narrative" and have subsequently appeared as an essay with the same title in *The D. H. Lawrence Review.* I am grateful to James Cowan, editor of the *Review,* for encouraging my work on that paper and for permitting me to reprint portions of it here.

[22] *The Complete Poems of D. H. Lawrence,* ed. Vivian de Sola Pinto and Warren Roberts (New York: Viking, 1964), p. 191. All references to Lawrence's poems (included hereafter in the text) will be to this edition.

[23] Kenneth Rexroth, Introduction to *D. H. Lawrence, Selected Poems* (New York: Viking, 1959), p. 14; Tom Marshall, *Psychic Mariner: A Reading of the Poems of D. H. Lawrence* (New York: Viking, 1970), p. 116.

[24] See "The Living Cosmos: Varieties of otherness," in my *Acts of Attention,* pp. 162-89.

[25] Rexroth, p. 14.

[26] See Marshall, p. 117.

[27] D. H. Lawrence, *The Lost Girl* (London: Heinemann, 1920), p. 347.

[28] *Paradise Lost,* IX, 782.

[29] See W. B. Yeats, *Collected Poems* (New York: Macmillan, 1955), "The Rose," pp. 31-49.

[30] *Samson Agonistes,* II, 99-102.

[31] Ibid., I, 41.

[32] See John Donne, "Good Friday. Riding Westward."

[33] D. H. Lawrence, *The Escaped Cock,* ed. Gerald M. Lacy (Santa Barbara, California: Black Sparrow, 1978), p. 43.

[34] D. H. Lawrence, *Apocalypse,* with an introduction by Richard Aldington (New York: Viking Compass, 1966), p. 39.

[35] Denise Levertov, *The Sorrow Dance* (New York: New Directions, 1967), p. 30.

[36] D. H. Lawrence, *Studies in Classic American Literature* (New York: Viking, 1924), p. 191.

Merle R. Rubin (essay date 1981)

SOURCE: "'Not I, but the Wind That Blows Through Me': Shelleyan Aspects of Lawrence's Poetry," in *Texas Studies in Literature and Language,* Vol. 23, No. 1, Spring, 1981, pp. 102-22.

[*In the following essay, Rubin discusses resemblances between the poetry of Lawrence and Percy Bysshe Shelley.*]

Despite Lawrence's strenuous denials of influence, specific influences upon his poetry are clearly discernible. In addition to Whitman, Wordsworth, and Blake,[1] other influences were the King James Bible, the Nonconformist hymns of Lawrence's chapel youth, and the poetry of the Pre-Raphaelites, Swinburne, and Hardy. The early love poems are faintly Pre-Raphaelite in their vivid attention to color and detail and more than faintly Swinburnian in their plangent use of small, simple words ("sweet," "cool," "pain," "ache," "darkness," "moon," "sun"). This strain in turn is traceable to the major tradition of English Romanticism,[2] and more specifically a certain aspect of it reverts to Shelley, who was among the first of Wordsworth's heirs to uncover in the Wordsworthian landscape the sexual elements which Wordsworth, for the most part, conceals. Lawrence himself speculates that fear of the body drove English painters—with the exception of Blake—into the realm of landscape,[3] but he does not evolve a parallel argument for English poets and certainly does not—as perhaps he should—credit Shelley with this kind of Blakean discovery. On the contrary, he includes him in his list of "escape artists."

Lawrence's view of Shelley is complex and revelatory. It reveals much about Lawrence, and it illuminates a significant, often neglected aspect of Shelley: what Lawrence calls his "maleness." But before proceeding to unravel the intricacies of this poetic relationship, we should dispel some of the lingering vague delusions which encumber our perceptions. There is a general impression that Lawrence hated Shelley, probably the result of the pronouncement on Shelley made by Mark Rampion, the character in Huxley's *Point Counter Point* who is based on Lawrence:

> "Oh, exquisite and all that. But what a bloodless kind of slime inside! No blood, no real bones and bowels. Only pulp and a white juice. . . . he was always pretending . . . that the world wasn't really the world, but either heaven or hell. And that going to bed with women wasn't really going to bed with them, but just two angels holding hands. . . . *So* spiritual. And all the time he was just a young schoolboy with a sensual itch like anybody else's."[4]

Rampion's objections certainly sound quite Lawrentian, and when he goes on to criticize "To a Skylark" for disembodying the bird to whom it is addressed, one might readily assume this to be Lawrence's verdict on that poem. In fact, however, Lawrence cites the first stanza of this poem for its wonderful "sense of conflict contained within a reconciliation." Far from denouncing Shelley as the author of some "dreadful lie in the soul," Lawrence proceeds to praise this stanza for its balance and truthfulness:

> Shelley wishes to say, the skylark is a pure, untrammelled spirit, a pure motion. But the very "Bird thou never wert" admits that the skylark *is* . . . a bird, a concrete, momentary thing. If the line ran, "Bird thou never art," that would spoil it all. Shelley wishes to say, the song is poured out of heaven: but "or near it," he admits. There is the perfect relation between heaven and earth. And the last line is the tumbling sound of a lark's singing, the real Two-in-One.[5]

So in fact, Lawrence credits Shelley with the ability to reveal the fullness of imaginative or spiritual power without losing sight of earthly limitations.

Unlike Rampion, then, Lawrence deeply admired Shelley and felt that his own poetry was linked with Shelley's. Even random remarks in his letters testify to this. Writing from Lerici in 1913, he recalls Shelley amid the buoyant waters,[6] describes himself as stunned by the subtlety of Shelley's meters,[7] and finds Shelley "a million thousand times more beautiful than Milton."[8] In a letter of 1916 thanking his correspondent for an edition of Swinburne, he says that Swinburne "is very like Shelley, full of philosophic spiritual realisation and revelation. . . . I put him with Shelley as our greatest poet."[9]

Lawrence's concern with revelation and the nature of creative processes animates his poetry and prose alike, and in the three areas, "religion, work, love" which he says "link us on to an eternity,"[10] Shelley's poetry provides him with vital insights into the realms of "singing," "influencing," and "being," while Shelley's person functions as a kind of exemplary figure of lyric inspiration. The Skylark sings, the West Wind (like the "winds of light" in *Adonais*) influences, and the rhapsodist of *Epipsychidion* explores the extent of love. And, like Lawrence, Shelley often blends the three areas in a single quest: a kind of sacramental vision of profane love, in which, we might say, two diverse meanings of the word "sacral" converge.

As a person, or rather as a poetic figure, Shelley (or the Shelley of Shelley's poetry) emerges for Lawrence as a being so "transcendently male" as to be a kind of angelic abstraction, surpassing even Spenser in degree of "pure maleness." For Lawrence there is no being in the world so transcendently male as Shelley: "He is phenomenal. The rest of us have bodies which contain the male and the female. If we were so singled out as Shelley, we should not belong to life, as he did not. . . . But it were impious to wish to be like the angels."[11] Shelley is here perceived as too male, too angelic to be quite human, a perception which seems to contradict Lawrence's other insight about the Skylark's combination of heaven and earth. Yet, like that master of exquisite balance, of a poised "tumbling," this angelic, male Shelley arouses emulous love as well as a kind of disdainful incredulity. Writing of the poet who "never lived," but "transcended life," Lawrence insists, "we do not want to transcend life, since we are of life." That is to say that we (Lawrence and his reader?) do not expect or want Lawrence to be like Shelley. Lawrence promises to shun such excessive spirituality, yet at the same time believes that a certain kind of "imbalance" is an essential component of the poetic constitution:

> A man who is well balanced between male and female . . . is, as a rule, happy, easy to mate, easy to satisfy, and content to exist. It is only a disproportion, or a dissatisfaction, which makes the man struggle into articulation. And the articulation is of two sorts, the cry of desire or the cry of realisation, the effort to prolong the sense of satisfaction, to prolong the moment of consummation.[12]

Thus, Lawrence's apparent irony at the expense of the spiritual Shelley is, as we might have suspected, in part an expression of envy. This ambivalence of feeling toward a poet who is in many ways his precursor may also help explain other inconsistencies in his expressed views. For instance, in the same **"Study of Thomas Hardy"** where later he praises "To a Skylark," he first reads the poem in a different spirit, berating Shelley for insisting on "the bodilessness of beauty, when we cannot know of any save embodied beauty."[13] But as we have seen, Lawrence knows Shelley better than this. "If the whistling skylark were a spirit, then we should all wish to be spirits. Which were impious and flippant," he concludes. Yet even here Lawrence (like Shelley) uses the subjunctive "were," and if "Bird thou never wert" marks the fine line between doubt and credence, wish and reality in Shelley's poem, Lawrence's "were" indicates his healthy skepticism about his own judgment of Shelley.

The burden of Lawrence's poem **"Manifesto"** is the poet's desire to be, if anything, more Shelleyan than Shelley:

> then I shall be glad, I shall not be confused with her,
> I shall be cleared, distinct, single as if burnished
>   in silver,
>
>   . . . . .
>
> two of us, unutterably distinguished, and in
>   unutterable conjunction.
> Then we shall be free, freer than angels, ah, perfect.[14]

If this postcoital, wished for state of being differs notably from Shelley's image of "the wells / Which boil under our being's inmost cells, / The fountains of our deepest life, . . . / Confused in Passion's golden purity" (ll. 568-71), the difference is in Lawrence's repudiation of love's confusion. Of the two states, Shelley's is really the more physical, elevating coition above separation. The lovers

in *Epipsychidion* "touch, mingle, are transfigured"; Lawrence's transfiguration occurs only after each lover has perished on the other's darkness, or in other words, understood that, *contra* Shelley, two persons or two passions cannot become "One."

Why does Lawrence reject the Shelleyan model of love? The simplest answer might be that he finds his own experience in love different from, if not indeed opposite to, the Shelleyan idea and so is merely describing what he has found to be true in his own case. But why, then, cast such an account in Shelleyan terms at all? And why, of all things, wish to be like the angels? Certainly the closing lines of the poem deliberately recall Shelley, with "music" and "sheer utterance" issuing out of the unknown, "the lightning and the rainbow appearing in us unbidden, unchecked." "We shall not look before and after. / We shall *be,* now," he continues. Once again Shelley is more "realistic," admitting that we do indeed "look before and after," that we cannot be as unencumbered as the skylark however much we might wish it. Lawrence more strenuously insists upon being where the skylark seems to be, so much so that his last line ("We, the mystic NOW.") veers toward the banality of the Living Theater, saved only by the poised opposition of what "we shall know in full" and how it will issue "straight out of the unknown." The "unknown" is darkness, the Other, whatever is not available to mental fingering, Being, perhaps, as opposed to consciousness. What "we shall know in full," however, is experience itself. The contrast is between two modes of consciousness: deliberation or reflection, on the one hand, and sensory or any other kind of perception, on the other.

This knowledge, rooted in perception and sensation, akin to inspiration, is symbolized by things that are utterly transitory: "the lightning and the rainbow," annunciatory flashes almost totally Lawrentian in origin. Or perhaps these "ambassadors" are Shelley's messengers, "angels of rain and lightning," further internalized, wedded to the music of the skylark and emanating from within. The manner in which they appear "in us unbidden, unchecked," recalls the images and ideas of creation in Shelley's *Defence of Poetry:* "the mind in creation is as a fading coal, which some invisible influence, like an inconstant wind, awakens to transitory brightness; this power arises from within, like the colour of a flower which fades and changes as it is developed, and the conscious portions of our natures are unprophetic either of its approach or its departure." Subtle, powerful, controlled, Shelley's conception seems to include Lawrence's understanding of the role of the unconscious in the process of inspiration and creation. Thus, Lawrence's attachment to the unknown, to nothingness, to darkness can be considered in the context of the Romantic struggle with Cartesian dualism.

When Lawrence expresses his idea of the creative process, he is less controlled, but never far from the poet who is, in his eyes, the lyric poet proper:

It seems to me a purely lyric poet gives himself, right down to his sex, to his mood, utterly and abandonedly, whirls himself round . . . till he spontaneously combusts into verse. He has nothing that goes on, no passion, only a few intense moods, separate like odd stars, and when each has burned away, he must die. It is no accident that Shelley got drowned—he was always trying to drown himself—it was his last mood.[15]

This description, offered by Lawrence as a salutary contrast to the activities of "half-lyric" poets, such as his contemporary, Richard Middleton, envisions "sheer utterance" as a relentlessly centrifugal divestment, a kind of kenosis. As Shelley is seen as the perfect type of this lyricism, perfectly able to give and to give up, Middleton is seen as an example of the blocked poet:

I think he always felt some obstruction. I think one has as it were to fuse ones [sic] physical and mental self right down, to produce good art. And there was some of him that wouldn't fuse—like some dross, that hindered him, that he couldn't grip and reduce with passion. And so he hated himself. Perhaps if he could have found a woman to love, and who loved him, that would have done it, and he would have been pure. He was always impure. I can't explain the word impure, because I don't know what it means.[16]

"Find a woman," incidentally, was the advice Lawrence and Frieda gave E. M. Forster; perhaps it was a standard remedy of theirs. But what Lawrence means by impurity here is anything in the self that obstructs creation. Shelley speaks of the "unwilling dross that checks the spirit's flight," those recalcitrant elements of the self that impede poetry. ("Thus poetry, and the principle of self, of which money is the visible incarnation, are the God and Mammon of the world.") Blake's natural selfhood is perhaps yet another version of this same unfusible dross: self-consciousness which leads to crippling self-hatred and the often corresponding tendency toward selfishness or self-aggrandizement. These, certainly, are the traits of Lawrence's mechanical men, trapped in the circular world of their revolving egos, like cogs in a machine.[17]

Escape from the vicious circle of selfhood is traditionally deemed possible through love, whether it be eros, caritas, or agape. Lawrence's triad of religion, work, and love is also a grouping of three activities which operate analogously. Additionally, Lawrence's writings suggest that "coming through" in the area of love is a prerequisite for achieving the desired effect in one's work, although I think we should be careful not to assume that he is proposing correspondences as causes and effects, simply because they are not derived arbitrarily. Outside the novels the most explicit record of Lawrence's explorations of love may be found in, *Look! We Have Come Through!* and a number of the poems in *Birds, Beasts and Flowers*. By the time we reach a poem like **"Tortoise Shout,"** however, we see the emergence of a more purely mythic approach to the question, which recalls in substance, if not in style, Aristophanes' discourse on the origins of sexual love in the *Symposium*.[18]

More personal in the sense that confession may be deemed more personal than any kind of mythopoeia, however individualistic or even idiosyncratic, is the testimony of *Look! We Have Come Through!* This story of "a man during the crisis of manhood," as Lawrence describes it in his "Argument," is basically an erotic history, a group of poems which he urges the reader to consider as forming a single "organic" whole. Precedents for such an enterprise are legion, Dante's *Vita Nuova* and Shelley's *Epipsychidion* being only two of the most obvious examples. *Epipsychidion* is a close ancestor. It certainly is the closest approach of its kind to a single organic whole; it is an erotic history, a confession, a celebration, a proposal (or proposition); yet it proceeds by fits and starts in an effort to prolong poetic utterance into a kind of endless rapture.

Just what do these poets, to use Lawrence's phrase, come through? One aim of sexual love is to break down the isolating barriers between people. Death and time are perhaps the ultimate barriers, but the most basic walls are our identities: both the limits of any single consciousness as well as the walls of one's own skin. Lawrence believes that the man and woman in his poems come to "some sort of conclusion"; indeed, in the original edition of *Look! We Have Come Through!* he goes so far as to say "they transcend into some condition of blessedness." Before attempting to understand if and how they accomplish this, let us regard the conclusion of Shelley's poem.

As Shelley and Emily are united, becoming one "spirit within two frames," sharing "one immortality, / And one annihilation," language itself seems to disintegrate with them: words, "chains of lead," fall downward as thought files upward, and the poet himself is left panting (a desperate kind of aspiration), sinking (his mere person cannot sustain such an effort), trembling (he shudders at extinction, yet quivers with life), and at last expiring. To expire is, of course, to die: if "die" held a double meaning for poets of the Renaissance, Shelley's term "expire" here conveys its second meaning even more strongly. Not only does it evoke ejaculation, but to expire, or breathe out, is also to perform the active counterpart of the more passive condition of having been inspired. Though the lovers share "one annihilation," Shelley's last word before his little envoi is "expire," and so instead of mere decimation, we are left with something less absolute and far more suggestive. Rather than sexual love as a form of annihilation, we see annihilation recast as a form of love. But words fail, even at their most suggestive, and it seems as if the failure of words tuned to so ethereal a pitch insures the poem's success, just as the transcendent quality of the love is heightened by the extinction of the lovers' identities.

Against Shelley's pattern of endless aspiration, the main thrust of Lawrence's idea of love is based upon an attempt to turn in some other direction. This he achieves by admitting hate as well as love into a vision which invokes separation even more strongly than it desires union. His wife believes in their union: "she thinks we are all of one piece. It is painfully untrue," he would tell her. Otherness is realized and incorporated into the sexual experience:

> I want her to touch me at last, ah, on the root and
>   quick of my darkness
> and perish on me, as I have perished on her.
>
> . . . . .
>
> when it has struck home to her, like a death, "this
>   is *him!*"
> she has no part in it, no part whatever,
> it is the terrible *other,*
> when she knows the fearful *other flesh,* ah,
>   darkness unfathomable and fearful, contiguous
>   and concrete,[19]

And on he proceeds until they become "freer than angels." But in no way has he evaded or altered the sense of extinction ("when she passes away as I have passed away"). He wants her to experience or know what he has known, as he says in the previous section: "What remains in me, is to be known even as I know. / I know her now: or perhaps, I know my own limitation against her." The other, perhaps, cannot be known—not as it knows itself and feels itself to be. It is known only as that which begins where the "I" leaves off. If she is to be more than the dark ground against which his "limitation" is outlined, then she must know as well as be known, or in other words, be a reciprocal "thou" to his "I." But what does an "I" or "thou" experience? A plunging "over the brink . . . upon sheer hard extinction," according to Lawrence, who says "I have come, as it were, not to know," or who has certainly abandoned one kind of knowing for another. Having "ceased from knowing," he claims to have "surpassed" himself. As in *Epipsychidion,* words become extremely suggestive here, making it hard to determine whether death and limits are the final kind of knowing or if knowledge of otherness is a new heaven and new earth. The problem is not deliberate obscurantism, but a genuine difficulty faced by poets seeking to conceptualize experience:

> It is a kind of death which is not death.
> It is a going a little beyond the bounds.
> How can one speak, where there is a dumbness on
>   one's mouth?

Both poets face the problem of how we perceive, understand, describe transcendence, even in its simplest sense. Or how can one know anything outside oneself? In Lawrence, transcendence has been made to reappear in the guise of transgression—as the crossing of a boundary. In order to feel one has gone "beyond," it is necessary to have felt the "definite, inviolable limitation" of a boundary. Lawrence seems to be suggesting that only limitation can save transcendence from collapsing back into nothingness.

Similarly, his insistence that he and she are "two and distinct" is not a vote for sexual equality (although it speaks against the rabid feminist view of Lawrence as a male chauvinist), but far more basically, an outcry against solipsism. The poet's horror of that state is vividly conveyed in Sections III and IV of **"New Heaven and Earth,"** which describe the "maniacal horror" of a world where "everything was me, I knew it all already": the creator regarding his creation regards himself and the lover kissing the woman he loves kisses himself. Lawrence's outcry indirectly evokes the whole tradition of the Solitary in Wordsworth, Byron, Shelley, and others, but finds a more immediate ancestor in Whitman, whose vast capacity for identifying himself with what he met provoked even in Whitman, at certain crucial moments, the sudden revulsion most vividly portrayed in "A Hand-Mirror" and "As I Ebb'd with the Ocean of Life." A more distant ancestor may be a figure like Blake's Urizen, the creator of a universe bounded absolutely by the limits of his own mentality. Closer still, perhaps, is the speaker of **"The Crystal Cabinet,"** who "bent to Kiss the lovely Maid / And found a threefold kiss returned." Trapped in a mirror world, here not of rationality but of sexuality, striving to seize the inmost form, he bursts the cabinet, which cannot sustain "ardor fierce" or "hands of flame," the true desire to touch what is other or the sheer distinctness of separate identities.

"New Heaven and Earth" concludes after the poet has touched the familiar flank of his wife, but suddenly and happily, found it strange, other, not-himself. Prior to this discovery of a new land, however, he has explored a phantasmagoric world of murder, war, and death, all the more phantasmagoric for being, in fact, the world in which we live. The real world and the one we conceive coincide: only by blotting out the deathly selfhood does the poet touch the freshness of a new birth, a resurrection. He finds himself "the same as before, yet unaccountably new." This idea of death and rebirth anticipates the later predominance of the theme in Lawrence's *Last Poems,* although a certain shrillness of tone present here and not heard in the death poems suggests that the discovery of a brave new world is still somewhat premature. Although Lawrence claims here that it is enough to have found the green new continent of his wife, two poems later in **"Manifesto"** he aims at more: that she become the discoverer of him.

This returns us to the problematic passage noted earlier, the core of which is "I want her to touch me . . . on the root and quick of my darkness / and perish on me, as I have perished on her." Here and in the following three poems, she does not actually do so; all is poised in a kind of waiting, and indeed the last poem, **"Craving for Spring,"** is written almost entirely in the future tense. Is Lawrence dealing with a circumstantial problem in his marriage or treating a more basic problem of ontological limitations? It is hard to say. This is the point at which the question of Lawrence's sexual proclivities is often raised, but those who have tackled it have come to conclusions at best only partially illuminating and at worst downright misleading. Initially viewed as a "priest of love" and, in some instances, as a sort of male maenad of unrestrained eroticism, Lawrence has also been called a puritan and even a prude. It is by now generally agreed that he was neither a prude nor a libertine, but something can be gained from considering him in the context of puritanism, a tradition which includes, after all, Spenser (curious artificer of the chaste and the perverse), Milton (champion of true marriage and, hence, of rightful divorce), Blake (who sought the lineaments of gratified desire, but distrusted the allurements of Beulah), and Shelley (advocate of free love who was shocked at Byron's promiscuity, defender of the strange customs of the Greeks, which, he knew, could not have included sodomy).

The complexity and seriousness of Lawrence's attitudes toward sex are very much in keeping with this tradition, and to assert that his profound interest in these matters bespeaks impotence, mother fixation, sublimated or thwarted homosexuality, an oral or an anal nature, or the class conflict is to miss the point and to reveal only one's own biases. As Lawrence himself says in **Psychoanalysis and the Unconscious,** to label every feeling, to assume a hierarchy of erotic stages is a mistake; it is a sin against the complexity of human feelings. Offering in place of Freud's mechanistic model his own fourfold myth of human development, Lawrence says, one does not have to believe this, the implication being that he at least is honest enough to present his myth *as* a myth. Random reading of Lawrence's work can provide evidence for almost anything,[20] but precisely this courage to expose his secrets constitutes his genius. Let the explicator beware then, not because literature is an inviolate preserve but because the instruments of such analysis are too small and crude for a vision as broad and complex as Lawrence's.

Not Lawrence's sexual proclivities, but the relationship of Lawrence to that tradition which emphasizes the importance of the sexual act is worth our efforts to determine. The diagnosis of sexual proclivities is highly inexact both in method and terminology, and the symptoms and impulses it purports to uncover are not finalities. The Romantic tradition in and against which Lawrence works as a poet provides a more suitable context for analysis, for it is the tradition he draws on when he envisions sexual love as an ultimate form of personal interchange, rather in the way that poetry is an ultimate form of linguistic communication. And as we see in Shelley's work, the two forms are closely interlinked.[21] In a single "moment" of perhaps aeonic duration, the lovers Laon and Cythna are united, "all thought, all sense, all feeling, into one / Unutterable power." Whatever this mysterious power may be, Shelley knows it as that which inspires, causes to tremble, and finally, makes sing. Poetic, erotic, and religious inspiration in Shelley's eyes are "one," or at the very least, analogous, a conclusion similar to Lawrence's linkage of the three in his letters of 1908.

By this, his twenty-third year, Lawrence has lost his faith in religion, yet still possesses a remarkably religious temperament, like Shelley's, at once skeptical and prophetic. Lawrence's sense of his vocation includes a deep awareness of the formidable limitations all but blocking his quest: "As true as I am born, I have the capacity for doing something delicately and well. As sure as I am poor, I am being roughened down to a blunt blade; I am

already rusting; I will not take the trouble to polish myself."[22] Where Shelley (aristocratic as well as angelic) can view what blocks his quest as "th' unwilling dross that checks [the spirit's] flight," which renders him, at worst, a man chained and bowed by a heavy weight of hours, Lawrence struggles with additional constraints. Is he a worthy instrument for the vatic Word? What kind of instrument is he anyway? Although he seems to abhor the "roughness" foisted upon him by the relative poverty of his circumstances, elsewhere in the same letter to Blanche Jennings, he has this to say about Mrs. Dax's objections to his style of writing: "I must flaw my English if I am to be anything but a stilted, starched parson. How can I be wilful and whimsical in good English? But wilful and whimsical I ought not to be, according to Mrs. Dax,—in a novel. How can a woman whose feelings flow in such straight canals follow me in my threadings, my meanderings, my spurts and my sleepings!"[23]

Yet Lawrence is aware of some risk in asserting his originality in such a way: "I am voluntarily wearing off the fine edge of my character. Had I been rich, I should have been something Ruskinian (—blessed poverty!). Now I shall be nothing—and am content."[24] "Ruskinian" here seems to imply a sensibility so susceptible to influence as to be capable of critical or reflective (secondary) effort only and not of the more original, self-assertive activity of creation.[25] Rather than be secondary, Lawrence claims he would prefer to be "nothing." As he elsewhere applies erotic terms to aesthetic matters, here he infuses a new (aesthetic) meaning into seemingly socioeconomic terminology. This is hardly surprising because for Lawrence life means his life as a poet, artist, and prophet. It is somewhat ironic that the hectic energy with which he pursued his vocation has given rise to the notion that Lawrence is first and foremost a "vitalist," for his vitalism is actually a concern for the vitality of art. Like Nietzsche (another misunderstood prophet who often and rightly reminds his readers that he is a "philologist"), Lawrence tends to assail all life which is not in accord with his aesthetics and all art which fails to subsume the whole of life's powers and complexities.

But the willfully assumed roughness, the poverty, the labyrinthine "meanderings" of the soul may also result in the poet's blocking himself and besmirching his authentic intentions. In the same letter Lawrence also remarks of his soul, "I am choking it with mud and stones; I am cooling it, or people are cooling it for me, by making it work, when it doesn't want, and for dirt." Reflected here, perhaps, are the sentiments of the poet who writes:

> So, shall I take
> My last dear fuel of life to heap on my soul
> And kindle my will to a flame that shall consume
> Their dross of indifference; and take the toll
> Of their insults in punishment?—I will not!—[26]

Rather than care whether his pupils "can write / A description of a dog, or if they can't," Lawrence has other concerns for his "soul." The poet's soul is the arena for what Lawrence calls "the conflict of Love and Law," a process he discusses in this passage from his richly suggestive and somewhat misnamed essay, **"A Study of Thomas Hardy"**:

> Each work of art has its own form, which has no relation to any other form. When a young painter studies an old master, he studies, not the form, that is an abstraction which does not exist: he studies maybe the method . . . but he studies chiefly to understand how the old great artist suffered in himself the conflict of Love and Law, and brought them to a reconciliation . . . so that he, the young artist, may understand his own soul and gain a reconciliation between the aspiration and the resistant.[27]

As "the aspiration and the resistant" recall Shelley's contending forces: imaginative flight and reality's "unwilling dross," so do the terms "Love" and "Law" echo the Shelleyan pair, "love and life," used in *Adonais* to describe the same phenomenon:

> . . . . When lofty thought
> Lifts a young heart above its mortal lair,
> And love and life contend in it, for what
> Shall be its earthly doom, the dead live there
> And move like winds of light on dark and stormy air.

This stanza, which begins "The splendours of the firmament of time / May be eclipsed but are extinguished not," points to a theory of poetic influence. The "stars" which are past poets not only have an "appointed height," but their presence cannot be evaded. Nor are these stars simply forms of light; they are *winds* of light, actively inspiring forces. Whether or not all inspiration is entirely composed of this starry influx,[28] past poetry seems to be an inevitable part of it.

In his essay of 1928, **"Chaos and Poetry,"** Lawrence again deals with this issue and also displays an intriguing confusion about the components of inspiration. Poets, he says, fear and desire "chaos," but Lawrence will not or cannot say if "chaos" is simply disorder, or natural wildness, or the sublime fluency of a great work of art.

> Man must wrap himself in a vision, make a house of apparent form and stability, fixity. In his terror of chaos he begins by putting up an umbrella between himself and the everlasting whirl. . . . Bequeathed to his descendents, the umbrella becomes a dome, a vault, and men at last begin to feel that something is wrong. . . . Then comes a poet, enemy of convention, and makes a slit in the umbrella; and lo! the glimpse of chaos is a vision, a window to the sun. But after a while, getting used to the vision, and not liking the genuine draught from chaos, commonplace man daubs a simulacrum of the window that opens onto chaos, and patches the umbrella. . . .

> This is the history of poetry in our era. Someone sees Titans in the wild air of chaos, and the Titan becomes a wall between succeeding generations and the chaos they should have inherited. The wild sky moved and sang. Even that became a great umbrella between mankind and the sky of fresh air; then it became a painted vault, a fresco.[29]

Here we may wish to interrupt long enough to ask just where the draft of chaos originates. The wild sky, the Titans in the air seem to have been made static by those who have tried to depict them, while a poet or an artist is a man who cuts an opening rather than one who paints what he sees. Yet the visionary chaos contains Titans, which are certainly forms, and in this sense "chaos" is the magnitude of past art. The umbrella which keeps us from chaos, Lawrence also calls a "vision," but so too is the glimpse of chaos "a vision" and "window."

Continuing, Lawrence describes the "umbrella" as having become so big and so full of tight, hard patches and plasters that it can no longer be slit:

> If it were slit, the rent would no more be a vision, it would only be an outrage. We should dab it over at once, to match the rest.

> So the umbrella is absolute. And so the yearning for chaos becomes a nostalgia. And this will go on till some terrific wind blows the umbrella to ribbons, and much of mankind to oblivion. The rest will shiver in the midst of chaos. For chaos is always there . . . no matter how we put up umbrellas of visions.

> What about the poets, then, at this juncture? They reveal the inward desire of mankind . . . the desire for chaos, and the fear of chaos. The desire for chaos is the breath of their poetry. The fear of chaos is in their parade of forms and techniques. Poetry is made of words, they say. So they blow bubbles of sound and image, which soon burst with the breath of longing for chaos, which fills them. But the poetasters can make pretty shiny bubbles for the Christmas tree, which never burst, because there is no breath of poetry in them, but they remain till we drop them.[30]

Ostensibly, Lawrence is describing how a work of art is perceived by succeeding generations: beheld in its infancy as a glimpse of wild, uncharted chaos, but later viewed as a convenient, then conventional, and finally clichéd, pattern. This is the ennui produced by culture: a reader may find Wordsworth conventional not because that reader has been poring over "I Wandered Lonely as a Cloud" for the past century or so but because his exposure to the multifold aftereffects of Wordsworthian-influenced poetry blinds him to the originality of the original. The aspiring artist, with his own interest in new creation, suffers more acutely than the reader. Although Lawrence writes as if the only problem were for the poet to get some fresh air, his complicated idea of the umbrella-vault-sky bespeaks a deeper anxiety about tradition. The apocalyptic violence he so casually summons forth, with its powerful imagery of ripping and tearing, is similar to that of Yeats, who found himself in a similar predicament of belatedness.

Problematic in this respect is the statement beginning: "But after a while, getting used to the vision, and not liking the genuine draught from chaos." This breezy assertion all but conceals a contradiction more difficult to resolve than the overt paradox the essay proposes (man's simultaneous desire and fear of chaos). For if man is "used to the vision," why is he disturbed by "the genuine draught from chaos"? Does the eye find customary prospects which chill the blood and nerves? Perhaps, but more likely, the "eye," in becoming "used to the vision" has already found a way of defending itself against the draft, already viewing previous visions as if they were commonplace.

The "fresh air," which ought to be each generation's inheritance, is the reviving breath of inspiration: Shelley's West Wind and Wordsworth's "correspondent breeze."[31] And, pragmatically, we could define "chaos" as the state which precedes creation and thus as the state into which the poet must descend prior to inventing the order of his own creation. Elsewhere in the essay, Lawrence says that absolute chaos is not human. But by identifying (a non-absolute?) chaos with "fresh air" and the "wild sky," he offers in place of absolute disorder a boundless heaven of Titans, Macbeth, and Wordsworthian primroses.[32] Human passions, the wilderness of nature, and the works of true poets are imbued with the same spirit. As the "eye" revises the vision, attempting to reduce the uncomfortable sublimity of inspiration (including past art), the poet continues to fear and desire this same wild breeze.

As expressed in the first ten lines of the **"Song of a Man Who Has Come Through,"** the wind that blows through him makes its way not only through the individual poet but also through the "chaos of the world." The wind is a chaotic force which imposes order, even on itself. In this poem Lawrence, like Shelley, seeks to become one with the afflatus or, at least, to contain it perfectly. For the poet to yield himself to and be borrowed by the wind is almost *the* Shelleyan stance; in assuming it Lawrence displays some interesting shifts of emphasis: he is especially concerned with being sufficiently "delicate" to bear the wind, yet not be overpowered by it or crushed against the rocks. Thus, he asks two questions: am I fine, delicate enough? and am I hard enough? The wind becomes for him "an exquisite chisel, a wedge-blade inserted," while the poet himself will be "the sheer tip of a wedge / Driven by invisible blows." The poet's stance is simultaneously male and female (or active and passive), more obviously so than in Shelley, because Lawrence stresses the axis of hard-soft, aggressive-receptive polarity more strongly than Shelley does. Yet the polarity exists in "Ode to the West Wind": "Thou / For whose path the Atlantic's level powers / Cleave themselves into chasms." Indeed, there is even an unidentified chisel.

Lawrence's images of hardness may seem to overcompensate for his fears about softness. "Hard" imagery is similarly characteristic of Yeats's middle period, while Nietzsche liked to proclaim that he philosophized with a hammer. Aside from impotence, prolonged virginity, and other personal explanations, there are subtler reasons for this late Romantic attitude: it compensates for what the poet (or philosopher) fears may be overreceptiveness and it helps to define individuality more distinctly. Lawrence's chief concern as expressed here is his fitness to be a vessel of the wind. Unquestionably, he feels the wind blowing through him, but he wonders whether he is fine enough to be its channel, strong enough to express what he feels. Shelley's poem expresses a more radical doubt, not about his fitness as a vessel but about the constancy and duration of the afflatus. Shelley does not worry about his personal or artistic abilities: "What if my leaves are falling like its own!" He wants only to continue to feel propelled: "If even / I were as in my boyhood, and could be / The comrade of thy wanderings over Heaven." But all too soon Shelley finds himself at the end of his quest: even in an early poem like *Alastor* (1815), the hero speeds daemonically toward a conclusion in which he is "quenched forever." For him, as for Wordsworth in the paradigm of loss set forth in the "Intimations" ode, inspiration is already on the wane as the task of writing begins. Thus, Shelley calls again to the wind, even as it is blowing around him, so that it will blow through him once again.

Lawrence more cautiously stations himself at the beginning of his quest. In his later poems, facing the new boundary of death, he still regards it as the *beginning* of a voyage. The **"Song of a Man Who Has Come Through"** is above all a promise. Just as the poet pledges to be a fit instrument, to "blur no whisper, spoil no expression," he is providentially interrupted by a knocking from without. Are clock time and the constraints of the quotidian world reasserting their claims here, as De Quincey remarks of the knocking in *Macbeth* and as Coleridge implies about all interruption? Or, as Lawrence more pointedly asks, does someone wish to do him harm? Is he now to be struck down just as he is most exposed, most extended, most vulnerable, suggestively caught just as he is about to come forth as a poet, as well as in flagrante delicto?

"No, no," we are told, "it is the three strange angels," and they are to be admitted. The interruption is discovered to be a sign of annunciation. The angels are "strange," outside, unknown, apparently new to Lawrence; yet he familiarly knows them as "*the* three strange angels," the messengers who always appear to announce a birth but whose appearance is always a surprise, even if one knows how to interpret it. Poised thus between expectation and surprise in the achievement of a kind of balanced imbalance, Lawrence has come through to what turns out to be yet another beginning, a stance not so much Shelleyan as Whitmanian. This is the Whitman who is always starting out from Paumonok, or from the cradle, or down the open road, and it is to him that Lawrence turns in search of an alternate poetic model. It is almost as if Lawrence comes through Shelley to arrive at Whitman (an odd version of the biological doctrine "ontogeny recapitulates phylogeny"), although it is probably more accurate to say that Lawrence misinterprets both his models in order to create a place for himself.

In this context we may wish to examine Lawrence's proclamation of a new poetry in the Introduction to the American edition of his *New Poems:*

> This is the unrestful, ungraspable poetry of the sheer present, poetry whose very permanency lies in its wind-like transit. Whitman's is the best poetry of this kind. Without beginning and without end, without any base and pediment, it sweeps past forever, like a wind that is forever in passage, and unchainable. Whitman truly looked before and after. But he did not sigh for what is not.[33]

In part, Lawrence defends *vers libre,* whose function he contrasts to more symmetrical forms, which he calls poetry of the beginning and of the end, where "the finality and the perfection are conveyed in exquisite form: the perfect symmetry, the rhythm which returns upon itself like a dance where the hands link and loosen and link for the supreme moment of the end. Perfected bygone moments, perfected moments in the glimmering futurity, these are the treasured gem-like lyrics of Shelley and Keats."[34] But is only Whitman's poetry windlike? Lawrence's portrayal of Whitman covertly employs the language of Shelley, while his picture of Shelley seems an attempt to remove him from the direct line of influence and place him in a category more remote.

The two "gem-like" lyricists also figure indirectly at the opening of the essay. Just before he is mentioned by name, Shelley appears as the lark of morning, the singer of the future who "may sound sad, but with the lovely lapsing sadness that is almost a swoon of hope." (Cf. *Prometheus Unbound:* "to hope till Hope creates / From its own wreck the thing it contemplates.") Contrasted with the voice of the future, "exquisite and ethereal," is the nightingale's song of the past, "rich, magnificent," a "triumph" that is "a paean, but a death-paean." This, surely, is Keats, although Lawrence does not say so. Instead he refers back to the two germinal poems of Western literature: the powerfully nostalgic *Iliad* and the painfully aspirant *Odyssey,* as he characterizes them. He then seems to suggest that all poetry is song of the horizon, the past or the future:

> Our birds sing on the horizons. They sing out of the blue, beyond us, or out of the quenched night. . . . Only the poor, shrill, tame canaries whistle while we talk. The wild birds begin before we are awake, or as we drop into dimness out of waking. Our poets sit by the gateways, some by the east, some by the west. As we arrive and as we go out our hearts surge with response. But whilst we are in the midst of life, we do not hear them.

What station could be more transitional than a gateway? What horizon could be less fixed than this bird-haunted region of liminal consciousness? But no sooner does Lawrence discuss the lyrics of Shelley and Keats than he suddenly announces the existence of yet another kind of poetry compared to the plasmic, vibrating quality of which all else (Homer, Shelley, Keats) seems static. Blooming like the living tissue of a rose, this poetry of

mutation becomes for Lawrence the "supreme" kind of poetry, truest to the "ever-present" flux that is life itself. Whitman is hailed as progenitor of this mode and praised for his ability to put into his work the quivering mystery of the *"pulsating, carnal self."* We "fear and respect" him because he is "so near the quick." This tribute to Whitman is rather like Shelley's to the skylark.

Lawrence reserves his criticism of Whitman for another occasion, and it is amusing to set against his "holy dread" of the Whitmanian mystery the insouciant treatment accorded the Singer of the Open Road in *Studies in Classic American Literature:* "As soon as Walt *knew* a thing, he assumed a One Identity with it. If he knew that an Eskimo sat in a kyak, immediately there was Walt being little and yellow and greasy, sitting in a kyak."[35] Whether or not this is fair to Whitman (or to the Eskimo) need not concern us here. What we recognize is the gesture of repudiation. As when granting Shelley's ability to accomplish what he set out to do, Lawrence is quick to insist that Shelley's goal cannot be Lawrence's; in the case of Whitman, Lawrence applauds his profound understanding of the balance needed between sympathy and individualism, but castigates him for failing to live up to the exigencies of his own credo. "Walt" is seen as a poet who falls victim to the temptation of identification; by identifying himself with everything else, Whitman throbs with a ceaseless, automatic "love" more like the unfeeling hum of a motor than the natural ebb and flow of passion's tide.

Lawrence's transformations of the Whitmanian mode (which can be observed in *Birds, Beasts and Flowers*) involve his emulation of traits like apostrophe and the incantatory, expansive use of free verse form, as well as his counter-Whitmanian insistence upon the otherness, the miraculous strangeness and unassimilable details of the objects he addresses and describes so attentively. This critique of Whitman in some ways parallels his critique of Shelley, for what Lawrence brings to the Shelleyan mode of love poetry is a concentration upon the recalcitrant, unassimilable aspects of sexuality.

Yet there are hazards in accepting Lawrence (or any other poet) only at his own estimation, as there are hazards in coming to hasty conclusions on the intricate matter of interpoetic relationships. Lawrence's characterization of Shelley is as much a beautiful fictive covering as it is a discovery or insight, while Lawrence's expressed image of his own work as plasmic and instantaneous may be undercut slightly—and enriched greatly—by such a poem as **"Fidelity,"** in which he seems to abandon flower for gem, only to recreate the gem as a kind of slow flower.

Lawrence's **Last Poems,** although beyond the scope of this essay, are continued evidence of Shelley's influence and Lawrence's ability to transform it. Particularly Shelleyan is the **"Ship of Death,"** while **"Lucifer"** recalls not only Shelley but Swinburne and Meredith. When we consider how the resplendent Romantic larks and nightingales of Shelley and Keats have tended to engender their ironic opposites, from Yeats's uncharacteristically "brawling" sparrow and Hardy's "little ball of feather and bone" to Frost's harshly plaintive "Oven Bird," we can appreciate just how remarkably expansive Lawrence's **"Phoenix"** truly is.

NOTES

[1] See D. H. Lawrence, *The Complete Poems of D. H. Lawrence,* ed. Vivian de Sola Pinto and F. Warren Roberts (New York: Viking, 1967), pp. 1-21 (hereafter cited as *Poems*), and Harold Bloom, "Lawrence, Eliot, Blackmur, and the Tortoise," reprinted in his *The Ringers in the Tower* (Chicago: Univ. of Chicago Press, 1971), pp. 197-204.

[2] See also Colin Campbell Clarke, *River of Dissolution: D. H. Lawrence and English Romanticism* (London: Routledge & Kegan Paul, 1969); Sandra Gilbert, *Acts of Attention: The Poems of D. H. Lawrence* (Ithaca: Cornell Univ. Press, 1972); Edward Lucie-Smith, "The Poetry of D. H. Lawrence—With a Glance at Shelley," in *D. H. Lawrence: Novelist, Poet, Prophet,* ed. Stephen Spender (New York: Harper & Row, 1973), pp. 224-33.

[3] D. H. Lawrence, *Selected Literary Criticism,* ed. Anthony Beal (New York: Viking, 1966), p. 64 (hereafter cited as *Criticism*).

[4] Aldous Huxley, *Point Counter Point* (New York: Harper & Row, 1928), pp. 119-20. It is interesting to juxtapose DHL's letter to Huxley written in October 1928 in which he says, "your Rampion is the most boring character in the book—a gas bag. Your attempt at intellectual sympathy! It's all rather disgusting, and I feel like a badger that has its hole on Wimbledon Common and trying not to be caught." Indeed, the entire letter is insightful about Huxley's book. See also Lawrence's response in poetic form: "I Am in a Novel," *Poems,* p. 489.

[5] *Criticism,* p. 187.

[6] D. H. Lawrence, *The Collected Letters of DHL,* ed. Harry T. Moore (New York: Viking, 1962), p. 231. Moore's edition is being superseded by the Cambridge edition edited by James T. Boulton. I cite letters from the latest available edition.

[7] *Letters* (Moore), pp. 244-45.

[8] *Letters* (Moore), p. 253.

[9] *Letters* (Moore), p. 474.

[10] *The Letters of D. H. Lawrence,* ed. James T. Boulton (Cambridge: Cambridge Univ. Press, 1979), I, 62.

[11] *Criticism,* p. 71.

[12] *Criticism,* p. 71.

[13] *Criticism,* p. 71.

[14] *Poems,* p. 267.

[15] *Letters* (Moore), p. 251.

[16] *Letters* (Moore), p. 251.

[17] See the poems beginning with "What Then Is Evil?" *Poems,* p. 712: "Oh, in the world of things / the wheel is the first principle of evil. / But in the world of the soul of man / there, and there alone lies the pivot of pure evil / only in the soul of man, when it pivots upon the ego."

[18] Geoffrey Hartman notes DHL's revival of the Platonic archetype in "Marvell, St. Paul, and the Body of Hope," *Beyond Formalism* (New Haven: Yale Univ. Press, 1970), p. 171, n. 33.

[19] Unless otherwise noted the quotations that follow are from the poem "Manifesto," *Poems,* pp. 262-68.

[20] Daniel A. Weiss, *Oedipus in Nottingham: D. H. Lawrence* (Seattle: Univ. of Washington Press, 1963), for example, finds evidence of nursing fantasy. Jeffrey Meyers, "D. H. Lawrence and Homosexuality," in Spender, p. 146, argues that DHL, like Birkin, "never really moves beyond homosexuality. He merely substitutes anal marriage for homosexual love." Barbara Hardy, "Women in D. H. Lawrence's Works," in Spender, pp. 90-121, disputes the idea of DHL's misogyny. On the principle of offering the simplest explanation for any given phenomenon, I cite the following from DHL's letter to Blanche Jennings, *Letters* (Boulton), I, 103: "By the way, in love, or at least in love-making, do you think the woman is always passive . . . enjoying the man's demonstration, a wee bit frit—not active? I prefer a little devil—a Carmen—I like not things passive. The girls I have known are mostly so; men always declare them so, and like them so; I do not."

[21] See stanzas 31-34 of *Laon and Cythna* for the relation of silence, words, passion, voice, etc.

[22] *Letters* (Boulton), pp. 53-54.

[23] *Letters* (Boulton), p. 53.

[24] *Letters* (Boulton), p. 54.

[25] Ruskinian, while not an entirely negative term for DHL, also connoted the condition of being overburdened with a tender social conscience and the consanguineous blight of self-righteous purity. See *Letters* (Boulton), pp. 80-81. Yet even here, DHL's own comments on the Gothic are—not surprisingly—Ruskinian.

[26] *Poems,* p. 74.

[27] *Criticism,* pp. 186-87.

[28] Influence both inspires and blocks creation, as Harold Bloom has discussed in his tetralogy beginning with

The Anxiety of Influence (New York: Oxford Univ. Press, 1973).

[29] *Criticism,* pp. 90-91.

[30] *Criticism,* pp. 91-92.

[31] On one level, DHL's essay could be read in light of Paul Goodman's reflection in *Kafka's Prayer* (New York: Vanguard, 1947; Stonehill, 1976), p. 83: "The harm that is done by greatness is a natural violence; it breaks down our defenses against our own natures; it drags up into actuality, against our inertia and resistance, the human powers that we did not know we had."

[32] *Criticism,* p. 91. DHL explicitly links Wordsworth to the primrose, and primrose to primavera. The authorless Titan may be Shelley's Prometheus. The whole passage contains a lot of Shelleyan imagery: domes and vaults in conjunction with wind recall stanza 2 of "Ode to the West Wind," another poem expressive of great impatience.

[33] *Poems,* p. 183.

[34] *Poems,* p. 182.

[35] *Criticism,* p. 395.

Roger Poole (essay date 1984)

SOURCE: "D. H. Lawrence, Major Poet," in *Texas Studies in Literature and Language,* Vol. 26, No. 3, Fall, 1984, pp. 303-30.

[*In the following essay, Poole attempts to defend Lawrence as a major poet fully in control of poetic technique.*]

Over the years, a number of studies of Lawrence's poetry have appeared, though by no means as many as his merits suggest, and it is astonishing that the Open University's third-level course on twentieth-century poetry[1] not only omits Lawrence from the poets studied, but manages to accord him little more than a passing mention.

Nevertheless, some good studies have appeared, but the emphasis has hardly been on Lawrence's technical artistry. In one way or another, most studies have been interpretative. One of the earliest was Horace Gregory, who, writing not long after Lawrence's death, makes statements which appear to have influenced later critics:

> Lawrence could not sit down to write poetry with the feeling of conscious effort behind him. Consciousness always spoiled the game. . . . The quarrel with poetry came to this: in writing a poem certain attention must be directed towards its formal structure—so much be said and no more—but Lawrence often had too much to say and could not wait for the moment when the emotion or idea became fully rounded into formal utterance.[2]

It is true that Lawrence disliked consciousness; yet Lawrence's power as a poet does not depend upon "formal structure" or "formal utterance." Lawrence had a marvelous feeling for diction and stress; he had deep poetic instincts and sheer intelligence so that even in so notably formal a poem as **"Cherry Robbers"** the success lies at least as much in the controlled cadences, the diction, the images, the color, the psychology, the drama, as in the form.

Referring to the preface Lawrence wrote for his 1928 *Collected Poems,* Gregory comments:

> His introduction to the **Collected Poems** of 1928 is an apology. He was not satisfied with the poems as they were written and to make matters worse he attempted in some cases to rewrite them. He insists at last that they are not poems at all, but a kind of biographical backdrop for his career.[3]

Gregory fails to notice that the apologetic element applies to Lawrence's comments on his early poems and on his autobiographical series, **Look! We Have Come Through!** To make a general comment out of a specific one is misleading. Also it is interesting to note that Richard Ellman, in his excellent essay, disagrees with Gregory, for Ellman comments that Lawrence's poems are not merely "personal and autobiographical" but "symbolic and representative," adding that Lawrence's revisions "necessarily improve upon form as well as content."[4]

There is in Gregory, too, the feeling that the poetry is second rate as compared with the prose. Still referring to the 1928 **Collected Poems.** Gregory observes: "Meanwhile, the strength of each poem he wrote had been drained off into another medium, the novel. The unfinished poem had been re-created and completed in a paragraph of prose."[5] Apart from the difficulty of comparing poetry with prose, such a comparison does the poetry less than justice, for, while one is glad to recognize the greatness of Lawrence as a prose writer, to regard the poetry as anything less than a successful art in its own right is totally unsatisfactory.

In my opinion, while Horace Gregory's essay may be viewed as an early recognition of Lawrence's merit as a poet, it is limited in its treatment and contains within it views or hints that later critics have taken up, much to Lawrence's disservice,[6] and even so scholarly a commentator as Gamini Salgado concludes his review of the 1964 **Complete Poems** by saying, "Perhaps we shall have to settle on the formula that it is magnificent but it is not poetry."[7]

Of course, critics have touched upon Lawrence's poetic artistry. Kenneth Rexroth, in his somewhat generalized account, mentions that "Lawrence was simply very sensitive to quantity and to the cadenced pulses of verse,"[8] but does not develop the point. Joyce Carol Oates's long essay[9] is a sympathetic and thoughtful interpretation of Lawrence the visionary artist, but it does not pretend to be an *explication de texte*. The notable full-length studies by Tom Marshall,[10] and

Sandra Gilbert,[11] do not much examine Lawrence's poetic technique, though there are a few small exceptions.

One critic, already mentioned, Richard Ellman, rightly notes that Lawrence concerns himself with rhythm and diction rather than with rhyme and pattern: "If stanzaic pattern was never a primary interest with him, diction was; if rhyme did not bother him much, rhythm did."[12] Within the modest space of fifteen pages, Ellman offers probably the most appreciative account of Lawrence's poetry, and his essay is distinguished by some treatment of Lawrence's poetic technique, but he does not pursue the matter to any great extent.

Therefore, however much or however little has been written on Lawrence's poetry, it is because Lawrence has been neglected as a poetic artist that this present essay seeks to make good the claim announced in its title.

It is a commonplace of popular opinion that poetry is a matter of "inspiration," and Shakespeare may be cited in support when he has Theseus, in his famous speech on the imagination in *A Midsummer Night's Dream,* speak the lines: "The poet's eye, in a fine frenzy rolling, / Doth glance from heaven to earth, from earth to heaven."

There is something almost Dionysiac in this vision of a poet and his poetry, and Lawrence might have been regarding himself in this kind of light when he wrote:

> A young man is afraid of his demon and puts his hand over demon's mouth sometimes and speaks for him. And the things the young man says are very rarely poetry. So I have tried to let the demon have his say, and to remove the passages where the young man intruded. So that, in the first volume, many poems are changed, some entirely rewritten, recast. But usually this is only because the poem started out to be something which it didn't quite achieve, because the young man interfered with his demon.[13]

What Lawrence means is that the young man knew he had the demon of true poetic fire within him but that, as a young, inexperienced writer, he was frightened of his latent powers and hindered their utterance, choosing instead to write more or less conventionally. This can be seen from two very early poems, **"To Guelder-Roses"** and **"To Campions,"** neither of which is at all inspired. Lawrence recognizes this limitation when he remarks on how he "perpetrated" them:

> I remember perfectly the Sunday afternoon when I perpetrated those first two pieces: **"To Guelder-Roses"** and **"To Campions"**; in spring-time, of course, and, as I say, in my twentieth year. Any young lady might have written them and been pleased with them; as I was pleased with them.[14]

It is interesting to observe that a little later the situation begins to change when he speaks of the demon's getting hold of him, just as a person is gripped, as we say, by some power or force: "But it was after that, when I was twenty, that my real demon would now and then get hold of me and shake more real poems out of me, making me uneasy."[15]

One does not wish to underestimate the role of inspiration in Lawrence's poetry, and certainly R. P. Blackmur's claim that Lawrence's demon was no more than an "outburst of personal feeling" is quite untenable.[16] There is no space here to pursue the inadequacies of Blackmur's outlook; it is sufficient to say that Vivian de Sola Pinto is far more understanding when he observes that Lawrence's poetry exists at a very deep level: "He means what he calls in the Foreword to *Fantasia of the Unconscious* 'pure passionate experience,'[17] or experience at a deeper level than the personal."[18]

It is far more than any mere "outburst of personal feeling" that comes through in many of Lawrence's poems. Time and again we are conscious of a riding force giving form, as it were, to the poems, and we begin to see that Lawrence is a maker and molder of words as well as a singer and prophet.

However, although we can admit wholeheartedly to the power of Lawrence as an inspirational force (a fundamental quality which has been treated with insight by Joyce Carol Oates),[19] the present essay emphasizes technique and form. Yet it is hoped that the inspirational Lawrence receives his due recognition; indeed, in practice it is often difficult to separate the two, and one thinks, for example, of the powerful and haunting line, "Orpheus, and the winding, leaf-clogged, silent lanes of hell" (*CP,* p. 281).

For Lawrence, conventional craftsmanship was not enough and could even be a barrier to true expression. As he puts the matter in a letter to Edward Marsh (18 August 1913): "I have always tried to get an emotion out in its own course, without altering it. It needs the finest instinct imaginable, much finer than the skill of the craftsmen."[20]

Alvarez brings out this point in his discussion of one of Lawrence's early poems, the deservedly well known, **"End of Another Home Holiday."** He speaks of the "toughness" of the poem, saying "The toughness, instead of being in the logic, is in the truth to feeling, the constant exertion of the poet's intelligence to get close to what he really feels, not to accept on the way any easy formulation or avoidance."[21] Alvarez talks about a "logic of sensibility," that is, the way the poem proceeds by a series of disparate yet harmonic personal recollections and images. There is present "a rigorous worrying, probing down to the quick of the feelings."[22] He continues, nothing the connection between inspiration and form:

> the inner pressure and disturbance gives to every one [i.e., to every poem] its own inherent form. . . . His poems are not effusions; they don't run off with him. Instead, the intelligence works away at the emotions, giving to each poem a finished quality, an economy in all the repetitions. It is a matter of the fullness with which the subject is presented.[23]

What Lawrence is offering us, then, in **"End of Another Home Holiday"** is not "an outburst of personal feeling" but an inspiration which feeds on personal memories to produce a poem in which the craftsmanship varies according to the needs of the utterance. The hand has been removed from the demon's mouth, and the demon has shaken out a real poem.

Lawrence's lack of regard for poetic conformity may be viewed as a determined attempt to cast off conventions, and in one letter to Ernest Collings (24 December 1912), he was fierce in expressing his attitude:

> These damned old stagers want me to train up a child in the way it should grow, whereas if it's destined to have a stub nose, it's sheer waste of time to harass the poor brat into Roman-nosedness. They want me to have form: that means, they want me to have *their* pernicious ossiferous skin-and-grief form, and I won't.[24]

In another letter (to Edward Marsh, 17 December 1913), he seems to grin to himself as he acknowledges his apparent shortcomings in the handling of meter: "About metres, I shall have to pray for grace from God. But (scissors!) I think Shelley a million thousand times more beautiful than Milton."[25]

It is clear from a number of fine poems (and one could cite, for example, **"Piano," "A Winter's Tale," "Discord in Childhood"**) that Lawrence could handle the traditional forms and meters very well, but it is equally true that the great majority of his best poems are not of this kind. In many of such poems Lawrence's sensitivity to rhythm, tone, image, feeling, and point of view is so acute that his free verse is, in reality, disciplined; it is rather as though the poem were obeying the laws of a creative force, and one thinks of a palm tree, for instance, which seems to be disciplined into its own particular shape by the discipline of conditioned growth.

In the following brief passage from **"Trees in the Garden"** from the *More Pansies* collection, we can see that Lawrence is trying to make us aware of his experiencing of the trees. What matters is not their geometrical perfection but the quality of "treeness" felt by the poet. The effect of the language is to make this experience luminous:

> Ah in the thunder air
> how still the trees are!
>
> And the lime-tree, lovely and tall, every leaf silent
> hardly looses even a last breath of perfume.
> (*CP*, p. 646)

Although one of the marks of Lawrence's greatness as a poet is an almost unfailing ability to portray things in themselves with a fidelity which amounts to inspiration, here the words reflect only the experience which the poet has of the trees. The exclamation mark makes us feel the poet's sense of wonder, while the form of the last two lines is cast in the same kind of exclamatory mood, for the poet, taken up in wonder at the lime tree, simply directs his and our attention toward it. It is so marvelous that he has no time to make a considered grammatical statement: he just grasps the thing itself and shows it and points it out to us, gasps out to us almost, the qualities he has sensed in it.

In the first two lines we can observe a stressed rhythm, with the emphasis, not conventionally regular, falling on major words and first syllables. There is, therefore, a preponderance of stressed syllables, so that two often come together, an effect which is continued in the last pair of lines. There is also a tendency for the stressed syllables to be long and the overall effect is one of measured, deliberate pace,[26] as though Lawrence's wonder is long lasting, which surely is what is intended. Hence the stress pattern coincides with the mood and meaning, and it is artistically satisfying that Lawrence impresses us in this way right from the beginning of the poem.

The single initial word "Ah" carries great weight as an exclamation (or as introducing the exclamation), and this word, along with its echoes "air" and "are," forms part of the pattern of wonder, exclamation, and lingering feeling that we have noticed. Yet we must remember that these three words are not just sound effects: the poem requires them.

Both pairs of lines are Lawrence's speaking voice. We can imagine him there, regarding the trees, and these are his spoken thoughts. Lawrence is a dramatic poet: he often presents poems in a kind of speaking voice. He is, as it were, telling us; or these are his thoughts and we magically overhear him. The result is a sense of immediacy and naturalism. There is, of course, alliteration strongly present in the repetition of the "l" sound, and while Lawrence could hardly have been unaware of the lissome grace which this adds to the lines, what predominates is the naturalness of Lawrence's response to the scene. He is not sculpting words or carefully measuring meters, but adopting language at its simplest and most transparent so that no single word, however well selected, no single phrase, however well crafted, obscures the felt response.

Lawrence admits to the ripple and jingle element in poetry at large, though, we should note, he equates this with poesy, a term he reserves to signify something less than poetry, which for him is concerned with vision:

> Poetry is a matter of words. Poetry is a stringing together of words into a ripple and jingle and a run of colours. Poetry is an interplay of images. Poetry is the iridescent suggestion of an idea. Poetry is all these things, and still it is something else. Given all these ingredients, you have something very like poetry, something for which we might borrow the old romantic name of poesy. And poesy, like bric-à-brac, will for ever be in fashion. But poetry is still another thing.
>
> The essential quality of poetry is that it makes a new effort of attention, and "discovers" a new world

within the known world. Man, and the animals, and the flowers, all live within a strange and for ever surging chaos. The chaos which we have got used to we call a cosmos. The unspeakable inner chaos of which we are composed we call consciousness, and mind, and even civilization. But it is, ultimately, chaos lit up by visions, or not lit up by visions.[27]

> On the part of the poet it [poetry] is an act of faith, pureattention and purified receptiveness. . . . The act of attention is not so easy. It is much easier to write poesy.[28]

Despite the talk about poetry as a ripple or jingle or a run of colors, these are the words of a man for whom poetry is a serious undertaking. Ripples, jingles, and runs of colors are only a part of poetry, even if an important part; and to attain the vision needs an "effort of attention" and a spirit of "purified receptiveness."

In an important letter to Edward Marsh (19 November 1913), Lawrence turns his attention to the art of poetry:

> It all depends on the *pause*—the natural pause, the natural *lingering* of the voice according to the feeling—it is the hidden *emotional* pattern that makes poetry, not the obvious form. . . .
>
> It is the lapse of the feeling, something as indefinite as expression in the voice carrying emotion. It doesn't depend on the ear, particularly, but on the sensitive soul. And the ear gets a habit, and becomes master, when the ebbing and lifting emotion should be master, and the ear the transmitter. If your ear has got stiff and a bit mechanical, *don't* blame my poetry.[29]

All this offers an acute insight into Lawrence's ideas on writing poetry. We continually find that Lawrence uses stress which coincides with the sense of what is being said, with the meaning, literal and figurative, with major words, with syllable length, with punctuation, and with natural breaks and phrasing. It is not something which is imposed upon the sense. Often we see that Lawrence opens a line with a stressed syllable, and not infrequently we see him deploying two or more stressed consecutive syllables. These practices, together with the general coincidence of stress with sense, produces a lingering effect, a slight lapse in the apparent passage of time, an ebb and flow of emotion, a sense of measured pace, and sometimes even a kind of spondee effect.

Lawrence objected to conventional stress patterns, disliking the impression they give of "footsteps hitting the earth," saying also that he preferred the term "length" to "stress": "I think I read my poetry more by length than by stress—as a matter of movements in space than footsteps hitting the earth.[30] This is very well said. There is in Lawrence's poetry a great sense of measured pace and length, and we are conscious of movement in space, as it were. There is no doubt that for Lawrence the term is an apt one, but unfortunately it can be confused with other applications of the term as, for example, the length of a line or syllable. Further, the term "stress" has an accepted

currency, and for these reasons the present writer has adopted it, despite Lawrence's persuasive objections. However, we need to think of it with Lawrence's "length" in mind and certainly not as banging footsteps hitting the earth.

The remarks we have quoted from Lawrence's letter to Marsh do demonstrate how Lawrence wants to "get an emotion out in its own course, without altering it," for it is this that makes the poetry and not the obvious or conventional forms and techniques. For Lawrence, it is the technically unobvious form that matters—the natural pause, the natural lingering of the voice. Lawrence is not saying that technical forms are unrequired or that merely feeling something intensely produces a satisfactory form, but that the pressing needs of the emotional pattern are the major considerations, and that this emotional pattern depends upon an instinctive ear for feeling: "the finest instinct imaginable, much finer than the skill of the craftsmen." We can regard what he is saying as a protest against form without feeling, against the necessity of form as a prior consideration.

If we apply Lawrence's words to the few lines above from **"Trees in the Garden,"** we see that they offer a perceptive description of what is happening there. We may ask ourselves, why not "the lovely and tall limetree" instead of "the lime-tree, lovely and tall"? The former is the natural word order for a prose statement, but Lawrence is not making a statement, whether in poetry or in prose: he is disclosing to the reader his excitement at what he can see. He wants to burst out that it is the lime tree (and other trees) that has caught his attention. They have provided the act of attention. Having accomplished this, Lawrence then describes them, partly objectively ("tall"), partly subjectively ("lovely"). Finally, in this verse, the line "hardly looses even a last breath of perfume" may be seen as the lingering of Lawrence's voice as he seeks to breathe perfume into the thundery air. We can see this if we scan the line: "hárdlỹ lóosĕs évĕn ă lást bréath ŏf pérfŭme" (*CP*, p. 646). The whole line is effectively slow and leisured as though Lawrence is breathing in and savoring the "treeness" which is before him. Though the first three pairs of syllables may be viewed as conventional trochees, we are given three regularly stressed syllables which are followed at "last" and "breath" by two consecutively stressed syllables, and which provide a kind of "climactic" lingering at this point. Even the last one, "fume," though unstressed, is yet another long syllable. The line pattern, scanned in this way, is not orthodox, but it achieves the effect of getting "an emotion out in its own course."

The next stanza shows Lawrence still speaking naturally as he comments on the scene, as if he were still there in the garden, present there, speaking his thoughts as they come into his head while he watches: "Ănd thĕ ghóstlỹ, créamỹ cólŏured līttle trées ŏf léaves / whíte, ívorỹ whíte ămŏng thĕ rámblīng greéns" (*CP*, p. 646). These fine lines, with their prevailing images of a sort of ghostly off-whiteness ("ghostly" because of that word's suggestion of unnaturalness, as occasioned here by the unusual silence in the thunder air), are basically steady iambic, though with an effective number of extra unstressed syllables which serve to run us on quickly to the stressed syllables which are so important in Lawrence's poetry. In this respect, we can notice the stress of the first word of the second line, "white," which draws attention to the key tone of the description: "white, ivory white." Lawrence likes to emphasize the initial syllable of a line (we can see the effect again in "hardly," above), so that starting a line with a stress can give just that hint of drama or strength which is often a feature of his best poetry.

Let us now consider this long, flowing line, still from **"Trees in the Garden"**: "and the balsam-pines that are blue with the grey-blue blueness of things from the sea" (*CP,* p. 647). The stress is basically anapest, a measure which is entirely in keeping with the running sense of excitement Lawrence feels at this point, but held up sensitively by three successive, stressed syllables at "grey-blue blueness" which form the natural climax of the line. After this the anapests slow down, so that we have a line which starts with rising excitement, reaches a plateau of emotion, and then slows, to be followed, in fact, in subsequent lines, by a further pattern of risings, plateaus, and fallings.

The line quoted is beautifully nostalgic, exciting yet reflective, harmonious, *and* lingering. The pines are seen through an aura of blueness (a color which is peculiarly suitable for the visual context of this poem), while the natural pauses and alliterations are perfect expressions for the visually conceived experience that Lawrence communicates. Indeed, the whole poem might be regarded as a piece of impressionistic word painting with blue, creamy white, and green as the abiding colors.

In so many of his poems, what Lawrence gives us is the living thing as he sees and feels it. He is not offering an overfinished product, but a creation which takes place almost before our eyes: "We do not speak of things crystallized and set apart. We speak of the instant, the immediate self, the very plasm of the self. We speak also of free verse."[31] In a letter written to Catherine Carswell (11 January 1916), Lawrence makes a similar point. He asks for "a free, essential verse, that cuts to the centre of things, without any flourish,"[32] telling her, with exacting directness, "Use rhyme *accidentally,* not as a sort of draper's rule for measuring lines off."[33] These comments match Lawrence's declared intention, already noted, of getting "an emotion out in its own course, without altering it." With Lawrence's various observations in mind, we can look at one of the best of his earlier poems, **"Pear-Blossom."**

It might be objected that the rhymes in **"Pear-Blossom"** tend to be repetitious, for, in self-rhymes—repetitions, really—"foam" is used twice, "ever" twice, and "me" four times. It is obvious from numerous poems that Lawrence could rhyme well; yet rhyme in itself was not important to him. He wanted the freedom to express what he had to say, and rhyme had to give way to this necessity. The repeated "me" is required by the central significance of the poem: the quality of the physical relationship between the man and the woman, as seen by the man. She crawls over him, then climbs back, then looks at him, and finally weeps, causing a trembling (which indicates the intensity of the weeping) of the bed under him. "Foam" is an admirable noun to use of pear blossom, and though to our ears it might have been preferable to change one or two of the rhyming words, it might also be that Lawrence wanted us to see the foam in two sorts; first, as a fountain and, second, as sprays and spurts, which latter carries a different picture into our minds. The off-rhymes "blossom" and "bosom" seem felicitous not only because of the echoing nature of the sound but because of the echoing imagery. The final two, "ever" and "ever," are totally acceptable as a clinching pair which bespeak the terror in the poet's mind at the prospect of everlasting separation.

It is interesting to observe that the form of the poem is a species of terza rima as far as the end of the sixth verse, though with varying line length, and that the last two verses effectively break this pattern with a definitive form of their own. The whole poem, therefore, combines elements of regularity and irregularity, for, while neither rhyme nor rhythm nor pattern can be measured with a draper's rule, even purely as a formal poem it holds together compactly.

Yet the poem is a success for other more important reasons. It marries objective details with subjective apprehension of those details, and these two aspects are sensitively linked by the pear blossom which, though something which exists as actual blossom, is also a symbol of the lovemaking which has taken place. The action of the woman in clambering across the man to reach the pear blossom is perceived with a naturalness of observation that is at once robust and delicate. The moment of terror at the end of the poem reminds us a little of the moment of fear at the end of one of Wordsworth's "Lucy" poems ("Strange Fits of Passion Have I Known"), where the descending moon fixes fear in the poet's mind, except that the mood and situation in the Lawrence poem is not deliberately vague and supernaturalistic as in the Wordsworth poem. Instead, Lawrence's poem suggests an immediate, natural, if irrational, flush of panic on the part of the poet that the death of the woman will bring separation and an end to the beauty and sensuality which the two have experienced and which have been prefigured by the lovely, but evanescent, pear blossom.

The whole spreading fountain of blossom at the beginning of the poem, symbolizing the rushing power of love, at the end is reduced to a few, isolated flowers cut off from the tree, their living source. The very helpless loveliness of the pear blossom becomes the objective correlative, thereby focusing attention on the passage of love between the man and the woman.

Lawrence supplies those little intimate details which make the poem so exactly right—the woman combing her hair or digging her knee into the man's chest. These details, together with the symbolic strength of the poem as revealed by the naturalistic experience, are what give the poem its power, and not just Lawrence's control of rhyme and prosody, though these are effectively present.

"Ballad of Another Ophelia" is one of Lawrence's most remarkable poems, though it has rarely caught the attention of critics.[34] It takes the form of a monologue in which the mad Ophelia speaks her thoughts. She is now an ordinary country girl, and we are to imagine that her sole interests have been reduced to the small world of the orchard and the farmyard with its hens and chicks. The monologue itself is subtly deranged as the poet allows the distressed girl to reveal the vision that lies within the vision. Throughout the poem Lawrence displays a fine awareness of rhyme and rhythm; it is superbly imagistic and is possibly the most intellectually formulated of all his poems.

The opening verse offers a cameo of farm life. The apples in the orchard are aptly seen out of focus through the rain-washed windowpane, and the hen is viewed affectionately and comically for the same reason, but the verse ends with the transmuting of the raindrops into tears, thus localizing for us Ophelia's grief.

The stark second verse provides a commentary on the first. There is no future for Ophelia, no ripeness to come. Images of disappointment are strongly present: "blackish"-tasting apples, "tears," "yellow dapples / Of autumn," "withered"; and the impression is suggested that the whole season is decayed and ruined. An examination of the stress pattern discloses some familiar Lawrentian features. The stress tends to fall on the first syllable of each line, making the emphasis made yet more emphatic, and on major words or syllables, especially in line 1 where three strong words in succession bear the stress, with pairs or even triples of unstressed syllables occurring at frequent intervals, except in the last line which is appropriately steady in its iambic meter. The overall impression is one of deliberate strength and steadiness:

> Nóthĭng nŏw wĭll rípĕn thĕ bríght gréen ápplĕs
> Fúll ŏf dĭsăppoíntmĕnt ănd ŏf ráin;
> Bláckĭsh thĕy wĭll táste, ŏf téars, whĕn thĕ yéllŏw
>   dápplĕs
> Ŏf aútŭmn téll thĕ wíthĕrĕd tále ăgáin.
>   (*CP,* p. 119)

In the third verse, the repetition of "Cluck!" sensitively suggests madness, and this characteristic is subtly present in other places throughout the poem, as, for example, in the anecdote of the "grey rat" and the "gold thirteen," with the associated disjointed syntax (in the third line of the fourthverse) centering around the broken-off comment "oh, the beast is quick and keen." Ophelia is talking to herself and of herself, and Lawrence is able to give us a picture of the pathetic girl whose former court of Denmark is now reduced to a farmyard, while the ravaging of the chick (here, "spark" and, later, "sparkles"—because the chicks are bright little creatures and are one of the few bright spots in her sad life) by a rat is emblematic of her own loss. The gray rat is suggestive of an ominous,

rapacious intruder, while the "gold thirteen," with which it is contrasted, carries with it the idea of wealth or fulfillment or harvest mingled with the inexplicit and ominously suggested "thirteen."

The fifth verse has an extra number of unstressed syllables, resulting in an open running effect which is suited to the change of tone and relaxation of tension as Ophelia remembers her lover, the Hamlet of better times. Hamlet is viewed in terms of blissful natural images, but this verse is succeeded by a seriously questioning one, even though the questions are lightly expressed as far as prosody is concerned, and in terms of Ophelia's madness. The poet ironically seeks to understand the so-called wisdom by which man diminishes the beauty of nature, while the sun, as overseer of all life, is envisaged as sarcastically inquiring about the nature of man.

The theme is developed in the penultimate verse where Ophelia's loss is encompassed by the images that stand for her. Hamlet has loved her, taken her, abandoned her, as we learn from the generalized tender imagery of the fallen blossom ("undressed is all the blossom") and the localized, direct, pathetic imagery of the shift ("And her shift is lying white upon the floor"). We recall how, in the play, Ophelia has to endure the taunts of Hamlet, and this verse is Lawrence's imaginatively realized enactment of what subsequently happens. The last two lines show the strong image clusters associated with the demanding, rapacious lover ("grey one," "shadow," "rat," "thief"), while "rainstorm" suggests an image of Hamlet's passion. This particular image seems also to suggest her shattered life and mind and harks back to the distorting rain and tears of the first verse.

Again, the meter is a combination of unstressed triples, stressed syllables at the beginning of a line, and stressed major words and syllables. We can observe the dramatic increase in pace as the climax is reached at the end of the third line, only to be succeeded by a slowing down of pace in the fourth line which, however, has a strong initial stress on "Creeps" and an even stronger emphasis on the first syllable of "ravishes." What we have in this fourth line is, in fact, two "action" phrases introduced by powerful verbs, the second of which is climactic to the first. Indeed, in these two lines, sense and prosody go so closely together that we seem to need some special indication of stress, and the present writer employs . . . [the stress marking (¯)] to indicate the needed emphasis: "Thăt ă gréy ŏne, līke ă shádŏw, līke ă rāt, ă thĭef, rāinstŏrm / Créeps ŭpŏn hĕr thĕn ănd rāvĭshĕs hĕr stóre!" (*CP,* p. 120).

The final verse continues the image of the store, but the apples are decayed and moldy ("grey" echoes the previous associations of this word), and we are told that all the chicks have been ravished ("O the golden sparkles laid extinct!"), so that now Ophelia has nothing left to her. Even the clouds are autumnal, and the poem concludes with the all-seeing sun winking, or so it seems to the crazed girl, in frivolous derision at the goings-on of man.

One poem, **"Cherry Robbers,"** may be taken as an example of Lawrence's ability to write more traditional verse. Punctuation, line length, vowel length, word order, rhythm, rhyme, tone—all are means whereby the message of the poem is expressed. It is interesting to observe the stress pattern, for this again demonstrates the poet's command of stressed syllables. Most of the lines open with a stressed syllable, thus affording such lines a firm start as, for example, each fourth line of the first two verses. In the first verse, in the case of the dominant image, "blood-drops," both syllables need to be stressed, while in the second line of the second verse, *each* word needs to be stressed. At this point Lawrence reaches the tocsinlike finality of the midnarrative climax which yet looks back to the first dramatic statement ("Hang strings of crimson cherries") and forward to the third and fourth dramatic statements ("Cherries hung round her ears" and "Offers me her scarlet fruit").

The whole poem has to be regarded as a splendid piece of phrasing, but we can notice also that the poet, with an acute awareness of language, enhances his drama by employing a predominantly Anglo-Saxon derived vocabulary, much of which consists of one-syllable words, as, for example, in the cutting directness of the poem's final statement. These last eight words are so totally unencumbered that the reader seems to experience within himself the sadistic male response to the girl who is both temptress and victim. The term "sadistic" is deliberately a little too strong, but as Lawrence reveals the element of macho-selfishness within the male's winning of the female, we can certainly contrast the almost detached clinical clarity of the male approach, as depicted in the last line and a half, with the vibrancy and color associated with the girl.

The totality of the poem is established in a series of connections: pleasure and pain, victor and victim, will and desire, sex and hurt. The cherries and the dead birds are vivid images forcing us to see life as red and flaming and yet associated with death. The young girl plays with the fruit of life, tempting the young man to take it. He does, but in doing so, realizes that he is also a marauder. The cold "I will see / If she has any tears" is a statement that sums up, vindictively, one feels, the main theme, which is, in general, that of the union of beauty with pain.

The poem is finely crafted with an absolute surety of touch for the rightness of words, but that sureness encompasses also Lawrence's instinctive "feeling" for the power of the image. The strength of the imagery gives the poem its richness and depth, but it is the finished, shapely formality of the poem that finally makes it art. I have discussed the matter of the stress pattern, and it is revealed below, as is also the exactness of the rhyming, the balance of long lines against shorter ones, and the way in which these shorter lines (the second and fourth of each verse) are cast as finishing statements to the preceding first and third lines. Repeated readings of **"Cherry Robbers"** serve only to underline its totality—language, technique, sound, image, feeling, sight, vision:

> Uńdĕr thē lóng dărk boúghs, līke jéwĕls réd
>   Ĭn thē háir ŏf ăn Eástĕrn gírl
> Háng stríngs ŏf crímsŏn chérrīes, ăs íf hăd bléd
>   Blóod-dróps bĕneáth ĕach cúrl.
>
> Uńdĕr thē glístenīng chérrīes, wĭth fóldĕd wíngs
>   Thrée déad bírds líe:
> Pále-brĕastĕd thróstlĕs ănd ă bláckbĭrd, róbbĕrlīngs
>   Stáined wīth réd dýe.
>
> Ăgáinst thē háystáck ă gírl stánds laúghĭng ăt mĕ
>   Chérrīes húng rŏund hĕr eárs.
> Ŏffĕrs mĕ hĕr scárlĕt frúit: Ĭ wĭll sée
>   Ĭf shĕ hás ăny téars.
>
>   (*CP*, pp. 36-37)

Despite the success of **"Cherry Robbers,"** the wide sweep of Lawrence's free verse commands most attention, and by contrast with **"Cherry Robbers," "The Song of a Man Who Has Come Through,"** for example, from the autobiographical sequence ***Look! We Have Come Through!,*** is a good example of what Lawrence has to say about poetry: "free verse is, or should be, direct utterance from the instant, whole man. . . . free verse has its own *nature,* that is neither star nor pearl, but instantaneous like plasm."[35]

In this poem, wind images reveal that love is a tremendous, fulfilling, creative force, capable of overcoming all obstructions. For the man in the poem love is not a light or romantic gift, but a possessing yet delicate power that blows through him, body and soul, transcending his limitations and forcing him exaltingly to surrender to the new directions involved in marriage. The repetitions and parallels, the beautifully placed, pausing semicolon after "inserted," the well-judged commas, the series of "if" clauses, the exciting exclamation mark—all lead in a fine rush to the first climax in line 10. A cluster of associated words carry through the idea of movement: "winged," "blows," "directions," "course," while others, finely tempered, turn around the idea of cutting: "fine," "exquisite," "chisel," "wedge-blade," "inserted."

In lines 8, 9, and 10 we see how Lawrence creates the huge image of a great rock split asunder by the force of a driven wedge, to demonstrate how power derived from marriage can smash the strongest obstruction to it. There are no rhymes, but there is rhythm, the rhythm demanded by what the poet needs to say, and not that of any precise meter. Indeed, Lawrence employs a recognizable meter only once in the poem, and that is in the tenth line climax to the first verse. Essentially it consists of two sets of iambics followed by a run of anapests: "The rock will split, we shall come at the wonder, we shall find the Hesperides" (*CP*, p. 250). It is doubtful if this were a conscious decision on Lawrence's part. It is far more likely that he instinctively selected the standard strong iambic pattern for the four strong monosyllables which provide the central point of the climax and a lilting, running meter to underpin the urgency and excitement of the man and woman's discovery of the nature of marriage.

The word "wonder" is then picked up and taken over into the second part of the poem. "Wonder" is associated, for Lawrence, with mystery and vision. He set it against knowledge and regarded it as the most precious element in life:

> and deny it as we may, knowledge and wonder counteract one another. So that as knowledge increases wonder decreases. . . . When all comes to all, the most precious element in life is wonder. . . . The one universal element in consciousness which is fundamental to life is the element of wonder.[36]

Life without wonder is a poor thing, and one constantly finds this sense of wonder abiding in the great moments of Lawrence's prose and poetry. In the present poem it constitutes our admittance of the mystery that exists in marriage.

From here on the poem changes. Verses and lines shorten, and language becomes compact and terse as the wonder the poet has caught sight of and felt makes demands on him, ending with the compelling admittance of the "three strange angels" (probably based on Genesis 18)[37] and probably symbolizing the forces spoken of in the poem that make marriage truly creative—sensitivity, strength, and wonder.

"Grapes" from the splendid ***Birds, Beasts, and Flowers*** collection is an undoubted triumph. Its aura is as rich and scented as that of the remarkable poem **"Fish"** is isolated and unattainable. **"Grapes"** centers upon the sense of touch, which for Lawrence is the supreme avenue of knowing, and we can mention here that the naturalness and immediacy of touch contrasts with the alien spirit of mechanistic materialism that Lawrence so fiercely opposed. In the poem even so famed an emblem as the rose is strikingly rejected by Lawrence because it opens out and is thus a symbol for the explicit and the conscious, whereas the dark grape represents the sensuous intoxication of an older order when men lived a more instinctive, tactile life, unclogged, as we are today, by civilization's "clothed vision." The poem as a whole is a marvelous evocation of Lawrence's belief that man needs avenues of communication other than the cerebral.

It is, perhaps, something of a paradox that such a reaching outward is actually the result of a highly intelligent man thinking about the nature of life, and we can observe that the word "tendril" (or "tendrilled"), which occurs five times, offers one more example of Lawrence's ability to select just that word which marries sensuous exactness with sympathetic import. This word provides a key concept in the poem, for it comes to stand for the primeval, noncerebral way of seeing, since it reaches out, orients, and locates by touch; no other term of such living, embracing sensibility could have taken its place.

There is in **"Grapes,"** as in other great poems by Lawrence, a rich vibrancy, a hypnotic, pulling undertow, a kind of slow, pulsing, cellolike music that is one particular feature of his poetry and gives him stature as a major poet. When we look at the lines quoted below, we can note again Lawrence's liking for a stressed initial syllable to give a line an impressive, firm start and see how his rhythm does not depend upon conventional meters; instead he selects for stress the main sense-carrying syllables, a process which often entails several running, intermediate nonstressed syllables. Further, some stressed words are imperatives. All this is combined with a rare sense of balance of word and phrase. The lines below demonstrate an intuitive sureness of handling such that form and meaning are mutually supportive:

> Reăchĭng ŏut ănd gráspĭng bў ăn ínstĭnct mŏre
>   délĭcăte thăn thĕ móon's ăs shĕ féels fŏr thĕ
>   tídes . . .
> Ănd áll ĭn nákĕd cŏmmúnĭŏn cŏmmúnĭcătĭng
>   ăs nów ŏur clóthed vísĭon căn névĕr
>   cŏmmúnĭcăte . . .
> Dúskў ăre thĕ ávĕnúes ŏf wíne,
>   Ănd wé mŭst cróss thĕ fróntĭers, thŏugh wĕ
>   wíll nŏt,
> Ŏf thĕ lóst, férn scĕntĕd wórld:
> Táke thĕ férn-séed ŏn ŏur líps,
> Clóse thĕ eyés, ănd gó
> Dówn thĕ téndrĭlled ávĕnŭes ŏf wíne ănd thĕ
>   óthĕrwórld.
>
>   (*CP*, pp. 285-87)

There is no room in the space of a short essay to dwell upon the complete range of Lawrence's poetry, but a consideration of **"Sicilian Cyclamens"** seems called for because it is one of Lawrence's most intelligent and delicately perceived poems.

The following verse, the concluding one of the poem, has a wonderful freshness:

> Greece, and the world's morning
> Where all the Parthenon marbles still fostered the
>   roots of the cyclamen.
> Violets,
> Pagan, rosy-muzzled violets
> Autumnal
> Dawn-pink,
> Dawn-pale
> Among squat toad-leaves sprinkling the unborn
> Erechtheion marbles.
>
>   (*CP*, pp. 311-12)

The tone is that of an exclamation, even an acclamation, the first line claiming our attention by the stressed initial syllable, with two stressed consecutive syllables providing a sustaining, dignified effect near the end of the line: "Gréece, ănd thĕ wórld's mórnĭng." The long second line bears the same sense of dignity. Stressed, important syllables carry the line sturdily along with intervening light, lifting unstressed syllables. As in the first line, a pair of consecutively stressed syllables, just after the midway point, gives the line a sustained, dignified, almost ringing strength: "Whĕre áll thĕ Párthĕnŏn márblĕs stíll fóstĕred thĕ roots ŏf thĕ cýclămĕn" (*CP*, p. 311).

Most of the lines are short, or very short, and may be viewed as leading in a series of statements to the conclusion, or climax, of "the unborn / Erechtheion marbles." Inspection of the series reveals that the stress pattern leads naturally toward this climax, for we have several stressed initial syllables (in the fourth line, each of the four words or part words is stressed initially), a repetition ("Dawn"), while the penultimate line exhibits as many as five consecutively stressed syllables. The total effect is of a pressing forward by a series of waves which sustain the meaning until the last statement is made.

We should have regard also for the imaginative power Lawrence displays here. The cyclamens are envisaged as being prior to the ancient Parthenon in that this great work of civilization was once only present as unearthed stone, fast in the ground, humbly fostering the little flowers.

The whole of the quoted verse, then, fits together in phrasing, in imaginative power, in form and artistry; but it is fascinating to turn to the remarkable opening of the poem, for it is that to which the concluding section artistically returns us. The words "pagan" and "cyclamen" in that section take us back to the opening, which offers a striking picture of Lawrence and his wife, who are first seen in their own house and then, by a natural domestic transmutation, seen as savages of the pagan Mediterranean world, aware for the first time of the beautiful little cyclamens at their feet.

> When he pushed his bush of black hair off his brow:
> When she lifted her mop from her eyes, and
>   screwed it in a knob behind
>   —O act of fearful temerity!
> When they felt their foreheads bare, naked to
>   heaven, their eyes revealed:
> When they felt the light of heaven brandishing
>   like a knife at their defenceless eyes,
> And the sea like a blade at their face,
> Mediterranean savages:
> When they came out, face-revealed, under heaven,
>   from the shaggy undergrowth of their own hair
> For the first time,
> They saw tiny rose cyclamens between their toes,
>   growing
> Where the slow toads sat brooding on the past.
>   (*CP,* p. 310)

The husband lifts back his hair, the wife pushes hers back into a knob behind. It is a marvelously ordinary domestic scene; yet we have the arresting comment, "O act of fearful temerity!," for this is the act by which, imaginatively and mythically, the two feel themselves to be kin to the people from an age far back in time when the sea and light were stronger (because the world was younger). Physical force contrasts with the opening domesticity, and the images of "blade," "knife," "savages," and "shaggy undergrowth" suggest a precivilized, barbaric state. At this stage these primitive people become suddenly aware of beauty: "They saw tiny rose cyclamens between their toes, growing," and we see that Lawrence makes them *feel* their awareness. This sensitive response to life and beauty is seen as entering the human consciousness for the first time and is set imaginatively against the unpleasant,

nonbeautiful or ugly images of the past as suggested by "slow toads" in the ominous, long-syllabled last line.

We can note, in passing, that it was partly because of this poem that R. P. Blackmur made one of his most extraordinary judgments when he remarked that "the hysteric mode carries the pathetic fallacy and the confusion of symbols beyond any resolution."[38] The pathetic fallacy is not necessarily a poetic failing. John Ruskin, in his famous discussion of the matter, essentially bases his acceptance or nonacceptance of the pathetic fallacy in poetry upon the poet's honesty of feeling: "But by how much this feeling is noble when it is justified by the strength of its cause, by so much it is ignoble when there is not cause enough for it."[39] It is my opinion that the pathetic fallacy in this poem is totally justified by the significance and the poetic truth of what Lawrence has to say, and I hope that this will become apparent in the further discussion.

There is nothing hysterical about **"Sicilian Cyclamens,"** nor does it exhibit any confusion of symbols. Lawrence gives us a controlled, delicate poem, full of fresh natural imagery which is matched by the speaking naturalness of the varying line length: "The hare suddenly goes uphill / Laying back her long ears with unwinking bliss" (*CP,* p. 311). The pathetic fallacy is present as in "And cyclamens putting their ears back," but the usage is wholly of this linked, sympathetic kind, for Lawrence is concerned throughout to emphasize the sensitivity, the freshness, the delicacy of the pre-Hellenic Aegean. Cyclamens, greyhounds, hares—all share this quality of alert life.

In the verses quoted below, the cyclamens and the greyhound buds (or the "delicate very-young greyhound bitches") are both symbols of the newness and youthfulness of nature. The cyclamen flowers fold back into a sleek, long, greyhoundlike bud. It has drawn itself out of the earth and is now in front of the "poet's" feet. It has an unreal quality, a dreaminess, for it is the first time that man has noticed the beauty of the newly emerging cyclamen. The day itself is so new that it is said to be "inexperienced," and the cyclamens are again compared to young greyhounds. They yawn as they half awaken into awareness, and the cyclamens similarly arch and awaken and prick their ears.

Cyclamens, greyhounds, and later, the hares (though the last two have no independent existence but are only part of the cyclamen metaphor) all relate to man's dawning consciousness of the beauty of nature—the young cyclamens themselves being symbols of nature's preeminence and priority, for they are "stone-engendered" from the uncut rocks out of which the Parthenon marbles are one day to be built. There is no confusion of symbols, for they are all part of one expanded but delicately worked out experience:

> The shaking aspect of the sea
> And man's defenceless bare face
> And cyclamens putting their ears back.

Long, pensive, slim-muzzled greyhound buds
Dreamy, not yet present,
Drawn out of earth
At his toes.

Dawn-rose
Sub-delighted, stone-engendered
Cyclamens, young cyclamens
Arching
Waking, pricking their ears
Like delicate very-young greyhound bitches
Half-yawning at the open, inexperienced
Vista of day,
Folding back their soundless petalled ears.

Greyhound bitches
Bending their rosy muzzles pensive down,
And breathing soft, unwilling to wake to the new day
Yet sub-delighted.

(*CP,* pp. 310-11)

The wonder-inspiring freshness of **"Sicilian Cyclamens"** can be met elsewhere in Lawrence's poetry, as for example in **"Middle of the World"** from the great post-humous collection, *Last Poems.* It is surely rare for a poem to open with such freshness and with such a sense of immediacy:

Thís séa wĭll névĕr díe, néithĕr wĭll ĭt évĕr grów óld
   nór ceáse tŏ bĕ blúe, nór ĭn thĕ dáwn
   céase tŏ líft ŭp ĭts hílls
ănd lét thĕ slím blăck shíp ŏf Dĭŏnýsŏs cŏme
      sáilĭng ĭn
wĭth grápe-vĭnes úp thĕ mást, ănd dólphĭns léapĭng.

(*CP,* p. 688)

The first three lines are cast in the form of a challenge which seems to rise and climax, like waves rolling in as phrase succeeds phrase. Its resonance comes from Lawrence's instinctive feeling for short Anglo-Saxon words with their biblical overtones. Opinions may differ, but the lines have something of the same staying power as, for example, Psalm 24:7: "Lift up your heads, O ye gates; and be ye lift up, ye everlasting doors; and the King of glory shall come in."

We can observe how the fourth and fifth lines of the first verse, with their easy slipping length not only contrast beautifully with the short, iterated challenges of the preceding three lines but are also, in their sense of motion, length, ease, and fecundity, redolent of vitality, richness, and naturalness; they need to be contrasted with the mechanistic, automatic image suggested by "clock-work" in the next verse. One may notice too, how, after the deliberately pausing comma, the last three words—"and dolphins leaping"—end the verse with a sense of excitement.

Scansion again shows Lawrence's grasp of emphasis. The stressed syllables sustain the dignity of the initial challenge, while the last two, by contrast, are basically steadying iambic as Dionysus' ship comes sailing in.

The last verse is also truly Lawrentian:

And the Minoan Gods, and the Gods of Tiryns
are heard softly laughing and chatting, as ever;
and Dionysos, young and a stranger
leans listening on the gate, in all respect.

(*CP,* p. 688)

Dionysus, latest of the gods, is also part of the youthfulness of the ancient Aegean, and the spirit of those times is still with us. For those who are aware, it is always being reborn, and the incarnate gods may still be seen, and the "music of lost languages" may still be heard. Even though modern ships pass to and fro (verse 2), in reality they diminish nothing, for "the distance never changes."

"Middle of the World" has a lingering beauty of image, word, and phrase combined with a part mythological, part historical insight. The distant figures are set before us here and now, and we see them in living detail. The "slim naked men from Cnossos" who are portrayed as "descending from the ships at dawn" or "kindling little fires upon the shores" are no mere abstractions, and we admire Lawrence's capacity to marry denotative language in phrases like these or in others ("laughing," "chatting," "listening") to the total imaginative and mythological conception.

When we try to account for Lawrence's ability to produce poetry that is marked with such a feeling awareness for the measures of word, phrase, and line, we find ourselves falling back on the explanation that Lawrence has absorbed the language of the Bible. We know from his essay **"Hymns in a Man's Life"** that he was brought up with a "direct knowledge of the Bible," that he had imbibed a "direct relation" with places like "Galilee and Canaan, Moab and Kedron," and that they were invested with a kind of wonder for him. It is this essay where he proclaims, as we have seen, that the most precious element in life is wonder.[40] So, although the language of the hymns may be banal, it involved Lawrence in a relationship with the Bible in general and with biblical language.[41] Everything was part of a sturdy Protestant tradition, and, above all, the sounds and the words were all invested with wonder.

It therefore does not seem accidental that when we turn to the Authorized Version, and especially perhaps to the Psalms, we encounter a rhythm and a phrasing that bear resemblance to passages from Lawrence's poetry. Psalm 92, for example, chosen at random, begins in this way:

Ĭt ĭs ă góod thíng tŏ gĭve thánks ŭntŏ thĕ Lórd, ănd
   tŏ sĭng práisĕs ŭntŏ thý náme, Ŏ mŏst Hígh:
Tŏ shéw fórth thý lóvĭngkíndnĕss ĭn thĕ mórnĭng,
   ănd thý fáithfŭlnĕss évĕry níght,
Ŭpón ăn ínstrŭmĕnt ŏf tén stríngs, ănd ŭpón thĕ
   psáltĕry̆; ŭpón thĕ hárp wĭth ă sólĕmn soúnd.

Or this from the opening of Psalm 94:s

Ó Lórd Gód, tŏ whŏm véngĕance bĕlóngĕth; Ó Gód,
   tŏ whŏm véngĕance bĕlóngĕth, shéw thýsĕlf.
Líft ŭp thýsĕlf, thŏu júdge ŏf thĕ eárth: réndĕr
   rĕwárd tŏ thĕ próud.
Lórd, hów lóng shăll thĕ wíckĕd, hów lóng shăll
   thĕ wíckĕd tríŭmph?

Hów lóng shăll thĕy úttĕr ănd spéak hărd thíngs?
ănd ăll thĕ wórkĕrs ŏf ĭnĭquĭtў bóast thĕmsélves?

What we have is a pattern of stresses usually consisting of some two or three unstressed syllables in combination with stressed syllables, the stressed syllables normally being major or important ones, with two or three stressed consecutive syllables also appearing from time to time as, for example, in "speak hard things," which has the effect, as we have seen in Lawrence's poetry, of slowing the line, strengthening, and emphasizing. There are too, in Psalm 94, stressed imperatives and the presence of the stressed syllable at the beginning of the line which, as in Lawrence's work gives the line a firm, bold start.

The Bible is also noted for its repetitions and balancings, as may be seen from the extract from Psalm 94. Lawrence's use is neither so extensive nor so pronounced as that found, say, in the Psalms, but it is clearly present in his poetry. It may take one of two forms. More generally it occurs as part of the poem's artistic development as, for example, in **"Cypresses"** where words like "cypresses," "Romans," "Etruscans" are repeated or where ideas and images essential to the poem's thought, such as viciousness, silence, suppleness, smiling, or darkness, occur and recur. Less frequently, but not infrequently, it forms part of the poet's technique as, for instance, in **"The Song of a Man Who Has Come Through,"** where "mere" words and phrases (e.g., "If only" or "What is the knocking?") are repeated and balanced, one against another.

Even in so unpropitious (from the point of view of biblical rhythms) a poem as the imagist, tightly rhymed, brilliant short poem **"Green,"** Lawrence's liking for balance, repetition, and consecutive stress may be seen:

> The dawn was apple-green,
>   The sky was green wine held up in the sun,
> The moon was a golden petal between.
>
> She opened her eyes, and green
>   They shone, clear like flowers undone
> For the first time, now for the first time seen.
> (CP, p. 216)

Lawrence's poetry is often of a dramatic kind; in it the poet is a thinker, presenting his thoughts and allowing us to overhear him. It is suggested that the following comparisons are reminiscent, one of another in tone of voice as well as in balance and repetition:[42]

> The Lord is my rock, and my fortress, and my
>   deliverer;
> The God of my rock; in him will I trust:
> He is my shield, and the horn of my salvation, my
>   high tower, and my refuge,
> My saviour; thou savest me from violence.
> I will call on the Lord, who is worthy to be praised:
> So shall I be saved from mine enemies.
> (2 Samuel 22:2-4)[43]

> Let the sea heave no more in sound,
> hold the stars still, lest we hear the heavens dimly

ring with their commotion!
fold up all sounds.
(from **"Silence,"** *CP,* p. 698)[44]

> Save me, O God, from falling into the ungodly
>   knowledge
> of myself as I am without God.
> Let me never know, O God
> let me never know what I am or should be
> when I have fallen out of your hands, the hands of
>   the living God.
> (from **"The Hands of God,"** *CP,* p. 699)

> And all the dark-faced, cotton-wrapped people,
>   more numerous and whispering than grains of
>   rice in a rice-field at night,
> All the dark-faced, cotton-wrapped people, a
>   countless host on the shores of the lake, like
>   thick wild rice by the water's edge,
> (from **"Elephant,"** *CP,* p. 391)

It is hoped that throughout this essay enough has been said to suggest that Lawrence is a poet of great imagination, even though concentration has been upon Lawrence, the artist in words. Over a whole range of many fine poems, he instinctively chooses the right word, the right phrase, the right rhythms. In him, word and insight are one. D. H. Lawrence is a major poet because he uniquely marries the texture of expression to the texture of the imagination.

NOTES

[1] P. N. Furbank and Arnold Kettle, *Modernism and Its Origins,* Arts, A Third Level Course, *Twentieth-Century Poetry,* Units 4-5 (Milton Keynes, Eng.: Open University Press, 1975). It is only fair to say that the substantial course reader does contain some twenty or so references to Lawrence, but most of these are only passing or minor references. The only major reference is a reprinting of Graham Hough's critique of "Snake." See Graham Martin and P. N. Furbank, eds., *Twentieth-Century Poetry: Critical Essays and Documents* (Milton Keynes, Eng.: Open University Press, 1975), pp. 113-15, and Graham Hough, *Image and Experience: Studies in a Literary Revolution* (London: Duckworth, 1960), pp. 94-97.

[2] Horace Gregory, *Pilgrim of the Apocalypse* (New York: Viking, 1933), rpt. with revisions in Frederick J. Hoffman and Harry T. Moore, *The Achievement of D. H. Lawrence* (Norman: University of Oklahoma Press, 1953), pp. 235-52, 246-47.

[3] Ibid., p. 246. In this, Gregory may be echoing the comment made a little earlier by Richard Aldington: "From the first sentence in *The White Peacock* to the last broken utterance . . . all this mass of writing forms one immense autobiography" (see Richard Aldington, "Introduction to *Last Poems* and *More Pansies*" [1932]). D. H. Lawrence, *The Complete Poems of D. H. Lawrence,* collected and edited with an introduction and notes by Vivian de Sola Pinto and Warren Roberts, 2 vols. (1964; rpt. London: Heinemann, 1967), p. 594. Hereafter referred to as *CP.*

4 Richard Ellman, "Barbed Wire and Coming Through," *New Mexico Quarterly,* 23 (Spring 1953), rpt. in Hoffman and Moore, pp. 253-67, 255, 256. A shorter and presumably earlier form of this essay appeared in Richard Ellman, "Lawrence and His Demon," *New Mexico Quarterly,* 22 (Winter 1952), 385-93.

5 Gregory, p. 247.

6 In addition to R. P. Blackmur's essay (see n. 16), these include Anthony West, *D. H. Lawrence,* 2d ed. (London: Arthur Barker, 1966), p. 135: "it is difficult to take his claims to the stature of a poet seriously"; James Reeves, "D. H. Lawrence," in his *Commitment to Poetry* (London: Heinemann, 1969), pp. 222-27, esp. p. 222: "[Lawrence] was not a great poet . . . he was not a good poet in the technical sense"; and Michael Schmidt, *A Reader's Guide to Fifty Modern British Poets* (London: Heinemann, 1979), p. 101: "Unlike most of Lawrence's poems, "The Ship of Death" is memorable in its actual phrases."

7 Gamini Salgado, review of *The Complete Poems of D. H. Lawrence,* ed. Vivian de Sola Pinto and Warren Roberts (London: Heinemann, 1964), in *The Critical Quarterly* (Winter 1965), pp. 389-92; quotation from p. 392.

8 Kenneth Rexroth, Introduction to *Selected Poems of D. H. Lawrence* (New York: New Directions, 1947), p. 2.

9 See n. 19.

10 See n. 37.

11 Ibid.

12 Ellman, "Barbed Wire and Coming Through," p. 258.

13 D. H. Lawrence, Preface to *Collected Poems* (1928), p. 28, rpt. in *CP,* pp. 27-29.

14 Ibid., p. 27.

15 Ibid.

16 R. P. Blackmur, "D. H. Lawrence and Expressive Form," p. 288, in his *Language as Gesture: Essays in Poetry* (London: Allen & Unwin, 1954), pp. 286-300.

17 D. H. Lawrence, *Fantasia of the Unconscious,* p. 9, in *Fantasia of the Unconscious and Psychoanalysis and the Unconscious* (London: Heinemann, 1961), pp. 5-192.

18 Sola Pinto, "D. H. Lawrence: Poet without a Mask," *CP,* p. 2.

19 Joyce Carol Oates, *The Hostile Sun: The Poetry of D. H. Lawrence* (Los Angeles: Black Sparrow Press, 1974).

20 D. H. Lawrence, *The Collected Letters of D. H. Lawrence,* ed. Harry T. Moore, 2 vols. (London: Heinemann, 1962), p. 221.

21 A. Alvarez, "D. H. Lawrence: The Single State of Man," pp. 291-92, in *Modern Poetry: Essays in Criticism,* ed. John Hollander (New York: Oxford University Press, 1968), pp. 285-300.

22 Ibid., p. 291.

23 Ibid., p. 292.

24 Lawrence, *Collected Letters,* p. 172.

25 Ibid., p. 253.

26 Ibid., p. 242.

27 D. H. Lawrence, "Preface to *Chariot of the Sun* by Harry Crosby," p. 255, in *Phoenix: The Posthumous Papers of D. H. Lawrence,* ed. Edward D. McDonald (London: Heinemann, 1936), pp. 255-62.

28 Ibid., pp. 260-61.

29 Lawrence, *Collected Letters,* pp. 243-44.

30 Ibid., p. 242.

31 D. H. Lawrence, "Poetry of the Present," Introduction to the American edition of *New Poems* [1918], p. 185, rpt. in *CP,* pp. 181-86.

32 Lawrence, *Collected Letters,* p. 413.

33 Ibid., p. 413.

34 For Lawrence's own comments see his letter to Harriet Monroe, 31 July 1914, in Lawrence, *Collected Letters,* p. 288.

35 Lawrence, "Poetry of the Present," in *CP,* pp. 181-86.

36 D. H. Lawrence, "Hymns in a Man's Life," p. 598, in *Phoenix II: Uncollected, Unpublished, and Other Prose Works by D. H. Lawrence,* comp. Warren Roberts and Harry T. Moore (London: Heinemann, 1968), pp. 597-601.

37 See Tom Marshall, *The Psychic Mariner: A Reading of the Poems of D. H. Lawrence* (London: Heinemann, 1970), p. 84. For me the case is clinched by the parallel reference in Lawrence's *The Rainbow* (London: Penguin Books, 1970), p. 292 (chap. 11), quoted by Marshall: "Once three angels stood in Abraham's doorway and greeted him, and stayed and ate with him, leaving his household enriched for ever when they went"; but see also Sandra M. Gilbert, *Acts of Attention: The Poems of D. H. Lawrence* (Ithaca: Cornell University Press, 1972), p. 107.

38 Blackmur, p. 297.

39 John Ruskin, "The Pathetic Fallacy," *Modern Painters,* III, 156, rpt. in John Ruskin, *Ruskin as a Literary Critic:*

Selections, ed. A. H. R. Ball (Cambridge: Cambridge University Press, 1928), pp. 146-60.

[40] See n. 36.

[41] This is not intended as an original statement. Rexroth, pp. 13-14, briefly touches on the subject.

[42] Theodore Robinson, in his study of Old Testament poetry, has a number of things to say which are of interest to the kind of verse Lawrence wrote. In one place he discusses balance and parallelism: "It is the speaker's thought which rouses an expectation, and this can be satisfied only by a repetition or by a balancing conception" (*The Poetry of the Old Testament* [London: Duckworth, 1947], p. 20). See also James L. Kugel, *The Idea of Biblical Poetry: Parallelism and Its History* (New Haven: Yale University Press, 1981).

[43] The text used is that of *The Reader's Bible: The Reader's Bible, Being the Authorized Version of the Holy Bible Containing the Old and New Testaments and the Apocrypha Translated out of the Original Tongues* (London: Oxford University Press, Cambridge University Press, Eyre & Spottiswoode, 1951). In this edition, verse numberings are omitted, and the text is printed as prose or verse.

[44] The fact that the last verse of the poem begins "Lift up your heads, O ye Gates!" indicates how closely Lawrence had the Bible in mind (see Psalm 24:7).

Frederic Vanson (essay date 1985)

SOURCE: "D. H. Lawrence—The Poetry," in *Contemporary Review*, Vol. 247, No. 1438, November, 1985, pp. 257-60.

[*In the following essay, Vanson argues that Lawrence was a master craftsman, and places him alongside such poets as Gerard Manley Hopkins, Percy Bysshe Shelley, and Robert Browning, while finding him not equal to Virgil, Dante, and Shakespeare.*]

At the time of the **Lady Chatterley** obscenity trial in an article for a provincial newspaper I suggested that in time to come (i.e. now!) the real fame of D. H. Lawrence would derive not from his novels but from his poetry. Time has proved me wrong, for there are today probably a hundred readers of **The Rainbow** or **Women in Love** to every one familiar with **"The Ship of Death."**

No doubt this is in part due to the Chatterley affair and its aftermath, but I do hold the view that if the fame of this brilliant writer (for brilliant he is for all his flaws) does not depend upon his poetry, nevertheless in some degree it ought so to do, for he was undeniably a considerable poet of great originality and power.

After all, *is* there a poet like David Herbert Lawrence? Does not his verse stand quite apart from the mainstream of English poetry and owe, as Blake's does, hardly anything to his forerunners? Is it not true that as he had no precursors so he has had to date no successor? The test of his claim to originality is surely that he cannot be successfully imitated.

In his early years as a poet he was associated with the Imagists, though only loosely so, but a comparison of a truly imagist poem like Ezra Pound's famous example with any poem of Lawrence's will prove that he does not belong with that school.

> The apparition of these faces in the crowd;
> Petals on a wet, black bough.
> ("In a Station of the Metro")

> Softly, in the dusk, a woman is singing to me
> Taking me back down the vista of years, till I see
> A child sitting under the piano, in the boom
>   of the tingling strings
> And pressing the small poised feet of a mother
>   who smiles as she sings.
> ("Piano")

In retrospect it seems absurd that the often prolix and sometimes rhapsodic Lawrence could ever be classified with such economic word spinners as T. E. Hulme or H.D. Was he then a Georgian poet? True, some of his early pieces were published alongside poems by such typical Georgian figures as Squire or Abercrombie, but other than being their contemporary there is scarcely any point of resemblance. He had no fellows in his one-man school.

Individual as his work was, it was certainly not ignored by those of other persuasions. Even so conservative a figure as J. C. Squire was quick to recognise the merits of Lawrence's verse, though their practice could hardly be more different, nor their philosophies more at variance.

If only one in a hundred readers of Lawrence know his poetry it is still a considerable number. *The Collected Poems* in two volumes as well as the handy Penguin selection are steady sellers. This poetry obviously still speaks, and speaks powerfully, to a large number of readers, a number far greater than that enjoyed by some of the best poets writing today. Why is this so? What are the strengths of his verse?

To begin with, he was a master craftsman. I have no doubt that had he decided to write in *terza rima* or to compose a sonnet sequence he could have done so with great efficiency. He chose in the main to use free verse forms, but he understood well that free verse should not be so free as to fall apart. Poetry differs from prose in its cadence and this he knew. It depends upon a certain heightening of language and this he exhibits to perfection without falling into rhetoric for rhetoric's sake. He was undoubtedly familiar with Whitman and his English disciple, Edward Carpenter, but his *vers libre* is not theirs. At its best it is beautiful, exact, balanced and memorable:

> It is a mountain lion,
> A long, long slim cat, yellow like a lioness.

Dead.
He trapped her this morning he says, smiling
    foolishly.

Lift up her face,
Her round, bright face, bright as frost.
Her round, fine-fashioned head, with two dead ears;
And stripes in the brilliant frost of her face,
                sharp, fine dark rays,
Dark, keen fine eyes in the brilliant frost of her
    face . . .

                        ("Mountain Lion")

Or, to take another example:

A woman has given me strength and affluence.
Admitted!
All the rocking wheat of Canada, ripening now,
has not so much of strength as the body of one
    woman
sweet in ear, nor so much to give
though it feed nations . . .

                        ("Manifesto")

So much for form; what of content? Much of Lawrence's poetry fairly obviously relates to events, external and subjective alike, in his life—his relationship with his mother, with 'Miriam', with his wife, Frieda. Much else is inspired by his travels in both the Old World and the New. These influences and sources are brought together with an intensity of emotion rare in English poetry. Later, his preoccupations widened out to embrace what we have come to think of as the Lawrentian philosophy—a belief that man has been corrupted unto death by civilisation and that the way back to a prelapsarian wholeness lies through sexual love between men and women seen as peers. Lawrence, in fact, is an intensely physical poet and presents us with a heightened awareness of animals, plants, trees; geographies come alive, zoology assumes a quasi-metaphysic. These things make his poetry intensely visual, sensual, tactual almost. They can also be his weakness.

But let us not cavil. What of its kind, if indeed it *has* a kind, is superior to **"Snake"**?

He reached down from a fissure in the earth-wall
    in the gloom
And trailed his yellow-brown slackness soft-
    bellied down, over the edge of the stone trough
And rested his throat upon the stone bottom,
And where the water had dripped from the tap, in
    a small clearness
He sipped with his straight mouth,
Softly drank through his straight gums, into his
    slack, long body . . .

How beautifully, accurately descriptive this is!

The same descriptive or evocative power (also, of course, abundantly present in the novels) is seen in a different and earlier context in the poem **"Love on the Farm."**

The rabbit presses back her ears,
Turns back her liquid, anguished eyes

And crouches low; then with wild spring
Spurts from the terror of his oncoming;
To be choked back, the wire ring
Her frantic effort throttling;
Piteous brown ball of quivering fears!
Ah, soon in his large, hard hands she dies,
And swings all loose from the swing of his walk!

Such passages as these give us Lawrence at his most powerful. In many of the small, late, embittered bagatelles of his last years we see a smaller spirit, a spiteful mind. The one real flaw in Lawrence as a poet is his occasional lapse into banality, spite or plain silliness. **"The Oxford Voice"**, for example, is a dreadful piece of spiteful inverted snobbery (and I write as a non-Oxonian!) and **"How Beastly the Bourgeois Is"** is a ridiculous piece of class prejudice.

It is interesting that in his recent anthology *The Penguin Book of English Christian Verse* Peter Levi includes Lawrence. Lawrence was, of course, no orthodoxly religious man, but his imagery is full of Judeo-Christian allusions. That he was a religious man is not in serious doubt, but no orthodoxy could have held his mind. The poem **"Phoenix"** may be seen as a restatement of the Christian doctrine that to gain your life you must be prepared to lose it, but this does not make him a Christian in any ordinary sense of the term.

Are you willing to be sponged out, erased, cancelled,
    made nothing?
Are you willing to be made nothing? dipped into
    oblivion?

If not you will never really change.

The phoenix renews her youth
only when she is burnt, burnt alive, burnt down
to hot and flocculent ash . . .

And if that poignant and beautiful poem **"The Ship of Death"** is not a religious poem then there is no such thing. In **"The Body of God"** Lawrence comes as near as he ever does to stating his credo—

There is no god
apart from poppies and flying fish,
men singing songs, and women brushing their hair
    in the sun.
The lovely things are god that has come to pass,
    like Jesus came.
The rest, the undiscoverable, is the demiurge.

To summarise, D. H. Lawrence is undeniably a poet of skill, of emotional power, of prolific if uneven achievement, a brilliant observer and delineator of people, creatures and places, a religious poet with no formal code of belief. Do these add up to greatness? Is he a minor poet, a major poet or a major-minor?

These value judgements seem to me very difficult and of dubious value. Lawrence was not one of the towering geniuses of poetry alongside Shakespeare, Dante, Homer,

Virgil. But is he less than, say, Browning, Shelley, Heine, Herbert, Hopkins? For my own part I think not, but in the last analysis such mensuration of genius is of no great value. A true poet is a unique and uniquely valuable human being and that, surely, is enough.

Let Lawrence's own words speak for him—

> I have been, and I have returned.
> I have mounted up on the wings of the morning
>   and I have dredged down to the zenith's reversal.
> Which is my way, being man.
> Gods may stay in mid-heaven, the Son of Man
>   has climbed to the Whitsun zenith,
> But I, Matthew, being a man
> Am a traveller back and forth.
> So be it.

("St. Matthew")

FURTHER READING

Criticism

Aiken, Conrad. *Collected Criticism (Formerly 'A Reviewer's ABC')*. London: Oxford University Press, 1935, 414 p.
> Essays written by Aiken on Lawrence between 1924 and 1929 that evidence Aiken's admiration for Lawrence as a prose writer as well as his reservations concerning the prosaic nature of Lawrence's verse.

Baker, James R. "Lawrence as Prophetic Poet." *Journal of Modern Literature* 3, No. 5 (July 1974): 1219-38.
> Discusses Lawrence's poetry and the works of W. B. Yeats, Robinson Jeffers, and T. S. Eliot, finding prophetic qualities in the work of all four poets.

Brashear, Lucy M. "Lawrence's Companion Poems: 'Snake' and *Tortoises*" *The D. H. Lawrence Review* 5, No. 1 (Spring 1972): 54-62.
> Analyzes "Snake" as part of a sequence including the separately published *Tortoises*, and notes the thematic and stylistic similarites of the works Lawrence eventually published under the heading "Reptiles."

Cipolla, Elizabeth. "The *Last Poems* of D. H. Lawrence" *The D. H. Lawrence Review* 2, No. 2 (Summer 1969): 103-19.
> Employs Lawrence's posthumously discovered notebooks to analyze the poems written in the last two years of his life.

Drew, Elizabeth and John L Sweeney. *Directions in Modern Poetry*. New York: Gordian Press, 1967, 290 p.
> Enumerates the inconsistencies the commentators perceive in Lawrence's poetry and finds that the poet was a chronicler of immediate emotions resulting in poetry that varied widely in quality.

Gilbert, Sandra M. *Acts of Attention: The Poems of D. H. Lawrence*. Ithaca, N.Y.: Cornell University Press, 1972, 327 p.
> Champions Lawrence as a writer fully in control of his poetic faculties, using evidence from Lawrence's own essays to support her claim.

Gomme, A. H., ed. *D. H. Lawrence: A Critical Study of the Major Novels and Other Writings*. New York: Barnes & Noble, 1978, 224 p.
> Compiles ten essays on Lawrence, including "D. H. Lawrence's Poetry: Art and Apprehension," by R. T. Jones, in which the author uses Lawrence's fiction to explain the themes of his poetry.

Henderson, Philip. *The Poet and Society*. London: Martin Secker & Warburg, Ltd., 1939, 248 p.
> Equates the collection *Birds, Beasts, and Flowers* in importance with T. S. Eliot's *The Wasteland*.

Hyman, Stanley Edgar. *The Critic's Credentials: Essays & Reviews by Stanley Edgar Hyman*, edited by Phoebe Pettingell. New York: Atheneum, 1978, 325 p.
> Categorizes Lawrence's work as alternately written by either a "Young Woman," "Tarzan," "Peepshow Barker," "Hedge Preacher," or "Spiteful Ted," while acknowledging that Lawrence was capable of poetic triumphs.

Mace, Hebe Riddick. "The Achievement of Poetic Form: D. H. Lawrence's *Last Poems*." *The D. H. Lawrence Review* 12, No. 3 (Fall 1979): 275-88.
> Responds to R. P. Blackmur's arguments against Lawrence's poetry by defending free verse as an honored English literary tradition.

Marshall, Tom. *The Psychic Mariner: A Reading of the Poems of D. H. Lawrence*. New York: Viking Press, 1970, 275 p.
> Presents an overview of Lawrence's career as a poet and the critical response that his poetry received.

Moore, Harry T., ed. *A D. H. Lawrence Miscellany*. Carbondale: Southern Illinois University Press, 1959, 395 p.
> Compiles essays dedicated to various aspects of Lawrence's writing which reinforce Moore's opinion of Lawrence as the major author of the twentieth century.

Murfin, Ross C. *The Poetry of D. H. Lawrence: Texts & Contexts*. Lincoln: University of Nebraska Press, 1983, 263 p.
> Divides Lawrence's poetry into three phases and places his entire body of work firmly in the Romantic tradition.

Oates, Joyce Carol. *The Hostile Sun: The Poetry of D. H. Lawrence*. Los Angeles: Black Sparrow Press, 1973, 60 p.
> Contends that Lawrence's poetry is superior to his prose, and that his poetry needs to be judged as a whole rather than as individual poems.

Solomon, Gerald. "The Banal, and the Poetry of D. H. Lawrence." *Essays in Criticism* 23, No. 3 (July 1973): 254-67.

Argues that Lawrence undermines the effectiveness of his poetry with less-than-adequate technique.

Steinberg, Erwin R. "'Song of a Man Who Has Come Through'—A Pivotal Poem." *The D. H. Lawrence Review* 11, No. 1 (Spring 1978): 50-62.
    Finds Biblical sources for Lawrence's poem, in contrast to previous critics who believed the work referenced Greek mythology.

Trail, George Y. "West by East: The Psycho-Geography of *Birds, Beasts, and Flowers.*" *The D. H. Lawrence Review* 12, No. 3 (Fall 1979): 241-55.
    Relies on information about Lawrence's travels to explicate the poems contained in *Birds, Beasts, and Flowers.*

Vickery, John B. "D. H. Lawrence's Poetry: Myth and Matter." *The D. H. Lawrence Review* 7, No. 1 (Spring 1974): 1-18.
    Places Lawrence's poetry between the mythopoetic verse of T. S. Eliot and the physical descriptiveness of the work of William Carlos Williams.

The following sources published by Gale contain further coverage of Lawrence's life and works: *Concise Dictionary of British Literary Biography,* 1914-1945; *Contemporary Authors,* Vols. 104, 121; *Dictionary of Literary Biography,* Vols. 10, 19, 36, 98, 162, 195; *DISCovering Authors; DISCovering Authors: British; DISCovering Authors: Canadian; DISCovering Authors: Modules, Most-Studied Authors Module, Novelists Module, Poets Module; Major 20th-Century Writers; Short Story Criticism,* Vols. 4, 19; *Twentieth-Century Literary Criticism,* Vols. 2, 9, 16, 33, 48, 61; *World Literature Criticism.*

Lloyd Osbourne

1868-1947

(Full name Samuel Lloyd Osbourne) American novelist, playwright, and short story writer.

INTRODUCTION

Osbourne is considered a gifted storyteller whose romantic adventure novels place him solidly in the tradition of Anglo-American escapist fiction. Bearing similarities to the popular writings of his stepfather and occasional collaborator, Robert Louis Stevenson, Osbourne's imaginative fiction features a blend of humor, excitement, and fantastic wonder and is frequently set in exotic locales. His 1908 novel *Infatuation* is counted among his more serious works, but it is for his relationship to Stevenson and for his popular novels, such as *The Adventurer*, that he is generally remembered.

Biographical Information

Osbourne was born in San Francisco, California, on 7 April 1868 to Samuel Osbourne and Fanny Van de Grift. While Osbourne was still quite young his mother married the well-known writer Robert Louis Stevenson. Osbourne accompanied his parents on their frequent travels, and was educated by private tutors in England, France, and Switzerland. He later attended Edinburgh University, where he studied civil engineering. Further travels with Stevenson after his departure from Edinburgh took Osbourne to Samoa. There he served as U.S. vice consul-general until 1897. In the late 1880s, Osbourne began his literary collaboration with his stepfather. Together the two produced three novels: *The Wrong Box*, *The Wrecker*, and *The Ebb-Tide*. After Stevenson's death, Osbourne wrote several more novels, including *The Adventurer*, *Infatuation*, and *A Person of Some Importance*, and produced a collection of short fiction, *Wild Justice: Stories of the South Seas*. Later in his career he wrote, along with his nephew Austin Strong, several dramas. Osbourne died in 1947.

Major Works

Osbourne's fiction includes a collection of romantic novels and adventure stories, many of them set in the South Pacific, where he spent a significant portion of his adult life. *Baby Bullet* is a light, humorous romance concerning the travels of a young American woman and her governess across Europe in an aging and unreliable automobile. *The Adventurer* recounts the voyages of the *Fortuna*, an enormous sailing ship that travels overland on wheels. Its captain, Lewis Kirkpatrick, directs the vessel across South America in search of the treasures of Cassaquiari, an ancient lost city. Accompanied by a cast of European and American characters—the scientific explorer Dr. von Zedtwitz, the inventor Westbrook, and the expedition's millionaire financier Mrs. Poulteney Hitchcock among them—Kirkpatrick and the *Fortuna* brave brutal storms, a mutiny, and the attacks of natives before recovering thousandsof gold ingots in remote Cassaquiari. Based on the actual disappearance of an Austrian archduke, *A Person of Some Importance* offers a fictionalized and fantastic account of this man's self-imposed exile on a tropical island. Discovered by a discharged U. S. Navy cadet, the archduke takes this American, Matthew Broughton, into his service for several years. After Broughton returns to New England he is tracked down by agents of the Austrian Emperor who coerce him into revealing the location of the missing duke. When the Emperor finally reaches the distant island he finds the missing man has very recently died. Osbourne's representative short story collection, *Wild Justice: Stories of the South Seas*, contains nine tales, ranging from peaceful idylls to accounts of jealousy and murder.

Critical Reception

Critical response to Osbourne's works amounts to reviews that assess the relative merits of his novels and short stories as entertainment. Reviewers have typically praised him for his imagination and inventiveness, as well as for his amusing plots and vivid presentation of exotic settings. Detractors have noted that, while exciting, Osbourne's stories fail to engage readers on a thematic level, and many have observed the lack of psychologically complex characters in his fiction. Nonetheless, critics generally acknowledge that Osbourne's works were simply intended as amusements, and most of his reviewers share an enthusiasm for his writing in this context.

PRINCIPAL WORKS

The Wrong Box [with Robert Louis Stevenson] (novel) 1889
The Wrecker [with Robert Louis Stevenson] (novel) 1892
The Ebb-Tide [with Robert Louis Stevenson] (novel) 1894
The Queen versus Billy (short stories) 1900
Baby Bullet (novel) 1905
Love, the Fiddler (short stories) 1905
The Motor-Maniacs (novel) 1905
Three Speeds Forward (novel) 1906
The Tin Diskers (novel) 1906
Wild Justice: Stories of the South Seas (short stories) 1906

The Adventurer (novel) 1907
Schmidt (novel) 1907
Infatuation (novel) 1908
Person of Some Importance (novel) 1911
Peril (novel) 1929

CRITICISM

The Bookman (essay date 1906)

SOURCE: A review of *Baby Bullet,* in *The Bookman,* London, Vol. XXIX, No. 173, February, 1906, p. 225.

[*In the following review, the critic characterizes* Baby Bullet *as a pleasant but essentially popular novel.*]

The fine literary quality that distinguished many of the stories in Mr. Lloyd Osbourne's *Love the Fiddler* and *The Queen versus Billy* is lacking in his *Baby Bullet,* which is a light readable novel of the more popular kind, written in the easy, agreeable, somewhat commonplace style that seems essential to popularity. Not that the story itself is commonplace—it is an amusing and ingenious romance of a pretty American girl and her governess who are making a walking tour through England, and come into possession of an obsolete-pattern motor-car, which is continually breaking down, and involves them in all manner of difficulties and delectable adventures, but carries them to an altogether idyllic happiness at last. There is enough technical motor talk to delight the expert, and not enough of it to worry the ignorant; the love episodes are touched in with a charming airiness; the humour of the book verges at times on the broadly farcical, but the interest of it never flags for a minute, and it makes very pleasing reading throughout.

The Bookman (essay date 1906)

SOURCE: A review of *Wild Justice,* in *The Bookman,* London, Vol. XXX, No. 176, May, 1906, pp. 75-6.

[*In the following review, the critic praises the stories of Osbourne's* Wild Justice *for their "vividness and beauty and straightforwardness."*]

The collective title of Mr. Lloyd Osbourne's nine tales refers apparently to the rough equity of the South Sea Islands; to the justice of sailors safely away from legal machinery, of natives, and of the two in their relations together. It also, we fancy, has reference to that deeper justice which makes a great passion worth while, whatever the tragic consequences, and which led Baudelaire to exclaim: "Mais qu'importe l'éternité de la damnation à qui a trouvé dans une seconde l'infini de la jouissance!" For in these stories where white man meets brown, the nature of the former is stirred to its primitive depths.

Many have been moved by the scene in *Westward Ho!* where the sailors are found living with native women in the wild. It will be remembered that Joseph Conrad has treated the interaction of black and white with matchless insight; has used it, indeed, as a searchlight on our civilisation. Mr. Osbourne is not so subtle a psychologist as the author of *Lord Jim.* He is more of a story-teller. In the best of this nine, Jack Haviland—yearning to leave the squalor aboard and the debauchery ashore of life in a tramp's fo'c'stle, and to have a home—deserts from "the sea, that took all and gave nothing." A Samoan girl and her kinsfolk develop all the good which was latent in his nature, and he works for them as they never could themselves. Their life is a successful idyll, until the Powers harry the islands, and then—the end. If the psychology of the story holds good—and we think it does—**"The Renegade"** is a very fine effort. It is told with the vividness and beauty and straightforwardness that distinguish this volume. *Wild Justice* is a book to be recommended. There are men in it.

The Nation (essay date 1907)

SOURCE: A review of *The Adventurer,* in *The Nation,* New York, Vol. 85, No. 2214, December 5, 1907, p. 518.

[*In the following review of* The Adventurer, *the critic praises Osbourne's versatile imagination and engaging storytelling.*]

Mr. Osbourne's new story is characteristically ingenious and fantastic. The centre of the stage is held by a wonderful land-going ship, the Fortuna, constructed for the purpose of treasure-hunting beyond the South American llaños. Supported on eight gigantic wheels, and carrying two lofty schooner-rigged masts, she drives, day after day, across the trackless plain, bounding, jolting, careening before the trade-wind—her goal a deserted city of unknown antiquity, where ingots of gold lie stacked in subterranean caverns. The voyage of the Fortuna is full of vicissitudes. There is mutiny among her crew; there are hurricanes and calms, and accidents to gear and canvas; worst of all, there are hordes of screaming, half-naked savages, from whom the good ship escapes only after deadly battle. The final success of the enterprise is due, in large measure, to Kirkpatrick, the resourceful young captain. At the opening of the story he appears as an unsuccessful jack-of-all-trades, looking for employment in London. Pertinaciously following up the clue of a mysterious newspaper advertisement, he is led into the midst of an adventure, the objective of which is completely hidden from him, until he finds himself under the very masts of the Fortuna, in the far interior of the Orinoco country. An entertaining and varied group of persons embark upon this expedition with him, among them a German archæologist, a wealthy dowager from Paris, a manufacturer from Jersey City and his plucky daughter. Vera, between whom and Kirkpatrick develops an engaging romance.

Mr. Osbourne's versatile imagination seems never to fail him. There is not a lull in the action, not a paragraph of dull writing. It is to be regretted that, in a tale so extravagantly fanciful, the author should have given himself free rein in the description of sickening carnage and violence. In spite of this defect of taste, and the too liberal amplification of a plot which is, at best, only a conceit, *The Adventurer* bids fair to take its place among a not too numerous company of Stocktonian and Stevensonian kindred.

The Bookman (essay date 1908)

SOURCE: A review of *The Adventurer,* in *The Bookman,* London, Vol. XXXV, No. 205, October, 1908, p. 58.

[*In the following review, the critic calls* The Adventurer *a "clean and invigorating tale."*]

Dr. von Zedtwitz, guiding a scientific expedition from the city of Quito into the unexplored regions of the Southern Llanos, fell into the hands of the savage aboriginals and spent three years in captivity. It was then that he happened by chance upon a place called Cassaquiari, and found the ruins of an antique city, and among the ruins the actual strong-room of the citadel, and in the strong-room five thousand ingots of pure gold. He escaped from captivity and one day met Mrs. Poulteney Hitchcock. She was a millionaire and was soon persuaded to finance an expedition to recover the buried treasure. Westbrook, the famous inventor, designed the vessel *Fortuna* that was to bear the weighty mass across the land—a topsail schooner running on gigantic wheels. And then a band of men was got together to make the great adventure. Lewis Kirkpatrick was one of these, before long captain of them, and he is the hero of this swinging tale. Other romancists have shrunk from the last mendacity and have called fire down from heaven or up from the bowels of the earth to prevent avaricious hands from wresting treasure from the grave where it has been buried. Not so Mr. Lloyd Osbourne. He works to a finish. With breezy courage he takes his gallant company out and leads them home again, bringing their golden tale behind them. Lewis Kirkpatrick's share of the sport was 437,000 dollars and a wife—Vera, the lovely daughter of Westbrook the inventor. That, it will be admitted, was fairly good hunting. "Corking—simply corking," was Wicks's description of the picture made by the treasure in the ancient vault, and "corking—simply corking" is the happiest label to attach to Mr. Osbourne's book *The Adventurer.* It is a clean and invigorating tale of adventure, the breeziest that has been written for many a day.

William Morton Payne (essay date 1912)

SOURCE: A review of *A Person of Some Importance,* in *The Dial,* Vol. LII, No. 613, January 1, 1912, pp. 23-4.

[*In the following review, Payne sees* A Person of Some Importance *as inventive but disappointing in style and characterization.*]

The romantic story of the Austrian archduke who separated himself from civilization some twenty years ago, his subsequent history and fate to remain a mystery, has been taken by Mr. Lloyd Osbourne for the groundwork of the tale which he entitles *A Person of Some Importance.* Last year, it will be remembered, the missing man was declared to be legally dead, and his estate settled. Mr. Osbourne's invention (for which there is some shadow of historical support) represents the archduke as having concealed himself, in company with the lady for whom he thought the world well lost, upon a remote island in the South Pacific, and as having died there after his twenty years of self-imposed exile. The name "John Orth," which he is known to have taken, here becomes "John Mort." The story is primarily concerned with one Matthew Broughton, in training for the navy, but dismissed in disgrace from the Annapolis Academy for participation in a hazing outrage. He ships before the mast, knocks about the seas for a while, and finally comes upon "John Mort," by whom he is made a sort of confidential agent. After some years of this life, he wearies of it, and returns to his home in New England, pledged to the profoundest secrecy by his late royal employer. This is where the real story begins, for agents of the Austrian court get upon Broughton's track, and seek to extort from him the secret which they are persuaded is in his possession. They resort in vain to cajolery, bribery, and personal violence. They thwart his every attempt to make a living, and when he elopes with the daughter of the local magnate, they track him to California, lure him on board a ship under their control, and carry him to the South Pacific. Here, it seems, an Austrian battle-ship, carrying no less August a passenger than the Emperor, is awaiting their arrival; and here, moved by the Emperor's own plea, Broughton discloses his well-kept secret. But when the mysterious island is reached it transpires that "John Mort" has died a few weeks before, and the hopes of his imperial father are crushed. Here is obviously the material for a good yarn, and as far as invention is concerned, the author has put it to fairly good use. But his style is so raw, and his characterization so wooden, that our chief feeling is one of disappointment that the theme has not fallen into hands capable of doing it more justice and of more fully realizing its romantic possibilities.

The Bookman (essay date 1922)

SOURCE: A review of *Wild Justice: Stories of the South Seas,* in *The Bookman,* London, Vol. LXII, 369, June, 1922, p. 143.

[*In the following review, the critic lauds* Wild Justice *as a fascinating blend of tragedy and humor.*]

It is not fair of Mr. Lloyd Osbourne. Here are we, packed more or less securely in some of the biggest cities of the world, taking shelter from rain, wearing clothes that afflict us in hot weather and are not particularly comfortable in cold weather, catching trains and colds and running offices and paying—or trying to pay—income-tax; and he considers this a suitable moment to call our attention to those South Sea isles where nature supplies every need and laughter and flowers and blue skies are the principal things that matter. Still, to do him justice, he describes several "affairs" which go to show that envy and murder, revenge and foul play have their setting in these lovely scenes, and that human nature, unchecked by law, can be very ugly indeed. To this new edition of his volume of stories [**Wild Justice**] some excellent additions have been made. Perhaps the best of them are those which deal with the white men who, for various reasons, are castaways on the shores of coral-girt and strangely-populated islands—castaways who have by no means lost their nerve, and who "carry on" their new life with the utmost cheek until discovery comes by a visiting ship whose message betrays them. Upon this foundation Mr. Osbourne has built some exciting yarns, and no reader will complain that he has not given good measure. He has the art of dramatist and novelist combined, and his methods are exactly right. Take as an example the incident of **"Old Dibs,"** the mysterious stranger who landed with "five large trunks and the clothes he stood in." Money, in hard cash, was in those trunks, and the two men whom he confided in rigged up a hiding-place in a giant tree in the middle of the island, where, in the event of a suspicious-looking vessel making a call, he could retire. For a long time nothing happened; then came an inquiring ship, and up the tree went the visitor, by the strenuous efforts of his friends. And the ship's company hunted in vain for the absconding banker and company promoter on whose head a big price was set. His end, after such a fine run for his money, was a sad one, but he retained his acuteness to the last, and took care that his money did not fall into other hands. The story is one that holds the reader to the finish, and it is a good example of the author's style and genius for an exciting plot. Humour and tragedy, inseparable as ever, go to the making of this fascinating book.

The Bookman (essay date 1929)

SOURCE: A review of *Peril*, in *The Bookman*, London, Vol. LXXVI, No. 451, April, 1929, p. 64.

[*In the following review, the critic recounts the plot of* Peril *and comments on the "charm and fragrance" of its love story.*]

There is a briskness about this latest story [*Peril*] by Stevenson's stepson and collaborator which quickly arrests the attention and retains it. For hero, Mr. Lloyd Osbourne presents in Hal Curwen—novelist, thirty-six, divorced—a portrait which may owe something to his own early New York experiences; but his setting and the other characters are wholly of the New York and Long Island and California of to-day. The delightful Nigma is certainly of the present. "She belonged to the new type of expensively educated young American women in whom femininity is guarded like a jewel; who can ride and swim and play games without impairing their essential charm; who can wear the appropriate clothes with elegance." And Tim Reardon, "one of the copper millionaires," is as decidedly of the nineteen-twenties. The Sherlock Holmes, too, is essentially of the United States and up-to-dateness. He is a dentist, and "blows in" to the coroner's inquest to prove that the body which had been accepted as that of Tim Reardon is nothing of the kind, for he was Tim's dentist and while Tim had not a single gold tooth in his head, the corpse had three. But Mr. Osbourne gives his readers more than mere smartness. The love story of Hal Curwen has charm and fragrance of rare quality.

FURTHER READING

Biography

Morley, Christopher. "An American Gentleman." In *The Ironing Board*, pp. 86-91. Garden City, N.Y.: Doubleday & Company, 1949.
    Anecdotal memoir of Osbourne.

Santiago Ramón y Cajal

1852-1934

Spanish histologist, essayist, and autobiographer.

INTRODUCTION

A seminal figure in the field of neuroanatomy, Ramón y Cajal is numbered among the world's finest scientists. For his isolation of the nerve cell, or neuron, as the fundamental unit of the nervous system Ramón y Cajal was awarded the 1906 Nobel Prize for physiology or medicine, an honor he shared with Italian anatomist Camillo Golgi. In addition to this groundbreaking achievement, Ramón y Cajal is recognized for his work relating to the structure of the brain and nervous system, the function of nerve impulses, the nature of vision, and the processes of neural degeneration and regeneration. He is likewise noted for his nonscientific writings, particularly his autobiography, *Recuerdos de mi vida* (*Recollections of My Life*).

Biographical Information

Ramón y Cajal was born in the village of Petilla de Aragon, Spain, on 1 May 1852, the son of Justo Ramón y Casasús, a barber and surgeon, and Antonia Cajal. A recalcitrant youth, Ramón y Cajal indulged his passion for drawing and neglected his studies. In time, his father persuaded him to study medicine. Ramón y Cajal was apprenticed to a barber, and later a cobbler, by his father, but continued to practice his art clandestinely. When he was somewhat older, Ramón y Cajal accompanied his father to a nearby churchyard where the two obtained bones for use in their study of anatomy. His interest in medicine piqued, he began to produce detailed sketches of the bones. At the age of sixteen, Ramón y Cajal embarked upon the formal study of medicine at the University of Zaragoza, graduating with a medical degree in 1873. His subsequent service as an army surgeon in Cuba was cut short when he contracted malaria and was returned to Spain. A long convalescence ensued, during which he earned a doctoral degree in medicine. From 1879 to 1883 Ramón y Cajal acted as director of the anatomical museum at the University of Zaragoza and began his work in cell biology. He accepted a position as professor of descriptive anatomy at the University of Valencia in 1883 and a professorship of histology at the University of Barcelona in 1887. He was named chair of histology at the University of Madrid in 1892.

In 1896 he produced his *Manual de anatomia pathologica general* and subsequently his *Textura del sistema nervioso del hombre y de los vertebrados* (*New Ideas on the Structure of the Nervous System in Man and the Vertebrates*) between 1899 and 1904. After years of relative

neglect by the international scientific community, Ramón y Cajal's research on the anatomy of the nervous system was recognized in 1906 by the Nobel committee. Together with the Italian anatomist Camillo Golgi, who had developed a cell-staining process employed in research, Ramón y Cajal shared the Nobel Prize for physiology or medicine in that year. In 1913 and 1914, he published his two-volume *Estudios sobre la degeneración y regeneración del sistema nervioso* (*Degeneration and Regeneration of the Nervous System*). His reputation as an international authority on the anatomy and pathology of the nervous system long since secured, Ramón y Cajal was honored in 1920 by King Alfonso XIII of Spain, who commissioned the Instituto Cajal in Madrid. Upon its completion in 1922, Ramón y Cajal resigned his position at the University of Madrid to continue his work at the Instituto until his death on 18 October 1934.

Major Works

Containing 1,800 pages and 887 original illustrations, *Textura del sistema nervioso del hombre y de los vertebrados* is Ramón y Cajal's principal work of neurohistology. The text offers considerable support for modern neuron theory, which describes the nervous system as a complex network of discrete nerve fibers separated by tiny gaps, or synapses. For his *Estudios sobre la degeneración y regeneración del sistema nervioso* Ramón y Cajal developed a new technique for staining neuroglia, the delicate connective tissue of the nervous system. This allowed him to classify several new types of cells and to examine the problem of regenerating damaged nervous tissue. He also produced a monograph on the procedures of science, *Reglas y consejos sobre investigación biológia* (*Precepts and Counsels on Scientific Investigation*). Among his nonscientific works, Ramón y Cajal published a notable autobiography, *Recuerdos de mi vida*, as well as a collection of anecdotes and aphorisms entitled *Charlas de café*.

Critical Reception

Since rising from relative obscurity following the recognition of his work by the Nobel Prize committee in 1906, Ramón y Cajal has been acknowledged as a principal figure in the field of neuroscience. The complete publication of *Textura del sistema nervioso del hombre y de los vertebrados* in 1904 did much to overturn the then-prevalent conception of the nervous system as a single, conjoined mass rather than as a system of differentiated cells. The research documented in his *Estudios sobre la degeneración y regeneración del sistema nervioso* has proved vital to the medical treatment of tumors and repair of severed nerve tissue. At the end of the twentieth century only a small portion of Ramón y Cajal's theoretical work is still disputed among neuroscientists, while his enduring contribution to science and medicine as the progenitor of modern neurobiology remains unquestioned.

PRINCIPAL WORKS

Manual de anatomia pathologica general (nonfiction) 1896
Textura del sistema nervioso del hombre y de los vertebrados [*New Ideas on the Structure of the Nervous System in Man and the Vertebrates*] (nonfiction) 1899-1904
Estudios sobre la degeneración y regeneración del sistema nervioso. 2 vols. [*Degeneration and Regeneration of the Nervous System*] (nonfiction) 1913-1914
Reglas y consejos sobre investigación biológia [*Precepts and Counsels on Scientific Investigation*] (nonfiction) 1916
Charlas de café (aphorisms) 1922
Recuerdos de mi vida [*Recollections of My Life*] (autobiography) 1923
Cajal on the Cerebral Cortex: An Annotated Translation of the Complete Writings [edited by Javier DeFelipe and Edward G. Jones] (nonfiction) 1988

CRITICISM

Raoul M. May (essay date 1926)

SOURCE: A review of *Recuerdos de mi vida* and *Charlas de café*, in *ISIS*, Vol. VIII, 1926, pp. 498-503.

[*In the following review, May recounts Ramón y Cajal's life and scientific accomplishments, then considers the aphorisms in* Charlas de café.]

Among living biologists there is certainly no greater genius than S. Ramón y Cajal, the eminent Spanish histologist and neurologist. And were genius to be judged not only by the results achieved, but also by the difficulties overcome, Ramón y Cajal would stand preeminent among them all.

Ramón y Cajal began his scientific career at a time when Spain was almost totally unproductive of any original scientific investigation. Urged as much by patriotic zeal as by the *feu sacré* of research, he has succeeded, in the forty-five years since his first publication, in creating a great Spanish school of histology and neurology, in actively stimulating investigators in related fields of science, and in foreign countries, and in pointing a way to Spain, by his noble example, to a new era of scientific endeavour.

The son of a country physician, a man who had risen by his own efforts and knew the value of work, Santiago Ramón y Cajal was born in 1852, in Petilla de Aragón, in the province of Navarra. He was brought up in small towns in various provinces of Spain. As is the case with so many men of genius, his early years were passed in open opposition to the formal education of books and masters, and in close study of nature. This early took the form of a great love for pictorial art, for which he appears to have had great talent. His aesthetic tendencies were actively combatted, however, by his parents, who saw in them merely the expression of laziness, especially as the young Santiago was known wherever he went as the leader of all the boyish pranks of the neighborhood. These pranks, under the energetic guidance of their son, ran the gamut from the explosion of wooden canons to stone fights with the police. To curb these youthful outbursts, Dr. Ramón placed his son as apprentice, first to a barber, then to a shoemaker.

Synchronous with his exuberant energy, however, the young Santiago Ramón was experiencing a great fever of romanticism. Guided by his love for art, and by French and Spanish authors of the romantic era, he was an ardent worshipper of Chateaubriand, Hugo and Quevedo. It is with these masters, and largely outside of the standard education of the schools, that he grew up to adolescence.

His father constantly urged him to take up the profession of medicine, and to get rid of his artistic ideas. To incite him to work along medical lines, he began with his son the study of anatomy, and more especially that of oste-ology. To Santiago, with his artistic idiosyncracy, osteol-ogy was but another pictoric theme, a theme which, although it dealt with hard and dry realities, he es-poused with far greater enthusiasm than the dialectics and metaphysic of his school masters. Here, so he says, working on dry bones in an attic, under the tutor-ship of his father, was laid the basis of all his future scientific activity.

Once he had finished with the secondary schools, the young man studied medicine in Zaragoza. There was at the time an almost absolute lack of laboratories in Spain, and medicine was merely a clinical study. Zaragoza, as one of the smaller medical schools, offered no particularly great advantages. Here, however, Ramón y Cajal made a profound study of gross anatomy, and soon became ex-tremely competent in this science.

His medical studies completed, he had to serve his coun-try in the army; he was accepted in the medical corps and, after a brief campaign in Spain, was sent to Cuba to serve in the war against the insurgents of 1874. There, under fearful sanitary conditions, he soon fell a victim to ma-laria, and was saved from death only through his extraor-dinary physique and resistance. He returned to Spain and, after his recovery, prepared himself for a professor-ship. Once more, however, disease laid a heavy hand on him, this time in the form of pulmonary tuberculosis. The extraordinary energy which he had stored up in his boy-hood and adolescence here again came to his rescue, and, because of his tremendous "élan vital," he triumphed a second time over disease. Having passed competitive examinations, he was appointed Professor of Descriptive Anatomy at the University of Valencia.

It was during his preparation for a professorship that he began to take an interest in microscopic anatomy and its technique; working always by himself, and pushed only by his own curiosity and enthusiasm, he founded a small laboratory of his own. Once a professor in Valencia, he began a series of investigations in histology which can be said to be the most brilliant of modern times. His maiden studies were on inflammation, nerve terminations, the structure of the cholera vibrio, that of stratified pave-ment epithelium, the crystalline lens, cartilage, bone, and muscle. He soon drifted over, however, to a study of various structures of the nervous system, and especially, at first, the retina. Using the newly discovered method of Golgi, which is specific for the nervous system, he modi-fied it so that in his hands it gave results which no one had been able to obtain before him. We can say that no part of the nervous system of vertebrates has been left unstudied by Ramón y Cajal. Beginning with a beautiful comparative study of the retina, which culminated in his publication, in 1892, of **"La rétine des vertébrés"** in *La Cellule,* he successively studied, throughout the verte-brate series, the spinal cord, the medulla, the cerebellum, the various integrating parts of the cerebrum, the sympa-thetic nervous system, the peripheral nerves, the sense organs. These studies, undertaken on embryos, young animals, and adults, found their completion in an elaborate investigation of the human cerebral cortex, which Cajal found to be quite different from that of lower mammals.

During this period of morphological investigation, Cajal did not leave aside theoretical considerations. Among the most important which he put forth, one may count his theory of neurotropism, to explain, in part, the growth and connections of the nervous system, and the theory of the dynamic polarisation of the nerve cell, according to which the dendrites carry cellulipetal impulses, while the axon is used for cellulifugal ones. This later theory was also expounded by Van Gehuchten, the celebrated Belgian neurologist. Ramón y Cajal also made most of the observations which finally led to the proposition of the neurone doctrine by Waldeyer. According to this theory, now universally accepted, the nervous system, except for very rare exceptions, is made up of discrete elements which are merely contiguous to each other, but never continuous.

Ramón y Cajal was professor, after leaving Valencia, at Barcelona, and finally at Madrid. Here he founded his *Revista Trimestrial Micrográfica,* which became, in later years, the *Trabajos del Laboratorio de Investigaciones Biológicas de la Universidad de Madrid.* In this review he and his students have published, and continue to publish, some of the most important contributions to biology of modern times.

Cajal's studies on the morphology of the nervous system of vertebrates are beautifully resumed and extended in his ***Textura del sistema nervioso del hombre y de los vertebrados*** (1897-1904), translated by L. Azoulay and amplified by Cajal in 1909-11 as ***Histologie du système nerveux de l'homme et des vertébrés.*** His later studies deal with: 1. The cytology of the nervous system. He developed for this study the method of impregnation which bears his name, and which is one of the very best specific methods for the nervous system. He studied the neurofibrillar system, the Golgi apparatus, the finer cyto-plasmic constituents of nerve cells, etc. 2. Degeneration and regeneration in the nervous system of vertebrates, especially mammals. This study covers once again the entire nervous system, and is an experimental counter-part of his earlier purely morphological studies. He shed much light on this much belabored, and yet badly known theme. His long studies are resumed in a book: ***Estudios sobre la degeneración y regeneración del sistema nervioso*** (1913-14) which has been translated into English by R. M. May, and is about to be pub-lished. 3. The nervous system of invertebrates, and more especially the visual structures; these highly important studies, still being continued, have helped to an immense extent in the understanding of the very complex nervous structures of the lower phyla, a field which had been but little studied by other investigators.

Besides these studies, which follow a general trend of investigation, Cajal has published numerous special stud-ies on neuroglia, ependyma, muscle fibers, blood, bacteria, special methods in neurology and photography, etc. Up to 1923 he had published 14 books and 252 original investigations. His work has been extensively translated into French and German, but little of it has seen the light in English.

Among the main honors which Ramón y Cajal has received one may cite the Moscow prize of the International Medical Congress, the Croonian Lectureship of the Royal Society of London, the lectures at Clark University in 1899, the Helmholtz Medal of the Berlin Academy of Sciences, the Nobel prize, doctorates and decorations from all parts of the world, fellowship in all important scientific societies, etc. His students have been numerous and excellent, and some of them, like F. Tello and Rio-Hortega, have now taken their place among the world's best investigators in biology. The list of their studies, as well as Cajal's own, up to 1923, are appended to *Recuerdos de mi vida.*

But besides being a very great biologist, Ramón y Cajal is also an able littérateur and philosopher. In the second book which we review here, *Charlas de café,* which may be liberally translated as *Café Conversation,* he exposes some of his ideas on friendship and hate, love and women, old age and pain, death, immortality and glory, genius and dumbness, conversation, polemics and opinions, character, morals and customs, pedagogy, literature and art, politics, war, society, humor, etc. The book is composed of more or less disconnected thoughts which have occurred to the author throughout his life, and especially in the stimulating atmosphere of the cafés which he was wont to frequent. A résumé of these thoughts is an impossibility, and we may give only some of the more outstanding and sagacious among them:

"Other conditions being equal, the coefficient of honorability of actresses and cabaret singers is in an inverse ratio to the diameter of their jewels."—"Although the case is rare, one sees bright and even beautiful women married to imbeciles. Is it to elevate them or to depress them? The latter appears more probable than the former. Unlike the donkey of Apuleius, who recovered the human form after eating a rose, these unhappy men eat a rose to become donkeys."—"When we are young we think: I 'am immortal'. When we are old we say: I 'die without having lived', or, sadder still, I 'have not known how to live'. And we would think the same if our life lasted the two hundred years of an elephant or the three hundred of a crocodile."—"Inexorable death sometimes surprises us as it does female Hymenoptera which, once they have terminated the nuptial flight, are often devoured by birds. If heaven reserves such a fate for us, let us pray that it may at least allow us to give birth to some noble and ideal creation. Nor should we fear to leave the work incomplete: once the egg of truth is laid, someone will be there to incubate it. The really tragic thing is to fall before the spiritual wings have sprouted, our brain swollen with immature germina."—"From the depths of eternity human heads must appear to the psychological principle of the universe like those bubbles which are formed

on the wave as it breaks against the shore. They shine a moment with polychrome hues, they copy in miniature the azure's blue and the magic of the landscape, and they break a second later, giving way to the new generation of iridescent globules."—"I have noted that even in the most deeply religious minds there remains a sediment of philosophic doubt. If they were absolutely persuaded of the immortality of the spirit, would they applaud the subtle allegations of intuitive philosophers, and would they be complacent concerning the pretended communications from the dead which are referred to by spiritualists, fakirs, and theosophists? Who looks for allies when he is certain of victory?"—"Glory is like a woman: we pursue her if she is disdainful of us, we disdain her if it is us whom she prefers."—"In countries of gray skies there is an abundance of gray matter."—"Like the highest peaks, which emerge only from mountain chains, scientific or artistic geniuses arise only from the high plateaus of general culture."—"May Heaven keep me from discussing philosophic or scientific questions with lawyers. This type of polemist is rarely interested in being right, but rather on defending his client. And the *client* may be God, free will, immortality of the soul, or else positivism, pantheism, spiritism, socialism, etc. Before these modern sophists, any adversary will have his rôle reduced merely to that of oratorical opponent or trainer."—"The greatest workers are those who have learned methodically to manage their laziness. Febrile, paroxysmical activity soon becomes fatigue and disillusionment; the machine breaks down before having been able to refine the product."

Charlas de café allows us to penetrate deeper still in Ramón y Cajal's mind than *Recuerdos de mi vida.* And one sees a great man indeed, great because he understands fully the futility of effort, and yet carries on.

William Carleton Gibson (essay date 1936)

SOURCE: "Santiago Ramón y Cajal (1852-1934)," in *Annals of Medical History,* Vol. VIII, No. 5, September, 1936, pp. 385-94.

[*In the following essay, Gibson details Ramón y Cajal's life, work, and influence on the field of medical science.*]

> The ideal of science is to elucidate the dark mysteries and unknown forces which invest us, for the benefit of our descendants, and to make the world more agreeable and intelligible, while we ourselves are forgotten like the seed in the furrow.—CAJAL.

The beginning of the second half of the nineteenth century saw Helmholz, Ludwig, Virchow and Claude Bernard laying the foundations of scientific medicine. The new discoveries in physiology had been the signal for a concerted study of the minute structures of the body. Little was it realized that a new figure, Ramón y Cajal, had appeared on the horizon, in the far-off village of Petilla in the Pyrenees.

Cajal was born of the hardy peasant stock of Upper Aragón and Navarre. His father, a "surgeon of the second class," was famed throughout the mountains for his surgery, and not less for his hunting. Despite the greatest hardships, he entertained the burning hope that he might some day achieve the doctorate in medicine and surgery, and that his son Santiago should become a good doctor. In a tribute to his father written years afterwards, Cajal has said:

> He bequeathed to me his moral qualities to which I owe what I am; the religion of the sovereignty of the will, faith in hard work, the conviction that a spirit of steadfast and unrelenting determination is capable of moulding and integrating everything from the muscle to the brain, making good the deficiencies of Nature and even overcoming the misfortunes of character, the most niggardly and refractory phenomena of life. It was from him also that I acquired the commendable ambition to be something, and the resolution neither to consider any sacrifice too great for the realization of my aspirations nor ever to change my course for any secondary considerations.

The earliest recollections of Ramón the younger were of the Spanish victories in Africa in the eighteen hundred and fifties, of a lightning storm which destroyed the school, killing some of the pupils, and of an eclipse of the sun. By the age of four he was learning French under his father's tutelage in a smoky shepherd's cave near his home in Valpamas. When only six years old he had, in addition to ideas of arithmetic and geography, a capacity for writing correctly, and on one occasion acted as scribe for his family during his father's absence in Madrid. An insatiable desire to observe and to sketch birds often led to the most dangerous excursions along the cliffsides, which, together with long absences from the village, caused his mother much anxiety. His ingenuity in fashioning cages of willows was rewarded in a collection of twenty kinds of birds and of innumerable eggs. In many ways Cajal's early years are reminiscent of the boyhood of another young naturalist, surveying ponds and woods for animal life in Ontario, William Osler.

When eight years of age the boy moved with his family to the town of Ayerbe; in order that his father might have a better practice and that the "children might have a better education." Santiago's artistic instinct came to the fore as he sketched the castles and the ravines of this quiet countryside, now a national park. Because his family abominated this "useless distraction" he was forced to buy his crayons and paper secretly, and to go out into the surrounding country to sit by the road; drawing the peasants passing by with their tiny mule carts. But when he could not buy colours he had the most ingenious methods of scraping paint off stone walls, or of soaking the bright dye stuffs out of the covers of books of cigarette paper. His artistic exploits were effectively stopped when an "authority" commissioned to decorate the church walls declared that Santiago's attempt at painting St. James the Apostle was a "crude daubing" and concluded "the boy will never be an artist."

He begged his father to send him to Huesca or to Zaragossa where he might attend a drawing school; but his father wanted him to study the classics in preparation for a medical training. The boy was sent off to the school of the Aesculapian Fathers at Jaca, a mountain town. The description of this school experience which Cajal has left us is too ghastly to bear repetition in the twentieth century. Memorizing Latin verbs was nauseating to him; and was like "hammering nails into a wall." He was shamefully flogged and beaten, and starved in a dungeon as an impetus to the loathsome work of memorizing. After five months of disgraceful torture he was withdrawn from school in a sorry condition.

During months of recuperation he planned a great wooden cannon with which to seek revenge. All the neighbourhood came to see a trial shot and the explosion was of such proportions that the boy was sentenced to jail for three days, and on the recommendation of his father was deprived of food. Unable to tolerate the jeering crowds outside his cell, he hurled stones at them through the bars.

Next he was given a trial at the Lyceum, Huesca, where mathematics and science were well taught. Safely placed in a family of the village by his father, he lost no time in finding subjects to paint, to the utter neglect of his studies. On passing his terminal examinations he returned home to Ayerbe where he retailed to his former comrades stories of his adventurous and unencumbered year "abroad." His father, however, decided that Santiago would do well to spend his vacation rereading all his school textbooks to make up the evident deficiencies, and to this end he allowed him to work in the solitude of an unused pigeon house. Needless to say a means of escape was found, leading through the granary outside, to freedom.

A friendly confectioner in the town had, in his attic, a large number of books which he allowed Ramón to peruse. How great was the boy's surprise and delight on finding "Don Quixote," "Robinson Crusoe," and the "Voyages of Captain Cook" along with several volumes of Hugo, Dumas, the comedies of Calderon, and the poems of Quevedo! In a short time he produced a miniature Robinson Crusoe, under the influence of these romantics.

Returning for his third year at Huesca, in company with his brother Pedro, Santiago was apprenticed by his father to a barber, while his brother was located in the usual manner with a town family. Ramón the elder was determined that should everything else fail, his son should at least have the status of a hairdresser, as well as an acquaintance with the phylogeny of the art of surgery. In later years Cajal often remarked how much he owed to this experience, but at the time it was irksome and hateful to be "a romantic apprenticed to a barber." Rebelliously he joined the town vandals and became a notorious ruffian with great agility at stripping orchards and scaling walls. After bating the professor of Greek for a term, and making little progress with his work, he returned to

Ayerbe to enter an apprenticeship under a rather dour cobbler. A more progressive shoe-maker induced the family to allow the boy to work with him for a year, and the former village ruffian became a most adept craftsman.

This year of interesting work was followed by another fling at school, this time at a drawing school. It was not long before all the stock models for drawing had been exhausted, and the art teacher, greatly taken with the boy, journeyed the considerable distance from Huesca to Jaca to try to convince the father that the boy's future lay in art. But it was not to be, and Santiago was again refused, with the result that he again became unruly at school. One night while passing along the Santa Domingo he saw by the light of the moon a freshly whitened wall, whose attraction he could not resist. With a piece of charcoal he drew a most malicious caricature of the much-disliked professor of psychology, with sad results in his *viva voce* examination. He became so defiant in the end that he joined a group of young adventurers and packed off in the bravado fashion into the hills to "begin anew," only to return in a short time a vanquished Don Quixote.

The father then capitalized on the boy's interest in drawing, and induced him to study osteology. After the manner of the time, this sixteen-year-old student made his first acquaintance with the bones of the human frame in a cemetery by moonlight. As he packed the white objects into a sack and climbed the wall he could hear the rattling voices of departed spirits screaming curses on these "profanateurs de la mort." In the granary the father gave all his leisure time to teaching Santiago, whose single purpose was to sketch bones, from every angle, and to try to explain their function. In two months he was able to name all the minute foraminae in the skull, together with the structures passing through them. With a truly amazing grasp of anatomy, he was matriculated at the medical school in Zaragossa, to study for the licentiate.

In a short time Ramón the elder moved to Zaragossa to join the staff of the medical school, where he became an ardent and renowned teacher of anatomy. His son, through diligent study and dissection, became an assistant in the anatomy laboratory in his third year, and prepared a large atlas of human anatomy. Because of the technical difficulties in printing such a large volume of colour plates, the book was never published. (Some of the plates are preserved at the Instituto Cajal, in Madrid, while the remainder are in the library of Cajal's brother, Pedro Ramón, professor emeritus of gynecology at Zaragossa.)

Eighteenth century vitalism still reigned in this medical school, the teaching in obstetrics was entirely oral, and to Cajal's dismay the greatest emphasis was still placed on book learning. His studies therefore contributed little to his development, and he had "three manias" outside the university: literature, gymnastics and philosophy. Of the first we know little except that he wrote, in company with many youthful spirits of this first liberal period in Spain, many poems, and even a novel under the spell of Victor Hugo.

Because he was defeated in a test of strength with a fellow student, Cajal took up gymnastics of the most vigorous sort, exchanging lessons in muscle physiology with the trainer of a local athletic club. Having developed his biceps to an unbelievable size, and his chest measurement to 45 inches, he found that on attempting to study at night his head "dropped on the books with the weight of a paper press." It seemed to him that individuals as well as nations tended to become bellicose as their physical forces increased.

His mania for philosophy was in part a reaction to his regime of gymnastics and their enforced solitude, and in part to the early revolution in the 1870's. After exhausting the university library in metaphysics he finally adopted what he describes as "absolute idealism."

After gaining the licentiate in medicine, without distinction, the young doctor joined the medical corps to serve his military year. After eight months of pursuing insurrectionists in Spain he was made a captain and sent to Cuba. But the New World presented no primeval forest and no freshness; in fact it was a sad scene of inefficiency and lack of organization, a waste of men and supplies. At the hospital at Puerto Principe Cajal contracted malaria and tuberculosis, and was forced to return to Spain in 1875.

For the next two years he carried on dissection and clinical work with his father, and was given a temporary appointment in the faculty at Zaragossa. For the doctorate of the University of Madrid he had to attend examinations in the history of medicine, analytical chemistry, and in normal and pathological histology. Having studied the last subject with the aid of textbooks only, he was somewhat overcome on being shown his first microscopic preparations in Madrid by Maestre de San Juan. Passing the doctorate with ease, he hastened back to Zaragossa to set up a histological laboratory, and for the purpose secured an old microscope, long forgotten in the Department of Physiology. A friendly professor showed him for the first time in his life the circulation of the blood, in a frog. Immediately his imagination was fired with the possibilities of microscopic study. He spent all his army pay from Cuba on a Verick microscope and a few reagents, to be followed later by a Ranvier microtome which he had seen in Madrid. His first books were Beale's "Microscope in Medicine" and "Protoplasm and Life," which, with Henley's "L'Anatomie Générale" and Ranvier's "Manuel de Technique d'Histologie," may still be seen in the Instituto Cajal. Despite the reproach of the professors at Zaragossa that microscopic anatomy was "celestial and fantastic," Cajal began his examination of the body tissues, beginning with muscle and skin, and leaving the nervous system to the last.

Hardly had he received the appointment as Director of the Anatomical Museum at Zaragossa than he was seized with three severe haemoptyses, and was forced to recuperate for an unbearably long time at San Juan de la Peña. Here he became completely absorbed in photography and discovered a method of making bromide plates, far superior to anything then existing in Spain. This method led to a photolithographic application used to illustrate his earliest publications in Zaragossa. These consisted of a study of tissues in inflammation (1880) and one on the nerve endings in voluntary muscle (1881).

The professors at Zaragossa considered the microscope an impediment to the future progress of biology and cared little for Cajal's research in the meagre laboratory in his home. Some even remarked, "Who is this Cajal to pass judgment on foreign savants?" Little wonder indeed that Cajal competed for the vacant chair of anatomy at Valencia. This he successfully won, and commenced his work at the small salary of five hundred dollars. Having already married on the merest pittance he now felt himself a man worthy of a larger microtome, and at least one new foreign microscopical journal.

Of these trying but hopeful days he has written in his *Recuerdos de mi vida* and has given us the following paragraph about his wife:

> Eulogies do not flow readily from my pen, but I delight to say that, with beauty which seemed formed to shine in promenades, visits and receptions, my wife cheerfully condemned herself to the obscurity of my lot, remaining simple in her tastes, and with few aspirations other than tranquil contentment, order and system in the management of the home, and the happiness of her husband and her children.

On taking up his post at Valencia he avowed his intention of gaining international recognition within ten years, saying: "It is a disgrace that among so many thousands of discoveries in anatomy, there is not one to which the name of a Spaniard is attached." With an inner urge and fury he threw himself into his investigations and his "inspired curiosity" unravelled many of the mysteries of the nervous system. Because he was miserably poor he used small animals, chiefly mice, and put a dozen different specimens on a slide.

The cholera epidemic of 1894 brought Cajal into prominence as a microscopist, and the Central Committee presented him with a fine Zeiss instrument for his work in his former home at Zaragossa. With a staining method of his own he was the first in Spain to show the causal relation of the Koch (comma) bacillus.

At the age of thirty-five he exchanged his professorship for the chair of histology at Barcelona. "Isolated by language and tradition from the main current of science he had grown and ripened in Spain in the leisurely tempo of life in Latin countries." From Dr. Luis Simarra, a psychiatrist in Madrid, Cajal learned of the Golgi chrome-silver method for staining nervous tissue, which Simarra had discarded as capricious. A modification of this technique, and its application to innumerable specimens, showed a new world for research. Cajal's systematic study and masterly drawings meant little to a doubting Europe. Recognition came only after a demonstration of his preparations, chiefly of retina and cerebellum, before

the German Society of Anatomists in Berlin. Kölliker was so impressed with what he saw, that he immediately took up the silver methods and confirmed Cajal's earlier work. Returning triumphantly from Germany, Cajal won the professorship of histological and pathological anatomy in the University of Madrid. At the age of forty he was just beginning. The next forty years were to be his best.

The Royal Society of London invited the newly appointed professor to give the Croonian Lecture for 1894, a very high honour following such men as Virchow and Kölliker. The lecture, which he gave in French, on **"La structure fine des centres nerveux"** was enthusiastically received by English physiologists. Visits were paid to the laboratories of Ferrier, Mott, and Horsley along with his host, Prof. Charles Sherrington. His visit occasioned much celebration, and he received an honorary doctorate at Cambridge, and was later made a Foreign Member of the Royal Society, the first Spaniard to achieve the honour in a century and a half. It has been recounted that while in London, Cajal converted his bedroom, in the home of Professor Sherrington, into a miniature laboratory with the cupboards full of specimen bottles and slides. On the day set for conferring his degree at Cambridge, Cajal arrived much earlier than was expected, and wandered into one of the beautiful college gardens, where he was lost until perilously near the degree ceremony.

In 1899, along with four other European savants, Mosso, Forel, Picard and Boltzmann, Cajal took part in the Decennial Celebration at Clark University, at Worcester, Massachusetts. He gave three discourses on **"The Comparative Study of the Sensory Areas of the Human Cortex"** and demonstrated his microscopic preparations to his interested admirers. Despite the fact that the Spanish-American war was but a year past, he characterized America as the "home of tolerance and freedom," and remarked upon the lack of prejudice in the new schools of scientific work. An honorary degree was conferred on him, not so much because of his position as rector of the University of Madrid and life senator of Spain, but rather as a distinguished investigator in the field of neurology.

Returning to Spain he was made the first director of the Instituto Nacional de Higiene de Alfonso XIII. Then there followed the "Moscow Prize" for medical research, presented at the International Medical Congress which met in Paris in 1900. In 1906 Cajal shared the Nobel Prize in Medicine with the brilliant Italian neurohistologist Camillo Golgi. The presentation in Stockholm was notable for the lecture which Cajal gave, in which he was profuse in his tributes to his elders, among them Golgi, Kölliker, Van Gehüchten, and especially the native Retzius.

Following these international honours came latent recognition at home. Although offered the Ministry of Public Instruction in the Spanish cabinet, Cajal wisely refused. Medals were struck in his honour by the Spanish medical students. In the Bueno Retiro Park, near his favorite walk, the citizens of Madrid erected a statue, depicting the great biologist gazing into the pool of everchanging life.

A stamp issue was proposed in his honour, but he opposed it as long as he lived. After his death in 1934, a very artistic stamp was produced, portraying the man and his microscope. Many pictures of Cajal have appeared at various times, but none so interesting as those which he always retouched with his pen before presenting them to visitors at his laboratory.

But these years marked by honours were also years of unceasing work. A Spanish school of histology was being built up, which has come to include such men as Rio-Hortega, the late Nicholas Achucarro, Villaverde, Sanchez, De Castro, Wilder Penfield, Director of the Montreal Neurological Institute, and Tello, Director of the Instituto Cajal, Madrid. By developing the silver nitrate and gold stains for the cells of the nervous system, Cajal brought our knowledge of the most delicate mechanism in the human body to a new level. "Years from now, investigators unfamiliar with them will no doubt continue to rediscover what Cajal found at the turn of the century." How often we have failed to give this man his due. With arduous and endless microscopic preparations he reduced the "forest" of the nervous system to an intelligible order, from which has emerged Cajal's greatest contribution, his "law of the polarization of the nerve cell." This is the fundamental conception underlying all our clinical and physiological work today.

The later years brought less laboratory work for Cajal but his restless pen elaborated former discoveries in support of his original hypothesis of the discontinuity between the units of the nervous system. Though the government built him the massive new Instituto Cajal, he would not leave the meagre laboratory in his home, where he had spent half his lifetime.

The publications of the man are perhaps his greatest and most lasting contribution to science and literature. Beginning in Barcelona he published the *Revista Trimestral de Histología Normal y Patológica* in which his own researches as well as those of his pupils were communicated. With the move to Madrid the journal became the *Revista Trimestral Micrográfica,* and has since become the familiar *Trabajos,* or *Travaux,* of the Laboratory of Biological Investigation of the University of Madrid. The change from Spanish to French in the publications was made in the hope that the work of his pupils would be more widely recognized than his own had been.

Among his 286 contributions the best known is the three-volume work, *Textura del sistema nervioso del hombre y de los vertebrados,* published first in 1904 and translated into French in 1909. His work, *Degeneration and Regeneration of the Nervous System,* is the most complete treatise on the subject ever written. Its publication was made possible by a large subscription collected by the Spanish physicians and surgeons in the Argentine. His monumental *Histology of the Nervous System* in two volumes contains 925 original illustrations. Besides a handbook of histology which he, like Osler, wrote for his first students, he has contributed many

original observations in his book on colour photography. It is to be hoped that with American and European support it will be possible to republish the early works of this benefactor, and to make his contributions to knowledge and literature more widely known.

Cajal's autobiography, *Recuerdos de mi vida,* has become a classic in Spain, and its early chapters are used as a Spanish text in many American colleges today. For his literary works, he was presented, along with Menéndez Pidal, for an honorary doctorate at the Sorbonne in 1924.

As a "diastole of rest" after a "systole of work," Don Santiago, as he was known, loved to sit with his friends in the sidewalk cafés, discussing the news of the capital. His pen often became restless and covered the table-cloth with sketches, just as it spattered his library wall with ink, when, in his last year, he was propped up in bed, writing polemics reminiscent of his younger days.

From his charming *Charlas de cafe* (Coffee-house Chatter) the following extracts have been made:

> Reality overruns every concise phrase, like liquid poured into a tiny cup.

> Grey matter abounds in countries with grey skies.

> Genius, like the inhabitants of the depths of the sea, moves by its own light.

> Only the doctor and the dramatist enjoy the rare privilege of charging us for the annoyance they give us.

> Let the vicious and idle say what they choose, agreeable and useful work remains the best of distractions.

> As long as our brain is a mystery, the universe, the reflection of the structure of the brain, will also be a mystery.

In his *Rules and Counsels for the Scientific Investigator* (translated into German by Professor Misckolczy) we find many interesting passages, a few of which follow:

> The emotion lights the cerebral machine which acquires by it necessary heat, the forge where fortunate intuitions and hypotheses will be wrought.

> No one ignores the fact that the one who knows and does is valuable compared to the one who knows and goes to sleep.

> The sincerest and the most devoted scientist remains profoundly human; in his life for his fellow beings he exceeds the best, expanding his usefulness beyond present and local conditions. Thanks to these men of singular talent whose sight penetrates into the shadows of the future, and whose exquisite sensibility makes them regret the errors and the stagnation of routine, in scientific progress, only the genius can have the privilege of opposing the

current and modifying the moral medium. His mission is not the adaptation of his ideas to those of society but the adaptation of society to his ideas, and if he is right (as he usually is) and proceeds with prudence and energy, without dismay, sooner or later humanity will follow him, applaud him and cover him with glory. Trusting in this pleasing tribute of veneration and justice, every investigator works with confidence because he knows that if individuals are capable of ungratefulness, communities very seldom are, if they reach full consciousness of the reality and utility of an idea.

Thus lived and wrote the colourful Don Santiago. Since his death in October, 1934, many tributes have been penned, none more aptly than that by Sir Charles Sherrington:

> He had come to stand in some sort as a symbol of national cultural rebirth. Despite, perhaps partly because of, his retired and simple life and his advanced years, he and his scientific devotion and prestige were taken to typify to many of his fellow countrymen what a new Spain might cherish and accomplish; he was taken as a sort of forecast of what a new Spain should stand for. In this sense he caught the national imagination.

This man, whose name was magic for the Spanish peasant as for the struggling research worker, has been fittingly memorialized:

> Where he found stagnation and a complete lack of interest in science he has left active universities, and a modern outlook. A true son of Spain, and the most modest of men, his chief, perhaps his only interest in the honours which he received was that through him, Spain was honoured.

Today there is rising a new University City on the edge of Madrid where 25,000 students will eventually come for an education, one-fifth of them in medicine. On a hill overlooking the capital, stands the new Laboratory of Normal and Pathological Histology, opened on the first anniversary of Cajal's death. Here are to be found men from the far corners of the earth, purusing post-graduate study under Pio del Rio-Hortega, one of the emerging national figures of the new Spain. A portrait of Cajal hangs in the large laboratory, with the following scrawled on it:

> "It has been said many a time that the problem of Spain is a problem of culture. It is necessary in fact, if we would enroll ourselves with the civilized peoples, that we must cultivate intensely the desert of our land and brain, thus rescuing by prosperity and mental vigour all those national riches that have been lost in the sea, and all those talents which have been lost in ignorance."

Thus his patriotic soul, that could not forget his Aragonese ancestry whose glorious exploits had filled entire pages of history, spent a moment in exultation and reflection looking through the great windows of the world, his face a little lengthened by his beard, faintly reminiscent of Don Quixote, saying to future generations, that in Spain one might still make science, and great science, everlasting.

REFERENCES

Addison, W. H. F. *Scient. Monthly,* 31:1930.

Cortezo, D. *El siglo med.,* 69:1922.

Garrison, F. H. *Bull. N. Y. Acad. Med.,* 5:483-508, 1929.

Hilton, W. A. *Scient. Monthly,* 36:225-235, 1933.

Obituary notice. *Lancet,* 2:959, 1934.

Penfield, W. *Arch. Neurol. & Psychiat.,* 16:213-220, 1926. *Ibid.,* 33:172-173, 1935.

Sherrington, C. S. *Obituary Notices, Roy. Soc. London,* 1:424-441, 1935.

Sprong, W. *Arch. Neurol. & Psychiat.,* 33:156-162, 1935.

Dorothy F. Cannon (essay date 1949)

SOURCE: "Summation and Appraisal—By Way of Epilogue," in *Explorer of The Human Brain: The Life of Santiago Ramón y Cajal (1852-1934),* Henry Schuman, 1949, pp. 263-75.

[*In the following excerpt, Cannon surveys Ramón y Cajal's scientific and literary work, and describes his character and influence.*]

> *What then remains? Courage, and patience, and simplicity, and kindness, and, last of all, ideas remain; these are the things to lay hold of and live with.*
>
> —A. C. BENSON

NEURONISM AND ITS IMPLICATIONS

That a man situated as Cajal was in a country where science was neglected and even despised should be the one to furnish modern neurology with so many new facts and such well-substantiated theories is the last thing one might expect. Study of the minute anatomy of the nervous system would seem to call for the finest of equipment and a delicacy of technique that is difficult to achieve even under the direction of a skillful teacher. Yet when Cajal began his work he had only the most meager equipment and nothing but foreign textbooks to guide him. The patience needed for the meticulous detail of preparing sections for microscopic study is enormous. Only those who have attempted many times to follow such directions as textbooks offer, and have failed again and again because they neglected some seemingly trifling matter, can fully realize how trying such work can be. In the early years, too, Cajal had to work without the stimulus and reward that come from original research and discovery. For he was occupied at first only in repeating the observations others had made. He worked for five years in obscurity without contact with the leaders in histology outside Spain and without the incentive of emulation. Yet his findings were to revolutionize neurology.

The core of Cajal's discoveries was his neuron doctrine. He pointed out to a skeptical world the fact that the basic unit of the nervous system is not the nerve *fiber,* as had been thought up to that time, but the nerve cell. Drs. Augusto and Jaime Pi-Suñer give a striking interpretation of the significance of this concept, which in the 'eighties was pure heresy:

> The thesis that "everything communicates with everything" could bear some appearance of truth and clearness, but would have made absolutely impossible the actual psychological notions about the nervous system with the concepts of facilitation, summation, and inhibition, which at that time were unknown terms. It particularly disagrees with the pregnant theory of the final common path. The valuable help lent by the learned Spaniard in destroying the reticular theory and laying the foundations for the theory of the final common path may well be considered his best contribution to the knowledge of physiology of the central nervous system. [Journal *of Nervous and Mental Disease* 84:525, 1936.]

In the years to follow, the neuron doctrine became an established part of nervous anatomy. It was soon substantiated by new evidence gained from studies of diseases of the nervous system and it at once proved useful in giving medical men a deeper understanding than they had formerly had of the physical basis of many types of nervous and mental disorders. Cajal's discoveries constitute the basis of our present-day knowledge of the development and structure of the neuron; of the way in which the nervous impulse is transmitted from sense organ to central nervous system and thence to muscle or gland; of the processes of degeneration and regeneration of nerve fibers; and of the localization of the various sensory and motor areas of the brain.

Carrying his studies of the nerve cells and of the neuroglia of the brain still further, Cajal offered a reasonable hypothesis to explain the phenomenon of sleep and of the loss of consciousness under certain pathological conditions of the body. A series of neurons connect the brain, the physical basis of consciousness, with the external surfaces of the body which receive the stimuli from the outside world. On occasion, these neurons contract— that is, the nerve cells draw in their prolongations, as living protoplasm always does when it is irritated. If the contraction is sufficient to cause the neurons to separate from one another, all consciousness of sensation is lost because the paths of conduction are broken. This occurs naturally in sleep. But the same contraction may result from a blow on the head severe enough to make one lose consciousness, or it may be due to toxic poisons within the body that affect the neurons. The same contraction occurs, too, when a person is fully anesthetized. Sometimes, however, only the more delicate neurons are affected—those through which intellectual processes are accomplished and sensations of pain are felt. These higher neurons are more sensitive to the action of narcotic drugs than are the lower neurons governing the vegetative functions of the body. The higher neurons continue in a state of contraction as long as the influence of the drug lasts, and therefore, by varying the amount given, the depth and length of the anesthesia can be regulated. Similarly, when a person is in a hysterical state, though the paths of conduction may not be interrupted, the neurons may make unusual and unintended connections. Such improper connection may leave parts of the body without sensation or may lead to abnormal sensations.

Cajal's neuron doctrine also helps to explain the mechanism of memory. Recalling one thing may block the pathway to another. It is a common experience for one to forget what he intended to say when his recollection of it is temporarily blocked by another thought that crossed his mind at something he may have just seen or heard. Various sorts of injuries to the nervous system may affect the memory of certain parts of one's past life, as may also the subconscious suppression of painful memories—a phenomenon that lies at the root of the modern treatment of certain nervous and mental disorders through psychoanalysis. Observation of disordered mental states such as illusions and hallucinations have confirmed Cajal's theory as to the contracting and expanding of the branchings of the nerve cells, the blocking of the normal connections, and the occurrence of accidental, unanticipated interconnections that produce abnormal nervous response.

Cajal himself did not fully work out all these hypotheses, but he did hint at many of them. The important thing is that he established the essential anatomical facts underlying them and that his discoveries led other men to do research along these lines—research that proved more fruitful because of the new direction his work had given it.

In evaluating his contributions to human knowledge, one must take into account the diverse fields his discoveries touched and illumined. The new data on the intimate structure of the nervous system that he brought to light are admittedly of greatest interest to the histologist, the physiologist, the pathologist, and the surgeon. But they are of immense concern also to psychologists and psychiatrists, since detailed information about the structure of the nervous system, coupled with observation of its normal and abnormal functioning in health and disease, gives useful suggestions as to ways of coping with nervous and mental disorders. To a considerable degree it was Cajal's work that made modern neurosurgery and neuropsychiatry possible. How important a contribution this was is at once apparent when one considers the vastness of the problem of nervous and mental disorders in the world today. In the United States alone probably more than three million persons are victims of severe nervous or mental disease. It is difficult to determine just how many more are afflicted with the milder form of disorder known as neurosis, but unquestionably it too causes an immense amount of incapacity and misery, representing an enormous economic burden and tragic human waste. Cajal's discoveries have a direct bearing on education because they offer telling hints as to effective methods of teaching and of learning. He has given a valid explanation of how we learn to perform certain acts more easily and quickly through practice and how the faculty of memory can be developed through training. The nerve cells involved in such learning do not increase in number, but the connections between them become more perfect through use. The pathways of interconnection become stronger and the cells may even acquire new branchings by which more diverse connections with other cells are made possible.

Cajal's law of dynamic polarization affirms that the cell body with its dendrites directs the impulse along a one-way course—toward the axon. The question at once suggests itself: What happens when several impulses coming from the dendrites compete with one another for right of way? In such cases, Cajal said, it is the cell body that determines which impulse shall have priority. He suspected that there might be a chemical action of some sort in this selectivity, but did not develop the idea. Years later, Sir Charles Sherrington and his colleagues of the Cambridge School of Physiologists offered a theory of chemical mediation of the nervous impulse.[1] The English physiologists also introduced the modern concept of the *synapse,* the contact point between the axon of one neuron and the dendrites of the next one in the chain of connection. At the synapse a resistance is set up to the passage of the impulse from one cell to the next. The resistance may vary in degree from an almost imperceptible slowing down to actual blocking (inhibition). However great the resistance may be, the course of the impulse is irreversible; it must go on toward its destination or drain away.

Cajal's theory of nervous conduction has been validated again and again, notably by Cannon's[2] animal experiments on the reflex arc and Pavlov's famous demonstration that a dog to whom food is given at the same time a bell is rung will learn to salivate when a bell is rung even though no food is offered—through the operation of the now well-known conditioned reflex. These concepts lie at the basis of all modern educational and psychological thought, explaining the mechanisms of animal instinct and habit formation as well as of all human learning. They help to explain, too, the phenomenon of integration, the "oneness" of our consciousness in spite of the fact that it is constantly being bombarded by infinitely diverse stimuli from both inside and outside the body.

THE PERFECTING OF NEW STAINING METHODS

Through the use of Golgi's discarded silver stain—perfected in 1888, so early in his career—Cajal was able actually to see more of the nervous system than had the anatomists before him. It was because of this

happy discovery in technique and his idea of applying it to very young or unborn animals whose nerve fibers had not yet myelinated that he was able to add so much in a field that had already been thoroughly worked over by the greatest anatomists of the century—a field so much worked over, in fact, that it seemed almost naïve to expect to find anything more.

Having made a startling beginning with Golgi's stain, Cajal proceeded to perfect Ehrlich's methylene blue and finally to devise new methods that were wholly his own. In 1903 he developed his reduced silver-nitrate stain; in 1913, the gold sublimate, by which the neurofibrils, hitherto elusive to microscopic study, could be clearly visualized and traced. This stain soon yielded valuable data on the structure of the astrocytes, star-shaped cells in the tissue of what Cajal called the "third element" of the nervous system. It was one of his followers, Pío del Rio Hortega, working with various adaptations of Bielschowsky's[3] method (staining axons and neurofibrils with ammoniacal silver), who invented the silver-carbonate stain and through its use obtained such clear pictures of the "third element" that he was able to make exhaustive studies of the microglia and oligodendroglia of which it is, in part, composed.[4] These researches threw new light on the gliomas, tumors of the glia, or supportive cells of the nervous system, and have been of inestimable help to neurosurgeons in their understanding of these growths and in their efforts to extirpate them.

Another direct medical application of Cajal's investigations—this one the outcome of his studies on nervous degeneration and regeneration and his procedures for producing expertly stained sections—is the modern technique by which the physician is able to aid the regeneration of injured nerve fibers and hasten the healing of a severed nerve. Instead of letting Nature work alone—slowly and often inefficiently—to repair traumatized axons, the doctor now puts them in direct contact with connective tissue or with the cut end of the nerve, if that is possible.

CAJAL'S WRITINGS

Most of Cajal's scientific works were written to serve as textbooks for students and they still rank among the best and the most authoritative. His chief treatises have become classics in histology and give completely original conceptions of cell structure in every part of the nervous system. For many years after his death investigators unfamiliar with his work continued to discover facts Cajal had already unearthed in the 'nineties. The best-known of his scientific writings is his ***Textura del sistema nervioso*** (Texture of the Nervous System) (1897-1904), which was revised and amplified in the French edition of 1909. After all the years that have passed since then, this is still the most complete and accurate description ever made of the more delicate nervous structures. His great treatise on the retina completes and supplements the investigations made in this field by such pioneers as Max Schultze, and his encyclopedic work on nervous degeneration and regeneration is the most comprehensive study of the subject to date.

His books and articles—scientific and literary—approximate 286. His literary writings, such works as the *Cuentos de vacaciones* (Holiday Tales), *Psicología de Don Quijote y el quijotismo* (The Psychology of Don Quixote and Quixotism), *Recuerdos de mi vida* (*Recollections of My Life*), *Reglos y consejos* (*Rules and Counsels*), *Cuando yo era niño* (When I Was a Child), *Charlas* and *Chácharas de café (Conversations* at the Café), *Pensamientos escogidos* (Selected Thoughts), *La mujer* (Woman), *El mundo visto a los ochenta años* (The World as Seen at Eighty), are of such merit that an honorary degree was given him, in company with another noted Spanish writer, Menéndez Pidal, by no less an institution than the French Sorbonne. Many of his writings have been regarded by competent critics as valuable additions to Spanish literature. *Reglos y consejos* illustrates his literary style at its best.

THE SPANISH SCHOOL OF HISTOLOGY

One of Cajal's most significant contributions is the school of Spanish histologists he founded and inspired through his teaching and example. To create such a school had been the ambition of his youth. And at that unpropitious time, this must have seemed a project worthy of a second Don Quixote. Even after the school had grown and prospered, he had fears—in the moods of despondency that came upon him with increasing frequency in his later years—that it would shortly cease to exist after he died. Far from it. On the first anniversary of his death, a new Laboratory of Normal and Pathological Histology was established at the University of Madrid. The enrollment of the university increased strikingly in the years to follow, with a large proportion of the students enrolled in medicine. Graduate study of scholarly caliber was made available to promising students under the direction of men who had been trained by Cajal, many of them outstanding figures in the new Spain. Nothing would have given Cajal greater satisfaction than to see how well his disciples, and their disciples, carried on his work.

Throughout all his scientific productivity and in the midst of the many bitter controversies that raged about it during his lifetime, saddening his days, he never forgot the true aim of science as he himself had once trenchantly expressed it in his *Charlas de café*—"to elucidate the dark mysteries and unknown forces which surround us for the benefit of our children, and to make the world more agreeable and intelligible while we ourselves are forgotten, like the seed in the furrow." He used often to say that the real problem of Spain was a problem of culture. He had once scrawled that thought on a picture of himself hanging in the university laboratory. And he had added: "If we Spaniards are to be numbered with the civilized peoples of the world, we must cultivate the desert of our land and the intellect of our people, thus salvaging through prosperity and mental vigor all those national riches that have been lost in the sea and all those talents lost in ignorance."

DON SANTIAGO THE MAN

Nature had given Cajal many gifts. He was the greatest scientist Spain had ever produced and one of the scientific leaders of the world. He was also an artist of distinction, an authority on color photography, and a precursor in the revival of art that took place in Spain before the outbreak of the Civil War. He was a witty talker, a dynamic teacher, an admirable writer. Among the fortunate faculties he possessed were his ingeniousness, his artist's deftness, and the sharp power of observation the scientist shares with the artist. All these were indispensable to successful work in such a science as histology. So too were his patience, his perseverance, his tirelessness, his urgent drive to do something of note. It is clear that his make-up combined the prime requisites for the work to which, reluctantly at first, he devoted his life.

His capacity for work and the scope of his achievement were immense. Someone of his own land summed it up wittily in the little verse:

> *A Castilla y Aragón, nuevo mundo dió Colón;*
> *A Castilla y Aragón, mundo interno dió Ramón.*[5]

Van Gehuchten once summed it up succinctly too, in more serious fashion: "Cajal has given us the key with which to open up the mysterious caverns of the brain, and with it he himself has unlocked a whole vast world— the world of thinking man."

Dr. Ernesto Lugaro, while professor of psychiatry at the University of Turin, wrote what is perhaps the most apt of all the evaluations of Cajal and his work:

> The case of Santiago Ramón y Cajal is certainly unique in history. In a backward environment that was indolent and almost hostile, this man succeeded, by sheer force of talent and will and by inspired, indefatigable work, in a colossal scientific achievement as harmonious as a work of art and solid enough to last for centuries. At the same time, he managed to stir up by his example and his teaching latent, unsuspected energies, creating a school in which the students in their turn were trained to become teachers of the first rank, changing the face of histology and medicine, and shaking the somnolence of the universities in his country. And that was not all. Almost without wishing it, scarcely paying any attention to politics, he exercised a tonic effect on the entire political life of his land, producing changes which, in the opinion of the world, refuted the old commonplaces derogatory to Spain and gave that nation a new faith in its own power. . . .
>
> The work of Cajal is monumental. Without exaggeration it can be said that modern neurology owes to him above all others the enormous progress realized in the last half-century: a gigantic complex of facts and ideas from which present-day neurology derives its characteristic physiognomy. Especially in the field of the

morphology of the nerves, it can truly be said that Cajal, by himself alone, has produced more than all the other neurologists together: methods, techniques of inexhaustible fruitfulness, work tools for all; numerous discoveries—even the least of which a scholar might be proud of; penetrating, synthesizing interpretations, both lucid and persuasive, that have worked like ferments on physiology and pathology. No matter what branch of his subject a neurologist chooses, he must always have Cajal's work constantly before him and must invoke his name in the exposition of any facts or ideas whatever. . . .

He has set an example of wholesome nationalism, a nationalism that is not nourished on jealousy of neighboring countries and on blind negation of foreign values but is concerned with raising the repute of one's own country through worth-while work. His was a strong and noble character without taint of self-seeking. [*Revista di patologia nervosa e mentale* 45:v, 1935.]

Cajal was not only admired by his colleagues and his followers—they loved him too. The very fact that he was known among them simply as "Don Santiago" tells something of their affection. Moreover, his students sensed keenly the greatness of the spiritual heritage he left them. Again and again they mention his endless kindness. They tell how ready he was with quick encouragement whenever the vicissitudes of life had made them downhearted about their own work, how ready he was with his help and protection when they needed it. "And to the greater glory of his spiritual excellence," wrote Fernando de Castro, "he always made it a point not to exert pressure on his pupils by influencing them with any ideas of his in their interpretations of the results they obtained from their own original researches."[6]

Sir Charles Sherrington in the obituary of Cajal that he wrote for the Royal Society of London pays him this warm homage:

> He has come to stand in some sort as a symbol of national cultural rebirth. Despite, perhaps partly because of, his retired and simple life and his advanced years, he and his scientific devotion and prestige were taken to typify by many of his fellow countrymen what a new Spain might cherish and accomplish; he was taken as a sort of forecast of what a new Spain should stand for. In this sense he caught the national imagination. Banknotes bore his effigy; a postal issue was to distribute his likeness millionfold as a national emblem. He deprecated the proposal at the time, but after his death it was done. We may well believe that such a memento, at once national and democratic, would have touched Don Santiago's virile heart. It is a tribute which gives evidence of the position accorded him by the Spanish, a position accorded him with the sympathy and applause, indeed, of the civilized world entire. [From *Obituary Notices of Fellows*, 1935. By permission of Sir Charles S. Sherrington and the Royal Society of London.]

It was also on the occasion of Cajal's death that Dr. Wilder Penfield wrote of him:

> Now that the end has come, his life and achievement loom large in the history of neurology. He was a many-sided genius impelled by that mysterious "whisper" that comes to God's chosen few that draws them ever onward to explore beyond the horizons of existing knowledge, without rest and with no need for recompense other than to know that they have entered the promised land of discovery. [From *Archives of Neurology and Psychiatry* 33:172, 1934. By permission of Dr. Wilder Penfield and the American Medical Association.]

There could be no more fitting epitaph.

NOTES

[1] Two theories compete for general acceptance today: the chemical and electrical. Perhaps both electrical and chemical elements are involved. Both theories postulate the accumulation at the synapse of an active principle—electrical or chemical—which, upon reaching a certain level, will stimulate the dendrites beyond the synapse. The delay at the contact point may be accounted for by the need to build up the required amount of electrical charge or the required concentration of chemical.

It has been observed that in the autonomic nervous system activity is accompanied by the production of chemicals—acetylcholine, sympathin, and related compounds—that stimulate muscles and glands. Acetylcholine is also found here and there in the central nervous system, particularly in those parts containing motor cells and axons.

[2] Walter Bradford Cannon (born 1871). Boston physiologist. Cannon's discoveries with reference to the physiological basis of emotion constitute one of the greatest contributions to psychology and psychiatry in this century. From studies of x-rays of digestive processes in cats, he found that fear and rage interfere with the normal functioning of the smooth muscles and glands. The bodily changes produced by fear and rage he found to be of a sort that temporarily allow the individual concerned to make greater effort than usual. The heart beats faster, blood pressure is raised, the adrenal glands secrete adrenalin, enabling the body to fight harder or to run away faster—in other words, giving the human machine greater power for a short period. But there are other changes, as, for example, the cessation of the activity of the stomach muscles. The body neglects its usual functions to concentrate its full energies on the emergency that produces the emotion. When such emergencies arise rarely, they do no harm to the healthy body. But in our life today emotional upheaval often becomes chronic, owing probably to the many frustrations modern life imposes, since our society seems to awaken more desire than it is able to satisfy.

[3] Max Bielschowsky (1869-1940). German neuropathologist.

[4] Important today in the diagnosis of nervous disorders are Rio Hortega's glia stain, which tints the cytoplasm of the neuroglia black, and Penfield's glia stain, which renders the oligodendroglia clearly visible. In studying a microscopic slide for diagnostic purposes, the physician or surgeon must follow an orderly procedure and hold to a definite point of view. After finding out what stain has been used on the tissue, he must look for the special structures that stain shows well. Tissue of the cerebral cortex tinted with Cajal's stain, for instance, shows only the glia cells; tissue stained by Weigert's method shows the myelin sheaths. To obtain a more complete picture, sections treated with different appropriate stains must be studied serially.

[5] To Castile and Aragon, Columbus gave a new world; To Castile and Aragon, Ramón gave the inner world.

[6] Translated from the Spanish of the article on Cajal in the volume of *Archivos de neurobiología* dedicated to his memory: 14:833, 1934. Cajal's last scientific paper had been written for this same journal and appears in 13:217, 1933.

Lloyd G. Stevenson (essay date 1953)

SOURCE: "1906: Camillo Golgi (1844-1926), Santiago Ramón y Cajal (1852-1934)," *in Nobel Prize Winners in Medicine and Physiology 1901-1950,* Henry Schuman, 1953, pp. 32-40.

[*In the following excerpt, Stevenson offers a brief summary of Ramón y Cajal's life and his Nobel Prize-winning research in neurophysiology.*]

Santiago Ramón y Cajal was born May 1, 1852, In Petilla, an isolated village in the Spanish Pyrenees, where his father was "surgeon of the second class." The elder Ramón later extended his studies and in time became professor of anatomy at Zaragoza. The son's unfortunate early schooling, under tyrannical teachers, failed to reveal his gifts. It was followed by apprenticeship, first to a barber, then to a shoemaker. His father then undertook to teach him, particularly in osteology, which revealed the boy's talent as a draftsman. Thereafter he studied medicine at Zaragoza and was graduated in 1873. Then came compulsory service in the Spanish army, chiefly in Cuba, until 1875; during this interval he suffered severely from malaria and dysentery. After taking a medical degree at Madrid, he became a demonstrator and then, in 1877, professor of anatomy at Zaragoza; but he was soon forced to interrupt his work because of pulmonary tuberculosis. He married in 1879 and in 1884 was called to the chair of anatomy at Valencia. For a time he worked at bacteriology and serology, but turned to his proper field, histology, and in 1887 was given a chair in that subject at Barcelona. Learning of the Golgi silver stain from Luis Simarra, a neuropsychiatrist of Madrid, Ramón y Cajal developed an improvement of his own which he began to use in the study of the nervous system. This was the first of his several important innovations in staining technique. In 1889 he demonstrated his work before the German Society of Anatomists, was praised by Kölliker, and was soon acclaimed by German histologists generally. In 1892 he was appointed professor of normal histology and pathologic anatomy at Madrid. International honors now accumulated. There followed many years of intensive labor. By 1923 he had already published 237 scientific papers. He also wrote a large number of books, including not only comprehensive works on the nervous system but popular essays, a treatise on color photography, etc. He died on October 18, 1934, at the age of eighty-two.

. . . . .

From the sum of my researches springs a general concept which comprehends the following propositions:

The nerve cells are morphologic units, the neurons, to use the word sanctioned by the authority of Professor Waldeyer. This had already been demonstrated, as regards the dendritic or protoplasmic extensions of the nerve cells, by my illustrious colleague Professor Golgi; but when our researches began there were only conjectures more or less tenable regarding the way in which the ultimate divisions of the axons and nerve collaterals are arranged. Our observations, with Golgi's method, which we applied first in the cerebellum, then in the spinal marrow, the brain, the olfactory bulb, the optic lobe, the retina, etc. of embryos and young animals, revealed, in my opinion, the terminal disposition of the nerve fibers. These, in their ramifications to several junctures, incline constantly toward the neuronal body and toward the protoplasmic expansions, around which arise plexuses, or nerve nests, very close-woven and very rich. The . . . morphologic dispositions, which vary in form according to the nerve centers one studies, attest that the nerve elements have reciprocal relations of *contiguity* and not of *continuity,* and that communications, more or less intimate, are always established not only between the nervous arborizations but between the ramifications of one part and the body and protoplasmic extensions of another part. . . .

These facts, recognized in all the nerve centers with the aid of two very different methods (Golgi's and Ehrlich's) . . . involve three physiological postulates:

(1) Since nature, in order to assure and amplify contacts, has created complicated systems of ramifications around the cells (systems which would become incomprehensible by the hypothesis of continuity), it is necessary to admit that the nervous currents are transmitted from one element to another by virtue of a sort of induction, or influence at a distance.

(2) It is also necessary to suppose that the cellular bodies and the dendritic prolongations, like the axis cylinders, are induction apparatus, since they represent intermediate links between the afferent

nerve fibers and the axons mentioned. This is what Bethe, Simarro, Donaggio, we ourselves, etc., have confirmed quite recently, in demonstrating, with the aid of neurofibrillary methods, a perfect structural concordance between the dendrites and the axis-cylinder prolongation.

(3) Examination of the transmission of nerve impulses in the sense organs, such as the retina, the olfactory bulb, the sensory ganglions and the spinal marrow, etc., show not only that the protoplasmic expansions play a conducting role but also that the movement of the nerve impulse in these prolongations is *toward the cell body,* whereas in the axons it is *away from the cell body.* This principle, called *the dynamic polarization of neurons,* formulated a long time ago by van Gehuchten and us as an induction drawn from numerous morphological facts, is not contrary to the new researches on the constitution of nerve protoplasm. In fact we shall see that the framework of neurofibrils makes up a continuous reticulum from the dendrites and the cell body to the axon and its peripheral termination.

[Translated from Santiago Ramón y Cajal, **"Structure et Connexions des Neurones,"** *Les Prix Nobel en 1906.*]

. . . . .

The quotation from Ramón y Cajal has been selected as the latter's attempt at a general summation of an important part of his work. The neuron theory, here presented in a condensed form, was firmly established by his researches. Its importance to subsequent investigators can hardly be assessed in a few words. It underlies the exceedingly important work of Sir Charles Sherrington. It guided the thought of Egas Moniz, who introduced prefrontal leucotomy (see below, pp. 264-270). It is one of the basic theories of modern biological science.

Ramón y Cajal's contributions are also too numerous and too complex for summary treatment. As he himself said, "Unfortunately it is absolutely impossible to condense in a few pages morphological facts the description of which occupies a large number of brochures with hundreds of drawings." It may be mentioned, however, that another Nobel laureate, Robert Bárány . . . , in attempting to connect the function of the labyrinth apparatus of the ear with cerebellar function, was initially dependent on the Spanish histologist's account of the nerve connections involved. It is safe to say that there is no neurologist or neuroanatomist of recent times who does not owe him a similar debt.

Even more lasting than his wealth of recorded observations will be the improved methods of Cajal and his disciples. First, in 1888, he increased the applicability of the Golgi stain. In 1903 he developed his own reduced silver nitrate strain. . . . In 1913 he introduced the gold sublimate stain. . . . His eminent pupils Achucarro and Hortega [introduced] the silver carbonate stains. . . .

These methods in the hands of Cajal and his students have clarified much of the embryology of each cellular element in the nervous system. Furthermore, the finer details of gliomas revealed by these stains, with the accumulating light from embryology, have given the neurosurgeon useful correlations of structure and biologic characteristics of brain tumors. [Wilbur Sprong, "Santiago Ramón y Cajal: 1852-1934," *Archives of Neurology and Psychiatry,* Vol. 33 (1935), pp. 156-162.]

REFERENCES

Cannon, Dorothy F. *Explorer of the Human Brain: The Life of Santiago Ramón y Cajal (1852-1934)* (New York: Schuman, 1949).

Ramón y Cajal, Santiago. *Recollections of My Life,* translated by E. Horne Craigie and Juan Cano (Philadelphia: American Philosophical Society, 1937), 2 vols.

Sprong, Wilbur. "Santiago Ramón y Cajal: 1852-1934," *Archives of Neurology and Psychiatry,* Vol. 33 (1935), pp. 156-162.

J. Z. Young (review date 1992)

SOURCE: "Nervous Starts," in *Nature,* Vol. 356, No. 6370, April 16, 1992, pp. 624-5.

[*In the following review, Young observes the significance of Ramóny Cajal's work to modern neuron theory.*]

Those who probe the nervous system with electrodes probably seldom stop to consider the history of knowledge of the cells they are impaling. Yet it would help them to think about the problems that have arisen in the search for units of nervous activity. Since the days of Santiago Ramón y Cajal, most neuroscientists have depended on a rather simple picture of the neuron, with dendrites, cell body and axon as the essential unit. This has also been the model mostly used in artificial intelligence. Shepherd's book [*Foundations of the Neuron Doctrine*] provides a survey of the history of the neuronal hypothesis. In his last chapter, he raises the question of whether we should now look for units both larger and smaller than the neuron.

The controversy at the end of the last century turned on the question of whether neurofibrils proceed from one cell to the next. It was conducted in fairly ferocious language. Cajal writes of his reticularist opponents, such as Golgi and A. Bethe, as "fanatics with haughty minds, inclined towards mysticism". Finally, in 1917, he is happy to write that "the unhorsed physiologist of Strasbourg [Bethe] decided to abandon the field. *Victis honos!*"

Cajal was, of course, correct in claiming that "connection is by contact", but his opponents were skilful light microscopists and not so far wrong as he supposed. Now that electron microscopy has shown the correct relationships at synapses, we can see that their interpretations were in a sense correct. The finest branches of a nerve fibre may indeed appear to enter the end organ, for instance in the groove at the surface of a muscle fibre. There is no evidence that Cajal realized that it is the completeness of the two membranes that is important. If the finer branches run in a trough, the most honest light-microscope interpretation may be that there is continuity. Cajal's opinion was right, but his figures are almost all drawings.

The advocates of the neuron theory were themselves quite "haughty" and hasty in their rejection of all possibilities of "continuity". We know now that gap junctions may allow passage of ions and small molecules between neurons. Furthermore, there may be complete fusion of nerve cells if they always function together. For instance, the two giant cells of the squid initiate contraction of the muscle sac—and they are completely joined by a bridge: for jetting, both sides of the mantle must contract together. But where impulses are initiated there are synapses. This is a system of "Fused neurons and synaptic contacts", as the paper in which it was described was called in 1939. The fusion is the exception that proves the rule. Nerve fibres *can* fuse, but where decisions are to be made they are separated by synapses. I remember explaining all this to Sherrington (in about 1938). He looked up at me quizzically and said, "I hope that you are right Young, but I find it hard to believe." It is ironic that the squid's giant fibre synapse, more thoroughly investigated than any other, involves a syncytial postsynaptic fibre. I hope that Cajal would have enjoyed the joke (but I'm not sure that he would).

This history of old doubts and quarrels shows how hard it is to arrive at secure knowledge. As more has been discovered it becomes clear that the classical neuron doctrine needs to be extended. Almost from the start there were doubts as to what the term should include. The word 'neuron', originally suggested by Waldeyer in 1891, comes from the Greek, meaning, literally, tendon or sinew, and was applied through confusion to nerve trunks. Some authors therefore wished to keep the term neuron for the axon, whereas others (paradoxically) tried to use it only for the nerve cell body. Kölliker and others emphasized that the word should be spelled 'neurone'. This usage is still insisted on by some British physiologists and by Cambridge University Press. Shepherd nowhere mentions the history of this spelling. Many people must be puzzled to know which form to use and the book could have given authorative guidance. Surely British physiologists and Cambridge University Press should now abandon this pretentious and unhelpful practice and follow the rest of the world.

More serious are the problems raised by the discovery that dendrites may have synaptic outputs and that axons can have inputs from other axons. Moreover, dendrites do not always have graded synaptic responses but may

carry voltagegated propagated action potentials, whereas, conversely, some axons do not carry these at all. Shepherd summarizes the effects of such processes: "there is not a fixed correlation of structure and function within the different parts of the neuron; axons and dendrites provide flexible substrates in which a variety of membrane channels and local organelles . . . can support different types of physiological properties and function operations. . . . So although the neuron remains a basic anatomical, physiological, genetic and metabolic unit . . . it contains several levels of local subunits, and is itself a part of larger multineuronal units." Such a neuron has several potentially modifiable parts. It will provide a truer picture for neuroscientists and theoreticians who are trying to model parallel computing systems (although there will be difficulty in constructing them).

It is useful to have, at the same time as this review of the neuron doctrine, a new issue of Cajal's own book on degeneration and regeneration of the nervous system. This was first published in Spanish in 1913-14, the cost of publication being covered by expatriate Spanish physicians in Argentina in honour of Cajal's Nobel prize. It was translated into English in 1928, but without several important sections that are included in the present edition. Complete with Cajal's excellent pictures of his preparations, the new edition makes a wonderfully full account of regeneration. Several of his most important ideas are developed here. Particularly relevant to modern work are the concepts of neurotropism and his studies of regeneration in the central nervous system. It is good to have this book, but it tempts one to complain that Cajal's greatest work, *Histology of the Nervous System of Man and the Vertebrates,* published in 1899 in Spanish and in 1909 in French, is still not available in English. Illustrated again by Cajal's beautiful figures, that book provides detail of every part of the brain and peripheral nervous system, and should be accessible to every neuroscientist.

Geoffrey Montgomery (essay date 1993)

SOURCE: "The Dark Room," in *Grand Street,* Vol. 12, No. 3, Fall, 1993, pp. 223-40.

[*In the following essay, Montgomery explores the impact of Ramón y Cajal's scientific research on the study of vision.*]

1. Ayerbe, Spain—1860

Unlike the other boys at school, Santiago Ramón y Cajal had no fear of solitary confinement. The dark detention center, a basement room set below the town square, into which light slashed only through cracks in the room's single shuttered window, was a place for Cajal to think: a quiet room in which to concentrate on what outrages to commit tomorrow. Cajal was then eight or nine. His fellow delinquents, locked in the blackness of the school prison, felt the presence of evil spirits. But Cajal had been raised a rationalist by his physician father, Don Justo. When one day he saw a spectral image hanging on the ceiling of his cell, the ghostly form inspired not superstitious terror, but the first of Cajal's scientific discoveries.

Cajal's troubles with the schoolmaster and his father—indeed, with all the authorities of Ayerbe, the Aragonese town to which his family moved in 1860—had begun in the square outside the shuttered window of his detention cell. The new boy in town, Cajal had been mocked by the young ruffians of Ayerbe upon his first appearance in the square for his unvillagelike dress and his Castilian accent. Subsequent visits brought beatings and a rain of stones. In Valpalmas, where his family had spent the four previous years, Cajal had been a loner; when not following the rigorous course of studies demanded by his father, he had delighted in taking long rambles through the countryside, collecting young animals and bird eggs. It was in Ayerbe that Cajal became socialized, and the society he entered was the same band of boys who had assaulted and stoned him.

Cajal became the master craftsman of the armaments used by these vandals and thieves. He made slingshots of hemp and goatskin, helmets and cuirasses of cardboard and old tin, bows of every kind of wood available in the district, arrows of bamboo and broken shoemaker's awls. His athletic prowess, especially his skill in scaling the walls of private orchards from which he stole first fruits, combined with his genius for military artifice, soon made Cajal the gang's captain. He was listed in the village's "Index of Bad Companions" and was blamed for every mischief performed by the gang, for every penned rabbit shot at and every chicken killed; every arrow left behind pointed back to its maker.

The second source of Cajal's delinquency was art. "A smooth white wall exercised upon me an irresistible fascination," Cajal would write of his "graphomania" in his autobiography, **Recollections of My Life (Recuerdos de mi vida)**. He felt impelled to apply a pencil to any blank surface he saw—whether smooth white wall or blank page—filling it especially with scenes of war from the age of swords and steeds and shining armor. Entirely self-taught, Cajal was a prodigiously gifted draftsman. But his father was irremediably opposed to this passion. Having lifted himself from poverty to a first-class degree in medicine and surgery, Don Justo was not about to see his firstborn waste his talents on such a precarious career as painting. His son would be a brilliant physician. That was the course laid out. When Don Justo came across his son's drawings and pencils, they were confiscated and his son whipped.

And so Cajal practiced his art in secret. He hid his drawings like illicit treasure. Escaping to the countryside, he would sketch the battles of the bullring and the bloody exploits of his name-saint, Santiago (St. James), the warrior apostle. Unable to buy paints, he extracted his own colors from wall scrapings and by soaking red and blue booklets of cigarette paper in water, then winding the wet papers into a stubby brush. In school, impossible as it

was to draw on blank sheets of paper in open view, Cajal used the wide margins of the catechism as his canvas. Particularly popular were caricatures of the schoolmaster, passed from hand to hand around the class with much hilarity. Eventually the harassed teacher would intercept these lampoons and, since beatings did not seem to intimidate the artist, lock Cajal in the catacomb-like prison cell below the town square.

It was in this dark chamber that the boy's true vocation was announced. The visitation came in the form of an image drawn by no human hand. Looking one day at where a beam of light from a hole in the shuttered window hit the low ceiling, Cajal saw to his amazement the inverted forms of the people and beasts of burden filling the sunlit square outside. Their images hung and moved in luminous color. Cajal, already tutored in some of the elements of physics by his father, went to the window shutters and began to play with this projection. When he widened the hole in the shutter, he saw the contours and colors of the figures dissolve. Narrowing this aperture with a piece of saliva-moistened paper made the forms on the ceiling grow sharper, more vivid. Despite his ignorance of optics, Cajal was able to understand the basis of the phantom. If one's eye is placed at the hole in the shutter, the field of its vision expands in a cone whose apex is the eye. Rays of light reflected from each point in the scene outside converge at this peephole; move the eye from its aperture, and these rays cross and enter the room. A second, inverted cone projects inside. The scene this cone of light carries is visible if the room is darkened and the cone intersected by a ceiling or screen.

"Proud of my discovery," Cajal would write in his memoir, "I became daily more attached to the realm of shadows." Cajal, the covert artist, stood on a chair, held a sheet of paper before the lightbeam, and "amused myself by tracing on paper the bright and living images which appeared to console me, like a caress, in the solitude of my prison." The world outside was distanced, reduced to a representation. He watched the fights and play of his classmates projected on the blank page, thinking, "All these luminous shades are a faithful reproduction of reality and better than it is, since they are harmless."

Finally, one schoolday when Cajal's cell was filled with other troublemakers, he decided to reveal his discovery. But instead of being astonished, his fellow delinquents only laughed. It was a trick of the light, they said, of no importance whatever. Not for the last time, Cajal was struck by this absence of wonder at the phenomena of nature. "It is strange to see how the populace, which nourishes its imagination with tales of witches or saints, mysterious events and extraordinary occurrences, disdains the world around it as commonplace, monotonous and prosaic, without suspecting that at bottom it is all secret, mystery, and marvel."

Cajal, of course, would later learn that he was not the first to unlock the secrets of the dark room, generally known by its Italian name, "camera obscura." This "tremendous discovery," Cajal wrote, has been "wrongly ascribed to [Giambattista della] Porta, though its real discoverer was Leonardo da Vinci." But in fact the phenomenology of the dark room has been known since antiquity, and first received sustained investigation by the Islamic scholar Alhazen and his European followers in the Middle Ages. The camera obscura did not become a truly useful instrument, however, until the sixteenth century, when it was discovered that the placing of a convex lens at the aperture in the window shutter would greatly enhance the clarity and vividness of the projected image. This was first reported by Daniele Barbaro in 1569, but became generally known only through the second edition of Porta's best-selling compendium, *Natural Magic,* published in 1589. "In a small circle of paper," wrote Porta, "you shall see as it were the Epitome of the whole world."

Porta defined four uses for the dark room that foreshadow its development through our own time. The camera can be used to project eclipses of the sun and moon on a wall for safe viewing; this astronomical use seems to date back at least to Alhazen. (Cajal had been first introduced to the marvels of physics through his observation of the 1860 eclipse with his father, who had described the basic principles by which the moon shed its shadow across the earth's surface.) Second, the camera can be used as a place of entertainment, of spectacle. People will pay to enter the room to watch projections of painted scenes of demons, monsters, and fabulous battles—scenes painted on semitransparent paper and held before the camera's aperture. This use was to lead to the development of the magic lantern show and of course the cinema.

The camera's third use, wrote Porta, is as a draftsman's aid. A real scene will be projected on a flat surface in perfect perspective, where its form can be traced. The camera was used in this way by Dutch artists of the seventeenth century, notably Vermeer. By the end of that century the dark room had been shrunk down to a portable draftsman's box, and it was the discovery of how to chemically record the image projected into such a box that led to the invention of photography.

Photography would become one of Cajal's lifelong infatuations. Forbidden by his father to practice art, Cajal used the photographic camera as an alternate means of satisfying his mania for making images. He mastered the chemistry of synthesizing photographic emulsions; in 1912 he would publish one of the first books on the making of color photographs. Yet it was by following the thread of Porta's fourth use for the dark room that Cajal would find his greatest fulfillment: the camera obscura as a model for the structure and function of the eye.

In 1589, when Porta wrote, scholars still disagreed whether vision was the result of visual rays somehow sent out to objects by the eye or of light reflected back into this organ. For Porta, the dark room provided proof of this latter theory. Just as images from the outside world were projected into the camera obscura, so too were images projected into the eye. Yet Porta, standing

on the murky threshold between Renaissance Neoplatonism and natural magic and the experimental natural philosophy of Galileo and Kepler, thought the light-sensitive element of the eye was its *lens,* whose crystalline transparence somehow made it suited for the faculty of sight. It was not until Kepler became acquainted with the dark room through his astronomical studies that the true isomorphism between eye and camera was identified: the aperture in the window shutter corresponded to the eye's pupil, the lens to the lens of the eye, and the room's projection screen to the retina lining the back of the eye's inner surface. "Thus vision is brought about," wrote Kepler in 1604, "by a picture of the thing seen being formed on the concave surface of the retina."

Santiago Ramón y Cajal would come to be generally considered the father of modern neuroscience. Nowhere was his revolutionary approach to the nervous system better displayed than in his study of the retina, that transparent sheet of neural tissue where light becomes transformed into the electrochemical language of the brain. It was in his analysis of the retina's exquisite cellular structure, wrote Cajal, that "I felt more profoundly than in any other subject of study the shuddering sensation of the unfathomable mystery of life." Yet Cajal's entry into the nervous system was in fact crucially conditioned by his occupation of the photographic dark room, and his revelations of the structure and function of retinal nerve cells were both guided and ultimately limited by his equation of eye and camera.

2. The Latticed Window

It was only in the summer of 1868, when Cajal was sixteen, that Don Justo realized that his son's passion for image-making might have some application in his training for medicine. That summer, Don Justo introduced his son to his beloved subject of human anatomy by climbing with him one moonlit night over a cemetery wall. There the two picked through a pile of exhumed bones for the most "perfect and least weathered crania, ribs, pelves, and femurs," which they took back for scrutiny in the family barn. Don Justo taught Cajal to overlook no detail in his observation of bone structure, and for Cajal's artistic leanings "osteology constituted one more subject for pictures." Within two months, to the amazement of his father, Cajal had formulated a detailed mental map of all the bones, muscles, arteries, and nerves of the human body.

That same year, in the city of Huesca, where Don Justo had sent his truant son for a solid dose of schooling and discipline, Cajal gained his first admittance to the photographic darkroom. A group of photographers known by a friend of his had set up a laboratory in the underground chambers of a ruined church. Here Cajal watched in wonder as the light-sensitive salts of silver were mixed into a colloidal film, which was then laid thinly over a plate of glass, and as albumen-covered paper for positive prints was sensitized. "All of these operations astonished me, but one of them, the development of the latent image by means of pyrogallic acid, positively stupefied me." The skin of the scene projected into the camera, the frozen forms of an instant of the past, gradually materialized within the developing bath, as if slowly surfacing from the depths of a dark lake. "The thing seemed simply absurd." Yet when Cajal questioned the practitioners of this magic on the "theory of the latent image," the laughter of his friends in the dark room of Ayerbe was audible again. The photographers had no knowledge of or interest in the mechanism behind this process; "the important thing to them was to take many portraits and to take in still more money."

It had been known since 1727 that certain compounds of silver blacken upon exposure to light. The first attempt to use a sheet of paper coated with silver nitrate to record a portable camera obscura image was made by Thomas Wedgwood, scion of the Wedgwood pottery family, around 1800. Wedgwood failed because his coatings of silver salts were insufficiently sensitive to the relatively weak camera image. Furthermore, he lacked a fixer: that is, he could lay a leaf directly on his coated paper under the sun and make a negative image, but any further exposure to sunlight spread a shadow of liberated silver across the white figure of the leaf. The whole paper turned black. Wedgwood had no way of stopping the light-recording process—of "fixing" his images.

The first fixed photograph was made by William Henry Fox Talbot in August 1835; it showed the view through a latticed window in his home at Lacock Abbey. "When first made," Talbot noted by the side of this paper negative, "the squares of glass about 200 in number could be counted, with help of a lens." In 1839 Daguerre announced his own method of fixing camera images on polished silver plates: a method dominant for the next two decades because of its greater rendering of detail, but ultimately without offspring, as Daguerre's negative images could not serve as a template for positive copies. Talbot was impelled to improve his process. The image of the latticed window had required a camera exposure of many minutes; it was only when the sun had visibly blackened the two hundred squares of light on the coated paper that Talbot ended the exposure. Such exposure times made portraiture impractical. But in 1840 Talbot discovered that a latent image could be formed on his photographic paper in a far shorter period of time and then developed into a visible image through the action of pyrogallic acid. This made possible such photographs as "The Open Door," published in his *Pencil of Nature,* in which the bright sun reflected from a stone stable is contrasted with the darkness of the room inside, at the far end of which is visible, through a half-open door, a dimly lit latticed window—a window that almost seems to refer back to the latticed glass in Talbot's 1835 composition.

The word "retina" derives from the Latin translation of a Greek term for the one-third-millimeter-thick sheet of transparent tissue lining the back of the eye: "netlike tunic." Two other Greek names for the retina compared it to a spiderweb and to glass; long before its light-sensing function was known, the retina itself was seen as a kind

of latticed window. Its transparence fitted Greek theories that tied the retina to the conveyance of the "visual spirit" flowing from the brain to the eye's crystalline lens—the place where mind and image supposedly met.

Yet by the nineteenth century, scientists realized that if the retina contained the eye's true light-receptors, elements within the tissue must be colored so as to absorb light. In 1876 Franz Boll discovered that the purple rod cells lying within a frog's retina bleached yellow upon exposure to light. Descartes had described how the imaging function of the retina could be proved by placing the eyeball of an ox or dead person in the aperture of a dark room; remove the white sclera from the back half of the eye, and one could see projected there the inverted scene outside. In 1878 Willy Kuhne of the University of Heidelberg set out to prove that a living retina could record such a scene using visual purple as its photographic pigment. Kuhne secured the head of an albino rabbit in place before a barred window for a three-minute exposure. The rabbit was then decapitated and its retina removed. In a yellow image against the purple of this gossamer tissue were the window's six skylit panes. Kuhne fixed this "optogram" in alum and then drew a copy for all the world to see—a curious complement to the latticed window of Talbot's first photograph. The three-century-old analogy between eye and camera seemed deeper than ever.

That year, Santiago Ramón y Cajal coughed up blood. The young physician had already been stricken with malaria during military service in Cuba, and now he had contracted tuberculosis. Cajal had by then begun his investigations with a microscope and was studying anatomy in hopes of gaining an academic appointment, for Don Justo felt that his malaria-weakened son would be unable to maintain a medical practice. Now consumption had seized him. Cajal saw his death foretold in the artificially encouraging manner of his father's questions and his own emaciated frame.

But a long interval in the country, with his sister as nurse, served to restore Cajal's strength. In his autobiography, Cajal also credits photography with reviving his spirits and will to live, as it "obliged me to take continual exercise and, by offering me the daily solution of artistic problems, it flavored the monotony of my retreat. . . . " After his marriage, when Cajal was beginning his academic career, his passion for photography led him to begin manufacturing ultra rapid gelatin silver-bromide plates; these fast emulsions were then unavailable in Spain. Indeed, Cajal's photographs of bullfights, "and especially one of the president's box crowded with beautiful young ladies . . . created a furor." Cajal was compelled to manufacture these fast emulsions—whose standard formula he had improved—for general distribution, and might have begun a new Spanish industry if not for his preoccupation as director of Zaragoza's Anatomical Museum.

Cajal had become entranced with the invisible universe revealed by the microscope; he once peered through his lens for twenty consecutive hours in order to observe a white blood cell crawling out of a capillary. In 1880 he began publishing his findings; by 1884 he had the chair of Anatomy at Valencia. He specialized in histology, the study of the microstructure of tissues, publishing a book on the subject in 1885 filled with 203 woodcuts—the first Spanish histology text to contain original illustrations. Just as he had found the formula for ultrarapid gelatin silver-bromide emulsions in a foreign journal and subsequently improved it, Cajal was always searching for new techniques to visualize the cellular composition of the tissues he studied. At the time, the standard stains for nerve cells colored only the cell bodies and the thick beginnings of their fibers. The fiber's tangled terminations and interlinkings were impossible to see. Commencing his analysis of the nervous system, "that masterpiece of life," Cajal borrowed the superior microdissection technique that Max Schultze had pioneered in the retina. The nerve tissue was softened in solution, and then, with a needle, the cells' spidery fibers were teased apart. In Cajal's hands, the method enabled the isolation of the larger nerve cells in the body. But for the fine transparent cells of tissue such as the retina, Cajal thought, the method required the patience of a Benedictine monk. One did not merely have to count the angels dancing on the head of a pin; one also had to dissect them.

3. The Black Stain

Cajal's first vision of the black stain anticipated T. S. Eliot's line in "The Love Song of J. Alfred Prufrock": " . . . as if a magic lantern threw the nerves in patterns on a screen." The magic lantern was silver nitrate—the same salt of silver first used by Talbot as a photographic pigment. And this lantern first shined for Cajal in 1887, in the house of Luis Simarros, a psychiatrist and neurologist in Madrid.

Cajal was in Madrid to serve as a judge in the examinations for anatomy professorships. While in the capital he paid visits to the laboratories of fellow microscopists. Luis Simarros had just returned from Paris with samples of several novel methods for preparing neural tissue, among them the "black stain" (*reazione negra*) discovered in 1880 by the Italian histologist Camilo Golgi. Cajal had read a brief, dismissive note about Golgi's stain but had never before witnessed its workings. The procedure for black staining was relatively simple: bathe tiny slices of brain tissue in potassium bichromate, and then treat this tissue with a solution of silver nitrate crystals. Many samples failed to stain. But in those that did, a latent image of spectacular appearance developed: individual nerve cells were blackened from their cell bodies to their finest branching twigs. Under the microscope, the dark-stained cells were framed against the surrounding tissue like wintry trees, stripped of leaves, standing black against the sky before dawn.

Finally Cajal had a method of penetrating the tangled thicket of the nervous system, of tracing ramifying fibers to their terminations. Within a year, Cajal had mastered and improved Golgi's black stain. Like Talbot increasing the sensitivity of his silver salt negatives, Cajal developed a method of double impregnation to maximize the chance of staining his cells. Just as importantly, still daunted by the crowded complexity of adult nervous tissue—"a forest so dense that . . . there are no spaces in it, so that the trunks, branches, and leaves touch everywhere"—Cajal reverted to the embryonic brains of birds and mammals. "Since the full-grown forest turns out to be impenetrable and indefinable, why not revert to the study of the young wood, in the nursery stage . . . ?" (Moreover, the insulating sheath of myelin that covers axonal fibers on adult nerves, which is not stained by the Golgi method, is largely absent in embryos and neonates.)

The pre-Cajal period in neuroanatomy had settled one important issue: all fibers ramified back to the bodies of nerve cells. But still unresolved was the nature of the relationships between these fibers. The dogma adhered to by Golgi and nearly all other researchers was that the fibers of the brain formed a unified whole, merging together in one vast and continuous plexus. For Cajal, this reticular theory was a "species of protoplasmic pantheism," precluding the specific nerve linkages required for reflex action and the doctrine of the association of ideas. According to the reticular hypothesis, nerve impulses could travel along no specific pathways, but instead fed into a "sort of unfathomable physiological sea, into which, on the one hand, were supposed to pour the streams arriving from the sense organs, and from which, on the other hand, the motor . . . conductors were supposed to spring like rivers originating in mountain lakes."

In a fever of graphically illustrated publications, Cajal showed instead that each nerve cell retained its individuality. Its branches did not merge with those of other trees of the neural forest, but instead communicated with them through intimate contact, across a narrow cleft that came to be called the synapse. Cajal's neuron theory underlies all modern attempts at a biological understanding of brain function. Synapses connect neurons along specific pathways, and the implications of this specificity of neural wiring were nowhere clearer than in the retina—for Cajal, "the oldest and most persistent of my laboratory loves."

Max Schultze had shown that we have in effect two retinas in each eye—one for day, and one for night. Night vision is mediated through the rod cells . . . and utilizes the visual purple studied by Kuhne; day and color vision works through the retina's cones . . . , which use three other related photopigments. Rod vision is color-blind and coarse, says Cajal, producing "an image with little detail, comparable roughly to an ordinary photograph out of focus." The cones, on the other hand, give "colored pictures, detailed and brilliant, like a photograph in colors on an autochrome plate."

Rods and cones occupy the retina's innermost layer. In order for their light-recording signals to be sent to the brain, they must pass their signal to bipolar cells, which in turn signal retinal ganglion cells, whose axonal fibers form the optic nerve connecting the eye and brain. Schultze had carried the cellular anatomy of the retina to its highest level before Cajal, but without the black stain he had been unable to trace the connections between rods, cones, and bipolar cells. He assumed, however, that they merged in a common plexus.

Cajal's first foray into the retina proved this view false. The cells of this outpost of the brain—for the retina is an outgrowth of the same embryonic tissue as the central nervous system—are independent and communicate through synaptic contacts. "This important point established," wrote Cajal, "I proposed a very simple question to myself. Since the impression received by the rod is different from that taken up by the cone, it is necessary from every point of view that each of these specific impressions should be conveyed through the retina by a specific channel." That is, the rod and cone signals must pass through separate classes of bipolar cells.

"Knowing what I was looking for, I began to explore eagerly and repeatedly the retina of fishes and mammals, . . . and finally, as the reward of my faith, there deigned to appear most clearly and brilliantly those two types of bipolar cells demanded by theory and guessed by reason." Cajal also found that in the fovea, the small cone-rich center of the retina that is the place of highest visual acuity (we read by flicking letters on a page across our foveas), bipolar cells synapse with single cones. This allows the foveal cones' fine-grained sensitivity to be transmitted individually to the brain.

Cajal spent the last years of his long life running the Madrid institute that had been constructed in his honor, extending his study of vision to the compound eye of insects. In 1906 he shared the Nobel Prize with his great adversary, Camillo Golgi, who, on the Stockholm stage, reportedly refused to speak to the Spaniard who had stolen his black stain. Golgi, though his grand vision of neural structure was utterly mistaken, felt the Nobel should have been his alone.

In his autobiography, Cajal laments his lack of progress in understanding the functional anatomy of the cerebral cortex, "enigma of enigmas." He predicted that "the supreme cunning" of the cortex "is so intricate that it defies and will continue to defy for many centuries the obstinate curiosity of investigators." And in a review published in 1933, a year before his death, Cajal revisited the retina, the place where his fascination with image-making and neuroanatomy had so happily converged. He had traced the pathways of day and night vision through the second layer of this transparent sheet and felt he understood well enough the vertical pathways leading from rods and cones through the optic nerve and brain. Yet two other classes of cells, whose fibers ran perpendicular to this direct pathway, continued to puzzle him. He had discovered and named these two cell types—"horizontal" and "amacrine." But their presence seemed a direct challenge to the specific retinal pathways he had delineated. For the horizontal cells seemed to pool together signals arriving from many contiguous cones—a design that seemed counterintuitive. It was as if the blackening of one silver crystal of fine-grained photographic film caused the blackening of neighboring crystals. Similarly, the amacrine cells contacted and apparently pooled signals from many contiguous bipolar cells. Cajal had hypothesized that these indirect connections might play a booster role in aiding neural transmission. But at the age of eighty-one, with only a year to live, he admitted that this was only a poor guess. The amacrine cells, he said, were an "enigma," the horizontal cells a "paradox."

4. The Open Door

The beginning of an answer to Cajal's enigma came a few years after his death, in the late 1930s, when someone flicked on the light of H. Keffer Hartline's dark lab. Hartline, then at Johns Hopkins University, had pioneered methods for electrically recording the impulses transmitted by individual optic-nerve fibers. He worked in the dark, stimulating elements of the giant compound eye of the horseshoe crab with small spots of light. What happened when the overhead lights came on in his dark lab had happened many times before: the firing of the optic nerve fiber he had been stimulating with his penlight drastically diminished. But why should flooding the room with light decrease instead of increase this light-sensing fiber's firing pattern? "I have no idea how often I had noticed this [phenomenon] unthinkingly," Hartline later wrote, "without grasping its perversity."

Until the day the light went on, Hartline had assumed that the thousand elements of the horseshoe crab's retina, like the silver crystals of photographic film, functioned independently. If a single receptor "saw" light, it sent an impulse to the brain, no matter what neighboring receptors saw. But what Hartline discovered was that neighboring retinal cells in fact talk to each other. Investigations of the cat and frog retinas in the early 1950s, by Stephen Kuffler and Horace Barlow, indicated that the pathways of this communication were the horizontal and amacrine cells that had so bewildered Cajal. If retinal elements surrounding a light-detecting cell are themselves excited by light, they send *inhibitory* signals to this central cell, preventing it from firing. The retina is wired to respond not to regions of uniform darkness or light, but instead to areas of contrast, to the edges and contours of shadows and objects.

The eye is not a camera. A light square sitting on a black background looks brighter than the same square on a gray background. The eye, unlike a camera, does not record absolute luminosity. It looks at patches of the scene through a kind of latticed window, and compares the light radiating through one tiny pane of glass with that radiating through the immediately surrounding panes.

It is now known that the latticed window of the retina is remapped over twenty times in the brain. And here the dark room continues to serve as a model and machine, as a metaphor and theater of exploration. Beginning in the late 1950s, two of Stephen Kuffler's young colleagues, David Hubel and Torsten Wiesel, began projecting patterns of light on a screen of a dark room while recording from cells in the cerebral cortices of cats and monkeys facing the screen. They found that within the gridlike arrangements within the visual cortex lie cells that detect contrast across different dimensions of the image—form, color, motion, and depth. The more complex response properties of these cortical neurons are generated through their specific connections with lower-order cells; such cells are regularly arrayed within the cortex according to their function. The brain perceives the world through a series of grids whose functions are defined by their neuronal structure. These latticed windows are not transparent; they begin to transform the image projected into the camera obscura of the eye as soon as light strikes the retina.

Ultimately, however, the neurons of the visual system must perform an interpretive task not unlike that of the photographer in Michelangelo Antonioni's film *Blow-Up,* who secretly takes pictures of a couple cavorting in a deserted London park. Developing one of these photographs, the photographer then becomes puzzled by the troubled gaze of the woman over her companion's shoulder. In his darkroom, he blows up the image of the woman's face—an act akin to the magnification of detail that occurs when we point our eyes at an object and thus place this segment of the visual scene on our fovea—the cone-rich, high-resolution center of our retinas. Able to see where the woman's pupils are pointed, the photographer then goes back to the original photograph and blows up the segment of the surrounding bushes that the woman is foveating. But for a long time the photographer sees nothing in this sun-dappled patch of shrubbery. It is like the image of interbranching nerve cells Cajal encounters before the application of the black stain—"a forest so dense that . . . the trunks, branches, and leaves touch everywhere": there is no separation of figure and ground. Then suddenly, in a true gestalt shift, the scene in the park bushes resolves itself before the photographer's eyes. The latent image emerges from the undifferentiated mass of foliage, the fractured patches of shadow and flickers of reflection from sunlit leaves: the face of an assassin, aiming a sleek gray gun, waiting to kill the man the woman has lured to that deserted meadow. The human visual system evolved in conditions not unlike this leafy picture, in which prey and predators lay hidden in verdant underbrush. Such camouflaged objects do not simply exist in the raw image projected on the back of an eye or camera: they must be extracted. How such gestalt perceptions are pieced together remains unknown. Form recognition, the creative process by which disparate elements of a two-dimensional retinal image are reconstructed by the brain into the objects of the four-dimensional world, is perhaps the central problem of modern neuroscience.

The great neurosurgeon Wilder Penfield, who studied briefly at the Instituto Cajal in the 1920s, wrote of Cajal's first vision of the true structure of the nervous system:

"Working alone, he was like a man who had lit a lantern in the dark, one who had a magic key. He opened the doors all along a dark street so others could see into the secret chambers where the brain meets the mind." No terminus to this street has yet been found. Each new discovery is a disclosure: a door opens to admit one. Beyond this threshold, at the dark room's far wall, stands a latticed window, palely lit.

William R. Everdell (essay date 1997)

SOURCE: "Santiago Ramón y Cajal: The Atoms of Brain, 1889," in *The First Moderns: Profiles in the Origins of Twentieth-Century Thought,* The University of Chicago Press, 1997, pp. 100-15.

[*In the following essay, Everdell discusses Ramón y Cajal's formulation of neuron theory, suggesting that he may be 'the most important progenitor of twentieth-century neuroscience.'*]

> But when classicism says "man," it means reason and feeling. And when Romanticism says "man," it means passion and the senses. And when modernism says "man" it means the nerves.
> —Hermann Bahr, *The Overcoming of Naturalism: Sequel to "Critique of the Moderns"*

In October 1889, at the Congress of the German Anatomical Society at the University of Berlin, a short, powerfully built Spaniard with penetrating black eyes set up a small exhibit of drawings done on paper with colored inks. For the past two and a half years, alone in a spare room behind his house in Barcelona, he had been drawing them from nature through the eyepiece of a Zeiss, the most powerful optical miscroscope yet made. His subject was the brain of the embryo of a small bird, its cerebellum to be exact, and each thin slice of it had been cut, prepared and dyed using his own improved version of a painstaking two-step process recently discovered in Italy. Because Spain was not a place where new science was published at the turn of the century, he had had to edit and print his own journal in order to make his results known. Some of the German biologists at the Congress had made the effort to read those articles when they arrived in the mail in 1888, but the Spanish language had given them trouble. Cajal had tried giving his talk to the Congress in halting French (which was not much of an improvement), but it was the drawings and slides around which the professionals now crowded, amazed. Seeing made it plain. Each stained cell stood out perfectly against a background of staggering complexity, and no matter how many times the tiny fibers of one nerve cell met those of another, there was clearly no physical connection between them. The basic unit of the brain—the neuron—had been isolated.

The maker of these mind-changing pictures was not Picasso, who would not strut the streets of Barcelona for another seven years, or paint its Avinyo Street prostitutes until 1906. Eight years old in 1889, young Pablo Ruiz was already making accomplished drawings of birds, but they were of whole-birds. No less diminutive, pugnacious, brilliant and ambitious than Picasso, this other Spanish artist, standing behind a laboratory table in Berlin beside his pictures of birds' brains, was thirty years older. His art was the one we now call neuroscience, one which, a century later, has begun to look like the most promising of all the twentieth-century sciences. The artist's name was Santiago Ramón y Cajal.

Cajal could not be a neuroscientist in 1889, for the field had yet to be staked out. He had made his scientific debut as a medical researcher in the area called histology, or the study of tissue structure, a field first laid out by Bichat in the early years of the nineteenth century. The job of a histologist was to use that supreme biological tool of the nineteenth century, the optical miscroscope, to find and describe the cell structure of a heart muscle or a stomach lining. The hope was to discover how they worked and how they might go wrong, but the basic task was simply to classify—that is, to offer a taxonomy of the different tissues and the cells within those tissues. Of all sciences, taxonomy—Adam's task of distinguishing among things and naming them—is probably the least glamorous. Ernest Rutherford was later to say that all science was "either physics or stamp-collecting." Taxonomy was stamp-collecting. A good taxonomist had to be humble, as well as extraordinarily thorough and persistent, like Linnaeus, who founded biological taxonomy in the eighteenth century by naming and classifying some 4,000 species of animals and 6,000 species of plants.

This kind of tireless single-mindedness was very much in the character of Santiago Ramón y Cajal. He was the sort of person who would teach himself how to play championship chess, how to drop animals with a slingshot, or how to use a camera and make his own photographic plates. He was capable of spending months in a gym building up his body; of stealing books, eagles' nests, and even the bones in a graveyard for study. Tempted by the glamorous new subspecialty of bacteriology in 1885, and by medicine's sudden fascination with hypnotism in 1886, he always came back to general histology and its vision of life as a function of matter. Not many could have watched through a microscope for two hours straight, fascinated, as he was, by a white blood cell oozing its way through the wall of a capillary.

Tenacity showed up early in Cajal. When he was a boy of eleven, according to his own irresistible account, he built a cannon in his back yard. Once the gun was ready, he loaded it with stones and blew a good-sized hole in a neighbor's garden gate. The constable jailed Cajal for three days, much to the satisfaction of the boy's outraged father; but the sentence, which would surely have deterred almost any other child, made no impression on Cajal. As soon as he was released, he proceeded to build another cannon; and when that one blew up in his face and nearly blinded one eye, Cajal went on to steal the flintlock blunderbuss his father kept for

show and shoot it off in secret with gunpowder he had made in a makeshift laboratory on the roof.[1]

Cajal described his motive in blowing things up as "a lively admiration for science and an insatiable curiosity regarding the forces of nature." Doubters may be reassured by the tale of how Cajal managed to hold on to his deepest vocation against the kind of fundamental and long-term opposition that would have discouraged almost anyone else. That vocation, Cajal's first love, was not science, but painting. At "eight or nine years old I had an irresistible mania for scribbling on paper, drawing ornaments in books, daubing on walls, gates, doors, and recently painted façades." He could not do this at home "because my parents considered painting a sinful amusement."[2]

> My father . . . was almost completely lacking in artistic sense and he repudiated or despised all culture of a literary or of a purely ornamental or recreative nature. . . . This somewhat positivistic tendency I believe to have been not innate but acquired. . . . [3]

Deprived of paper and pencils by his family's poverty and his father's positivism, Cajal saved his centavos for them. Growing up in the classically rural town of Ayerbe in the shadow of the Pyrenees, he found color "by scraping the paint from walls or by soaking the bright red or dark blue bindings of the little books of cigarette paper, which at that time were painted with soluble colours."[4]

Such persistence finally wore down Cajal Senior, to the point where he was willing to take advice as to his son's vocation. He went straight to the town's leading painter-plasterer with Santiago in tow, showed him one of the boy's drawings and asked him whether it showed any talent. The contractor looked the picture up and down and pronounced it "a daub! . . . the child will never be an artist."

"'But does the boy really show no aptitude for art?' 'None, my friend,' replied the wall scraper. . . . " But it would be years before Cajal himself could be convinced of this expert's wisdom. His father's dream was for Cajal to become a doctor, but Cajal remained an artist no matter what he did with him. Why, Cajal demanded, "exchange the magic palette of the painter for the nasty and prosaic bag of surgical instruments! The enchanted brush, the creator of life . . . be given up for the cruel scalpel, which wards off death. . . . " And so Cajal engaged his parents in what he called "a silent war of duty against desire" that went on for years. At his first school, Cajal neglected his classical subjects and caricatured the master with such persistence and skill that school administrators concluded the only way to stop him was to lock him up. The lockup was "the classic dark chamber—a room almost underground, overrun with mice," but even there Cajal found a way to make art. There was a tiny hole in the wall facing the town, and on the wall opposite the hole there appeared, to the boy's delight and astonishment, a moving picture of what was going on in the town square. It was upside down, but it was quite clear enough to draw.

Thus Cajal, prohibited from going to the square, found that science could arrange for the square to come to him. He had discovered the camera obscura, "a tremendous discovery in physics, which, in my utter ignorance, I supposed entirely new."[5]

The discovery gave Cajal "a most exalted idea of physics," but his teachers continued to find him hopeless. Eventually he was sent away to the town of Jaca to learn his Latin from friars. Under the friars, who beat students and threw them at blackboards, Cajal quickly "conceived a loathing for Latin grammar" and a recurrence of his "madness over art." He didn't blame the friars much, for he knew his mind "wandered continually." Cajal judged his own understanding to be about as mediocre as his diligence, and his "verbal memory" to be less reliable than his "memory for ideas." When he reached age twelve his father tried him in another school in a larger town called Huesca—so large that Cajal later seriously opined that it had altered and enriched the neural connectivity of his brain. Within hours of arriving he had spent lunch money on paper and a box of paints. Within a week he was "drawing on the walls with chalk," and not long after, he remembered, he was able to draw a map of Europe for homework freehand and from memory. Proudly he included the many scores of noncontiguous states in the old German Confederation. After that the basket cells in a cerebellum would be child's play.[6]

In later years, Cajal professed to be happy he had not become an artist. His early drawings, he concluded, had shown an anatomical ignorance and a caricatural understanding of his subjects—"a tendency which many modernist and futurist painters to-day cultivate systematically with rapturous applause from superficial critics." He considered himself to have been an indifferent colorist who never understood the basic insight of his contemporaries, the impressionists, "that nature seldom presents an absolutely pure colour," or that gray is less a color than it is a scale of brightness. Here again he found the necessary self-deprecatory language in the Modern art that had since arisen in spite of him. "Who does not detect at first glance, by the loudness of its colouring, the unfortunate product of the unskilled painter or the dissident modernist, who from snobbery pays homage to the 'loud' school, slipping back unwittingly to the infantile phase of art?" Cajal finally extracted a year of artistic training from his father by spending a year as apprentice to a cobbler, but that year was the finish of his ambition. Once his slow and reluctant abandonment of art was complete, he remembered its lessons as lessons of failure. It had, he wrote, "led me to sharpen my observation of nature and to distrust memory;" or, in short, to become an observational scientist.[7] Cajal often called himself modern but never Modernist, and he used the word "modern" as a synonym for realistic, scientific, and materialistic. He seems never to have become aware of the literary and artistic movement turn-of-the-century Spanish critics were calling *Modernismo,* which was a Spanish version of French *Décadence* and symbolism. He became, in the end, more of a positivist than his father, intent on erasing every trace of the transcendent and mysterious in the study of nature, of mind, and of brain. If the true vocation of the artist is simply to see, Cajal's great discovery was that of an artist; but it was as a medical researcher, an analyst, a phenomenologist of the discrete that Cajal was to become a Modernist.

Taxonomy actually requires more than tenacity. It is more epistemologically challenging than any other science, more so even than fundamental physics.[8] It makes more innocent assumptions, and rarely examines them from the perspective of phenomenology—the mind's take on the putative outer world. What, in fact, are you seeing when you classify a thing and give it a name? Why are the edges that mark one thing off from another found in one place and not in another? Why are some categories appropriate for bringing things together and not others? If categories dictate or are dictated by a hypothesis, then why that hypothesis and no other? The mere act of distinguishing one thing from another raises the phenomenological problem. Worse, it raises the problem of infinites. Linnaeus, for example, had subscribed to the basic assumption we have come to call the great chain of being, including the so-called "plenitude" principle that there was no vacant place or "missing link" in the chain. If the principle were true, then nature would have to be a continuum, and if nature were a continuum, then the differences between species would have to be infinitesimal and the number of species infinite. This objection never seems to have occurred to Linnaeus, who died expecting the number of species in the world to top out at around 15,000. It did not take the nineteenth century long to show that there were more than twelve times that number of beetle species alone, and of course that is nothing compared to infinity.[9] As we shall see, it was only in 1900 that the concept of finite numbers of simple parts was brought in to solve the problem of species.

One might have expected it sooner. Mendel had in fact proposed it in 1865. As for the hypothesis that reduced all living things to a concatenation of similar parts—the celebrated "cell theory"—it was even older, dating from an article by Schleiden and Schwann back in 1839. Cells themselves had been found much earlier than that. In 1837, for example, Jan Purkinje had found the prominent cerebellum cells now named for him. Within the nervous system proper, histology had placed several kinds of cells before 1888, and some of the classic nineteenth-century textbooks of general histology, like Albrecht von Kölliker's in 1853 and Ranvier's in the 1870s, actually began with an exemplary nerve cell as the best way to introduce a student to the cell concept. Nevertheless, most of the central nervous system looked to nineteenth-century scientists as if it were mostly a partless, continuous mass.

Of course, the nerves were the object of intense attention in the old century, especially in Germany. There the universe that Hegel and the Hegelians had filled with spirit was being rapidly reduced to mere matter. Karl Marx was out of school. For young scientists, the goal that emergent positivism and fashionable materialism seemed most of all to demand was scientific proof that consciousness was only a byproduct of electricity and chemistry in the nervous system. It was in 1842 that four students of the great biologist Johannes Müller—Carl Ludwig, Hermann Helmholtz, Emil DuBois-Reymond, and Ernst Brücke—had sworn their oath never to admit that any "other forces than the common physical chemical ones" were needed for life.[10] That same year Helmholtz had submitted as his doctoral thesis measurements of the speed of an electrical impulse along the nerves of a frog. DuBois-Reymond would go on to publish the standard work on electrical transmission in the nerves, called *Studies on Animal Electricity.* Brücke would bring the neural materialist faith to Vienna, where he eventually passed it on to his lab assistants, including an aspiring young neuroscientist named Sigmund Freud.

For a while the brain seemed to yield to this latest attempt to associate it with mind. It was in 1861 that French anthropologist Paul Broca discovered the area in the temporal lobe of the human brain that, when injured, seemed to prevent a patient from using grammar. Carl Wernicke found his own language "area," complementing Broca's, in 1874. For a while phrenology, the fashionable therapy of the 1840s that read mental function from the bumps on one's skull, looked like something more than junk science. In 1881 Freud's colleague Sigmund Exner wrote the standard text on the localization of functions in the brain, and in 1884 Exner's teacher, Theodor Meynert (who also taught Wernicke, Freud, and Auguste Forel), built his own general psychiatry text on his former student's localizations. Next to these philosophically adventurous experiments in physiology, collecting, observing, and describing nerve tissue—mere neurohistology—lost a lot of its glamor. It became an exercise for students and a subspecialty for cheerful toilers like Cajal.

The ancient discipline of psychology was powerfully affected by neural materialism. Professors of psychology, especially in Germany, began to worry that if the materialists were to achieve their goal of proving that the human psyche had no autonomy, no selfhood, then the psychology profession, the study of mind as a whole, might have to be abandoned. Both Wilhelm Wundt, a former Müller student who founded the first experimental psychology laboratory in Leipzig in 1879, and William James, the trained physiologist who founded the first U.S. Department of Psychology at Harvard in 1875, were driven by this anxiety.[11] Both found themselves in the 1880s writing their way toward philosophy and out of physiological psychology. By 1913, the American intellectual descendants of Wundt and James would find a paradigm for psychology that was both more materialistic and less, one that allowed the mind its wholeness by simply disallowing any questions as to how it worked. For vain efforts to understand mind and inconclusive investigations of brain function "behaviorism" substituted a bare input-output model, called the mind a "black box," and cut the whole subject of psychology loose from neuroscience for a century.

These sorts of attitudes meant that in the 1880s, as Cajal was beginning to publish his researches and before the microbe hunters had made their mark, neurohistologists were pretty solidly ensconced in a small corner of the learned world. Their territory was vast and various but no longer galvanizing for other scientists, since none of their new findings seemed to offer a major philosophical challenge. The decade's new terms—"cytoplasm," "nucleoplasm," and "mitosis" (complete with "prophase," "metaphase," and "anaphase")—and its new tool, the microtome tissue-slicer, invented by von Gudden, Mad King Ludwig's psychiatrist, presaged no new paradigm. The single great problem for the field was how to distinguish one structure from another in any nervous system larger than a snail's. Some worked with leeches, crayfish, and lampreys, dauntingly complicated but simpler than mammals or human beings. The central nervous system in *Homo sapiens,* which we now know contains something on the order of ten billion nerve cells with perhaps a trillion connections, appeared to histologists like Kölliker to be an inextricable tangle of fibers, interrupted only occasionally by cells with a recognizable structure. The fibers often thinned down beyond the resolving power of microscopes, and teasing them apart with dissecting tools seemed "an undertaking for a Benedictine."[12] Massed fibers seemed to form a good part of the cerebrum and spinal cord, which the professionals dubbed "gray matter;" and there was also a lot of "white matter," which some were beginning to understand took its color from the myelin sheathing around nerve fibers. Under the cerebrum there was even a patch of black matter, learnedly called, in Latin, *substantia nigra.* Differentiation of parts, or what the histologists called the "fine structure" of this great tangle, came with frustrating slowness. Between 1836 and 1838, a Müller student named Robert Rémak had suggested that most of these myriad fibers in the brain were processes attached to cells. In 1839 J. B. Rosenthal had described the *Achsencylinder* or axon, an extended fiber on some cells of the central nervous system, and in 1855 Rémak had proposed that each nerve cell had only one of them—though most of Rémak's students, including Kölliker, found the conclusion too bold. Otto Deiters, who died young after years of dissecting the neural tangle with threadlike needles and staring at it through his microscope, had left notes asserting that though axons were single and did not branch, other parts of the nerve cell did have tiny "protoplasmic processes" (we call them "dendrites") branching out from them.[13]

Optical microscopes had their limits, even with oil-immersion lenses; microdissection seemed beyond human skill; and dyes and stains were fuzzy, unpredictable, and unreliable. Locked away from the "fine structure" of the nervous system in the heroic age of chemistry, histologists fixed on the dyes and stains. They tested nearly every kind of chemical that came along in the nineteenth century, trying to find an elixir that would make nerves stand out against their impossibly undifferentiated background by coloring only one or two at a time. Their first historian, Gustav Mann, wrote in 1902 that "to be an histologist became practically synonymous with being a dyer," except that "the professional dyer knew what he was about, while the histologist with few exceptions did not know, nor does he to the present day."[14] The carmine dye pioneered by Joseph von Gerlach in the mid-1850s had one advantage: it was red. Aside from that it could not stain a single nerve with precision, and it could not stain all its processes, in particular the long axon, out to their ends. Indigo proved a little harder to work with and not much of an improvement. The new aniline dyes, tried out in 1859, were brilliant but they had much the same limitations, as did the methylene blue first applied by the soon-to-be famous bacteriologist Paul Ehrlich in the 1870s, or the "haematoxylin" he pioneered in 1886.

To the workers most involved, like Carl Weigert, who had invented several staining methods, it soon became clear that it was not just the dye that made a difference, but the preparation of the tissue both before and after the dye was applied. Tissue had to be "fixed" or it would alter or decay, but it shrank in some fixatives and lost features in others. Tissue's refractive index had to be chemically "cleared" or optical microscopes wouldn't work. Some procedures had to be done in the dark; some in acid-clean test tubes without metal touching the contents. Some dyes were oxidizing agents and had to be reduced in order to work; some were reducers that needed oxidizers; some worked better if they were allowed to deteriorate for a while. The relationships of reagents were so close and so hard to understand that the task of histologists became not to make a stain work, but to figure out how it had worked the first time—that is, to make it work more than once. Chromic acid, pioneered as a stain in 1843, eventually turned out to be more useful as a tissue bath, preparing cells to absorb more distinctive stains. In the 1860s Deiters and his teacher Max Schultze successfully used a salt of chromic acid, potassium bichromate, to give cells that had been fixed with the acid a purplish color, and tried the old carmine stain to make the result stand out further. Exner had found in the 1870s that "osmic acid" (osmium tetroxide in water) worked both as a preperation and as a stain, but that it only colored the sheathing of a fiber—the myelin—which meant that an axon's all-important terminations, which were unmyelinated, could not be seen. The extra time all these measures took is a good measure of the size of the dye obstacle. In the spirit of trying everything, someone was bound to try gold, and in 1872 Gerlach, the inventor of carmine, did so. He used the chloride, gold's only generally available salt, and found that it stained cells well enough to be worth its price. Gold quickly earned a place in the repertoire and inspired a long string of efforts to improve it. Freud's sixth published paper, in 1884, was a report on the improvements he had made in gold chloride staining.

In the end, however, it was not gold that did the trick, but silver—silver nitrate, in fact, which was one of the family of chemicals that had made photography possible at the beginning of the nineteenth century. The man who first used it correctly was a histologist named Camillo Golgi,

from the Italian city of Pavia, who began publishing his observations "on the structure of the gray matter" in the *Italian Medical Gazette* in the summer of 1873.[15] He made it work by soaking the gray matter in potassium bichromate as before, but then he added a dilute solution of silver nitrate to the bath. The potassium bichromate already in the cells reduced the silver nitrate to metallic silver, which fell out as a precipitate. Silver stained the inside of the entire cell black, magnificently distinct against the yellow left by the chromates; but the real beauty of the new substance was that somehow it could stain cells in the middle of a three-dimensional cube of tissue, one cell at a time, all the way out to their ends, so that they stood out "like trees in a winter mist."[16] With it Golgi could make out a dendrite only 30 millionths of a meter long. Under proper conditions Golgi found he could even see the long axon of a nerve cell stained almost as far as the axon extended, and could at last distinguish between long- and short-axon nerve cells.

The idea was not altogether new, silver nitrate having been used by one histologist along with ammonia to stain nervous tissue,[17] and by another preceded by acetic acid to stain motor nerves, but the stain was very temperamental. So much depended on what you did to prepare the tissue before adding the silver that Golgi never stopped working on it. His papers began appearing in French and English journals in the 1880s, and his most comprehensive work, published in 1886, would eventually win him a Nobel Prize. By then the new staining method was being tried in histology labs all over Europe.

Spain, however, seemed not to be in Europe at all. In the nineteenth century Spanish medical researchers never considered the brain without leaving room for the soul, and it often took whole decades to naturalize a new technique. As an assistant in the Zaragoza Medical Faculty in 1880, Cajal had had to learn the art of lithographic engraving in order to get his papers illustrated accurately. He had been advanced enough to use gold chloride staining in his first published paper, and to suggest ammoniacal silver nitrate in his second, but no one else in Zaragoza had ever tried silver. At the University of Valencia where Cajal had secured his first professorship in histology in 1883, researchers were still innocent of Golgi and his stain. When Cajal had interrupted his own researches to return to Zaragoza and pitch in as a bacteriologist on the cholera epidemic in 1885, he was still using the older stains himself. Cajal didn't get his first chance to see the silver-bichromate technique in use until 1887, when he paid a visit to Madrid as a judge for the national exam in descriptive anatomy and visited Luís Simarro, who had just come back from France. Simarro showed Cajal some examples of Golgi staining he had in his house, and later took him down to his lab in the unofficial biological institute in Gorguera Street to show him more. Cajal remembered being so impressed that he gave up all other methods, and began not only to apply the new staining technique but to tinker and improve on it. Soon he had added an extra step to the preparation sequence by making two separate soaks out of what had been a continuous procedure. His great discoveries were less than a year away.

Cajal had found his method just in time. The extraordinary hypothesis that the entire mass of the central nervous system was composed of the extensions of separate and distinct cells had already been advanced. In October 1886, Wilhelm His of Leipzig had asserted that there was no continuity between nerves, just as (recent research had shown) there was no continuity between nerves and the muscle cells they controlled. In January 1887 Auguste Forel, the Director of the Burghölzli Asylum in Zurich who would in the same year begin his work on hypnotherapy, published a paper on brain anatomy pointing out that "no one has yet seen" any such continuous connections between "outgrowths of the ganglion cells, the fibres [axons], or the protoplasmic processes [dendrites]" of one cell and those of another. Four months later in Oslo, Norway, Fridtjof Nansen, about to set off on the first expedition to cross Greenland, put a finishing touch on his neuroanatomy Ph.D. thesis and made the same observation. "A direct combination between the ganglion cells, by direct anastomosis of the protoplasmic processes does not exist."[18] Cajal had only just gotten his first look at the Golgi-stain lithographs in Luís Simarro's biology lab in Madrid and already there had been three separate attacks on the old theory of brain histology. Of course now, a century after the fact, it seems like an edifice was crumbling, but in 1887 the old hypothesis that all the nerve fibers of the gray matter were mutually connected in a single network was in no real trouble. This so-called reticular hypothesis (*reticulum* is the Latin word for network) was in fact vigorously promoted by Joseph von Gerlach, the man who had brought carmine and gold chloride to histology, and Theodor Meynert, the formidable Viennese. Its great champion was in fact none other than the discoverer of silver-chromate, Camillo Golgi himself. "Ruled by the theory," Cajal remembered, "we who were active in histology then saw networks everywhere." It was a beautiful theory and, he wrote, "As always, reason is silent before beauty."[19]

The way was therefore open to Cajal. He was the only one working on the problem who had both the technique and a mind that was ready to change. In November 1887, when he took up his new professorship in Barcelona, the first thing he did after moving his growing family into their new house in Riera Alta street was to set up his laboratory and start staining brain tissue. First came a two- to four-day soaking in 1 percent osmic acid and 3 percent potassium bichromate solution to harden the tissue and pervade it with chromate; then the 20 percent silver nitrate solution and thirty more hours of soaking to precipitate the silver. Next he would put the specimen in pure alcohol to harden it, mount and slice it with a microtome, then soak the slices in six to eight changes of pure alcohol to get rid of all the water. Finally he would clear their refractive index with oil of clove or bergamot, wash out the oil of clove with a solvent, varnish with a resin, and mount the specimen.[20]

Early the next year, after moving to a larger house in Bruch Street, Cajal began to work on the nervous system in earnest. 1888 was to be "my greatest year, my year of fortune."[21] Sensing the commitment it would require, he gave up chess, in which he had made himself an expert, for the next twenty-five years. In the back room he used as a laboratory Cajal had made one more change in the methods used by Golgi and the earlier researchers, one that had been missed by all his contemporaries, including His, Forel, and Nansen. He had decided to use embryos. "Since the full-grown forest turns out to be impenetrable and indefinable, why not revert to the young wood, in the nursery stage . . . ?"[22] was how he explained coming up with the rather off-putting idea of using unfledged, unhatched chicks to study the central nervous system. Its brilliance lay in the fact that the nervous system in almost all vertebrates is incomplete at birth. Though the nerves have grown dendrites and axons, not all of these are fully extended. Moreover, the "glial" cells have hardly begun their task of covering the nerve extensions with the ubiquitous white insulation called myelin.

Best of all, the silver-chromate stain works better in embryos. When Cajal looked at the first chick cerebellum, what he saw was a lot of extraordinarily long axons, completely uncovered and stained brownish-black to their very tips, exposed to his objectifying gaze. It was obvious to him that every fiber belonged to a particular cell. They did not go through the wall of any other cell; they came up close enough to touch it, but they never actually did. He could see where they ended. Obvious as always were the Purkinje cells with their many thick branches and prominent cell bodies, but now it became clear that the fuzzy structures enclosing those bodies were the branching ends of the axons of entirely different nerve cells whose own cell bodies were tiny. They enclosed the Purkinje cell like a basket around a melon, but they never penetrated it. Cajal stared through the microscope and drew exactly what he saw. Then he drew his conclusion: the famous central network, "that sort of unfathomable physiological sea, into which, on the one hand, were supposed to pour the streams arising from the sense organs, and from which, on the other hand, the motor or centrifugal conductors were supposed to spring like rivers originating in mountain lakes" did not exist at all. "By dint of pretending to explain everything [it] explain[ed] absolutely nothing." The truth was that the entire central nervous system was like a telephone exchange in which each nerve cell communicated only with such other nerve cells as were touched by the ends of its axon. The alternative was "protoplasmic pantheism . . . pleasing to those who disdain observation. . . . "[23]

Today Nansen is remembered as an Arctic explorer and statesman; Forel as Jung's predecessor at Burghölzli, Kokoschka's portrait subject, and one of Freud's sources on hypnotism. As for His, he is best remembered as the doctor who stood by when they exhumed the body of Johann Sebastian Bach, and made careful measurements of the great man's skull. The reason is that they had only guessed at Cajal's conclusion. They had not proved it.

Proof required that patient, endless work with chemicals, needles, microtomes, microscopes, and lithographic plates, the sort of work Freud had learned how to do long before he became a doctor, when Brücke had set him to study the nervous system of the lamprey in 1876. In 1882 Freud gave a lecture on "The Structure of the Elements of the Nervous System" based on what he had learned from the lamprey and later the eel and the crayfish. At the point in this lecture, published in 1884, where he had taken up the implications of the network theory, three of Freud's biographers pronounced that he had proposed the neuron and anticipated Cajal.[24] They were wrong. Freud had not seen through the network and, as we shall see, had a very different professional destiny.[25] Soon he would abandon the psychological microcosm for what he hoped was the Big Picture. In 1889, two months before Cajal traveled to Berlin to convince the Congress of Anatomists of his new idea, Freud went to Paris to learn from the Experimental and Therapeutic Hypnotists, whose Congress coincided with the World's Fair. (The Congress of Physiological Psychology also met in Paris during the Fair, and there, just to compound the irony, was William James.) Thus Cajal brought his new idea, together with the indispensable hard-won proof, to a rather small gathering of men who practiced a well-established but not very fashionable discipline. Perhaps because of that, they treated him extremely well. The Belgian van Gehuchten, who had been Cajal's faithful correspondent, withdrew his opposition to the new hypothesis on the spot, as did, soon after, the Basel professor, Lenhossék. The Swede, Retzius, was skeptical but kind. Even Wilhelm His marveled and applauded, and the formidable Berlin expert, H. Wilhelm G. von Waldeyer-Hartz, was unexpectedly welcoming. As for the patriarch of the Society, Albrecht von Kölliker, he swept Cajal into his carriage, took him to his hotel, and gave him a dinner. Promising to have everything Cajal wrote published in Germany, Kölliker said, "I have discovered you and I wish to make my discovery known in Germany."[26]

In November, Cajal returned to Spain and got back to work; but the rest of the histological world continued to reverberate. Between October and December 1891, the great Waldeyer published a series of six long articles in the *German Medical Weekly* on the whole state of the question of the fine structure in neuroanatomy. There he attributed the new gray-matter-discontinuity hypothesis to Cajal and gave it the name "neurone doctrine." These articles gave rather more credit to Waldeyer than Cajal thought he deserved, but there is no doubt they secured Cajal's scientific reputation for the rest of his life.[27] News of his discovery passed beyond the small world of histology and became an example of "science," ever progressing in the nineteenth-century manner. Soon people who knew no science to speak of would have some inkling of what Cajal had found. Never again would he be anonymous and unsupported, though he never stopped behaving as if he were. In 1894 the British Royal Society offered him its most prestigious award in biology, the Croonian Lectureship.[28] England's leading neuroanatomist, Charles Sherrington, invited Cajal to stay with him in his home in

London when he gave the lecture. There Sherrington was amazed to discover that Cajal would clean his own bedroom, hang out his sheets, and lock his bedroom door in order to prevent the traveling laboratory he had set up there from being disturbed.[29]

In the 1890s Cajal advanced and provided evidence for four additional hypotheses about the nervous system. The first of these, which has acquired the name of the "Law of Dynamic Polarization," asserts that the axons of nerve cells are always outputs for nerve impulses and that dendrites are always inputs. Signals did not, therefore, spin around in an endless circuit, but instead went only one way until they stopped and were received.[30] The second of Cajal's later hypotheses is the idea that neurons grow from the ends of the axons at a point analogous to the root hair of a plant. Cajal found this in chick embryos in 1890 and called it the "cone of growth."[31] The third of these ideas Cajal advanced in 1892 and eventually called the "Chemotactic Hypothesis." Wondering why the growth cones of axons followed one trajectory instead of another and how growing axons could go such long distances to make the "right" connections, Cajal suggested they found their way by following trails of chemicals already laid down among the other nerves.[32] These three hypotheses are now conventional wisdom so taken for granted that Cajal's name has become completely detached from them, and they are taught as if anatomists had always known them. Fair enough, since Cajal never found a proof for them and indeed there was never anything in his experimental repertory that could have provided one. The fate of the fourth hypothesis, as we shall see, is not yet known.

In 1899, when Clark College in Worcester, Massachusetts celebrated its tenth anniversary, its president, William James's first Ph.D. student, G. Stanley Hall, invited the stars of European science to give lectures to celebrate. Ludwig Boltzmann arrived to discuss the paradoxes of physical and mathematical continuity. The mathematician M. E. Picard talked of Peano's foundations of arithmetic. The three other speakers were all brain scientists: Ramón y Cajal, Forel, and Angelo Mosso, who had all sailed over together on a French Line ship from Le Havre. Cajal spoke first, trying to sum up in three lectures what was then known about the structure of the cerebrum. Using large colored placards, he described all the new neurons and neural fibers he had isolated, the consequences of their separate existence, the direction of impulses in the fibers, and the curiously precise way in which the fibers extended themselves into the numbingly complex space made up of the cells and fibers that were already there. Forel followed with a flamboyant talk on the possibilities of brain science in which he claimed that he and Wilhelm His had been first with the neuron doctrine. Of this claim Cajal says nothing in his autobiography beyond profuse references to Forel's intelligence and charm.

What struck Cajal more than Forel's belated claim was the astonishing attitudes the Americans demonstrated on the subject of his homeland. When the invitation came in the mail, Cajal had asked his government whether he ought to accept it. It was, after all, only a few months after San Juan Hill and the devastating defeat of Spain by the United States in the Spanish-American War—a war the United States claimed had been fought to free Cuba from Spanish cruelty. Cajal knew exactly what Spain had done in Cuba, because he had seen it for himself. In 1874, doing his military service in the Spanish army's medical corps during an earlier colonial war, he had watched as the Spanish Governor-General tried to cut Cuba into three pieces with two barbed-wire fences running north and south, the better to control the insurgent population. In Cajal's view, the scheme, which inspired a later Governor-General named Valeriano Weyler to develop the concentration camp, had been not only cruel but impractical. As skeptical of Spanish intentions as he had been of Spanish strategy, Cajal hadn't liked having his patriotism called on to endorse the incompetence, peculation, and stupidity of Spanish imperialism in Cuba. Indeed, soon after this trip, in order to reconcile his deep and continuing loyalty to Spain with honest criticism, Cajal would begin writing his memoirs. But the Americans he met during his east coast tour struck him as obtusely simple and bewilderingly oblivious of the effect they had had on so many of the world's peoples. In the unexpected heat of a New York City hotel in July as he waited to go on to Worcester, Cajal found triumphant modernity in the sixteen-year-old Brooklyn Bridge, but a touch of irony in the newer Statue of Liberty. To insistent questions from the American press about how he would improve the United States, Cajal tactfully offered little beyond uniform praise of democracy, except a Victorian put down of feminism and a suggestion to build laboratories for bacteriology and histology. He reserved for a footnote in his memoirs the point he had wanted to make about American imperialism. "One cruelty never justifies another [and] those who argue thus seem to forget that only powerful nations can commit certain excesses with impunity."[33] He arrived in Worcester with a raging headache on the eve of the Fourth of July, and was treated next day to twenty-four hours of songs, cheers, rocket explosions, and citizens firing rifles into the air.

As Cajal dealt with his increasing fame, the "neuron doctrine" was becoming orthodoxy with histologists, neuroanatomists and psychologists, and Cajal's extraordinary pictures began to enter the ken of nonscientists. In 1900 northern Europe's greatest early Modern artist, the Norwegian Edvard Munch, painted a picture of his sister Laura, wrapped in a shawl and seated forlornly in a chair. She was chronically insane and Munch would paint her many times; but in the foreground of this painting, now called *Melancholy (Laura)*,[34] there is a table with a strange design in dark blue, red, white, and gray. As the viewer comes in for a closer look she realizes that the strange design has come out of the sketch book of Santiago Ramón y Cajal. It is a sagittal section of cerebral nerve tissue viewed in tight perspective and painted in the colors of histological stain.

In 1906, the sixth Nobel Peace Prize was awarded to Rough Rider Theodore Roosevelt, a decision which, as Cajal wrote drily, "produced great surprise, especially in Spain."[35] Cajal was himself in Stockholm to see Roosevelt accept the prize, because the Swedish Academy had awarded Cajal the 1906 Nobel for medicine. Half of it, anyway. The other half had gone to Camillo Golgi, "very justly adjudicated to . . . the originator of the method with which I accomplished my most striking discoveries,"[36] wrote the ever tactful Cajal. They met for the first time when they were introduced at the ceremony. The next day Golgi gave his Nobel acceptance lecture, and the day after that Cajal gave his, both in French. Cajal's lecture, **"The Structures and Connections of Nerve Cells,"** was a sustained defense of the independence of the neuron. Golgi's, "The Neuron Doctrine, Theory and Fact," was a sustained attack on the same idea.[37] To the end of his life, Golgi, the inventor of the reduced silver nitrate stain, would maintain his faith in undifferentiated neural networks. Cajal, who had made the stain his instrument for discovering the neuron, was unable to convince Golgi of the truth of his discovery even as they shared a Nobel Prize for it.

It was in the year 1906 that Cajal's disciple Sherrington coined the word "synapse" to describe the junction between one nerve cell and another.[38] Cajal was increasingly lionized as evidence continued to mount for his central doctrine of neural atomism, and for the Dynamic Polarization, Growth Cone, and Chemotactic hypotheses. Cajal's fourth hypothesis, however, never proved out in his lifetime and remains in dispute at this moment. This is the view that the phenomenon we call memory is a product of particular states of the entire brain or neural network. Memory, thought Cajal, was not the effect of some chemical or of changes in one or a few nerve cells; it was, he thought, a global property of the entire brain. Such a view is very much in the center of debate in the last decade of the twentieth century—the Decade of the Brain—and, if it turns out to be true, could make Cajal the most important progenitor of twentieth-century neuroscience, and turn Freud (who was the star attraction at Clark University's twentieth anniversary ten years after Cajal) into an artifact.[39] The brain may not govern, as the nineteenth century thought. It may simply "emerge," an undetermined consequence of the simple interactions of more than ten billion cells making a trillion connections. The mind may not govern either, as Freud would insist ten years after Cajal had found the neuron. It may emerge instead, conscious and unconscious, in the same way, a way that never occurred to the nineteenth-century mind of Sigmund Freud, but did occur to the nineteenth-century mind of Santiago Ramón y Cajal once he had made a twentieth-century hypothesis about the atoms of brain.

NOTES

[1] Santiago Ramón y Cajal, *Recollections of My Life* (Cambridge: MIT Press, 1989), 69-75.

[2] Ibid., 36.

[3] Ibid., 37.

[4] Ibid., 36.

[5] Ibid., 40-42, 44-46.

[6] Ibid., 45, 53, 55, 58, 78, 82-83.

[7] Ibid., 40-41, 92-93.

[8] "Naming is an extremely important act in science." Steven Rose, *The Making of Memory: From Molecules to Mind* (New York: Anchor Books/Doubleday, 1992), 41.

[9] "[T]axonomy . . . is a murky endeavor, for nothing in science raises so much controversy as attempts to classify and order the universe of observables. From the days of Linnaeus. . . . This disputatiousness is partly because the universe is a continuum, and our endeavors to identify discontinuities owe as much to our own human ingenuity and determination as they do to the material reality of what is being classified." Rose, *The Making of Memory,* 118.

[10] Quoted in Siegfried Bernfeld, "Freud's Earliest Theories and the School of Helmholtz," *Psychoanalytic Quarterly* 13, no. 3 (1944),348. The date is given as 1847 rather than 1842 in Gordon M. Shepherd, *Foundations of the Neuron Doctrine* (New York: Oxford University Press, 1991), 31.

[11] Cajal had no anxiety on this score, but he understood the question. "And our much talked of psychological unity? What has become of thought and consciousness in this audacious transformation of man into a colony of polyps?" (Cajal, *Recollections,* 296). Modern neuroscience glories in addressing just this question.

[12] Cajal, *Recollections,* 305.

[13] Otto Deiters, *Untersuchungen über Gehirn und Rückenmark des Menschen und der Säugethiere* (Brunswick: Vieweg, 1865); in Shepherd, *Foundations,* 42-44, 47.

[14] Gustav Mann, *Physiological Histology* (London: Oxford University Press, 1902); in Arthur Smith and John Bruton, *Color Atlas of Histological Staining Techniques* (Chicago: Year Book Medical, 1977), 9.

[15] Camillo Golgi, "Sulla struttura della grigia del cervello," *Italian Medical Gazette,* 2 August 1873; trans. in Shepherd, *Foundations,* 84-88.

[16] Rose, *The Making of Memory,* 259.

[17] The ammoniacal silver nitrate occasionally exploded if left standing around in the lab.

[18] In Shepherd, *Foundations,* 122. Cf. Cajal, *Histology,* trans. M. Fernán-Núñez (Baltimore: Williams and Wilkins, 1933), 413.

[19] Cajal, *Recollections,* 303.

[20] Ibid., 306; Cajal, *Histology,* 681; Dorothy F. Cannon, *Explorer of the Human Brain* (New York: Henry Schuman, 1949).

[21] Cajal, *Recollections,* 321.

[22] Ibid., 324.

[23] Ibid., 336-38.

[24] In *Freud, The Biologist of Mind* (New York: Harper, 1983), 16, Frank J. Sulloway cites without examination the assertions of R. Brun ("Sigmund Freuds Leistungen auf dem Gebiete der organische Neurologie," *Schweizerische Archiv für Neurologie und Psychiatrie* 37 [1936], 200-207), Smith Ely Jelliffe ("Sigmund Freud as a Neurologist," *Journal of Mental and Nervous Diseases* 85 [1937], 696-711), and Ernest Jones (*The Life and Work of Sigmund Freud,* vol. 1 [New York: Basic Books, 1953], chapter 14).

[25] "If we assume," said Freud at the point in his lecture where the neuron idea would have been most likely to come up, "that the fibrils of the nerve have the significance of isolated paths of conduction, then we should have to say that the pathways which in the nerve are separate are confluent in the nerve cell: then the nerve cell becomes the 'beginning' of all those nerve fibers anatomically connected with it. . . . " Freud, "Die Struktur der Elemente des Nervensystems," *Jahrbücher für Psychiatrie* 5 (1884); in Shepherd, *Foundations,* 72-73. Freud is clearly talking about a network whose connections lie within cells rather than of independent neurons.

[26] Cajal, *Recollections,* 357.

[27] "Waldeyer, the illustrious biologist of Berlin . . . giving a resumé of Cajal's ideas and discoveries in a German weekly only baptized them with a new word, 'neurone'. . . . " Cajal, *Histology,* 287.

[28] Cajal, "La fine structure des centres nerveux," Croonian Lecture at Royal Society, Burlington House, London, *Proceedings of the Royal Society, London,* Series B, 55 (1894), 444-67.

[29] John C. Eccles, *The Physiology of Nerve Cells* (Baltimore: Johns Hopkins University Press, 1957), 10.

[30] Cajal, "Leyes de la morfologia de las celulas nerviosas," *Revista trimestriel del micrografia* 1 (Madrid, 1897). Referenced in Cajal, *Histology,* 454. Arthur van Gehuchten helped Cajal pursue this hypothesis.

[31] Cajal, "A Quelle époque apparaissent les expansions des cellules nerveuses de la moëlle épinière du poulet?" *Gaceta médical Catalana* 13 (1890), 737-39. Cf. Cajal, *Histology,* 461.

[32] An article by Cajal in *Anales de la Sociedad Española de Historía Natural* (1892) describes neural pathways from the olfactory area (smell) to the hippocampus (memory), chemical "neurotropism" of growth cones, and a proposal for a "neurotropic" theory of nerve growth. Cf. Cajal, *Histology,* 482; also Cannon, *Explorer of the Human Brain,* 157.

[33] Cajal, *Recollections,* 488.

[34] Now in the Munch-Museet, Oslo.

[35] Cajal, *Recollections,* 550.

[36] Ibid., 546.

[37] *Les Prix Nobel 1904-1906* (Stockholm: Norstedt, 1906).

[38] Charles Scott Sherrington, *The Integrative Action of the Nervous System* (New Haven, Conn.: Yale University Press, 1977).

[39] "Of broader interest is the potential significance of the neuron doctrine as one of the great ideas of modern thought. One thinks here for comparison of such great achievements of the human intellect as quantum theory." Shepherd, *Foundations,* 9.

FURTHER READING

Biography

Craigie, E. Horne, and William C. Gibson. *The World of Ramón y Cajal: With Selections from His Nonscientific Writings.* Springfield, Ill.: Charles C. Thomas, 1968, 295 p.
   Contains a biography of Ramón y Cajal in the form of a travelogue and excerpts from his collection of aphorisms and sketches, *Charlas de café,* and other nonscientific works.

Ramón y Cajal, Santiago. "Recollections of My Life." *Memoirs of the American Philosophical Society* VIII, Parts I-II (1937): 3-638.
   English translation of Ramón y Cajal's autobiography. Includes a list of Ramón y Cajal's publications, titles, decorations, and prizes.

Williams, Harley. *Don Quixote of the Microscope: An Interpretation of the Spanish Savant Santiago Ramón y Cajal (1852-1934).* London: Jonathan Cape, 1954, 255 p.
   Biography designed for nonscientific audiences that emphasizes Ramón y Cajal's universal appeal.

Franklin Delano Roosevelt

1882-1945

American statesman.

INTRODUCTION

The thirty-second president of the United States of America, Roosevelt is considered among the greatest political leaders of the twentieth century. Elected to the office of president for an unprecedented four consecutive terms, he served as U.S. chief executive from 1933 to his death in 1945. The economic reforms implemented by Roosevelt in response to the Great Depression of the 1930s—known collectively as the "New Deal"—are thought to have transformed the role of the federal government as a regulator of social and economic security. For his leadership of the United States during the Second World War, Roosevelt is acknowledged as a champion of liberal democracy. Furthermore, among his numerous impacts on world politics in the twentieth century, Roosevelt's actions late in his administration are viewed as instrumental in the creation of the United Nations.

Biographical Information

Roosevelt was born on 30 January 1882, the only child of James and Sarah Delano Roosevelt, members of a wealthy and influential New York family. He was educated privately until the age of fourteen, when he entered Groton. He attended Harvard University beginning in 1900, and there was engaged to Anna Eleanor Roosevelt, a distant cousin. He studied law at Columbia University, passed the bar, and became a law clerk at a Wall Street firm. In 1910, Roosevelt entered politics, winning the New York state senate race as a Democrat. He was reelected in 1912, and that year offered his support to the successful presidential campaign of Woodrow Wilson. In return for his aid, Wilson named Roosevelt assistant secretary of the navy, a position he retained throughout the First World War. Roosevelt entered the 1914 United States Senate race in New York, but was defeated by Tammany Hall. His 1920 vice-presidential hopes on the Democratic ticket with James Cox were likewise disappointed. In the summer of 1921 Roosevelt was stricken with poliomyelitis, a disease that left him completely paralyzed for a time. A long period of convalescence followed, during which Roosevelt retreated to Warm Springs, Georgia, where his condition significantly improved, though he never regained the use of his legs. He returned to politics in 1928, waging a successful campaign for the governorship of New York. While governor, Roosevelt witnessed the disastrous 1929 stock market crash and the beginning of the most severe economic depression in U.S. history. He won reelection in 1930, and two years later ran his first presidential campaign, defeating the Republican incumbent Herbert Hoover.

Roosevelt's first term as U.S. President was a period of frenzied activity in response to the extreme economic crisis that gripped the nation. Roosevelt's program of relief measures, the New Deal, was designed to provide assistance to suffering Americans and to spur the stagnant economy through a series of federal expenditures and initiatives. Among the programs instituted were the creation of the Federal Deposit Insurance Corporation, the Agricultural Adjustment Administration, the Civilian Conservation Corps and the Works Progress Administration; the implementation of a social security program for the unemployed and elderly; and the establishment of the Securities and Exchange Commission, the Tennessee Valley Authority, and the National Recovery Administration. Roosevelt was reelected in 1936, despite the fact that certain portions of the New Deal, including the National Industrial Recovery Act, were declared unconstitutional by the Supreme Court. As the Great Depression continued through the 1930s, Roosevelt's attentions were increasingly drawn toward Europe, where the aggression of Nazi Germany could no longer be ignored. Large-scale war had broken out with Adolf Hitler's 1939 invasion of

Poland. In 1940 Roosevelt was reelected for a third term. Meanwhile, military preparations had already begun in the United States, and Roosevelt initiated the "Lend-Lease" Bill, which granted Great Britain much-needed munitions and supplies for the war with Germany. The Japanese surprise attack on Pearl Harbor, Hawaii, on 7 December 1941 prompted the U.S. to declare war, drawing the nation into battle in Europe and the Pacific.

Roosevelt's principal activities during wartime, aside from his position as commander-in-chief of the U.S. armed forces, included his diplomatic role in the alliance with Britain and the Soviet Union. Roosevelt's meeting with Soviet Premier Joseph Stalin at Teheran in 1943 resulted in a U.S. promise to provide a second front in the European theater via an invasion of German-controlled France. A second historic summit between Roosevelt, Stalin, and British Prime Minister Winston Churchill occurred in February, 1945 at Yalta. By this time, the war in Europe was nearing its end and Allied victory appeared imminent. Roosevelt, Stalin, and Churchill entered negotiations concerning the occupation of Eastern Europe and other war-torn areas following the end of hostilities. While many of the assurances made by both Roosevelt and Stalin were never realized, the U.S. leader did succeed in winning international support for the development of the United Nations. Two months after his return to the United States, on the morning of 12 April 1945, Roosevelt suffered a cerebral hemorrhage and died at Warm Springs.

Major Works

During his life Roosevelt produced very little in the way of written works, save for his personal correspondence and the mass of documents that have been collected in *The Public Papers and Addresses of Franklin D. Roosevelt.* Among the texts contained in this work are transcripts of Roosevelt's well-publicized "fireside chats"—radio addresses to the American people that he conducted throughout his presidency. Roosevelt's speeches of note include his acceptance speech for the 1932 U.S. presidential nomination, his first inaugural address of 1933, and his 1937 "Quarantine" speech calling for a check on the aggression of the Axis Powers, Germany, Italy, and Japan. While scholars acknowledge that these speeches were composed in large part by professional speechwriters, Roosevelt had the final say as to their content, and frequently made emendations to their texts. Critics of the speeches have since analyzed their rhetorical merit and technique, as well as their historical significance in order to achieve a broad understanding of Roosevelt as a politician and orator.

Critical Reception

While Roosevelt's historical significance as a U.S. president and a world leader has never been doubted, the progress of critical reevaluation undertaken in the years since his death has produced a somewhat more balanced view of Roosevelt and his accomplishments. In terms of his domestic policies, commentators have observed that

New Deal legislation largely failed to improve the stagnant U.S. economy, which did not strengthen until 1941 and the consequent shift to wartime production. As a defender of democracy, it has been noted that Roosevelt properly recognized the menace of Hitler's Fascist expansionism, but was unable to discern the similar threat of Soviet totalitarianism—a fact borne out by what contemporary critics see as Stalin's extensive diplomatic manipulation of Roosevelt at the Teheran and Yalta conferences. Further estimations of Roosevelt have portrayed him as elusive and dissembling, qualities that he may have used to his advantage in diplomatic negotiations, but which called into question previously held perceptions of his impeccable moral character. Others have remarked that Roosevelt often vacillated in or delayed his decisions, with untold consequences. Despite his faults, however, contemporary scholars generally concur in their assessment of Roosevelt as a formidable figure in world history whose profound commitment to justice and the traditions of American democracy are unsurpassed.

PRINCIPAL WORKS

The Public Papers and Addresses of Franklin D. Roosevelt (1928-1936). 5 vols. (memoranda, speeches, and miscellany) 1938
The Public Papers and Addresses of Franklin D. Roosevelt (1937-1940). 4 vols. (memoranda, speeches, and miscellany) 1941

CRITICISM

David S. Muzzey (review date 1942)

SOURCE: "Public Papers of Franklin D. Roosevelt," in *Political Science Quarterly,* Vol. LVII, No. 3, September, 1942, pp. 426-31.

[*In the following review of* The Public Papers and Addresses of Franklin D. Roosevelt, *Muzzey considers the comprehensiveness and accuracy of this collection of presidential documents.*]

Supplementing the five volumes which covered the years of the governorship and the first presidential administration of Franklin D. Roosevelt, these four volumes[1] (compiled and collated, like the previous ones, by Samuel I. Rosenman) cover the exceptionally important years of the second administration. As the titles suggest, the first two of these volumes are concerned primarily with our domestic situation and "dedicated," as President Roosevelt says in the opening sentence of the 1937 volume, "to the continuance of faith in democracy as the world's best hope." The last two volumes, in the same spirit of Lincolnian dedication, find the president increasingly concerned with the international problems confronting the nation as the war clouds gathered and finally broke over Europe in the greatest struggle in history for the preservation of freedom and the democratic way of life.

Any attempt to analyze these volumes in detail would be impossible in a review article. But we may point to several features which distinguish them from such other collections of presidential papers as we have. The first feature is their completeness. It is not alone formal presidential messages and proclamations that we have here, as, for example, in the old standard compilation of J. D. Richardson, but letters, speeches, fireside chats, interviews on a variety of subjects which give us a more intimate appreciation of the president's thought and policy than we have in the case of any of his predecessors. Again, 197 of the 663 Items are supplemented by Notes of comment and explanation by the president himself, sometimes running to several double-column pages of fine print. A third outstanding feature is the inclusion of over eighty press conferences, nearly a fourth of the total number held during the administration. These conferences, carefully selected for their importance and reported stenographically in full, are perhaps the most valuable, and certainly the most interesting, items in the volumes. Here the president in his informal give and take with the reporters (most of whom he calls by their first names) lays his cards on the table with a trust in his crowded room-full of interlocutors which we could not imagine in a Hoover or a Coolidge. Nor can we estimate the value for future historians of the administration of the matters of policy discussed in these conferences.

Not only, then, do we have in these four volumes and their predecessors a more complete record of the Roosevelt administrations than we have for any other president, but we also have the assurance that this valuable record will be preserved intact for the use of coming generations. While the papers of other presidents are widely scattered, some lost, some destroyed, and some still held jealously from the public (like the papers of the two Adamses in vaults in Boston until 1955, or the Lincoln papers in the Library of Congress which will not be available to the public until 1947), the Roosevelt papers, and, if the urgent incitation of the president himself is accepted, the papers of other public servants high in the administration, will be deposited in the new Roosevelt Library at Hyde Park, New York, and will be immediately accessible to all who wish to study them. At his 508th press conference on December 10, 1938 (1938 volume, p. 629) President Roosevelt outlined the plan which he had recently discussed with a group of scholars, mostly historians, at a luncheon at the White House. Let us quote his own words in the Note to the item of the press conference:

> I came to the conclusion that, as soon after I left the White House as possible, they [my papers] should all be turned over to the United States as public property rather than as a private collection. . . .

Accordingly, after consulting with an advisory committee consisting of leading historians, statesmen, and scholars in the United States, I decided to try to create a central library for study and research into the history of this particular period of time in American life. . . . I decided to construct this public institution at Hyde Park, New York. . . . Furthermore, the location of the library near my own residence will enable me in later years to assist in the arrangement, maintenance and development of the collection.

The land for the library was donated to the United States by the president and his mother. The funds for the construction of the stone fireproof and air-conditioned building were contributed by private subscription. The cornerstone was laid by the president in a felicitous speech on November 19, 1939 (1939 volume, p. 580), and the completed library was dedicated on June 30, 1941. It will take its place with such institutions as the Clements Library at Ann Arbor and the Huntingdon Library at Pasadena as a treasure house for American historians.

But to return to the volumes. A large part of the 1937 volume is devoted to the fight for judicial reform which was precipitated by Roosevelt's "bombshell" message to Congress on February 5, 1937 (1937 volume, p. 51). As this plan of reform, especially in the feature which called for the "infusion of new blood" into the Supreme Court by the appointment of six new judges, was perhaps the most unpopular move of the whole administration and was rejected by the Senate, it was not strange that the president was earnest and explicit in his defense of his action. The disallowance of nine of the first eleven measures of the New Deal by the Supreme Court had convinced him, especially after "the election returns of 1936 left little room for doubt" that the people of the United States wanted the fight for the New Deal to go on, that "the reactionary members of the Court had apparently determined to remain on the bench as long as life continued, for the sole purpose of blocking any program of reform." (Introduction, p. lxi) Time, he said, would not allow us to wait for vacancies. The process of amendment to the Constitution to curb the Court would be too cumbersome and such amendment could be defeated by one more than one fourth of the states. Roosevelt was accused of wishing to "pack" the Court, to render it subservient to his dictatorial will, to destroy the "palladium of our liberties," and to wreck the balance of power in our tripartite government as consecrated by the Constitution. He lost the fight legally; but he believed that he had won it virtually, because thenceforth the Court ceased to nullify the acts of Congress. "I feel convinced," he wrote (Introduction, p. lxvi), "that the change would never have come, unless this frontal attack had been made upon the philosophy of the majority of the Court. That is why I regard the message of February 5, 1937, as one of the most important and significant events of my administration on the domestic scene. That is why I regard it as a turning point in our modern history." This language will seem rather unconvincing even to many of the president's admirers. What really gave Roosevelt the victory was not so much the "frontal attack" on the aged justices as the fact that resignations and deaths soon created enough vacancies on the bench to afford him the opportunity of appointing most of the members of the Court. At present Justices Stone and Roberts are the only members not originally appointed by Roosevelt, and Stone's promotion to Chief Justice was the president's act.

President Roosevelt exposed himself to further criticism in the summer of 1938, when he exerted his personal influence to have certain Democratic Senators (and Representative O'Connor of New York) who were opposed to the New Deal eliminated from Congress. The economic "recession" of 1937 had caused some reaction against the administration and filled the Republicans with hope of winning the midterm elections of 1938 and perhaps the presidential election of 1940. Under these circumstances the president, "as head of the Democratic Party, charged with the responsibility of carrying out the definitely liberal declaration of principles set forth in the 1936 Democratic platform," believed that it was his duty to urge support of the opponents of the disaffected candidates—though George Washington had indignantly refused to interfere in a congressional election. "I am not asking the voters of the country to vote for Democrats next November as opposed to Republicans [the mistake of Woodrow Wilson in 1918] . . . nor am I, as President, taking part in the Democratic primaries," said the president in his fireside chat of June 24, 1938 (1938 volume, p. 399). But the line between Mr. Roosevelt "as president" and as "head of the Democratic Party" was a little too fine for the public to grasp; and the net result of his attempt to "purge" the offending Senators was their easy victory in the primaries and at the polls.

Though reference to foreign affairs is not lacking in the first two volumes, as is witnessed by the president's "quarantine" speech at Chicago on October 5, 1937 (1937 volume, p. 406) and the assurance, in the Kingston speech of August 18, 1938, that the United States would "not stand idly by if the Dominion of Canada's soil were threatened by any other Empire" (1938 volume, p. 491), it is only in the last two volumes that the emphasis shifts decidedly to the international situation. The president, never blind to the danger which the tense situation in Europe and the Far East boded for the United States, became more and more anxious for the modification of the neutrality legislation of 1937, which he believed a hindrance rather than a help to the preservation of our neutrality. "The issue really is," he declared in an address to the Pan-American Union on April 14, 1939 (1939 volume, p. 195), "whether our civilization is to be dragged into the tragic vortex of unending militarism punctuated by periodic wars, or whether we shall be able to maintain the ideal of peace, individuality and civilization as the fabric of our lives." On the same day he sent telegrams to Hitler and Mussolini asking them to coöperate in bringing a peaceful solution of the tense situation in Europe, to which he received

no reply. Again, on August 24, when the Polish crisis was coming to a head, he begged Hitler not to resort to war (1939 volume, p. 444). A week later Hitler's invasion of Poland precipitated the second world war.

President Roosevelt realized from the outbreak of the war that the eventual safety of the United States depended upon as complete as possible coöperation with the democracies; and the 1940 volume, as its title indicates, is devoted chiefly to the measures calculated to prepare us for such coöperation. "There can be no appeasement with ruthlessness," he said in a fireside chat of December 29 (1940 volume, p. 633). "We must be the great arsenal of democracy." To this end, he urged (against bitter opposition from many quarters) large appropriations for national defense (1940 volume, pp. 230, 250, 286), introduced conscription (p. 428), promised the support of material resources to the nations fighting the dictators (p. 259), and began to make good his promise by turning over to Great Britain fifty over-age cruisers in return for the lease of certain naval bases on the Atlantic coast (p. 391). Though we maintained a technical neutrality until more than a year after Roosevelt's election for a third term, that neutrality was wearing thin, as was the case in the months preceding our entrance into the first world war. The next volume in this remarkable series will have to furnish the story of cumulative provocations of the Nazis and the Japanese, culminating in the dastardly attack of the latter on Pearl Harbor, which united our nation in the determination to join the democracies in putting an end to the totalitarian menace.

These volumes are no less distinguished for their accuracy than for their importance. Only a few slips have been noticed by the reviewer. On page 93 of the 1937 volume the Bonneville project is located 60 miles from Portland, Oregon, instead of 40 miles, as corrected on page 98. The Buenos Aires conference should be dated December 1936, not December 1937 (1937 volume, p. 227). The Sherman Antitrust Act of 1890 is spoken of as passed "nearly forty years ago," instead of nearly fifty years (1938 volume, p. 314). The world's population is underestimated at "a million and a half human beings" on page xxvii of the 1939 volume. Perhaps the most serious criticism of President Roosevelt's statements is his repeated pledge that no American boys would be sent abroad to fight. To the "mothers and fathers" of the American youth he declared in an address at Boston on October 30, 1940 (1940 volume, p. 517): "I have said this before, but I shall say it again and again and again—your boys are not going to be sent into any foreign wars." Again, on December 29, he said in his fireside chat (1940 volume, p. 640), "You can nail any talk about sending armies to Europe as deliberate untruth." The fact that most of these assurances were given during a presidential campaign in which Mr. Roosevelt's opponents were constantly charging him with the desire to lead the country into war may partially explain, but hardly justify, pledges which he must have realized did not lie within his own power to fulfill.

NOTE

1 *The Public Papers and Addresses of Franklin D. Roosevelt.* With a Special Introduction and Explanatory Notes by President Roosevelt. Four volumes. 1937: *The Constitution Prevails,* 659 pp.; 1938: *The Continuing Struggle for Liberalism,* 686 pp.; 1939: *War—and Neutrality,* 635 pp.; 1940: *War—and Aid to Democracies,* 741 pp. New York, the Macmillan Company, 1941. $30 the set.

Bessie C. Randolph (essay date 1943)

SOURCE: A review of *The Public Papers and Addresses of Franklin D. Roosevelt,* in *American Journal of International Law,* Vol. 37, No. 1, January, 1943, pp. 172-74.

[*In the following review, Randolph favorably assesses* The Public Papers and Addresses of Franklin D. Roosevelt.]

In 1938 the compiler of [***The Public Papers and Addresses of Franklin D. Roosevelt***] published five volumes which contained the papers of Franklin D. Roosevelt issued during his two terms as Governor of New York, 1929-1933, and also during his first term as President of the United States—from March 4, 1933, to January 19, 1937. He has now compiled the papers for the President's second term, one volume being devoted to each of four periods and having its own title: 1937—The Constitution Prevails; 1938—The Continuing Struggle for Liberalism; 1939—War and Neutrality; 1940—War and Aid to Democracies. The last volume closes at the date January 16, 1941. Mr. [Samuel I.] Rosenman had had the distinct advantage of being approved and practically appointed by the President to undertake this important task for which he was so peculiarly fitted by his experience as Counsel to the Governor of New York for both terms and by his continuing and intimate relations with Mr. Roosevelt after the latter became President.

The physical features of these four large volumes, which make a total bulk of well over 3,000 pages, are admirable. They are strongly and attractively bound in soft stone blue and the type is unusually clearcut and well spaced. Every paper is numbered, each volume having its own separate series. At the beginning of Volume I is included a striking feature—a table which lists alphabetically for all four volumes a number of topics, including Agriculture, Banking, Civilian Conservation Corps, Courts and Constitution, Democratic Party, Education, Foreign Affairs (European Relations, Pan American Affairs, Far Eastern Relations, Foreign Trade, Neutrality, etc.), Health, Hours and Wages, Insular Possessions, National Defense, Reorganization of Executive Branch of Government, Social Security, etc. These listings give page references in each of the four volumes in order that the reader may follow through at a glance. Immediately after these reference groupings is a long alphabetical list of smaller topics by each of which is set down the larger topic under which it may be found. Hence there is for the student a preliminary,

comprehensive index to supplement the index placed at the end of each volume. Especially useful in Volume I is a complete list of "Proclamations and Executive Orders" with numbers and exact dates as found in the United States Statutes at Large for the 75th and 76th Congresses, *i.e.,* from January, 1937, to January, 1941.

Particularly vivid and instructive are the notes appended to numerous papers by Mr. Rosenman and in some cases by President Roosevelt himself. They give a volume of information and carry on, sometimes to a conclusion, the story begun by the paper itself. Thus there is in fact a sort of connected narrative between the papers and even the volumes. In these notes comment is limited almost entirely to fact, very little opinion being expressed. As to the selection of contents, no attempt was made to include all papers, and the selection is apparently objective and fair. In length, the items range all the way from a brief paragraph or so to long and detailed statements which fill many pages. Most valuable and vividly interesting is the introduction written for each volume by the President himself. His introduction to Volume I (1937) gives his own story of the fight for the reform of the federal judicial system, proper emphasis being placed on the proposed reform of the lower and intermediate courts, although the public was apparently more interested in the dramatic fight over the Supreme Court. These introductions give the story of many of his political aspirations and struggles over four years of critical and stormy politics at home and abroad.

Among the papers, the speeches are most significant, the most important, of course, being those addressed to Congress. These speeches contain a mass of information concerning executive acts and the reasons therefor, as, for example, those which support the policy of exchanging over-age destroyers for bits of British territory in the Western Hemisphere where naval and air bases could be established by the United States. There are progress reports on all sorts and sizes of federal enterprises. A number of speeches are made for the encouragement of various undertakings in the amelioration of human suffering. Speeches over the radio—those famous fireside chats—deal with every possible topic on imminent problems, domestic and foreign, and throw a light on our international affairs which could come from no other source. They will be for all present and future students of American foreign policy a source of priceless information from a period of global war and reconstruction.

An ordered reading of the various declarations or proclamations of neutrality beginning in 1939 will save confusion. The declarations distinguish carefully between neutrality under general international law and that under our domestic "laws of neutrality" which are not neutrality laws at all. Immediately following the proclamations under both headings are the innumerable executive orders necessary to implement the law.

Of outstanding value are the numberless press conferences (about 370) in dialogue form—the familiar chatty exchanges between the President and press representatives. These chats cover a multitude of topics which could not be touched upon anywhere else.

In this collection of papers is reflected a breadth and vitality of interest in men and movements befitting the head of a great democratic republic. There is indicated also a power of continuous growth and change which—according to the views of a particular reader—may be for better or for worse. In no single field, with possibly one or two exceptions, is this more apparent than in the field of diplomatic relations. These four books will be a source of instruction and inspiration to countless students in our own and foreign lands: We hope that Mr. Rosenman may begin before long the collecting and editing of the papers of President Roosevelt's third term.

Robert T. Oliver (essay date 1945)

SOURCE: "The Speech That Established Roosevelt's Reputation," in *The Quarterly Journal of Speech,* Vol. XXXI, No. 3, October, 1945, pp. 274-82.

[*In the following essay, Oliver examines Roosevelt's delivery of his 1932 presidential nomination acceptance speech as the turning point in his political career.*]

Chicago was the scene of the most dramatically staged speech of Franklin D. Roosevelt's career—his acceptance of the nomination for the presidency, in the Chicago Stadium, on Saturday, July 2, 1932.

This speech marked the real turning point in his political reputation. It ended the "Frank is good natured but lacks brains and leadership" period and ushered in the "Franklin Delano Roosevelt—Fighting Liberal" era. From that moment (rather than from the time of the nomination itself, or of his election, or of his inauguration) the public feeling about Roosevelt began to crystallize into the pattern it has largely maintained ever since. For the first time he began to emerge into the public consciousness as a bold experimenter, aggressive fighter, breaker of traditions.

Some liked and some feared these characteristics. His foes had but a short wait before they could point out that his experimenting led him in an apparently zig-zag course of broken promises and inconsistencies; whereas his friends were assured that the general progression was all in one direction. But after the acceptance speech, friend and foe began to unite on the basic picture of Roosevelt which this incident etched on their minds.

The tremendous interest in Roosevelt's acceptance speech was due partly to circumstance.

The Democrats had a much better show to put on the air than that staged by the G.O.P. two weeks earlier. This did not demand much of the Democrats, for the Republican convention had been spun of dull stuff.

The renomination of Herbert Hoover was a foregone conclusion, albeit a reluctant one for the seasoned politicians of the Old Guard, who knew how to read the writing on the wall. A feeble effort was made to chuck Charley Curtis off the ticket, but was dropped when Hoover made it known that he would not permit the sacrifice of his running mate. With this much settled even before the convention met, the platform was the only business to be debated.

It was the platform which caused the most general dismay. Partly by misjudgment of the public temper, and partly because of a vigorous campaign staged by both wets and drys, the G.O.P. platform makers let themselves be maneuvered into picking prohibition as the chief issue of the presidential campaign. This in as catastrophic a year as 1932!

Two newspaper men noted for their dispassionate and balanced analyses registered their amazement as they arrived at Chicago and found what the party leaders had in mind. Mark Sullivan, sampling the sentiment of the Chicago crowds and delegates, wrote: "One would suppose that depression does not exist. . . . " Walter Lippmann found it "astonishing that in the midst of such great economic distress there should be no rumbling here of social discontent. . . . It may be that conservative Republicans are too deaf to hear the discontent and that the progressive Republicans are too bewildered to express it." Throughout the country fifteen million unemployed and all of the additional millions who depended on them echoed this surprise at the Republican preoccupation with the issue of drink.

Then, as a fitting anticlimax to this anticlimatic situation, the platform finally adopted a compromise proposal so involved and ambiguous that, as one observer sardonically declared, the "wet" portion was cheered by the drys, and the "dry" section was cheered by the wets. With this done, the G.O.P. quickly nominated its candidates, and went home.

From the audience point of view, the chief virtue of the convention had been its brevity. The Democratic reaction was epitomized in a wry comment by Jouett Shouse: "We'll put on a show that will make the Republican shindig look like child's play."

The situation confronting the Democrats was much different from that of the G.O.P. and much more inherently interesting. The prohibition issue had indeed been raised, but had been practically settled in a pre-convention exchange. Al Smith staked his main fight for the nomination upon his straightforward demand for repeal of the eighteenth amendment. This demand the Roosevelt forces took over and made their own, thus eliminating any possibility of fireworks by guaranteeing its inclusion in the platform.

Roosevelt himself had made clear his own selection of issues in his **"Forgotten Man"** speech, delivered on April

7. The phrase had done precisely what it was intended to do: it struck sharply into the public mind. It had drawn from Al Smith his first direct attack upon his old friend and political co-worker, and had identified Roosevelt unmistakably in the public mind with the unemployment and depression issue.

The nomination battle promised to be good. The Roosevelt forces had a clear majority of votes, but not enough to win the nomination under the traditional two-thirds rule. For a time Roosevelt's advisers toyed with the idea of ditching this requirement (as they could by obtaining a simple majority vote for a change of rules) and riding to victory upon their assured delegate strength. The chance that this would breed resentment and lead to a party split, however, caused this plan to be abandoned on the eve of the convention.

Meanwhile, Smith and Garner, the two other leading candidates, worked desperately to increase their strength. The "Stop Roosevelt" movement looked anxiously for a compromise candidate. Walter Lippmann thought he had one, and, on the day before the convention met, he tried to stampede the delegates with a whole-souled eulogy of Newton D. Baker.

James Farley and Louis Howe worked night and day, buttonholing delegates and pleading for additional support. When the frail Howe became too tired to stand the pace, he stretched on the floor of his hotel room, surrounded by fans and ice water, while Jim Farley lay down beside him to discuss the strategy of their campaign.

At Albany Roosevelt sat by his radio, listening to every word that came from the convention, conferring often via the telephone with his managers, and making it known that if a deadlock threatened he would fly to Chicago to try to break it with his presence.

When the call to order came at 1:00 P.M. on June 28, no one knew what would happen to the nomination. Farley tried to postpone the platform debate until after the nominee was selected—and failed. He thereupon announced that the nomination of Roosevelt was assured on the first ballot.

But the "Stop Roosevelt" forces knew better. They also knew that Roosevelt, despite his delegate strength, was in a dangerous spot. If after the first ballot he began to lose votes, even a few, his cause would probably be lost. Then there would be a chance for one of the other leaders, or, if necessary, a "dark horse" could be rounded up.

What actually happened is history now, but it was packed with suspense at the time, and thus helped to build up the radio audience for the acceptance speech. The first ballot did not nominate Roosevelt. Neither did the second, nor the third—although, instead of losing votes, his total very slowly crept up. It was still far from the two-thirds requirement.

After the second vote Farley and Howe fought for an adjournment that would give them time to try anew for more support before the balloting could proceed. They lost this fight, and the roll call for the third vote proceeded wearily.

Then, at 9:15 A.M., the delegates demanded a halt till evening. Farley, worn as he was, sought out Sam Rayburn and proposed that the vice-presidency be given to Garner in exchange for the Texas and California votes. "I'll see what can be done," was Rayburn's response, and Farley went back to his room to sleep.

At 9:30 that evening the fourth ballot was just commencing when William Gibbs McAdoo, leader of the California delegation, asked for the platform to explain his vote. "California," he declared, "came here to nominate a candidate. When any man comes into this convention with popular will behind him to the extent of almost 700 votes . . . [At this point the galleries and the delegates sensed what was coming and drowned out McAdoo's voice with a roaring bedlam of boos and cheers. Then his words emerged again.] California casts 44 votes for Franklin D. Roosevelt."

Thus was the nomination settled. But it was not—as is customary—made unanimous. The 190 votes pledged to Al Smith remained adamant and the final total read: Franklin D. Roosevelt, 945; Alfred E. Smith, 190. Nonetheless the candidate was named as Permanent Chairman Thomas J. Walsh rolled off in his best political baritone the name of the winner—"Franklin Delano Roosevelt, the next President of the United States."

Thereupon Al Smith, the erstwhile "Happy Warrior," went up to his hotel room, packed his bags, and went home. Many thought he was on his way to split the party and allow the Republicans to slip back into office. Few realized how completely he was simply walking out of the national political scene.

Meanwhile, back in Albany, Roosevelt was making up his mind to fly to the convention to accept the nomination at once. His decision was not wholly surprising. As early as June 12, when Farley and Howe arrived at Chicago, it "became known" that Roosevelt might fly to the convention if a deadlock developed, and might come on anyway, for a conference with the leaders, after the convention adjourned. Both possibilities were promptly denied.

Then, on June 23, an enterprising reporter sent out the forecast (unauthorized) that "no one need be surprised if the Governor swoops down on the embattled hosts of Democracy here next week in an airplane." On June 29, before the balloting began, it was discovered that by Roosevelt's request the American Airways had sent a trimotored Ford fourteen passenger plane, capable of cruising at 130 miles an hour, to the Albany Airport. Still, the news that the Governor would start out the next morning after the nomination swept around the country with a thrill of speculative interest.

"It isn't true, then, that he's an invalid?" "How has he had time to prepare a speech?" "What will he say?" "How will he look?" "Will he compromise with the Smith forces?" "Will he hedge on repeal of prohibition?" "Will he merely smile, and mouth platitudes, and say practically nothing at all?"

The tradition, of course, was for the nominees of both parties to slide back into a decent obscurity for several weeks after the conventions. They were supposed to retreat to secluded vacation spots, recover from the fury of the primaries battle, formulate their programs in conferences with their party leaders, make whatever deals might be demanded in the interest of party harmony, and lay out their strategy for the election campaign of the late summer and fall. Usually the nominees needed this rest, and so did the country. To provide it, the convenient fiction had been invented of "notifying" the nominees of their selection some weeks after they already knew it, whenever it should be deemed expedient to commence the campaign.

While the country wondered and murmured, its interest simmering to a boil, Roosevelt disposed of this tradition with casual aplomb.

From the moment his decision to fly to the convention was announced, every detail of the trip became front page news. It was recalled that this was the first time Roosevelt had been in an airplane since his wartime days as Assistant Secretary of the Navy, when he had used a plane regularly on inspection trips around the country.

Feature writers searching for means of depicting the adventurous quality of the flight compared the daring of the nominee to that of his fifth cousin. While Theodore Roosevelt was president he had wanted to submerge in a submarine, to call attention to the practicality of the new underseas craft. This his body guards had refused to let him do. Now another Roosevelt was launching into another stratum, the air.

It was pointed out that the day was cloudy, with squalls of rain along the route. Newsmen noted that the plane would have to buck head winds for the entire trip. Bulletins were flashed from along the way: "The Roosevelt plane is flying low, skirting cloud banks along Lake Erie"; "The candidate is flying over Toledo, with scattered showers reported." At Buffalo, and again at Cleveland, the plane was forced to stop to refuel.

At both stops reporters crowded in for interviews with the entire personnel of thirteen: Governor Roosevelt, his wife—who was generally referred to as Eleanor—his son Elliott, his secretaries Guernsey T. Cross, Marguerite Le Hand and Grace Tully, his friends Judge and Mrs. Samuel I. Rosenman, his body guards Earl Miller and Gus Gennerich, and the three members of the crew.

The country was informed that the departure of the plane from Albany was delayed for half an hour, until 8:30; that the candidate worked on his acceptance speech between

Albany and Buffalo; that thereafter he read telegrams and newspapers, looked at the scenery, and chatted easily with the other occupants of the plane. The roar of the airplane's motors en route was recorded in a national broadcast. The time when the wheels of the plane grounded at the Chicago Municipal Airport was clocked at 4:27 P.M., just nine hours after the flight started.

The brief greeting which Roosevelt gave to the crowd of 5,000 at the Airport was broadcast to the convention hall and around the country. Reporters noted that the Roosevelt glasses were jolted off by the press of the crowd (and not broken); that an hour was consumed in driving the fifteen miles to the Stadium, through street crowds estimated at 20,000; that at Grant Park the nominee was constrained by an insistent crowd to stop for a few words—though all he told them was that he would be making his speech in a few minutes at the convention. Finally, at 5:50 the party pushed its way into the hall, through another crowd, to appear before a body of weary delegates who had been marking time for the past two hours.

While the convention proceedings had purposely been drawn out during the day, workmen had pounded away building an inclined runway up to the platform. Others had brought in a huge banner with the words, OUR NEXT PRESIDENT—FRANKLIN ROOSEVELT, and hung it from the first gallery behind the rostrum.

The temporary chairs set up for the delegates were in wild disarray, with little trace left of their once orderly arrangement in neat sections. The floor was littered with 60 tons of waste paper. Visitors in the galleries and delegates on the floor were alike worn out by their five days of frenzied session, were wilted by the heat, were sickened by irregular meals and frequent indulgence in mustard-spread hot dogs and insipid soft drinks.

The trains that were to take the delegates home were scheduled to have left, but were being held at the stations until the final adjournment. Into this scene of disorder and discomfort walked the candidate, at ten minutes to six, leaning on the arm of his eldest son, James.

The huge convention organ burst into the strains of "Anchors Aweigh," while the delegates roared. The demonstration, in the words of a spectator, "was like a cyclone swooping down from the crowded galleries and whistling through the sections of delegates who stood on their chairs shouting and waving."

Roosevelt had heard just such ovations on behalf of the nominees in the Democratic conventions of every quadrennium since 1912. In '20, '24, and '28 he had received enthusiastic ovations himself. But this time he was the nominee, and, as he fully expected, was on the way to becoming President of the United States.

His first thought was for the friends who had fought and won this battle of the nomination. In serious mien, with the famous smile gone, he gave thanks to John E. Mack, who had nominated him, and to the chairman, Senator Thomas J. Walsh. James Farley had met him at the plane, and Louis Howe at the Stadium door. While the organswung into "The Star Spangled Banner," Roosevelt and his wife remained in solemn mood, standing at attention.

Then the strains of "Happy Days Are Here Again" rang out, and Roosevelt turned toward the crowd to receive its greeting and to wave and smile his own. His handsome face aglow with impish pleasure in the excitement caused by his unprecedented flight, Roosevelt took the measure of the crowd before him and naturally, easily, assumed the frame of mind of a major figure in American history.

Another mother's son was headed for the White House; one of the one hundred and thirty million was in process of elevation to the role of First Citizen. Another Rubicon had been crossed. A new era in the life of Roosevelt (and, though few guessed it, in the life of America) was being born.

After thirteen minutes the ovation broke off, and Chairman Walsh presented the candidate to the convention. Then smoothly, effortlessly, the best modulated radio voice in public life slipped into the opening paragraph of the acceptance speech:

"I appreciate your willingness after these six arduous days to remain here, for I know well the sleepless hours which you, and I [loud laughter and cheers] have had. I regret that I am late, but I have no control over the winds of Heaven and could only be thankful for my Navy training." [Cheers and laughter.]

Already some of the impatient galleryites, their curiosity satisfied and their dinners waiting at home, slipped away. The candidate went on. "The appearance before a National Convention of its nominee for President, to be formally notified of his selection, is unprecedented and unusual, but these are unprecedented and unusual times. I have started out on the tasks that lie ahead by breaking the absurd tradition that the candidate should remain in professed ignorance of what has happened for weeks until he is formally notified of that event many weeks later.

"My friends, may this be the symbol of my intention to be honest and to avoid all hypocrisy or sham, to avoid all silly shutting of the eyes to the truth in this campaign. You have nominated me and I know it, and I am here to thank you for the honor." [Loud and prolonged cheers.]

There followed an acceptance of the platform "100 per cent," and a pledge that "I will leave no doubt or ambiguity on where I stand on any question of moment in this campaign." Thence he launched a plea for non-partisanship and support by independent voters which was to become a major feature of the campaign: "Note well that in this campaign I shall not use the words 'Republican Party,' but I shall use, day in and day out, the words 'Republican leadership.'"

A few paragraphs further on he was urging: "Here and now I invite those nominal Republicans who find that their conscience cannot be squared with the groping and the failure of their party leaders to join hands with us; and here and now in equal measure, I warn those nominal Democrats who squint at the future with their faces turned toward the past, and who feel no responsibility to the demands of the new time, that they are out of step with their Party."

To implement this plea for support by all independent voters, Roosevelt offered a definition of his own political position as standing midway between the Old Guard reactionism and the Utopian radicals. "Wild radicalism has made few converts," he declared, "and the greatest tribute that I can pay to my countrymen is that in these days of crushing want there persists an orderly and hopeful spirit on the part of the millions of our people who have suffered so much. To fail to offer them a new chance is not only to betray their hopes but to misunderstand their patience."

By this time the gallery exits were crowded and even a few of the delegates were slipping out. Roosevelt had no magic great enough to hold these weary auditors longer in their seats. For them the great moment had passed when the nominee started his speech. Their function as greeters was over.

But the speech did not drop on inattentive ears. In every section of the nation families and groups of neighbors crowded intently around living-room radios and listened with a growing wonder and a growing faith. Here was veritably a new voice, a new personality, a new hope. Here at the very least was a fresh symbol of their own faith and desires; at the most, a fearless leader came in the nation's hour of bitterest trial to lead a new fight for freedom and security.

In friendly, social tones—neighborly, yet with a patrician assurance of born leadership—the voice came into their own homes from the familiar radio grill they had dusted with their own hands; it spoke of "the simple economics, the kind of economics that you and I and the average man and woman talk."

"Translate that into human terms," the radio voice quietly urged. "See how the events of the past three years have come home to specific groups of people. . . . Picture to yourselves. . . . My friends, you and I as common-sense citizens know. . . . " Here was surely no ordinary politician speaking; here was homey talk the people could understand, yet talk with an elevation and a dignity that inspired trust and confidence. When the speaker used the phrase, "statesmanship and vision," it seemed to belong as a fitting characterization of what was being said.

Back in the hall the galleries continued to empty, and in the homes the listeners grew more silent and attentive. Roosevelt gripped the rostrum hard, and swung into a theme that was nearest to his heart; a unifying thread upon which the diverse aspects of his political philosophy all were strung; the interdependence of all the people.

"Never in history have the interests of all the people been so united in a single economic problem. . . . That is why we are going to make the voters understand this year that this Nation is not merely a Nation of independence, but it is, if we are to survive, bound to be a Nation of inter-dependence—town and city, North and South, East and West. That is our goal, and that goal will be understood by the people of this country no matter where they live."

"My program," the nominee continued, "is based upon this simple moral principle: the welfare and the soundness of a Nation depend first upon what the great mass of the people wish and need; and second, whether or not they are getting it.

"What do the people of America want more than anything else? To my mind, they want two things: work, with all the moral and spiritual values that go with it; and with work, a reasonable measure of security—security for them-selves and for their wives and children. Work and secu-rity—these are more than words. They are more than facts. They are the spiritual values, the true goal toward which our efforts of reconstruction should lead. These are the values that this program is intended to gain; these are the values we have failed to achieve by the leadership we now have."

By now at least half the gallery seats were vacant, many delegates had left the floor, and the constant shuffling of chairs and feet added to the vast confusion of the con-vention hall. Roosevelt swung earnestly into his perora-tion, the last five paragraphs of his speech, into which he had put more effort than in all that went before. Here was the authentic voice of the democratic patrician, speaking with utmost earnestness to his people, to his friends. An appealing combination of idealism and common sense, it proved to have a projective power rare in the history of political campaign speaking. As these words sank home in the minds of millions of voters, the election results of 1932 began to assume definitive shape.

"One word more: Out of every crisis, every tribulation, every disaster, mankind rises with some share of greater knowledge, of higher decency, of purer purpose. Today we shall have come through a period of loose thinking, descending morals, an era of selfishness, among indi-vidual men and women and among Nations. Blame not Governments alone for this. Blame ourselves in equal share. Let us be frank in acknowledgement of the truth that many amongst us have made obeisance to Mammon, that the profits of speculation, the easy road without toil, have lured us from the old barricades. To return to higher standards we must abandon the false prophets and seek new leaders of our own choosing.

"Never before in modern history have the essential differ-ences between the two major American parties stood out in such striking contrast as they do today. Republican leaders not only have failed in material things, they have failed in national vision, because in disaster they have held out no hope, they have pointed out no path for the people below to climb back to places of security and of safety in our American life.

"Throughout the Nation, men and women, forgotten in the political philosophy of the Government of the last years, look to us here for guidance and for more equitable op-portunity to share in the distribution of national wealth.

"On the farms, in the large metropolitan areas, in the smaller cities and in the villages, millions of our citizens cherish the hope that their old standards of living and of thought have not gone forever. Those millions cannot and shall not hope in vain.

"I pledge you, I pledge myself, to a new deal for the American people. Let us all here assembled constitute ourselves prophets of a new order of competence and of courage. This is more than a political campaign; it is a call to arms. Give me your help, not to win votes alone, but to win in this crusade to restore America to its own people."

All over the country the earnest, reassuring overtones of this confidently calm voice fell upon listening ears. In the nation's capital it was heard by the fifteen to twenty thousand world war veterans who had stormed into the city as the "Bonus Expeditionary Force" and set up their camp on the Anacostia flats—until they were later dis-persed by presidential decree with tear gas, machine guns, bayonets and clubs. It was heard in President Hoover's own study by a tight-lipped, bitter critic, whose heart ached with dread lest this political infidel would overturn all for which he had fought.

It was heard in "Hooverville" shanty towns, in the drab and cheerless homes of the growing number of unem-ployed, in the simple living rooms of farmers, school teachers, white collar workers, and of those factory workmen who still had jobs. It was pondered in the more ornate homes of the well-to-do, who thoughtfully considered abandoning their old political allegiance in the hope that here, perhaps, was the answer to the country's economic ills.

The speech was heard by Milo Reno's Midwest Farmer's Holiday Association, organized to stop by violence the movement of food supplies until the price should be raised; it was heard by residents of rural county seats, where grim-mouthed farmers gathered to prevent by force the sale of mortgaged farms; it was heard by Howard Scott and his following of Technocrats, ready to make over America in the pattern of an engineer's dream; it was heard by Coughlinites, and disciples of Huey Long, by college intellectuals, and by the Mencken-denominated "booboisie," by sharecroppers and Wall Street brokers.

It was heard by ardent partisans who were "For Roosevelt before Chicago"; by Al Smith Democrats; by rock-ribbed Republicans; and by Norman Thomas Socialists. It was heard with skepticism, with scorn, and with scoffing; with enthusiastic acceptance; and with dubious reservation. But heard it was and, as events were to show, it won votes.

It is altogether possible that this speech, coming just at the crest of the wave of interest in the Democratic convention, just at the nadir of disillusionment with the Republican offering, may have been the most influential utterance of the entire campaign. There is some ground for believing that the only effective campaigning (except for the organizational work of "getting the vote to the polls") is that which is done very early.

Almost as soon as the nominees are selected, the independent voters begin making up their minds. Tentatively or decisively they align themselves with one candidate or the other. It is highly doubtful whether any amount of political oratory after that has much effect. Hooverites would listen to Roosevelt—but only to belittle and refute; New Dealers would tune in Hoover—but merely to jeer. Once the minds of the voters were made up, they simply became more and more set. The few who continued to waver could scarcely affect the final result.

If this theory is sound, Roosevelt's early bid for votes, made even before the convention adjourned, was a master stroke of policy. It set up a standard around which his warm supporters could rally; it gave newsmen and cartoonists a subject for their pens; it served as a focal point for public discussion and private thought.

The candidate could leave the hall, could with comparative quietness entrain for home, could withdraw for a few days of sailing along the New England coast; but never thenceforth could he be ejected from the public mind.

His dramatic flight to Chicago had ensured him of one thing; whether favorably or unfavorably, whether for obloquy or praise, he was in the public's eye and on the public's lips from that time on. The campaign came inevitably to center on F. D. R.

Arthur Schlesinger, Jr. (essay date 1950)

SOURCE: "Roosevelt and His Detractors," in *Understanding the American Past: American History and Its Interpretation,* edited by Edward N. Saveth, Little, Brown and Company, 1950, pp. 514-28.

[*In the following essay, originally published in 1950, Schlesinger responds to revisionist critics of Roosevelt's wartime foreign policy.*]

The storm of controversy around the foreign policy of Franklin D. Roosevelt is already as furious and looks to be as enduring as that which has raged around the foreign policy of Woodrow Wilson since 1919. War brings an almost inevitable aftermath of disillusion; and the failure of this last war to produce even an approximation of peace has charged our contemporary disillusion with a bitter sense of betrayal. As the revisionists of the Twenties turned on Wilson, so the revisionists of the Forties are today turning on Roosevelt.

The Wilson policies had only to face the relatively uncomplicated attacks of the outright isolationists—men like Harry Elmer Barnes and the early Walter Millis, who had a naïve conviction that the United States could live safely apart from the world. Such naïve isolationism is not, of course, wholly absent from revisionism today. Charles A. Beard, the intellectual leader of the isolationist wing of the revisionists, dedicated two volumes to a trenchant attack on the very foundations of Roosevelt's prewar policy—a scorching indictment which a number of isolationist journalists, such as John T. Flynn and George Morgenstern, have lived off ever since, and which, one understands, Professor C. C. Tansill of Fordham is planning to extend into the war years. Even an intimate member of the Roosevelt circle like Admiral Leahy could believe in 1945, *after* World War II, that "involvement in European politics would inevitably bring us into another European war," and that "there still remained a hope that we might succeed in avoiding entangling ourselves in European political difficulties."

But contemporary revisionism is on the whole a far more complex phenomenon. In its more serious aspects, it entirely accepts the necessity of American intervention into world affairs. It attacks Roosevelt, not for having intervened at all, but for having intervened unwisely, inadequately, or ineffectively. A whole series of critics—William C. Bullitt, Edgar Ansel Mowrer, Richard H. S. Crossman, Henry Luce, Raymond Moley, and most recently, Hanson Baldwin in his book *Great Mistakes of the War*—have argued that Roosevelt's foreign policies, particularly his insistence on subordinating politics to strategy during the war, have made the postwar problems even more exasperating and hopeless than they would have been anyway.

Into this embattled atmosphere Judge Samuel Rosenman has now released the last four volumes of his invaluable collection, *The Public Papers and Addresses of Franklin D. Roosevelt*. To these Judge Rosenman has contributed introductions and notes containing a crisp and informed defense of Roosevelt's wartime policies. The series is a model of editing and bookmaking; and the last four volumes in particular are essential for anyone concerned with the politics of the Second World War.

Judge Rosenman's volumes make available much material which is essential for a judgment of Roosevelt's foreign policy. At the same time, Basil Rauch, whose *History of the New Deal* is the best short volume on the legislative and administrative record of Roosevelt's first few years in office, has now completed *Roosevelt: from Munich to Pearl Harbor,* a survey of Roosevelt's prewar policies. And our knowledge of the war policies, and in particular of the Yalta conference, has been increased by the publication of Walter Johnson's book for Edward R. Stettinius, Jr., *Roosevelt and the Russians,* and by Admiral William Leahy's *I Was There.*

How does Roosevelt's foreign policy stand up in the barrage of defense and attack? The first clear point is that much of the crossfire obscures what may go down as Roosevelt's grand contribution to the strengthening of democracy: his insight into the military conditions of democratic survival. In the dark and bloody world of the mid-century, we forget the fact that a generation ago peace was accounted the normal and natural state of man. The liberal and democratic movements of the West, forgetting that they had themselves come to power through violence, had been lulled by the placid nineteenth century into thinking that wars could be localized and, in the not too distant future, eliminated entirely. The First World War was considered to be an unfortunate accident, the exception that proved the rule; and no drastic conclusions were drawn from it. An atmosphere of pacificism and proto-pacifism settled over the democratic left.

This atmosphere left Roosevelt singularly untouched. His sea-going background, his admiration for his jingo cousin Theodore Roosevelt, his own exciting tour of duty as Assistant Secretary of the Navy in the First World War—all these immunized him against the malaise which overtook the George Lansburys and the Oswald Garrison Villards. He recognized that free society could not endure on good will alone—that it must be prepared to face up to the military requirements of survival. At an early stage he disappointed the pacifist wing of his liberal admirers by slipping rearmament into the recovery program, blandly initiating the program of naval construction in 1933 "as a means of furthering national recovery."

This was the period when the fatuity of the Kellogg Pact was still the complacent expression of altogether too much liberal purpose. Stuart Chase had terrified the left in 1929 with his picture of "the two-hour war" in which a surprise air attack would blot out civilization by gas bombs: "not even a rat, not even an ant, not even a roach, can survive. . . . There is no defense." The reflex was the Oxford Oath: young men in Britain swearing never to take up arms for king or country, and young men in the United States avidly following their dubious example. Even the rise of Nazism could not dent the pacifist fantasies. Somehow the fascist challenge to civilization would be met in any way except on the field of battle.

We have forgotten too quickly the tenacity of pacifism in the left at this time. In March 1935 Clement Attlee, leading the Labor Party in its fight against the mild rearmament proposals recommended by the National Government as insurance against Hitler, could lecture the House of Commons, with sublime irrelevance: "We are told in the White Paper that there is danger against which we have to guard ourselves. We do not think you can do it by national defense. We think you can only do it by moving forward to a new world—a world of law, the abolition of national armaments with a world force and a

world economic system." An honorable member rudely interrupted: "Tell that to Hitler."

By whatever fortune, Roosevelt knew about Hitler; he was spared this particular form of the great illusion of pacifism. The liberals who admired the TVA but disliked the construction of the aircraft carriers *Enterprise* and *Yorktown* accordingly denounced Roosevelt or made preposterous excuses for him: the Navy, they said, was a kind of hobby, and the President must be indulged in it. Six years later the whole world could only regret that Roosevelt had not indulged himself with far less deference to pacifist opinion. The Navy, instead of being too large for democratic survival, was too small. The odious *Enterprise* turned out, in the words of Bernard Brodie, to be "the undisputed champion of all American warships in terms of combat record." Young men who had signed the Oxford Oath now fought in Normandy or in the South Pacific. There seemed to be a more direct connection between democracy and national defense than it had been fashionable for liberals to admit a decade before.

The United States was lucky in having as President a liberal who, in this respect at least, was unfashionable. Roosevelt's basic insight into the military conditions of democratic survival was, it is true, often overlaid in the Thirties by concessions, vain hopes, and bad inconsistencies. He retreated before the pressures incited by the Nye investigation and signed neutrality legislation designed to secure what he must have known, in other moods, was beyond the possibility of securing. He remained detached before the challenge of the civil war in Spain. Doubtless a fear of alienating Catholic support explained Roosevelt's Spanish policy in part; but more important, one feels, was the fact that he never really grasped the moral or even the strategic issues in Spain.

Professor Beard, marshaling his evidence with the skill and the selectivity of a master prosecutor, has made the most of the ebb and flow of Roosevelt's prewar policies. Yet there can be no serious doubt that Roosevelt had a basic and steady purpose, revealed first in the "quarantine" speech in Chicago in 1937. The rise of fascism had revived Roosevelt's insight into the fact that the United States would not long survive as a free nation in a totalitarian world. With the means at his disposal, he began the long labor of educating the people to the dimensions of the fascist threat to America.

Basil Rauch's *Roosevelt: from Munich to Pearl Harbor* provides an extremely able, clear, and fascinating account of this process of education. Rauch's cogent narrative has as only an incidental purpose the correction of Beard's manifold distortions and omissions; but rarely in the process of incidental commentary has one historian more effectively destroyed the work of another. Professor Rauch's revision of the revisionists brings much needed sense and proportion into the discussion of the period from Munich to Pearl Harbor. His book accentuates the personal tragedy which led one of the great American historians into succumbing in his last days to the "devil theory of war" which he had once himself so effectively exposed.

War itself brought new perplexities. Roosevelt was always a pragmatist, playing by ear, as he liked to say, his improvisations controlled, not by logical analysis nor by an explicit moral code so much as by a consistency of emotion and instinct. In domestic affairs this was fine: the crisis was less inexorable, the margin of error greater. But war lined his pragmatism up against the wall. "It is common sense to take a method and try it," he had said in ushering in the New Deal. "If it fails, admit it frankly and try another." This may indeed have been common sense in peace. It certainly was not in war, where the price of failure was defeat. Roosevelt simply could not shuffle his strategic plans the way he had shuffled programs for domestic recovery.

No one knew this better than Roosevelt himself. The insouciant cigarette holder and the press conference flippancies served only as an easy means of distracting attention from the eyes ever more shadowed, the cheeks ever more hollow, the expression ever more careworn and somber. And, in this dilemma, his pragmatism—even a pragmatism so superbly grounded in a brilliance of instinct and a generosity of emotion—tended to betray him. Had he been a man committed to abstract and explicit principles, like Wilson, he might have developed a specific political strategy for the war. But as a pragmatist, reluctant to sacrifice American lives to apolitical strategy of whose value he temperamentally could have no doctrinaire certitude, he had no choice but opportunism and expediency.

The four new volumes of *The Public Papers and Addresses* give a full if oblique reflection of Roosevelt's political dilemma. He did not direct the war in a political vacuum, of course. He set forth what he hoped would be the framework of the peace in such extremely general statements as the Atlantic Charter and the Four Freedoms. But these were essentially moral rather than political expressions: they were statements of hope rather than of decision. His world political strategy, as a consequence, was compounded of sentiments rather than of ideas.

Some of the sentiments which tempered the basic pragmatism were wise and commendable: Roosevelt's deep faith in the "massed, angered forces of common humanity"; his hatred of colonial imperialism; his genuine and capacious internationalism. Other sentiments were more ambiguous, such as the profound detestation of Germany which committed him to German policies of an impractical harshness, or his delight in what Isaiah Berlin has called the "royal cousin" approach to international diplomacy. At its best, Roosevelt's exultant sense of himself as the embodiment of a nation dealing with other archetypal heads of state could lead to a rich working relationship with men like Churchill and Mackenzie King. At its worst, it involved him in an entirely unworthy and cheapening preoccupation with crowned heads and royal families, so that the Archduke Ottos and the King Peters and the other bargain-basement remains of European monarchies could command a disproportionate amount of his time and his interest.

But his essential approach to the politics of war remained negative. And, as one main result, when he came to particular decisions, he often had little definite to insist on against the very clear, specific, and intelligible criterion of the military: the belief that any political decision was good which would shorten the war. Now this is not a bad criterion; it is certainly one not to be lightly overridden except where the political advantages of the longer way around are indisputable and conclusive. Hanson Baldwin has recently argued that Churchill was right in advocating the invasion of Europe through the Balkans rather than through France; but this is surely an instance where we would have paid a much higher military cost without gaining very clear or certain political advantages—indeed, with the possible result of producing a third world war before the second was over.

Yet, with a political strategy, so general and undefined, the criterion of military expediency became increasingly important. The day-to-day politics of the war grew increasingly to be a function, not of the State Department, but of the theater commanders. In his press conference after the Darlan deal in North Africa, Roosevelt quoted what he said was a Balkan proverb: "My children, you are permitted in time of great danger to walk with the Devil until you have crossed the bridge." But often in the smoke of war no one knew where the bridge was, or it constantly receded, while the Devil remained close and familiar. It was ironical that General Marshall, when he became Secretary of State, found himself the impatient prisoner of a system of military initiative in foreign policy which he himself had exacted from Roosevelt five years before.

The two areas of Roosevelt's wartime policy which have received special criticism are the policy of "unconditional surrender" and the policy toward the U.S.S.R. Both were in a peculiar sense personal policies; and both proceeded directly from the lack of specific content in his political objectives. The first, oddly enough, was opposed by the military and constituted one of the few cases of Roosevelt's overruling the military on political questions; the other was supported by the military and, indeed, in the Yalta phase was pushed to extreme lengths by the Army's passionate desire to insure Soviet participation in the war against Japan.

Hanson Baldwin recently called the unconditional surrender policy "the biggest political mistake of the war." Mr. Churchill evidently agrees, judging by his efforts to get out from under responsibility for it; contemporary records, however, give him a larger role in its formulation than his present memory will concede. But it remains clear that "unconditional surrender" was exclusively a Roosevelt inspiration; and that he alone continued to insist on it, after the Russians, the British, and the U. S. State Department and Army had done their separate bests to get him to forget it. It has become evident, in addition, that Roosevelt's infatuation with "unconditional surrender" derived in part from an entirely garbled recollection of American history. Roosevelt had an *idée fixe* that Grant had called for "unconditional surrender" at Appomattox and then had responded to such a surrender by acts of generosity to the defeated foe. "Lee surrendered unconditionally to Grant," Roosevelt actually wrote to Hull at one point, "but immediately Grant told him that his officers should take their horses home for spring plowing. That is the spirit I want to see abroad." Thus "unconditional surrender" had for Roosevelt the connotation of magnanimity to a helpless enemy. Yet the facts are that Grant talked of "unconditional surrender" at Fort Donelson and at Vicksburg; he said nothing about it at Appomattox. If the term had any historical connotation for most people, it was certainly not the amiable connotation which it incorrectly had for Roosevelt.

Still there was more to "unconditional surrender" than a foolish slip of memory on Roosevelt's part. He was looking hard in 1943 for a formula which would achieve two objectives: on the one hand, reassure the Russians against their fear that the West might seek a separate peace; and, on the other, make absolutely certain this time that the Germans would not escape the full consciousness and stigma of defeat. At the same time he wanted to keep the question of the terms of peace open, because, with his basic pragmatism, he could not know what the exact terms should be until the moment of peace had arrived. The principle of "unconditional surrender" seemed a perfect answer to the triple dilemma. And, while it is clear that Roosevelt tended to push the principle too far, particularly in regard to the satellite states, it is not at all clear to me that the principle itself, as Mr. Baldwin has argued, "discouraged opposition to Hitler, probably lengthened the war [and] . . . cost us dearly in lives and time."

Mr. Baldwin's assumption evidently is that "unconditional surrender" deterred the German people from an anti-Hitler revolution. Yet such a theory is surely based on a musket-over-the-fireplace conception of revolution, altogether irrelevant to a totalitarian state where police controls were reasonably intact. And there is no reason to believe in any case that the failure to gain terms from the Allies deterred any serious anti-Hitler movement; it certainly did not discourage the heroes of the 1944 *Putsch* from making their courageous attempt on Hitler's life. What "unconditional surrender" may have deterred is the attempt on the part of someone like Goering to win special terms for himself. While the defection to the Allies of Goering and part of the *Luftwaffe* might conceivably have shortened the war, it is not clear that it would have simplified the peace. It was a correct desire to guard against some such contingency as this which led Roosevelt to favor "unconditional surrender" in the first place. On the point of the effect of "unconditional surrender" the arguments of Wallace Carroll (in *Persuade or Perish*) and H. R. Trevor-Roper (in *The Last Days of Hitler*) seem far more convincing to me than the more modish views of Hanson Baldwin.

The question of the U.S.S.R. puts Roosevelt's pragmatism to the most severe of tests. As a pragmatist, Roosevelt reacted to the Soviet Union in terms of specific situations. When the U.S.S.R. was invading Finland, it seemed to him "a dictatorship as absolute as any other dictatorship in the world." But when the Red Army was beating back the Nazis at Stalingrad, the U.S.S.R. took on for him a more genial aspect—as it did for most of the free world. It was in this mood that he told Sumner Welles that both the U.S.A. and the U.S.S.R. were modifying their systems and that, though American democracy and Soviet Communism could never meet, they would become enough alike to keep the peace.

Thus the pragmatism which prevented Roosevelt from assessing the theoretical implications of a totalitarian system was one factor in his Russian policy, as another was his instinctive generosity in the face of Russian courage and sacrifice. His pragmatism—his refusal to anticipate the terms of peace—affected his Russian policy in another way. "People all over the world are shell-shocked," he wrote to George Norris in 1943—"and they will require a period of recuperation before final terms are laid down in regard to boundaries, transfers of population, free intercourse, the lowering of economic barriers, planning for mutual reconstruction, etc." But what was to happen in the interim? "I have been visualizing," Roosevelt told Norris, "a superimposed—or if you like it, superassumed—obligation by Russia, China, Britain, and ourselves that we will act as sheriffs for the maintenance of order during the transition period. . . . It will be so much easier to enter into lasting agreements after the transition period." Thus the conception of the big-power partnership—the Big Three, as it soon became—emerged as an easy substitute in Roosevelt's mind for more specific political objectives. And another factor encouraging this conception was surely his affable relations with his "royal cousin" Stalin.

Some revisionists, following the lead of William C. Bullitt, have criticized Roosevelt for not conditioning lend-lease aid to Russia in 1941 upon the acceptance of postwar political commitments. This argument overlooks the fact that it was almost as essential to us as to the Russians—and fully as essential to Mr. Churchill and the British—that the Red Army continue to kill Germans. It overlooks the even more crucial fact—which these same people, still following the lead of Bullitt, are always the first to assert in other contexts—that the U.S.S.R. would certainly not have kept such agreements, particularly when exacted under duress. Roosevelt, indeed, had very little choice but to postpone political discussions until the military crisis began to recede.

The test of his Russian policy thus came at Yalta; and Yalta, in the minds of many revisionists, has become the pat and comfortable explanation for everything that has gone wrong since the end of the war. There can be no question that Yalta represented the downfall of Rooseveltian pragmatism. For such pragmatism in international relations could succeed only among nations and leaders sharing the same or similar moral and social values; it was useless in dealings with men of opposed and hostile values. Thus pragmatism was a means of working out problems with Churchill, but it was an exposure of weakness to Stalin; and this Roosevelt did not know till after Yalta. Richard Crossman has argued persuasively that Roosevelt's foreign policy was obsessed by a desire to avoid the "mistakes" of Wilson; yet that herein Roosevelt was wrong, and that Wilson's narrow and zealous faith in abstract principle, rather than Roosevelt's limitless flexibility, was what was needed to counter Communism. "There can be little doubt," writes Crossman, "that Woodrow Wilson would have been a far more formidable adversary for Stalin than Franklin D. Roosevelt."

In general, this is a just criticism. But in detail, and as applied to Yalta, it can be much exaggerated. The actual import of that conference, indeed, has been recklessly distorted, including the really vicious attempt to blow up Alger Hiss into having been a major Presidential adviser. Edward R. Stettinius, Jr., and Walter Johnson in *Roosevelt and the Russians,* and Judge Rosenman in his cogent and admirable brief note on the Yalta conference (pages 537-548 in the last volume of *The Public Papers and Addresses*), dispose conclusively of the central misunderstandings and misrepresentations of the Yalta transactions.

It seems fairly clear that the so-called Yalta "concessions" were both justified in terms of the information available to Roosevelt and Churchill and without decisive practical effect on subsequent developments. The Yalta agreement on Eastern Europe, far from being a concession at all, represented an extension of democratic principles so far in advance of democratic power that there was no possibility of enforcing it once the U.S.S.R. decided to ignore them. The agreements on the UN were, on the whole, minor and inconsequential; who cares today how many votes the U.S.S.R. commands in the General Assembly?

As for the concessions in the Far East, these were made with the specific purpose of assuring Soviet entrance into the Japanese war by a designated date. The Army, not knowing at the time whether the Manhattan Project would ever produce anything and determined to reduce the hundreds of thousands of casualties anticipated in the invasion and subjection of Japan, pressed upon Roosevelt the absolute necessity of getting a firm commitment from Stalin. Even to someone like Admiral Leahy, who disagreed with the military estimate of the Far Eastern situation, the final arrangements seemed "very reasonable." "No one was more surprised than I," Leahy writes in *I Was There,* "to see these conditions agreed to at Yalta labeled as some horrendous concessions made by President Roosevelt to an enemy." Nor is it easy to argue convincingly that the situation in the Far East is any different as a result of the concessions. It is hard to see that anything short of the commitment of American troops to China could have averted the Communist triumph over Chiang Kai-shek.

Stalin probably negotiated in good faith at Yalta—in good faith, that is, within terms of the Soviet wartime policy of collaboration. That policy was not to be abandoned until military developments in the weeks after Yalta showed conclusively that the military crisis in Europe was over, and that collaboration was no longer necessary. At this point, Soviet policy rapidly switched to its postwar objective of the political conquest of Europe—a switch manifested in March 1945 by the tough Soviet interventions in Eastern Europe by the instructions through Jacques Duclos to the Communist Parties of the West to cease their "Browderite" tactics of collaboration, and by Stalin's own fantastic charges against Roosevelt. Ever the pragmatist, Roosevelt reacted swiftly to the new direction of Soviet policy. It is a misfortune that his death came in April before he had had occasion to embody his rapidly growing misgivings over Soviet policy in anything but secret cables to Stalin and to Churchill and in private conversations.

But, even if the consequences of Yalta have been rashly overstated, it still can be argued that Roosevelt's basic pragmatism throughout the war betrayed the democratic cause and lost the peace. This judgment seems to me, however, essentially mistaken. The fact is that the ambiguities in Roosevelt's attitude toward the Soviet Union corresponded precisely to the ambiguities in the whole Western attitude toward the U.S.S.R.; and this is a fact the historian cannot ignore, whatever subsequent wisdom hindsight may have given to the commentators.

The central reason for Wilson's failure had been that he incarnated convictions which the American people did not share; and that as a consequence Presidential policy outran the possibilities of national support. This error Roosevelt took great care to avoid. I happen to have been one of those myself who mistrusted Russia even in the glowing days of Stalingrad, but my argument for mistrust was essentially an intellectual one; and no one in control of democratic foreign policy could have assumed the responsibility for initiating an anti-Soviet policy in advance of demonstrated Soviet purposes of systematic hostility toward the West. Such purposes were not demonstrated during the war till March 1945.

Roosevelt described his policy toward the U.S.S.R. as a "great gamble." But it was a gamble which the American people were prepared to make. How much greater the gamble would have been, and how much less the chances of popular support, had U.S. policy based itself on the opposite hunch—the theory of Soviet noncollaboration—before the evidence was in to convince the people of the correctness of that theory! André Malraux, no friend of the Soviet Union or of Communism, has stated the problem with precision. Roosevelt went to Yalta, Malraux writes, "for reasons which, even today [1948], do not seem so bad to me. Our attempt to reach an agreement with the Russians entailed a liability which was, for France, very heavy. But would it not have been still heavier if we had refused even the attempt? I do not think that anyone could have remained in power in

France, or even in the United States, if he had brought about a break with Russia, which at that time would have seemed to have no justification."

Given the pragmatic genius of the American people, Roosevelt's policy toward Russia was the only possible policy. The problem of whether the West had a community of values with the Soviet Union could only be solved pragmatically. And it was not solved pragmatically till the period after Yalta.

The defects in Roosevelt's wartime policy thus seem to be reflections of the defects in the American climate of opinion. With his superb political instincts, Roosevelt knew, as Wilson did not know, that the American people learned by experience, not by logic. And, because he learned by experience himself, he could not anticipate what had not happened. He rallied a nation broken and dispirited by depression; he led it successfully through the greatest war of our history; he left it morally strong and materially prosperous. He was not a worker of miracles. To demonstrate that he was not a deity is hardly to build up a case against his greatness as a democratic leader.

Eleanor Roosevelt (essay date 1954)

SOURCE: "On My Husband," in *It Seems to Me*, W. W. Norton & Company, Inc., 1954, pp. 164-72.

[*In the following excerpt from* It Seems to Me, *a collection of questions and answers from letters addressed to Roosevelt's wife, Eleanor Roosevelt discusses some of the personal qualities of her husband.*]

Do you think your husband had any premonition that he might not live to complete his last term in the White House?

No, I do not think my husband had any premonition that he would not live to finish his term in the White House. Four years previously I think he had a feeling that any man well might not live through a third term. But, having lived through the third term, he believed, I think, that if it was right for him to run he would be able to win and he would live as long as he was needed to do his work.

Would you tell me what books and authors your illustrious husband most frequently mentioned as having influenced his vision and action?

I am afraid he never mentioned books in this connection. He always talked of Mahan's Naval History as having been one of the books which he found most illuminating when he read it. He liked historical biographies primarily, and read very widely.

He had a very catholic interest in many subjects, and of course read a great deal of history, though I do not remember hearing him say at any time that particular writings or particular books had influenced his point of view.

I should say that Woodrow Wilson had a great influence upon him, and Theodore Roosevelt, partly in their writings and much as individuals. My husband frequently talked about them, but not as inspirations.

I have just read **F.D.R.: His Personal Letters**. *In one or two letters he refers to his engagement to you but says nothing about how or when you became engaged. If this isn't too intimate a subject, I'd like to know a little more about how and where this happened.*

I became engaged to my husband on a weekend which we spent at Groton School, where we were visiting my young brother. I imagine, since my husband was writing personal letters, he thought that anyone concerned would probably know when we became engaged.

You remarked in your column recently that the "work as usual" way Governor Dewey spent his birthday didn't seem a very happy way of celebrating the occasion. I thought your husband was a "work as usual" man on his birthday too. Am I wrong?

My husband always had to work during the day on his birthday because he was always engaged in work that could not be laid aside, but his birthday was a day of much celebration. There was family celebration in the morning before going to work, and every year we had a particular group of friends who celebrated with him at dinner and in the evening.

Was your husband a regular churchgoer?

My husband was senior warden in our church at Hyde Park when he died. He went to church as often as it was possible for him to do so. It was extremely difficult for him to do this regularly in the last years of his life, and therefore I could not say that he was a regular churchgoer, but he performed his duties as senior warden and was extremely interested always in the church.

Is it true that your husband, the late President Roosevelt, never wrote his own speeches?

No. My husband wrote a great many speeches in his own hand. When he became President, however, he developed a regular routine. First of all he decided on the subject with which he was going to deal, then he called in the Government officials charged with the responsibility for the work on this particular subject: for instance, if it was to be a fiscal speech, the Treasury Department and the Federal Reserve Board were consulted; if agriculture, the Department of Agriculture and allied agencies, and so on.

After he had all the facts, he usually sat down with two or three people and explained his ideas of what he wished said. They made a first draft and brought it back to him. He then went over it, and sometimes there were as many as six or eight or ten drafts of the same speech. One member of this small group was usually someone adept at phrasing, another was good at cutting, because in any speech which is made over the radio one is apt to put a great deal too much into it to fit the time. In between each rewriting my husband went over it again, and if you ever go to the library at Hyde Park you will see the collection of speeches with corrections on the various copies in my husband's own handwriting.

When a speech was finally written, my husband always practically knew every word that was in it by heart, as he had gone over it so often. It was the final expression of his original thoughts. I have, however, seen my husband take a speech which his advisers thought was completely finished, tear it up and dictate an entirely new speech because he felt it was not simple and clear enough. He retained the facts, but he was particularly adept at putting thoughts into simple and clear enough words so that even I, who might not know anything on the subject, found I could comprehend what he was talking about.

They say that many great men's wives have a feeling of intuition, before the men become well known, that their husbands are marked for greatness. Did you have any feeling like that about your husband when you were first married?

No, but I am not given to going much beyond the things that have to be done each day. I have always been so busy that, if I thought I had adequately met the demands day by day, what was going to happen in the future never received a great deal of thought.

It is a mystery to me how a man from a conservative, wealthy home like Mr. Roosevelt ever became such a great liberal. What do you think influenced him most in this direction?

Very often a social conscience is more easily awakened in one who has not been hardened by having to battle for every advantage in life. My husband's parents brought him up with a sense of obligation to other people. He had a chance to travel and make contact in a simple way with people in other parts of the world. His mind was open and intelligent, and as his contacts broadened his sense of justice deepened. He was a liberal because he believed in social justice.

What people besides President Roosevelt's parents and yourself had the most important personal influence on his life?

I think Louis Howe had a great influence on my husband's life, and also his two uncles, Mr. Warren Delano and Mr. Frederic Delano—and my uncle, Theodore Roosevelt, made a deep impression on him as a young man, as he did on so many other young men of that generation.

What did President Roosevelt plan to do when he retired from the Presidency to private life again?

My husband had planned when he retired to write regularly for one magazine and to devote himself to putting his papers in order and to enlarging and making more interesting the library at Hyde Park.

Your husband never wrote pointed personal letters, as President Truman does, but he certainly must have needed to let off steam at times. What kind of safety valve did he have in periods of terrible tension and pressure?

My husband disliked writing longhand letters, except for brief business or personal memos. Temperaments differ. He was very slow to anger, but when he was angry it shook him to the bottom of his soul and he was more apt to take his anger out in cold and never-to-be-forgotten words than in any impulsive way.

To the ordinary criticism affecting him and his family he rarely paid any attention. He taught us all to believe that it was better to ignore criticism. He lost respect for some writers and critics and then rarely read what they said, so, of course, they bothered him little. He also advised us to look with care for any constructive criticism, but if it became particularly carping to ignore it and never answer it.

His illness had given him extraordinary self-control in personal matters. When matters affecting affairs of the country were at stake, and in periods of tension and pressure, he practiced this same self-control. He suffered when things went wrong with the family, though those personal things were quickly swallowed up in the much more important things that touched the country as a whole.

Did your husband ever describe his personal impressions of Stalin? I seem to have heard that they got on very well, exchanged jokes, etc.

Yes. When my husband came home he always talked over his trip. When he came home from his first meeting with Mr. Stalin in Tehran, he told us he sensed a great suspicion on the part of the Marshal but formal relations were always polite. He felt no warmth of understanding or of normal intercourse. My husband determined to bend every effort to breaking these suspicions down, and decided that the way to do it was to live up to every promise made by both the United States and Great Britain, which both of us were able to do before the Yalta meeting.

At Yalta my husband felt the atmosphere had somewhat cleared, and he did say he was able to get a smile from Stalin.

I understand that President Roosevelt used to have a couple of cocktails before dinner. What did he drink?

I do not think that my husband often had a couple of cocktails before dinner. Sometimes he did, but not always, and many times he had none. When he made cocktails, he liked a Martini, a rum cocktail or an Old-Fashioned. It was more a question with him of a time to relax and have a few friendly minutes with people than of caring very much what he drank or even whether he had a drink. The doctors approved of it because they thought it helped his circulation.

We would like to serve your husband's favorite menu at a dinner to open the polio drive and commemorate his birthday on January 30. Could you tell us some of his favorite dishes?

My husband was very fond of curried chicken. He also liked scrambled eggs, corned-beef hash or roast-beef hash, any kind of game and especially terrapin, Maryland style. Waffles with maple syrup was a favorite dessert.

Which of the books about your husband do you feel gives the most accurate picture of him, and which the least accurate?

If you are interested in my husband's labor record, Miss Frances Perkins' book, *The Roosevelt I Knew,* is excellent. *Roosevelt and Hopkins,* by Mr. Robert Sherwood, gives an extraordinarily good picture of the general times. Perhaps my husband's own letters, edited by my son Elliott, would give you a more intimate picture of his personality than anything else. The book I like least, and which is the least accurate, is John T. Flynn's; but, of course, there are many books about my husband which I have not had time to read.

In This I Remember *you stated that our late President was advised to eliminate the famous "stab in the back" from his speech after Mussolini attacked France, and that he refused to do so. Miss Grace Tully said that it was not in the President's script and that he ad libbed it. Which of you is right?*

Miss Tully is quite right. The phrase "stab in the back" was not in the President's script. It had been discussed beforehand, and his advisers urged him not to put it in. He put it in on his own initiative when he was making his speech. He did this sort of thing quite often, so there is nothing contradictory between what Miss Tully said and what I said.

I wish to know if the quotation "We have nothing to fear but fear itself" is an original saying of the late President. If not, from whom did he quote?

It was an original saying, if there is anything really original!

Do you feel that your opinions ever changed your husband's political decisions?

Never.

Waldo W. Braden and Earnest Brandenburg (essay date 1955)

SOURCE: "Roosevelt's Fireside Chats," in *Speech Monographs,* Vol. XXII, No. 5, November, 1955, pp. 290-302.

[*In the following essay, Braden and Brandenburg explore the significance and effectiveness of Roosevelt's direct communication with the American people via radio with his so-called "Fireside Chats."*]

At a tense moment in his career Franklin D. Roosevelt opened one of his speeches with these sentences:

> Our government, happily, is a democracy. As part of the democratic process, your President is again taking an opportunity to report on the progress of national affairs to the real rulers of this country—the voting public.[1]

Herein Roosevelt expressed succinctly a major tenet of his political creed. Throughout his career when he needed support, he frequently took his case to the people, hoping to create sufficient pressure to assure the success of his program. Grace Tully, his private secretary for many years, noted that he "had a profound respect for the judgment of the American people and the power of public opinion."[2] Out of this philosophy grew a remarkable set of speeches that have become known as the Fireside Chats.

These speeches found their beginning in Franklin Roosevelt's experiences with radio during his governorship of New York. The increase in the number of home radio sets and the extension of far flung radio networks coming simultaneously with Roosevelt's return to politics in the late twenties, after he had been stricken with poliomyelitis in 1921, provided him with a most effective and far reaching means of influencing public opinion. Personal visits to his constituents were no longer necessary. When a recalcitrant legislature opposed revision of existing utility legislation, Roosevelt spoke to the people over a state radio chain with gratifying results; mail came "flooding into Albany, most of it in support of Roosevelt's position and most of it addressed to the working level of the legislature."[3]

Roosevelt continued to speak directly with the people of the state, via the new medium of radio, about once every ten days during his governorship. This, he later explained, was "to enlist their support on various occasions when a hostile legislature declined to enact legislation for the benefit of the people."[4]

Prior to Roosevelt's "intimate talk" of March 12, 1933, the first Fireside Chat, a President traditionally spoke to the people only in "formal addresses."[5] The success of this first talk, his previous successes with radio while governor of New York, and the advantages of the new medium to a man with his physical handicap and with his excellent radio voice, made obvious to him and his advisers the desirability of continuing these presentations. As a result, Roosevelt delivered twenty-eight addresses commonly identified as Fireside Chats, in addition to his numerous other appearances on the air as President. Following is a chronological list of the Fireside Chats with their titles as given in Roosevelt's ***Public Papers and Addresses***:

> 1. Sunday, March 12, 1933, **"An Intimate Talk with the People of the United States on Banking."**

2. Sunday, May 7, 1933, **"What We Have Been Doing and What We are Planning to Do."**

3. Monday, July 24, 1933, **"The Simple Purposes and the Solid Foundations of Our Recovery Program."**

4. Sunday, October 22, 1933, **"We Are on Our Way, and We Are Headed in the Right Direction."**

5. Thursday, June 28, 1934, **"Are You Better Off Than You Were Last Year?"**

6. Sunday, September 30, 1934, **"We Are Moving Forward to Greater Freedom, to Greater Security for the Average Man."**

7. Sunday, April 28, 1935, **"Fear Is Vanishing, Confidence Is Growing, Faith Is Being Renewed in the Democratic Form of Government."**

8. Sunday, September 6, 1936, **"We Are Going to Conserve Soil, Conserve Water, Conserve Life."**

9. Tuesday, March 9, 1937, **"Discussing the Plan for Reorganization of the Judiciary."**

10. Tuesday, October 12, 1937, **"Discussing Legislation to be Recommended to the Extraordinary Session of the Congress."**

11. Sunday, November 14, 1937, **"Requesting Cooperation in the Taking of the Unemployment Census."**[6]

12. Thursday, April 14, 1938, **"Dictatorships Do Not Grow Out of Strong and Successful Governments, but Out of Weak and Helpless Ones."** Fireside Chat on Present Economic Conditions and Measures Being Taken to Improve Them.

13. Friday, June 24, 1938, **"*I* Have Every Right to Speak [in connection with political primaries] Where There May Be a Clear Issue Between Candidates for a Democratic Nomination Involving Principles, or a Clear Misuse of My Own Name."**

14. Sunday, September 3, 1939, **"As Long as it Remains Within My Power to Prevent, There Will Be No Blackout of Peace in the United States."** Fireside Chat on the War in Europe.

15. Sunday, May 26, 1940, **"At This Time When the World Is Threatened by Forces of Destruction, It Is My Resolve and Yours to Build Up Our Armed Defenses."**

16. Sunday, December 29, 1940, **"There Can Be No Appeasement with Ruthlessness. We Must Be the Great Arsenal of Democracy."**

17. Thursday, September 11, 1941, **"When You See a Rattlesnake Posed to Strike You Do Not Wait Until He has Struck Before You Crush Him."** [Maintaining freedom of the Seas]

18. Tuesday, December 9, 1941, **"We Are Going to Win the War and We Are Going to Win the Peace That Follows,"** Fireside Chat to the Nation Following the Declaration of War with Japan.

19. Monday, February 23, 1942, **"We Must Keep on Striking our Enemies Wherever and Whenever We Can Meet Them,"** Fireside Chat on Progress of the War.

20. Tuesday, April 28, 1942, **"The Price for Civilization Must Be Paid in Hard Work and Sorrow and Blood."**

21. Monday, September 7, 1942, **"If the Vicious Spiral of Inflation Ever Gets Under Way, the Whole Economic System Will Stagger,"** Fireside Chat on the Cost of Living and the Progress of the War.

22. Monday, October 12, 1942, **"The President Reports on the Home Front."**

23. Sunday, May 2, 1943, **"There Can Be No One Among Us—No One Faction—Powerful Enough to Interrupt the Forward March of Our People to Victory,"** Fireside Chat on the Federal Seizure of the Coal Mines.

24. Wednesday, July 28, 1943, **"The Massed, Angered Forces of Common Humanity Are on the March. The First Crack in the Axis Has Come,"** Fireside Chat on the Progress of the War and Plans for Peace.

25. Wednesday, September 8, 1943, **"Fireside Chat Opening Third War Loan Drive."**

26. Friday, December 24, 1943, **"Keep Us Strong in Our Faith That We Fight for a Better Day for Humankind,"** Christmas Eve Fireside Chat on Teheran and Cairo Conferences.

27. Monday, June 5, 1944, **"Fireside Chat on the Fall of Rome."**

28. Monday, June 12, 1944, **"Review of the Progress of the War—Fireside Chat Opening Fifth War Loan Drive."**

The term Fireside Chat was introduced during the preparations for Roosevelt's second direct talk to the American people. While working out the mechanical details for broadcasting from the White House, Harry C. Butcher, manager of the Washington office of the Columbia Broadcasting System, gained considerable understanding of the President's purposes in these speeches. When he read a proposed press release announcing the broadcast of May 7, 1933, Mr. Butcher sensed that his program director "had not quite grasped the idea"; consequently he inserted the words "Fireside Chat" and some "additional corrections" in order to convey what he believed to be a more accurate interpretation of the President's forthcoming message.[7] The term was immediately accepted by the press and the public. Roosevelt obviously approved. His *Public Papers* identify addresses in those terms; a note accompanying the original "chat" refers to the expression: "The following is the first so-called fireside chat, which has been applied by the Press to the various radio reports I have made to the people of the Nation."[8] On two occasions the president used the term in his later addresses. On June 24, 1938, he began, "The American public and the American newspapers are certainly creatures of habit. It is the warmest night I have ever seen in Washington and yet this talk will be referred to as a fireside talk." On December 29, 1940, his first words were, "This is not a fireside chat on war."

The Fireside Chats typically were delivered from the Diplomatic Reception Room on the ground floor of the White House.[9] This room was large enough to accommodate a small audience, which usually consisted of a few members of Roosevelt's family, some of his close advisers, and a few other friends or associates who happened to be in Washington at the time. Its atmosphere "bore little relationship to the quiet and secluded atmosphere generally associated with a real fireside. There happened to be a real fireplace in the room, but it was empty. At it the President sat before a desk on which were bunched three or four microphones, a reading light, a pitcher of water, and glasses."[10] Sufficient space was available to permit each of the radio networks to have its own announcer in a separate cubicle.

> There were some thirty uncomfortable folding chairs for those who had been invited to listen. . . . The audience was seated about ten minutes past ten for a ten-thirty broadcast (the usual hour), and the President was wheeled in at about ten-twenty, carrying his reading-copy and the inevitable cigarette.
>
> Radio announcers for the major broadcasting chains would huddle about, testing their microphones. The radio engineers would test their equipment, which was spread all over the room from wall to wall, making it difficult to move about. . . .
>
> The President, once seated at his desk, exchanged greetings and pleasantries for a few moments with the guests and the announcers. As the minute of ten-thirty approached, the atmosphere got more tense. The President would put out his cigarette, arrange his reading copy, and take a drink of water, as nervously as when he was about to address a visible audience. Then, on signal, complete silence, a nod from the chief radio engineer, the usual announcement from each announcer stating tersely that the broadcast was coming from the White House and introducing "The President of the United States"—and finally the clear, resonant voice: "My friends."[11]

The President's "intimate talk" with the people only eight days after he assumed office set the pattern for his subsequent Fireside Chats. Each of these talks was intended to concern only one fundamental issue, which at the moment was of much immediate interest to the American people. Addresses for such Democratic party affairs as Jackson or Jefferson Day dinners, routine observances of the March of Dimes or Red Cross campaigns, or situations with large immediate audiences were not occasions for Fireside Chats and were not called by that name. The "chats" were informal, simple presentations to be listened to and comprehended by the great mass of American voters.

The Fireside Chats varied in length from about 1200 to 4500 words and required from fifteen to forty-five minutes for delivery. The typical one took thirty minutes on the air.[12] For these talks with the people Roosevelt ordinarily chose to speak between nine and eleven p.m. (E.S.T.). A notable exception was his Christmas Eve Fireside Chat, delivered December 24, 1943, from 3:00 to 3:30 p.m. (E.S.T.). Seemingly he preferred broadcasts on the first three days of the week, for twenty-one of the twenty-eight were presented on Sunday, Monday, or Tuesday.[13] Prior to the war he usually spoke over the facilities of at least two of the networks; but of course upon our entrance into World War II his audience increased, and he always had at his disposal the three major networks as well as overseas broadcasts by short wave. Each one of these talks was presented at a moment when it would seem most timely and dramatic. Roosevelt and his advisers attempted to select the "logical occasion for each talk."[14] Hence they coincided with the bank holiday, the opening of the congressional elections, a return from a trip through the drouth stricken areas, the outbreak of war in Europe, the declaration of war on Japan, and the launching of a war bond drive. The talks, referred to by Roosevelt as "heart to heart talks"[15] were presented under the guise of informational reports to the people, but in truth most of them were highly stimulating and on occasion truly persuasive.

It would be difficult to rank these twenty-eight talks in terms of their significance. Each in its own way, highly important at the time of delivery, was accorded a dramatic significance in the melee of political events. The setting, ideas, and effectiveness of a select few will be considered.

FIRESIDE CHAT OF MARCH 12, 1933

"An Intimate Talk With the People of the United States on Banking"

Two days after he became President, Roosevelt sought to meet the banking crisis by the temporary closing of all banks. Only six days later, with the banks of the entire nation still closed, Roosevelt delivered a radio message described in his *Public Papers* as an "intimate talk with the people of the United States on banking." He began: "I want to talk for a few minutes with the people of the United States about banking. . . . I know that when you understand what we in Washington have been about I shall continue to have your cooperation as fully as I have had your sympathy and help during the past week." The President explained the crisis in "A.B.C. fashion" and urged the people "not to repeat their own extraordinary [previous] behavior . . . when they attempted to convert their bank deposits into currency, [thus] precipitating crisis."[16] In concluding his address, Roosevelt made the following direct appeal:

> Confidence and courage are the essentials of success in carrying out our plan. You people must have faith; you must not be stampeded by rumors or guesses. Let us unite in banishing fear. We have provided the machinery to restore our financial system; it is up to you to support and make it work. It is your problem no less than it is mine. Together we cannot fail.

"The talk made a tremendous popular hit."[17] Confidence was restored. "The worst of the crisis had been weathered. [The next day] solvent banks began to reopen . . . all over the nation."[18] Large volumes of currency were deposited as the banks were reopened.[19] Moreover, this "return flow of money came principally from hoarded funds rather than from active circulation."[20] As one popular writer expressed it,

> The people listened . . . and felt that the man in the White House was their friend, as well as leader, who would save them from further catastrophe no matter what. Almost audibly, a sigh of relief went up through the entire land.[21]

The first Fireside Chat had accomplished its basic purpose and still more, for "the average citizen had [so] warmed to this appeal, [that] the most successful medium of publicity [and persuasion] for the New Deal had been discovered."[22]

FIRESIDE CHAT OF MARCH 9, 1937

"Discussing the Plan for Reorganization of the Judiciary"

Franklin Roosevelt's personal prestige had risen higher than ever before at the beginning of 1937. In the election of the previous year, the most one-sided election since 1820, he had carried every section of the country; his party had won a greater majority in Congress than any modern president's; many Congressmen were well aware that they had "ridden Roosevelt's coattails into office." Moreover, the campaign of 1936 had been "primarily concerned with the personality and principles of . . . Franklin D. Roosevelt."[23]

The overwhelming mandate from the people convinced the President that he could carry out the remainder of his policies without delay. He was convinced that his "Congressional program, which had pulled the nation out of despair, had been fairly completely undermined" by the courts.[24] Hence, in early 1937 Roosevelt launched a direct attack upon the judiciary.[25] He went before Congress, February 5, with a plan for the "reorganization of the Judicial Branch" which sought, primarily, a judiciary of younger men.[26] Then pending was a bill to permit federal justices to retire at the age of seventy at full pay, providing they had held commissions for at least ten years. Roosevelt urged that for each qualified justice who failed to take advantage of this retirement provision,

the President should be authorized to appoint an additional justice.[27] Other changes were also proposed, but the one issue of great interest to both the President and the people was the proposal affecting the Supreme Court.[28]

Taking their cue from ex-President Hoover who accused his successor of wanting to "pack the Supreme Court," the Republicans immediately attacked the bill. Gradually powerful opposition also developed among Democrats. Senator George of Georgia, who had played an important part in writing the 1936 Democratic platform, accused Mr. Roosevelt of repudiating that platform. Wheeler of Montana, a Democrat and then widely known as a liberal, launched a speaking campaign to convince the country that the proposed bill would make the Supreme Court subservient to one man.

When opposition continued to develop, the President took over direct leadership of the campaign for his bill. On March 4 he spoke by radio to Victory Dinners of Democrats throughout the country. And then he carried the issue to the people in a Fireside Chat. He repeated historical precedents for his plan and attempted to answer charges that he sought to destroy the balance of power among the three branches of the Federal government. The President's primary purpose, however, was to convince the people that the courts were deliberately, and unfairly thwarting his program.[29]

Instead of the popular support which the recent election had given him reason to expect, the response to the court speeches was not favorable. Liberals were divided in their opinions. Some of his advisers, for example, Farley, Frankfurter, Rosenman, and Corcoran, thought the President had erred in this attack. Most newspapers vigorously defended the Court. It became increasingly clear that the President's overwhelming Congressional majorities had melted away on the court issue as the debate, called "the bitterest since the League of Nations struggle,"[30] continued.

Roosevelt faced the problem of convincing the nation that his judicial reform bill was essential to the welfare of the country. The people who had come to venerate the Supreme Court were shocked by references to "nine old men." They had no desire for experimentation with the Supreme Court of the land, especially in light of Roosevelt's admission that some of his experiments would probably fail and be discarded. Roosevelt, the practical man of politics, could not convince the American people that his court proposals would harm no sacred traditions. "Practical politics" seemed an insufficient reason for tampering with the courts. Moreover, the President did not succeed in calming the misgivings of those who knew that the court proposals had been recommended without consultation with the Democratic congressional leaders. Many thought they sensed an element of executive trickery in the whole proposal. John Gunther's evaluation is typical:

> If Roosevelt had been more candid, if he had explored opinion more subtly and taken Congress

into his confidence, the result might have been different. But people could not get over the feeling that the proposal had been cooked up in an underhanded way. If he had said without equivocation, "It has become necessary to pack the Court, and I am going to pack it," he might have won. Many men of good will agree that something had to be done to stop usurpation by the courts of the legislative function; but they could not stomach the way Roosevelt did it.[31]

Roosevelt's Fireside Chat and other addresses on the Court issue did not calm the doubts of the public and as time passed his support on the issue decreased.[32]

The degree of Roosevelt's success or failure on the court issue is clouded, however, by the fact that Supreme Court decisions began to go in favor of New Deal philosophy.[33] "The Senate has been evenly divided on the [Supreme Court] issue with eight or ten members undecided, [but] now the waverers joined the opposition, believing that the necessity for the Bill had passed, and even the ranks of its supporters showed signs of breaking."[34] Roosevelt did not hesitate later to claim a clear-cut victory on the basis of the changed attitude of the Court,[35] but the end result was considered a defeat for the President.[36] He signed a compromise bill August 24 which retained most of the procedural reforms he had recommended, but made no mention of the appointment of new justices and judges.

FIRESIDE CHAT OF SEPTEMBER 3, 1939

Outbreak of World War II

The Nazis began their invasion of Poland in September, 1939. England and France declared war on Germany, September 3. That same Sunday evening, Roosevelt delivered a Fireside Chat to the American people who were overwhelmingly desirous of keeping the United States out of the war.[37] The President's argument on the direct issue of war or peace was that the best method for the American people to preserve their peace was to subscribe to his policies, for he was determined, so he said, that the United States should not go to war.

> I have said not once but many times that I have seen war and that I hate war. . . .

> I hope the United States will keep out of this war. I believe that it will. And I give you assurance and reassurance that every effort of your government will be directed toward that end.

> As long as it remains within my power to prevent, there will be no blackout of peace in the United States.

Roosevelt's statement that he desired peace for the United States demanded ethical support. His foreign policy had received its most severe criticism because many persons thought his condemnations of European aggressors and his proposals to "quarantine" the "disease" of war had endangered, rather than helped preserve, peace

for the nation. Public opinion polls indicated that more than a two to one majority favored stricter neutrality laws in preference to leaving the job to the President.[38] To meet these attitudes and to inspire faith in his ability to keep the nation out of war, the President reviewed the specific instances in which he had attempted to preserve world peace.[39] Newspapers praised the speech of September 3, 1939, primarily for that sentiment.[40]

President Roosevelt did not follow Woodrow Wilson's example of asking Americans to remain neutral in thought and deed. Instead, he declared:

> This nation will remain a neutral nation, but I cannot ask that every American remain neutral in thought as well. Even a neutral has a right to take account of the facts. Even a neutral cannot be asked to close his mind or his conscience.

This line of thought prepared the way for the President to argue later that the existing arms embargoes should be lifted as contrary to American concepts of neutrality. Roosevelt was clearly inconsistent in advocating "neutrality" at one time "without reservations" and at another time as not requiring that Americans be "neutral in thought."[41] His concept of neutrality involved: first, a declaration of nonparticipation in the conflict; second, refraining from acts which might be called warlike under strict interpretation of international law; and third, the right to give moral support and to set up conditions making it easier for the favored belligerents to obtain critical materials. Such a policy was a far cry from what neutrality as a principle of international law had come to mean to authorities on the subject,[42] but there is no doubt that Roosevelt's recommendations were far more successful with both Congress and the American people than were those of his opposition.[43]

The President was particularly anxious to forestall any attempt to label him or his party as the "war" group or to designate any group to which he did not belong as the "peace" bloc. He successfully handled that issue, for the American people, eighty-four to ninety-five per cent of whom consistently opposed becoming involved in war[44] approved his attitudes and policies with regard to the European situation.[45]

FIRESIDE CHAT OF DECEMBER 29, 1940

"We Must be the Great Arsenal of Democracy"

The might of the German war machine, as it crushed Western Europe, convinced the President and the American people of the desirability of aiding the British and of assuming the role of a non-belligerent. Although many in the United States were still determined to keep their country from entering the war,[46] they gradually came to believe that helping England was more important than staying out of the conflict.[47] Roosevelt decided to speak to the American people on Sunday evening, December 29, 1940. According to Robert Sherwood:

Roosevelt really enjoyed working on this speech for, with the political campaign over, it was the first chance he had had in months and even years to speak his mind with comparative freedom. He had indulged himself once, six months previously, in the "stab in the back" reference, but the consequences of that were so awkward that he had felt compelled subsequently to confine himself to the most namby-pamby euphemisms in all references to the international situation. Now, for the first time, he could mention the Nazis by name. He could lash out against the apostles of appeasement. . . . He could speak plainly on the subject which was always in his mind—the disastrous folly of any attempt at a negotiated peace.[48]

The President declared that his purpose in this speech was to avoid the necessity of a "last ditch war" for the preservation of American independence. He advocated increased aid to the Allies who were holding the "aggressors from our shores now." He assured his listeners that acting as the "arsenal of democracy" would "keep war away from our country"; this "arsenal of democracy" phrase was tremendously successful with the American people.[49] Through it, the President was able to shift his arguments. While the United States was maintaining a policy of "neutrality," he had not directly urged aid for the Allies. His original proposal to repeal the neutrality acts had been to make the United States "truly neutral."[50] In contrast to his previous stand, the President contended in his Fireside Chat of December 29 that the United States must provide aid to the Allies because such aid was essential to the defense of this country. He declared:

> The Nazi masters of Germany have made it clear that they intend not only to dominate all life and thought in their own country, but also to enslave the whole of Europe, and then to use the resources of Europe to dominate the rest of the world.

As he stirred Americans' fear of destruction, Roosevelt argued that the United States should aid Germany's opponents because the Axis was "being held away from our shores" by the Allies. This approach coincided with a shift of public opinion.[51] The American people supported the President in his plea that the United States should be the "arsenal of democracy." Press Secretary Stephen Early said that messages sent to the White House approved the Fireside Chat of December 29, 1940 in a ratio of one hundred to one.[52] The Lend-Lease Bill, presented to Congress in January by the President, was hotly debated, but those favoring aid to the democracies clearly were on the side more popular with the great majority of American citizens.

FIRESIDE CHAT OF SEPTEMBER 11, 1941

"Maintaining Freedom of the Seas"

On June 20, 1941, the President delivered a speech revealing that an American merchant vessel, the *Robin Moor*, had been sunk May 21 by a German submarine in the South Atlantic while *en route* to South Africa.[53] In August,

1941, the President and Prime Minister Churchill met secretly and agreed upon the joint declaration of August 14, 1941, which became known as the "Atlantic Charter." As American determination to see that Great Britain got sorely needed supplies increased, and as American armed patrols moved farther into the Atlantic, "warlike" incidents multiplied.[54]

His entire address of September 11, 1941, delivered by radio to his "fellow-Americans," dealt with the Nazi menace in the Atlantic; it broke the news to the public that to enforce "freedom of the seas" United States warships had orders to "shoot first" at any Nazi vessels seen within certain areas of the Atlantic designated as American "defensive waters." Roosevelt had stressed since May, 1941, that America's historic policy had insisted upon "freedom of the seas." This policy justified, according to his arguments to the American people in September, 1941, "a naval and air patrol [operating] over a vast expanse of the Atlantic" which would "protect all merchant ships—not only American ships but ships of any flag—engaged in commerce."

The American people[55] and the press[56] heartily endorsed the President's speech and his arguments for "freedom of the seas." Roosevelt was given credit not just for voicing an already established sentiment for freedom of the seas, but for creating that sentiment. He denied the rights of the Nazis to prescribe areas of the high seas into which no ships could enter without "peril of being sunk," even though he had argued at the beginning of World War II that "American merchant vessels should . . . be restricted from entering danger zones" and that those vessels which did enter "danger zones" be warned that "all such voyages are solely at the risk of the American owners themselves."[57] Similarly, he had argued early in the war that munitions should not be "carried to belligerent countries on American vessels."

Roosevelt was clearly inconsistent concerning "freedom of the seas," but the more significant fact seems to be that "freedom of the seas" as a line of argument was stressed by the President only during that particular period when the doctrine happened to coincide with Roosevelt's own desires for immediate American foreign policy and when an appeal to this "historic American policy" would forward public support of the President's actions. During the earlier period when this country endeavored to commit no hostile acts or make any breeches which could be clearly labeled warlike, the President made no mention of "freedom of the seas."

Franklin Roosevelt's arguments for America's "historic policy" of "freedom of the seas" were highly successful with his American audience. Those who favored increased aid to the Allies, those who were most vociferous in their condemnations of the fascists were, of course, ready to support the doctrine. But from no group was there any organized disagreement. Since the President had not concerned himself with the issue until late in 1941, and since his advocacy of the doctrine then implemented his avowed "primary task" of "providing more and more arms" for the Allies, he, apparently, used the doctrine to bring about his desired foreign policy rather than as an end in itself.

Roosevelt's plea for "freedom of the seas" gave the American people a moral principle with which to support a view they wanted to find reasons to uphold. By autumn of 1941, sentiment against the Axis was overwhelming. Roosevelt was the one person primarily responsible for using the phrase "freedom of the seas" during World War II to make possible the ever increasing aid to the Allies which both he and his listeners desired.

Mr. Roosevelt firmly believed it the duty and right of the executive to deal directly with the American voters. He schooled the people to anticipate and to enjoy his talks with them. Only the conviction of his advisers that he ought not use the Fireside Chat too frequently[58] prevented the delivery of far more such "intimate talks." The subjects of his Fireside Chats were the critical issues of his Presidency. After American entrance into World War II, however, he typically used his "chats" not to win support for his own policies in opposition to others in this country, but primarily to report on the progress of the conflict and to lift the morale of the American people.[59]

The language of the Fireside Chats reflects Roosevelt's eagerness to communicate his ideas to the voters. Samuel I. Rosenman suggests this spirit when he tells about the preparation of the first of these talks:

> The Treasury Department prepared a scholarly, comprehensive draft of the speech. The President saw that it would be meaningless to most people, tossed it aside without any attempt at rewriting, and proceeded to write his own instead. He dictated it in simple, ordinary language—he looked for words that he would use in an informal conversation with one or two of his friends. He found the kind of language that everyone could understand. And everyone did understand. Confidence was restored. And in those dark days, confidence was essential for a panic of bewilderment could have meant chaos and collapse.[60]

Roosevelt achieved directness and intimacy by the frequent use of the first and the second persons. He almost always referred to himself as "I" and to the voters as "you." This spirit is reflected in many of his openings:

> It is three months since I have talked with the people of this country about our national problems. . . . (Oct. 22, 1933.)

> It has been several months since I have talked with you concerning the problems of Government. (June 28, 1934.)

> Three months have passed since I talked with you shortly after the adjournment of the Congress. (Sept. 30, 1934.)

> Since my Annual Message to the Congress on January 4th, last, I have not addressed the general public over the air. (April 28, 1935.)

He likewise used many devices to make his thoughts clear and to emphasize the simplicity of his ideas. These talks with the people abound in phrases and sentences like the following: "let me state the simple fact," "let me make clear," "one more point before I close," "I want to talk with you very simply," "let me give you an example." He included as supporting material numerous simple illustrations and homely analogies taken directly from his daily conversations and from his frequent trips throughout the nation. Rosenman suggests that the efforts of many persons went into these speeches in order to capture this intimate quality.

When Roosevelt spoke to the nation on these occasions, he adopted a warm, friendly, direct, conversational mode of speech. Rosenman characterizes this manner on one occasion:

> I heard Roosevelt deliver this speech. His voice seemed to reach out right into every home in the United States. Those paragraphs, spoken badly, could have sounded very "corny"; but, as he delivered them, they expressed the deep, sincere, warm emotions of a leader who was terribly concerned about the millions of human beings whose welfare was so greatly affected by the policies of the government he led.[61]

The Fireside Chats demonstrated Roosevelt's ability to "bring the people right into the White House."[62] Perhaps for the first time in American history the people of the nation were made to feel that they knew their President personally and that they were receiving inside information first hand on important events. They were stirred and stimulated by Roosevelt's friendly informal manner; they somehow felt that they had a direct part in shaping the policies of the federal government and that Washington was no farther away than the radio receiving sets in their living rooms. Unquestionably, his continued acceptance by the majority of the American people, despite the frequent opposition of the press[63] and his occasional troubles with Congress[64] was due in important measure to Roosevelt's outstanding success whenever he carried issues directly to the people in his Fireside Chats.

NOTES

[1] Fireside Chat of June 23, 1938.

[2] Grace Tully, *F. D. R., My Boss* (New York, 1949), p. 86.

[3] Tully, *F. D. R.,* p. 88.

[4] *The Public Papers and Addresses of Franklin D. Roosevelt,* ed. Samuel I. Rosenman (New York, 1938), II, 60.

[5] Robert Sherwood, *Roosevelt and Hopkins* (New York, 1949), p. 43.

[6] There is some question as to whether this address should be listed as a Fireside Chat. It is not so listed in Roosevelt's *Public Papers and Addresses* (see Vol. VI, 483), but Sharon quotes "the editors" as explaining that they "made an 'oversight.'" (See footnote 7.) This address was delivered on a Sunday evening and began "I am appealing to the people of America tonight"; it concerned the single issue of the desirability of cooperation in the taking of the unemployment census; the success of the President's appeal in the speech was obviously of less importance to him than public reaction to his typical Fireside Chat.

[7] John H. Sharon has gathered much interesting information on procedures in these broadcasts. The authors of this paper acknowledge their indebtedness to him. See "The Fireside Chat," *Franklin D. Roosevelt Collector,* II (Nov. 1949), 2-30.

[8] *Public Papers and Addresses,* II. 60.

[9] Roosevelt's report on the Teheran and Cairo conferences, Dec. 24, 1943, was delivered from his study in the Roosevelt Library at Hyde Park.

[10] Samuel I. Rosenman, *Working With Roosevelt* (New York, 1952), p. 93.

[11] Rosenman, *Roosevelt,* p. 93.

[12] Eight required 15 minutes; nineteen, approximately 30 minutes; and one, 45 minutes.

[13] Eleven of the twenty-eight were presented Sunday evenings.

[14] See letter from F. D. R. to Frank C. Walker, February 13, 1936, *F. D. R., His Personal Letters,* ed. Elliott Roosevelt (New York, 1950), III, 554.

[15] F. D. R., *His Letters,* III, 554.

[16] "The Roosevelt Week," *Time,* XXI (March 20, 1933), 7.

[17] James Truslow Adams and Charles Garrett Vannest, *The Record of America* (New York, 1949), p. 558.

[18] Dixon Wecter, *The Age of the Great Depression, 1929-1941* (New York, 1948), p. 66.

[19] By the middle of April, deposits in the reporting member banks had increased by one billion dollars.

[20] *Public Papers and Addresses,* II, 60.

[21] John Gunther, *Roosevelt in Retrospect* (New York, 1950), p. 278.

[22] Wecter, *Depression,* p. 65.

[23] Laura Crowell, "Franklin D. Roosevelt's Audience Persuasion in the 1936 Campaign," *Speech Monographs,* 17 (1950), 48-64.

[24] Introduction to the 1937 volume of *Public Papers and Addresses,* VI, lviii.

[25] For Roosevelt's review of court rulings which had been "major blows" to his administration, see the Introductions to the 1935 and 1937 volumes of his *Public Papers and Addresses,* IV, 3-14, and VI, liii-lviii.

[26] At that time, Justice Louis D. Brandeis was 80; Willis Van Devanter, 77; James Clark McReynolds, 75; George Sutherland, 74; Charles Evans Hughes, 74; Pierce Butler, 70; Benjamin Cardozo, 66; Harlan F. Stone, 65; and Owen J. Roberts, 61. Van Devanter, McReynolds, Sutherland, and Butler had been invariably conservative in their opinions.

[27] A draft of the proposed bill submitted to Congress set fifteen as the maximum number of Supreme Court justices at any time.

[28] During his first term in office, Roosevelt had no opportunities to make appointments to the Supreme Court. Preceding presidents had usually been more fortunate in influencing the Court. Taft had named five members; Wilson, three; Harding, four; and Hoover, three.

[29] ". . . . There is no basis for the claim made by some members of the Court that something in the Constitution has compelled them regretfully to thwart the will of the people. . . . We have, therefore, reached the point as a Nation where we must take action to save the Constitution from itself. . . . We want a Supreme Court which will do justice under the Constitution—not over it. . . . We must have judges who will bring to the courts a present-day sense of the constitution—judges who will . . . reject the legislative powers which the courts have today assumed."

[30] Jeanette P. Nichols and Roy F. Nichols, *The Republic of the United States* (New York, 1942), p. 549.

[31] Gunther, *Roosevelt,* p. 296.

[32] Gallup polls indicated no successes on the part of the President, and a slight trend in favor of his opposition.

"Would you favor curbing the power of the Supreme Court to declare acts of Congress unconstitutional?" (Dec., 1936): No, 59%; "Would you favor a compromise on the Court plan which would permit the President to appoint two new judges instead of six?" (May, 1937): No, 62%; "Should Congress pass the President's Supreme Court plan?" (June, 1937): No, 58%; "Would you like to have President Roosevelt continue his fight to enlarge the Supreme Court?" (Sept., 1937): No, 68%; "Do you believe the Roosevelt administration should try to defeat the reelection of Democratic congressmen who opposed the Supreme Court plan?" (Sept., 1937); No, 73%. George

Gallup and Claude Robinson, "American Institute of Public Opinion—Surveys, 1935-38," *Public Opinion Quart.* II (1938), 378-79.

33 March 22, 1937, the Washington State Minimum Wage Act was found constitutional although it raised almost identical issues with the New York measure declared invalid in 1936. (Justice Roberts switched sides on the two decisions.) April 12, the Court found the Wagner Labor Relations Act constitutional. May 18, Justice Van Devanter, who had been conservative in most of his opinions, announced his retirement to take effect June 1 under the new Retirement Act. May 24, the Supreme Court validated the Social Security Act.

34 Basil Rauch, *The History of the New Deal, 1933-1938* (New York, 1944), p. 281.

35 "The Court yielded. The Court changed. The Court began to interpret the Constitution instead of torturing it. It was still the same Court, with the same justices." No new appointments had been made. And yet, beginning shortly after the message of February 5, 1937, what a change! " . . . I feel convinced that the change would never have come, unless this frontal attack had been made upon the philosophy of the majority of the Court. That is why I regard the message of February 5, 1937, as one of the most important and significant events of my administration on the domestic scene." Introduction to *Public Papers and Addresses,* VI, p. lxvi.

36 "[Roosevelt's] scheme for changing the trend of decisions by changes in Court personnel other than in the usual manner was completely defeated." Carl Brent Swisher, *American Constitutional Development* (Boston, 1943), p. 946. "The Court stood victor, for the principle of judicial review remained intact and unrestricted; the Court's authority as an institutional force had not been surrendered." Louis M. Hacker and Benjamin B. Kendrick, *The United States Since 1865* (New York, 1949), p. 574. "The Defeat of Roosevelt's reorganization plan was a great moral victory for the opponents of the New Deal." Oscar Theodore Barck, Jr. and Nelson Manfred Blake, *Since 1900, A History of the United States in Our Times* (New York, 1947), p. 576.

37 The American Institute of Public Opinion asked: "Should we send our army and navy abroad to fight against Germany? 84% of those questioned answered "No" after World War II had broken out in September, 1939. 95% said "No" in October, 1939. "Gallup and Fortune Polls," *Public Opinion Quart.* IV (1940), 111.

38 *Public Opinion Quart.* II (1938), 376.

39 "It is right that I should recall to your minds the consistent and at times successful efforts of your government in these crises to throw the full weight of the United States into the cause of peace."

40 "Press Indorses Roosevelt on U. S. Neutrality," *New York Herald Tribune,* Sept. 5, 1939. Ernest K. Lindley commented, "If newspaper editorial reaction is accepted as the acid test, the President's radio address of Sunday night was an overwhelming success." "Not Neutral in Thought," *Washington Post,* Sept. 8, 1939.

41 Addresses of Sept. 3 and Sept. 21, 1939.

42 Following is a typical definition of neutrality: "Neutrality . . . is the obligation to hold the scales even, to remain a friend of both belligerents, to lend support to neither, to avoid passing judgment on the merits of their war." Edwin Borchard and William Potten Lage, *Neutrality for the United States* (New Haven, 1940), p. vi.

43 His address of September 21, 1939 recommending changes in the neutrality laws was endorsed by the great majority of newspapers, regardless of political affiliation. "Majority of Papers Endorse Roosevelt Neutrality Message," *Washington Star,* Sept. 22, 1939. Prior to the President's speech of September 21, 57% of the voters with opinions in an American Institute of Public Opinion survey were in favor of changing the neutrality law. After the President's speech, a new survey found that sentiment for lifting the embargo had increased to 62%. The latter survey was taken before Congressional debate began on the issue. George Gallup, "The Gallup Poll," *Washington Post,* Oct. 4, 1939.

44 *Public Opinion Quart.* IV (1940), 111.

45 Do you approve or disapprove of Roosevelt's policies with regard to the European situation up to now? Approve, 69.2%; Partly approve, 11.7%; Disapprove, 5.8%; Don't know, 13.3%. *Public Opinion Quart.* IV (1940), 105, a *Fortune* poll released in Nov., 1939.

46 About 85% of the Americans questioned consistently answered "No" to the Gallup query of whether the United States should enter the war. "If you were asked today to vote on the question of the United States entering the war, how would you vote—to go into the war, or to stay out of the war?"

47 "Which of these two things do you think is the more important for the United States to do—to keep out of the war ourselves, or to try to help England win, even at the risk of getting into the war?"

Further evidence of the opinion of Americans in 1939 and early 1940 has been supplied by Philip E. Jacob, of Princeton University, who analyzed the "Influence of World Events on U. S. 'Neutrality' Opinion." He concluded, "On the one hand, an overwhelming majority of the American public want the Allies to win the war. At the same time, the American people are more determined than ever to stay neutral as regards military participation or financial aid to those who have not paid their debts." *Public Opinion Quart.* IV (1940), 63-64.

48 Sherwood, *Roosevelt,* p. 226.

[49] "Hopkins provided the key phrases which had already been used in some newspaper editorials: 'We must be the great arsenal of democracy.' I have been told that the phrase was originated by William S. Knudsen and also by Jean Monnet, but whoever originated it, Roosevelt was the one who proclaimed it. There was some debate at first over its use by the President, since it might seem to preclude the eventual extension of aid to the Soviet Union or to certain Latin American 'republics,' but the phrase was too good to be stopped by any quibbles." Sherwood, *Roosevelt*, p. 226.

[50] Message to Congress, Sept. 21, 1939. He boasted later, however, that repeal had been instituted as "a policy of aid for the democracies . . . [which] had its origin in the first month of the war, when I urged upon the Congress repeal of the arms embargo provisions in the Neutrality Law." Address of March 15, 1941.

[51] According to Gallup polls, December 1940, was the first time a clear-cut majority of Americans believed helping England win was more important than keeping the United States out of the war. From 60% in December, the percentage increased to 68% in January, 1941.

[52] "Wires 100-1 Favor Roosevelt's Stand," *Washington Post*, Dec. 31, 1940.

[53] The facts were a bitter condemnation of submarine warfare and Nazi methods. The vessel had been sunk within thirty minutes from the time of the first warning. It was sunk without provision for the safety of the passengers and crew, who were left afloat in small lifeboats from two to three weeks until they were accidentally discovered and rescued by friendly vessels. Roosevelt branded the act as "outrageous," as that of "an international outlaw."

[54] For brief details of the sinking of eight merchant vessels by the Nazis between August 17 and October 19, 1941, see Wheeler B. Preston, "American Involvement," *American Year Book, 1941* (New York, 1942), p. 75.

[55] More than twice as many people approved as disapproved when the Gallup poll asked them, after the speech of September 11, 1941, whether "the United States navy [should] shoot at German submarines or warships on sight." "Gallup and Fortune Polls," *Public Opinion Quart.* VI (1942), 140-174.

[56] "Press Comments on Roosevelt's Speech," *New York Times*, Sept. 12, 1941. "Editors Appraise F. D. R.'s Address," *United States News*, XI (Sept. 19, 1941), 16.

[57] Message to Congress, Sept. 21, 1939.

[58] Stephen Early, Roosevelt's Press Secretary, explained: "Mr. Roosevelt would call in his staff and tell us, 'I think I'll go on the air next week and talk about such and such.' There would be a discussion to see if it would be advisable for him to speak on such a subject at that particular time. Nine times out of ten we advised against his going on the air for we didn't want the Fireside Chat to lose its appeal to the people. The President wanted to go on the radio many more times than we would allow him." Sharon, *Franklin D. Roosevelt Collection* II (Nov. 1949), 10.

[59] Roosevelt delivered approximately the same number of Fireside Chats after the entrance of the United States into World War II as before. Although some of these attracted tremendous listening audiences (such as the address of Dec. 9, 1941, following the attack upon Pearl Harbor, and his report, Dec. 24, 1943, of his conferences at Teheran and Cairo), in no one of them did the President support a point of view opposed by a significant number of his listeners. His address May 2, 1943, following Federal seizure of the coal mines, was delivered to an American audience containing a relatively small but extremely hostile minority.

[60] Rosenman, *Roosevelt*, pp. 92-93.

[61] Rosenman, *Roosevelt*, p. 175.

[62] Sherwood, *Roosevelt*, p. 42.

[63] In 1940, for example, Roosevelt won the election with a popular vote of 27,000,000 to Willkie's 22,000,000 and an electoral vote of 449 to 82. However, the "700 daily newspapers that thus far have declared their support of Wendell Willkie for President have a combined circulation of 16,387,145 against an aggregate circulation of 5,332,905 for the 216 that have come out for President Roosevelt." "Willkie Holds Heavy Lead in Press Backing," *New York Times*, Aug. 31, 1940.

[64] Note, for example, the relatively minor fluctuations in Roosevelt's popularity as determined by public opinion polls about every three to six months from late 1937 until December 1939. (*Public Opinion Quart.*, II (1938), 377; III (1939), 583; and IV (1940), 85. Yet within this period, from January to August 1939, Congressmen were far more critical of Roosevelt and much less inclined to follow his wishes than at any previous time during his Presidency. The Congressional session was typically described by such headlines and articles as: "Congress Opens Fight to Take Back Powers," *New York Times*, July 2, 1939; "Congressional Revolt Dominates National News of the Summer," *Scholastic*, XXXV (Sept. 18, 1939); "Congress Checks Up at Box Office, Dramatic First Act in its Fight with Roosevelt, *Business Week*, Aug. 12, 1939; "Adjournment Ends a Chapter of Presidential Defeat," *Newsweek*, XIV (Aug. 14,1939), 11, and "Congress Quits, . . . Clash Marks End," *New York Times*, Aug. 6, 1939.

Rexford G. Tugwell (essay date 1956)

SOURCE: "Franklin D. Roosevelt on the Verge of the Presidency," in *The Antioch Review*, Vol. XVI, No. 1, March, 1956, pp. 46-79.

[In the following essay, Tugwell surveys the challenges faced by Roosevelt at the beginning of his first term of presidency in 1933.]

Early in the day on 4 March 1933 Franklin D. Roosevelt with his new official family, asked the blessing of God on the administration which was about to begin. He might well ask for Divine assistance; no other seemed adequate to the national exigency. The degeneration of the economic system had not been stayed by the prospect of a change in Washington. If anything, conditions were worse; and they were certainly worse in the whole financial structure. In fact the sickness which, until February, had been kept fairly far away from the centers of finance by one means or another[1] was now reaching those well-defended citadels, the metropolitan banks. The trouble was like a flood which rose higher and higher, inundating one after another of the supposedly safe islands of the economy. Just during the few days preceding 4 March, the governors of additional states had proclaimed what were euphemistically called "bank holidays"—which meant, in ordinary language, that the banks were closed to prevent the drawing out of funds by depositors; they were no longer considered safe, and withdrawals had reached such proportions that further out-payments would be impossible.[2]

Many of the anticipatory Democrats who had invaded Washington to celebrate the taking-over were unable to pay their way and there was some embarrassment. The spectacle of silk-hatted and formal-coated politicians scrounging around for the cash they needed to meet their bills had its comic side. But it can hardly have seemed comic to Franklin[3] and those with him who were now picking up responsibility as Hoover, Mills and others of the outgoing crowd laid it down. He may well have prayed more earnestly for assistance on that day than on any of the other occasions when he had assumed new public duties.

He had a choice to make; or, rather, he *had* had a choice to make, for about certain matters his mind was already made up. He was praying for help, not for guidance. He had concluded that it would be best to attempt the restoration of confidence, gradually reopen the solvent banks, and wait until later for reform. It is credible that he might have used the crisis in another way. He might have set up a substitute for the old system which had broken down under pressure. It was time for a genuine national banking structure: the semi-private one had failed disastrously. He chose not to do that for reasons known only to himself; they were not confided to anyone. I can only venture here the suggestion that the restoration of some order in the economy was, in his mind, so urgent a matter that he adopted the quickest and easiest means to this end. The American people needed a renewed confidence in their institutions. This was something he could give them. A new banking system might not be perfectly designed; it might not work well at first, and might have to be tinkered with. This was not a time for risking doubt of the new administration's competence or of his own wisdom.

It may seem to a later generation absurd that there can have been such urgency. To suppose that in the United States known to them there can have been a genuine danger of civil violence, a breakdown of discipline, so that familiar institutions—police and justice, supply and distribution, transportation and communication—might so largely cease to function as to create an emergency, seems to them a fantastic exaggeration. But those who lived through that time and had some responsibility will always be conscious of the narrowness of their escape.

What do people do who have no money? There were those who had been wondering about that for several years. There were now upwards of twelve millions who were unemployed, and who had been out of work for a long time. They had no income as of a right. They might get something from the local authorities and they might participate in the sporadic and scattered efforts to start public works, but there was nothing to be counted on. Their provision for their families might break down altogether; perhaps, on occasion, it had already broken down. There were many, indeed, who had had to learn what to do without money. There were many interim makeshifts—selling household goods, borrowing from usurers, applying for private charity—but when these failed there was a last resort—the soup and bread lines for food and the Hoovervilles for shelter. The bread lines by now had lengthened until they stretched down streets and around corners; and often supplies ran out before the hungry had all been fed. And the Hoovervilles were sprawling obscenely on the garbage dumps and wastelands of every city periphery.

The terrible strain on people's bodies and minds from endless insecurity and hardship had tended to intensify and to spread. Unemployed men and women could not pay rent unless they were helped; nor could they buy food or clothes or provide shelter unless they were helped. The help, even when it came, was never enough. And when landlords and storekeepers were not paid, neither were the builders of houses nor the manufacturers of goods. When these could not collect, they could not repay loans at the bank or meet their other liabilities. This was why factories were closed or working part-time; it was why building had stopped; it was why, finally, the economic sickness had spread to the banks.

It was no longer only the unemployed workers who had to learn what to do when they had no money. People much further up the scale of living were within sight of having to find out too. There was still a vast difference between them and the unemployed. They had claims on income, at least; and the poor had none.

Both, on inauguration day, were in fact equally moneyless—the one group because they had none coming, the other because their claims were not honored.

Two resorts were used in various localities when currency was no longer available because banks were shut: these were barter and the issuance of script. Barter was useful when there could be direct exchanges; but it was only by the merest chance that in so highly specialized an economy as that of 1933 sellers and buyers could make direct contact. People who lived in cities hardly ever had any goods useful to the producers of food in the countryside. Industrial goods came from factories and individuals seldom had them to dispose of. But barter was used to a certain limited extent where the conditions permitted it to be organized. Script was found to be somewhat more useful. It could represent goods and could pass easily from hand to hand. When, however, too much was expected of it, exchange broke down. It had to be guaranteed. And when it got too far from the source of issue, recognition for it was only doubtfully granted.

Both these extra-legal devices gradually declined in use as the emergency passed and the banks reopened. There was a time, however, at the worst of the currency shortage, when in rather wide areas they proved indispensable.[4]

Conservatives were indeed worried almost as much by the various ingenious devices for meeting the emergency as by their actual troubles. It was an added reason for demanding that something be done at once. Their voices, as a matter of fact, were louder than those of the workers, who, on the whole, had undergone their ordeal with amazing patience. The President-elect knew about the unemployed. If, in his travels, he had not noted the smokeless factory chimneys, seen the idle on the street-corners, and glimpsed the empty railroad trains, he had those by him who could tell him about the amazing state to which the proud democracy had fallen. His wife, Eleanor, for instance, suffered in sympathy with the involuntary poor; so did Frances Perkins; and Franklin's own state relief organization (whose assistant director was Harry L. Hopkins) had been swamped with the rising demands for assistance.

So he knew. He knew also about the farmers. They had tired of poverty, of debts they could not pay, of losing their land and their homes by foreclosure. They were strongly inclined to approve the *status quo ante*; they wanted nothing changed except their own present inability to make a profit from farming. They were also die-hard individualists, the thorniest of all citizens for bureaucrats to organize. And a majority of them were Republicans, as befitted citizens with such predilections, even if many of them had, in anger and resentment, voted against Hoover. Conservative as they might be, their resentments now had the upperhand, and it was they who were showing most generally the symptoms of a riotous indiscipline, their usual preference for order making the protest much more terrifying than it otherwise would have been. Many a foreclosure sale, undertaken with all due process, was stopped by threats of violence. Until a conspiracy among the newspapers to maintain optimism got under way, there were many available accounts of such happenings during the winter. At sales in Pennsylvania, the auctioneers were bid five cents for a cow, five cents for family furniture, and five cents for the farm buildings. Hard-faced neighbors circulated among the crowd to see that

no one bid more. Out in Iowa milk-trucks were stopped on the highway and dumped. Not for starvation prices, the farmers said, would they furnish any more produce to the city markets.

Incidents of this sort had multiplied. They were now a daily occurrence in many neighborhoods.[5] It was true that Hoover had proposed, and the generally hostile Congress had agreed to pass, a bill to ease bankruptcies. It would have some effect; but it had not yet taken hold. The Reconstruction Finance Corporation was lending to states so that the furnishing of relief should not entirely stop. Furthermore, large loans were being made to businesses, to railroads, and to manufacturers, as well as banks, to keep them going. And all these measures might have had some effect except that the spreading paralysis all the time outran the measures taken to check it. Unemployment increased, loans were soon exhausted; and more and more were called for. There was no end in sight, not even any visible slowing of the decline. The enormous loan funds seemed to disappear without trace, leaving only an unpayable obligation.

II

In such circumstances those who knew best how fast the degeneration was spreading could hardly be blamed for grasping at immediate remedies and forgetting for the moment any hope of reform. That, at least, was the reaction Franklin had. It was he, more than anyone else, on whom responsibility was descending with the momentum of a juggernaut. He may well have prayed, in the old church across Lafayette Square from the White House, for time as well as for wisdom. But of time there was none. Such wisdom as could be managed must be used instantly. And wisdom to be of use must already have been available for several days.

One rather skeptical historian, Richard Hofstadter, has remarked that what seemed to the nation on that day the inspired and winged words of the inaugural address were actually trite and commonplace. Exhorting Americans to abjure excessive caution and once more to be bold and forthputting; telling them they had nothing to fear but fear itself—this was, as can be seen in the chilly light of later scholarly assessment, only another version of that "restoration of confidence" which had been Hoover's ruinous theme. It was the same idea businessmen were always harping on.[6] It was what Baruch had counselled as a campaign device. It had been the burden of the Pittsburgh speech during the campaign. Restore confidence, it had run, and business will recover. When business recovers, unemployment will disappear and the banks will again be secure![7]

How was it that when Franklin asked for confidence, courage began to reinfuse the whole nation? There can be no doubt that it happened. Even those who were no better off than they had been before stopped feeling sorry for themselves and looked around for opportunities to improve their lot. There was an unmistakable renewal of hope and optimism. The access of good feeling was, it must be admitted, largely just that—a feeling. But it was traceable to the relief people felt in knowing there was to be a change. No one, for a long time, had believed that Hoover knew what to do, or that, if he did, he would be able to do it. He was discredited. But Franklin would at least make new efforts without being controlled by stifling preconceptions. Also—and this was important—he had the power to act, because the Congress was Democratic too. Moreover, he had given an impression of vitality and initiative from the moment of his nomination when he had broken precedent, flown to Chicago to accept the party's designation, and spoken heartening words.

There was a most astonishing improvement from one week to the next. The week before inauguration was one of despair. The sinking spell seemed to be more and more beyond any human control and fright was almost palpably present in the air. The week after inauguration, the reversal was like the change of an ocean tide in high latitudes. Confidence did come flooding back and its return had the same irresistible volume as the outward flow. Did Franklin cause the change? Why, if this was to be so, did not the *prospect* of his accession have more effect? The historian dislikes having to answer such questions as these. He dislikes especially making the admission that the trite words of a man, flung out into the ears of a listening people, could so change the course of events, yet the facts of those March days have to be dealt with.

Such a change as happened at once is certainly not easy to start, since it requires a reversal of feeling throughout a whole nation; but it is even more difficult to sustain and to enlarge. The words of the inaugural may have been only another version of the "threadbare" confidence theme, but there was this difference between what Franklin had to say and what his predecessor had been saying: Hoover had addressed his exhortations to businessmen; Franklin addressed his words to others in the community. In fact businessmen could find little comfort in what he said; to them it sounded as though he was making promises to others which would require of them some novel humiliations. Others, however, very obviously found new hope in what he had to say even though it might be difficult for later analysts to detect just what it could have been. They, however, lacked the impression of the strong, warm voice speaking to the multitude before him and to all those who sat by their radios and waited with faint hope. A miracle was so much desired that perhaps they created it; but it must be said that Franklin's *élan,* his soaring vigor, his conveyance of a cheerful unafraidness—all these—played a great part.

Then, too, the accusations he made undoubtedly helped. The devils were whipped again as they had been during the campaign. Business, he said, had been the cause of all the trouble. And businessmen had abdicated their responsibilities. He would shoulder these. And no one henceforth would be allowed to carry on as the wicked ones had in the years just past. "We are," he said, "stricken by no plague of locusts . . . plenty is at our doorstep, but a generous use of it languishes in the very sight of supply." This was because "the rulers of the exchange of mankind's goods have failed through their own stubbornness and their own incompetence. . . ."

He went even further. There was the much-quoted passage about the "money changers" who had "fled their high seats" in the temple of civilization. "We may now," he said, "restore that temple to the ancient truths." He then went on to speak of ethics and of those who had betrayed their sacred trust. To such conduct there must be an end. There could be no confidence while it was tolerated, for confidence "thrives only on honesty, on honor, on the sacredness of obligations, on faithful protection, on unselfish performance."

This was one needed change, but it was only one of attitude; actual reconstruction required more drastic changes. Above all, "this nation asks for action," he said, "and action now." Then he got down to the hard policy. He summarized it in two paragraphs:

> Our greatest primary task is to put people to work. This is no unsolvable problem if we face it wisely and courageously. It can be accomplished in part by direct recruiting by the Government itself, treating the task as we would treat the emergency of a war, but at the same time, through this employment, accomplishing greatly needed projects to stimulate and reorganize the use of our natural resources.
>
> Hand in hand with this we must frankly recognize the overbalance of population in our industrial centers and, by engaging on a national scale in redistribution, endeavor to provide a better use of the land for those best fitted for the land. The task can be helped by definite efforts to raise the values of agricultural products and with this the power to purchase the output of our cities. It can be helped by insistence that the Federal, State, and local governments act forthwith on the demand that their cost be drastically reduced. It can be helped by the unifying of relief activities which today are often scattered, uneconomical, and unequal. It can be helped by national planning for and supervision of all forms of transportation and communications and other utilities which have a definitely public character. There are many ways in which it can be helped, but it can never be helped merely by talking about it. We must act and act quickly.

If it is said—as it has been said—that this was not much of a program to offer an almost fatally sick nation, that, I think, must be admitted to be true. Part of it was inoperable, part was trivial, and none of it went to the heart of the matter in a remedial way. It is, however, a fact, which everyone who lived through that time can attest, that the sick nation enlarged the words and the intentions far beyond their face value. Their therapeutic effect was just next to miraculous. The cure, whatever it was, then and there began to take effect. It must have been, when all is said, the magic of leadership which was responsible.

III

Franklin that morning had called at the White House. He and Hoover had ridden together in the big black limousine to the Capitol, Franklin chatting cheerily, Hoover tired almost to death from his long immolation, hardly responding at all. Later, Hoover had sat among those who listened while Franklin took the oath on the old Dutch family Bible, repeating after Chief Justice Hughes the solemn words of consecration (instead, as was customary, of only saying "I do"). Hoover's face was a study in distrust as Franklin launched into his speech. He almost visibly winced as the "money changers" were referred to. There was only dull resignation as the "program" was elaborated. Afterward, he made his way, forgotten and alone, back to the White House and presently out of Washington, while Franklin rode triumphantly down Pennsylvania Avenue through madly cheering crowds to take possession of the Presidency. There was a New Deal.

What the biographer has to acknowledge at this juncture—beginning on this day—is that he begins now to deal with entirely different phenomena than he has dealt with before. The man whose career he has been following has, up till now, been an entirely accountable person. He has got where he now is by scheming, by conforming and compromising, by hard work, by faithful performance of his political business—and all of this attended by good luck. Every step can be understood, even the recent election to the Presidency, which was much more a vote against Hoover than for Franklin. Now, however, the man who recited the uninspired inaugural was transformed into an almost unimaginable embodiment of American hopes. From now on he became a symbol. And the person was gradually lost in the President.

Naturally when, by election, the people had chosen a new leader, he had begun to move in a heightened glare of publicity. There had been endless curiosity about him and about his family for months before inauguration. The smallest detail had been news. The Governor of New York had had little privacy; but he had had a good deal more than the President-elect. And that well-enforced sense of ownership which people feel about their chief executive is a far more demanding sentiment than is centered in any governor. On the morning after election, the Secret Service of the United States had taken charge of his person. Thereafter the security controls would never be lifted until his death. The alert young men always near, trying to be inconspicuous, but watchful of his safety, were evidence that he was public property.[8]

What Americans saw was a man well-schooled in being a public figure and well-equipped to become the symbol of great office. They were prepared to approve the inaugural even before it was heard; and this receptivity accounts for easily half its effect. Since July there had been a show of energy, of fearlessness in the face of adversity, and even of gaiety, which contrasted with what they had seen in Hoover. The contrast was in fact about as complete as it was possible to conceive. Cold aloofness was being exchanged for an eloquently expressed sympathy; and they liked it. Even the normally hostile press was kind; the reporters were always mostly friendly; and even the publishers knew how much their readers longed for a change. They compromised with principle for the time being.

The reporters know, being shrewd analysts, that the air of confidence and cheerfulness was partly assumed, that actually Franklin could not possibly be so sure of himself as he seemed. But they could not be certain how far into the causes of distress he actually saw, or the extent to which a program of action had actually been shaped. He might be better prepared than they had thought; he seemed not to be uneasy. The truth was that some preparations were further along than they guessed by inauguration day. Others were far from being ready for action; only their outlines were beginning to be visible.

Normally the Congress would not have met until the following January; and in the usual circumstances the new President would have had months in which to prepare a program of legislation. Until the last moment Franklin anticipated such an interval. For effect, it had been supposed, he would call a special session, but it would be limited to a few matters which were well along—relief, mostly, and public works. Even when the banking crisis made a special session imperative, there was not at first any intention of asking for the kind of performance which would be put on during the hundred days. That spectacle would be pretty much improvised as events developed. But although it thrilled the whole nation, it did not exactly come as a surprise. The economic situation had by then become so acute that it was more a fulfillment than an expectation.

The man who had been a successful governor, who sailed his own craft along the foggy New England shore with his big and handsome sons for a crew, who received important men and ordinary men with the same tolerance and good nature,[9] who was at home in Warm Springs with his numerous family of convalescents, who went off with his friend Vincent Astor for a cruise in Caribbean waters, on the fabulous *Nourmahal*, apparently unconscious of any possible criticism, and who, on landing, was shot at by an assassin whose bullets missed miraculously, and who exhibited thereafter no nervousness whatever—such a man might well be expected to meet the exigencies of office intrepidly. No, his performance after 4 March would be no real surprise.

It would, however, be accepted with profound gratitude as a kind of fortunate blessing. Once more the nation had found a champion in time of need. There was even a little complacency mixed with the prevalent adulation. Good fortune was a blessing which did not have to be deserved; the nation was inclined to feel that a change of luck was justified by the years of very bad luck which had been undergone without abandoning balance and humor.

The psychology of accession, and specifically of accession to the Presidency, has two well-marked sides: what happens to the public is one phenomenon; what happens to the new President is the other. There nearly always tends to be a general euphoria, intensified when the new incumbent has been elected after an exciting campaign in which strong contenders have been engaged. There is something about a democratic majority which impresses even those who do not belong to it; the general impulse is to believe that the choice is right. Consequently inauguration is very often attended by a hope that for once representation will prove to be a salutary principle. Regardless—or very nearly regardless—of the start made by the incumbent, good wishes flow to him and he is borne along into his first term on a tide of approval.

Reciprocally he discovers, sometimes quite suddenly, that he is president not of his party, or of those who voted for him, but of all the people. In this discovery there is a kind of exhilaration which, if he is well-prepared and knowledgeable, will stir him to the formulation of an actionable program in a hurry. If he is not prepared, and not a quick learner, the period may pass without any real accomplishment, and disillusion will settle over the political scene which so short a time ago shone with optimism.

The initial months of new administrations have long been called "honeymoons" for lack of a better term to describe the bemused mutual regard of people and president. Political writers apply the term more narrowly to the temporary abatement of the perennial quarrel between the executive and the legislative branches. They are apt to ascribe it rather cynically to good behavior in hope of favors. And favors from the executive are certainly to be had, patronage being among the most important. But the real secret of Congressional tameness is the uneasy sense among the Representatives that they are outside the mystical union of president and people which they dare not invade. He has, after all, been elected by all citizens, they by only a comparatively few. In his single person there is concentrated the very principle of representation. Legislators, being politicians, are impressed, in spite of themselves, by the latent power implied in this oneness. They are afraid, initially, to challenge it, or to risk its invocation even to a small degree. They behave, for the moment, with almost comical circumspection.

They watch, however, with hard and experienced eyes for the inevitable weakening of this bond, ready to assert their own powers at the first signs of weakness. They will go as far in attrition on the executive, then, as they dare to go. Infrequently they trespass too daringly, rouse his ire, cause him to "go to the people." They retreat sullenly from their positions if he succeeds—and almost invariably he does succeed.

Presidents differ enormously in their initial understanding of their situation. Many in the past have come to office without appreciating its complexities. These have wasted the honeymoon period, have lowered the leadership level of the Presidency, and have passed into history as "weak" incumbents. The presidents who, on the contrary, loom large in history have been those who were identifiable

as "strong." What this means is that they were leaders, that they understood their representative nature, understood, also, the inherently divisive nature of the legislative branch, and that they used the power flowing to them from popular regard to coerce all the converging but diverse interests into yielding consent to a program in the public interest.

There have been presidents who started off badly and then recovered; and the measure of their intelligence is usually said to be the rapidity and extent of recovery. Those who were initially worst are sometimes supposed to have been made that way by legislative experience. Being schooled in opposition to the executive, they are ambitious, as they take office, to "get along with the Senate," as several of them have said. Truman was one of these. But there have been presidents without this experience who have started out in the same way—Cleveland was one of these and Eisenhower was another. So the source is doubtful; but the fact is not. Presidents do differ in their conception of the office as they assume it. The best reputed presidents have been the ones who have had an initial understanding of the necessity for leadership; but there have been several who did make quick and complete recoveries—the kind made so conspicuously in recent times by Truman.

These general remarks are made to place Franklin at the time of his inaugural. Obviously he falls into the category of those who understood the realities of the situation before entering on it. He was prepared to exercise leadership at once and without more mealy-mouthed equivocation than was necessary to comply with the amenities. A good legislator to him would be one who would go along: a bad one, a reluctant cooperator. He did not expect that policies, or the laws to effect them, would originate in the legislature. They would originate with him, or in his neighborhood, and it would be his responsibility to see that they were accepted. More perfectly than any president of all the long line, except his predecessor Theodore, and, further back, Jefferson, he grasped the fact that presidents are first of all Chief Legislators. One who senses this can follow much more intelligibly his actions during the interval between election and inauguration as well as the occurrences of the hundred days.

IV

The interval did not result in the settlement of all difficulties and the arrival at policies governing all the attitudes to be assumed; but much more was done than is usually realized. Some of what was done was not wise and was not permanent, but that it was done at all goes further to show how well the new President understood his responsibility. It is true that everything was, so to speak, compressed or syncopated, and decisions were hurried because of a fiscal crisis so demanding that much else which might have progressed to decision was delayed or neglected. But there was never any doubt about the decision-making power or about the forthcoming of essential directives.

Garner, of Texas, feeling his oats a bit as Vice President-elect, was persuaded by his business friends to head a movement for a national sales tax, something they had hoped and worked for ever since the income tax had become burdensome; and now that even Hoover's budgets were unbalanced, and there were obvious new obligations coming up to be paid for, they tried again through Garner. Franklin, without such emphasis as would embarrass Garner too much, let it be known that he expected to balance the budget by reductions of expense and by enlargements of the income tax. Half of this was distressing to the conservatives; the other half they probably were too realistic to believe. But all the Progressives rejoiced aloud.

There was, however, an intimation, in this difference, of a schism among Franklin's followers. It was not created at this moment; it had been latent and inevitable all along; but it would enlarge and become more and more difficult to compromise. It would be impossible to estimate the proportion of his time for the next decade that Franklin would have to spend holding together the uneasy, mutually hostile, elements of his support; but it would be very high. It would be exhausting too. Both sides would be unreasonable and demanding. But Franklin would never quite reach a position where he could do what he must have longed to do innumerable times—make his choice and let the reactionaries go.[10]

He could see what was happening well enough, but it was part of his talent for finesse that he prevented an outright split even so early. It is arguable whether the resulting compromises paid; but they were inherent in the Roosevelt political method.

The conservatives may have been made suspicious by the small evidence of intransigency furnished by the sales tax rejection; but there were other issues about which they had no real complaint. One of these was the solution of the banking crisis. The measures determined on would not solve the problem. There would be a long struggle about inflation—or, rather, about the means taken to inflate, during which the shades of Silver Dick Bland and Cross-of-Gold Bryan would seem to haunt Washington. And throughout the monetary crisis Franklin's temporizing would rate as a miracle of compromise. But the conservatives would in the end be more unhappy than the inflationists. The debts owed to them would be repaid in cheapened dollars. This grievance would rankle and erupt repeatedly for years to come.

This inflationary policy was not yet settled on. But it was obvious to financially sensitive watchers that a decision of sorts was moiling about in Franklin's head. They could not pin it down; he was evasive; he sometimes seemed, even, to be on the other side—had he not made that speech at Pittsburgh during the campaign which castigated Hoover for having an unbalanced budget and for not having reduced governmental expenses? This seemed to lead straight to acceptance of the "restoration of confidence" principle for which Baruch, Young, and others stood.

On the other hand, the Progressives in the Senate and the House were waiting with obvious impatience to renew the push for federal relief, for enormous public works undertakings, and, what was perhaps worse, for economic planning councils. These would not only require higher taxes, and, even with that, very likely an unbalanced budget, but would also set up a system for bringing business into some sort of discipline to be administered by the government.

Old Carter Glass, "father" of the Federal Reserve Act, had a revision of the act almost at the passage point in the lame-duck session. His bill had been explored earnestly by Franklin who had promised support for its passage. But somehow Glass did not trust him. He had heard disquieting rumors; and ever since the election he had taken a sour view of Franklin's passages through Washington during which he had "sent for" Democratic leaders. Cordell Hull might comply with such requests; but Glass regarded Franklin as an upstart, and said so. He was probably amazed when Franklin, in February, offered him the secretaryship of the Treasury. So, when they heard of it, was everyone close to Franklin. It was even more inexplicable than the offer to Hull of the secretaryship of State. Glass grumpily refused. Whether Franklin was relieved or not, no one knows. But Hull accepted. And whether Franklin was gratified or not, no one knows. One thing is certain. With both Glass and Hull in his cabinet, it is impossible to think of him doing what was subsequently done, and what, even then, he must have been considering.

Why then did he ask Glass to be a member of his cabinet? This and other selections can only be understood—and then not altogether—by exploring somewhat more at length the theory on which he must have been acting in putting together his official family. I say "must have been," because I do not know; I can only infer. But that is all anyone will ever be able to do. In this, as in so many similar important issues, Franklin allowed no one to discover the governing principle. He might have to change principles and it would be embarrassing to admit such inconsistency. It was much better to make no commitment, to act without saying why. He was sometimes annoyed by the resultant guessing and generalization, especially among the newspapermen—he told one once to put on a dunce cap and stand in the corner—but his freedom was maintained even if with some difficulty and embarrassment.

His first group, however, was pretty obviously intended to consolidate his coalition and to make it likely that even the most reluctant members would accept his directions. It was weighted heavily with the Southerners whose support he had to have—they would have control of the Congressional committees—and who were likely to have the most difficulty in swallowing the medicine he expected to prescribe. It must be said, however, that Franklin had less anticipation of difficulty with the Southerners than he ought to have had. His confidence in his own ability to get along with people, which was almost illimitable, led him to underestimate the differences in opinion between North and West and South. Actually antagonisms would prove to be so irreconcilable that he could only occasionally find a modus vivendi. But trouble of this sort would not begin until after the honeymoon period was over. During the crisis and the good feeling of the first few months, only such Southerners as Cotton Ed Smith, Chairman of the Agricultural Committee of the Senate, showed their true colors. It was Cotton Ed who had prevented the bill for farm-relief from passing in the lame-duck session before inauguration, although it had passed the House and had been endorsed by Franklin.

Most of the Southerners were amenable to party discipline. They were first of all party men; they were experienced in Washington because they had been there even in Republican times. And if they could never hope to rise to the Presidency, they could control the legislative branch through seniority. Moreover, they had a strong hold on the party machinery for the same reason. They influenced nominating conventions, in a kind of negative way, through the two-thirds rule. That is, they could usually prevent the nomination of any candidate of whom they disapproved and could trade strongly for second place on the ticket—which might, sometime, yield the Presidency through death.[11]

No Northern Democrat in the White House could afford to ignore such strength; he had to compromise with it. That compromising had begun in the trading at Chicago which had yielded the Vice-Presidency to Garner of Texas. It was no more than an extension of it which yielded the Southerners three cabinet posts, and would have yielded four if Glass had not happily refused. These three were Hull, Swanson, and Roper. Of these Hull and Swanson were out of the Senate (and Glass would have been; so, also, Walsh, if he had not died on the eve of becoming Attorney General) and could be supposed to be influential in that body. This was especially true of Hull, who had been so long a faithful party man.[12] It is probable, however, that Franklin at this time—although he confided in no one—did not think of this as compromising but rather as a gathering in of resources to fortify his own position. His other selections emphasize that probability. Ickes was, as is known, the choice of the Congressional Progressives. He was suggested to Franklin by Senators Johnson, Cutting, Wheeler, Norris, and Costigan, after at least two of these—Johnson and Cutting—had refused. The secretaryship of the Interior was especially valued by Westerners because of its implications for land and water development; and to the Western Progressives because of their fear of the power interests, and their hostility to financiers and other traditional Eastern enemies. Dern, from Utah, was not so well known as a Progressive, nor was Henry Wallace. But neither could be thought of as conservative; and Henry Wallace embodied, because of his father's martyrdom to Hoover in the Harding cabinet, the whole agricultural movement of the Mid-West. Cummings, who was substituted for Walsh at the last

moment, was a stop-gap; he had been intended as Governor General of the Philippines—but he was a Connecticut politician with solid party ties.

The most difficult of the cabinet posts to fill, because of the current fiscal troubles, was the secretaryship of the Treasury. William H. Woodin, who was finally chosen, was a kind of compromise among many possible choices. He was a businessman and a financier but he was not a banker and he was untouched by the contemporary scandals. Moreover, he was one of the small group who had made early contributions to the Howe-Farley activities which had given Franklin's presidential bid its momentum. He added nothing to Franklin's strength; but also he was not vulnerable and not so averse to unorthodox procedures that he could be expected to make trouble if some of the measures fermenting in Franklin's mind should actually be decided on.

This was the list, except for Farley and Perkins. The Postmaster Generalship does not have the importance which should belong to a Cabinet post; but by tradition it had gone almost invariably to the political manager who had acted for the President. He sat with the others less as the head of the postal service than as the vice-head of the party. Farley's reputation was, at the moment, high; and his widespread organization was ideologically neutral. He was as favorable to Southerners, for instance, as to Democrats from New York, when it came to party matters. The one difficulty was in the West, where Progressivism was at least half Republican even when it was wholly Rooseveltian. Farley found it impossible to understand that the La Follettes, the Wallaces and others like Norris in Nebraska and Olson in Minnesota, were more important to Franklin than the Democrats in their respective states. The coalition of West and South in his mind was all within the Democratic party. He could not comprehend mavericks. This, in the end, would prove to be one of the reasons why he and Franklin would have to part company. For the moment it was only a lesser problem among many which, Franklin could see, would require some attention; but he had no real apprehension about this or any other political difficulty. He could depend, at any rate, on himself.

In the matter of the secretaryship of Labor there were several considerations. The first of these was that Franklin was not really sympathetic to organized labor. He did not trust labor leaders and had none of the rapport with them which he felt at once when farm leaders sat down across the desk from him. He said to the farm leaders at the very first: "Make up your minds what you can agree on and that we will do." That was the line he followed throughout. But he felt no such trust in labor men. Moreover, he had to deal with the schisms represented by several claimants to labor's prerogatives. In other recent administrations the secretaryship of Labor had gone to a union official, as the secretaryship of Commerce had gone to a businessman, and that of Agriculture to a representative of farmers.

Franklin could not choose a union man without offense to his rivals; but also, what was more important, he obviously did not consent to the theory which would require the choice of any union leader. Cabinet members should not represent interests—except a political interest. They should represent the public as the President did. This difference between Franklin's attitude and that of some of his predecessors was fundamental.

This difference accounted, also, for his not choosing some of those for cabinet posts who seemed to commentators at the time the most likely selections. As a matter of fact, his cabinet list was not foreshadowed by any of the wiseacres. Those who were prominently suggested included those who had been his rivals for the nomination, starting with Al Smith and including Baker, Ritchie, and Byrd. Also prominently mentioned were Owen D. Young and Norman Davis, both of whom had been well-publicized visitors since election. But, also, most often mentioned of all was Bernard Baruch, who had been so prominent in Wilson's administration and who was still known to control a bloc in the Congress.

When the cabinet came to be announced the two omissions most noticed were Smith and Baruch. For both these it had been expected that a place would be made. And Franklin at once began to betray some uneasiness about Baruch. Concerning Smith he had no qualms. Smith's backing he thought could be reached in other ways. Of Baruch, however, he was afraid. Baruch was a kind of myth. He was supposed to be a wise and disinterested statesman—a thought carefully cultivated by the clever propaganda of publicity agents. Actually, Franklin knew, he used his power over Congressional votes for at best whimsical purposes, and at worst ones not unrelated to his business interests. Franklin was determined not to have the disposer of such influence present in his intimate counsels. Cabinet members could be troublesome enough when they began to be thrust forward by the groups which gathered naturally behind their departments; it would be intolerable to have as Secretary of State, for instance, a person who could be suspected of manipulating the international exchanges and who had intimate Wall Street connections.

Franklin paid a certain tribute in favors to Baruch's power, but not probably such a price as he would have had to pay if he had been inside the cabinet. Baruch maintained an apartment at the Carlton Hotel which was something of a headquarters, already, for his intimates among the politicians and administrators. Congressmen foregathered there with business lobbyists; there also many government administrators went to be blessed and to forestall opposition. Franklin would know what he was doing when he made Hugh Johnson and George Peek heads of the two most important recovery agencies. He was reckoning to gain Baruch's support and still keep control of Baruch's henchmen. It may have been a mistake. Inside a year both had gone or were going amid a vast hullaballoo. And Baruch was doing a good deal of harm in setting up opposition to Franklin's program. The

consequences of Baruch's influence will never be calculated. Progressive measures of all sorts suffered; many of them had to be abandoned; and favors went to those whose opposition in principle to all Franklin stood for was notorious. But Franklin pretended to be oblivious. Occasionally he had Baruch to lunch or asked him to do some special job. But never until the final stages of the war did he consider inviting him into the official family, and then he changed his mind before making the offer.

Baruch, or Young, or even Baker, as Secretary of State or of Commerce would have been regarded as fronting for an interest. If Franklin would not have a representative of labor or of agriculture, but rather chose "experts" in each field, how much less would he have a representative of business when business was so low in the public regard, and was, as a matter of fact, about to be brought under investigation and discipline. For the Commerce post he chose Daniel C. Roper, who was an old-time Democrat from South Carolina. Roper was a smooth and effective politician of conservative bent. He was not suggested for the post by anyone except possibly himself; but he had been one of the early and expectant visitors to the President-elect who had been marked by the reporters.

Franklin's holistic principle did not prevent an interesting deployment of the businessmen who had been Roosevelt supporters even though none were asked to join the cabinet. Straus, who wanted terribly to be Secretary of Commerce, and who could see no reason why he should not follow the tradition which had landed other businessmen in that post, had to be satisfied with the embassy in Paris. Similarly Morris went to Belgium, and Bingham to London. In quite another vein Franklin repaid an old debt by sending Josephus Daniels to Mexico. But on the whole, Franklin could be seen to have chosen an official family representative of Democratic and Progressive strength which yet did not personify any interest inimical to general or public interest centered in himself. His attempt would not prove to be wholly successful; but it served well enough during the earliest stage of his administration.

v

Franklin understood, even if he did not accept, the prevalent additive attitude. To an extent he shared it, as who would not, having had his education and experience. There was very little in all he had been taught to impress on him the principle of social unity, especially as concerned the obligations of individuals or corporate enterprises. Every one around him all his life had been of the view that general well-being was arrived at by the separate achievements of many contributors, his teachers no less than the politicians and businessmen with whom he had associated. His teachers expressed it by accepting and elaborating the theory of free competition in economics and rights without obligations in politics. The putative hidden hand, spoken of by the economists, which led individual enterprisers to establish the good of the whole, was basic. It was, in fact, a euphemism for nature; and the processes of competition were supposedly controlled by natural law.

The nineteenth-century economists had derived these conclusions from observing the operations of business enterprise. They formalized the practice of competition. They also justified that practice by pointing out that fairness to all was achieved when sellers and buyers, producers and consumers, workers and employers carried out free bargaining. The market, when it was not restricted in any way, would tend toward stability. Every bargainer would get not only all he was entitled to but all he could get in the long run; therefore the system deserved defense. It was an ethical as well as an economic concept. It was translated into political principle as laissez faire. The state would only upset the natural balance by any interference. Matters would come right only if left alone.

Throughout Franklin's life this had been the accepted doctrine of all those to whom he had owed regard. Yet some instinct from time to time seemed to make him doubtful. It will be recalled how little respect he had as governor for some businesses, particularly the utilities. He was clear, certainly, that much regulation was justified in revisionist competitive theory as keeping competition really free. But practical considerations—in the field he had studied most, electric power—had led him to think government ownership often necessary. It could not be said that he had become a socialist. No one ever heard him advocate public ownership of *all* business or even all the power business. But even outside the utility field, he had concluded that drastic regulation might be needed, so drastic as to run beyond merely the establishment of freedom. The stringent protections for workers in New York State were one example. But the depression had enforced the same lesson concerning banking and finance. Just now there were turning over in his mind various approaches to these problems which would not be found in the books of laissez-faire believers.

One of the phenomena of American life which would doubtless puzzle the historians of the future was the persistent clinging to a philosophy of individualism in the midst of progress toward collectivism. That philosophy was not, for instance, allowed to interfere with the development of businesses into empires of embracing extent. One of the necessary characteristics of this progress was the swallowing up or destruction of competitors, and those who were thus swallowed or destroyed could not have regarded themselves as possessing the freedom they heard about and believed in. The anti-trust laws had been intended to stop this kind of thing; but they had notoriously not succeeded. Not even the most convinced laissez-faire believers had been able to say how big an enterprise would be beyond toleration. Growing could, therefore, not be stopped, and incidents along the way, such as the elimination of competitors, could not be stopped either. Because they were small they could not survive. They were comparatively inefficient; and efficiency too was an American objective.

But, theoretically and officially, Americans clung to laissez faire. Socialism was a word with opprobrious connotations. Even collectivism was a dangerous idea. No politician could survive who did not praise free enterprise, proclaim his devotion to the small businessman, and denounce big businessmen and socialists alike. Their leaders had emphatically not told Americans that they were, in fact, members of a collectivity, that each lived in a close and necessary association with others, and that the good of one had become the good of all. This was the more remarkable because of the particular experiences of that generation, the most startling of all being the very depression they were now in the midst of. There can hardly ever have been lessons more thoroughly misunderstood. Because this was so the remedy most favored was more of what had caused the illness.

The depression had affected more than one or a few persons and enterprises; it had touched all of them; its miasmic influence had indeed reached far beyond the confines of one nation. The whole world was involved. This had not happened because of anything one or a few individuals had done. It was a sickness of the whole. And nothing could be clearer than that general remedies, not those directed to individual rescues, would be needed to effect a cure. They were being considered even now. And Franklin's consideration was not only of ways to relieve hardship—although he often spoke of that—but also of ways to reactivate the economy. If the economy "recovered," there would be employment, higher incomes, improved well-being, better business. Such was his reasoning.

The industrial system was just beginning to be regarded—largely as a result of the depression—as an organism subject to curable illnesses. Those who so regarded it might be a small circle, but they were influential. The Taylor Society, for instance, made up of efficiency engineers, had lifted their eyes from shop management to business policy. And academic economists were extremely knowledgeable about business cycle theories. There was current talk about stimulation, stabilization, and other similar means for recovering. And each had its own devices. Stimulation, it was argued, could be administered by direct additions to purchasing power, and it might be better to find the funds for this by inflating, since this raised the price level and enabled debtors to get more dollars with which to pay off their creditors. Getting rid of the current load of debt was an important preliminary to the resumption of loaning; and until loaning began, business would be restricted. Stabilization was to be reached, it was said, by getting prices into balance again so that each industrial group could make fair exchanges with other groups—so that each could work for the other and each would be the other's consumers.

Franklin probably had been exposed to more theory during the last year—proposals for recovery involving general principles—than he had heard before in all his life. And although the end sought was practical, still the ideas were inclusive and had to do with the general good rather than that of any individual or group. The national economic health was in question. If it improved, everyone and every group would improve along with it. This was the holistic view.

Franklin was not really very much at home in the realm of ideas. His was a mind which dealt much more pleasurably with arrangements of people and things. And he had a predilection for hanging on to concepts he had at some pains thought out in the past. This, however, was not so strong a leaning that he failed to see facts or to grasp the obsolescence which often overcomes concepts. He knew that some fairly precious notions had to give way to others which were more precious. On the whole, it has to be said that, by the time he became President, he had an equipment of traditions, preferences, attitudes, and values—as well as an array of talents and a fund of experience—peculiarly suited to the tasks before him. Perhaps as important as any item of his equipment was his vigorous instinctive reaction to challenge. This was a kind of driving force. It forbade inaction when there was something to be done. Then there was the noblesse his father had taught him and which was part of the Christianity he professed. It was wrong to tolerate injustices. Then too he had a politician's attitude toward inconsistency. He knew the public memory was short and that he could change his mind without penalty if he had not made—as he seldom did—embarrassing commitments on principle.

So he considered the nation as a whole but also had a genuine outgoing concern for disadvantaged men and women. He thought of agriculture; but he remembered that there were farmers. He saw that finance was a system; but it was one which financiers ran—well or badly as the case might be. His holistic or collective thinking ran concurrently with his older sympathies and understandings. It was pleasant to think that relief for the unemployed put a stop to hunger and cold at the same time that it stimulated the production of goods. He was inclined to revert to suspicion that men's and women's characters were undermined if they were not required to earn the income they received, and so he favored work relief rather than grants.[13]

This and other illustrations of a similar sort show how varied and mixed Franklin's ideas and preconceptions were. His make-up, although it had been given structure and substance by Groton, Harvard, and his other experiences, was such a generally open one that new facts, thoughts, and experiences flowed into it and were tested quite readily and quickly for their values. Sometimes they were rejected, sometimes accepted; the bias was not—as in so many minds—toward rejection. Yet there is no understanding him if it is not always recalled that what was accepted *had* been evaluated and that the evaluation had been in terms of the ends to be served.

Those ends were political and moral. There was the good of the nation to be considered. The nation should be fair, even generous in dealing with its citizens; but they too should be just to their nation; people should have duties as well as privileges; they owed something to each other

and to their country. He saw his own immediate duty as a multiple one; to find ways which led to recovery, and, beyond that, to improvement. So he consented to a system of temporary relief, both for individuals and businesses—and this meant not only grants to the poor, but also loans to distressed businesses, moratoria on old debts, and assistance to home owners, all of which would be attended to in the first rush of legislation. But he went further. Presently he would urge the Civilian Conservation Corps to improve forest resources, as well as to take youths off the city streets; would set up the Tennessee Valley Authority as a sample attack on the various ills of a distressed region, and begin to outline a system of public works which would improve all the facilities of common life. And following on, much more general ends would be sought through the AAA and the NRA. The American people were not going merely to recover; they were going to be lifted toward new levels of living, toward stability and security. Nothing less would discharge the obligation the new President felt to be his.

This seemed to be a complicated enough task, although its elements, if not its details, had become fairly clear by inauguration; but there were others of which hardly anyone as yet seemed conscious. Americans, most of them, were struggling with disaster, and there were few of them who could spare consideration for anything beyond economic recovery—for themselves and for the country. But the President of the United States must consider the nation's security along with its well-being. Almost alone among his countrymen Franklin was beset in 1933 with uneasiness about events occurring abroad. Almost alone he understood that their implications for the nation's future were very serious indeed. It should be remembered that Hitler came into power in Germany just thirty-three days before Franklin was inaugurated in Washington.

VI

As he looked about the world with which he would have to deal as the constitutional shaper of foreign policy, there were strange phenomena to evaluate. There was Communism in Russia, Fascism in Italy, Nazism in Germany, and totalitarianism in Japan—all aggressive and all activated by fanaticism. There was, in fact, very little governmental democracy left anywhere except in Britain, France, and other Western European nations, and this was complicated by imperial glories which were fast fading and, as they departed, were ingloriously muddied by disputes with colonial peoples. And even the nearest neighbors of the nation were dictatorships, many of them naked and cruel ones. South of the Rio Grande there were few practicing democracies.

The New Deal would also inherit many ongoing arrangements made in accordance with tradition or with Republican interpretations of it. These he must appraise; but he was usually clearer in his own mind about these than he was about domestic problems. A representative instance of this was the Disarmament Commission which had been at work in Geneva for several years. This had been a matter of real concern to Hoover, who was a Quaker, and who had hoped for some achievement which would mark his administration as having made a notable contribution to peace. But progress had been disappointing. It happened that one delegate of the United States was an experienced diplomat and was also a Democrat. This was Norman Davis; and soon after election Franklin began to explore with him the probability of further progress. The prospects did not seem favorable, especially since the League of Nations was evidently in process of disintegration. The aggressors—especially Japan, Italy, and Germany—were in no mood to submit to sanctions even if the other powers had had the courage to impose them. Armaments seemed more likely to increase than to diminish. It was true that a treaty limiting navies had been negotiated and signed in 1930; but land armaments, although the Treaty of Versailles had called for reduction, had been, for twelve years, the subject of temporizing committee meetings which had got nowhere.

Hoover's move to reactivate negotiations had been made early in 1932, through Ambassador Gibson. These proposals called for "the reduction of armies in excess of the level required to preserve internal order by one-third, together with the abolition of certain 'aggressive' arms."[14] Concerning this, years later, Hoover had to remark sadly that: "The conference adjourned to meet again late in the year, by which time I had been defeated in the election and was without power to carry on."[15]

Franklin rather hoped to pursue Hoover's beginnings to a conclusion. He would keep Davis on the job; and he himself, after studying carefully the possibilities, would make a new appeal, not through the somnolent League, but directly to the heads of states.[16]

But it was all too obvious that the totalitarian nations were intent on objectives which were utterly inconsistent with disarmament. They meant to have their way, by force if necessary. And it was this intention which Franklin felt he might well have to oppose. It was not clear in the winter of 1933 that aggression at any cost was an irrevocable determination of Hitlerians, although in August 1932, Germany had withdrawn from the disarmament compact. But the signs were ominous, and Franklin studied them with intent concern. About Japan there could be no doubt; and he did not hesitate to associate himself openly and without reservation with what was called "the Stimson Doctrine." This was the first glimpse Americans had of the approach to foreign policy of the incoming President. Some of them liked it, but more did not—those who paid any attention at all. It required no particular foresight to anticipate that ultimately much more serious differences would arise from the decisions just now in the making. These might even bring war. This too Franklin accepted without hesitation as probable. From the very first he felt that war might come; but he felt, also, that only appeasement would avoid it, and that perhaps only temporarily.[17]

These decisions were only shaping; and just possibly there might be a change in Germany or Japan. Franklin in any case was determined also that the nation should steadily oppose the totalitarian aggression he feared was developing. These were the beginnings of fateful policies. But, terrible as their implications were, Franklin entered on them at this time without hesitation. They must have been ones he had pondered over in the past and thoroughly settled on without anyone having been consulted. He came to them quickly and decisively; they could not possibly have been improvised.

Another ongoing matter needing immediate attention was the London Economic Conference. But to this he had been alerted since his first meeting with Hoover soon after election. Gradually his differences with the old policy had become clearer; and by now he knew that in these negotiations the war debts owing the United States could not be thrown into a general bargain with monetary stabilization, trade relations, and disarmament. Hoover had agreed with the Europeans that they made one package. Franklin was determined not to jeopardize the rest by bringing in the debts about which American opinion was bitter. And all of Hoover's efforts to commit him had failed. There were at the moment negotiators in Geneva working on the agenda for this London conference in the spring. He must take them over, revise their instructions and, before the meeting actually took place, devise a comprehensive economic foreign policy. It was no slight task for an economic amateur who had as many confusing advices as were coming to Franklin. Still it must be done. Here too, however, he was further along toward a conclusion than anyone realized—or would realize until he sent the "bombshell" message to the conference itself. Where the conclusions came from puzzled everyone. But there can be no doubt that he had them.

This was much more characteristic than was usually recognized. The propensity for arriving at settled attitudes without consultation was hidden by the extensive consulting he carried on all the time. What was missed about this was that when he opened subjects for discussion he was often already far along in making up his mind, and that, anyway, he had reached a stage at which he did not mind having it known that his interest was engaged. It is sometimes important to people to know what a president is considering. He has to be secretive to a degree for public reasons. Added to these, in Franklin's case, there were private ones. Exposure was repugnant to him if it led to the opinion that he was weak or uncertain; he must always appear to have confidence in his own judgment. It will be recalled that this was true when as governor he made the utilities the object of a long-run political persecution. When he talked with his advisers about the behavior of the power companies it was only to stock his armory. He had already come to his conclusion. It was so about Japan. When he talked with Stimson on 9 January at Hyde Park, he was not open to conviction; his conviction had already been arrived at. It might surprise the Secretary; but it would not surprise him more than others who had thought themselves in Franklin's confidence.[18]

Many times as President he would "spring" decisions on the public and even on those close to him. But he had been doing this for a long time. It had not been noticeable when he had been a lesser figure and the decisions of lesser consequence; but in a governor, and even more in a president, it was a notable, even a genuinely fateful, characteristic. It ran to the process of judging. It tended to remove decisions from rationality, to enlarge the role in them of instinct, of gathered values, of preconception. Franklin was certainly an exaggerated example of non-rational decision-making.

It was of moment, therefore, what were the values, the attitudes, and the stores of experience from which he arrived at policy. This is something difficult to reduce to generalization. It is, however, easily illustrated. Consider, for instance, his instant but persistent reaction to Hitler, as he too made his bid for world leadership. It is not only striking how concurrent their emergence into national leadership was; but also that their estimates of each other were made once for all as they were first ranged in opposition.[19] Throughout the ensuing years, as each gathered power in his own way, each was also to fix his nation in a position of such implacable opposition to the other's that trial by force could not in the end be avoided.

How much an antagonism of traditions, tastes, and personalities this was can be seen now by looking back along the era which was just opening in 1933. A merely casual examination of the incidents involving both nations during that time reveals a steady deepening of repugnance, a gathering of resolution, and a growing unwillingness to seek accommodation. But this design, so apparent to the backward look, was not apparent then. Franklin was not well enough understood, for one thing, for many people to have judged the meaning of his apparently casual comments or his oblique references. Nor, in fact, was there enough attention being paid to any of the developments abroad so that a president's concern would be much noticed. When it was noticed, there was no premonition that ultimate war might be involved. Americans took leave, as they always did, to make fun of foreign peculiarities; and Hitler almost at once became a comic figure. He was never comic to Franklin, whose approach to him was, in fact a curious mixture of detestation and dread. He disliked Hitler so much that he could not see him as a serious collaborator in leadership; yet he understood the mighty force such a man of malice might ultimately have at his disposal.

The active antagonism, it must be said, was mostly on Franklin's side. Hitler was in process of making the same double mistake his predecessors had made before 1917, of first ignoring and then misunderstanding the American temper, and of underestimating the current American leader.

Wilson had gone to war for reasons quite other than had developed in Franklin's mind, and, as will be recalled, much more reluctantly than the younger man had approved. Franklin, when he first sized up Hitler, saw in him a personification of the same traits he had regarded as so revolting two decades earlier. And this time they appeared in exaggerated form: Hitler seemed to Franklin almost a caricature of the insensitive, overbearing, gross, unsportsmanlike, and aggressive German. This was the picture which would be so endlessly detailed in later years by cartoonists and correspondents; it was seen at once—long before American reactions had become stereotyped—by the new American President.

There was, however, one difference between Franklin's and most others' estimates. He had a healthy respect for the organizing genius of the Germans even under the control of so fantastic a character as Hitler; he had, after all, been a schoolboy in Germany for some time. He noticed, and spoke of, something not many others saw—that behind Hitler was the whole of German industrialism. The great capitalists gave him financial backing; his national socialism was oligarchical. They regarded him as a perhaps unsavory but still a useful front for their designs. And this connection meant a good deal to Franklin, who was already sensitized to the sinister machinations of the international financial system and the world-wide cartels which centered in Germany.

Another thing: Franklin understood from the first, also, that there were allies and collaborators in the United States who would find totalitarianism congenial. Many of them for years had been admiring Mussolini for seeing to it that "the trains ran on time," a kind of symbol in their minds for a discipline they thought the United States could do with more of. These admirers were of various sorts: for one instance, those who had some actual association, perhaps well hidden, with the Germans; and for another, those who had ideological sympathies with Nazism. The first were powerful but few; the second were, however weak at the moment, potentially many. There are always the ignorant, the malicious, the unstable, and the envious to whom appeals of the Hitlerite sort can be made with effect—appeals to racial prejudice, to jealousy, or simply to hate and to vengeance for fancied wrongs.

Huey Long, Father Coughlin, Milo Reno, and John Simpson were plying the trade of agitation; and they had many lesser collaborators. America was far from immune to the virus working in Europe. It may well be that Franklin dreaded, more than anything else, as he surveyed the presidential job, the inevitable encounters with this spreading disease. He knew how difficult it would be to counter it; but he would, he knew, have to try—not directly, at least at first; but indirectly. He studied the means at his disposal with the dispassionate eye of the expert.

One thing can be said—and it was a matter of immense importance to the country after the winter they had just lived through—he was not awed or paralyzed by the complexity or the vastness of the task he faced. He was like a strong swimmer in a rushing stream. He liked the opposition. It was something to overcome with joy because he was so much alive and so competent to meet the challenge.

NOTES

[1] Mostly by allowing the banks in small communities to fail. Their assets were heavily weighted with foreign bonds and other doubtful obligations sold to them by the metropolitan banking houses.

[2] Not all the banks were insolvent; that is to say many of them had assets enough to cover their obligations. But these assets could not be realized immediately and the demand for cash had exhausted the available reserves of currency.

[3] The subject here is spoken of by his first name somewhat as his pastor might do in speaking to Higher Authority of Thy Servant, Franklin.

[4] Part of the same improvised machinery were the self-help workshops set up in various places. Some were naturally more successful than others, depending on the management. That in Ohio finally began to look something like a system within a system. The unemployed working to produce things which other unemployed could use; and these, in turn, producing to exchange—this was clearly an alternative to formal capitalism. It was viewed with the expected suspicion by conservatives and tended to wither as relief became more easily available and as works projects were developed. But it was one of the chief counts of the critics of Harry Hopkins' successive organizations to care for the unemployed that in various places these improvisations had been encouraged. Those who managed the local relief agencies, however, were usually undoctrinaire folk. Anything, they felt, which would assist those beaten down by the failure of industrialism was to be fostered. These were the heroes of the long depression. They were already hard at work before Franklin came to Washington or Harry Hopkins had been heard of outside New York.

[5] The following paragraphs are quoted from *Time* (6 February 1933, p. 17):

Near Bowling Green, Ohio, 800 ugly-tempered farmers last week assembled at Wallace Kramp's place to watch a finance company foreclose its $800 mortgage. Bidding began at 15¢ for a spring harrow. When the company's representative raised it to $1.55, somebody shouted: "That's the guy what holds the mortgage." Promptly the bidder was marched well out of the bidding range where he was rescued by a sheriff. Wallace Kramp's neighbors bought in all his things for $14, handed them back to him.

At Nampa, Idaho, where a United Farmer's League was in process of organization, one William Ai Frost jumped up and shouted: "Just give me a six-shooter and four red-blooded men who will have the nerve to follow me and a will to make the legislature put through any law we want."

At Overton, Neb., any outsider who dared to bid at the foreclosure sale on Mike Thinnes' farm was threatened with a ducking in the horse trough at the hands of 200 farmer friends. Mrs. Thinnes bought in cows for 10¢, horses for 25¢, tractors for 50¢—at a total cost of $15.

At Perry, Iowa, approximately the same prices prevailed at the foreclosure on George Rosander's place when 1500 of his friends collected to restrict the bidding. The holder of a $2,500 mortgage collected precisely $42.05.

At Le Mars, Iowa, 25 farmers gathered to block foreclosure of a mortgage on the home of Dentist George Washington Cunningham. They explained that they all owed Dr. Cunningham for professional services.

Events such as the above were what John Andrew Simpson, president of the National Farmer's Union had in mind last week when he told the Senate Committee on Agriculture: "The biggest and finest crop of revolutions is sprouting all over the country right now."

[6] It was what a whole parade of business leaders counselled before a lame-duck investigating committee of the Senate over which the retiring Reed Smoot of Utah presided, but which, after 4 March, would be chaired by Pat Harrison of Mississippi. It was as pitiful an exhibition of futility as can ever have been displayed by the responsible men of a leading nation. *Cf.* for an extended reporting *The New York Times* of various February dates.

[7] *The American Political Tradition,* Chapter XIII, p. 312, 1951:

When Hoover bumbled that it was necessary only to restore confidence, the nation laughed bitterly. When Roosevelt said: "The only thing we have to fear is fear itself," essentially the same thread-bare half-true idea, the nation was thrilled. . . .

[8] Two chiefs of the White House detail during Franklin's Presidency have written accounts of their stewardship: Colonel Starling and Michael Reilly who succeeded him.

[9] Including such varied contemporary giants as Owen D. Young, Cardinal Mundelein, Huey Long, and Thomas Lamont.

[10] Not, at least until his third term was ending and Willkie had been rejected as a Republican candidate. He would then feel the time right and begin negotiations with Willkie. Willkie's death—and his own shortly afterward—would intervene and nothing would result. *Cf.* Rosenman, *Working with Roosevelt,* N.Y., 1952.

[11] The attack on the two-thirds rule in 1932 was withdrawn from with some embarrassment by Farley; but in 1936 it was abrogated without any great difficulty. So, often, are consequential changes made if the right time is waited for.

[12] He had, for instance, been chairman of the National Democratic Committee back in the '20's.

[13] He clung to this notion even when it was less practical, certain that he was right when trusted friends differed with him. On this very point, as it would happen, Frank Walker, one of the most loved of them, would feel strongly enough to leave his official family later on—but still without changing Franklin's determination.

[14] *Cf. The Memoirs of Herbert Hoover; The Cabinet and the Presidency*, p. 340ff.

[15] *Op. cit.*, p. 356.

[16] This would be done on 16 May 1933. Hoover always considered that Franklin had done something unethical in not acknowledging that he—Hoover—had invented the formula for abolishing offensive land arms. In a rather sour note in the *Memoirs (op. cit.,* p. 357) Hoover said: "The nations apparently ignored the proposal, and I was informed that they considered the League should not be so sidetracked. In any event, all American pressure was discontinued, and all American interest was allowed to die."

[17] An account of Secretary Stimson's concern that his Far Eastern policies should be perpetuated will be found in his memoir *On Active Service in Peace and War*, N.Y., 1948, pp. 282ff. Franklin was quite ready to check Japanese aggression directly. Perhaps I may note that I was one of those who objected seriously. I thought the liberal forces in Japan ought to be built up; and the Stimson doctrine played directly into the militarists' hands, making war much more likely than it might otherwise have been. I thought it was not our business to intervene between the Japanese and the Chinese. The Chinese in the long run would take care of these invaders as they had so many others.

[18] *Cf. op. cit.,* p. 293: "The most important point to Stimson was Mr. Roosevelt's quick understanding and general approval of his Manchurian policy. Stimson warned him that the League was approaching a final statement; Mr. Roosevelt promptly agreed and promised that he would do nothing to weaken Stimson's stand. The following week the President-elect went even farther in a public statement in support of the administration's Far Eastern policy. 'It was a very good and timely statement and made me feel better than I had in a long time.' (Diary, January 17, 1933). In a second meeting in Washington on January 19 Mr. Roosevelt remarked 'that we are getting so that we do pretty good teamwork, don't we?' I laughed and said 'yes'."

[19] Hitler was allowed to form a cabinet by the aged Von Hindenburg early in February, and, as Franklin was choosing his cabinet, Hitler was also choosing his. It may be worth while to recall Hitler's list, considering how much its names were to mean: Vice Chancellor, Von Papen; Foreign Minister, Von Neurath; Interior, Frick; Defense, Von Blomberg; Finance, Von Krosigh; Economics, Hugenberg; Labor, Seldte; without Portfolio, Goering.

There was a general election on 5 March the day after Franklin's inauguration. This election had been preceded by a campaign of outrageous violence, including the Reichstag fire, and was won by the Nazis—that is they gained 92 Reichstag seats, so that with collaborators, they had a clear majority. Hitler then assumed dictatorial powers, suspended by decree most of the Republican constitution and entered fully on that desperate career of international aggression and internal hoodlumism which was to alienate most of the world and finally bring a belated retribution. Hitler had been rising since the '20's on a tide of German resentment against the Treaty of Versailles. He now considered himself loosed from all restraints and the loosening approved by his people.

Dorothy Borg (essay date 1957)

SOURCE: "Notes on Roosevelt's 'Quarantine' Speech," in *Political Science Quarterly*, Vol. LXXII, No. 3, September, 1957, pp. 405-33.

[*In the following essay, Borg focuses on the political contexts of Roosevelt's 1937 "quarantine" speech—an address aimed at checking the aggression of the Axis powers—and examines the domestic response to U. S. involvement in restraining belligerent nations.*]

The "quarantine" speech which President Roosevelt made at Chicago on October 5, 1937, is generally assumed to have been a landmark in our foreign policy, showing the point at which the President made a definite decision to take a strong stand against the Axis Powers. It is also widely supposed that, because of evidence at every hand of the country's hostility to the speech, Mr. Roosevelt, quite justifiably, felt compelled to relinquish his determination to deal firmly with the totalitarian states. Yet the further one examines these assumptions, the more they seem to invite rethinking.

I

Turning to the speech itself, the most popular interpretations are that the President was announcing that he had decided: to reverse his foreign policy, abandoning the isolationism of our neutrality legislation for a Wilsonian type of collective security; or to use sanctions against Japan to stop the hostilities in China; or to initiate forthwith a program for the application of sanctions against future aggressors—meaning the Axis Powers. However, a consideration of the events surrounding the speech, and of its text, suggests that the President was probably only engaging in a groping and intermittent effort, which he had been making for some time, to find some sort of a plan which would avert war between the dictatorships and the democracies. If so, the "quarantine" speech should not be regarded as an indication that, in the autumn of 1937, Mr. Roosevelt resolved to embark upon some strong and specific policy toward the Axis countries but rather as indicating that he was still pursuing a variety of nebulous schemes for warding off catastrophe.

In order to discuss further both the popular interpretations of the speech and the interpretation just advanced, it is necessary first to look at the two areas where the material lies which make more detailed discussion possible: the President's search for a program to avoid war and the story of the writing of the Chicago address.

As the international crisis deepened in the 1930s, Mr. Roosevelt was intensely concerned over the aggression of the Axis nations. In keeping with a pattern he tended to follow almost instinctively, he seems to have felt that, if he advanced notions of his own about possible means of meeting the crisis, he might stimulate others to build on his suggestions until a solution was found. His first great effort to dramatize the concept of searching for a program to stabilize the world situation was made in connection with the Buenos Aires Conference of 1936. It will be recalled that this conference was convened at his suggestion to strengthen the Inter-American peace system. However, both the President and Secretary Hull proclaimed over and over again that the purpose of the conference was not just to work out a scheme for the maintenance of peace in the Americas but to evolve a program which, speaking in general terms, could be copied by the rest of the world. And it was precisely to draw the attention of as many people as possible to the universal significance of the proceedings at Buenos Aires that Mr. Roosevelt made his own dramatic trip to the conference.

Two features of the developments at Buenos Aires have a special significance in connection with later efforts to formulate a program to deal with the problem of war and peace.[1] One was the over-all character of the Buenos Aires agreements. The sixty-seven agreements arrived at by the Conference constituted a comprehensive plan divorced from any commitments to sanctions. They emphasized the value of a so-called constructive approach to peace, by which was meant an attempt to settle the underlying causes of friction that give rise to wars. They also emphasized the need to develop machinery to adjust disputes by peaceful means or, if this proved impossible, to limit hostilities once they occurred.

The second significant factor was the discussion about plans for organizing, in wartime, the countries that were not parties to the dispute. One idea was that an arrangement should be made so that these nations would adopt a collective neutrality that went further than anything as yet embodied in the Inter-American peace system. This view was vigorously pushed by Secretary Hull in his famous Eight Pillars of Peace speech delivered at the outset of the Conference.[2] It was incorporated in the draft convention presented to the Conference by the United States Delegation; for the convention would have committed neutral American countries, in case of war between two or more American republics, to apply laws comparable to the neutrality legislation existing in the United

States.[3] While the United States proposal was not adopted, the determination to develop the concept of collective neutrality in the Americas remained a fixed part of our policy.

Another idea was that there should be what, for lack of a better term, may be called a collective nonbelligerency. This concept became a center of discussion at Buenos Aires because the Central American nations introduced a draft treaty based on a plan, advanced by Uruguay during the First World War, for the creation by the American states of a moral front which would adopt measures, such as the severance of diplomatic relations, that were noncoercive but not neutral.[4] In the process of watering down the Central American draft the closeness of this type of a collective nonbelligerency and a common neutrality was underscored. The purpose of both was to have the nations, not parties to the conflict, form a community for their own protection and to influence the course of the hostilities. (It was thought that a collective neutrality could, if necessary, be manipulated to favor one side or the other, as was indeed done after the outbreak of war in Europe.)[5] Moreover both the ideas of collective neutrality and of collective nonbelligerency were regarded as preventive in that, if either were incorporated in an agreement, they would serve to deter would-be aggressors.

Following the Buenos Aires Conference, the President continued to look for a program to relieve the international tension, suggesting frequently that the nations of the world might get together to work out something comparable to the achievements reached at Buenos Aires. Secretary Hull spoke similarly, both men often stressing the noncoercive character of the Buenos Aires agreements. When, for example, Prime Minister King of Canada visited Washington in the spring of 1937, Mr. Hull told him that, in his estimation, the only way of stopping the drift toward war was for England to seek the coöperation of other European countries in developing a constructive and comprehensive scheme for the stabilization of peace like the Buenos Aires program.[6] The President himself discussed at length with Mr. King the possibility of calling an international conference to set up a new world organization which would seek to maintain peace by peaceful means rather than by economic or military sanctions.[7] He suggested that new methods of achieving peace be tried such as "going after the root causes of war" so as to establish a "collective security based on the removal of war causes." Also wars should be prevented or cured by "public opinion" not by "penalty." A few weeks later the President talked along similar lines to Norman Davis, who was about to leave on a mission to Europe, indicating that Mr. Davis might explore some of these ideas with European statesmen informally.[8]

At the same time the President was groping for other means of getting the dictatorships and the democracies to make a concerted effort to ensure peace. Even before the Buenos Aires Conference, Mr. Roosevelt had spoken to friends of the possibility of stopping the trend toward war by some dramatic action such as inviting the heads of the big European nations to a meeting on board a battleship at sea where they would evolve some plan for a "lasting peace" to be achieved without commitments to coercion.[9] Word of the President's scheme reached the *New York Times* which printed a front-page article under a streaming headline: "ROOSEVELT IF ELECTED MAY CALL KINGS, DICTATORSHIPS AND PRESIDENTS TO GREAT POWER CONFERENCE."[10]

The net result of all this talk of a program to resolve the existing crisis was that, by the spring of 1937, there were repercussions even in the European dictatorships. Mussolini, in a highly publicized interview, virtually invited the President to take the initiative in bringing the statesmen of the world together to settle some of the outstanding causes of tension.[11] Hitler was rumored to have said that he would attend a conference for the improvement of the international situation if Mr. Roosevelt convened it.[12]

Perhaps encouraged by signs of possible coöperation from the Axis nations, Mr. Roosevelt, in the spring and summer of 1937, tried to take some concrete steps toward a general international agreement that would make for peace.[13] Norman Davis, on his trip to Europe in May, had long conversations on this subject with various European statesmen, primarily British and French—conversations of which he kept detailed records that have turned up in his files.[14] Mr. Davis spoke first with Mr. Spinasse, then French Minister of National Economy, and with Anthony Eden. All agreed that a comprehensive program should be developed that would tackle the three most important sources of the growing international crisis: political and economic conditions and the race in armaments. It was assumed that the United States would have to take the initiative in starting such a program but that President Roosevelt would want to limit himself to economic and disarmament problems, leaving the European Powers to settle their political controversies among themselves. In the end it was agreed that some plan might be launched, probably by calling a large international conference, in a few months—possibly September.

When Mr. Davis approached Neville Chamberlain, the latter proved to be more than sympathetic to the idea that the dictatorships and the democracies should try to adjust their differences but considerably less interested in the American concept of bringing this about through a comprehensive program undertaken by many nations. Mr. Chamberlain thought it impractical "to do everything at once" and declared that, in his opinion, political appeasement would have to precede economic appeasement and the limitation of armaments. He told Mr. Davis that the British government was doing what it could toward a "beginning of political appeasement" and had just instructed its Ambassador in Berlin to impress upon Hitler that the British wanted to establish "more friendly relations and a sound basis for peace" as soon as they were convinced that Germany genuinely desired the same thing. Mr. Davis indicated that he was quite in favor of England's trying to reach an understanding with Germany; he only wondered whether tackling the problem of

peace on a wider scale could await the outcome of Britain's efforts. In addition Mr. Davis raised the question of the possibility of Mr. Chamberlain's coming to the United States to talk with the President directly.

The President decided, after Mr. Davis's return home, to go on from where the latter had left off. Early in June, Mr. Davis wrote the Prime Minister, in the strictest secrecy, that Mr. Roosevelt would like him to visit the White House around late September.[15] The President, he explained, was ready to make arrangements immediately to have an agenda drawn up for their meeting. Mr. Davis stated also that he thought England and America should pave the way for a "broader move" to ensure peace and hoped that, within a few months, it would be possible to start a "concerted and comprehensive effort to achieve economic rehabilitation, financial stability, a limitation of armaments and peace." The Prime Minister replied that he did not believe the time ripe for a meeting with the President.[16] The British government was, he asserted, still trying to open talks with the Germans and these might provide a "valuable indication" of the direction in which it might be possible to advance, thereby serving as a useful preliminary to discussions between himself and Mr. Roosevelt.

The President was, however, too intent upon his course to drop matters here. At the end of July he wrote personally to the Prime Minister saying that he appreciated his desire to make such progress as was possible along other lines but nevertheless would like suggestions for steps that might be taken to expedite their meeting.[17] Mr. Chamberlain did not answer until two months later when he informed Mr. Roosevelt that he had no suggestions to make.[18] The international situation, he declared, was changing so quickly that any plans were likely to be obsolete almost as soon as they were made. While the tension in Europe was easing somewhat, things were still a "long way from the resumption of cordial relations between the totalitarian states and the democracies."

It was precisely at the time that the Prime Minister rejected the President's second invitation to open discussions that Mr. Roosevelt delivered the "quarantine" speech. Presumably he felt that, if an advance toward peace was to be made, he would have to try some method less dependent upon Mr. Chamberlain's initiative. Perhaps it was to encourage others to supply the necessary impetus that the President renewed his efforts to dramatize publicly the idea of searching for a plan to avert war. Parts of the "quarantine" speech (for reasons that will be clearer later) appear to have constituted one of these efforts. Another effort was started on the day following the "quarantine" speech when Sumner Welles wrote a memorandum for the President outlining a new peace program.

So much has been written about Mr. Welles's scheme that it does not seem necessary to do more than recall its essentials.[19] Mr. Welles believed that it would be easier to get the democracies and dictatorships together to seek a solution of political, economic and armament problems if they first succeeded in reaching an understanding on less explosive issues. He therefore suggested trying to achieve a general agreement on questions such as the fundamental rules which ought to govern international behavior. The President himself proposed holding a dramatic meeting of diplomatic representatives accredited to Washington, in the White House on Armistice Day, at which he would read a message designed to set in motion procedures leading to an agreement of the kind Mr. Welles envisaged. Mr. Welles thereupon put his scheme into more concrete form but the entire matter was dropped before Armistice Day because of Secretary Hull's objections. It was revived, however, in early January 1938 when it was hoped that it would, among other matters, lend support to Great Britain's continued attempt to arrive at an understanding with Germany.[20] Perhaps the best-known part of the story is that which deals with the submission of the Welles plan to Mr. Chamberlain; the latter's rejection of it during Mr. Eden's absence from England; and Mr. Eden's successful efforts to get the Prime Minister to reverse his stand around the middle of January. In the end the matter was dropped for a number of reasons but in the Hyde Park files there are revised drafts with notations by Mr. Roosevelt which show that the President and Mr. Welles continued working on the scheme until at least mid-February.[21]

It would seem therefore that the President was searching for a program to reduce the danger of war over a period which started considerably before and continued for some time after the "quarantine" speech. The programs that Mr. Roosevelt acted upon differed in many respects but all aimed at getting the various conflicting nations to coöperate in the interests of peace at the least by entering into some sort of initial agreement. The emphasis was mainly on a constructive approach to maintain peace. But it was also on arrangements which were designed: to prevent the outbreak of war by providing for a collective neutrality or nonbelligerency, the mere threat of which would act as a restraint upon aggression; or to make possible the use of pressure, through such a neutrality or nonbelligerency, in case hostilities could not be averted.

This then was Mr. Roosevelt's search for a plan which could be used to cope with the international situation. The story of the writing of the speech starts with Mr. Hull. The Secretary, on learning that the President was to make an extensive trip in late September, urged him to deliver an address, in some large mid-western city, for the purpose—according to Mr. Hull's own account—of counteracting the growing trend toward isolationism throughout the country.[22] One may take for granted that Mr. Hull also believed that an expression of the moral outrage felt in the United States against the Axis nations would be welcome at home and have a salutary effect abroad. Mr. Roosevelt, no doubt wholly in sympathy with the Secretary's views on this matter, at once agreed and asked Mr. Hull and Norman Davis to furnish him with the necessary material.

The record—pieced together from the Hyde Park files and what has recently emerged from the Davis files—shows that Mr. Davis sent the President four separate memoranda.[23] Two were mailed from Washington where, judging by a statement in Mr. Hull's *Memoirs,* the Secretary and Mr. Davis wrote them jointly.[24] Mr. Davis appears to have written the other two in New York and read them over the telephone to Mr. Dunn in the State Department before mailing them to the President. It is these four memoranda which the President took on his Western tour and, during the course of his journey, put together to make up the "quarantine" speech.

The first two memoranda (those in which the Secretary must have had a hand) contained the familiar opening passages of the speech. Without naming the Axis Powers, but obviously referring to them, they described with great forcefulness the brutal chaos being created in parts of the world by certain nations. They went on to make two points repetitiously: that disorder in any segment of the globe could not fail to affect every country; and that peace-loving nations must make a concerted effort to maintain peace. Among the statements in the original draft were:

> There is a solidarity and interdependence about the modern world, both technically and morally, which makes it impossible for any nation to isolate itself from what goes on in the rest of the world or to secure itself through indifference, isolation, or neutrality from economic and political upheavals in the rest of the world. . . .

> An overwhelming majority of the peoples and nations of the world today want to be left alone to live in peace. Nevertheless, the peace, the freedom and the security of these peoples and nations are being jeopardized by the remaining ten per cent, who are threatening a breakdown of international order and law. Surely the ninety per cent who want to live in peace under law and according to moral standards that have received universal acceptance can and must find some way to make their will prevail. . . .

> If we are to have a world in which it is possible to breathe freely and live in amity, the peace-loving nations must make a concerted effort to uphold laws and principles on which alone peace can exist.

The President used the whole of the first two memoranda with the exception of one paragraph which will be referred to later.[25] In places, he altered some of the wording and freely rearranged the sentences. One gets the impression that Mr. Roosevelt was trying to edit the text to conform to his usual terse and brilliantly vivid style of writing. But this is only an impression and certain changes may have been designed to convey a stronger meaning. The only additions Mr. Roosevelt made were a few relatively brief passages apparently inserted to supply either color or clarity.[26]

The other two memoranda, which must have been written by Mr. Davis alone, proclaimed at the outset:

It is my determination to pursue a policy of peace. . . . We recognize, however, that if we are unable to or unwilling to defend our rights and interests we will lose the respect of other nations and we will also lose our own self-respect.

This nation was dedicated to certain principles which our forebears considered to be of greater value than life itself and without which life would not be worth living. If the time ever comes when we are no longer willing or able to defend to the utmost of our ability the principles which are the foundation of freedom and progress we will sacrifice our great national heritage and will cease to have the' vitality and stamina to keep this nation alive.

The President omitted these paragraphs and in their place wrote the famous "quarantine" passage:

It seems to be unfortunately true that the epidemic of world lawlessness is spreading.

When an epidemic of physical disease starts to spread the community approves and joins in a quarantine of the patients in order to protect the health of the community against the spread of the disease.

The remainder of the Davis draft featured the sentence, "War is a contagion"—a sentence which may have suggested the word "quarantine" to the President[27]—and emphasized that "There must be positive endeavors to preserve peace." It closed with a moving statement that there was a tendency in the welter of conflicting ideologies battling for control of the modern world to overlook one basic truth: that "man, the human being is . . . the supreme end of society." But, despite its eloquence, the President discarded this passage and wrote the following ending:

There must be positive endeavors to preserve peace. America hates war. America hopes for peace. Therefore, America actively engages in the search for peace.

No doubt some of the reasons for thinking that the popular interpretations of the "quarantine" speech should be reconsidered are already evident. Nevertheless it seems desirable to discuss briefly these interpretations and the conclusion advanced here, one by one.

1. Those who believe the President planned the speech as an announcement of a decision to revert to the type of collective security embodied in the League Covenant rely mainly on two arguments: that the tone of the address was so threatening it must have been designed to indicate a drastic move of this kind; that the speech conspicuously emphasized the idea of nations maintaining peace by a "concerted effort."

But the tone of the speech existed in the original memoranda where it was clearly not meant to go beyond fulfilling Mr. Hull's purpose of awakening the American people to the dangers of isolationism and voicing moral indignation at the destructiveness of the Axis countries. It might be argued, as already suggested, that Mr. Roosevelt strengthened the meaning of the original in places but he does not seem to have sharpened the tone of the draft as a whole and, in one very important instance, he moderated it. The passage of the Davis text which Mr. Roosevelt discarded and replaced with his "quarantine" statement could certainly be construed as a warning that, if pushed too far, the United States would fight. The first version was even stronger, for it included, "We recognize, however, that a policy of peace at any price will not ensure peace. . . . This nation was born fighting for certain principles which our forebears considered to be of greater value than life itself. . . . " President Roosevelt may have seen the initial draft but, even if he did not, the interpretation to which the revision opened itself could scarcely have escaped him and it seems probable that he omitted it as too menacing.[28] This thesis is further supported by the fact that the one paragraph (referred to earlier) which the President did not use out of the memoranda sent from Washington had similar overtones.

The reference to a "concerted effort" was also in the drafts forwarded from Washington and, read in context, clearly meant that peace-loving nations should coöperate to arouse the conscience of the world to ensure the maintenance of high moral standards in the conduct of international relations. The presence of this theme is indeed not surprising, for, of all themes, it was most frequently used by Mr. Hull at this time and was also often employed by the President.

2. The idea that the "quarantine" speech was an advance notice of a declaration of sanctions against Japan resulted, to a large extent, from the circumstances under which the speech was given. The day after Mr. Roosevelt's appearance at Chicago, the League of Nations blamed Japan for the hostilities which had started in China in July and called for a conference of the Nine Power Treaty nations. Within a matter of hours, the State Department endorsed the League's position. The fact that these events happened hard upon each other gave rise to the belief that they were all part of one piece of political strategy which would culminate in the Nine Power nations adopting sanctions against Japan. However, we know today that there was no such direct connection between the President's Chicago address and the League's actions. And there is no convincing evidence to suggest that the President had decided to use coercive measures against Japan.

Sumner Welles, writing in the 1950s, seemed indeed to supply such evidence.[29] He said that in the summer of 1937 the President was far more preoccupied with the Far East than with Europe and that Mr. Roosevelt had, on several occasions, talked to him about the possibility of stationing units of the American and British navies at certain points in the Pacific to enforce an embargo against Japan. Mr. Welles stated further that, as he was in Europe during most of September 1937, he knew little about the writing of the "quarantine" speech but believed the President had in mind the embargo and quasi blockade he had mentioned earlier.

However, on further inspection, it would seem that Mr. Welles's recollections (in common with those of many others) had altered over the years; for in 1944 he had written:

> Partly because of the issues involved in the Spanish war, and partly because the real nature of Hitlerism was becoming increasingly apparent, the President determined to make a vigorous effort to persuade public opinion that in its own interest the United States should propose some constructive plan for international action to check the forces of aggression before they succeeded in engulfing the world. For this effort he selected the very heart of isolationism—the city of Chicago.[30]

Mr. Welles then went on to quote the "quarantine" speech. His recollection closer to the event does not therefore bear out the thesis that the Chicago address reflected Mr. Roosevelt's determination to use sanctions against Japan but instead supports the interpretation that the President was thinking of some program to stabilize the world situation.

3. There is a contemporary record which suggests that the President planned the "quarantine" speech to introduce a program involving sanctions against future aggressors (meaning the Axis states) which he expected to launch immediately after his return from Chicago. Secretary Ickes, in his diary entry of September 19, 1937, described a talk with the President in which the latter said he was considering addressing a letter to all the countries of the world, except possibly the "three bandit nations," proposing that all peace-loving peoples isolate those who invaded the rights of others. "What he had in mind," Mr. Ickes wrote, "is to cut off all trade with any such nation."[31] According to the Secretary, Mr. Roosevelt said further that his proposal would not apply to the current situations in Spain and China, as what had been done could not be undone; that he wanted to "evolve a new policy for the future." Mr. Ickes himself commented that "of course, if he should do this, it would be a warning to the nations that are today running amuck." The Secretary wrote further that Mr. Roosevelt asked him whether he should send this letter before or after his trip out west, to which Mr. Ickes replied that he should wait until his return.

It would seem, however, that Mr. Roosevelt could not have settled upon this plan more than momentarily, for he appears to have been considering a variety of other schemes with equal seriousness. Just before his talk with Secretary Ickes, the President told two other members of the Cabinet—Hull and Morgenthau—that he was thinking of publicly declaring his readiness to act as a clearing house for peace—a suggestion which on the surface does not sound the same as the one discussed with Mr. Ickes. Further, the day after his talk with Mr. Ickes, the President told Mr. Morgenthau that he had dropped the

idea of making such a public declaration and had decided to do nothing that would call for any response or action from any quarter, the whole thing being a matter of long-term education. It should also be recalled that at this time the President was considering still another course, not having as yet received a response from Prime Minister Chamberlain to his proposal for opening discussions which were partly intended to lead to an agreement between the democracies and the Axis countries. Moreover it is clear that he did not abandon the desire to get the democracies and totalitarian states together, for he started working on the Welles plan only three days after his Chicago speech.

4. The theory that the "quarantine" speech was not a vital landmark in Mr. Roosevelt's foreign policy but part of a groping attempt to find some means of forestalling war is based on various pieces of evidence (some already mentioned) including Mr. Roosevelt's own statements.

Immediately after the delivery of the "quarantine" speech, Mr. Roosevelt went to Cardinal Mundelein's house in Chicago where they had a long talk which was—and has remained—confidential. However, there appears in the Roosevelt files a letter written, on the following day, by Cardinal Mundelein to the Apostolic Delegate to the United States which says in part:

> Yesterday the President of the United States delivered here in Chicago a strong and important address which may affect the future peace and tranquillity of the world. Afterwards, in my own house, he continued discussion of the subject to which he had given considerable thought. He asked me whether he might invite participation of the Holy See in the movement and, as it is for the purpose of establishing permanent peace in a war-torn world, I answered him that I thought he should. . . .

> His plan does not contemplate either military or naval action against the unjust aggressor nation, nor does it involve "sanctions" as generally understood but rather a policy of isolation, severance of ordinary communications in a united manner by all the governments of the pact.[32]

The rest of the letter indicated that the President hoped such a movement for the creation of a "permanent peace" would arrest the wave of lawlessness already submerging parts of the world.

About two weeks after the "quarantine" speech, Norman Davis, who was about to leave for the Brussels Conference where he was to represent the United States, went to see the President for oral instructions.[33] Mr. Davis's notes show that Mr. Roosevelt used language similar to that of the "quarantine" speech and of his talk with Cardinal Mundelein. They state that the President remarked that, if all other procedures failed at Brussels, the countries wanting to stop the Sino-Japanese conflict and safeguard themselves from its consequences—"or in other words the so-called neutral nations"—should "band together for their own protection against this contagion." The other Powers might, for example, give China every facility for acquiring arms; or an alternative might be for "the neutrals to ostracize Japan, break off relations."

Side by side with his notes on this interview, there is, in Mr. Davis's files, a paper marked: "Handed to me by President as of possible use." This contains what must be an excerpt from an article or book which says, in substance, that the Inter-American principle of neutral coöperation, short of force, would seem to offer a useful formula for the United States in the existing situation; and it urges the President to apply this formula so as to develop a "constructive program" in which a group of neutrals, acting in common, might make their influence felt.

It would seem therefore that, immediately after delivering his address at Chicago, Mr. Roosevelt spoke to Cardinal Mundelein, not as though he had just proclaimed some drastic policy, but as though, as in the past, he were throwing out the germ of an idea with the hope that it might grow. From the tenor of his remarks and the paper he gave Mr. Davis, it appears likely that the President thought the Inter-American concepts of collective neutrality or nonbelligerency contained the seeds of some method for dealing with the world-wide situation. He suggested that "so-called neutrals" might develop a common program but he seems to have been very vague about the nature of that program. It was not to involve military action nor "'sanctions' as generally understood." But it might include, among other matters, the "severance of ordinary communications in a united manner" or a "break off" of relations. Perhaps in talking to Cardinal Mundelein, Mr. Roosevelt had in mind the possibility of developing a plan which would provide for the creation, under certain circumstances, of a moral front limited to such matters as the severance of diplomatic relations—a plan which, it might be added, would seem to furnish appropriate grounds for an appeal to the Pope. Or perhaps he was looking for a scheme which would, if necessary, permit the extension of the concepts of collective neutrality or nonbelligerency so that they might embrace a wide range of pressures up to and including economic pressures.[34] The mere existence of arrangements of this character was, as stated earlier, regarded as likely to discourage aggression so that they might be considered as a sound basis for the establishment of a "permanent peace." It is just possible that the President also thought some technique might be developed whereby if "neutrals" exercised pressures, which were not regarded as sanctions in the ordinary sense but as measures taken for their own protection against the contagion of war, they would avoid the risk of having to resort to military action inherent in systems like that of the League.[35]

Somewhat curiously, in addition to Cardinal Mundelein's letter and Mr. Davis's notes, a document which has long been familiar to historians seems to support the idea that the President had no definite policy at this stage but was contemplating a variety of possibilities including ways of embroidering on the Inter-American system. This document

is a transcript of the off-the-record press conference he held the day after he spoke at Chicago.[36] It is usually assumed that Mr. Roosevelt, anxious to avoid being questioned, was deliberately confusing in his answers to the correspondents; but it seems quite possible that the President's replies were meant to be taken at their face value.

The reporters, over and over again, asked the President to define the meaning of his Chicago address and especially of the word "quarantine." The President stuck to the following explanation of the speech as whole:

> P: . . . the lead is in the last line, "America actively engages in the search for peace." I can't tell you what the methods will be. We are looking for some way to peace. . . .
>
> Q: Foreign papers put it as an attitude without a program. . . .
>
> P: It is an attitude and it does not outline a program; but it says we are looking for a program.

At the outset a reporter had asked the President whether he would not admit that a "quarantine" must involve a repudiation of our neutrality legislation. Mr. Roosevelt declared, "Not for a minute. It may be an expansion." The correspondent asked, "Doesn't that mean economic sanctions anyway?" to which the President answered, "No, not necessarily." Later the President remarked that there were many methods of attaining peace which had as yet never been tried. A correspondent asserted that, in his opinion, to quarantine aggressors was no longer neutrality. The President stated that "On the contrary, it might be a stronger neutrality." The conference ended with this exchange:

> Q: Do you agree . . . that sanctions mean war?
>
> P: No. Don't talk about sanctions. Never suggested it. . . . Don't get off on the sanction route.
>
> Q: I meant that in general terms; going further than moral denunciation.
>
> P: That is not a definition of "sanctions."
>
> Q: Is a "quarantine" a sanction?
>
> P: No.
>
> Q: Are you excluding any coercive action? Sanctions are coercive.
>
> P: That is exactly the difference.
>
> Q: Better, then, to keep it in a moral sphere?
>
> P: No, it can be a very practical sphere.

For whatever reasons, Mr. Roosevelt seems thereafter to have shunned entering into any explanations of the "quarantine" speech. But in a Fireside Chat, on October 12, he referred to his remarks at Chicago, saying in part that it was the duty of a president to think in terms of peace not only for one but for many generations.[37] Peace, he declared, must be "sound and permanent," built on a "cooperative search" for peace by all nations desiring this end.

To me it would seem that throughout the period, before and after the "quarantine" speech, Mr. Roosevelt was moved by a deep inner feeling that it must be possible to find a formula which would avoid as unthinkable a catastrophe as another world war. In retrospect it may look to many as though nothing could have averted tragedy short of a clear-cut and determined policy against the Axis. But the chances are that the Chicago speech reflected no such policy. What governed Mr. Roosevelt's behavior could be fully understood only by a grasp of the whole history of the times illuminated by that rarest of things, a wise and informed feeling for the President's personality. Nevertheless one influence is blatantly obvious, namely, the political situation in the United States, a matter which prompted the rest of these notes.

II

The second assumption referred to at that outset is that Mr. Roosevelt, with full justification, felt that the American people wholly repudiated the "quarantine" speech and that he therefore abandoned his decision to adopt a firm policy against the Axis Powers. If Mr. Roosevelt made no such decision, obviously he did not abandon it. But this does not rule out the possibility that the President, Mr. Hull, and others in the Administration believed that the country almost uniformly rejected the speech and were influenced by their belief. Indeed there is a good deal to suggest that this was the case. Sumner Welles has described the President as "dismayed by the widespread violence of the attacks" following his appearance at Chicago.[38] Mr. Hull has stated in his *Memoirs* that the "reaction against the quarantine idea was quick and violent" and set back by many months the Administration's efforts to educate public opinion away from isolationism.[39] Judge Rosenman has likewise spoken of the nation's response to the speech as "quick and violent—and nearly unanimous."[40] The effect of this evaluation of the country's attitude upon the Administration's policy is inevitably an elusive matter. But certainly during the main international event that followed—that is, the Brussels Conference—the Administration's policy was exceedingly cautious, and cables from Washington to Norman Davis, during his conduct of the negotiations at Brussels, are marked by a worried preoccupation with public opinion at home.[41] As will be seen later, Mr. Roosevelt himself introduced this note of concern in his original instructions to Mr. Davis.

However, even a limited look (such as that which follows) at the kind of material—mainly leading newspapers and weeklies—which the Administration must have used to assess the popular reaction to the "quarantine" speech raises a question which may well be worth more intensive study.[42] Were the President and those around him, in fact, justified in concluding that the country reacted with speed, vehemence and solidarity against the speech; or were they perhaps so responsive to the criticisms of certain isolationists that they equated these with the opinions of the country as a whole?

A reading of a group of leading publications, of the type that members of the Administration must have seen, shows that the controversy over the "quarantine" speech lasted until the end of the Brussels Conference in late November. Because the speech was immediately followed by the League's denunciation of Japan and its call for a Nine Power Conference, and because we supported the League's action, many believed that these events had been planned to introduce a new, forceful foreign policy which would be fully revealed at Brussels.

In this group of publications, estimates of the country's reaction to the speech went through two phases. Pierrepont Moffat, writing in his diary, described the initial phase—the immediate response to the speech—as a "burst of applause."[43] A similar impression was recorded in comment after comment in the publications surveyed. On October 6, the *New York Times* printed excerpts from sixteen editorials from all parts of the country and indicated their trend in its headline: "ROOSEVELT SPEECH WIDELY APPROVED."[44] The *Christian Science Monitor,* on the 7th, declared that observers were surprised at the degree of enthusiasm evoked by the speech, with even papers hostile to the Administration finding words of praise.[45] In a review of the week on Sunday (the 10th), the *San Francisco Chronicle* wrote that the average citizen had responded to the President's message like a "cavalry horse to a bugle call."[46] It said that Roosevelt had appealed to the nation much as Wilson had taken the case for the League to the country to "whip a little group of Senators"—only, where Wilson failed, Roosevelt succeeded. *Time* magazine stated at about the same time that the Chicago address had elicited more words of approval, ranging from enthusiastic to tempered, than anything Mr. Roosevelt had done in many a month.[47] He had regained the support of many whom he had alienated earlier and provided himself with an active peace issue which promised to remain popular unless it threatened to involve us in war. Meanwhile he kept the country guessing whether his proposed "quarantine" meant diplomatic pressures, voluntary boycotts, or economic sanctions.

The marked tendency to agree that the initial response to the speech was positive disappeared in the second phase. Fundamentally, the question was whether the American people were initially enthusiastic about the speech largely because they were glad to have the President openly express disapproval of the Axis Powers; and, if so, whether their enthusiasm had changed after the idea became widespread that the "quarantine" speech would be translated into strong action against Japan at the Brussels Conference. Publications, such as *Newsweek,* felt that, influenced by increasing cries of alarm from leading isolationists, the tide of opinion soon began to turn.[48] Publications like *Time,* on the other hand, believed that popular sentiment remained firmly behind the President.[49] Most of the comments in other publications ranged between these extremes. In general they agreed that the original enthusiasm for the speech had been tempered by anxiety that, at the Brussels Conference, Mr. Roosevelt's new foreign policy would not stop short of war. This was by no means intended, however, to imply that the country would not support punitive measures against Japan, including economic sanctions. For the view was constantly expressed that boycotts, embargoes, etc. against the Japanese would not involve military action. In short, it would seem that the feeling in this group of journals was that the "quick" reaction to the "quarantine" speech, far from being hostile, was decidedly favorable, and it would seem that, in the long run, their opinions differed too widely to justify any definite conclusion.

Turning to the question of editorial policies, an expansion of a study by Lawrence Kramer of eight newspapers, selected to represent different parts of the country and different political convictions, shows six approving the speech and two opposing.[50]

Among the favorable papers were two published on the west coast: the *San Francisco Chronicle* and the *Los Angeles Times.* The *Chronicle* at the outset welcomed Mr. Roosevelt's statements at Chicago as meaning that he had decided to join in coöperative economic sanctions against Japan. It believed the Navy would have to be held in readiness but that there would be no necessity to use it. But, even before the Brussels Conference, the *Chronicle* stated with considerable bitterness that the hopes placed in Mr. Roosevelt's declarations were apparently unjustified. The President had spoken "brave" words at Chicago but there was no indication that he himself knew what he meant by them.[51] The *Times* went through a similar process of expectation and disillusionment. It first supported the "quarantine" speech on the assumption that it foreshadowed the adoption at Brussels of economic and financial measures against the Japanese; but when no such measures materialized, it asked sharply why the speech had ever been made. What originally looked like a statesmanlike utterance, it said, appeared very different in the light of the lack of any effort to implement it.[52]

In the middle of the country, the *Milwaukee Journal* expressed itself, at the close of the Nine Power Conference, with even greater vehemence. It scathingly described the delegates departing from Brussels utterly beaten, their tails between their legs. "Where do we go from here?" it asked, and declared, "Nowhere. There wasn't any bright new dream when the President spoke at Chicago . . . only rhetoric."[53]

The *Cleveland Press,* a Scripps-Howard paper, while hailing the "quarantine" speech and believing it implied more than moral pressure, pursued a cautious policy, never definitely advocating any course.

On the east coast, the *Christian Science Monitor* at the beginning expected the warm response to the President's message to lead to an arms embargo or possibly economic sanctions. But ultimately it, too, became disappointed and concluded that Mr. Roosevelt had grown more afraid than ever of his isolationist critics. The *New York Times,* on its part, saw in the "quarantine" speech and subsequent events the need for reconsidering its editorial position. While applauding the speech as ushering in a more internationalist foreign policy, the *Times* took no definite stand throughout the Brussels Conference. At the end of November, however, it attracted widespread attention by calling on the Administration to overcome its fear of isolationist groups, in and out of Congress, whom it held responsible for undermining our leadership in world affairs and turning the Brussels Conference into a fiasco. A few weeks later the *Times,* in a dramatic editorial, came out in favor of withholding raw materials and credits from Japan.[54]

While these six papers seem sufficiently representative to assume that their views, or equivalent ones in similar publications, came to the attention of the Administration, it may be well to mention the editorial policies of the Washington papers which Mr. Roosevelt seems to have frequently scanned.[55] The *News,* being a Scripps-Howard publication, followed the cautious policy already noted. The *Post* issued a sensational front-page editorial on October 6 endorsing the "quarantine" speech as a first step toward economic measures against Japan. The *Star* not only advocated such measures but declared that, unless they were boldly applied, the signatories of the Nine Power Treaty would deserve nothing better than the contempt which they would certainly get from the Axis countries.[56] The *Times* and *Herald,* both Patterson papers, were in favor of a long-range, Anglo-American blockade of the Japanese.[57] It cannot be stated too often, however, that no matter what actions were recommended it was believed, with few exceptions, that they would not and must not lead to war.

If the editorial opinions of the above newspapers suggest considerable evidence of support for the "quarantine" speech, so, it should be added, did the President's mail. The great majority of the letters on the Chicago address, which fill several boxes in the Hyde Park files, are messages of appreciation, often written with deep emotion.

The other side of the coin is the nature of the opposition to the speech and its influence upon the Administration including the President. The two hostile papers in Mr. Kramer's study were the *Chicago Tribune* and a Hearst publication. Nothing demonstrated the attitude of the *Tribune* better than its account of Mr. Roosevelt's appearance at Chicago on October 5. It described thousands of Chicagoans turning out to greet the President, expecting to hear a message of peace, and being plunged by his words into a "world-hurricane of war fright." Throughout October and November the *Tribune* harped upon two themes: that a "quarantine" must mean economic sanctions and economic sanctions must mean war; that we were merely puppets of the British, serving as saviors of their Empire in the Far East.

The same themes were emphasized by the Hearst press. But Mr. Hearst went much further. He issued a questionnaire to members of Congress which, leading off from the "quarantine" speech, asked whether we should take sides in the Sino-Japanese conflict or steer clear of all wars. The answers were published in a series of articles which began on October 17 and ran for about two weeks. The introduction stated that Congressmen from the "Atlantic to the Pacific, from Canada to the Gulf" had "roared back their determination for today, to-morrow, and forever to keep the United States out of foreign wars."

Many of the published replies came from important political leaders, mainly well-known isolationists.[58] Senator Borah said he was utterly opposed to the United States participating in sanctions against Japan which would be "just the same as initiating war." Senator Vandenberg declared that any move toward naming aggressors, using sanctions, etc., would lead us in the direction of entangling alliances—the one thing we were determined to avoid. Senator George of Georgia wrote that he would not, under any circumstances, favor action which might risk war with Japan. Senator Richard Russell asserted that, instead of policing the world to maintain peace, we should rely upon our neutrality legislation to "quarantine" us against war. Senator La Follette stated that he was opposed to anything which, by implication or otherwise, might ultimately require the United States to use force.

The statement which received the widest publicity was that issued by Hiram Johnson on October 19, the eve of Norman Davis's departure for Brussels.[59] Speaking of the coming conference, the Senator said, "We want no union with welching nations who will . . . tell us we must lead mankind to save the world." Mr. Davis, he insisted, would not be going to Europe unless an agreement had been reached in advance between England and the United States. Mr. Roosevelt had no right to make a mystery of what he meant by a "quarantine" and, unless he intended nothing but words, the inevitable result would be war.

Even a cursory look at the record shows that the Administration observed Mr. Hearst's tactics closely from the outset. At his press conference on October 6, Mr. Roosevelt made some remarks about excerpts from editorials around the country, presumably those in the *New York Times*. He failed, however, to mention that they were mostly in his favor but concentrated instead upon the editorial written by—to use his own words—"the old man of the seas—old man Hearst." This, he declared, was "the silliest ever . . . perfectly terrible—awful. Says it means this is getting us into war and a lot more of that." A few days later, Mr. Ickes recorded in his diary that the Hearst press was after Mr. Roosevelt "full cry" for his Chicago address and that the President had said he wanted to remind Hearst that he had been responsible for an absolutely unjustifiable war with Spain.[60] At about the same time, Pierrepont Moffat noted in his diary that Hearst was "alleged to be about to start a campaign against the idea of a 'quarantine'."[61] When the campaign got underway,

Mr. Roosevelt clearly showed his concern. On the day Norman Davis sailed, the President issued a statement which was generally accepted as a reply to Senator Johnson's attack.[62] Obviously addressing himself to the accusation that we had an understanding with the British, Mr. Roosevelt asserted that we were "of course" entering the Nine Power Conference without any prior commitments. He also emphasized that the purpose of the meeting was to seek a *peaceable* solution of the Sino-Japanese conflict. Off the record, the President dictated some instructions to guide Mr. Davis in his relations with the British.[63] The British Cabinet, these said, must recognize that there was such a thing as American public opinion. Mr. Davis must make clear, "at every step," that the United States would neither take the lead at Brussels nor be made a "tail to the British kite as is now being charged by the Hearst press and others."

There can be little doubt therefore that the "quarantine" speech provoked a barrage from prominent isolationists and that this barrage had its effect upon the Administration. There can also be little doubt that considerable evidence of approval of the speech came to the attention of the Administration but was not accepted as weighing substantially in the balance. Perhaps an extensive study would reveal a wider tide of opinion against the address to support the Administration's view. But until such a study is made, it seems pertinent to continue asking whether the Administration's judgment was not unduly governed by its sensitivity to the attacks of leading isolationists.

NOTES

[1] Stenographic report of the conference in *The Inter-American Conference for the Maintenance of Peace, Proceedings* (Buenos Aires, 1937); *Report of Delegation of the United States to the Inter-American Conference for the Maintenance of Peace* (Washington, 1937), Department of State Conference Series 33.

[2] *Peace and War: United States Foreign Policy, 1931-41* (Washington, 1943), p. 342; *The Memoirs of Cordell Hull* (New York, 1948), I, 498.

[3] *Documents on International Affairs, 1936* (London, 1937), p. 77.

[4] Martin, Percy Alvin, *Latin America and the War* (Baltimore, 1925), pp. 361 *et seq.*, 381. *Inter-American Conference for the Maintenance of Peace, Proceedings*, pp. 138, 221, 739.

[5] Bemis, Samuel Flagg, *The Latin American Policy of the United States* (New York, 1943), p. 287, chapter xxi. Welles, Sumner, *The Time for Decision* (New York, 1944), p. 204.

[6] The memorandum of this conversation was an unusually comprehensive statement of Mr. Hull's views and was sent to the President. See *Foreign Relations of the*

United States, 1937, I, 641, and Hull, *Memoirs,* I, 546. Even after the outbreak of the Sino-Japanese war, Mr. Hull was urging Japan to join the United States in the leadership of a peace movement based on the Buenos Aires agreements. See *Foreign Relations of the United States: Japan, 1931-41,* p. 331.

[7] *F.D.R.: His Personal Letters, 1928-45* (New York, 1947), I, 664. Based on notes of their discussion written by Mr. King while talking with the President and shown to the latter.

[8] Memorandum by Mr. Davis on telephone conversation with the President on March 19. Davis files.

[9] Hull, *Memoirs,* I, 546.

[10] August 26, 1936, story by Arthur Krock.

[11] *Foreign Relations of the United States, 1937,* I, 655.

[12] *Ibid.,* pp. 29, 638, 640, 649.

[13] Apparently in March, Secretary Morgenthau told Mr. Chamberlain that the United States wanted to help in finding some way of preventing the outbreak of war. For correspondence on this see *ibid.,* I, 98-106.

[14] The following accounts of Mr. Davis's conversations are all based upon his memoranda.

[15] Davis files. Draft in Roosevelt files, P. S. F. Great Britain, 1933-38, Box 7.

[16] *Ibid.*

[17] *Foreign Relations of the United States, 1937,* I, 113.

[18] *Ibid.,* p. 131.

[19] *Ibid.,* pp. 665-670. Mr. Welles's own accounts of his plan are in *The Time for Decision,* p. 64, and *Seven Decisions That Shaped History* (New York, 1950), chapter i. See also discussion in *The Challenge to Isolation* by William L. Langer and S. Everett Gleason (New York, 1952), p. 22.

[20] *Foreign Relations of the United States, 1938,* I, 115-126.

[21] Roosevelt files, P. S. F. State—1938.

[22] Hull, *Memoirs,* I, 544-545.

[23] The four memoranda are in both the Roosevelt and the Davis files. There is one difference in the texts (noted below) and some differences in the accompanying letters and notations.

[24] Hull, *Memoirs,* I, 544.

[25] *The Public Papers and Addresses of Franklin D. Roosevelt* (New York, 1941), *1937,* p. 406.

[26] The paraphrase of a recent author is from James Hilton's *Lost Horizon;* the quotation from a Bishop was taken from a letter written to the President by Bishop Frank W. Sterrett (Roosevelt files); the paragraph beginning "the situation is definitely of universal concern" is quoted from the State Department's instructions to the Minister in Switzerland in regard to the League's consideration of the Far Eastern crisis, September, 28. *Foreign Relations of the United States, 1937,* IV, 43.

[27] There are various stories about the President's use of the word "quarantine." Mr. Ickes thought the President took it from a talk in which he (the Secretary) said that neighbors had a right to "quarantine" themselves against the spread of infection such as existed in the international situation. See *The Secret Diary of Harold L. Ickes* (New York, 1954), II, 221. Mr. Welles has stated that the President used the word "quarantine" in talking to him about the possibility of drawing a line in the Pacific to form a quasi blockade against Japan. See Rosenman, Samuel I., *Working with Roosevelt* (New York, 1952), p. 164. For an account by William Phillips see footnote 34.

[28] The original version of this memorandum is in the Davis files and is marked "N.Y. September 17, 1937" with a further notation "Phoned to Mr. Dunn." Presumably the State Department suggested the changes which appeared in the revised version in the Roosevelt files.

[29] Welles, *Seven Decisions That Shaped History,* pp. 8, 13-14, 70-75, 91-93; Rosenman, *op. cit.,* p. 164, has letter from Mr. Welles on the "quarantine" speech.

[30] Welles, *The Time for Decision,* p. 61.

[31] This statement leaves open to question whether Mr. Roosevelt actually stated he had in mind cutting off all trade with the aggressor or whether Mr. Ickes thought that was what the President had in mind. The document which indicates most clearly that one of the President's ideas was to find some means of using coöperative economic pressures is cited in footnote 34.

[32] Roosevelt files.

[33] Davis files.

[34] The President must have mentioned a plan including economic pressures to Clark Eichelberger in early July 1937. In mid-July Mr. Eichelberger sent the President a memorandum based on a talk which they had had some two weeks earlier. The discussion seems to have centered on the possibility of evolving a comprehensive international program which would provide for far-reaching economic measures, drastic disarmament, and a renovation of the existing peace machinery. In connection with the last, Mr. Eichelberger, evidently recapitulating some of the points which had been made during the course of the conversation, wrote that the principle of consultation among nonbelligerents embodied in the Buenos Aires agreements might be extended to the entire world. Once

the world had adopted such principles, he continued, the American people would be willing to accept the idea of denying trade to the aggressor. "Instead of sanctions being voted piecemeal, they would take the form of a denial of the economic benefits of the more nearly just international society to the nation that would make war." Also at some point during this meeting, the President intimated that he might someday make a dramatic speech which—to quote Mr. Eichelberger—would "lead the world on the upward path." Roosevelt files, O.F. 20 State Department, Box 6.

One further account of a conversation with the President at this time should be mentioned, though the whole tenor of the talk, in addition to the vagueness of the language, makes it hard to evaluate. William Phillips, in his autobiography, describes a visit with Mr. Roosevelt on October 6, and states that he asked the President what he meant in using the word "quarantine" in his speech the day before. The President replied that he had searched for a word which was not "sanctions" and had settled on "quarantine" as a "drawing away from someone." Mr. Phillips adds that as the discussion proceeded, Mr. Roosevelt indicated his willingness to "go very far in drawing away." See *Ventures in Diplomacy* (Boston, 1952), pp. 206-207.

[35] Based partly on a remark to this effect said to have been made by Mr. Roosevelt some months later. (Talks with John M. Blum who is working on a book with Mr. Morgenthau based on the latter's diaries.)

[36] *The Public Papers and Addresses of Franklin D. Roosevelt, 1937,* pp. 414-425.

[37] *Ibid.,* p. 429.

[38] Welles, *Seven Decisions That Shaped History,* p. 13. See also p. 73 and Welles, *The Time for Decision,* p. 63.

[39] Hull, *Memoirs,* I, 545. One cannot help wondering whether the severely critical attitude which Mr. Hull is known to have developed toward the "quarantine" speech did not arise only after he saw the attacks in the isolationist press. Pierrepont Moffat recorded in his diary on October 5, 1937, that a meeting of State Department officials was being held on that day in the Secretary's office when the ticker service brought in the text of the President's Chicago address. "The Secretary was delighted at the speech," Mr. Moffat wrote, "and the majority thought it would be strongly approved by the public." See *The Moffat Papers* (Cambridge, 1956), p. 153.

[40] Rosenman, *op. cit.*

[41] Statement based on a study of our Far Eastern policy during this period which the writer is making.

[42] There do not seem to be any polls that show any particular shift in opinion right after the "quarantine" speech. See *Public Opinion, 1935-1946* (Princeton, 1951) which includes exact dates on which polls were issued.

Some of the evidence Mr. Hull cites in his *Memoirs* (p. 545) to prove that the country reacted against the "quarantine idea" is unconvincing. He states, for example, that the A. F. of L. passed a resolution, following the speech, to the effect that "American labor does not wish to be involved in European or Asiatic wars." But he fails to mention that the day after the "quarantine" speech William Green at a convention of the A. F. of L. proposed a boycott of Japanese goods and was, according to all press accounts, overwhelmingly applauded. Moreover about a week later the A. F. of L. and the C.I.O. both passed resolutions to boycott Japan.

[43] *The Moffat Papers,* p. 155.

[44] P. 17.

[45] P. 1. Article by the Washington Bureau of the *Monitor.*

[46] Magazine section, p. 3.

[47] October 18, p. 19. The article was obviously written before the Fireside Chat of October 12.

[48] December 20, p. 11.

[49] November 1, p. 17.

[50] Lawrence I. Kramer, Jr., then at Harvard, wrote a long manuscript summarizing all the editorials in these papers dealing with the major developments in our Far Eastern policy from 1933 to 1937. The above is based on the section on the "quarantine" speech with additions and analyses made entirely on my own responsibility.

[51] November 5. The editorials in each newspaper are too numerous to cite except where reference is made to a specific editorial.

[52] November 26.

[53] November 26.

[54] These two editorials appeared respectively on November 30 and December 24.

[55] Mr. Roosevelt's scrapbook at Hyde Park is full of clippings from the Washington press. Grace Tully lists eleven newspapers which the President looked through customarily for editorial opinion. Of these, four opposed the "quarantine" speech: *The Chicago Tribune,* a Hearst paper, the *New York Herald Tribune,* and the *New York Sun.* See *F.D.R.: My Boss* (New York, 1949), p. 76.

[56] October 7.

[57] October 10 and 12 respectively. The *New York Daily News,* also a Patterson paper, had come out on October 3 for such a blockade (magazine section, p. 6).

[58] The references in this paragraph are to articles printed on October 17 and 18.

[59] *San Francisco Examiner,* October 20, p. 1.

[60] Ickes, *Secret Diary,* II, 227.

[61] *The Moffat Papers,* p. 155.

[62] *New York Times,* October 20, p. 15.

[63] *Foreign Relations of the United States, 1937,* IV, 85. The memorandum was also sent to Ambassador Bingham in London who conveyed its contents to Mr. Eden (*ibid.,* p. 114).

Richard L. Watson, Jr. (essay date 1958)

SOURCE: "Franklin D. Roosevelt in Historical Writing, 1950-1957," in *The South Atlantic Quarterly,* Vol. LVII, No. 1, Winter, 1958, pp. 104-26.

[*In the following essay, Watson offers a critical overview of historical monographs on Roosevelt of the 1950s.*]

Almost ten years ago, David Potter contributed an article to the *Yale Review* entitled "Sketches for the Roosevelt Portrait."[1] Potter pointed out that rarely had there been an opportunity to document so well the life of a public figure as prominent as Franklin D. Roosevelt. Almost all the major figures associated with him save Stalin, Marshall, and, of course, the President himself, had already contributed their memoirs. Roosevelt had made his contribution by providing for a magnificent research center at Hyde Park in which an almost unbelievable cubic footage of documents on the Roosevelt era had been housed. Since then, although Stalin has died almost as inscrutably as he lived, Marshall has agreed to the establishment at Lexington, Virginia, of a depository for his own papers, where an able professional is already in charge.

In 1949, when Potter wrote his article, many of the books on Roosevelt consisted of the memoirs of his associates. Of these, most were highly favorable in their appraisal of the New Deal and of F. D. R.'s part in it. This is not to say that they were entirely uncritical. Indeed, the most useful of these, those by Frances Perkins, Raymond Moley, Jim Farley, and Robert Sherwood, clearly pointed to weaknesses in character and procedures. However, the most consistently hostile of F. D. R.'s critics was John Flynn, whose books combine research with waspishness, and who showed, as Potter pointed out, some amusing inconsistencies in his selection of illustrations to prove the points that he wanted to make.

In addition to the memoirs were many monographs concerning the Roosevelt story, written before 1949. These include histories of New Deal agencies, which vary from slick-paper officials to the coldly objective analyses of the Brookings Institution. There were also at least three important general works, which continue to be useful references for any student of twentieth-century American history. Of these the one of perhaps the most general interest, because of its skilful organization and straightforward literary style, is Dixon Wecter's *The Age of the Great Depression* (1948), the last volume to date in the History of American Life Series. Another book equally thoughtful, more indicative of the author's predispositions, more detailed on the economic implications of the New Deal, and more pessimistic as to its accomplishments, is Broadus Mitchell's *Depression Decade* (1947). Perhaps most significant in its contribution, although more pedestrian in its approach, is Basil Rauch's *The History of the New Deal* (1944). Rauch's significance in New Deal historiography lies in his careful development of the thesis of the "Two New Deals," the "First" stressing recovery through increased prices and catering to large industry and the "big farmer," the "Second" emphasizing reform, partial to labor and all farmers, and aiming at social security and increased purchasing power. This thesis, or variants thereof, has crept into the textbooks, and has been generally accepted by most writers on the New Deal. If used cautiously it makes good sense and is a useful teaching device, although some of the similarities between the two "New Deals" are just as important as the differences.

The coming of the Second World War not only changed the direction of the Roosevelt administrations, but also shifted the emphasis of the writing about F. D. R. Most of the significant writing during the forties was on questions relating to foreign policy. Indeed writing became so brisk that schools of historians developed, and bitterness was created which probably was more acute than after the First World War. Revisionism has, in fact, become sufficiently controversial to inspire a number of historiographical articles; consequently, it would be mere repetition to devote much space to foreign policy here. Of the four principal historiographical articles, the one by William Appleman Williams (*Oregon Historical Quarterly,* September, 1956) is itself a highly opinionated yet stimulating critique of the course of twentieth-century American foreign policy. Robert H. Ferrell, writing on "Pearl Harbor and the Revisionists" in the *Historian* (Spring, 1955) is somewhat more favorably inclined. Louis Morton is firmly objective in writing "Pearl Harbor in Perspective, A Bibliographical Survey," for the *United States Naval Institute Proceedings* (April, 1955), while Wayne S. Cole's excellent article in the *Mississippi Valley Historical Review* (March, 1957) is analytical and equally objective.

Although in the fifties fewer memoirs of those intimately associated with Roosevelt have been published, there have been several which have made a significant contribution to an understanding of his administration. Of these probably the most important is a series of articles written by Rexford Guy Tugwell, one of the original brain trusters.[2] Tugwell's articles unfortunately do not form any easily recognizable sequence. They are repetitious; occasionally, the organization is difficult to follow, and the wording requires alert reading lest the subtleties seem to be contradictory. At the same time, Tugwell, perhaps more than any of the Roosevelt associates, exhibits a brilliant mind grappling with the economic, social, constitutional, and political problems that Roosevelt faced. Indeed, he implies that these problems were partly intellectual and that their solution required a psychological adjustment. In other words, according to Tugwell, the problems of the depression could not be solved by simply using past remedies. Obviously, the twenties offered no solution, and even though Tugwell acknowledges a relationship between the earlier Progressive Movement and the New Deal, he could see few precedents in progressivism which would help solve the problems of the depression and the postdepression years.

Perhaps more important, the Tugwell articles bring out the differences among the Roosevelt advisers. Tugwell quite frankly admits that he differed with many of the decisions that F. D. R. made. Roosevelt, though an experimenter, was more conservative and more of a compromiser than was Tugwell. Yet the latter concludes that Roosevelt was the master in his house, that he had general objectives toward which he was heading, and that he knew that many of his compromises were inglorious. Tugwell concludes: " . . . he would be the last to gloss over the ordeals he underwent, to belittle the baseness of the struggles he often had to carry on, or to claim that his ends were not more noble than his means."

Less important for an understanding of Roosevelt than Tugwell's articles, but perhaps equally important for an understanding of the New Deal, is Marriner Eccles's *Beckoning Frontiers* (1951). This book must have enraged Eccles's fellow-bankers, because it describes one of them whom the depression had made into a Keynesian before he had read Keynes. This intellectual shift makes fascinating reading, as does Eccles's account of the effect of the depression upon banks, of his joining the New Deal, and of his activities on the Federal Reserve Board.

Several other memoirs of Roosevelt advisers throw light on various aspects of the New Deal. Jesse H. Jones's *Fifty Billion Dollars, My Thirteen Years with the R. F. C.* (1951) reflects the point of view of a self-assured conservative. Samuel I. Rosenman's *Working with Roosevelt* (1951) is somewhat disappointing as a book by one who was closely associated with F. D. R. for many years, but at the same time, in addition to what it shows about speech-making, it does illuminate some little known events. Perhaps of greatest interest in this respect was Roosevelt's approaching Willkie to organize a new liberal party. Harold L. Ickes's three-volume diary (1953, 1954) is one of the most amazing documents of all because of its success in at times enlightening and at other times obscuring the events and the man it describes. Louis B. Wehle's *Hidden Threads of History: Wilson through Roosevelt* (1953) provides trenchant comments upon his association with Roosevelt. Here is a somewhat critical appraisal of the TVA and a balanced character sketch of Roosevelt himself. Finally, Donald Richberg's *My Hero, the Indiscreet Memoirs of an Eventful But Unheroic Life* (1954), is important for its treatment of the NRA.

One of the most revealing memoirs could have been that of Roosevelt's earliest political advisor, the "gnomelike" Louis McHenry Howe. Unfortunately Howe was not interested so much in posterity as he was in "making Franklin President," and thus he wrote little if anything about their association. However, Lela Stiles, a newspaper columnist who joined the Roosevelt entourage in 1928, has written a biography of Howe, *The Man behind Roosevelt: The Story of Louis McHenry Howe* (1954). Because of Miss Stiles's close association with Howe and Roosevelt, her book has more the flavor of a memoir than a biography. It is useful in describing the techniques of the little man who as a twentieth-century political adviser has yet to meet his match. At the same time, it is chiefly revealing as a document describing the enthusiasm and loyalty of the little-known personal retinue which became attached to Roosevelt from time to time through the years, of which Miss Stiles herself was one.

Memoirs have done more to illuminate the roles of advisers of Roosevelt and the administrative figures of the New Deal than of the congressional leadership of the era. Too frequently, the New Deal is thought of simply in terms of F. D. R. and the brain trust, with little realization of the role that Congress played in it. Or, if Congress is considered, the Roosevelt critic frequently describes it as a rubber stamp. Yet both houses of Congress during the Roosevelt era were dominated by tough-minded politicians, most of whom had emerged from the jungle of local politics upon the national scene many years before and had kept themselves on the national scene by being ever responsive to the demands of their local constituencies. A surprising number of New Deal measures were originated by Congressmen; and each enactment had to receive the approval of Congress, else it would not become law. Unfortunately, few of the congressional giants of the New Deal era have written their memoirs.

Since 1950, however, three of importance have been published. Of these, *The Private Papers of Senator Vandenberg* concentrates only on the period of the war where Vandenberg obviously made his greatest contribution. However, the autobiographies of Alben Barkley and Tom Connally do indicate something of the problems of a Democratic Congressman throughout the Roosevelt regime. Barkley's *That Reminds Me* (1954) does not provide a detailed narrative of congressional activity during the New Deal. It is important in indicating the scope of the economic disaster; it discusses the "Dear Alben" letter and criticizes Roosevelt's tactics at the time of the Supreme Court fight. It describes Barkley's support for the third term, his disagreement with F. D. R. over wartime tax policy, and the vice-presidential nomination of 1944. Critical of Roosevelt at several points, Barkley nevertheless concludes that, although not a profound thinker, Roosevelt "had a deep and penetrating insight into both the philosophy and the mechanics of government," "had the instinct of a virtuoso for playing practical politics," and was "one of the most fascinating personalities" that he (Barkley) had ever known.

My Name is Tom Connally (1954), written by Alfred Steinberg in collaboration with the Senator, gets more to the heart of congressional relationships during the New Deal than does the Barkley volume. Connally, a congressman from Texas since 1917, a senator since 1928, was in a strategic place to see what went on in the maneuvering for the Democratic presidential nomination of 1932. Later he worked closely with Vice-President Garner, who, according to Connally, considered his own beliefs less important than the Roosevelt program. Connally obviously had little affection for insurgents such as Norris and Wheeler, but respected the solid party men such as Ashurst, McKellar, and even Republican McNary. He broke with Roosevelt over the Supreme Court measure, in part, because the latter ignored the congressional leadership in preparing the bill. In general, he turned up his nose at the brain trust and insisted that Roosevelt unquestionably made his own decisions. But there is no question that the legislative was the most important branch of the government in Connally's opinion. As he said about the first years of the New Deal:

> My afternoons on the Senate floor during the early period of the recovery program were a hectic conglomeration of debate and politicking. President Roosevelt originated much of the program with the advice of his Brain Trust and cabinet officers. But there were also many bills that stemmed directly from Capitol Hill. Besides, all of the legislation had to be passed by Congress, and this required constant prodding from the White House plus a smooth-working congressional leadership.

But, even though the student of the New Deal will continue to hope for more memoirs of participants, the principal contributions since 1950 have been biographies and monographic studies. Of these, the earlier ones were based largely on interviews or printed sources. In this group, two biographies are for different reasons highly rewarding books. John Gunther does not himself consider his *Roosevelt in Retrospect* (1950) a biography. It is not written chronologically or in narrative form. In fact, it is written so much in the same chummy style of Gunther's other popular volumes that it can quite aptly be given the subtitle "Inside F. D. R." Perhaps it can best be described as a sympathetic character sketch with profuse illustrations. Here is a partial description of the President: too eager to please, devious, garrulous, patient, energetic, self-confident, optimistic, politically skilful, with a broad but not subtle sense of humor, simply but not introspectively religious, tolerant, intuitive rather than logical, curious, casual, practical, ingenious, flexible—and the adjectives could go on and on. Perhaps more sensitively than anyone else, Gunther has brought out the impact of polio upon the Roosevelt career, an episode which provides an opportunity for the author quite cautiously to introduce a touch of psychology. In short, although Gunther makes little effort to examine the era historically, and although some of his evidence is somewhat uncritically accepted, the Roosevelt portrait as he paints it will be very difficult to forget.

It is perhaps unfair to compare Harold F. Gosnell's *Champion Campaigner, Franklin D. Roosevelt* (1952) with the Gunther volume. Whereas the latter is thick and rich in detail, the former is pared down to the bones. Although Gosnell's purpose is to use the Roosevelt career to explain "what makes for success in American politics," he uses the historical approach and provides a comprehensive narrative. The focus, however, is upon Roosevelt, not upon the New Deal. His conclusions are not startling and boil down quite simply to the contention that Roosevelt's political success was based in part upon certain qualities as a campaigner, of which some were "inherited" and others were acquired by experience. Most important, through these qualities and through his skill in putting them across to the electorate he came to exemplify the American tradition; thus he won popular confidence and, through his powers of persuasion, the acceptance of his program.

Neither Gunther nor Gosnell have attempted to provide any comprehensive analyses of the New Deal or of the diplomacy of the Roosevelt Era. The new volumes in the Chronicles of America series, now edited by Allan Nevins, have attempted to do this. Of the four volumes that cover the Roosevelt era, Denis W. Brogan's *The Era of Franklin D. Roosevelt* (1950) is probably the most satisfactory. Concerned almost exclusively with political and economic developments, it nevertheless moves into the war period, but only in as far as political questions such as the election of 1944 are concerned. The gaps left by Brogan in foreign policy and wartime activities are filled by Allan Nevins's *The New Deal and World Affairs* (1950), a skilfully written, comprehensive, completely sympathetic survey of Roosevaltian foreign policy to the founding of the United Nations; Fletcher Pratt's *War for the World* (1950) is concerned exclusively with military (principally naval) operations, and Eliot Janeway's *The Struggle for Survival* (1951) takes a highly subjective view of wartime administration. Of these, the volume by Pratt should not have been written, being a model of bad historical writing; the volume by Janeway, though thought-provoking and intelligent, does not belong in the series because of its lack of understanding of what constitutes historical writing (*South Atlantic Quarterly*, L, January, 1951, 109-121).

In a sense, the Gosnell biography marks the transition from the Roosevelt books of the early 1950's to those coming out later in the decade. The distinguishing feature of the more recent books is the exploitation of the manuscripts and documents now made available in the Roosevelt library at Hyde Park. The fact that these and other masses of government manuscripts are generally available has made it possible for scholars to be much further ahead in exploring the career of a public figure of such importance than would normally be the case. Roosevelt scholarship, for example, has almost reached the same stage today as that of Wilson scholarship, with the notable exception that more scholarly articles are available on Wilson.

The two most formidable undertakings of the decade in Roosevelt scholarship are those by the Harvard historians,

Arthur Schlesinger, Jr. and Frank Freidel. Schlesinger is projecting a multi-volume work on "The Age of Roosevelt" of which the first volume, *The Crisis of the Old Order,* was published in 1957. Freidel contemplates several more volumes in his biography of Franklin D. Roosevelt, of which three have already appeared. At first glance, it might seem that the two works must necessarily duplicate one another, but actually it is obvious from a study of Schlesinger's first volume that he is interpreting his project in quite different terms from the strictly biographical approach of Freidel.

Indeed one could almost say that Roosevelt's part in *The Crisis of the Old Order* is purely incidental. Schlesinger's thesis appears to be that the New Deal was rooted firmly in earlier twentieth-century experience and that "the crisis of the old order" brought about by the Depression offered an opportunity to work out a reform program. This thesis, it should be noted, is somewhat different from the position of Richard Hofstadter in his Pulitzer-prize-winning *The Age of Reform* . . . (1955), who considers the New Deal a "new departure" in American reform movements. Schlesinger's thesis is, of course, not a particularly novel one: the question as to whether the New Deal was "evolutionary" or "revolutionary" has been argued almost as vigorously as has World War II revisionism; nor will readers of Link, Gabriel, Commager, Mowry, Goldman, Fine, F. A. Allen, and a few other writers on early twentieth-century America find most of Schlesinger's subject matter sensationally new. He has, however, provided a neat synthesis of the political and intellectual currents of progressivism which support his thesis. His story broadens as it reaches the twenties, where he describes "the economics of Republicanism" and the age of business together with the rumblings of discontent among labor groups, reformers, and intellectuals. But the Depression provides the crux of his story, and 400 pages of a 500-page book are devoted to the onset of the depression and the election of 1932, with a 100-page flashback on the Roosevelt pre-presidential career.

Schlesinger's most telling contribution is to keep alive for this generation the sense of horror at the effects of the depression. As the forties brought a wartime prosperity and as the postwar boom and the Iron Curtain maintained it, economic disaster has seemed remote. To the generation of the fifties the New Deal is simply Roosevelt and a mass of no longer particularly controversial legislation. The idea that the economic heart of the nation could stop beating not much more than twenty-five years ago is unbelievable. The fact that it did stop beating, that people were freezing and starving, that ominous sounds of revolt were being heard not only from those physically suffering but from businessmen who so far were still receiving dividends must be sensed, if one is to understand the New Deal. Schlesinger has chosen his statistics and his incidents skilfully; he has not exaggerated, and the climate of the Depression, at least by one who has lived through it, can be sensed again through his pages.

A more difficult question to determine, however, is whether Schlesinger, in his obvious sympathy for the New Deal, has been fair to Hoover. Schlesinger acknowledges that Hoover "brought great areas of the economy . . . into the orbit of national action," and that "he breached the walls of local responsibility as had no President in American history." But, aside from these observations, his appraisal of the unfortunate Republican is devastating. "Infatuation with the balanced budget." "Gloom and insecurity." "Dragged despairingly along by events." "His was the tragedy of a man of high ideals whose intelligence froze into inflexibility and whose dedication was smitten by self-righteousness." These are characteristic expressions of the indictment, and it is time that someone took direct issue with the Hoover biographers, who have seen no weaknesses in Hoover economics. At the same time, it is perhaps unfortunate that Schlesinger, whose political activities have made him suspect by many, is the one who has taken such strong issue with these writers.

The case for Hoover can be more strongly stated. It is not fair to assert unequivocally, as Schlesinger does, that Hoover considered the economy without defect in 1929 and 1930. He had been critical of the economic structure, especially the banking system, when he became President, and he continued to be. To say that "few men had seemed to care less about the Sherman Act" is also unfair. Hoover may not have been a crusader for small business, but he believed firmly in competition. He was a trust-buster rather of the Theodore Roosevelt school than that of Brandeis. Nor does Schlesinger give Hoover his due on the critical unemployment-public-works issue.

Admittedly, Hoover developed an "obsession" for a balanced budget; admittedly also, the stress upon the sound economy, the skepticism toward the efficacy of public works, the misinterpretation of statistics on the number of unemployed left him open to accusations of inflexibility and heartlessness. At the same time, Hoover did launch an unprecedented program of public works. Moreover, it is a questionable assertion (p. 232) that "in December, 1931, he formally repudiated the contention, once his own, that further expansion of public works would aid recovery." The evidence for this statement appears to be the report of a special committee appointed by Hoover to study "the desirability of the further expansion of public works as an aid to recovery." Hoover himself did not take quite this position, although he did rule out public works that were not self-liquidating. Moreover, Schlesinger does not put sufficient stress upon such statements of Hoover as that of February 3, 1931, in which he pledged that if voluntary and local agencies were unable "to prevent hunger and suffering in my country, I will ask the aid of every resource of the Federal government because I would no more see starvation among our Countrymen than would any Senator or Congressman. . . ."

Schlesinger's flashback upon the Roosevelt career and his discussion of the election of 1932 are the areas in which there is considerable overlapping with other recent writers. But in most instances the writers differ so fundamentally in scope and objective that the duplication is not significant. Only Frank Freidel, for example, is attempting a biography of Roosevelt that will certainly run to six volumes. Probably no one will ever again attempt one in such detail, since it is unlikely that the manuscripts and memoirs which will become available in the future will materially change Freidel's interpretation, at least of the pre-presidential years.

His is not flashy biographical writing, but it is more than just methodical. Schlesinger's style is more brilliant, but that very fact leaves him open to charges of exaggeration or misinterpretation. Freidel's style is appropriate to the nature and scope of the subject. It is simple, clear, and direct. He has combed periodicals and newspapers and has used the unique Oral History Project at Columbia University. Most important of all are his finds in the large manuscript collections open to researchers on twentieth-century politics topped by those at the Roosevelt Library. The style, the depth of the research, perhaps above all the tone, mark this as a distinguished biography.

The work, moreover, demonstrates the value of such biographical studies in providing the basis for historical synthesis. A study of the Progressive era, for example, must be based upon the way in which it manifested itself on the local level. In other words, countless studies of local "progressivism" are necessary even to make it possible to define the term. Roosevelt began as a local politician who was fortunate in many things, such as his name and background, who combined his good fortune with attention to detail and an awareness of the popular issues of the day. Before the war, he rode the tide of progressivism, which brought him at times to a break with Tammany, but he was careful never actually to sever his ties, and the regulars found it difficult to describe him as a bolter. The Roosevelt career exemplifies Democratic progressive politics in New York state.

The Freidel biography also illuminates the preparedness campaign, a facet of the Wilson administration hitherto obscure. Somewhat ironically perhaps, after becoming Assistant Secretary of the Navy, F. D. R. sometimes found his relations with the Wilson administration similar to his former relations with Tammany. His views in the bitter preparedness agitation more closely paralleled those of his uncle, of Lodge, and of the Navy professionals than those of his superiors, Wilson, Bryan, and Daniels. Freidel's treatment, particularly if read in conjunction with the much more subjective half-memoir, *The End of Innocence* (1954), by Jonathan Daniels, clearly brings out the bitter controversies that developed. Wilson and Daniels at times became furious with the youthful interventionist, yet when the chips were down, he always fell back into line; to him the Administration and the Party came first.

Freidel's second volume picks up the story with the end of the war and carries it until 1928. The subject matter of the book is somewhat thinner than in the first volume, for these were the years during which Roosevelt was almost entirely immobilized by polio. Freidel keeps the focus on Roosevelt, his painfully slow recovery from the disease, his dabbling in business, yet always keeping in close touch with the political scene. Again, however, the Roosevelt story is almost as important in emphasizing an aspect of twentieth-century American politics which usually remains obscured in the inadequate general histories of the twenties: what was happening to the Democratic party in the post-Wilson years of national defeat. The Democratic party was in fact struggling for existence, and F. D. R.'s fertile brain was active in formulating schemes for its rehabilitation, while Louis McHenry Howe was planning Roosevelt's part in the process. By the mid-twenties Roosevelt was already widely respected in his party; only his physical disability prevented him from being a serious contender for the presidency both in 1924 and 1928.

With 1928 Roosevelt's public career becomes complicated once again. Now, in addition to being Governor of the State of New York, itself one of the most difficult of executive positions, he was also running for President of the United States. For the accomplishments of the governorship, Freidel's third volume may be supplemented by Bernard Bellush's *Franklin D. Roosevelt as Governor of New York* (1955). Based upon newspapers, periodical articles, memoirs, and the Roosevelt papers, this volume is a well documented, clearly written narrative. Bellush's assessment is highly favorable, although he is critical of Roosevelt's initial handling of Tammany, and he concludes that much of the Governor's program originated with Al Smith. At the same time, he insists that Governor Roosevelt educated the public, dealt skilfully with obstinate Republican legislatures, handled Tammany with "unusual executive ability and political acumen," and pushed through much constructive legislation. Indeed Bellush is convinced that through his activities as governor, Roosevelt "had already formulated the basis for a program when he campaigned for the presidency in 1932."

In spite of the clarity of the study, *Franklin D. Roosevelt as Governor of New York* has a certain air of unreality because it is devoted so exclusively to the governorship. The reader is quite apt to overlook the fact that, at the same time, Roosevelt was running for the presidency. In this aspect of the political story Freidel's skill is perhaps most notable. In fact, one of Freidel's major theses is that F. D. R. was at the same time acting as governor and running for the presidency. Within a few weeks of his election as governor, Freidel concludes, Roosevelt had "without waste effort quietly erected . . . the scaffolding for both the governorship of New York and the candidacy for President in 1932."

This scaffolding consisted of a program and a tightly knit political organization. The program included more emphasis upon the farmer than did Al Smith's and a continued emphasis upon conservation and public power. Immediately after the market crashed, F. D. R. no more than Hoover was at first particularly concerned. In fact, he criticized Hoover's radicalism and preached Manchester liberalism. As conditions became worse, however, New York experienced many of the elements that were to go into the New Deal. As Freidel points out, for example, F. D. R. was a pioneer in working on the problem of relief for the unemployed.

Freidel shows that the building-up of the Roosevelt political organization was a masterpiece of co-operation, foresight, detailed planning, and timing. Here old line Democrats such as House, Hull, and Baruch combined with politicians more closely associated with the Roosevelt name such as Ed Flynn, Farley, and Howe and brain trusters such as Rosenman, Moley, and Tugwell. Letters, tours, speeches, physical examinations, public opinion polls, somewhat questionable maneuvers about Tammany and the League of Nations—all had their part in making Roosevelt President.

In spite of serious criticism of his methods at several of these points, Freidel's general conclusion is that Roosevelt's record indicated that greatness lay ahead. Roosevelt, Freidel concludes, clearly was in command of his forces as they advanced into the campaign. In retrospect, his qualifications for political office seem clear: "his years of careful training in practical politics," his familiarity with foreign affairs and defense policy acquired during World War I, "his superb administration of the State of New York" under adverse circumstances, his "humble willingness to learn," his "phenomenal capacity for hard work." In comparison with these, his principal weaknesses—"his tendencies to compromise and to accept things on the surface"—seem very small indeed.

Another indication of the direction which the Roosevelt presidency might follow and which is implicit in both Freidel and Schlesinger may be found in an important book, *The Economic Thought of Franklin D. Roosevelt and the Origins of the New Deal* (1956), by Daniel R. Fusfeld. Unlike most writers on Roosevelt, Fusfeld insists that Roosevelt was quite knowledgeable on things economic, that in fact he studied with considerable care the economic literature on a subject which at the moment concerned him. At the same time Fusfeld argues that Roosevelt's knowledge was not primarily theoretical, but largely derived from experience.

In short, Fusfeld would contend that by the time Roosevelt was elected President, he was well educated economically in "progressive" economics. A family background that accepted social reform, moderately liberal courses in economics at Harvard, debating economic issues as a candidate for local office and as a supporter of Theodore Roosevelt and Woodrow Wilson, being forced to make decisions on controversial questions involving business, labor, and government during World War I, self-education during the twenties culminating in the complexities of the New York governorship—all this, Fusfeld clearly implies, puts the burden of proof on those who have asserted that Roosevelt had no understanding of economics.

But Fusfeld's study ends with Roosevelt's election to the presidency in 1932, the same date at which Freidel chose to end the third volume of his biography. Such a tantalizing ending has undoubtedly caused many of their readers to speculate as to whether Fusfeld would find the same consistency in Roosevelt's economic thought during the presidential years, and whether Freidel will modify his essentially favorable appraisal as he proceeds through the thirties and into the forties. If the conclusions of two other recent writers on Roosevelt and the New Deal are any criteria, no objective writer would be able to find consistency, and favorable conclusions would have to be seriously qualified.

The writer of a general work who in recent years has provided the most serious indictment of the New Deal is a distinguished American historian of Stanford University, Edgar E. Robinson. Robinson assumed the task of providing an appraisal of the New Deal as the result of the will of Mr. J. Brooks B. Parker, a Philadelphia businessman. The will left $25,000 to be used in subsidizing a study of the impact of Roosevelt "without fear, favor, or prejudice." Robinson's earlier studies of elections made him a logical candidate for this assignment, although his association with Hoover at Stanford raises the question of the wisdom of his selection.

The result of Mr. Robinson's labor is important even though hardly as objective as a literal interpretation of the terms of the will would seem to require. Its importance lies principally in an exhaustive (70-page) bibliographical essay prepared by Vaughn D. Bornet, Mr. Robinson's associate in the project. Divided into sections, with works cited listed chronologically within the sections, this essay constitutes what is perhaps the most useful bibliographical aid to the writings by and about Roosevelt. Moreover, the objectivity of the critical comments goes far to meeting the terms of the will.

Robinson's text, on the other hand, is important rather for its criticism of the Roosevelt leadership from the "conservative" (that is roughly equivalent to the Hoover) point of view. Roosevelt's "transcendent power," according to Robinson, came because "he represented fairly well the level of conception, understanding, and purpose that characterized the mass of the American people of his time." This appeal was rooted deep in America's "rebel" past, in "the heritage of the masses of Americans who have always been radical in outlook . . . though infrequently in action." Roosevelt was able to provide them "for a time" with the practical results that the people wanted because of the initial crisis and because an "unusual combination of radical elements . . . repeatedly returned him to power."

So far the argument is clear. But its conclusion is less so. Robinson goes on:

> We shall see that in these years there were other "revolutionaries" at work. Roosevelt's leadership was the façade behind which a less understanding

but profoundly convinced revolutionary leadership was provided in the Congress, in administrative departments. in the press, on the radio, and in the colleges and schools. It was rarely a leadership pledged to doctrines alien to American soil.

Indeed this other leadership arose directly from American experience. . . . It was a revolutionary leadership in the sense that it was the work of fairly small groups dedicated to making over American society. And it used the slogans that found ready response in the hearts of Americans, in particular those associated with freedom of thought and expression. Eventually these advocates of fundamental change found their counterparts in other nations, and America was plunged into a world conflict of ideas, as well as of armies.

Franklin Roosevelt, possessing indomitable courage and will power, won the allegiance of innumerable enthusiasts, and by an incomparable sense of timing, he won continuing support of a huge body of voters.

This gave him control of a nation, and direction of the greatest striking force in the world. For a time he was the most powerful leader of the twentieth century, and in fact the most powerful in the history of mankind. A man of good intention cast in the role of hero, he was overwhelmed by the inexorable forces of his time. This was his tragedy, the tragedy of his people, and the tragedy of the world.

What is Robinson trying to show as to the affinity between Roosevelt and totalitarian revolution elsewhere in the world? This is never explicitly put, but he does state that "*Government* under Roosevelt, and particularly the Executive, was to be all-powerful," and that "on the whole, this leadership—in method and result—was injurious to the slow working of democracy as Americans know it. . . . "

This is a serious indictment, and there is much in Robinson's vigorous writing that is worthy of careful consideration. But the indictment is relegated to the realm of argument when placed beside another more important contribution to Roosevelt literature, James M. Burns's *Roosevelt: The Lion and the Fox* (1956). Burns's conclusions, although considerably more favorable to Roosevelt than are Robinson's, present an equally serious indictment with similar conclusions as to his baleful lasting effect. More significant than the similarity of conclusion, however, is that the two authors arrive at their conclusions from diametrically opposite points of view. Robinson is worried because Roosevelt was "radical"; Burns, because he was "conservative."

Burns's approach, somewhat like that of Gosnell, is that of the political scientist interested in political leadership. It takes as its basic hypothesis "the central findings of social scientists that leadership is not a matter of universal traits but is rooted in a specific culture." In a seven-page note Burns summarizes certain findings made by the behavioral sciences in the study of leadership and shows how "promising developments" in the general field have at the same time "enormously increased the complexities" of such studies.

The main trends in the general field of leadership study, according to Burns, have been first of all to place an increased emphasis upon environmental factors rather than heredity and secondly to de-emphasize universal traits as determining leadership and to emphasize instead "a reciprocal relationship between personality and culture . . . specific to a given situation." Moreover, Burns follows T. N. Whitehead in insisting upon emphasizing the difference between a leader who plays any role necessary to conform to the demands of society and "the creative leader who assumes roles . . . only as a tactical means of realizing his long-term strategic ends, and in the long run seeks to broaden the environmental limits within which he operates." This concept is basic to an understanding of Burns's interpretation of Roosevelt, for his appraisal is that F. D. R. "failed to exercise creative leadership."

Although Burns's interest in explaining the development of Roosevelt, the leader, is clear, it is injected subtly enough not to detract from a chronological narrative of his life. In a consideration of his boyhood, for example, Burns concludes that one cannot find "any foretoken of Franklin D. Roosevelt the politician" in his ancestry; nor is there any evidence that his parents "fashioned a world for their son that would encourage an interest in politics"; as for Groton, "none of his political battles" was won there, and at Harvard he showed less "political craft" than Hoover had displayed at Stanford ten years before.

The Progressive era and World War I, Burns concludes, were decisive influences. F. D. R. could not "escape the pervasive atmosphere" of reform, but he became a Democrat by chance. At first he was interested only in political progressivism, but, influenced by his Uncle Theodore, by his studies of official reports, and by the social consciousness of Tammany, he became concerned with economic and social causes. In response to specific conditions, he moved toward a New Deal position twenty years before the New Deal. Yet, withal, he sensed from his own political experiences that working with existing political organizations generally was more successful in achievement than risking all in "a knightly onslaught." The war provided experience in administration. His long hours, innumerable conferences, and "hard bargaining" not only brought him to political maturity but interested him in the working of the Federal government and how to improve it. His continuing progressivism is indicated by his prediction in 1919 of a new party consisting of liberals from both parties. In surveying his career to this point, Burns finds grounds for cautious generalization. First of all, from his youth on F. D. R. "was usually willing to come to terms easily with the dominant forces in his environment." He was fortunate, moreover, in his name, his associations, his income, "and in the assurance he gained from all these." But most important in explaining his future achievements, according to Burns, were his "keen ambition and his capacity to learn."

The period of the twenties to 1932 constitutes the second section of the Burns biography. One might expect a behavioral scientist to make much of the polio episode, but Burns does not believe that it brought any significant change in Roosevelt's political thought, although it altered the political picture considerably. In some respects his legs became a political asset: they brought him sympathy and compelled Eleanor to enter politics. Of most importance, however, his physical weakness kept him out of politics during the years of Democratic inadequacy. This was just "luck," and through good fortune too he was elected governor at a strategic moment, a success which pushed him further up the political ladder. Although Burns's appraisal of the governorship is somewhat less favorable than that of Bellush, it is similar to that of Freidel, adding up in Burns's book to an "impressive record," and "truly an apprenticeship in politics and statecraft."

With Roosevelt's presidency, the direction in which Burns's conclusions are taking him assume clearer form. The essence of his appraisal is that although Roosevelt provided "a leadership of frankness and vigor," he had no "master program." He boasted of "playing by ear," but in fact, according to Burns he was influenced by his party, his advisers, and Congress. Almost all the early legislation was embodied in either platform or campaign addresses; his advisers were numerous and diverse in philosophy; and Congress was equally diverse and effective enough to make Roosevelt believe that he must compromise with it. Yet he kept control over his advisers, Burns concludes, almost singlehandedly giving "pace and direction to the New Deal battalions," and "rarely lost the initiative with Congress."

Furthermore, according to Burns, a notable feature of the first term was Roosevelt's essential conservatism. Many of his advisers and "Congress" were more radical than he. Roosevelt's earnest desire was to stay above party battles. He did not work out a program of radical reform; he did not seek to build up voting strength among minority groups by promptly endorsing civil rights legislation and supporting underprivileged farm or labor groups. He was slow to do these things, because he continued to play by ear.

At this point Burns breaks with the standard interpretation of the Second New Deal. This interpretation sees Roosevelt coming to terms with radical elements in Congress and the demagogues of the left. Fearing the economic effects of a radical legislative program and the political effects of a radical coalition in 1936, he "stole their thunder" and marched leftward himself in order to remain in control of the program and to assure re-election. Burns insists that this interpretation is much too simple. Roosevelt's shift occurred partly because Congress had moved leftward after 1934, but in addition, he says cogently, the leftward shift was merely coincidence, a salvaging of those elements in the First New Deal which the court had not ruled out. However, Burns concludes, "the main reason for the new posture was the cumulative impact of the attacks from the right . . . the desertion of the right . . . automatically helped shift Roosevelt to the left."

This desertion was paradoxical, because, Burns insists, Roosevelt was still essentially conservative. He talked about the general rather than party or group interest; he believed in the unity of the past, present, and future; he was religious, and conducted himself as a gentleman of culture; he upheld personal property rights; and, of most significance, he believed in change "as essential to holding on to the values of national importance." Yet the right deserted him, according to Burns, because it was no longer in the conservative tradition. Business was narrowly self-interested and was a "prisoner" of laissez-faire; and of most importance was the psychological fact that Roosevelt had deprived business men of their position of preeminence—"he had sapped their self-esteem"; "he had disassociated the concept of wealth from the concept of virtue."

Deserted by the right, he appealed to the left. This was tactical rather than strategic, and as a tactical maneuver it met with overwhelming success in 1936. However, since it was not strategic, since there was no program or philosophical shift involved, according to Burns, disaster was to follow. "Creative leadership" was lacking. The United States drifted in foreign affairs, Supreme Court reform fizzled, a political purge was badly planned, and, perhaps most important, recession struck in 1937 and 1938.

The recession, in fact, is the crux of the Burns indictment. It symbolizes to him Roosevelt's failure:

> Roosevelt's fumbling and indecisiveness during the recession showed his failings as an economist and thinker. His distrust of old and doctrinaire economic theories freed him from slavery to ideas. . . . But at the same time . . . cut him off from the one economist and the one economic idea that might have provided a spectacular solution to Roosevelt's chief economic, political and constitutional difficulties.

That economist, Burns asserts, was John Maynard Keynes.

Why did not Roosevelt accept Keynes? Burns argues that it was not simply because of the political situation or because of divided advisers, but that it was an intellectual failure. "A Keynesian solution . . . involved an almost absolute commitment," concludes Burns, "and Roosevelt was not one to commit himself absolutely to any political or economic method."

Equally important and related to the failure to accept "absolute commitment," Burns adds, was Roosevelt's lack of concern with the means used to gain laudable ends. He had moral objectives: "man's responsibility for his fellow man," and government's responsibility for the general welfare. But he had few illusions about man's nature and felt that power was necessary in order to win out over man's foibles. He was morally certain that his aims were right; hence "he was willing to use Machiavellian means" to win the elections indispensable for keeping him in power: "He would use the tricks of the fox to serve the purpose of the lion."

Both Robinson and Burns would agree, then, that Roosevelt failed as a creative leader. Both would agree that this failure was partly intellectual, that it resulted from an unwillingness to make "principle" the guide of method. They are in fundamental disagreement, however, as to the alternatives to failure. To Robinson the alternative was apparently something that resembled Hoover's individualism. To Burns it was a positive program for the benefit of the common man symbolized by a whole-hearted endorsement of Keynesian economics. Yet, in spite of this failure, Burns can still look "at the man as a whole" and "see the lineaments of greatness—courage, joyousness, responsiveness, vitality, faith, and, above all concern for his fellow man . . . sensitive but not weak, considerate but not fussy, plucky in his power to endure, capable of laughing and of taking a joke."

Thus the dilemma for the thoughtful reader of the Roosevelt literature remains. Not only do the scholars differ fundamentally in their interpretation of the past; but each one of them carefully hedges his own indictments. Thoroughly documented and thoughtfully conceived though *Roosevelt: The Lion and the Fox* is, the dilemma will not be resolved by establishing a preconceived standard of creative leadership and placing the Roosevelt record beside it. Nor will the dilemma be resolved by those, such as Robinson, who refuse to face the fact that nineteenth-century liberalism is inadequate for twentieth-century America.

Those who criticize the New Deal from that point of view are guilty of de-emphasizing the significance of the Depression. Moreover, in spite of the hypotheses concerning the effect of environment and changing situations, neither Burns nor Robinson sufficiently considers the realities of the political situation in its local, sectional, and party aspects. Finally, too few writers on the New Deal have sufficiently stressed the magnitude of the specialized administrative problems created by depression and war in contrast to the number of people trained to be specialized administrators.

The first three volumes of Freidel's biography give promise that subsequent ones will show an understanding of such questions as these. Moreover, his own comment in a review of *Roosevelt: The Lion and the Fox* indicates his awareness of the need for an historical approach to Roosevelt and the New Deal. He is complimentary about Burns's thorough research, smooth style, and the persuasive force of his indictment of Roosevelt, but his final sentence in the review is a model of understatement: "Measured by what his New Deal advisors ideally desired, he fell miserably short; measured by what other possible presidents might have achieved in the 1930's—Baker, Garner, or Smith, for example—he might receive higher marks."

NOTES

[1] Although this essay is designed to give some idea of the books published since 1950 about Franklin D. Roosevelt and the New Deal, it is concerned primarily with the following: *Franklin D. Roosevelt: The Apprenticeship, Franklin D. Roosevelt: The Ordeal,* and *Franklin D. Roosevelt, The Triumph.* By Frank Freidel. Boston: Little, Brown and Company, 1952, 1954, and 1956. Pp. 456, 320, and 433. Each volume $6.00. *The Age of Roosevelt: The Crisis of the Old Order, 1919-1933.* By Arthur M. Schlesinger, Jr. Boston: Houghton Mifflin Company, 1957. Pp. xiv, 557. $6.00. *Franklin D. Roosevelt as Governor of New York.* By Bernard Bellush. New York: Columbia University Press, 1955. Pp. xii, 338. $5.00. *The Economic Thought of Franklin D. Roosevelt and the Origins of the New Deal.* By Daniel R. Fusfeld. New York: Columbia University Press, 1956. Pp. 337. $5.00. *The Roosevelt Leadership, 1933-1945.* By Edgar Eugene Robinson. Philadelphia: J. B. Lippincott Company. 1955. Pp. 491. $6.00. *Roosevelt: The Lion and the Fox.* By James MacGregor Burns. New York: Harcourt, Brace and Company. 1956. Pp. xvi, 553. $5.75.

[2] "The Preparation of a President," *Western Political Quarterly* I (June, 1948), 131 ff.; "The New Deal in Retrospect," *ibid.* (Dec., 1948), 373 ff.; "The New Deal: The Available Instruments of Governmental Power," *ibid.,* II (Dec., 1949), 545 ff.; "The New Deal: The Progressive Tradition," *ibid.,* III (Sept., 1950) 390 ff.; "The New Deal: The Decline of Government," *ibid.,* IV (June and Sept., 1951), 295 ff. and 469 ff.; "The Two Great Roosevelts," *ibid.,* V (March, 1952), 84 ff.; "The New Deal, the Rise of Business," *ibid.* (June and Sept., 1952), 274 ff. and 483 ff.; "The Compromising Roosevelt," *ibid.,* VI (June, 1953), 320 ff.; "The Protagonists: Roosevelt and Hoover," *Antioch Review* XIII (Winter, 1953), 419 ff.; "Franklin D. Roosevelt on the Verge of the Presidency," *ibid.,* XVI (Spring, 1956), 46 ff.; "The Experimental Roosevelt," *Political Quarterly,* XXI (July, 1950), 239 ff.; "The Progressive Orthodoxy of Franklin D. Roosevelt," *Ethics* LXIV (Oct., 1953), I ff.; "Fallow Years of F. D. R.," *ibid.,* LXIV (Jan., 1956), 98 ff. After the type was set for this article, a full-length biography of Roosevelt by Tugwell was published: *The Democratic Roosevelt* (Garden City: Doubleday and Co., 1957), 712 pp., $8.50. This is an important book. It is based upon considerable research in both printed and unprinted sources as well as upon Tugwell's own experiences. It has at points psychological overtones with a unique and quite subjective interpretation of Roosevelt's motivation.

Morton J. Frisch (essay date 1962)

SOURCE: "Franklin D. Roosevelt and the Problem of Democratic Liberty," in *ETHICS: An International Journal of Social, Political, and Legal Philosophy,* Vol. LXXII, No. 3, April, 1962, pp. 180-92.

[In the following essay, Frisch discusses Roosevelt's efforts to preserve American democracy during the Great Depression.]

The literature on Franklin D. Roosevelt generally reflects praise from those who call themselves liberals and criticism from those who call themselves conservatives.[1] Both major factions in American politics have been so preoccupied with the intricacies of the class struggle that a proper understanding of Roosevelt as a democratic statesman has been prevented. The significance of Roosevelt's contribution to the American political tradition will be largely missed, we believe, unless we remove the dark glasses of the class struggle. The intention of this paper is to present a view of Roosevelt's statesmanship which moves away from the limits of partisan considerations, whether they be liberal or conservative. Such a move will enable us to see whether the actions he took as a statesman were based on a serious and considered understanding of what democracy is all about, for the literature, whether praising or blaming him, usually regards his actions as merely "shrewd." Of course, Roosevelt was shrewd. But that artificial distinction between shrewdness and idealism overlooks the more important questions as to whether he was shrewd for good or for ill ends, and whether he was conscious or thoughtful about the relationship between shrewd actions and ultimate objectives. In order to answer these questions, we shall need to consider his understanding of the problem of democratic liberty as it developed in the crisis of the Great Depression. We shall not attempt here to carry the problem further by discussing the character of the society which Roosevelt preferred. Indeed, all the important political controversies in his career, whether they be the court-packing crisis of 1937, the attempted purge of Democratic congressmen in 1938, or the third-term issue in 1940, were related to the fundamental question of the kind of society he desired to achieve. But, for the moment, it will simply be sufficient to see whether Roosevelt seriously considered the problem of democratic liberty and indicate the manner in which the relation between these considerations and his actions as a statesman can be understood.

The United States is the oldest extensive republic in history[2] (until the founding of our country all large countries were monarchical and all republics were of the order of size of city-states). This country has preserved the same regime for more than 180 years. Certainly the stability of the American Republic must be regarded as a positive political attribute,[3] and the question naturally arises as to how our Constitution has been able to survive for so long. The following explanation is offered: the United States has been confronted in its history with three paramount domestic emergencies or crises, namely, the collapse of the Articles of Confederation, the Civil War, and the Great Depression, and they all were successfully met from the point of view of the continued existence of democratic liberty. These successes were due in large part, we believe, to the presence of superior or creative statesmanship, more specifically, the Founding Fathers,

Abraham Lincoln, and Franklin D. Roosevelt. And when we consider how these statesmen influenced the course of our national political life, we are irresistibly drawn by these considerations to the thought concerning political fundamentals upon which their actions rested. The study of political events properly points always to the thought related to those events, and it is with this consideration in mind that we propose to consider the manner in which the problem of democratic liberty presented itself to Franklin D. Roosevelt during the Great Depression.

At the beginning of his fourth year as President, Roosevelt characterized his Administration as "the writing of a new chapter in the history of popular government," with marked assurances that it was the intention of that Administration to build upon "essentially democratic institutions."[4] But we must try to understand more precisely what the President meant when he stated that his Administration was engaged in the writing of a "new chapter" in the history of popular government. Just one year earlier, at the beginning of his third year in that office, he had remarked that "in every Nation economic problems, long in the making, have brought crises of many kinds for which the masters of old theory and practice were unprepared."[5] But why should the crisis of the 1930's be considered as different from those already faced and overcome? The answer is that there were then new circumstances which had not existed before, and in this connection it would be worth our while to consider the observations of the great nineteenth-century commentators on American political institutions.

In 1840, when the Industrial Revolution was still in its earlier stages (in the United States), Alexis de Tocqueville had remarked that the "manufacturing aristocracy" which was growing up under our very eyes was "one of the harshest that ever existed in the world." The friends or partisans of democracy, he counseled, "should keep their eyes anxiously fixed in this direction; for if ever a permanent inequality of conditions and aristocracy again penetrate into the world, it may be predicted that this is the gate by which they will enter."[6] By the 1880's, when the Industrial Revolution had gathered considerable momentum, Lord Bryce commented upon the growing dissatisfaction of educated men with the economic liberalism of Adam Smith which, as he stated, conceives of the laws of demand and supply as a kind of self-regulatory mechanism upon which society can prosper. There are necessary benefits, said Bryce, which these laws do not procure, and unlimited competition seems to press too hard upon the weak. In fact, that very freedom of association which was the fruit of the democratic development prepared the ground for "a new form of tyranny," corporations acting in combination in unexpected ways, to suppress democratic liberty.[7] To quote Bryce:

> The power of groups of men organized by incorporation as joint-stock companies, or small knots of rich men acting in combination with unexpected strength in unexpected ways, overshadowing

individuals and even communities, and showing that the very freedom of association which men sought to secure by law when they were threatened by the violence of potentates may, under the shelter of the law, ripen into a new form of tyranny. . . . He who considers the irresponsible nature of the power which three or four men, or perhaps one man, can exercise through a great corporation, . . . the cynical audacity with which they have often used their wealth to seduce officials and legislators from the path of virtue, will find nothing unreasonable in the desire of the American masses to regulate the management of corporations and narrow the range of their action. . . . The next few years or even decades may be largely occupied with the effort to deal with these phenomena of a commercial system far more highly developed than the world has yet seen elsewhere.[8]

These industrial enterprises seemed to Bryce to have developed the characteristics, not simply of an economic undertaking, but of a kind of governing body.

In the early 1930's Roosevelt described the spirit of his program as a "new deal" which, as he explained it, represented a "changed concept" of the duties and responsibilities of government toward the economic life of the nation,[9] and that changed concept was necessarily the result of a changed world, which had become transformed by the potentialities of technology. The President characterized this "modern economically interdependent community" of ours as "governed by rules and regulations vastly more complex than those laid down in the days of Adam Smith or John Stuart Mill." In those days (that is, in the days of Smith and Mill), "private businesses . . . were conducted solely by individuals or by partnerships."[10] But, with the increase in the scale of industrial enterprise, individuals competing against others have refused to remain individuals. Instead, competing individuals have replaced themselves by corporate groups, and the result has been the emergence of a comparatively small group of corporations as "great uncontrolled and irresponsible units of power" within the state. Indeed, private enterprise had materially changed. It had become privileged enterprise rather than free enterprise. But "clearsighted men" (like Theodore Roosevelt and Woodrow Wilson) "saw with fear the danger that opportunity would no longer be equal; that the growing corporation . . . might threaten the economic freedom of individuals to earn a living."[11] Where Jefferson had feared "the encroachment of political power on the lives of individuals," it was Woodrow Wilson who saw, in the highly centralized economic system, "the despot of the twentieth century, on whom great masses of individuals relied for their safety and their livelihood, and whose irresponsibility and greed (if they were not controlled) would reduce them to starvation and penury." The concentration of financial power had proceeded far enough in 1912, said the President, for Wilson to realize fully its implications—"in a closer [i.e., more interdependent] economic system the central and ambitious financial unit is no longer a servant of the national desire, but a danger."[12] We cannot help

noticing here Roosevelt's marked departure from the older liberal view and, more particularly, from the views of Thomas Jefferson.

Roosevelt shared the older view as far as it went. That is, he was willing to defer, and did defer, to the principles of Jefferson. He meant with full seriousness that it was in the field of "political philosophy" that "Jefferson's significance is transcendent."[13] It was his considered judgment that the author of the Declaration of Independence was the "chief builder" of the "foundation principles" on which rests "the social and political structure of the Republic,"[14] and the spiritual father of the American democratic faith. But if Jefferson were to return to the councils of his party today, he would find among other things that the "economic changes of a century have changed the necessary methods of government action."[15] Jefferson, it is true, realized that "the exercise of property rights might so interfere with the rights of the individual that the Government, without whose assistance the property rights could not exist, must intervene, not to destroy individualism, but to protect it."[16] But, as was previously indicated, Wilson saw the situation more clearly than Jefferson. Jefferson did not seem to anticipate that the economic changes of a century, the growth of financial power, might necessitate increased regulations and controls over the nation's economy for the preservation of our democratic liberties. There is no more *Hamiltonian* a remark in the whole corpus of Roosevelt writings and speeches than his counsel to the nation at the "horse-and-buggy" press conference of 1935, in the wake of the adverse NRA decision by the Supreme Court, that "we have got to decide one way or the other . . . whether in some way we are going to turn over or restore to the Federal Government the powers which exist in the national Governments of every Nation in the world to enact and administer laws that have a bearing on, and general control over, national economic and national social problems."[17] And in his Second Inaugural Address in January, 1937, he declared that "the essential Democracy of our Nation and the safety of our people depend not upon the absence of power, but upon lodging it with those whom the people can change or continue at stated intervals through an honest and free system of elections."[18] Just a few months later, in the midst of the President's struggle with the Supreme Court over controversial New Deal legislation, Senator Mills Logan of Kentucky shrewdly observed: "On the one hand we have a Democratic Administration fighting for the constitutional interpretation advocated and sustained by Marshall and Hamilton, and on the other hand we have a Republican Party which has gone over to the Jeffersonian side of the question, and is standing up and fighting for the views of Thomas Jefferson."[19] This switchover in viewpoints here commented upon marks the extent of Roosevelt's departure from the older liberal view that liberty consists almost exclusively in security against restraints by the state. In a message to the Congress, delivered in April, 1938, the President declared that "private enterprise is ceasing to be free enterprise and is becoming a cluster of private collectivisms," that "the liberty of a democracy" was not secure if that democracy were willing to tolerate "the growth of private power to a point where it had become stronger than [the] democratic state itself," and that "big business collectivism in industry compels an ultimate collectivism in government."[20] Here the tension between the old and new liberalism becomes fully apparent.

Our first task has been to consider the new circumstances in America since the Civil War which necessitated the increased concern on the part of the national government for the proper functioning of our economic life. But, of course, the national government had always exhibited a considerable amount of interest in economic affairs, and in this sense the attachment to the doctrine of "let alone" was always an attachment to a theoretical purity which was impossible of practical application. As the President explained, even in the pristine age of individualism, "the United States passed protective laws designed, in the main, to give security to property owners, to industrialists, to merchants, and to bankers."[21] It has been shown that, as a result of the Industrial Revolution, economic power became concentrated in the hands of a comparatively small group of corporations rather than dispersed, and free competition on which the earlier liberal economists had so heavily relied was drastically reduced in the process. Also, it has been suggested that these concentrations of economic power prepared the ground for "a new form of tyranny" acting to suppress democratic liberty. We must now consider, as precisely as we can, the *consequences* of these new circumstances as they relate to the problem of democratic liberty.

To understand the problem of democratic liberty more precisely within the context of modern industrial America, we must remind ourselves of the plight of the factory-worker in the grip of the Industrial Revolution. In this connection the observations of Tocqueville are pertinent, for even prior to the Civil War the liberties of free wage-laborers had been considerably affected by technological advances.

> I think that, on the whole, it may be asserted that a slow and gradual rise of wages is one of the general laws of democratic communities. . . . But a great and gloomy exception occurs in our time. I have shown, in a preceding chapter, that aristocracy, expelled from political society, has taken refuge in certain departments of productive industry and has established its sway there under another form; this powerfully affects the rate of wages. As a large capital is required to embark in the large manufacturing speculations to which I allude, the number of persons who enter upon them is exceedingly limited; as their number is small, they can easily concert together to fix the rate of wages as they please.
>
> Their workmen, on the contrary, are exceedingly numerous, and the number of them is always increasing; for from time to time an extraordinary run of business takes place during which wages are inordinately high, and they attract the surrounding population to the factories. But when men have once embraced that line of life, we have already seen that they cannot quit it again, because they soon contract habits of body and mind which unfit them for any other sort of toil. These men have generally but little education and industry, with but few resources; they stand, therefore, almost at the mercy of the master.
>
> When competition or some other fortuitous circumstance lessens his profits, he can reduce the wages of his workmen at pleasure and make from them what he loses by the chances of business. Should the workmen strike, the master, who is a rich man, can very well wait, without being ruined, until necessity brings them back to him; but they must work day by day or they die, for their only property is in their hands. They have long been impoverished by oppression, and the poorer they become, the more easily they may be oppressed; they can never escape from their fatal circle of cause and consequence. The state of dependence and wretchedness in which a part of the manufacturing population of our time lives forms an exception to the general rule, contrary to the state of all the rest of the community; but for this very reason no circumstance is more important or more deserving of the attention of the legislator.[22]

As Tocqueville observes, in the absence of deliberate restraints imposed by the state, the peculiar aristocracy of industrial nations is in an unusually favorable position to exercise an enormous amount of control over the lives of free wage-laborers. What does it avail the wage-laborer to be free if he will starve without work, and is therefore driven to accept work on terms which the industrialist dictates? In such circumstances, the wage-laborer must rely altogether on the benevolence of the industrialist, and what frequently results is not liberty, but tyranny. The wage-laborer simply does not have equal bargaining power with the industrialist. To give more substance to a contract signed between them, there would need to be an equality of the contracting parties, and, as Tocqueville states, there is no circumstance more important or deserving of the attention of the legislator than the deprivation of the factory worker. In other words, it is the business of the legislator to make such rules and regulations for the conduct of society which shall add most to the security (and hence enjoyment) of those liberties for the sake of which the society was formed. And among those rules which democratic societies may properly make for their better preservation are those dealing with equality of economic rights and opportunities. As the President stated in his acceptance speech for the presidential renomination in June, 1936: "Liberty requires opportunity to make a living—a living decent according to the standard of the time, a living which gives men not only enough to live by, but something to live for. For too many of us the political equality we once won was meaningless in the face of economic inequality."[23] Roosevelt repeated this thought in many variants. In his Greeting to the Economic Club of New York in December, 1940, he stated: "The freedoms that we must and will protect in the United States are the freedoms which will make the individual paramount in a true democracy. In our American way of life political and economic freedom go hand in hand."[24] Therefore, the President would say, democratic liberty includes not only liberty of expression, security of person and property, the rights of public meeting and association, but the liberty to organize and bargain collectively, to pursue useful and remunerative employment commensurate with one's ability, and so on. And a regime which fosters these things is a good regime. Accordingly, and in this spirit, the President declared that he was not for "a return to that definition of liberty under which for many years a free people were being gradually regimented into the service of the privileged few." Instead he preferred "that broader definition of liberty under which we are moving forward to greater freedom, to greater security for the average man than he has ever known before in the history of America."[25]

In his Commonwealth Address, delivered in San Francisco during the 1932 presidential campaign, the President remarked: "We have learned a great deal [about liberty and the pursuit of happiness] in the past century. We know that individual liberty and individual happiness mean nothing unless both are ordered in the sense that one man's meat is not another man's poison."[26] There is, of course, a large and important truth in this assertion that the liberty of an individual is only valid insofar as it does not infringe on the proper liberties of other individuals. The price of liberty therefore is the restraint of liberty, and the price of liberty for everyone is the restraint on the greater liberties of some. As Justice Harlan Fiske Stone indicated in a letter to Herbert Hoover, written in March, 1934:

> Today what the Wall Street banker does may have serious consequences on the fortunes of the cotton planter in Mississippi and the farmer in Iowa. The textile manufacturer of New England is at the mercy of the employer of child labor or underpaid labor in the South. He must yield either to the pressure or abandon his business, with all the consequences to his employees and to his community—unless, perchance, the freedom of action of the employer of child labor is to some extent curtailed in the interest of the larger good.[27]

Liberty, as distinct from the liberties of special persons and classes, is the liberty that can be enjoyed by all members of the political community, and that kind can exist only insofar as it is restrained by rules. The restraint on the exploiter becomes the liberty of the exploited, and only through restraint on the actions by which individuals exploit other individuals does the whole political community gain political liberty. In this sense, restraint must be contrasted not with liberty but only with a narrow interpretation of it.

The argument just stated suggests that liberty is not necessarily opposed to restraint. Instead, all political liberty rests on restraint and, as we have previously stated, the restraints imposed on one individual or group of individuals become the condition of the liberties of other individuals. As the President stated in his Commonwealth

Address: "Every man has a right to his own property; which means a right to be assured, to the fullest extent attainable, in the safety of his savings. . . . In all thought of property, this right is paramount; all other property rights must yield to it. If, in accord with this principle, we must restrict the operations of the speculator, the manipulator, even the financier, I believe we must accept the restriction as needful, not to hamper individualism, but to protect it."[28] It is of some importance that Roosevelt's conception of a defined and limited liberty has its parallel in the writings of Edmund Burke. In a letter to the Sheriffs of Bristol on the Affairs of America, although written in another context, Burke made the same point:

> The extreme of liberty (which is its abstract perfection, but its real fault) obtains nowhere, nor ought to obtain anywhere; because extremes as we all know, in every point which relates either to our duties or satisfactions in life, are destructive both to virtue and enjoyment. Liberty, too, must be limited in order to be possessed. The degree of restraint it is impossible in any case to settle precisely. But it ought to be the constant aim of every wise public counsel to find out by cautious experiments, and rational, cool endeavors, with how little, not how much, of this restraint the community can subsist; for liberty is a good to be improved, and not an evil to be lessened. It is not only a private blessing of the first order, but the vital spring and energy of the state itself, which has just so much life and vigor as there is liberty in it.[29]

The liberty which is good is not the liberty of one individual or group of individuals gained at the expense of others, but the liberty which is dependent upon the completeness with which all members of the political community are restrained from injuring one another. Indeed, as the President observed, the Declaration of Independence, not to mention the very purposes of the American Revolution itself, "while seeking freedoms, called for the abandonment of privileges."[30] To the extent that privileges are misconstrued as freedoms, the regime is that much less democratic.

We have been led, as was to be expected, to the awareness that individuals are free to direct their own activities only insofar as other individuals are prevented from injuring and exploiting them. So far there is no real departure from the fundamental tenets of individualism, and it is with this old-fashioned understanding of the word in mind that Roosevelt declared that "we must go back to first principles; we must make American individualism what it was intended to be—equality of opportunity for all, the right of exploitation for none."[31] Moreover, in a message to the Congress in June, 1934, on the objectives of the Administration, the President assured the legislators that "this seeking for a greater measure of welfare and happiness does not indicate a change in values. It is rather a return to values lost in the course of our economic development and expansion."[32] In short, this seeking for a greater measure of economic security is not destroying liberty but confirming it. In Roosevelt's own words: "What the American people demanded in 1933 was not less democracy but more democracy,"[33] and this obviously necessitated, as he explained it, modifying and controlling private economic enterprise. And as a result of these restraints the whole political community experiences not a diminution, but an increase of their democratic liberties. Indeed, private enterprise had become too private. For private enterprise had lost its sense of directedness toward the public good. Certainly the founders of the doctrine of private enterprise had never allowed themselves to become entranced by the mechanics of the market and matters of mere self-interest. Only a small boy could be entranced by such considerations.

But there is one massive objection to the foregoing argument. In brief, this objection amounts to the charge that, if the government does for the individual in the interest (the very real interest) of his own welfare and security what he has previously done for himself, what effect will all this have on his character, initiative, and enterprise? Tocqueville gave serious attention to this matter, and in fact sketched a kind of paternalistic welfare state which would gradually rob the individual of all the uses of himself; "it would degrade men without tormenting them."

> I think . . . that the species of oppression by which democratic nations are menaced is unlike anything that ever existed in the world; our contemporaries will find no prototype of it in their memories. I seek in vain for an expression that will accurately convey the whole of the idea I have formed of it; the old words *despotism* and *tyranny* are inappropriate: the thing itself is new, and since I cannot name, I must attempt to define it.

> That power is absolute, minute, regular, provident, and mild. It would be like the authority of a parent if, like that authority, its object was to prepare man for manhood; but it seeks, on the contrary, to keep them in perpetual childhood: it is well content that the people should rejoice, provided that they think of nothing but rejoicing. For their happiness such a government willingly labors, but it chooses to be the sole agent and the only arbiter of that happiness; it provides for their security, foresees and supplies their necessities, facilitates their pleasures, manages their principle concerns, directs their industry, regulates the descent of property, and subdivides their inheritance; what remains but to spare them all the care of thinking and all the trouble of living? Thus it every day renders the exercise of a free agency of man less useful and less frequent: it circumscribes the will within a narrower range and gradually robs a man of all the uses of himself.

> After thus having successfully taken each member of the community in its powerful grasp and fashioned him at will, the supreme power then extends its arm over the whole community. It covers the surface of society with a network of small complicated rules, minute and uniform, through which the most original minds and most energetic characters cannot penetrate, to rise above the crowd. The will of man is not shattered, but softened, bent, and guided; men are seldom forced to act, but they are constantly restrained from acting. Such a power does not destroy, but it prevents existence; it does not tyrannize, but it compresses, enervates, extinguishes and stupefies a people, till each nation is reduced to nothing better than a flock of timid and industrious animals, of which the government is the shepherd.[34]

The President did of course make such statements as "Americans do not wish to see a permanent extension of purely Government operations carried to the extent of relieving us of our individual responsibilities as citizens"[35] and "any paternalistic system which tries to provide for security for everyone from above calls for an impossible task and a regimentation utterly uncongenial to the spirit of our people,"[36] and they were meant with full seriousness. But we are somewhat inclined to believe that his liberalism, enlightened though it was, prevented him from fully appreciating the dangers of the kind of paternalistic state which Tocqueville had so clearly outlined.

Still Roosevelt's liberalism may not have been quite so naïve on this score. Needless to say, he abhorred both fascism and communism, but precisely for the same reason. He considered both these extremes as distinct threats to individualism. In this connection, we must mention the President's exchange with representatives of the American Youth Congress (in June, 1940), a group that regarded the war in Europe as hardly more than a struggle for power and not, as the President himself believed, a conflict between different forms of government or different ways of life. Roosevelt asked one of the youths whether he would prefer living in France or Germany, and the youth replied that he would much prefer living in the United States. But the President insisted that the choice was between France and Germany, that is, between a poorly ordered democracy and an efficiently ordered tyranny. As for himself, the President remarked, he "would rather live in France than in Germany," and that was because the French have "a pretty free method of life" and "a great deal of civil liberty."[37] We could further underscore this attitude of mind with the President's observation nearly two years earlier that "the conflict is still sharpening throughout the world between two political systems. The one system represents government by freedom of choice exercised by the individual citizens. In the other, and opposing system, individual freedom and initiative are all made subordinate to the totalitarian state."[38] In other words, individualism and civil liberties were such crucial considerations for the President that the choice between regimes, between democracy and tyranny (or totalitarianism), could be made on this basis. In Roosevelt's thinking, the great alternative of our times is between democracy and tyranny, and tyranny as a form of government embraced both the Fascist and Communist variations.[39] But since democracy and tyranny, as they are so called, are essentially different, the one correct and the other faulty,[40] how indeed did they differ? Individualism is present in the one and absent in the other. And it is in this sense that the President considered individualism to constitute the core of the democratic form. As he stated in his address to the Pan-American Scientific Congress in May, 1940: "We, and most of the people of the world, still believe that men and women have an inherent right to hew out the patterns of their own individual lives, just so long as they as individuals do not harm their fellow beings. We call this ideal by many terms which are synonymous—we call it individual liberty, we call it civil liberty and, I think, best of all, we call it democracy."[41] From these accumulated considerations, it is quite possible that Roosevelt may have been far more appreciative of the dangers of paternalism than we were at first inclined to believe.

The President was deeply concerned about the danger to our liberties caused by economic inequality, and as a result of that concern there emerged in his own mind an understanding of the problem of democratic liberty which went beyond the Jeffersonian understanding. The problem of democratic liberty, as Roosevelt suggested, is necessarily concerned with economic as well as with political considerations. In other words, democratic liberty must be construed as consisting not only of security for political rights, but also in guaranties that the economically weak will not be at the mercy of the economically strong. In the circumstances of a modern industrial democracy, the President believed, the defined and limited liberty which alone can be generally enjoyed is most likely to be secured by a regime which restrains economic inequalities as well as one which concerns itself with the virtues of individual enterprise. It is in this broadened sense (as Roosevelt asserted) that "our ideal is democratic liberty,"[42] and this constitutes a marked departure from the older liberal view. But we are compelled to move a step further for, without recourse to a deeper principle than that which we have thus far had, we seem unable to really transcend the individualism of the older liberal view. We have already seen that democratic liberty rests on restraint, and the enlargement of that liberty may necessitate increased restraints on the particular liberties of some individuals. But when such restraints are denounced as infringements on liberty, we are forced to ask: for what purpose are the restraints intended? The restraints derive their justification from the kind of action that they curtail, or in the kind of society in which such restraints (and liberties for that matter) are exercised. In this sense, it is no longer a matter of increasing or decreasing restraints, but of organizing them in such a fashion so as to secure conditions which are believed necessary for the common good. Hence the clue to a deeper understanding of liberty is indicated by our recourse to the notion of the common good, and our concern for liberties and restraints recedes as our concern for the common good or justice comes into view.

In a campaign address at Detroit, Michigan, in October, 1933, Roosevelt used the theme of "social justice." In that address, he stated that the followers of the doctrine of "let alone" maintain that a system of employment insurance interferes with individualism, and that the remedy for the causes of poverty are beyond the control of any individual, whether he be "a czar of politics or a czar of industry." But the followers of the doctrine of "social action," Roosevelt continued, maintain that if we set up "a system of social justice" we shall have little need for the exercise of "mere philanthropy." "Justice, after all, is the first goal we seek. We believe that when justice has been done individualism will have a greater security to devote the best that individualism can offer."[48] Now, if as Roosevelt seems to suggest, individualism cannot be realized without justice (or something like that), it follows that all definitions of individualism or liberty must presuppose some conception of justice. The very idea of justice or the common good presupposes an area in which one individual's liberty is not in conflict with another's. Liberty is not at all "a license to climb upwards by pushing other people down,"[44] but rather the opportunity to choose among those lines of activity which do not involve injury to others. And every injury is an injustice. As the President explained: "The thing we are all seeking is justice—justice in the common-sense interpretation of that word—the interpretation that means justice against exploitation on the part of those who do not care much for the lives, the happiness and the prosperity of their neighbors."[45] The connection between *liberty* and *justice* is nowhere more succinctly expressed than in Burke's letter to M. Dupont written during the period of the French Revolution, and which we may appropriately reproduce in this connection.

> Of all the loose terms in the world, liberty is the most indefinite. It is not solitary, unconnected, individual, selfish liberty, as if every man was to regulate the whole of his conduct by his own will. The liberty I mean is social freedom. It is that state of things in which liberty is secured by the equality of restraint. A constitution of things in which the liberty of no one man, and no body of men, and no number of men, can find means to trespass on the liberty of any person, or any description of persons, in the society. This kind of liberty is, indeed, but another name for justice; ascertained by wise laws, and secured by well-constructed institutions. I am sure that liberty, so incorporated, and in a manner identified with justice, must be infinitely dear to everyone who is capable of conceiving what it is. But whenever a separation is made between liberty and justice, neither is, in my opinion safe.[46]

Like every other principle, liberty for Burke depended upon the circumstances. He was opposed to theoretical, unconnected liberty, and could never conceive of it stripped of all its relations. The circumstances, he counseled, give liberty its "distinguishing color" and its "discriminating effect." Liberty is not identical with justice, but it may be a part of it. Liberty without justice is only a theory, and theories are not safe guides in politics. As far as his own principles were concerned, Burke had "no idea of a liberty unconnected with honesty and justice."[47] In short, liberty is the liberty to act according to what is permitted, and what is permitted presupposes a conception of what is just.

In the course of this essay, we have been carried beyond the horizon of liberty. Liberty implies restraint, but the *purposes* for which governments choose to exercise those restraints is the crucial political consideration, for those choices determine to a large extent the character of the society in which we live. In a speech delivered in November, 1938, the President stated that "we cannot carelessly assume that a nation is strong and great because it has a democratic form of government." Also, in that same speech, he indicated that democracies of late have been weakened by the dissensions and suspicions created by "social injustices," thereby conceding that democracies could act unjustly, or that a democratic order is not necessarily a just order simply by virtue of its democratic form.[48] But he was absolutely convinced that only democracies could be truly just, that is, that the good or just regime was a democratic regime properly ordered. In this sense, he went on to say that "too many of those who prate about saving democracy are really interested in saving things as they were." But, he counseled, "democracy should concern itself also with things as they *ought to be.*"[49] It was precisely at this point that the President came face to face with these paramount political questions: Is the American democracy a good or just democracy? And in recognition of its deficiencies (which obviously were present),[50] how can the American democracy become a better or more just democracy? Interestingly enough, what Roosevelt suggests here is far more indicative of conservative than liberal thinking. Be that as it may, one cannot really understand the Social Security Act, the National Labor Relations Act, the Fair Labor Standards Act, and other crucial pieces of New Deal legislation if one does not consider them in terms of their intention to secure a better quality of life for the members of our democratic political community. As he stated to the Congress upon recommending wages and hours legislation: "A self-supporting and self-respecting democracy can plead no justification to the existence of child labor, no economic reason for chiseling workers' wages or stretching workers' hours."[51] Indeed, Roosevelt's quest for a broader understanding of democratic liberty, a liberty which includes equality of economic rights as well as equality of political rights, has carried us in a somewhat unexpected way to deeper questions (of which the President himself was perhaps only dimly aware) relating to the aims and justifications of a democratic political order. At any rate, we have learned that the problem of liberty is inseparable from the problem of justice, since liberty is the liberty to act in ways which are either just or unjust. As Burke wisely remarked: "The effect of liberty to individuals is that they may do as they please; we ought to see what it will please them to do before we risk congratulations, which may be soon turned into complaints."[52] Mere liberty may produce majority tyranny, and in order to have democratic relevance liberty must ultimately be understood in terms of what is just. Liberty therefore is a means to justice or the just ordering of society and not an end in itself.

The Great Depression, which had reached its peak in 1933, was as perilous a crisis in the life of the nation as the deterioration of the regime under the Articles of Confederation or the Civil War. Needless to say, it was the most serious economic emergency in American history. In May, 1857, Lord Macaulay, writing to an American friend, Henry Stephens Randall, predicted that "the time will come when New England will be as thickly populated as old England. . . . You will have your Manchesters and Birminghams. And in these Manchesters and Birminghams hundreds of thousands of artisans will assuredly be sometimes out of work. Then your institutions will be fairly brought to the test."[53] Roosevelt placed that crisis in its larger perspective: "When I became President, I found a country demoralized, disorganized, with [labor, business, and agriculture] seeking to survive by taking advantage of the others. As in the time of George Washington in 1787, when there was grave danger that the state would never become a Nation—as in the time of Abraham Lincoln, when a tragic division threatened to become lasting—our own time has brought a test of the American Union."[54] And, we may properly ask, in such a crisis will democratic government be able to preserve itself or will America turn to other forms as, for example, fascism or communism? This is a question which no experience of previous crises can answer, and at such a time creative statesmanship is imperative. The creative task of democratic statesmanship is the preservation of the regime under the changing conditions of newer generations. This task assumes different shapes at different times, but the challenge is always the same. The crucial problem in each instance is one of preservation, and that means the preservation of properly or justly ordered democratic institutions.[55]

NOTES

[1] In its original form, this paper was presented before the Teacher's Summer Institute on Government under the auspices of the College of William and Mary in Williamsburg, Virginia, in July, 1961. I am indebted to Professor Richard G. Stevens, of the College of William and Mary, for a critical reading of this paper and for several extremely important suggestions concerning matters of presentation.

[2] See Franklin D. Roosevelt, "Preface to a Projected Book on the Machinery of Government" (Franklin D. Roosevelt Library, Hyde Park, N.Y., 1922 or 1923): "Of all the great nations of the world the United States has the oldest continuous form of government, if one considers the democratization of the British Parliament a change."

[3] See Lord Bryce, *The American Commonwealth,* ed. Louis Hacker (2 vols.; New York, 1959), II, 433: "As one test of a human body's soundness is its capacity for reaching a great age, so it is high praise for a political system that it has stood no more changed than any institution must change in a changing world, and that it gives every promise of durability."

[4] Roosevelt, *The Public Papers and Addresses of Franklin D. Roosevelt,* compiled by S. I. Rosenman (13 vols.; New York, 1938-50) (hereinafter cited as FDR, *PPA*), V, 13.

[5] *Ibid.,* IV, 15.

[6] Alexis de Tocqueville, *Democracy in America,* trans. H. Reeve (2 vols.; New York, 1959), II, 171.

[7] Bryce, *op. cit.,* II, 400-401.

[8] *Ibid.,* pp. 400-401, 599.

[9] FDR, *PPA,* I, 782.

[10] *Ibid.,* IV, 339.

[11] *Ibid.,* I, 748.

[12] *Ibid.,* p. 749.

[13] *Ibid.,* VII, 579.

[14] Roosevelt, *Public Papers of Governor Franklin D. Roosevelt* (4 vols.; Albany, N.Y., 1930-39), 1932 vol., p. 577.

[15] *Ibid.,* p. 583.

[16] FDR, *PPA,* I, 746.

[17] Roosevelt, "Press Conference No. 209, May 31, 1935," *Press Conferences of Franklin D. Roosevelt* (Hyde Park, N.Y., 1956), V, 333.

[18] FDR, *PPA,* VI, 2.

[19] *Congressional Record* (75th Cong., 1st sess., July 7, 1937), LXXXI, Part 6, 6877.

[20] FDR, *PPA,* VII, 305, 308, 313.

[21] *Ibid.,* p. 479.

[22] Tocqueville, *op. cit.,* II, 201-2.

[23] FDR, *PPA,* V, 233.

[24] *Ibid.,* IX, 597.

[25] *Ibid.,* III, 422.

[26] *Ibid.,* I, 755.

[27] Harlan Fiske Stone to Herbert Hoover, March 27, 1934. Quoted in A. T. Mason, *Security through Freedom* (Ithaca, N.Y., 1955), p. 77.

[28] FDR, *PPA,* I, 754.

[29] Edmund Burke, *The Works of the Right Honourable Edmund Burke* (11 vols.; Boston, 1869) (hereinafter cited as Burke, *Works*), II, 229.

[30] FDR, *PPA,* XII, 163.

[31] *Ibid.,* I, 681.

[32] *Ibid.,* III, 292.

[33] *Ibid.,* XIII, 404.

[34] Tocqueville, *op. cit.,* II, 336-37.

[35] FDR, *PPA,* II, 356.

[36] *Ibid.,* IV, 342.

[37] "Press Conference No. 649A, June 5, 1940," *op. cit.,* XV, 488-89.

[38] FDR, *PPA,* II, 356.

[39] See *ibid.,* VII, 399: "Communism . . . is just as dangerous as Fascism."

[40] Roosevelt described democracy as "the best instrument of government yet devised by mankind" (*ibid.,* IX, 10), and tyranny as "the oldest and most discredited rule known to history" (*ibid.,* p. 301).

[41] *Ibid.,* IX, 185.

[42] *Ibid.,* VII, 221.

[43] *Ibid.,* I, 776-77.

[44] *Ibid.,* IV, 341.

[45] *Ibid.,* pp. 489-90.

[46] Burke, *Correspondence of the Right Honourable Edmund Burke,* ed. C. W. Fitzwilliam and R. Bourke (4 vols.; London, 1844), III, 106-7.

[47] Burke, *Works,* II, 416.

[48] FDR, *PPA,* VII, 585.

[49] *Ibid.,* VII, 586. (My italics.)

[50] See *ibid.,* V, 579: "We who live in a free America know that our democracy is not perfect."

[51] *Ibid.,* VI, 210-11.

[52] Burke, *Works,* III, 242.

[53] T. B. Macaulay to Henry Stephens Randall, May 23, 1857, *The Reader's Macaulay,* ed. W. French and G. Saunders (Chicago, 1936), p. 63.

[54] FDR, *PPA,* VII, 520.

[55] See *ibid.,* p. 419: "The task [of preserving popular government] assumes different shapes at different times. Sometimes the threat to popular government comes from

political interests, sometimes from economic interests, sometimes we have to beat off all of them together."

Thomas W. Benson (essay date 1969)

SOURCE: "Inaugurating Peace: Franklin D. Roosevelt's Last Speech," in *Speech Monographs*, Vol. XXXVI, No. 2, June, 1969, pp. 138-47.

[*In the following essay, Benson investigates various drafts of Roosevelt's final speech, which was to be delivered in April of 1945.*]

> *The only limit to our realization of tomorrow will be our doubts of today. Let us move forward with strong and active faith.*

In the spring of 1945 it was evident to the nation that the war in Europe would soon end in victory for the Allies. It was also evident to some that Franklin Roosevelt was failing. In early April Roosevelt, weary from his recent trip to Yalta, went to his Warm Springs retreat. On Wednesday, April 11, working on a speech to be delivered by radio to Jefferson Day Dinners on Friday, April 13, Roosevelt added in his own handwriting a concluding sentence to a ghostwritten draft: "Let us move forward with strong and active faith." These were the last words, other than his signature, that he was to pen. On Thursday, April 12, while sitting for a portrait, Roosevelt suffered a cerebral hemorrhage and died a few hours later.

The 1945 Jefferson Day speech, although it was never delivered, has taken its place as the last speech in the Roosevelt canon, and has been singled out as having special significance.[1] And yet much that has been written about the speech is inaccurate or misleading, and several questions of importance to Roosevelt scholarship are unanswered. Who wrote the speech? Of what significance are the changes Roosevelt made in drafts submitted by his writers? And, since the speech was never delivered, can we be confident that the draft Roosevelt left was in finished form?

At the Franklin D. Roosevelt Library in Hyde Park, New York, a thin box numbered 1577 contains four typewritten drafts of the last speech.[2] The first, written by a heretofore unknown author at the Democratic National Committee, was received at the White House sometime before April 9, 1945, on which date Robert Sherwood forwarded it, together with a draft he had written, to Jonathan Daniels, who in turn wrote a third draft and sent the accumulated materials to William D. Hassett, Roosevelt's secretary. The fourth draft was written by Roosevelt himself, dictating to Mrs. Dorothy Brady, a stenographer, at Warm Springs on the afternoon of April 11.[3]

In all previous references to the authorship of the last speech, the writer of the draft prepared at the Democratic National Committee was unknown. It was by chance that

I met a man who, learning of my interest in public address, mentioned that he had worked on Roosevelt's last speech. That man is Josef Berger, an author and speechwriter currently residing in Brooklyn Heights, New York, but in 1945 the chief speechwriter for the Democratic National Committee. Some of Berger's writings have been published under the pseudonym of Jeremiah Digges, under which name he was listed in the 1945 edition of *Who's Who in America.*[4]

Josef Berger is probably the model ghostwriter. A modest, sensitive man, he is a skillful writer who does not need to establish a claim to literary status by revealing his authorship of others' speeches. Although not reticent about his work on Roosevelt's speech, he had never bothered to make public his authorship, on the grounds that

> Although I am proud of the little assist I was able to give President Franklin D. Roosevelt, I really don't care who knows about it—or doesn't know about it. The credit a ghostwriter can take for the job he does must be, as I see it, a wholly personal matter, within himself, . . . The only thing that matters to me is that I think it was a good speech and belongs now to the late President, and to his memory.[5]

But despite the modesty and general credibility of Berger, some documentation is needed to support his designation as the author of the first version of the speech. Inquiries to the Democratic National Committee turned up no support. Luckily, other sources of evidence were available. In 1938 Josef Berger had won a grant from the John Simon Guggenheim Memorial Foundation to write a book about the Portuguese fishermen of America. In 1946, he applied for a second grant, this time to "do a book for American teenagers about teenagers of the Soviet Union, and follow that with one about American teenagers for young readers in the Soviet Union."[6] Included in the material supporting Berger's 1946 application was a letter from the late Sam O'Neal, Director of Publicity for the Democratic National Committee. The letter, on the letterhead of the Democratic National Committee, was addressed to Henry Allen Moe of the Guggenheim Memorial Foundation. It read:

> For the confidential information of yourself and members of your board of selection, this is to certify that Josef Berger prepared, at my request, the original draft of the Jefferson Day Address which was to have been delivered by the late President Franklin D. Roosevelt on April 13, 1945, and which was published posthumously; and that although the late President made certain revisions, much of the original draft was retained.[7]

There is at least one other witness to Josef Berger's authorship of the original draft. George F. Willison, an American historian and a former chairman of the classics department at St. John's College in Annapolis, Maryland, was in a position to observe the creation of the speech.[8] In 1944-45, Willison served as a writer at the Democratic

National Committee, and shared a two-man office with Berger. He recalls:

> I well remember the circumstances under which Joe drafted FDR's "last speech." . . . As Joe was drafting the speech, he and I talked about it frequently, and I read many pages of the final draft.[9]

How did it come about that a Roosevelt speech would be originated by an author of whom no mention existed in the White House records of the speech? An account of the origin and development of the speech reveals a departure from Roosevelt's usual methods of preparation. As Berger recalls it:

> We all knew the President was ill, but I don't think anyone realized just how ill. Robert E. Hannegan, then Chairman of the Democratic National Committee and U.S. Postmaster General, very much wanted FDR to address the party's Jefferson Day Dinner scheduled for April 13, and made a strong bid for the President's acceptance. The answer was No. Hannegan then told Sam O'Neal, a Washington newspaperman who had succeeded Paul Porter as head of the Committee's Publicity Division, to have me do a draft anyhow. I think he hoped that if the President liked it well enough he might still change his mind.

> O'Neal told me to keep it down to five minutes. I decided not to spend any part of these precious minutes on Jefferson, but to keep it on the task of building a lasting peace. The next I heard was that the President had changed his mind and would address the gathering for the dinner.[10]

Although the President commonly used help in writing his speeches, that help seems in most cases to have come from sources sought out by the President himself.[11] But in this case the initiative for the speech came from beyond the White House, and so it is not surprising that no effort was made by the White House staff to determine who had written the draft which led to the acceptance of the speaking engagement, particularly when Roosevelt would have no further use of his services, making his identity of historical interest only.

Robert Sherwood, who wrote the second draft of the speech, was a frequent and well-known contributor to Roosevelt speeches. His recollection of the period helps to date Berger's draft and the decision of the President to go ahead with the speech. Sherwood mentions a meeting with the President on March 24, 1945, at which Roosevelt brought up the subject of the Jefferson Day speech and asked Sherwood to "look up some Jefferson quotations on the subject of science."[12] If both Sherwood and Berger recall the circumstances accurately, Roosevelt must have read and tentatively approved of Berger's draft before March 24, and he must have had some specific ideas about revisions, since the Berger draft does not mention either Jefferson or science, subjects which Roosevelt makes relevant to the theme of the Berger draft. One possible snag in the chronology of the speech's

development is the letter from Sherwood to Daniels accompanying Sherwood's version of the speech. In it, Sherwood mentions that the speech—the Berger draft—was referred to him by Daniels.[13] But the two Sherwood documents are not irreconcilable, since Roosevelt might well have spoken with Sherwood about the speech and left it to Daniels to forward the manuscript.

Jonathan Daniels, author of the third draft, was at the time of Roosevelt's death the Presidential Press Secretary, having been promoted a short time before from his post as administrative assistant. Daniels was the son of Josephus Daniels, Secretary of the Navy under Wilson when Franklin Roosevelt had served as Assistant Secretary. Jonathan Daniels was a journalist and author of fiction and nonfiction books, including later writings on Roosevelt.[14]

These three men—Berger, Sherwood, Daniels—submitted to Franklin Delano Roosevelt drafts of a speech that might have been regarded as a minor, if excellent, ceremonial address had it been delivered, but which was to become uniquely significant as Roosevelt's last statement to his countrymen on the new world which was to follow the war.

II

Having answered the question of who worked on the President's last speech, we must next ask who wrote how much of what appears in the draft prepared by Roosevelt himself.

The Roosevelt draft contains thirty sentences, the last of which is the only sentence contributed by Roosevelt alone. Roosevelt copied twenty-three sentences without revision, and incorporated in his draft six sentences from earlier drafts which he revised. None of the sentences which Roosevelt used from the Daniels draft had failed to appear in earlier drafts, leading to the conclusion that Roosevelt rejected altogether the Daniels version. The first twenty-two sentences of Roosevelt's draft appear to have been taken from the Sherwood draft. Of the twenty-two, Roosevelt copied eighteen without revision and revised sentences eight, nine, ten, and eleven. Sentences one and fifteen had originated in the Berger draft, had been revised by Sherwood, and were used without further revision by Roosevelt. Sentences twenty-three to twenty-nine were from the Berger draft. Roosevelt revised sentences twenty-seven and twenty-nine. In all, nine of Berger's original sentences appeared in the Roosevelt draft, four of them revised by either Sherwood or Roosevelt.

Reproduced below is the Roosevelt version of the speech, with sentence numbers added. Footnotes reproduce earlier versions of sentences which were revised.

RADIO ADDRESS OF THE PRESIDENT
JEFFERSON DAY DINNER
APRIL 13, 1945

(1) Americans are gathered together this evening in communities all over the country to pay tribute to the living memory of Thomas Jefferson—one of the greatest of all democrats; and I want to make it clear that I am spelling that word "democrats" with a small "d."[15]

(2) I wish I had the power, just for this evening, to be present at all of these gatherings.

(3) In this historic year, more than ever before, we do well to consider the character of Thomas Jefferson as an American citizen of the world.

(4) As Minister to France, then as our first Secretary of State and as our third President, Jefferson was instrumental in the establishment of the United States as a vital factor in international affairs.

(5) It was he who first sent our Navy into far distant waters to defend our rights. (6) And the promulgation of the Monroe doctrine was the logical development of Jefferson's farseeing foreign policy.

(7) Today this nation which Jefferson helped so greatly to build is playing a tremendous part in the battle for the rights of man all over the world.

(8) Today we are part of the vast Allied force—a force composed of flesh and blood and steel and spirit—which is today destroying the makers of war, the breeders of hatred, in Europe and in Asia.[16]

(9) In Jefferson's time our Navy consisted of only a handful of frigates headed by the gallant U.S.S. CONSTITUTION—"OLD IRONSIDES"—but that tiny Navy taught nations across the Atlantic that piracy in the Mediterranean—acts of aggression against peaceful commerce and the enslavement of their crews was one of those things which, among neighbors, simply was not done.[17]

(10) Today we have learned in the agony of war that great power involves great responsibility.[18] (11) Today we can no more escape the consequences of German and Japanese aggression than could we avoid the consequences of attacks by the Barbary Corsairs a century and a half before.[19]

(12) We, as Americans, do not choose to deny our responsibility.

(13) Nor, do we intend to abandon our determination that, within the lives of our children and our children's children, there will not be a third world war.

(14) We seek peace—enduring peace. (15) More than an end to war, we want an end to the beginnings of all wars—yes, an end to this brutal, inhuman and thoroughly impractical method of settling the differences between governments.[20]

(16) The once powerful, malignant Nazi state is crumbling. (17) The Japanese war lords are receiving, in their own home-land, the retribution for which they asked when they attacked Pearl Harbor.

(18) But the mere conquest of our enemies is not enough.

(19) We must go on to do all in our power to conquer the doubts and fears, the ignorance and the greed, which made this horror possible.

(20) Thomas Jefferson, himself a distinguished scientist, once spoke of "the brotherly spirit of Science, which unites into one family all its votaries of whatever grade, and however widely dispersed throughout the different quarters of the globe."

(21) Today, science has brought all the different quarters of the globe so close together that it is impossible to isolate them from one another.

(22) Today we are faced with the preeminent fact that, if civilization is to survive, we must cultivate the science of human relationships—the ability of all peoples, of all kinds, to live together and work together in the same world, at peace.

(23) Let me assure you that my hand is the steadier for the work that is to be done, that I move more firmly into the task, knowing that you—millions and millions of you—are joined with me in the resolve to make this work endure.

(24) The work, my friends, is peace. (25) More than an end of this war—an end to the beginnings of all wars. (26) Yes, an end, forever, to this impractical, unrealistic settlement of the differences between governments by the mass killing of peoples.

(27) Today, as we move against the terrible scourge of war—as we go forward towards the greatest contribution that any generation of human beings can make in this world—the contribution of lasting peace, I ask you to keep up your faith.[21] (28) I measure the sound, solid achievement that can be made at this time by the straight-edge of your own confidence and your resolve. (29) And to you, and to all Americans who dedicate themselves with us to the making of an abiding peace, I say:

The only limit to our realization of tomorrow will be our doubts of today.[22] (30) Let us move forward with strong and active faith.

III

Of what significance are the changes that Roosevelt made in the drafts presented to him? The Berger draft, although only nine of its sentences found their way into the President's draft, set the theme for the speech. Berger's draft was a vigorous denunciation of war and a challenge to work for peace. Roosevelt removed much of the most hard-hitting language, such as:

Even as I speak these words, I can hear, in my mind's ear, an old, old chorus. You have heard it too. You will hear more of it as we go forward with the work at hand.

It is the chorus coming from the defeatists, the cynics, the perfectionists—all the world's sad aggregation of timid souls who tell us, for one reason or another, it can't be done.

They have been afraid to come along with us as we approached this task of destiny. And they will shrink, they will pull back and try to pull us back with them, as we get further into it.

Oh yes, they will agree, war is horrible. War is hell.

And yet, in their pale, anaemic minds there is a kind of worship of this same horror of war. They tell us there can be no end of it. They endow it with immortality. They certify it to us as the ultimate fate of mankind on earth.

Now, you and I don't stand in such awe and adoration. We don't think war deserves it.

You and I are not willing to concede that we were put here on earth for no better purpose. And from here on, the wars that would come if we let them would leave precious few of us to argue to the contrary!

You and I call war stupidity—not plain stupidity, but enormous, brutal stupidity, a crime that makes no more sense to its perpetrator than it does to its victim.

Well, today that cult of the faint-hearted, the credo of those cringing adorers of a criminal precedent, is on its way out. And in a span of time as far back as history goes, that is something new under the sun.

To me, there is no greater hope for humanity, there is no better sign in the world of our time, than the fact that this abject worship of war has become—for the first time—a minority belief. We have struck boldly forward in the inner world of our thinking, in the world that we project for our kind, and we have discovered that the world is not flat.

True, if there are new corporals who will want to become rulers of the earth, we cannot legislate wild fancies out of their minds. And if there are other impractical dreamers who must indulge themselves in their private nightmares—the pipe-dream that war is inevitable—we cannot pass laws abridging the freedom to dream.

But we can and we will stop these murderous hallucinations from reaching us. We can and we will keep them confined to the dream-world of would-be conquerors and of the defeatists who are their accessories before the fact. We can stop them from wrecking the lives of sane, sound, peace-loving, practical humanity. This we can do. And this we will do.

I say "we," for I know that I am only one in many millions who share this belief and are so resolved. We have had it proved abundantly to us in America

that our people, whether Democrats or Republicans, want to strike boldly against the threat of war. They have demanded a sane, practical end to it. And they have their feet on the ground.

The Sherwood draft, in contrast to Berger's, was not so much a condemnation of war as it was a celebration of victory, couched in terms of homage to Jefferson, with a final gesture of commitment to peace. Roosevelt put together his first draft out of the warlike passages from Sherwood followed by the milder peace-seeking passages from Berger. The President thus achieved a balanced impression of peace through strength, and omitted Berger's monolithic—but rather militant—condemnation of war in all its aspects. It must be left to historians to conclude whether in creating that ambiguous balance between peace and strength, Roosevelt was looking forward in his last days to a world regulated by the United Nations, or to one committed to an unending arms race.

Other Roosevelt omissions from the Berger draft are significant. In opening the speech and referring to the President's wish that he could be with each of his listeners, Berger wrote:

> I have spoken to my doctor about my inability to be in more than one spot at a time, but he tells me the condition is chronic. There is nothing he can do about it.

Both Sherwood and Daniels made use of this paragraph in their introductions. Roosevelt undoubtedly struck out the paragraph in accordance with his policy of not referring to his health, in the belief that it would draw attention to his partial paralysis. This policy had been violated only once, in the address to the Congress on March 1, 1945, after Roosevelt's return from Yalta:

> I hope that you will pardon me for this unusual posture of sitting down during the presentation of what I want to say, but I know that you will realize that it makes it a lot easier for me not to have to carry about ten pounds of steel around on the bottom of my legs.[23]

This reference to his leg braces in the speech to Congress was not a part of the written text, but was interpolated at the moment of speaking. When the President's health was a vital factor in maintaining public morale, hence the war effort, it is evident why even a tangential reference to Roosevelt's health should have been struck out of the Jefferson Day speech. In addition, the paragraph contains an unintentional irony that might have violated wartime security. The draft apologized for an "inability to be in more than one spot at a time," when the President *was* going to be in more than one spot at a time. It was common for Roosevelt to maintain the appearance that he was at the White House when in fact he was at Warm Springs, and the address on April 13, to have been delivered from Warm Springs, was so set up that it would appear to be coming from the White House.[24]

The Berger draft began with a partisan gesture which Sherwood eliminated. Berger's second paragraph reads: "I, too, feel the old need of a homecoming, the old urge to show up among the folks, and to take pride with you in the fact that we are Democrats." Both this paragraph—and a later reference by Berger to the unity of Democrats and Republicans in wartime—were omitted from Roosevelt's draft. Sherwood's first paragraph makes a striking gesture of nonpartisanship—a form of partisanship—by referring to Thomas Jefferson as a democrat "with a small 'd'." Stinnett has made it clear in his work on the Democratic National Committee Dinners that the occasions were always highly partisan, always directed at an ingroup, but that non-partisanship was one of thirteen dominant strategies employed by Roosevelt, Harry Truman, and Sam Rayburn, the major speakers from 1936 to 1958. In the speeches of FDR delivered at the dinners from their beginnings in 1936 through 1943, the strategy of nonpartisanship ranked fifth out of thirteen (for Rayburn and Truman, it ranked eleventh out of thirteen).[25] Roosevelt's preference for nonpartisanship is partly explained by his long-standing struggle with conservatives in his own party, a struggle which led him in 1944 to consider dumping them and forming a liberal democratic party with Wendell Willkie.[26]

Comparisons have been made between the Roosevelt draft of the speech, as published, and his First Inaugural. Both Frances Perkins and Ben Zevin have noted the parallel between "The only thing we have to fear is fear itself," and "The only limit to our realization of tomorrow will be our doubts of today. Let us move forward with strong and active faith."[27] What has not been previously commented upon is that Berger quite intentionally echoed the First Inaugural:

> Several commentators said that there was a curious kind of rounding out of his ideas, probably in the knowledge that this was the last speech that he would ever make to the public. And the reason they said this was that, you know in his First Inaugural Address, his first public utterance as President, he said, "the only thing we have to fear is fear itself." And he wound up this speech with "our doubts of today will be the only limitation on our achievements of tomorrow." Several people said that this construction reminded them of his First Inaugural. Well, it was deliberately put in that way to do that.[28]

Berger's draft of the speech made the parallel with the First Inaugural even more explicit. In a passage most of which was omitted by Roosevelt, Berger wrote:

> I remember saying, once upon a time in the long, long ago when I was a freshman, that the only thing our people had to fear was fear itself. We were in fear then of economic collapse. We struck back boldly against that fear, and we overcame it.
>
> Today, as we move against an even more terrible scourge, and as we go forward towards the greatest contribution that any generation of human beings

can make in this world—the contribution of lasting peace—that little admonition of thirteen years ago comes back to me.

Roosevelt muted the resonances of his First Inaugural, but he allowed them to remain. What had been written to suggest a second embarkation—a moving from war to peace that paralleled the moving from depression to abundance—became not an embarkation but a rounding off.

The President saw victory on the horizon and meant to direct the thinking of the nation beyond the immediate need of winning the war to the larger need of preserving a hard-won peace. As one of the very few who could anticipate the power of atomic weapons, Roosevelt could appreciate the urgency of his message as the hearers of his speech could not have done. An attitude of pacifism would certainly have seemed to Roosevelt a dangerously sentimental one at this point in history. Nevertheless he prepared for his countrymen a message of positive determination to keep the peace—a peace he did not live to see.

IV

One final question about Roosevelt's last speech remains to be answered. Did the President intend to deliver the speech in the "first draft" form that he had completed at the time of his death, or would he have revised it? Although the answer cannot be stated with certainty, the weight of the evidence seems to support the conclusion that Roosevelt did not intend to deliver the speech in the form that we know it. Let us examine the arguments on both sides of the question.

What evidence supports the conclusion that the President intended to deliver the speech as it has been published in his papers? The present opinion of the Franklin D. Roosevelt Library is that the "first draft" is the final draft. In a letter of August 7, 1951, the then director of the Franklin D. Roosevelt Library, Herman Kahn, concluded that: "This so-called 'First Draft' was in reality the final version of the speech in the form in which he would have delivered it had he lived, as is shown by the fact that he had it typed up in final form."[29] That Kahn's position is still that of the Library is shown by the repetition of his words in a letter to me from Elizabeth B. Drewry, present Director, on May 24, 1967. The existence of the speech in its "final form," would be convincing. And in fact there *is* a copy in the Library on 8½ x 11-inch 3-hole looseleaf paper, the form used for reading copies. But the statement by Kahn is misleading. It is extremely doubtful that "he had it typed in final form," since there appears to be no evidence that Roosevelt himself ordered the typing in final form. In fact, a check of that "final form" reveals the heading:

THE LAST ADDRESS OF THE PRESIDENT
Prepared For Delivery Over The Radio
At The Jefferson Day Dinner
April 13, 1945[30]

It is absurd to suppose that the President would have ordered the typing of anything entitled his *last address*. It is much more reasonable to account for the existence of the speech in final form by hypothesizing that Roosevelt's staff wished to make a final copy of the speech for the press and for history. But in exposing as an error the "final form" argument, we have only removed the major support from the argument that Roosevelt intended his "first draft" as his final one; we have not demonstrated, and we cannot, that he meant to revise it.

External evidence can be of very little help. It is clear that if he meant to revise the speech, Roosevelt would have had to do so in the slightly more than twenty-four hours between his death and the scheduled delivery of the speech. It has so far been impossible to determine just how Roosevelt intended to spend those hours. Certainly the time was not great, and it may be that Roosevelt intended to let the speech stand without revision. But there is some evidence to the contrary.

William D. Hassett, Roosevelt's secretary, among whose duties was the handling of Roosevelt's papers, recorded in his diary for April 11, 1945, that the President, "in the afternoon, dictated the first draft of his Jefferson Day speech to Dorothy Brady."[31] Audrey Turner, in a White House memo of April 18, 1945, requested that Augustus Giegengack prepare a box marked "F.D.R. *Draft* of Jefferson Day Dinner Speech—April 13, 1945."[32] Turnley Walker claims that Roosevelt planned to work on the speech on Friday, April 13.[33]

Samuel Rosenman, compiler of Roosevelt's papers and addresses, and a man familiar with Roosevelt's habits of speech composition, describes the "first draft," with which he concludes his collection, as "the latest draft of the President's proposed speech. . . . The draft was not the final one; the preparation of the final draft was prevented by death."[34]

Rosenman's position can be supported by one piece of internal evidence which is in my view conclusive. In making use of the drafts of Berger and Sherwood, Roosevelt created a draft in which two paragraphs came very close to repeating each other. The paragraphs in question had originated in a single paragraph in the Berger draft. Sherwood had revised the paragraph, and Roosevelt included both Sherwood's and Berger's versions in his draft. Paragraph twelve of Roosevelt's draft is from Sherwood:

> We seek peace—enduring peace. More than an end to war, we want an end to beginnings of all wars— yes, an end to this brutal, inhuman, and thoroughly impractical method of settling the differences between governments.

Paragraph twenty of Roosevelt's draft is directly from Berger:

> The work, my friends, is peace. More than an end of this war—an end to the beginnings of all wars.

> Yes, an end, forever, to this impractical, unrealistic settlement of the differences between governments by the mass killing of peoples.

It must be a matter of opinion whether Roosevelt intended to include in his speech two paragraphs so nearly identical. My opinion is that the repetition is clumsy and unlike Roosevelt, who often employed repetition of words or phrases, but who seldom if ever repeated such a large section in such a small speech, especially without working a significant variation or acknowledging that he was repeating himself.[35] Admittedly my judgment may be wrong, or it may be that Roosevelt was so weak, so near death, that he overlooked an obvious stylistic blunder and would, had he lived, have read it as written. But his other stylistic alterations, and his purposeful combining of the points of view of the Berger and Sherwood drafts indicate an alert mind, even if his handwriting was extremely shaky. He was exhausted but not inattentive. In my view, Roosevelt committed an oversight which he would have noticed and corrected had he had a chance to read over the typed "first draft." We know that the President put the speech together from two earlier drafts, from which he used more or less uninterrupted sections—the first section from Sherwood and the second from Berger. But it is not known that Roosevelt ever saw a copy of his compilation. I am not arguing that Roosevelt must have meant to correct it because there was a mistake in the speech—if he had known of the mistake he would not have left it in. I am saying that the mistake was so obvious that if Roosevelt had completed his normal process of speech preparation, he would have noticed and eliminated the repeated paragraph. That the repetition appears at all indicates to me that Roosevelt had not completed the process of composition, review, and approval commonly employed in the preparation of his speeches. From all available reports of his habits of composition, it appears that Roosevelt always reviewed drafts which he had dictated before he approved them for delivery.[36]

It is vital to the preservation of democratic decision making that society possess a detailed knowledge of influences upon public opinion. Rhetorical scholars in particular have an obligation to illuminate the processes by which public discourse is originated, disseminated, and received. In the case of Roosevelt's speech of April 13, 1945, a relatively minor address was elevated to importance by the very fact that it was not delivered. The sudden elevation of the speech has called to our attention a form of ghostwriting *by consignment* heretofore not given the attention it may deserve.

NOTES

[1] Gail W. Compton, "Franklin Delano Roosevelt: An Annotated Bibliography of His Speaking" (unpubl. Ph.D. diss., University of Wisconsin, 1966), p. 178; Frances Perkins, *The Roosevelt I Knew* (New York, 1946), p. 6; Samuel I. Rosenman (ed.), *The Public Papers and Addresses of Franklin D. Roosevelt* (New York, 1938-50),

XIII, 613-616; Ronald Floyd Stinnett, "A Pentadic Study of Democratic National Committee Dinner Speaking, 1936-1958" (unpubl. Ph.D. diss., University of Minnesota, 1961), pp. 195-196; Ben D. Zevin (ed.), *Nothing to Fear: The Selected Addresses of Franklin Delano Roosevelt, 1932-1945* (New York, 1961), pp. 463-465.

[2] The Papers of President Franklin D. Roosevelt, Record Group 13. The President's Master Speech File, Item Numbered 1577. Hereinafter cited as Item 1577. I wish to acknowledge the generous assistance of the director and staff of the Franklin D. Roosevelt Library when I was conducting my research. Compton, p. 178 refers to a "longhand draft" of the speech at the Library, apparently referring to a typed first draft to which Roosevelt added some words in his own hand. In addition to the four drafts there are several later copies of the latest draft.

[3] Grace Tully, *F.D.R.: My Boss* (New York, 1949), p. 360; William D. Hassett, *Off the Record with F.D.R., 1942-1945* (New Brunswick, 1958), p. 333. In the F.D.R. Library the Roosevelt draft is headed "First Draft," since it was the first version prepared by Roosevelt.

[4] *Who's Who in America* (Chicago, 1944).

[5] Letter from Josef Berger, Brooklyn, New York, August 23, 1967.

[6] *Ibid.*

[7] Letter from Sam O'Neal to Henry Allen Moe, Washington, D. C., March 10, 1946, from a copy supplied to me by the John Simon Guggenheim Memorial Foundation.

[8] Author of such works as *Saints and Strangers* (New York, 1945); and *Behold Virginia: The Fifth Crown* (New York, 1952).

[9] Letter from George F. Willison, Ballston Spa, New York, September 29, 1967.

[10] Letter from Berger, Brooklyn, New York, August 23, 1967.

[11] Earnest Brandenburg, "The Preparation of Franklin D. Roosevelt's Speeches," *QJS,* XXXV (1949), 214-221; Earnest Brandenburg and Waldo W. Braden, "Franklin Delano Roosevelt," in *History and Criticism of American Public Address,* ed. Marie K. Hochmuth (New York, 1955), III, 464-482; Laura Crowell, "The Building of the 'Four Freedoms' Speech," *SM,* XXII (1955), 266-283; Samuel I. Rosenman, *Working with Roosevelt* (New York, 1952), pp. 1-12.

[12] Robert E. Sherwood, *Roosevelt and Hopkins: An Intimate History* (rev. ed., New York, 1950), pp. 878-879.

[13] Letter from Sherwood to Daniels, April 9, 1945. Item 1577, Franklin D. Roosevelt Library.

[14] "Franklin Delano Roosevelt and Books," *Three Presidents and Their Books* (Urbana, 1955), pp. 89-105; *Frontier on the Potomac* (New York, 1946); and *The End of Innocence* (Philadelphia, 1954), which tells the story of Roosevelt and the elder Daniels during the Wilson administration.

[15] The Berger draft begins:

"My friends:

Knowing that you are gathered tonight in cities, in towns, from one end of the country to the other, to give expression to your loyalty, I wish that I had the power, just for an evening, of being in a thousand places at once.

I, too, feel the old need of a homecoming, the old urge to show up among the folks, and to take pride with you in the fact that we are Democrats."

[16] Roosevelt inserted "Today" in the sentence submitted by Sherwood.

[17] Sherwood draft reads: "In Jefferson's time, our Navy consisted largely of one warship—the gallant U.S.S. 'Constitution'—'Old Ironsides'."

[18] Roosevelt inserted "Today" in the sentence submitted by Sherwood.

[19] Sherwood draft reads: "We can no more escape from that responsibility than we could avoid the consequences of German and Japanese aggression."

[20] The Berger draft reads: "The work, my friends, is peace. More than an end of this war—an end to the beginnings of all wars. Yes, an end, forever, to this impractical, unrealistic settlement of the differences between governments by the mass killing of peoples." The Roosevelt draft here incorporates without change the paragraph as it was revised by Sherwood.

[21] Berger draft reads: "Today, as we move against an even more terrible scourge, and as we go forward towards the greatest contribution that any generation of human beings can make in this world—the contribution of lasting peace—that little admonition of thirteen years ago comes back to me."

"I ask you to keep up your faith."

[22] Berger draft reads "doubt" rather than "doubts."

[23] Rosenman (ed.), *Public Papers,* XIII, 570.

[24] Bernard Asbell, *When F.D.R. Died* (New York, 1961), pp. 12, 19-20, 25. The New York *Times* for April 12, 1945, contains on page 12 a letter from Roosevelt to the Congress dated "The White House, April 11, 1945." Such items were frequently released to obscure Roosevelt's movements when he was out of town. See also Roosevelt's comments on the difficulty of finding a vacation retreat in "The Nine Hundred and Forty-eighth Press Conference (Excerpts). . . . May 6, 1944," Rosenman (ed.), *Public*

Papers, XIII, 117-118. Zevin's anthology places the speech in Washington, D. C.: Zevin, p. 463.

[25] Stinnett, pp. 106, 308-309, 367-368.

[26] Rosenman, *Working with Roosevelt,* pp. 463-470.

[27] Perkins, p. 6; Zevin, p. 463.

[28] Josef Berger, interview with the author, Brooklyn, New York, December, 1965. This interview is printed, in part, in *Today's Speech,* XVI (1968), 74.

[29] Letter from Herman Kahn to Mr. C. F. Palmer, Chairman, Franklin D. Roosevelt Warm Springs Memorial Commission, Palmer Building, Atlanta, Georgia, August 7, 1951. Item 1577, Franklin D. Roosevelt Memorial Library.

[30] Item 1577, Franklin D. Roosevelt Memorial Library.

[31] Hassett, p. 333.

[32] Item 1577, Franklin D. Roosevelt Memorial Library. Italics mine.

[33] *Roosevelt and the Warm Springs Story* (New York, 1953), pp. 288-289.

[34] Rosenman (ed.), *Public Papers,* XIII, 616. But Rosenman does not cite any evidence to support his position, and he does commit one bit of editorial sloppiness when he reproduces photographically the last page of the *Berger* draft, on which the President had written in longhand, as "Facsimile of last page of the draft for address President Roosevelt planned to deliver on Jefferson Day, 1945." See also Rosenman, *Working with Roosevelt,* p. 551.

[35] For descriptions of Roosevelt's use of repetition see Brandenburg and Braden, pp. 510-512; Joseph A. Schiffman, "Observations on Roosevelt's Literary Style," *QJS,* XXXV (1949), 222-223; Stinnett, pp. 336, 337.

[36] Brandenburg and Braden, pp. 464-465, 473-479.

Athan Theoharis (essay date 1972)

SOURCE: "'Roosevelt and Truman on Yalta': The Origins of the Cold War," in *Political Science Quarterly,* Vol. LXXXVII, No. 2, June, 1972, pp. 210-41.

[*In the following essay, Theoharis examines United States policy toward the Soviet Union in the 1940s, contrasting Roosevelt's ambivalence and largely conciliatory approach with Truman's more rigidly anti-Soviet stance.*]

Only recently has the question of the origins of the cold war seriously divided American historians, the emergence of a "revisionist" school coinciding with intensive research into primary sources. Yet, revisionists do disagree over whether there existed a discontinuity between President Roosevelt's and President Truman's policies; they disagree in their evaluations of the relative influence of economic and political considerations and in their estimates of the role of key advisers in shaping the decisions and priorities of the two presidents.

This paper will emphasize the tactics and personalities of Roosevelt and Truman, their specific responses to Soviet policy and influence. Focusing on Yalta, I shall examine the Truman administration's commitment to the agreements concluded at the conference and Roosevelt's and the State Department's responsibilities for the development of the Cold War. Conceding that the trend of the Open Door ideology was inimical to accommodation with the Soviet Union, I, nonetheless, contend that the discretion available to policy makers did not demand the specific policies adopted after April 1945 that led to the cold war. Put simply, the thesis of this paper is, to quote Lloyd C. Gardner, that "the United States was more responsible for the *way* in which the Cold War developed."[1]

At issue for American diplomats during the 1940s was how to deal with the progress and consequences of World War II. Given the Soviet Union's strategic political and geographic position and its inevitable physical presence in non-Soviet territories after the war, the development of U.S. policy toward Eastern Europe, Germany, and the Far East would influence the climate of Soviet-American relations. Indeed, the diplomacy of the Roosevelt and Truman administrations in the 1941-46 period was the product, in part, of their conceptions of the Soviet role in Eastern Europe, and especially in Poland; of Soviet involvement in the Far Eastern war and its consequences for postwar China and Japan; and of the status of postwar Germany as determined by decisions concerning the level of German reparations payments.

The dominant role of the post-New Deal presidency in the formulation of foreign policy, the consistency of Truman's policies with those of Roosevelt, and the extent to which either president determined policy or followed recommendations of ostensibly subordinate advisers, furthermore, had crucial significance for U.S.-Soviet relations. During the war, and in the postwar years, U.S. policy was made by the president or his advisers, and not simply at the major summit conferences. At best, the role of the public or of Congress had become that of a potential restraint; policy makers did operate on the premise that Congress or the public might seek to counteract policy decisions. Yet, these were possible deterrents; they did not control policy. As one result of the Executive Reorganization Act of 1939, the president had acquired a bureaucratic apparatus that increased his independence and authority. The post-New Deal president, by resorting to public relations and *fait accompli,* had, as a result, greater freedom to create public opinion and structure the policy debate.

Soviet responses, moreover, were based on an appraisal of the policies of the president, and not on the differing priorities of advisers, the Congress, the public, or the press. While, admittedly, the president, especially Roosevelt, might invoke public, congressional, or press opinion during negotiations with Soviet leaders, this bargaining ploy did not lead Stalin or other leaders in the Kremlin to view U.S. policy as determined by domestic considerations. Concessions might be made in the wording of communiques to make an agreement more palatable to the American public or press, but Soviet policy makers operated on the assumption that they were dealing with the president and that his policy was based upon understood commitments. For this reason, the nature of presidential leadership influenced immediate postwar relations between the United States and the Soviet Union. Most significantly, the Truman administration's attempts to "undo" the Yalta commitments led to the Cold War.

What was involved was not only the enigmatic and ambiguous nature of Roosevelt's policies, substantial as these ambiguities were, but the noncommitment of key personnel in the State Department to the "soft" line that Roosevelt had adopted at Yalta. A perusal of the pre-Yalta briefing papers demonstrates both the conservatism of these men on the key questions affecting U.S.-Soviet relations and their sense almost of American omniscience and omnipotence. These attitudes are dramatically revealed in their various recommendations concerning: the creation of an Allied control commission for Eastern Europe; political conditions in postwar liberated Europe; and the Tito-Subasic agreement.[2] Specifically, a November 10, 1944 memorandum of James C. Dunn, director of the office of European affairs, to then Undersecretary of State Stettinius (accompanying the briefing book that the department had prepared for the use of the secretary of state and the president) captures this sense of omniscience. In this memo, Dunn emphasized:

> You now have the policy papers on U.S. policy and attitudes toward Eastern Europe, the Balkan area, and the Near East. . . These policy papers include the general position of the U.S. . . . and have specific recommendations with regard to the policy and attitudes we *should* pursue. . . . I think these memoranda *should be* brought to the President's attention. . . . On the trip to the [Yalta] conference would be the ideal time to bring them to his attention as there would be an opportunity to discuss these situations and the positions we *should* adopt in order to protect American interests.[3]

The reiteration of "should" conveys the concerns of key State Department personnel that their priorities were not shared by the president. The rigidity of their position, in contrast to Roosevelt's at Yalta, contained the seeds of possible conflict with the Soviet Union after Truman's accession to the presidency. Truman's limited understanding, of both international affairs and Roosevelt's specific commitments, would enable policy advisers to become policy makers after April 1945 when determining the meaning of the Yalta agreements. Thus, the State Department's briefing paper to Truman of April 13

emphasized that the stalemate over the reconstruction of the Polish provisional government stemmed from "the Soviet authorities consistently sabotaging Ambassador Harriman's efforts in the Moscow Commission to hasten the implementation of the decisions at the Crimea Conference."[4] This interpretation of Roosevelt's differences with Stalin diverged substantively from the deceased president's most recent position. In a March 29 note to Churchill, Roosevelt had contended that the Yalta agreement on Poland had represented a compromise between the Western demand for a new government and Soviet insistence that the Lublin government merely be enlarged. Roosevelt added, "but if we attempt to evade the fact that we placed, as clearly shown in the agreement, somewhat more emphasis on the Lublin Poles than on the other two groups . . . I feel we are exposing ourselves to the charge that we are attempting to go back on the Crimea decision."[5]

Nor was this April 13 briefing by State atypical. On May 12, when lend-lease to the Soviets was abruptly terminated (with Truman, despite his denial in his memoirs, having been fully briefed by Lend-Lease Administrator Leo Crowley and Acting Secretary of State Joseph Grew),[6] the State Department also recommended reconsidering the U.S. commitment to implement the Yalta Far Eastern agreements.[7] On that same day, Truman advised the U.S. ambassador to China, Patrick Hurley, that "it was not appropriate at the present time" to fulfill the Yalta Far Eastern agreements and, therefore, that Chiang Kai-shek need not be informed of their existence.[8]

Just what agreements had been concluded at Yalta? What objectives underlay Roosevelt's policy at Yalta and how were they related to his earlier diplomacy and to U.S. policy toward the Soviet Union after April 1945? In the remainder of this paper, I intend to discuss, first, Roosevelt's pre-Yalta policy, then, the commitments he accepted at the Yalta Conference, and, lastly, the nature of Truman's commitment to the vaguely worded Yalta agreements.

I

During the war years, Roosevelt's policies toward the potential problems concerning the postwar status of Eastern Europe, Germany, and the Far East were strikingly vacillating and ambivalent. The president, like his conservative secretary of state, Cordell Hull, sought to postpone difficult political decisions until after the war. For a time, he refused even to enter serious discussions with the Soviet Union over territorial and other political matters. Roosevelt's stance on German reparations particularly dramatize this ambiguity of policy and preference for postponement. Thus, although Hull had agreed both to the principle of reparations in kind and not in money at the Moscow foreign ministers conference of October 1943 and to the establishment of an European Advisory Commission to outline Allied policy toward postwar Germany, no efforts were made to determine the level or basis of reparations payments and to develop plans for postwar occupation. In October 1944, indeed, Roosevelt halted any planning for postwar Germany. Significantly, while the debate between Treasury and State was raging over the level of German reparations, Roosevelt wrote to Hull that "I do not think that at this present stage any good purpose would be served by having the State Department or any other Department sound out the British and Russian views on the treatment of German industry."[9]

But a "policy of no-policy," if viable for Germany, at least during the war years, could not be sustained in every instance. Decisions had to be made early over the handling of the Italian surrender and the Allied administration of Italy until a peace treaty could be concluded. In the U.S.-British military theatre, Italy was liberated exclusively by Western troops. In this sense, Anglo-American policy provided a test of Western openness and cooperation with the Soviet Union and a possible future model for Soviet responses in Eastern Europe, which would be liberated by Soviet troops. The Italian surrender and the wartime supervision of Italian politics was directed exclusively by the United States and Great Britain. Following discussions with the Badoglio government over the terms of Italian surrender and cobelligerency, the United States and Britain simply informed the Soviet Union of the proposed terms. Before Stalin could reply and express his view that leniency was not required, Roosevelt and Churchill had already acted.

The terms of the Italian capitulation of September 3, 1943, moreover, acknowledged the Allied commander-in-chief's authority to establish a military government. In response, Stalin pressed for the creation of an Allied control commission to administer Italian political affairs, one in which the Soviet Union would have an important role. Since the Soviet request could not be denied, Roosevelt and Churchill agreed to establish a Military-Political Commission (MPC), though one stationed in Algeria and not Italy and with its authority strictly circumscribed.

Stalin sent Andrei Vyshinsky as the Soviet representative to the MPC and later protested when General Eisenhower, following Roosevelt's directions, established an Allied control commission under his command. In the end, an arrangement was reached, published in the foreign ministers' declaration on Italy of October 30, 1943, that led to Vyshinsky's return to Moscow, his rank being inappropriate to what was essentially an advisory position. The foreign ministers' declaration affirmed:

> [the] three Foreign Secretaries recognize that so long as active military operations continue in Italy the time at which it is possible to give full effect to the principle set above will be determined by the Commander-in-Chief [U.S.] on the basis of instructions received through the Combined Chiefs of Staff [Anglo-American]. The three Government parties to this declaration will at the request of any one of them consult on this matter.[10]

The establishment in Italy of the principle that military occupation should have precedence over political matters, including the right of military authorities to determine who should be allowed to form local governments and when normal politics might resume, provided the justification (if any were needed) for Soviet intervention in the politics of Eastern Europe. This precedent had particular importance for Soviet actions in Poland and Romania where the prewar regimes' hostility toward the Soviet Union would have complicated Soviet military occupation and military operations against Germany. Seemingly, in the various armistice agreements concluded by the Soviet Union with Romania, Hungary, and Bulgaria in 1944, the Roosevelt administration accepted this consequence.[11]

These precedents made U.S. wartime policy toward Poland doubly unrealistic and provocative. Initially, difficulties stemmed from the Katyn Forest incident and from Soviet insistence on Western recognition of her territorial borders of 1941, specifically the Curzon Line. The refusal of the Polish government-in-exile (in London) either to countenance boundary changes in the east, to recognize the legitimacy of Soviet insistence on friendly relations, or to accept the Soviet direction of political developments during the course of military operations against Germany further complicated the situation. When British Foreign Minister Anthony Eden visited Washington in 1943 and informed Roosevelt of his views—that Soviet territorial demands were correct and moderate and that the Soviets genuinely favored a strong Poland, but that Polish aspirations were the primary obstacle to good Soviet-Polish relations—Roosevelt expressed agreement, particularly on the proposed Curzon Line. Roosevelt, however, remained silent on these questions in his dealings with the London Poles. The London Poles, in turn, interpreted his silence as U.S. disapproval of the Soviet claims.[12]

Throughout 1943 and 1944, Roosevelt sustained this noncommital course, thus strengthening the resistance of the London Poles to serious negotiations and thereby contributing to the deterioration of Soviet-Polish relations. Following the Soviet incursion into Polish territory in January 1944, Roosevelt offered his good offices to Mikolajczyk, the prime minister of the London Polish government, to mediate but not guarantee a solution of the Polish border difficulty. Roosevelt abandoned this stance of studied ambiguity only on November 17, 1944, and then after Soviet troops had crossed the Curzon line (July 22) and after Moscow Radio had announced the formation of a Polish Committee on National Liberation (July 22) and the subsequent signing of a military and political agreement between this committee and the Soviet Union. At that time and with the American presidential election over, Roosevelt informed Mikolajczyk that whatever agreement the Poles and the Soviet Union concluded would be acceptable to the United States but that the United States could not guarantee Poland's frontiers.[13]

U.S. policy had not been simply the product of domestic politics; key policy advisers had continually counseled a firm stand against the Soviets and the need to sustain the London Poles. Indeed, within State, John Hickerson, deputy director of the office of European affairs, recommended, on January 8, 1945, that the United States secure the establishment of a Provisional Security Council, in which the United States would have a major voice, to supervise political developments in Eastern Europe.[14] And, on January 18, 1945, Secretary of State Stettinius made the same recommendation to Roosevelt. Significantly, Stettinius's proposal provided not only for a rotating chairmanship, thereby implying the equality of the powers, but also for establishing the headquarters in Paris.[15]

Nor was this January proposal inconsistent with Stettinius's earlier recommendations. In a memo dated November 15 and in a telegram dated November 25, 1944, discussing the crises created by Mikolajczyk's resignation from the London government and Soviet organization (and possible recognition) of the Lublin Poles, Stettinius had recommended that the United States continue to pressure Stalin to make territorial concessions to the Poles. Since the Lubin committee had "very little support inside Poland," he argued, "for the moment our best policy is to take no action but carefully watch developments."[16] And, in a December 13, 1944, letter to the U.S. ambassador to Moscow, W. Averell Harriman, advising him that the United States continued to recognize the London government, Stettinius expressed the unrealistic hopefulness on which he based U.S. policy. In an estimate predicated on a series of "ifs," Stettinius conjectured:

> *It is possible* that the present Polish Government [in London] will be unable to make any headway in solving Polish problems and therefore *may* fall. Mikolajczyk *may* then be induced to form a new Cabinet composed of persons who fully support his policies, which eventually *might* make it possible for us to take a more positive attitude in favor of the Polish Government in London.[17]

Even at this late date, Roosevelt remained unwilling to embark on a new course. Instead, on December 15, 1944, he sent a telegram to Churchill requesting his views on the possibility of Mikolajczyk's returning to power and on what actions the United States and Great Britain jointly should take in the event of Soviet recognition of the Lublin committee. On December 16, 1944, Roosevelt cabled Stalin unsuccessfully urging him not to recognize the Lublin Poles until the forthcoming Big Three meetings.[18]

Nor was Roosevelt's wartime policy toward the future Soviet role in the Far East any more definite. At Teheran and in discussions with Harriman during 1944, Stalin had made known Soviet political and territorial demands in Asia; he indicated that once the Soviet Union entered the war against Japan, she would not play a secondary role. At the same time, he had expressed his deference to the U.S. desire to keep China, including her political system, intact and had denied any intent to infringe upon Chinese sovereignty in Manchuria.

Throughout, Roosevelt attempted to secure Soviet military involvement in the war against Japan. He continued to operate on the premise that U.S. policy—to make China a great power—was correct and attainable. A Sino-Soviet accord, he believed, would minimize Soviet intervention in

China and force the Chinese Communists to come to terms with Chiang Kai-shek. At the same time, Roosevelt never consistently backed General Stillwell's efforts to reform the Chinese Nationalist regime or to alter its military policy. A sense of wishfulness characterized Roosevelt's estimates of the internal strength of the Nationalist regime, of the prospects for resolving the civil conflict between the Nationalists and Communists without civil war, and of the simply military consequences of Soviet involvement in the war against Japan.[19]

II

Roosevelt's decision to go to Yalta constituted, in essence, a change from wishful thinking and postponement. By early 1945, military developments, and prospective military and political developments, ensured that the Soviets would play a dominant role in Eastern Europe, that Soviet unilateral actions in Germany would complicate Allied occupation policy, and that the Soviet role in the Far East possibly could frustrate the attainment of U.S. objectives. To postpone matters to a postwar peace conference might contribute to the establishment of spheres of influence, to the breakdown of Allied unity and cooperation, and to the further radicalization of politics throughout Europe and the Far East.

Roosevelt's diplomacy at Yalta, therefore, reflected not so much overconfidence in his ability to placate Stalin through personal diplomacy, though this was a factor, as his recognition of the weakness of the U.S. diplomatic position and the reality—even legitimacy—of Soviet influence in Eastern Europe, the Far East, and Germany. Although the language is vague, the Yalta agreements did confirm this acceptance of Soviet postwar influence and the importance of accommodation to avert disharmony and conflict.

The most troublesome issue confronting the conferees was Poland. Roosevelt's phrasing of his requests at Yalta clearly conceded the weakness of the Western bargaining position. He emphasized his need to "save face" when pressing for slight territorial concessions to the Poles from the Curzon Line, emphasized the domestic importance of the Polish-American vote when urging Stalin to make other concessions over the status of the Polish government, and requested "some gesture" to satisfy the demand of the six million Polish-Americans that the United States be "in some way involved with the question of freedom of elections." By basing his requests on American domestic political considerations, Roosevelt undermined his effect on the decisions of the conference. The final communiqué could simply be worded to gloss over what in fact had been conceded. In many respects, this was the result of the negotiations on Poland: Stalin merely agreed to a formula for the formation of a Polish provisional government and the holding of free and democratic elections under tripartite supervision that would not contradict Soviet objectives yet would enable Roosevelt and Churchill to appease the public opinion that they had so regularly cited during conference proceedings.[20]

Moreover, Roosevelt's February 6 demand that a new Polish government be established, maintaining that the Lublin government "as now composed" could not be accepted (a statement which Churchill immediately endorsed), was not pressed at the conference. The reference to Lublin "as *now* composed" and the further assurance to Stalin that the United States would never support in any way any Polish government "that would be inimical to your interests," significantly reduced the impact of this demand. Stalin replied that Poland did not involve merely honor or domestic public opinion, but the security of the Soviet Union. Second, indirectly recalling the example of the Italian surrender, Stalin also emphasized the importance for the Red Army of secure supply lines in its advance into Germany that only a stable, nonhostile local administration could provide.[21]

The result, incorporated in the Declaration on Liberated Europe and the agreement dealing with Poland, amounted to face-saving formulas for the West. The Lublin government was not to be scrapped for a wholly new government, but rather enlarged to provide the basis for the new government. Stettinius's proposal for reorganizing the Lublin government—"fully representative Government based on all democratic forces in Poland and abroad"—was amended by Molotov to "wider democratic basis with the inclusion of democratic leaders from Poland and abroad." And, the language of the amended Declaration on Liberated Europe, by providing for unanimity even before consultations could begin, acknowledged Soviet authority and her right to veto her allies' objections. Further, the initial State Department proposal for "appropriate machinery for the carrying out of the joint responsibilities set forth in this declaration" was also amended by Molotov to provide instead that the three governments "will immediately take measures for the carrying out of mutual consultations." Nor was observation of the proposed future elections by the three governments guaranteed, since, "in effect," ambassadors alone would observe and report on elections.[22]

The Eastern European agreements, one-sided and a tacit repudiation of earlier U.S. policy, indirectly served to create the potential for subsequent U.S.-Soviet problems. The vagueness of the language, the seeming lack (at least as existing published papers of the proceedings reveal) of intensive discussion over significant changes that amounted to U.S. acceptance of the Soviet position, as well as the exclusion of State from a central negotiating role and the implicit rejection of its policy recommendations at Yalta meant that implementation of the agreements would be determined by the commitment of U.S. policy makers to accept the reality of Soviet influence and the spirit underlying the conference.

A similar situation occurred in the Yalta discussions on Germany. Most important matters involving Germany were postponed, though even then it was implicitly agreed that the Big Three would jointly determine occupation and reparations policy. The level of German reparations payments did divide the Allies at Yalta. The final agreement, though, provided for the creation of a reparations commission to discuss this question; the commission was instructed, with Roosevelt and Stalin concurring and Churchill dissenting, that during its deliberations the figure of $20 billion with one-half going to the Soviet Union should provide "the basis for discussion."[23]

At Yalta, Roosevelt had no clearly formulated German policy. Supporting simply a harsh peace, but no longer committed to dismemberment and sizable reparations, he nonetheless remained unwilling to force a dispute with Stalin and accepted the postponement of these issues. Roosevelt's agreement to a stated sum as the basis for discussion, however, could be construed as a commitment in principle to a fixed figure if not to that sum. The only merit of Roosevelt's temporizing was in avoiding division and disharmony. By not providing clear guidelines for future discussions, it served to complicate future U.S.-Soviet relations.

The Yalta discussions on the Far East were characterized by the same imprecision of agreement and absence of thorough negotiations. The general terms of Soviet involvement had tacitly been agreed to at Teheran and during discussions between Stalin and Harriman in 1944. Both Roosevelt and Stalin remained interested, nonetheless, in a more specific understanding. At Stalin's insistence, the conditions for Soviet involvement were set forth in writing at Yalta and agreed to by the three powers (though Britain did not participate in the discussions). Specifically, the Soviet Union was to receive South Sakhalin and the Kurile Islands from Japan. In addition, Russia secured "lease" rights to Port Arthur; her "preeminent interests" were to be safeguarded in an internationalized port of Dairen and in a "jointly operated" Sino-Soviet commission for the Chinese-Eastern Railroad and the South-Manchurian Railroad; and the status of Outer Mongolia was to be "preserved." Roosevelt admitted not having discussed the matters of Outer Mongolia, the ports, or the railroads with Chiang Kai-shek and conceded that, for the moment, military considerations required continued secrecy. Stalin then informed Roosevelt that Chinese Foreign Minister T.V. Soong was coming to Moscow in April, that it might be appropriate at that time to inform him of this matter. Ultimately, it was decided that Roosevelt would take the initiative to inform the Chinese and would make this move when so directed by Stalin, the determining factor to be military developments in Europe. In return for these concessions, Roosevelt secured two qualified Soviet commitments: to enter the war against Japan two or three months after the termination of the war in Europe and to conclude a pact of "friendship and alliance" with the Nationalist government.[24]

The Far Eastern agreements, however, had not defined the extent of the Soviet role in Manchuria, particularly in the area surrounding the ports and railroads; the reference to the "pre-eminent interests" of the Soviet Union could result in the establishment of a Soviet sphere of influence. Moreover, whether Roosevelt had accepted the German or Italian model as the basis for joint occupation policy in postwar Japan was not clear from the discussions or agreements reached at Yalta. No specific agreement had been made concerning this matter—the outright cession of South Sakhalin and the Kuriles to the Soviet Union did not establish physical occupation of Japanese territory and a right to have an equal voice in occupation policy. Roosevelt's attempt to secure Soviet involvement, however, and the spirit of mutual assistance and cooperation provided justification for Soviet insistence on equal participation in occupation policy.

In sum, at Yalta, Roosevelt adopted a conciliatory policy, accepting the reality of Soviet power and the legitimacy of her postwar involvement in Eastern Europe, Germany, and the Far East. He did not reverse this policy upon returning to Washington. Thus, in late February 1945, when Molotov forced King Michael of Romania to establish a new government, Roosevelt and Churchill only mildly protested, suggesting that consultation among the Allies might bein order. When the Soviet Union rejected this appeal by pointing out the consistency of Soviet action with the 1944 armistice agreements, Roosevelt, much to the dismay of the State Department, refused to press the matter.[25]

Moreover, in the impasse that emerged during the Moscow discussions between Harriman, Clark Kerr, and Molotov over the reorganization of the Lublin government, Roosevelt's position diverged significantly from that of Churchill. He urged Churchill to have Mikolajczyk endorse the Yalta agreements and thereby remove what had been one basis for Soviet opposition to his inclusion in a new provisional government. At the same time, Roosevelt refused to endorse Churchill's proposal that the United States and Britain jointly demand that any Pole nominated by any one of the three governments be invited to Moscow for consultation and that the Soviet Union use her influence to prevent "any further legal or administration action [in Poland] of a fundamental character." Such demands, Roosevelt insisted, would ensure a stalemate. In his own protest to Stalin, Roosevelt instead emphasized that "while it is true that the Lublin Government is to be reorganized and its membership play a prominent role, it is to be done in such a fashion as to bring into being a new government." Despite his strongly worded protest and his insistence that the Moscow negotiations were to create a different government, Roosevelt's only concrete demand was that the Lublin Poles could not claim to reject "what Poles are to be brought to Moscow by the Commission for consultation. Can we not agree that it is up to the Commission to select the Polish leaders to come to Moscow to consult in the first instance."

By this protest, Roosevelt was not rejecting Soviet dominant interest, but dissociating the United States from acquiescence to the demands of Lublin, which would have implied recognizing its authority and its right to speak for the Polish people. In itself, this position did not contribute to the resolution of the stalemate then existing in Moscow.[26]

III

Roosevelt's death significantly changed the diplomatic setting, by introducing, for one thing, an element of uncertainty about future U.S.-Soviet relations. More important, it introduced Harry S. Truman, a man more rigidly anti-Soviet and, given also his noninvolvement in Roosevelt's policymaking, more responsive to the suggestions of policy advisers whose recommendations had been ignored at Yalta. His personal political style would have far-reaching consequences for the Yalta understandings: Truman would not feel compelled to honor the commitments and would seek to exploit the vague language of the agreements to avoid compliance.

In part, the Truman administration in 1945 bore the legacies of Roosevelt's earlier policy of postponing and avoiding clearly defined commitments and the partial continuing of that policy at Yalta. Despite Yalta, doubt remained over Roosevelt's position on, among other things, German reparations and dismemberment, the character of the postwar governments of Eastern Europe, and the nature of the Soviet postwar role in the Far East. More important, in making concessions to the Soviet Union, Roosevelt had acted unilaterally, without securing the understanding or acquiescence of his subordinates. The imprecision of Roosevelt's administrative leadership thereby provided an opportunity for these subordinates to take advantage of the policy vacuum created by Roosevelt's death and Truman's woeful ignorance of both international politics and the Yalta commitments to secure the eventual adoption of their recommendations.

In April, Harriman had a conversation with Stalin that, because it coincided with Roosevelt's death, permitted him to affirm Truman's intention to continue the policies of his predecessor. Capitalizing on Stalin's statement of willingness to work with Truman as he had with Roosevelt, Harriman extracted from the premier a pledge to have Molotov, on his way to San Francisco, stop off in Washington to consult with Truman. Such a move, Harriman insisted, would promote collaboration. Stalin acceded. Intended as a friendly gesture, Molotov's trip was initiated to provide the opportunity for an exchange of views and a testing of cooperation.[27]

Harriman's move, though not necessarily intentionally, coincided with an intensive policy reexamination in Washington involving Truman and key advisers who had urged Truman not to compromise to reach accommodation.

Truman, in fact, adopted a less conciliatory approach in April 1945. On April 16, he and Churchill sent a joint note to Stalin outlining their proposal for resolving the Polish impasse. Their note placed the Western-oriented Polish political leaders on the same basis with the Lublin Poles. Understanding that even the vague language of the Yalta agreements did not support his position, Truman, nonetheless, remained confident that a strong stand would not precipitate a break with the Soviet Union.[28]

The same attitude also prevailed at his meeting with Molotov on April 23. Truman's language at that meeting was blunt and undiplomatic, specifically rejecting the Yugoslav formula (expanding the existing government by adding a new minister for every four already in the cabinet) as the basis for composing the new Polish provisional government. An agreement had been concluded, Truman self-righteously affirmed, and only required Soviet compliance. In response to Molotov's protests, Truman conceded the vagueness of the language of the agreements (the president had earlier been advised by Leahy, among others, that the Soviet position was consistent with the Yalta agreements). Molotov denied that any agreement had been broken and stressed the need for cooperation, to which Truman reiterated his insistence that the U.S. interpretation was the only one possible.[29]

The result of this meeting, if possibly psychologically satisfying to the frustrated Americans, did not lead to diplomatic resolution. Responding to the April 16 note and the April 23 meeting, Stalin emphasized Poland's importance to Soviet security and protested Western efforts to dictate to the Soviet Union. Truman's refusal to accept Lublin as the core of the new government was inconsistent with the Yalta agreements. Soviet actions in Poland were comparable to those of Britain in Belgium and Greece; the Soviet Union had not sought to interfere in these countries or to ascertain whether British actions made possible representative government. The United States and Great Britain were combining against the Soviet Union and the United States was attempting to secure Soviet renunciation of her security interests.[30]

On May 19, in a seeming about-face, Truman consulted Stalin on Harry Hopkins's proposed mission to Moscow for mutual consultations. Significantly, when the Hopkins mission was first considered in early May, Byrnes and the State Department opposed the idea, recognizing that it meant that Truman had decided to make some concessions to the Soviets.[31]

Truman's objectives for the Hopkins mission remain obscure. The trip did not eliminate the tensions that had surfaced in April, though an agreement worked out on the composition of the Polish provisional government did essentially follow the Yugoslav formula, and on July 5, the Truman administration did recognize the reorganized government.[32]

The Eastern European question, however, had not been amicably resolved. At Potsdam, Truman refused to recognize either the Oder-Neisse line as the western boundary of Poland or Soviet primacy in Bulgaria, Hungary, and Romania. In his public report of August 9 on the results of the conference, Truman declared that Bulgaria and Romania were not to be within the sphere of influence of any one power. And earlier on June 1, 12, and 14, the administration had instructed Harriman to propose to Stalin that the United States and Great Britain be accorded veto power over the actions of Soviet commanders in Hungary, Romania, and Bulgaria.[33]

The Truman administration's decision to accept confrontation rather than seek accommodation also underlay its often shifting and confused, but unbending, German policy. Thus, even though, at the time, these decisions did not necessarily reflect a conscious strategy or policy, on May 10, 1945, Truman unilaterally approved Joint Chiefs of Staff (JCS) directive 1067 and replaced Roosevelt's representative to the Moscow Reparations Commission, Isadore Rubin, with Edwin Pauley. The vagueness of JCS 1067 and the unilateral nature of its promulgation, without consultation with the British, Russians, or French, marked a shift toward a softer policy toward Germany. The directive simply provided general discretion to U.S. military zonal authorities to determine the level of German industrial production and, indirectly thereby, German reparations payments.[34]

During the June discussions in Moscow on reparations, Pauley had adopted an uncompromising line on Soviet requests for specific agreement on German reparations levels, thereby effectively averting progress toward any agreement. The Truman delegation adopted the same stance at Potsdam, indirectly avoiding the issue of joint policy. While paying lip service to the Yalta agreement on reparations, Secretary of State Byrnes refused to respond to Soviet efforts to determine the specific reparations sum that the United States would accept. Dismissing the Yalta figure of $10 billion as "impractical," Byrnes supported a policy whereby, in Molotov's words, "each country would have a free hand in their own zone and could act entirely independently of the others." Despite Assistant Secretary of State Clayton's warning that Byrnes's insistence that reparations come from the zone of the occupying power "would be considered by the Russians as a reversal of the Yalta position," Truman did not alter this position. Potsdam, then, contributed to the division of Germany along zonal lines. In addition, Truman's willingness to reject the Yalta formulas, while publicly proclaiming his commitment to them, added the element of distrust to diplomatic relations. The further complication to joint planning provided later by French obstruction heightened this distrust. A high Soviet official told James Warburg in the summer of 1946 that "after six months of French obstruction, we began to suspect that this was a put-up job—that you did not like the bargain you had made at Potsdam and that you are letting the French get you out of it."[35]

This element of deception inherent in Truman's reparations diplomacy is elaborated in John Gimbel's study of U.S. reparations and occupation policy in Germany. Emphasizing the disparity between the administration's public position and its private actions Gimbel points out:

> A cable from the War Department to Clay on January 3, 1946 . . . added that Clay's freedom of action was not limited by JCS 1067. It said that formal policy change would result in unfavorable comment in the press to the effect that the United States had abandoned its firm stand on the treatment of Germany. . . . Apparently influenced by all

these pressures to hold to the original "hard" line, American officials gave out "explanations of policy" and "restatements of policy" and generally interpreted their own actions to the public and their allies as fulfillment of, rather than deviations from, the directive and the Potsdam agreement.[36]

Gimbel describes the essence of Truman's diplomatic method as a crafty attempt to have it both ways: to disown earlier concessions without accepting the responsibility of overtly repudiating them and establishing new relations. This aspect of Truman's diplomacy constituted an important element of his response to the Soviet Union and was as crucial to the deterioration of Soviet-American relations as the specific policy differences over Poland and Germany. It was revealed as well in the administration's policy toward the Yalta Far Eastern agreements.

The vague wording of the Far Eastern agreements presented formidable unresolved diplomatic problems for the entering Truman administration. On the surface, the concessions did not seem major. In fact, however, the extent of the postwar Soviet role in either China or Japan had not been clearly defined. Thus, as soon as he became president, Truman was beset by pressure from key advisers in State, the Foreign Service, and his cabinet to reappraise the Far Eastern agreements.[37] At an April 23 cabinet meeting, the president himself raised the issue of reappraisal. Distressed over Soviet actions in Eastern Europe, Truman suggested that the failure of a Yalta signatory to fulfill any of its commitments might free the other signatories from fulfilling theirs. The main opposition to this position came from the military. General George C. Marshall, then chairman of the Joint Chiefs of Staff, argued that the concessions had to stand because the Far Eastern war could not be won without Soviet military assistance.[38]

While no formal decision on the concessions was reached in the cabinet then, the German surrender on May 8 led to further administration reevaluation of Yalta. During a May 11 meeting in Forrestal's office, Harriman, who was about to return to Moscow, contended that "it was time to come to a conclusion about the necessity for the early entrance of Russia into the Japanese war." He reiterated this case at State on May 12, and it was agreed that Harriman's views should be formulated precisely "for discussion with the President."[39]

On May 12, though perhaps not the consequence simply of Harriman's initiative, two actions occurred. Responding to a cable from Hurley sent on May 10 stating his view that the time had come to inform Chiang of the Yalta terms, Truman stated that "it was not appropriate at the present time" to fulfill the Yalta Far Eastern agreements and therefore Chiang ought not to be informed of their terms. Second, Acting Secretary of State Grew sent memorandums to Secretary of War Stimson and Secretary of Navy Forrestal requesting that the military services state their views on the Far Eastern agreements. The memorandums detailed the State Department's objections

to the Yalta concessions as well as its suspicions of Soviet aims and questioned whether the United States should remain committed to the enactment of the Yalta terms and, if so, in whole or in part. Before informing Chiang of the Yalta concessions, Grew further suggested, the U.S. should first secure Soviet agreement to influence the Chinese Communists to achieve unity under Chiang.

In a May 21 reply, Secretary Stimson reiterated the importance of Soviet military assistance to the early defeat of Japan. Stimson went on to say that Soviet influence in the Far East was inevitable and that a Big Three conference to discuss and possibly revise the Yalta concessions would be undesirable. While remaining suspicious of Soviet objectives and committed to a policy of limiting Soviet influence, Stimson still believed that the administration could not successfully renegotiate the terms set at Yalta. Furthermore, he argued, any such effort could only delay the timing of Soviet military intervention without reducing postwar Soviet influence in the area.[40] As yet committed neither to repudiation nor to fulfillment, Truman in a meeting with Soong on May 14 failed to inform him of the Yalta agreements, refusing also to respond to Soong's query about the Soviet role in the Far East. Moreover, Truman successfully dissuaded Soong from flying to Moscow to secure Soviet assistance against the Chinese Communists. Soong agreed to postpone this trip to a later date.[41]

The Hopkins mission to Moscow, however, raised anew the issue of the Yalta Far Eastern agreements. On May 28, Stalin reaffirmed his government's intention to enter the Far Eastern war and the expectation that Soviet troops would have a role in the occupation of Japan. The time was right, Stalin advised Hopkins, to initiate discussions between the Soviet Union and the Chinese Nationalists on the Yalta concessions to Russia; these talks should begin no later than July 1. The Soviet Union would be ready to enter the war against Japan by August 8, but only on the condition that a Sino-Soviet treaty had been successfully concluded by then.[42]

In response to the Hopkins mission, on June 9, Truman personally informed Soong of the Yalta provisions concerning China and urged him to initiate negotiations with the Soviet Union. Hurley also was instructed to inform Chiang Kai-shek of the Yalta terms. In a June 14 meeting with Soong, Truman specifically reported the substance of Hopkins's May 28 conversation with Stalin. Concerned about the ramifications of the Yalta concessions and the weakness of the Chinese negotiating position vis-à-vis the Soviet Union, Soong then and in earlier discussions with Grew sought a definite U.S. commitment to China. First, he pressed for a U.S. pledge to cosign, and thereby to accept the obligation to act upon, any treaty concluded between China and the Soviet Union. Second, he suggested that the status of Port Arthur be guaranteed by the four powers. Third, he asked Truman to define the U.S. interpretation of the Yalta provisions ceding "preeminent interests" to the Soviet Union in the areas surrounding the railroads and Dairen. Truman refused to consider any of these requests. Thus, as he left Washington for Moscow, Soong had no firm understanding of the extent of U.S. support for China during the ensuing negotiations.[43]

The administration's initial position during the Soong talks had been to inform the Chinese of the Yalta terms and suggest that discussions be initiated—and no more. Subsequently, in both the first phase of the Moscow negotiations (June 30-July 14) and the final stage preparatory to the conclusion of a formal treaty (August 1-14), the administration assumed an ambivalent stance, never formally denouncing Soviet demands and always refusing to clarify the U.S. position.

The administration's noncommittal position deeply troubled the Chinese throughout their difficult discussions with the Soviets. At the inception of formal talks on June 30, Stalin stipulated as the Soviet condition for a pact of friendship the resolution of outstanding Sino-Soviet differences, including Chinese acceptance of the independence of Outer Mongolia, the Soviet right to administer jointly the Manchurian railroads, and Soviet "lease" rights to and "pre-eminent interests" in Dairen and Port Arthur. During the June 30-July 14 meetings, the status of Outer Mongolia was amicably resolved. But Soong and Stalin continued to differ over Soviet rights in Dairen and Port Arthur. Seeking U.S. support for his efforts to limit Soviet demands, Soong pressed Harriman for a clarification of the U.S. interpretation of these rights. Harriman, in turn, requested advice from the Truman administration, which, on July 4, repeated its refusal to be bound by any specific interpretation of the Yalta terms on the grounds that clarification would indirectly involve the United States in the negotiations and hence implicitly bind it to fulfilling the resulting settlement. While eager to sustain its independence of the negotiations, the administration, nevertheless, did not wish to disavow interest; thus, on July 6, Secretary of State Byrnes instructed Harriman to inform the Russians that, as a signatory to the Yalta agreements, the United States wanted to be fully consulted before a final agreement was concluded between the Soviet Union and China.

Still pressured by Soong about America's seeming indifference to the fate of China, on July 9, Harriman again urged the administration to report its understanding of the Yalta terms, this time directly to Stalin. Simultaneously, the State Department drafted a memorandum urging U.S. support of China at the Moscow negotiations. The administration, however, made no formal decision either on the State Department's recommendation or on Harriman's request.[44] The Sino-Soviet talks finally reached a stalemate. After stressing his inability to accede to Stalin's demands on port rights, Soong broke off the negotiations on July 14 and returned to Chunking for further consultations with Chiang Kai-shek.

The United State's seeming ambivalence throughout this preliminary negotiating period was indicative not of indifference but of the desire to forestall Soviet involvement in the Far East. Since the Soviet Union had declared its

unwillingness to enter the war against Japan until a treaty had been concluded with China, by stalling negotiations on that treaty, the administration could avert the inevitable extension of Soviet influence in China and Japan without formally repudiating the terms laid down at Yalta.

By June, the administration's options had increased as the result of the defeat of Germany. Thereafter, the administration operated on the premise that Soviet military involvement against Japan was not imperative. This shift was revealed on June 18 in another change of position by the Joint Chiefs of Staff, who now described Soviet aid as desirable but not indispensable and recommended that the United States not bargain for Soviet involvement.[45]

With all this in mind, Truman and Byrnes discussed the Far East with Stalin and Molotov at the Potsdam Conference on July 17. First the Soviet leaders informed Truman and Byrnes of their willingness to accept Chinese control of Manchuria as well as to recognize the Nationalists as the sole leaders of China. In reply, Byrnes affirmed that the United States held to a strict interpretation of the Yalta terms. Then, feigning ignorance of the recently concluded Soong-Stalin talks, Byrnes sounded out Stalin about the areas of Sino-Soviet disagreement. On the basis of Stalin's reply, Byrnes and Truman concluded that the differences between the Soviet and Chinese positions were so fundamental that, at least in the immediate future, a Sino-Soviet treaty was highly unlikely.[46]

The Potsdam discussions between the U.S. and Soviet military staffs provided further assurances for the administration that a Sino-Soviet treaty was still a necessary precondition for Russia's entering the Japanese war.[47] Moreover, at Potsdam, the administration remained in contact with the Chinese Nationalists. On July 20, Chiang Kai-shek informed Truman about Soong's mission, arguing that the Chinese had bargained in good faith and could make no further concessions to secure the treaty. Truman agreed—in fact, he directed Chiang specifically to make no more concessions. Despite this, Truman insisted on the implementation of the Yalta terms and urged Chiang to have Soong return to Moscow to continue negotiations.[48]

While the administration continued formally to support the Yalta commitments, in view of the July 17 meeting with Stalin and Molotov, Truman's instructions to Chiang—if Soong followed them—would effectively stymie the conclusion of a treaty. Moreover, the successful testing of the atomic bomb led Marshall to concede to Stimson and Truman on July 23 that Soviet entry into the war against Japan was no longer necessary, but Marshall again maintained that the Soviet Union could enter anyway and obtain "virtually what they wanted in the surrender terms." Byrnes came away from the discussion hoping only that the Sino-Soviet discussions might be stalled and thereby "delay Soviet entrance and the Japanese might surrender." Finally, instead of consulting the Soviets, the administration unilaterally drafted the formal declaration demanding unconditional Japanese surrender; it also decided unilaterally to accept the Japanese request of August 10 for clarification of the surrender terms.[49]

Moreover, once the second phase of the Sino-Soviet discussions began, the United States adopted a more rigid stance, advising the Chinese to stand firm even if that firmness prevented agreement. On August 5, Byrnes asked Harriman officially to inform Soong that the United States opposed concessions beyond those agreed to at Yalta. He specifically warned the Chinese not to make further concessions over the status of Dairen or Soviet reparations demands. The essence of this new administration position was to support the Chinese at the same time that it opposed concessions needed to conclude the treaty; only if the Soviet Union reversed its attitude and radically changed its demands would a treaty result prior to Japanese surrender.[50]

Truman's policy failed to forestall the Soviet Union's entrance into the Japanese war. Although a formal Sino-Soviet treaty had not been concluded and although the United States finally neither requested nor encouraged Soviet intervention, the Russians nonetheless declared war on Japan on August 8 and moved troops into North China and Manchuria. Simultaneously, Stalin warned Soong on August 10 that, should a formal Sino-Soviet agreement not be concluded, Chinese Communist troops would be permitted to move into Manchuria. Fearful of Soviet support of the Chinese Communists, Chiang Kai-shek acceded to the Soviet demands on the unresolved issues. The formal Sino-Soviet treaty was then quickly concluded, and its terms announced on August 14.[51]

The administration's indirect opposition to the Yalta provisions created the potential for U.S.-Soviet division once the war with Japan ended. The rapidity of the Japanese surrender and the last-minute Soviet entry into the war had complicated surrender proceedings. The administration had had little time to devise formal terms indicating to whom Japanese troops should surrender. Indeed, until Soviet entry, there had been no discussion about Soviet rights to direct or control Japan during the period of occupation. Thus, when unilaterally issuing General Order #1, the United States directed Japanese troops to surrender to the Nationalists in all areas of China south of Manchuria and to the Russians in Manchuria, Korea north of the thirty-eighth parallel, and Karafutu. These surrender orders were intended to achieve two purposes: to preclude Japanese surrender to Chinese Communist troops and to minimize the Soviet occupation role in China and Japan.[52]

Immediately, on August 16, the Soviet Union protested that these surrender provisions violated the Yalta agreements. Stalin demanded that the Soviet surrender zone include the Kuriles and Hokkaido (the northern sector of Japan). Unwilling to create the opportunity for Soviet military presence in Japan, Truman on August 18 acceded to the Soviet request for the Kuriles but not for Hokkaido. At the same time he pressed for an American air base on the Kuriles. In a sharp rejoinder on August 22, Stalin reiterated his earlier demand for Hokkaido and opposed Truman's request for the air base.

This was no mere territorial conflict; it involved the more basic question of the Truman administration's policy toward the Soviet occupation of Japan. At issue was whether the administration was formally prepared for confrontation. Truman at the time hesitated to reject the prospect of a negotiated settlement and replied to Stalin's sharp note of August 22 that the United States had not sought air base but only landing rights on the Kuriles. Truman further pointed out that the Kuriles were not Soviet territory. Yalta had only permitted Soviet occupation, he said; their final status would have to be determined at a future peace conference. On August 30, Stalin acceded to the request for landing rights. He denied, however, that the status of the Kuriles was unclear, contending that the cession had been permanent and that future peace talks would merely ratify this fact.[53]

Directly or indirectly, the objective of limiting Soviet influence in the Far East underlay administration policy toward the Yalta agreements. Truman and Byrnes cunningly, but shortsightedly, here too sought to have it both ways: to avert the effect of the agreements without formally repudiating or renegotiating them.

IV

This clearly contradictory policy required the administration to continue to refrain from publishing the Yalta agreements on the Far East. Publication would have bound the administration to fulfilling them and would have established earlier U.S. insistence on Soviet involvement, negating the limited Soviet military contribution to defeating Japan. Therefore, the Truman administration neglected to publish the Far Eastern agreements on three ostensibly favorable occasions: when the Soviet Union declared war on Japan on August 8, when the Sino-Soviet treaty was announced on August 14, or when Soviet troops occupied the Kurile Islands on August 27.

The U.S. troop withdrawal that permitted Soviet occupation of the Kuriles precipitated bitter protests by conservatives in both Congress and the press, who charged that Soviet possession of these "strategic" islands would directly threaten the security of the United States and Japan.[54] In a September 4 press conference, on the eve of his departure for the London Foreign Ministers Conference, Byrnes attempted to allay this protest. The decision leading up to U.S. withdrawal, he informed the press, had resulted from "discussions" (as opposed to "agreements," he implied) conducted at Yalta, not Potsdam. Byrnes, claiming that his attendance at Yalta had provided him with "full" knowledge of these "discussions," attributed the responsibility for them to Roosevelt rather than Truman. He then announced his intention to review them at London; a final agreement on the status of the Kuriles, he concluded, could be made only at a forthcoming peace conference.[55]

Byrnes dissembled in two respects at this press conference: first, in implying that the status of the Kuriles had not yet been defined and, second, in failing to report the existence of the other Far Eastern agreements. His statements were to have serious ramifications for the Truman administration.

Byrnes's secretiveness on the second point stemmed from the administration's desire to prevent the Soviets from assuming a controlling role in China and in the occupation of Japan. This objective necessarily conflicted with Soviet policy and contributed to the atmosphere of distrust that prevailed during the September meetings of the Council of Foreign Ministers in London. Although Molotov then protested the unilateral character of U.S. occupation policy in Japan, demanding the establishment of an Allied control commission, Byrnes equivocated and, in the end, succeeded in postponing any final decision on Japan.[56]

This strategy and the attendant necessity not to publish the Far Eastern agreements—or even, for that matter, admit their existence—would seriously compromise the administration's position. The first public hint of the existence of the agreements occurred in November 1945 during the controversy surrounding the resignation of Hurley as U.S. ambassador to China. In resigning, Hurley charged that U.S. foreign policy had been subverted by "imperialists" and "communists" in both the State Department and the Foreign Service, charges which led to special hearings by the Senate Foreign Relations Committee in December.

The tone of the committee's questioning of Hurley was sharp, at times even hostile. Attempting to defend Hurley, who had repeated his charges of employee disloyalty and insubordination, a sympathetic Senator Styles Bridges asked whether at Yalta—given the absence of Chinese representatives—any agreement concerning China had been concluded. Although he had not attended the conference, Hurley claimed knowledge about the China discussions. He added that Secretary of State Byrnes was a better authority on that subject.

In his prepared statement the next day, Byrnes dismissed Hurley's charges against the personnel of the State Department and the Foreign Service as wholly unfounded. Senator Bridges, however, was much more concerned with the Truman and Roosevelt administrations' China policy. Repeating his question of the day before, he asked Byrnes whether any agreement concerning China was concluded at Yalta in the absence and without the consent of Chiang Kai-shek. Bridges's confident tone, and the possibility that he had secured access to the Yalta text through Hurley or another source in the State Department, complicated Byrnes's reply. To admit that agreements had been concluded at Yalta without advising or consulting Chiang and had not yet been published would put the administration on the defensive and possibly expose its earlier dissembling. Faced with this dilemma, Byrnes neither affirmed nor denied that an agreement had been made:

I do not recall the various agreements [of the Yalta Conference]. It is entirely possible that some of the agreements arrived at Yalta affected China some way or another, and I have told you that I would gladly furnish you the communique and then you could decide whether or not they affected China. If they were made they certainly were made by the heads of government and certainly only the three Governments were represented there.

Bridges then observed that had any agreement on China been concluded, the secretary could not have been unaware of its existence.[57] Thus, when the administration would publish the Far Eastern agreements, it would have to offer a convincing rationale both for its earlier failure to publish them and for Byrnes's seeming ignorance of the matter.

This situation came to pass in February 1946. The event precipitating the publication of the Far Eastern agreements was the administration's announcement in January that it had turned over to an international trusteeship certain Pacific islands the United States captured from Japan during World War II. During a January 22 press conference, Acting Secretary of State Dean Acheson was asked whether the Soviet Union would similarly be required to turn over the Kuriles to an international trusteeship. In answer, Acheson pointed out that the Yalta agreements had provided only for Soviet occupation of the Kuriles; the final disposition would have to be determined at a future peace conference. Acheson conceded, however, that such a conference might simply affirm Soviet control. On January 26, Moscow Radio challenged Acheson's remarks, denying that Soviet control of these territories was temporary or that Soviet occupation was related only to the prosecution of the war against Japan.[58]

At a press conference on January 29, Byrnes announced that the Kuriles and South Sakhalin had in fact been ceded to the Soviet Union at Yalta. He further disclosed that agreements concerning Port Arthur and Dairen had also been concluded. But these agreements would become binding only after the formal conclusion of a peace treaty with Japan.

The most dramatic aspect of Byrnes's press conference was not the disclosure of the agreements themselves but his attempts to explain the Truman administration's earlier failure to release them or indeed even to admit their existence. What Byrnes did was to tell the press that although he had been a delegate to Yalta, he had left the conference on the afternoon of February 10, before the concluding session the next day. He had not learned about the specifics of the Far Eastern agreements until August 1945, a few days after the Japanese surrender. In response to further questions, Byrnes said he did not know whether former Secretary of State Stettinius knew about the agreements or where, in fact, the text was deposited. It was not, he stated, in the State Department archives, but it might be in the White House files.[59]

Once again, Byrnes had adroitly covered his tracks. He had shifted responsibility for both the Yalta agreements and the failure to publish them to the Roosevelt administration's tactics of secrecy. His statement did, however, raise two important questions: first, had the agreements been privately concluded by Roosevelt without the knowledge of other White House or State Department personnel and, second, where was the text.

During a January 31 press conference, Truman sought to resolve these questions. The text, he claimed, had always been in the White House files, except when under review either by members of the White House staff or other administration personnel. While he had always known the whereabouts of the text, Truman said, he had not reviewed it until he began to prepare for the Potsdam Conference. Asked when the agreements would in fact be published, Truman answered that it would be necessary first to consult the British and the Russians. Most of the agreements, he added, had already been made public; the others would be disclosed at the "proper" time.[60]

The Truman administration's policy toward the Yalta Far Eastern agreements and other administration tactics strained the already uneasy relations between the United States and the Soviet Union. It was in the area of tactics and personality that the rigidity and moralistic tone of postwar U.S.-Soviet relations derived important substance, and not simply from conflicting ideologies and objectives. In this sense, the cold war was an avoidable conflict: the "way" it evolved being a product of shortsighted political leadership. The opportunities for détente provided by Yalta were effectively subverted by the Truman administration, and U.S.-Soviet relations suffered until a change in presidents brought an administration less rigidly bound to the self-righteous politics of confrontation. Eisenhower's politics remained conservative; but, with the Geneva summit conference of 1955, his presidency marked a new, less militant phase of the cold war.

NOTES

[1] Lloyd C. Gardner, *Architects of Illusion: Men and Ideas in American Foreign Policy, 1941-1949* (Chicago, 1970), x.

[2] See *Foreign Relations of the United States—Diplomatic Papers: The Conferences at Malta and Yalta* (Washington, D.C., 1955), 43, 93-108, 202-66 (hereafter, *Yalta Papers*).

[3] *Ibid.,* 42 (emphasis added).

[4] Harry S. Truman, *Memoirs: Year of Decisions* (Garden City, N.Y., 1955), I, 15.

[5] Herbert Feis, *Churchill, Roosevelt, Stalin: The War They Waged and the Peace They Sought* (Princeton, 1957), 575.

[6] Barton Bernstein, "American Foreign Policy and the Origins of the Cold War," in Barton Bernstein, ed., *Politics and Policies of the Truman Administration* (Chicago, 1970), 28.

[7] Tang Tsou, *America's Failure in China: 1941-1950* (Chicago, 1963), 256.

[8] Gar Alperovitz, *Atomic Diplomacy: Hiroshima and Potsdam* (New York, 1967), 96.

[9] Quoted in Diane Shaver Clemens, *Yalta* (New York, 1970), 31-34, 37-39.

[10] William L. Neumann, *After Victory: Churchill, Roosevelt, Stalin and the Making of the Peace* (New York, 1967), 105, 110-11; Feis, 178; Clemens, 30; Martin Herz, *Beginnings of the Cold War* (Bloomington, 1966), 114-15.

[11] Bernstein, 20.

[12] Clemens, 14-15.

[13] *Ibid.,* 17-27; *Yalta Papers,* 208.

[14] *Ibid.,* 93-96; James MacGregor Burns, *Roosevelt: The Soldier of Freedom* (New York, 1970), 535-36; Gabriel Kolko, *The Politics of War: The World and United States Foreign Policy, 1943-1945* (New York, 1968), 149; Gardner, 49.

[15] *Yalta Papers,* 97-100.

[16] *Ibid.,* 209, 212.

[17] *Ibid.,* 214 (emphasis added).

[18] *Ibid.,* 216, 218.

[19] Tsou, 33-34, 38-39, 58-59, 74-87, 95-105, 162-68, 192-94, 244; Feis, 404; *Yalta Papers,* 378.

[20] Clemens, 179; *Yalta Papers,* 846; Herz, 84; Burns, 584.

[21] *Yalta Papers,* 727-28; Clemens, 183-86.

[22] *Yalta Papers,* 977-78, 980; Clemens, 186-92, 198-99, 201-12; Burns, 584; Herz, 82, 84, 104-05; Alperovitz, 135.

[23] *Yalta Papers,* 570-72, 619, 629-30, 634; Clemens, 137-39, 141-42, 146-47, 159-65, 172.

[24] *Yalta Papers,* 768-70, 894-95, 984.

[25] Alperovitz, 136.

[26] *Ibid.,* 248-54; Herz, 89-91

[27] Herz, 94.

[28] Alperovitz, 19-26, 32; Bernstein, 25; Gardner, 57, 60; Truman, 80-81.

[29] Alperovitz, 28, 33; Herz, 95-96, 109-10; Feis, 578.

[30] Alperovitz, 34; Herz, 97-98.

[31] Alperovitz, 69, 70-71.

[32] *Ibid.,* 72, 73, 76; Herz, 21-26, 29-30, 32-36.

[33] Alperovitz, 140-43, 147-52; Kolko, 576, 578; *Public Papers of the Presidents: Harry S. Truman, 1945* (Washington, D.C., 1961), 214 (hereafter, *Truman Papers*).

[34] Alperovitz, 79; Kolko, 512-13.

[35] Bernstein, 49; Clemens, 271; Alperovitz, 85-86, 152-58, 162-63,166-69; Lloyd Gardner, "America and the German 'Problem,' 1945-1949," in Bernstein, ed., *Politics,* 120-22; William A. Williams, "A New View of American Omnipotence," in Robert A. Divine, ed., *Causes and Consequences of World War II* (Chicago, 1969), 329-34.

[36] John Gimbel, *The American Occupation of Germany: Politics and the Military, 1945-1949* (Stanford, 1968), 4.

[37] Feis, 639; Tsou, 254-55; Alperovitz, 94.

[38] Tsou, 255.

[39] Alperovitz, 31-32, 95; James V. Forrestal, *The Forrestal Diaries,* ed. Walter Millis (New York, 1951), 56.

[40] Alperovitz, 96, 99, 100; Tsou, 256-57; Lloyd Gardner, *Economic Aspects of New Deal Diplomacy* (Madison, 1964), 253-54; Richard G. Hewlett and Oscar E. Anderson Jr., *The New World, 1939/1946* (University Park, Pa., 1962), 350-51; Kolko, 535.

[41] Alperovitz, 96-97; Kolko, 535.

[42] *Ibid.,* 547; Alperovitz, 102; Hewlett and Anderson, 351-52; Tsou, 271; Gardner, *Economic Aspects,* 255, U.S. Dept. of Defense, *The Entry of the Soviet Union into the War against Japan: Military Plans, 1941-1945* (Washington, D.C., Sept. 1955), 72; Herbert Feis, *Contest Over Japan* (New York, 1967), 13-14.

[43] Gardner, *Economic Aspects,* 256; Alperovitz, 120-21; Kolko, 537.

[44] Truman, 315-19; Alperovitz, 123-25; Gardner, *Economic Aspects,* 256; Tsou, 274, 279.

[45] Alperovitz, 119; Tsou, 265; Hewlett and Anderson, 363-64.

[46] Tsou, 268, 278; Gardner, *Economic Aspects,* 257; Kolko, 558-59; Hewlett and Anderson, 385-86.

[47] Hewlett and Anderson, 393; Kolko, 561.

[48] Tsou, 278-79, 282; Gardner, *Economic Aspects,* 258; Kolko, 560; Hewlett and Anderson, 391.

[49] Gardner, *Economic Aspects,* 258; Kolko, 560, 562; Hewlett and Anderson, 370, 381, 383, 392, 395, 397, 398; Tsou, 268; Forrestal, 78; Alperovitz, 181-82, 190-91; Feis, *Contest,* 14, 16.

[50] Hewlett and Anderson, 398; Tsou, 282-83.

[51] Feis, *Contest,* 8; Hewlett and Anderson, 403; Tsou, 269, 283; Alperovitz, 189.

[52] Feis, *Contest,* 7, 17-19; Alperovitz, 189-91; Tsou, 308; Kolko, 600.

[53] *Ibid.,* 600-01; Feis, *Contest,* 19-20.

[54] *Chicago Tribune,* Aug. 29, 1945, p. 2; Sept. 6, 1945, p. 18.

[55] *Ibid.,* Sept. 5, 1945, p. 1; *New York Times,* Sept. 5, 1945, pp. 1, 9; *New York Herald-Tribune,* Sept. 5, 1945, p. 1.

[56] Feis, *Contest,* 12, 28, 34-37.

[57] U.S. Senate, Committee on Foreign Relations, *Hearings on the Investigation of Far Eastern Policy,* 79th Cong., 1st Sess., 1945, pp. 123-24, 231-33.

[58] *Chicago Tribune,* Jan. 23, 1946, p. 12; Jan. 27, 1946, p. 1. *Newsweek,* XXVII (Feb. 4, 1946), 46.

[59] *Chicago Tribune,* Jan. 30, 1946, p. 5; U.S. Dept. of State, *Bulletin,* XIV (Feb. 10, 1946), 189-90.

[60] *Truman Papers* (1946), 102-05.

Halford Ross Ryan (essay date 1979)

SOURCE: "Roosevelt's First Inaugural: A Study of Technique," in *The Quarterly Journal of Speech,* Vol. 65, No. 2, April, 1979, pp. 137-49.

[*In the following essay, Ryan analyzes the rhetorical technique of Roosevelt's first inaugural address.*]

Historian David Potter's observation that, by historical hindsight, the critic might not perceive events as contemporaries comprehended them[1] is germane to a study of Franklin Delano Roosevelt's First Inaugural Address. Although Roosevelt had large majorities in the Congress, he could not know the "Hundred Days" legislation would pass without Congressional demurral or difficulty. To assume that FDR knew of his forthcoming legislative successes when he fashioned his first inaugural is mistaken, and such an assumption causes the critics to miss some valuable insights concerning FDR and his speech.

FDR's first inaugural is one of his best known and most important speeches. If for no other reason, it was a significant speech because FDR believed it contained all of the elements of his New Deal.[2] Samuel I. Rosenman ranked the speech among FDR's best: "This was one of the President's truly great speeches, not only in form and substance but in accomplishment."[3] And Harry Hopkins thought it was FDR's best speech: "For myself I think his first inaugural address was the best speech he ever made. . . . With that one speech, and in those few minutes, the appalling anxiety and fears were lifted, and the people of the United States knew that they were going into a safe harbor under the leadership of a man who never knew the meaning of fear."[4] But surprisingly little rhetorical attention has been paid the speech.[5]

My primary purpose in this essay is to examine three rhetorical techniques that FDR used in his speech. Before discussing them, however, I wish to establish that they were indeed *his* techniques; and after discussing them I shall observe their similarity to Adolph Hitler's rhetorical techniques in response to the *zeitgeist* of March, 1933.

THE PRODUCTION OF THE SPEECH

In this section, I wish to examine three general areas: the nature of the texts, who was responsible for the original draft and the famous fear statement, and selected textual emendations by FDR.

The following extant drafts are in the Roosevelt Library, Hyde Park, New York: the first draft, which is in FDR's handwriting; the second draft, a typed copy of the first with a variety of emendations; the third draft, also typed, which includes the emendations from draft two and additional emendations; and a final typed reading copy from which FDR delivered his speech.[6]

The existence of Roosevelt's handwritten draft, in conjunction with a note which FDR had attached to this draft (the note stated that he wrote the first draft at Hyde Park on 27 February 1933), has led some to conclude that FDR authored his own inaugural address.[7] Although FDR wrote this first draft, he was not responsible for its authorship.

Rather, Raymond Moley composed the first draft. In fine, Moley has related how he prepared the first draft, how FDR copied his draft in longhand at Hyde Park, and how Moley tossed his own draft into the fire, with the words "This is your speech now," after FDR had finished copying his draft.[8] Moley's version is independently verified by an investigation of FDR's handwritten draft. Several of FDR's handwritten pages do suggest that he did copy them from another source. Instead of the speech text's filling each successive page, there are lacunae on pages three, five, and seven. These lacunae suggest that FDR took more pages to write than did Moley, or to put it another way, the ten pages of copy could be reduced to approximately eight pages if FDR had written his text seriatim on each page.[9]

As for the famous fear statement, "the only thing we have to fear is fear itself," a variety of sources have implied that it was somehow FDR's.[10] However, the phrase was undoubtedly Louis Howe's handiwork. Howe was FDR's personal secretary and Howe dictated a whole beginning paragraph for the third draft in which the phrase appears *de novo*.[11] If the phrase were not original with Howe, then his original source has eluded later researchers.[12]

I turn now to selected emendations made in the texts. But I shall deal only with FDR's revisions, and then only those revisions which are germane to my study.

Only one major relevant revision appears on the handwritten draft (FDR's copy from Moley's draft). In the second paragraph, Moley wrote of leadership in past national crises—the Revolution, the early emergence of the nation, and the Civil War—and how the people's support of that leadership "on every occasion has won through to." FDR crossed out the quoted phrase and substituted "is an essential to victory."[13] Not only is FDR's phrase more concise, but it also links leadership with victory in a military-like sense, about which I shall note more later.

A variety of minor emendations are made in the second draft (the first typed one), but I pass them by because they are not in FDR's bold, print-like handwriting.

The third draft (the second typed one) is replete with FDR's handwriting and contains some significant alterations. In his paragraph that contained his fear statement, Howe had written, "nameless, unreasoning, unjustified terror which paralyzes the needed efforts to bring about prosperity once more." With a definite emphasis on military-like words, FDR produced, "which paralyzes *needed* efforts *to convert retreat into advance*" [hereafter, italicized words indicate FDR's emendations]. Later on, the text read: "The standards of the money-changers stand indicted"; however, FDR wished further to denigrate the bankers by writing: "*Practices* of the *unscrupulous* money-changers stand indicted." *Practices* somewhat sullies the loftiness of "standards" and *unscrupulous* quite speaks for itself. Treating the bankers in the same vein a bit later, FDR changed "They know of no other ways than the ancient rules" to "They know *only* the rules *of a generation of self-seekers*." A little later on, FDR further strengthened the text to cast additional ridicule on the bankers. "The moral stimulation of work must no longer be submerged in the sham of evanescent profit scouring" became "The moral stimulation of work *no longer* must be *forgotten* in *the mad chase of* evanescent profits."[14] All of these emendations demonstrate that FDR took particular pains (pleasure?) to denigrate and deprecate the bankers more than Moley's draft had done. Later, I shall demonstrate why.

In the latter part of his address, FDR turned to his personal leadership as President. In a number of places in this draft FDR strengthened or clarified Moley's language in order to enhance the positive nature and vigor of his intended leadership style. The following examples illustrate the point. "Because without such discipline no progress can be made, or any leadership really led" became "Because without such discipline no progress *is* made, *no* leadership *becomes effective.*" The future tense of Moley's thought is brought into the present tense by FDR's change and stresses the immediacy of his leadership, and *effective* looks for immediate and tangible results. "I am prepared under my constitutional duty to indicate the measures" became "I am prepared under my constitutional duty to *recommend* the measures." *Recommend* has a stronger sense of positive advocacy than "indicate," which suggests merely pointing out. The point is that FDR wanted to stress his leadership role by taking the lead in recommending to Congress his measures rather than merely indicating to Congress what measures he thought were appropriate. But, interestingly, FDR deleted "sword of" in the following passage: "With this pledge taken, I assume unhesitatingly the sword of leadership of this great army of our people." Perhaps the term "sword" sounded too militaristic, and perhaps he wanted to stress his personal leadership rather than his assuming a symbolic sword of leadership. All of these emendations demonstrate that FDR wanted clearly to state and to show the active personal leadership with which he would assume the presidency, and that he wished to strengthen Moley's draft in those respects.[15]

The fourth draft, his actual reading copy, contained only one emendation. While waiting in the Senate Committee Room for the ceremonies to begin, FDR added in longhand an opening sentence: "This is a day of consecration." When he delivered the speech, he verbally inserted "national" before "consecration."[16]

In summary, one might have wished that FDR had authored his own first inaugural, but he did not; and that the famous fear statement, which is so intimately associated with him and his inaugural, was his also, but it was not. Nevertheless, FDR did make emendations on three of the four drafts, and most of those changes demonstrated his desire to use militaristic words to evoke military-like associations in his listeners. He paid special attention to the bankers by utilizing language which purposefully defamed them and their practices. Lastly, he managed his language to strengthen his leadership role. He would act immediately to lead the nation in its crisis. The philosophical significance of this textual investigation is that, although the forthcoming exegesis of FDR's rhetorical purposes is concerned with some of Moley's and Howe's ideas, FDR was satisfied with the text to make it his inaugural address, and many of the points I shall later make were expressly his word choices. What follows, then, is based on the assumption that "the President's speech is the President's speech."[17]

THE TECHNIQUES

Before discussing FDR's three rhetorical techniques, I wish to comment briefly on his speech as one in the genre of inaugural addresses. Wolfarth has isolated four major issues on which presidents traditionally speak: Domestic Issues, International Issues, American Traditions, and Other.[18] FDR's first inaugural pays tribute to American Traditions. Some typical examples are "This great nation," "the American spirit of the pioneer," "seeking old and precious moral values," "essential democracy," and so forth. A handful of sentences centered around the "good neighbor" policy comprise his treatment of International Issues. But FDR's predominant theme was Domestic Issues. In an accompanying notation for his inaugural address, FDR wrote that in his speech he attempted primarily to allay the nation's fear: "I sought principally in the foregoing Inaugural Address to banish, so far as possible, the fear of the present and of the future which held the American people and the American spirit in its grasp."[19] Indeed, his famous fear statement made an indelible impression on the American mind. Yet, however popularized and catchy FDR's famous fear statement was, it was not the crux of his speech. Nor was it the solitary theme on which commentators based their evaluations of his speech's efficacy with his reading and listening audiences. A close examination of FDR's first inaugural reveals that he used three rhetorical techniques to aid him in announcing his implementation of his New Deal. In this section, I shall examine these techniques in relationship to the American people and the Congress within the inaugural context of March, 1933.

The Scapegoat Technique

In early 1933, America's preeminent concern was the banking crisis. Almost 5,000 banks had failed since 1929, and twenty-two states had closed their banks prior to March 4 of FDR's inaugural year.[20] The spiraling effects of margin and then more margin, stock losses, foreclosures, and, ultimately, bank failures probably had at their epicenter the bankers and the brokers. Tugwell specifically indicted them: "Wall Street was again the wicked place it had been during the progressive era. The financial establishment was being blamed for what had happened."[21] And Farr concurred with Tugwell's analysis: "It was true that most of the guilt belonged to the money changers, who probably had something to do with the Stock Exchange."[22]

FDR's coup in his inaugural was to make the money-changers the scapegoat[23] for the Depression. It has already been demonstrated, via the textual emendations, how FDR purposefully used language to denigrate the moneychangers. In his speech, he unflinchingly proclaimed what was believed by the average American—the money-changers were culpable for the Depression. The efficacy of his using the scapegoat technique ensued from his ability to channel the American people's anxieties and frustrations from themselves to the money-changers. The speech text leaves no doubt that FDR utilized the scapegoat technique to blame Wall Street for the Depression: "the rulers of the exchange of mankind's goods have failed through their own stubbornness and their own incompetence, have admitted their failure, and have abdicated. Practices of the unscrupulous money-changers stand indicted in the court of public opinion, rejected by the hearts and minds of men." And, again, "Yes, the money-changers have fled from their high seats in the temple of our civilization. We may now restore that temple to the ancient truths."[24] Leuchtenburg noted that FDR's delivery matched the mood of his language: "Grim, unsmiling, chin uplifted, his voice firm, almost angry, he lashed out at the bankers."[25] Having castigated Wall Street, FDR then indicated that he would direct his New Deal measures toward checking it and its practices. In order to stop a return to the "evils of the old order," FDR announced that there would be banking reform: "There must be a strict supervision of all banking and credits and investments. (Applause.) There must be an end to speculation with other people's money. (Applause.) And there must be a provision for an adequate but sound currency. (Applause.)"[26] To this end, Congress passed FDR's Emergency Banking Act on March 9.[27] The task of putting "people to work" began with the Civilian Conservation Corps, March 31; the fear of foreclosure was alleviated by the Emergency Farm Mortgage Act, May 12, and the Home Owner's Loan Act, June 13.[28]

Various contemporary signs indicated that FDR struck a responsive rhetorical chord by utilizing his scapegoat technique. When he said that he would restore the "temple to the ancient truths," his inaugural audience applauded for the first time.[29] Editors from Universal Films and Pathe News included FDR's attack on the bankers in their news film.[30] Tugwell noted that FDR "tramped hard on those who were responsible."[31] Morison observed that FDR gave the money-changers an "excoriation."[32] The news-print media also supported FDR's use of the scapegoat technique. The *Christian Century* noted, "The 'false money-changers' deserve all the condemnation that can be heaped upon them."[33] *The Nation* observed that Roosevelt dealt the money-changers a "verbal scourging."[34] *News-Week* stated, "It was an assault on the bankers, against whom the voices of the distressed are raised in an ever-swelling chorus as the depression endures."[35] The scapegoat technique also had FDR's desired effect on the business community. *The Times* (London) noted that FDR was "likely to rouse the opposition of a good many vested interests."[36] FDR used the scapegoat technique to blunt the expected opposition from those *laissez-faire* sympathizers who might attack his New Deal banking and investment measures.[37] Rauch observed that FDR was somewhat successful in disarming his banking critics: "The bankers were in a chastened mood. . . . They had lost the cohesion of a vested group."[38]

FDR, then, used the scapegoat technique to blame Wall Street for the Depression and the banking crisis. Available evidence from the inaugural audience, from contemporary news-films and news-print media, and from later commentators suggests that FDR was successful in obtaining his end.

Military Metaphor

Although Americans had elected FDR and his New Deal, questions still remained about the nature of his personal leadership. Granted, FDR and the Democratic party platform had advocated reform and recovery through lower tariffs, unemployment relief, the protection of investments and agriculture, the repeal of the Prohibition amendment, etc.; yet Americans avidly awaited his inaugural address, which should cue the nation to how he planned to lead the country out of the Depression.[39]

Knowing that his program would need mass support and that the New Deal would bring broad and at times radical departures from conducting government as it had been until 1933, Roosevelt endeavored to garner that support by using military metaphor. Osborn has argued that an examination of metaphor can "permit a more precise focusing upon whatever values and motives are salient in society at a given time."[40] Leuchtenburg studied the Depression era values and motives and concluded that FDR purposefully responded to the Depression crisis by using military metaphor: "Roosevelt's inaugural address . . . reflected the sense of wartime crisis,"[41] and "President Roosevelt sought to restore national confidence by evoking the mood of wartime."[42] The careful listener or reader would have noted that FDR had deployed an advance guard of military metaphor in the early parts of his address: "retreat into advance," "victory," "direct recruiting," and "emergency of war." But when FDR directly urged support for and acceptance of his New Deal leadership in the latter three-fourths of his speech, his language was replete with military metaphor:

> if we are to go forward, we must move as a trained and loyal army, willing to sacrifice for the good of a common discipline, because without such discipline no progress can be made, no leadership becomes effective. We are, I know, ready and willing to submit our lives and our property to such discipline because it makes possible a leadership which aims at the larger good. This I propose to offer, pledging that the larger purposes will bind upon us, bind upon us all a sacred obligation, with a unity of duty hitherto evoked only in times of armed strife. With this pledge taken, I assume unhesitatingly the leadership of this great army of our people dedicated to a disciplined attack upon our common problems.[43]

There can be little doubt that FDR purposefully used the military metaphor to create the symbol of a great American army. This army, organized under the personal leadership of its new Commander-in-Chief, would wage war on the Depression. In fact, a certain Rev. Hicks from Yonkers, New York, had urged in a letter to FDR that he call for a "mobilization as if the United States were at war."[44] The repetition of "discipline" four times and of "leadership" three times, and other value laden words, such as "duty," "sacred obligation," and "armed strife," should reinforce those salient values and desires which yearned for action against the Depression. If Conkin was correct when he argued that "The situation invited a surrender of power to some leader,"[45] then FDR's military metaphor facilitated Americans' surrender of power and liberty, much as one does in the real Army, to their Commander-in-Chief.

The effect-oriented responses from private persons and the press were favorable to FDR's military metaphor appeals. From all quarters came support for FDR's bid for quasi-military leadership power, and that support was often couched in Roosevelt's infectious military metaphor. Republican Alfred M. Landon of Kansas affirmed, "If there is any way in which a Republican governor of a midwestern state can aid the President in the fight, I now enlist for the duration of the war."[46] Myron C. Taylor, chairman of United States Steel Corporation, declared, "I hasten to reenlist to fight the depression to its end."[47] James Hagerty wrote in the *New York Times,* "In the phraseology which ran all through his speech he indicated that he regarded the United States as in an economic war."[48] The *New York Times* capsulized other leading newspapers' comments, parts of which are included here: The *Constitution* in Atlanta said Roosevelt gave a "straight-from-the-shoulder attack"; the *News-Age Herald* in Birmingham labeled the speech "a clarion call for nation unity in the face of a crisis"; the *Plain Dealer* in Cleveland responded to FDR's military metaphor and characterized the speech as "fighting words, fit for a time that calls for militant action"; in Des Moines, the *Register* believed "it is the rallying of the country to renewal of a courageous and sustained war on the depression."[49] The New York *Daily News* had not supported Roosevelt, but it pledged itself "to support the policies of FDR for a period of at least one year; longer if circumstances warrant."[50] In its inimitable manner, *The Times* (London) also took notice of Roosevelt's military metaphor: "What is important to note is the spirit which inspired it throughout. A high and resolute militancy breathes in every line."[51]

But this successful use of military metaphor—as gauged by private and media reaction—could also hurt FDR if Americans misperceived his intent. Therefore, in what seems to be an effort to reassure Americans that they had little to fear of a nascent executive dictatorship in his New Deal, FDR hastened to allay the American people: "Action in this image, action to this end, is feasible under the form of government which we have inherited from our ancestors. Our constitution is so simple, so practical, that it is possible always to meet extraordinary needs by changes in emphasis and arrangement without the loss of essential form."[52] The critic might have challenged FDR's assertion that "changes in emphasis and arrangement" can ensue without a "loss of essential form," but Farr believed the assertion sounded fine to about 99 percent of FDR's listeners and, anyway, there was little time to raise that question because FDR's confident voice continued on.[53]

However, Adolph Hitler's Fuehrer-principle was fresh in some Americans' minds and they were not so easily beguiled. Partially indicative of this thinking was William Randolph Hearst's *New York Mirror* issue of 6 March, which headlines its story, "ROOSEVELT ASKS DICTATOR'S ROLE."[54] Edmund Wilson, editor of the *New Republic,* believed that FDR's military metaphor signaled a dire warning: "The thing that emerges most

clearly is the warning of a dictatorship."[55] Rauch has written that, even among liberals, the military metaphor caused some concern: "Liberals were later to profess they found the germs of fascism in the First New Deal. Perhaps they found cause for suspicion in the evocation of the 'regimented' moods of wartime."[56]

Although some contemporary, and especially later, critics were less comfortable with FDR's military metaphor than were most of his contemporaries, Roosevelt's military metaphor successfully evoked in the American people a patriotic duty and discipline to support his quasi-military leadership in his symbolic war on the Depression. Lest this military metaphor might smack too much of an incipient, executive dictatorship, FDR took pains to assure his audience that the Constitution would survive, that mere changes in emphasis would not affect its essential form.

Carrot-and-Stick Technique

During the interregnum (November 1932 to March 1933), Roosevelt received advice from many quarters, including even President Herbert Hoover, on how he could help to stop the deepening Depression. Of particular concern here is the advice FDR received on how to cope with the new Congress, about which some predictions were not particularly encouraging. Rollins has given an accurate picture of Congress *before* FDR's inaugural was delivered: "The new Congress was already divided and confused. Some wanted inflation, some a sound gold dollar. Some wanted a 30-hour week, some employment guaranteed. Some looked for a new Mussolini, some for a new Jefferson."[57] Political commentator Walter Lippmann wrote that it would take a strong President to lead a boisterous Congress: "The new Congress will be an excitable and impetuous body, and it will respect only a President who knows his own mind and will not hesitate to employ the whole authority of his position."[58] FDR received from Senator Key Pittman of Nevada a letter (11 February 1933) in which Pittman warned FDR about the Congress: "your leadership . . . is going to be exceedingly difficult for a while. Democrats have grown . . . individualistic, they have lost the habit of cooperation, they have grown unaccustomed to discipline."[59] Of these typical warnings, Patterson has written, "Such predictions of an unruly Congress in a time of social and economic crisis were commonplace in the months prior to Roosevelt's inauguration."[60] FDR had enlisted the country in his symbolic army with the military metaphor; he had used the scapegoat technique to subdue Wall Street; he had a favorable press;[61] he had now only to deal with the Congress.

Accordingly, FDR resorted to the carrot-and-stick approach to move the Congress to follow his executive leadership. His carrot was a clever cajoling of Congress to act either on its own or in tandem with him:

> And it is to be hoped that the normal balance of
> executive and legislative authority may be wholly
> equal, wholly adequate, to meet the unprecedented

task before us. But it may be that an unprecedented demand and need for undelayed action may call for temporary departure from that normal balance of public procedure. I am prepared under my constitutional duty to recommend the measures that a stricken nation in the midst of a stricken world may require. These measures, or such measures as the Congress may build out of its experience and wisdom. I shall seek within my constitutional authority to bring to speedy adoption.[62]

But if the carrot were not motivation enough, then the stick would be:

> But in the event that the Congress shall fail to take one of these two courses, in the event that the national emergency is still critical, I shall not evade the clear course of duty that will then confront me. I shall ask the Congress for the one remaining instrument to meet the crisis: broad executive power to wage a war against the emergency, as great as the power that would be given to me if we were in fact invaded by a foreign foe.[63]

The tumultuous applause which immediately followed, and it was the greatest applause of any passage in the speech,[64] could not have been mistaken by the listening members of Congress. Eleanor Roosevelt thought the applause was "a little terrifying. You felt that they would do *anything*—if only someone would tell them *what* to do."[65] The *News* in Dallas supported FDR's carrot-and-stick technique by suggesting that, "if Congress fails him, the country will strongly back him in his demands for virtual war powers."[66] The conservative Boston *Transcript* even agreed with FDR: "The President's program demands dictatorial authority. This is unprecedented in its implications, but such is the desperate temper of the people that it is welcome."[67]

In hindsight, the Congress was anything but intransigent, but FDR did not know that when he fashioned his speech. Conkin observed, "Almost any legislative proposal would pass."[68] Patterson believed that Congress' willingness to cooperate with FDR stemmed from its wish to delegate responsibility, its eagerness to spend, and because FDR was actually more conservative than was the Congress.[69] Although the carrot-and-stick technique admittedly did not directly cause Congress to cooperate, it did nevertheless serve a vital function. The carrot-and-stick's efficacy ensued from FDR's willingness to use the stick if it were necessary. Rollins believed that if FDR had not demonstrated his ability to act and to lead, he might have failed on inauguration day: "What Roosevelt did do, with monumental success, was to preserve the faith which vague commitment or partial action might have shattered."[70]

ROOSEVELT AND HITLER COMPARED

The *zeitgeist* of March, 1933, manifested some similar conditions in Germany and the United States,[71] and these conditions were utilized by their respective leaders. Humphrey has outlined the conditions and their causes:

> The same world-wide economic collapse which brought Hitler to power in Germany in 1933, brought Roosevelt and the New Deal to America. . . . [I]n the month of March, 1933, the positions of Roosevelt and Hitler were strangely similar. Both had risen to power on the crest of a wave of protest against things as they were. Both men and both nations faced problems of unemployment, financial collapse, and the task of inspiring a bewildered and despairing people.[72]

Toland believed that Hitler's *Weltanschauung* originated "in New York City's Wall Street."[73]

In reacting to similar conditions, the two leaders used similar language. Hitler blamed the Jews and other half-hearted lukewarm people (*die Halben*) for the Depression.[74] The historical originators of the scapegoat became under Hitler the very object of his attack. Hitler also used militaristic terms in his speeches. Words such as "blood, authority of personality, and a fighting spirit," as well as "victory" and "fight," interspersed his speeches.[75] On 23 March 1933, Hitler used the carrot-and-stick technique in opening the Reichstag. He offered the Reichstag an "opportunity for friendly co-operation"; but his stick was, "It is for you, gentlemen of the Reichstag, to decide between war and peace."[76] Chancellor Hitler demonstrated that he appreciated the efficacy of Roosevelt's various techniques in his inaugural address by the language Hitler chose to express his congratulatory cable:

> The Reich Chancellor is in accord with the President that the virtues of sense of duty, readiness for sacrifice, and discipline must be the supreme rule of the whole nation. This moral demand, which the President is addressing to every single citizen, is only the quintessence of German philosophy of the State, expressed in its motto "The Public Weal Before Private Gain."[77]

Mussolini's *Il Giornale d'Italia* saw in FDR's inaugural a reaffirmation of its views:

> President Roosevelt's words are clear and need no comment to make even the deaf hear that not only Europe but the whole world feels the need of executive authority capable of acting with full powers of cutting short the purposeless chatter of legislative assemblies. This method of government may well be defined as Fascist.[78]

With similar circumstances in which they came to power, with similar reactions via their similar rhetorical techniques, would not one expect their personal leadership to be similar? Under Hitler, Germany became a Nazi dictatorship. The possibility certainly existed for FDR to become a dictator. Gunther has wisely observed that possibility: "We are apt to forget nowadays the immense, unprecedented, overwhelming authority conferred on FDR by an enthusiastically willing Congress during the first hundred days of his first administration. The Reichstag did not give Hitler much more."[79] Farr has observed that FDR's "proposed charter of authority, as we read it today, was simplicity itself: the President was king."[80] And Robinson noted, "Clearly, semi-dictatorial powers had been granted the President."[81] Yet, the United States did not have a Mussolini or a Hitler in Franklin Delano Roosevelt.

One reason was the nature of their respective countries. Halasz has argued that the United States had a long history of constitutional democracy which Germany did not have; moreover, FDR was not asking for a sacrifice of political freedom, as was Hitler; nor were the American people, as were most Germans, convinced that the Depression demanded such a sacrifice.[82] The Democratic party did not utilize intimidation and physical force to bully others, as did the Nazis, and the Republican party could and did oppose FDR, whereas Hitler stifled dissent and suppressed opposing political parties.

Also, Hitler and Roosevelt had critical differences in their conceptions of leadership and the framework in which it should be exercised. On the first day he assumed the office of Reich Chancellor, Hitler said he would never relinquish it: "No power in the world will ever get me out of here alive."[83] Juxtaposed to that statement is an interesting FDR emendation of the third draft, which suggests that FDR had a more reasonable and limited conception of his leadership tenure. On the draft, FDR added *present* to the following sentence: "They have made me the *present* instrument of their wishes."[84] The term "present" implies the four-year term, and it does not preclude some other president four years later—nor is a permanent Roosevelt presidency thereby suggested. In the 1934 Nuremburg rallies, Hitler's minion Rudolph Hess proclaimed, "The party is Hitler. Hitler, however, is Germany just as Germany is Hitler. Heil Hitler!"[85] No such language has been adduced to FDR's most ardent supporters. While Hitler was the embodiment of Louis XIV's popularly ascribed dictum *l'etat c'est moi*, FDR clearly was not. By philosophy and practice, FDR preferred to work within accepted constitutional channels. Although he threatened Congress in his inaugural, he indicated that he would rather work with them. As Gunther wrote, "Roosevelt, it might be mentioned parenthetically, always strove to work *with* Congress; this is a point often forgotten these days, but it was vital."[86] Moreover, FDR had a respect for the Constitution and its essential democracy. Although Sherwood granted that "No President since Lincoln tested the elasticity of the Constitution as he [FDR] did," Sherwood also held that FDR did not equal "Lincoln's record in circumventing the Constitution."[87] Manchester opined that "Roosevelt preferred to work within the Constitution."[88] In the final evaluation, then, Freidel was probably correct in his conclusion that FDR did not intend to assume the role of a Hitler because "that was too repugnant to his basic thinking."[89]

CONCLUSION

In his First Inaugural Address, FDR's main concern was Domestic Issues. An investigation of his textual emendations has demonstrated that he selected words to effect certain ends. He used the scapegoat technique to blame the bankers and brokers for the Depression, an efficacious technique because FDR used it to adapt to and to speak for the existing and prevalent attitudes against Wall Street. He marshaled a military metaphor to evoke in the American people a sense of duty and discipline—values salient and needed in a time of national crisis—to persuade the citizens of the nation to support his quasi-military leadership in his war on the Depression. For the members of Congress he used the carrot-and-stick technique to demonstrate to them and the country his desire to act either in tandem with the Congress or alone if it failed him. FDR successfully used these techniques because their potential efficacy was available in attitudes of the immediate inaugural audience, of most of the contemporary news media, and, perhaps most importantly, of the members of Congress and ultimately the American people. Rodgers realized the successful effect that FDR's address had on the American people, that it "first won for him the support of the great masses of people and put behind his efforts the full force of an overwhelming public opinion."[90]

The *zeitgeist* of March 1933 produced Hitler and Roosevelt, who utilized similar rhetorical techniques in reacting to the Depression. Although their rhetorical means were similar, basic dissimilarities in their respective countries, their leadership roles, and their expected tenure of rule accounted for their diametrically opposed ends as national leaders.

Closing remarks are perhaps best left to Roosevelt, himself. His three rhetorical techniques coalesce in his inaugural conclusion: "The people of the United States have not failed. In their need they have registered a mandate that they want direct, vigorous action. They have asked for discipline and direction under leadership. They have made me the present instrument of their wishes. In the spirit of the gift, I take it."[91]

NOTES

[1] David M. Potter, *The Impending Crisis 1848-1861,* ed. Don E. Fehrenbacher (New York: Harper & Row, 1976), p. 145.

[2] *The Public Papers and Addresses of Franklin D. Roosevelt,* ed. Samuel I. Rosenman (1928-1936, 5 vols.; New York: Random House, 1938), II, 16.

[3] Samuel I. Rosenman, *Working with Roosevelt* (New York: Harper, 1952), p. 89.

[4] Harry L. Hopkins, "Foreword" in *Nothing to Fear,* ed. B. D. Zevin (Boston: Houghton Mifflin, 1946), p. viii.

[5] Although the following rhetorical works on FDR are helpful, they do not explicate FDR's first inaugural nor its significance: Earnest Brandenburg, "The Preparation of Franklin D. Roosevelt's Speeches," *Quarterly Journal of Speech,* 35 (1949), 214-21; Earnest Brandenburg and Waldo W. Braden, "Franklin D. Roosevelt's Voice and

Pronunciation," *Quarterly Journal of Speech,* 38 (1952), 23-30; Harold P. Zelko, "Franklin D. Roosevelt's Rhythm in Rhetorical Style," *Quarterly Journal of Speech,* 28 (1942), 138-41; Hermann G. Stelzner, "'War Message,' December 8, 1941: An Approach to Language," *Speech Monographs,* 33 (1966), 419-37; Earnest Brandenburg and Waldo W. Braden, "Franklin Delano Roosevelt," in *A History and Criticism of American Public Address,* ed. Marie Kathryn Hochmuth, III (New York: Longmans, Green, 1955), 458-530.

[6] Inaugural Address, 1933, Master Speech File, Box 0610, Roosevelt Library. The first draft is on legal paper. The second draft was typed on Tuesday, February 28. The third draft was retyped on Wednesday, March 1. The reading copy was typed on March 3 in Washington. Hereafter, references to the Roosevelt Library holdings on the first inaugural will be cited as Master Speech File.

[7] James MacGregor Burns, *Roosevelt: The Lion and the Fox* (New York: Harcourt, Brace, 1956), p. 162; Edgar Eugene Robinson, *The Roosevelt Leadership 1933-1945* (Philadelphia: Lippincott, 1955), p. 104; Rosenman, *Working with Roosevelt,* p. 89; Ernest J. Wrage and Barnet Baskerville, eds., *Contemporary Forum: American Speeches on Twentieth-Century Issues* (New York: Harper, 1962), p. 136.

[8] Raymond Moley, *The First New Deal* (New York: Harcourt, Brace & World, 1966), p. 114. Moley gives a general description of his composition of the address and discusses his and Louis Howe's role in subsequent drafts (pp. 99-115). Moley includes photographs of the handwritten draft, but he does not picture the other three critical drafts. Moley advises that in his earlier book, *After Seven Years* (New York: Harper, 1939), he made only casual reference to the authorship of the first inaugural because his "function as a collaborator was well known" and everyone knew he "would be involved in the preparation of this speech" (p. 116).

[9] Master Speech File, first handwritten draft, pp. 1-10.

[10] Gunther thought the phrase was uniquely FDR's, John Gunther, *Roosevelt in Retrospect* (New York: Harper, 1950), p. 124. Rosenman thought FDR read it in Thoreau: "Nothing is so much to be feared as fear," Rosenman, *Working with Roosevelt,* p. 91; Henry David Thoreau, *The Journal of Henry David Thoreau,* ed. Bradford Torrey and Francis H. Allen (New York: Dover, 1962), 7 Sept. 1851, p. 261. Wecter suggested it might have come from the *Ladies' Home Journal:* "There is nothing to fear—except fear." Dixon Wecter, *The Age of the Great Depression 1929-1941* (New York: Macmillan, 1948), p. 44; "It's Up to the Women," editorial, *Ladies' Home Journal,* Jan. 1932, p. 3.

[11] Moley, *The First New Deal,* p. 115.

[12] Asbell believed that Howe filched the phrase from a newspaper department store advertisement, Bernard Asbell, *The F. D. R. Memoirs* (Garden City: Doubleday,

1973), p. 32; however, Freidel has complained that the piece has eluded later researchers: Frank Freidel, *Franklin D. Roosevelt Launching the New Deal* (Boston: Little, Brown, 1973), p. 203. My search of Howe's papers provided nothing.

[13] Master Speech File, first handwritten draft, p. 1.

[14] Master Speech File, draft number three (typed), pp. 1-4.

[15] *Ibid.,* pp. 10-11.

[16] Master Speech File, reading copy, pp. 1-2. Those sources, including government printings and Rosenman's edition of FDR's personal papers and speeches, which relied on the advanced text are thus in error.

[17] Arthur Larson, *Eisenhower: The President Knowbody Knew* (New York: Scribner's, 1968), p. 150. Although Larson said this of President Eisenhower, the statement probably can be generalized to all presidents, and it is specifically applicable to FDR. See Rosenman, *Working with Roosevelt,* for his analogous role as speech writer for FDR to Larson's for Eisenhower, and Rosenman's analogous conclusion: "the finished product was always the same—it was Roosevelt himself" (p. 12).

[18] Donald L. Wolfarth, "John F. Kennedy in the Tradition of Inaugural Speeches," *Quarterly Journal of Speech,* 47 (1961), 130.

[19] *The Public Papers and Addresses of Franklin D. Roosevelt,* II, 16.

[20] Samuel Eliot Morison, *The Oxford History of the American People* (New York: Oxford Univ. Press, 1965), p. 949.

[21] Rexford G. Tugwell, *Roosevelt's Revolution* (New York: Macmillan, 1977), p. 6.

[22] Finis Farr, *FDR* (New Rochelle: Arlington House, 1972), p. 182.

[23] The scapegoat has its derivation in Jewish antiquity, when the people symbolically placed their sins on a goat's head and then allowed the goat to escape into the wilderness, thus relieving them of their guilt.

[24] Franklin D. Roosevelt, "First Inaugural Address," in *Great American Speeches 1898-1963,* ed. John Graham (New York: Meredith, 1970), pp. 51-52. I utilize this text because it is a verbatim printing from a recording of the inaugural address, Caedmon Record, TC 2033-A. Hereinafter the address is cited as First Inaugural.

[25] William E. Leuchtenburg, *Franklin D. Roosevelt and the New Deal: 1932-1940* (New York: Harper & Row, 1963), p. 41.

[26] First Inaugural, p. 53; Caedmon Record, TC 2033-A.

[27] Morison, p. 954.

[28] *Ibid.*

[29] Caedmon Record, TC 2033-A.

[30] Universal Films, Film MP 77-5, Roosevelt Library; Pathe News, Film 201-29-1, Roosevelt Library. Complete news-film footage of FDR's first inaugural is not extant; there-fore, what the news editors retained in their truncated versions is significant.

[31] Rexford G. Tugwell, *In Search of Roosevelt* (Cambridge: Harvard Univ. Press, 1972), p. 222.

[32] Morison, p. 950.

[33] "The Inaugural Address," *Christian Century,* 15 Mar. 1933, p. 351.

[34] "The Faith of Roosevelt," *The Nation,* 15 Mar. 1933, p. 278.

[35] "Roosevelt Takes Oath in Crisis," *News-Week,* 11 Mar. 1933, p. 9.

[36] "The President's Speech," *The Times* (London), 6 Mar. 1933, p. 13, col. 2.

[37] Conkin has argued that the end of government *laissez-faire* was, in hindsight, actually a boon to busi-ness. Paul K. Conkin, *The New Deal* (New York: Crowell, 1967), p. 34.

[38] Basil Rauch, *The History of the New Deal: 1933-1938* (New York: Creative Age Press, 1944), p. 61.

[39] Approximately 50,000,000 Americans listened to FDR's address on the radio, and the immediate inaugural audi-ence numbered approximately 150,000.

[40] Michael Osborn, "Archetypal Metaphor in Rhetoric: The Light-Dark Family," *Quarterly Journal of Speech,* 53 (1967), 126.

[41] William E. Leuchtenburg, "The New Deal and the Analogue of War," in *Change and Continuity in Twentieth-Century America,* ed. John Braeman, Robert H. Bremner, and Everett Walters (n. p.: Ohio State Univ. Press, 1964), p. 104.

[42] *Ibid.*, p. 105.

[43] First Inaugural, pp. 53-54.

[44] Letter from the Rev. William C. Hicks, St. Andrew's Memorial Church, Yonkers, New York, 24 Feb. 1933, PPF 10, Box 1, Roosevelt Library.

[45] Conkin, p. 30.

[46] Quoted in Cabell Phillips, *From the Crash to the Blitz: 1929-1939* (London: Macmillan, 1969), p. 107.

[47] "Leaders Here Praise Address as 'Strong,'" *New York Times,* 5 Mar. 1933, p. 6, col. 6.

[48] James A. Hagerty, "Roosevelt Address Stirs Great Crowd," *ibid.*, p. 2, col. 2.

[49] "Comment of Press on Roosevelt's Inaugural Address," *ibid.*, p. 6, cols. 4-5.

[50] Quoted in Phillips, p. 107.

[51] "The President's Speech," *The Times* (London), 6 Mar. 1933, p. 13, col. 2.

[52] First Inaugural, p. 54.

[53] Farr, p. 182.

[54] Quoted in *ibid.*, p. 191.

[55] Quoted in William Manchester, *The Glory and the Dream* (Boston: Little, Brown, 1973), p. 77.

[56] Rauch, p. 59.

[57] Alfred B. Rollins, Jr., *Roosevelt and Howe* (New York: Knopf, 1962), p. 367.

[58] Quoted in James T. Patterson, *Congressional Conser-vatism and the New Deal* (Lexington: Univ. of Kentucky Press, 1967), p. 1.

[59] *Ibid.*

[60] *Ibid.*, pp. 1-2.

[61] Manchester, p. 81.

[62] First Inaugural, p. 54.

[63] *Ibid.*

[64] Caedmon Record TC 2033-A; Freidel, p. 205; Pathe News and Universal Films both included this important segment (see n. 30).

[65] Joseph P. Lash, *Eleanor and Franklin* (New York: Norton, 1971), p. 360.

[66] "Comment of Press on Roosevelt's Inaugural Address," *New York Times,* 5 Mar. 1933, p. 6, col. 6.

[67] Quoted in Phillips, p. 107.

[68] Conkin, p. 30.

[69] Patterson, pp. 4-5.

[70] Rollins, p. 366.

[71] Fred L. Casmir, "The Hitler I Heard," *Quarterly Journal of Speech,* 49 (1963), 9-10.

[72] Hubert H. Humphrey, *The Political Philosophy of the New Deal* (Baton Rouge: Louisiana State Univ. Press, 1970), pp. xx-xxi.

[73] John Toland, *Adolph Hitler* (Garden City: Doubleday, 1976), I, 239.

[74] Robert Payne, *The Life and Death of Adolph Hitler* (New York: Praeger, 1973), p. 232.

[75] *Ibid.,* p. 234.

[76] Toland, I, 322.

[77] Quoted in Toland, I, 340-41.

[78] Quoted in Freidel, p. 208.

[79] Quoted in Manchester, p. 80.

[80] Farr, p. 183.

[81] Robinson, p. 107.

[82] Nicholas Halasz, *Roosevelt Through Foreign Eyes* (Princeton: Van Nostrand, 1961), pp. 44-55.

[83] Paul Preston, "The Burning of the Reichstag," in *Sunrise and Storm Clouds,* Vol. X of *Milestones of History,* ed. Roger Morgan (New York: Newsweek Books, 1975), p. 137.

[84] Master Speech File, draft number three (typed), p. 13.

[85] Quoted in Toland, I, 381.

[86] Gunther, p. 278.

[87] Robert E. Sherwood, *Roosevelt and Hopkins: An Intimate History* (New York: Harper, 1948), p. 41.

[88] Manchester, p. 81.

[89] Freidel, p. 205.

[90] Cleveland Rodgers, *The Roosevelt Program* (New York: Putnam, 1933), p. 16.

[91] First Inaugural, p. 54.

Lord George-Brown (essay date 1979)

SOURCE: "Franklin Delano Roosevelt, 1882-1945," in *The Voices of History: Great Speeches of the English Language,* Stein & Day, 1979, pp. 202-08.

[*In the following excerpt, George-Brown introduces selections from Roosevelt's most historically significant speeches.*]

Governor of New York before he became the thirty-second President of the United States in 1932, Roosevelt was a powerful speaker. He won the Presidency in four consecutive elections, and during this long period in office was the first President to broadcast directly to the people.

In 1932, the country was in the thick of unprecedented depression. Roosevelt's first Inaugural Address on 4 March 1933 set out his New Deal programme of reform, and concluded as follows:

If I read the temper of our people correctly, we now realize, as we have never realized before, our interdependence on each other; that we cannot merely take, but we must give as well; that if we are to go forward we must move as a trained and loyal army willing to sacrifice for the good of a common discipline, because, without such discipline, no progress is made, no leadership becomes effective.

We are, I know, ready and willing to submit our lives and property to such discipline because it makes possible a leadership which aims at a larger good.

This I propose to offer, pledging that the larger purposes will bind upon us all as a sacred obligation with a unity of duty hitherto evoked only in time of armed strife.

With this pledge taken, I assume unhesitatingly the leadership of this great army of our people, dedicated to a disciplined attack upon our common problems.

Action in this image and to this end is feasible under the form of government which we have inherited from our ancestors.

Our Constitution is so simple and practical that it is possible always to meet extraordinary needs by changes in emphasis and arrangement without loss of essential form.

That is why our constitutional system has proved itself the most superbly enduring political mechanism the modern world has produced. It has met every stress of vast expansion of territory, of foreign wars, of bitter internal strife, of world relations.

It is to be hoped that the normal balance of executive and legislative authority may be wholly adequate to meet the unprecedented task before us. But it may be that an unprecedented demand and need for undelayed action may call for temporary departure from that normal balance of public procedure.

I am prepared under my constitutional duty to recommend the measures that a stricken nation in the midst of a stricken world may require.

These measures, or such other measures as the Congress may build out of its experience and wisdom, I shall seek, within my constitutional authority, to bring to speedy adoption.

But in the event that the Congress shall fail to take one of these two courses, and in the event that the national emergency is still critical, I shall not evade the clear course of duty that will then confront me.

I shall ask the Congress for the one remaining instrument to meet the crisis—broad executive power to wage a war against the emergency as great as the power that would be given to me if we were in fact invaded by a foreign foe.

For the trust reposed in me I will return the courage and the devotion that befit the time. I can do no less.

We face the arduous days that lie before us in the warm courage of national unity; with the clear consciousness of seeking old and precious moral values; with the clean satisfaction that comes from the stern performance of duty by old and young alike.

We aim at the assurance of a rounded and permanent national life.

We do not distrust the future of essential democracy. The people of the United States have not failed. In their need they have registered a mandate that they want direct, vigorous action.

They have asked for discipline and direction under leadership. They have made me the present instrument of their wishes. In the spirit of the gift I take it.

In this dedication of a nation we humbly ask the blessing of God. May He protect each and every one of us! May He guide me in the days to come!

On 29 December 1940, Roosevelt broadcast an appeal for aid to the Allies fighting Nazi aggression, ending with the words:

But all of our present efforts are not enough. We must have more ships, more guns, more planes— more of everything. And this can be accomplished only if we discard the notion of "business as usual". This job cannot be done merely by super- imposing on the existing productive facilities the added requirements of the nation for defence.

Our defence efforts must not be blocked by those who fear the future consequences of surplus plant capacity. The possible consequences of failure of our defence efforts are now much more to be feared.

And after the present needs of our defence are past, a proper handling of the country's peacetime needs will require all of the new productive capacity, if not still more.

No pessimistic policy about the future of America shall delay the immediate expansion of those industries essential to defence. We need them.

I want to make it clear that it is the purpose of the nation to build now with all possible speed every machine, every arsenal, every factory that we need to manufacture our defence material. We have the men—the skill—the wealth—and above all, the will.

I am confident that if and when production of consumer or luxury goods in certain industries requires the use of machines and raw materials that are essential for defence purposes, then such production must yield, and will gladly yield, to our primary and compelling purpose.

So I appeal to the owners of plants—to the managers—to the workers—to our own Government employees—to put every ounce of effort into producing these munitions swiftly and without stint. With this appeal I give you the pledge that all of us who are officers of your Government will devote ourselves to the same wholehearted extent to the great task that lies ahead.

As planes and ships and guns and shells are produced, your Government, with its defence experts, can then determine how best to use them to defend this hemisphere. The decision as to how much shall be sent abroad and how much shall remain at home must be made on the basis of our over-all military necessities.

We must be the great arsenal of democracy. For us this is an emergency as serious as war itself. We must apply ourselves to our task with the same resolution, the same sense of urgency, the same spirit of patriotism and sacrifice as we would show were we at war.

We have furnished the British great material support and we will furnish far more in the future.

There will be no "bottlenecks" in our determination to aid Great Britain. No dictator, no combination of dictators, will weaken that determination by threats of how they will construe that determination.

The British have received invaluable military support from the heroic Greek Army and from the forces of all the Governments in exile. Their strength is growing. It is the strength of men and women who value their freedom more highly than they value their lives.

I believe that the Axis powers are not going to win this war. I base that belief on the latest and best of information.

We have no excuse for defeatism. We have every good reason for hope—hope for peace, yes, and hope for the defence of our civilization and for the building of a better civilization in the future.

I have the profound conviction that the American people are now determined to put forth a mightier effort than they have ever yet made to increase our production of all the implements of defence, to meet the threat to our democratic faith.

As President of the United States, I call for that national effort. I call for it in the name of this nation which we love and honour and which we are privileged and proud to serve. I call upon our people with absolute confidence that our common cause will greatly succeed.

On 8 December 1941 Roosevelt addressed a joint session of Congress requesting a declaration of the existence of a state of war between Japan and the United States.

Yesterday, December 7th, 1941—a date which will live in infamy—the United States of America was suddenly and deliberately attacked by naval and air forces of the empire of Japan.

The United States was at peace with that nation, and, at the solicitation of Japan, was still in conversation with its Government and its Emperor looking toward the maintenance of peace in the Pacific.

Indeed, one hour after Japanese air squadrons had commenced bombing in the American island of Oahu the Japanese Ambassador to the United States and his colleague delivered to our Secretary of State a formal reply to a recent American message. And, while this reply stated that it seemed useless to continue the existing diplomatic negotiations, it contained no threat or hint of war or of armed attack.

It will be recorded that the distance of Hawaii from Japan makes it obvious that the attack was deliberately planned many days or even weeks ago. During the intervening time the Japanese Government has deliberately sought to deceive the United States by false statements and expressions of hope for continued peace.

The attack yesterday on the Hawaiian Islands has caused severe damage to American naval and military forces. I regret to tell you that very many American lives have been lost. In addition, American ships have been reported torpedoed on the high seas between San Francisco and Honolulu.

Yesterday the Japanese Government also launched an attack against Malaya.

Last night Japanese forces attacked Hong Kong.

Last night Japanese forces attacked Guam.

Last night Japanese forces attacked the Philippine Islands.

Last night the Japanese attacked Wake Island.

And this morning the Japanese attacked Midway Island.

Japan has therefore undertaken a surprise offensive extending throughout the Pacific area. The facts of yesterday and today speak for themselves. The people of the United States have already formed their opinions and well understand the implications to the very life and safety of our nation.

As Commander in Chief of the Army and Navy I have directed that all measures be taken for our defence, that always will our whole nation remember the character of the onslaught against us.

No matter how long it may take us to overcome this premeditated invasion, the American people, in their righteous might, will win through to absolute victory.

I believe that I interpret the will of the Congress and of the people when I assert that we will not only defend ourselves to the uttermost but will make it very certain that this form of treachery shall never again endanger us.

Hostilities exist. There is no blinking at the fact that our people, our territory and our interests are in grave danger.

With confidence in our armed forces, with the unbounding determination of our people, we will gain the inevitable triumph. So help us God.

I ask that the Congress declare that since the unprovoked and dastardly attack by Japan on Sunday, December 7th, 1941, a state of war has existed between the United States and the Japanese Empire.

Isaiah Berlin (essay date 1980)

SOURCE: "President Franklin Delano Roosevelt," in *Personal Impressions*, edited by Henry Hardy, The Hogarth Press, 1980, pp. 23-31.

[*In the following essay, Berlin gives his impressions of Roosevelt and his influence, characterizing him as "the greatest leader of democracy, the greatest champion of social progress in the twentieth century."*]

I never met Roosevelt, and although I spent more than three years in Washington during the war, I never even saw him. I regret this, for it seems to me that to see and, in particular, to hear the voice of someone who has occupied one's imagination for many years, must modify one's impression in some profound way, and make it somehow more concrete and three-dimensional. However, I never did see him, and I heard him only over the wireless. Consequently, I must try to convey my impression without the benefit of personal acquaintance, and without, I ought to add, any expert knowledge of American history or that of international relations. Nor am I competent to speak of Roosevelt's domestic or foreign policies: or the larger political or economic effect. I shall try to give only a personal impression of the general impact of his personality on my generation in Europe.

When I say that some men occupy one's imagination for many years, this is literally true of Roosevelt and the young men of my own generation in England, and probably in many parts of Europe, and indeed the entire world. If one was young in the 30s, and lived in a democracy, then, whatever one's politics, if one had human feelings at all, the faintest spark of social idealism, or any love of life whatever, one must have felt very much as young men in Continental Europe probably felt after the defeat of Napoleon during the years of the Restoration, that all was dark and quiet, a great reaction was abroad: and little stirred, and nothing resisted.

It all began with the great slump of 1931, which undermined the feeling, perhaps quite baseless, of economic security which a good many young people of the middle classes then had. There followed the iron 30s, of which the English poets of the time—Auden, Spender, Day Lewis—left a very vivid testament: the dark and leaden 30s, to which, alone of all periods, no one in Europe wishes to return, unless indeed they lament the passing of Fascism. There came Manchuria, Hitler, the Hunger Marchers, the Abyssinian War, the Peace Ballot, the Left Book Club, Malraux's political novels, even the article by Virginia Woolf in the *Daily Worker,* the Soviet trials and purges, the conversions of idealistic young liberals and radicals to communism, or strong sympathy with it, often for no better reason than that it seemed the only force firm enough and strong enough to resist the Fascist enemy effectively; such conversions were sometimes followed by visits to Moscow or by fighting in Spain, and death on the battlefield, or else bitter and angry disillusionment with communist practice, or some desperate and unconvinced choice between two evils of that which seemed the lesser.

The most insistent propaganda in those days declared that humanitarianism and liberalism and democratic forces were played out, and that the choice now lay between two bleak extremes, communism and Fascism—the red or the black. To those who were not carried away by this patter the only light that was left in the darkness was the administration of Roosevelt and the New Deal in the United States. At a time of weakness and mounting despair in the democratic world Roosevelt radiated confidence and strength. He was the leader of the democratic world, and upon him alone, of all the statesmen of the 30s, no cloud rested—neither on him nor on the New Deal, which to European eyes still looks a bright chapter in the history of mankind. It was true that his great social experiment was conducted with an isolationist disregard of the outside world, but then it was psychologically intelligible that America, which had come into being in the reaction against the follies and evils of a Europe perpetually distraught by religious or national struggles, should try to seek salvation undisturbed by the currents of European life, particularly at a moment when Europe seemed about to collapse into a totalitarian nightmare. Roosevelt was therefore forgiven by those who found the European situation tragic, for pursuing no particular foreign policy, indeed for trying to do, if not without any foreign policy at all, at any rate with a minimum of relationship with the outside world, which was indeed to some degree part of the American political tradition.

His internal policy was plainly animated by a humanitarian purpose. After the unbridled individualism of the 20s,

which had led to economic collapse and widespread misery, he was seeking to establish new rules of social justice. He was trying to do this without forcing his country into some doctrinaire straitjacket, whether of socialism or state capitalism, or the kind of new social organisation which the Fascist regimes flaunted as the New Order. Social discontent was high in the United States, faith in businessmen as saviours of society had evaporated overnight after the famous Wall Street crash, and Roosevelt was providing a vast safety valve for pent-up bitterness and indignation, and trying to prevent revolution and construct a regime which should provide for greater economic equality and social justice—ideals which were the best part of the tradition of American life—without altering the basis of freedom and democracy in his country. This was being done by what to unsympathetic critics seemed a haphazard collection of amateurs, college professors, journalists, personal friends, freelances of one kind or another, intellectuals, ideologists, what are nowadays called eggheads, whose very appearance and methods of conducting business or constructing policies irritated the servants of old-established government institutions in Washington and tidy-minded conservatives of every type. Yet it was clear that the very amateurishness of these men, the fact that they were allowed to talk to their hearts' content, to experiment, to indulge in a vast amount of trial and error, that relations were personal and not institutional, bred its own vitality and enthusiasm. Washington was doubtless full of quarrels, resignations, palace intrigues, perpetual warfare between individuals and groups of individuals, parties, cliques, personal supporters of this or that great captain, which must have maddened sober and responsible officials used to the slower tempo and more normal patterns of administration; as for bankers and businessmen, their feelings were past describing, but at this period they were little regarded, since they were considered to have discredited themselves too deeply, and indeed for ever.

Over this vast, seething chaos presided a handsome, charming, gay, very intelligent, very delightful, very audacious man, Franklin Delano Roosevelt. He was accused of many weaknesses. He had betrayed his class; he was ignorant, unscrupulous, irresponsible. He was ruthless in playing with the lives and careers of individuals. He was surrounded by adventurers, slick opportunists, intriguers. He made conflicting promises, cynically and brazenly, to individuals and groups and representatives of foreign nations. He made up, with his vast and irresistible public charm, and his astonishing high spirits, for lack of other virtues, considered as more important in the leader of the most powerful democracy in the world—the virtues of application, industry, responsibility. All this was said and some of it may indeed have been just. What attracted his followers were countervailing qualities of a rare and inspiring order: he was large-hearted and possessed wide political horizons, imaginative sweep, understanding of the time in which he lived and of the direction of the great new forces at work in the twentieth century—technological, racial, imperialist, anti-imperialist; he was in favour of life and movement, the promotion of the most generous possible fulfilment of the largest possible number of human wishes, and not in favour of caution and retrenchment and sitting still. Above all, he was absolutely fearless.

He was one of the few statesmen in the twentieth or any other century who seemed to have no fear at all of the future. He believed in his own strength and ability to manage, and succeed, whatever happened. He believed in the capacity and loyalty of his lieutenants, so that he looked upon the future with a calm eye, as if to say 'Let it come, whatever it may be, it will all be grist to our great mill. We shall turn it all to benefit.' It was this, perhaps, more than any other quality, which drew men of very different outlooks to him. In a despondent world which appeared divided between wicked and fatally efficient fanatics marching to destroy, and bewildered populations on the run, unenthusiastic martyrs in a cause they could not define, he believed in his own ability, so long as he was at the controls, to stem this terrible tide. He had all the character and energy and skill of the dictators, and he was on our side. He was, in his opinions and public action, every inch a democrat. All the political and personal and public criticism of him might be true; all the personal defects which his enemies and some of his friends attributed to him might be real; yet as a public figure he was unique. As the skies of Europe grew darker, in particular after war broke out, he seemed to the poor and the unhappy in Europe a kind of benevolent demigod, who alone could and would save them in the end. His moral authority—the degree of confidence which he inspired outside his own country—and far more beyond America's frontiers than within them at all times—has no parallel. Perhaps President Wilson, in the early days, after the end of the First World War, when he drove triumphantly through Paris and London, may have inspired some such feeling; but it disappeared quickly and left a terrible feeling of disenchantment behind it. It was plain even to his enemies that President Roosevelt would not be broken as President Wilson was. But to his prestige and to his personality he added a degree of political skill—indeed virtuosity—which no American before him had ever possessed. His chance of realising his wishes was plainly greater; his followers would be less likely to reap bitter disappointment.

Indeed he was very different from Wilson. For they represent two contrasting types of statesmen, in each of which occasionally men of compelling stature appear. The first kind of statesman is essentially a man of single principle and fanatical vision. Possessed by his own bright, coherent dream, he usually understands neither people nor events. He has no doubts or hesitations and by concentration of will-power, directness and strength he is able to ignore a great deal of what goes on outside him. This very blindness and stubborn self-absorption occasionally, in certain situations, enable him to bend events and men to his own fixed pattern. His strength lies in the fact that weak and vacillating human beings, themselves too insecure or incapable of deciding between alternatives, find relief and peace and strength in submitting to the leadership of a single leader of superhuman size, to whom all issues are clear, whose universe consists entirely of primary colours, mostly black and white, and who marches towards his goal looking neither to right nor to left, buoyed up by the violent vision within him. Such men differ widely in moral and intellectual quality, like forces of nature, and do both good and harm in the world. To this type belong Garibaldi, Trotsky, Parnell, de Gaulle, perhaps Lenin too—the distinction I am drawing is not a moral one, not one of value but one of type. There are great benefactors, like Wilson, as well as fearful evildoers, like Hitler, within this category.

The other kind of effective statesman is a naturally political being, as the simple hero is often explicitly anti-political and comes to rescue men, at least ostensibly, from the subtleties and frauds of political life. The second type of politician possesses antennae of the greatest possible delicacy, which convey to him, in ways difficult or impossible to analyse, the perpetually changing contours of events and feelings and human activities round them— they are gifted with a peculiar, political sense fed on a capacity to take in minute impressions, to integrate a vast multitude of small evanescent unseizable detail, such as artists possess in relation to their material. Statesmen of this type know what to do and when to do it, if they are to achieve their ends, which themselves are usually not born within some private world of inner thought, or introverted feeling, but are the crystallisation, the raising to great intensity and clarity, of what a large number of their fellow citizens are thinking and feeling in some dim, inarticulate, but nevertheless persistent fashion. In virtue of this capacity to judge their material, very much as a sculptor knows what can be moulded out of wood and what out of marble, and how and when, they resemble doctors who have a natural gift for curing, which does not directly depend upon that knowledge of scientific anatomy which can only be learned by observation or experiment, or from the experiences of others, though it could not exist without it. This instinctive, or at any rate incommunicable, knowledge of where to look for what one needs, the power of divining where the treasure lies, is something common to many types of genius, to scientists and mathematicians no less than to businessmen and administrators and politicians. Such men, when they are statesmen, are acutely aware of which way the thoughts and feelings of human beings are flowing, and where life presses on them most heavily, and they convey to these human beings a sense of understanding their inner needs, of responding to their own deepest impulses, above all of being alone capable of organising the world along lines which the masses are instinctively groping for. To this type of statesman belonged Bismarck and Abraham Lincoln, Lloyd George and Thomas Masaryk, perhaps to some extent Gladstone, and to a minor degree Walpole. Roosevelt was a magnificent virtuoso of this type, and he was the most benevolent as well as the greatest master of his craft in modern times. He really did desire a better life for mankind. The great majorities which he obtained in the elections in the United States during his four terms of office, despite mounting hostility by the press, and perpetual prophecies on their part that he had gone too far, and would fail to be re-elected, were ultimately due to an obscure feeling on the part of the majority of the citizens of the United States that he was on their side, that he wished them well, and that he would do something for them. And this feeling gradually spread over the entire civilised world. He became a legendary hero—they themselves did not know quite why—to the indigent and the oppressed, far beyond the confines of the English-speaking world.

As I said before, he was, by some of his opponents, accused of betraying his class, and so he had. When a man who retains the manners, style of life, the emotional texture and the charm of the old order of some free aristocratic upbringing revolts against his milieu and adopts the ideas and aspirations of the new, socially revolted class, and adopts them not out of expediency but out of genuine moral conviction, or from love of life, inability to remain on the side of what seems to him narrow, mean, restrictive—the result is fascinating and attractive. This is what makes the figures of such men as Condorcet or Charles James Fox, or some of the Russian, Italian and Polish revolutionaries in the nineteenth century so attractive; for all we know this may have been the secret also of Moses or Pericles or Julius Caesar. It was this gentlemanly quality together with the fact that they felt him to be deeply committed to their side in the struggle and in favour of their way of life, as well as his open and fearless lack of neutrality in the war against the Nazis and the Fascists, that endeared him so deeply to the British people during the war years. I remember well, in London, in November 1940, how excited most people were about the result of the Presidential election in the United States. In theory they should not have worried. Willkie, the Republican candidate, had expressed himself forcibly and sincerely as a supporter of the democracies. Yet it was absurd to say that the people of Britain were neutral in their feelings *vis-à-vis* the two candidates. They felt in their bones that Roosevelt was their lifelong friend, that he hated the Nazis as deeply as they did, that he wanted democracy and civilisation, in the sense in which they believed in it, to prevail, and that he knew what he wanted, and that his goal resembled their own ideals more than it did those of all his opponents. They felt that his heart was in the right place, and they did not, therefore, if they gave it a thought, care whether his political appointments were made under the influence of bosses or for personal reasons, or thoughtlessly; or whether his economic doctrines were heretical or whether he had a sufficiently scrupulous regard for the opinion of the Senate or the House of Representatives, or the prescriptions of the United States' constitution, or for the opinions of the Supreme Court. These matters were very remote from them. They knew that he would, to the extent of his enormous energy and ability, see them through. There is no such thing as long-lived mass hypnotism; the masses know what it is that they like, what genuinely appeals to them. What the Germans thought Hitler to be, Hitler, in fact, largely was, and what free men in Europe and in America and in Asia and in Africa and in Australia, and wherever else the rudiments of political thought stirred at

all, what all these felt Roosevelt to be, he in fact was. He was the greatest leader of democracy, the greatest champion of social progress in the twentieth century.

His enemies accused him of plotting to get America into the war. I do not wish to discuss this controversial issue, but it seems to me that the evidence for it is lacking. I think that when he promised to keep America at peace he meant to try as hard as he could to do so, compatibly with helping to promote the victory of the democracies. He must at one period have thought that he could win the war without entering it, and so, at the end of it, be in the unique position, hitherto achieved by no one, of being the arbiter of the world's fate, without needing to placate those bitter forces which involvement in a war inevitably brings about, and which are an obstacle to reason and humanity in the making of the peace. He, no doubt, too often trusted in his own magical power of improvisation. Doubtless he made many political mistakes, some of them difficult to remedy: some would say about Stalin and his intentions, and the nature of the Soviet state; others might justly point to his coolness to the Free French movement, his cavalier intentions with regard to the Supreme Court of Justice in the United States, his errors about a good many other issues. He irritated his staunchest supporters and faithful servants because he did not tell them what he was doing; his government was highly personal and it maddened tidy-minded officials and humiliated those who thought the policy should be conducted in consultation with and through them. He sometimes exasperated his allies, but when these last bethought them of who his ill-wishers were in the U.S.A. and in the world outside, and what *their* motives were, their respect, affection and loyalty tended to return. No man made more public enemies, yet no man had a right to take greater pride in the quality and the motives of some of those enemies. He could justly call himself the friend of the people, and although his opponents accused him of being a demagogue, this charge seems to me unjust. He did not sacrifice fundamental political principles to a desire to retain power; he did not whip up evil passions merely in order to avenge himself upon those whom he disliked or wished to crush, or because it was an atmosphere in which he found it convenient to operate; he saw to it that his administration was in the van of public opinion and drew it on instead of being dragged by it; he made the majority of his fellow citizens prouder to be Americans than they had been before. He raised their status in their own eyes—immensely in those of the rest of the world.

It was an extraordinary transformation of an individual. Perhaps it was largely brought about by the collapse of his health in the early 20s and his marvellous triumph over his disabilities. For he began life as a well-born, polite, not particularly gifted young man, something of a prig, liked but not greatly admired by his contemporaries at Groton and at Harvard, a competent Assistant Secretary of the Navy in the First World War; in short, he seemed embarked on the routine career of an American patrician with moderate political ambitions. His illness and the support and encouragement and political qualities of his wife—whose greatness of character and goodness of heart history will duly record—seemed to transform his public personality into that strong and beneficent champion who became the father of his people, in an altogether unique fashion. He did more than this: it is not too much to say that he altered the fundamental concept of government and its obligations to the governed. The welfare state, so much denounced, has obviously come to stay: the direct moral responsibility for minimum standards of living and social services, which it took for granted, are today accepted almost without a murmur by the most conservative politicians in the western democracies; the Republican Party victorious in 1952 made no effort to upset the basic principles—which seemed Utopian in the 20s—of Roosevelt's social legislation.

But Roosevelt's greatest service to mankind (after ensuring the victory against the enemies of freedom) consists in the fact that he showed that it is possible to be politically effective and yet benevolent and human: that the fierce left- and right-wing propaganda of the 30s, according to which the conquest and retention of political power is not compatible with human qualities, but necessarily demands from those who pursue it seriously the sacrifice of their lives upon the altar of some ruthless ideology, or the practice of despotism—this propaganda, which filled the art and talk of the day, was simply untrue. Roosevelt's example strengthened democracy everywhere, that is to say the view that the promotion of social justice and individual liberty does not necessarily mean the end of all efficient government; that power and order are not identical with a straitjacket of doctrine, whether economic or political; that it is possible to reconcile individual liberty—a loose texture of society—with the indispensable minimum of organising and authority; and in this belief lies what Roosevelt's greatest predecessor once described as 'the last, best hope of earth.'

Kenneth S. Davis (essay date 1984)

SOURCE: "FDR as a Biographer's Problem," in *The American Scholar,* Vol. 52, Winter, 1983/84, pp. 100-08.

[*In the following essay, Davis presents a profile of Roosevelt's character.*]

When, more years ago than I like to count, a publisher approached me with the proposal that I do a book about Franklin Delano Roosevelt, only the accompanying offer of what was for those days a quite large advance against royalties was tempting to me. It was a temptation I resisted. The flood of Rooseveltiana already in print, including several established classics, was overwhelming; I saw no need to add to it. The risks and difficulties of the proposed project were formidable. There was the danger, for instance, of becoming bogged down in interminable research (it crushed my spirit to learn that there were forty-five tons of documents in the Roosevelt Library at Hyde Park). Finally, conclusively, as I thought at the time, FDR, though I'd read with much interest a great many books about him and his administration, was devoid of interest to me as a writing subject of my own.

Earlier I had dealt with three very different biographical subjects. With each of these I had felt a considerable measure of personal rapport.

Long ago I did a biography of Dwight Eisenhower. I liked him personally when I was in contact with him in England and France. I understood his background, for I was a friend and colleague of his brother Milton, who was then president of Kansas State University, and I had been born and raised just forty miles or so from Ike's hometown of Abilene. It was only after he became president that I found it possible to dislike Ike—and my book about him was completed some years before he (mistakenly, I think) entered politics.

Adlai Stevenson, with whom I also had personal contact and of whom I wrote my second biography, I actually loved as a human being. He had great sweetness and warmth and wit, and it seemed to me we had many of the same priorities, the same basic values, the same unfashionable view of history as essentially a moral drama. I often felt, when I was writing about him, that I understood Stevenson from the inside out, better than most who were much more intimately associated with him; and though he'd not be likely to say so to anyone else (with the possible exception of his sister Buffie), he gave me oral and documentary reason to believe *he* thought I understood him too.

I never met Charles Lindbergh. It wasn't necessary for the kind of book I wrote about him, whose essential subject was heroism and hero worship in twentieth century America. But with Lindbergh, too, I had a certain empathy. His small-town midwestern background had similarities to my own; he was half-Swedish, as I am; I share some of the "gloomy Swede" withdrawal tendencies that were his and his father's; I could understand his kind of courage, a precisely calculated risk taking, a cold-nerved willingness to bet one's life on an estimate of odds; and I could certainly empathize with his profound aversion to the incredible mass adulation of which he became the victim.

Toward Franklin Roosevelt, however, I had initially no personal sympathetic attraction: indeed, as a biographical subject, and quite apart from the bristling difficulties he presented in that aspect, he repelled me.

How and why was this so?

For one thing—despite all I'd read of his warm heart and concern for the welfare of common folk, and despite the impression he conveyed of these things when he talked on the radio or appeared in newsreels—I could never quite have for him a genuinely *human* feeling. He was to me more a symbolic movement than a person, and a movement about whose meaning and direction I had frequent grave doubts. I cast my first presidential ballot for him. My first professional employment was a lowly post in a New Deal agency, from which vantage point he often appeared a radiant godlike figure who was not only America's saviour from the glooms and despairs of the Great Depression but my own personal saviour as well. On many an occasion he also appeared the one indispensable barrier to a flood of reaction into some form of American fascism, and for that reason I was forever defending him in argument, always vehement and often acrimonious, with my otherwise beloved father and with other Roosevelt-hating Republicans. Awesome was his manifest genius (evidently a unique blend of intuition, calculation, confidence, charm, and personal force) for locating, seizing, then actively holding the focal points of countervailing political power, a genius whereby he achieved and maintained through a dozen years of crisis a decisive centrality in the historical process of America, of the world as a whole. He was central to everything! Wherever he was seemed the capital of the universe simply because he was there! But by all this I was not encouraged to believe I had any understanding of, or could ever empathetically understand, Franklin Roosevelt as a living, breathing, feeling, thinking man. He was in all respects remote. His background as a member of the Hudson River aristocracy, his Groton-Harvard schooling, his polio crippling, his subsequent and consequent environmental experience, these were all so alien to anything I myself had experienced that I might never be able to depict them accurately, however hard I tried, much less comprehend and accurately describe their shaping influence on him. As for his basic motives, his ultimate aims, his actual feeling about himself and the world, his sense of reality—these things, I was sure, lay forever beyond my ken.

Nor were these the sum—they were not even the most important—of my initial objections to the publisher's proposal.

Just suppose I was mistaken about the impossibility of my ever finding and depicting the *real* Roosevelt. Suppose, after the arduous search that would evidently be required, I did find him. Would he prove to be a man in whose company I could live comfortably through the years required for a serious biography of him? I doubted it. About the FDR whom I observed across a vast social distance, but with a close attention, all through the years of my young manhood—about the FDR who later emerged for me out of the published works of people who had had contact with him—there was a great deal that was to me personally antipathetic. I happen to be an idealist in philosophy (my great teacher was Alexander Meiklejohn): I'm convinced that ideas are determinants of history and that long-term consistency, not immediate practical efficacy, is the test of the truth of ideas. With pragmatism and pragmatists, therefore, I have little imaginative sympathy—and FDR in action seemed almost wholly, purely pragmatic. He who was only too aware of the separateness of things had apparently little or no awareness of the connections and connectedness whereby organization (organismic wholeness) is created. His concern for consistency, if any, appeared minimal, which meant from my point of view that his concern for truth, for truthfulness, must also be nonexistent or minimal. And such a conclusion seemed justified by a good deal of evidence. Out of what I observed and read about him there emanated, along with a wonderfully animating life-affirming radiance, a faint (sometimes not so faint) odor of the sly, the slippery, the excessively clever.

Consider the published testimony: "Franklin Roosevelt was not a simple man," writes Frances Perkins. "That quality of simplicity which we delight to think [which I myself *do* think] marks the great and noble was not his. He was the most complicated human being I ever knew." Walter Lippmann, disgusted by the "intricate game" that FDR as New York governor and presidential candidate "elected . . . to play . . . with Tammany," suggested on several occasions that the "complicatedness" descried by Perkins was not unrelated to the arts and morality of an opportunistic confidence man. "The trouble with Franklin D. Roosevelt is that his mind is not very clear, his purposes are not simple, and his methods are not direct," concluded a famous Lippmann column. "A clear-headed, simple and direct man would not have landed himself in the confusion [Lippmann elsewhere calls it a "squalid mess"] which now prevails between Albany and City Hall." Much of the poignancy of Eleanor Roosevelt's memoirs derives from her expressed yearning to reach out and touch the essential self of the man she had married; her second volume aches with the frustration of her effort to reach him—a frustration leading to the bleak conclusion, after he had died, that she had been merely one of those whom he found "useful." Roosevelt "loved secrecy," writes Sam Rosenman, yet he "was often the one guilty of letting facts get out about which he had sworn others to secrecy." And both Rosenman and Ray Moley, also Rex Tugwell and Jim Farley, record instances of Rooseveltian mendacity, often employed merely to embellish a good story but sometimes with regard to major issues, and of his preference for the devious over the frankly straightforward, even on occasions (notably at the outset of his 1937 Supreme Court battle) when plain speaking and dealing would have far better served his ends.

At the very time I was considering the publisher's offer, Rosenman and James MacGregor Burns suffered acute public embarrassment for having accepted at face value FDR's claim (found in a memorandum in the Roosevelt Library) to have composed the first draft of his first inaugural address between the hours of 9:00 P.M. and 1:30 A.M., at Hyde Park, on the night of February 27, 1933. Moley's just-published *First New Deal* made scornful comment upon Rosenman's failure to check with him the account, in Rosenman's *Working with Roosevelt*, of the inaugural's making, since Rosenman well knew that Moley was at that time involved in the preparation of every Roosevelt speech. And Moley proved up to the hilt, with incontrovertible documentary evidence, that he himself wrote the first draft, which meant that not a word was true of Burns's vividly circumstantial story of this drafting, in *Roosevelt: The Lion and the Fox*—a book I continue greatly to admire. Moreover, reading *The First New Deal,* I could not but conclude that FDR's copying in his own hand of Moley's typed draft, in Moley's presence, on the night of February 27, was probably done with deliberate *intent* to deceive posterity. Obviously any historian ran grave risks who accepted as literally true, without further checking, anything FDR said about his own experience. The most primary source of information, in the case of FDR, was by that very token the most suspect.

Consistent with this was the fact that it was FDR who introduced the Big Smile to presidential politics, where it has since stuck (note the difference of standard facial expressions of photographed presidential politicians before and after 1932) and who institutionalized ghost-writing in presidential politics (Hoover, Coolidge, Harding, Wilson, and the presidents before them wrote most or all of their own speeches), thereby increasing the difficulty of knowing for whom or what one is voting in the polling booth.

In the face of all this, I'm reasonably sure I would never have signed that publishing contract had the idea not occurred to me, one day, of giving the proposed project a working title of "Franklin D. Roosevelt: A History" rather than "Franklin D. Roosevelt: A Biography" and then assigning to "history" the same weight I gave "Roosevelt" in my overall conception.

Every biographical work is of necessity, to greater or less degree, a "life-and-times." In most biographies, however, even those written about major political figures whose lives are absorbed in public affairs, the "times" are presented as a background or temporal setting for the "life." Insofar as history moves through such books, it is only as changing circumstance, which is to say that it remains essentially passive and static, environmental, scenic in the stage-metaphorical sense. But must the proposed work, if I agreed to do it, be done in this usual way? I saw no iron necessity. Instead of dealing with history as mere occasion or necessary condition for a story of Roosevelt's life, why not make it the very substance of the book—make *it* the story, having FDR as the central character or hero? This opened exciting possibilities. I might be enabled, if I chose, to shape a kind of "nonfiction novel" (Capote's phrase was not then overused), which, though scrupulously accurate in every biographical-historical detail, made use of a novelist's sense of drama, a novelist's feeling for character and place, a novelist's narrative and descriptive techniques. My aim and attempt could be to achieve an actual fusion of history and person in a single flowing process—a process, moreover, having a clear central theme, so that it became the development of a basic pattern of significance, or the working out of a definite program of meaning. Just possibly (against painful hazard one drugs oneself with impossible dreams) a work of art might be created having a Tolstoyan sweep and force—a work of necessarily vast scope, with great crowds of people and events, yet with the tightness, the essential unity of a short story.

And what would be the unifying theme? It must of course be no grand a priori concept arbitrarily imposed upon objectively existent data; it must instead logically derive from these data. But in point of fact I found it already derived in my mind as part and parcel of a long-perceived central theme of Western history—found it there as a general thematic conclusion that must be (has been) reached, I suppose, by every mind that has tried seriously to understand what has been *basically* happening in Western civilization since the Renaissance.

For obviously the most basic causal force operating in Western, and thence world, history, from the early seventeenth century till today, has been the accelerating advance of science and technology and its increasingly strong impact on social, cultural, economic, and political institutions and on the lives of individual men and women. Every major decisive historical event of the last two centuries has had at its heart the dynamic relationship (that of challenge and response) between man's personal and institutional life on the one hand and the growing power of his technology on the other. But since the latter has increasingly become the prime mover of the whole process, the question arises as to whether man's technology is truly his in the sense of ownership and control. Does he possess it, control it—or does it possess and control him? The question was no by means wholly fanciful when Mary Shelley published her *Frankenstein.* It had become wholly realistic by the time Henry Adams published his *Education.* And it was one of Adams's striking metaphors that set me thinking about all this, that day, in terms of FDR. Adams tells how, in November 1904, sailing up New York harbor at the end of a crossing from Cherbourg, he saw the "outline of the city" as "frantic." It was as if "power . . . [had] outgrown its servitude" and "asserted its freedom." It was as if "the cylinder had exploded, and thrown great masses of stone and steam against the sky." And when Adams had debarked and was again upon the streets of New York, the city seemed to him to have "the air and movement of hysteria"; its citizens "were crying, with every accent of anger and alarm, that the new forces must at any cost be brought under control."

But they were not brought under control. Instead, they continued to grow out of control, distorted into monstrous shapes by the political and economic arrangements of a preindustrial age. They imposed intolerable strains on social walls and vastly overflowed economic channels that had never been designed to contain them. They created global interdependencies that were increasingly frustrated by the prevailing system (or anarchy) of national sovereignties. Blind responses to them increasingly submerged individual lives and liberties in vast collectives, essentially mindless in their direction—giant organizations of which the nominal administrator was more puppet than master and in which human lives and purposes were more and more subordinate to the machine's laws of operation, the machine's convenience. In sum, a gap was opened and widened between power and intelligence (out of it came World War I, the Great Depression, World War II, the atom bomb) as the former advanced by leaps and bounds while the latter, whose firm grasp alone could make technology the servant of humane ends, limped farther and farther behind.

Here, then, was my central unifying theme. The struggle to close the power-intelligence gap, which was a struggle for emergence of a new kind of American community out of individualistic chaos and of at least minimal world government out of international anarchy, was for me the essential dramatic conflict, the plot, of the story having FDR as central character. By this perceived story line I would be provided with a selective principle (one was absolutely necessary) for choice and emphasis among the myriad items and possibilities anyone must consider who writes of Roosevelt and his years.

There remained the problem of FDR himself—that multifaceted, mercurial, enigmatic man. How was I ever to penetrate his thick and evidently swiftly changing disguises to reach any understanding of his essential being—of his basic attitudes and motives? I'd have to do that if I were to present him as other than a symbolic person or cardboard figure, all brilliant smiling surface. And I remember that, on the day of my final decision to sign the publishing contract, I made a list of published facts and surmises about him out of which I might possibly draw clues to a solution of this problem, clues possibly pointing the way toward a valid theory of personality.

Thus:

FDR was the only child of highly privileged parents, and his formidable mother, in a strange little book entitled *My Boy Franklin,* reports that he as a child, playing with other children, was always the one who gave orders. When she remonstrated with him one day, saying he should let others run things sometimes, he replied, "Mummie, if I didn't give the orders, nothing would happen!" And, surprisingly, significantly, his playmates seemed not often to resent his bossiness; they generally obeyed with willing alacrity. His mother also tells of the day when he came up to the Hyde Park house from woods along the river, which is quite a long walk uphill, to get his collector's gun. He'd seen a winter wren in "one of the big trees down there" and wanted it for his bird collection. She laughed at him. Surely he didn't expect that wren to sit there waiting for his return! "Oh, yes," he replied confidently, "he'll wait." The dead bird was in his hand when he came back to the house sometime later.

He was from early boyhood an inveterate collector, not just of birds but of stamps (this became his major lifelong hobby), naval prints, historical documents, and rare books (he specialized in Americana). He lived amid a clutter of ship models, figurines, and mementos of all kinds.

He was mildly but genuinely superstitious. He was superstitious about the number thirteen and would go to considerable trouble to avoid eating at a table of thirteen or beginning a journey on the thirteenth day of a month. "Occasionally this meant pulling a train out at 11:50 P.M. on the twelfth or 12:10 A.M. on the fourteenth," writes Grace Tully, who also reports that "one of the few occasions I know of when the President actually reprimanded someone brusquely in public involved the superstition of lighting three cigarettes on a match." On the evening when he waited at Hyde Park for a phone call from Chicago that would tell him whether or not he would win presidential nomination on the fourth ballot of the 1932 Democratic convention, he had the dining table moved so that the telephone cord would reach him at his accustomed place at the table's head, though it would have been less trouble for him to move to a side of the table that the cord would easily reach: to change chairs at table would be bad luck. He became addicted to certain articles of clothing as lucky—an old felt hat, an old sweater—and averse to others as unlucky.

He was notably ear-minded rather than eye-minded; he learned by listening, not by reading. Ed Flynn, who was as intimate an associate of his between 1928 and 1945 as any man, with the exception of Louis Howe and Harry Hopkins, writes that he "never saw him read a book" or even "read a magazine unless a particular portion was called to his attention." Moley, Tugwell, and many others who were for periods close to him testify that he seldom, if ever, read a serious book all the way through during the time they were associated with him. At Harvard, where his academic record was undistinguished, all his classes were in history, political science (only thoroughly orthodox economic theory was taught to him), and English, save for single courses in geology, general paleontology, Latin literature, and French literature. He had no exposure to mathematics, physics, chemistry, or philosophy (the philosophy faculty at Harvard, with James and Santayana as members, was exceptionally brilliant during his undergraduate years). He did enroll in a general introduction to philosophy, taught by Josiah Royce, but dropped it after three weeks. At the close of his last college year he complained to his roommate that his Harvard studies had been "like an electric light that hasn't any wire. You need the lamp for light but it's useless if you can't switch it on."

He was fond of gambling, but for small stakes. He played poker with more enthusiasm than skill, losing more than he won. He bet impulsively, was overinclined to bluff and, when dealer, was likely to raise howls of protest around the table by calling a game in which so many cards were wild that no one could estimate the odds. His business speculations during the 1920s were of the same "wild card" variety. He was attracted to the novel, the daring, and though he seldom invested much in any one such venture, he lost most or all of what he did put in when, as almost always happened, the venture quickly failed. Yet in elective politics, though he often seemed daring to the point of recklessness, he was, in reality and in general, shrewd and cautious. It is true that his very first campaign (for the New York legislature in 1910), his immediately following legislative battle over "Blue-eyed Billy" Sheehan, and his 1914 primary bid for the United States Senate were all extremely hazardous ventures. The latter was actually foolish: he suffered a predictable defeat of humiliating proportions. But thereafter he planned his political moves with care (and with Louis Howe), estimated the risks as precisely as possible, did what he could to minimize them, and paid close attention to relations between his immediate tactical objectives and his long-term strategic goal. Sometimes he miscalculated badly—he did so repeatedly in 1937, a year of disaster for him and the New Deal—but almost never did he proceed with no calculation at all.

He was constantly described, in public prints, as a "consummate actor"—and the published letters of his boyhood and youth do reveal a strong element of the histrionic in him. (This is often characteristic of unusually shy, sensitive people who learn to hide or overcome their insecurities through role playing; and his mother insists, as photographs of him suggest, that he was as a young boy very shy.) No letters he wrote home from Groton were more heavily underlined, more studded with exclamation points, than those he wrote in the spring of his VI Form year (he was then eighteen) about the part assigned him in W. S. Gilbert's *The Wedding March,* which was that year's school play; and from all accounts he was a hit in the part. A shared love for things theatrical was one of the bonds between him and Howe. He loved to mimic (he could take off Cal Coolidge hilariously), loved to act parts (*presiding* parts) in the costume skits that Howe composed for the Cuff-links Club dinners held annually on FDR's birthday. The histrionic in him greatly aided his delivery of speeches, which he made with maximum effectiveness. His physical presence at the lectern—leonine head tossed back or from side to side, strong jaw outthrust, an extraordinarily mobile countenance registering a great range and subtlety of emotion—was of itself alone powerfully communicative to his immediate audience; and he had a superb speaking voice, a vibrant tenor that could at his will become hard or soft in tone, cold or warm, harsh with scornful anger or gentle with affectionate intimacy. Often he rendered eloquent to the radio-listening ear, and sometimes soaringly so, lines that to the normal reading eye lay flat and dull upon the page.

He proclaimed himself a "snap-judgment man." Interviewed by Marquis Childs in early April 1944, he asserted that the "burden of responsibility" about which Childs questioned him was not really a burden for him because he made decisions so easily. ("You mean, sir, it is . . . not ever difficult?" asked a somewhat incredulous Childs. Replied FDR, "No, I should say, no.") Yet the evidence is abundant that he had a profound aversion to clear-cut irrevocable decisions and went to great lengths to avoid them, in his private as in his public life.

His wife and his mother were essentially antipathetic personalities. Eleanor was primarily animated by generous instincts, Sara by selfish ones, and between the two was a constant tension that broke, now and then, into open quarrel. When this happened, FDR seems seldom if ever to have taken sides. Generally he pretended unawareness that anything had gone wrong. And certainly he never made any sharp distinction between the loyalties he owed his mother and those he owed his wife, much less any clear-cut decision as to which set of loyalties had priority. In the case of his love affair with Lucy Mercer, about which I had been told one evening in Raleigh by Jonathan and Mrs. Daniels (the story was not yet generally known), he was forced by Eleanor to make a flat choice between divorce and a total renunciation of Lucy. He chose the latter (a divorce would end his political career; his outraged mother threatened to disown him), but he evidently did so with secret reservations, for he kept close track of her, may even have been in touch with her through the following years, and certainly renewed relations with her in the closing years of his life. When the issue facing him was whether or not to fire an unfit subordinate, he almost always postponed the decision unconscionably or avoided it altogether through false-compromise arrangements—a procedure doubtless dictated by his wish to avoid giving pain but which had the frequent effect of prolonging and increasing it. When the issue was between antagonistic public policy proposals, his initial effort was generally to try to weave them together, as in the famous case of the two tariff-policy speech drafts during the 1932 campaign. He was a Whitmanesque yea-sayer who could speak a firm no with only the greatest difficulty. Hence his natural tendency toward omnibus statutes and administrative agencies wherein sharp differences between ideas and men would (he hoped) be dissolved by a common bureaucratic label and goal statement, the latter so broad as to be practically meaningless.

One would expect such avoidance of sharp definition, such preference of "both/and" over "either/or" (as Kierkegaard put it), to be a manifestation of cowardice—and indeed the accusation of moral cowardice, of mental timidity, was leveled against him on occasion. But consider the indisputable evidence, the numerous crucial instances, of this man's magnificent courage!

His capacity to bear physical pain, hiding it from others behind a calm, cheerful demeanor, was almost incredible. He did so as a boy when an accident broke off one of his teeth, leaving the nerve nakedly exposed: only the sight of his pale drawn face, joined with his inability to speak in other than monosyllables, revealed to his mother that an accident had occurred and he was in agony. He did so as a man, over and over again, during his polio ordeal and the subsequent long, arduous struggle to walk again. Rare is the man who demonstrates such fortitude, such tenacious hold on long-term purpose through thick and thin, as he did during the 1920s. Even more rare is the crippled man who in his dealings with the world manages, as he did, to give no impression of lameness, physical or psychological, but radiates instead the zestful good cheer of a supremely healthy man. Nor was stoic courage the only kind he possessed. He was utterly fearless in the face of sudden, unexpected mortal danger. When a madman fired five revolver shots at him from barely twenty feet away, in Miami on the night of February 15, 1933, he, who perfectly realized that his enforced physical immobility made him an unusually easy target, seemed scarcely to have flinched. Certainly he remained calmly, precisely observant, almost as if the whole episode were witnessed by him from a safe distance—an episode he found intensely interesting but from which he was personally detached—as the remarkably clear, detailed, chronological account he gave newsmen a few hours later reveals. He gave no sign of letdown after the immediate excitement had passed either. Writes Moley: "I never in my life saw anything more magnificent."

In his talk about crises and their resolutions, he almost always referred to God, or God's beneficence. In his account to newsmen of the shooting, he said it was "providential" that the car in which he was riding had moved immediately after the shooting, since it would otherwise have been hemmed in by the excited crowd. When he later sent a telegram of thanks to the woman who had saved his life by grabbing the gunman's shooting arm, he spoke of the "Divine Providence" whereby (as it then appeared) "the lives of all the victims . . . will be spared." To Frances Perkins he once said that, in the ultimate crisis-hours of his polio attack, he felt that God had abandoned him—which suggests that, when he recovered, he felt that God had spared him after testing him for some divine purpose. On the night of March 2, 1933, when he rode a B&O train down from New York to Washington for his first inaugural, he summoned Jim Farley to his stateroom and there talked to him, a devout Catholic, not of the multitudinous problems whose solutions would be his responsibility in two days' time, but of faith in God. More important than any planned operation for the solution of the present crisis was a great people's religious faith, he said; ultimately the salvation of America depended upon the American people's active belief in divine providence, their seeking and acceptance of divine guidance. He himself proposed, had made the arrangements, to launch the New Deal with a prayer: his first public act on inauguration day would be his attendance at a worship service conducted at Saint John's Episcopal Church by the Reverend Endicott Peabody, rector of Groton, headmaster of Groton School.

It was this last of my listed items—the fact that Franklin Roosevelt was a man of great and evidently remarkably simple religious faith—that seemed and still seems to me the most potent of clues to the innermost workings of his psyche. His kind of superstitiousness, his kind of decision making (a feel for the relative weights of opposing external pressures), his kind of gambling—his opportunism, his optimistic courage under extreme pressures, his otherwise incredible manifestations on crucial occasions of a personal irresponsibility—all these were explicable in terms of what appeared to be his kind of plain, simple, matter-of-fact Christianity. "He felt that human beings were given tasks to perform and with these tasks the

ability and strength to put them through," Eleanor Roosevelt has written. "He could pray for help and guidance and have faith in his own judgment [thereby informed by divine will] as a result."

My own summation, on that day of my own decision making, was somewhat as follows: Born an only child into a highly privileged position, bearer of a name made immensely famous by a distant relative, Franklin Roosevelt had early inculcated within himself a sense of his own importance in the total scheme of things. Innately abnormally sensitive to other people (therefore originally shy of strangers), eager to please, anxious to serve, yet with an innate instinct for power, he was early encouraged into role playing, for which he had a natural talent, by his need for defense against the demands of a strong-willed, thoroughly selfish, domineering mother whom he loved. Possessed of an intellect that was broad but shallow, he collected facts and ideas as he did stamps and naval prints, letting them lie flat, distinct, separate in his mind, never attempting to combine them into any holistic truth. Indeed, he shied away from generalized thinking and abstract ideas. If never openly contemptuous of pure thought (certainly he was never assertively so), he had nothing to do with it personally, feeling it to be not merely irrelevant to his vital concerns but even hazardous to them insofar as it might distract his attention from small but important signs or cues presented him by and through his immediate environmental situation. For at the root and core of his conception of self and world was the inward certainty that he was a chosen one of the Almighty, his career a role assigned him by the Author of the Universe, and that the part he must act or play to the best of his ability, feeling himself into it, even identifying with it (up to a point), was a very great one.

Believing absolutely in God the Father and Jesus Christ as the Son of God; believing that God, caring for each individual human being, was infinitely kind and good as well as all-wise and all-powerful; believing or feeling that history was a working out of divine purpose, that every truly fundamental historical force was a manifestation of divine will—believing all this, he must and did believe that history, though it had at any given extended period of time a tidal ebb and flow, had, in the long run, a surging flow in one direction. It was away from polar evil toward polar good. This was the essential progress, from worse to better, a progress that was inevitable because it was God's will. As a chosen one, he himself was an instrument of progress, a special agent on earth of divine beneficence. But *only* an instrument. *Only* an agent. The notion of attempting a mystical union with God, becoming one with him, had it ever occurred to FDR, would have been rejected as an absurd, outrageous presumption—and similarly with regard to efforts to understand God in any deep metaphysical sense. What his heart accepted should not be questioned or even examined by his mind. "I never really thought much about it," he said to his wife when she pressed him (too hard) to say whether or not he was really convinced, intellectually convinced, that

Christian doctrine was true. "I think it is just as well not to think about things like that too much."

Thus, Roosevelt's attitude toward power, his attraction to it and exercise of it, was characterized by a humility, a selflessness wholly foreign to a Napoleon, a Mussolini, a Hitler, or a Stalin. By his religious faith and his self-conception in terms of it (his sense of his role in history), he was required actively to seek great power—the greatest earthly power. But he never did so with the feeling that he himself would *become* the power he exercised, or even that it would become his personal property, to be used in service of his purely personal will. It was assigned, imposed from on high. It remained God's. And the ultimate responsibility for his use of it was therefore also God's. This conviction enabled him to act, often, as if he were possessed of what Spengler called a "dreamlike certainty" of decision. Often he moved swiftly, boldly, with a seemingly fully informed decisiveness, as if he knew exactly what he was doing and what the results would be (though in reality he did not and could not know), when others in posts of decision—more cerebral than he, more weighed down by a sense of personal responsibility for large-scale consequences—were paralyzed by doubt and fear. His inward experience of such moments, however, was very different from a Napoleon's or a Mussolini's in that his act was not at all the exercise of an iron and conquering will. It was almost the opposite of it. Role and game playing fused: his experience became that of a pious gambler whose risk taking, teleologically motivated, is a form of prayer and an act of faith.

Robert Nisbet (essay date 1986)

SOURCE: "Roosevelt and Stalin (I)," in *Modern Age,* Vol. 30, No. 2, Spring, 1986, pp. 103-12.

[In the following essay, the first in a series of two, Nisbet examines Roosevelt's "uncritical, unconditional adulation" of Joseph Stalin from 1941 through the Yalta summit in 1945.]

It is unlikely that history holds a stranger, more improbable and unequal political courtship than President Roosevelt's courtship of Marshal Stalin in World War II. The very idea is arresting: Roosevelt, patrician, born with the silver spoon, Groton- and Harvard-educated aristocrat in American politics; Stalin, low-born revolutionist and bandit from early years, successor by sheer ruthlessness to Lenin as absolute ruler of the Soviet Union, liquidator of the kulak class in the Ukraine, purger of his own party, and totalitarian to the core. That a liaison of any kind should have existed between these two men is barely credible. That the liaison was a political courtship, initiated and pursued by the patrician and exploited by the revolutionist, is the stuff of political fantasy.

Roosevelt's pursuit of Stalin is well known after forty years of diaries, memoirs, letters, and biographies since the war. But on the evidence of a rising amount of writing

by scholars and journalists, it is seemingly not known well or not remembered well. More and more we find the Roosevelt courtship denied altogether, or dismissed as trivia, or otherwise deprecated. This is negligence compounded with ideology. For however we choose to assess the courtship—as the work of idealism and Olympian vision, or as appalling naiveté and credulity, it is a significant episode in the war: one that had effect on Roosevelt's relationship with Churchill, on actual war strategy and the politics of the peace settlement, and, not for a moment to be missed, on patterns of foreign policy opinion in the United States during the four decades following the war.

Moreover, Roosevelt's indulgence of Stalin has been noted and judged by too many close observers to be questioned as fact. Averell Harriman—close friend, wartime adviser, and envoy—writes: "He was determined, by establishing a close relationship with Stalin in wartime, to build confidence among the Kremlin leaders that Russia, now an acknowledged power, could trust the West. . . . Churchill had a more pragmatic attitude. . . . He turned pessimistic about the future earlier than Roosevelt and he foresaw greater difficulties at the end of the war."[1] So, it must be added, did Harriman himself.

George Kennan's view of Roosevelt's performance during the war is considerably harsher than Harriman's.[2] After commenting bitterly on the "inexcusable body of ignorance about the Russian Communist movement, about the history of its diplomacy, about what had happened in the purges, and about what had been going on in Poland and the Baltic States," Kennan turns more directly to FDR alone:

> I also have in mind FDR's evident conviction that Stalin, while perhaps a somewhat difficult customer, was only, after all, a person like any other person; that the reason we hadn't been able to get along with him in the past was that we had never really had anyone with the proper personality and the proper qualities of sympathy and imagination to deal with him, that he had been snubbed all along by the arrogant conservatives of the Western capitals; and that if only he could be exposed to the persuasive charms of someone like FDR himself, ideological preconceptions would melt and Russia's cooperation with the West could be easily arranged. For these assumptions there were no grounds whatsoever; and they were of a puerility that was unworthy of a statesman of FDR's stature.[3]

Churchill was not blameless during the first weeks following the Soviet entrance into the war. It was not necessary for him to hail so extravagantly the Soviet Union in its forced position—that of a "whipped dog," said one commentator—as adversary of Hitler and ally of Britain and the United States. To say that "the cause of any Russian fighting for his hearth and home is the cause of free men and free peoples in every quarter of the globe" was nonsense and hardly mitigated by his follow-up that he would league himself with the devil in hell against the "filthy guttersnipe" Hitler.

Churchill was an old student of war and a particularly keen student of Communist Russia, which he had warned against ever since the Bolshevik Revolution. He knew, and Roosevelt should have known, the desperate position Stalin was in. His army had been proved ill-organized and ill-led in Finland; his equipment was scarce and often inferior. His political and moral record was not one bit better than Hitler's. He was as much the totalitarian as the Nazi leader was. He had joined Hitler only two years before as ally against the West. Why then welcome him now as long-lost democrat and freedom-fighter? He would have had to accept aid under any restrictions or conditions they chose to set down. Churchill was as much a part of the hysterical welcome to Stalin as was Roosevelt at the very beginning. But it can be said for Churchill what can never be said for Roosevelt in World War II: he got over his hysteria quickly and by late 1943 was aware, as Roosevelt never was once in the war, of just what kind of "ally" the Soviet Union really was. Churchill tried throughout the war to apprize, to alert, Roosevelt to the Soviet menace that was growing daily out of the war against Hitler. To no avail.

"I know you will not mind my being brutally frank," wrote Roosevelt to Churchill early in their alliance, "when I tell you that I can personally handle Stalin better than either your Foreign Office or my State Department. Stalin hates the guts of all your people. He thinks he likes me better, and I hope he will continue to."[4] Roosevelt was being boastful, of course, but in the very act of boasting being also fatuous and credulous, to say the least. He knew nothing really about European, much less Soviet, affairs. He had never met Stalin or shown much interest in him throughout the 1930s, when Stalin was engaged in liquidating, purging, and exterminating. He had shown no interest in Soviet affairs, beyond giving diplomatic recognition to the Soviets shortly after he was first elected; nor, for that matter, much interest in any foreign affairs during two terms of office. China and the Pacific seemed to engage more of his interest than Europe; certainly this had been the case prior to about 1940. What could possibly explain, then, so arrant a claim to mastery of one of the two most formidable dictators in the world?

Very probably it was a visit to Moscow made by Roosevelt's closest and most trusted aide, Harry Hopkins, at the president's direction in July 1941. Roosevelt had written Stalin to ask that he treat Hopkins with the same degree of candor and fullness of thought that he would Roosevelt himself. Stalin was only too happy to do so. His embassy in Washington had informed him of the unique bond between the president and Hopkins. It was closer than that between Wilson and Colonel House in the First World War.

Stalin needed no further request. The red carpet was unrolled for Hopkins as though he were a head of state, and he was fêted accordingly. Stalin talked frankly to Hopkins about his need for vast quantities of war supplies, his hope that the United States would join the Soviets in their war against Hitler, in which case they could have their own autonomous units and their own commanders. Repeatedly he pressed upon Hopkins his conviction that President Roosevelt had greater influence upon the common man in the world than anyone else alive. It was vital to have his influence at work actively in the war against Hitler.[5]

Over several hours of confidential talks—with no one but the interpreter present—Stalin and Hopkins had an opportunity to review the whole picture of the war. In reply to Hopkins's request, Stalin gave him a detailed account of exactly the kinds of weapons, vehicles, and planes the Soviets needed from America and Britain. He expressed his personal confidence that the Soviet soldiers could hold the German troops back from overrunning Moscow and Leningrad. Naturally, Stalin made it plain, however, that direct military assistance to the Soviet Union on the Western front, however arranged, was imperative at the earliest possible moment. Above all, the quantity and the speed of Anglo-American military aid to the Soviet Union were crucial to Russian success.

Hopkins was deeply impressed. His long report of his talks with Stalin, given to the president upon Hopkins's return, concluded with some striking personal impressions of Stalin:

> Not once did he repeat himself. He talked as he knew his troops were shooting—straight and hard. He smiled warmly. There was no waste of word, gesture, nor mannerism. It was like talking to a perfectly coordinated machine, an intelligent machine. Joseph Stalin knew what he wanted, knew what Russia wanted, and he assumed that you knew. . . . He said good-by once just as only once he said hello. And that was that. Perhaps I merely imagined that his smile was more friendly, a bit warmer. . . .
>
> No man could forget the picture of the dictator of Russia as he stood watching me leave—an austere, rugged, determined figure in boots that shone like mirrors, stout baggy trousers, and snug-fitting blouse. . . . He curries no favor with you. He seems to have no doubts. He assures you that Russia will stand against the onslaughts of the German army. He takes it for granted that you have no doubts either. . . . [6]

Indeed, Roosevelt did not have any; not after Hopkins's glowing report. Hopkins's entranced mind became Roosevelt's. As James McGregor Burns has pointed out about Hopkins: "He had almost an extrasensory perception of Roosevelt's moods; he knew how to give advice in the form of flattery and flattery in the form of advice; he sensed when to press his boss and when to desist, when to talk and when to listen, when to submit and when to argue."[7] Hopkins was, of course, the perfect ideal-type of the American liberal-progressive in the 1930s—and after. A social worker initially, he was an early recruit to the New Deal, where he clearly found his Promised Land. He could adopt the pose of the playboy at the race tracks whose deepest, most consuming passion was the welfare of the common people, for whom he would gladly tax and tax and spend and spend. It was an effective pose; he was invited by Roosevelt to live in the White House in 1940; there he became without much question the president's *éminence grise*, almost constant companion, and ever-ready envoy.

For Roosevelt, after Hopkins's return from the Kremlin, the first order of the day was the immediate enlargement and expediting of Russian lend-lease. Prior to Hopkins's report, Roosevelt had been cautious about offending a substantial number of Americans who disliked godless Russia and were cold to its support even in the war against Hitler. Now the president threw caution aside. He appointed a high official whose sole responsibility was Russian lend-lease and who could report to the president directly. He told his cabinet, speaking specifically to Stimson, that he was "sick and tired" of excuses and from now on wanted to know what was on the water moving, not what was merely scheduled.[8]

Unhappily, the religious odium of the Soviets refused to go away. A very large number of Americans were deeply troubled by Soviet denial of religious freedom. Roosevelt tried to persuade the pope to persuade American Catholics to drop their objections to aid to Russia. He also took a hand in working up a list of a thousand Protestant theologians and clergy calling for full aid to the Soviets. Finally, he even adopted the stratagem of insisting that, appearances in the Russian Constitution notwithstanding, the Soviets did have religious freedom. Robert Dallek writes:

> Roosevelt knew full well there was no freedom of religion in the Soviet Union. Nor was he blind to the fact that he could extend Lend-Lease to Russia without demonstrating her devotion to religious freedom. But his concern to associate the Soviets with this democratic principle extended beyond the question of aid to the problem of American involvement in the war. Convinced that only a stark contrast between freedom and totalitarianism would provide the emotional wherewithal for Americans to fight, Roosevelt wished to identify the Russians regardless of Soviet realities with Anglo-American ideals as fully as he could. The effort to depict the Soviet Union as reformed, or reforming, on the issue of religious freedom was chiefly an expression of this concern.[9]

In this sadly misplaced effort. Roosevelt was of course violating every iota of Kennan's warning, on June 23, 1941, to the State Department from Berlin.

Roosevelt appears to have charmed himself eventually into belief that Stalin's nature partook of the religious. After returning from the Yalta conference in early 1945, he described Stalin to his cabinet as having "something else in him besides this revolutionist, Bolshevik thing." The president thought it might have something to do with his early training for the "priesthood." "I think that something entered into his nature of the way in which

a Christian gentleman should behave."[10] There is no record, unfortunately, of the faces of the cabinet members who were listening.

Roosevelt's passion to please Stalin at all costs reached even the extremely dangerous waters of the Arctic Ocean and convoys to Archangel and Murmansk. The first obvious disagreements between Churchill and Roosevelt in their correspondence were rooted in the contrasting views the two leaders took of the horrifying casualties in men and ships and materiel which were exacted by Nazi planes, submarines, and surface vessels. Churchill, following Admiralty advice, wanted to cut down on the number of convoys until safer arrangements could perhaps be arranged. Roosevelt was disinclined and through Hopkins sent an urgent telegram to Churchill to the contrary. He wanted shipments *increased* in number and size. Stalin, needless to say, responded nastily to any thought of cutting down on his lend-lease, no matter what the casualty rate might be. His own naval experts, he said, saw nothing to be concerned by.

Matters continued to worsen; on July 14, 1942, Churchill wrote Roosevelt that only four ships out of a convoy of thirty-three had reached Archangel, that Allied shipping losses for one recent week had reached 400,000 tons, "a rate unexampled in either this war or the last, and if maintained evidently beyond all existing replacement plans." Roosevelt was still seemingly untroubled; all that was important was getting what was possible to the Soviets. Not until his own naval adviser, Admiral King, looked into the British Admiralty reports and threw his personal weight behind them, did the president relent. He was not happy, though. He wrote Churchill that he was troubled by possible "political repercussions" and "even more that our supplies will not reach them promptly." "We have always got to bear in mind the personality of our ally," he wrote Churchill; "we should try to put ourselves in his place."[11]

Another matter on which Roosevelt and Churchill differed that involved Stalin's desires and demands was the creation of a second front on the French coast across the English Channel from Britain. There was no disagreement whatever so far as a cross-Channel front as such was concerned; that was as much a part of British strategy as American. It was the timing that was crucial. The British remembered Dunkirk only too well, and, after August 1942, their Dieppe invasion-experiment on the northern coast of France, one in which more than 5,000 British and Canadian soldiers were thrown back with 70 percent casualties in total defeat. They did not see how a second front across the Channel was possible until a huge build-up in England of soldiers, landing craft, weapons, planes, floating harbors, and the like made it realistically possible. Churchill knew very well how solidly and massively the Nazis were emplaced across the water—itself one of the most treacherous and storm-beset bodies in the world. And he knew that failure would be a devastating experience, one more than likely fatal to the Anglo-American war effort.

Roosevelt was impervious to British counsel. Stalin demanded a second front across the Channel in 1942, and Roosevelt did the same. When he sent Hopkins and Marshall to London in early 1942 for their first full conference with British counterparts, it was with instructions not to discuss but to press for such a front in later 1942. Whatever his real feelings might have been, General Marshall went along with his commander in chief. It was with only great reluctance and presumably apology to Stalin that Roosevelt relented on his demand for a second front in 1942, a demand, needless to say, that the Communist parties of Britain and the United States were pushing ardently and clamantly—their total opposition to the war against Hitler less than a year ago now a thing banished from the mind.

Roosevelt, having given up on 1942, now turned his full authority and eloquence to 1943—first early in the year, then the middle, finally the end. All the while Stalin—whose bare existence as a genuine adversary of Hitler owed almost everything to Britain and the United States—never hesitated to pin the white feather on Churchill, to accuse him of lack of true commitment to the war against Hitler for his refusal to be catapulted into a premature invasion of the Continent.

Today, looking back on D Day, June 6, 1944, and thinking of the astronomical numbers of men and weapons required and the sheer luck also needed, as things turned out, one can only marvel that Roosevelt and his American chiefs could have been as ignorantly opinionated as they were about an earlier second front. The answer, of course, is largely Roosevelt's courtship of Stalin. Politics and ideology, not strict military strategy, became sovereign.[12]

This courtship was not long in becoming obvious to both British and Americans. One of the latter, William Bullitt, an old friend, and Roosevelt's ambassador, first to Russia in the early 1930s, then to France through the outbreak of the war, did his best to steer Roosevelt away from his uncritical, unconditional adulation and generosity. In a long and detailed letter in early 1943, Bullitt suggested "more of the old technique of the donkey, the carrot, and the club" to the president. But Roosevelt was unmoved. That letter, with its detail of both political and military brief, has been called by George Kennan "among the major historical documents of the time . . . unique in the insights it brought."[13] Once, according to Bullitt's recollection in 1948, he made the same suggestion to the president in conversation. The reply was: "I think that if I give him [Stalin] everything I possibly can, and ask nothing from him in return, *noblesse oblige,* he won't try to annex anything, and will work with me for a world of peace and democracy."[14]

Roosevelt became almost obsessed, after Hopkins's magical visit to the Kremlin, by the thought of a visit of his own with Stalin, one without Churchill, without staffs, one simply for the purpose of a "meeting of minds" between the two of them. He was certain that "he was more likely to charm Stalin than Churchill." Sir John

Wheeler-Bennett has written of his desire for such a meeting.[15] At last, on May 5, 1943, Roosevelt wrote a very special letter to Stalin, one that would be carried to the marshal by a personal envoy whom, as Roosevelt well knew, Stalin liked and had the utmost confidence in.

The envoy was Joseph E. Davies, who had been Roosevelt's ambassador to the Soviet Union for a brief period ending in 1939. One reason, it should be noted, that Roosevelt wanted Davies to bear his invitation to Stalin was that the current ambassador, Admiral Standley, had recently angered Roosevelt by some remarks to the press that suggested his impatience with Soviet surliness and utter want of appreciation of American lend-lease. Davies was therefore ideal. After all, his *Mission to Moscow* was something of a best seller, as was, especially, the Hollywood movie made of the book, an even more extravagant idyll of Soviet humanitarianism than the book, one in which Stalin, Molotov, and others became surrogates of the American Founding Fathers. For Davies almost everything in the Soviet Union in the 1930s was milk and honey; he knew of no liquidation of kulaks, no Soviet murders by the thousands of Old Bolsheviks; the Moscow trials for Davies were all on the up and up, dealing with real traitors. It is no wonder Davies was greeted warmly and with royal attention. The main banquet in his honor was featured by the movie of *Mission to Moscow,* a copy of which Davies just happened to have brought with him on his joyous return to Moscow.

"In his letter to Stalin," Wheeler-Bennett writes, "Roosevelt made it quite clear that he wanted it *tête-à-tête* with the Russian leader. Mr. Churchill was not to be present. The president had urged that the meeting should be informal and free from 'the difficulties . . . of the red tape of diplomatic conversations.' It was to be a 'meeting of minds.' It was hoped that the meeting could be arranged for July or August.

"Stalin does not seem to have reacted with enormous enthusiasm to the suggestion of a purely bilateral meeting, although President Roosevelt felt obliged to tell Mr. Churchill that the initiative for such an exclusive arrangement *had come from the Russians.*"[16]

As it happened, Churchill was at that very time engaged in one of his hottest, most strenuous altercations with Stalin, who had just fired another of his charges of cowardice and faint-heartedness at the prime minister over the Western second front.

Not until late November 1943, did Roosevelt get at last his dreamed-of private "meeting of minds" with Stalin. The wait was worth it, for he got three such meetings—at the Teheran conference and in the Soviet embassy. By use of a purely contrived report by the Soviets that there was imminent danger of a Nazi parachute-assassination attempt, Roosevelt was persuaded by the Russians to occupy a suite in the Soviet embassy in Teheran rather than either the American or the British. The security, he was told, would be much better, as indeed it was from one point of view, that of the NKVD in full attendance as "servants" and "technicians."

The first of the private sessions between Roosevelt and Stalin took place just before the first plenary session.[17] Only Stalin's and Roosevelt's personal interpreters were permitted in the room. Roosevelt's was Charles E. Bohlen, on his way to a diplomatic career, with a near-perfect command of Russian, and the official American interpreter for the whole conference. Harmony ruled from the outset. Stalin, impressively courteous throughout, asked the president to feel free to bring up any subject he chose. And this Roosevelt did, throughout three intimate meetings.

Poland was extensively dealt with; it was not long or difficult to reach a complete meeting of minds on Poland and the rest of Eastern Europe. Roosevelt had what can most charitably be called a blind spot for East Europeans. He had informed Beaverbrook that he favored a plan for rounding up all dispossessed Europeans and sending them to Central Africa after the war. He also assured Churchill's adviser that boundaries were not really of concern to those people, that all that mattered was security and employment.[18] When a Hyde Park visitor mentioned the growing alarm of the Poles, in Europe and in America, about their future, Roosevelt replied: "I know it. I am sick and tired of these people. . . . I'm not sure that a fair plebiscite, if ever there was such a thing, wouldn't show that these eastern provinces would prefer to go back to Russia. Yes, I really think those 1941 frontiers are as just as any."[19]

There was thus no predisposition on Roosevelt's part to try to block Soviet plans for Poland. He was quite agreeable to the cartographic lifting of Poland and setting it down a few hundred miles to the west, and thus giving Russia the parts of Eastern Poland it wanted. Roosevelt did ask for one concession. He explained that he was probably going to run for a fourth term in the next year, 1944, and if so he would need the votes of the millions of Polish-Americans. Could Stalin therefore remain publicly silent about this agreement until after the election? Stalin indicated that he could. Wheeler-Bennett observes: "Roosevelt's words were of tremendous importance. On the one hand they virtually guaranteed to Stalin the territorial prizes he had been seeking in Eastern Poland. On the other, they removed all necessity for the Soviet Union to make its peace with the Polish government."[20]

There was little of genuine significance to the war and the postwar circumstances that was not dealt with by Stalin and Roosevelt in their three private sessions. They agreed on the very earliest possible cross-Channel second front as well as on a diversionary operation, so called, in the south of France, to be manned by divisions transferred from Italy. When Japan was brought up by the president, Stalin agreed that after a brief period of rest following Hitler's surrender, the Soviets would join the Pacific war. Roosevelt made evident that there would be generous territorial prizes for the Soviet Union. It was agreed that France should be reduced to a third-rate

power and its empire scattered. Stalin did not want possible French challenges to his anticipated power over Western as well as Eastern Europe. Roosevelt seems to have had no other reason beyond personal dislike of de Gaulle and suspicion of French morality and culture. Roosevelt introduced his Wilsonian dream—a United Nations organization after the war, one worldwide in scope. Stalin looked doubtful until the president assured him of his hope that it would be governed in fact by "the four policemen" of the world—the United States, the Soviet Union, Britain, and China, with the first two the great superpowers.

India came up, thanks to Roosevelt. He warned Stalin that Churchill was "prickly" on the subject. He, FDR, proposed "reform from the bottom, along the Soviet line." Bohlen was aghast at hearing the president exhibit such ignorance of the nature of the Bolshevik revolution—as far removed from a "bottom-up" revolution as anyone might imagine.[21] Stalin himself, who by this time could only have been satisfied that in Roosevelt he had a benign dunce, at least in military and peace strategy, for a companion, observed immediately, and somewhat drily, that India was a "complicated problem" and furthermore (Could Stalin's eye have had a twinkle?) that such drastic reform just might entail revolution.

Roosevelt and Stalin reached essential understanding in their three private meetings on all the main topics on the agenda for the official sessions. Churchill was not blind to what was going on; he begged Roosevelt for a private session, but once again Roosevelt pleaded his fear that if the two of them met privately, Stalin might become discouraged and suspicious. The result of the private meetings was to convert the public sessions into little more than sharp exchanges between Stalin and Churchill, with Roosevelt sitting mute a good deal of the time. Bohlen later wrote: "I did not like the attitude of the President, who not only backed Stalin but seemed to enjoy the Stalin-Churchill exchange. Roosevelt should have come to the defense of a close friend and ally, who was really being put upon by Stalin."[22]

Far from that, however, Roosevelt seems to have relished the confrontation and even hatched a little scene in which he could demonstrate to Stalin his feelings about Churchill. As he described it later to Frances Perkins back in Washington, he pretended, just as the official session began, to whisper loudly in Stalin's ear to the effect that "Winston is cranky this morning, he got up on the wrong side of the bed. A vague smile passed over Stalin's eyes. . . . I began to tease Churchill about his Britishness, about John Bull. . . . Winston got red and scowled and the more he did so, the more Stalin smiled. Finally Stalin broke into a deep guffaw, and for the first time in three days, I saw the light. I kept it up until Stalin was laughing with me, and it was then I called him 'Uncle Joe.'"[23]

Keith Eubank, commenting on this extraordinary episode, writes: "If his tale is true, Roosevelt had insulted

Churchill, who admired him, and demeaned himself before Stalin, who trusted neither man. In his craving for Stalin's approval and friendship, Roosevelt imagined the joke had been on Churchill and that Stalin had laughed with him. More probably Stalin had laughed at the President of the United States belittling an ally to find favor with a tyrant."[24]

All in all, it was a virtuoso performance for Stalin. There was little of the slightest strategic or geopolitical value to him that he did not nail down at Teheran or else put within easy position for action later. Hopkins had told Sir Alexander Cadogan on the way over that "you will find us lining up with the Russians."[25] At the end Admiral King said: "Stalin knew just what he wanted when he came to Teheran, and he got it."[26] At the very beginning of the conference, General Brooke told Cadogan: "This conference is over when it has just begun. Stalin has the President in his pocket."[27]

The notorious Yalta conference came a little over a year later. Once again it was Stalin who set the time and place. Churchill said that if ten years' research had been done, "we couldn't have found a worse place in the world than Yalta." The NKVD, uniforms often showing under the assumed clothing of servants and technicians, were everywhere. Despite the outcry after the war about Yalta, it really did little more than to reaffirm, this time in writing, what Teheran had produced with respect to Poland, its boundaries, its coming election, its Soviet-created Lublin government, the status of Russian relations with the Baltic and the Balkan states, the United Nations with the special representation in the Assembly allowed the Soviet Union, and the expansive, specifically designated areas of the Far East that would go to Stalin for his willingness to join the Anglo-American war against Japan—once the European war was safely and securely ended, of course. All in all, as Professor Eubank describes in detail, Yalta was more ceremony and reaffirmation than it was new substance. Teheran—most especially its three private Roosevelt-Stalin meetings—had done all the real work.[28]

Roosevelt and Stalin enjoyed a reunion. This time Stalin met alone with Churchill once, but clearly the zest was in further meetings with Roosevelt. Again, as at Teheran, Roosevelt shied away from any danger of being thought by Stalin to be ganging up with Churchill against him. "The Teheran format was repeated," writes Eubank; "Stalin waited for Roosevelt to bring topics up for discussion. Yet to Roosevelt this was a meeting of old friends who had met previously and corresponded ever since. At Yalta they were only renewing old contacts."[29]

Churchill had known from the Teheran conference that he was out of it, really. In his characteristic, impish way, he described his position to an old friend as that of a little donkey, alone knowing the way, but caught between the Russian bear and the American buffalo. There were times during the year following Teheran when it was feared that Churchill might even resign as prime minister over differences in military and political strategy with Roosevelt and the American chiefs. But General Brooke seems to have

persuaded Churchill to imbibe some of his own philosophy toward the Americans: "All right, if you insist upon being damned fools, sooner than fall out with you, which would be fatal, we shall be damned fools with you, and we shall see that we perform the role of damned fools damned well."

Thus armed philosophically, Churchill could endure more of Yalta folly than he might otherwise have been able to: for example, Roosevelt's assurance to Stalin, in Churchill's hearing, that all U.S. troops would be out of Europe within two years[30]; Roosevelt's chilly rejection of Churchill's proposal for a European Emergency High Commission to superintend Polish elections and the formation of a new government, saving Stalin the necessity of a word against the idea; and the almost wanton showering upon the Soviets of Far Eastern territorial treasures for Stalin's agreement to join the Pacific war. In substance, all of this had been done at Teheran more than a year before.

"In the end," writes Eubank, "Yalta became more notorious because this conference produced written documents which seemed to prove betrayal of Poland, a deal with Stalin over Eastern Europe, and a written pact over the Far East that changed the balance of power."[31] Additionally, there was the vaunted Declaration on Liberated Europe, solemnly signed by the Big Three at Yalta, in which assurances were duly registered of forthcoming democracies all over Eastern Europe.

Stalin did not acquire Eastern Europe from Yalta, for he had already occupied it by force during the months following Teheran. The true crime of Yalta is the legal and moral capital it gave Stalin—to draw on in Europe, Asia, and elsewhere.

Churchill recovered quickly from his immediate post-Yalta delirium; within a matter of days he was back at work alerting, advising, warning, and beseeching Roosevelt on the rising threat to the postwar world that the Soviet Union was becoming. For his part the president, it may be fairly said, had been no different at Yalta or after Yalta than he had been for a long time, since at least Teheran, with respect to Stalin and the Soviets. He had made a habit of counseling patience or providing justification for most of what the Soviets did. In one instance only did he depart from his norm. That was when Stalin, in a tone of rude insult, accused the president and the prime minister of participating in a scheme hatched in Bern, Switzerland, of effecting a special, negotiated surrender of the German military forces. Roosevelt drafted the telegram of denial and outrage, and Churchill commended him. It is hard to avoid the feeling that mixed in with the statesman's outrage is a tincture of a lover's feeling of betrayal.[32]

Apart from the Bern incident, the exchange of letters between the two leaders after Yalta is a largely faithful mirror of their sharply contrasting attitudes on Stalin and on the politics of the Soviet Union. On March 8 Churchill sent to Roosevelt a detailed listing of the specific derelictions of the Soviets, with special emphasis on Poland. He recommended strongly a direct confrontation by the two of them, enclosing a draft telegram to Stalin. Roosevelt's reply was: "I very much hope . . . that you will not send any message to Uncle Joe at this juncture—especially as I feel that certain parts of your proposed text might produce a reaction quite contrary to your intent." To which Churchill responded: "Which parts?" "We might be able to improve the wording, but I am convinced that unless we can induce the Russians to agree to these fundamental points of procedure, all our work at Yalta will be in vain." Churchill also indicated that he must shortly appear before Parliament. "I do not wish to reveal a divergence between the British and United States governments, but it would certainly be necessary for me to make it clear that we are now in the presence of a great failure and an utter breakdown of . . . Yalta."

In his response on March 15, Roosevelt made a show of indignation that Churchill should think their two countries to be in divergence: "From our side there is certainly no evidence of divergence of policy. We have merely been discussing the most effective tactics and I cannot agree that we are confronted with a breakdown of the Yalta agreement."

On April 5 Churchill wrote a very fireball of a letter to Roosevelt on Soviet behavior. It called for a "firm and blunt stand" without delay, and it concluded with the pregnant words: "If they are ever convinced that we are afraid of them and can be bullied into submission, then indeed I should despair of our future relations with them and much else." Roosevelt's reply was written by Admiral Leahy for his signature. It suggests concurrence with Churchill's position. But Professor Kimball, editor of the *Correspondence,* correctly writes: "So cryptic a message as this does not mean that the President had finally accepted the idea of a postwar Soviet threat and was advocating an early form of military containment. . . . One wonders if the President gave this message any consideration at all."[33]

Roosevelt's true feeling was written in his own hand on April 11, the day before he died: "I would minimize the general Soviet problem as much as possible because these problems, in one form or another, seem to arise every day and most of them straighten out as in the case of the Bern meeting. We must be firm, however, and our course thus far is correct."

(To be concluded)

NOTES

[1] Averell Harriman, *Special Envoy to Churchill and Stalin* (New York, 1975), p. 170.

[2] George F. Kennan, *Russia and the West Under Lenin and Stalin* (Boston, 1960), chap. 23 *passim.*

[3] *Ibid.,* p. 355.

[4] *Churchill and Roosevelt: The Complete Correspondence,* ed. Warren F. Kimball (Princeton, 1984). Roosevelt to Churchill, March 18, 1942. Kimball comments: "The President's belief that he could 'personally handle' Stalin lasted until Roosevelt's death." Vol. 1, p. 420.

[5] Robert E. Sherwood, *Roosevelt and Hopkins* (New York, 1948), chap. 15.

[6] *Ibid.,* pp. 343-44.

[7] Cited in Robert Dallek, *Franklin D. Roosevelt and American Foreign Policy, 1932-1945* (New York, 1979), pp. 279-80.

[8] *Ibid.,* p. 280.

[9] *Ibid.,* p. 298.

[10] *Ibid.,* p. 521.

[11] *Correspondence.* Churchill to Roosevelt, July 14, 1942; Roosevelt to Churchill, April 26 and July 29.

[12] See Mark A. Stoler, *The Politics of the Second Front . . . 1941-1943* (Westport, Conn., 1977).

[13] *For the President: Personal and Secret: Correspondence Between Franklin D. Roosevelt and William C. Bullitt,* ed. Orville E. Bullitt (Boston, 1972). Kennan's appreciation is contained in his laudatory introduction to the book. Bullitt's long letter to the president is dated January 29, 1943.

[14] This well-known citation from Bullitt's conversation with Roosevelt in the White House appeared under Bullitt's name in an article in *Life* magazine, August 30, 1948. Its reliability has been questioned by some on the basis of the estrangement between Bullitt and the president over Sumner Welles. But Orville Bullitt refers (p. 554) to a book by a French writer, Laslo Havas, *Assassinat au sommet,* in which the identical conversation reported by Bullitt in his article is described, even with some of the same Roosevelt phrases, by Havas. Most assuredly, there is no discrepancy between Roosevelt's spoken sentiment to Bullitt and his recorded behavior toward Stalin throughout the war.

[15] Sir John Wheeler-Bennett and Anthony Nicholls, *The Semblance of Peace* (London, 1972), p. 81.

[16] Wheeler-Bennett, pp. 81-82. (Emphasis added.)

[17] My treatment of the private conversations is based on Keith Eubank's account in his *Summit at Teheran* (New York, 1985), which in turn is largely drawn from Charles E. Bohlen's official notes as Roosevelt's interpreter during the conversations.

[18] Quoted in A. J. P. Taylor, *Beaverbrook* (London, 1972), p. 397. Taylor adds: "The report which Beaverbrook

brought back . . . revealed little but the strange workings of Roosevelt's mind."

[19] Cited by Dallek, pp. 436-37.

[20] Wheeler-Bennett, p. 162.

[21] Charles E. Bohlen, *Witness to History* (New York, 1973), p. 141.

[22] *Ibid.,* p. 146.

[23] Frances Perkins, *The Roosevelt I Knew* (New York, 1946), p. 84.

[24] Eubank, p. 351.

[25] Sir Alexander Cadogan, *Diaries* (New York, 1972), p. 581.

[26] Eubank, p. 311.

[27] Cadogan, p. 582.

[28] Eubank, pp. 472 ff.

[29] *Ibid.,* p. 474.

[30] Churchill, *Triumph and Tragedy* (Boston, 1953), p. 353. The Brooke words are cited by Kimball as commentary in *Correspondence,* vol. 3, p. 226.

[31] Eubank, p. 479.

[32] *Correspondence.* Churchill to Roosevelt, April 4, 1945.

[33] Vol. 3, p. 617.

Robert Nisbet (essay date 1986)

SOURCE: "Roosevelt and Stalin (II)," in *Modern Age,* Vol. 30, Nos. 3-4, Summer/Fall, 1986, pp. 205-17.

[*In the following essay, Nisbet continues his analysis of Roosevelt's credulity toward Stalin.*]

President Roosevelt's World War II courtship of Stalin reached its heights, as I have indicated, in the two summit meetings at Teheran and Yalta. At the first, during the course of three private talks with Stalin from which Churchill was excluded, FDR made clear that he would go along with Stalin's territorial desires in Eastern Europe and assured Stalin also that America would put up little if any protest over annexation of the Baltic states. He also gave his personal assurances of a rich reward in the Far East for Russia for its agreement to join in the war against Japan once Hitler was defeated.

Yalta added little of actual substance to Teheran. What Yalta did give Stalin was not East European territory, which he had already taken by force during the months following Teheran, but, equally important, all the documentary materials of a justification of Stalin's military aggressions in the whole of Eastern Europe. As Chester Wilmot pointed out more than thirty years ago in his path-breaking *The Struggle for Europe,* the real crime of Yalta was the moral cloak it gave Stalin for all the heinous depredations upon Poland and other Eastern states—starting with the pact with Hitler, including the Katyn Forest slaughter of many thousands of Polish officers, and continuing down to the cruel and blatant perfidy of the Soviets in the tragic Warsaw Uprising of August 1944—and for all that he would subsequently do by ruthless aggression first in the Far East and then in Eastern Europe and the Middle East. The Declaration on Liberated Europe, perhaps the greatest single piece of duplicity in World War II, carrying, alas, Churchill's as well as Roosevelt's and Stalin's names, was all Stalin needed to undergird a foreign policy and military strategy that reaches down to the present moment. With its calculated ambiguities covering such matters as human rights, democracy, and peace, the declaration read as if it had been written by Lenin and Stalin for the official Soviet canon. Needless to say, this fact did not prevent Roosevelt, upon his return from Yalta, from celebrating Yalta as a setting worthy of comparison to Philadelphia and the signing of the Constitution. Churchill was scarcely better.

But the saga of Roosevelt's courtship of Stalin is by no means confined to the Teheran and Yalta summits. There is no want of other, separate and distinct, demonstrations of ardor toward Stalin. There was Roosevelt's sudden gift—without any prior notification of Churchill—of one-third of the Italian navy to Stalin. All Stalin had asked for at Teheran was a loan of half a dozen ships for use in northern and southern waters. Churchill was thunderstruck when word of FDR's public announcement reached him in London, and he was quick to refuse his assent. But he was equally quick to take steps that would save FDR from a potentially embarrassing, even explosive, situation. Churchill's superior wisdom had once again come to the rescue.

Another incident that reveals Roosevelt's alacrity in accepting of Stalin's suggestions—and the necessity of being once again overruled by better judgment—is the "pastoralization" of Germany after the war. We are best acquainted with this horrendous proposal through the Morgenthau Plan, which seriously proposed the total stripping from Germany of its industry and capital technology and reducing it to arable and pasture. But Stalin had thought of the possibility and recommended it earlier: during one of the private sessions with Roosevelt at Teheran he broached it. Germany, he said, should be pastoralized and also dismembered into five or six new, small countries. The strategic importance of such geo-political mutilation from the Soviet point of view is obvious—as is the related recommendation that France too be reduced to a third-rate power. Russia would then have uncontested power over Western Europe, as well as Eastern.

At Teheran Stalin also proposed the immediate execution of 50,000 German officers once the war was over. Churchill was offended and said so. Roosevelt, playing the role of mediator in elaborately comic fashion said Stalin was too high: 49,000 would be better. Later in the evening Elliot Roosevelt argued for the execution of between 50,000 and 100,000 German officers. Churchill, in visible anger and disgust, left the room. Stalin came over and put his arm around Elliot's shoulder in a gesture of affection.

Thus Roosevelt was fully prepared in mind for the infamous Morgenthau Plan, and put his name to it at the second Quebec Conference in September 1944. The gist of the plan is contained in the mandate that industrial Germany "should not only be stripped of all presently existing industries but so weakened and controlled that it cannot in the foreseeable future become an industrial area." Wheeler-Bennett accurately observes: "Marshal Stalin could scarcely have gone further."

So, by a neat trick, was Churchill brought to sign the plan. It was linked inextricably with desperately needed credits for Britain amounting to six billion dollars. Churchill probably shrugged, knowing that so appalling and geopolitically cretinous a measure would never get through Roosevelt's chief advisers in Washington. And Churchill was right. When Roosevelt returned to Washington, he was confronted by a grim Stimson, Hull, McCloy, and even Hopkins, who explained just what the plan meant. Roosevelt was overcome, and the plan was allowed to die quietly. At least, he may well have thought, Stalin knew he had tried.[34]

The Warsaw Uprising in August 1944, with its massacre by the Germans of thousands of Poles, many of high station, is another unsavory illustration of Anglo-American, chiefly American, cravenness before Stalin. But to appreciate this horror, we are obliged to go back to an earlier one: that of the slaughter-execution by the Soviets of thousands of Polish officers in the Katyn Forest in 1939 after Stalin had divided shares of Poland with Hitler. Some 15,000 Polish officers were rounded up by the Soviets; about a third were cruelly executed on the edges of pits they had been forced to dig themselves. The rest of the captive officers were shipped to the gulag, never to be heard of again, presumably destroyed by the Russians. Despite repeated efforts by the Polish government-in-exile in London to obtain information about them from the Soviet government, nothing was ever disclosed by the Kremlin.

In 1943 the German army came across the shallowly buried Polish corpses. Naturally the Nazis publicized to the world their grisly discovery, using it as anti-Soviet and also anti-British and -American propaganda. The Polish government in London exile called for an international commission to investigate the charges, which the Soviets promptly denied, accusing the Polish government of collaborating with the Nazis. There was no question in any responsible person's mind of Soviet guilt in the massacre of the Polish officers, but from the day of the call for an international commission, the Soviets kept up a perpetual barrage of hatred against the official Polish government.

Then, in August 1944, the Soviets cruelly widened their attack. Germans were still in occupation of Warsaw but preparing to retreat from the city. Moscow Radio for days secretly called upon the Polish Home Guard in Warsaw to revolt on a certain day, promising that the already-advancing Soviet army would move in immediately to engage the Germans. Instead, after the Polish uprising in Warsaw began, the incoming Soviet troops suddenly stopped at a river a few miles from Warsaw and watched the spectacle over several days of Nazi massacre of the rebelling Home Guard.

This ugly display of Soviet barbarism took place, it must be realized, three months after the Normandy landing, after Paris had been freed, and after there was only the slightest threat to Russia from the German armies. The world was shocked, and when the British and Americans asked Stalin for permission to use Soviet air fields if any of their own planes were crippled and forced to land in their mission of dropping supplies for the Warsaw Poles, the answer was a sharp no. The reactions by Churchill and Roosevelt were individually characteristic. Churchill, on August 25, sent Roosevelt a draft telegram to Stalin for Roosevelt's concurrence, one begging for a relenting of the Soviet decision in order that the British and Americans, on their own responsibility alone, might help. Roosevelt, on the very next day, replied stiffly: "In consideration of Stalin's present attitude in regard to relief of the Polish underground . . . . I do not consider it advantageous to the long-range, general war prospect for me to join with you in the proposed message."[35]

It was about this time that Churchill wrote Roosevelt to say that Chaim Weizmann (head of the World Zionist Organization) had asked that the Jews be allowed to organize a brigade of their own, with their own commanders, uniform, flag, et cetera, to join in the war against the Germans. Churchill was all for it, and he was obviously eager to have Roosevelt join him. But the President's reply was a model of brevity and coldness: "I perceive no objection to your organizing a Jewish brigade as suggested."[36] End of message. But, then, as we have seen, FDR had never been able to bring himself to serious concern about Poles, East Europeans, *et al.*

A particularly important consequence of Roosevelt's almost abject devotion to Stalin is to be seen in his reaction to the British Mediterranean strategy. It was, predictably, as negative as Stalin's had been from the outset. This strategy was never declared by the British a substitute for the second front across the Channel, though both Stalin and Roosevelt chose to see it in this light.[37] Churchill and the British chiefs simply recognized the absolutely vital role of the Mediterranean in both military and political contexts. To lose it to the Soviets would be ruinous to Western civilization. Hence the necessity of shoring up Greek, Italian, and also Yugoslavian approaches to the

Mediterranean. Hence too the attractiveness of mounting campaigns from Italy especially which would additionally carry, if successful, the Allies into Central Europe, where they could wound the German armies and also, as Churchill put it, "shake hands with the Russians as far east as possible." But the Americans were blind, willfully so, to all such strategy.

It was this American blindness to the importance of the eastern Mediterranean, together with a lack of sympathy for any part of the "soft underbelly" strategy Churchill supported, that led the Prime Minister to begin thinking in 1944 about a private arrangement with Stalin out of which could come the strong influence he needed in Greece. In early June he proposed indirectly to Stalin that in return for Stalin's allowing him the measure of influence he wanted in Greece, he, Churchill—together with FDR—would grant the same to Stalin in Romania.

Roosevelt did not like this; it conformed with his distaste for anything suggesting imperialism and colonialism and would lead, he was certain, to "spheres of influence" in the postwar period instead of the single, unalloyed international order he cherished. He wrote Churchill precisely to this effect. Churchill was unconvinced. By August it was apparent to Churchill that Stalin was secretly considering an arrangement whereby he would have, through the operations of the Greek Communist guerrillas and their possible overthrow of the Greek monarchy, control of the Balkans, including Greece with its window on the Mediterranean.

Thus, when the Third Moscow Conference was held in October, Churchill, in a private meeting with Stalin—Roosevelt did not attend the conference—proposed his famous, or notorious, "percentages" agreements, to which Stalin readily agreed. Percentages were guidelines to the degree of permitted Soviet versus British and American influence in the Balkan countries. Thus, in return for a 90-10 percent proportion in favor of Britain in Greece, there was a 90-10 percent proportion favoring Russia in Romania and a 75-25 proportion for Russia in Bulgaria. More equal proportions were agreed upon for Hungary and Yugoslavia. For Churchill, the gain of Greece was clear net; after all there was not much that could have been done anyhow about Russia in Romania and Bulgaria. Three months after the agreements were reached by Churchill, he went to Greece, at Christmas, where he propped up the faltering monarchy with a strong regent and rallied the Greek army to repulse the Greek Communist guerrillas. He saved Greece and also the Mediterranean from highly probable Soviet domination after the war.

None of this "sphere of influence" operation was palatable to Roosevelt, who, in Sir John Colville's words, shook "in impotent fury" at Churchill's "imperialistic" behavior. So did other Americans, including some at the State Department and major newspapers. Churchill was undisturbed. To Roosevelt's critical reaction and complaint about high-handedness, Churchill wrote:

"Action is paralyzed if everybody is to consult everybody about everything."[38]

Stalin understood strategy very well. He wanted to be certain that his Western allies did not get themselves into central and eastern areas of Europe while the war against Germany was still under way and thus be in the Soviets' way when the time for postwar "stabilization" came. Stalin saw very clearly, and very early, the potentiality the Italian campaign had for this undesirable development. The defeat of Italy was an easy matter and of no real consequence. But Stalin knew well what Churchill had in mind: the advance of the victorious Allied armies past Rome, up into the Po Basin and thence in due time into Central Europe above the Alps. Not surprisingly, then, Stalin began counteraction at Teheran. General Brooke noted that "Stalin, to the delight of the Americans, championed a suggestion . . . that the Italian campaign should be abandoned in favor of a landing of the Mediterranean coast of France."[39]

Churchill, depressedly, had foreseen this on his way to the Teheran conference. He told Harold Macmillan: "Germany is finished, though it may take some time to clean up the mess. The real problem is Russia. I *can't* get the Americans to see it." Wheeler-Bennett after thus citing Churchill, adds about the Prime Minister:

> Throughout the Teheran conference Mr. Churchill's depression increased. He was depressed at the all too apparent rapacity of Soviet claims, at the degree of acquiescence with which these were received by the President, and at his own dilemma. For although he alone realized the magnitude of the danger involved, he knew too that alone he was powerless to avert it. Committed by inclination and policy to maintaining a solidly unified Anglo-American front, he was faced with a situation in which American policy chimed in more often with that of Stalin than with his own. He was thus compelled, usually against his better judgment, to concur in decisions which he felt to be inimical to the interests of Europe in general and Britain in particular.[40]

To this must be added the inescapable fact that the United States was rapidly becoming the dominant partner in the alliance—in number of troops and in amount of material. It could call the tune.

The more notable U.S. strategic follies in the European theater are almost always derivatives of Roosevelt's policy of deferring to Stalin. Thus the absurd insistence on a cross-channel second front in 1942; the complete failure ever to grasp the importance of Britain's Mediterranean strategy; the effort to give Stalin a third of the Italian navy; the belief in a last-ditch Nazi "national redoubt" in southern Germany, with troops duly dispatched; and, far from least, ANVIL.

This is the name given the purportedly diversionary Allied invasion of southern France. Stalin first thought of it; he had the best of reasons to see Italy robbed of valuable divisions to make ANVIL possible. For, as noted, these divisions were pointed through the north of Italy directly toward Central Europe, toward Vienna and Prague, and he wanted none of that. Hence Stalin's strong suggestion at Teheran—with Roosevelt's immediate endorsement—of the southern France operation, one assertedly to assist the larger Allied landing across the Channel in the north of France. The British were not taken in. They knew that such an operation was unnecessary to protect the flanks of the Normandy landing and the march east. And the British were to be proved right. Almost no opposition was met by the eight largely prime grade Anglo-American divisions transferred from Italy to ANVIL, and within a few weeks these troops had been quietly enfolded within Eisenhower's massive army to the north, their actual military value in the south nonexistent.

Churchill suffered more perhaps from Roosevelt's blind insistence upon emasculation of the Italian campaign— and of all hopes of beating the Russians to Vienna and Prague—than from any other single act by Roosevelt during the war. "What can I do, Mr. President," he wrote despairingly to Roosevelt, "when your Chiefs of Staff insist upon casting aside our Italian offensive campaign, with all its dazzling possibilities?"[41] Ambassador Winant wrote an urgent note to Roosevelt to say that he had never seen Churchill as badly shaken.[42] Only the pleas of his military chiefs seem to have prevented Churchill from resigning his role of British leader. For he believed completely in his plan to use Italy as the way to Central Europe and thus to putting a check on a Russian monopoly of the area after the war as well as on Nazi war operations.

But Roosevelt was immovable and doubtless would have been even if Churchill had resigned. He had given his full support at Teheran to Stalin in the ANVIL matter. He would not be, not then or later, any apparent threat to Stalin's sole, uncontested mastery of almost everything east of Berlin and Prague. To give Stalin as much as possible was, as he was quite willing to say openly, a part of his plan to get Stalin's full cooperation in the postwar reordering of the whole world, in the interest of peace and democracy. Churchill never forgot ANVIL. In his war memoirs he wrote: "The army of Italy was deprived of its opportunity to strike a most formidable blow at the Germans, and very possibly reach Vienna before the Russians, with what might have followed there." Mark Clark, commanding American general in Italy, felt exactly as Churchill did. "A campaign that might have changed the whole history of relations between the Western world and the Soviet Union was permitted to fade away. . . . The weakening of the campaign in Italy in order to invade Southern France, instead of pushing on into the Balkans, was one of the outstanding mistakes of the War."[43]

Even the notorious decision, solely on his own, by Eisenhower at the very end of March 1945 to make direct contact with Stalin by telegram with the message that he himself saw no value in an occupation of Berlin—the showcase as well as command center of all Nazi Germany—

and would bypass it, was a product at bottom of Roosevelt's policy, well known to Marshall and the other American chiefs, of deferring to Stalin in all possible matters. It is inconceivable that Eisenhower would have violated the military chain of command and failed to consult the combined chiefs in advance about his message had he not been sure beyond the slightest doubt that his action was in complete accord with Roosevelt's and Marshall's political views of the Soviets. Eisenhower, like most other American generals in U.S. history, had a passion for confining himself solely to military matters, leaving everything with political overtones to the President alone. As Forest Pogue has concluded: Eisenhower's wartime decisions "hewed strictly to Roosevelt's political desires."

Political policy was Roosevelt's alone to make, Ike insisted, and he was hardly in any doubt of what Roosevelt's policy toward the Soviets was. As Stephen Ambrose has written: "There can be legitimate debate about the wisdom of the President's policy, but there can be no doubt . . . what the policy was; it is equally clear that Eisenhower was trying to act within the context of the wishes of his political superior."[44]

Precisely. Of course Eisenhower might at least have allowed his closest staff to draft the message to Stalin to ensure clarity. For, as the result of Ike's own hasty drafting of the telegram to Stalin, twenty-four hours were lost while the American Military Commission under General Deane in Moscow frantically sought, by messages to SHAEF, the precise meaning of Eisenhower's original telegram, which the Commission was required to translate. General Deane was well aware of the agreed upon strategy by the Anglo-American forces to take Berlin for both military and political reasons. Now, this sudden, badly written message to Stalin—in violation of the chain of command—could only throw confusion into General Deane's mind. And of course into Churchill's and the British chiefs' minds.

The British had not even had the courtesy of an advance notice of what Eisenhower planned to write Stalin. Only after the telegram was dispatched to Moscow were the British notified, and accordingly stunned. Churchill pleaded with Ike to cancel his message to Stalin; but to no avail. It was, declared Eisenhower, a strictly "military" communication to Stalin, and he, Eisenhower, deferred to Roosevelt, his commander in chief, in all political affairs: or rather, to Roosevelt and Hopkins. There was not the slightest question in his or General Marshall's mind that he had conformed utterly and completely to the President's political wishes.

American General Simpson of the Ninth Army was probably the severest casualty—that is, he and his entire confident and eager army. By early April, a few days after Eisenhower dispatched his telegram to Stalin, the Ninth Army stood poised on the bank of the Elbe, a few crossings already achieved, waiting for the order from headquarters to march into Berlin, less than a two-days' operation, what with generally receptive Germans along the way only too happy to welcome Anglo-Americans instead of the feared and hated Russians. But instead of the order to proceed, there came an order to stop permanently—an order from Ike himself. "Nothing ever shook him [General Simpson] from the belief that the only thing standing between the Ninth Army and Berlin was a wide open autobahn,"[45] writes Ambrose. And with every reason. Berlin was a gift to Stalin by Eisenhower in the name of Franklin D. Roosevelt.

Churchill, echoing his chiefs' consternation, started to protest strongly to Roosevelt, but he desisted shortly; by this late date in the war, he knew only too well the hopelessness of countering decisions and actions which were stimulated by the President's desire to assure Stalin of his unwavering trust. Churchill thought a Latin quotation was in order. What he might have sent FDR was the chilling Lucretian *Concede: Necessest* ("Relax: it's inevitable") directed at himself in irony. But what he did send was *Amantium irae amoris integratio est,* translated by the President's staff as "Lovers' quarrels always go with true love."[46]

By the spring of 1945 there could not have been many in the higher councils of the British and the Americans who were unaware of Roosevelt's almost compulsive strategy of reassuring and pleasing Stalin at just about any cost. General Deane and Averell Harriman in Moscow were high among the initiated in this respect. Both sent telegrams to the President or to Hopkins seeking to warn the White House of the by now naked Soviet policy of exploiting the Anglo-American aid program for all it was worth. "I have evidence," Harriman wrote, "that they have misinterpreted our generous attitude toward them as a sign of weakness and acceptance of their policies. . . . Unless we take issue with the present policy, there is every indication that the Soviet Union will become a world bully."[47] But Harriman, by this time, had little confidence that he could succeed, at least lastingly, in his effort to warn. The President "consistently shows very little interest," Harriman wrote in his diary, "in Eastern European countries except as they affect sentiment in America."[48]

Two incidents suggest that occasionally at least the light shone through to Roosevelt's inner mind. Once at lunch in the White House, when one of Harriman's cables was brought to him, he reacted angrily: "Averell is right. We can't do business with Stalin. He has broken every one of the promises he made at Yalta."[49] And about the same time he uttered a similar remark to Anne O'Hare McCormick of *The New York Times,* declaring that although he continued to believe in the Yalta agreements, he had since found out that Stalin was "no longer a man of his word; either that or he was no longer in control of the Soviet government."[50]

No doubt such stories reflect a part of the truth; even FDR and perhaps Hopkins had moments when Stalin's actions became too blatantly self-serving or antagonistic

for easy assimilation. But, on balance, the fairest judgment is that Roosevelt remained serenely confident to the very end that he could "personally handle" Stalin, as he had boasted to Churchill as far back as March 1942. His final letter to Churchill, written by his own hand at Warm Springs a day before he died, read in part: "I would minimize the general Soviet problem as much as possible." This after months of Soviet rapacity, duplicity, and brutal subjugation of occupied East European countries!

In conclusion, the question must be asked once and for all: what led Roosevelt to embark as early as 1941 on the course of pleasing Stalin, a course that sometimes came close to disaster? It is easy to agree with George Kennan that the course Roosevelt took was "puerile," that it was by any accounting credulous in the extreme. But we need to know why, by what ideals or hopes, he was driven to such transparently puerile and credulous behavior. What were the strings pulling on his will? He thought himself a politician of the order of Churchill and doubtless Lincoln and Washington. But in all truth he was not; he did not come very close.

Whatever he might have been or become, his political vision, especially though not exclusively in foreign matters, was shaped by one of the most powerful democratic forces of the twentieth century: Woodrow Wilson and Wilsonianism. It is likely that even if the young FDR had not managed to become assistant secretary of state under Wilson in World War I, he would have still become an ardent follower of the author of the League of Nations. Young men of breeding, wealth, and education in Eastern private schools and colleges were prone to becoming Wilsonians during the 1920s and 1930s. In the United States Wilson became invested, even before his death, with all the martyrdom and the piercing vision of the good and eternal that any Christian saint might yearn for. It is hardly too much to say that in the eyes of many millions of Americans, Wilson *was* a saint: Christian and American in equal proportions.

President Roosevelt wanted, in the depth of his being, to do what Wilson had failed at: that is, make the world safe for democracy—American-style of course—and peace for all men. Roosevelt's interest in the European war, and in America's involvement in that war, rose out of a growing envisagement of himself as a Wilson resurrected to meet yet another world crisis. He had given America the New Deal; why not now a New Deal for all the world? Roosevelt seems to have been indifferent when the rumblings of approaching war in Europe began to be heard. Not indifferent, though, to America's interests. These he saw stoutly in the beginning as calling for strict neutrality. So had Wilson through most of 1916. Only when it came to Wilson like a thunderbolt that so crass and repugnant a war as that taking place across the Atlantic was exactly the opportunity sent him by God to vouchsafe himself in the interests of all mankind, did Wilson change—and so very suddenly—from neutrality and isolation to intervention.

Roosevelt, with fewer dramatic pawings of the air and clutchings at his breast, did very much the same between 1939 and the beginning of 1941. That was when he gave his Four Freedoms to the world. Here, he said in effect, are the real and the true objectives of the war now going on in Europe between Great Britain and Nazi Germany. FDR was exactly like his saint, Wilson, in this respect. It simply was not enough that great powers should fight for mere survival, and then military victory, against a dangerous and marauding "guttersnipe" like Hitler. Larger ideals and visions had to come into the picture in order to transfigure mere national interest into a shining crusade for mankind.

It was thus inevitable that Roosevelt would seek his historic meeting with Churchill in August 1941 in Argentia Bay, off Newfoundland. For Roosevelt had another message from heaven to present: the Atlantic Charter. He had had it drafted before he left Washington, but thought to have Churchill, after a long talk, do a fresh draft. The United States was not even in the war at that point, except as noncombatant ally and purveyor of Lend-Lease. But that did not faze Roosevelt. He knew that he was walking in Woodrow Wilson's footsteps when to a surprised Churchill he presented the idea, and indeed most of the details, of a charter that would at once define and elevate this war between Great Britain—and now, by just a couple of months, the Soviet Union—and Hitler's Germany.

The next step, as we have seen, was that of remaking the image of the Soviet Union, even to the point of endowing it magically with religious freedom—the mere thought of which must have nauseated Stalin and the Politburo. Somehow Americans must be shown the light: that is, the overwhelming truth that beneath the Soviet veneer of purges, genocides, and pervasive terror, there lay a different Russia; the Russia that had been captured by Joseph Davies in his *Mission to Moscow* and the Hollywood producers in their movie of the book—a movie that FDR loved to see repeatedly in the White House. This was a Russia in which men like Stalin and Molotov resembled America's own Founding Fathers; it was a Russia, deep down, of equality, social justice, and fraternity.

Everything followed of course from this master perception which had been generated in FDR's mind by Harry Hopkins' fateful visit to Moscow in the late summer of 1941. It was after Hopkins' return to the White House with his glowing report that things began to move, almost like events in a drama: the frenetic speeding up of Russian relief; the easy inclusion of the Soviets in the Atlantic Charter; the obsessive desire for private meetings with Stalin; Teheran and its massive gifts by FDR to Stalin; the volunteering of a third of the Italian navy to Stalin; acceptance of Stalin's ANVIL strategy; the occupation of Berlin by the Russians alone; everything. We must not forget unconditional surrender, another divine message, just like the Four Freedoms and the Atlantic Charter, as far as Roosevelt was concerned. With it the peace process could be hygienically postponed until the war was

over and the peacemakers, under FDR's stern gaze, could work from reason and justice, with all mankind the object of deliberation rather than sordid "spheres of influence" and other products of the imperialistic past. Also the doctrine of unconditional surrender would be a nice screen for FDR's rather primitive knowledge of geopolitics. That such a doctrine was detested by almost all military strategists and that it cut the ground from under the brave resistance movements in enemy territory mattered not to Roosevelt.[51]

Roosevelt's ignorance of not only the political geography of the world but also the peoples of the world was vast. His life had not made possible the kind of knowledge that was mere routine in Churchill's and even Stalin's *modus operandi*. Roosevelt confessed to Frances Perkins one day that while he knew "good" Italians and Frenchmen from "bad" ones, he was not sure about Russians. This, the reader must be advised, was spoken after he had come back from Teheran, where, as we know, he had quite literally given away the store to the Russians. FDR asked Miss Perkins if she would help him out by taking special note in her ordinary reading of any characterizations of the Russian people.[52]

But such confessed ignorance of Russians did not hinder Roosevelt's open-mouthed appreciation of the Soviets and their consecration to the good society. He told the Secretary that there was an "almost mystical devotion" in the Soviet leaders' attitude toward their people. "They all seem really to want to do what is good for their society instead of wanting to do for themselves. We take care of ourselves and think about the welfare of the people afterward."[53] If that particular piety were not still alive and well in American liberal thought, we could stop a moment and marvel at it in Roosevelt.

There was simply no restraining Roosevelt when it came to the Russians. At Yalta, according to the Alanbrooke diaries, he declared: "Of one thing I am certain, Stalin is not an imperialist."[54] In the strict Marxian sense, Stalin of course was not. But that bit of Marxist writ surely was not in Roosevelt's mind when he spoke. The question is, what *was* in it? He had, as we have seen, an uncanny ability to overlook Soviet annexations and depredations in Eastern Europe, once the tide of war had changed and the Germans were retreating westward, all the while he was ever-censorious about British and French protectiveness of their dependencies.

Once Roosevelt confronted Churchill in person about his and Britain's imperialism. "Winston, this is something you are not able to understand. You have 400 years of acquisitive instinct in your blood, and you just don't understand how a country might not want to acquire land somewhere if they can get it. A new period has opened in the world's history and you will have to adjust to it.[55]

Here we have the very essence of Roosevelt's envisagement of the war. It was a war against Hitler, of course; but it was something a great deal more in Roosevelt's strange mind. It was a war, in the main, against something that European countries—with Britain in the ignoble vanguard—had practiced for too long: imperialism and with it colonialism. Roosevelt might, just might, have seen the greater enemy as totalitarianism, as Churchill had ever since the Bolshevik Revolution. After all, FDR had the evil common denominator between the Soviets and the Nazis before his very eyes. But he was prevented by his peculiar idols of the mind from seeing it.

In all his performance during World War II, there is little evidence that Roosevelt ever reached an understanding of either the totalitarian state or the profound role of communism in the creation and development of this novel form of political order. Churchill may have lacked a full understanding of the totalitarian process, but with his usual instinctive genius he had recognized Bolshevism as a new type of despotism and the natural enemy of democracy and civilization in the West. He lauded the White Russian armies, and he sought with every means he had to give them the fullest possible support. And he relaxed his personal war on communism only when, as he saw it, its equally evil twin, nazism, came on the scene and became, by the middle 1930s, the more pressing enemy of the West.

Roosevelt was totally unable to see nazism as a creed drawn from an almost identical worship of collectivist power and Hitler as a demagogue who had unabashedly learned from Lenin and Leninism. For Roosevelt the Soviets had a "mystical" devotion to the commonweal. He liked that. The Nazis, however, in the President's weird mind, were really recrudescences of German imperialists like Bismarck, Treitschke, and Moltke. They were really, sad to say, like the British and French imperialists, only somewhat more militaristic.

He called General Patrick Hurley to him on one occasion. He wanted Hurley to hear him out on the evil of imperialism, no matter what its national color, and particularly on British imperialism. And he then wanted Hurley to take those Rooseveltian insights and expand them into a report on the subject. Hurley was something of a laughingstock, "half uniform, half buffoon," some said, but Roosevelt had immense confidence in him. We learn from Kimball, editor of the *Correspondence,* that Hurley was an agent of the Sinclair Oil Company and actively seeking oil concessions in Iran. But this did not bother Hurley, or Roosevelt either, assuming he was aware of it. Hurley furnished the President with a report, using Iran as his ideal-type of the imperialist victim of the Britains and Frances.

"We are approaching the irrepressible conflict between world-wide imperialism and world-wide democracy," declared the General. He added that British imperialism was being defended with the blood "of soldiers of the most democratic nation on earth," the United States. "Britain," he announced, "can be sustained as a first class power, but to warrant support from the American people she must accept the principles of liberty and democracy and discard the principles of oppressive imperialism."

On the other hand, declared Hurley, "Soviet Russia has earned for herself an assured place as a first class world power. Friendship and cooperation between the United States and the U.S.S.R. are essential to peace and harmony in the postwar world." Moreover, "Soviet prestige has benefited from their own well-ordered conduct and by their direct and positive relations with the Iranians."

Roosevelt sent a copy of the full Hurley report to Churchill on February 29, 1944, indicating that "I rather like his general approach." Poor Churchill. Two months passed before he could bring himself to reply to Roosevelt. "The General seems to have some ideas about British imperialism which I confess made me rub my eyes. He makes out that there is an irrepressible conflict between imperialism and democracy. I make bold, however, to suggest that British imperialism has spread, and is spreading, democracy more widely than any other system of government since the beginning of time."[56]

If someone had attempted to tell Roosevelt that the kind of aristocrats and monarchs he feared were the prime prey of the totalitarians, Communist or Nazi, that the very essence of the total state was its accolades to the "people," "masses," "workers," and "democracy" and, all the while, the extermination of aristocratic imperialists of the old mold, the President would surely have called the Secret Service for protection from such a madman. Or he would have telephoned Stalin to give him the flavor of the joke.

Roosevelt's sense of what the true enemy of the world was corresponded perfectly with Woodrow Wilson's in World War I: in a word, capitalist imperialism. He was therefore largely insensitive to the massive change in the world represented by the rise of totalitarianism, first in Russia, then Italy, Germany, and in time many other states. As Roosevelt had indicated to Stalin at Teheran, much to Charles Bohlen's dismay and incredulity, the Russian Revolution was one of the masses, one from the bottom up, not top down. At bottom the Bolshevik was a populist, a friend of the common man, a worker for justice.

Hence Roosevelt's virtual blindness to the horror of the Soviet massacre at Katyn Forest, to the Warsaw rising—betrayed by the Soviets—, to the brutal Sovietization of Romania and the Baltic states even before the war had ended, to Stalin's and Molotov's cynical, doubtless amused, double-crossing of their Polish guarantees at Yalta, and the equally cynical exploitation of FDR's United Nations organization.

But hence also FDR's instantaneous sensitivity to British and French acts of "imperialism," to Britain's failure to liberate all India as a war measure, to Churchill's bold and prescient assumption of command in Greece at Christmas 1944. That act so bothered Roosevelt, so tore at his Wilsonian conscience, that in the spring of 1945, at a time when the great and overriding problem was the Soviets' riding roughshod, brutally and terroristically, over Eastern Europe, he proposed a high-level commission, one with Trade Minister Mikoyan of the Soviet Union a prominent member, to visit and advise Greece immediately on its economic future. That, Roosevelt observed, "might have a constructive effect on world opinion at this time."[57] As it happened, at this same time Churchill was pleading with Roosevelt to set up a high-level commission to go to Poland immediately to report on the already corrupted elections taking place. Roosevelt thought it better, however, to settle for "low-level observers already there."[58]

Twice Roosevelt mentioned to Stalin, once in Churchill's hearing, the importance of the two of them meeting to reach a decision about the future of Hong Kong. India of course loomed up in FDR's mind as the very showpiece of British imperialism. He urged several times to Churchill that Britain give India its independence immediately. Once he sent a report by Chiang Kai Shek, of all people, urging this course. Churchill had to inform Roosevelt that the Congress Party in India represented only high caste Hindus, mostly intellectuals; it did not represent untouchables, Sikhs, Moslems, and the subjects of the royal states. Moreover, the Indian army, a million strong, was largely Moslem.[59]

Soviet political power fascinated Roosevelt. The attribute that seems to have interested him along with what he saw as the Communist devotion to society, was its unmediated, direct, and highly personal character. He once spoke half humorously, half-enviously of the favored position Stalin had by virtue of the absence of Congress to interfere and hinder. To Stettinius he said: "Woodrow Wilson said we are making the world safe for democracy; but can democracy make the world safe for it?"[60]

A nice question. But Roosevelt knew the answer. He had learned it during his second term, when the New Deal had suffered not only increased opposition from Congress but also irremediable setbacks by the Supreme Court. His effort to pack the Court—necessarily by congressional action—failed, and Roosevelt came face to face with the monumental obstacle the American Constitution is to eruptions of Caesarian or Napoleonic power. He had no difficulty in recalling Wilson's lamentable experience with the Senate over the League and the loss of the League to America. But Wilson had made the mistake of going it alone; and, with the presence of Stalin on the world scene, Roosevelt did not have to. Wheeler-Bennett writes:

> President Roosevelt's ambition was to establish the United Nations but to superimpose upon it an American-Soviet alliance which should dominate world affairs to the detriment of Britain and France, and to this end he made copious concessions to Marshal Stalin.[61]

Here too, in a way, FDR was taking Wilson as guide. Wilson had had no true or potentially true ally. He was left with only Britain, France, and Italy as his partners in the making of the new world. And Wilson had from the beginning of the whole war distrusted the motives of the Allied governments. It is of Wilson that Devlin writes here:

> Indeed he never lost his distrust of Allied motives. . . . The Allies did not, he believed, genuinely care about democracy and the right to self-government. He did; and he could proclaim his faith as they had not truly and sincerely done. In his mind it was then, and not before, that the war to rid the world of tyranny and injustice really began. What America touched, she made holy.[62]

Wilson had had no Stalin; Roosevelt did. Not a perfect partner, to be sure: crude and excessive in uses of power, cruel, too quick to seize and subjugate, but not an imperialist. If, as Hurley said, the future was to be a race between imperialism and democracy, then it would be better to settle for Stalin; unlike Churchill, the very epitome of imperialism, Stalin could be in time educated to the niceties of world democracy.

In the end Roosevelt succeeded only in starting another war: the Cold War. Not that Stalin would not have started it one way or another under any circumstances short of total defeat by Germany. Of course he would. The dynamic of Leninism was as strong in his veins as Trotsky's—only stated differently. But it was Roosevelt's abject courtship of Stalin that awoke the buds of war and revolution in the West, temporarily dormant under the demands of Hitler's war against the Soviets. It was, let us grant immediately, Wilsonian idealism that Roosevelt believed he was serving; Stalin was only an instrument to be played upon. But no one can doubt that in the way it came out, Roosevelt was the instrument and Stalin the player.

Roosevelt believed and said that by showering kindness and generosity upon Stalin he could get Stalin to work with him in the postwar years for good things. Kindness does sometimes turn away wrath. But in political history—state to state—it is more likely to turn *on* wrath, or such related emotions as hate and covetousness, more especially if there is a philosophy of history held by the recipient of kindness that foretells the necessary destruction of the benefactor.

Roosevelt triggered Stalin's exploitative reaction and his Cold War against the United States and Britain, even while the war against the Nazis was at full tide, in almost exactly the same way that Neville Chamberlain triggered Hitler's invasion of Poland and the start of World War II. Chamberlain too had said in effect that although others had dismally failed in the attempt, he could handle Hitler. That was just after Munich. Hitler had not incorrectly interpreted Chamberlain's affability and manner of accommodation as signs of weakness. Teheran was in a sense Stalin's Munich, as Munich was Hitler's Teheran. The two despots had the identical experience of seeing for the first time clearly and brilliantly just how weak and divided their enemies were. Perhaps Stalin needed nothing more than the repellent spectacle of Roosevelt's humiliating Churchill to cause him to declare war—cold war, but war—on the West immediately. Certainly it was Teheran, not the later Yalta, that was the setting of the beginning of the Cold War.

Roosevelt left two powerful legacies. They are as visible to those who condemn them as to those who love and follow them. The first is domestic: the legacy of the New Deal. The history of the American economic and political order during the past fifty years is the history of a constantly expanding New Deal with its native attributes of bureaucracy, collectivism, and centralization.

The second is the double standard so many Americans use when they look out at the world and judge its diverse political orders.[63] One standard is used for traditionalist, authoritarian, and friendly states such as South Viet Nam, South Korea, and South Africa. The Roosevelt legacy directs us to be relentless in our castigation of these "corrupt," "decadent," and "tyrannous" orders. It does not, must not, matter that they are often vital military bases for us. Perish the bases rather than our standard of judgment—drawn directly from Never-Land. The other half of the double standard is of course what we apply to the Soviet Union—or to Communist totalitarianism in Cambodia, Cuba, Nicaragua. Here there is no corruption, no decadence, no exploitative capitalism, no class system, and no ethnic or racial tensions. Here, the Roosevelt-born idyll continues; there is a good deal of power to be found; but it is applied to people "who seem really to want to do what is good for their society instead of wanting to do for themselves," to apply Roosevelt on Russia to Cuba, Nicaragua, Cambodia *et al.*

Moreover, the Soviet Union is "progressive," on the track of history, rather than "reactionary." It has broken clean of the ancient aristocracies and the modern capitalist rulers. Its power may seem harsh on occasion, but it is a "clean" power compared with that wielded by a Syngman Rhee or a Marcos; and from Soviet, unlike "reactionary," power, democracy will grow like grass—in time, if we are patient. The reason is perhaps the "almost mystical devotion" the Pol Pots, Castros, and Ortegas—not to forget the Lenins—havetoward their peoples.

The farce begun March 18, 1942, goes on and on.

NOTES

[34] Wheeler-Bennett, pp. 178, 181, 184.

[35] *Correspondence.* Roosevelt to Churchill, August 26, 1944.

[36] *Ibid.* Churchill to Roosevelt, August 23, 1944; Roosevelt to Churchill, August 28, 1944.

[37] Michael Howard, *The Mediterranean Strategy in the Second World War* (London, 1968) is the definitive study.

[38] *Correspondence.* Roosevelt to Churchill, June 10, and Churchill to Roosevelt, June 11, 1944.

[39] Sir Arthur Bryant, *Triumph in the West: Based on the Diaries of Lord Alanbrooke* (New York, 1959), pp. 64-65.

[40] Wheeler-Bennett, p. 290.

[41] *Correspondence.* Churchill to Roosevelt, July 1, 1944.

[42] Cited by Eubank, p. 442.

[43] Churchill, *Triumph and Tragedy* (Boston, 1952), p. 96; Mark Clark, *Calculated Risk* (New York, 1950), pp. 348-49.

[44] Stephen E. Ambrose, *Eisenhower and Berlin, 1945* (New York, 1967), p. 30.

[45] Ambrose, p. 92.

[46] *Correspondence.* Churchill to Roosevelt, April 5, 1945.

[47] Sir John Colville, "How the West Lost the Peace in 1945," *Commentary,* September 1985, pp. 43-44.

[48] *Ibid.,* p. 44.

[49] Cited by Wheeler-Bennett, p. 298.

[50] Harriman, p. 444.

[51] Kennan, pp. 366-67.

[52] Frances Perkins, p. 87.

[53] *Ibid.*

[54] Bryant, p. 304.

[55] Edward R. Stettinius, *Diaries* (New York, 1975), p. 40.

[56] *Correspondence.* Roosevelt to Churchill, February 29, 1944, Churchill to Roosevelt, May 21, 1944.

[57] *Ibid.* Roosevelt to Churchill, March 21, 1945.

[58] *Ibid.* Churchill to Roosevelt, March 8 and Roosevelt to Churchill, March 11, 1945.

[59] *Ibid.* Roosevelt to Churchill, July 29, 1942 and Churchill to Roosevelt, July 30, 1942.

[60] Cited by Dallek, p. 606 n.

[61] Wheeler-Bennett, p. 8.

[62] Patrick Devlin, *Too Proud to Fight: Woodrow Wilson's Neutrality* (London, 1975), p. 686.

[63] No one has written more eloquently on this double standard than Ambassador Jeane Kirkpatrick. See her *Dictatorships and Double Standards* (New York, 1982).

John Duffy (essay date 1987)

SOURCE: "Franklin Roosevelt: Ambiguous Symbol for Disabled Americans," in *The Midwest Quarterly*, Vol. XXIX, No. 1, Autumn, 1987, pp. 113-35.

[*In the following essay, Duffy maintains that Roosevelt was not an advocate for disabled Americans, calling this a myth perpetuated by Roosevelt's biographers.*]

President Franklin D. Roosevelt provides an ambiguous symbol for disabled people. In spite of his work on behalf of Warm Springs, the rehabilitation institute in Georgia he helped to found, Roosevelt, by his failure to act to reduce physical barriers, retarded the social and economic progress of his fellow disabled Americans. Instead of assisting disabled people to overcome the physical barriers and consequently the social prejudices they faced, he hid the reality of his disability and presented himself to the public as a man who was recovering from or who had recovered from an illness, a myth perpetuated by his biographers.

When Roosevelt took office, the nation faced an economic depression affecting all Americans, including the disabled. The Roosevelt administration promised to take action to help all Americans in their efforts to overcome the barriers to their economic and social well-being. Roosevelt, because of his special knowledge of the problems faced by disabled Americans, combined with his powers as President of the United States, was in an unique position to enable disabled Americans to share in the progress which his government helped other Americans to achieve. He failed to use that knowledge and power to benefit other handicapped Americans.

What manner of man was Roosevelt? He is given credit, and justly so, for the establishment of a major rehabilitation and treatment center at Warm Springs. He was properly proud of his role as "doctor" Roosevelt when Warm Springs was being established. Theo Lippman, in *The Squire of Warm Springs,* describes how Roosevelt used his position to promote the treatment and research done at Warm Springs. At Warm Springs there was an "FDR Special Fund" to help the needy. Most of the others distributed the funds, but sometimes he ordered that certain disabled people be helped. Some disabled people did not have to go through the admissions office or be placed on a waiting list. The stories of political favoritism surrounding the funds and Roosevelt's actions were probably exaggerated. It is true Roosevelt's work on behalf of Warm Springs aided some handicapped people.

Roosevelt presented himself to the public as a man who had recovered from an illness, arguing that what was done in his case could be done for others. At Rochester,

New York, on October 22, 1928, FDR said he was interested in the care of disabled children. He went on to say he was a good example of what could be done. He was on his feet because of proper care. What private wealth did for him, state funds could do for others, and the cost of restoring cripples to useful roles would be comparatively cheap. Rexford Tugwell, in *The Democratic Roosevelt,* while noting FDR's use of humor to deal with rumors about his health, argues also that Roosevelt made his speech at Rochester on October 22 to promote the extension of welfare services for the disabled. Theo Lippman, in *The Squire of Warm Springs,* takes a different view. The point of FDR's speech at Rochester, Lippman argues, was to present himself as a "recovered cripple." FDR continued to promote that image after he became governor, saying that society has a moral obligation to help cripples, and it was wasteful to allow them to remain unproductive.

Roosevelt also expressed the contradictory view that private, not public funds, should be used to deal with the handicapped. In a speech to the Banker's Club on June 4, 1929, inviting its members to contribute to his pet project, Warm Springs, he said there were 50,000 cripples in New York. Very few of them, he continued, received adequate medical treatment. He did not intend that the state do a great deal about it; it was not a governmental function. Neither the state nor the national government could look after the needs of the nation's 350,000 cripples. It had to be done by private charity, but the state would make a complete census and would investigate the possibility of developing spas.

Both as private citizen and public official, Roosevelt had to deal with functional problems—problems of disabled people, particularly people in wheelchairs—such as transportation and access to and within buildings. In his private life he learned quickly about some of the difficulties of moving about. His wealth and social position enabled him to overcome many problems, including those of transportation and access. The lack of mobility made household duties cumbersome. Many such duties were handled for him by a secretary, Missy LeHand. When FDR was staying at Val-Kil Cottage, he crawled along the sand to exercise when no one was watching. When he was exercising with Dr. McDonald, FDR had to crawl along the sand to go to the outhouse, and when he needed to use the bathroom, his son helped him. Frank Freidel reports that FDR was not able to walk up the many steps to his law office at 52 Wall Street in New York City, and he did not want to be carried in public; furthermore, he could get up the single step at the Fidelity and Deposit Company, his business office, only with difficulty, and he arranged to be whisked unobtrusively in and out of the building in a wheelchair after falling in the lobby on his crutches. His wealth and social position enabled him to avoid the humiliation of being carried into one building and enabled him to get help to enter the other. FDR's home in Hyde Park was equipped with an elevator and internal ramps to enable him to use a wheelchair. When FDR purchased a boat in Florida, he knew he needed a boat so designed that he could crawl back on deck from his fishing skiff. He also needed a boat in which he did not have to go down a ladder to reach the cabin. In addition to owning a boat which enabled him to exercise and swim in warm water, FDR, when he was at Warm Springs, had Tim Bradshaw, a blacksmith, equip his model T Ford with levers and pulleys so he could drive around Warm Springs. Almon Jones, who helped make much of the special equipment used by President Roosevelt, confirms that Roosevelt also had his 1938 Ford equipped with hand controls.

Governor Roosevelt was helped with many of the functional problems in public life. His lunch was brought to him because it was hard for a cripple to go to lunch. There was an elevator in the governor's Executive Mansion, which was fortunate because Eleanor assigned him a bedroom on the second floor. After Roosevelt became Governor of New York, Earl Miller, Al Smith's former bodyguard, became a state trooper and aide to Roosevelt. Miller lifted Roosevelt into and out of places where he could not lift himself. When Governor Roosevelt visited some of New York's state prisons, mental institutions, and hospitals, Eleanor entered the facilities to inspect them because it was difficult for FDR to do so.

When FDR became President, he frequently used the wheelchair for short distances on specially constructed permanent and portable ramps. For inaugurations he drove to the Capitol and went under the main stairway to the Rotunda. At the Rotunda door, the ramps enabled him to be pushed to the elevator which took him to the office of the Sergeant-at-Arms for the Senate. He waited there until the preparations for the inaugural were complete. Then he went to the inauguration stand in a wheelchair with a board wall marking the passageway to the Rotunda. At the last door, he rose from his chair and walked the 35 feet to the inaugural stand. In addition to the elevator in the Capitol, there was one in the White House—a small, squeaky one—which FDR first used to go to his second floor study to swear in his Cabinet.

FDR regularly used his wheelchair at the White House. The second floor of the White House is cut by a large east-wall hall with steps at the higher eastern end. A ramp with a rubber mat was made for the President's wheelchair. His valet pushed him in an armless wheelchair from the bedroom to the Oval Office where the President swung himself into an office chair to work. For his radio talks, FDR was wheeled to his doctor's office where his throat was sprayed, and then he was pushed to the Oval Office to give his speech. FDR was pushed to his pool when he wanted to use it. After using it, he was lifted into his wheelchair. At the end of the day, at about 6 in the evening, the President was wheeled to Dr. McIntire's office for his sinus checkups.

Early in his presidency, FDR approved plans for the expansion of the Executive Office. FDR told Eric Augler, the architect, he needed the room because he was disabled. In public FDR said the White House needed to be renovated to meet governmental requirements. He assured the public that the artistry of the Founding Fathers would be retained.

The Secret Service helped FDR with many of his functional problems. They built chutes to enable FDR to leave the White House in case of fire. When FDR went to vote, as he did in 1942, Secret Service agents carried FDR up the steps of the election hall. Then FDR stood in his braces and walked into the hall to vote. When he had to enter a car, FDR turned his back to it. He was then lifted by Secret Service men into the jump seat, and then he pulled himself into a rear seat. The procedure was performed so easily that thousands of people never realized his condition.

When FDR travelled, special aids, as well as manual assistance, were provided for him. Elevators were built into the President's special railroad car. Jones states, in a letter to the author, that he helped to construct "a series of railings throughout the President's railroad Pullman car which was named the Ferdinand Magellan. These railings allowed the President to swing himself about and to travel throughout the car. This car was, from all outward appearances a standard Pullman car. . . . " In fact,

> The President was most sensitive about public information concerning his disability and would allow no photographs to be made of him while he was being transported or loaded or in any way assisted. For that reason, we constructed an elevator on the rear of the train car which would allow the President to be loaded onto the train in his wheelchair very rapidly. The elevator was equipped with sensors that would detect the top platform and the corner platform and shut off the elevator lift mechanism so as to bring the President to a level position either at the top or bottom of the elevator. All of this equipment, when it was constructed, had to be made so that a person casually seeing the train in passing would not note any difference between it and another standard Pullman car. So these items of assistance had to be constructed in somewhat of a camouflage manner.

On his way to board *Amberjack II,* a Presidential yacht, in June 1933, Roosevelt came by train from Washington, D.C. to New Haven. To accommodate the Presidential party, the fence and gates separating the track from the Rotunda were taken down. The doors connecting the station and the Rotunda were removed, making an opening from the street to the waiting room. In an isolated part of the station, the President was put in a black car. After the Democratic National Convention in 1944, special ramps were put on the cruiser *Baltimore,* docked at San Diego, so the President could be pushed on board and go from the deck to the captain's quarters while enroute to Hawaii. FDR used a ramp and assistance to go from the *Potomac* to the *Augusta* in August, 1941, and during the Atlantic Charter Conference, FDR saw as much of the *Prince of Wales* as possible from a wheelchair. The Presidential Plane had a folding electric elevator between the outside skin and the floor for FDR's use, and when he took extended sea voyages, the ship was equipped with special elevators between at least two decks.

Roosevelt experienced both failure and success in dealing with problems of access and transportation. The failures and frustrations he faced are common to all people similarly disabled. His successes, however, were due largely to his high social and economic position. He did not have to go to a law or business office. He had hand controls on his car at least 20 years before they became available to the general public. He was able to obtain all kinds of personal assistance to move about. He had special devices built for his use when he needed them to deal with a functional problem.

Roosevelt must have known that many of these same aids could have helped thousands, if not millions, of disabled Americans. There is no evidence that he acted upon that knowledge. In fact, he hid knowledge about advances in technology for the disabled from them. One of the most common types of wheelchairs in use at that time was of rigid wood and wicker construction. Roosevelt had created for his own use, according to Jones, a collapsible, portable wheelchair made of stainless steel and leather.

It is true that if he had been candid about his disability at the beginning of his career, he would probably have had no career. In a series of letters to his friend Louis Wehle, Roosevelt made it clear that being seen with a disability would be fatal to anyone's political aspirations. But even after he became President, he failed to act directly or through subordinates to change the public view of disability or sponsor legislation to help remove physical and functional barriers which were, and still largely are, preventing the vast majority of disabled Americans from leading creative and productive lives.

Roosevelt and his alterego, Louis M. Howe, hid the reality and manipulated the image of the former's condition to enable FDR to obtain and retain political office. In 1912, when FDR experienced a bout with typhoid fever, Howe presented him to the public as a selfless public servant working from his sick bed against his doctor's orders. When FDR contracted polio in 1921, Howe at first said nothing, then said FDR was recovering from an illness, and finally admitted he had polio but stated FDR would experience no lasting injury. When Howe realized FDR was not going to recover soon, he laid down the rule that FDR was not to be carried in public. If FDR were to be seen as an invalid, it would ruin his political prospects. By joining various organizations, FDR kept his name before the public in the 20s. Eleanor served the same purpose, and she also kept the public from knowing about his disability. In his correspondence, FDR described his condition as one which was improving. He only permitted his condition to be seen under controlled positive conditions, avoiding any situation where the severity or permanence of his disability would become a matter of public knowledge. When running for public office, he campaigned hard and obtained the cooperation of the press in order to present himself to the public as a vigorous and healthy man—which he was—while, at the same time, hiding his disability. Once in office, he continued to be careful of his public image, presenting himself as a "recovered cripple," and he used a variety of special aids—some of which he had used as a wealthy private citizen—to deal with his functional problems.

During his lifetime, Roosevelt became a positive symbol for disabled Americans both because of his work for Warm Springs and his image as a "recovered cripple." Disabled Americans, like other Americans, did not know the full story. Even after his death, Roosevelt remains a positive symbol for disabled Americans because both they and nondisabled Americans still do not believe how well Howe and Roosevelt deceived them.

When Howe released the story that FDR had polio but would not be permanently injured, he defined FDR's condition either intentionally or accidently, in effect, as an illness rather than a disability. This public perception of FDR's condition was a boon to both Howe and Roosevelt because they both proceeded to describe Roosevelt's condition as an ailment from which he appeared to be recovering or had recovered rather than as a disability, which is a condition that results in a permanent impairment or loss of an important human function, or is a condition wherein one is perceived to have a permanently injured or lost function. It is true that Roosevelt's condition began as a disease but when he was presenting his condition to the public it was no longer a disease. The disease had run its course. It was a disability but he could not define it as such so he described it as an illness.

Howe's action had another important consequence. The vast majority of FDR's biographers make no distinction between illness and disability; they use the terms interchangeably, and they accept the view, which I do not, that FDR was concerned about the public perception of his health. Certainly questions about his condition were posed in terms of health, but I believe he and Howe defined the question in those terms so that is how the public and his biographers saw the question. A man regaining his health or who has recovered from an illness presents an acceptable public image; a cripple does not.

FDR and Howe defined the former's condition in terms of health in order to hide his disability. Even those biographers who make a distinction between illness and disability fail to realize the significance of that distinction. Theo Lippman was the first of FDR's biographers to write that FDR hid his disability, which, according to Lippman, Roosevelt did to dispel public concern about his health. I believe Lippman's view is wrong.

Several of Roosevelt's biographers argue he overcame his illness by means of the power of his spirit. Eleanor Roosevelt, in *My Days,* writes that FDR did not have a soft philosophy because he recovered from invalidism to physical strength and activity. Mrs. Roosevelt knew and admitted her husband did not recover complete use of his legs; clearly she means FDR spiritually overcame his illness and returned to active life. Frances Perkins puts the matter directly in *The Roosevelt I Knew.* She writes that FDR was spiritually transformed by his battle with pain.

Modern scholars do not accept the unprovable metaphysical explanation for FDR's success. They argue he did not do a great deal of reading or writing and that his political and economic views had been shaped and developed by his political experiences during the Wilson era. Elliott Roosevelt and James Brough characterize as a myth the idea that polio changed his character. He did not identify himself with other cripples as one might expect if his views had become more democratic. James Roosevelt, who was a young man when his father contracted polio and who accompanied him on many of his political trips, also writes in *My Parents* that his father's disability did not alter his character.

James M. Burns provides a more detailed analysis in *The Lion and the Fox.* He describes as a legend the view that polio transformed FDR into a more humane person. The qualities he needed to overcome polio were already within him. At best it gave him an opportunity to strengthen those qualities. Polio did not, for example, give him patience. He had already acquired that ability while maneuvering and battling with the politicians of Tammany Hall and New York State. He was already cocky and brought that optimism to his fight against polio. His progressivism was formed in the Wilson period. He never considered retiring from politics both because he was a man not given to meditation and because he was enjoying the political game. His condition had one important advantage: it allowed him to avoid political campaigning until Smith requested his help in 1928, although Howe did not want him to run even then. The 20s were bad times for Democrats.

Frank Freidel, in *The Ordeal,* believes polio increased Roosevelt's power of self-control and made it easier for FDR to make decisions. Roosevelt did not worry about things he could not change. Freidel believes the delay imposed by the disability afforded Roosevelt the opportunity to play the role of distant elder statesman, keeping on friendly terms with all sections of the party, until he was ready to play a more active political role.

John Gunther, viewing *Roosevelt in Retrospect,* states FDR developed his upper body to compensate for the weakness in his legs. In a fit of perverse logic, Gunther argues FDR's illness made him healthy and robust. Alfred Rollins, in *Roosevelt and Howe,* succinctly describes the few advantages Roosevelt acquired by contracting polio. The disability removed him from close public association with Democratic party failures. His illness did not affect his ideas but did influence the timing of his career.

The idea that FDR was spiritually transformed by his illness is, I believe, a dubious view. FDR's sons (James and Elliott), who were closely associated with Roosevelt's political campaigns, particularly the early ones, deny the

reality of such a transformation. Many modern scholars have severely criticized the idea, but they, as the preceding discussion on the views of Gunther and Rollins indicates, still confuse the terms "illness" and "disability." If the terms are interchangeable—and they are not—modern scholars do not explain how FDR could have been disabled yet could have recovered from his illness. They regard Roosevelt, in Lippman's phrase, as a "recovered cripple."

Louis Wehle, a friend and biographer of Roosevelt, who had long been interested in his political career, asked Ray Howard of the Scripps-Howard newspaper chain to counteract the rumors about FDR's health which were circulating during FDR's first campaign for the governorship of New York. The New York *World Telegram* published several articles about FDR's condition. Yet the rumors persisted. Wehle arranged for an interview to be given to Kents Speed of the New York *Sun* to enable him to write about FDR's health. FDR talked to Speed while the former was in his wheelchair. Under a headline describing FDR as "Roosevelt, Titan of Energy, Runs Multifarious Enterprises," the Speed article referred to a "list of activities he's heading [which] reads like a business directory—requiring use of legs by exercises," and finally, it mentioned FDR was "Built Like a Harvard Guard."

Kenneth Davis, in *FDR,* refers to FDR as ill and states that, as soon as everyone knew of the gravity of the illness, Howe became concerned about the effect of public awareness on Roosevelt's career. Davis relates Howe released stories saying FDR was ill but would recover. He notes that no mention was made in these stories of polio or paralysis, but he fails to make anything of the fact.

James Burns, in *The Lion and the Fox,* takes a curiously ambiguous view of Roosevelt's condition. He argues Roosevelt deceived himself into thinking a cure was possible, which he sought for seven years before finally admitting he would never walk again. Yet Burns also sees FDR's condition as one of illness. He notes that after FDR decided to run for Governor of New York in 1928, Republicans charged the crippled FDR was being sacrificed for Smith's benefit. FDR stated he would continue Smith's programs, but he knew his best reply to Republican charges was a vigorous campaign by train and by car. He kidded people about the hard campaign he was conducting, saying it was too bad a sick man must campaign so hard. Burns also notes that FDR instructed his staff not to send out any mail that mentioned disability or health during the 1932 Presidential campaign. FDR wanted, Burns reports, to conduct a vigorous campaign in order to attack Hoover, show his physical vitality, and crush the whispering campaign against his health. Burns does not question Roosevelt's presentation of his problem as one of health.

Frank Freidel accepts Roosevelt's presentation of his condition as one of illness. Freidel notes without adverse comment that the novelist Thomas Wolfe reflected the view of many of Roosevelt's contemporaries in *Of Time and the River* that his illness ended his career. He would not get better. His disease forced him to retire. In order to counteract such a view, FDR liked to appear well in public. Freidel notes that a Republican paper called Roosevelt the Boy Scout of Democracy, which pleased FDR because it would not have written about him if it had thought he was terribly ill. Freidel mentions two letters in which FDR told friends he was improving, and Freidel notes also that FDR told the same thing to James Cox, his former Presidential running mate.

During the Coolidge Presidency, FDR sought to advance the party and his own interests. He believed he could do that by helping Smith. During this period, he kept telling people what he would do when he could walk without braces. He told people he planned to resume an active political role in the future, but he avoided the nomination because he would be forced to take sides on controversial issues. He would, Freidel notes, also lose the immunity from attack and the glamour provided by illness. FDR said he could not run then, but his legs would be in such great shape within two years that he would be able to walk without braces. He went on to state he preferred executive work to being a member of an uninteresting social club. Howe told FDR to make the party delegates believe he was still too ill to run for political office for two more years. "Look pale, worn, and weak," Howe advised Roosevelt.

Freidel fails to note what a curious condition FDR had. He was improving when he made public statements, but in order to avoid a nomination to an office where it would be difficult to hide his disability, he became suddenly ill again. Howe and Roosevelt were willing to manipulate the image of his health in any fashion which would promote his political prospects and hide his disability.

In 1928 FDR conducted a vigorous campaign for Governor and displayed a masterful use of humor to counteract the image of invalidism. He said in a speech in Yonkers that if he were able to campaign for a year he could throw away his canes. Republicans who had been portraying FDR as dangerously ill changed their tactics for fear of arousing public sympathy for him. He told the press he was not in condition to run for Governor, but he was counting on his friends to walk into the Governor's chair. On his upstate tours, FDR created an image of himself as vigorous and healthy by standing erect in locked braces in his cars, often causing his audiences to laugh and inviting them to look at him and decide about his health. But Freidel notes that FDR sought primarily to keep his audiences' attention on issues other than his condition.

Theo Lippman, in *The Squire of Warm Springs,* takes a different view from that of FDR's other biographers, who believed Roosevelt was trying to respond to Republican charges directly by means of hard campaigning and humor. Lippman believes FDR's humor was designed to distract people from the fact that he could not walk because he was worried about public knowledge of his health. He was not concerned about it in private. Indeed,

he was playful about being carried in private, but when he ran for Governor of New York in 1928, Roosevelt drafted a reply to Republican doubts about his health in which he admitted to having a disability which he believed would go away. He never used that reply. Lippman also points out FDR went beyond trying to distract people about his health. In order to dispel public concern about his health, FDR hid his crippled legs. A healthy man who cannot walk, cannot lead, but he who is unhealthy and can walk can give confidence.

Roosevelt portrayed himself as recovering or recovered while hiding from public view any evidence of a permanent disability. Lippman argues he hid the disability to silence public concern about his health, but Lippman's account makes it clear Roosevelt declined to clarify the distinction between the terms. Roosevelt knew he was fine. Even before engaging in vigorous campaigns for the governorship, he had led an active life, traveling to Florida and Georgia. As long as the public believed his condition was an illness, he could persuade them he was improving or was in good health, but a disability is a permanent condition which presents an image of helplessness. Lippman's point that a healthy man who cannot walk cannot lead is true only if he is seen as disabled. Disability, not health, is the real problem. Lippman's other point, that an unhealthy man can give confidence, is at least paradoxical if not contradictory. If a person is unhealthy, he will have to recover if he is going to inspire confidence for any appreciable length of time.

In *Triumph Over Disability,* a work written in 1981, Richard Goldberg presents the same old points. He argues polio changed FDR and helped him to become President. The onset of polio, Goldberg believes, was a time of spiritual struggle for Roosevelt. According to Goldberg, FDR had paralytic polio, an incurable disease, and Louis Howe was sick and suffering from chronic bronchial asthma. To say both men had the named conditions is true. To say both men were ill is ridiculous in view of their long and active careers.

The evidence that FDR had a disability, not a disease, is to be found in Goldberg's own work. Roosevelt had his last visit with Dr. Lovett between May and June of 1923. At that time, his condition was characterized as follows: his arms are normal; his face and neck are normal; his bladder, bowel, and sexual functions are normal; his back is normal; his abdominal muscles range from poor to fair; he is paralyzed from the waist down; he has poor ability to bend from the hip; there is a loss of motion in his right quadriceps and none in his left; there is no hamstring motion; and there is no toe motion. To meet these problems, FDR developed new functional techniques. As Almon Jones states:

> Much of what we were involved with was preserving the illusion that the President did have some function in his lower extremities. It may be noted that the President was often seen to be walking with his son, Elliott. They were always arm in arm

with Elliott giving support to the President. In order for the President to do this, he used a walking stick and had a specially designed set of stainless steel braces which were made by me and were of all-welded construction. Because he lacked control over his ankle joint I made them spring loaded so that he would not drag his foot as it was swinging through stride. The spring loaded braces did give the impression of function by flexing the foot and making it appear that the President had some flexion function in his ankle joint.

There is another interesting apparatus which we designed and contracted for the President and that was the platform from which he spoke in the rear of the train. As I said, we were involved in creating illusions and we constructed the microphone stand such that when the President came to speak, a post-like saddle was slid out from under the microphone stand and a harness-type arrangement was quickly clipped into either side of the microphone platform, thus giving the illusion that the President was standing. He would be able to move from the left and right and lean to give emphatic statements, all the while, sitting astride this saddle and tied to the microphone platform with a harness.

Goldberg, like FDR's other biographers, states FDR gave the impression of being well, but he describes FDR's political activity at this time—inaccurately I believe—as nothing more than a facade. But his polio gave him a chance to become acquainted with other sufferers and to broaden his awareness of other social problems, a point not accepted by Roosevelt's major biographers. Despite the fact that FDR liked to give the appearance of being well or on the road to recovery, it was Dr. Draper's opinion that Roosevelt had achieved the limit of his recovery in the summer of 1923, and he informed Dr. Lovett in February 1924 he believed that FDR would make no further appreciable progress. What is strange is that in spite of the clinical evidence and the medical opinion that FDR's condition was a permanent disability, capable of improvement only by retraining of other muscles to take over the functions of the damaged ones, Goldberg still accepts without question FDR's opinion expressed in 1928 that he believed he could learn to walk without canes or crutches.

Hugh Gregory Gallagher's recent work entitled *FDR's Splendid Deception* contributes little of value to this topic. Gallagher re-states information already known from other sources, such as the pains the Secret Service took to hide Roosevelt's disability and the voluntary silence of the newspapers. Gallagher argues that FDR changed the way Americans viewed the handicapped, but Gallagher does not say how Roosevelt accomplished that while keeping his disability hidden. He makes no attempt to clarify the difference between illness and disability. Gallagher refers to Roosevelt as one who was "confined to a wheelchair" and as a "polio." The use of such prejudicial language by one who, because of his disability ought to know better, destroys what little value the book

may have for someone unfamiliar with Roosevelt. In my view the book presents Roosevelt not as a human being who dealt successfully with his handicap but as an object, a condition, a cause for pity. Gallagher reinforces some of the worst myths about disability and in doing so damns all disabled people.

As I have mentioned before, it would have been fatal to Roosevelt's political ambition to have been perceived as permanently disabled. Yet, even after he obtained the Presidency, he still did not use his power and special knowledge to benefit the disabled. He could not have proposed such comprehensive legislation as the Rehabilitation Act of 1973, which forbids discrimination in federally funded programs. Such legislation could only have been advocated in an age concerned with civil rights. But he might have proposed legislation to eliminate physical and functional barriers that prevented persons with disabilities from using public housing, public buildings, trains and buses.

Roosevelt's administration was pragmatic. It was open to new ideas and new programs. That was a chief reason for his success, yet he was not open to change for disabled people. Imagine how much the problem of accessibility to and within buildings could have been reduced or eliminated if work on the problem had begun in the Roosevelt presidency instead of only in the last decade. President Roosevelt had a special elevator which lifted him on and off his train. Imagine how much more accessible public transportation would be if Roosevelt had either directly or indirectly obtained passage of legislation mandating that similar devices be installed on all buses and trains. Roosevelt did not support directly or indirectly the passage of progressive legislation in either instance. Nor did he attempt privately to influence members of the business community to advocate or adopt such changes for humanitarian reasons. Had such legislation passed, Roosevelt would have made it possible for persons with disabilities to participate more fully in the life of the nation. That would have enabled citizens with disabilities and citizens without disabilities to know each other better. That fact would not have done away with social and economic inequalities, nor would it have eliminated prejudice. It would have made it possible for greater progress towards ending these evils.

Roosevelt could have done all this without endangering his position. He could have acted indirectly through friends and supporters. It was the age of radio, and no member of the public could see his disability, but they could be charmed by the power of his voice to support the improvement of disabled people. By the time he gained the presidency, Roosevelt had the press in his pocket at least where this subject was concerned. In fact, after the first presidential election not even the Republican opponents made an issue of his condition until the rumors about his fading health at the time of the 1944 elections. Even if he had directly advocated legislation of the kind that I suggested, I believe he would have run no risks. One does not have to belong to a special group to advocate legislation that would benefit them. Consider the case of U.S. Senator Lowell Weicker of Connecticut. He is undoubtedly the foremost legislative champion of the rights of persons with disabilities. Today no one calls him a cripple or questions his health. If Roosevelt had done the same he would have run the same risk—none. If he was asked why he supported such legislation, he could have said with perfect candor that it was because of his previous experience with the problems faced by people who have polio.

From all that has been said before, it is, I believe, clear that Roosevelt had knowledge and power that he could have used during his Presidency to benefit the disabled. He used that power only to benefit Warm Springs. While President, he never attempted either directly or indirectly to promote legislation to benefit citizens with disabilities or to use his private influence to assist them. His failure to do so means that the disabled community is living in a society which is full of physical barriers instead of living in a society which is largely free of them. If he had acted, we would be living with greater understanding and less prejudice between citizens with disabilities and those without them.

It may be argued that Roosevelt should not be blamed for his failure to act because the legislation might not have received congressional approval and his voice in public or in private might have gone unheeded. That seems improbable considering the many legislative accomplishments of his presidency and his personal charm in private conversation. Yet even if the record indicated that he had attempted it and failed, he could then be justly regarded as a proponent of the rights of disabled citizens. Instead his reputation as a friend of the disabled is based largely on a myth. It is a myth begun by Louis Howe and Roosevelt for the purpose of enabling him to obtain and retain political office. They knew that public knowledge of his permanent disability would be fatal to Roosevelt's political ambition. Roosevelt was presented to the public as one who is recovering or has recovered from an illness—one who has triumphed over his condition. This myth perpetuated by FDR's biographers sustains Roosevelt's reputation as a friend of the disabled. The reality of his actions and his omissions show him to be an ambiguous symbol at best for persons with disabilities.

SELECT BIBLIOGRAPHY

Bellush, Bernard. *Franklin D. Roosevelt as Governor of New York.* New York, 1958.

Bishop, Jim. *FDR's Last Year, April 1944-April 1945.* New York, 1974.

Burns, James. *Roosevelt: The Lion and the Fox.* New York, 1956.

———. *Roosevelt: The Soldier of Freedom.* New York, 1970.

———. *FDR: The Beckoning of Destiny, 1882-1928, A History.* New York, 1972.

Davis, Kenneth. *Invincible Summer: An Intimate Portrait of the Roosevelts Based on the Recollection of Marian Dickerman.* New York, 1974.

Feidel, Frank. *Franklin D. Roosevelt Launching the New Deal.* Boston, 1970.

———. *Franklin D. Roosevelt: The Ordeal.* Boston, 1954.

———. *Franklin Roosevelt: The Triumph.* Boston, 1956.

Gallagher, Hugh. *FDR's Splendid Deception.* New York, 1985.

Goldberg, Richard. *The Making of Franklin D. Roosevelt: Triumph Over Disability.* Cambridge, Massachusetts, 1981.

Gunther, John. *Roosevelt in Retrospect: A Profile of History.* New York, 1950.

Lash, Joseph. *Eleanor and Franklin: The Story of Their Relationship Based on Eleanor Roosevelt's Private Diaries.* New York, 1971.

Lippman, Theo. *The Squire of Warm Springs: FDR in Georgia, 1924-1945.* Chicago, 1977.

Looker, Erol. *This Man Roosevelt.* New York, 1932.

Perkins, Frances. *The Roosevelt I Knew.* New York, 1945.

Reilly, Michael. *Reilly of the White House.* New York, 1947.

Rollins, Alfred. *Roosevelt and Howe.* New York, 1962.

Roosevelt, Eleanor. *My Days.* New York, 1938.

Roosevelt, Elliott and James Brogh. *A Rendezvous with Destiny: The Roosevelts of the White House.* New York, 1975.

———. *An Untold Story: The Roosevelts of Hyde Park.* New York, 1973.

Roosevelt, James. *My Parents: A Differing View.* Chicago, 1976.

———. *Franklin D. Roosevelt on Conservation, 1911-1945.* Compiled and edited by Edgar B. Nixon. Vol. I. General Services Administration, National Archives and Record Services, Franklin D. Roosevelt Library. Hyde Park, 1957.

Rosenman, Samuel. *Working With Roosevelt.* New York, 1952.

Schlesinger, Arthur, Jr. *The Crisis of the Old Order.* Boston, 1957.

Sherwood, Robert. *Roosevelt and Hopkins: An Intimate History.* New York, 1948.

Smith, A. Merriman. *Thank You Mr. President: A White House Notebook.* New York, 1946.

Starling, Edmond and Thomas Sugone. *Starling of the White House: The Story of the Man Whose Secret Service Detail Guarded Five Presidents From Woodrow Wilson to Franklin Roosevelt as told to Thomas Sugone.* New York, 1946.

Tugwell, Rexford. *The Democratic Roosevelt.* Garden City, New York, 1957.

Wehle, Louis. *Hidden Threads of History: Wilson Through Roosevelt.* New York, 1963.

Richard P. Adelstein (essay date 1991)

SOURCE: "'The Nation as an Economic Unit': Keynes, Roosevelt, and the Managerial Ideal," in *The Journal of American History,* Vol. 78, No. 1, June, 1991, pp. 160-87.

[*In the following essay, Adelstein studies Roosevelt's economic policy during the Great Depression in view of John Maynard Keynes's economic theory and American managerialism of the twentieth century.*]

In a penetrating essay written in 1979, Robert Skidelsky directed attention to the political dimension of John Maynard Keynes's achievement and located its historical significance in the fundamental tension between this century's two great paradigms of social organization—"Freedom" and "Planning."[1] The Great Depression, he argued, starkly exposed the vulnerability of the industrial democracies to impersonal market forces, producing unemployment and misery that challenged the legitimacy of democratic political institutions. To many who were drawn to the radical solutions of planners of both the Right and the Left, it seemed that the West's economic agony would yield only to a thoroughgoing reconstruction of its political order; if Adolf Hitler would preserve capitalism by destroying liberty and democracy, then Joseph Stalin premised the achievement of democracy on the destruction of liberty and capitalism. But if the friends of freedom shrank from these extremes, they remained paralyzed by the apparent incompatibility of effective measures to end the distress with the preservation of traditional liberties that the vast majority still cherished.

It is in this context that Skidelsky measures Keynes's greatness. Aware that improvement in economic technique was the only alternative to political change whose consequences he despised, Keynes so defined the economic problem that its solution required neither the substantial diminution of personal liberty nor a reordering of the property relationships at the foundation of democratic capitalism. He thus postponed the day of reckoning between freedom and planning by offering a technical solution to the political problem, a solution that promised not only economic stability but also the preservation of both the price mechanism and the institutions of liberal democracy. But with the Keynesian consensus now in tatters, Skidelsky argued, in a world of new economic problems that urgently pose the old alternatives of freedom and planning, "we return to the original question. Can we look once more to an improvement in economic technique to solve the political problem? Or must we rely on political and social change to solve the economic problem?"[2]

Skidelsky's thoughtful assessment is grounded in the intellectual and political history of Keynes's own Britain, though its claim that Keynes helped "save" capitalism in its hour of greatest crisis reflects a view widely shared on both sides of the Atlantic. My purpose is to propose an alternative interpretation that not only draws on Skidelsky's useful, if rather apocalyptic, dichotomy of freedom and planning but also captures more closely the meaning of *The General Theory of Employment, Interest, and Money* for the history of ideas and institutions in the United States. I shall argue that the significance of Keynes's work for this country lies in his creation of a practical tool for welding the powers of the national state to the maturing ideology of managerial control, a pragmatic collectivism that had by 1930 become the principal manifestation of planning in American life. Like its collectivist counterparts in Europe, American *managerialism* vigorously asserted the primacy of an abstract, reified collective against the philosophical and political claims of living men and women. But to this it added a distinctive commitment to social engineering—the conscious, scientifically informed control of complex social processes and outcomes in the service of a collectively defined purpose.[3] By 1900, this managerial ideology had been firmly rooted in the private sector by new technologies of production and distribution and the innovative forms of business organization that integrated them into the American economy. Deeply impressed by the success of the huge new corporations in harnessing the labors of thousands and turning them to the achievement of a single purpose, American managerialists sought for half a century to extend the ideal of managerial control to the larger political economy, to achieve an effective merger of state and economy based on scientific principles of administration employed in the public interest.[4] But their efforts were frustrated by their continuing inability, even in the midst of the depression, to articulate a sufficiently clear and politically acceptable conception of national purpose, short of total war, toward which the techniques of management science might be directed.

It was precisely this definition of collective purpose, cast in compelling economic terms and divorced from the terrors of war, that *The General Theory* provided. Far from postponing the decision between freedom and planning, Keynes offered Americans the means to realize the managerial ideal of peaceful social engineering by defining a single, aggregated variable that could plausibly be identified with the public interest and manipulated by the state through the techniques of economic science. During the Great War itself, the almost universal subscription of the American people to the objective of victory and their readiness to subordinate individual interests to it had proved sufficient to support a regime of national economic planning. But after 1918, the efforts of such men as Herbert Hoover to build on the experience of the war and to turn a rationally organized economy to the pursuit of prosperity—in Hoover's phrase, "to synchronize socially and economically this gigantic machine that we have built out of applied science"—failed because of the rapid evaporation of the lubricating consensus and cooperation on which the success of wartime planning had been based.[5]

Now the "national income" defined by Keynes could become the object of conscious national policy, and the "nation" itself an "economic unit" whose collective interest could be persuasively articulated and pursued without the presence of war or the suffocating hand of coercive central planning looming over it. Still, a second world war was required before the Keynesian experiment could be initiated, and not just for the pervasive spirit of national unity and willingness to sacrifice for an easily perceived common interest that it fostered. The war itself, and not daring and imaginative statecraft, produced a national government with sufficient powers to tax and spend to perform effectively in the role Keynes assigned to it—a truth whose implications for both the political culture and the economic organization of the United States in our own time we have not yet fully understood or appreciated. It need not have been this way. The opportunity to create such a state without war, to reconstruct the federal bargain so as to make the sustained pursuit of Keynesian policy possible in peace, was surely there to be seized in 1933. Only the will to do so was missing.[6]

Instead, President Franklin D. Roosevelt, committed by inclination to the organic collectivism of the managerialists and by his own National Industrial Recovery Act (NIRA) to their vision of economic coordination and social harmony through central planning, consciously rejected the political economy of Keynes in favor of an attempt at deep structural reform of the American economy. Swayed by the potent but essentially false analogy of the depression to the Great War, he sought to re-create the spirit of national unity and common purpose of the war years by declaring war on the depression itself, and to use that unity to support a vast and potentially dangerous planning mechanism. But Roosevelt was no tyrant. He intuitively grasped the fundamental problem of central planning in a free society—how to imbue the people with a spirit of common purpose sufficiently powerful to win their submission to the ends of the planners and their consent to the intrusive control of day-to-day economic affairs that planning must entail. To solve it, he built a formidable planning machine, put the force of law behind it, and then tried to preserve the fragile unity he had created by standing above the policy battle, by with-holding his personal support and prestige from any

overall strategy or agenda of specific choices and offering instead his own personality as the unifying focus of the planning effort. To construct a managerialist state that was never needed, he devoted his considerable energies in the 1930s to a bruising but ultimately successful effort to use the model of total war to establish the constitutional basis for national economic planning in peacetime. In choosing to fight a constitutional revolution for the power to plan rather than another, far less radical and institutionally rending campaign that, under the same banner of national authority, would have transferred to the federal government the fiscal powers that the Framers had originally placed in the states, Roosevelt spurned the Keynesian promise of a true macroeconomics of peace and, in that crucial moment, turned his country to planning the macroeconomics of war.

The corporation is not a person, but an abstraction, a form of organization. Its essence is the intricate set of relationships between its owners, managers, and employees, and not those men and women themselves. Each of these people comes to the corporation with unique capacities and a distinctive welter of motives. But none can achieve their purposes without the cooperation of the others. This mutuality of dependence induces each to abide by various rules of conduct so that the others can predict his behavior in specific situations and adapt their own to it. The resulting order is a contract, based on consent, that regulates the behavior of participants by rules governing specified activities associated with the production of goods. But not all production contracts embody the combination of limited liability and legal independence characteristic of the corporation, and only in the corporation does the law grant legal personality to the coordinating abstraction itself, a continuous existence independent of the identity or interests of any of its temporal human constituents. Breathing life into a real but intangible social order that living men and women use to pursue their diverse purposes in the common enterprise of production, the law transforms their contract into a "corporate person," endowed with rights and interests of its own and guaranteed the protection of the Constitution, just as if it too were a living man or woman.[7]

As limited liability and technological breakthrough produced industrial combinations of unprecedented size and power in the nineteenth century, the reification of the corporation took on increasing significance. The logic of growth demanded the conscious planning and administration of entire domains of economic life, and managers in large firms increasingly assumed the tasks of coordination that were once performed spontaneously by the market. The necessary administrative talent was supplied at first almost entirely by engineers, who brought to the construction and management of business organizations the same confident intellectual style they had applied so successfully to the design of bridges and dynamos, and their approach complemented and reinforced the emerging legal ideology of corporate personality. They saw the firm as a machine, its operation manifesting the purposes of its designer, its parts constrained to move in concert at the command of a single will. The raw materials might be different, but the objective of control was the same. The task of the engineer was to manipulate stone and metal according to the laws of physical science in the interests of men; the task of the manager was to manipulate men according to the laws of social science in the interests of the corporation.[8]

The problem inherent in such a view stems from the purposive nature of the engineer's task, which is necessarily directed toward the achievement of specific ends that the engineer must know before he or she undertakes the job of design. The attempt to ascribe specific interests or purposes to forms of organization posed a hard question for the proponents of the new human engineering. Before the emergence of the great corporations, the "interests" of business enterprises were never an issue; partnerships and proprietorships were simply legal devices through which easily identifiable individuals pursued their own interests in the marketplace.[9] But if managers were to serve the interests of the new corporate person with the emerging techniques of industrial administration, they first had to know what those interests were. In their earliest days, the corporations, like the small businesses on which they fed, projected the personalities of their creators. What the Carnegie Company "wanted" or "needed" was nothing more or less than what Andrew Carnegie wanted or needed. But the corporations' newly won legal personality ensured that they would survive their creators to be run by anonymous managers committed to the ideal of scientific administration. By 1901 the Carnegie Company had become the United States Steel Corporation, its shares dispersed among thousands of stockholders and effective control of the firm severed from its ownership. With the tangled, personal motives of an Andrew Carnegie no longer at stake, toward what end was that control to be directed?

In its most general form, this central question would confront all forms of economic planning, public and private, in the age of concentration just then beginning. Where the interests of a thousand relatively autonomous working people had once been mediated by the spontaneous forces of an impersonal, disinterested market, with flexible prices directing the resources controlled by each toward the uses most highly valued by the others, order in the corporation had to be created by command instead. But with individual interests now subordinated to those of the corporation, what end would this visible hand serve? Was there a collective purpose sufficiently compelling to turn independent artisans and tradesmen into reliable employees, to induce them to trade their freedom of action and the autonomy of their interests for the rigorous hierarchical discipline necessary to organize production at the scale required by the new technologies?

The answer was profits. The more there were, the more could be distributed to owners, managers, and workers alike, so it could plausibly be said that larger profits served the interests of all the corporation's constituents. Less obvious but equally significant was the ease with

which profits could be visualized and, with increasingly sophisticated techniques of cost accounting, quantified.[10] Reducing the myriad ends of an organization's constituents to the maximization of a single number offered a perfect complement to the engineer's metaphor and a natural basis for both a theory of the firm and an applied science of management modeled on Newtonian mechanics. Theorists would now conflate the peculiarities of human knowledge and experience, the idiosyncrasies of machines, and the subtle value of long-term relationships between colleagues performing specialized tasks—all the qualitative dimensions of working life that give context to the activity of production and influence its organization—into an abstract "production function" that turned faceless, perfectly substitutable "inputs" into equally homogeneous "outputs." The firm, its parts moving in harmony toward the single, unifying objective of maximum profit, could become at once the object and the instrument of control, a fictitious personality of concentrated purpose through which the behavior of real men and women could be disciplined.

In the late nineteenth century, the new values epitomized by the ideal of managerial control found their way into American politics. Before the Civil War, political order was generally understood in Lockean terms; legitimate authority was the product of an agreement between free individuals whose validity, like that of any other contract, depended on the continuing consent of those it bound. The state itself had neither life nor purpose of its own. Instead, like the older forms of business association, it was simply an organizational device to be used by individuals for the promotion of their own welfare, its limited powers, indeed its very existence, conditioned on the prior existence and autonomy of its subjects. Now this view too came increasingly under attack. Led by such thinkers as Lester Ward, Herbert Croly, and John B. Clark, American managerialists began to conceive of social and political order much as the law was coming to see the corporation. Society became an "organism," a concrete, living entity whose existence preceded that of individuals and whose welfare gave meaning to their lives. The purposes and interests of this living collective were entirely its own, distinct from those of its human constituents and superior to them in the arena of politics. The American managerialists, strongly influenced by the "social physics" of Auguste Comte and Henri de Saint-Simon and the idealistic statism of Georg W. F. Hegel and the German historicists, saw the democratic state as the voice and active agent of the social being in the world of affairs. The democratic state must express the interests of the collective and be given pervasive powers to direct individual behavior and manipulate social outcomes to promote them.[11]

The new, empirical social sciences and the techniques of control derived from them would show the way. Once the laws that governed modern civilization were understood, humankind could turn them to the collective good, "precisely," wrote Ward, as people had "taken advantage of the physical forces of nature." Politics could be separated from administration; while the former concerned itself with articulating the common good, the latter could draw upon neutral theories of management science to bring it about.[12] Still, the obstacles along the way to this American utopia were formidable. The intrinsic collectivism of the managerial vision met with strong resistance in an individualistic culture still deeply distrustful of central government. An equally pervasive hatred of monopoly and concentrated economic power led to the Sherman Act of 1890 and bespoke a widespread uneasiness with the apparently inexorable advance of large-scale organization.[13] But the ideal of scientific administration in the interest of society posed a still more basic issue, the solution to the planner's problem in the public sphere. What *was* the collective purpose that could weld individuals together and whose expression could be the object of politics? What, that is, was the public analogue to corporate profits, the end to which the technique of the state's human engineers would be applied?

Some reformers, such as Walter Weyl, were deeply impressed by the productive capacity of the United States economy and sought an answer in the pursuit of material prosperity. Here, they believed, was a uniquely American source of solidarity, one that could both bring the people together and finance their common action through the state. But to contemporary eyes, the contradictions in such a view were obvious; the origins of prosperity, the reigning theory made clear, lay in the state's benevolent passivity toward the natural rhythms of economic life. The state that nourished the creation of wealth by its inactivity could scarcely manipulate its human creators to this very end. Something else was required, and as the effects of a war in which tightly organized industrialized societies hurled themselves en masse against one another drew closer to home, more and more Americans began to see participation as a way of extending the ideals of democracy and self-determination to a weary and reactionary Europe. The nation, Croly argued in supporting Woodrow Wilson's preparedness program in the summer of 1916, "needs the tonic of a serious moral adventure." In a crusade for peace and democracy, John Dewey wrote the following year, America would come of age at last, finding her cultural independence from Europe in the discovery of "a national mind, a will as to what to be."[14] Both Dewey and Croly recognized the dangers of the venomous pursuit of "disloyalty" and national purity total war would unleash but, in the face of this terrible solution to the planner's dilemma, repressed their doubts. For them, the sense of community and national purpose created by the war was a major justification for fighting it, and while they could offer no practical way to restrain the irrational underside of the popular mood, they remained hopeful that proper leadership could preserve the impulse to unity once the war was over and direct it toward peace and reform. Events seemed to give cause for optimism as increasingly effective techniques of coordination and control were devised and refined. With the elevation of Bernard Baruch to the chair of a now-strengthened War Industries Board in March 1918 and the passage of the Overman Act in May 1918, the power

to plan industrial production and distribution passed for the first time to a single, centralized federal organization.[15]

Industrial production climbed, distribution became more efficient, the war itself was won, and all this with property still nominally in private hands. Engineers, economists, and management scientists stood for an exhilarating moment at the center of an administered economic system devoted to the achievement of a clearly defined public purpose, certain that they had glimpsed the future. But, although what a bitter Randolph Bourne called the "herd instinct" persisted in red scares and extended immigration restrictions, the more rational elements of the wartime mood soon evaporated, taking with them the popular support they had engendered for the government's managerial apparatus.[16]

Still, the experience of planning left a deep impression on the planners and their allies in the disciplines of engineering and social science. Wesley Mitchell could speak with authority for both groups. Author of a pathbreaking treatise on business cycles that stressed the statistical analysis of quantitative evidence, Mitchell had worked in the Planning and Statistics Division of the War Industries Board and helped lead the unsuccessful effort to institutionalize a similar agency in the executive branch after the war. The war, he said in 1918, had shown that statistics were an essential ingredient in intelligent social and economic planning for the postwar years. But if their potential was to be realized, the social sciences must emulate the objective, mathematically precise methods of physical science and engineering. Mitchell harbored no doubts as to what these methods were to achieve. "In economics as in other sciences," he wrote six years later, "we desire knowledge mainly as an instrument of control. Control means the alluring possibility of shaping the evolution of economic life to fit the developing purposes of our race. It is this possibility, of which we catch fleeting glimpses in our sanguine moments, that grips us."[17]

The engineers who had participated in the planning enterprise, led by the universally admired Hoover, were gripped by the same dream. Elected president of the new Federated American Engineering Societies in 1920, Hoover began to articulate a vision of economic stability and prosperity based on rational management within individual firms and linkage between firms through associations for the exchange of information and coordination of production decisions. As secretary of commerce after March 1921, he moved decisively to build an integrated, scientifically administered system of cooperative private management with the indirect support of the federal government. Hoover, like Weyl, saw permanent prosperity and a resulting social reconciliation as the unifying public purposes toward which the disciplines of the engineer could be applied. But though he joined Mitchell and his professional allies in their successful assault on the theory of laissez-faire that had trapped Weyl in contradiction, he could never bring himself to accept the political corollary of the new economics, his enthusiasm tempered by opposition to outright federal control and a corresponding reliance on the voluntary cooperation of an enlightened private sector in achieving stable prosperity. He would encourage the proponents of the new science to design an economic machine capable of serving the public purpose and use the state to help build it. Yet he would deny the state the power to define that purpose clearly and leave control of the machine itself in private hands. This attempt to reconcile the economics of a new century with the politics of the old was the hallmark of his public life, and in the crisis of the depression, its contradictions were his ruin.[18]

These stresses were apparent in both of Hoover's major policy initiatives at Commerce. The first, a commitment to the collection and publication of data on costs, prices, outputs, and inventories throughout the economy, would not only assist the invisible hand by disseminating essential information to both large and small firms but contribute to stability as well by offering a sound basis for business planning and a psychological ballast of fact to prevent uncertainty and panic. During the war, the federal government, with the power to command information from firms and fix prices and outputs for its own well-defined ends, had been able to enforce a similar cooperation without the abuse traditionally associated with cartels. But Hoover shared the people's distaste for state-sponsored cartels without war, consistently and courageously resisting the efforts of corporate managers to secure a revision of the antitrust laws that would allow them to enforce private price and output agreements in the style of German cartels. But without rigged markets and oligopoly profits, how was cooperation with the state's information brokerage to be secured?[19]

Hoover's answer was to throw the government's support behind the controversial network of private trade associations catalyzed by the war economy of 1917 and 1918. Businessmen were quick to see that the war had created a vocabulary that could justify collusive practices once seen as simply pernicious. To this was added a seeming transformation of values, a new professionalism and public-spiritedness among those charged with operating the great concerns. But if the managers' bald attempt at cartelization gave him cause to suspect their motives, Hoover nonetheless placed his confidence in these men, in the values of science and objective rationality they professed and the institutions of voluntary cooperation they seemed to be building. He saw the key to both economic efficiency and social harmony in a "competitive" economy privately organized to suppress "disruptive competition" and administered in the public interest by a professional elite.[20]

The sharp recession that greeted the Harding administration was the inspiration for Hoover's second major initiative at Commerce. Early in 1921, he asked a committee of leading economists and other experts to advise him and the president on the problem, and in September of that year, he convened the President's Conference on Unemployment to consider their recommendations. These were strongly influenced by the ideas of Mitchell, now

research director of the National Bureau of Economic Research (NBER), and Otto T. Mallery of the Pennsylvania State Industrial Board. Like Hoover, Mitchell and Mallery believed that studies like one just completed by Mitchell at the NBER made it possible to estimate the maladjustments and distortions created by the business cycle, and that informed, active cooperation between business and government could tame the business cycle. The policy the conference endorsed was Mallery's. In 1919, he had colorfully described the rippling multiplier effect on income and employment of expenditures on public works. Now, he and the conference proposed that governments at all levels set aside a portion of the normal volume of spending on public works as a reserve for use during periods of distress. Since state and local government accounted for over 75 percent of all public spending and 90 percent of that devoted to construction, Washington could hardly take the lead in this regard. But it could exhort the other echelons of government, encouraging spending at low points in the cycle and urging restraint at its peaks.[21]

More important, the federal government might alert firms to the crucial role they could play in achieving economic stability. Hoover saw clearly that mass production required mass consumption, that ordinary people had to be able to buy the goods pouring out of the factories, so he consistently preached the gospel of high wages, not as a matter of abstract justice or even of industrial peace, but as a practical measure to ensure the adequacy of demand. Throughout the decade, he advocated the creation of several voluntary stabilizing mechanisms in the private sector, including unemployment insurance, wage maintenance, export management, and construction reserves. The sustained period of rising real income, stable prices, and nearly full employment that followed seemed to vindicate his ideas, and the affluence of the New Era cast a warm glow on his visible leadership of the associational economy and carried him to the White House in 1929. But when the cycle turned once again, its catastrophic virulence exposed the fragility of the edifice Hoover had helped build. His calls for voluntary unemployment insurance and similar stabilizers had largely gone unheeded, and as the slump deepened, large firms could not hold the line on wages despite massive layoffs and cutbacks in production. He tried to encourage private investment, but lenders would not lend, nor borrowers borrow. He talked of federal public works, but his heart was not in it, and though he understood that any real solution to the crisis must be based on increasing purchasing power, he led the fight in 1931 to balance the federal budget by raising taxes.[22]

Like the managerialists before him, Hoover was caught in the problem inherent in the idea of human engineering. He believed in managerial control and devoted his public life to cultivating techniques to achieve it. But he could see no public purpose short of war simple enough to mobilize a complex system of authority in a single direction and powerful enough to command the people's assent to it. His solution to the planner's problem relied upon the emergence of a new class of professional managers for whom the pursuit of corporate profit by scientific means was to be a virtue and a public calling. He would use the leverage of the state to encourage a vast, interconnected system of private control and trust its leaders to recognize the public interest and act on it. When they failed him, Herbert Hoover was lost.

It is sometimes said that before *The General Theory,* there was only "economics," but thereafter, "economics" became "microeconomics," joined now by the new "macroeconomics" of Keynes, and since the publication of Paul A. Samuelson's *Economics* in 1948, almost every elementary text used in the United States has presented the subject in just these terms.[23] Microeconomics, students are taught, is concerned generally with how independently defined goods are allocated to various uses and specifically with the role of prices in determining the output and distribution of each good. In this view, competitive markets, systems of pure central planning, and all the variants in between are seen as alternative approaches to the microeconomic problem, differing primarily in the reliance each variant places on prices in solving that problem. Macroeconomics is usually said to deal with relations between "aggregated" variables, such as consumption or investment, so that individual prices (except for interest rates) and the quantities of specific commodities produced and consumed (except for money) assume little importance.

So understood, the adage is certainly true, although the essential components of such a macroeconomics had been put in place by such men as Mitchell, J. A. Hobson, William T. Foster, and Waddill Catchings well before 1930. Still, it was Keynes who put the pieces together by constructing a theory in which the aggregates of income, consumption, and investment were mathematically related to one another and, by simple extension, to government spending and taxation. At the heart of this system lay the national income, which was also the focus of Mitchell's research at NBER. But in Keynes's scheme national income took on a theoretical and practical role it never played in Mitchell's. Where Mitchell had conceived of the national income as a *descriptive statistic,* a measure of the economy's performance at any moment and a signal that action of some sort might be desirable, Keynes allowed it to become a *dependent variable,* an object of policy that could be scientifically predicted and manipulated by the politically neutral technique of the state's economic engineers.[24]

The significance of this achievement becomes clearer if we recast the usual distinction between micro- and macroeconomic styles of thought in terms of the idea of purpose. Now the fault line is the one separating the individual from the collective, and the alternatives it poses encompass both the economic and political dimensions of social life. On one side lie the "micro" systems, competitive markets in the economic sphere and the liberal, limited state of Lockean theory in the political, in which only the purposes of real men and women are

recognized. On the other are "macro" systems, whose characteristic feature is the ascription of purpose and will to abstract forms of organization constructed by the human mind. The corollary of this collectivism is control—the subordination in principle of individual ends and desires to the single purpose of the whole and the creation in practice of corporate, hierarchical systems in which complex social processes can be rationalistically manipulated to achieve that purpose. And if from this new perspective his successors' assertion that Keynes was the first macroeconomist can no longer be sustained, we can nonetheless better appreciate the irony in his own far more important and truthful claim that his work now made it "possible by a right analysis of the problem to cure the disease [unemployment] whilst preserving efficiency and freedom," an irony whose bitterness he soon came to recognize.[25]

Fifty years before, the teleology of profit had given life to the modern corporation as a macroeconomic unit and formed the basis of a new science of management by fusing the interests of owner, manager, and worker into a simple, quantifiable expression of collective purpose. But where the managerialist dream of an analogous macroeconomy on a national scale had seemed possible only under the horrifying conditions of total war, Keynes now offered the hope of economic engineering in the service of peace and prosperity. The Keynesian system, in its exclusive reliance on aggregated variables and its apparent deference to the allocational functions of the price mechanism, separated the idea of economic management in the public interest from the detailed specification of prices and outputs that had always been associated with it and that so many dreaded. The planner's problem was solved by simply eliminating the need for "planning." But in politics as in biology, history makes real only a small part of the possible, and both the personalities and the institutional realities of the critical years between 1932 and 1934 conspired against the Keynesian promise. The ideas themselves were certainly in the air. Yet despite their own rather more sophisticated conceptions of the matter, neither Hoover nor his challenger Franklin D. Roosevelt believed the election of 1932 could be won by a man who did not swear loyalty to the "sound finance" of a balanced budget.[26]

Unlike Hoover, Roosevelt was deeply skeptical of public spending as a solution to the depression and firmly rejected the multiplier theory, the idea that the government's initial expenditure would stimulate its recipients to increase their own spending and thus magnify its effect on national income, as an "illusion of economic magic."[27] But given the enormity of the crisis, the economics of Roosevelt or Hoover, or of Keynes himself, was of little consequence in 1933. For a bit of simple arithmetic makes clear that the idea that the federal government could have done anything at all to end the depression was the real illusion. Measured in billions of 1929 dollars, the national income of the United States, which in 1929 had been $104.4, had fallen by 1933 to $72.7, a loss of $31.7. If we assume a multiplier of three, new public spending of some

$10.6 billion would have been required to restore the income of 1929. But in 1933, *total* federal expenditure on goods and services was $2.6 billion. Thus the federal government would have had to increase spending by over 400 percent to reach the national income of 1929, at a time when almost all the traditional functions of government were performed at the state or local level.[28] Distrustful of central authority and jealous of the prerogatives of the states, the Framers had in 1787 created a federalism in which primary responsibility for the construction and finance of local public works (roads, bridges, waterworks, and later, sewers, power systems, and mass transit) gravitated naturally to the states and municipalities. Presaging Bourne, they envisioned a national government that would come fully into its own only when it declared war. In the crisis of 1933, amid despair and urgent calls for action from all sides, that is precisely what Roosevelt did.

In this he reflected the mood of the nation. Despite his own allusions to a state of national emergency analogous to war, Hoover had to the end resisted deploying the full power of the federal government against the depression as Wilson had against the kaiser. But Hoover had been decisively rejected by a desperate and impatient people ready to experiment with its charter and to explore the potential of a truly national state. The experiences of the Great War were still fresh in the minds of many, and if memories of an ennobling sense of national community seemed sharper than those of malevolent social coercion and tight administrative control, this was only natural. "Why not," asked Gov. Alf Landon of Kansas in February 1933, "give the President the same powers in this bitter peacetime battle as we would give to him in time of war?"[29]

Such was the new president's inclination. "Our Constitution," Roosevelt said in his inaugural address, "is so simple and practical that it is possible always to meet extraordinary needs by changes in emphasis and arrangement without loss of essential form." It would have to be. For now, he said, the nation must move

> as a trained and loyal army willing to sacrifice for the good of a common discipline, because without such discipline, no progress is made, no leadership becomes effective. We are, I know, ready and willing to submit our lives and property to such discipline, because it makes possible a leadership which aims at a larger good. This I propose to offer, pledging that the larger purposes will bind upon us all as a sacred obligation with a unity of duty hitherto evoked only in time of armed strife.

Congress, he hoped, would cooperate in the struggle to come. But if it did not, "I shall ask the Congress for the one remaining instrument to meet the crisis—broad Executive power to wage a war against the emergency, as great as the power that would be given to me if we were in fact invaded by a foreign foe."[30]

Congress proved quite ready to recognize Roosevelt as commander in chief in the war against the depression. In June, over the objections of those who believed it would promote industrial cartels and feared the great increase in governmental power it implied, Congress created the National Recovery Administration (NRA), giving the president sweeping discretion to fix prices, outputs, and working conditions across the economy by establishing codes of "fair competition" with the force of law.[31] Under a single authority, with lines of command drawn even more sharply than those of the War Industries Board that was its model, the NRA conscripted the forces of production and placed them at the disposal of a commander given the maximum flexibility to respond to the situation as he saw it. Helping to speed the National Industrial Recovery Act through the House, Sam Rayburn of Texas expressed the feelings of many: "It is very true that under this bill . . . the President of the United States is made a dictator over industry for the time being, but it is a benign dictatorship. . . . For my part, I am proud to trust him and proud to follow him." Mobilized for war once again, the economy awaited its marching orders.[32]

But the NRA was a planning mechanism without a plan. The drafters of the NIRA, with no clearer idea than anyone else of what to do and hoping through vagueness to mask internal conflicts and encourage experimentation, refused to express any guidelines or objectives for the codes. It thus became an enabling act, placing unprecedented powers in the executive without any stated purpose or limitation on their use. Since the president declined to take command, this meant that whoever got control of the machine would get to define the plan. When the heirs to Hoover's vision of industrial self-regulation came forward with a policy not plainly at odds with the goal of increased purchasing power, they were able to claim the prize. As the professional managers saw it, the problem was competition itself, unscrupulous "chiseling" on prices and wages that drained the pockets of working people and drove honest businessmen to ruin. The remedy, they argued, was cooperation in the establishment of prices and outputs, and if such cooperation could not be secured through the voluntary methods of the 1920s, the present crisis demanded the strong hand of the state to enforce it.[33]

As some saw clearly at the time, a properly applied analogy to war in 1933 might well have brought recovery without (or in spite of) the huge expansion of federal control represented by the NRA.[34] Then as in 1917, the problem was insufficient production, but its source, and thus its solution, differed greatly in the two cases. The entry of the United States into the war meant an avalanche of new orders dropped on an economy already operating close to capacity, which resulted not only in widespread scarcity and dislocation but in a general inflation as well. Left to its own devices, the market might in time have induced the necessary adjustments, but time too was scarce, and the profits that the invisible hand would have distributed would certainly have been unacceptably divisive. The centralized controls of the war years, lubricated by a general willingness to cooperate before a threat everyone could understand, helped reduce the confusion and smooth the transition to war production while preserving the politically essential environment of visible sacrifice and common purpose.

Massive spending, contributing to increased output and employment, and only then, if necessary, central control in the face of scarcity and inflation—this was the line of causation drawn by real war. But the war of 1933 was declared by a president who would not spend and whose strategy was to attack the deflated economy and its demoralized army of unemployed with pervasive economic controls explicitly intended to reduce output and raise prices. Reflecting the thinking of the businessmen at its helm, the NRA sought to expand purchasing power by creating artificial scarcity in the midst of overcapacity, setting minimum prices in some industries and limits on production in others. But it soon became apparent that enforcing scarcity meant putting men out of work, men who then could not pay high prices for scarce goods. By October, the contradictions of its policy had become obvious, and the NRA was increasingly seen by the public as a simple producers' cartel enforced by the government, conspiring to fix prices in the usual way, and for the usual reasons, under the protective wing of the NRA's symbolic Blue Eagle. Neither the symbolism of war nor the resort to intimations of disloyalty could save the NRA in so poisoned an atmosphere, and the nation's first experiment in central planning in times of peace dissolved with the cohesive spirit of war that had given birth to it. With them was lost the unique political opportunity presented by the nation's overwhelming rejection of Herbert Hoover and the readiness of a vast majority to make common cause with a confident new president in his call to arms. Never again in his struggles for recovery and reform would Roosevelt be able to draw upon reserves of unity and cooperation quite so deep.[35]

He had not chosen this course for want of alternatives. As conditions worsened after 1930, and despite their inability to embed their prescriptions in a new, conceptually satisfying theory of the business cycle, professional economists increasingly joined Foster and Catchings in calling for substantial expenditures on public works as a means of restoring purchasing power. In the Congress, Democrats and Republicans had continuously urged public works on a reluctant Hoover, and during the First Hundred Days, Sen. Robert M. LaFollette, Jr., offered a plan that would have appropriated the staggering (and surely unspendable) sum of ten billion borrowed dollars for public works. The gospel had its propagators inside the New Deal as well. In the fluid days of April 1933, as the administration's initial strategy was being formulated, senior officials, including Frances Perkins, Henry Wallace, and George Dern, argued strongly for some variant of LaFollette's proposal. By the summer of 1934, the still more unsettling idea that it was the purposeful creation of public debt itself, and not the new employment directly created by public works, that was the key to solving the depression had found an institutional home in the Federal Reserve under Marriner Eccles, an

unschooled Utah banker and disciple of Foster, and his protégé Lauchlin Currie.[36]

But the most persuasive of the "Keynesians" who had the president's ear was Keynes himself. In an open letter solicited by the *New York Times* and published on December 31, 1933, Keynes candidly expressed his disappointment in the NIRA; it was, he said, "essentially Reform and probably impedes Recovery, [and] has been put across too hastily, in the false guise of being part of the technique of Recovery." Artificial scarcity was not the answer. "The object of recovery is to increase the national output," and insofar as "the volume of output depends on the amount of purchasing power . . . expected to come on the market," the attempt to raise prices by limiting output represented a "serious misapprehension as to the part which prices can play in the technique of recovery. The stimulation of output by increasing aggregate purchasing power is the right way to get prices up; and not the other way round."

> I lay overwhelming emphasis on the increase of national purchasing power resulting from governmental expenditure which is financed by Loans and not by taxing present incomes. Nothing else counts in comparison with this. . . . In the past orthodox finance has regarded a war as the only legitimate excuse for creating employment by governmental expenditure. You, Mr. President . . . are free to engage in the interests of peace and prosperity the technique which hitherto has only been allowed to serve the purposes of war and destruction. . . . Could not the energy and enthusiasm, which launched the NIRA in its early days, be put behind a campaign for accelerating capital expenditures, as wisely chosen as the pressure of circumstances permits?[37]

Roosevelt, to whom a sympathetic Felix Frankfurter had sent a copy of Keynes's letter three weeks before its publication, seemed receptive to its call for public works and deficit spending, though he did cite "a practical limit to what the Government can borrow—especially because the banks are offering passive resistance in most of the large centers." Encouraged, Frankfurter urged Roosevelt to see Keynes during his trip to the United States in June 1934. Keynes, "full of faith that we in the United States would prove to the world that [he had] the answer," saw the president alone at the White House and "delivered himself of a mathematical approach to the problems of national income, public and private expenditure, purchasing power, and the fine points of his formula." Roosevelt was uncomprehending. "I saw your friend Keynes," he told Perkins afterward. "He left a whole rigamarole of figures. He must be a mathematician rather than a political economist."[38]

Frankfurter kept the faith, continuing to urge the Keynesian solution on the president whenever he could. But despite Roosevelt's brief dalliance with the heresy of deficit finance in 1920 (when he and Louis Howe had included in proposals for the Democratic platform an explicit call for countercyclical federal spending financed by "Prosperity Bonds" issued at the discretion of the president), for five full years after his inauguration Roosevelt held fast to the ideal of a balanced budget and remained the chief opponent within the administration of an aggressive program of public works. In the campaign, he had excoriated Hoover for his inability to close the deficit and pledged himself to deep spending cuts to put the government in the black, and once in office, he moved quickly to show his resolve. Within a month, he had signed the Economy Act of 1933 and used it to issue a series of executive orders reducing benefits to veterans. As sentiment for increasing the money supply spread through Congress during the spring, Roosevelt resisted as best he could, confiding to Col. Edward M. House that "it is simply inevitable that we must inflate and though my banker friends will be horrified, I still am seeking an inflation which will not wholly be based on additional government debt." And when congressional enthusiasm for public works forced him to include a provision in the NIRA authorizing the expenditure of $3.3 billion on them over two years, he made sure that control over these funds rested with him rather than Congress, so that by separating the administration of the industrial codes from that of the public works program and entrusting the latter to the "stingy and meticulous" Harold Ickes, he was able to hold actual expenditures to a trickle.[39]

Roosevelt's indifference to public works was not the result of simple conservatism or timidity but rather the consequence of his deep commitment to another, more radical agenda. In speeches at Atlanta in May 1932, at the Commonwealth Club of California in San Francisco in September, and in a radio address to his supporters in business in October, he stressed the interdependence of all sectors in a mature industrial economy and spoke vaguely of the need for planning to ensure "such balance among productive processes as will tend to a stabilization of the structure of business." But if specificity was lacking in his persistent call for a fundamental reconstruction of the American political economy in which cooperation would replace competition under the watchful eye of a government devoted to the good of all, the philosophical root of his vision was clear enough. "Business," he said, "must think less of its own profit and more of the national function it performs. Each unit of it must think of itself as a part of a greater whole; one piece in a large design." Speaking to a convention of bankers in Washington in October 1934, Roosevelt left no doubt as to the agent of this "greater whole":

> You will recognize, I think, that a true function of the head of the Government of the United States is to find among many discordant elements that unity of purpose that is best for the Nation as a whole. This is necessary because government is not merely one of many coordinate groups in the community or the Nation, but government is essentially the outward expression of the unity and the leadership of all groups. . . . Government . . . must be the leader, must be the judge of the conflicting interests of all groups in the community.[40]

Roosevelt had not been driven to this way of thinking by the crisis of the depression. His unapologetic subordination of the interests of the individual to the purposes of "the Nation as a whole" and his identification of the national state as the voice and active hand of this larger entity reflected precisely the organic collectivism at the heart of the managerial ideal. He had made this clear more than twenty years before, in an address to the People's Forum of Troy, New York, on March 3, 1912:

> Conditions of civilization that come with individual freedom are inevitably bound to bring up many questions that mere individual liberty cannot solve. This is to my mind exactly what has happened in the past century. We have acquired new sets of conditions of life that require new theories for their solution. . . . I have called this new theory the struggle for the liberty of the community rather than liberty of the individual. . . . The right of any one individual to work or not as he sees fit, to live to a great extent where and how he sees fit is not sufficient.

We must, he went on, emulate the Germans, who in matters that put the ends of the individual at odds with the needs of the community have "passed beyond the liberty of the individual to do as he pleased with his own property and found it necessary to check this liberty for the benefit of the freedom of the whole people."[41]

It is easy to see why a mere program of public spending on roads and bridges, however substantial, that left the institutional foundations of the American economy otherwise undisturbed would have little appeal to a president deeply skeptical of Keynesian theory and presented with an historic opportunity to experiment with a thoroughgoing reordering of American economic and political life. But if Roosevelt was, as Otis L. Graham, Jr., has argued, an "instinctive collectivist" who by 1932 had come to share "an organic view of society which assumed the need for continuous public intervention to compensate for imbalances," why did he shrink from aggressively using the planning mechanism he had created to achieve the structural reform and redistribution of income that he thought so important? Rather than diffusing the immense potential of the NRA as an instrument of power and refusing to commit his prestige fully to any clearly defined plan, why did he not simply consolidate the agency's authority and turn it over to Rexford Tugwell, a colleague of Mitchell's at Columbia University in the 1920s and surely the one man in the administration who would most faithfully adapt the managerial ideal to the needs of a new age and make the NRA a model of scientific planning in the public interest?[42]

Part of the answer can be traced to the constraints of the economic and political culture of the moment, with its campaign for relaxation of the antitrust laws by the captains of industry and its still widespread, potent hostility to planning in the service of the redistributive ideals that Tugwell would have brought to the NRA. But more, I think, lies in the complex character of the president himself, the juxtaposition of a muted but genuine collectivism that attracted him to the possibilities of reform and the struggle to achieve it and a countervailing genius for ameliorating conflict that drew him from the battle and enabled him not only to manage an administration often at odds with itself but also to unite behind his own cheerful and confident personality a diverse, unruly people among whom consensus on actual policy was impossible. Roosevelt instinctively grasped what Friedrich A. Hayek would make explicit in 1944, that the essence of central planning, and the source of the immense political problem it poses, is its imposition of a single organizing objective on the multitude of individual purposes and desires characteristic of a free society. A mood of genuine solidarity or a sufficiently powerful collective purpose can command the people's consent to the inequalities of treatment and denial of personal interests large-scale planning entails. In their absence, such planning is intrinsically so divisive that any detailed plan must either be inflicted by the state on a sullen population or fail for want of acquiescence to the objectives and direction of the planners.[43]

Roosevelt's invocation of emergency powers without a declaration of war, his unwillingness to commit himself personally to an explicit and consistent strategic plan for the NRA, and his disinclination to bring the full weight of the law to bear in enforcing the codes all suggest his awareness and understanding of this dilemma. As Al Smith had said, an informal doctrine of emergency executive power had indeed been established during the Great War, when Congress had without serious challenge vested unprecedented discretionary authority in the president as commander in chief of the armed forces. But the formal declaration of war against a foreign state made an explicit statement of legislative policy unnecessary. The national interest for which domestic liberties and the separation of powers would temporarily be sacrificed was clear enough, and the existence of an easily perceived threat and its creation of an effective national consensus behind the objective of victory induced both the voluntary submission of most Americans to the rigors of economic planning and a mood that tolerated or encouraged informal social coercion of the rest. In a real war, when penal law *can* be invoked effectively and with broad public support against those who do not conform to the plan, it is not often necessary to employ so blunt an instrument to ensure cooperation. But now, at Roosevelt's request and relying upon his view of the flexibility of the Constitution in the face of an emergency to legitimate the extraordinary peacetime authority of the NRA, Congress once more delegated sweeping powers to the president to use as he saw fit, this time against a foe no one could see and few could understand.

Roosevelt was no despot. He wanted the genuine cooperation of the people in his efforts to "balance" the national economy through central planning, not to dictate to them or to compel their compliance with a plan that, once articulated, could not fail to arouse controversy and dissent, whatever its specifics might be. His experiences in the Navy Department during World War I and in the trade association movement in the 1920s had taught him that planning without coercion was possible only in a general atmosphere of common purpose and voluntary cooperation like that of the war years.[44] But in the war against the depression, where the casualties were everywhere but the enemy invisible and elusive, a common objective was much harder to formulate and far less likely to win the needed universal cooperation without coercion. Unlike Hoover, Roosevelt was prepared to place the federal government at the controls of a vast, rationalistically constructed economic machine. But, if for different reasons than his predecessor, he too shrank from defining the ends to which that machine would be put and tried to solve the planner's problem by rallying the people behind him and relying on the public-spiritedness and professionalism of the self-appointed leaders of the business commonwealth to steer it toward the collective good. If they succeeded in mastering the crisis, there would be credit enough for all to share; if not, the president could dissociate himself from the policy of his own administration and live to fight another day.

> Many good men voted this new charter with misgivings. I do not share these doubts. I had part in the great cooperation of 1917 and 1918 and it is my faith that we can count on our industry once more to join in our general purpose to lift this new threat and to do it without taking any advantage of the public trust which has this day been reposed without stint in the good faith and high purpose of American business. . . . As in the great crisis of the World War, [the NRA] puts a whole people to the simple but vital test:—"Must we go on in many groping, disorganized, separate units to defeat or shall we move as one great team to victory?"[45]

And so, from the beginning, he sought to recall the spirit of voluntary cooperation of the war years, hoping to win it by carefully avoiding commitment to any explicit plan and applying the new instruments of coercion he had created as gently as possible, as if the spirit were already there. For a time, it seemed to work. Gen. Hugh Johnson, the administrator of the codes, had served his apprenticeship at the War Industries Board and displayed a sure hand for the symbolic politics of war. Under the banner of the Blue Eagle, parades were held in cities across the nation, badges of compliance appeared in shop windows everywhere, and businessmen who refused to sign on were, at the general's urging, boycotted and stigmatized as "disloyal." But there was cheating too; from the start, violations of price and output provisions of individual codes appeared here and there, particularly in small businesses on the edge of ruin that were hard put to survive the consequences of artificial scarcity. Those who had made the sacrifices asked of them began to demand discipline of those who had not, a demand that put the NRA's leadership in an impossible position. They had not anticipated the sympathy that violations of the codes by those most vulnerable to them would evoke and were not prepared to risk destroying the fragile consensus they had won by punishing such "chiselers" to the full extent allowed by the NIRA. "Without more enforcement," as Donald Richberg, a leading NRA official, sadly put it, "we would lose the support of those willing to comply. With more enforcement we would increase the number and vigor of our opponents."[46]

It was just this planner's dilemma, brought on by the president's own inapposite analogy of the depression to war, that the Keynesian strategy would have avoided. It too offered a national purpose to legitimate and direct the government's efforts at economic engineering, while leaving the price mechanism largely intact, obviating the need to plan prices and outputs in detail, and preserving the ability of the invisible hand to allocate gains and losses spontaneously, without credit or blame. Keynes appreciated "the advantages of decentralisation and the play of self-interest" and believed that despite "the enlargement of the functions of government" it would require, the cardinal virtue of his macroeconomics lay precisely in its rejection of comprehensive planning and its preservation of the "free play of economic forces" in a context of full employment.[47] But if the attempt at central planning would cause problems a politician as astute as Roosevelt might reasonably have foreseen, in the United States of 1933 Keynes's prescription had still other virtues, both political and constitutional, that even its author did not recognize.

On the political side, the key to those virtues lay in the desperate financial situation of the states and municipalities. Throughout the 1920s, with little assistance from the federal government, state legislatures had responded to rapidly rising public school enrollments and the explosion in automobile ownership by spending heavily on schools and roads; total state expenditures, which had been $400 million in 1913, rose to $1.2 billion in 1921 and to almost $2.1 billion in 1929, with highway and school construction accounting for the bulk of the new spending. But despite a doubling of state tax revenues during the same period, resistance to new taxes often caused income to lag behind expenditures. By the end of the decade, counties and municipalities, which in the 1920s disbursed some 60 percent of all public funds, had accumulated a gross debt of $9 billion, and many state governments were deeply in the red. After 1929, as a steadily rising demand for unemployment relief was added to existing claims on falling tax revenues, the states drew closer to bankruptcy. Hoover's response was an offer of loans and advances on revenues to the states, but those were administered parsimoniously by the Reconstruction Finance Corporation and, given the size of the federal budget, were far too small to stem the tide. The states, unable to print new money, their creditworthiness—like that of their citizens—gravely in doubt, had little choice but to slash spending where they could. The stream of public works, which had flowed so freely in the prosperity of the New Era, was now shut down almost completely.[48]

Here was an opportunity for the new president both to attack the slump and to recast the traditional relationship between Washington and the states to make the fiscal power of the federal government commensurate with the national scope of the emergency. To be sure, the opposition to such an attempt to rewrite the federal bargain, generated on both the elevated level of constitutional theory and the more common ground of practical politics, would have been formidable indeed. But for so sensitive a political intelligence as Roosevelt's, there were clear signs that this opposition could have been overcome.[49] And in fact, even an aggressive federal program of public works would have interfered far less with the procedures and day-to-day operations of state government than the experiment in central planning actually did. Concerned that the interstate commerce limitations of the NIRA would enable small firms to evade the codes, General Johnson organized a staff of federal agents to monitor compliance in the field and, in an effort to extend the reach of federal authority that aroused much political resentment, urged the states to legislate "little NRAs" to prosecute code violators in the state courts.[50] Land reclamation projects and the construction of sewers and power systems across the nation would have offered tangible relief to stricken communities everywhere and, if administered sensitively, would have interfered only minimally with the institutions and politics of state governments, which might well have undertaken those projects themselves had they been able to. But the intrusiveness of an ineffective central plan, whose ultimate direction remained obscure, gradually made enemies of the very "army" it was meant to conscript.

The Supreme Court's rejection of the president's war analogy followed closely on the public's disenchantment with it, and the profound hostility and institutional violence of the ensuing constitutional revolution illuminate perhaps the greatest of all the blessings a Keynesian strategy might have conferred upon Roosevelt's America, and our own. In May 1935, observing that "extraordinary conditions may call for extraordinary remedies [but] extraordinary conditions do not create or enlarge constitutional power," the Court in *Schechter Poultry Corporation v. United States* unanimously struck down the NIRA on two grounds: its illegal delegation of congressional power to the president and its improper assertion of the authority to regulate economic affairs under the commerce clause. The demise of the NRA left the president at a loss and his administration without any economic policy at all, and despite Roosevelt's own inclinations in the matter, purposeful deficit spending seemed to many the only serious alternative left. Still unconverted to the Keynesian faith, the president nonetheless relented in April 1938.[51] His advisers had estimated full employment national income to be $88 billion, and with current income some $32 billion below that, they argued that the expectation of even $4 billion in new private investment was optimistic. But the constitutional constraints of 1787 still bound the federal government, and as the strains created by the $3 billion program Roosevelt sent to Congress made plain, it was not yet possible for it to spend in time of peace at the rate required to fill the gap. Despite the failure of the NRA, the president's belief in the need for structural reform and federal control remained unshaken. Convinced that stability required planning and coordination, he declared early in 1935 that abandoning the NRA was "unthinkable" and proposed a two-year extension of the agency and a strengthening of its authority. After *Schechter* he began to explore the possibility of relaxing the antitrust laws to permit voluntary coordination of business activities along the lines Hoover had resisted so strenuously.[52] When these came to naught, he turned again to direct regulation of prices and outputs, this time without even the NRA's nod to voluntarism. With the passage in 1938 of a Fair Labor Standards Act that provided for criminal sanctions against violators and a second Agricultural Adjustment Act, the hand of the federal government was again extended across the entire economy.

With the departure of the "Four Horsemen" (the four justices who had consistently voted to strike down New Deal legislation) in the wake of the harrowing Court-packing episode and their replacement by justices more in sympathy with Roosevelt's views, the Court's resistance to comprehensive peacetime planning crumbled. The Fair Labor Standards Act was upheld as a legitimate exercise of the commerce power in *United States v. Darby,* and by 1942 the constitutionality of mechanisms of central control whose authority reached even further than that of the NRA was firmly established. In *Wickard v. Filburn,* the Court upheld an order by the secretary of agriculture denying a farmer the right to grow wheat in excess of the department's quota, even though the excess was to be consumed entirely on the farm. However small the amount, reasoned the Court, home consumption withdrew some element of demand from the market, and if individual farmers were permitted to act in this way, the aggregate effect of their behavior would be to depress market demand and thus affect the price of wheat in interstate commerce. For 150 years, congressional authority under the commerce clause had waxed and waned, subject in the Court to the normal pressures of politics and circumstance. But *Filburn* marked a decisive, even revolutionary break with the past. Even *Darby* had required that some tangible commodity actually cross state lines before the power to regulate interstate commerce could properly be invoked. But after *Filburn,* all that was necessary was an assertion that the price of some good, somewhere, traded in interstate commerce would be altered by sufficiently extensive behavior of the kind the government sought to require or prohibit, a condition that in principle characterizes *every* individual decision to buy or sell any good. Exceeding the vision of even the most Hamiltonian of the Framers, the Court thus wrote its own version of the general equilibrium theory into the commerce clause and brought virtually all forms of private activity, "economic" or otherwise, within the regulatory reach of the federal government. If enthusiasm for its exercise had flagged since 1933, the power to plan now clearly resided in Washington. It remains there still, awaiting a new emergency and, perhaps, a leader less noble than Franklin D. Roosevelt.[53]

Within a single decade, Roosevelt's determined efforts to subject the undisciplined forces of economic life to rational

control and to re-create the merger of state and economy that had existed in the heady years of the Great War had resulted in a vast expansion of the regulatory powers of the national state. Yet even as real war erupted once more in Europe, the statecraft of the Framers still denied the federal government the means to stabilize the economy through public expenditure without the expedient of war. They had made the preservation of personal liberty the organizing principle and first obligation of the limited government they constructed, and a tightly constrained national state and faith in the efficacy of local government formed an environment within which the microeconomics of individual purpose and free exchange could flourish. But the enlargement of government of which Keynes now spoke was real and would have presented difficult practical and political problems even to a president eager to construct the apparatus necessary to manage demand effectively while maintaining the "free play" of individual interests in markets. Simply adapting existing budgetary procedures and creating the new disbursement machinery needed to enable a national government of traditionally circumscribed powers and with almost no experience in demand management to increase its taxing and spending authority fourfold would be daunting. And as Keynes recognized (and our own experience confirms), stabilization by purposeful fiscal policy appears possible only at some cost in popular control; guarding against the distortions that follow undisciplined deficit spending in periods of high employment seems to require either placing the ultimate authority to determine aggregate levels of expenditure and tax revenue in a board of technicians insulated from political pressures or the raising of constitutional barriers to permanent deficits.

All this would certainly have created great political tension, not just between Congress and the executive, but between the state and a people still unaccustomed to government by experts. But in 1933, an American Keynesianism without war would have required still more, a controversial reconstruction of the constitutional relationship between the states and the federal government. The issue would not have been, as it was in *Schechter,* the regulatory powers conferred by the commerce clause, but the division between Washington and the states of the authority to tax and spend, a contest that would turn on the meaning of the congressional power to provide for the "general welfare of the United States." As the Framers had intended, the states and municipalities built roads and bridges, constructed hospitals and schools, reclaimed land, and offered relief to the poor and sick. The creation of a new federalism that largely relocated these responsibilities in the federal government would certainly have demanded both an invocation of emergency powers at the outset and the persistence and political leadership necessary to make them permanent. Still, a president willing to lead this battle, to expend on this revolution the energy and political resources Roosevelt devoted to establishing the power to plan, could surely have won the day with far less violence to the constitutional order. Where the commerce clause had been a constant field of struggle since the time of John Marshall, and layers of interpretive doctrine stood between Roosevelt and the powers he sought for the national government, the boundaries of the general welfare clause were still unexplored, and what doctrine there was seemed far more favorable to an expansion of federal authority. But Roosevelt's commitment to the macroeconomics of war precluded the institutional experimentation and reform that would have made possible the far more modest control implied by Keynes's macroeconomics of peace. To build a government capable of comprehensive planning that was never needed, he declared a war where there was no enemy, and not until Dr. New Deal was replaced by Dr. Win the War was his reluctance to incur the deficits necessary for real recovery overcome. In fighting the wrong battle at the wrong time, he made real war the prerequisite to economic recovery and enabled his successors to make the Cold War that followed a bulwark of stable prosperity.[54]

Historians are properly skeptical of even the most sensitive, circumspect counterfactual discourse and the speculative form of argument it demands. But the generation of hypotheses about events not yet observed, the analysis of things that have never been, is the essence of all science, and perhaps an economist can best contribute to historical inquiry precisely by attempting to understand what did happen by asking what did not, and why. Given the political, constitutional, and cultural obstacles in its way, the achievement of the American Keynesianism I have described would have been a formidable task, and one may reasonably question Roosevelt's capacity to accomplish that task, even had he wanted to. But the best evidence of what he could have done is the magnitude of what he actually did. Perhaps because it succeeded so completely, it is easy to lose sight of the significance of Roosevelt's constitutional revolution, the speed and thoroughness with which it reordered the institutional foundations of the American political economy against powerful, principled resistance, and the dedication and expenditure of political capital required to see it through. In a period of fluctuating, almost aimless economic policy, a federal power to plan remained the president's only consistent, energetically pursued objective, and as the Court-packing struggle made clear, he was fully prepared to shed the blood his revolution demanded. Had he been able to break free of the weakening constraints of the reigning political and economic culture and the blinders of his own collectivism and to persuade himself that a revolution for the power to spend was as worthwhile as one for the power to plan, we might well have been spared the distortions of the "military Keynesianism" that are part of his legacy.

As his open letter of 1933 intimates, Keynes had feared precisely this result. With his characteristic flair, he made clear in *The General Theory* that the importance of compensatory spending by the state lay not in what the money bought but simply that it was *spent*. But by 1940, with war a reality, he was considerably more subdued. Writing in Croly's journal, the *New Republic*, he betrayed

the depth of his fears as he expressed his hopes for the future. Let him have the last word.

> It is, it seems, politically impossible for a capitalistic democracy to organize expenditure on the scale necessary to make the grand experiments which would prove my case—except in war conditions. It is thus that, not for the first time in the fluctuating fortunes of mankind, good may come out of evil. If the United States . . . steels itself to a vast dissipation of resources in the preparation of arms, it will . . . learn a lesson that can be turned to account afterward to reconstruct a world which will understand the first principles governing the production of wealth and which can endeavor—a harder task—to put it to good use. . . .

> Is it vain to suppose that a democracy can be wise and sensible? Must the poison of popular politics make impotent every free community? So much hangs on the issue that it is our duty to believe that we can do what we should, until the opposite is proved.[55]

NOTES

[1] Robert Skidelsky, "Keynes & the Reconstruction of Liberalism," *Encounter,* 52 (April 1979), 29-39.

[2] *Ibid.,* 39.

[3] John Maynard Keynes, *The General Theory of Employment, Interest and Money* (London, 1936). Citations here are to D. H. Moggridge and Elizabeth Johnson, eds., *The Collected Writings of John Maynard Keynes* (30 vols., London, 1971-1989), VII. Throughout this essay, I shall use the label *managerialism* for the coupling of a broadly collectivist ontology with a commitment to scientific administration, an outlook shared by a wide range of social theorists (such as Lester Ward, Simon Patten, Henry Carter Adams, Richard T. Ely, and the young Woodrow Wilson), influential publicists (among them Edward Bellamy, Herbert Croly, and Walter Weyl), and politicians (such as Theodore Roosevelt and Elihu Root).

[4] *Cf.* James Gilbert, *Designing the Industrial State: The Intellectual Pursuit of Collectivism in America, 1880-1940* (Chicago, 1972), 8-9, 18-22, 50-53.

[5] Ellis W. Hawley, *The Great War and the Search for a Modern Order: A History of the American People and Their Institutions, 1917-1933* (New York, 1979), 55.

[6] The phrase "nation as an economic unit" appears in the announcement of the award of the 1984 Nobel Prize in economics to Sir Richard Stone, an assistant to John Maynard Keynes in the British Treasury during World War II who there began to develop the modern system of national income accounts. Royal Swedish Academy of Sciences, "The Nobel Memorial Prize in Economics 1984," *Scandinavian Journal of Economics,* 87 (March 1985), 1. On World War II as a catalyst of national unity, Skidelsky, "Keynes & the Reconstruction of Liberalism," 36.

[7] *Cf.* Ronald Coase, "The Nature of the Firm," *Economica,* 4 (Nov. 1937), 390-92. *Santa Clara County v. Southern Pacific Railroad Co.,* 118 U.S. 394, 396 (1886). On the changing status of corporations in American law, see *Liggett v. Lee,* 288 U.S. 517, 541-80 (1933) (Brandeis, J., dissenting); James Willard Hurst, *The Legitimacy of the Business Corporation in the Law of the United States: 1780-1970* (Charlottesville, 1970); Morton J. Horwitz, "*Santa Clara* Revisited: The Development of Corporate Theory," *West Virginia Law Review,* 88 (Fall 1985), 173-224; and Richard P. Adelstein, "Islands of Conscious Power: Louis D. Brandeis and the Modern Corporation," *Business History Review,* 63 (Autumn 1989), 614-56.

[8] Alfred D. Chandler, Jr., *The Visible Hand: The Managerial Revolution in American Business* (Cambridge, Mass., 1977), 464-66; David F. Noble, *America by Design: Science, Technology, and the Rise of Corporate Capitalism* (New York, 1979), 263. *Cf.* Samuel Haber, *Efficiency and Uplift: Scientific Management in the Progressive Era, 1890-1920* (Chicago, 1964), x, 2-3, 19-24; Hugh G. J. Aitken, *Taylorism at Watertown Arsenal: Scientific Management in Action, 1908-1915* (Cambridge, Mass., 1960), 16, 21-28, 35-38; and the strikingly explicit articulation of the mechanical metaphor in Louis D. Brandeis, *Scientific Management and Railroads* (New York, 1911), 8.

[9] *Cf.* F. A. Hayek, *The Counter-Revolution of Science: Studies on the Abuse of Reason* (1952; reprint, Indianapolis, 1979), 165-73; and Glenn Porter, *The Rise of Big Business, 1860-1910* (Arlington Heights, 1973), 20-21.

[10] Chandler, *Visible Hand,* 464-65.

[11] On society as an organic unit, see Woodrow Wilson, *The State: Elements of Historical and Practical Politics* (Boston, 1894), 597; Richard T. Ely, *Socialism* (New York, 1894), 351; Henry C. Adams. "Relation of the State to Industrial Action (1887)," in *Two Essays by Henry Carter Adams,* ed. Joseph Dorfman (New York, 1954), 82-83; John B. Clark, *The Philosophy of Wealth* (Boston, 1886), 56; Simon N. Patten, *The New Basis of Civilization* (New York, 1907), 43; Frank Tariello, Jr., *The Reconstruction of American Political Ideology, 1865-1917* (Charlottesville, 1982), 53-69; and Robert H. Wiebe, *The Search for Order, 1877-1920* (New York, 1967), 140-42. On the historicists, see *ibid.,* 140; Joseph Dorfman, "The Role of the German Historical School in American Economic Thought," *American Economic Review,* 45 (May 1955), 17-28; and Jurgen Herbst, *The German Historical School in American Scholarship* (Ithaca, 1965). On "social physics" generally, see Hayek, *Counter-Revolution of Science,* 235-400. For the managerialist view of the role of government, see Wilson, *State,* 598; and, for Lester Ward's version of it, Henry Steele Commager, *The American Mind: An Interpretation of American Thought and Character since the 1880's* (New Haven, 1950), 211.

[12] For Ward's statement, see R. Jeffrey Lustig, *Corporate Liberalism: The Origins of Modern American Political Theory, 1890-1920* (Berkeley, 1982), 166. For managerialist

attitudes on the relationship of science to administration and political organization, see *ibid.,* 150-94; Woodrow Wilson, "The Study of Administration," in *The Papers of Woodrow Wilson,* ed. Arthur S. Link (62 vols., Princeton, 1966-1990), V, 359-80; and Robert B. Reich, *The Next American Frontier* (New York, 1983), 61-63.

[13] Hans B. Thorelli, *The Federal Antitrust Policy: Origination of an American Tradition* (Baltimore, 1955), 567-68; William Letwin, *Law and Economic Policy in America: The Evolution of the Sherman Antitrust Act* (Chicago, 1965), 59-70.

[14] Walter Weyl, *The New Democracy: An Essay Concerning Certain Political and Economic Conditions in the United States* (New York, 1912). See also Charles Forcey, *The Crossroads of Liberalism: Croly, Weyl, Lippmann, and the Progressive Era, 1900-1925* (New York, 1961), 61-64, 78-87; and Wiebe, *Search for Order,* 158. Herbert Croly, "The Effects on American Institutions of a Powerful Military and Naval Establishment," *Annals of the American Academy of Political and Social Science,* 66 (July 1916), 162. Arthur A. Ekirch, Jr., *The Decline of American Liberalism* (New York, 1955), 198-206, esp. 205.

[15] Ekirch, *Decline of American Liberalism,* 205-6; Arthur A. Ekirch, Jr., *Progressivism in America: A Study of the Era from Theodore Roosevelt to Woodrow Wilson* (New York, 1974), 268; Robert D. Cuff, *The War Industries Board: Business-Government Relations during World War I* (Baltimore, 1973), 135-47; Hawley, *Great War and the Search for a Modern Order,* 22-27; Barry D. Karl, *The Uneasy State: The United States from 1915 to 1945* (Chicago, 1983), 40-44.

[16] Randolph S. Bourne, *War and the Intellectuals: Essays by Randolph S. Bourne, 1915-1919,* ed. Carl Resek (New York, 1964), 67-79; Hawley, *Great War and the Search for a Modern Order,* 46-48, 71-73; David A. Shannon, *Between the Wars: America, 1919-1941* (Boston, 1965), 26-30.

[17] Wesley C. Mitchell, *Business Cycles and Their Causes* (Berkeley, 1913); Guy Alchon, *The Invisible Hand of Planning: Capitalism, Social Science, and the State in the 1920s* (Princeton, 1985), 27-32, 35-38; Wesley C. Mitchell, "Statistics and Government," *Quarterly Publication of the American Statistical Association,* 16 (March 1919), 229-30; Wesley C. Mitchell, "The Prospects of Economics," in *The Trend of Economics,* ed. Rexford G. Tugwell (New York, 1924), 25.

[18] On Herbert Hoover's economic and political philosophy, see Herbert C. Hoover, *American Individualism* (Garden City, 1922); and Albert U. Romasco, *The Poverty of Abundance: Hoover, the Nation, the Depression* (New York, 1965), 10-23.

[19] William J. Barber, *From New Era to New Deal: Herbert Hoover, the Economists, and American Economic Policy, 1921-1933* (Cambridge, Eng., 1985), 8-13; Robert F. Himmelberg, *The Origins of the National*

Recovery Administration: Business, Government, and the Trade Association Issue, 1921-1933 (New York, 1976), 10-12, 67-72, 88-109, 151-65. On Hoover's opposition to the Swope Plan and similar proposals, see Arthur M. Schlesinger, Jr., *The Age of Roosevelt*, vol. I: *The Crisis of the Old Order, 1919-1933* (Boston, 1957), 235.

[20] Hawley, *Great War and the Search for a Modern Order,* 83-84; Reich, *Next American Frontier,* 69-73; Ellis W. Hawley, "Herbert Hoover, the Commerce Secretariat, and the Vision of an 'Associative State,' 1921-1928," *Journal of American History,* 61 (June 1974), 116-40; Albert U. Romasco, "Hoover-Roosevelt and the Great Depression: A Historiographic Inquiry into a Perennial Comparison," in *The New Deal: The National Level,* ed. John Braeman, Robert Bremner, and David Brody (Columbus, 1975), 24.

[21] Barber, *From New Era to New Deal,* 16-22; Alchon, *Invisible Hand of Planning,* 59-63, 74, 79. For the National Bureau of Economic Research data, see National Bureau of Economic Research, *Income in the United States, Its Amount and Distribution, 1909-1919* (New York, 1921). On the controllability of the business cycle, see Herbert C. Hoover, "Introduction," in *The Stabilization of Business,* ed. Lionel Edie (New York, 1923), v; and Romasco, *Poverty of Abundance,* 32-38. Otto T. Mallery, "A National Policy—Public Works to Stabilize Employment," *Annals of the American Academy of Political and Social Science,* 81 (Jan. 1919), 57. For the report and recommendations of the conference on unemployment, see President's Conference on Unemployment, *Business Cycles and Unemployment* (New York, 1923), esp. xxvii-xxix, 231-61. Hawley, *Great War and the Search for a Modern Order,* 69; Barber, *From New Era to New Deal,* 18-19.

[22] Romasco, *Poverty of Abundance,* 24-65, 125-42, 187-201; Ellis W. Hawley, "The New Deal and Business," in *New Deal,* ed. Braeman, Bremner, and Brody, 55; Hawley, *Great War and the Search for a Modern Order,* 94-97; Barber, *From New Era to New Deal,* 170-73; Schlesinger, *Age of Roosevelt,* I, 203-34; Herbert Stein, *The Fiscal Revolution in America* (Chicago, 1969), 18-24, 26-38.

[23] Paul A. Samuelson, *Economics: An Introductory Analysis* (New York, 1948).

[24] For Keynes's generous acknowledgment of his debt to J. A. Hobson, and to earlier articulations of the under consumptionist hypothesis, see Moggridge and Johnson, eds., *Collected Writings of Keynes,* VII, 358-71. William T. Foster and Waddill Catchings, *The Road to Plenty* (Boston, 1928), 134-35; William T. Foster and Waddill Catchings, "Mr. Hoover's Road to Prosperity," *Review of Reviews,* 81 (Jan. 1930), 50-52. On Keynes's belief that public affairs should be managed by "an elite of clever and disinterested public servants," insulated from the political pressures of popular democracy, see Skidelsky, "Keynes & the Reconstruction of Liberalism," 36.

[25] Moggridge and Johnson, eds., *Collected Writings of Keynes,* VII, 381.

[26] On Hoover's views on the budget, see Schlesinger, *Age of Roosevelt,* I, 231-32; Romasco, *Poverty of Abundance,* 222-29; Stein, *Fiscal Revolution in America,* 26-38. On Roosevelt's position during the campaign and the first months of his presidency, see *ibid.,* 43-47; Daniel R. Fusfeld, *The Economic Thought of Franklin D. Roosevelt and the Origins of the New Deal* (New York, 1956), 202-3, 230; and William E. Leuchtenburg, *Franklin D. Roosevelt and the New Deal, 1932-1940* (New York, 1963), 37, 47-48.

[27] Radio Address, April 7, 1932, in *The Public Papers and Addresses of Franklin D. Roosevelt,* ed. Samuel I. Rosenman (13 vols., New York, 1938-1950), I, 625. See also Schlesinger, *Age of Roosevelt,* I, 136.

[28] The national income figures are based on data compiled by the U.S. Department of Commerce, in Lester V. Chandler, *America's Greatest Depression: 1929-1941* (New York, 1970), 4, 24, 121. On the infeasibility of effective fiscal policy during the early years of the depression, see *ibid.,* 121-22; and Stein, *Fiscal Revolution in America,* 14, 22-24. See also Walter S. Salant, "The Spread of Keynesian Doctrines and Practices in the United States," in *The Political Power of Economic Ideas: Keynesianism across Nations,* ed. Peter A. Hall (Princeton, 1989), 50-51. Keynes's estimate of the multiplier, based on figures he called "very precarious," was roughly 2.5. He believed the value to be somewhat greater during the slump. Moggridge and Johnson, eds., *Collected Writings of Keynes,* VII, 127-28. Total expenditures by state and local governments on goods and services during 1933 were $7.8 billion; they would thus have had to more than double their spending to provide the necessary stimulus. Apart from the infeasibility of such concerted action, they would have had great difficulty borrowing the requisite funds. Unlike the federal government, they could not print new money. Chandler, *America's Greatest Depression,* 121-22.

[29] Carl N. Degler, "The Ordeal of Herbert Hoover," in *The Shaping of Twentieth Century America: Interpretive Essays,* ed. Richard Abrams and Lawrence Levine (Boston, 1971), 363; Romasco, *Poverty of Abundance,* 175-81. Cf. Peter A. Gourevitch, "Breaking with Orthodoxy: The Politics of Economic Policy Responses to the Depression of the 1930s," *International Organization,* 38 (Winter 1984), 99. William E. Leuchtenburg, "The New Deal and the Analogue of War," in *Change and Continuity in Twentieth-Century America,* ed. John Braeman, Robert H. Bremner, and Everett Walters (Columbus, 1964), 103. Al Smith found the war analogy equally compelling; see *ibid.*

[30] Rosenman, ed., *Public Papers and Addresses of Franklin D. Roosevelt,* II, 13, 14, 15-16.

[31] Leuchtenburg, "New Deal and the Analogue of War," 118; Ellis W. Hawley, *The New Deal and the Problem of Monopoly: A Study in Economic Ambivalence* (Princeton, 1966), 29-34. Though subscription to the National Recovery Administration (NRA) codes was voluntary, those

who subscribed were subject to a complex sanctioning mechanism if they did not meet code provisions. Violations of a code approved by the president were to be treated as "unfair methods of competition," with enforcement assigned in the first instance to the code authorities, then to the Federal Trade Commission and, ultimately, to the federal courts. The president might compel compliance by licensing individual businesses and was granted an open-ended authority to modify or abolish existing codes at any time. Karl, *Uneasy State*, 114; Albert U. Romasco, *The Politics of Recovery: Roosevelt's New Deal* (New York, 1983), 189. On the recovery act's provisions, see Charles L. Dearing, Paul T. Homan, Lewis L. Lorwin, and Leverett S. Lyon, *The ABC of the NRA* (Washington, 1934), 16-24. On the NRA, see Himmelberg, *Origins of the National Recovery Administration*, 181-218; Arthur M. Schlesinger, Jr., *The Age of Roosevelt*, vol. II: *The Coming of the New Deal* (Boston, 1958), 87-102; Bernard Bellush, *The Failure of the NRA* (New York, 1975); John Kennedy Ohl, *Hugh S. Johnson and the New Deal* (DeKalb, 1985); and Donald R. Brand, *Corporatism and the Rule of Law: A Study of the National Recovery Administration* (Ithaca, 1988).

[32] Leuchtenburg, "New Deal and the Analogue of War," 117-35; Gerald D. Nash, "Experiments in Industrial Mobilization: W.I.B. and N.R.A.," *Mid-America*, 45 (July 1963), 157-74; Brand, *Corporatism and the Rule of Law*, 82-83, and esp. 268. *Cf.* David M. Potter, *People of Plenty: Economic Abundance and the American Character* (Chicago, 1954), 126. See also *ibid.*, 114-15, 204-6.

[33] Dearing, Homan, Lorwin, and Lyon, *ABC of the NRA*, 23; Hawley, *New Deal and the Problem of Monopoly*, 19-21, 31-34; Romasco, *Politics of Recovery*, 192-93; Himmelberg, *Origins of the National Recovery Administration*, 181, 197; Louis Galambos, *Competition and Cooperation: The Emergence of a National Trade Association* (Baltimore, 1966), 173-202; Robert M. Collins, *The Business Response to Keynes, 1929-1964* (New York, 1981), 28-32.

[34] The idea was expressed not only by such economists as Keynes, William T. Foster, Paul Douglas, and E. R. A. Seligman but also by Thomas Lamont of the House of Morgan and Sen. Robert LaFollette of Wisconsin. Leuchtenburg, "New Deal and the Analogue of War," 96-97, 125-26, 128.

[35] Hawley, *New Deal and the Problem of Monopoly*, 53-129; Himmelberg, *Origins of the National Recovery Administration*, 197, 209, 211-12; Schlesinger, *Age of Roosevelt*, II, 152-76. *Cf.* Leuchtenburg, "New Deal and the Analogue of War," 120, 132-33. For an argument that the industrial codes helped prolong economic stagnation after the trough of the Great Depression, see Michael W. Weinstein, "Some Macroeconomic Impacts of the National Industrial Recovery Act, 1933-1935," in *The Great Depression Revisited*, ed. K. Brunner (Boston, 1981), 262-81.

[36] J. Ronnie Davis, *The New Economics and the Old Economists* (Ames, 1971); Joseph Dorfman, *The Economic Mind in American Civilization* (5 vols., New York, 1946-1959), V, 664-77, 691-93; Jordan A. Schwarz, *The Interregnum of Despair: Hoover, Congress, and the Depression* (Urbana, 1970), 23-44, 141-47; Romasco, *Politics of Recovery*, 196; Frances Perkins, *The Roosevelt I Knew* (New York, 1946), 268-70; Schlesinger, *Age of Roosevelt*, II, 95; Arthur M. Schlesinger, Jr., *The Age of Roosevelt*, vol. III: *The Politics of Upheaval* (Boston, 1960), 237-41; Alan Sweezy, "The Keynesians and Government Policy, 1933-1939," *American Economic Review*, 62 (May 1972), 116-24; Byrd L. Jones, "Lauchlin Currie, Pump Priming, and New Deal Fiscal Policy, 1934-1936," *History of Political Economy*, 10 (Winter 1978), 509-24.

[37] For the letter, see Max Freedman, ed., *Roosevelt and Frankfurter: Their Correspondence, 1928-1945* (Boston, 1967), 178-83.

[38] Roosevelt to Frankfurter, Dec. 22, 1933, *ibid.*, 183-84; Frankfurter to Roosevelt, May 7, 1934, *ibid.*, 213-14. On Frankfurter's support for a program of public works, see Nelson Lloyd Dawson, *Louis D. Brandeis, Felix Frankfurter, and the New Deal* (Hamden, 1980), 28-35. Perkins, *Roosevelt I Knew*, 225. An equally disappointed Keynes told her he had "supposed the President was more literate, economically speaking" and offered a simple verbal example of the operation of the multiplier. "I wish he had been as concrete when he talked to Roosevelt, instead of treating him as though he belonged to the higher echelons of economic knowledge." *Ibid.*, 226.

[39] See, for example, Frankfurter to Roosevelt, memoranda, Nov. 21, 1934, Dec. 28, 1935, in *Roosevelt and Frankfurter*, ed. Freedman, 240-42, 296-300. Fusfeld, *Economic Thought of Franklin D. Roosevelt*, 73-75. Rosenman, ed., *Public Papers and Addresses of Franklin D. Roosevelt*, I, 659-69, 795-812, II, 49-54, 99-143, III, 173-81; Collins, *Business Response to Keynes*, 3; Romasco, *Politics of Recovery*, 35-51, 67; Schlesinger, *Age of Roosevelt*, II, 109; Himmelberg, *Origins of the National Recovery Administration*, 189-90, 196-201; Stein, *Fiscal Revolution in America*, 49-70.

[40] Rosenman, ed., *Public Papers and Addresses of Franklin D. Roosevelt*, I, 639-47, 742-56, 780-86, esp. 783. On the need for "rebuilding many of the structures of our economic life and reorganizing it in order to prevent a recurrence of collapse," see also his Message to the Congress, June 8, 1934, *ibid.*, III, 287-93; *Ibid.*, I, 784, III, 436.

[41] Fusfeld, *Economic Thought of Franklin D. Roosevelt*, 49-50.

[42] Otis L. Graham, Jr., *Toward a Planned Society: From Roosevelt to Nixon* (New York, 1976), 20. On Rexford Tugwell's views, see Fusfeld, *Economic Thought of Franklin D. Roosevelt*, 210-12; R. G. Tugwell, "The Principle of Planning and the Institution of Laissez Faire," *American Economic Review*, 22 (Supplement, March 1932), 75-92;

Rexford G. Tugwell, *The Industrial Discipline and the Governmental Arts* (New York, 1933), esp. 200-16; and R. G. Tugwell, "The New Deal: The Progressive Tradition," *Western Political Quarterly,* 3 (Sept. 1950), 390-427. On the influence of the "national planners" in the NRA, see Schlesinger, *Age of Roosevelt,* III, 214-15, II, 92-94, 179-84; and Hawley, *New Deal and the Problem of Monopoly,* 43-46.

[43] *Cf.* Romasco, *Politics of Recovery,* 3-12, 241-47. Friedrich A. Hayek, *The Road to Serfdom* (Chicago, 1944), 56-71, 105-7.

[44] Fusfeld, *Economic Thought of Franklin D. Roosevelt,* 58-71, 101-8.

[45] Rosenman, ed., *Public Papers and Addresses of Franklin D. Roosevelt,* II, 252-53, 256.

[46] Schlesinger, *Age of Roosevelt,* II, 114-16; Hawley, *New Deal and the Problem of Monopoly,* 53-55, 105-10; Leuchtenburg, *Franklin D. Roosevelt and the New Deal,* 68-69. On the problems associated with enforcing the codes, see Brand, *Corporatism and the Rule of Law,* 92-105, *Ibid.,* 104.

[47] Moggridge and Johnson, eds., *Collected Writings of Keynes,* VII, 380.

[48] James T. Patterson, *The New Deal and the States: Federalism in Transition* (Princeton, 1969), 7-10, 13-16, 26-49. Given the stance of the federal government, the states were forced to raise taxes and did so largely by way of regressive sales and consumption levies. The taxes depressed purchasing power when it was most needed and counteracted the mild stimulative effect of Washington's unintentional deficits. See *ibid.,* 95-99; and E. Cary Brown, "Fiscal Policy in the 'Thirties: A Reappraisal," *American Economic Review,* 46 (Dec. 1956), 857-79.

[49] Thus, for example, the campaign for federal public works quietly waged in the administration's earliest days by Louis Brandeis, the most faithful living champion of the states against the claims of the federal government, and the obvious distress of the states themselves suggested the strong possibility of broad acquiescence to an increased federal role in fiscal matters. See Dawson, *Louis D. Brandeis, Felix Frankfurter, and the New Deal,* 28-35; and Patterson, *New Deal and the States,* 158, 91.

[50] Patterson, *New Deal and the States,* 112-18.

[51] *Schechter Poultry Corporation v. United States,* 295 U.S. 495, 528 (1935). Four months earlier, the Court had signaled its views on the delegation issue in *Panama Refining Co. v. Ryan,* 293 U.S. 388 (1935). For an account of Roosevelt's outlook two days after the *Schechter* decision, see Romasco, *Politics of Recovery,* 214. The combination of extraordinary relief expenditures and falling tax revenues had forced a mild course of deficit spending on Roosevelt, and by 1936, this involuntary

fiscal policy had begun to bear fruit; unemployment remained high, but production had regained the level of 1929, and with some prices starting to rise, a few speculators began to invest in inventory. But the president saw only the possibility of balancing the budget at last and moved to cut spending. He almost succeeded. The budget deficit was $3.6 billion on expenditures of $8.7 billion for 1936; $2 billion in new revenues and $1.3 billion in spending cuts slashed this figure to $358 million in 1937. In August 1937, the economy responded by registering the sharpest decline in industrial production ever measured. Stein, *Fiscal Revolution in America,* 91-95; Salant, "Spread of Keynesian Doctrines," 42-45.

[52] Romasco, *Politics of Recovery,* 211, 225-40; Stein, *Fiscal Revolution in America,* 103-18; Leuchtenburg, *Franklin D. Roosevelt and the New Deal,* 248-49, 254-64.

[53] William B. Lockhart, Yale Kamisar, and Jesse H. Choper, *Constitutional Law* (St. Paul, 1970), A1-A10; *United States v. Darby,* 312 U.S. 100 (1941), *Wickard v. Filburn,* 317 U.S. 111 (1942).

[54] U.S. Const., art. I, sec. 8, cl. 1. On the general welfare clause, *Cf.* David E. Engdahl, *Constitutional Federalism* (St. Paul, 1987), 162-73. Roosevelt used these terms in a press conference late in 1943. Rosenman, ed., *Public Papers and Addresses of Franklin D. Roosevelt,* XII, 569-75.

[55] "If the Treasury were to fill old bottles with banknotes, bury them at suitable depths in disused coal mines which are then filled up to the surface with town rubbish, and leave it to private enterprise on well-tried principles of *laissez-faire* to dig the notes up again . . . there need be no more unemployment. . . . It would, indeed, be more sensible to build houses and the like; but if there are political and practical difficulties in the way of this, the above would be better than nothing." Moggridge and Johnson, eds., *Collected Writings of Keynes,* VII, 129; J. M. Keynes, "The United States and the Keynes Plan," *New Republic,* July 29, 1940, pp. 158-59.

Amos Perlmutter (essay date 1993)

SOURCE: "The President's Style and World View," and "Roosevelt and His War Strategy," in *FDR & Stalin: A Not So Grand Alliance, 1943-1945,* University of Missouri Press, 1993, pp. 25-56.

[*In the following excerpt, Perlmutter probes Roosevelt's enigmatic worldview and evaluates the merits and faults of his wartime strategy.*]

THE PRESIDENT'S STYLE AND WORLD VIEW

How did Roosevelt arrive at decisions? What was the nature of the process? What or who influenced him? What information did he consider in making key decisions? What was his frame of reference at Teheran and Yalta? How did the president conduct the war day by day? What personal experience did he bring to the war? How did he perform as war leader, and how did he come to the decisions that shaped the postwar world?

Franklin Delano Roosevelt became a legend in his time, but beyond the legend lies an enigma. Roosevelt left little for historians to rummage through: there are no diaries, no autobiography; and the letters that exist do not reveal feelings, private observations, philosophical outlook or theories. It is doubtful that Roosevelt would have written his story even if he had lived longer. He epitomized the modern man of action—living in the moment, not inclined to introspection or reflection. He did not analyze his actions, and he offered no great theory of politics or presidential power. He was not a thoughtful man, compelled to record his thoughts on paper.

It is instructive to compare him with Winston Churchill, an equally gregarious and accessible man, but one who could never resist the invitation of a blank sheet of paper. In books, histories, diaries, reportage, fiction, and letters, Churchill wrote about anything that interested him— which was almost everything—through the prism of his own perspective. If Roosevelt continues to intrigue biographers at least partly because he left so little written material behind, Churchill achieves the same effect because he left so much. Whether writing about his ancestor the Duke of Marlborough, his tragically flawed father Lord Randolph, the English people, generals, or yeomen, Churchill's hero was always Churchill, with the wealth of material serving as a defense against understanding the man within.

A researcher will find nothing in the archives that reveals a personal Roosevelt. His letters are informational, devoid of emotions. What is striking about the fragments of communications and messages in Hyde Park is the absence of reflection on history or people. Interoffice memos to aides do not reveal strategies, goals, tactics, or his views on the meanings of the office he occupied.[1]

The man who appeared so generous with his energy, and so accessible, was also elusive. He was a friend to the whole world, but intimate with few, if any. He could inspire affection and loyalty, even though he was never really close to any person, not even the mother who adored him and lived her life for him. His relationship with his wife and fourth cousin Eleanor lacked real closeness. They admired each other's talents and intelligence, but did not provide each other with emotional fulfillment. Roosevelt was not very concerned about or affectionate toward his children. Lewis Howe and Harry Hopkins, his closest aides, could not claim personal closeness to the president.

Roosevelt resisted being known because he lacked confidence in the abilities of others. He found it difficult to delegate authority and was often frustrated by outside sources of power. In spite of the "happy warrior" face he presented to the world, his presidency was characterized by suspicion and mistrust. He made most of his decisions alone.

Operating on the strength of his personality, FDR radiated power and the joy of using it. "His habits were practical, rather than analytical."[2] Neville Chamberlain called him a "windbag," while Walter Lippmann suggested that "the trouble with Franklin D. Roosevelt is that his mind is not very clear, his purposes are not simple and his methods are not direct."[3] The consensus among those who knew him well was that he was secretive and made solitary decisions, even though he was surrounded by advisers who constituted a kind of medieval court.

Roosevelt identified with his cousin Theodore Roosevelt and, to a lesser degree, with Woodrow Wilson. Historians often compare FDR to Wilson, noting that Roosevelt was a junior member of the Wilson administration as assistant secretary of the navy and that he studied Wilson a great deal. There is something of Wilson in Roosevelt's United Nations organization, a resurrection of Wilson's League of Nations; and Wilson's moralistic international outlook is echoed in Roosevelt's approach to world affairs. Both shared a certain internationalist naiveté.

But Franklin Roosevelt resembles his great uncle Teddy the most. The resemblance is not just one of family, although this surely must have entered Franklin's mind when he compared himself to his illustrious predecessor in the presidency. FDR was born into the age of navalism, of the strategic theories of sea power and its influence upon history. America's coming of age did not at first mean that it would spread its power over the Atlantic and challenge the Old World in Europe. Power for America first meant the Far East, China, Japan, and the Pacific; and this meant sea power, a navalist orientation. China, Japan, and the Pacific caught Franklin Roosevelt's mind when he became interested in international matters; cultural nationalism, Anglo-Saxon and Pacific imperialism informed the young Roosevelt. The new American spirit was in the air that he breathed.

In 1890, Captain Alfred T. Mahan, an American naval historian, published *The Influence of Seapower in History,* emphasizing the importance of naval strategy for a continent bounded by two oceans. He viewed the oceans as strategic highways for the advancing industrial state America was becoming. Theodore Roosevelt was an enthusiastic convert to navalism, as were Henry Cabot Lodge, Henry Adams, and others.[4] Theodore also possessed an irrepressible personality, which, along with his enthusiasm for navalism and Americanism, became a tacit legacy for the young Franklin. Teddy was larger than life, even if he sometimes appeared juvenile in his poses. He was a voracious reader, a thinker, and a writer from whom FDR learned the importance of the sense of power and the relationship between power and responsibility. But Franklin never understood Theodore Roosevelt's concept of the balance of power.

It is not clear why Franklin Roosevelt joined the Democratic party, breaking family and class tradition. The influence of Wilsonianism on Roosevelt is also a subject worthy of some discussion. "Roosevelt's first administration was much less a Wilsonian restoration than might have been expected."[5] He took on only two of the party's Wilsonians, Cordell Hull and Daniel C. Roper, both of whom had little influence in his administration. Louis Brandeis, one of the old architects of Wilson's "New Freedom," was skeptical of FDR, while Wilson's critic William Bullitt became a close friend. Harold Ickes and Henry Wallace represented Republican and progressive factions, and leading New Dealer Donald Richberg also came from this group. Roosevelt remembered well Wilson's dilemma in attempting to get the American people to intervene in the Great War in Europe, and the subsequent struggle for the peace treaty that broke Wilson's spirit. With the experience of Wilson to guide him, Roosevelt became more circumspect when faced with the same dilemma in the late 1930s.

Roosevelt's legacy of the imperial presidency was "derived from a genuinely imperialist source."[6] Projecting Wilsonian idealism, Roosevelt was the offspring of the old expansionists. The Calvinist origins of Wilsonian idealism were congenial with Roosevelt's own strain of protestantism; but his instincts governed his foreign policy, and those instincts were patrician and expansionist. Roosevelt was not a disappointed Wilsonian, but rather a combination of both Wilson and Theodore Roosevelt. FDR, not Henry Luce, authored the American century; and Roosevelt's vision, centered on the Far East rather than the decaying Old World, was hardly humanitarian. It was the vision of the American mercantilists, the expansionists of the Gilded Age, the Mahans, Lodges, and Theodore Roosevelt. In the words of Protestant clergyman Josiah Strong, author of the best selling *Our Country,* God was "preparing mankind to receive our impress."[7]

FDR had had considerable administrative experience in his four years as governor of the most populous state in the Union between 1928 and 1932, and then nine years as president before the war. His administrative style combined confidence in himself and an unorthodox method of operations that shunned daily routines and detailed work. Arthur Schlesinger, Jr., claimed that "little fascinated Franklin Roosevelt more than the tasks of presidential administration,"[8] but the opposite was the case. Roosevelt believed in executive reorganization and improving management, but his style was antithetical to all the accepted norms of classical administration. He created many agencies and bureaucracies, but his unorthodox management style prevailed, at the expense of efficient administrative practices. The president's efforts to achieve greater government efficiency were compromised by the inherent inertia of the American political system and by his own work habits.

White House decision-making was characterized by confusion and the presence of many aides who believed they had the president's ear. He received little intelligence on the development of the Munich crisis and on the events leading up to Pearl Harbor.[9] He had unfounded anxieties about the Soviet Union's loyalty to the alliance, worried needlessly about Nazi and Fascist penetrations into Latin America, and allocated military resources that were needed elsewhere to that area.[10] He overreacted to Japanese expansion without understanding that country's needs. While pursuing the war, he also pressured the British and the French to relinquish their empires. The result was chaos, indirectness, and constant overlapping of authority.[11] Friendly historians have seen touches of political genius in Roosevelt's famous habit of assigning "overlapping and competing authority and jurisdiction to his subordinates."[12] But Roosevelt's method could just as easily be seen as carelessly inefficient. It assured only that, in the end, despite the influence of others, the president made the final decision.

This method had succeeded in domestic politics, but it was not suited for the conduct of the war. Wartime decision-making suffered from a plurality of channels of information from which key advisers and assistants were at least partially blocked. Seeing himself as the ultimate poker player, Roosevelt felt that he could hold all the cards and always produce a hand that would win the game. "These methods led to frustration among his subordinates and to complaints of a lack of coordination."[13]

The conduct of the war constantly demanded that important decisions, determining crucial operations and affecting the outcome of battles, be made. Roosevelt's inclination was to wait and see, to vacillate before reaching critical decisions that required action with unpredictable outcomes. He abhorred unpredictability, and as a result avoided as much as possible making decisions on issues about which he knew little. Instinct repeatedly prevailed over long-term planning.

With Churchill and Stalin, FDR's instinct was to use his powerfully persuasive personal charm and engaging manner, hoping that his rhetoric would persuade or hypnotize. He sought to convey an image of himself as the arbitrator, the conciliator, so that he could by turns placate Stalin and mollify the increasingly despairing Churchill. Instead, what he did was engender confusion and doubt about the strength of his commitment and the direction of his strategy. Both Churchill and Stalin saw Roosevelt as indecisive, and Stalin thus believed he could use Roosevelt to advance Stalin's ends.

Internationalist, Isolationist, Reformer, or Appeaser?

Franklin Roosevelt has been portrayed as an early foe of Hitler, prevented from combating the evil that Hitler represented by an isolationist Congress. Roosevelt's rhetoric at the time may have given this impression, but his actions sought to mollify the isolationists and, in the process, sent mixed signals to European leaders. This is not surprising, as Roosevelt had essentially a nineteenth-century outlook, with no understanding of what fueled modern mass movements outside the United States, no conception of their impact on international stability. The consolidation of Nazi power in Germany and the increasing anti-Semitic legislation had little effect on Roosevelt.

He remained silent when, on April 1, 1933, the Nazis boycotted all Jewish establishments, the first of many steps that would lead to the Final Solution.[14] In 1933, Hjalmar Schacht, president of the Reichsbank, met with Roosevelt, but Roosevelt's admonitions about the Nazi treatment of the Jews struck Schacht as mild.

> After dinner, exactly half an hour remained for a private conversation between the President and me. He began with the Jewish question, which had undoubtedly done a great deal of harm, probably not out of particular sympathy for the Jews, but from the old Anglo-Saxon sense of chivalry toward the weak. But he did not elaborate on this theme and said that this hurdle would be cleared even if its importance should not be underestimated.[15]

The president's early policy toward Nazi Germany amounted to appeasement, though he did not pursue it with the enthusiasm of European appeasers. Indeed, Roosevelt's slowness in formulating a realistic and effective response to Hitler was not unusual for a time when many Western political leaders pursued a policy of appeasement. Roosevelt's intentions in the early and middle 1930s were to restore prosperity and protect threatened nations from military aggression, yet not upset his domestic recovery or frighten isolationists.[16] Historian Wayne Cole is right to conclude that Roosevelt needed the support of the isolationists in Congress to realize his domestic New Deal. They generally supported his domestic policy but were firmly opposed to developing an internationalist, let alone an interventionist, policy.[17] The recurrent military and political crises in Europe and elsewhere were secondary to FDR's domestic reforms. He found no contradictions between his commitment to economic nationalism and mild internationalism which spilled over into foreign affairs.

The New Deal entailed an internationalist view of American interests. A global New Deal meant exporting the great American domestic experiment abroad to inspire the yearning for a "universal democracy, [and] for the abolition of colonialism."[18] Some of these ideas would find their way into the Atlantic Charter of 1941 and the United Nations charter in 1945, and be voiced strongly at Yalta. But in the mid-1930s, Roosevelt's pronouncements about the Good Neighbor policy and calls for international disarmament were not followed by action. European diplomats, comparing Roosevelt's rhetoric to his actions, concluded that he was a closet appeaser. "To the British government," D. C. Watt writes, "especially to Premier Neville Chamberlain, he seemed to have appeared as an unreliable windbag in charge of a country whose friendship and support Britain simply had to have."[19]

Intellectual Roots of the New Deal and Other Domestic Policies

Cole notes that "Roosevelt's relations with American isolationists from 1932 to 1945 had enduring significance for the history of American foreign policy." He also writes that "[Roosevelt] decisively triumphed over the isolationists" and that "his victory over them marked a watershed in the history of American foreign policy."[20] The issue, however, is not who won—Roosevelt or the isolationists—but when Roosevelt finally prevailed. How much support for his domestic programs was Roosevelt willing to sacrifice for his interventionist foreign policy? This persuasive politician could have found a way to minimize such loss of support, but instead, he vacillated, procrastinated, and wavered. The combination of interventionist rhetoric and delay that amounted to inaction failed to prepare the nation for the war. It fostered a material and psychological unpreparedness which led to the prolongation of the war and to unequal postwar arrangements between the United States and the Soviet Union.

Professor Cole writes that isolationists opposed American intervention in European wars, but not necessarily in Asia, the Pacific, or Latin America, areas they considered natural American spheres of interest. They believed "the United States could more effectively lead the world to the good life by building and sustaining democracy, freedom, and prosperity at home."[21] By Cole's definition, Roosevelt was a functional isolationist. Like the isolationists, he believed in a defensive foreign policy and opposed significant military preparation. It was not until the late 1930s that Roosevelt actually supported a gradual and entirely insufficient form of military preparedness.

Historians have stressed the differences between Roosevelt and the isolationists, their differing viewpoints over legislation that created overseas entanglements. But these differences didn't show until near the end of the decade, when Roosevelt pushed legislation to help the beleaguered British.

European appeasement was motivated by the wish to satisfy Hitler in order to prevent immediate war, even if it meant the sacrifice of small Central European states. The American form of appeasement was the result of isolationism. Europeans never understood the distinction, not grasping that isolationism, which they detested, was tantamount to appeasement, which they pursued. British and German statesmen thought Roosevelt an isolationist, and, to a degree, so did the French. The policies of one's allies and potential enemies are based on such perceptions. Appeasers like Chamberlain and Lord Halifax thought they saw in the president a kindred spirit.

Differing Goals for Appeasement

The president's policy of aid short of war, projecting "positive and active roles in efforts to preserve the peace and guard security in international affairs,"[22] may have been good enough to overcome the isolationists at home. But his calls for disarmament, trade reciprocity, and conference diplomacy, along with supporting Britain's balance of trade and industrial growth, were insufficient to deter Chamberlain from his policy of appeasement. Without repealing the Neutrality Act, such talk left Chamberlain with little confidence in the president and reassured him in his impression that Roosevelt favored appeasement.

If Roosevelt intended for the British and the French to stand up to Hitler, the effect of his policies was the opposite. British historian C. A. MacDonald writes, "The United States began to use its influence to stimulate appeasement in Europe."[23] The president's globalist New Deal and his interventionist rhetoric were contributing to appeasement, not discouraging it. Washington was hoping for a final settlement of European problems through the rule of law in international affairs, through "the liberalization of world trade."[24] But the Roosevelt-Hull policy of free trade, disarmament, and the rule of law was unrealistic given the climate of the times. Somehow, Roosevelt hoped that the aggressors would be quarantined in this way. "The president was neither well informed nor very well equipped to understand what was happening in Europe."[25] Roosevelt's and Hull's idealistic and anti-imperialist views meant that both men were almost naturally hostile to the British conservative ruling class in the cabinet.[26]

Although both the United States and Great Britain were inclined toward a policy of appeasement, they operated at cross purposes because they saw appeasement as a way to achieve different ends. Chamberlain hoped to rearm Great Britain by buying time, while Secretary of State Cordell Hull was simultaneously calling for a disarmament conference. The American version of appeasement was crafted by Sumner Welles who, in July of 1937, called for a revision of Versailles. "In effect, this was an implicit statement of American support for German revisionist demands."[27] It also had the effect of weakening Chamberlain's strategy of achieving appeasement with Hitler.

Roosevelt's famous 1937 Quarantine speech, hailed as the beginning of the end of American isolationism, was received with dismay in England, where it was seen as another obstacle to appeasement. The speech, according to Prime Minister Chamberlain, "by condemning the aggressors, threatened to lock the democracies into confrontation with all three 'dissatisfied' powers, Germany, Italy and Japan." Chamberlain's policy was to divide them. The speech, however, was hailed by Foreign Secretary Anthony Eden, who saw in it evidence that America was finally abandoning its "psychological withdrawal" from world affairs. This served only to irritate Chamberlain.[28]

After the speech, the Roosevelt administration continued to sound like an appeaser, with Welles, in 1938, offering an even more elaborate plan for world peace, a plan that called for an international conference to discuss new rules of international conduct, arms limitations, and tariff reductions. Welles saw the plan as providing "valuable parallel action"[29] for Anglo-German negotiations, and the president accepted Welles's recommendations. Chamberlain rejected the plan without consulting Eden, who would soon resign from the government. To the Americans, MacDonald writes, Chamberlain's rejection, which shocked Welles and the White House, meant "exclusion from all participation in European settlement."[30] But Reynolds suggests something closer to the truth when he says that Chamberlain's rejection didn't "sorely disappoint Roosevelt." The president, he argues, had never

really been "very enthusiastic about Welles's plan" in the first place, and had only been giving it lip service.[31] To fill a diplomatic vacuum was one thing, but actually to coordinate a plan of action with the British was quite another. It was not the president's style to work with people he did not personally know, and he would hardly have relished the prospect of having to coordinate with Chamberlain a mutually agreeable policy.

And so, the two leaders, both favoring appeasement, failed to coordinate their policies. "Whatever F.D.R.'s private scruples, he had no alternative policy to offer, and he waited to see if Chamberlain's would succeed."[32] Chamberlain personally disliked Roosevelt, but what governed his attitude toward the president was the president's inability to match rhetoric with action. He was, as he confided to one of his trusted ministers, deeply suspicious "not indeed of American good intentions, but of American readiness to follow up inspiring words with any practical action."[33]

The Munich or Czech-Sudeten crisis, from March through September of 1938, underlined the lack of understanding or cooperation between the two men. To the active prime minister, the president was an observer who provided commentary. The president failed to articulate his concepts of deterrence or appeasement. Though disturbed about the turn of events in Czechoslovakia, he would not violate the Neutrality Act. As Chamberlain saw it, Roosevelt had adopted a position of benevolent neutrality, which constituted neither appeasement nor determined support for Chamberlain's policy. This strengthened the prime minister's view that in the absence of a clear American policy toward Europe, he must conclude a deal with Hitler himself, which meant handing Czechoslovakia over to him. Hitler's threat to Great Britain was immediate, whereas to the United States Hitler seemed removed, almost unreal. The asymmetry between the two nations, their leaders, and peoples strengthened the aggressive powers.

> In retrospect the Munich crisis marked the last phase of one American policy and the beginnings of another. Roosevelt's intervention in the final stages of the crisis was a final attempt to pursue the appeasement line which had characterized policy before the anschluss, a line based on the assumption that Hitler's aims were limited and that Germany could be reintegrated into the international system by a policy of judicious concessions. When it was revealed later in October that Hitler did not regard Munich as a final settlement, the President abandoned the policy. The failure of appeasement brought him back to the idea first evolved during the Czech crisis, of containing further German expansion by placing the economic resources of the United States behind Britain and France. This approach was based on the assumption that Hitler's aims were unlimited and that Germany could only be restrained by the threat of force. The conception of the United States as the "arsenal of democracy," a limited liability role which envisaged the deployment of American economic rather than

military power against the axis, was to characterize American policy until 1941.[34]

The object of American intervention in European affairs thereafter "would be to precipitate a movement for a general political and economic settlement which would obviate the necessity for Germany to strike out to obtain sources of raw materials in markets deemed by the German leaders necessary to maintain the living standard of the German people."[35]

. . . . . .

ROOSEVELT AND HIS WAR STRATEGY

President Roosevelt brought to the war America's immense economic energy together with considerable naiveté about the implications of the task involved. He had a single purpose: to win the war. But he had no grand strategy to apply to that effort.

To evaluate Roosevelt's strengths and weaknesses as a strategist, we must first understand what strategy is. It is not the management of specific military campaigns. Strategy is not the civilian management of the military, nor is it political leaders managing military leaders. No matter how destructive or sophisticated weapons become, *strategy* has remained the same since Machiavelli and Clausewitz defined the term. Strategy is grand strategy; it is the rationale for a nation going to war, the motives behind engaging in violent struggle and/or using diplomatic means to resolve conflicts. The conduct of warfare is not the ultimate goal of grand strategy. Rather, as Machiavelli and Clausewitz have taught us, strategy encompasses the political and diplomatic struggle to resolve conflict and fulfill national aspirations. Grand strategy is not a military skill, but a political one. It speaks of both aims and reasons for diplomacy and war. It is the planning of what one intends to achieve in the execution of warfare. Grand strategy requires a set of clear goals rather than mere beliefs. The grand strategist must have a gift for timing.

The qualities required in a peacetime coalition are intensified in wartime, during which the maintenance of coalitions demands constant assessment of the changing purposes of allies and enemies. Success requires staying ahead of both rivals and allies, taking the lead in critical situations, but also exercising patience in order not to precipitate events unnecessarily. Coalition partners are likely to be more cooperative at the beginning of a crisis. But in the course of the war, alliances tend to weaken as circumstances change. Maintaining alliances requires a strategist able to perceive problems before they result in disaster or missed opportunities.

Roosevelt failed in that task because of his work habits and his disinterest in world politics before 1937 and 1938. He was further hampered by the traditions, institutions, and ideology of the country he led. The society Roosevelt represented was unsuited to negotiate the

great power alliances necessitated by World War II. The United States, even as it expanded, had remained instinctively isolationist. It distrusted the Old World, subscribing to the theory that, in World War I, it had saved Europe from itself. The checks and balances inherent in the American political system, the unrestrained press, frequent elections, and the force of public opinion made it difficult for any president to adopt great strategies. Roosevelt, although the senior partner in the alliance because of his country's power, was at a disadvantage from the start when dealing with Stalin and Churchill.

Unlike Churchill, FDR was not by inclination or experience a seasoned strategist. Churchill's accomplishments as a war leader were considerable. He fought the war with the limited resources of a declining empire, an army that failed more often than it succeeded; and yet, until 1943, he was the primary mover behind the Anglo-American alliance. He prevailed over the American generals and sometimes over the president himself. But Roosevelt's relationship with Churchill was complicated by the fact that the two countries faced different problems and saw the war in different terms. England faced the threat of invasion and occupation, whereas the United States felt no such urgency and in fact did not become fully mobilized until the latter part of the war.

Stalin was different from Churchill. His country had been invaded, his regime faced with annihilation. He was deeply involved before the war, and much more so during it, with grand strategy; even though the strategy of the first years of the war, 1941 to 1943, was simply survival for his country and his regime. In domestic and party politics he was very different from either Churchill or Roosevelt. To Stalin, politics meant total political control, achieved by eliminating or exiling his political opponents. He was not hampered by an electorate, by checks and balances, or by powerful political rivals. His only restraint was the prospect of total failure. Nothing in Roosevelt's limited study of history or in his personal experience prepared him for Stalin's practice of politics. Churchill, with more experience but with less power in the alliance, took a more realistic stance toward Stalin.

When Japan attacked in 1941, the nation did not have any grand strategy to guide it in the war. The military had begun to seek policy guidance from the president only in May, 1940, after watching Germany's easy victories in France.[1] When preparations began, New Dealers headed the War Resources Board, Export Control, the Selective Services System, and some three hundred other emergency agencies run by civilians or joint civilian military officials.

Before 1940, Roosevelt had appeared committed to using his influence in Europe without having to resort to force. The United States was not a belligerent and was prevented from becoming one by the Neutrality Act. However, after Great Britain and France declared war in the wake of the Nazi invasion of Poland, the United States was perceived as a de facto belligerent by the Germans.

As the threat to Great Britain became imminent, a strategy evolved. Between 1937 and 1940, President Roosevelt's goals remained unclear, except for his articulation of a search for alternatives.[2] This vagueness and vacillation over choices continued until the Japanese attack on Pearl Harbor on December 7, 1941.[3]

Roosevelt's failure of leadership might be explained by multiple factors, according to Utley: FDR was "deeply suspicious of Japanese intention"; he faced pressing matters in Europe; and he "did not have time to devote to Asian Affairs." Furthermore, "he liked to think in terms of a quarantine, naval blockades, and simple economic sanctions; the stuff of which the negotiations with Japan were made did not suit him."[4]

An examination of President Roosevelt's decision-making style and strategy formulation after 1941 requires a look at the process that led to Lend-Lease and, later, to the Allied policy of "Unconditional Surrender."

Lend-Lease: Generosity or Reciprocity?

During the summer of 1940, events forced the U.S. to consider action. The fall of France, Great Britain's isolation and the possibility of its being invaded and defeated, and the threat against the Atlantic by German U-Boats, all of these matters made the question of what to do about the war urgent for Roosevelt. Churchill looked to the United States for help. In the U.S., however, the debate was about aid to Britain, not entry into the war. This debate was a "unique crisis in the American experience."[5]

The underpinnings of America's security policy—its separation from the European and Asian powers by two oceans; the balance of power in Europe and Asia; and American free markets—were being threatened. The debate over what to do about "Britain standing alone" stirred questions about the policy of isolation that had been forged during the 1930s. America was unprepared for war and now feared what would happen if Britain should fall to the Nazis. The privileged position of the U.S. in the world seemed vulnerable.

Roosevelt understood that he could not bring America directly into the war, especially not in an election year. He moved slowly, unenthusiastically; he was reluctant to be forced into decisions by events he could not control. The debate centered on how to help Great Britain, even though it was known that an intensification of support to any extent would make the United States a de facto belligerent. The initial step on May 10, 1940, was to have American military equipment released to Great Britain and France. Roosevelt circumvented the Neutrality Act by selling the equipment back to its manufacturers, who then sold it to the Allies.

The next step, after the fall of France in June, was a strategic decision to increase aid to England to keep it from losing. The president moved to respond to Churchill's almost desperate plea for a "loan" of forty or fifty old destroyers, striking a deal by August. Churchill later wrote that he thought the transaction brought the two countries closer together, but there, he misread the president. "These were not the president's intentions, for the president was still hedging his bets, responding pragmatically to events and probably still hoping to avoid American belligerency if he could achieve his ends by less extreme means."[6] With the Atlantic threatened, Great Britain under attack, and Europe under Hitler's domination, it was a late date to hedge; but there simply was no American strategy for war.

In 1940, the president, without a policy or sense of direction, *was being slowly and reluctantly pushed into the war*. The turning point would be Lend-Lease, prompted by a carefully crafted letter from Churchill to Roosevelt. Churchill and Roosevelt biographer, Warren Kimball, says it "may have been the most carefully drafted and redrafted message in the entire Churchill-Roosevelt correspondence."[7] In a plea which Churchill called one of "the most important [letters] I ever wrote," he asked Roosevelt for immediate aid in cash and sizable military supplies to offset British losses in shipping to U-Boats in the Atlantic.[8] The president never answered the letter directly,[9] but communicated his decision to help Britain through a press conference on December 17, 1940.

Lend-Lease was a characteristically Rooseveltian New Deal idea, an untraditional form of financing "to devise a give-away program that did not look like one."[10] The negotiations with Congress over the bill saw Roosevelt at his best, circumventing the isolationists and mobilizing public support. On March 11, 1941, the president signed into law the Lend-Lease Act. Lend-Lease was a key event of the war, marking the first institutionalization of the Anglo-American relationship. The subsidy was also taken by Hitler as a U.S. declaration of war against the Axis powers. Kimball is right when he asserts that "more than any other single event prior to the declaration of war against Germany, the Lend-Lease Act signalled that participation."[11]

Before Pearl Harbor, Roosevelt was unwilling to go beyond Lend-Lease. Lord Halifax, the British ambassador to the United States, was frustrated, writing that dealing with Roosevelt "seems like hitting wads of cotton wool." The president remained reluctant to use his powers as Commander-in-Chief "so long as national security is not imperatively compromised." The president "was attempting to work within the democratic structure as fully as he could without endangering American national security."[12]

Lend-Lease's approval by Congress demonstrated that Roosevelt could employ his political skills to great effect. "His legislative tactics in and around congress proved virtually errorless." But the short-of-war approach represented by Lend-Lease backfired. "Anyone could see that the Act (Lend-Lease) gave Hitler an excuse to declare war on the United States,"[13] but Roosevelt did not, leaving America unprepared for war.

Nevertheless, Lend-Lease helped forge one of the most enduring and successful war alliances in history, making it one of the singular achievements of the war. The Anglo-American alliance was strengthened in a series of conferences in Washington and in the Atlantic, creating a military instrument that would defeat the Axis powers by the end of 1945.

The August, 1941, Atlantic Conference typified Roosevelt's methods of operation, involving the deception and maneuverings in which he delighted. He deceived the press by appearing to go off on his pleasure yacht, the *Potomac,* then returned to the White House to board a special train at Union Station; the train took him to New London, Connecticut, where the *Potomac* was anchored, waiting to take him to the USS *Augusta,* the flagship of the U.S. Atlantic fleet. He met Churchill in Placentia Bay, Newfoundland.

The Placentia Bay conference between Churchill and Roosevelt produced what is known to history as the Atlantic Charter, which shaped the course of the war. The Charter, offering Roosevelt a forum for idealistic pronouncements, was not a plan for grand strategy.[14] In the Wilsonian tradition, it proclaimed the purpose of the war, stressing that no secret diplomacy would be conducted and that territorial arrangements and "other political bargains should await a universal peace conference."[15]

The State Department campaigned to include the abolition of "imperial preferences," a slap at the British, and the creation of a general international organization. Churchill was not too keen on a joint declaration of lofty principles, which were difficult to uphold during the course of a lengthy war; but in August, 1941, he was not in a position to argue too strongly. For the high-minded Roosevelt, though, this was not much of a concern; and he would later try, mostly unsuccessfully, committing Stalin to the Charter's "universal" principles.

The proposal that emerged from the conference came from a British working draft, and, as a result, had an "Old World outlook." The Charter was a hindrance to the successful conduct of the war, and it poisoned the Anglo-American-Soviet relationship. Its influence was "severely limited,"[16] especially when it came to Stalin, who treated the Charter with hostility. It did not serve the Grand Alliance.

Yet, the Anglo-American summits produced some remarkable results. Churchill's grand strategy undergirded the military alliance between partners unequal in strength, military capacity, and economic resources. The greatest accomplishment was the creation of a U.S.-British Combined Chiefs of Staff, headquartered in Washington, D.C., thus coming under the control of the president, but still crucial for winning the war.

The Allies remained firmly committed to a policy. Although constantly challenged, this policy was strictly adhered to throughout the war, much to the anger of American military chiefs operating in the Pacific theater, especially General Douglas MacArthur and the naval chiefs, Ernest J. King and William Leahy. But Roosevelt never wavered. He remained constant to the Europe First policy to the end of his life. The Europe First policy should not be confused with a grand strategy, though any number of historians have treated it as such.[17]

The Unconditional Surrender Formula

The Allied policy of unconditional surrender, proclaimed at Casablanca in January, 1943, applied to all the Axis belligerents, but was seen and applied differently by the Americans, British, and Soviets. The policy, an American innovation, was embraced by Stalin and supported rather indifferently by the British. It was first and foremost a typical Rooseveltian proclamation, simultaneously vague and inflexible. "The announcement," Professor Howard is quoted by A. E. Campbell as saying, "was made without any of the forethought and careful consideration which should have gone to the framing of so major an act of Allied policy."[18]

Roosevelt was motivated by memories of the outcome of World War I, when parties rushed to negotiate with each other and make secret arrangements and territorial concessions even as the war was still going on, plaguing postwar relationships. Unconditional surrender, giving the war the appearance of a moral crusade, calling the nation to a total war against enemies not deserving the usual diplomatic considerations, would avoid a repetition of post-World War I intrawar diplomacy, while offering the generals no specific strategic guidance. Unconditional surrender was successful as an inspiration, mobilizing the peoples' energies for a war of the democracies against the forces of totalitarianism. It was less successful as a strategic concept. It did not terrorize the enemy; instead it served Joseph Goebbels's propaganda machine as the massive bombings of civilian population centers stiffened German resistance. It also hampered the anti-Nazi resistance within the German military, which, faced with the Allied policy, could hope for little public support for its actions against Hitler.

As a practical policy, unconditional surrender yielded inconsistent results, often handcuffing military commanders and restricting their flexibility. The policy of not dealing with the enemy on any level was violated by Churchill, for example, when he came up with the "percentages formula" for a division of Eastern Europe between the West and the Soviets in 1944. Unconditional surrender was not applied to Italy. Churchill insisted that it apply only to Germany in order to secure the support of the Italian people, some still under German occupation after the 1943 Italian surrender.

The principal merit of unconditional surrender was that it had the president's absolute commitment even though it lacked any attention to specifics or possible consequences. As a policy, it reverberated through the postwar world, but it may have had little effect on the eventual outcome of the war itself. "With the advantage of hindsight, it may appear that the policy made little difference to the future of Italy or Japan."[19]

In my view, it also had little effect on Germany during the war. Churchill had clearly stated that he was fighting against Hitler and Hitlerism, not against Germany and Germans; but the policy of unconditional surrender did not allow for such distinctions. It aimed to punish an entire population and to destroy a country. Massive bombing did not distinguish between soldiers and civilians, Nazis and anti-Nazis, the actively ideological and the war-weary. All were killed indiscriminately, and there is no evidence that such a policy helped end the war a day sooner.

The failure to develop a policy for dealing with Germany after surrender created an occupation nightmare. As late as 1944, when the war's outcome was no longer in doubt, Roosevelt still had not made up his mind about how to deal with a defeated Germany. Policy, he suggested, depended "on what we and the allies find when we get into Germany—and we are not there yet."[20] This was just another example of Roosevelt's penchant for not making decisions, and it was not challenged by Churchill or Stalin. It was another instance of the policy of muddling through, of conceiving strategy as he went along.

The Commander in Chief and the Concept of Coalition Warfare

More than anything, Roosevelt liked to be called the Commander in Chief.[21] His military staff, including Chief of the Army General George C. Marshall, acted as presidential advisers. Marshall initially had doubts about the president's unorthodox ways and secretive decision-making, but he came to trust and respect Roosevelt, a trust and respect that was mutual. Marshall believed that however undisciplined the president's methods were, he was a man of considerable political acumen.

In the crucial years of 1942 and 1943, Roosevelt was deeply involved in strategic military issues. According to Kent Roberts Greenfield, who edited many of the official U.S. war series, including the famous Green Books, the president made close to fifty crucial decisions against the advice or over the protests of his senior military advisers. Yet, as Greenfield notes, military historians and others, including, for example, Robert Sherwood and General Alan Brooke, chief of the imperial general staff, had conflicting impressions as to whether it was Roosevelt or Marshall who conducted strategy.[22]

Strategic conduct should not be confused with strategic thinking. The chief American strategic thinker was Marshall, but it was Roosevelt who conducted the coalition. In that sense, he was the supreme commander in the Lincoln tradition; but unlike Abraham Lincoln, he never carefully followed the military campaign.[23]

Roosevelt's singular contribution to the Allied war effort was adherence to the concept of a Joint Chiefs of Staff and the coordination between the American and British Joint Chiefs. But Marshall had been the originator of the Joint Chiefs concept and its guiding light. The role played by Marshall conformed to the president's preferred style. In addition to his specific command authority, Marshall acted as chief of the Joint Chiefs, a presidential surrogate in a manner similar to Harry Hopkins and other presidential staff members who acted as surrogate diplomats.

When it came to alliance strategy, Marshall, in early 1942, tried unsuccessfully to defeat the British preferred strategy in the Mediterranean. The Joint Chiefs and Marshall advocated opening a second front in Europe as early as that year, but Roosevelt at first forced Marshall to accept the British staff strategy. In April, 1942, Marshall changed his mind and persuaded Churchill to do so, a testimony to Marshall's persistence. Plans went ahead for the Second Front to alleviate pressure on the Soviets. As it turned out, this proved unnecessary after the Soviet counteroffensive late in 1942, but it showed Roosevelt's tendency to listen to his chief military adviser.

Overall, however, Roosevelt offered almost no specific strategic guidance. The president ran the war as a coalition strategist, but it was a very strange coalition, with members of unequal status and two distinct parts. One alliance was the Anglo-American, another was the American-Anglo-Soviet. The first was highly institutionalized, with a permanent military advisory body, the Anglo-American Joint Chiefs of Staff in Washington, to coordinate military effort. Stalin fought his own war, independent of his allies, not sharing military intelligence or strategic thinking with them.

Not surprisingly, most historians have taken for granted that World War II was a great coalition war against fascism and Japanese expansionism. If we keep to the loose meaning of coalition as an alliance of distinct parties combining to fight a common foe, then World War II was an example of coalition warfare. But if coalition warfare means that the parties unite their efforts into a coordinated strategy as represented in the summits, then the coalition was fragile. At best, the World War II coalition was an *entente cordiale* between Great Britain, the USSR, and America. All three participants had a common goal of defeating Germany, Italy, and Japan, but this did not amount to a Grand Alliance. The two alliances were each pursuing separate policies, and certainly Stalin never truly coordinated them. Even their separate military offensives never became a triangular military effort. For Churchill, the goal, after assuring Britain's survival, was to save the British Empire and bargain the Russians out of parts of Eastern Europe through his "percentage" deal with Stalin. Roosevelt's eye was on the Pacific, and he hoped to establish a liberal international order in Europe with Stalin's help. Stalin's larger goal was expansion into Eastern Europe at the expense of the wartime alliance. The three did not alter these basic goals at any point.

The experience of war was also different for each participant. The United States certainly suffered in the Pacific, but events such as the loss of the Philippines did not threaten U.S. survival. The territorial integrity of the United States was never at risk during any part of the war. Great Britain and the Soviet Union, however, fought for their very existence. Both desperately needed American military, political, and material support, while Roosevelt never needed his allies for material aid.

The alliance was subject to changes by developments in the military situation. Stalin was generally accommodating in 1941 and 1942, when Hitler still occupied most of European Russia. Beginning with his counteroffensive in Moscow and especially after Stalingrad, with the defeat of Hitler a given, Stalin's concept of the relationship began to change. The Soviet army's march into Eastern and Central Europe reshaped his strategy into an expansionist one.

The Churchill-Roosevelt relationship also changed after 1943, with Churchill increasingly becoming the weaker partner, a change reflected in their letters. After 1943, Churchill would, on the average, send Roosevelt two-page letters, and Roosevelt would reply by cable or through Hopkins or Harriman.[24] David Kaiser writes that "many important military questions hardly found their way into their exchanges at all."[25] In the summer of 1943, Roosevelt flatly lied to Churchill rather than admit that he had hoped to see Stalin alone before he and Churchill met.

The politics of the alliance was conducted at the great summits of Casablanca, Cairo, Teheran, and Yalta. Roosevelt and Churchill continued to pursue a global war, whereas Stalin's participation remained limited to the Soviet Union and Eastern Europe. Roosevelt did not have a strategy beyond the defeat of Germany and Japan. Roosevelt and his generals confined themselves to winning the war and did not consider the political consequences of specific military operations in their deliberations. Stalin, especially after Stalingrad, operated on two tracks—defeating Hitler and expanding the boundaries of the Soviet Union.

NOTES

The President's Style and World View

[1] John M. Lewis, "Franklin Roosevelt and the United States Strategy in World War II," 134.

[2] *Ibid.*

[3] *Ibid.*, 158-59.

[4] Henry Adams, *The Letters of Henry Adams,* vol. 4.

[5] Lewis, "Roosevelt and World War II," 345.

[6] *Ibid.*, 361.

[7] Quoted in David F. Healy, *U.S. Expansionism: The Imperialist Urge in the 1890's,* 38.

[8] Quoted in Lewis, "Roosevelt and World War II," 136.

[9] See Donald Cameron Watt, *How War Came: The Immediate Origins of the Second World War, 1938-1939,* 193-96.

[10] Donald Watt, "Roosevelt and Neville Chamberlain: Two Appeasers," 201-3; and David Reynolds, *The Creation of the Anglo-American Alliance, 1937-41: A Study in Competitive Co-operation,* 69-72.

[11] Lewis, "Roosevelt and World War II," 135, 137.

[12] *Ibid.*, 159.

[13] *Ibid.*, 234, 235.

[14] *Ibid.*, 235.

[15] Schacht report to the German Foreign Ministry quoted in Frank Friedel, *Franklin D. Roosevelt,* vol. 4, *Launching the New Deal,* 396.

[16] Wayne S. Cole, *Roosevelt and the Isolationists, 1932-45,* 10-11, 298-300.

[17] *Ibid.*, 8-11.

[18] Willard Range, *Franklin D. Roosevelt's World Order,* 137.

[19] Watt, "Roosevelt and Chamberlain," 203.

[20] Cole, *Roosevelt and the Isolationists,* 3.

[21] *Ibid.*, 7.

[22] *Ibid.*, 297.

[23] C. A. MacDonald, *The United States, Britain, and Appeasement, 1936-1939,* 1.

[24] *Ibid.*

[25] Watt, "Roosevelt and Chamberlain," 185.

[26] *Ibid.*, 186-87.

[27] *Ibid.*

[28] MacDonald, *United States, Britain, and Appeasement,* 43, 48.

[29] Quoted *Ibid.*, 66.

[30] *Ibid.*, 62-65, 69.

[31] Reynolds, *The Creation,* 32.

[32] *Ibid.*, 33.

[33] Quoted in William R. Rock, *Chamberlain and Roosevelt: British Foreign Policy and the United States, 1937-1940,* 69.

[34] MacDonald, *United States, Britain, and Appeasement,* 105.

[35] *Ibid.*

. . . . .

Roosevelt and His War Strategy

[1] Maurice Matloff and Edwin Snell, *Strategic Planning for Coalition Warfare, 1941-1942,* 11-31.

[2] Mark M. Lowenthal, "Roosevelt and the Coming of the War: The Search for United States Policy, 1937-1942," 433.

[3] For FDR's Japanese-Far Eastern policy, see the excellent analysis by Jonathan G. Utley, *Going to War with Japan, 1937-1941* (Knoxville: University of Tennessee Press, 1985), 3-42.

[4] *Ibid.,* 181.

[5] Reynolds, *The Creation,* 105.

[6] *Ibid.,* 132.

[7] Letter from Churchill to FDR, 12/8/40, in Warren F. Kimball, *Churchill and Roosevelt: The Complete Correspondence,* 1:88.

[8] Kimball, *Churchill and Roosevelt,* 1:101; see also Reynolds, *The Creation,* 150-68.

[9] Kimball, *Churchill and Roosevelt,* 1:102.

[10] Warren F. Kimball, *The Most Unsordid Act: Lend-Lease, 1939-1941,* 124.

[11] *Ibid.,* vi.

[12] *Ibid.,* 231, 240.

[13] *Ibid.,* 233.

[14] The best American study is Matloff and Snell, *Strategic Planning, 1941-1942.*

[15] Theodore A. Wilson, *The First Summit: Roosevelt and Churchill at Placentia Bay, 1941,* 174-76.

[16] *Ibid.,* 187, 202.

[17] See Matloff and Snell, *Strategic Planning, 1941-1942,* and others.

[18] Quoted in A. E. Campbell, "Franklin Roosevelt and Unconditional Surrender," 219.

[19] *Ibid.,* 231.

[20] Quoted *Ibid.,* 238.

[21] Author's interview with Joseph Alsop, Washington, D.C., 1986.

[22] Kent Roberts Greenfield, *American Strategy in World War II: A Reconsideration,* 80-84, 50-51.

[23] See the outstanding classic study by General Colin Ballard, *The Military Genius of Abraham Lincoln* (London: Oxford University Press, 1926), which argues that Lincoln had a tremendous sense of grand strategy.

[24] See Kimball, *Churchill and Roosevelt,* vol. 3.

[25] David E. Kaiser, "Churchill, Roosevelt, and the Limits of Power," 204.

Louis Auchincloss (essay date 1994)

SOURCE: "The Inner FDR," in *The Style's the Man: Reflections on Proust, Fitzgerald, Wharton, Vidal, and Others,* Charles Scribner's Sons, 1994, pp. 37-45.

[*In the following essay, Auchincloss speculates on Roosevelt's elusive inner character.*]

Along the walls of the main hall of the classroom building of Groton School were hung, in chronological order, the framed autographed letters of the presidents of the United States. Since Theodore Roosevelt, whose sons had attended the school, these letters had all been addressed to the headmaster. As a fourth-former in the winter of 1933, I eagerly awaited the hanging of the letter of Franklin Delano Roosevelt, Groton '00. Would he write that he had been inspired by this same collection in his student days to become in afterlife the great statesman that he had become? What a climax!

But when the letter arrived, it seemed, at least to a fifteen-year-old, rather an anticlimax. The newly inaugurated president recorded that the collection had indeed inspired him to become what he had later become—a collector. I did not realize how neatly he was spoofing the general expectation.

Later in my academic career I discovered that the FDR twist could work the other way just as neatly. He came to the University of Virginia in the spring of 1940 to deliver the address at the law school graduation of his son Franklin. Professor Leslie Buckler of the law faculty boarded the official train to greet the Roosevelts and sit with them while the ramp for the president's wheelchair was put in place. It was natural that the topic of law degrees should be introduced, and the president, while expressing his satisfaction at Franklin's graduation, nonetheless pointed out that in his day a degree had not been a requisite to taking the New York Bar Examinations and that he had become a practicing attorney without finishing at Columbia Law. After a pause, Leslie Buckler replied that his own situation had been similar: returning from the war in Europe, he had been allowed to take the Maryland

Bar without going back to school. There was a moment's silence, and then the famous laugh rang out. "But you're not president of the United States!"

If one were to take a national poll asking which were the three greatest presidents, I think it likely that Washington, Lincoln, and Franklin Roosevelt would be the ones chosen. Jefferson, according to many historians, left us too shockingly unprepared for the War of 1812; Jackson's reforms seem mild enough in the light of social changes to come; and a greater modern awareness of Theodore Roosevelt's jingoism has tended to trivialize his once heroic image. But Washington's unchallenged position as our founding father has saved him from later carping; Lincoln has been deified and FDR continues to dominate the chronicle of our century.

When the young FDR, then Assistant Secretary of the Navy, called on Henry Adams, it is ironic that the venerable sage of Lafayette Square should have said to him: "Young man, I have lived in this house many years and seen the occupants of that white house across the square come and go, and nothing that you minor officials or the occupants of that house can do will affect the history of the world for long." Adams was talking to a future occupant of that house who would disprove the claim.

Obviously, there were factors that helped to establish the enduring fame of FDR other than his peculiar genius. The greatest depression and the greatest war of the century occurred in his administrations, and that we pulled out of the first and were victorious in the second was not entirely his doing. Also he had the luck of having a First Lady more loved and more active than any other to that date. And, of course, he was elected president four times, twice as many as any other. But it was still his broad smile, his jaunty air of optimism, his confident and silver-toned speeches that gave the world hope, and justified hope, in its darkest hours.

Both the stories with which I started this piece suggest FDR's persistent consciousness of the excitement and drama of his great position, and a study of the three excellent additions to the swelling body of literature about him—*Before the Trumpet,* by Geoffrey C. Ward; *FDR: The New York Years,* by Kenneth S. Davis; and *FDR,* by Ted Morgan—has led me to speculate that a peculiar and very private sense of personal drama and destiny may be the key to the elusive character of the thirty-second president.

Ward quotes Eleanor as writing, somewhat resentfully, after her husband's death: "I was one of those who served his purposes." FDR had no real confidants, she maintained, certainly not herself. No human being ever fully shared his inner life.

This was true, even from his boyhood. Morgan writes:

> He had to fight to get his locks trimmed and to graduate from dresses and kilts. He learned that

there was a part of himself he could not reveal to his mother, and acquired an opaque core, a sort of inner armor. It was a matter of survival. . . .

> It was at his mother's knee that he learned the protective ambiguity that so many of his associates would later comment upon. As the brain truster Rexford Tugwell put it, "He was the kind of man to whom those who wanted him convinced of something—usually something in their own interest—could talk and argue and insist, and come away believing that they had succeeded, when all that happened was that he had been pleasantly present."

After his affair with Lucy Mercer, FDR's relationship with Eleanor became more of a political partnership than a marriage. His children he always loved, but they were usually away and apt to give him more headaches than help with their divorces and speeding tickets and business problems. Louis Howe—in Davis's phrase that "untidy, irritable, asthmatic, chain-smoking little man"—and his secretary "Missy" LeHand were obsessively devoted to their boss, but idolatry does not make for true intimacy. The president accepted the offer of their lives gratefully, knowing that his success was all the return they expected. The Brain Trust, Moley, Tugwell, Berle, et al., representing, as Davis puts it, "a historic attempt to bridge the gap between Intelligence and Power," stimulated and excited him, but they were essentially co-workers. As for his friends, they were for relaxation: Vincent Astor for fishing, his old college friend Livingston Davis for jokes and (in earlier days) for girls. FDR liked people in quantity, at parties, for banter, for story swapping, for general hilarity. Harry Hopkins came nearest to establishing a closer tie, but even that was mostly professional.

Yet I suspect he was not lonely: he did not need intimacy. He may even have shunned it. A satisfaction greater than that offered by people may have been supplied by a romantic vision of himself in history, a sense of his destiny that never left him, even in the terrible days of polio, a vision in which America was seen lapped by the blue waves of seas on which rode beautiful naval vessels and covered with rich valleys and streams and productive farms—he was always more of a Jeffersonian than a Hamiltonian, inclined to find the "good life" in the agricultural countryside as opposed to the wicked city. It was a vision, I suspect, whose setting was reproduced in prints and paintings and stamps, most of all stamps, so clear, so precise, so detailed yet so idealized, affirming America as a peaceful and democratic polity, an America that was waiting for a successor to Cousin Theodore.

This sustained inner identification of himself with the nation could have been a kind of artistic creation. He conformed himself to it, in appearance, in language, in manner, surrounding himself with beautiful and appropriate props: naval paintings and prints, fully rigged ship models, English political cartoons, a million stamps. The knowledge of history that he accumulated was prodigious. Adolf Berle said that he could tell you about naval construction, constitutional law, the story of coins, the ability of white men to live in the tropics—he could tell you about any concrete subject, it seemed, but had little interest in abstract ideas, their analysis, their contradictions. It was only natural that he should turn to people like Howe and LeHand who may have glimpsed the vision behind the style. Did any of his family really sense it? How could the verve of his conversations or the brilliance of his speeches have been appreciated by the author of "My Day"? For even the banalities of that column failed to exhaust the armory of clichés that Eleanor had amassed to combat the social evils of her time.

At first things came too easily for FDR. It must have seemed that the vision of himself in history could almost be left to realize itself. As Morgan puts it: "Before polio he walked along flower-strewn paths. Men came to him offering valuable prizes: Would he like to be state senator, or assistant secretary of the Navy? Would he like to run for vice president? There was an embarrassment of riches." And as Eleanor once said: "If something was unpleasant and he didn't want to know about it he just ignored it. I think he always thought that if you ignored a thing long enough, it would settle itself."

It was not only the polio that brought him to deeper revaluations of his character and destiny; it was the affair with Lucy Mercer when for the only time in his life he found himself tempted to throw up his political career and family for the gratification of a passion. He resisted it, gaining some of the strength that he was to need a few years later in the struggle with infantile paralysis. And when he emerged from the temptations of despair it was to find his old vision enhanced, even more powerful, as we can infer from Morgan's description of him at the Democratic Convention of 1924 when he nominated Al Smith in the "Happy Warrior" speech:

> Then came the moment when he had to walk alone. Releasing Jimmy's arm, he took the second crutch and moved across the stage, the crowd almost holding its breath as it watched. Putting aside his crutches, he grabbed the lectern, threw back his head and smiled into the spotlight's glare.
>
> Here was a man of American ancestry older than the nation itself, a man with a background of Cambridge Square, bearing a famous name, who had dragged his crippled body into the steaming convention hall to make a bid for a second-generation American born and bred in the East Side slums—surely this was what the framers of the Constitution had had in mind.

It was, anyway, what FDR had had in mind. A man who lives alone with a vision will be tempted to be his own moral judge. FDR believed in God, but religion to him was a very private matter; he avoided public worship because he did not like people to stare at him while he prayed. He may have regarded God as a kind of senior partner who did not really want to be consulted in pragmatic political decisions where the end (the vision) justified a very broad category of means.

Certainly FDR went very far with the latter. It is sad to learn that he denied Judge Joseph Proskauer any credit (except for the quotation from Wordsworth) in the writing of the "Happy Warrior" speech, his own greatest triumph up to that time. It now appears that Proskauer not only wrote every word of the address, but that FDR objected strongly to the text and agreed very reluctantly to use it at the last minute. He lied in a speech where he claimed to have written the constitution of Haiti. When he was Assistant Secretary of the Navy he lied in a congressional investigation of the navy's use of its men to entrap homosexuals, denying that he knew that the entrappers were instructed, if necessary, to engage in sexual acts with suspects. And as president he did not hesitate to use the tax power to smite his enemies while shielding his friends from its impact. Thus he spared Lyndon Johnson from prosecution by the Internal Revenue Service in the very smelly audit of the Brown & Root construction firm, which had surreptitiously financed Johnson's campaign for the Senate in 1941. But he pressed for an all-out investigation of Moe Annenberg for tax fraud, which resulted in the old man's conviction and jail sentence. When Annenberg rose from publishing the *Daily Racing Form* to become the owner of the *Philadelphia Inquirer,* he attacked the New Deal. Roosevelt told J. Edgar Hoover that Annenberg's group was out to "get" Harold Ickes if he came to Philadelphia. "I want Moe Annenberg for dinner," he told Henry Morgenthau, Jr., and he got him.

Of course, this protean side of FDR's nature could be a great political asset. As Morgan says, he adopted a position of deliberate changeability that allowed him to hold contradictory views simultaneously, juggling apples and oranges until the time was ripe for decision. Norman Thomas, who regarded him as the greatest threat to socialism of the century, charged that he failed to make essential, internal connections between facts. Davis's reply to this is that as an essential man of action FDR had less faith in the need to correlate items of information than he had in the signs and portents presented to him through his senses. "He collected facts, including other people's expressed ideas, as he did stamps and naval prints." There they were, stored away in his remarkable memory, to be used when circumstances called, rather than woven into a systematized body of knowledge.

FDR's ultimate protection against the extremes to which his pragmatism might otherwise have led him lay in his sense of the nature and fragility of his own power. He knew, as Morgan expresses it, that he could maintain this power only so long as he made himself "the embodiment both of the collective will and the moral compact." Perhaps that is what I have called his "vision." Davis offers a touching picture of this usually self-sufficient and practical romantic turning at last to his "spiritual partner." When his son James was helping him to bed shortly after his election in 1932 he uttered one of his rare expressions of innermost feeling, "an almost unique revelation that what he felt was a fear of personal inadequacy in the face of personal challenge":

"I'm just afraid I may not have the strength to do this job," he said. "After you leave me tonight, Jimmy, I am going to pray. I am going to pray that God will help me, that He will give me the strength and the guidance to do this job and to do it right. I hope you will pray for me, too, Jimmy."

Cliff Lewis (essay date 1995)

SOURCE: "Art for Politics: John Steinbeck and FDR," in *After The Grapes of Wrath: Essays on John Steinbeck in Honor of Tetsumaro Hayashi,* edited by Donald V. Coers, Paul D. Ruffin and Robert J. DeMott, Ohio University Press, 1995, pp. 23-39.

[In the following essay, Lewis explores John Steinbeck's efforts on behalf of Roosevelt during the Second World War.]

The Nazi attack in Europe led to many American artists' participation in government war projects. Writer John Steinbeck was among those whom the Roosevelt administration called upon for assistance. Steinbeck's war contributions to the Roosevelt Administration included suggestions for an espionage program, recommendations to trust Japanese-Americans, and propositions for post-war domestic and foreign policy. And after the war Steinbeck was asked to write a farewell address to a New Deal leader. In Steinbeck's Washington eulogy (1946) for Roosevelt assistant Harry Hopkins, Steinbeck artfully defines a new myth in America's public consciousness— government exists to improve citizens' lives—for which Roosevelt and Hopkins are the symbols. Steinbeck, who kept his political efforts secret, became for FDR loyalists a hidden spokesman for New Deal principles. Drawing largely from unexamined manuscripts,[1] this essay will argue that in the period under discussion, 1939-1946, Steinbeck evolved as an astute yet visionary political writer and, for the innermost circle of the FDR election team, a respected advisor.

The journey that brought Steinbeck to Washington from Salinas, California, began indirectly with his 1936 newspaper articles "The Harvest Gypsies," whose research introduced him to the wretched conditions of migrant workers and to the relief efforts of federal workers. Steinbeck revised the articles in spring 1938 as a pamphlet titled *Their Blood Is Strong*; the pamphlet was one of several projects that evolved into *The Grapes of Wrath* (DeMott xxxiv-xli), the novel that brought Steinbeck in 1939 to the attention of Eleanor Roosevelt and the nation.

Steinbeck's realization that the federal government could alter the appalling migrant conditions, along with the influence of politically active artists Pare Lorentz and Paul de Kruif among others,[2] induced Steinbeck to appeal to Washington to intervene in reactionary California politics. The Roosevelts had been concerned about the serious labor problems in California. When a Democratic governor replaced a conservative Republican, FDR initiated further federal support to the state. Eleanor Roosevelt, moreover, welcomed personal letters drawing her attention to poverty and corruption, and she directed federal authorities to investigate the reports. With FDR's commitment to correct injustices and Eleanor Roosevelt's proclivity to answer personal appeals, reformers felt the White House welcomed their ideas.

Steinbeck first contacted the President in a cryptic telegram from "The Steinbeck Committee to Aid Agriculture Organization," February 9, 1939, protesting the threatened "curtailment of the FSA [Farm Security Administration] Camps and relief program"[3] (RL). The Steinbeck Committee also in February telegraphed a one-sentence request to the President asking "for the continuation and extension of the LaFollette Civil Liberties Committee" (RL). The LaFollette Hearings, which opened in San Francisco in 1939, exposed the abuse of American migrant workers and as well the tactics of the Communist Party to organize them.[4] But Steinbeck also used his name to seek help for a friend. On June 14, 1939, Steinbeck telegraphed a request to Eleanor Roosevelt asking the government to continue funding the U.S. Film Service, the organization Pare Lorentz had created in 1938 to fund his documentaries. Perhaps Steinbeck's trip to Washington around June (Benson 402) was for a meeting with Mrs. Roosevelt. Mrs. Roosevelt brought Steinbeck's request to the President's attention. FDR instructed the Director of the Budget to reply to Mrs. Roosevelt; despite Mrs. Roosevelt's support the funding ended (RL). Nevertheless, Steinbeck had committed himself to a project for someone in Washington. On October 16, 1939, he wrote, "I have one little job to do for the government," and, two days later, "Sorry I committed myself to the Washington thing" (*Working Days* 106, 107). The nature of "the Washington thing" is unknown. A subsequent appeal for another favor resulted in an intriguing relationship between Steinbeck and Washington.

Steinbeck's next request from Washington was self-serving. To acquire quickly Mexican permission for a "marine ecology" trip into its coastal waters, Steinbeck in the fall of 1939 persuaded Paul de Kruif to contact the State Department (RL). For some reason FDR himself reviewed the request and on December 13 sent a memorandum to an aide to determine whether the Navy could employ the John Steinbeck expedition "in connection with information for ONI [Office of Naval Intelligence]." The note specifically directs ONI chief Admiral Andersen to see if he can use Ricketts and Steinbeck "for this [intelligence gathering] purpose" (RL). The Mexican permits arrived without aid from the State Department. No existing correspondence indicates that Steinbeck and Ricketts collected naval intelligence in Mexico. But a few months later, while on a movie project in Mexico, Steinbeck, as we shall see, sent political intelligence to Washington. And since Steinbeck and Ricketts corresponded with Naval Intelligence after Pearl Harbor, it seems safe to assume that the subject of spying must have come up previously.[5] Thus within a year after Steinbeck began asking the Roosevelts for favors, a year in which war started in Europe, Steinbeck began collecting foreign intelligence.

II

Forwarding intelligence about Mexico and recommending a propaganda bureau to influence American public opinion constituted one phase of Steinbeck's war effort. In Mexico to film his documentary *The Forgotten Village,* assisted by Herbert Kline (who directed *Lights Out in Europe* (1940), a film about the Nazi attack on Poland), Steinbeck worried that the lights were dimming in Mexico. There Steinbeck observed the growing influence of Germany. He responded with a typed three-page letter to his uncle Joe Hamilton, Information Officer of the Works Project Administration, warning that deteriorating political conditions required an American response.

Steinbeck's letter of May 1940 described the many levels of fascist threat in Mexico's forthcoming election: "The other candidate is General Almazan. He is a fascist, is being backed by Hearst, by Harry Chandler, and by the [American] oil companies, and by the business interests of Mexico. . . . Unfortunately, he also has the backing of the German element and the German propaganda office. . . . He has promised to raise a rebellion if he isn't elected . . ."(RL).

Steinbeck offered explanations as to why American economic interests supported a fascist system. Steinbeck wrote, "Hearst . . . still has a lot of land down there which he hopes won't be taken from him . . . [and] there is a strong interventionist group in the United States who would like to take over Mexico for . . . Hearst and the Standard Oil Company."

Harry Chandler had huge land investments in the San Fernando Valley, along the Colorado River in Mexico, and exerted influence through his *Los Angeles Times.* According to Daniel Yergin, when the Mexican Government nationalized American oil production in that country, American companies would not purchase Mexican oil. Mexico was forced to trade with Japan, Germany, and Italy. In this dispute, FDR aligned the U.S. with Mexico against the oil companies (276-77).

American public opinion was the second issue Steinbeck believed Washington should consider. Steinbeck warned that the American public received false information from its media about Mexican political events. According to Steinbeck, columnist Walter Winchell wrote that Mexican communists and fascists were cooperating when, Steinbeck said, they battled in the streets. Further, Steinbeck commented, *Life* magazine published pictures of labor marches with captions claiming that the laborers wore storm trooper uniforms, but which Steinbeck identified as their "work uniforms."

Inept American government bureaucracies were the third problem Steinbeck outlined to his uncle. "Ten FBI men arrived lately in Mexico [City]. They are all known . . . [and] they are regarded as spies. They are so obviously FBI men that it is funny. They pose as tourists . . . a hammer [hammier] bunch of flat feet never existed." By

contrast, "The Germans have absolutely outclassed the Allies in propaganda." To these problems Steinbeck added a fourth, one of attitude: "Our businessmen" are arrogant and "Our young diplomats get drunk and express their contempt . . ." for Mexicans (RL). In Steinbeck's view the United States faced a political crisis on its southern border partly of its own making.

Steinbeck recommended that "a propaganda office be set up which, through radio and motion pictures, attempts to get this side of the world together. Its method would be to make for understanding rather than friction." Steinbeck then offered the use of his film crew and volunteered to recruit Hollywood experts who would share the work (RL). Although the letter to Joe Hamilton proposed a propaganda agency, he did not directly advocate an intelligence-gathering organization to replace the incompetent FBI, but the implication exists. Nor does he explain how to deal with the fascist-leaning American businesses.

The letter alerted Washington. Steinbeck traveled to the capital. There on June 24, 1940, he sent Roosevelt a one-paragraph summary reporting that "a crisis in the western hemisphere is imminent, and is to be met only by an immediate, controlled, considered, and directed method and policy" (RL). Roosevelt instructed an aide to bring Steinbeck to the White House "for twenty minutes" the next day. Persuaded by Steinbeck's argument for an American response, FDR offered Steinbeck some form of job. Steinbeck declined. Several weeks after returning to California, Steinbeck wrote of the June meeting: "I hope I made some of it stick" (*Working Days* 114). It did. This meeting confirmed Roosevelt's fears about Nazi penetration, and he "made hemispheric defense a priority." Consequently, in "August 1940 he created by executive order the Office of the Coordinator of Inter-American Affairs (CIAA)" with Nelson Rockefeller its head, with John Hay Whitney chief of the Motion Picture Division (Koppes and Black 51). Neither position was salaried.

A year went by before Roosevelt formed his international intelligence and propaganda units. Steinbeck was one among many to suggest a failure in our gathering of foreign intelligence. For instance, in August 1940 William Donovan, whom the British were training to administer an American spy network that did not yet exist, discussed with FDR speechwriter Robert Sherwood the need for a spy organization.[6] Finally, a year later, FDR accepted Donovan's argument for a "central enemy intelligence organization" and then appointed Donovan the unsalaried Coordinator of Information of what was later designated the OSS and then renamed the CIA (Brown 164-65). When Donovan formed the Foreign Information Service as a propaganda branch of the CIO, Sherwood was in charge of "radio propaganda" and had "800 journalists, broadcasters, and writers" helping him the first year (Brown 170). According to Jackson Benson, Steinbeck's work for that organization in its first year was immense (487). As a result of the June meeting, moreover, Steinbeck had FDR's confidence.

An economic proposal Steinbeck sent FDR two months later also received a hearing. On August 13, 1940, Steinbeck forwarded a scheme to destroy Germany's economy. Noting to Roosevelt that "I find I have a job whether or not I want one," (referring to the June meeting) Steinbeck suggested that FDR meet a friend "with imagination . . . a remarkable scientist" who will "put forth an analysis and a psychological weapon . . ." (RL). In September FDR and the U.S. Treasurer met with Dr. Melvyn Knisley but decided not to act upon his scheme of dropping counterfeit money into the European war zone (Benson 465). Nearly a year passed before Steinbeck returned to Washington.

After working for a year in California on various film and book projects, Steinbeck traveled to Washington in the fall of 1941 to meet with newly appointed CIO Director Donovan to discuss organizing a propaganda unit (Benson 487). A subsequent report from Steinbeck to Donovan leads me to believe that they discussed organizing a Foreign Nationalities Branch within the CIO to collect information from European refugees about their homelands for propaganda or for spying purposes. These refugees, Steinbeck's biographer informs us, were Steinbeck's inspiration for his novel about the Norwegian Resistance, *The Moon Is Down* (Benson 487-88). The function of this branch as a spy network might explain the contents of an extraordinary Steinbeck-Donovan correspondence in December 1941.

Donovan sent FDR on December 15, 1941—eight days after Pearl Harbor—a typed summary of Steinbeck's recommended treatment of Nisei or Japanese-Americans. The arguments of Steinbeck's report suggest that he was aware of California and Washington officials' mistrust of the Nisei. The Hyde Park document demonstrates Steinbeck's confidence in Nisei loyalty; his scheme to assure their continued wartime loyalty is shrewd and wise. As the internment decision remains topical, I quote the entire document.

Memorandum for the President:

The following suggestions have been made to us by John Steinbeck:

1. The Nisei or native born Japanese have condemned the action of Japan and have reiterated their loyalty.
2. In every community the Nisei have very close organizations.
3. Every Japanese foreign born or native born is known to these organizations.
4. There is no reason so far to suspect the loyalty of Japanese-American citizens.

IT IS SUGGESTED:

1. That local civilian defense authorities make contact with these Japanese.
2. That they be given auxiliary status in controlling sabotage.
 (1) They know the language.
 (2) They would be more likely to know of illegal gathering places than whites.

 (3) They have very close check on unknown or strange Japanese.
 (4) Such evidence of trust would be likely to cement the loyalty of inherently loyal citizens.
3. No information need be given them. It can all come from them.
4. Any valuable information coming from them would do much to overturn a distrust of themselves.
5. This can all be done by local authorities.
6. A failure to cooperate would be indicative of disloyalty.

CONCLUSION:

A. By instituting this cooperation, some actual information may be gained and since the Japanese community is settled, such a plan would in effect make the loyal Japanese responsible for the disloyal.

B. In case valuable work were done by the Nisei, it should be published, thus cementing loyalties and driving a wedge between loyal and disloyal Japanese.

C. Organization of this cooperation by the local Civil Defense organizations should be very easy to accomplish.

D. It would constitute a test of loyalty (RL).

In strategic positions throughout this document emphasis is upon the loyalty of these Americans. But Steinbeck acknowledges that "unknown or strange Japanese"—not Americans—should be watched. And before condemning a priori "our inherently loyal citizens," we could administer a loyalty test. However unfair to ask for such a test, it was a shrewd request—given the current distrust and the subsequent judgment—that the Nisei no doubt would have welcomed. The audience was not the Nisei but one suspicious of and unfamiliar with these West Coast citizens. In a few words Steinbeck had tried to educate the President about their community and to persuade him to follow a benign policy.

Consequently Steinbeck's report is organized into three parts: Part one affirms Nisei loyalty and indicates that Steinbeck well understood their insular community. Part two suggests the ways the government officials can use the Nisei community to spy upon "unknown or strange Japanese." His third section reaffirms that the spy system will both succeed in uprooting possible enemies and offer further proof of patriotism.

Today it seems like an extreme proposal even to set before paranoid officials. Over the last forty years we have come to distrust domestic surveillance. We recall the results of McCarthyism and the House Un-American Activities Committee: innocent lives ruined, the loss of our Chinese diplomatic corps. Neither the government's spying upon Vietnam war protesters nor the Church Committee's revelations about the C.I.A.'s abuse of power prepares us for Steinbeck's proposal. We must, instead, recall that fifty-two years ago, when Steinbeck offered his proposal, just a week had passed since the Japanese had destroyed our Pacific fleet and its supporting air power in Hawaii and the Philippines. However unsavory Steinbeck's recommendation that Americans spy on one another, under the circumstances Steinbeck's views show that while he does not doubt the loyalty of Japanese-Americans, he must go to extremes to protect them from those who do. Better to acknowledge that a few traitors might exist and should be caught, and try to protect the rest, Steinbeck may have reasoned.

Steinbeck's "loyalty test" was not offered. In February, 1942, at the insistence of California and Washington political leaders and such prominent Americans as Walter Lippmann, the Nisei lost their freedom. They also lost businesses, homes, and reputations under the Internment Program. Disregarding Steinbeck's knowledge of his employees and neighbors brought national disgrace. A play that he coauthored, *A Medal for Benny,* begun in December, 1942, protested the discrimination against an Hispanic war hero, but it could easily be read in retrospect as a response to the abuse of the Nisei.[7]

Steinbeck's war efforts consisted of more than recommending policies. As Jackson Benson has described Steinbeck's wartime writing thoroughly, I limit my remarks to an outline of Steinbeck's activities. Commencing in the fall of 1941 and into 1943 Steinbeck worked without pay for the CIO, "the Office of War Information, the Writers' War Board, and the [Army] Air Force" (487). In that period he wrote two books for the government: *The Moon Is Down,* which promoted guerrilla warfare, and *Bombs Away,* the result of an exhaustive national tour of air bases, which encouraged the enlistment of citizens into the air force.[8] It is ironic and sad that despite Steinbeck's work on the behalf of the intelligence and military services, other government bureaucracies blocked his application for an officer's rank in Army Air Force Intelligence, and for a while interfered with his freedom to travel abroad because his loyalty was suspect (Benson 508-09).

The F.B.I. questioned Steinbeck's loyalty. From 1936 until his death in 1968 it collected a file on his political life (Robins 96). Because he denounced economic injustice, many Californians thought Steinbeck sympathetic to communism. Communist Party member Howard Fast made this shocking statement: "[Steinbeck] was a CP member when he wrote *In Dubious Battle* . . . we all knew he was a Party member" (Robins 97). (The Communist Party in Poland, as I observed while I was there in 1976, interpreted that novel as hostile, and had banned it.) Fast and J. Edgar Hoover little understood Steinbeck's politics. Nor did Steinbeck at first understand Hoover. In 1939 Steinbeck had forwarded a particularly threatening letter on his life to the F.B.I. with a request for help. But Steinbeck's view changed. As we saw in his 1940 letter, Steinbeck did not respect the professional work of the F.B.I. Nor did he send Hoover his report on the Nisei. It went instead to Donovan to be forwarded to FDR. By 1943, around the time of his application for military service, Steinbeck knew Hoover was investigating him. Steinbeck asked Attorney General Biddle, Hoover's superior, to demand that Hoover discontinue the spying. Hoover lied and said

Steinbeck was mistaken to believe he was under investigation (Robins 96). How could Steinbeck have known? Very likely during the army's review of Steinbeck's application, Hoover's agency sent its confidential file on Steinbeck to military authorities. And someone of authority in a military or civilian agency who read it probably reported the file's existence to Steinbeck. Pare Lorentz, an Army Air Force Officer, recalls a meeting with Air Force Intelligence at the Pentagon in 1943 where Lorentz learned that Naval Intelligence recommended Steinbeck be turned down for a military commission. And Lorentz adds that shortly thereafter he warned Steinbeck of the Navy's letter (106). Nonetheless, Steinbeck's letter to Biddle addressed Hoover and not Naval Intelligence. If Steinbeck had an enemy in Hoover, he had friends in Army Intelligence, in the spy chief Donovan, and in the White House. Finally his passport was approved, and he covered the European war for four months as a journalist in 1943. Although his war work for the government had ended, still ahead were two White House campaign projects to write.

Had Steinbeck been unusually patriotic during this two-year period? No. A few names will serve to represent the thousands of notable Americans who served for patriotic reasons as did Steinbeck. We noted that Rockefeller and Whitney and Donovan (who could not afford it) served without pay. Dollar-a-year men left business to serve in capacities such as organizing military production of war supplies. The authors of *Hollywood Goes to War* inform us that John Houseman, Thornton Wilder, and Stephen Vincent Benet worked for the Foreign Information Service for little money (55-56). Film producers Frank Capra and John Ford enlisted in the service (122); actor Douglas Fairbanks, Jr., whom Steinbeck fictionalized in his war reports, led commando missions against Germans. Steinbeck's reputation of a public spirited citizen is more visible than others because of the written records he left behind. The history of millions of Americans who served longer in or out of uniform is still being written.

III

In 1944, Steinbeck escaped from war and politics by working on his novel *Cannery Row.* In June he agreed to help reelect FDR. We learn of Steinbeck's campaign role in a memorandum from Oscar R. Ewing, Assistant Chairman of the Democratic Committee, who on June 29 sent a note and a Steinbeck "Letter" to Steve Early, FDR Press Secretary. Ewing wrote, "Appropos of the possibility of the President in advance of the Convention, indicating that he will accept the nomination, the Chairman [Robert E. Hannegan] asked me to send to you the enclosed suggestion for a statement that he might make. This was prepared by *John Steinbeck.*"[9] The intent of a "Letter" to the Democratic Party—really to the American public—is to explain why FDR sought a fourth term. Roosevelt slightly revised Steinbeck's "Letter" and sent it to Party Chairman Hannegan on July 10, 1944. The next day the revised "Letter" appeared in the newspapers.[10] The "Letter" intended to blunt the Republican criticism of

Roosevelt's presumed dictatorial ambition. Steinbeck opened his "Letter" by saying that during wartime the President's "superior officer—the people of the United States" is ordering him through the Democratic Party and the electorate to "serve" again in office. Steinbeck compared the thought of Roosevelt's refusal to serve a fourth term to that of a soldier who wanted "to leave his post in line." As soldiers each must serve his country in wartime (HRC).

The "Letter" noted, however, that FDR "will not run, in the usual partisan, political sense" out of respect for those suffering in combat. Then Steinbeck added a further argument for not campaigning because "I have not the time nor the inclination." Perhaps Roosevelt's health was not up to a strenuous campaign, but the question of whether the President would be nonpartisan was answered in this attack upon Republicans: "And I shall hesitate to abandon the country and the war to a group whose last experience in public power reduced the nation to panic, economic hysteria and leaderless anarchy. . . . " The concluding paragraph reiterates in military language that FDR would serve as the public "ordered" (HRC).

Roosevelt included most of Steinbeck's prose in the newspaper "Letter" or in his Democratic Convention "Address" a month later. Omitted from both was Steinbeck's graphic description of the battlefield: "the young men of America . . . dying in the hell of the beaches and the islands" became in FDR's acceptance speech "days of tragic sorrow."

The success of Steinbeck's June "Letter" brought another request. This time Steinbeck corresponded with Harry Hopkins's aide Howard O. Hunter, who requested platform ideas in 250 words or less for FDR's July 20, 1944, "Convention Address."[11] The exact number of words was not accidental. Roosevelt in a July 15 memo to Hannegan asked for a "Gettsyburg Address type of platform" because "People are tired of the old type—don't read them—don't remember them if they do" (RL). Steinbeck wrote a poetic yet visionary Lincolnesque platform. He sent Hunter the typed page with eleven items titled "Manefesto" [sic]. An accompanying note apologized for his having written 300 words but warned that the ideas were arranged and written for dramatic impact and therefore should not be altered (RL). FDR, who had little feel for language, rewrote it and so erased from history an eloquent political document.

The rhythmic flow of ideas is indeed memorable. Using declarative and parallel sentences, Steinbeck opened each of the eleven statements with the pronoun "We" followed by the verbs "intend," "propose," "believe," and in one instance "will not." The first ten items fall roughly into the categories of either foreign or domestic policies; point eleven asserts that technology and science will make an "abundance" of food and goods available and therein lies "the greatest promise of comfort and security the world has ever seen." Steinbeck's eleven points effectively define what was to become the Truman Presidency,

although Truman's policies, as David McCullough's *Truman* shows, had other sources:

Manefesto

1. We intend to win the war quickly and decisively.

2. We propose to create and to help direct a militantly peaceful world organization with the strength to prevent wars.

3. We believe that no people can long prosper in isolation, that all must rise together or sink separately.

4. We propose to cooperate with other nations through trade, association and understanding in order that all people may climb to the new peak of security and comfort which technical developments have made possible.

5. We will not permit methods of production or destruction to be used or controlled by men or nations for the exploitation or enslavement or [sic] peoples.

6. We believe that a free flow of goods and of ideas are [sic] the foundations of world peace and world development.

7. We believe that a thoughtful and controlled economy can support the farmer on his land, the workman in his job and the merchant behind his counter and we know from brutal experience that uncontrolled economy can and will bring us to the edge of destruction.

8. We propose that our returning fighting men shall be secure in their futures—that they shall have jobs in private industry if possible, but we insist that they shall have jobs.

9. We propose to lower taxes when possible but not at the expense of the welfare, security or strength of the nation.

10. We intend to protect our racial, religious and political minorities from those who would deny them their right to live and develop in our democracy.

11. We believe that in the techniques of abundance lie the greatest promise of comfort and security the world has ever seen. We propose to encourage, develop and control those techniques to the end that the greatest good may indeed come to the greatest number and that peace and plenty may live not only in our nation but in the whole world (HRC).

Roosevelt and his speechwriters absorbed only parts of the poetry into their dreary prose and so lost the moment. Let me cite one example of how the revision muddled items 7 and 10 by hiding them in the middle of the FDR "Address":

Improvement through planning is the order of the day. Even in military affairs, things do not stand still. An army or a navy trained and equipped and fighting according to a 1932 model would not have been a safe reliance in 1944. And if we are to progress in our civilization, improvement is necessary in other fields in the physical things that are a part of our daily lives, and also in concepts of social justice at home and abroad (Rosenman 204).

Although many of the policies, especially the controlled economy and the plans for a U.N., were those of the New Deal, nowhere else are they stated so eloquently. Other goals, such as civil, political, and human rights at home and abroad, and a sharing of our wealth and technology internationally became the hallmarks of Truman's Presidency. FDR's "Address" pointedly omitted references to the civil rights (#10) Steinbeck advocated, other than blandly asserting the need for "social justice." Although Steinbeck's proposal to battle international economic and political totalitarianism anticipated Cold War diplomacy, the proposal today has become an honored one. Altogether, Steinbeck's vision for America is, a half century later, inspiring.

Steinbeck's spelling variation of the word "Manifesto" intended perhaps to offer the modern world a vision equal to one Marx expressed in his *Communist Manifesto*. Yet in style and tone it combines the language of Lincoln that FDR requested, certain policies of FDR, and the civil and human rights view of John Steinbeck. The "Manefesto" represents, I believe, the height of Steinbeck's political expression. More important than his Stevenson correspondence because it was written for a sitting president, the Manefesto's domestic ideas are possibly the base for policies Steinbeck worked into President Johnson's Great Society Program address (Hayashi). It was Steinbeck's last work for FDR.

IV

To most people the death of FDR in spring 1945 followed months later by that of his confidant Harry Hopkins, signaled the end of the New Deal. Steinbeck's praise for the achievements of the New Deal and a statement about its place in the nation's psyche occurred in a memorial service in Washington for Harry Hopkins on May 22, 1946.[12] Three speeches totaling two and a half typewritten pages were delivered at the ceremony. Dorothy Thompson's talk came to one page; Steinbeck's eulogy, delivered by Burgess Meredith, covered less than half a page; and Sam Rayburn's speech about public service consumed the final pages (HRC). It is Steinbeck's original three typewritten pages only, however, that I wish to discuss.

Steinbeck never mentioned Hopkins's name until the middle of the eulogy and then twice after that; he mentioned Roosevelt's name once. The omission of the names shifts the focus from the mundane to the thought that "the man was also an idea." It is the immortal concept of the New Deal that Steinbeck wished the audience to recognize, not the man-symbols for it. Paragraph two resembles in rhythm and tone the *Gettysburg Address* he had studied two years before: "Fourteen years ago the

nation lay tortured with fear . . . its industry in ruins . . . [with] a growing cynicism toward government. . . . The nation slowly fought its way out of the wreckage . . . this nation was attacked . . . leadership continued. . . ." It is evident that Steinbeck perceived his subject as a form of political-economic civil war that the New Deal, represented by Roosevelt and Hopkins, had won over their laissez-faire enemies. The battle over, the burial commences: "Then, within a year of one another, the great leader and his friend and advisor died. And no enemy has forgiven these two men. They cannot be allowed to rest because— only the smallest part of them is dead" (HRC). The ideas that prevailed, we understand, transcend the grave.

Steinbeck described the governmental principles that won: in Washington "welfare took precedence over profit . . . it became rooted in the minds of the people. . . . People should come before [*sic*] profit. . . . The idea is a flame in the eyes of the people." Then Steinbeck denounced the recent weakening of New Deal policies: "Even the legislation designed to protect the nation from plunder was cut off at its source by a powerful, greedy and rich fifth column." In defense of Truman he added, "It is true that the new leadership has endorsed the great idea but it is being mawled [*sic*] and shouldered and attacked" (HRC).

Next, Steinbeck's purpose became clearer—his address, modeled upon Lincoln's, was a call for rededication:

> We should be here today not to celebrate the memory of Harry Hopkins but to try to determine within ourselves how much of him is dead and how much lives. . . . Have we become weak and cowardly because two brave free men are dead? . . . Must the nation come to know that without a fight compromise will be permitted with the public welfare . . . ? They are not questions Franklin Roosevelt or Harry Hopkins would have considered since to them there was only one answer.

Steinbeck then listed New Deal economic weapons that brought victory in this political Civil War: "dams . . . new forests . . . highways . . . public buildings . . . saved people by the process of building" (HRC).

Steinbeck argued that future Americans would expect a public-spirited government because the New Deal's political-economic emancipation had been planted within Americans' consciousness: "The administration which will ever again permit one third of its citizens to be ill housed, ill clothed and ill fed cannot survive." The memorial to Harry Hopkins and to his "great friend," Steinbeck concluded,

> is carved in the generations. It is chizeled [*sic*] in the hardest most enduring material we know—the Idea. It flows in the veins and shines in the eyes of the people and it will be there just as enduring in their children. HUMAN WELFARE IS THE FIRST AND FINAL TASK OF GOVERNMENT. IT HAS NO OTHER.

> The graves cannot be closed. The men are not dead. (HRC)

Steinbeck's final words as literary executor of the New Deal defined the new federalism for which this civil war had been fought. Unlike Lincoln's Gettysburg dedication, Steinbeck's graveside dedication did not get a hearing. Ceremonial managers failed to appreciate Steinbeck's unspoken comparison between the Roosevelt-Hopkins era and that of Lincoln. The latter assigned the federal government to protect civil rights; the former assigned the federal government economic responsibility for its citizens. If Steinbeck were bitter about the mismanagement of his eulogy, he had the right to be, for the Steinbeck Washington Address was a fitting response to the burial of the New Deal warriors.

In the writing period discussed, Steinbeck's political transformation is startling. From writing about local poverty in 1936, Steinbeck in 1946 defined for a Washington audience the mythic presence of the New Deal. As an unpaid government employee, Steinbeck composed perhaps some of the best and least-known political prose in our century. Persuaded to spy, to write propaganda, to draft Roosevelt speeches, Steinbeck's political writing nevertheless demanded respect for Mexican citizens, liberty for Japanese Americans, civil rights at home, human rights abroad, and a government that served humanity.

The Steinbeck-Roosevelt connection, however slight, is a commentary upon the access artists had to Washington before the war. As a consequence of war, government grew so large that "experts" replaced amateur consultants such as Steinbeck. Afterwards, writers had presidential access for different purposes: John Hersey attended Truman cabinet meetings for historical documentation; Norman Mailer interviewed candidate Kennedy and wrote a glowing account; but for a writer to submit, as Steinbeck did, domestic and foreign programs is unlikely to occur again. Washington, as David Brinkley has shown, used to be a small town. The Roosevelts reached out to controversial people. And John Steinbeck had the intelligence to blend the practical and the ideal in concise prose. A willingness to listen to people such as Steinbeck may in part explain the ideals for which the Roosevelt Presidency stands.

NOTES

[1] Steinbeck's correspondence is on file in the Franklin D. Roosevelt Library in Hyde Park. References to that correspondence are abbreviated *RL* in the text. I wish to thank Robert Parks for his generous help at the Library. Steinbeck's political writing is to be found at the Harry Ransom Humanities Research Center (abbreviated *HRC*) in Austin, Texas. An earlier version of this essay on speech writing appeared previously in Lewis.

[2] Steinbeck apprenticed in the film business with Pare Lorentz, creator for the New Deal of the classics *The Plough That Broke the Plains* and *The River* in the late thirties. He met Paul de Kruif, biologist and coauthor with Sinclair Lewis of *Arrowsmith,* about the same time he met Lorentz, and he retained lifelong friendships with both.

[3] Charlie Chaplin and Helen Douglas asked Steinbeck for the use of his name in their relief organization. As a Congresswoman Douglas lost an election to Richard Nixon, who implied that she supported communism. Weedpatch, where the Joads go for aid and are introduced to ideas about economic democracy, is modeled after a federal camp.

[4] For material Steinbeck might have used for his novel *In Dubious Battle,* see U.S. Senate Committee Report on the Violations of Free Speech and Rights of Labor, 1939, in Part I of *Report* no. 1150 titled "Employees Association and Collective Bargaining" (11). Exhibit 8307, p.18183, containing the March 28, 1934, "Monthly Handbook for Functionaries," describes the process of recruiting for the Party; its diction is altered slightly in the novel. Handbook: "The unit membership committee . . . passes on him." Mac to Jim: "The committee passes on the report and the membership votes on you." Mac's recruitment of Jim and Mac's organization of the strike follow the directions from the Handbook.

[5] In Steinbeck's *The Log from the* Sea of Cortez he acknowledges that with Ed Ricketts's help, the two of them offered priceless information to Naval Intelligence about the coastal waters around Japanese occupied Pacific Islands (lix–lxi). Such an offer suggests that discussion about collecting marine information along Mexican shores for Naval Intelligence occurred.

[6] Anthony Cave Brown states that the FBI Director "had established a Special Intelligence Service for work in South America . . ." (159) that Donovan and others recognized as ineffective. Steinbeck's name is not mentioned by Brown or by an earlier Donovan biographer, Corey Ford.

[7] A scene dramatized in the play has some similarities to an actual clash between civilians and an army general in California in 1945. The play's climax features an army general threatening to use tanks against an Anglo community who refused to bury an Hispanic Congressional Medal of Honor winner in the town cemetery. The actual clash Bill Hosokawa described involved Anglos and a Japanese-American. On December 8, 1945, General Stilwell presented Mary Masuda a Distinguished Service Cross awarded posthumously to her brother Staff Sgt. Masuda at her California home, where despite threats, she had returned from an Internment Camp. General Stilwell intended the ceremony to be a strong rebuke to the "barfly commandos" who discriminated against Nisei heroes (414).

[8] See Coers for the influence of Steinbeck's novel on citizens of German occupied countries. Benson relates the story that Steinbeck stalled writing *Bombs Away* because of the guilt he felt in sending soldiers to their deaths. Summoned to Roosevelt's office, Steinbeck was convinced by the President's command performance that he had no choice but to write the book. Steinbeck to himself: "I am not going to do this. They will have to get somebody else." After FDR talked about Steinbeck's writing: "Now John, you are going to do what I want you to do—

what I want you to do, John." And then Steinbeck: "Yes, Mr. President, I am . . ." (508).

[9] I discovered two political documents, the handwritten "Letter" and the typed "Manefesto," in the Steinbeck Collection at the HRC, and with help from Robert Parks at RL. I discovered a typed version of the "Letter" (minus a page) and also located the "Manefesto," confirming that Steinbeck indeed worked on the campaign.

[10] Rosenman contains the final version of Roosevelt's July 10 "Letter" (197-98).

[11] Documents at Hyde Park show that Rosenman had written a long acceptance speech for FDR to deliver July 20; FDR rejected it and asked for an "Address." So the call went out through Hunter to Steinbeck for a short speech. An aide and FDR hastily stitched together the Rosenman essay and Steinbeck's "Manefesto" on a train from Chicago to San Diego for the broadcast.

[12] Harry Hopkins had died in the winter, but the memorial service occurred in Washington on May 22, 1946, at the Sylvan Theatre. Of the three eulogies Steinbeck's alone deserves recognition. Someone decided wrongfully that his first two and a half pages were too historical, too descriptive, and used only the last two paragraphs.

WORKS CITED

Benson, Jackson J. *The True Adventures of John Steinbeck, Writer.* New York: Viking, 1984.

Brown, Anthony Cave. *The Last Hero: Wild Bill Donovan.* New York: Times, 1982.

Coers, Donald V. *John Steinbeck as Propagandist:* The Moon Is Down *Goes to War.* Tuscaloosa: U of Alabama P, 1991.

DeMott, Robert. Introduction. *Working Days.* By John Steinbeck. New York: Viking, 1989. xxi-lvii.

Hayashi, Tetsumaro. *John Steinbeck and the Vietnam War (Part I).* Steinbeck Monograph Series, No. 12. Muncie: Steinbeck Society, 1986.

Hosokawa, Bill. *Nisei: The Quiet Americans.* New York: Morrow, 1969.

Koppes, Clayton R., and Gregory D. Black. *Hollywood Goes to War.* New York: Free Press, 1987.

Lewis, Cliff. "Steinbeck: The Artist as FDR Speechwriter." *Rediscovering Steinbeck—Revisionist Views of His Art, Politics and Intellect.* Ed. Cliff Lewis and Carroll Britch. Lewiston: Mellen, 1989. 194-217.

Lorentz, Pare. *FDR's Moviemaker Memoirs and Scripts.* Las Vegas: U of Nevada P, 1992.

McCullough, David. *Truman.* New York: Simon, 1992.

Robins, Natalie. *Alien Ink: The FBI's War on Freedom of Expression.* New York: Morrow, 1992.

Rosenman, Samuel I. *The Public Papers and Addresses of Franklin D. Roosevelt, XIII.* New York: Russell, 1969.

Steinbeck, John. *The Log From the* Sea of Cortez. 1951. New York: Compass, 1964.

———. *Working Days: The Journal of* The Grapes of Wrath, *1938-1941.* Ed. Robert DeMott. New York: Viking, 1989.

U.S. Senate Committee Report on the Violations of Free Speech and Rights of Labor. *Report* 1150, 1939.

Yergin, Daniel. *The Prize: The Epic Quest for Oil, Money, and Power.* New York: Simon, 1990.

FURTHER READING

Biography

Davis, Kenneth S. *FDR: The Beckoning of Destiny, 1882-1928: A History.* New York: G. P. Putnam's Sons, 1972, 936 p.
  Examines Roosevelt's life prior to his presidency.

———. *FDR: The New Deal Years, 1933-1937: A History.* New York: Random House, 1986, 756 p.
  Biography of Roosevelt during his first presidential term that investigates the nature and effectiveness of his New Deal policies.

Morgan, Ted. *FDR: A Biography.* New York: Simon and Schuster, 1985, 830 p.
  Comprehensive study of Roosevelt's life and political career.

Criticism

Campbell, A. E. "Franklin Roosevelt and Unconditional Surrender." In *Diplomacy and Intelligence during the Second World War: Essays in Honour of F. H. Hinsley,* edited by Richard Langhorne, pp. 219-41. Cambridge: Cambridge University Press, 1985.
  Considers the consequences of Roosevelt's commitment to the unconditional surrender policy during World War II.

Cashman, Sean Dennis. *America, Roosevelt, and World War II.* New York: New York University Press, 1989, 402 p.
  Historical study of United States involvement and policy in the Second World War.

Edmonds, Robin. *The Big Three: Churchill, Roosevelt, and Stalin in Peace & War.* London: Hamish Hamilton, 1991, 608 p.

> Analysis of diplomatic relations between Roosevelt, Winston Churchill, and Joseph Stalin during the war years 1939 to 1945 that makes extensive use of available documentary sources and provides a detailed bibliography.

Frankfurter, Felix. "Franklin D. Roosevelt." In *Of Law and Men: Papers and Addresses of Felix Frankfurter, 1939-1956*, edited by Philip Elman, pp. 359-64. New York: Harcourt, Brace and Company, 1956.

> Tribute to Roosevelt by his former advisor occasioned by Roosevelt's death in 1945.

Heinrichs, Waldo. *Threshold of War: Franklin D. Roosevelt and American Entry into World War II.* New York: Oxford University Press, 1988, 278 p.

> Detailed investigation of political events and foreign policy from March 1941 to the Japanese surprise attack on Pearl Harbor on 7 December 1941.

Lowenthal, Mark M. "Roosevelt and the Coming of the War: The Search for United States Policy, 1937-42." *Journal of Contemporary History* 16, No. 3 (July 1981): 413-40.

> Assesses Roosevelt's equivocal and uneven prewar foreign policy.

Nolan, Cathal J. "'Bodyguard of Lies': Franklin D. Roosevelt and Defensible Deceit in World War II." In *Ethics and Statecraft: The Moral Dimension of International Affairs*, Cathal J. Nolan, ed., pp. 57-74. Westport, Conn.: Greenwood Press, 1995.

> Defends Roosevelt's practice of diplomatic deceit during the Second World War.

Ryan, Halford R. *Franklin D. Roosevelt's Rhetorical Presidency.* Westport, Conn.: Greenwood Press, 1988, 206 p.

> Evaluates Roosevelt as "a preeminent presidential persuader."

Schlesinger, Arthur M., Jr. *The Age of Roosevelt: The Crisis of the Old Order 1919-1933.* Boston: Houghton Mifflin Company, 1957, 557 p.

> Establishes the contexts of American leadership prior to Roosevelt's election to the presidency.

—————. *The Age of Roosevelt: The Coming of the New Deal.* Boston: Houghton Mifflin Company, 1958, 669 p.

> Views Roosevelt's political actions in regard to the American economic crisis of the 1930s.

Steele, Richard W. "The Pulse of the People: Franklin D. Roosevelt and the Gauging of American Public Opinion." *Journal of Contemporary History* 9, No. 4 (October 1974): 195-216.

> Probes Roosevelt's response to public opinion during his presidency.

Thompson, Robert Smith. *A Time for War: Franklin Delano Roosevelt and the Path to Pearl Harbor.* New York: Prentice Hall Press, 1991, 449 p.

> Enumerates the events leading up to the American entrance into World War II.

Warren, Sidney. "Franklin Delano Roosevelt." In *The President as World Leader*, pp. 165-282. New York: McGraw-Hill, 1964.

> Explores Roosevelt's global impact as a twentieth-century U. S. president.

Winfield, Betty Houchin. *FDR and the News Media.* Urbana: University of Illinois Press, 1990, 276 p.

> Examines presidential press relations during the Roosevelt era and the influence of the Roosevelt administration on mass media.

The following source published by Gale contains further coverage of Roosevelt's life and career: *Contemporary Authors,* **Vol. 116.**

"The Second Coming"

William Butler Yeats

Irish poet, dramatist, essayist, critic, short story writer, and autobiographer.

The following entry presents criticism of Yeats's poem "The Second Coming." For information on Yeats's complete career, see *TCLC*, Volumes 1, 11, 18, and 31.

INTRODUCTION

Yeats is considered one of the finest poets in the English language. He was devoted to the cause of Irish nationalism and played a significant part in the Celtic Revival Movement, promoting the literary heritage of Ireland through his use of material from ancient Irish sagas. Magic and occult theory are also important elements in Yeats's work, as many of the images found in his poetry are derived from his occult researches. Such is the case in regard to Yeats's lyric poem, "The Second Coming." The work is generally viewed as a symbolic revelation of the end of the Christian era, and is one of Yeats's most widely commented–on works. Thought to exemplify Yeats's cyclical interpretation of history, "The Second Coming" is regarded as a masterpiece of Modernist poetry and is variously interpreted by scholars, whose principal concern has been to unravel its complex symbolism.

Biographical Information

Yeats was born in Dublin to Irish-Protestant parents. His father was a painter who influenced his son's thoughts about art. Yeats's mother shared with her son her interest in folklore, fairies, and astrology as well as her love of Ireland, particularly the region surrounding Sligo in western Ireland where Yeats spent much of his childhood. Educated in England and Ireland, Yeats was erratic in his studies, shy, and prone to daydreaming. In 1884 he enrolled in the Metropolitan School of Art in Dublin. There he met the poet George Russell, who shared Yeats's enthusiasm for dreams and visions. Together they founded the Dublin Hermetic Society to conduct magical experiments and "to promote the study of Oriental Religions and Theosophy." Yeats also joined the Rosicrucians, the Theosophical Society, and MacGregor Mather's Order of the Golden Dawn. In 1885 Yeats met the Irish nationalist John O'Leary, who was instrumental in arranging for the publication of Yeats's first poems in *The Dublin University Review*. Under the influence of O'Leary, Yeats took up the cause of Gaelic writers at a time when much native Irish literature was in danger of being lost as the result of England's attempts to anglicize Ireland through a ban on the Gaelic language. By the early years of the twentieth century Yeats had risen to international prominence as a proponent of the Gaelic Revival and had published numerous plays and

collections of poetry. In 1917 Yeats married Georgiana Hyde-Lees. Through his young wife's experiments with automatic writing, Yeats gathered the materials on which he based *A Vision*, his explanation of historical cycles and theory of human personality based upon the phases of the moon. Yeats began writing "The Second Coming" in January 1919, in the wake of the First World War and the Bolshevik Revolution in Russia. It was first published in November 1920 in *The Dial* and later appeared in his collection *Michael Robartes and the Dancer*, one of several works of the period that exemplify the rhetorical, occasionally haughty tone that readers today identify as characteristically Yeatsian. In 1922 Yeats became a senator for the newly formed Irish Free State. The following year he was honored with the Nobel Prize for literature. Ill health forced Yeats to leave the Irish senate in 1928. He devoted his remaining years to poetry and died in France in 1939.

Major Themes

"The Second Coming" is viewed as a prophetic poem that envisions the close of the Christian epoch and the violent birth of a new age. The poem's title makes reference to the Biblical reappearance of Christ, prophesied in Matthew 24 and the Revelations of St. John, which according to Christianity, will accompany the Apocalypse and divine Last Judgment. Other symbols in the poem are drawn from mythology, the occult, and Yeats's view of history as defined in his cryptic prose volume *A Vision*. The principal figure of the work is a sphinx-like creature with a lion's body and man's head, a "rough beast" awakened in the desert that makes its way to Christ's birthplace, Bethlehem. While critics acknowledge the work's internal symbolic power, most have studied its themes in relation to Yeats's *A Vision*. According to the cosmological scheme of *A Vision*, the sweep of history can be represented by two intersecting cones, or gyres, each of which possesses one of two opposing "tinctures," *primary* and *antithetical*, that define the dominant modes of civilization. Yeats associated the primary or solar tincture with democracy, truth, abstraction, goodness, egalitarianism, scientific rationalism, and peace. The contrasting antithetical or lunar tincture he related to aristocracy, hierarchy, art, fiction, evil, particularity, and war. According to Yeats's view, as one gyre widens over a period of two thousand years the other narrows, producing a gradual change in the age. The process then reverses after another twenty centuries have passed, and so on, producing a cyclic pattern throughout time. In the early twentieth-century Yeats envisioned the primary gyre, the age of Christianity, to be at its fullest expansion and approaching a turning point when the primary would begin to contract and the antithetical enlarge. Yeats wrote: "All our scientific, democratic, fact-accumulating, heterogeneous civilisation belongs to the outward gyre and prepares not the continuance of itself but the revelation as in a lightning flash . . . of the civilisation that must slowly take its place." Thus, in "The Second Coming" scholars view the uncontrolled flight of the falcon as representative of this primary expansion at its chaotic peak, while the coming of an antithetical disposition is symbolized in the appearance of the "rough beast" in the desert, a harbinger of the new epoch.

Critical Reception

The general relationship of *A Vision* to "The Second Coming" has been accepted by most critics, yet the elusive nature of Yeats's imagery has prompted varying interpretations of the poem. Many scholars have focused on its political character and especially on the sphinx-like beast of the poem's second half, seeing it as representative of the general forces of violence and anarchy, or more specifically of the Russian Revolution, World War I, the Irish Civil War of 1916, Fascism, or communism. Such views typically emphasize the horrific and ominous nature of the beast, and associate its appearance with the decline of western civilization. Critics who have used *A Vision* extensively in their interpretations of the poem, however, have occasionally noted that the sphinx is not necessarily intended as a negative image—and that Yeats himself was not displeased to witness what he viewed as the close of the Christian era. Commentators have also

seen "The Second Coming" in the context of other poems by Yeats that elicit similar or parallel themes, such as "Leda and the Swan" and "A Prayer for My Daughter." Additional areas of critical interest concerning the work include study of the symbolic nature of the falcon, exploration of the lengthy process of revision undertaken by Yeats, and consideration of the poet's ironic use of religious allusion in the poem. Others critics have also observed significant influences on the work, which contains echoes of Percy Shelley's *Prometheus Unbound*, and have examined its philosophical underpinnings, particularly in relation to the conception of alternating cycles of human history proposed by Friedrich Nietzsche. Overall, "The Second Coming" has been well-received as one of the most evocative visionary lyric poems of the twentieth-century and widely praised for its technical excellence and extensive symbolic resonance.

CRITICISM

Donald Weeks (essay date 1948)

SOURCE: "Image and Idea in Yeats's 'The Second Coming'," in *PMLA*, Vol. LXIII, No. 1, March, 1948, pp. 281-92.

[*In the following essay, Weeks seeks to trace the images, thoughts, and associations alive in Yeats's mind while he was writing "The Second Coming."*]

There are poets whose art is an accumulating cluster of images that become more and more identified with specific ideas. I believe Yeats to have been such a poet, in whom a cluster of images grew in significance to produce the great poems of the period from the first World War to the second. Generally accepted as one of Yeats' finest lyrics is **"The Second Coming."** I believe that the poem gains in richness by being considered in the light of associations that had long preoccupied Yeats, and that are frequently found together in his writings: Shelley, and especially his *Prometheus Unbound;* the Great Memory; and the Second Coming.

Yeats came by his admiration of Shelley from his grandfather, who "constantly read Shelley,"[1] and from his father, J. B. Yeats, who used to "read out the first speeches of the *Prometheus Unbound*" at a time when the father's influence upon the son's thoughts "was at its height." Yeats had already begun to play the rôle of the poet which he sustained all his life. He chose as his first model Alastor, "my chief of men and longed to share his melancholy, and maybe at last to disappear from everybody's sight as he disappeared drifting in a boat along some slow-moving river between great trees." His "mind gave itself to gregarious Shelley's dream of a young man, his hair blanched with sorrow, studying philosophy in some lonely tower, or of his old man, master of all human knowledge, hidden from human sight in some shell-strewn cavern on the Mediterranean shore."[2] Because his father exalted dramatic poetry above all other kinds, Yeats began to write play after play in imitation of Shelley, and of Edmund Spenser. The result was that his poetry became "too full of the reds and yellows Shelley gathered in Italy,"[3] a condition which Yeats then tried to cure by fasting and sleeping on a board.

Prometheus Unbound was the first book which Yeats in a mood of romance "possessed for certain hours or months" as the book he longed for. It became for him "my sacred book." When Yeats was twenty (1885), he proposed to the members of the Hermetic Society "that whatever the great poets had affirmed in their finest moments was the nearest we could come to an authoritative religion, and that their mythology, their spirits of water and wind were but literal truth. I had read *Prometheus Unbound* with this in mind and wanted help to carry my study through all literature."[4] When Yeats wrote in 1900 his essay on the *Philosophy of Shelley's Poetry,* he was spending his fourth summer at Coole. The chief poem of this summer was the *Shadowy Waters.* Yeats says in his essay, "I have re-read *Prometheus Unbound,* which I had hoped my fellow-students would have studied as a sacred book, and it seems to me to have an even more certain place than I had thought, among the sacred books of the world."[5] He was then thirty-five. It is a psychological cliché to say that any poem so profoundly admired by a man growing into a great poet himself has made an ineradicable impression.

In the same essay Yeats tell us when and where he re-read *Prometheus Unbound:* "I have re-read his *Prometheus Unbound* for the first time for many years, in the woods of Drim-da-rod, among the Echte hills, and sometimes I have looked towards Slieve-nan-Orr, where the country people say the last battle of the world shall be fought till the third day, when a priest shall lift a chalice, and the thousands of years of peace begin."[6] Here for the first time in Yeats I find the association of *Prometheus Unbound* with the second coming. In her *Poets and Dreamers,* published in the same year as *Ideas of Good and Evil,* Lady Gregory begins her essay on "Mountain Theology" with the same legend:

> Mary Glynn lives under Slieve-nan-Or, the Golden Mountain, where the last battle will be fought in the last great war of the world; so that the sides of Gorteveha, a lesser mountain, will stream with blood. But she and her friends are not afraid of this; for an old weaver from the north, who knew all things, told them long ago that there is a place near Turloughmore where war will never come, because St. Columcill used to live there. So they will make use of this knowledge, and seek a refuge there, if, indeed, there is room enough for them all.[7]

This essay is not dated, but others in the book are, and none is dated later than 1902. It does not seem unreasonable to assume that here was a legend which Yeats learned when Lady Gregory took him, for the sake of his health and his art, collecting folklore among the neighboring cottages. Since Mary Glynn lived about ten miles from Gort, she was among the neighbor folk.

In the *Philosophy of Shelley's Poetry* Yeats for the first time associates Shelley with the idea of the Great Memory, which becomes so important in Yeats' work: "He seems in his speculations to have lit on that memory of nature the visionaries claim for the foundation of their knowledge." Later in the essay Yeats writes:

> I imagine that, when he wrote his earlier poems, he allowed the subconscious life to lay its hands so firmly upon the rudder of his imagination, that he was little conscious of the abstract meaning of the images that rose in what seemed the idleness of his mind. Any one who has any experience of any mystical state of the soul knows how there float up in the mind profound symbols, whose meaning, if indeed they do not delude one into the dream that they are meaningless, one does not perhaps understand for years. Nor I think has any one, who has known that experience with any constancy, failed to find some day in some old book, or on some old monument, a strange or intricate image, that had floated up before him, and grown perhaps dizzy with the sudden conviction that our little memories are but a part of some great memory that renews the world and men's thoughts age after age, and that our thoughts are not, as we suppose, the deep but a little foam upon the deep. Shelley understood this, as is proved by what he says of the eternity of beautiful things and of the influence of the dead, but whether he understood that the great memory is also a dwelling house of symbols, of images that are living souls, I cannot tell. He had certainly experience of all but the most profound of the mystical states, of that union with created things which assuredly must precede the soul's union with the uncreated spirit.[8]

Previously Yeats had made an observation on *Queen Mab* which illustrates this passage and throws light on what happened to Yeats himself.

> The passage where Queen Mab awakes 'all knowledge of the past,' and the good and evil 'events of old and wondrous times,' was no more doubtless than a part of the machinery of the poem, but all the machineries of poetry are parts of the convictions of antiquity, and readily become again convictions in minds that dwell upon them in a spirit of intense idealism.[9]

Neither Yeats' poetry nor his prose shows any special preoccupation with Shelley or the Great Memory from 1903 until January 1918, when *Per Amica Silentia Lunae* was published. In a letter to his father, Yeats described *Per Amica* as a "little philosophical book—60 pages in print perhaps—'An alphabet.' It is in two parts: **"Anima Hominis"** and **"Anima Mundi"** and is a kind of prose backing to my poetry. I shall publish it in a new book of verse, side by side, I think. Reviewers find it easier to write if they have ideas to write about—ideas like those in my *Reveries*."[10] The essays were published with one accompanying poem, **"Ego Dominus Tuus,"** the ideas in which are pertinent to **"Anima Hominis."** The prologue to *Per Amica* is dated May 11, 1917. The "Maurice" addressed in it must be Ezra Pound, with whom Yeats lived in Sussex during the summer of 1916. Yeats tells how on his return to London their conversations had so obsessed him that he had to write the book to have his say. The importance of *Per Amica* in the development of Yeats is that it shows the beginning of the dominant ideas of the later *Vision,* at this stage still general, still poetic.

"Anima Hominis" is dated February 25, 1917. The essay develops the ideas of the mask and the opposite. It explains the beginning of what is to be one of Yeats' most persistent images.

> Many years ago I saw, between sleeping and waking a woman of incredible beauty shooting an arrow into the sky, and from the moment when I made my first guess at her meaning I have thought much of the difference between the winding movement of nature and the straight line, which is called in Balzac's *Seraphita* the "Mark of Man," but comes closer to my meaning as the mark of saint or sage. I think that we who are poets and artists, not being permitted to shoot beyond the tangible, must go from desire to weariness and so to desire again, and live but for the moment when the vision comes to our weariness like terrible lightning, in the humility of the brutes. I do not doubt those heaving circles, those winding arcs, whether in one man's life or in that of an age, are mathematical, and that some in the world, or beyond the world, have foreknown the event and pricked upon the calendar the life-span of a Christ, a Buddha, a Napoleon: . . . [11]

In **"Anima Mundi"** Yeats tells how he had experimented with dreams and visions and had come to believe in a Great Memory. He quotes much from Henry More's *Anima Mundi.* He cites Shelley, "A good Platonist," as having "set this general soul in the place of God," and as having said wise things about the nature of dreams. Later in the essay Yeats says, "When I remember that Shelley calls our minds 'mirrors of the fire, for which all thirst,' I cannot but ask the question all have asked, 'What or who has cracked the mirror?' I begin to study the only self that I can know, myself, and to wind the thread upon the perne again."[12] Yeats had previously used this cracked mirror image in **"Rosa Alchemica"** (1897). Its appearance in the midst of a mystic experience makes it seem relevant at this point. The I of the story accuses Michael Robartes, who wants him to become initiated into the Order of the Alchemical Rose:

> "You would sweep me away into an indefinite world which fills me with terror; and yet a man is a great man just in so far as he can make his mind reflect everything with indifferent precision like a mirror." I seemed to be perfectly master of myself, and went on, but more rapidly "I command you to leave me at once, for your ideas and phantasies

are but the illusions that creep like maggots into civilisation when they begin to decline and into minds when they begin to decay."[13]

The speaker is angry. He is about to rise and strike Robartes with an alembic from the table when he is drowned in a wave of peacock feathers, a wave that becomes flame and is full of voices. He knows that he has struggled for hundreds of years and is now at last conquered. He hears a voice over his head crying, "'The mirror is broken in two pieces,' and a more distant voice cry with an exultant cry, 'The mirror is broken into numberless pieces' . . ." He swirls up through space, through forms caught in the eternal moment, until "All things that had ever lived seemed to come and dwell in my heart, and I in theirs . . ."[14] He then falls through a starry space, awakes, and says to Michael Robartes that he will go wherever Robartes wills. Whether the experience of **"Rosa Alchemica"** was fiction or reality, it seems related to *Per Amica* exactly as such early lyrics of Yeats as those on the rose are related to later lyrics like **"The Second Coming."** In *Per Amica,* after remembering that Shelley had called our minds "mirrors of the fire for which all thirst," Yeats goes on to describe personal experiences that suggest the episode from **"Rosa Alchemica"** and, it seems to me, the philosophy of Prometheus in the first act of *Prometheus Unbound.*

> At certain moments, always unforeseen, I become happy, most commonly when at hazard I have opened some book of verse. Sometimes it is my own verse when, instead of discovering new technical flaws, I read with all the excitement of the first writing. Perhaps I am sitting in some crowded restaurant, the open book beside me, or closed, my excitement having over-brimmed the page. I look at the strangers near as if I had known them all my life, and it seems strange that I cannot speak to them: Everything fills me with affection, I have no longer any fears or any needs; I do not even remember that this happy mood must come to an end. It seems as if the vehicle had suddenly grown pure and far extended and so luminous that one half imagines that the images from **"Anima Mundi,"** embodied there and drunk with that sweetness, would, as some country drunkard who had thrown a wisp into his own thatch, burn up time.

> It may be an hour before the mood passes, but latterly I seem to understand that I enter upon the moment I cease to hate.[15]

As Yeats put the matter in the epigraph to his 1914 volume of poems, "In dreams begin responsibilities." In the epilogue to *Per Amica,* addressed to "Maurice," Yeats quotes Mallarme: "All our age is full of the trembling of the veil of the temple."[16] "The trembling of the veil" was to become not only the title of the second volume of Yeats' autobiography, but also the serious theme which was to lift to greatness Yeats' next two volumes of poetry, *The Wild Swans at Coole* (1919) and *Michael Robartes and the Dancer* (1921), in which **"The Second Coming"** appeared.

I do not know precisely when **"The Second Coming"** was written. It appears in print for the first time in the *Nation and Athenaeum* for November 1920, and in the *Dial* for the same month. That same autumn the poem appeared in the ***Michael Robartes and the Dancer*** printed at the Cuala Press. The poem which follows **"The Second Coming," "A Prayer for My Daughter,"** is dated June 1919, but there is no way of determining the relation of **"The Second Coming"** to this date. From internal evidence which I shall discuss later, I believe Yeats must first have written the poem in the summer of 1918 at Ballinamantane House near Coole and Ballylee, or in the summer of 1919 at Ballylee. It is perfectly clear from reading the ***Collected Poems*** that **"The Second Coming"** is one of the group of poems which was written out of Yeats' *Vision,* several of which, as Yeats admitted, are unintelligible without the reader's knowing ***Michael Robartes and His Friends.***

The story of Yeats' *Vision* is well-known: how four days after his marriage in October 1917 (***Per Amica*** was written in the spring of that year) Yeats discovered his wife to be a medium, how out of the record of her communications came the ***Discoveries of Michael Robartes,*** which he later expanded into *A Vision.* It was dissatisfaction with what he called his earlier "unnatural story of an Arabian traveller"[17] that led Yeats to the exposition called "Great Wheel." To me, the necessity for Yeats' exposition is clearly foreshadowed by the statement in ***Per Amica Silentia Lunae,*** "I do not doubt those heaving circles, those winding arcs, whether in one man's life or in that of an age, are mathematical. . . . "[18] "The Great Wheel" is the mathematics of Yeats' vision; it was "finished at Thor Ballylee, 1922, in a time of Civil War,"[19] Mrs. Yeats' exposition having ended in 1920. The additional books of the *Vision* were finished by 1925.

"The Great Wheel" is rich in suggestions of Shelley, especially in the chapter on the "Twenty-eight Incarnations," in which Yeats discusses the double personalities of many historical figures. Shelley appears under phase 17, the Daimonic man. But it is more important to keep in mind the theme of the *Vision* as Michael Robartes puts it in the ***Stories of Michael Robartes and His Friends,*** "Have I proved that civilizations come to an end when they have given all their light like burned-out wicks, that ours is near its end?"[20] Without elaborating unnecessarily Yeats' exposition of the Great Wheel, I want to point out two statements which Yeats makes about the Thirteenth Cone. He says:

> The cone which intersects ours is a cone in so far as we think of it as the antitheses to our thesis, but if the time has come for our deliverance it is the phaseless sphere, sometimes called the Thirteenth Sphere, for every lesser cycle contains within itself a sphere that is, as it were, the reflection or messenger of the final deliverance. Within it live all souls that have been set free and every *Daimon* and *Ghostly Self;* our expanding cone seems to cut through its gyre; spiritual influx is from its circumference, animate life from its centre. "Eternity also," says Hermes in the

Aeslepius dialogue, "though motionless itself, appears to be in motion." When Shelley's Demogorgon— eternity—comes from the centre of the earth it may so come because Shelley substituted the earth for such a sphere.[21]

There is an interesting footnote to this passage, which I think further demonstrates the point I have been making that *Prometheus Unbound* was always available to Yeats' mind for illustration of an argument: "Shelley, who had more philosophy than men thought when I was young, probably knew that Parmenides represented reality as a motionless sphere. Mrs. Shelley speaks of the 'mystic meanings' of *Prometheus Unbound* as only intelligible to a 'mind as subtle as his own'." I think the appeal of such a statement as Mrs. Shelley's to Yeats is obvious. He took her at her word.

Later in the *Vision* Yeats discusses the changes which came from the birth of Christ and the changes which will come with the Great Year—1927, as Yeats had figured it out. The Great Year must "reverse our era and resume past eras in itself; what else it must be no man can say, for always at the critical moment the *Thirteenth Cone,* the sphere, the unique intervenes."[22] Yeats then quotes the five lines of **"The Second Coming"** beginning, "Somewhere in the sands—"

I hope I have shown that three ideas and their associated images remained in Yeats' mind for some thirty years: the Second Coming, the Great Memory, and *Prometheus Unbound.* I feel that these ideas gained intensity and complexity as they became part of Yeats' vision. Now I want to suggest the chain of associations that led to **"The Second Coming."** I think it is obvious that poems popped from Yeats in emotional excitement and were then subjected to that technical refinement of which he became a great master. What I am giving as possible successive steps in the creation of a poem must have been, with Yeats, lightning-swift associations that seemed simultaneous. Lest I have given the impression that **"The Second Coming"** was written while Yeats was working on *A Vision,* I will repeat the statement that Mrs. Yeats' exposition ended in 1920. Then Yeats began to examine the fifty some copy-books of automatic writing preparatory to writing the system. I have already said that **"The Second Coming"** was first published in November 1920. But in discussing poetry, I believe that when one has shown certain associations to be of long standing in the poet's mind, one may safely use to throw light on the poem the same associations in the poet's writing after the creation of the poem. I have at all times assumed the persistence of certain ideas and images in Yeats.

1. I begin with the fact that since his late teens Shelley, and especially *Prometheus Unbound,* had been of great interest to Yeats.

2. From 1916 at the latest Yeats was increasingly concerned with the decline of the west, the trembling of the veil, the Great Year, the Second Coming, and the warnings

of the end which came to man from the Great Memory. I think these ideas gained greater intensity with Mrs. Yeats' exposition of the Great Wheel.

3. Among the fuses which set a poem off may be its dominant idea, its dominant image, or its first image. Since the first paragraph of the poem can be explained as having arisen from the first image, I assume the falcon to be the beginning of the creation of the poem. There are three possibilities here. The simple explanation that Yeats had recently seen a falconer and his bird is too simple, and not in accord with the richness of associations in Yeats' work of this period. The second possibility goes back to a practice of Yeats. In the **"Cold Heaven"** from the 1914 volume of poems, *Responsibilities,* Yeats speaks of staring into the "cold and rook-delighting heaven" until "imagination and heart were driven so wild" that only memories were left. In the third poem after, the **"Magi,"** Yeats sees the wise men "in the blue depths of the sky." Yeats wrote in *Per Amica Silentia Lunae* of the desirability of passing into a slight trance to allow images and associations free play in one's mind. He himself had cultivated this practice. A poet dreaming on his tower, a bird across the sky, the memory of the **"Magi"**—here is a possible chain of associations.

The third possibility involves associations with the hawk. In the Cuala Press edition of the *Wild Swans at Coole* (1919) appeared one of Yeats' Noh plays, *At the Hawk's Well.* It was the third of a series linked psychically; the fourth of the series was *Calvary.*[23] Among the lyrics in the *Wild Swan* is the **"Hawk,"** in which the bird also will "not hear the falconer." Later in a note to **"Meditations in Time of Civil War"** written at Thor Ballylee in 1922, Yeats says of the seventh poem:

> I suppose that I must have put hawks into the fourth stanza because I have a ring with a hawk and butterfly upon it, to symbolize the straight road of logic, and so of mechanism, and the crooked road of intuition: 'For wisdom is a butterfly and not a gloomy bird of prey.'—1928.[24]

That Yeats was not always consistent in his use of images is clear from a note on **"Calvary"** in *Four Plays for Dancers:* "Certain birds, especially as I see things, such lonely birds as the heron, hawk, eagle, and swan, are the natural symbols of subjectivity, especially when floating upon the wind alone or alighting upon some pool or river. . . . "[25] The hawk as symbol of subjectivity seems less relevant to **"The Second Coming"** than the hawk as symbol of logic. Since the poem moves at once to a picture of the age of mechanism, the hawk seems not improbable as symbol of logic. But the three possibilities I have suggested are not exclusive.

Although I am not saying that these associations happened just so, I must insist that in a poet who treasured subtlety as Yeats did, there is a clear flickering of similar images from poem to poem in work of the same period.

4. The association of the hawk with mechanism and the phrase, "the widening gyre," may have brought into Yeats' mind a passage from the first act of *Prometheus Unbound,* with all the implications of **"The Second Coming"** which that poem has. I refer to the torture of Prometheus by the woeful sight of "a youth with patient looks nailed to a crucifix" (1, 585-586). The Fury taunts Prometheus with this emblem of those who endure wrong for man. He tells Prometheus (the italics are mine):

> In each human heart terror survives
> The ruin it has gorged: the loftiest fear
> All that they would disdain to think were true.
> Hypocrisy and custom make their minds
> The fanes of many a worship, now outworn.
> They dare not devise good for man's estate,
> And yet they not know that they do not dare.
> *The good want power,* but to weep barren tears.
> *The powerful goodness want;* worse need for them.
> The wide want love; and those who love want
>   wisdom;
> *And all best things are thus confused to ill.*
> Many are strong and rich, and would be just,
> But live among their suffering fellow-men
> As if none felt; they know not what they do.
>   [1, 618-631]

In **"The Second Coming"** Yeats wrote:

> Things fall apart; the centre cannot hold;
> Mere anarchy is loosed upon the world,
> The blood-dimmed tide is loosed, and everywhere
> The ceremony of innocence is drowned;
> The best lack all conviction, while the worst
> Are full of passionate intensity.
>   [3-8]

I find these passages alike not only in idea but also in rhythm. The superiority of Yeats seems demonstrated by the difference between the last line of the Shelley and the last line and a half of the Yeats, the passionate intensity of the worst having more terror than Shelley's "they know not what they do," in spite of the allusion here to Jesus' "Forgive them, for—"

5. If the unbinding of Prometheus can logically give rise to the thought of **"The Second Coming,"** I think it likely that the idea of **"The Second Coming"** was reinforced by the sight or memory of "Slieve-nan-Or, the Golden Mountain, where the last battle will be fought in the last great war of the world." Since the memory would do as well as the sight, it makes little difference whether the poem was written at Ballylee during the summer of 1918 or 1919, or in London or Oxford during 1920.

6. The "vast image out of *Spiritus Mundi*" came, I think, from the last poem in the *Wild Swans at Coole.* It is the **"Double Vision of Michael Robartes,"** a poem which John Aherne wrote Yeats accorded with Robartes diagrams.

> On a grey rock of Cashel I suddenly saw
> A sphinx with woman breast and lion paw,

A Buddha, hand at rest,
Hand lifted up that blest . . .

[II, 1-4]

Later in the *Vision* Yeats pointed out that he should have said *Christ* not *Buddha*, since Buddha was a Jupiter Saturn influence and therefore bad.[26] Whether Yeats actually had this double vision I do not know. The poem says that he did.

Although I saw it all in the mind's eye
There can be nothing solider till I die;
I saw by the moon's light
Now at its fifteenth night.

[II, 9-12]

And after that arranged it in a song
Seeing that I, ignorant for so long,
Had been rewarded thus
In Cormac's ruined house.

[III, 17-20]

Cormac's house was the home of the Gaelic gods on the grey rock of Cashel.

But Yeats had had a single vision, the vision of the beast. Yeats explains in the introduction to **"The Resurrection"** in *Wheels and Butterflies* the origin of this vision: "Had I begun *On Baile's Strand* or not when I began to imagine, as always at my left side just out of the range of the sight, a brazen winged beast that I associated with laughing ecstatic destruction?" Yeats wrote a footnote to the phrase *brazen winged beast:* "Afterwards described in my poem **'The Second Coming.'"**[27] This would indicate that Yeats kept the image in mind from about 1904, when *On Baile's Strand* was first produced, until 1918-19. He seems to have dropped in **"The Second Coming"** the laughter of the beast.

Of course the Book of Revelations has associations that might have enriched the meaning of the image "out of Spiritus Mundi." There is nothing in Revelations to suggest that the beast was a sphinx. Yeats changes the Greek female sphinx to the Egyptian male sphinx, more appropriate perhaps to the "sands of the desert." The beast of Revelations with its number, 666, has a history related to the Great Year, a history which Yeats must have known.

The image of the rough beast slouching toward Bethlehem with which **"The Second Coming"** concludes needs no special explanation. It is quite plainly an association of the idea of the beast, the Anti-Christ, with the birthplace of Jesus. There may be some association with Yeats' earlier poem, **"The Magi,"** in which the wise men, "by Calvary's turbulence unsatisfied," hope to find again in Bethlehem the "uncontrollable mystery on the bestial floor." The phrase, "the bestial floor," suggests a kind of uncontrollable mystery different from the Second Coming of Christ.

It is not easy to exaggerate the associations current in a poet's mind at the time of his finest work. **"The Second Coming"** belongs to such a period in Yeats' life. Although it is not possible ever to say that associations arose only in a certain order, it is possible to describe the ideas and images alive in the poet's mind at the time of the writing of the poem. I hope I have done this with **"The Second Coming."**

Finally, a note on Yeats and *Prometheus Unbound.*

Yeats stayed at Coole during Lady Gregory's last illness. Here in the winter of 1931-33 Yeats read again Balzac and *Prometheus Unbound,* "for the third time," Hone says, a statement which seems meaningless to me.[28] The reading apparently inspired Yeats to write his essay, **"Prometheus Unbound,"** in which Yeats acknowledges that Shelley "and not Blake, whom I had studied more and with more approval, had shaped my life. . . . " But the shaping was not altogether good: " . . . and when I thought of the tumultuous and often tragic lives of friends or acquaintances I attributed to his direct or indirect influence their Jacobin frenzies, their brown demons." Yeats decided that Shelley was nightmare-ridden, afraid of death, and therefore not a true mystic, because "his system of thought was constructed by his logical faculty to satisfy desire, not a symbolical revelation received after suspension of all desire." Yeats concludes his essay with a tribute to Balzac:

When I was thirteen or fourteen I heard somebody say that he changed men's lives, nor can I think it a coincidence that an epoch founded in such thought as Shelley's ended with an art of solidity and complexity. Me at any rate he saved from the pursuit of a beauty that seeming at once absolute and external requires, to strike a balance, hatred as absolute.[29]

The reader, while glad that Balzac had such influence, may also agree with Yeats that "we are never satisfied with the maturity of those whom we have admired in boyhood; and, because we have seen their whole circle— even the most successful life is but a segment—we remain to the end their harshest critics."[30]

NOTES

[1] Joseph Hone, *W. B. Yeats* (New York: Macmillan, 1943), p. 7.

[2] *The Autobiography of William Butler Yeats* (New York: Macmillan, 1938), pp. 58, 150.

[3] *Ideas of Good and Evil* (New York: Macmillan, 1903), p. 4.

[4] *Autobiography,* pp. 273, 78, 80.

[5] *Ideas of Good and Evil,* p. 91.

[6] *Ibid.,* pp. 110-111.

[7] *Poets and Dreamers* (Dublin: Hodges, Figgis, 1903), p. 104.

[8] *Ideas of Good and Evil*, pp. 105, 112-114.

[9] *Ibid.*, p. 105.

[10] J. B. Yeats, *Letters to His Son W. B. Yeats and Others* (London: Faber and Faber, 1944), p. 238.

[11] *Per Amica Silentia Lunae* (New York: Macmillan, 1918), pp. 45-46.

[12] *Ibid.*, pp. 66, 90.

[13] *Early Poems and Stories* (New York: Macmillan, 1925), pp. 476-477.

[14] *Ibid.*, p. 477.

[15] *Per Amica*, pp. 91-92.

[16] *Ibid.*, p. 95.

[17] *A Vision* (New York: Macmillan, 1938), p. 19.

[18] *Per Amica*, p. 46.

[19] *Vision*, p. 184.

[20] *Ibid.*, p. 50.

[21] *Ibid.*, pp. 210-211.

[22] *Ibid.*, p. 263.

[23] Hone, *op. cit.*, p. 362.

[24] *The Collected Poems* (London: Macmillan, 1935), p. 448.

[25] *Four Plays for Dancers* (London: Macmillan, 1921), p. 136.

[26] *A Vision*, pp. 54, 207-208.

[27] *Wheels and Butterflies* (London: Macmillan, 1934), p. 103.

[28] *Op. cit.*, p. 455.

[29] *Essays 1931 to 1936* (Dublin: Cuala Press, 1937), pp. 61-62, 58, 62.

[30] *Autobiography*, p. 211.

Edward A. Bloom (essay date 1954)

SOURCE: "Yeats's 'Second Coming': An Experiment in Analysis," in *The University of Kansas City Review*, Vol. XXI, No. 2, Winter, 1954, pp. 103-10.

[*In the following essay, Bloom analyzes "The Second Coming" in light of Yeats's philosophical writings, calling the poem "a masterpiece of complexity."*]

Turning and turning in the widening gyre
The falcon cannot hear the falconer;
Things fall apart; the centre cannot hold;
Mere anarchy is loosed upon the world,
The blood-dimmed tide is loosed, and everywhere
The ceremony of innocence is drowned;
The best lack all conviction, while the worst
Are full of passionate intensity.

Surely some revelation is at hand;
Surely the Second Coming is at hand.
The Second Coming! Hardly are those words out
When a vast image out of *Spiritus Mundi*
Troubles my sight: somewhere in sands of the desert
A shape with lion body and the head of a man,
A gaze blank and pitiless as the sun,
Is moving its slow thighs, while all about it
Reel shadows of the indignant desert birds.
The darkness drops again; but now I know
That twenty centuries of stony sleep
Were vexed to nightmare by a rocking cradle,
And what rough beast, its hour come round at last,
Slouches towards Bethlehem to be born?[1]

It is truistic that all of the best poets use symbols of one kind or another to represent attitudes or emotions or situations. Now the reading of poetry is a matter of skill as well as of taste. Most poets presuppose a certain amount of skill in reading and even knowledge of some allusions, be they topical, mythical, or religious. Enjoyment comes, in Wordsworth's phrase, from "the sense of difficulty overcome." There is pleasure in recognizing a challenge and then satisfactorily answering it. Some poets, like Blake, or Yeats, or Eliot, find artistic advantage in the use of symbols frequently designated as "private." The word "private," however, is inaccurate when, with the passage of time and through critical clarification, the symbols become clear enough to discriminating readers. Private symbolism becomes even less of a charge when a poet like Yeats creates works that have a satisfying meaning regardless of the reader's knowledge of his philosophical, introspective processes. To understand these processes, of course, is to enlarge the connotative value of what he has said. But even with knowledge derived only from a close reading of the individual works, we may still derive enjoyment from his poetry.

Assuming that we have never read Yeats' philosophical system, **"The Second Coming"** will lend itself to interpretation for the average trained reader who desires to understand. First let us see what paraphrase reveals. The poem opens with concrete statement: The falcon, a savage hawk trained to aid in hunting, flies in increasing circles or spirals (*gyres*). A difficult bird to keep in captivity, the falcon responds to a primitive urge to return to its savage state. Despising civilized restraint, it kills for the joy of killing. In the second stanza Yeats makes a prophecy couched in the more abstract language that marks the concluding lines of the preceding stanza. He prophesies that the falcon is a harbinger of a revelation, of a Second Coming. Now the Second Coming, we know, is an orthodox concept of the reincarnation of Christ. But the specific details which conclude the stanza and the poem anticipate not the coming of Christ, even as avenger, but of a monster which, like the falcon, suggests destruction; at the same time it suggests something mysterious or unknown. This knowledge comes to the poet in a vision as an omen—in which the Egyptian Sphinx rises to life and *Slouches towards Bethlehem to be born.*

The image evokes terror: If the falcon returns to a state of wild nature we can understand that it is responding to certain instincts, subhuman though they be. But the Sphinx, a thing of sand and stone, having had no existence—at least as we would understand existence during the recorded history of mankind—is now incarnated. The vision is all the more terrifying because the Sphinx has come to life for some grotesque, unknown purpose, and because, unlike the falcon, it is of such monstrosity that we feel it can never be held in check by any human agency. Upon the evidence of the poem itself, we might be inclined to interpret Yeats as saying that Christianity has failed to sustain mankind and that an ominous, larger principle is about to replace it. Barbaric paganism of which the Sphinx is mutely symbolic (it might be construed from the details immediately available to us) was restrained by the birth of Christ. Paganism, however, never really died; it was merely kept in check by an abiding principle which, temporarily, was stronger than it, and under which it chafed, awaiting an opportunity to rebel. Continuing from the surface evidence of the poem, we might interpret Yeats as arguing that the Christian principle has meaning only while its tenets are in operation. But as soon as Christianity breaks down, permitting *mere anarchy* to be *loosed upon the world,* there can be no restraining of this monstrous symbol of seeming evil, since evil can be subjugated only by good. Later in this analysis, however, we shall introduce additional testimony by Yeats that must cause some qualification of these statements.

The word *gyre* is an uncommon one and consequently captures the attention at the very beginning of the poem. Not only does it fit the metrical objective more easily than, say, *circle* or *spiral,* but it also lends at least a subconscious preparation for some unusual occurrence or thought to follow. In the same line, also, we find three polysyllabic words, *turning - turning - widening,* whose denotations of slow movement and gradually increasing distance are enhanced by vocalic repetition and by the identical *-ing* suffixes. There is further significance in the *i-* assonance, which closely reinforces the linkage between *widening* and *gyre,* and in the consonantal association between *turning* and *gyre;* the metrical relations are essential to the full meaning of the line. The thought runs on to the second line, where the effect is enlarged by the completed clause. Here the slow-motion pattern is maintained by the repetition of *falcon* and *falconer,* with the addition of *cannot,* whose vowels are in assonance with the vowels of the two nouns. (This relationship, however, is essentially visual rather than auditory, because falcon is generally pronounced *faulkon* or *faukon.*) Up to this point we are thoroughly clear about the nature of the image, which is self-sufficient: the bird is escaping

its captor. Yeats demands no further knowledge of his readers. The image, nevertheless, takes on an even more intensive connotation if we have read other works by Yeats and have some understanding of his attitudes.

This is not the place for an intensive examination of Yeats' philosophic system, but an outline of the major features will provide the key to his intention. In a work called *A Vision* Yeats recorded two pertinent ideas. One is that the human life goes through phases of subjectivity and objectivity, at one time or another the two qualities merging, and then the one or the other becoming predominant. The second is that history, comparably, goes through phases or cycles—each of 2,000 years duration—in a regular, deterministic manner. Both human life and history are represented by double cones or gyres operating in contrary directions. The narrow end of each cone illustrates the subjective and the wide end the objective phases of life and history. Yeats demonstrated this notion—not original with him—in unpublished notes to **"The Second Coming."**[2] "The mind whether expressed in history or in the individual life has a precise movement which can be quickened or slackened but cannot be otherwise altered, and this movement can be expressed by a mathematical form," the double cone. The discovery of "a fundamental mathematical movement" which marks each mind leads to an ability (by those properly qualified, of course) to prophesy "the entire future of that mind." Yeats explains the mathematical figures thus:

> . . . the human soul is always moving outward into the objective, or inward into itself and this movement is double because the human soul has consciousness only because it is suspended between contraries, the greater the contrast the more intense the consciousness. The man in whom movement inward is stronger than the movement outward, the man who sees all life reflected within himself, the subjective man reaches the narrow end of a gyre at death which is always . . . preceded by an intensification of the subjective life. . . . The objective man on the other hand, whose gyre moves outward receives at this moment [of death] the revelation not of himself seen from within . . . but of himself as if he were somebody else.

The same is true of history. When one age is coming to an end "the revelation of the character of the next age is represented by the coming of one gyre to its place of greatest expansion and of the other to that of its greatest contraction." Yeats uses the gyre in other poems, such as **"Demon and Beast,"** which appeared in the same volume as **"The Second Coming"** (*Michael Robartes and the Dancer,* 1921), **"Sailing to Byzantium"** (in *The Tower,* 1928) and **"The Gyres"** (in *Last Poems and Plays,* 1940). Its specialized consistency and its explication by Yeats himself preclude suspicions of accident or eccentricity and, hence, merits such application as we may later be able to include in the meaning.

Following the almost languorous introduction, Yeats provides a sharp, shocking contrast in the third line by use of two abrupt clauses. This is the culmination of the physical action. The statement is now more general, even abstract, so that we know the falcon image is only a symbol for a larger philosophic idea. It is the bursting of the floodgates which leads to submergence of identity and to absolute objectivity. In this confusion we have the highly impersonal, objective, even ineffable *Things*. While he was restrained by man, the falcon flew in a regularly described circle or spiral, his *widening gyre* still limited by an invisible axis or center. But with the inevitable bursting of bondage the arbitrary limitation becomes impossible, since the act is deterministically inevitable. In other words a phase has ended and man once more has succumbed to savagery and *mere anarchy*. Each cycle of civilization must come to a disastrous close. As Yeats writes in *A Vision:*

> Each age unwinds the threads another age has wound, and it amuses me to remember that before Phidias and his westward moving art, Persia fell, and that when full moon came round again, amid eastward moving thought, and brought Byzantine glory, Rome fell; and that at the outset of our westward moving Renaissance Byzantium fell; all things dying each other's life, living each other's death.

The implication, of course, is that each new cycle—if the pattern is repetitive—opens barbarically and without order. *Mere,* on the surface, is an ambiguous reference. Its connotation is slighting or trivial, as though Yeats were saying ironically, anarchy doesn't amount to much. But *mere* also has an obsolete denotation, which is more clearly the one intended by Yeats; that is, *absolute, sheer,* and *unqualified* anarchy.

To impress his point Yeats lengthens and emphasizes line 5, resorting to both consonance and assonance, which are paralleled (at least the assonance is) in line 4, where the new action has begun. Notice, also, the return to concrete statement, the poet wishing to dramatize the issue which now clearly relates to mankind: anarchy, after all, is human not animal violation of order at the end of one cycle and the beginning of a new one. The situation, then, obviously warlike, provokes an attack upon established morals and, more exactly, upon established order. Yeats, in delicate syntactical counterpoint, returns to expository and then abstract statement. Throughout the poem he has used Christian symbols because he considers himself a specific part of the present Christian cycle—now coming to a close.

Christianity, however, is only typical of all the other historical cycles. Thus, *the ceremony of innocence* has an immediate Christian reference that is paradoxical: an orthodox purifying symbol is the sacramental rite of baptism, but the purification is washed away by the blood of war. In another sense, however, *the ceremony of innocence* may be said to apply to similar rites in non-Christian cycles when sacrificial blood was let for religious purposes and when, again, wars negated the meanings of those rites. There is also in this phrase an implicit irony.

If the above interpretation of *the ceremony of innocence* is acceptable, then Yeats seems to say that as man grows more mature and civilized, he grows more beastly. *The ceremony of innocence* should suggest purity and beginning, but the purity and beginning are negated by a collapsing civilization.

The *passionate intensity* of the first stanza appears at first to signify both exposition and physical action which bring the poet to his prophetic thematic conclusions in the second stanza. Such collapse of moral order, the poet intimates, must have far-reaching spiritual consequences. Ever since Christ, in the present cycle, there has been a theological premise that at some future time man will be called upon to account for his sins. But this assumption has had something of optimism in it for the virtuous, the belief being that judgment will be rendered by a God of justice and mercy. Now, however, we are prepared to look for a more esoteric meaning in this phrase. Christianity, as Yeats sees it, is simply one historical phase, and when he says

> The best lack all conviction, while the worst
> Are full of passionate intensity . . .

he may be speaking in general terms of the overt attitudes which precipitate the collapse of a civilization. This, of course, is also an ironic reversal of values as well as a realistic attitude. In his notes, however, Yeats says that it is a supreme act of faith to fix the attention upon the gyre (apparently to determine the degree of subjectivity or objectivity)

> until the whole past and future of humanity or of an individual man shall be present to the intellect as if it were accomplished in a single movement. The intensity of the Beatific Vision when it comes depends upon the intensity of this realization.

It is a temptation to ignore this statement, a seeming contradiction of the idea as stated in the poem. If we relate *passionate intensity* to Yeats' philosophy, however, it seems to celebrate his notion of the reconciliation of opposites. While "the worst" are fanatically bent on pressing the destruction of civilization, the visionary philosopher is endowed with an insight denied to ordinary people. The *widening gyre* is the state of objectivity just prior to the completion of the cycle. The *passionate intensity* is the human action that accelerates the completion of the wheel, but it may also be interpreted as the *Beatific Vision* of the subjective philosopher who has reached his most subjective, introspective state, when he is most profoundly capable of prophesying the impending catastrophe. We can argue, of course, that the catastrophe, according to Yeats' philosophy, is inevitable. But Yeats impresses upon us in the first stanza that man has also had an active hand in the collapse. Any justification for this notion is provided by Yeats himself, since the last two lines of the first stanza become a transition to the second prophetic stanza, which states the vision and the resolution.

With the flagrant rejection of humanitarian conduct, *Surely some revelation is at hand;/Surely the Second Coming is at hand.* Repetition of *Surely* and the virtual identity of the two lines establishes an urgent, inescapable mood and a warning tone. So imperative is the poet's feeling that he repeats *The Second Coming!* sharply, and then pauses for the most emphatic caesura in the entire poem in order to enforce consideration of this crucial idea. In familiar orthodoxy the Second Coming would be the reincarnation of Christ for the purpose of rendering judgment on man. Yeats' philosophy, however, complicates this interpretation. Now he seems to say that a Second Coming takes place at the conclusion of every cycle. It is easy to over-emphasize the Christian elements of the poem, but the Christian symbolism—even if only representative—is too consistent to be dismissed. It is perhaps no distortion of Yeats' thinking to infer his condemnation of those who precipitate a collapse, inevitable though that collapse may be. The thought seems to come to Yeats that chaos which is urged out of a former moral state can hardly be rewarded by the mercy of a Christ. Thus he envisions a monstrous substitute for Christ, one that has some divine (*Spiritus mundi*) but foreboding source, and that has been sent to render harsh judgment on man.

The Sphinx is the symbol for a transformation from known to frightening and unknown values. Supposedly inanimate, this *shape with lion body and the head of a man* has merely lain dormant since a previous cycle, nursing its latent capacity for evil destruction and biding its time. The horror is enforced by its objectivity and merciless singleness of vengeful purpose. Yeats creates a terrifying and hypnotic image through the use of understatement as he envisions the awakening of the beast-god. The *desert birds* are *indignant* rather than terrified because they have no rational understanding of what is happening. Lacking insight, they associate only a temporal consequence with this action and are annoyed by an unaccountable change in their tranquillity. They are a symbol for those men who likewise fail to comprehend and who regard the disruption of an established order as an unwarranted personal inconvenience. They represent also those innocents who must be affected by crimes which they have not committed, and by the inevitable cyclical course of history. The image is particularly good because of the contrasts it provides. These birds are wilder than the falcon; yet their flight, too, is circular, as the word *reel* connotes. But the word also suggests an unevenness, the chaos and disorder that have already begun; whereas *widening gyre* suggests that there is still regularity, that it is the moment before disintegration. The movement of the desert birds also provides a striking contrast with the sluggish, implacable progress of the Sphinx.

The conclusion comes with the poet's emergence from the dream-state. He has returned to reality, but, paradoxically, the only reality is the vision which has just hypnotized him. The world of which he is part is not one of illumination but of enveloping, hopeless darkness and disaster. Only when Yeats awakens does he understand the reality. The barbarism has been quelled by the Christian phase during *twenty centuries of stony sleep* since the birth of Christ (represented by the *rocking cradle*), but it has never expired. Its own period of quiescence has been disturbed into a *nightmare* by some other passionate yet temporary force of salutary faith. Now with man himself turned barbarian, it is time for the God of barbarians to reassert himself. Once again it is necessary to turn to the unpublished notes for clarification, for there is more to the association than the twenty centuries since the birth of Christ. Generally, according to Yeats, all the gyres complete their historical cycles in 2,000 years. At the moment of writing the gyre is attaining its widest, hence more objective expansion, unlike the period preceding the birth of Christ, in which the gyre was narrowing. The new phase, we may assume, will last approximately another 2,000 years, even as the phase which opened with the creation of the Sphinx and ended with the birth of Christ lasted 2,000 years. The new phase, furthermore, promises to be a barbaric one at its inception. Hence, Yeats conceives of an ironical transvaluation in which a cruel beast-deity will supplant a humane and just deity at Bethlehem, the source of Christianity.

We have already witnessed how the poem's meaning, though enlarged and enriched by the additional information about the gyres, supports interpretation without it. But that information, we have also seen, proves essential for a really satisfactory interpretation. Now it is pertinent to incorporate one more allusion, this time a topical one, for **"The Second Coming"** owes much of its creation to the Irish struggle for independence. The Easter Rising of 1916 took Yeats by surprise, when the Irish nationalists rebelled against English rule. Although his sympathies were for a free Ireland, he disliked the Bohemian society of Dublin and the revolutionary political beliefs which motivated the uprising. He revered the "big houses" of the country aristocracy, whose society was for him an achievement of civilization which symbolized for him an absolute of which he approved. The mob, as he wrote in **"The Leaders of the Crowd,"** would *Pull down established honour;* and yet he felt compelled to support their action, however passively, for the future hopes of Ireland. Practically, also, he recognized that the execution of the rebel leaders, the "Sixteen Dead Men," had made martyrs of them and that the purpose of the Rising could not be discussed dispassionately. So torn by his conflicting sentiments, Yeats wrote **"The Second Coming"** as the culmination of a series of political poems: **"September, 1913," "Easter, 1916,"** and **"The Rose."**

Considered from this point of view, **"The Second Coming"** is an indication that for Yeats the noble aspirations of the Easter Rising had degenerated into the aimless brutal warfare of the Blacks and Tans and that, in turn, into the fight between the Free-Staters and the Republicans. Ultimately, political ideologies seemed to have little significance. The poem, thus, may be read as a prophetic commentary upon the decay of modern civilization. But it may also be read for its historical-topical significance as it reflects the blood-letting of civil upheaval. Note, then, that the *widening gyre* may be related to the sanguinary events in Ireland, because in Yeats' philosophy objectivity also applies to the moment in the historical cycle when political activity denies the integrity of the individual. We are now able to see that Yeats protests against the dissolution of order in Ireland as *Mere anarchy,* and that *The blood-dimmed tide* may be interpreted with reference to that conflict. Supplemented by our new information, The *ceremony of innocence* may be read as a direct allusion to political grievances; in this phrase is encompassed the notion that the innocent as well as the guilty are sacrificed. The somber closing lines lead to the conclusion that a new absolute—the *rough beast*—perhaps not so salutary as the old established order, is coming to dominate the next cycle of man's history.

Both the "private" and supplementary details have immediate topical bearing only upon the first stanza, which is expository and dramatic, and which sets the mood and tone; they also clarify the intention of prophetic warning. To re-emphasize the point, the poem has no absolute dependence of meaning on these augmenting details. Knowledge of these matters, however, ultimately becomes indispensable, since it gives the poem tremendous depth and exploits the imagery to its fullest. With these elements in mind, further, we come close to the full meaning of **"The Second Coming,"** which is a masterpiece of complexity.

NOTES

[1] "The Second Coming" (from *Michael Robartes and the Dancer,* 1921) is reproduced with the kind permission of The Macmillan Company. The present text is from *The Collected Poems of W. B. Yeats* (New York, 1940).

[2] Yeats' previously unpublished notes and other illuminating data about the gyres are available in *W. B. Yeats, Man and Poet,* by A. Norman Jeffares (London, 1949), pp. 196 ff. See also T. R. Henn, *The Lonely Tower* (London, 1950), pp. 182 ff.

Bernard Levine (essay date 1970)

SOURCE: "Vision and 'Responsibility'," in *The Dissolving Image: The Spiritual-Esthetic Development of W. B. Yeats,* Wayne State University Press, 1970, pp. 81-101.

[*In the following essay, Levine considers "The Second Coming" in the context of several earlier poems by Yeats, seeing the work "as proof of the speaker's journey toward psychological equanimity" and humankind's imaginative acceptance of responsibility.*]

The heroic quest for Yeats was a perdurable subject for poetry, explored first in the longest and one of the earliest of his poems, **"Oisin"** (1889). Almost immediately after **"Oisin,"** love, the longing for everlasting union with the beloved, became the poet's principal concern; and after

that Yeats dealt with the lover's anguish and disillusionment (1897-1905). This in turn became the basis for reaffirmation of an heroic discipline, evidence in poems which made the immortal beloved an epical rather than an ethereal figure, the personification of a martyred ideal, noble and solitary in her ways (1908-1915). The lover's adoration of the beauty of the Rose of Ireland had given way to a worshipful respect for the fading beauty of a latter-day Helen, the "phoenix" whose country betrayed her romantic zeal and whose defeat seemed to her admirer only to increase her stature.

From about 1910 the speaker himself (with his "Helen" as an example) adopts the heroic pose, sounding the clarion call of "joy in defeat," learning to exult in spite of the seemingly insurmountable opposition of the petty and frenetic world around him. The magnetic core of Yeats's poetry deepens as the poet's horizons broaden. The social and political world is taken on as a challenge to the soul, and if conflict leads to defeat, that is what strikes the spark of enlightenment, the spiritual reserve that holds against violence and destruction. Personal hatred and bitterness are best exorcised, Yeats suggests, by making the self "the world's servant" (*P,* 376), through self-surrender becoming "self-possessed" (*E,* 524). Yeats's poetry in this respect can be read as a "sacred book," reflecting in its highest moments the Self-illuminating process.

In the present [essay] we shall consider Yeats's "public poetry" from 1910 to 1921, concentrating on the way in which the speaker transforms his identity in the course of addressing himself to his social "responsibility." We shall consider first those poems in which the speaker makes "Helen" the paragon of nobility, and then the several poems of "exultation." **"The Second Coming"** will serve as our terminal point of reference.

In the "Helen" poems the old image of the immortal beloved has been replaced by the image of a woman whose mystery braves the crassness and injustice of this world. Her majestic bearing, despite her having fallen from favor, is what commends her to the speaker; and he memorializes her heroic quality while confirming his own sense of solitude. It is as though the unrequited lover had recouped his loss by sympathetic avowal of the beloved's innate dignity.

The speaker in the "Helen" poems seems to be what Yeats in *A Vision* calls "The Daimonic Man." He is a person in search of his transpersonal Self, but someone who has tried sharing the awareness of his spiritual counterpart (potentially his daimonic being) with the woman he loves. In renouncing his desire for the woman, therefore, he finds himself better able to realize his own destiny. What he is deprived of he can accept as "proof" of spiritual gain. Because he substitutes for the object of his desire a Self-inspired image, "The Daimonic Man" is obviously endowed with creative insight; but because he is in a state of transition his convictions may not be expressed with the greatest possible intensity.

The Body of Fate [the outcome of circumstance] . . . is "loss," and works to make impossible "simplification by intensity." The being, through the intellect, selects some object of desire for a representation of the *Mask* as Image, some woman perhaps, and the *Body of Fate* snatches away the object. Then the intellect (*Creative Mind*), which in the most *antithetical* phases were better described as imagination, must substitute some new image of desire; and in the degree of its power and of its attainment of unity, relate that which is lost, that which has snatched it away, to the new image of desire, that which threatens the new image to the being's unity. (*V,* 142)

Unlike the speaker in Yeats's poems of exultation, the speaker in the "Helen" poems finds himself at cross purposes. He cannot rejoice in his vision without first arguing with himself, or with the insensitive world, for *her* sake. His grasp of his subject and its conceptual core is thus weakened because his point of view is divided. Indeed it would seem the speaker in these poems is looking for his proper subject. Consider this poem called **"Words,"** published in 1910:

> I had this thought a while ago,
> 'My darling cannot understand
> What I have done, or what would do
> In this blind bitter land.'
>
> And I grew weary of the sun
> Until my thoughts cleared up again,
> Remembering that the best I have done
> Was done to make it plain;
>
> That every year I have cried, 'At length
> My darling understands it all,
> Because I have come into my strength,
> And words obey my call';
>
> That had she done so who can say
> What would have shaken from the sieve?
> I might have thrown poor words away
> And been content to live.

In his diary for January 22, 1909, Yeats, in talking about his twenty-year relationship with Maud Gonne, accounts for his having written this poem. "How much of the best that I have done and still do is but the attempt to explain myself to her. . . . If she understood I should lack a reason for writing and one can never have too many reasons for doing what is so laborious."[1]

Is it for her sake, for his sake, or for the sake of writing that the speaker in **"Words"** makes poetry of his thoughts? Each stanza turns upon a different aspect of this leading question. In stanza 1 the speaker makes ready to reassure "my darling" that he has learned to live in a country where people are "blind" and "bitter"; in stanza 2, he suggests that simply clarifying his position should be enough, making it clear to himself and her that he accepts his unequal relationship with others; and yet in stanza 3 he is dismayed that, no matter how well he reconciles himself to his situation, "my darling" will never be able to understand—him or the means by which he is able to put up with the world.

The three-way problem, then, is only partially resolved: the speaker finds strength in being able to express his thoughts about a land that otherwise would seem alien to him; but he cannot quite reconcile himself to the fact that he must live *alone* with this redeeming insight. In stanza 4 he copes with the irony only by redoubling it. Because the one person that inspires him cannot really understand him, he thinks himself cut off from life; and he thinks himself cut off because of his continuing need to express himself. He is caught in a trap of his own making, thinking that "words" would finally release him from any obsessive concern he had for those he loved or hated. But in the end "words," indeed, are all he has left, the ability to make poetry of his discontent.

When the speaker says "I might have thrown poor words away / And been content to live," he does not imply he will be satisfied living alone; he wants to be alone with his beloved, who at last would understand him. And yet the poem is not actually addressed to the beloved, as were the early love lyrics (see *P,* 157), or as was **"Adam's Curse."** **"Words"** is a discursive poem, ostensibly about a man's relationship to a woman, his compatriots, his art; but it strikes our attention more for its manner than for its specific content—the gentle, meditative tone that shows us a man struggling with his own understanding, being made to acknowledge a fate he had never asked for.

In **"Words"** and in other of the "Helen" poems the speaker nonetheless looks to the figure of Helen to resolve his quarrel with country and countrymen. He makes of Homer's paragon a personal example—the image of a woman who is noble enough to disregard the slights, the abuse, the intolerance, and forgetfulness of those who once held her in esteem. She is the model for the tragic joy the speaker soon after comes to feel in his own right. And from her image he soon learns to fashion a mask for himself, in the process growing more flexible in his manner of expression.

In **"No Second Troy,"** the earliest of the "Helen" poems (1908, written, as Hone observes, after Yeats had visited Maud Gonne in Paris) the speaker takes "ignorant men" to task for not being equal to his heroine's zeal. Indignant at their common perversion of her gospel, he lauds her "most violent ways," investing her image with a nobility—"That nobleness made simple as a fire"—which consequently makes what she does of epical import.

> Why, what could she have done, being what she is?
> Was there another Troy for her to burn?

The speaker shows self-righteous anger on her behalf, not blaming her even "that she filled my days / With misery" nor attentive to that more cautious voice of the poet: Yeats himself disapproving of Maud because she gave assent to violence.[2] The speaker embraces Helen's cause with the conviction of a man who has shared her experience; and his own feelings echo as a paean to her passionate, Dianesque aloofness.

> What could have made her peaceful with a mind
> That nobleness made simple as a fire,
> With beauty like a tightened bow, a kind
> That is not natural in an age like this,
> Being high and solitary and most stern.
>
> (*P*, 256-57)

In the poem **"Peace,"** published in series with **"No Second Troy"** but written a year and a half after the latter (again in relation to Yeats's visit to Maud Gonne, this time in Normandy[3]), the speaker takes a reverse stand. Instead of his headlong devotion in the earlier poem, the speaker is entirely circumspect in **"Peace."** He views his heroine with a more penetrating eye, modifying what he supposes to be the heroic ideal.

> Ah, that Time could touch a form
> That could show what Homer's age
> Bred to be a hero's wage.

The speaker is considerably more deliberate in his testimonial to the modern-day Helen. He is not as straightforward as he might be in his appraisal of her, but it is quite obvious that he does not condone her stormy involvement in life. It may have been that Helen's fiery temperament had been at one time commensurate with her beauty. But when Time preys on her beauty the external effects gradually are shed and what then would remain is her radiant composure. Had she indeed been as the speaker imagines, she would have served him, and those like him, as someone to emulate. Even in her youth, he conjectures, some painter might have foreseen her overwhelming virtue: her "'delicate high head / All that sternness amid charm, / All that sweetness amid strength'" until (as was expressed in a line later deleted) "'they had changed us to like strength. . . . '"

The speaker is no mere worshipper of feminine beauty. He is strong-willed enough to conceive of Helen as the image of what he himself would become. Worth noting in this respect is his attempt to identify Helen as "half lion, half child," (a therianthropic image which with **"The Second Coming"** becomes a correlative for the speaker's own, transpersonal solitude and visionary insight). This composite image, as first used in **"Against Unworthy Praise,"** describes the unspoiled virtue of a woman whose ideals have been misread, distorted, by unconscionable "knaves." The speaker argues away his indignation by claiming to share with his heroine a secret placing them above the ordinary run of men.

> O heart, be at peace, because
> Nor knave nor dolt can break
> What's not for their applause,
> Being for a woman's sake.
> Enough if the work has seemed,
> So did she your strength renew,
> A dream that a lion had dreamed
> Till the wilderness cried aloud,
> A secret between you two ["her" and his "heart"],
> Between the proud and the proud.

The speaker communes with this woman because he is assured they are, together, in touch with the heroic world of the imagination. Their lion's dream thus gives them strength to render ineffectual the everyday world around them.

But just how convincing is the speaker's claim to be privy to an abiding mystery? He does not, cannot, focus squarely upon eliciting an image from *Anima Mundi,* because his attention is divided: he is more intent on reconciling his own differences with the world and trying to establish at the same time the spiritual ascendancy of his heroine. The speaker does not concentrate with the intensity of the speaker in **"The Second Coming"** upon creating, or invoking, a transformational image. The dual image of the woman—" she, singing upon her road, / Half lion, half child"—becomes a unitive symbol only because of a juxtaposition of words, not because of any profound poetic process. As a result the terminal figure in the poem seems merely a by-product of the imagination and not a direct, daimonic source of inspiration.

In the sequence of poems addressed to Helen, the titular heroine is meant to be a symbol of inner strength for having suffered defeat in the external world. But so long as the speaker cultivates that image in its own right, independent of his own being, and without primary emphasis upon the change he undergoes contemplating that image, he will be able to make only minimally effective his use of image as symbol. The burden of the poem is not to prove itself a moment of stasis or to crystallize a sequence of images, but rather to suggest the poem's dynamic inscape—the power of the word to draw in toward a single symbolic center.

"The Second Coming" does this. And it appears that the transformation symbol in that poem (the sphinx) is anticipated in the "Helen" poems. **"Against Unworthy Praise,"** written in 1910, ends with a pristine form of such a symbol. **"His Phoenix"** (*P*, 353-54) written four and a half years later (January 1915) makes use of an intermediate figure, a cross between the "child" and the "sphinx": "I knew a phoenix in my youth," reads the refrain; she has "the simplicity of a child. / And that proud look as though she had gazed into the burning sun [*cf.* **"The Second Coming,"** l. 15], / And all the shapely body no nittle gone astray." The speaker mourns, he says, "for that most lonely thing." There is regret mixed with admiration as he recalls her untainted beauty. She had her heyday when she was young. Now she is a victim of "that barbarous crowd," isolated and alone. But her "proud look" and indomitable eye still haunt the speaker.

However, it does not seem the person speaking has gone through too great an effort to picture his phoenix. She is an image out of the immediate past,[4] not out of the larger context of *Anima Mundi.* She seems to have been born whole, not evolved through the process of the poem. Only slightly does she share in that elemental world from which the "rough beast" in **"The Second Coming"** originates. This latter image derives from an in-felt psychological matrix; in **"His Phoenix"** the speaker looks back in time, more intently than he looks within, for his controlling image.

Most of the "Helen" poems, no less than **"The Second Coming,"** show the speaker attempting to maneuver the central image in such a way as to make it serve as a buffer between himself and his outrage—a solvent for the indignant attitude he has toward "the barbarous crowd." In **"The People"** (*P*, 351-53), written at about the same time as **"His Phoenix,"** and published together with that poem and five others in *Poetry*, February 1916, the speaker engages his transfigured heroine in a dialogue concerning the people. Unlike other of the "Helen" poems, this is a poem of self-reproof. The man who has spent a good part of his life working for "this unmannerly town" questions the value of his sacrifice. He might as well have given in to his tendency to withdraw from the thankless world, he says, and move instead "among the images of the past / . . . unperturbed and courtly images" of Quattrocento Italy "where the Duchess and her people talked / The stately midnight through until they stood / In their great window looking at the dawn." But that kind of intellectual and esthetic isolation is only a halfway house, his twentieth-century lady tells him. There are those, of course—the "drunkards, pilferers of public funds"—who thrive upon dishonesty, but do they constitute "the people," she asks, do they make up the real body of the country? Despite what wrong had been done her, she tells him, "'never have I, now nor at any time, Complained of the people.'" He counters the simplicity of her faith. She is ruled by her heart, he says, not by any "analytic mind." And then he recoils from his words. Meeting his indignation head-on, her generosity puts him to shame. He suddenly recognizes the truth of her words.[5]

The "Helen" poems contrast markedly with the early poems of exultation, in that the latter are more directly concerned with the self-illuminating intensity of the speaking voice. They seem indeed the antithetical counterparts of the "Helen" poems—visionary rather than devotional in manner. Let us examine now the poems of exultation and determine in what way they, like the "Helen" poems, anticipate the premonitory tone of **"The Second Coming."**

"Life is not lived," Yeats wrote in 1907, "if not lived for contemplation or excitement" (*E*, 252). Visionary excitement indeed may be induced by contemplation. The contemplative mind is able to symbolize, intensify by simplifying its comprehension of reality, and as a result grow free of nonessential impressions. It is different from the "analytic mind" which multiplies by dividing in that it tends to magnify partial aspects of reality into representations of the whole: coloring what it sees with its own bias.

Tom O'Roughley, the titular figure of a poem Yeats wrote in 1918, focuses upon the differences between the two states of mind: "Wisdom is a butterfly," he says, "and not a gloomy bird of prey." The analytic mind feeds upon

rather than frees itself of the world—imposes meaning, sets goals, establishes rules, in short, perpetuates by delimiting its range of reference. "Logic-choppers rule the town" is how Tom sums it up. But Tom does not bank upon the wayward world for his direction in life: "'An aimless joy is a pure joy,'" he says. And to show his joyous indifference, he turns a lively heel upon all speculation concerning life and death:

'If little planned is little sinned
But little need the grave distress.
What's dying but a second wind?
How but in zig-zag wantonness
Could trumpeter Michael be so brave?'
Or something of that sort he said,
'And if my dearest friend were dead
I'd dance a measure on his grave.'

(*P*, 337-38)

The linear movement of the poem, accelerating to its final statement by rhetorical questioning, accords nicely with Tom's startling final gesture, his gay dismissal of any speculative faith. His attitude is not unlike that of Yeats writing in 1907: "That we may be free from . . . sullen anger, solemn virtue, calculating anxiety, gloomy suspicion, prevaricating hope, we should be reborn in gaiety" (*E*, 252). Tom envisions his own transformation: and his espousal of a "zig-zag wantonness" seems a felicitous correlative of the speaker's visionary excitement.

Tom has the last word, but we wonder if the author has not after all been overly deliberate in structuring the poem, in writing about his sense of exultation and in using the too mindful indirection of a persona. The more characteristic of Yeats's poems feature the first-person narrator, who makes us feel the immediacy of his subject.

In **"The Dawn,"** similar in theme to **"Tom O'Roughley,"** the speaker contemplates directly his subject and then rises to the full strength of his controlling image. The ironic first eight lines, telescoping the world he takes exception to, prevent any progressive concentration of mood; but the lines nonetheless seem to provide a springboard for his excitement, as reflected in the culminating image.

I would be ignorant as the dawn
That has looked down
On that old queen measuring a town
With the pin of a brooch,
Or on the withered men that saw
From their pedantic Babylon
The careless planets in their courses,
The stars fade out where the moon comes,
And took their tablets and did sums;
I would be ignorant as the dawn
That merely stood, rocking the glittering coach
Above the cloudy shoulders of the horses;
I would be—for no knowledge is worth a straw—
Ignorant and wanton as the dawn.

Again (*cf.* **"Tom O'Roughley"**) the speaker expresses his desire to be free of that peddling intellect which can "measure a town" or reduce to a piece of slate the incalculable mystery of the cosmos. The speaker holds thumbs down on products of the analytic mind, himself having recourse to the larger, yet self-contained, world of the imagination.

> I would be ignorant as the dawn
> That merely stood, rocking the glittering coach
> Above the cloudy shoulders of the horses. . . .

His insight takes the form of an image of static intensity, signifying, as he hopes, his would-be transformation.

Yeats used over and again the images of animals and "dawn" to express the consecrated energy of the moment of vision. It is not until the very late poem **"High Talk"** that the speaker blends these images into the perfect climax for a poem of exultation . . . : but we may profitably pause, I think, over the use of these images in the earlier poems. In **"The Dawn"** the conjunction of horses and sun is perhaps the most memorable composite image of transfiguration in Yeats's early poetry. In three other poems, all written before **"The Dawn"**—**"At Galway Races"** (1908), **"Upon a House shaken by the Land Agitation"** (1909), and the poem to which Yeats gave his longest title, **"To a Wealthy Man who promised a Second Subscription to the Dublin Municipal Gallery if it were proved the People wanted Pictures"** (1912)—we have the visionary images of horse and sun dealt with separately. We might look at these three poems before passing on to the more emotionally ambivalent poems of exultation.

Unlike the narration in **"Tom O'Roughley,"** **"The Dawn,"** and other later poems describing the speaker's elation, the narrator in these three early poems rides dauntlessly high because of his sense of aristocratic pride. **"At Galway Races,"** the first of Yeats's poems of exultation, shows the narrator boldly articulating his triumphal vision. The spectacle of the race is regarded as the spirit of the country as a whole, the brave riders setting an example for the people to follow:

> There where the course is,
> Delight makes all of the one mind,
> The riders upon the galloping horses,
> The crowd that closes in behind. . . .

There is not a bit of scorn in the speaker's words. His optimism rings with the sense of *noblesse oblige*. With "horsemen for companions" he may look down on "the merchant and the clerk," but nonetheless holds out some hope for their redemption. All life, he supposes, can be refashioned from the vision of "men / That ride upon horses." And their concerted response to an apocalyptic trumpeting is what sustains the imagination of such men:

> Sing on: somewhere at some new moon,
> We'll learn that sleeping is not death,
> Hearing the whole world change its tune,
> Its flesh being wild. . . .

No feeling of separation or defeat here. The vibrant tread of horsemen is meant to be felt in this stirring image of a world potentially transformed.

In **"At Galway Races"** there are foreshadowings of **"The Second Coming,"** but the buoyant tone of this early poem is a far cry from the probative vision of the speaker in the later poem. For all his gallantry the speaker in **"At Galway Races"** cultivates too broad a view, extending himself without sufficient check upon his imagination: he seems hellbent on a vision of unity-of-being among all men. And this vision, the poet realizes later, is impossible (*A*, 235-36). The relation of man to men is too problematic to allow the visionary anything finally but the promise of his own solitude.

A new note is sounded in a poem Yeats wrote a year after **"At Galway Races":** it is addressed to Lady Gregory, who numbered among the last of Ireland's landed aristocracy. Quizzically the speaker asks:

> How should the world be luckier if this house,
> Where passion and precision have been one
> Time out of mind, became too ruinous
> To breed the lidless eye that loves the sun?

The speaker is concerned with the problem of preserving from destruction the invaluable emblems of nobility. The external effects (the material dwelling) may become common property, he says, but that will never endow the new owners with the character of the people the dwelling once housed; and how can the actual possession ever compare with the spiritual resolve of those who had lived there? Yet, however much the speaker regrets the fall of the physical structure, he wonders if its demolition will really keep the tradition from being perpetuated. It should, he supposes, serve only to inure the spirit, allow the self-liberating mind to discover above all else "gradual Time's last gift," what no man of mean wealth can ever understand: "a written speech / Wrought of high laughter, loveliness and ease." The noble mind finds in lofty repose enduring strength: "sweet laughing eagle thoughts that grow / Where wings have memory of wings, and all / That comes of the best knit to the best." The proud heights inherited by "the best" are those "eagle thoughts" signified by the hieratic symbol of the "eye that loves the sun."

In **"To a Wealthy Man . . ."** the sun's eye is a symbol for those aspiring to be remembered among "the best."

> Let Paudeens play at pitch and toss,
> Look up in the sun's eye and give
> What the exultant heart calls good
> That some new day may breed the best
> Because you gave, not what they would,
> But the right twigs for an eagle's nest!

"Eagle" and "sun" are matched in dignity, symbols of an aristocratic pride. But they are not symbols entirely pared of reference to the material world; the speaker is asking the wealthy man to give money (in spite of the money-minded Paudeens) in order to further the cause of art. Art, "whose end is peace," would presumably set the proper tone for the city and, in its conspicuous stillness, would seem to triumph over the rankling crowd.

It was a year before the speaker would address another patron of the arts and assure her that noble souls are "Bred to a harder thing / Than Triumph." He advised her to "take defeat": "turn away / And like a laughing string / Whereon mad fingers play / . . . Be secret and exult, / Because of all things known / That is most difficult" (*P*, 291).

The speaker comes around to acknowledging that the real challenge for the beleaguered soul is to evolve a discipline of laughter, feeding elation not on splendiferous visions or bright arrays of possibility but on the more salient issue of broken hopes and unrealized dreams. What's desired is the free feeling that comes of having been purged of personal bitterness, indignation, and pride. It is a humbling and a revelation, the shock of illumination in the wilderness, a stigmatic release of emotion. The three poems which most aptly convey the mixture of pain and elation, **"Paudeen," "The Cold Heaven,"** and **"Demon and Beast,"** contrast therefore in tone with the three "aristocratic" poems of exultation. And they contrast as well with **"The Dawn"** and **"Tom O'Roughley,"** poems in which the innocence and quicksilver quality of the speaker prevail.

In the three, what we may call "stigmatic" poems of exultation, the speaker traverses an emotional spectrum from pain, indignation, or hatred, to self-enlightenment.[6] He is lifted, it seems, in the process of transcribing his vision. In **"Paudeen"** and **"The Cold Heaven"** the cumulative excitement of the words virtually imitates the ecstatic heightening that the speaker professes to undergo. With the culminating moment in each poem something flashes upon the mind's eye of the speaker, an image shivering with visionary intensity. The image of the sun, evident in most of the poems we are considering, in these two poems seems to show through an inner light, refulgent with the speaker's own articulate energy.

> Indignant at the fumbling wits, the obscure spite
> Of our old Paudeen in his shop, I stumbled blind
> Among the stones and thorn-trees, under
>   morning light;
> Until a curlew cried and in the luminous wind
> A curlew answered; and suddenly thereupon I
>   thought
> That on the only height where all are in God's eye,
> There cannot be, confusion of our thought forgot,
> A single soul that lacks a sweet crystalline cry.
>
>   (*P*, 291)

> . . . And I took all the blame out of all sense and
>   reason,
> Until I cried and trembled and rocked to and fro,
> Riddled with light.[7]
>
>   (*P*, 316)

In both poems, as well as in **"Demon and Beast,"** the image of the birds helps bring about a catalytic change in the speaker. It is significant that in none of these poems do we get the proud image of hawk or eagle. They are common birds—the curlew, the rook,[8] the gull or "some absurd / Portly green-pated bird"—which touch upon the speaker's emotions, filling him at once with remorse and joy; for him the sight of them, their free-flying and yet humble forms, induces tears that are gladly shed, feelings which whelm up when grievance gives way to forgiveness and pride dissolves in benediction. "Being no more demoniac / A stupid happy creature / Could rouse my whole nature" (*P*, 400).

The conflict described in these three poems is the conflict between a man's demonic and daimonic natures. The speaker's quarrel with the world can result only in disdain or hate, or else erupt in some act of violence; but if the quarrel is contained and the self becomes the principal target of the speaker, then the latter is able to project over and beyond any demonic assertion the mystery of his spiritual Daimon.

The stigmatic poems are the outcome of this recurrent struggle, the moment of poetic vision translating the emotional experience. The speaker can celebrate his triumph because he has found momentary release from his shadow—the selfish, delimiting aspect of his being. The dissociated images of beast and bird are thus used to describe an unwinding, "contraconic," experience: the way antipathetic (animal-spiritual) elements are resolved through enlightened understanding of the self and others. The idea is expressed in the opening lines of **"Demon and Beast"**—

> For certain minutes at the least
> That crafty demon and that loud beast
> That plague me day and night
> Ran out of my sight;
> Though I had long perned in the gyre,
> Between my hatred and my desire,
> I saw my freedom won
> And all laugh in the sun.

This first stanza ends with reference to the sun as an image of unfettered happiness; the next stanza is concerned with the manifestation of an inner light.

The speaker finds himself in the "sweet company" of dead men, portraits that speak out to him the vital wisdom of *Anima Mundi*. Having comprehended those nodding and smiling figures on the wall—"glittering eyes in a death's head"—he is able to rout the blatant "beast" and thereby feel the spiritual purity which makes him at one with all men: "For all men's thoughts grew clear / Being dear as mine are dear." His understanding now is of the heart as well as the head, and presumably he resolves for the moment that antinomy which, in **"The People,"** keeps the speaker from realizing the possible "purity of a natural force" ("his phoenix's" unconditional belief in "the people").

The speaker's humanity is not proved until a pervading joy is able to make him surrender his intellectual and egotistic pride. That done, his example might serve the people: for "never yet had freeman / Right mastery of natural things." For the speaker freedom is evidenced by passionate self-control, and once the demon has been exorcised, that freedom allows a more profound sensitivity. His entire being is engaged by two "stupid happy creatures"—a gyring gull splashing down beside a floating duck. The birds express for him "aimless joy" and bring "a tear-drop" to his eye. Apparently he feels the release that comes from a sudden conjunction of opposites, the felicitous melding of instinct and insight. For the moment his "whole nature" responds to the world around him with primordial innocence.

The speaker thus discovers the exquisite "sweetness" of life, having "no dearer thought / Than . . . [to] find out a way / To make it linger half a day." A man's life, though, is necessarily bound by a self-conscious existence; as a result the natural world is seen at its purest only when death is regarded, not as an ironic or absurd fate, but as a means of spiritual release—

> O what a sweetness strayed
> Through the barren Thebaid,
> Or by the Mareotic sea
> When that exultant Anthony
> And twice a thousand more
> Starved upon the shore
> And withered to a bag of bones!
> What had the Caesars but their thrones?

The life of Saint Anthony is interpreted by what Yeats in "Phase 27" of *A Vision* calls the "Emotion of Sanctity," the realization of a "contact with life beyond death." "It comes," Yeats maintains, "when synthesis [of facts and ideas] is abandoned, when fate is accepted" above the strictures of reason and intellect.

The vision of Anthony exulting at his death consummates the sequence of images (i.e., light-sight-liquid images) in this discursive poem. It completes the experience of the speaker whom we see first "laughing in the sun," then communing with "glittering eyes in a death's head," finally feeling "a tear-drop start . . . up" as he watches a bird by "the little lake . . . take / A bit of bread. . . . " Like the saint of "Phase 27" the speaker seems to allow "the total life, expressed in its humanity, to flow in upon him and to express itself through his acts and thoughts." What the speaker sees, thinks, and does thus makes for a composite emotion, reflecting his understanding of that extraordinary scene "by the Mareotic sea."

The poem, worked out in terms of this daimonic vision of Saint Anthony, is the last of Yeats's three stigmatic poems of exultation. It is a fitting conclusion to the cycle. The contritional intensity of **"Paudeen"** and **"The Cold Heaven"** is relaxed in **"Demon and Beast"**; the moment of revelation is extended in such a way as to allow the speaker to comprehend the human condition, the "total life" clarified for him in the emotion aroused by a sympathetic, because transpersonal, awareness.

We have considered thus far groups of poems which describe a progressive internalization of image. The "Helen" series, which succeeds the adorational and apocalyptic love lyrics of the early years, projects the heroic ideal of the poet in the image of a woman; the heroine has an almost divine nobility, and is endowed with spiritual beauty. In the poems of exultation it is the speaker himself who commands our attention; and the key images in the poem are those which reveal the nature of his spiritual state. Like **"The Gift of Harun Al-Raschid,"** the last of the marital love poems, the early poems of exultation conclude with the figural representation of a mysterious (daimonic) reality. The stigmatic poems differ from the other poems of exultation, as well as from the "Helen" poems, the marital love poems, and the spiritual and sensuous love lyrics, in that they express a more embracing, human love; the speaker is shown struggling to overcome the daimonic pride and hatred that plagues the soul; and, as we have seen, he emerges from the struggle with a more charitable vision of mankind—a brand of social "responsibility" which allows him to "respond" to, and by this means accept, the human condition as a measure of his personal effort at Self-fulfillment.[9]

A man's actions, Yeats realized, should relate to his social "responsibility." If hatred is "the common condition of our life," as he says in the essay **"Anima Mundi"** (*M*, 365), then it must be consciously controlled. The demon cannot be thought merely to have run away in a moment of enlightenment. The struggle for self-mastery is wholly internal, and it continues as long as there is one's self to think about.

The ideal that makes life livable cannot be conceived to lie outside the human mind. It is a self-sustaining force. "When I remember that Shelley calls our minds 'mirrors of the fire for which all thirst,' I cannot but ask the question all have asked, 'What or who has cracked the mirror?' I begin to study the only self that I can know, myself, and to wind the thread upon the pern again" (*M*, 364). It is when the mind fastens upon some reality beyond itself that the "thread" is likely to snap and thereby scotch the vision of life. Unlike Shelley, Yeats learned to take the living world for proof of his own intensity, and not consider it merely a perversion of reality. Because, as Yeats claimed in his essay **"Anima Mundi,"** a poem could be its own revelation (once the imagination burned free of self-consciousness), then the world itself, from which the poem is drawn, would seem a revelation: it would be allowed its own rhythm, coexisting, curiously enough, with the unresolved images of *Anima Mundi*, the "soul of the world" which haunts the visionary mind.

The vision for Yeats is its own solvent, reducing to a common denominator seemingly disparate images. "I look at the strangers near," Yeats reports in describing this state of mind, "as if I had known them all my life . . . : everything fills me with affection, I have no longer any fears or any needs." And he goes on to explain, in the essay **"Anima Mundi,"** that this affection makes him susceptible to the intelligence of some higher being, casting for him a mysterious image. (The kind of autochthonous love Yeats describes here, one may note, is the antithesis of Shelley's ethereal, Platonic love.)

I have something about me that, though it makes me love, is more like innocence. I am in the place where the Daimon is, but I do not think he is with me until I begin to make a new personality, selecting among those images, seeking always to satisfy a hunger grown out of conceit with daily diet; and yet as I write the words 'I select,' I am full of uncertainty, not knowing when I am the finger, when the clay. Once, twenty years ago, I seemed to awake from sleep to find my body rigid, and to hear a strange voice speaking these words through my lips as through lips of stone: 'We make an image of him who sleeps, and it is not he who sleeps, and we call it Emmanuel.' (*M*, 365-66)

The image Yeats talks about, no less than the condition attending its inception, anticipates the visionary image effected in **"The Second Coming."** "Emanuel," Hebrew for "God be with us," is meant by Yeats to signify not the messianic figure of a man, as the Old Testament tradition would have it, but an unconscious presence. At the critical moment between sleeping and waking, when the subconscious weighs in often precarious balance with the conscious mind, the ghostly voice all but paralyzes personal will, and projects upon the subliminal imagination the unsatisfied will of the dead; the body becomes a suspended form, transfigured momentarily by atavistic images impressed upon the mind.

"The Second Coming," written about eighteen months after **"Anima Mundi,"** objectifies an autohypnotic state, showing the speaker in the process of eliciting from *Spiritus Mundi* the transformational image. More so than any previous lyric, even the three stigmatic poems, **"The Second Coming"** demonstrates what Yeats meant by "responsibility." The speaker "responds" transpersonally to the threat of destruction. A cool intensity replaces the "wild" excitement and elated agony of the early poems of exultation. Anarchic events are accepted as manifestations of man's impending fate; they are not regarded simply as a challenge to the speaker's defense of an heroic order. Aristocratic pride, personal bitterness, indignation toward the ungovernable crowd no longer are the vital issues. Prophetic insight has more than offset the prospect of social upheaval.[10]

There is an apparent reversal in the point of view of the poem. The dissolving center of the phenomenal reality gives way to a startling image of concentration so that, as a result, the centrifugal demon seems to have been brought under control of a daimonic intelligence. The animal form that slowly evolves in the mind's eye—an organic, yet entelic, energy—heralds, therefore, the watchful release of the body. The speaker may thus be said to have struck a radical balance, evoking the symbol of a potentially interchangeable (physical-spiritual) reality.

That unformed image of the beast was formerly contained by the unconscious, confined by—but now, under the aspect of violence—ready to break from, any rational order.[11] And from the cultural devotion of the past twenty centuries, it would appear, will emerge for the uninitiated

a subterranean terror; for the visionary that terror, however, is subliminal, and may be brought to light not in fear but out of a complementary, immanent wisdom. The manifestation of force would seem to breed a vision of final destruction; but for the speaker it becomes an occasion for spiritual revelation, bringing on a flash of insight which intimates a change, gradual and deliberate, as natural as the mystery of any emerging form. It is a psychogenic emancipation. And it is made possible through metamorphosis, not through any retaliatory exchange of power. Any action in the external world, as Schopenhauer claimed, will have served to mirror back upon the doer the extravagant energy of his own will, forcing the individual to recognize the self, and not some outside power, as the unpurged source of evil in the world.

The contemplative vision results from surrender of the will. It leads to dissolution of the energy of the self by dissolving into daimonic symbol images which have taken hold on the mind and whose assertive force has not yet been exhausted. Symbolic form results from a concentration which purifies by relaxing the conscious mold of organic form: breaking up (without destroying its reticulate core) any rigidified, specific pattern of thought. Under the influence of its own generative power, mind and body operate more equally upon each other, re-forming the self, making it progressively less insistent upon proving its will upon other selves, other forms of being. Once circumstances in the surrounding world can be accepted as its own fate, then the self enlarges its capacity for being.

In this consists the commanding mystery and solitude of the visionary. In **"The Second Coming"** the speaker appears to have let himself be overshadowed by his image of the sphinx, allowing it to proliferate, by religious and historical association, while converging toward an instinctive unity, the elemental ground of the imagination. The living-stone is assigned no specified locale; the sands of the desert, suggesting the slow passing of time, become a correlative for the ineffectual world the stone image will displace; but that image takes shape as a phantasmagoria, calculated to rephrase the historical question in the form of a spiritual enigma: "what rough beast . . . ?"

It is curious that none of the existing critiques of **"The Second Coming"** have focused squarely upon the state of mind of the speaker. What the poem says about the world and beast is not meant as simply a projection of the formidable state of affairs today, and the prospect of some equally formidable antidote. With the above discussion I have been suggesting that the poem be read as proof of the speaker's journey toward psychological equanimity. The images, while certainly gathered from the real world (history and culture), reflect control of an inner world, the untried recesses of the self. And again, unlike previous critics of the poem, I take for my verifying text "Phase 22" of *A Vision*: the pivotal point in the transition from the subjective to the ghostly self.[12] In "Phase 22," Yeats muses, "we seem to have renounced our ambition under the influence of some strange, far-reaching impartial gaze." The evolving image of the sphinx returns just this kind of impartial gaze—"blank and pitiless as the sun" (the most memorable perhaps of Yeats' eye-sun images): its indifferent wisdom seeming to confront us with the inherent justice of man's fate. However the world mayfare, a man's acceptance of his "responsibility" makes available to him the redeeming strength of his imagination. He may "use the *Body of Fate* to deliver the *Creative Mind* from the *Mask* [Yeats describes this as "self-immolation"] . . . , so using the intellect upon the facts of the world that the last vestige of personality disappears." At this point "the desire to dominate has so completely vanished, 'amalgamation' [the resolving power of the imagination] has pushed its way into the subconscious, into that which is dark, that we call it a vision." The man of action is the antithesis of the visionary; he cannot internalize his sense of mission, he cannot amalgamate through art or language what he feels must be expressed. Action, Yeats observes, "is a form of abstraction that crushes everything it cannot express." "Men will die and murder for an abstract synthesis, and the more abstract it is the further it carries them from compunction and compromise; and as obstacles to that synthesis increase, the violence of their will increases. . . . Before the point of balance has been reached" [the moment of vision] a man who is "out of phase" (yet identified with "Phase 22") may "become a destroyer and persecutor, a figure of tumult and of violence." The imaginative mind confronts such a demonstration of self, opposing to license and havoc a spiritual vision which is ominous, appalling. But before some actual Armageddon, it is visionary insight which is most instructive: "life, the balance reached, becomes [for men of "Phase 22"] an act of contemplation. There is no longer a desired object, as distinct from thought itself, no longer a *Will,* as distinct from the process of nature seen as fact. . . . Intellect knows itself as its own object of desire; and the *Will* knows itself to be the world" (*V,* 157-63).

Individuation triangulates itself into self, spirit, world; it is the conscious separation of a spiritual whole. Not until the self foresees its identity with the world and can so refine its desire as to understand the troubled soul of the world—the residual consciousness of "Anima Mundi"—not until then will the imagination be able to conjure any embracing vision of reality.

The sphinx may offer only a glimpse of the underlying truth, but its momentary appearance is sufficiently edifying. The poet submits his will to the innervating fire of his imagination. No longer is he content with the prefigured beatitude of heroic Helen, "his phoenix," "half-child," fit to be despoiled, perhaps, by a centaur; nor, after 1913, is he moved to scale terrestrial heights, raising his voice in the *peine et joie* of illumination. In **"The Second Coming"** the poet's imagination is felt to move through the image, the speaker's voice vibrant with the intimation of something a part of, though mysteriously removed from, himself.

The unconscious is rendered in **"The Second Coming"** in terms of common experience, half-revealed, but shared on our part by some twinge of recognition. Coupled with that strange, lurking image of the beast is the guiding hand of the speaker, holding in counterpoise the claims of personal assertion and social violence. The speaker braces with the threat of utter destruction a petrifying construct of the psyche—so that as a result the cause of man's inhumanity is made over into a millennial symbol of transformation. That symbol for the moment obliterates all attention to the images which circumscribe it—images of blood, water, sun, stone, sand. The *trompe l'oeil* of the sphinx moving impresses itself upon the mind with the sudden curtain-drop, followed by the speaker's unresolved question at the end. And the shadow of that harrowing beast seems to linger after the last words in the poem are spoken.

NOTES

[1] Jeffares, *Yeats, Man and Poet,* p. 141.

[2] *Ibid.,* pp. 59-60.

[3] Hone, *Yeats, 1865-1939,* p. 252.

[4] Yeats first makes reference to the "phoenix" in his diary for January 1909. He is greatly agitated when he writes about the uncertain terms of his relationship with Maud Gonne. "Of old she was a phoenix and I feared her, but now she is my child more than my sweetheart. . . . Always since I was a boy I have questioned dreams for her sake—and she herself always a dream and deceiving hope . . . the phoenix nesting when she is reborn in all her power to torture and delight, to waste and to ennoble" (Moore, *The Unicorn,* pp. 202-203). In the poem he wrote in 1915 Yeats no longer suggests her cruelty or her transforming, redemptive power.

[5] Thomas Whitaker traces her words to those of Coventry Patmore and Plutarch—*Swan and Shadow: Yeats's Dialogue with History* (Chapel Hill, 1964), pp. 159-60.

[6] The poems suggest the process of enlightenment as undergone by a saint or Christ, contracting pain or stigmata ("riddled with light") as an antidote to pride and as a means of inducing a sense of charity, or love.

[7] I would agree with Peter Ure in saying that the phrase "riddled with light" is "the highest point to which the poem mounts in its restless rush of movement and rising rhythms" (*Yeats,* p. 58). The word "riddled" suggests both the ecstatic—stigmatic—pain of physical transfiguration and the speaker's dumbfounded questioning of self-justifying motives, his faculties having momently been transfixed by the enigmatic disclosure of his own, absolute self-enlightenment.

[8] T. R. Henn contends that "The Cold Heaven" "has the clarity and vehemence of a visionary moment: made credible and vivid by the epithet *rook-delighting.* The stark

visual impression of the black rooks, in the wild acrobatics* [Henn's note: *Rooks and green plovers are among the few birds which seem to do this, in a kind of ecstasy] in which . . . they sometimes revel . . ." ("'The Green Helmet' and 'Responsibilities,'" in *An Honoured Guest*, p. 51).

9 My reading of Yeats's word "responsibility" as deriving from the earlier connotation of "respond," "responsiveness," is not the reading applied by any critics, so far as I am aware, who have dealt with the volume *Responsibilities*. Stephen Spender's reading comes closest to my interpretation in that he relates the conventional sense of the word to the poet's awareness of his inherent, imaginative response to reality: "What does Yeats . . . ultimately feel responsible towards? The answer is, perhaps, to an abstraction, to the imagination which creates. But nevertheless this abstraction is a quality within ourselves"—"The Influence of Yeats on Later English Poets," *Tri-Quarterly*, IV (1965), 89. Compare also Priscilla Shaw's statement: Yeats was "both moral and responsible, and the surface irresponsibility or 'aestheticism' of some of his poems is clearly a reaction to the impossibility of adequate moral action, rather than some unthinking impulse" (*Rilke, Valéry and Yeats*, pp. 218-19).

10 The proleptic intent of the poem, to paraphrase a remark of Hart Crane's, is best construed with regard to poetic or psychopoetic, not historical, necessity—"Modern Poetry," in *Collected Poems of Hart Crane*, ed. Waldo Frank (Garden City, 1958), p. 182. Compare Thomas Parkinson's remark about one of the five possible "modes" in which the narrator in Yeats's poems speaks: "poems of pure revelation—what Yeats himself would have considered pure poetry—are possible only within the impure content of the life of the divided self struggling through successive nightmares of deceptive lures"—*W. B. Yeats: The Later Poetry* (Berkeley, 1964), p. 54. Is it necessary to conclude, therefore, as does R. P. Blackmur (among others) that the "magic" of revelation in "The Second Coming" "promises . . . exact prediction of events in the natural world" ("The Later Poetry of W. B. Yeats," in *Permanence of Yeats*, p. 49)?

11 Johannes Kleinstück has dealt in greatest depth with the psychological implications of the poem: " . . . *der Bezugspunkt, um es so zu sagen, war der Mensch in seiner Gottebenbildlichkeit; das Unmenschliche am Menschen war zwar nicht ohne Wirkung und Wirklichkeit, aber man erkannte es nicht als Ideal an. Jetzt ist es, als ob sich das Unmenschliche für diese Nicht-Anerkennung rächen wollte; was unterdrückt war, kommt nach oben.*" ["The point of relation, as it were, has to do with man in his likeness to God; the unhuman man was not indeed without consequence or reality, but it was not recognized as an ideal. Now it is as if for this lack of recognition the unhuman would take revenge; what was repressed comes to the surface."] Suppression of brutish qualities, Kleinstück implies, before the elevated ideal of God, is symbolized in Western consciousness by obeisance of the three kings from the East (*"grausamsten Tyrannen"*) before Jesus; and the reverse movement would be symbolized quite naturally by the figure of a beast slouching, ready to spring—"W. B. Yeats: *The Second Coming. Eine Studie zur Interpretation und Kritik," Die Neuren Sprachen* (July, 1961), 306. John Unterecker also takes cognizance of the unconscious tendency in men to make their own mortality reason for wishing upon the world universal destruction (*A Reader's Guide to Yeats*, pp. 164-65).

12 Cleanth Brooks makes the puzzling statement that the poem is seen in the context of "Phase 23"—offering no substantial argument for his proposition ("Yeats: The Poet as Mythmaker," in *Permanence of Yeats*, p. 72). T. R. Henn, regarding what the poem describes rather than the state of mind of the narrator, assigns "The Second Coming" to the "primary" phases 2 to 7, *The Lonely Tower: Studies in the Poetry of W. B. Yeats* (London, 1949), p. 190.

WORKS CITED

A. *The Autobiography of William Butler Yeats, Consisting of Reveries over Childhood and Youth, the Trembling of the Veil and Dramatis Personae*, Garden City, 1958.

E. *Essays and Introductions*. London, 1961.

M. *Mythologies*. New York, 1959.

P. *The Variorum Edition of the Poems of W. B. Yeats*, ed. Peter Allt and Russell Alspach. New York, 1957.

V. *A Vision*. (A reissue with the author's final revisions.) New York, 1961.

Russell E. Murphy (essay date 1981)

SOURCE: "The 'Rough Beast' and Historical Necessity: A New Consideration of Yeats's 'The Second Coming'," in *Studies in the Literary Imagination*, Vol. XIV, No. 1, Spring, 1981, pp. 101-10.

[*In the following essay, Murphy turns to Yeats's A Vision for an indication of the meaning of "The Second Coming." Murphy contradicts typical readings of the poem by focusing on its positive qualities when viewed in this context.*]

On April 8, 1938, William Butler Yeats, commenting on the world political scene in a letter to his friend Ethel Mannin, wrote:

> If you have my poems by you, look up a poem called **"The Second Coming."** It was written some sixteen or seventeen years ago and foretold what is happening. I have written of the same thing again and again since. This will seem little to you with your strong practical sense, for it takes fifty years for a poet's weapons to influence the issue.[1]

"The same thing" was the emergence not only in Nazi Germany, but in Italy, Spain, Russia, and China of strongman dictators, all of them potential avatars for that "rough beast" whose own impending appearance in a desperate and chaotic world Yeats's **"The Second Coming"** had not so much prophesied as anticipated in that note of questioning dread on which the poem concludes: "And what rough beast, its hour come round at last, / Slouches towards Bethlehem to be born?"[2]

By now those fifty years and more have elapsed since that poem's original publication in November, 1920 (**Variorum,** p. 401n.), and history has provided numerous candidates in answer to the question, not the least among them the figure of Adolf Hitler, who visited his own demonic wrath upon any ethnic, religious, and political group which did not fit into his concepts of racial purity or share his vision of a thousand-year *Reich*. While those various candidates for the distinction have hopefully proved themselves to the world-at-large to be sufficient answer to Yeats's question (and no doubt would have been sufficient proof of the poem's predictive powers for Yeats himself, had he lived to see World War II), they have not proved to be answer enough for the critics of the poem. Rather, attempting to read the poem on more cosmically apocalyptic levels than the mere mundane of heinous atrocities and intolerable tyrannies and oppression, and seeing as well the obvious potential for a connection to be made between Yeats's "rough beast" and the Beast of Revelation 13, they would have us face ultimate meanings and answer the question with our own worst fears. Thus, Morton Irving Seiden can write that Yeats "concludes his poem with a warning that the Second Coming of Western tradition is to be not the expected return of Christ, but the Second Coming of the Antichrist"; and that "we are profoundly stirred not so much by Yeats's joy as by his horror and his fear . . . [in the face of] the terror of anarchy, the burden of nightmare, and the tragedy of a hope so far removed from the discordant present as to be almost meaningless."[3] For Richard Ellmann, meanwhile, "'**The Second Coming**' gives no hint of the redeeming or even salutary qualities of the new dispensation,"[4] and "the final intimation that the new god will be born in Bethlehem, which Christianity associates with passive infancy and the tenderness of maternal love, makes its [the beast's] brutishness particularly frightful" (Ellmann, p. 260). Finally, although Harold Bloom identifies "the Egyptian Sphinx . . . [as] the rough beast who slouches toward Bethlehem to be re-born, not born, in place of the rebirth of Christ," he at least has the good sense to admit that that would occur "not literally, but [as] . . . what would actually be a demonic epiphany."[5]

Even those critics who regard Yeats's beast on less cosmically awful levels have to concede that any positive values assigned to its coming are matters of faith, while all of the negative associations are supported by historical actualities. For Frank Tuohy, then:

> The identity of the "rough beast" is part of a question which the poet leaves unanswered.

Anarchy brings forth its antithesis, which may be exceedingly nasty, but for the poet, who looks at history aesthetically rather than morally, may also be exciting and stimulating and not necessarily unwelcome. If the "rough beast" suggests the Black and Tans or the Fascists, this is a piece of good fortune that Yeats could not have foreseen.[6]

John Unterecker, though he, like Bloom and Ellmann, focuses on the poem's cosmic implications, admits likewise some positive value to the concluding vision:

> Yeats . . . explicitly prophes[ies] the reversal of the world's gyres, the birth of a new, violent, bestial anti-civilization in the destruction of the two-thousand-year Christian cycle. His rough beast, compounded from Christ's Matthew 24 prediction of His future return and St. John's vision of the coming of the Antichrist, the beast of the Apocalypse, gives a double meaning to the "revelation" that is at hand.[7]

Unfortunately, Unterecker does not go on to explicate the nature of that "double meaning," assuming, apparently, that it is all too obvious.

Oddly enough, many of the critics refer to the cosmology which Yeats expounded in *A Vision* to support their readings of the threatening dimensions of the beast, since **"The Second Coming"** with its opening image of the falcon "turning and turning in the widening gyre" makes use of a key symbol from that cosmology, i.e., the gyres or intersecting cones. As we have already seen, Unterecker makes specific reference to "the reversal of the world's gyres" in his discussion of the beast's significance, while Ellmann, in his discussion of the same topic, in addition to quoting from a pertinent note to the poem, merely notes that "*A Vision* paint[s] a pleasanter picture of the new god than might be expected, and . . . [is] not wholly consistent with the poem" (Ellmann, p. 258). Finally Bloom legitimately, albeit parenthetically, gripes at a key juncture in his own treatment of the poem that he does not know "how to keep *A Vision*'s terms out" (Bloom, p. 323). What is odd, however, is that they all seem to have missed the point, for, as I shall demonstrate in the remainder of this paper, not only do *A Vision*'s terms clarify the dimensions of Yeats's rough beast, but they give that otherwise cryptic utterance a resoundingly positive value compatible with other relatively contemporary evaluations of the direction in which mankind is moving.

Put simply, all that the gyres mean is that human history can be symbolized in two continuously intersecting cones, one primary or solar or objective (e.g., Apollonian), the other antithetical or lunar or subjective (e.g., Dionysian). In those terms, Christ Jesus was a primary dispensation, and the coming new dispensation—*not* covenant—will be antithetical. Read "antithetical" as Antichrist and the source of much of the confusion—including Yeats's own from time to time—can be seen instantly. The movement of the gyres, however, while they must be seen as being in cyclical conflict, is complementary, not so much as

white complements black or positive complements negative or good complements evil, but as goings complement
comings, reintegration complements disintegration, and
reconciliations complement sunderings. To begin with,
Yeats's own extended note to **"The Second Coming"**
ought at least to clarify that poem's visionary underpinnings apropos of the gyres:

> At the present moment the life gyre is sweeping
> outward, unlike that before the birth of Christ which
> was narrowing, and has almost reached its greatest
> expansion. The revelation which approaches will
> however take its character from the contrary
> movement of the interior gyre. All our scientific,
> democratic, fact-accumulating, heterogeneous civili-
> zation belongs to the outward gyre and prepares not
> the continuance of itself but the revelation as in a
> lightning flash, though in a flash that will not strike
> only in one place, and will for a time be constantly
> repeated, of the civilization that must slowly take
> its place (*Variorum,* p. 825).

What, then, according to *A Vision,* will that new civilization be like? For surely it is only in attempting to answer
that question by working directly from within rather than
generally from outside the very cosmology that fostered
the Yeats poem that the symbolic identity of the rough
beast can be rendered, if not as positive as the Second
Coming of Jesus, then at least as positive as the processes of historical necessity which oblige mankind to
endure his goings forth as surely as his comings hither.

Yeats's claims for *A Vision,* which was first published in
1925, were perhaps too extravagant. In a dedicatory
epistle to Ezra Pound he writes: "I send you the introduction of a book which will, when finished, proclaim a new
divinity."[8] Though *A Vision*'s system of symbols and
their geometric interactions may not in fact proclaim a
new divinity, it would not be misleading to say that they
do describe a process of societal and spiritual evolution
whereby individuals and the race collectively move
through twenty-eight so-called phases, each like hours
on a clock—called the Great Wheel—ticking out the
comings and the goings of the gyres, and each phase
defined in terms of human types. Each defined that way,
that is, except for Phases One and Fifteen, which are also
the two key phases for our immediate purposes. They are
both discarnate or supernatural phases representing, respectively: the dark of the moon and the full of the moon;
the perfection of the soul and the perfection of the body;
wisdom (*Sapientia*) and beauty (*Pulchritudo*); and the
fine point of the antithetical cone (the perfection of the
world or collectivity) and the fine point of the primary
cone (the completion of the Christ or individuation).
According to that same schemata, Western civilization
in 1927 was passing through Phases Twenty-three,
Twenty-four, and Twenty-five (*cf.* diagram, *A Vision,* p.
266); and in the poem **"The Phases of the Moon,"**
Michael Robartes, a fictitious adept and *alter ego* invented by Yeats in early attempts to publicize his own
system (purportedly given to him by spirit communicators
through the medium of his wife Georgie between 1917 and
1921), makes it clear that "Hunchback and Saint and Fool"
are the final key to the mystery which the student of the
occult in his shadowy tower (as likely Yeats himself at
Thoor Ballylee as any other novitiate) cannot unravel (*A
Vision,* pp. 59-64).

Another portion of *A Vision,* however, unravels the
mystery whose only mystery for us should be the obscure occultisms in which it is phrased. In the section
entitled "The Great Wheel," Yeats goes into undisguised
detail about each of the twenty-eight phases or incarnations. It is in that section that we learn that the Hunchback, the Saint, and the Fool are the typological embodiments of the characteristics of Phases Twenty-six,
Twenty-seven, and Twenty-eight respectively, those
phases, in other words, which Western civilization, as of
Yeats's writing, would shortly be entering (*A Vision,* pp.
176-82). Still, it is Phase One that we must focus on in our
consideration of **"The Second Coming,"** for it is in that
phase, which follows Phase Twenty-eight, that the antithetical influx to replace the dissipating primary dispensation will occur; that is to say, in Phase One that the rough
beast will be born. Thus, in another, earlier treatment of
the cosmology, while Yeats was still speaking through
the fictitious Robartes, we learn that: "After an age of
necessity, truth, goodness, mechanism, science, democracy, abstraction, peace, comes an age of freedom, fiction,
evil, kindred, art, aristocracy, particularity, war . . . " (*A
Vision,* p. 52).

At this juncture there is a slight confusion, however, for
Robartes had introduced his postulation by mentioning
"'the third antimony of Immanuel Kant, thesis: freedom;
antithesis: necessity . . . '" (*A Vision,* p. 52). If "antithesis" equals antithetical, then "thesis" must equal primary; thus the incoming "age of freedom" would be primary, not antithetical. Because of such a confusion in the
terminology, it is not made clear if that new "age of
freedom" which Robartes predicts was the Christian era,
which itself fostered as much superstition as it fostered
faith, replacing the rationalties of the classical Greco-
Roman civilization which it supplanted, or the truly coming new age which will supplant our own Christian era.
Fortunately, it is the fictitious Robartes' Watson, Owen
Aherne, who clarifies matters somewhat by asking:
"'Even if the next divine influx be to kindred [i.e., that age
of freedom] why should war [which concludes the list of
that age's characteristics] be necessary?'" (*A Vision,* p.
53). Despite the inadvertent crosswiring of terms like
thesis and antithesis with the far more key terms, primary
and antithetical, then, the next divine, antithetical influx
will be that age of freedom, and the rough beast shall be
the avatar of that coming age's characteristics.

Still, how rough and how a beast, for certainly as much
as we are asked to anticipate an age of evil and war, we
are also encouraged to anticipate an age of freedom and
kindred and art. Too, we should keep in mind that, as
opposed to our age's stultifying preoccupations with the
levelling forces of democracy, it shall be an age of some
manner of aristocracy. Once more, it is when Yeats speaks

openly, as he does in his treatment of the twenty-eight incarnations, that a measure of clarity and logic replaces the obscurantisms of occult jargon. Here, then, is his description of Phase One, i.e., of the coming antithetical influx anticipated questioningly in **"The Second Coming":**

> This is a supernatural incarnation . . . there is complete passivity, complete plasticity. Mind has become indifferent to good and evil, to truth and falsehood . . . the more perfect be the soul, the more indifferent the mind . . . [for it is] the final link between the living and more powerful beings. . . . All plasticities do not obey all masters, and . . . those that are the instruments of subtle supernatural will differ from the instruments of cruder energy; but all, highest and lowest, are alike in being automatic (*A Vision,* pp. 183-84).

The key, perhaps, is in its being a discarnate phase in which "acts can no longer be immoral or stupid, for there is no one there that can be judged" (*A Vision,* p. 183). It is for one thing, then, *not* the Last Judgment of the Apocalypse which the Beast will precede, but more a shifting and sifting from one level of being to another, as well as a period clearly "beyond good and evil."

Yeats was familiar with the works of Friedrich Nietzsche from as early as 1902, and critics have traced much of *A Vision*'s postulations on alternating cycles of human history back, by implication, to similar theories of Nietzsche's.[9] The following is, I think, a pertinent passage from his *Beyond Good and Evil,* a work which, among other things, argues for the necessary development of a human aristocracy of the spirit. Note, too, the allusions to a war-like, barbarian culture ruled foremost by concepts of kindred and caste:

> Let us tell ourselves without indulging ourselves how every superior culture on earth got its *start!* Men whose nature was still natural, barbarians in every frightful sense of the word, men of prey, men still in possession of unbroken strength of will and power-drives—such men threw themselves upon weaker, better-behaved, more peaceable races, . . . in which the last life powers were flickering away in flashing fireworks of intellect and corruption. The distinguished caste in the beginning was always the barbarian caste; their superiority lay primarily not in their physical but in their psychic power; they were more whole as human beings (which on every level also means "more whole as beasts").[10]

Phrases and images from this passage reverberate strikingly against similar passages previously quoted from Yeats, particularly his note on **"The Second Coming"** and Robartes' predications for the coming age; but the significance of the passage is better told by ignoring sources and analogues for the sake of focusing on their shared view of the human element in history as being primarily a psychic or spiritual element. I for one am painfully aware that one of history's most bitter ironies will be to link forever Nietzsche's concepts of the *Übermensch* with

Hitler's crack-pot racial theories and his policies of mass genocide. A far more interesting though far less noted irony, however, can be found in those astounding similarities between Nietzsche and Yeats's comments in poetry and prose on the dimensions of the human element in the coming age, not the least astounding among those similarities being that Nietzsche too envisions the human as beasts, but makes his the more wholly human, while the critics, as I have amply illustrated, would have us see Yeats's beast as anything but. Does Yeats himself, however, even if he might not have been fully aware of the furthest implications of his own cosmology, do likewise? Does *A Vision* view the coming human as essentially bestial, and if it does, does it do so in positive or in negative terms?

Phase Two is, obviously, the subsequent phase to Phase One; more important, it is, rather than supernatural and discarnate, natural and human. If the rough beast is to emerge from the divine antithetical influx of Phase One, his characteristics will be defined for us in Yeats's description of the human type embodying the spiritual qualities of Phase Two. Here is that description. If that coming creature lives in conflict with his fate, Yeats says that "he gives himself only to violent animal assertion and can only destroy; strike right and left." Unquestionably, the rough beast of **"The Second Coming,"** with all of that image's negative connotations intact, comes to mind; but those are only the negative aspects of the embodiment of Phase Two. His positive aspects—that is, what he achieves if he lives in accordance with his fate, giving "himself to Nature as the Fool . . . gave himself to God"—are no less suited by that phrase, rough beast; nor, however, is he any less that wholly human—and not in either case demonic—figure than the *Übermensch* which Nietzsche anticipates and argues for the spiritual release of. Describing those aspects with which fate will thus endow the creature, Yeats writes:

> He is neither immoral nor violent but innocent ["beyond good and evil"]; is as it were the breath stirring upon the face of the deep; the smile on the face of a but half-awakened child . . . remembered as a form of joy, for he would seem more entirely living than all other men, a personification or summing up of all natural life.

And no less christic, we might add, since earlier critics of the poem have persistently asked us to regard the rough beast in the most eschatologically christocentric terms. No less christic, if the Christ is always the anointed one, the chosen vessel carrying God's perfected Will among a still-to-be-perfected mankind. A divinely human creature, as Christ Jesus was the humanly divine, is then, in Yeats's own words, as likely, if not more likely, an apt description of the "rough beast . . . slouch[ing] towards Bethlehem to be born"; for so much is the embodiment of the characteristics of Phase Two according to *A Vision.* "The new *antithetical tincture* (the old *primary* reborn) is violent," Yeats goes on to admit, continuing the description, but "it forces upon the *primary* and upon itself a beautiful form" with "the muscular balance and form of an animal good-humour with all the appropriate comeliness of the Dancing Faun." Furthermore, should "the rare accident [of wholly accepting one's fate] . . . not occur, the body is coarse, not deformed, but coarse from lack of sensitiveness, and is most fitted for rough physical labour" because "if [he is] born amid a rigid mechanical order [such as we have seen the old *primary* become], he would make for himself a place, as a dog will scratch a hole for itself in loose earth" (*A Vision,* pp. 106-107). Finally, it is interesting to note that one of the last images called forth in *A Vision* is of "a Communist . . . ploughing on the Cotswold Hills, nothing on his great hairy body but sandals and a pair of drawers, nothing in his head but Hegel's *Logic*" (*A Vision,* p. 301). For that as well is the "rough beast" questioningly anticipated in **"The Second Coming"**; but in no case is he represented as anything the human should fear or despise or disown, for he is, to repeat Yeats, that "summing up of all natural life," the perfection of the human animal to this point.

It is understandable that Yeats, a poet simultaneously working within the implications of the system expounded in *A Vision* as well as living the very history that seemed to have brought all of **"The Second Coming"** 's most dreadful possibilities to fruition, might have missed the very point which I contend that *A Vision* makes in response to the question on which the poem ends. We should not, however, be so willing to forgive the incredible lapses of judgment which subsequent critics are guilty of, for others besides Nietzsche and Yeats have spoken within the last century and a half and less of an emerging new age which would not so much require as necessitate by the sheer force of biological, psychological, spiritual, and historical evolution the concomitant emergence of a new mankind. Nor need we look as far back as to Whitman's *Democratic Vistas* and his hopes for America's sons becoming New Adams, creatures of a transcendent joy for life and with an inner power and quality of spirit; or for that matter to the prophetic aspects of Tennyson's *In Memoriam* or to the visionary conclusion to Shelley's *Prometheus Unbound.* More recently, and far more scientifically, Teilhard de Chardin, speculating on the logical possibilities of the Omega of the Apocalypse by tracing the direction of biological evolution within a christocentric framework, began writing, at virtually the same time that Yeats was worrying through *A Vision* with its proclamation of a new divinity, a work entitled *The Phenomenon of Man.* De Chardin writes:

It is . . . a mistake to look for the extension of our being . . . in the Impersonal. The Future-Universal could not be anything else but the Hyper-Personal—at the Omega Point.[11]

For the failure that threatens us to be turned into success, for the concurrence of human monads to come about, it is necessary and sufficient for us that we should extend our science to its farthest limit and recognize and accept . . . not only some vague future existence, but also, as I must now stress, the radiation *as a present reality* of that mysterious centre of our centres which I have called Omega (de Chardin, p. 267).

It seems perfectly logical, even if not necessarily permissible, to see in de Chardin's Omega Point the Phase One of Yeats's schema, and to see in that intensely personalized and radiant *"present reality"* or Omega the Natural Man, radiating joy wholly and innocently and summing up all of life, of Yeats's emergent Phase Two.

Finally, Carl Jung, also writing with this same chaotic period for Hebraic-Christian, Greco-Roman Western civilization in view, a culture which Oswald Spengler during the 1920's had relegated to the ashheap of outworn modes and tired ritual, noted that:

There are no longer any gods whom we can invoke to help us. The great religions of the world suffer from increasing anemia, . . . the so-called conquest of nature overwhelms us with the natural fact of overpopulation and adds to our troubles by our psychological incapacity to make the necessary political arrangements. It remains quite natural for men to quarrel and to struggle for superiority over one another. . . .

If so much sounds like Nietzsche, it is when Jung suggests the only possible outlet from such a dilemma that he sounds like Yeats:

As any change must begin somewhere, it is the single individual who will experience it and carry it through. The change must indeed begin with an individual; it might be any one of us.[12]

Whether that individual be seen as the Communist on Cotswold Hill or the rough beast of **"The Second Coming"** or the man of Phase Two or de Chardin's Omega, the individual must be seen as the wholly human; otherwise—and only otherwise—there would indeed be no common human value to either our hopes or our fears.

If the foregoing was the barest inkling of the expressed hopes of the finest thinkers and men of letters of the last few preceding generations, those concurrent fears that it might in fact all turn out rather quite badly were simply given poetic voice by Yeats in his conclusion to **"The Second Coming"**—and even then they were stated as a question. To accept that the breakthrough, as terrified as we might be that we may lose the best as well as the worst of the old in doing so, must be made by sheer necessity in any event and that, when it is, it will signal no loss whatsoever and will rather be the true "prize of the spirit,"[13] one which this race has labored to earn, is the only way, to paraphrase other lines from the Yeats poem, to restore to the best the unsentimental conviction that mankind is perfectible and to allow the worst to turn their own passionate intensity, if not into plough-shares, at least into less deadening realities and demeaning fictions. For our enduring is

Proof that there's a purpose set
Before the secret working mind:
Profane perfection of mankind
     (**"Under Ben Bulben,"** *Variorum,* p. 639).

NOTES

[1] Allan Wade, ed., *The Letters of W. B. Yeats* (New York: Macmillan, 1955), p. 851.

[2] W. B. Yeats, "The Second Coming," in *The Variorum Edition of the Poems of W. B. Yeats,* ed. Peter Allt and Russell K. Alspach (New York: The Macmillan Company, 1957), pp. 401-02. All references to the text and notes will be made from this edition.

[3] Morton Irving Seiden, *William Butler Yeats: The Poet as Mythmaker* (New York: Cooper Square Publishers, 1975), pp. 235-36.

[4] Richard Ellmann, *The Identity of Yeats,* 2nd ed. (New York: Oxford University Press, 1964), p. 258.

[5] Harold Bloom, *Yeats* (New York: Oxford University Press, 1970), p. 323.

[6] Frank Tuohy, *Yeats* (New York: Macmillian, 1976), p. 169.

[7] John Unterecker, *A Reader's Guide to William Butler Yeats* (New York: Farrar, Straus & Giroux, 1959), p. 165.

[8] W. B. Yeats, *A Vision* (New York: The Macmillan Company, 1956), p. 27. All references to the text will be made from this edition.

[9] Seiden, p. 49; Ellmann, pp. 91-92.

[10] Friedrich Nietzsche, *Beyond Good and Evil,* trans. Marianne Cowan (Chicago: Henry Regnery Company, 1955), pp. 199-200.

[11] Pierre Teilhard de Chardin, *The Phenomenon of Man,* trans. Bernard Wall (New York: Harper and Row, 1959), p. 260.

[12] Carl G. Jung, "Approaching the Unconscious," in *Man and His Symbols,* ed. C. G. Jung and M.-L. von Franz (New York: Dell, 1967), p. 91.

[13] Wallace Stevens, "Imagination as Value," in *The Necessary Angel* (New York: Random House, 1951), p. 142.

James Lovic Allen (essay date 1985)

SOURCE: "What Rough Beast?: Yeats's 'The Second Coming' and *A Vision*," in *REAL: The Yearbook of Research in English and American Literature,* Vol. 3, 1985, pp. 223-63.

[In the following essay, Allen interprets "The Second Coming" as a political poem associated with the rise of communism.]

"The Second Coming," one of Yeats's three or four most famous poems, is also one of his most frequently explicated or analyzed. It is, furthermore, one of the most variously interpreted, perhaps *the* most variously interpreted. There is no generally accepted reading or any significant degree of consensus about meaning or meanings. One reason for this situation is that the poem's broadly suggestive imagery and apocalyptic tone suited or matched the age from which it sprang—a period of cultural and political upheaval between two world wars, to which it might seem to apply descriptively or prophetically. In colloquial terms, the piece "caught a wave," lending it an apparent generality of theme or significance perhaps well beyond its author's immediate concerns or interests at the time of composition. Evidently pleased with the poem's popular appeal and appearance of prophetic validity, Yeats himself made comments which helped to contribute to such wide-ranging interpretations. Circumstances like these along with critical trends in this century have led a number of prominent authorities to argue that the piece need not be associated with anything so arcane or specific as the details of Yeats's private "system" or the theories of history developed in his "cranky" prose volume *A Vision.*[1]

In the most general poetic or critical sense, perhaps it is proper to let a poem mean whatever it can or will. By no means is the purpose here to limit the richness or potential of Yeats's poem. However, in scholarly terms it is also frequently useful, informative, and rewarding to know what can be learned of a poem's genesis and of the author's intention when the piece was created—theories and principles of the now old "new criticism" to the contrary notwithstanding. This more academic approach to **"The Second Coming"** has also been much pursued, but not exhaustively or satisfactorily. With **"The Second Coming,"** even more than is usually the case with difficult poems by Yeats, the materials are confusing and parts of the puzzle sometimes ill-fitting. In fact, the present study itself, though extensively and productively exploratory, probably should not claim definitive status.

The issues of chief concern here are the extent to which and the ways in which **"The Second Coming"** is related to Yeats's notoriously elaborate and esoteric prose volume *A Vision.* The first question to be considered involves dates. **"The Second Coming"** was written in January, 1919[2], and was initially published in November, 1920[3]. The first edition of *A Vision* was published in 1925, with the revised version appearing not until 1937. Initial impressions might be, then, that the poem's composition could not have been influenced by a book whose earliest version was published six years later, although almost none of the exegetes who ignore *A Vision* have chosen to cite this situation as a reason for its neglect. The facts are, however, that the source materials for *A Vision*— Mrs. Yeats's automatic writings—began late in 1917, and Yeats states that the so-called instructors "drew their first symbolical map of history, and marked upon it the principal years of crisis, early in July 1918. . . ."[4] Thus, on the one hand, the basic raw materials on history in *A Vision* were available in ample time to permit significant relationships to exist between them and a poem with historical implications written in the first part of 1919. On the other hand, what must be constantly guarded against is the tendency to assume too uncritically connections between the poem and historical materials in either edition of the book, for numerous enlargements, developments, and refinements of those materials naturally occurred between 1919 and 1937. However, still another complicating—though also potentially clarifying—factor may be involved. It is possible, or even probable, that the success and impact of the poem was such that in certain respects *it,* once written, may have had some influence upon the development of certain aspects of the book rather than the other way around. This possibility should neither be overemphasized nor ignored.

Two other facts unequivocally relate **"The Second Coming"** to *A Vision.* The one of most long-standing visibility is the note to the poem which Yeats included in the 1921 publication of **Michael Robartes and the Dancer** at his sisters' small Cuala Press in Ireland. Although this text may have been relatively inaccessible to most scholars before 1949, it was reproduced in that year by A. N. Jeffares in his book *W. B. Yeats, Man and Poet*[5], a source which also asserts (perhaps mistakenly) that the note was *written* in 1919.[6] This note was made even more prominent a few years later in the first printing of the **Variorum Poems** (pp. 823-25). It explicitly and unequivocally associates **"The Second Coming"** with the historical cones and gyres which were to appear in more detail subsequently in both editions of *A Vision.* More recently revealed connections between poem and book, which most scholars and critics of the 1950's, 1960's, and 1970's had no way of knowing about, are those provided in the notes of *A Critical Edition of W. B. Yeats's A Vision (1925).*[7] Various materials there indicate, from pre-1919 scripts and notations, an anticipated apocalyptic reversal of historical eras involving Christ or a counterpart of some kind.

PROBLEMS IN A VISION'S SYSTEM OF HISTORY

One of the chief difficulties encountered in the attempt to discover significant relationships between **"The Second Coming"** and *A Vision* is that the sections of the book dealing with history are almost hopelessly flawed and inconsistent, not to mention their inherent complexity even where they momentarily seem systematic or orderly. All scholarly and critical attempts to elucidate adequately the historical system have foundered on this stumbling block. How much Yeats was aware of the incongruities is difficult to determine. Why he did not more forthrightly acknowledge them is equally unclear. All that is certain is that they exist.

One confusing aspect of the system that Yeats himself clearly did understand (although he is inconsistent about it, as will become apparent later) has been fully perceived and dealt with in print by only one commentary other than mine, to my knowledge. In addition to the bifurcation of all culture into the opposite *tinctures* of *antithetical* and *primary,* familiar to virtually all Yeatsians, each of the interlocked gyres in an era is distinguished by predominantly religious or secular features as well. Then the two

sets of qualities are joined into four possible combinations; these are *antithetical* religion, *primary* religion, *antithetical* secular life or politics, and *primary* secular life or politics. Thus, when Yeats sets up his opposing interlocked gyres of history, he not only contrasts an *antithetical* cone to a *primary* cone, but, further than that, he also counterpoises an *antithetical secular* (and political) cone to a *primary religious* one.[8] Only the two-thousand-year cones or gyres of so-called "eras" are involved in this present consideration.[9] The two-thousand-year cones, gyres, cycles, or eras are called "civilizations" if they are secular and political, or "religious dispensations" if they represent major spiritual or theological movements. The extent of misunderstanding in these matters is indicated by the fact that some commentators have spoken of the system's "Christian civilization." There is no such unit or concept in *A Vision,* and Yeats virtually never uses the two words *Christian* and *civilization* in direct combination with each other.[10] The Christian *era* or "religious dispensation" is the period from the birth of Christ to a point somewhere between AD 2000 and 2100. Counterpoised to it, in its first 1000 years at any rate, is "classical civilization," represented chiefly by the Roman Empire. In the first century AD this *antithetical* civilization's gyre is at its widest expansion, with the interlocking Christian cone *(primary)* at its narrowest point because that religious dispensation would naturally be at its merest beginnings immediately after the birth of Christ. Commentary on the situation in the *second* half of the Christian religious dispensation (AD 1000 to about 2000) must be reserved until later since that is one of the main places at which Yeats's exposition ceases to be self-consistent.

Almost without question, the most confusing element of the entire situation is that in both editions of *A Vision* Yeats has articulated at different places two incompatible and irreconcilable versions of the system just discussed. No one appears to have recognized this fact. One of the two versions involves a so-called interchange of the *tinctures,* a sudden and violent switch of the *antithetical tincture* from the smallest point of the dwindling cone to the widest expansion of the counterpoised one and vice versa for the *primary tincture.* The passage in the earlier edition is actually the clearer of the two:

> . . . this figure differs in form from that which preceded it and symbolised the preceding period of two thousand years. This difference is caused by a movement analogous to the exchange of the *Tinctures* but instead of the words *primary* and *antithetical* we substitute Solar and Lunar. . . . Before the birth of Christ, for instance the Lunar gyres came to the narrow end of their cone, and at His birth passed into the broad end of the other cone and so continued to converge. The Solar gyre upon the other hand passed from broad to narrow. . . . This means that as the civil life [secular and political] grew more and more *antithetical* in nature the religious grew more and more *primary.* . . . At [the midway point], however, there is no interchange, but a return, a change of direction, the gyres which diverged now converge and vice versa. . . . (*CEVA,* pp. 168-69)[11]

The corresponding passage in the later version reads as follows:

> At the birth of Christ took place, and at the coming *antithetical* influx will take place, a change equivalent to the *interchange of the tinctures*. . . . Before the birth of Christ religion and vitality were polytheistic, *antithetical,* and to this the philosophers opposed their *primary,* secular thought. At the birth of Christ religious life becomes *primary,* secular life *antithetical.* . . . (***Vision*** B, pp. 262-63)

After having explained this feature of the system's cones in earlier nonhistorical contexts, however, Yeats says, "The diagram is sometimes so used by my instructors and gives them a phrase which constantly occurs, 'the interchange of the *tinctures,*' but it is inconvenient" (***Vision*** B, p. 75). His next sentence indicates that the interchange is "for this reason" "generally" *disregarded.* That the same kind of lack of consistency applies to the historical gyres is suggested by a careful reading of the following passage:

> . . . the automatic script generally [shows] that each civilisation and religious dispensation is the opposite of its predecessor. . . . For instance, classical civilisation [is] 1000 B.C. to A.D. 1000 let us say . . . and our own civilisation is now almost midway in [its] movement. . . . At or near the central point of . . . classical civilisation . . . came the Christian *primary* dispensation. . . . At or near the central point of our civilisation must come *antithetical* revelation. . . . (***Vision*** B, p. 204; see also pp. 254-55)

Although it is difficult to compare the two versions of Yeats's historical system without diagrams, it is fairly clear that the one just described has no sudden change of *tinctures* from the widest expansion of one cone to the narrowest point of the other, nor vice versa. On the other hand, instead of a mere reversal or "change of direction" at the narrowest part of each civilization's gyre, as in the other structure, there is a non-violent change of tinctures where the cones simply touch point to point, *antithetical* classical civilization having expired and our present *primary* one having begun at AD 1000. In this version of the system, a religious cone and the counterpoised civilization's cone are opposite to each other in *tincture* only half the time instead of all the time. If necessary, the reader can, with patience, work out a diagram for himself to see how and why this is so. Such an interpretation is apparently the one that Harper and Hood have in mind when they say, " . . . a religious dispensation . . . lead[s] into a secular civilization of the same type; the primary religious dispensation beginning with Christ thus gives way to a primary secular civilization beginning at 1000 AD . . ." (*CEVA* notes, p. 45).

If **"The Second Coming"** relates to the system of history in *A Vision,* but the system in *A Vision* has two differing versions or interpretations, then the obvious question— never before articulated—becomes, "To which version does the poem correspond?". As for the birth to come at about AD 2000, it would seem to be the same in either interpretation: a new *antithetical* religious dispensation is expected at that point in both cases. However, the outward-sweeping gyre of the poem's famous opening lines—assuming that that gyre represents our present civilization—would be different in the two versions. It would be *antithetical* in the interpretation, with a drastic interchange of the *tinctures* every two thousand years. The reason is that the Roman Empire represented the widest expansion of an *antithetical* secular cone that began to dwindle at the year zero, and at the midway point, in this version, "there is no interchange, but a return, a change of direction."[12] Therefore, our new civilization would remain *antithetical* until AD 2000, when the cataclysmic interchange would occur. In the other version, though, where any change of *tinctures* occurs simply when one cone succeeds another, touching point to point, our present civilization would be *primary,* contrasting in *tincture* since AD 1000 to its *antithetical* predecessor, the Roman Empire. This delineation represents, believe it or not, an oversimplification of the problems and difficulties involved, but it provides as much as needs to be considered for present purposes.[13]

PROBLEMS IN "THE SECOND COMING"

"The Second Coming" constitutes the culmination of a considerable heritage of apocalyptic pieces in Yeats's work. These include the early story **"The Adoration of the Magi,"** the uncollected play ***Where There Is Nothing*** as well as its successor ***The Unicorn from the Stars,*** the poem **"The Magi,"** and to some degree the section of ***Autobiographies*** entitled "The Trembling of the Veil." The interrelationships between these and other pieces have been studied by several commentators, who show that anticipation of an impending new era was a continuing thematic element in Yeats's thought long before the advent of Mrs. Yeats's automatic writing.[14] There is, however, a fundamental difference between **"The Second Coming"** and most of the predecessors just mentioned, a difference of tremendous importance whose inadequate recognition, by Melchiori as well as virtually all others, has been one of the greatest causes of misunderstanding and misinterpretation of the poem. The predecessors tended to have a religious emphasis, looking forward to the birth of a new god or gods who would replace the outworn Christianity for which Yeats had so little use. Both the title and the allusion to Bethlehem in **"The Second Coming"** deceptively suggest that it also has a religious theme. However, it is, in fact, a *political* poem that achieves much of its power and impact from Yeats's adroitly *ironic* implementation of religious imagery and tradition. Admittedly, determination of this fact might have been difficult—though not impossible—before Jon Stallworthy's initial publication of the poem's working drafts in 1963.[15] These drafts, though, especially in the later transcription, leave no question whatever that the poem's genesis was completely political. Furthermore, certain similarities of theme and image (not to mention dates of composition) between **"The Second Coming"**

and **"Nineteen Hundred and Nineteen"** suggest that the one poem is as politically oriented as the other, while a number of authorities have noted similar kinships between **"The Second Coming"** and political elements in the piece which follows it in *Collected Poems,* **"A Prayer for My Daughter."**[16]

However, **"The Second Coming"** might also be said to share the most crucial of all its images—the fabulous-beast icon—with one of the earlier apocalyptic pieces. This misleading circumstance probably would have created trouble enough in any event. But it has been exacerbated almost beyond comprehension, especially as far as exegeses of the already difficult poem are concerned, by Yeats's own identification with each other of the two works involved. In *Wheels and Butterflies* he says, "Had I begun *On Baile's Strand* or not when I began to imagine, as always at my left side just out of the range of the sight, a brazen winged beast that I associated with laughing, ecstatic destruction?" To this more or less rhetorical question he appends the following footnote: "Afterwards described in my poem **'The Second Coming.'**"[17] Then in his next sentence Yeats speaks of *Where There Is Nothing,* in which just such a brazen beast appears. Despite their creator's implied equation, though, the beasts from play and poem are not really alike at all, either literally or figuratively. Unlike the later one, the earlier monster is sharp-toothed and winged as far as visual appearances are concerned.[18] As for thematic implications, the beast in *Where There Is Nothing* is specifically identified with "Laughter" (*loc. cit.*), in marked contrast to the grim and foreboding figure in **"The Second Coming."** Why Yeats ever made his association between the two is irksomely difficult to understand unless—or until—their common heritage in Biblical and occult traditions of apocalypse is fully recognized and explained, as is done later here.

The opening lines of **"The Second Coming"** constitute another problem. A number of commentators have held that the "widening gyre" is *primary* or objective. I once thought that they were wrong, for I was convinced that the historical scheme that includes a point-to-circle interchange of the *tinctures* was the one on which **"The Second Coming"** was based. Further research has led me to realize that I was mistaken on this point. The most obvious indication of my error is that the 1921 note for the poem—despite internal inconsistencies of its own—is explicit about the *tincture* of this widening cone: "At the present moment the life gyre is sweeping outward . . . and has almost reached its greatest expansion. . . . All our scientific, democratic, fact-accumulating, heterogeneous civilization [*primary* qualities] belongs to the outward gyre . . ." (*Variorum Poems,* p. 825). Though more diffuse and less easy to illustrate with quotation of a single sentence, the last portion of the essay **"A People's Theatre"**—published in the year in which **"The Second Coming"** was written—also indicates that the present outward-whirling spiral is "objective" or *primary* (*Explorations,* pp. 258-59). Finally, a careful reading of the "Dove or Swan" section of *A Vision* reveals that Yeats's prepossession in the period from AD 1000 to the

present is so much with the growing dominance of *primary* civilization and politics that he fails to dwell on religion's corresponding decrease, whereas in the first half of the section he had carefully sustained the balance between *primary* Christianity's growth and the *antithetical* Roman Empire's decline. This unit of the book is the same in both editions except for excision of a few pages at the end in the 1937 version. This means that all three prose sources emphasizing a widening *primary* gyre of civilization in the present age are close to **"The Second Coming"** in dates of composition. The only reasonable conclusion is that the poem must almost certainly portray the same phenomenon and that the alternative version of the history system with an expanding *antithetical* secular cone ("civilization") approaching a sudden interchange of *tinctures* at AD 2000 is not relevant to its interpretation. This point will be of considerable importance in another connection presently.

In his journal article that reproduces the drafts of **"The Second Coming,"** Stallworthy says, "The falcon has long been a problem.[19] Then he refers to the early draft line that used the word *hawk* instead of *falcon* and cites the well-known note for **"Meditations in Time of Civil War"** about hawks—gloomy birds of prey—being emblems of logic and mechanism as opposed to the butterflies of wisdom. He seems to feel that with this reference he does away with the problem because logic and reason are qualities of the *primary* tincture and therefore should neatly associate the falcon symbolically with the outward-sweeping objective gyre.[20] Unfortunately for such a reading, whereas Yeats had indeed used hawks as images of reason or mental ability, as in the poem **"The Hawk,"** his use of symbolic birds was in a stage of transition at the time of **"The Second Coming,"** and an alternative symbolism could be equally applicable. Not only is the hawk imagery in *At the Hawk's Well* (1917) probably more subjective than objective, but in the play *Calvary* (1920) a whole congeries of bird emblems is developed, with large noble birds like hawks made explicitly *antithetical* in an extended note to the play:

> I use birds as symbols of subjective life, and my reason for this . . . cannot be explained fully till I have published some part at any rate of those papers of Michael Robartes, over which I have now spent several years [a semi-private allusion to the automatic scripts of Mrs. Yeats]. . . . Certain birds, especially as I see things, such lonely birds as the heron, hawk, eagle, and swan, are the natural symbols of subjectivity, especially when floating upon the wind alone or alighting upon some pool or river, while the beasts that run upon the ground, especially those that run in packs, are the natural symbols of objective man. (*Variorum Plays,* p. 789)

As far as interpretational suggestions for **"The Second Coming"** are concerned, matters are further complicated by the fact that in *Calvary* the birds' subjectivity is dramatically contrasted throughout to the *primary* qualities of Jesus Christ.

If hawks and falcons were consistently symbols of *primary* logic and reason, then it would be appropriate enough to conclude that the falcon in the opening lines of **"The Second Coming"** is an objective emblem, in keeping with the widening objective gyre that its flight delineates. Or, on the other hand, if the historical system involving an interchange of the *tinctures* were apposite (and thus the widening gyre were *antithetical*), then again there could be perhaps emblematic accord between a subjective bird and its *antithetically* spiraling flight. But since the widening gyre approaching the year 2000 might be *antithetical* or *primary* depending on the version of the history system in mind and since hawks at the time in question might be either objective or subjective, then the falcon very much remains a problem, especially in light of the further bird imagery later in the poem, to be considered presently. Personally I think that the falcon itself must be taken almost "unsymbolically," if such a thing is possible in Yeats, though its widening gyre is almost certainly *primary*. The bird in its outward-spiraling flight was the poem's earliest germinal element; the first three lines of the first draft read as follows:

> Ever more wide sweeps the gyre
> Ever further hawk flies outward
> from the falconer's hand.[21]

Evidently the image simply struck Yeats's imagination with such vividness and immediacy from the very outset that he was loath to relinquish it and, in fact, did not throughout all the draft's progressions toward the poem's finished form.[22]

WHAT ROUGH BEAST?

Stallworthy indicates that the beast in **"The Second Coming"** "has been hunted by numerous critics and commentators, but has always eluded capture."[23] With minimum concern for what dismay may be created among interpretatively oriented critics, the present study has intentionally mounted an intensive scholarly expedition, the chief purpose of which has been finally to capture Yeats's monster. The leader of the excursion, though not totally happy about some uneasy moments here or elusive movements there, is generally not dissatisfied with the outcome of the long and arduous venture.[24]

Almost certainly the greatest cause of confusion about the beast is the fact that *A Vision*'s historical system—in either of the two versions already reviewed—predicts somewhere near the year AD 2000 the annunciation or birth of a new *religious* dispensation, an "*antithetical* influx" that will be contrary to the *primary* birth of Christ in the year zero and, to one degree or another, will be a counterpart or near equivalent of the *antithetical* annunciation to Leda at approximately 2000 BC. Everyone who has read *A Vision*—as well as many who have not—knows that Yeats regarded himself and his sympathetic personae like Cuchulain and Michael Robartes as *antithetical* men, whereas Christ and Christianity were unfavorably *primary* in *tincture*. Why, then, would Yeats portray the birth of the new *antithetical* dispensation at the end of the outgoing *primary* era with a symbolic figure as horrible and repugnant as the one in the poem? Some commentators have attempted to answer this question by pointing out that Yeats's *antithetical* characters were often men-of-war, that the *antithetical tincture* is characterized as "masculine, harsh, surgical" (**Vision** B, p. 263), that there comes "After us the Savage God."[25] But such *antithetical* figures in his other poems and in his plays are at least aristocratic, gallant, or heroic. They are not characteristically associated with anarchy, pitiless blank eyes, the drowning of ceremony and innocence in tides of blood, or frighteningly bestial qualities. Resolution of the apparent enigma here comes with realization that the rough beast in **"The Second Coming"** is neither *antithetical* nor emblematic of a new religious dispensation. It is, rather, *primary* and representative of a secular or political entity.[26]

Perhaps the two parts of this thesis should be examined independently, at least at first. What evidence suggests that the rough beast might be *primary* rather than *antithetical*? First of all, there is the symbolism of subjective birds versus objective beasts already cited from the note for the play **Calvary**, which was written almost contemporaneously with **"The Second Coming."**[27] Second, in the introductory stories about Michael Robartes in both versions of *A Vision*, the book of Giraldus contains "a number of curious allegorical pictures; . . . a man whipping his shadow; a man being torn in two by an eagle and some kind of wild beast . . ." (*CEVA*, p. xvii; see also **Vision** B, p. 38). The two-word expression "wild beast" should be kept in mind, for it will become important later. One reading, of course, might be that the eagle represents spirit and that the beast represents flesh or the physical world, but in light of what follows in Yeats's book itself, it would probably make much more sense to interpret the eagle as *antithetical* and the beast as *primary*. For, in the non-historical sections of *A Vision*, these are the two qualities of which each human personality is composed in varying proportions or the disparate aspects of human nature between which man is divided or "torn."

Next, the beast in **"The Second Coming"** is doubly related to the sun. It is explicitly so related in the poem itself, with its "gaze blank and pitiless as the sun," and it is indirectly so related by virtue of its "lion body." In tradition, one of the strongest symbolic connections for the lion is with the sun.[28] In *A Vision* itself Yeats seems to have in mind the association between lion and sun when he says, "When I think . . . of Salome . . . delicately tinted or maybe mahogany dark—dancing before Herod . . . I see her anoint her bare limbs according to a medical prescription of that time, with lion's fat, for lack of the sun's ray, that she may gain the favour of a king . . ." (**Vision** B, p. 273). Although in the body of his work as a whole Yeats's sun and moon symbolism are almost hopelessly inconsistent, within the confines of *A Vision* the term *solar* usually means *primary* and *lunar* means *antithetical*. Thus, both the lion-like body and the solar eye of the beast increase its *primary* implications.[29]

The suggestion that the rough beast in **"The Second Coming"** might represent a political entity has been relatively commonplace, even among critics not thoroughly familiar with *A Vision*'s marked distinction between religious dispensations and civilizations (secular or political movements). Early and late, some critics have identified the figure with fascism. This makes no sense, however, for the same reasons that interpreting the beast as *antithetical* makes no sense; for, politically speaking, fascism would be an extreme form of the *antithetical.* Such is indicated in *A Vision* itself: "*Primary* means democratic. *Antithetical* means aristocratic" (*Vision* B, p. 104). These lines of demarcation are indicated at various other places throughout the book. Yeats was, of course, briefly intrigued by fascism at one point in his career. However, **"The Second Coming"** was written before the development of that interest and also, for that matter, before the emergence of fascism as a political phenomenon. Unless the poem was indeed presciently prophetic, it can have nothing to do with fascism as an organized political system.[30]

Other commentators have identified the rough beast as emblematic of communism, and there can be little question that these theorists are on valid ground. For one thing, one of them cites a statement by Mrs. Yeats that socialist movements inspired the poem.[31] More importantly, the drafts indicate that similarities between the French Revolution and the Bolshevik Revolution were the ideological seeds for the poem in Yeats's thought. Torchiana transcribes some of the drafts himself (rather differently from either of Stallworthy's versions), and his remarks and supporting evidence constitute a reasonably strong case for the communistic interpretation, especially as to Yeats's concern that the Ireland of 1919 might be a dangerously inflammatory tinderbox for the spread of Bolshevik politics.[32]

Communism makes more sense than fascism as a political referent for the beast image for two additional reasons. One of these is the date of composition. Whereas fascism developed after the poem was written, the Bolshevik Revolution occurred just a little more than a year before. Two essays published in the year in which **"The Second Coming"** was written—**"A People's Theatre"** and **"If I Were Four-and-Twenty"**—are clearly marked by indications of Yeats's concern at the time with "the Red Terror."[33] The other main reason why communism makes more sense than fascism as a meaning for the icon is that communism, if truly achieved, would be the absolute or ultimate form of democracy—a mass-oriented *primary* political system which the aristocratic-minded Yeats would naturally abhor with exactly the kind of horror evoked in the poem by the slouching-beast image. In support of this point is the fact that the word *mob* occurs several times in the drafts; and, of course, the term *anarchy* appears in the poem itself.

Another key word that appears several times in the drafts is *murder.* Yeats habitually used this word elsewhere in connection with communism, which strengthens ties between that political system and the imagery of **"The**

Second Coming" (*Explorations,* pp. 429-30).[34] Furthermore, in a section of **"The Trembling of the Veil"** first published in the year after **"The Second Coming,"** Yeats quotes the opening lines of the poem to express his feelings about "the growing murderousness of the world" (*Autobiographies,* pp. 192-93). Perhaps the most telling of all such usages, however, comes from a debate held not only in the same year as the poem's composition, but even in the very month: "Mr. W. B. Yeats . . . said that Russia had, in the name of progress and in the name of human freedom, revived tyranny and torture of the worst description—had, in fact, resorted to such a mediaeval crime as burning men for their opinions."[35] The drafts of **"The Second Coming"** have far more explicit and unequivocal language about Bolshevism than *murder* and *mediaeval crime,* however: "The Germany of Marx has led to Russian Com."[36] This leaves little doubt. Torchiana transcribes the line in exactly the same way, incidentally.[37] The development of widely divergent interpretations of **"The Second Coming"** prior to the publication of these drafts is easily understandable. But it is difficult to comprehend how critics can contend since their publication, as many have done, that such specific language and pointed meanings were "generalized," refined away, or cast aside in the process of the poem's development so that the finished piece has sometimes been taken, even recently, as not about anything so topical as communism or political systems at all.[38]

There is considerable further evidence to indicate that the late drafts and the final poem are just as much about the advent of communism as the early drafts. For example, in the last pre-publication draft as reproduced by Stallworthy, after a couple of false starts with the word *jealous* in connection with the beast's rousing from its "stony sleep," Yeats has the somewhat strange-sounding expression "by jealousy stung awake." That combination of words sounds less strange, however, when one finds a passage written some years later in which Yeats is still pondering what his "instructors" had told him about "the end of any age," the "final phase" of a "civilisation," and Swift's view that such things are brought about "by the jealousy . . . of the many" (*Explorations,* p. 316). In context, the word *jealousy* here is obviously meant in the sense of revolutionary resentment against the wealthy few. And the passage from the drafts sounds less strange still when, in another place, speaking against the same kind of things depicted in the earliest drafts of **"The Second Coming,"** Yeats says that eighteenth-century "America . . . had neither the wealth nor the education of contemporary Ireland; no such violence of contraries . . . had *stung* it into life. [In Ireland] the influence of the French Revolution *woke* the peasantry from the medieval *sleep,* gave them ideas of social justice and equality . . ." (*Variorum Poems,* p. 833; my italics). The "stony sleep," of course, survived even into the final poem.[39]

Careful examination of the drafts from another, though related, perspective reveals that instead of changing his subject, as some have suggested, what Yeats so characteristically did was to make it simultaneously more subtle and more powerful by discovering ways to express it through symbol and allusion rather than direct statement. Dealing with violent revolution in late eighteenth-century France and in twentieth-century Russia, he was understandably cast into an apocalyptic frame of mind, and at the end of the first prose draft he wrote, "Surely the second Birth comes near."[40] The "second Birth" (as opposed to "Second Coming") is clearly an expression welling up from the massive automatic scripts that had spoken repeatedly of a new "Avatar," "the Second Master," a "New Messiah," and so forth (see *CEVA* notes, pp. 20, 45, 46). But in 1919 the apocalyptic event associated with those terms was only "near" (first draft), not "at hand." This "second Birth" was to be the annunciation of a new religious dispensation "at about 2100" (p. 45). Yeats's poem, by contrast, is about a *political* development manifesting itself in the final outward-moving spirals of the *present* era's cone or gyre. Under the influence and excitement of months of epochal terminology and imagery from his "instructors," Yeats appears to have confused or combined these two phenomena in the early stages of his drafts, either unconsciously or semi-consciously. Even so, neither the words *second Birth* nor the idea occurs again for a number of lines. Then appears, "Surely the great falcon must come," which is immediately replaced by "Surely the hour of the second birth is here."[41] At this point Yeats's thoughts evidently drifted momentarily even further in the direction of the scripts' religious annunciation, though, as Stallworthy notes, the use of the falcon as an emblem of the new birth is out of keeping with the poem's opening.[42] He then fumbled with the "second birth" for three or four more attempts before coming up all at once with a shift to "the second coming" (not deleted) and the first mention of Bethlehem. It is with this combination that **"The Second Coming"** achieved that magical click, like the closing of a box, with which the major pieces of a poem suddenly fall into place according to Yeats.[43] For it was rather clearly at this point that Yeats realized the tremendous advantage for his poem of the vast storehouse of Biblical and traditional imagery of apocalypse over the arcane materials in the automatic scripts and card files of his private system, especially since his poem was not really about the *antithetical* religious annunciation there predicted anyway. In the same momentary flash of creative genius, or just before or after, he must also have recognized the symbolic and imaginative possibilities of the concept of a *secular* Christ, of associating all the detested levelling religious dogmas of *primary* Christianity with the detested levelling political doctrines of *primary* communism. Throughout the final drafts of the poem the constant central objective is development of the grotesquely repugnant beast icon and effective handling of its powerfully ironic relationships to the unequivocally allusive image of Bethlehem.[44]

Secular Christ the beast, then, a levelling socialism which is the final extreme manifestation of the outward-sweeping *primary* political gyre, is to *precede* the new *antithetical* religious dispensation.[45] Specific materials exist

in support of this analysis of the situation and interpretation of the poem. Originally, "Dove or Swan"—written, it will be recalled, before 1925 and therefore relatively close in time to **"The Second Coming"**—concluded with a segment which Yeats deleted from the 1937 edition of *A Vision*. It deals with what the system predicts to come in the last part of the present cycle (after Phase 22) and in the first part of the new one. It indicates rather clearly that something like communism or socialism will occur *before* the dawning of the new age. The imagery is even sometimes reminiscent of that in **"The Second Coming"**:

> Then with the last gyre must come a desire to be ruled or rather, seeing that desire is all but dead, an adoration of force spiritual or physical, and society as mechanical force be complete at last. . . .
>
> A decadence will descend, by perpetual moral improvement, upon a community which may seem like some woman of New York or Paris who has renounced her rouge pot to lose her figure and grow coarse of skin and dull of brain, feeding her calves and babies somewhere upon the edge of the wilderness. . . . What awaits us [is] democratic and *primary*. . . .
>
> When the new era comes . . . it will, as did Christianity, find its philosophy already impressed upon the minority who have, true to phase, turned away at the last gyre from the *Physical Primary*. (*CEVA*, p. 213)

A similar source is Yeats's 1921 note for the poem itself. In it a fictitious desert tribe, the Judwalis, tell Michael Robartes, "*For a time* the *power* will be with us, who are as like one another as the grains of sand [ultra-democratic, socialistic, or *primary*], but when the revelation comes it will not come to the poor but to the great and learned and establish again for two thousand years prince & vizier [*antithetical* types]" (*Variorum Poems,* p. 825; my italics). Finally, in a more well-known passage at the end of the second edition of *A Vision,* Yeats indicates that even in 1937 he is still concerned about the possibility of Communism spreading dangerously far in the final phases of the present cycle before the advent of the new era:

> How far can I accept socialistic or communistic prophecies? I remember the decadence Balzac foretold to the Duchesse de Castries. I remember debates [on socialism] in the little coach-house at Hammersmith or at Morris' supper table afterwards. I remember the Apocalyptic dreams of the Japanese saint and labour leader Kagawa, whose books were lent to me by a Galway clergyman. I remember a Communist described by Captain White in his memoirs ploughing on the Cotswold Hills, nothing on his great hairy body but sandals and a pair of drawers, nothing in his head but Hegel's *Logic*.
>
> What discords will drive Europe to that artificial unity . . . which is the decadence of every civilisation? How work out upon the phases the gradual coming and increase of the counter-movement, the *antithetical* multiform influx . . . [?] (*Vision* B, pp. 301-02)

The final portion of this last quotation indicates still another kind of reason why it does not make sense in terms of the system to interpret the cataclysmic birth of the beast in **"The Second Coming"** as the beginning of the new *antithetical* cycle. There, as in several other places, Yeats's indications are that the coming *antithetical* influx will have only its barest beginnings somewhere near AD 2000 to 2100, with its development to maturity or fullest expansion not until considerably later.[46] Like Christianity at the year zero, the new religious dispensation will be just at the tip of its cone at the time of annunciation. According to the apposite version of the system, nothing either *antithetical* or religious will be so wide-sweeping near AD 2000 as the phenomenon symbolized by the imagery in **"The Second Coming,"** but rather some *primary* secular power or political movement.

Two related points about other parts of **"The Second Coming"** should be made in the light of the analysis just presented. One involves the lines "The best lack all conviction, while the worst / Are full of passionate intensity." Donald Weeks and others have suggested that these lines strongly echo a passage from Shelley's *Prometheus Unbound,*[47] while some commentators have suggested even other parallels or possible sources outside Yeats's own work. Such parallelisms may be interesting to speculate about, but there are quite a few similar passages from Yeats's own work which provide better elucidation of these lines. The just-quoted passage about the minority in the old era having already the philosophy of the new age is one. Yeats felt that he and a few other distinctly *antithetical* types were born out of phase, so to speak, in the final stages of a strongly *primary* civilization. Unfortunately members of this minority, surrounded by vocal or even violent masses, were all too often something less than staunch or united in their views (the words *uncertain* and *wavering* occur in the drafts). One of the most helpful parallel passages from Yeats's own works comes from that *aquiline-visaged antithetical* persona Michael Robartes, who, in an introductory story from the second edition of **A Vision,** speaks to a small group of pupils or disciples as follows: "Dear *predatory birds,* prepare for war. . . . Love war because of its horror, that belief may be changed, civilisation renewed. *We desire belief and lack it.* Belief comes from shock . . ." (**Vision** B, pp. 52-53; my italics).[48]

This same passage sheds light on the second of the two related points, which has to do, rather obviously, with the "indignant desert birds" whose shadows are reeling all about the poem's rough beast (in the drafts occurs the line "an angry crowd of desert birds"). Very clearly in operation here is **Calvary**'s symbolism of *antithetical* birds versus *primary* beasts, even though the falcon imagery in the poem's opening lines may be inconsistent or muddled in this connection. Although members of the *antithetical* minority may lack conviction, they would naturally be at least "indignant" over the threatening advent of a vast *primary* majority, as was Yeats himself when he wrote this poem. The appearance in the finished piece of only the shadows of the birds may be meant to suggest their ineffectual minority situation in contrast to an inundating "blood-dimmed tide" of anti-aristocratic masses.

During the 1920's and 1930's, both communism and Yeats's attitude toward it changed, although his concerned interest did not entirely disappear. Any number of passages from those intervening years reveal, however, that he realized at a rather early date that the Bolshevik state as it was actually being run was much more an inhumane oligarchy than a truly socialistic system. This no doubt accounts for his tendency in later years to lump most of the chief European governmental structures together for equal disapprobation and may help to explain why and how in 1936 he felt at liberty to say that **"The Second Coming"** had predicted more than a decade and a half previously what was currently happening on the Continent (**Letters,** p. 851). If one wants truly to understand the original thematic implications of **"The Second Coming"** and its rough beast, however, he must remind himself constantly that the poem was written in 1919, slightly before the advent of fascism and very shortly after the Bolshevik Revolution and the earliest instances of inhumane political executions in Communist Russia.

WHY A SPHINX?

Some commentators do not even consider or mention the fact that Yeats specifies a sphinx as the monster in his nightmare vision. Before publication of the drafts, some may have felt that the line "A shape with lion body and the head of a man" was too indefinite to make the identification certain. A few, in fact, have even stressed the likelihood of intentional indefiniteness. But the first transcription of the drafts in 1963 provided new evidence—"breast & head"[49]—and the second in the early 1970's added "& with woman's" before the word *breast.*[50] These details leave virtually no question. In fact, they even tell us that Yeats's first impulse was to depict the Greek or female form of the fabulous creature, after which he settled upon the Egyptian or male version. This very change itself will be of significance in efforts to answer the tantalizing question, "Why a sphinx?"

A series of futile attempts to arrive at a satisfactory answer to this question almost thwarted efforts to capture Yeats's beast. Only with last-minute assistance from an unexpected source was failure averted. Unlike many of Yeats's other important symbols, the sphinx makes very few appearances elsewhere in his work, contrary to the impression given by some commentators.[51] It appears in none of the plays (except for passing references in the translations of Sophocles, of course), in only one poem other than **"The Second Coming,"** (**"The Double Vision of Michael Robartes,"** also written in 1919 and so presumably of potential relevance), and only here and there in the prose, usually in references either to visual portrayals by Charles Ricketts or to Hegel's use of the image in his *Philosophy of History*. This last, however, even though its occurrences include **A Vision**'s sections on history, can have no bearing on **"The Second Coming,"** since Yeats did not read Hegel's book until after 1919. Statements of traditional meanings in sources like Cirlot are of little assistance except for associations between the Egyptian sphinx and the sun, as between lion and sun. Usual significances are of such dubious relevance (for example, "enigma," "the great mystery," and so on) or multiple diversity that they remain next to useless. Only the fellow sphinx in **"The Double Vision of Michael Robartes"** would seem to be of much potential aid.

However, **"The Double Vision of Michael Robartes"** is not a readily understandable poem, and explications of it are few and conflicting in their suggestions of meanings. Yeats himself says in *A Vision* that he used the main symbols in the poem "in ways I am not yet ready to discuss" and that the piece was written "in the first excitement of discovery," with clear indications that more considered thought or later experience might have led to a different handling of the symbology (B, pp. 207-08). The passage also says that of two main contrasted images, the sphinx and Buddha, one is associated with "the outward-looking mind, love and its lure" and the other "with introspective knowledge of the mind's self-begotten unity, an intellectual excitement" (p. 207). Since the poem itself describes the sphinx as gazing upon all things known or unknown "In triumph of intellect," the latter description from *A Vision* would seem to be the relevant one. Although little or no assistance beyond this can be gained from the appearance again of that virtually indefinable word *intellect* in Yeats's vocabulary, the description "introspective knowledge of the mind's self-begotten unity" certainly sounds subjective or *antithetical* rather than objective or *primary.* However, in terms of consistency between the two poems, the present analysis of **"The Second Coming"** would be benefitted more if the sphinx in **"The Double Vision"** could somehow be glossed as *primary.* Thus, the need for evidence in support of such an interpretation becomes apparent.

Further investigation brings to light two sources of possible assistance. In an essay entitled "The Buddha as Symbol in W. B. Yeats: A Study of Two Poems," T. R. S. Sharma argues urgently, if not always completely convincingly, that in Yeats's poems **"The Double Vision of Michael Robartes"** and **"The Statues"** the Buddha figure is subjective or *antithetical* and the sphinx in the former poem and the grimalkin in the latter (a miniature sort of sphinx, it is suggested) are objective.[52] Sharma pursues his argument by associating the sphinx with the "outward-looking mind, love and its lure" from the passage in *A Vision,* despite the fact that the other description, "introspective knowledge," and so forth, is the one that includes "intellectual excitement" to tie in with the poem's "triumph of intellect." The basis for some doubt is, therefore, apparent. The other source is F. A. C. Wilson's book already cited. In one note it says, "In this study I have assumed that Yeats *originally* meant his Buddha to typify subjectivity and his Sphinx to typify objective intellectualism, despite his difficult note in *A Vision. . . .*"[53] But then he later says of that sentence, "This is perhaps the statement in the present book about

which I feel most doubtful; though not doubtful enough to delete it."[54] Not very reassuring materials. If they convince anyone that the sphinx in **"The Double Vision"** is *primary,* so much to the good. If, not, then the only line of thought would seem to be agreement with Richard Ellmann, who could conceivably be said to be following Yeats's own comments previously quoted. Ellmann states that the images in **"The Double Vision"** are troublesome because they are used differently there from any other place in the poet's work.[55] As far as **"The Second Coming"** is concerned, that leads back to the original question, "Why a sphinx?"

Conclusions based on much investigation and contemplation are that Yeats used a sphinx figure in **"The Second Coming"** for three interrelated reasons, or one might say rather that, in characteristic fashion, he syncretized in his imagination meanings and implications from three relatively separate sources. Two of these sources involve the initially indicated female Grecian sphinx. One of the main associations for this figure in ancient tradition is, of course, the Oedipus myth, and that is—virtually certainly—just exactly one of the sources upon which Yeats drew. In the myth the sphinx was identified with death, pestilence, and famine. Until its riddle was answered, the city of Thebes could not thrive. Death, pestilence, and famine, along with war and bloodshed, tie in directly with the body of apocalyptic Biblical lore that Yeats elected to draw upon the moment that he settled upon "the second coming" and an allusion to Bethlehem instead of "the second Birth" and notions of a new "Avatar" from his automatic scripts.[56] The sphinx image first appears in the same verse draft as that dual Biblical allusion, only some six lines or so removed if deletions and trial repetitions are not considered. One momentary objection might be that Yeats's mind was not very significantly involved with the Oedipus story in 1919, since his translations of Sophocles' two plays came later; but a bit of sleuthing reveals that he had indeed been quite interested in the tale for a number of years. In fact, he had been involved in efforts to arrange a performance of *Oedipus Rex* at the Abbey Theatre from a date as early as 1904 or 1905.[57] There is no question, in short, that on the basis of his theatrical experience alone the riddling sphinx of the Oedipus myth would have been an immediately apprehended image of pestilence and famine in the mind of W. B. Yeats in the year 1919.

Yeats was also thoroughly familiar with the story of Oedipus and the sphinx from another source as well, however. The mythic motif had been appropriated as a favorite subject by a group of symbolist artists and poets so familiar and akin to Yeats that the scarcity of sphinx images in his own work is, in fact, somewhat anomalous. His closest associate among the pictorial artists involved was Charles Ricketts, one or more of whose pictures depicting a sphinx Yeats referred to in very admiring terms in at least two places (*Vision* B, p. 298, *Autobiographies,* p. 550). Actually, the impact on Yeats of this circle of artists' interest in the sphinx figure may have been somewhat overstated by commentators. In addition to Melchiori, already mentioned, D. J. Gordon and Ian Fletcher, in their catalogue of an exhibition of art works with supposed relationships to Yeats's writing, list and discuss perhaps a disproportionate number of items. The material is helpful, nevertheless, in its suggestion of possible associations.[58] Some of Ricketts' pictures were illustrations for Oscar Wilde's poem on the subject, a lush Edgar-Allan-Poeish sort of thing with possible influences from Swinburne. Even Yeats's friend T. Sturge Moore wrote a poem—far less impressive than Wilde's—entitled "The Sphinx." In his recent book on Yeats's songs and choruses, David Clark includes a collection of plates which reproduce some of these paintings and drawings that depict from varying perspectives the encounter between the mysterious riddler and Oedipus.[59] What becomes apparent from an examination of these and other renderings[60] is that both the sphinx and the dancing Salome became favorite subjects for quite a few symbolist artists in the late nineteenth century, with the usual theme in both cases being the femme fatale. Salome or some surrogate in that role appears rather frequently in Yeats's own work. Certainly such implications for the female sphinx are in no way foreign to Yeats's concern in **"The Second Coming"** and may help to explain his initial use of that figure rather than the masculine Egyptian image. For what could be a better way to portray communism than as a heartless seductress luring the unsuspecting masses into harm's way? In his book with the plates already mentioned—which any reader interested in the subject should definitely see if unable to view the originals or other copies elsewhere—one of Clark's chief interests is associations of the sphinx with death, another shade of meaning by no means foreign to Yeats's concerns in **"The Second Coming."** However, the conception of death postulated by Clark is much "warmer" and more alluring than that suggested by the imagery of Yeats's apocalyptic poem, except to the extent that the femme fatale motif may be involved in both cases.[61]

For a matter of weeks, reasons like these were the only ones that I could come up with in answer to the question, "Why a sphinx?" While they may well be contributory, they clearly cannot be exclusive, because they all involve the female Grecian sphinx, whereas Yeats almost immediately modulated to the male Egyptian icon in the drafts of his poem. Then the fuller answer came, like one of Yeats's lightning strokes, from a source to which I cannot possibly acknowledge adequately the degree of my indebtedness.[62] The key to understanding as fully as possible Yeats's "rough beast" in all its richly manifold symbolic implications is knowledge of the roles of the sphinx in various occult traditions and of the interrelationships between those and the long-standing body of orthodox and quasi-orthodox Christian eschatology, apocalypse, and second adventism in western culture. I do not understand why someone—especially myself—has not recognized this circumstance and researched this subject before now. Although many of the connections are iconographic, associational, and poetic rather than logical and discursive, there can be little doubt that they were quite real in Yeats's mind when he wrote the poem.

The main two lines of association can best be presented initially for discussion by reference to their symbolic identification with two cards from certain versions of the tarot deck, although both also exist in occult tradition independently of that set of "magic" cards, especially in cabalistic lore. The cards in question are the Chariot and the Wheel of Fortune. Both include a sphinx or sphinxes in some versions of the deck, and, in such versions, both have connections with the Old Testament Book of Ezekiel as well as with "the Wheel of Ezekiel" and the throne of God.[63] All of these associations and many others are interrelated with each other in a very intricate and complex esoteric symbology. Ezekiel is one of the two most prophetic and apocalyptically oriented books in the Old Testament (the other is Daniel), and it has both direct and indirect connections with the New Testament book of similar kind, The Revelation of St. John the Divine, with its imagery of Christ's second coming and his role as a destructive warrior and death-dealer at the day of judgment and advent of a new dispensation. As will become apparent, Yeats did not have to imagine or invent such associations between the sphinx and a warlike Christ. They existed ready to hand in the two intertwined traditions, orthodox and heterodox. All he had to do was sharpen the focus by means of that allusive juxtaposition whose manner and tone are the central concern of his final two drafts—Bethlehem and beast.

Several versions of the tarot deck depict a sphinx atop or above the Wheel of Fortune, with the four "living creatures" of Ezekiel's vision in the four corners of the card, or in some cases just their heads: lion, man, eagle, and ox.[64] On the cards four separate animals or "living creatures" are shown. However, in Ezekiel there are four creatures, *each* of which has four heads of the kinds just indicated, as well as wings (see 1.6, 10). An occult attempt to represent pictorially such a monster appears in W. Wynn Westcott's translation of Eliphas Lévi's *The Magical Ritual of the Sanctum Regnum*, evidently on the page facing the title page. There is a photographic reproduction of the two pages in Kathleen Raine's *Yeats, The Tarot, and the Golden Dawn* (illustration 15).[65] As indicated there, such a "living creature" from the prophetic book of the Old Testament is sometimes called "The Cherub of Ezekiel," or in other places the creatures are designated simply as cherubs or cherubim (occasionally spelled with a *k*). But they are also sometimes called sphinxes, and in some esoteric sources the terms *cherub* and *sphinx* are used almost interchangeably.[66]

The extraordinary four-headed "living creatures" or "sphinxes" in the Book of Ezekiel are further identified there with some very strange wheels which follow them about and which contain their spirits (1.19-21). Anyone at all acquainted with the various interrelated bodies of occult lore is familiar with the propensity in esoteric tradition for quaternities and the tendency for quaternities to develop into four-sectioned circles or wheels. It was probably inevitable that this kind of thing should happen with the four four-headed living creatures of Ezekiel, who were already associated with wheels anyway. Thus the so-called "Wheel of Ezekiel" is such a divided circle with one of the four animals represented in each of the four quarters or at each of the dividing lines.67 It takes no special ingenuity to perceive that this wheel and any number of others like it are prototypes, to one degree or another, for Yeats's great wheel in *A Vision,* whose phases correspond to gyres, cones, and cycles throughout the book but especially in the sections on history. Thus beasts or sphinxes could easily be identified with cardinal points in the cycles, particularly one like the conclusion of an era. This kind of association, of course, tends to become too generalized to be a major element of meaning in poem or system. On the other hand, however, neither Yeats nor a responsible critic could very well associate his "rough beast" with the "living creatures" of Ezekiel without being reminded of the various kinds of wheels of process or progress with which those creatures are sometimes linked in esoteric tradition.

The other tarot card related to the sphinx is The Chariot. Originally this card had horses pulling the vehicle, but in the nineteenth century some decks replaced the horses with sphinxes.68 The chariot is much like a wheeled throne in many instances with a king, prince, or some other figure representing triumph in it. The occult symbology is often quite detailed and complicated.69 The chariot is sometimes even associated with the throne of God in the vision of Ezekiel. Of course, for Yeats's symbolic purposes the figure could readily be related associatively to the triumphant armed Christ at his apocalyptic return to earth in the corresponding New Testament book, Revelation.70

That the sphinxes on the Chariot card are also sometimes associated with the "living creatures" of Ezekiel is made unequivocal by the fact that, in at least one version of the tarot pack, instead of two sphinxes pulling the chariot there are all of Ezekiel's beasts (four separate animals, as in Revelation 4.7) before the vehicle, either pulling it or else protecting it.71 In the versions with two Egyptian sphinxes, usually one is white and the other is dark or partly black, with them apparently pulling in opposite directions.72 This fact brings the whole congeries of sphinx tradition and occult apocalypse into direct connection with an import laden icon which Harper and Hood take to be the very seminal image of the automatic scripts' entire dual-natured system itself—a chariot pulled by opposite-colored horses (*CEVA* introduction, pp. xii-xvii, xlix). Thus, if a horse (or a sphinx) of one color is associated with the subjective or *antithetical tincture* and an animal of the other color with objectivity or the *primary,* what could be more natural than to represent by such a beast the point where a *tincture,* in its final expansion, inundates all culture—by a horse or, more in keeping with apocalyptic lore, a sphinx? Some readers may feel that this last-mentioned possibility pushes esoteric interpretation a bit far. Perhaps. But once again, how could Yeats possibly have been unaware, or his informed critic be silent?

Another area of occult lore in which the sphinx plays an important role is the complicated system of meditation known as Enochiana or Enochian magic, which is discussed and described at considerable length in sources like Regardie73 and Francis King.74 Initiates of the Inner Order of Yeats's Rosicrucian society, The Golden Dawn, were introduced to this method of achieving visions, and Yeats would have been thoroughly familiar with its principles and terminology.75 In this esoteric activity one of the chief attributes of the sphinx emblem is power, which is also in fact one of its attributes in certain aspects of the tarot deck and in ancient tradition as well.76 While power would clearly seem to be an appropriate quality for association with the beast in **"The Second Coming,"** it and certain other meanings tend to be positive or favorable more than negative and foreboding, for which reason their applicability to Yeats's poem might be questionable.77 Almost certainly Yeats's chief reason for using the sphinx icon was to evoke through associational links all the graphic imagery of pestilence, bloodshed, warfare, and destruction inherent in Ezekiel, Revelation, and post-Biblical traditions of Christian Armageddon or quasi-Christian apocalypse.

Such lines of implication, of course, raise momentarily the question of Yeats's familiarity with the Bible in general and with the Book of Ezekiel in particular. But the question is quickly laid to rest: in fact, with a vengeance. In addition to three references to Ezekiel in the poetry, there is a very telling one in the Yeats-Ellis edition of Blake, which says that the four Zoas "are identical with the wheels of Ezekiel and with the four beasts of the Apocalypse."78 The words in this passage are almost certainly Yeats's rather than Ellis'; but even if not, both editors insisted that they each approved all passages written by the other. Also, in Yeats's play *The King's Threshold,* the poet Seanchan says in his death speech: "I need no help. / He needs no help that joy has lifted up / Like some miraculous beast out of Ezekiel" (**Variorum Plays,** p. 309). While this passage removes any question about Yeats's knowledge of Ezekiel and its beasts, its tone would seem to be out of keeping with what has been said here of the "living creatures" and their awesome import in apocalyptic tradition. However, in the play Seanchan is very clearly a type that would have been labelled subjective or *antithetical* in the terminology of *A Vision.* Therefore his defiant final speech would have to be in sharp contrast to the connotations for death in **"The Second Coming."** Also, the beast appears in the play only as part of a simile. Though the beast is designated "miraculous" and "lifted up," as it might well be in virtually any context, Seanchan is the one who is "joyous," not the beast. In accord with such a reading, the "living creatures" are "lifted up"—wheels and all—in Ezekiel (1.19-21, 10.17-19).

What is perhaps more telling about the appearance of Ezekiel's beast in *The King's Threshold,* in relationship to **"The Second Coming,"** is the date rather than possibilities of meaning. The passage did not exist in the original play (1904). Instead, it appeared for the first time in "A New End for *The King's Threshold"* written in 1921.79 This means that the beast or beasts from Ezekiel were unequivocally in Yeats's mind at a time not far removed from the composition of **"The Second Coming."** In fact, it is quite likely that associations in the poet's mind from the recently published poem help to account for the reference in the play.[80] That a difference in meaning from the image in **"The Second Coming"** should not be considered beyond the realm of possibility is suggested by the fact that a few lines later in his new conclusion for the play Yeats also employs the moon symbolically in a way contrary to its *antithetical* usage in the historical system:

> O, look upon the moon that's standing there
> In the blue daylight—take note of the complexion,
> Because it is the white of leprosy
> And the contagion that afflicts mankind
> Falls from the moon.
>
> (***Variorum Plays,*** p. 309)

In short, Yeats clearly felt that symbolism in the new conclusion for the play had to be kept consistent with the tone and meaning of imagery and usages in the original work rather than shifted or altered in light of the iconography that had developed in his system between the piece's original composition and its revised conclusion. In fact, Bushrui, who identifies the beast image as an echo from **"The Second Coming,"** comments briefly on ways in which the "New End for *The King's Threshold*" could in 1921 incorporate certain elements of meaning from the emerging system of *A Vision* without violating in spirit or intent the play originally written almost two decades earlier.[81]

A SECULAR CHRIST

"The Second Coming" is not about the annunciation of some new avatar or religious dispensation. Neither is it about the influx of some new *antithetical* civilization or hierarchical social structure of "kindreds" or "covens," though Yeats thought about and wrote about such things in other places during and after the advent of his system. It is about precisely what its title indicates that it is about, the *second* coming of *Christ*. This second Christ, however, will be secular and political rather than spiritual and religious. Yeats in various places identified certain attributes of Christ or Christianity with those of such political systems as democracy or socialism. Chief among such qualities in common were two: the supposed equality of all humans—not surprisingly—and the dominance of reason or logic, perhaps somewhat less expectedly. One illustrative passage is the following: " . . . Christ came at the Graeco-Roman meridian . . . was the first beginning of the One—all equal in the eyes of One. . . . Equal rights and duties before the One—God with the first Christians, Reason with Rousseau" (***Explorations,*** p. 311). In another place Yeats's identification of Christ with reason is startlingly explicit, even if the element of egalitarianism is present only through reverse implication, by virtue of the speaker's being that most *antithetical* and autocratic of personae, Michael Robartes: " . . . I said to myself, 'Jesus Christ does not understand my despair, He belongs to order and reason'" (***Vision*** B, p. 41).[82] For present purposes, probably the most striking of such passages on reason is one which was published in the same year as **"The Second Coming"** was written. Not only does it associate Christianity with logic and egalitarianism, but it also labels logic a "wild beast": "Logic is loose again, as once in Calvin and Knox, or in the hysterical rhetoric of Savonarola, or in Christianity itself in its first raw centuries, and because it must always draw its deductions from what every dolt can understand, the wild beast cannot but destroy mysterious life" (***Explorations,*** p. 277; cf. the "wild beast" of Giraldus' book). Very significantly, in light of this contemporaneous passage, one of the late drafts of **"The Second Coming"** momentarily labelled the monster slouching toward Bethlehem as a "wild thing", before Yeats settled upon his now famous turn of phrase "what rough beast."[83]

However, the most explicit and emphatic revelation of a secularized Christ in Yeats's imaginative thought, a political phenomenon characterized by all the aspects of Christianity which he most disliked, comes in **"A Packet for Ezra Pound"** (1929), which eventually became a part of the introductory materials for the 1937 version of *A Vision*. There Yeats not only articulates the idea of a secular Christ, but also chooses as his *antithetical* type or symbolic persona opposite to Christ the mythic hero Oedipus: "What if Christ and Oedipus . . . are the two scales of a balance, the two butt-ends of a seesaw? What if every two thousand and odd years something happens in the world to make one sacred, the other secular; . . . one divine, the other devilish?" (***Vision*** B, pp. 28-29). After twenty centuries of dominance by the sacred Christ, the time has arrived in **"The Second Coming"** for that "something" to happen, for the appearance of that other Christ, the secular one. Here, I think, we have a case in which the poem helped to shape the subsequent book rather than the other way around. For if in 1919 the sphinx was the emblem used to image the birth of that secular Christ, in the form of egalitarian revolutions (French and Bolshevik), what could be more fitting than to choose an autocratic ruler, Oedipus, the sphinx's traditional antagonist and opposite, as representative of the *antithetical* being who becomes sacred when the *primary* one becomes secular? Furthermore, since the *primary political* gyre will reverse its movement and dwindle during the next thousand years while the *antithetical* religious one spirals outward, Oedipus, the aristocratic avatar in Yeats's historical scheme just as in the myth, will eventually vanquish the sphinx, the secular Christ of communism.[84]

Finally, not only could—and did—Yeats conceive of a secular Christ, but he was also capable of discussing in surprisingly explicit prose ideas much akin to those intimated by elliptically allusive poetry in **"The Second Coming."** The height of the *primary* era of civilization is imaged as Christ's impending return in the role of apocalyptic avenger and ruthless arbiter at a horrible day of doom, with reason and egalitarianism once again emphasized as dominant characteristics:

> What has set me writing is Coleridge's proof,
> which seems to me conclusive, that a civilisation
> is driven to its final phase . . . by "pure thought,"
> "reason," . . . by that which makes all places and

persons alike. . . . "Pure thought" . . . finds all alike, leaves all plastic, and its decisions, did it dwell equally in all men, would be a simultaneous decision, a world-wide general election, a last judgment, and for judge a terrible Christ like that in the apse at Cefalù. (***Explorations,*** pp. 316-17)

Possibly Yeats is here confusing Cefalù with Monreale, which he mentions simultaneously with Cefalù in ***Vision*** B (p. 285), or perhaps both with Daphni, where "Christ is revealed in the aspect of Jehovah, a heavy Semitic judge with thick nose and full, cruel mouth, the thickbrowed eyes gazing pitilessly to one side, . . . one sinewy hand . . . raised in blessing but conveying also menace and condemnation."[85]

While Christ may be alternately sacred or secular in Yeats's imaginative thought, He is virtually always "objective" or *primary,* as is clearly indicated again and again by passages inside and outside ***A Vision.*** What Yeats anticipates with foreboding and horror in **"The Second Coming"** is the *"physical primary"* of our civilization's "last gyre," with its "adoration of force" and "society as mechanical force," *not* the subsequent *antithetical* "new era" with its "Second Fountain [which] will arise after a long preparation" (*CEVA,* pp. 211, 213-14). His famous prophetic poem is, then, in fact about the second coming of Christ, though Christ in a frighteningly unfamiliar worldly guise. In opposition to the mass-oriented and anti-individualistic spiritual teachings of the sacred Christ Jesus, this new secular Messiah will espouse a mass-oriented and anti-individualistic political materialism. After twenty centuries of religious equality urged by Christ the Lamb, a cataclysmic and levelling social anarchy is to be loosed upon the world by Christ the Lion.

NOTES

[1] The list of commentators who have neglected, belittled, or ignored the relationships between "The Second Coming" and *A Vision* is too long to be given here. Perhaps three representative examples will suffice. Donald Weeks's treatment of *A Vision,* in just three paragraphs of an article on the poem that is eleven and a half pages long, would certainly seem to constitute neglect ("Image and Idea in Yeats' 'The Second Coming,'" *PMLA,* 63 [1948], 286-87). Balachandra Rajan is among those who feel that "The Second Coming" is "capable of standing on its own text," although he makes a few references to the system in his exegesis (*W. B. Yeats: A Critical Introduction* [London: Hutchinson University Library, 1965], pp. 119-22). Certainly Patrick J. Keane's study is an extreme instance of rejection: in an elaborate and extended commentary which is evidently intended to be definitive, at least in its own terms, *A Vision* is mentioned only once ("Revolutions French and Russian: Burke, Wordsworth, and the Genesis of Yeats's 'The Second Coming,'" *Bulletin of Research in the Humanities,* 82 [1979], 19).

[2] See Richard Ellmann, *The Identity of Yeats,* 2nd ed. (New York: Oxford Univ. Press, 1964), p. 290; A. Norman

Jeffares, *A Commentary on* The Collected Poems of W. B. Yeats (Stanford: Stanford Univ. Press, 1968), p. 238.

[3] See Jeffares, *Commentary; The Variorum Edition of the Poems of W. B. Yeats,* ed. Peter Allt and Russell K. Alspach (New York: Macmillan, 1957), p. 401. Subsequent references to this edition will appear in the text.

[4] *A Vision* (1937; rpt. London: Macmillan, 1962), p. 11. Subsequent references to this edition (the so-called *Vision* B) will appear in the text.

[5] 2nd ed. (London: Routledge and Kegan Paul, 1962), pp. 197-98.

[6] Jeffares, *Yeats,* p. 197.

[7] Ed. George Mills Harper and Walter Kelly Hood (London and Basingstoke: Macmillan, 1978). Subsequent references to this edition (the so-called *Vision* A) will appear in the text alongside the abbreviation *CEVA.*

[8] George Mills Harper and Walter Kelly Hood deal with these combinations and constructions briefly in one of the notes in *CEVA,* p. 45. The present essay assumes most readers' familiarity with technical terms and concepts from *A Vision* like *antithetical* (or subjective), *primary* (or objective), *gyres,* etc.

[9] Another potential source of confusion is that within every two-thousand-year pair of interlocked gyres there are two one-thousand-years cycles, while each two-thousand-year era is itself half of a larger four-thousand-year period. However, Yeats is quite explicit about this matter at the beginning of the section entitled "Dove or Swan," and most serious scholars have understood the situation.

[10] At least three commentaries have mistakenly used the expression "Christian civilization": Cleanth Brooks and Robert Penn Warren, eds., *Understanding Poetry,* 3rd ed. (New York: Holt, Rinehart and Winston, 1960), p. 407; Helen Vendler, *Yeats's* Vision *and the Later Plays* (Cambridge, Mass.: Harvard Univ. Press, 1963), p. 101; and Robert O'Driscoll, "'The Second Coming' and Yeats's Vision of History," in *A Festschrift for Edgar Ronald Seary: Essays in English Language and Literature Presented by Colleagues and Former Students* (St. John's: Memorial University of Newfoundland, 1975), p. 173. At least three others use the words *Christian* or *Christianity* and *civilization* in close proximity to each other and appear to have in mind the concept that would be denoted by a direct combination: A. Norman Jeffares, "Gyres in Yeats's Poetry," in his *The Circus Animals: Essays on W. B. Yeats* (London: Macmillan, 1970), p. 109; Edward A. Bloom, "Yeats' 'Second Coming': An Experiment in Analysis," *University of Kansas City Review,* 21 (1954), 106; and Hazard Adams. In Adams the equation is all but explicit. He says that Salome's "dance takes place upon the verge of phase I of the Christian millennium," that her "movements are prophetic of . . . the appearance of a new civilization," and that "she sends the new

civilization on its way" (*Blake and Yeats: The Contrary Vision* [1955; rpt. New York: Russell and Russell, 1968]), pp. 218-19.

[11] This passage and some subsequent ones might be made somewhat clearer through the use of diagrams, but the prohibitive expense of reproducing such visual aids precludes their use here.

[12] Whether or not reference to "the year zero" is technically acceptable (there being no year between 1 BC and AD 1), the expression is used here and later because Yeats implies it (with the numeral *0*) on his large "historical cones" diagram with dates that relate to the various phases in the present era (*Vision* B, p. 266).

[13] Readers interested in clarification of at least one further major difficulty in *A Vision's* system of history may see my recent note about the large diagram with dates and phases just mentioned in note 12 ("The Red and The Black: Understanding 'The Historical Cones' in Yeats's *A Vision," Yeats Annual,* 3 [1984]). One reason why information on the problems treated there is not urgently needed here is that, as Yeats says of the illustration, his instructors "have adopted a system of cones not used elsewhere in this exposition" (*Vision* B, p. 256). There are even inconsistencies not resolved by my note, however, that I did not fully recognize at the time. The main one is that the diagram, once understood, clearly indicates that the gyre which widens at the approach of AD 2000 (part of the "hour-glass" shaped figure) should be that of an *antithetical* civilization or secular movement, according to *Vision* B, p. 262. But as the discussion here will show, the *text* of "Dove or Swan" and at least two earlier sources stress the growth and expansion of a *primary* secular or political phenomenon at the end of the current era. I give the subject attention here for two reasons. One is that present concerns are with the historical portions of the book as well as with the poem. The other is that final concession should be made (though others enough have done likewise on less evidence): there simply are no resolutions to some of the discrepancies and incongruities in *A Vision.*

[14] A careful study, with more emphasis upon Yeats's prose and certain symbols or figures than on particular poems or plays, is Donald Pearce's "Philosophy and Phantasy: Notes on the Growth of Yeats's 'System,'" *University of Kansas City Review,* 18 (1952), 169-80; see especially 173-79. Giorgio Melchiori focuses on creative pieces and their imagery (*The Whole Mystery of Art: Pattern into Poetry in the Work of W. B. Yeats* [New York: Macmillan, 1961], pp. 35-72), but commits a major error in his explication of certain animal emblems, as becomes apparent here. Ellmann treats the subject concisely but quite instructively, drawing the black pig of Irish legend into Yeats's evolving cluster of apocalyptically symbolic "beasts" (pp. 50-51).

[15] Stallworthy's first publication of the drafts was in his book *Between the Lines: Yeats's Poetry in the Making*

(Oxford: Clarendon Press, 1963). He subsequently published a revised and fuller transcription in a journal article, which is almost identical to the chapter in his book except for improvements in the transcriptions. All further references here will be to the later publication ("The Second Coming," *Agenda,* 9/10 [1971/72], 24-33) unless otherwise noted.

[16] Politically suggestive images shared by "Nineteen Hundred and Nineteen" and "The Second Coming" are nightmare, a "monster" with blank eyes, and gyres and spirals in connection with things breaking up and one epoch replacing another. "Nineteen Hundred and Nineteen" and "A Prayer for My Daughter" also share the levelling wind, which might well be considered analogous to the levelling tide in "The Second Coming."

[17] *Explorations,* sel. Mrs. W. B. Yeats (New York: Macmillan, 1962), p. 393. Subsequent references to this edition will appear in the text.

[18] See *The Variorum Edition of the Plays of W. B. Yeats,* ed. Russell K. Alspach, assisted by Catherine C. Alspach (New York: Macmillan, 1966), pp. 1099, 1102. Subsequent references to this edition will appear in the text.

[19] p. 25.

[20] Stallworthy's apparent satisfaction on these points is somewhat surprising in view of the fact that Yeats's inconsistencies with the bird symbolism (to be dealt with at greater length here) were pointed out by Donald Weeks as early as 1948 (pp. 288-89).

[21] Stallworthy, p. 24.

[22] The word *hawk* is deleted and replaced by *falcon* in the next draft. In this same draft the outward-sweeping cone is called "the intellectual gyre" (p. 24). Stallworthy clearly takes *intellectual* to relate to logic (pp. 25, 28), which would make the gyre *primary,* though he does not say so explicitly. Such a connection may have some validity; which would mean that Yeats has simply been contradictory with his bird symbolism in the poem since, as will be seen, the indignant desert birds are almost certainly *antithetical.* However, the equation of intellect with logic is very tenuous. Both in *A Vision* and elsewhere, Yeats uses the word *intellect* in so many ways and contexts that settlement upon any consistent denotation or set of connotations is virtually impossible. In one place, for example, he replaced the word *intellect* with *reason* when revising a typescript that was ultimately excluded from *A Vision* (see Walter Kelly Hood, "Michael Robartes: Two Occult Manuscripts," in *Yeats and the Occult,* ed. George Mills Harper [Toronto: Macmillan, 1975], p. 223). In another, by sharp contrast, he associates intellect with imagination, especially in the *antithetical* phases of the system (*Vision* B, p. 142).

[23] Stallworthy, p. 30.

[24] There is neither space nor inclination to review here all the numerous previously proposed prototypes or "sources"—inside and outside Yeats's own works—for the famous beast image. Most of the more potentially relevant ones are probably familiar to readers of this essay anyway.

[25] See William Butler Yeats, *Autobiographies* (London: Macmillan, 1955), p. 349. Subsequent references to this edition will appear in the text.

[26] The only two scholars or critics that I have found who agree with this designation of the beast as *primary* are Donald Pearce (p. 177) and Thomas Parkinson (*W. B. Yeats: The Later Poetry* [Berkeley and Los Angeles: Univ. of California Press, 1964], p. 166). However, neither of these identifies the beast as a political phenomenon or movement. The list of commentators who have mistakenly taken the rough beast to be *antithetical* is long. It includes, among others, Harold Bloom (*Yeats* [New York: Oxford Univ. Press, 1970], p. 318), Elizabeth Cullingford (*Yeats, Ireland and Fascism* [New York and London: New York Univ. Press, 1981], p. 161), Harper and Hood (p. 45), O'Driscoll (p. 178), Rajan (pp. 121-22), Peter Ure (*Towards a Mythology: Studies in the Poetry of W. B. Yeats* [Liverpool, 1946; rpt. New York: Russell and Russell, 1967], and Vendler (p. 101).

[27] In connection with this play and its note, F. A. C. Wilson expands briefly on objective beast symbolism in Yeats's work (*Yeats's Iconography* [New York: Macmillan, 1960], pp. 166-67).

[28] See J. E. Cirlot, *A Dictionary of Symbols,* trans. Jack Sage, 2nd ed. (New York: Philosophical Library, 1971), pp. 189-90.

[29] Like so much in this poem, the line in question is not without some inconsistencies, however. One of the *primary* qualities of Christ so intensely disliked by Yeats was His particular kind of pity. If, then, there are to be associations between the beast and Christ, as later suggested, the "pitiless" sun-like gaze tends to be symbolically anomalous, even if imagistically effective.

[30] Commentators who have identified the beast as fascism include John Heath-Stubbs (*The Darkling Plain: A Study of the Later Fortunes of Romanticism in English Poetry from George Darley to W. B. Yeats* [London: Eyre and Spottiswoode, 1950], pp. 208-09), D. S. Savage ("Two Prophetic Poems," *Adelphi,* 22 [1945], 26), Conor Cruise O'Brien ("Passion and Cunning: An Essay on the Politics of W. B. Yeats," in *In Excited Reverie: A Centenary Tribute to William Butler Yeats, 1865-1939,* ed. A. Norman Jeffares and K. G. W. Cross [New York: St. Martin's Press, 1965], pp. 275-78), and Cullingford (pp. 161-62). The last of these identifications is apparently the result of an illogical backlash effect from the author's overwrought efforts to disprove O'Brien's theses about Yeats's affinities with fascism. Louis MacNeice states (*The Poetry of W. B. Yeats* [1941; rpt. New York: Oxford

Univ. Press, 1969], p. 119) that Stephen Spender also identifies the rough beast as fascism in his book *The Destructive Element,* However, I can find no such ascription in Spender's book. But MacNeice himself comes quite close to just such an equation (pp. 119-20).

[31] See Donald T. Torchiana, *W. B. Yeats and Georgian Ireland* (Evanston: Northwestern Univ. Press, 1966), p. 214.

[32] Torchiana, *W. B. Yeats and Georgian Ireland,* pp. 214-19.

[33] These essays appear in *Explorations,* pp. 244-59 and pp. 263-80. The quoted phrase occurs on the first page of the first essay, which is the more explicit and uniform of the two.

[34] See also *The Letters of W. B. Yeats,* ed. Allan Wade (London: Rupert Hart-Davis, 1954), p. 656. Subsequent references to this edition will appear in the text.

[35] This material, printed in the *Irish Times,* 30 January 1919, is quoted by both Torchiana (p. 216) and Cullingford (p. 116). Cullingford's treatment of Yeats's politics is extraordinary, as already intimated in reference to her equation of the rough beast with fascism. Her chapter "Visionary Politics" drastically overstates the connections between Yeats's interests in governmental systems, especially Marxist ones, and *A Vision:* "Composed between 1917 and 1925 and continually modified thereafter, *A Vision* is Yeats's attempt to understand the calamitous events of that time. . . . [It] is founded on, and inspired by, one fundamental antithesis: '*Primary* means democratic. *Antithetical* means aristocratic.' Conceived and written while the Bolsheviks were consolidating their power in Russia, *A Vision* offers an alternative to the Marxist interpretation of history" (p. 121). Cullingford's data is massive, but much of it appears to have been shaped to suit the author's preconceptions. If assessed without prejudice, it would strongly support the view that Yeats's beast represents communism. Instead, the conclusions are ambivalent and unconvincing: " . . . the destruction of innocence by socialist revolutions . . . was the motive force behind 'The Second Coming' . . ." (p. 117), but "socialism both repelled and attracted [Yeats]; *A Vision* was his way of holding these contrary impulses in balance" (p. 140).

[36] Stallworthy, p. 25.

[37] Torchiana, p. 214.

[38] Rajan exemplifies the theoretical tendency described here: " . . . Stallworthy's presentation of the various drafts shows how specific references to Pitt, Burke and the German advance to Russia were discarded and how, in its evolution, the poem moved steadily to its twin objectives of universality and immediacy" (p. 121). O'Driscoll's essay constitutes an extreme example of such theory put into practice (*despite* his initial attention to *A Vision*'s system of history): "The Second Coming for Yeats is not the coming of Christ or Communism or

Fascism or Democracy, but the coming of a free and expressive religion of art and the imagination . . ." (p. 177).

[39] Related to this sleep is still another image which has often been glossed in general terms rather than with reference to the language and ideas of Yeats's system. A number of commentators have spoken of the "rocking cradle" that "vexed to nightmare" the "stony sleep" as an emblem of infantile innocence in ironic contrast to the beastly horror of the poem's vision. There can be no doubt that the cradle image bears connotations of birth. However, the Christ-child is traditionally associated with a stable manger (pun intended), not a "rocking cradle." The image was much more probably related in Yeats's mind to an expression and concept from his poem "The Phases of the Moon" (1918), which is used as a verse prologue in both versions of *A Vision:* "Twenty-and-eight the phases of the moon, / . . . The cradles that a man [or era] must needs be rocked in . . ." (*Vision* B, p. 60, *Variorum Poems,* p. 373). These "cradles" are, of course, the phases of the wheel or of the gyres in Yeats's system. The incessant alternations of the opposed historical eras—*antithetical, primary, antithetical, primary*— might also be thought of as rocking cradles, especially since the noun *cradle* in the poem is singular instead of plural. In such an interpretation, the cradle of the present era has rocked to the extreme of its tilt in the *primary* direction, the widest fluctuation of the objective gyre.

[40] Stallworthy, p. 24.

[41] Stallworthy, p. 27.

[42] See Stallworthy, p. 28. Actually, Stallworthy generally agrees with a good deal of what has just been said and with what follows in this note—or vice versa. Yeats quickly realized and corrected his drift toward the revelation of a new religious annunciation. Nevertheless, this brief appearance of the "great falcon," presumably as an *antithetical* deity figure, constitutes an interesting prototype in view of subsequent appearances of other divinely annunciatory birds in "Leda and the Swan," "The Mother of God," and *The Herne's Egg.*

[43] *Letters on Poetry from W. B. Yeats to Dorothy Wellesley* (1940; rpt. London: Oxford University Press, 1964), p. 22.

[44] The numerous exegeses which associate Yeats's rough beast with the "Antichrist" of orthodox and heterodox tradition would seem to be somewhat simplistically off the mark. The Antichrist concept and second adventism constitute related but different bodies of religious lore in and "around" Christianity. In view of Yeats's title and the Bethlehem allusion, his beast cannot properly be identified with the former, because the Antichrist is supposed to appear at some time *before* the second coming and, in some versions, is to be defeated and displaced by Christ upon His reappearance on earth. Yeats's poem and its beast emphatically *are,* however, related to the extensive and pervasive tradition of second adventism. As will be seen even more fully, the ironic allusions to that

iconographically rich body of apocalyptic lore are clearly among the chief evocative features contributing to the piece's almost supernatural immediacy and impact, as well as to its widespread critical acclaim and even popular renown. For valuable further information on both traditions, see W. Bousset, "Antichrist", and S. J. Case, "Second Adventism," *Encyclopaedia of Religion and Ethics* (New York: Charles Scribner's Sons, 1961), I, 578-81, and XI, 282-86, respectively.

[45] While there are materials in the automatic scripts about Christ being *antithetical* at certain times or in certain senses (see *CEVA* notes, p. 79), He and Christianity are unequivocally *primary* throughout virtually all of Yeats's published works.

[46] One passage draws a parallel between the height of Christianity and Christ's influence at AD 1000 and the greatest influence of his predecessor two thousand years before at 1000 BC (*Vision* B, p. 285). By logical implication, then, Christ's successor and his dispensation would have their fullest development two thousand years *after* A. D. 1000, at AD 3000.

[47] Weeks, p. 289.

[48] Relevant to the points just made and to those which follow is the fact that Yeats in one place explicitly describes Robartes' face as "hawk-like" (*CEVA,* p. xv).

[49] Stallworthy, *Between the Lines,* p. 22.

[50] Stallworthy, p. 29.

[51] See, for example, Melchiori, p. 36.

[52] *The Literary Criterion,* 7 (1967), 33, 35, 39-40. Sharma concedes that Frank Kermode and Giorgio Melchiori differ with his opinion (p. 32).

[53] Wilson, p. 311.

[54] Wilson, p. 322.

[55] See Ellmann, p. 255.

[56] Actually, such calamities also tie in with at least some of the scripts' predictions about impending events as well. For example, Harper and Hood speculate that one passage about the future may have been excluded from *A Vision* "because the prophetic tone was . . . too harsh . . . : 'I find in my documents a statement that population will decline through pestilence and famine and accidents of nature . . . '" (*CEVA* notes, p. 63).

[57] In 1904 Yeats commented in *Samhain* on London's ban against staging *Oedipus Rex* (*Explorations,* pp. 131-32). About the same time, he evidently asked Gilbert Murray to consider translating the play for the Irish Theatre; Murray declined in a letter written on January 27, 1905 (see Richard J. Finneran, George Mills Harper, and

William M. Murphy, eds., *Letters to W. B. Yeats* [New York: Columbia Univ. Press, 1977], I, 145-46). There are seven references to the possibility of staging the play in letters among the Directors of the Abbey dating from 1906 to 1908 (Ann Saddlemyer, ed., *Theatre Business: The Correspondence of the First Abbey Theatre Directors: William Butler Yeats, Lady Gregory and J. M. Synge* [University Park and London: Pennsylvania State Univ. Press, 1982], pp. 127, 147, 151-52, 159, 178, 216, 295). By November, 1909, Yeats was contemplating translating the play himself and had "gone through translations and [found] Jebb's much the best" (*Letters*, pp. 538-39). Then, when censorship of the play in England was withdrawn, Yeats's interest in the project lapsed, even though he had purportedly "finished the dialogue in the rough" (p. 537). This had to be in 1910 or afterwards, since he was still reviewing translations late in 1909. Wade reproduces in full a note entitled "Plain Man's *Oedipus*" (originally published in the *New York Times*, 15 January 1933) in which Yeats outlines both his initial (pre-1919) and subsequent (post-1919) interest in Sophocles' play *(loc. cit.)*. That the piece did not fade entirely from his thoughts in the interim period is made clear by a sentence from the "People's Theatre" essay published in the year that "The Second Coming" was written: "You [Lady Gregory] and I and Synge, not understanding the clock, set out to bring again the theatre of Shakespeare or rather perhaps of Sophocles" (*Explorations*, p. 252).

⁵⁸ *W. B. Yeats: Images of a Poet* (Manchester: Manchester Univ. Press; New York: Barnes and Noble, 1961), pp. 96-98, 109-10.

⁵⁹ *Yeats at Songs and Choruses* (Amherst: Univ. of Massachusetts Press, 1983), pp. 197, 199-201.

⁶⁰ See Robert L. Delevoy, *Symbolists and Symbolism* (New York: Rizzoli, 1978), pp. 39-43, 131-35, and passim.

⁶¹ See Clark, pp. 192-202. The materials in Clark's book may support the theses of the present study even further in several ways. Clark points out, for example, that Yeats, like D. G. Rossetti ahead of him, "calls the Sphinx a Fate" (p. 193; see also *Variorum Plays*, p. 844). If the possibility can be entertained that Yeats might have conceived of the sphinx in the same way as readily in 1919 as almost a decade later, then the idea of "a Fate" might relate to and reinforce suggestions of doom and apocalypse in "The Second Coming." Further than that, Clark points out that Rossetti's picture portrays a sphinx "whose eyes look past [its interrogators] without answering the question they seem to ask" and that the artist had said his drawing was about "the pitiless eyes of Fate" (pp. 192-93). While the odds that Yeats would have known and recalled such a remark may be slight, the picture and the phrase are both startlingly evocative of the line in Yeats's poem, "A gaze blank and pitiless as the sun."

⁶² A young Australian Yeats scholar, one of the few in his country, attended the International Yeats Symposium at Winthrop College, South Carolina, in April, 1983, where I presented a paper which was an embryonic version of the present essay. (An expanded model of that presentation is in print for anyone who may be interested in knowing what its major theses were ["William Butler Yeats," in *Critical Survey of Poetry*, ed. Frank N. Magill (Englewood Cliffs, N. J.: Salem Press, 1982), VII, 3194-99]. Other than an enormous disparity in volume and detail, one of the chief differences between those two essays and this study is that I then believed that the version of the history system involving an interchange of the *tinctures* was the one appropriate to the poem. The earliest prototype of those analyses is a master's thesis on "The Second Coming" and *A Vision* deposited somewhere in the stacks of the Howard-Tilton Memorial Library at Tulane University, in which I identified Yeats's rough beast as *primary* and communistic nine years before Stallworthy's initial publication of the poem's drafts, when Heath-Stubbs, Savage, and others were interpreting it as fascism. Unfortunately, the two of these three precursors that dealt with the question "Why a sphinx?" answered it in a way that turned out to be anachronistic for "The Second Coming." Their answer is not at all irrelevant for *A Vision*, however, as will be seen later in connection with part of the introduction to the 1937 edition.) The Yeats scholar from Australia, Colin McDowell, who also made a presentation on *A Vision* at the Winthrop Symposium and who is a specialist on both Yeats's occult interests and occultism in general, continued to discuss my theories with me via correspondence after the conference. When I foundered on the issue of the sphinx in the poem, he generously sent some tentative suggestions and a collection of photocopies from sources on occultism not available in libraries to which I have convenient access, with revelatory and productive consequences the scope and impact of which not even he will know until he reads what follows.

⁶³ Virginia Moore says that the Wheel and Chariot cards with their sphinxes "fascinated" Yeats (*The Unicorn: William Butler Yeats' Search for Reality* [New York: Macmillan, 1954], p. 60), which may well be believed in light of what unfolds in the sequel here.

⁶⁴ I have placed these figures in the present sequence intentionally in order to indicate immediately the obvious basis for associations between the sphinx as depicted in Yeats's poem and the four "living creatures" of Ezekiel, even if there were no extant traditional connections. This list also reveals at least one reason why Yeats had to change from the female Greek sphinx to the male Egyptian one—"head of a man." Another reason for that change may have been greater proximity, geographically and thematically, to Bethlehem, while still another may have been a desire to intensify the desert imagery for poetic effects much like those that function in Eliot's *The Waste Land*. I suspect also other purposes for desert imagery, such as associations with Michael Robartes' travels in the Near East, with the land of the fictional Judwalis, etc., although I am not sure that I understand all the reasons for Yeats's preoccupation with those things themselves (mystery, civilization's origins, "Babylonian starlight"?). However, a virtually certain further reason for desolation imagery in

"The Second Coming" itself is practically self-explanatory when one recalls Yeats's figurative use of the expression "the Christian desert" (*Vision* B, p. 271). Christianity is also associated with desert imagery elsewhere in the book, with emphasis on its making all things and all men equal and indistinguishable, "featureless as dust" (p. 274). This, in turn, is reminiscent again of the *primary* Judwalis, who are "as like one another as the grains of sand" in the 1921 note to "The Second Coming" (*Variorum Poems*, p. 825). Incidentally, in the tarot-deck portion of occult tradition the sphinx has become a blend of the Greek and the Egyptian in many cases. Most versions—though not all—depict female breasts, but also most—again, not all—portray the characteristic "King Tut" type of headdress. Some show wings but most do not. The Greek sphinx is winged, whereas Egyptian ones vary in this particular. For differing versions in the tarot, see Paul Foster Case, *The Tarot: A Key to the Wisdom of the Ages* (1947; rpt. Richmond, Va.: Macoy Publishing Company, 1975), p. 118; Robert Wang, *The Qabalistic Tarot: A Textbook of Mystical Philosophy* (York Beach, Maine: Samuel Weiser, 1983), pp. 195, 210; Eliphas Lévi, *Transcendental Magic: Its Doctrine and Ritual,* trans. and ed. A. E. Waite (London, 1896; rpt. New York: Samuel Weiser, 1974), p. 389.

[65] (Dublin: Dolmen Press, 1972).

[66] Wang (p. 198) and Israel Regardie (*The Golden Dawn: An Account of the Teachings, Rites and Ceremonies of the Order of the Golden Dawn* [1937-40; rpt. St. Paul: Llewellyn Publications, 1971], IV, 310) suggest that the sphinx is a "combination" or synthesis of the cherubs, but in at least one place Lévi uses the terms *cherub* and *sphinx* simply as alternates for each other (p. 273). Such usage accords with, and clearly derives from, Chapter 10 of Ezekiel, in which the "living creatures" appear again and are called "cherubim."

[67] See Wang, p. 196, or Raine, illustration 26.

[68] See Richard Cavendish, *The Tarot* (London: Michael Joseph, 1975), p. 90; Wang, p. 210; A. E. Waite, *The Pictorial Key to the Tarot* (London, 1910; rpt. New York: Samuel Weiser, 1973), pp. 96-97, or Lévi, pp. 388-89.

[69] See the sources just cited.

[70] On the one hand, it would be easy to overlook or understate the emblematic connections articulated here. On the other hand, however, it would perhaps be almost impossible to overstate their power and significance for the success and impact of Yeats's poem. An important iconographic detail that reinforces the multiple-levelled interrelationships involved is the bared or flashing sword. Recognition of its various appearances in the congeries draws into clearer identification with each other the triumphant charioteer, the militant and judgmental Christ of doomsday tradition, the sphinxes of occult and Biblical lore, and the rough beast of Yeats's poem (a sphinx). In a number of versions of the Chariot card, the victorious

king or warrior holds what appears to be a sceptre, but the object in his hand is sometimes a sword held by the blade, with the handle at the top. This observation is verified by those packs in which the sword is instead held by its handle (as in the middle illustration in Cavendish, p. 90) and by verbal rather than visual portrayals: "An erect and princely figure carrying a drawn sword" (Waite, p. 96). Also, most versions of the Wheel card that have a sphinx at the top show a sword held in the crook of one arm or else in one hand, as in three of Wang's four examples (p. 195). Moreover, the gatekeeper of Eden with a fiery sword is sometimes identified as a sphinx in occult lore, probably from the previously mentioned sphinx-cherub equation (see Lévi, p. 273; Cavendish, pp. 90, 102). Finally, the Christ of Revelation and second adventism is prophesied to strike down in vindictive carnage the nations of the earth when "out of his mouth goeth a sharp sword" (19.15; see also 19.11, 21).

[71] See Wang, p. 210, second illustration.

[72] See Lévi, p. 389, and Wang, p. 210, third illustration.

[73] IV, 310-22.

[74] *Astral Projection, Magic and Alchemy* (London: Neville Spearman, 1971), pp. 81-87.

[75] See Moore, pp. 142, 151, 203, 257, 277.

[76] See Cavendish, p. 90, and Wang, p. 197.

[77] For example, the Egyptian sphinx, especially atop the wheel of fortune, is often taken to represent a resolution of the four elements or signs with which the four creatures are sometimes associated, much like the phoenix in alchemy (Wang, pp. 198, 213; Cavendish, pp. 92, 102). In other contexts the sphinx is a fearful gatekeeper or guardian of entryways to newer or higher realms of knowledge or being (Wang, p. 197). Such roles clearly accord with the sphinx's representation of mystery and enigma and might also conceivably relate in similar ways to the entry of a new historical era. However, those roles involve synthesis and stasis more than seems appropriate to the imagery and themes of flux and catastrophic dynamism in "The Second Coming." Probably, therefore, such suggestions of meaning should be given relatively little emphasis here.

[78] *The Works of William Blake, Poetic, Symbolic and Critical,* ed. William Butler Yeats and Edwin J. Ellis (London: Bernard Quaritch, 1893), I, 251.

[79] See S. R. Bushrui, *Yeats's Verse-Plays: The Revisions 1900-1910* (Oxford: Clarendon Press, 1965), p. 109.

[80] The "living creatures" are not called "beasts" in Ezekiel itself. Thus, Yeats's expression "beast out of Ezekiel" in "A New End for *The King's Threshold*" suggests that he probably picked up the term *beast* for use in "The Second Coming" from tradition or Revelation (4.7) or both. More

importantly, the expression in the play demonstrates that in the poet's imaginative thought Ezekiel's "creatures" were equatable with "beasts." This point validates the thesis that adequate understanding of the nature and iconographic function of Yeats's famous image in "The Second Coming" depends upon recognition of its demonstrable associations with the prophetic book's "living creatures" and all of the apocalyptic symbology and import deriving from those associations.

[81] Bushrui, pp. 114-15.

[82] This declamation is strongly reminiscent of the play *Calvary* (published in the same year as "The Second Coming") and its dramatic opposition of subjective desert birds to Christ's objectivity. Yeats's note to the play states: "I have surrounded Him [Christ] with the images of those He cannot save, not only with the birds, . . . but with Lazarus and Judas. . . . 'Christ,' writes Robartes, 'only pitied those whose suffering is rooted . . . in some shape of the common lot. . . . ' I have therefore represented in Lazarus and Judas types of that intellectual despair that lay beyond His sympathy . . ." (*Variorum Plays*, p. 790). In a different way, Robartes' outcry echoes and accords with a passage on the Church's decline as the cycles of history approach the rationalistic eighteenth century: "The gyre ebbs out in *order* and *reason*, the Jacobean poets succeed the Elizabethan, Cowley and Dryden the Jacobean as belief dies out. Elsewhere Christendom keeps a kind of spectral unity for a while . . ." (*CEVA*, p. 205, *Vision* B, p. 295; my italics).

[83] See Stallworthy, p. 30.

[84] Yeats's discussion of Oedipus as the "new divinity" begins on page 27 of *Vision* B, and on page 28 the sphinx is mentioned as an antinomical figure in the myth, though not exactly in the role suggested here. On the same page Oedipus is also contrasted to abstraction, to Plato's One, and (by clear implication) to reason. He is instead designated as "an image from Homer's age;" this obviously aligns him with the system's previous *antithetical* annunciation, which theoretically occurred 4000 years ago. That annunciation, of course, is graphically portrayed in Yeats's poem "Leda and the Swan," which was written in the interim between "The Second Coming" and "A Packet for Ezra Pound." Incidentally, associations between Oedipus and the sphinx are strong in occult tradition as well as in ancient mythology (Levi, pp. 15-16, Wang, p. 198).

[85] John Beckwith, *Early Christian and Byzantine Art* (Baltimore: Penguin Books, 1970), p. 120. One should see also pp. 123 and 131 as well as plates 215, 223, and 231 for evidence in support of the proposition that in his prose passage Yeats might perhaps have confused Cefalu with Monreale, or maybe even both with Daphni. The passage from *A Vision* suggests that after Christianity's powerful domination of culture in the middle ages, Christ's image will "grow more like ourselves, putting off that stern majesty [of] . . . Cefalù and Monreale. . . . " But the text and plates in Beckwith's book make unmistakable

the fact that the mosaics at Cefalù and Monreale depict Christ much more sympathetically than the awesome portrayal at Daphni. Cefalù's depiction, the least "stern" of the three, hardly seems to bear the iconographic burden put upon it by the passage from *Explorations*. If Yeats never visited Daphni nor saw a reproduction of its Pantocrator, then the mosaic at Monreale (in the apse, as is Cefalù's) may well be the memory image inspiring his "terrible Christ."

Jewel Spears Brooker (essay date 1986)

SOURCE: "'The Second Coming' and 'The Waste Land': Capstones of the Western Civilization Course," in *College Literature*, Vol. XIII, No. 3, Fall, 1986, pp. 240-53.

[*In the following essay, Brooker examines "The Second Coming" and T. S. Eliot's* The Waste Land *as these poems confront the decline of western civilization.*]

"The Second Coming" by W. B. Yeats and *The Waste Land* by T. S. Eliot are ideal companion poems to use as a capstone experience in a course in Western Civilization. Both poems deal powerfully with the state of civilization in the twentieth century; both suggest that civilization is falling apart and each in its own way reveals the cause of the crisis. Both poems (especially *The Waste Land*) allude to central events and major texts of the last several thousand years of Western (and Eastern) Civilization. *The Waste Land*, furthermore, suggests that the main activity of general humanities courses, *i.e.*, systematic study of great texts, has value as a means of redeeming civilization from ruin.

In his most famous critical essay, "Tradition and the Individual Talent," Eliot argues that a poet must write with Western Civilization, so to speak, in his bones. He calls this presence of the past within a poet "the historical sense," and argues that it is "indispensable for anyone who would continue to be a poet beyond his twenty-fifth year."

> The historical sense involves a perception, not only of the pastness of the past, but of its presence; the historical sense compels a man to write not merely with his own generation in his bones, but with a feeling that the whole of the literature of Europe from Homer and within it the whole of the literature of his own country has a simultaneous existence and composes a simultaneous order.[1]

One can disagree with the idea that the historical sense is a universal requirement for poets, but not with the fact that Eliot used it as a standard for himself and conscientiously prepared himself to be a poet by saturating himself in the great texts of Western Civilization. Next to Milton, Eliot is probably the English language's most learned poet; his mind includes most of the great classics of Western Civilization and is like the "mind of Europe" described in "Tradition and the Individual Talent,"—a "mind which changes, . . . but which abandons nothing *en route*" (6). The great texts hover over everything that he wrote, but in a special and obvious sense, they literally and conspicuously constitute *The Waste Land.* Yeats was not learned in the same classical sense as Eliot, but he too was well educated, particularly in the great myths of Western Civilization. As a repository of the myths of the Greeks, Hebrews, Romans, Christians, and especially the Celts, as well as a representative of his age, Yeats is invaluable in a general humanities course.

The reason for using **"The Second Coming"** and *The Waste Land* as capstone texts in a Western Civilization course, then, is that they gather within themselves many of the texts included in early parts of the course. In that they focus on the same crisis from very different standpoints, they tend to be reciprocally interpreting and are more valuable used together than alone. Moreover, Eliot's particular mode of re-collecting texts provides students with the joy of re-cognizing and re-interpreting the past texts at the same time that they are beginning to understand the present ones. These poems enable students to understand another point that Eliot makes in the "Tradition" essay: the new changes the old as much as the old influences the new. The *Divine Comedy,* for example, not only influenced and became a part of *The Waste Land,* but for a student who studies first Dante and then Eliot, *The Waste Land* actually makes a difference in the *Divine Comedy.*

In spite of the fact that the two modern poems seem made to order for use as companion capstone texts, they are seldom so used. The main reason is that they are considered too difficult for such courses. Many faculty feel uncomfortable with them; many more feel that they are simply too advanced for general education courses, courses usually taught in the first two years and often as requirements. But even though both poems are in some ways endlessly complex, both are remarkably accessible to students, especially if introduced into a course which anticipates them by including great works which they in a sense recapitulate. In my experience, students find **"The Second Coming"** mysteriously powerful, even before they have any idea of what it means. And today's students, brought up on rock music rather than on books, are in one way more prepared than their more literary elders to read *The Waste Land.* Unhampered by expectations of narrative form, they bring an immediate appreciation of discontinuous form. In fact, to the astonishment of teachers, students often take to *The Waste Land* far more naturally than to the "easier" poems of, say, Wordsworth or Frost.

In the conviction that the poems by Yeats and Eliot are both invaluable and accessible, I have written the following guide for students (and faculty), especially for those in general humanities courses of the kind so often taught in American colleges. The first part of my essay provides the context for these poems and offers a reading of **"The Second Coming"**; the second part focuses on *The Waste Land.* Both parts assume that students bring to the twentieth-century materials some experience with central texts of Western Civilization, specifically including Sophocles's *Oedipus Rex,* St. Matthew's gospel, St. Augustine's *Confessions,* Dante's *Purgatorio,* Shakespeare's *Hamlet,* Darwin's *Origin of Species* (selections), Nietzsche's *Birth of Tragedy,* Freud's *Interpretation of Dreams,* and Frazer's *Golden Bough* (selections).

I THE AGE OF ANXIETY

The importance of such poems as *The Waste Land* and **"The Second Coming"** is inseparable from their value as pictures of modern man and modern civilization; and they should be considered, first of all, in the context of the civilization and the crisis which they document. At the core of this crisis is a fear that Western Civilization is on the edge of disaster and, in fact, may be wiped out entirely. One reason that these poems continue to speak to us so powerfully is that we are still in this crisis. There is a real danger that contemporary man will destroy his universe and everything in it, that he will literally annihilate himself and his civilization. Our anxiety is an extension of Eliot's and of Yeats', for both have the same roots. Around 1920, when these works were written, and in 1986, the danger is related to incredible advances in knowledge and at the same time a loss of cultural memory, a collective forgetfulness about basic spiritual and humanistic resources and values.

The massive collapse of traditional values and the lamentable failures in brotherhood characteristic of our century have resulted in a pervasive cultural uneasiness. W. H. Auden calls the modern crisis a breakdown of liberal humanism, by which he means a breakdown of faith in the existence of God, in the goodness of man, and in the possibility of progress. This breakdown produced what Auden in a fine poem calls "The Age of Anxiety." In that "anxiety" is distress or uneasiness caused by the apprehension of some certain but vague disaster, Auden's term seems appropriate. The Age of Anxiety is often said to have begun in August, 1914; and it is true that the First World War had an incalculable effect on the modern mind. In that war, Western Civilization began literally tearing itself to pieces on the battlefields of Europe. The war, however, was not primarily a beginning; it was, rather, a culmination, not a cause of the modern spiritual crisis, but a result of it.

The pervasive disillusionment characteristic of the Age of Anxiety should be associated with a radical revision, during the second half of the nineteenth century, of ideas and principles which had long served as the foundation of Western Civilization. Among those most responsible for the revision are Charles Darwin, Friedrich Nietzsche, Sigmund Freud, and Sir James G. Frazer. In *Origin of Species* (1859) and *The Descent of Man* (1871), Darwin removed mind (human or divine) from the origin and development of life. He maintained that God, if he existed, had been absent in history; and implied that man, merely a creature among creatures, is not justified in considering himself endowed with inalienable "human" rights. Like all other organisms, he is a creature of environment and chance. In *Birth of Tragedy* (1872), Nietzsche argued that Dionysus, the dark god of wine and irrationality, is more basic to art and to life than either Socrates or Apollo, symbols of reason and light. And in a famous boast, Nietzsche proclaimed that "God is dead." Sigmund Freud, in *Interpretation of Dreams* (1899), suggested a model of human nature in which the irrational and the unconscious and the violent are foundational. In *Civilization and its Discontents* (1930), he summed up his findings that man is not a gentle loving creature who simply defends himself when attacked but an innately aggressive one opposed to culture. The anthropologist Sir James Frazer also contributed much to the shape of the Age of Anxiety. In *The Golden Bough* (1890), a great encyclopedia of primitive religion, he argued that religion evolved from magic and is in turn being replaced by science. He meant to recover respectability for Christianity by bringing it into line with Darwinian evolution, but ended by suggesting that all religions are the same religion, all heroes (Christ and Dionysus) the same hero. The disquiet produced by these thinkers was compounded around the turn of the century by physicists who called into question or denied notions of reality which had supported the Western mind for millennia. In the place of an ordered universe, scientists such as Max Planck and Niels Bohr postulated one ruled by chance, a universe consisting of tiny and unpredictable bits of energy. All of this is part of the intellectual background leading to the Age of Anxiety, to the disease associated with the fear that Western Civilization was falling apart.

The conviction that a major dispensation in history was quickly drawing to a close was not limited to artists. German historian Oswald Spengler argued in *The Decline of the West,* published in German in 1918 and in English a few years later, that civilizations are organisms which go through stages of youth, maturity, decay, and that then, like all organisms, they die. As Greece and Rome flourished and disappeared, so shall we. Western Civilization, in his diagnosis, is in a very late stage of decay, and death is being hastened by neglect of the spiritual (philosophy, religion, art) and cultivation of the merely material. In the 1930s and 40s, the famous British historian Arnold Toynbee, in *A Study of History,* also argued that Western Civilization is breaking down. He did not believe that civilizations automatically move through stages of growth and decay, but that civilizations stand or fall insofar as they meet or fail to meet environmental and moral challenges. Toynbee argued that Western Civilization is breaking down because we resort to violence and war to solve our problems. He was part of a chorus of intellectuals who claimed that in abandoning our spiritual and humanistic values, we have lapsed into barbarism.

Yeats and Eliot were not alone, then, in their feeling that a major era in civilization was coming to an end. Eliot is often described as having expressed in *The Waste Land* the disillusionment of his age. He himself hated this sort of talk, and once quipped that maybe he expressed his readers' illusion of being disillusioned, but never meant to do so. He was, he claimed, expressing his own disillusion; he was just "grumbling." But whether he meant to or not, he transformed his personal grumbling into art, expressing in a new form what many of the most intelligent and sensitive people of this century have felt. In *Ulysses* (1922), published the same year as *The Waste Land,* James Joyce put it this way, "History is a nightmare from which I am trying to awake."

II THE SECOND COMING

The conviction that Western Civilization is falling apart, important in most twentieth-century art, is perhaps most memorably expressed in Yeats' **"The Second Coming,"** written in 1919 and published in 1920.[2]

> Turning and turning in the widening gyre
> The falcon cannot hear the falconer;
> Things fall apart; the centre cannot hold;
> Mere anarchy is loosed upon the world,
> The blood-dimmed tide is loosed, and everywhere
> The ceremony of innocence is drowned;
> The best lack all conviction, while the worst
> Are full of passionate intensity.
>
> Surely some revelation is at hand;
> Surely the Second Coming is at hand.
> The Second Coming! Hardly are those words out
> When a vast image out of *Spiritus Mundi*
> Troubles my sight: somewhere in sands of the desert
> A shape with lion body and the head of a man,
> A gaze blank and pitiless as the sun,
> Is moving its slow thighs, while all about it
> Reel shadows of the indignant desert birds.
> The darkness drops again; but now I know
> That twenty centuries of stony sleep
> Were vexed to nightmare by a rocking cradle,
> And what rough beast, its hour come round at last,
> Slouches towards Bethlehem to be born?

The title of this poem is taken from the Christian religion. The first coming was the birth of Christ, the Incarnation; it marked the end of one major historical dispensation and the beginning of another. According to the New Testament, Christ's second coming, to be preceded by a time of troubles and sorrow, will mark the end of this present age. In many interpretations, the second coming is also to usher in a new age, a millennium in which Christ will reign on earth and in which there will be peace. This doctrine of the second coming as a turning point in history can be found in Matthew 24 and other parts of the Bible.

Yeats strongly believed that civilization as we know it is coming to an end. He had a theory of history similar in some respects to that of Spengler. Like Spengler, he believed that history moves in large cycles of growth and decay. Yeats believed that these cycles last about two thousand years and that the present cycle, which began with the birth of Christ, is about to end. The second coming of Christ, traditionally considered as a major historical intersection, as the end of this age and the beginning of the next, is thus a useful image for him.

The first stanza begins with an image of a falconer who has lost control of his hawk. Communication and control are lost, and things fall apart. This image is followed by a description of the historical situation when Yeats was writing this poem, a time of unprecedented violence and barbarism. These were the days of the First World War, the Russian Revolution, and civil war in Yeats' own country of Ireland.

St. Matthew's gospel describes the days just before the second coming in the following terms: "For then shall be great tribulation, such as was not since the beginning of the world to this time, no, nor ever shall be. And except those days be shortened, there should no flesh be saved." Surely, the poet cries, this anarchy and violence and moral collapse in history must be the sign that the second coming is at hand. The mention of the second coming triggers a vision. It arises from the *Spiritus Mundi,* that is, from the "Spirit of the World." (For Yeats, the *Spiritus Mundi* is the storehouse of primitive and archetypal images, images likes that of the Sphinx.) One would expect that the vision triggered by the phrase "the second coming" would be the same as that described by Matthew: "And they shall see the Son of man coming in the clouds of heaven with power and great glory." And one would expect that the vision of the new age would be an image of the Biblical kingdom of God, where swords (implements of war) have been recycled as plows (implements of agriculture), where love and pity have banished hate. But Yeats' vision is not the Christian vision. This turning point in history will not be the second coming of Christ the Prince of Peace, but the appearance of another god, a successor to Christ. Like Christ, this god will come from the Mediterranean world. But whereas Christ was a combination of the divine and the human, a perfect man, his successor in Yeats' vision is a combination of the bestial and the human, a monster with the head (intelligence) of a man and the body (passions, instincts) of a lion. In this ultimate nightmare, Yeats sees a god with a blank gaze and slowly moving thighs, a god who is the antithesis of love. This new master will be "pitiless as the sun"; that is, he will be morally neutral and radically democratic. The sun, as the Bible says, shines alike on the just and the unjust. This blind god sheds his beams equally on murderer and victim; he smiles at the same time on the gluttony of despots and the starvation of children.

Yeats interprets his vision by saying that the Greek world was vexed to nightmare by the birth of Christ in Bethlehem. And now, interpreting contemporary history, he sees the Christian era in its own nightmare. In the famous closing image, he wonders about Christ's successor, the rough beast now slouching towards Bethlehem to inaugurate the next era of human history.

III THE WASTE LAND

T. S. Eliot is of towering significance in the aesthetic and moral life of this century. The first half of the century, in fact, is often referred to as the "Age of Eliot," and the publication in 1922 of *The Waste Land* is the most important event in twentieth-century poetry.[3] As the distinguished critic Richard Ellmann has said, *The Waste Land* became so famous that for much of this century, the latest poetry in Arabic, Swahili, or Japanese was far more likely to have been influenced by Eliot than by earlier poets in those languages or by any other poet in English. After *The Waste Land,* Eliot turned to a different kind of poetry, of which the masterpiece is *Four Quartets,* published during the Second World War.

A waste land, of course, is a desert or any place inhospitable to life and health. Some waste lands, such as deserts or icebergs or rocky mountains are natural; but others, such as the used part of a coal mine, a trash dump, a city slum, or a bombed countryside, are man-made. And of course some waste lands are symbolic, that is, they are not "lands," but states of being. For example, a college or a marriage may be a waste land. Eliot's poem includes references to all of these waste lands. The literal desert may be seen in such lines as "What are the roots that clutch, what branches grow/ Out of this stony rubbish?" The man-made waste lands may be seen in such lines as those describing the polluted river banks where the "flowers" of summer consist of "empty bottles, sandwich papers, / Silk handkerchiefs, cardboard boxes, cigarette ends." The symbolic lands can be seen in the two families of part II—the miserable and fruitless couple from the upper classes, and the literally fruitful but loveless Lil and Albert, whose children are the expensive and unwanted by-product of Albert's lust.

The most important waste land in Eliot's poem, however, is the comprehensive one that includes all of the others— Western Civilization in the twentieth century, a place which is sterile and hostile to health and flourishing. Eliot's poem is his metaphor for the state of man and culture in the twentieth century. Like Yeats and many others of his generation, he interpreted the contemporary situation in Europe and the United States as one of moral and cultural decay. He felt that the basis of cultural unity had disappeared, that the glue which had held Western Civilization together had dissolved. As Yeats describes this crisis in **"The Second Coming,"** "Things fall apart, the centre cannot hold." The center of which Yeats writes is Christianity, which for two thousand years had held things together. But in the late nineteenth century, Christianity lost its power to unify culture, and for the first time in two thousand years, the non-existence or irrelevance of God was consciously taken as a cultural assumption. *The Waste Land* is a picture of what remains when the center is removed; it is a picture of civilization with no moral or cultural or religious center, no god-concept, no glue. It consists quite literally of hundreds of fragments of the western present and of the western past insofar as it had survived into the twentieth century. The text of the poem is in some ways comparable to what Bloomsbury would look like if a bomb should drop on the British Museum.

Some of the fragments in *The Waste Land* are preserved exactly. For example, "Those are pearls that were his eyes" is a line from Ariel's song in Shakespeare's *The*

Tempest; and "Poi s'ascose nel foco che gli affina" a line from Dante's *Purgatorio.* Other fragments in the poem have been changed by evolution through time, but are still recognizable. The pathetic song of Ophelia in Shakespeare's *Hamlet,* for example, has evolved into the popular song "Good night, ladies, we're going to leave you now" and also into the final words which contemporary people say as they're leaving the pub after an evening of drinking together, "Goonight Lou. Goonight May. Goonight."

Eliot's fragments may appear at first to be more or less independent, related only by the fact that all can be connected on some level to a waste land. But in fact, the fragments fall naturally into groups, with a number of fragments falling into several groups at once. These fragment clusters, then, are not mutually exclusive and do not have firm boundaries. Part of the poem's meaning derives from the juxtaposition of these clusters. For example, there are many fragments dealing with wasted landscapes, and also many dealing with city scenes. By simply placing these fragments side by side without comment, Eliot suggests that the modern city is a waste land. This idea is reinforced by portraying the city dwellers as sterile, loveless, and isolated. He does not actually state: "London (or Paris or New York) is a waste land," but he clearly suggests that these cities are places where life does not flourish. The accuracy of Eliot's depiction of modern urban existence may account in some part for the power of his poem.

The single most important group of fragments in Eliot's poem are those having to do with literal waste lands, for these references refer to an ancient myth, and it is this myth which provides Eliot with his title and his major symbol. The myth describes a land cursed with sterility, a land in which crops will not grow, women cannot bear children, cattle cannot reproduce, etc. The sterility in the land and its occupants is connected in some mysterious way to impotence in the ruler of the land. The ruler, who is both a god and a king, has been wounded in his genitals (as a result of war, sickness, old age, or whatever), and this sexual incapacity affects his entire kingdom, depriving it of regenerative power. Just as the curse on the divine ruler has blighted his people and land, so would his healing lead to their health. The curse can be lifted if (1) a hero will come and undergo certain trials in order to find the wounded ruler and ask him certain ritualistic questions, and if (2) the healed ruler is allowed to die, a circumstance which would permit his resurrection or revitalization.

The waste land myth is part of the background of the Greek tragedy *Oedipus Rex.* The following description of the city of Thebes, from the translation by Dudley Fitts and Robert Fitzgerald, is one of many ancient versions of the myth of the cursed land and its suffering inhabitants.

> Thebes is tossed on a murdering sea
> And cannot lift her head from the death surge.
> A rust consumes the buds and fruits of the earth;

> The herds are sick; children die unborn,
> And labor is vain. . . . Death alone
> Battens upon the misery of Thebes.
> . . . The noble plowland bears no grain
> And groaning mothers cannot bear—

The curse on the land and its inhabitants is directly related to the king's sexual health. Oedipus is guilty of the great sexual taboo of incest (as well as the sin of patricide), and this situation reacts on his land. For healing to occur, certain questions have to be asked and answered. The horrible irony of this version of the waste land myth is that Oedipus is at once the sexually unclean king and the questor who must ask the questions and purge the land.

Eliot was particularly well-educated in philosophy, literature, and religion, and he must have encountered this myth in innumerable versions. In a note to *The Waste Land,* he reveals two special sources of his understanding of the myth.

> Not only the title, but the plan and a good deal of the incidental symbolism of the poem were suggested by Miss Jessie L. Weston's book on the Grail legend: *From Ritual to Romance.* . . . To another work of anthropology I am indebted in general, one which has influenced our generation profoundly: I mean *The Golden Bough;* I have especially used . . . *Adonis, Attis, Osiris.*

The Golden Bough by Sir James Frazer is a twelve-volume collection of thousands of myths from all times and all places. Frazer began his work in the generation after Darwin, and as Darwin had attempted to discover the origin of the species and chart the descent of man, so Frazer tried to discover the origin of religion and chart the descent of the gods. He discovered that most myths have certain features in common, and as Darwin had postulated a common ancestor for man, so Frazer postulated a single ancestor for all religions. By putting together the common features of many myths, he was able to construct what he considered to be the parent myth. This myth had broken up over time, but its fragments persist in the myths and religions that we know from history and in the present world. According to Frazer, all religions, including Christianity, are fragments of this one great myth. The myth which Frazer constructed out of all his fragments is the myth of the waste land, outlined above and taken by Eliot for the main symbol of his poem.

Jessie Weston was a student of the legends having to do with the Holy Grail, the cup Christ is said to have used at the last supper. In studying these legends and fragments of legends, most of which date from the early middle ages, she came to the conclusion that the legends of the Holy Grail had also descended from a single parent. Like Darwin and like Frazer, she used the fragments she had to construct what she thought to be the parent legend. She argued that the legends of the Holy Grail are, in fact, fragments of the pre-Christian waste land myth.

Eliot's interest in the waste land myth, unlike that of Frazer and Weston, is not in the myth itself, but in its power to suggest truths about contemporary life, and also in its claim to support an underlying unity for modern society. Post World I London, in which Eliot was living at the time he wrote the poem, contained all sorts of people, all sorts of beliefs. They seemed to have nothing in common with each other or with the poet; and although crowded together in a modern city in which they literally touched and smelled each other daily, they all seemed alone, isolated. But in terms of Frazer's thesis, all people, regardless of how separate they seem to be, are brothers; all beliefs, no matter how bizarre, are one belief. *The Waste Land* is a collection of human voices and mythic fragments such as is found in any modern metropolis. The human and mythic odds and ends of a modern city seem unconnected, but they are all related because of the myth of the waste land.

Eliot works mainly by suggestion, and so he does not say precisely what causes a flourishing place to become a waste land. By using the myth, he suggests that there is a mysterious but certain relationship between the wounding of God and the existence of a waste land. In wounding or sterilizing our God, we have wounded ourselves. His decay and ours are intertwined. Fruitfulness in a family or a city or a civilization is dependent on connections between people who know and love each other, who share traditions and beliefs. The physical or sexual connection by itself, however, without the traditions and beliefs and the love, generates not a garden, but a different type of waste land. By using the myth, Eliot also suggests a connection between human love (*caritas*) and divine love (*agape*). The Bible makes the same connection by stating that a man who cannot love his brother, whom he has seen, cannot truly love God, whom he has not seen.

The background myth, then, suggests that the cause of the waste land is a failure to connect, a lack of love. The myth also suggests that it is possible to get rid of the curse. In the myth, the healing of the land is tied to the healing of the king. His healing, death, and revitalization would lead to ours. This healing could be accomplished by undergoing certain trials and by asking certain questions about the meaning of life. The healing, interestingly, happens because the questor asks the right questions rather than because he receives the right answers. God cannot heal himself; he is dependent on a person who will conceive of and ask certain questions.

Whether *The Waste Land* is experienced as difficult or easy depends to a great extent on the expectations brought by the reader. If the reader demands a story or plot, a hero or main character or main speaker, an argument or lesson; if the reader demands an understanding of every line; if he demands any or all of these things, he will have a difficult time indeed. But if (as Eliot expects) the reader suspends these demands and accepts the poem as an arrangement of fragments of western culture, he will have an easy time. To return to my example of Bloomsbury after a bomb has fallen

on the British Museum: if one came upon such a scene, he would be able to make sense out of it without understanding every fragment. In fact, he could get the basic idea just by experiencing the scene, even if he did not at first recognize any specific fragment. And then he could start reconstructing by identifying a few fragments and finding complementary fragments and so forth. And he would find meaning, not just in the reconstructed fragments, but more important, in the act of reconstructing them.

Eliot's poem has suffered from the work of teachers who try to explain it line by line, layer by layer. It is often introduced by presenting the reader with a list of fragments with tags showing where Eliot got them. Such a list overwhelms most readers and constitutes a barrier to understanding the poem. A better approach is a simple reading, noticing the fact that the poem is made up of fragments of Eliot's own verse and fragments of Western Civilization, knowing that these fragments (according to Frazer and Weston) were once part of one myth, trying to understand what has happened and why. Simply knowing the myth and experiencing the bits and pieces of meaning in the poem is to most readers at once illuminating and unforgettable.

A second stage in reading this poem has to do with the recognition of specific fragments. Many of the fragments are pictures and sounds of contemporary life, familiar because we see and hear them every day. Others are from other times and places; some, we instantly notice, are in foreign languages. These fragments of contemporary and historical life have been carefully selected and arranged by the poet so that the more one knows, the richer the poem becomes. Most people will recognize some of the fragments of myth and religion and history and literature, even on a first reading. But since getting the main point of the poem does not require understanding all of the fragments and does not require immediate understanding of any specific fragment, the best procedure is to focus on the familiar ones and, for the time being, forget about the others.

The richness which comes from retrieving fragments (and the works from which they came) can be suggested by considering the lines "To Carthage then I came/ Burning burning burning burning," lines which can be understood simply as part of a scene of contemporary life. The first part of this passage from *The Waste Land,* however, is a translation of the opening phrase of chapter 3 of St. Augustine's *Confessions,* which reads (in Edward Pusey's translation):

> To Carthage I came, where there sang all around me in my ears a cauldron of unholy loves. I loved not yet, yet I loved to love . . . I sought what I might love, in love with loving . . . For within me was a famine of that inward food, Thyself, my God, yet, through that famine I was not hungered . . . my soul was sickly and full of sores, it miserably cast itself forth, desiring to be scraped by the touch of objects of sense. . . . [4]

If recognized as part of Augustine's autobiography, if recovered as part of his quest for love and knowledge and truth, if understood as part of his attempt to put his loves in order, if then returned to the context of the modern city, the fragment in Eliot's montage takes on profound suggestiveness. This process of recognizing and recovering fragments and bringing them to bear on Eliot's poem will be rewarding in itself and will lead to the heart of his deeply moral vision of Western culture. In asking such questions as why the line from Augustine exists only as a fragment, why Eliot thought it and the tradition of which it is a part were worth recovering, and why he put it at the end of a contemporary scene of sterile lust, a reader will have begun the work of reconstruction that might lead civilization beyond the waste land.

Some readers are disquieted by the foreign phrases scattered throughout *The Waste Land.* The fact that they are jibberish to most of us and to most of the modern characters in the poem is more important than any meaning they have in themselves. A main point in the poem is that we are so split up by nationalism and other "isms" that we do not understand each other's languages, much less each other's masterpieces. Most of us would not recognize lines in English from Tennyson, much less lines in Italian from the *Inferno* or in German from *Tristan und Isolde;* and Eliot claims that this inability to connect to our past and to each other is the main cause of the waste land. A mere translation of foreign phrases, such as appears in the footnotes of many teaching editions of the poem, does not solve the problem, because simply knowing the translation of a line does not permit the reconnection which Eliot considered essential. In the final analysis, recovery of meaning and reconstruction of bridges will not be accomplished by editors, but by readers who take Eliot and his landmark poem seriously.

As parts of classic works available in ordinary libraries, most of the waste land fragments are in a literal sense not really fragments. But Eliot is not concerned with what exists in libraries, but with what exists in the heads and hearts of modern man. And to most modern people, Plato, the Bible, Augustine, Dante, Shakespeare, and most of our noblest ancestors exist only as a name or as a part of a line heard in an advertising jingle or as part of a popular song ("O O O O that Shakespeherian Rag—"). Fragments in themselves have no power to unify and revivify culture, but as part of the great traditions of our common history, they have the power to help us turn our waste land into a garden.

NOTES

[1] T. S. Eliot. "Tradition and the Individual Talent." *Selected Essays.* 2nd ed. New York: Harcourt Brace, 1950.

[2] W. B. Yeats. "The Second Coming." *The Poems of W. B. Yeats.* Ed. Richard J. Finneran. New York: Macmillan, 1983.

[3] T. S. Eliot. *The Waste Land. The Complete Poems and Plays: 1909-1950.* New York: Harcourt Brace, 1952.

[4] Augustine. *The Confessions of St. Augustine.* Trans. Edward B. Pusey. New York: Washington Square Press, 1951.

Robert F. Fleissner (essay date 1988)

SOURCE: "On Straightening Out Yeats's 'Rough Beast'," in *CLA Journal,* Vol. XXXII, No. 2, December, 1988, pp. 201-8.

[*In the following essay, Fleissner speculates on the nature of the "rough beast" in "The Second Coming."*]

The bestial image at the tail end of William Butler Yeats's **"The Second Coming"** is described there as a "rough" one indeed and so deserves some critical straightening out. Hence yet another note on this famous poem may be justified.

I

As a starter, let us consider a surprising, recent news release, which was boldly captioned, at least in the local papers, as follows: "Move Over, Tarzan: Anthropologist says army of apemen slaves only a test tube away." Composed by Uli Schmetzer of the Knight-Ridder News Service, the essay depicted a dean at Florence University, Brunetto Chiarelli, who had announced that "biogenetic scientists, using refined techniques of artificial fertilization, are capable of creating a new breed of slave, an anthropoid with a chimpanzee mother and a human father." If true, it would appear that the half-man, half-beast figure from Yeats's apocalyptic poem is now about to be born indeed (or toward the end of this century, at any rate, as the poem decrees). Was Yeats, then, being proleptic in more ways than one?

Before refining the possible validity of such an analysis of the poem, we might scrutinize more closely the seemingly science-fiction ambience for this unusual prediction. Evidently, the news release was expected to have rather sensational impact, as revealed in the opening, one-sentence paragraph: "The image of the mad scientist with the white beard concocting an apeman in his laboratory is no longer a science fiction fable but a 1987 possibility." The reader is likely to recollect not only such a film as *Planet of the Apes,* but all the commotion in the past about a presumed "missing link," a likewise conjectured creature in the evolutionary chain containing substantial characteristics of both beast and human. This hypothesis most probably formed part of the background for Yeats's anthropoid-like effect, as did a somewhat comparable poem by Browning, "Caliban upon Setebos."

After the initial, attention-getting claim, the news report then provided an important (and probably mainly expected) qualification: that "the experiments on the new subhuman species had been interrupted at the embryo stage because of 'ethical problems,'" These vague *desiderata* were not formally spelled out, but most readers may well posit what they could be, particularly for Christians wary of accepting evolutionary or Darwinian principles. Indeed, as a university colleague of mine somewhat conservatively yet pointedly expressed it: "Would the Pope allow such a creature to have an abortion?" When I acquainted others with this news item, responses were, for the most part, skeptical. Yet Dr. Chiarelli had added that genetic researchers have now successfully crossed species which actually are "genetically more diverse than man and ape," so that such an embryo may in fact already have been created in this country. (No evidence for the second assertion, however, was produced.) Another reader revealed to me no real surprise at the revelation, having only this dry, rather captious response: unemployment is bad enough already; anthropoids doing odd jobs, as it were, would succeed only in making conditions worse. Finally, the obvious analogy of modern interest in cloning humans also came to mind, even as such experimentation is also still tentative and open to some doubt.

The real problem to be confronted in this paper is not how to arrive at any finalized verdict about the feasibility of such a creation, but rather to see what propitiatory illumination it might indirectly shed on Yeats's symbolic image. Ethical concerns about a potential anthropoid reflect critical concerns about the rough beast's identity. How mythical, for example, is it? Although many readers, perhaps most, upon first perusal have associated the monstrous image with evil, specifically with the Anti-Christ (so described in the Apocalypse), others have pointed rather to the grotesque connection poetically established between this symbol and the birthplace of the Savior. In a word, the conflated image is also bewildering, not a clear-cut case of something wicked.

The effect upon some readers has been curiously unaesthetic for that reason, even repugnant. (For what it may be worth, the same latter term was incidentally also used in the news release to cite what a noted Italian scientist felt about the proposed anthropoid.) To those purists who would object to any presumably wholesome collocation of "rough beast" and "Bethlehem," though, it can be objected, in turn, that Yeats's style allowed for just this sort of juxtaposition. In other words, if the adjective "rough" strikes some readers as pejorative, others can defend him for his clever use of Expressionistic style. In short, one's aversion to the beast's roughness may be deemed too precious, let us say, to be in keeping with modernist poetic experimentation; it too easily can reflect a penchant for prettiness, for the sentimentally picturesque instead of for the strong, bold, masculine, and innovative. So, in terms of the modernity of the image, to associate the "rough beast" and the potential anthropoid may be to cope with analogous aversions, but at the same time such a conjunction could be looked at more objectively as advancing man's knowledge of the unknown, both imaginatively and scientifically; from this perspective, the beast might well be taken as a metaphor even for science itself—not to mention, at the same time, strong

humanistic reaction to the encroachments of "scientism." Thus the bestial effect can be paradoxical in more ways than one.

In any event, Yeats's rough image may rightly be termed notorious. Because he himself most probably did not consciously envisage precisely an anthropoid in creating his provocative poem, we ought first to try to look at it figuratively from his artistic perspective. Whereas the standard scholarly gloss relates it to his peculiar, cyclical understanding of history (one rather akin to Spengler's),[1] to which he allowed himself to accommodate certain occult features of Christian lore (without thereby assuming a formal religious stance), the creature at the end need not be contained in his personal brand of mysticism alone. For that would be too reductive. Clearly it has a distinctive bearing on the biblical Anti-Christ, but as mentioned earlier, this poetic beast is not only antithetical to the gentle Jesus, but is to be born at His very birthplace—a seemingly tasteless correlation.[2]

In answer to this criticism, we might note first that by using vague qualifiers like "some" and "somewhere" Yeats deliberately blurred his imagery, thus not allowing the reader to pinpoint the overall effect in too theologically exact a manner. Another possible response is that even though the beast travels to Bethlehem to be "born," this itinerary represents only a way by which the Anti-Christ is to make others try to follow him (thereby having them infer that he is the real Christ come again). A further reply is that the beast will not turn into the Anti-Christ (thereby be "born") until he comes into conflict with the real Christ at Bethlehem (which would then be renamed Armageddon). In any event, whether Yeats's enlisting of apocalyptic raw material necessarily motivated his own final effect has now to be determined. For example, his conception of Christ's "rocking cradle" having already vexed "to nightmare" the Classical Age preceding Him would not so easily be in strict keeping with traditional Christian interpretation. For the Savior went on record resolutely assuring His followers that He came to fulfill and not deny in the process. Hence, in one sense, Yeats's conception of Christ here is as off-kilter as his Anti-Christ.

In my previous, brief explication of the "rough beast,"[3] I have contended that the image was probably meant more symbolically in modern terms than biblically. Because it relates to the sphinx in Egypt, it very likely stood for something characteristically African, indeed even for the "dark continent" itself as coming into its own as a power to be reckoned with toward the latter part of this century. True, the seemingly negative images associated with the animal, at first glance, might not pay much of a compliment to the emergence of the Third World; nonetheless, a clear precedent for such a romanticized reading is discernible already in Blake's "The Tiger," even as both Blake and Yeats can easily provide useful glosses on Eliot's similarly provocative image of "Christ the tiger" in *Gerontion*. (It is, further, a commonplace that Yeats's beast was partially based on Blake's.)[4] Again, if such a correlation is apt, Yeats might again be taken to task for it because of its primitive approach to the Third World. Whatever the case, his own later verdict, that his beast was symbolic of totalitarianism, has been construed as a "dubious afterthought" of his.[5] Perhaps this is so because there is nothing necessarily "socialistic" about his beast and because both fascism and communism have condemned the sort of Expressionistic art Yeats was constructing, preferring "calendar art" in its place. Moreover, he is well known for advancing his own "crypto-fascist, neo-feudalist" program,[6] so it would be a bit ironic, to say the least, if he was condemning such reactionary tendencies in his most famous poem.

II

In order to come to better terms with the "rough beast," which in the final analysis may not be fully intellectualizable, admittedly, I should like to propose first an interpolative amendation and thereby closer connotative study of the key name *Bethlehem* (in contrast with *Babylon*, the locale traditionally linked with the Anti-Christ). The proposed interpolation offered is the implicit insertion of the word *his* in brackets before *Bethlehem* in the final lines. Such a qualifier would set off the traditional birthplace of Christ with the "new" locale set forth in the lyric. An inserted *his* was most probably understood implicitly anyway, but, obviously because of the meter, would not be actually allowed. The point of the emendation would then be to suggest that the beast's own poeticized Bethlehem will hardly be quite the same as Jesus's.

As for the names themselves, let me offer a few pointers which may be instructive, ones not put in print before, to my knowledge. The first is that *Babylon* conjures up "baby lion" (the letter "i" being another interpolative emendation, one silently understood). Because the beast is described as part lion, even as the name of Babylon is linguistically "part - 1(i)on," that city has its claim to the "rough" aspects of Yeats's final image. But then, why, it might well be asked, did not he write *Babylon* here instead of *Bethlehem*? Evidently he did not because his effect was meant to be more than biblical. Or, in another sense, the beast was to be construed as relating to Christ Himself! It may do so if the familiar "Lion of Judah" "slouches" into the final scene. That view may appear a bit extravagant, but it has by no means gone by the board,[7] and because Ethiopia has been termed the land of the Lion of Judah, the symbol of Africa again would come into the poetic picture.

The question here is whether something only *part* lion, like the rough beast, qualifies at all for consideration as the full-fledged Lion of Judah. It would seem at first that a being which is half-man and half-beast would make more sense as a *contrast* to Christ as truly man and truly God. Still, whether contrast or simple analogy is more pertinent is hard to say.

In short, then, a final connotative association, one related more to occasion and intent, seems in order. Perhaps the

Bethlehem involved referred not so much to the Near Eastern purlieu as to one much closer to home geographically. In the British Isles the label commonly designated a well-known hospital for the insane, one shortened, in ordinary parlance of course, to *Bedlam*. If Yeats had had that commonplace connection on the back of his mind, it would explain a lot. And the association was then so obvious that it would hardly need to be proven in black and white. The poem as a whole details a state of chaos extant suggesting a psychotic atmosphere rather than the calm haven of the Prince of Peace. Further, because of Yeats's Irish background, he may have wished to convey thereby a tone of confusion, what is popularly called Irish blarney, in his tantalizing, riddling image as well. At least such a modernist reading would have the net effect of saving the end of the verse from being seemingly contradictory in its apparently ruthless juxtaposition of antithetical elements from Scripture alone. And it is not quite a canard that way either, the Irish element notwithstanding. Although the emendation proposed before *Bethlehem*, namely *his*, can be silently understood and not introduced into an oral presentation, the locale itself might well be read as *Bedlam* without altering the orthography.

As a final code, somewhat corroborating this point is another recently suggested to me, namely that the speaker's bewilderment is expressed not only in the riddling final line, but in the repetitive quality of his doing a double-take in citing the phrase "the Second Coming" twice earlier (11. 11-12). This almost nervous effect would point, I submit, to imaginative accommodation of biblical material to other sources, not to mere exegesis of dogma (which would call for simple assertion). In any case, Yeats was not himself Christian in any orthodox sense. In his ***Autobiography***, he tells of giving instead "much time to what is called the Christian Cabala"; he insists that modernist souls like his had "hearts that Christianity, as shaped by history, cannot satisfy."[8] It would seem rather reductive therefore to limit the "rough beast" and its Bethlehem merely to orthodox Christian antecedents.

NOTES

[1] It is helpful to read the poem in connection with *A Vision*. See also Russell E. Murphy, "The 'Rough Beast' and Historical Necessity: A New Consideration of Yeats's 'The Second Coming,'" *Studies in the Literary Imagination,* 14 (1981), 101-10 (from a special issue on the occult). Murphy related Yeats's vision cogently to Nietzsche's, noting that national socialism had perverted the German philosopher's philosophy.

[2] Richard Ellmann, in *The Identity of Yeats* (New York: Oxford Univ. Press, 1964), finds it "shocking" (p. 257).

[3] "The Second Coming of Guess Who?: The 'Rough Beast' as Africa in 'The Second Coming,'" *Notes on Contemporary Literature,* 6 (November 1976), 7-9. Comparable is Richard P. Wheeler, "Yeats' 'Second Coming': What Rough Beast?" *American Imago,* 31 (1974), 233-51. Wheeler also takes a psychological approach. On the

poem's sphinx as symbolic of Africa, cf. Chancellor Williams, *The Destruction of Black Civilization: Great Issues of a Race from 1450 to 2000* (Chicago: Third World Press, 1974), p. 74. Much as I admire the spirit behind this book, I confess that to ascribe the sphinx's flat nose to a black man and thereby to reject "Caucasoid" features is to demote the standard view that the Pharaoh's nose was broken off or worn away with time. But he may be right.

[4] Hazard Adams, *Blake and Yeats: The Contrary Visions* (Ithaca: Cornell Univ. Press, 1955), pp. 236-40.

[5] Harold Bloom, *Yeats* (New York: Oxford Univ. Press, 1970), pp. 320-21. Yeats referred to the poem in 1938 as having "foretold what is happening." See his letter of 8 April 1938 to Ethel Mannin, in *The Letters of W. B. Yeats,* ed. Allan Wade (New York: Macmillan, 1955), p. 851.

[6] See Martin Seymour-Smith, *Who's Who in Twentieth Century Literature* (New York: McGraw Hill, 1976), p. 406. John Harrison, in *The Reactionaries: A Study of the Anti-Democratic Intelligentsia* (New York: Schocken Books, 1967), is harsh on Yeats for his political views but goes too far. See my review article in *Journal of Human Relations* (Central State University), 17 (1969), 138-45.

[7] For what it is worth, this leonine connection was first brought to my attention by a Catholic nun, a Sister who happened to have previously delivered a paper on the "rough beast" image as a distinct allusion only to the Anti-Christ. Even she was subject to second thoughts on this issue, to creatively new second comings.

[8] References are to Walter E. Houghton and G. Robert Stange, eds., *Victorian Poetry and Poetics,* 2nd ed. (New York: Houghton Mifflin, 1968), pp. 773, 776.

Edward Proffitt (essay date 1991)

SOURCE: "Yeats's 'The Second Coming'," in *The Explicator,* Vol. 49, No. 3, Spring, 1991, pp. 165-6.

[*In the following essay, Proffitt contends that the "rough beast" of "The Second Coming" refers to the offspring of the sphinx-like desert creature in the poem.*]

Yeats's **"The Second Coming"** must be one of the most widely explicated and paraphrased of poems. Still, its closure remains a mystery. If the "rough beast" spoken of at the end is the sphinx-like creature of lines 13-17, how can it be going to be born in Bethlehem when it has already been born in the desert? Indeed, how could any creature slouch toward the place where it is to be born?

Readers of the poem characteristically fudge this difficulty. For instance, in his otherwise exhaustive treatment, Richard P. Wheeler gets around the problem (ironically, because part of his title comes from line 21) by saying nothing about it at all or about the last two lines ("Yeats'

'Second Coming': What Rough Beast?" *American Imago* 31 [fall 1974]: 235-51). I, too, have fudged the matter when teaching the poem by saying, as other readers have held, that the beast is physically born in the desert but is to be born spiritually in Bethlehem. But that is a most unsatisfying conclusion. A. M. Gibbs comes closer to a satisfying solution in speaking of the "sexual hint in the ominous description of the beast 'moving his [*sic*] slow thighs'" ("The 'Rough Beasts' of Yeats and Shakespeare," *Notes and Queries* 17 [fall 1970]: 48-49). By focusing on the desert creature and its thighs, I have come, I think, to a tolerable solution.

In *The Riddle of the Sphinx* (London: Hogarth Press, 1934), Geza Roheim states that "The Sphinx . . . is the father and mother in one person" (22). There is our clue. Yeats's creature, though specified to have "the head of a man" (no such specification, of course, would be needed if the creature were simply to be taken as male), is female—as the focus on the "slow thighs" suggests—as well as male, or "the father and mother" at once. So, what "Slouches towards Bethlehem to be born" is not the desert creature but its child, slouching *in utero* in the fetal position. That makes sense. Moreover, this reading is much more frightening than any other I know, and Yeats clearly intended to convey a sense of fright. For we are left with no idea as to what the creature to be born will be. We are given a glimpse of the parent, but then "The darkness drops," and we are left to wonder how much more terrible its offspring might be. This reading also uncovers a symmetry between Mary and the creature that reflects the poem's title and makes it particularly appropriate.

All in all, by taking the poem's last line—"Slouches towards Bethlehem to be born"—to refer to the offspring of the desert creature rather than to the desert creature itself, we can conclude that Yeats's closure both makes sense and is satisfying. Its complexity, once understood, makes the poem seem especially rich and worthy of our attention.

Seamus Deane (essay date 1992)

SOURCE: "'The Second Coming': Coming Second; Coming in a Second," in *Irish University Review,* Vol. 22, No. 1, Spring/Summer, 1992, pp. 92-100.

[*In the following essay, Deane studies "The Second Coming" in relation to the accompanying poems of Michael Robartes and the Dancer, concentrating on its combined sexual and historical themes.*]

Yeats's famous poem **"The Second Coming"** is concerned with an ending and a beginning, both of them so interfused that it is scarcely possible to say where the distinction between them can be found.[1] The poem does indicate the moment when they appear to disengage. "Hardly are those words out / When. . . . " The phrase

"The Second Coming" has just been completed for the second time when the action of that coming commences with the "vast image". Indeed these first eleven lines have several repeated words and phrases: "Turning and turning", "falcon / falconer", "loosed", "surely", "at hand".[2] Further, the definite article, used eleven times, is strategically important in the establishment of the pattern of repetition. It insinuates a complicity with the reader, a knowingness. We can specify what the falcon, the tide, the ceremony, the best, the worst are because the surrounding poems of the volume *Michael Robartes and the Dancer* (1921) tell us. In the vicinity of **"The Second Coming"**, poems like **"The Leaders of the Crowd"**, **"Towards Break of Day"**, **"Demon and Beast"**, **"A Prayer for my Daughter"**, **"A Meditation in Time of War"**, **"To be Carved on a Stone at Thoor Ballylee"** provide a narrative sequence of which **"The Second Coming"** is an integral part. They help us to know what "the ceremony of innocence", "the worst" and all other agents and conditions of the poem's action are. As is always the case, a Yeats poem is, in a sense, a quotation from the volume in which it appears. *Michael Robartes and the Dancer* has a group of poems at its centre about Easter 1916 and **"The Second Coming"** is reputedly about the Russian Revolution of 1917. Both of these political moments are dramatised as part of a larger theatrical dispute that dominates the whole volume. It takes the usual Yeatsian form of a collision between opposites out of which might come unity or, more likely and less heroically, release from the trial of strength between them into a limp, exhausted freedom. It is the sort that he writes of in **"Demon and Beast"**, when a floating (not a soaring) bird could please him:

> Being no more demoniac
> A stupid happy creature
> Could rouse my whole nature.

The "freedom" he wins from "hatred and desire" is not gratifying.

> Yet I am certain as can be
> That every natural victory
> Belongs to beast or demon,
> That never yet had freeman
> Right mastery of natural things,
> And that mere growing old, that brings
> Chilled blood, this sweetness brought;

Freedom is a poor thing compared to the bestial and/or demonic energies that create the force field in which we live most vitally. This casts some light on the group of poems about the Easter rebellion (**"Easter 1916"**, **"Sixteen Dead Men"**, **"The Rose Tree"**, **"On A Political Prisoner"** and, less directly, **"The Leaders of the Crowd"**). It is not freedom, its legitimacy or otherwise, that concerns Yeats. It is the energies that fought for it, the demonic return to Ireland of what he believed to have been effectively repressed, even though the last two poems in this sequence would seem to indicate that he believed the repression had been renewed in the intervening five years and that the abstract mind had taken over again. But **"Easter 1916"** is, in an ambiguous,

questioning way, wondering if the rebellion had been a Second Coming of the daemonic that had then yielded to its malign intimate, the Bestial, represented by the Black-and-Tan atrocities in the War of Independence and by the era of bloodshed that included the First World War and the Russian Revolution. The ambiguity is not wholly centred on the Easter Rebellion as such. It arises from the distinction that this book struggles to make between Demon and Beast, between a violence that is renovatory and one that is destructive. These impulses are so intertwined that they can scarcely be separated. But it is in such a struggle that humankind achieves its greatness. Freedom is what is left after the struggle is over, "mere growing old".

"The Second Coming" poses a question in the form of a prophecy; equally, it proposes a prophecy in the form of a question. The prophetic element, the vision of the stirring to life of the Rough Beast from its two-thousand year long sleep, almost overrides the question, since it implies catastrophe in so unmistakable a fashion that there is no room left to doubt that this is a demonic energy that has, through repression, become bestial. The echoing of the Book of Revelation (in specific words and phrases like "loosed" and "at hand" as well as in the title, repeated twice in the poem, and in the biblical geography) confirms the impression of terror. But the Beast is not imitating Christ's Second Coming at all. It is imitating his first coming, by going to Bethlehem to be born. The second coming is a rerun of the first, not an analogue for the biblical Second Coming. It is, in a very specific sense, like the Beast of Revelation, an Anti-Christ, a reverse image of the First Coming but not a prelude to the Second.

It is here that the element of questioning begins to reassert itself against the element of prophecy. This "Egyptian" beast is going out of bondage over to Palestine to be born. The double biblical reference here—the liberation of the Jews from Egypt and the Flight into Egypt of the Holy Family—collaborates with the tropes of secondness and of reversal of direction that dominate the poem. The manner of the Beast's going ("slouches") is important. But it has already come to life; in what sense then will it be born—or born again? Will it be reborn as the thing it is, or will it be reborn as something different? It would seem that this nightmarish vision can only be known for what it is when it is interpreted, when the Rough Beast of the dream is born again as something which represents what was "vex'd to nightmare" by the "rocking cradle". The manger, mutated into a rocking cradle, a domestic and familial object, emblematic of a nursery peace and comfort, is, in this guise, an oppressive emblem. Christianity oppressed, suppressed or repressed demonic energies that have now gone bad. In their release they bring destruction with them. But it *is* a release. This peculiar version of the second coming may, after all, have its redemptive component within it because the therapeutic moment has arrived. The unconscious has finally spoken. The phrase that, in Christian belief, signalled the end of human history, has precipitated the beginning of another phase, one dominated by those very energies that had been hitherto occluded. It is a very potent question after all what this Rough Beast is or what it will become when it reaches its Bethlehem, its symbolic place, to be born again in the human imagination. Yeats spent so much of his life in the pursuit of those deep energies of the occult, almost cancelled in the modern world, that he could scarce forbear to cheer their sudden rearrival, however apocalyptic the form it took.

The second coming is bestial but it is also vague. It is "a vast image", "a shape"—the first nouns in the poem preceded by the indefinite article. Just as the definite article worked its effect by insinuating a complicity with what is known, so the indefinite article conversely achieves its contrasting effect by enhancing the sense of something unknown, the more sinister for being indefinite. It is also the more sinister for being a private, personal symbol. Yeats's own presence comes into the poem at the strategic moment when the first eight lines of what could have been a sonnet like **"Leda and the Swan"** are resumed, not into a sestet, but into a full sonnet. We not only have a sonnet and a half, we have an aborted sonnet that is then reborn as a full one, as the poem itself comes for the second time, brought to its full formal strength by the sudden intervention of the poet who now reveals himself to be the speaker:

> The Second Coming! Hardly are those words out . . .

The words are spoken and suddenly, in a flash, the vision comes. It comes in that second after speech and belongs to sight. The poem began with the falcon that "cannot hear"; it breaks at a critical point into speech and then continues as sight, vision. But the vision is, paradoxically, the more indelible for its vagueness. It is a personal vision but it is also public, since it is both a shape that is emerging from "somewhere" in the desert, and it is also recognisably the Egyptian Sphinx. At least, it is Sphinx-like, traditionally mysterious and yet known. But it is also a repetition. This creature too, like the apocalypse that has seized Europe, is announced by the wheeling birds, whose punning action ("Reel shadows") reiterates that of the falcon.

Still, this is not only a second coming, it is a coming that is second to a previous one—or, rather, to several previous comings that belong both to this poem and to the volume in which it appeared. In **"Solomon and the Witch"**, **"An Image from a Past Life"** and **"Under Saturn"** images return, prophesying something ominous. The cockerel in "Solomon and the Witch" that "Crew / Three hundred years before the Fall" crows again because he thought

> 'Chance being at one with Choice at last,
> All that the brigand apple brought
> And this foul world were dead at last.'

The cockerel may be mistaken. As the Witch points out,

> 'Yet the world stays.'

So, replies Solomon,

> 'Maybe an image is too strong
> Or maybe is not strong enough.'

The female lover in **"An Image from a Past Life"** puts her hands over her beloved's eyes to conceal from him the female image from a past life that she cannot understand, knowing only

> . . . I am afraid
> of the hovering thing night brought me.

In **"Under Saturn"**, the return image is that of an ancestor who died "before my time" and is yet "like a vivid memory". The labouring man "who had served my people" cried out:

> 'You have come again,
> And surely after twenty years it was time to come.'

It would seem that the cry was addressed to the poet himself, reincarnated as his ancestor, returning now to "that valley his fathers called their home." Later in the volume, **"Towards Break of Day"** the lovers dream, he of a waterfall on Ben Bulben, she of the white stag of Arthurian legend. The question is,

> Was it the double of my dream
> The woman that by me lay
> Dreamed, or did we halve a dream
> Under the first cold gleam of day?

What all these poems have in common is a questioning of the status of the vision. They are enactments of the issues raised in the fictional correspondence between Michael Robartes and Owen Aherne that Yeats cited in his 1921 note to this volume. In his analysis of dreams, Robartes claims that "the followers of Kusta-ben-Luki"

> . . . distinguished between the memory of concrete images and the abstract memory, and affirm that no concrete dream-image is ever from our memory.

In a later passage, Yeats cites Robartes writing to Aherne in a letter dated 15 May 1917:

> 'No lover, no husband has ever met in dreams the true image of wife or mistress. She who has perhaps filled his whole life with joy or disquiet cannot enter there. Her image can fill every moment of his waking life but only its counterfeit comes to him in sleep; and he who classifies these counterfeits will find that just in so far as they become concrete, sensuous, they are distinct individuals; never types but individuals. They are the forms of those whom he has loved in some past earthly life, chosen from *Spiritus Mundi* by the subconscious will, and through them, for they are not always hollow shades, the dead at whiles outface a living rival.'

These forms he calls the Over Shadowers. The same "subconscious will"

. . . selects among pictures, or other ideal representations, some form that resembles what was once the physical body of the Over Shadower, and this ideal form becomes to the living man an obsession, continually perplexing and frustrating natural instinct. It is therefore only after full atonement or expiation, perhaps after many lives, that a natural deep satisfying love becomes possible, and this love, in all subjective natures, must precede the Beatific Vision.

Yeats goes on to say that he does not think he "misstated Robartes' thought" in allowing the woman and not the man of **"An Image from a Past Life"** to see the "Over Shadower or Ideal Form". Images, he says, "in moments of excitement . . . pass from one mind to another with extraordinary ease." Thus,

> The second mind sees what the first has already
>   seen, that is all.

As a commentary on the love poems of **Michael Robartes and the Dancer,** this is all quite helpful. Robartes and the Dancer, Solomon and the Witch, the "He" and "She" of **"An Image from a Past Life"**, are engaged in a very Yeatsian kind of love talk—post-coital discussion of how to overcome the sense of imperfection and separation that has been exacerbated by a dream, a vision, an allegory:

> In this altar-piece the knight,
> Who grips his long spear so to push
> That dragon through the fading light,
> Loved the lady; and it's plain
> The half-dead dragon was her thought,
> That every morning rose again
> And dug its claws and shrieked and fought.

This is a dragon that has to be killed over and over; Solomon and the Witch must also make love again in the hope that the language of a real, not a false coming (or crowing) may be heard. Repeated love, repeated sexual climax is part of the process of atonement, the purgation that will perhaps some day make the Beatific Vision available. But Robartes has not completed his system. Aherne has to be shocked into the further realisation that

> The mind, whether expressed in history or in the individual life, has a precise movement . . . and this movement can be expressed by a mathematical form. . . . A supreme religious act of their (the Judwalis') faith is to fix the attention on the mathematical form of this movement until the whole past and future of humanity, or of an individual man, shall be present to the intellect as if it were accomplished in a single moment. The intensity of the Beatific Vision when it comes depends upon the intensity of this realisation.

This passage leads on to the well-known characterisation of the intersecting cones and gyres, outward and inward sweeping, with the contemporary world reaching its greatest and fatal expansion, preparing

not the continuance of itself but the revelation as in a lightning flash, though in a flash that will not strike only in one place, and will for a time be constantly repeated, of the civilization that must slowly take its place.

The historical turn, like lovers, has to come again and again; with each flash of contact, the images appear, slowly emerging out of phantasmagoria to achieve their full form in a mathematically defined system. These images have to keep coming. They are never originary, since they have taken their form, inverted, from what has gone before and is now at the point of exhaustion. They are always coming second, and they come in a second, in a flash, and each sexual-historical lightning strike produces an image that may or may not be sufficient to represent the end of life and history. The only vision that can represent that is, *per impossibile,* the Beatific Vision which does not represent anything but itself, which simply is.

Nevertheless, the poem **"The Second Coming"** is clearly a hellish vision. Just as it has its anticipations within the volume in which it occurs, it also has its anticipations in history, some of which are visible in the early drafts. The Russian Revolution of 1917 has, as its great prefiguration, the French Revolution. The degree to which Yeats drew upon and concealed his sources in Burke, Blake, Shelley, Wordsworth, Nietzsche and others has been well-documented as has the contribution of his early experiments with MacGregor Mathers in the Order of the Golden Dawn.[3] He envied the women of the circle for their capacity to form vivid mental images. Patrick J. Keane tells us that in the experiments with Mathers, Yeats reported that for him

> . . . 'sight came slowly, there was not that sudden miracle as if the darkness had been cut with a knife, for that miracle is mostly a woman's privilege.' This simile reappears in the drafts of the clairvoyant section of **'The Second Coming'**. Groping for figurative language with which to introduce the mysterious moment just prior to the vision of the vast image rising up out of *Spiritus Mundi'*, Yeats first wrote: 'Before the dark was cut as with a knife.'[4]

The "woman's privilege" is repeated in the vision of this poem. We know that Yeats was deeply affected by Burke's lament for Marie Antoinette in his *Reflections on the Revolution in France* and that the sexual mutilation of the Princesse de Lamballe's body was one of the horrific moments of the Terror of September 1792 that registered deeply on him. The murder of the Tsar's family in Russia, the monstrous rebirth there of German Marxism, the drafts that speak of the "second birth" rather than the second coming, the reference to Bethlehem and the inevitable association with the Virgin birth (later reimagined in the Greek fable of **"Leda and the Swan"**), the fact that the phrase "Rough Beast" is applied by Shakespeare to Tarquin in *The Rape of Lucrece*[5] all give to the second stanza of the poem a more specific inflection of sexual violation, threatened by

> A shape with lion body and the head of a man.

Between the idea of a second "coming" and that of a second "birth", the poem reveals its conflict. There is a welcome given to the male coming, to its brute strength, its renewable energy, its destructive power. But there is also a horror at the consequences of its emergence, the suffering of the female figure who is represented only by contextual reference and echo and yet who is the reigning figure over "the ceremony of innocence" celebrated in the succeeding poem, **"A Prayer for my Daughter"**. The second coming of this male force will be a violation that results in a monstrous birth. The hand that rocked the Bethlehem cradle may have, like the Virgin, or Marie Antoinette, or the Tsarina of Russia, ruled the world in some sense. But now the mob-beast has risen in male fury to put an end to all that Christian, family-centred ceremony in a threatening, slouching rapist's walk into the Holy Land that is a dreadful parody of its biblical antecedents.

How differently might we read the poem had Yeats made it, as he made the opening poems of the volume, a dialogue between a "He" and a "She". In this instance, it is the second stanza, the born-again sonnet, that would be spoken by the "She". However, the central point is that the vision of history and the vision of love relationships, both of which are part of Yeats's preoccupation in this book of poems, are superimposed one upon the other in **"The Second Coming"** and that Yeats's contradictory emotions of horror and welcome are ultimately visible in the poem's inner dialogue between a highly present male voice and an almost wholly concealed female one.

From 1910 onwards, Yeats remained loyal to a double narrative that generated conflict and regenerated energy in his poems. One was the narrative of revival, especially associated with Ireland and the occult; the other was the narrative of degeneration, especially associated with the modern world and science. **"The Second Coming"** is a poem that produces both narratives simultaneously. It is about the return of barbarism and about the return of the lost energies of the occult. In some respects, the poem wishes to interfuse these, to make one the function of the other; in other respects, it wishes to distinguish them and, further, to dwell on that moment, that split-second, when the distinction becomes clear. The poem (orits final question) is itself lacking in all conviction and full of passionate intensity. The Beast's hour has "come round at last" and this is a matter for celebration. But it is also a ravening beast that threatens violation and endless monstrosity. Caught between two value systems, Yeats represents one as male, the other as female, one as triumphant, the other as horrified, imbricating into the form of the poem itself the ironic admission that the best that can be said is second-best. "Things" could hardly be worse. But the threatened rape, when it does take place in **"Leda and the Swan"**, answers the final question of **"The Second Coming"** with a question of its own. If the knowledge of the occult is to be reintroduced to the world, then that might be compensation for the destruction that it, vengefully and necessarily, has to bring with it. But in the coming of the Swan,

Did she put on his knowledge with his power
Before the indifferent beak could let her drop?

If not, the darkness drops again. It all depends on that sexual-historical second in which knowledge comes with power. Otherwise, it will have to wait again for its second coming. And the daemonic, when it comes second, comes as the Bestial. Can the Bestial find a Bethlehem in which it can be born again as the daemonic? That would truly be a second coming.

NOTES

[1] A version of this essay was delivered as the Judith Wilson Annual Lecture on Poetry at Cambridge University, March 1991.

[2] All references to Yeats's poems and his commentary upon them are from Richard J. Finneran (editor), *W.B. Yeats: The Poems* (Dublin: Gill and Macmillan, 1984). The poems of *Michael Robartes and the Dancer* are on pp. 175-190 and the commentaries on pp. 642-645 and pp. 646-648.

[3] Patrick J. Keane, *Yeats's Interactions with Tradition* (University of Missouri Press, Columbia, 1987), pp. 72-105.

[4] Keane, p. 565.

[5] Keane, p. 64.

A. Raghu (essay date 1992)

SOURCE: "Yeats's 'The Second Coming'," in *The Explicator*, Vol. 50, No. 4, Summer, 1992, pp. 224-5.

[*In the following essay, Raghu addresses Edward Proffitt's 1991 explication of "The Second Coming." Raghu argues that the "rough beast" of the poem is a mental image or vision, and that the final lines of the poem should not be read literally.*]

Edward Proffitt's very original thesis, that the rough beast mentioned in the penultimate line of Yeats's **"The Second Coming"** is the offspring of the sphinx-like creature of lines 13-17, which was propounded in his note on the poem (*Explicator* 49.3, spring 1991), definitely makes sense but does not seem to be as wholly satisfying as he claims it to be.

If one accepts the postulate of Geza Roheim, cited by Proffitt, that "The Sphinx . . . is the father and mother in one person,"[1] one has necessarily to reject Proffitt's thesis, as it is only the mother who can carry her child in her womb. The "sexual hint in the ominous description of the beast 'moving his [sic] slow things,'"[2] which is seen by A. M. Gibbs and by Proffitt, does not appear to be sufficient to impart the female sex to it. On the other hand, if at all the creature has a sex, it seems to be male: Yeats says that it possesses the head of a man and the body of a lion, not a lioness. Besides, to ascribe the female sex to it, or even to add a female element to its sex, would dilute the terrifying nature of the creature. To see the rough beast slouching *in utero* in the fetal position, as Proffitt suggests, imposes a rather heavy strain on the reader's imagination.

The twelfth line of the poem makes it explicit that the sphinx-like creature is little more than "a vast image," a mighty mental picture seen by the speaker. This mental picture emanates from *Spiritus Mundi,* the Yeatsian counterpart of the Jungian collective unconscious, the general storehouse of images common to the race. It is therefore only natural that the speaker cannot specify the exact location of the creature; all that he can say is that he sees it moving "somewhere in sands of the desert." It is not quite accurate to say, as Proffitt does, that we are given a glimpse of the creature. It is the speaker who has a glimpse of the creature, and we are only told about it. The speaker states that the creature "Troubles my sight" making it clear that the vision, notwithstanding its roots in racial memory, is a personal one, something that he shares with no one else.

As the vision comes to an end and "The darkness drops again," the speaker realizes that he has had a preview of things to come. He now knows that the "stony sleep" of each civilization, normally lasting two thousand years, is "vexed to nightmare," that the security offered by every civilization contains within itself the seeds of its own destruction, and that the specific nemesis of the civilization to which he belongs is the sphinx-like creature seen in his vision, which he now alludes to as a "rough beast."

The two concluding lines of the poem do not form a statement but constitute a question, as is unambiguously indicated by the punctuation mark that brings the poem to its close. The physical identity of the creature is beyond doubt, as the speaker has already seen it in his vision, but he is not certain of its place of birth. Bethlehem, because of its association with Christ, whose second coming is prophesied in the Bible (Matt. 24.3-44, Mark 13.3-37, Luke 21.7-36, and Revelation 6.12-17), appears to be an ironically appropriate birthplace for the beast. Pointing out that a civilization lasts two thousand years from nadir to nadir and that Christ came at the Greco-Roman meridian, Yeats wrote in his diary, "Our civilisation which began in A.D. 1000 approaches the meridian and once there must see [sic] the counter-birth."[3]

The closure of the poem need not be given too literal a reading. Keenly aware of the physical appearance of the beast, the speaker feels that slouching is the movement most natural to it, and he wonders whether it is now on its way to the town of Bethlehem in order to make its appearance.

NOTES

[1] Geza Roheim, *The Riddle of the Sphinx* (London: Hogarth, 1934) 22; qtd. in Edward Proffitt, "Yeats's 'The Second Coming,'" *Explicator* 49.3 (1991): 165.

[2] A. M. Gibbs, "The 'Rough Beasts' of Yeats and Shakespeare," *Notes and Queries* 17 (1970): 48-49; qtd. in Proffitt 165.

[3] W. B. Yeats, "Pages from a Diary in 1930," *Explorations,* selected by Mrs. W. B. Yeats (London: Macmillan, 1962) 311.

Karen Marguerite Moloney (essay date 1993)

SOURCE: "Re-envisioning Yeats's 'The Second Coming': Desmond O'Grady and the Charles River," in *Learning the Trade: Essays on W. B. Yeats and Contemporary Poetry,* edited by Deborah Fleming, Locust Hill Press, 1993, pp. 135-47.

[*In the following essay, Moloney reads Desmond O'Grady's poem "Professor Kelleher and the Charles River" as a response to the ideas expressed in "The Second Coming."*]

In "Professor Kelleher and the Charles River" (*Contemporary Irish Poetry* 260-62), the narrator, Desmond O'Grady as a young Harvard graduate student, engages in conversation one April afternoon with John Kelleher, professor of Celtic Studies. Nearby runs the gentle but polluted Charles River, whose meandering course assumes, in these stanzas, apocalyptic dimensions: as O'Grady asserts in the poem's first line, the Charles "reaps here like a sickle." The image recalls both the sickle-shaped curve the river makes as it flows past the campus and the tendency of that curve to "harvest" floating debris. The phrase also alludes to a larger harvest, in which death acts the role of "the grim reaper."

This dramatically charged image resides at the heart of O'Grady's setting, in turn the unequivocal center of the poem. Indeed, each succeeding stanza contributes further details to the development of the initial scene. Stanza two introduces us to "the ivy wall,/ The clock towers, pinnacles, the pillared university yard," and the adjacent Protestant cemetery. In stanza three, we learn that student crews are rowing down the river; stanza four focuses on "a leafing tree" rooted at the edge of the water; and stanza five mentions that "beyond" can be seen "some scraper, tower or ancestral house's gable end." Stanza six anchors its action "there by the blood-loosed tide"; and in the seventh stanza "The saffron sun sets." Taken together, such details increase our sense that this conversation between professor and student is actually occurring at a particular place and moment. More meaningfully, though, O'Grady's images—remarkably resonant and often, as we shall see, deliberately opposed to one another—stimultaneously assert the poem's challenge to Yeats's prophetic pronouncements in **"The Second Coming."**

David Perkins notes that largely because Yeats's "achievement and reputation were too great and too much in everyone's mind" (474), he actually had "relatively little" influence on other Irish writers of this century. More accurate, however, is Robert Garratt's assessment that "so essential was the role Yeats played in determining the direction of modern Irish poetry that those poets who followed him, try as they would, could neither ignore him nor escape his influence" (16). Indeed, Garratt's *Modern Irish Poetry* is largely a study of the various responses of post-Yeatsian poets to the insistent, imperious presence of "the great Yeats, whose long and prolific literary career changed modern literature and made Ireland a land of imagination for readers all over the world" (17). Certainly, even Perkins concedes that while its style may not be Yeatsian, "the work of contemporary Irish poets frequently alludes to specific phrases of Yeats or to his attitudes and opinions" (474). Still, Perkins groups Desmond O'Grady with Joyce, Beckett, Denis Devlin, and Thomas MacGreevy as "Irish poets who lived abroad and adopted international styles" (474-75), and one might therefore expect O'Grady to affect indifference to the earlier poet. Instead, O'Grady invites deliberate comparison with Yeats in his frequently anthologized poem set by the Charles River—and patently validates Garratt's thesis in the process.

Should we be surprised? Yeats himself, after all, did not choose to ignore his own predecessors. Indeed, Harold Bloom's study of Yeats's Romanticism devotes a full five chapters to questions of influence; the pervasive influence of Blake and Shelley is "studied throughout" (vii). Particularly relevant for our analysis here is Bloom's comment that

> As much as any other poem by Yeats, **"The Second Coming"** bears its direct relation to Blake and Shelley as an overtly defining element in its meaning. The poem quotes Blake and both echoes and parodies the most thematically vital passage in Shelley's most ambitious poem, *Prometheus Unbound.* (*Yeats* 317)

Specifically, as first pointed out by Margaret Rudd (119, noted in turn by George Bornstein 202, 207), Urizen's "stony sleep" in *The Book of Urizen* (III.57) reappears in **"The Second Coming"** as the sphinx's "stony sleep" (19). Even more tellingly, Bloom demonstrates that Shelley's "central insight" (320) in *Prometheus Unbound*—

> The good want power, but to weep barren tears.
> The powerful goodness want: worse need for them.
> The wise want love; and those who love want
>   wisdom;
> And all best things are thus confused to ill
>   (I.626-629)

—is echoed in Yeats's poem: "The best lack all conviction, while the worst / Are full of passionate intensity" (187).

As Bloom notes, however, what for Shelley was "an insight of the Left . . . Yeats proceeds to appropriate for the Right" (320). "His mind," Bloom explains further,

> [was] on the Russian Revolution and its menace, particularly to aristocrats. . . . But unlike his Romantic precursors, Yeats is on the side of the

counter-revolutionaries, and his apocalyptic poem begins by seeing the intervention against revolution as being too late to save the ceremoniously innocent. (318)

It would be a neat twist to announce now that O'Grady re-adopts the cause of the left in yet another rewriting of the original Shelley: would that it were *quite* so simple.

Set side by side, Yeats's rewriting of Shelley and O'Grady's reworking of Yeats do provide the most direct point of comparison between **"The Second Coming"** and "Professor Kelleher and the Charles River." Consider, first, these lines from **"The Second Coming"**:

> The blood-dimmed tide is loosed, and everywhere
> The ceremony of innocence is drowned;
> The best lack all conviction, while the worst
> Are full of passionate intensity.
> Surely some revelation is at hand;
> Surely the Second Coming is at hand.
>
>   (187)

Compare them, next, with their transformation in "Professor Kelleher and the Charles River":

> Locked in their mute struggle there by the blood-
>   loosed tide
> The two abjure all innocence, tear down past order—
> The one calm, dispassionate, clearsighted, the other
> Wild with ecstasy, intoxicated, world mad.
> Surely some new order is at hand;
> Some new form emerging where they stand.
>
>   (261-2)

The echoes here of Yeats's well-known lines naturally also adapt Shelley's. More importantly, O'Grady's lines suggest a fundamentally different approach to "apocalypse" than does Yeats's poem.

Perkins may define O'Grady as working outside the traditions of modern Irish poetry, but even O'Grady takes on the master, countering Yeatsian transcendence with echoes of the very language—and techniques, as we shall see—Yeats used to create it. Indeed, both **"The Second Coming"** and "Professor Kelleher and the Charles River" contemplate a new world order, but with a crucial difference. Where Yeats prophesies the demise of the ruling classes and an age of horrifying violence, O'Grady celebrates personal realization, awareness, and responsibility—for the historically marginalized as well as for the elite, for the left *and* for the right. More precisely, O'Grady rejects Yeats's vision of a Second Coming, the superimposition of a new historical gyre upon an old, to favor perennially renewable personal vision, as available to the peasant as to the aristocrat. To understand the exact nature of this challenge to Yeats, it becomes helpful now to examine the quality and purpose of the tension generated in the poem among sets of sharply antithetical images.

As in the likening of the Charles River to a sickle, O'Grady's images are often multi-layered. Even more frequently they are also at odds with each other and thus embody the struggle in which Kelleher and his student are caught. In fact, tension and conflict, in my estimate, are the primary source of the poem's rhetorical energy. For example, in the second stanza, the scene to the west is contrasted with the scene to the east, and the cemetery dead vie in our imagination with the living Irish farmer. In stanza three, student rowing crews are juxtaposed against the memory of O'Grady's father on the Shannon, just as John Kelleher's lecturing is set against the memory of earlier history lessons at home in Limerick; and in stanza four, the water and the land are linked in hostile partnership: "The secret force/ Of the water worries away the live earth's under-surface" (261). The oxymoronic phrase, "dying conceptual motion," chosen to epitomize the wave's erosive power, also epitomizes the poem's thematic preoccupation with antitheses. The poem is, after all, a record of a conflict between an aging professor's and a young student's views of the past, one contender "dispassionate," if not "lack[ing] all conviction," the other "full of passionate intensity," to characterize both using Yeats's counterpart phrases.

Such a pointed interest in opposites is, of course, yet another invocation of Yeats, who, believing with Blake that "without contraries is no progression" (*A Vision;* see Olney 86-124), muses in poem after poem on the opposing energies of "nature and art, youth and age, body and soul, passion and wisdom, beast and man, creative violence and order, revelation and civilization, poetry and responsibility, and time and eternity" (Perkins 596). O'Grady's knack for mimicry, however, is subordinated in "Professor Kelleher and the Charles River" to a much more intriguing rhetorical purpose, a purpose brought into clearest focus by an analysis of the conflicts pervading the religious imagery in the poem.

The Charles River is described approvingly in stanza one as "living water," and more neutrally but still with respect in stanza four as a "secret force," as well as dismissively in stanza five as a "bitch river" and menacingly in stanza six as a "blood-loosed tide." The Atlantic itself, into which the Charles flows, is, we learn in stanza two, "godless." If "living water" did not so strongly imply a vital, life-giving, spiritual sustenance, reconciling the remaining four descriptive phrases would not be so difficult. One could acknowledge, for example, that "secret force" might suggest, on one level, a classified military unit, or at least an unspecified form of strong and insidious power. "Living water," on the other hand, calls to mind connotations of eternal sustenance and rebirth, certainly to include the Christian rite of baptism; indeed, the phrase can even allude to Christ himself. What is so positively charged a phrase doing in such close conjunction to the more negative descriptions of the river and ocean?

Assuming, as I am, that such an odd juxtaposition does not represent simple Yeatsian parody, the puzzle is further compounded by the poem's seasonal setting. The action of the poem, of course, occurs during spring, the traditional month of resurrection, yet every contemporary poet knows also that "April is the cruellest month" (Eliot 63),

and O'Grady embraces this dichotomy. It is April in his poem, yet the sun "sweeps flat as ice," and although "the spring air . . . thaws," it is "still/ Lean from winter." Moreover, the thawing graveyard clay and "harvesting" river of stanza one actually host a resurrection in stanza seven: "The great dim tide of shadows from the past/ Gathers for the end—the living and the dead"; but the resurrection occurs in darkness, processioning shadows among stars. Although the poem's final, climactic line, "All shadows procession in an acropolis of lights," commands rhythmic majesty, the fact remains that shadows are processioning—and shadows, especially a "great dim tide of shadows," however majestic, connote the solemnity and gloom of Hades. Just as spring in the poem is not unequivocally warm and life-affirming, resurrection in the poem is not unquestionably good.

> Another disturbing religious crosscurrent emerges when
>   Overhead, far from the wave, a dove
> White gull heads inland.

Of course, the dove is a traditional symbol of peace, innocence, and gentleness, as well as a widely recognized emblem of the Holy Ghost; the appearance of the word *dove* in its prominent position at the end of line three is clearly designed to elicit such associations. However, this emphasis is immediately undercut by enjambing "dove/ White gull," and the reader realizes with some disappointment that it is a gull, not a dove, that flies inland—a scavenger bird, not Noah's harbinger of hope.

Tension is heightened, then, in stanza four when the ominous shadow of the "leafing tree," "With all its arms, crawls on the offal-strewn meadow." Certainly, the shadow's steady lengthening indicates much more than the passage of time: the tree is also the cross (both crucifix and burden) of traditional Christianity, and its shadow falls over the age, slowly advancing like a rifle-carrying soldier crawling across a battlefield.

What purpose is served by such religious allusions and images as these—including the explicit, venerable-in-this-context, Protestant past of Cambridge and the implicit, plebeian-in-this-context, Catholic heritage shared by O'Grady, Kelleher, and the ploughing Irish peasant, their "common [both shared and proletarian] brother"? The answer to this question, I must emphasize, is central to the poet's vision; the key to the answer is the poem's last stanza.

No line in the poem is more straightforward than the line, "All force is fruitful. All opposing powers combine." Neither is another line more weighted with meaning. Here O'Grady declares that the conflicts he depicts in the poem like a fervent Yeatsian apprentice—conflicts between west and east, the dead and the living, memory and the present, water and land, youth and age, water-as-life and water-as-destruction, spring and winter, dove and gull, tree and cross, Protestantism and Catholicism, aristocracy and peasantry—merge, unite, combine, and do so with

O'Grady's blanket endorsement that "All force is fruitful." But can one stanza in which direct statements of resolution are made resolve six stanzas of images at war with each other? Perhaps not, if there existed no rich literary tradition for O'Grady to build upon, no Blake, Shelley, Yeats—or Joyce—to whom to add his voice. Such voices, of course, do exist.

"All force is fruitful. All opposing powers combine" is surely a restatement of Blake's "Without contraries is no progression"; recognizing this, we are at once in touch with the familiar existential discussion about the necessity of opposites, not to mention the Jung-prescribed need to integrate the shadow within our own natures. Even so, if O'Grady were to rely solely on this restatement to resolve the ambiguities of the poem's religious images, the conclusion would be disappointingly weak; I would argue, in consequence, that there is no resolution in the poem. In actuality, though, the line is integrated carefully within a final stanza whose striking images and lyrical majesty transcend the conflicts at hand and conclude the poem on a powerfully unifying note:

> Dusk. The great dim tide of shadows from the past
> Gathers for the end—the living and the dead.
> All force is fruitful. All opposing powers combine.
> Aristocratic privilege, divine sanction, anarchy at last
> Yield the new order. The saffron sun sets.
> All shadows procession in an acropolis of lights.

In **"The Second Coming,"** Yeats's pronouncement that "Surely some revelation is at land;/ Surely the Second Coming is at hand" is followed immediately by his vision of the rough, sphinx-like beast slowly approaching Bethlehem. In O'Grady's poem, his own pronouncement that "some new order is at hand;/ Some new form emerging where they stand" immediately precedes a great gathering of shadows, "the living and the dead." This is perhaps the ultimate antithetical pair, at least for Yeats, for whom "the ultimate antithesis is that between antithesis itself, as the moral structure of human existence, and a realm or state of being in which all antitheses are annihilated" (Perkins 596).

Another echo in these lines, however, deepens their richness and underscores their ability to reconcile the conflicts of preceding stanzas. In the concluding scene of James Joyce's "The Dead," as Gabriel Conroy lies quietly in his hotel room contemplating that "one by one they [friends, family, acquaintances] were all becoming shades" (223), he himself experiences a powerful form of vision:

> . . . he imagined he saw the form of a young man standing under a dripping tree. Other forms were near. His soul had approached that region where dwell the vast hosts of the dead. . . . the solid world itself which these dead had one time reared and lived in was dissolving and dwindling (223).

The final, climactic paragraph of the story, then, describes the soft fall of snow over all of Ireland, "like the descent of their last end, upon all the living and the dead" (224).

The snow of Joyce's conclusion is absent from the last stanza of "Professor Kelleher and the Charles River," but both scenes link the living with the dead. Apparently, both authors are comfortable with the interdependence of the two forms of entities, perhaps because interdependence can represent a particularly fruitful form of interaction between opposites.

The Joyce passage, certainly, has generated markedly divergent interpretations. Some critics hear in it only a death knell for Gabriel Conroy; "others read the conclusion as a moment when Gabriel is gifted with the self-recognition and selfless awareness of all humanity denied to the other characters in *Dubliners*" (Scholes and Litz 303). I personally am persuaded by Florence Walzl, who argues for the validity of both interpretations. In her view, the ambiguity of the passage is utterly intentional. "Every image in it," she writes,

> is a symbol, and since each symbol is multi-faceted in reflecting earlier ambiguities, the epiphany allows for either a life or death interpretation. Paradoxical images of arrest and movement, darkness and light, cold and warmth, blindness and sight, are used in this conclusion to recall both the central paralysis-death theme of *Dubliners* as a collection and the rebirth-life theme of "The Dead" as a narrative. (431)

According to Walzl, in order to achieve this complex rhetorical purpose, Joyce deliberately creates paradoxical pairs of images. For example, "in some contexts [Joyce] equates the east with dawn and life and the west with sunset and death, but in other contexts [he] associates the east with the old and sterile and the west with the new and vital" (433).

An equal complexity operates in "Professor Kelleher and the Charles River." In stanza two the Irish peasant is ploughing, "East, over the godless Atlantic." *East* typically suggests dawn, awakening, resurrection, images associated with viable Christianity; yet, eastward also lies an ocean which is "godless," a term which defies religion. In fact, each of O'Grady's positive religious images is undercut by their darker, religion-defying contraries. The living water becomes a "bitch river," the dove is in fact a gull, and the shadow of the cross crawls menacingly over the two men's conversation, aware somehow that its influence is threatened. The resurrection itself is godless, irreligious. And along with the aristocratic privilege which O'Grady did not inherit (even if he has qualified for a Harvard education) and the anarchy loosed in **"The Second Coming,"** divine sanction (far too often a weapon in traditional Christianity) is superseded in stanza seven by the new order immediately at hand. Religion is superseded in O'Grady's vision of new order.

O'Grady's vision, then, is steeped in irony. Indeed, how could so momentous an event as the ushering in of a new world order be preceded by a mere conversation, even a significant conversation, on the banks of the Charles River in Cambridge? Admittedly, O'Grady has endowed the incident with cosmic ramifications by describing it as an "ageless," "mute struggle" initiated "as in some ancient dance." Even so, one strains to visualize a new order ushered in by an incident introduced with a statement like "Walking, John/ Kelleher and I talk on the civic lawn." The lines, "Surely some new order is at hand;/ Some new form emerging where they stand," result from a professor and student's dismantling of "past order." The irony here satirizes the whole idea of resurrection and religious rebirth into a new world. Really, is it a new world being ushered in? Is a Second Coming presaged?

The answer is, "No." The poem instead recalls the setting for a moment of heightened personal awareness for a young student "mad" for change—and his acceptance, even if only temporary, of personal responsibility for that change as he "abjure[s] all innocence." The "new form" to replace "Aristocratic privilege, divine sanction, [and] anarchy" is an order as personal to the poet as his struggle with Kelleher while they walk on Harvard's civic lawn. The vision is not Yeats's vision of an apocalyptic Second Coming, but an intensely personal realization, "selfbounded and selfcontained upon the immeasurable background of space or time" (*Portrait* 212), and, like Gabriel Conroy's, "initiated by a moment of deep, if localized sympathy" (Loomis 417). For O'Grady, this is the only valid order, order which can be renewed not only every two thousand years, but as perennially as the seasons themselves renew and as often as a young man conflicts with an old.

Despite, then, the profound Yeatsian echoes in the poem, O'Grady ultimately aligns himself with Joyce—with whom he shares not only his early Catholic education, but his need as well to leave Ireland and adopt an international outlook. In a way, in fact, O'Grady—with Joyce—represents the achievement of a class of people whose insensitivities and materialism the great Protestant Ascendancy poet railed against and for whom he predicted only disaster. Indeed, if **"The Second Coming"** prophesies the unfortunate demise of the world's aristocracy with all the customs and ceremonious privileges Yeats so openly valued, then Joyce and O'Grady—in particular the latter with his humble Limerick beginnings—represent in many ways the new men whom Yeats feared. Need Yeats have been so wary? O'Grady may invert the Yeatsian vision, appropriating Yeats's own methods in the process, but he does so with an aplomb that Yeats himself could not have failed to acknowledge. If, in O'Grady's new order, primacy is given to the common man, surely Yeats would have admitted that *this* common man, at least, deserves it.

"Professor Kelleher and the Charles River" is a vivid, memorable depiction of Desmond O'Grady's version of "new order." His vision emerges out of conflicting images which embody struggle, religious undercutting which vivifies the need at the helm for something other than traditional Christianity, and irony which pushes for the validity of personal experience and insight. This vision may not be as powerful or far-reaching as Yeats's in **"The Second Coming,"** but it is not meant to be. O'Grady's vision is a response to a contemporary, post-Yeatsian

world, and although "Professor Kelleher and the Charles River" might be said to chronicle the demise of Christianity that Yeats predicted in his more famous poem, the slouching beast whose reign Yeats also prophesied is conspicuously absent from O'Grady's stanzas. The two poets thus agree that the old ways are coming to an end, but they diverge sharply on the question of what comes next. I for one believe that O'Grady's emphasis on the validity of individual epiphany, particularly in a postmodern world where one can do no better than perennially create new personal order, represents, ultimately, the more relevant response.

WORKS CITED

Blake, William. *A Vision. The Complete Writings of William Blake.* Ed. Geoffrey Keynes. London: Oxford UP, 1972.

———. *The Book of Urizen. The Complete Poems.* Ed. Alicia Ostriker. New York: Penguin Books, 1981, 242-58.

Bloom, Harold. *Yeats.* New York: Oxford UP, 1970.

Bornstein, George. "Yeats and the Greater Romantic Lyric." *Critical Essays on W. B. Yeats.* Ed. Richard J. Finneran. Boston: G. K. Hall and Co., 1986, 190-207.

Eliot, T. S. *Collected Poems 1909-1962.* London: Faber and Faber, 1963.

Garratt, Robert F. *Modern Irish Poetry: Tradition and Continuity from Yeats to Heaney.* Berkeley: U of California P, 1986.

Joyce, James. "The Dead." *Dubliners: Text, Criticism, and Notes.* Ed. Robert Scholes and A. Walton Litz. New York: Penguin Books, 1981, 175-224.

———. *A Portrait of the Artist as a Young Man: Text, Criticism, and Notes.* Ed. Chester G. Anderson. New York: Penguin Books, 1982, 5-253.

Loomis, C. C., Jr. "Structure and Sympathy in 'The Dead.'" *Dubliners: Text, Criticism, and Notes.* By James Joyce, et al. Ed. Robert Scholes and A. Walton Litz. New York: Penguin Books, 1981, 417-22.

O'Grady, Desmond. "Professor Kelleher and the Charles River." *Contemporary Irish Poetry.* Ed. Anthony Bradley. Rev. ed. Berkeley: U of California P, 1988, 260-62.

Olney, James. *The Rhizome and the Flower: The Perennial Philosophy—Yeats and Jung.* Berkeley: U of California P, 1980.

Perkins, David. *A History of Modern Poetry: From the 1890s to the High Modernist Mode.* Cambridge, MA: The Belknap P of Harvard UP, 1976.

Rudd, Margaret. *Divided Image: A Study of William Blake and W. B. Yeats.* London: Routledge and Kegan Paul, 1953.

Scholes, Robert, and A. Walton Litz. Editors' Introduction. *Dubliners: Text, Criticism, and Notes.* By James Joyce, et al. New York: Penguin Books, 1981, 297-303.

Shelley, Percy Bysshe. *Prometheus Unbound. Anthology of Romanticism.* Ed. Ernest Bernbaum. 3rd ed. New York: The Ronald Press Company, 1948, 883-935.

Walzl, Florence L. "Gabriel and Michael: The Conclusion of 'The Dead.'" *Dubliners: Text, Criticism, and Notes.* By James Joyce, et al. Ed. Robert Scholes and A. Walton Litz. New York: Penguin Books, 1981, 423-33.

Yeats, William Butler. "The Second Coming." *The Poems of W. B. Yeats: A New Edition.* Ed. Richard Finneran. New York: Macmillan, 1983.

———. *A Vision.* New York: Collier, 1965.

Nathan Cervo (essay date 1995)

SOURCE: "Yeats's 'The Second Coming'," in *The Explicator,* Vol. 53, No. 3, Spring, 1995, pp. 161-3.

[*In the following essay, Cervo explores the prophetic implications of "The Second Coming" with regard to Christian millennarianism.*]

Yeats's poem **"The Second Coming"** was published in **Michael Robartes and the Dancer** (1921), a few years after Oswald Spengler's *The Decline of the West,* which appeared just after the close of World War I and the Balfour Declaration (1917). In a long note on the widening "gyre" (line 1) mentioned in the poem, Yeats observed: "All our scientific, democratic, fact-accumulating, heterogeneous civilization belongs to the outward gyre and prepares not for the continuation of itself but the revelation as in a lightening flash . . . of the civilization that must slowly take its place."[1] The outward gyre, Yeats tells us, is unlike the gyre before the time of Christ, which was narrowing. Under the expansive centrifugal force of the outward gyre, "the centre cannot hold" (3): "Mere anarchy is loosed upon the world" (4).

Although the "anarchy" has been linked to the Russian Revolution of 1917 and the "rough beast" (21) slouching "towards Bethlehem to be born" (22) has been spoken of as a prophetic embodiment of Fascism,[2] an explication of the word "beast" may show that, in this poem, Yeats foresaw the state of our present culture in the United States ("scientific, democratic, fact-accumulating, heterogeneous") and associated the wordly success of this culture with chiliasm.

It is in this connection that the Balfour Declaration may be brought into play to shed some light on the nature of the "beast." In 1917, assisted by the eccentric English colonel T. E. Lawrence, discontented Arabs wrested Jerusalem from the Turks, and in 1918 Turkish resistance collapsed. (Lawrence's revolt in the desert is chimed in the poem by

"shadows of the indignant desert birds" [17; the Turks].) The Arabs aimed at a Middle East that was exclusively Arabian. "But in 1917 the British government, trying to rally Jews throughout the world to the Allied cause, issued the Balfour Declaration (named for the foreign secretary) favoring 'the establishment in Palestine of a national home for the Jewish people.' Zionist aspirations and Allied promises thwarted Arab hopes."[3]

Within the context of the history of Christian millennarianism, Zionism may be said to have a decisive role: "One view of the Antichrist was that he would be a Jewish messiah who would promise to bring the people back to their land. If Christians put any stock in this hope, it was viewed as the Jews' final mistake. Their restoration would be but the prelude to the second coming of Christ and the destruction of the Antichrist."[4] The rejudaicization of Jerusalem would amount to a definitive split between the Old and New Testaments. Ironically, its effect would be the same as that envisioned by Marcion, who insisted on an exclusively christianized reconstituted Jerusalem. For Marcion (died c. 163), a wealthy shipowner of Sinope in Pontus who went to Rome (about 140 CE) and founded the semi-Gnostic Marcionites (144 CE), "the historical destruction of Jerusalem meant the final death of the Jewish Creator-God of the Old Testament,"[5] a moralistic, yet capricious, despot akin to the Antinomian William Blake's Nobodaddy.

The christology of the Marcionites is of some moment in this explication. In their view, the body of Christ was a mere phantasm. Not only were they anti-Judaic, they were anti-matter, espousing asceticism as their way of essentially spiritual affirmation. Yeats, who assumed the name "Demon Est Deus Inversus" (The Daimon Is God Turned Upside Down) upon his initiation into the Golden Dawn, an esoteric cult, points to the Marcionite nature of the "beast" in his poem **"Demon and Beast,"** which immediately precedes **"The Second Coming"** in **Michael Robartes and the Dancer.** In **"Demon and Beast,"** both the ascetic and antinomian notes are struck when Yeats praises the "exultant Anthony [of Egypt]" (46) "[a]nd twice a thousand more [hermits]" (47). Contemptuous of civil society, supported in the West by Roman law, Yeats ends **"Demon and Beast"** thus: "What had the Caesars but their thrones?" (50). Earlier, Yeats had declared:

> Yet I am certain as can be
> That every natural victory
> Belongs to beast or demon,
> That never yet had freeman
> Right mastery of natural things[.]
>
> (34-38)

"Right mastery" comes from living out the archetypes, from sustaining oneself on the rhizome of the Gnostic Pleroma, the Collective Unconscious, or Platonic anamnesis, of that spiritual race cast into matter and into human boundaries (bondage to matter). The "vast image out of *Spiritus Mundi*" (12) is such an archetype. Specialized spiritual knowledge is viewed as an instinct of the elite.

In light of the above, the "rough beast" slouching "towards Bethlehem to be born" (21-22) may be identified, within the context of the tremendous dialectic between conventional and unconventional christology that is the subject of **"The Second Coming,"** as "the man of lawlessness" (*ho anthropos tes anomias;* II Thessalonians 2:3), the "man" (*anthropos*) here signifying the hermaphroditic, gender-inclusive Gnostic transcendental ideal of the Self. Paul fully teaches (II Thessalonians 2:3-12) that before the second advent, or coming, "the *anthropos* of lawlessness" must be revealed.

The "rough beast" is pointedly described as a sphinx, an Egyptian monument, "with lion body and the head of a man" (14), because, by means of the poem's ideational dialectic, Yeats wishes to show that "our scientific, democratic, fact-accumulating, heterogeneous civilization" is begging for a backlash, "a lightning flash": "The revelation which approaches will . . . take its character from the contrary movement of the interior gyre"[6] (that is, from the conventional Christian dispensation). The Judeo-Christian foundation of Western civilization, imitating Jesus ("And he was with the wild beasts"; Mark 1:13), will encounter the amalgamized theosophy of Egyptian esoteric alchemy and transfigure its defiance, producing "the civilization that must slowly take [our present governing culture's] place."

NOTES

[1] *The Collected Poems of W. B. Yeats,* ed. Richard J. Finneran (New York: Macmillan, 1989) 493.

[2] *The Norton Anthology of English Literature,* vol. 2. (New York: W. W. Norton & Company, 1962) n. 2, 1355.

[3] Crane Brinton, John B. Christopher, and Robert Lee Wolff, *Civilization in the West* (Part 2: 1600 to the Present) (Englewood Cliffs: Prentice-Hall, 1981) 466.

[4] Robert B. Eno, rev. art. of Stefan Heid, "Chilasmus und Antichrist-Mythos: Eine fruhchristliche Kontroverse um das Heilige Land," *The Catholic Historical Review* 80:1 (January 1994): 127-128.

[5] *Ibid.*

[6] *Collected Poems* 493: Yeats's note.

John R. Harrison (essay date 1995)

SOURCE: "What Rough Beast?: Yeats, Nietzsche and Historical Rhetoric in 'The Second Coming'," in *Papers on Language and Literature,* Vol. 31, No. 4, Fall, 1995, pp. 362-88.

[*In the following essay, Harrison focuses on Nietzschean suggestions in the language and imagery of "The Second Coming."*]

In the absence of a thorough examination of the impact on **"The Second Coming"** of Yeats's historical thought, it is arguable that the meaning the poet intended has not only been consistently overlooked, but that in general the poem has been taken to mean the opposite of what he intended. This essay offers a reassessment of the thought and imagery, of the response Yeats wished to evoke, and of the antithetical rhetoric of his dialectical view of history.

The text provides a striking example of the synthetic technique which produced some of Yeats's finest poems, one which condenses into imagery as much of the poet's thought as is possible but which also creates interpretative problems of which he was fully aware and which he attributed to the compressed, logical rigor of the ideas: "It is hard for a writer, who has spent much labor upon his style, to remember that thought, which seems to him natural and logical like that style, may be unintelligible to others" (**Variorum** 853). However, Yeats did not believe his philosophy to be either obscure or idiosyncratic; in fact he found confirmation of it in the work of Boehme, Heraclitus, Jung, Nietzsche, Spengler, and Vico and in Neoplatonism and the Upanishads. More surprisingly, he considered the intellectual equivalent of his own imaginative richness of suggestion to be the "packed logic," the "difficult scornful lucidity," of Alfred North Whitehead, Professor of Applied Mathematics at Imperial College, London, and subsequently of Philosophy at Harvard, and Bertrand Russell's collaborator on the *Principia Mathematica* (**Letters** 714). Russell's "plebeian loquacity" infuriated Yeats who admired "something aristocratic" in Whitehead's mind, a combination of terse clarity and suggestive complexity in thought and expression which he labored assiduously to attain, nowhere more so than in this poem.

Yeats wrote **"The Second Coming"** at the time he was collecting, from his wife's automatic writing, the material from which he created the philosophical system later set out in *A Vision,* the "very profound, very exciting mystical philosophy" which was to change radically the nature of his verse, and make him feel that for the first time he understood human life: "I live with a strange sense of revelation. . . . You will be astonished at the change in my work, at its intricate passion" (**Letters** 643-44). In reality this philosophy was neither completely new nor entirely mystical in origin, but rather a crystallization of what Yeats had read, thought, experienced and written over many years, the result of the process whereby he had "pieced [his] thoughts into philosophy" (**"Nineteen Hundred and Nineteen,"** *Variorum* 429). Despite Yeats's own conviction that this had produced a striking change in his writing, many critics have demurred. There has often been a reluctance to take Yeats's thinking seriously and, partly as a consequence of this, a refusal to accept that he successfully expressed his beliefs in his poetry, especially a skepticism regarding what Graham Martin has called his "cryptic symbolism" (230). In fact the symbolism in **"The Second Coming"** is anything but cryptic, except in the limited sense that it embodies some of the most profound elements of his philosophy in a concentrated and complex form which he recognized might prove not immediately intelligible to the reader, but which is entirely logical and consistent. Moreover, it mines a deep and rich vein—literary, philosophical, historical, political and mythical—which has little, if anything, to do with the occult.

The most fundamental question which has to be addressed in any interpretation of the poem concerns the response Yeats invites to the sphinx symbol, which is awesome, frightening, at last seemingly repulsive, yet which I shall contend paradoxically embodies much to which he was intellectually and emotionally committed. Critical opinion has predominantly interpreted the rough beast as a comfortless vision of horror, symbolizing the birth of a "violent, bestial anti-civilization" (Unterecker 165), while often suggesting that the poem as a whole consists of generalizations which do not require, or would not benefit from, detailed analysis.[1] Two recent commentaries have underlined the need for a critical reassessment by reiterating such views. In the first Thomas Kinsella asserts that the rough beast is related, visually and verbally, to the imagery and the "brutal diction" of **"Nineteen Hundred and Nineteen."** The passage he quotes refers to atrocities committed by the Black and Tans at Gort in County Galway:

> Now days are dragon-ridden, the nightmare
> Rides upon sleep: a drunken soldiery
> Can leave the mother, murdered at her door,
> To crawl in her own blood, and go scot-free;
> The night can sweat with terror.
> (Variorum 429)

In fact there is only a superficial resemblance between these lines and the imagery and "brutal diction" associated with the rough beast of **"The Second Coming,"** in which the contemporary Irish context is inseparable from the wider context of Yeats's intellectual, social and historical perspectives. In the second, Nicholas Drake states that "the rhetorical phrases, repetitions . . . and metaphors are generalizations lacking any specific context" (52-54). On the contrary, this poem is a compelling example of the movement in Yeats's verse towards the concrete and particular, and the perspectives referred to above provide for the language and imagery the specific context which Drake denies exists.

Those critics who have attempted to provide such a context have not pursued the implications of the imagery with the rigor and fearlessness Yeats demanded of himself, which ultimately took him "Ravening, raging and uprooting . . . / Into the desolation of reality" (**"Supernatural Songs,"** *Variorum* 563).[2] To explore these implications fully one needs clearly to identify, and make intelligible, the "natural and logical" thought process incorporated in the language and imagery, and to explore the poem's "imaginative richness of suggestion," what may aptly be called its "difficult scornful lucidity."

Yeats's thought is here compressed into images with an intensity rare even in his work and with a deliberately provocative Nietzschean element of paradox.[3] Yeats's interest in Nietzsche was aroused at least as early as September 1902, when his American lawyer friend, John Quinn, sent him his own copy of *Thus Spake Zarathustra* together with copies of *The Case of Wagner* and *A Genealogy of Morals.* The first mention in Yeats's letters is dated by Wade 26 September 1902. He wrote to Lady Gregory: "You have a rival in Nietzsche, that strong enchanter. . . . Nietzsche completes Blake and has the same roots—I have not read anything with so much excitement since I got to love Morris's stories which have the same curious astringent joy" (*Letters* 379). It was shortly after this, and not I believe coincidentally, that he began to reconstruct his poetic style to give it more "masculinity," more "salt," and to make it more idiomatic. Yeats also annotated John Quinn's copy of Thomas Common's *Nietzsche as Critic, Philosopher, Poet and Prophet,* which appeared in 1901. Most of his annotations are on passages from *A Genealogy of Morals, Beyond Good and Evil* and *Thus Spake Zarathustra.* According to Professor Donald Torchiana Yeats's library contained at least the following texts (the dates of English translations are given in brackets): *The Case of Wagner* (1895), *A Genealogy of Morals* (1899), *The Dawn of Day* (1903), *The Birth of Tragedy* (1909), *Thoughts out of Season* (1909), and *The Will to Power* (1909-10). He also possessed Daniel Halévy's *Life,* translated by his own biographer, J. M. Hone. Professor Torchiana's inspection of the library was hurried and by no means thorough and he acknowledged that there may have been other works by Nietzsche (Thatcher 143). With such a consuming and lasting interest in Nietzsche's work, and considering that he possessed three texts published between 1909 and 1910, it is unlikely that Yeats was not acquainted with Nietzsche's last work to appear, *Ecce Homo,* first published in German in 1908 and in English in 1911. In the course of this discussion of **"The Second Coming"** I shall point to some remarkable resonances between the work of these two writers in both language and meaning, while the critical emphasis will of course be on Yeats, not Nietzsche. Moreover, the question of literary influence is far too complex to be addressed here, and I am not in any way suggesting that either Yeats's language or meaning is directly derived from his reading of Nietzsche.

From the outset the poet invites, indeed demands, reference to his philosophic system, the central symbol of which contains two interpenetrating gyres or cones, perpetually in conflict and alternately victorious.[4] Whatever mystical origins Yeats may have claimed for this idea, it is a recognizably dialectical, and not necessarily an occult, concept. Despite the importance of this symbolism in Yeats's thought, it is rarely introduced into his poetry as explicitly as it is here; its use is thus a direct pointer to what he intended to be the poem's specific philosophical and historical context:

> Turning and turning in the widening gyre
> The falcon cannot hear the falconer,
> ("The Second Coming" lines 1-2)

and throughout the poem bird imagery contributes to a coherent pattern, though not explicitly. In Jon Stallworthy's view the confusion which has surrounded the falcon image is dispelled once we realize that it was originally "hawk," but other connotations suggest that Yeats made the substitution precisely to avoid any association with "a gloomy bird of prey" (Stallworthy 18). Yeats adapted the dramatic description of the eagle that "stares on the sun by natural right" from Chaucer's *Parlement of Foules:*

> Ther mighte men the royal egle finde,
> That with his sharpe look perceth the sonne.
> (330-31)

In the next few lines Chaucer describes the goshawk as "the tyraunt with his fethres donne / And greye" (a distinctly "gloomy bird of prey") while the falcon is "the gentil faucon, that with his feet distreyneth / the Kinges hond." The "falcon-gentle," Middle English "faucon gentil," is the female or young of the goshawk, while in modern falconry the word "falcon" tends to be used only of the female of the species. This does not necessarily make her any less predatory in reality but Yeats would have been familiar with these nuances. The "brazen hawks" of **"Meditations in Time of Civil War"** are of an entirely different species. There are several falcon echoes throughout the poem but the opening lines have undertones which are typical of Yeats's thought and poetry. The peregrine falcon was the most popular of the birds of prey when falconry was the sport of kings, its fierce alertness and lofty bearing earning its reputation as a bird of nobility. (Chaucer links it specifically with the highest-born.) Thus the separation of man and bird offers a striking image of social and cultural disintegration, not from a simple loss of communication, in itself redeemable and lacking the symbolic dimension required for the anarchic forces it heralds, but from Yeats's anguish at the disruption of the order and cohesion, the homogeneity of the aristocratic society he so admired.

There follows a subtle interplay between this disintegration of the aristocratic ideal, anarchy and violence. Successive drafts of the poem indicate that Yeats had in mind the First World War ("bloody frivolity"), the Bolshevik Revolution (the most striking instance of the destruction of an aristocratic society by egalitarian forces), the threat of anarchy and widespread violence in Ireland, all of which seemed to confirm Nietzsche's predictions, and the prophecies of Macgregor Mathers in the late 1890s, of immense wars accompanied by and followed by anarchy (Stallworthy 18-19). Moreover, Yeats's interlocking gyres are in part an attempt to present his cyclical view of history in visual terms. The cone representing the next and imminent era, the "antithetical dispensation," rises from its base to its apex, and similar pyramidal structures have been widely used to symbolize aristocratic, hierarchic societies; while the inverted cone representing the previous two thousand year cycle, the Christian era, rises to its point of greatest expansion, a widening gyre like the one in which the falcon loses its point of reference. The

Christian era had culminated in the egalitarian mass society which Yeats found so distasteful. Historically the "centre," the nadir of the inverted cone, is the birth of Christ, the "first coming." However, "Things fall apart; the centre cannot hold" because Christianity had "dwindled to a box of toys" (*Autobiographies* 333). In those drafts of the poem which Stallworthy managed to decipher, the blanket-word "things," which seems to have a looseness uncharacteristic of Yeats's drive towards greater precision of statement, is the only word that never changes its form. While it implies that literally everything, the whole social and cultural superstructure, is falling apart, there are other more compact and personal associations which echo the themes already mentioned. Yeats would also have had in mind the disintegration of material objects such as his own Thoor Ballylee, itself a crumbling monument to a threatened culture and incorporating a "gyre" in the form of a spiral staircase.

Violence, which for Yeats was symptomatic of the end of one era and the birth of another, becomes widespread as the inverted cone reaches its point of greatest expansion: "Mere anarchy is loosed upon the world" as the mass society promulgates its disruptive ideologies, a line that creates a singular effect from the inherent ambiguity of the word "mere" and its surprising juxtaposition with "anarchy." Here it has a primary meaning as a superlative in the sense of "sheer anarchy," suggestive of vastly destructive forces, and a secondary meaning as a scornful understatement, as in the phrase "a mere bagatelle." In an early draft Yeats had written "vile anarchy," which is more emphatic but which lacks the ambiguity and internal tension of the final version. The change was completely successful and provides for the first stanza a controlled center which does hold, and which allows the subsequent images of violence to intensify. It is interesting to identify the thought process by which in successive drafts of the poem the passing of innocence gradually assumes the social and cultural dimensions of the associated imagery, from the straightforward "some innocent has died" through "Old wisdom and young innocence," "The gracious and the innocent," "ceremonious innocence," to the greater complexity of "The ceremony of innocence is drowned." It is clear that Yeats increasingly associated this lost innocence with traditional values ("Old wisdom"), graciousness and ceremony, with what he was later to describe as his chosen theme—"traditional sanctity and loveliness" (**"Coole Park and Ballilee, 1931"**). Immediately after **"The Second Coming"** in the *Collected Poems* Yeats placed **"A Prayer for my Daughter"** whose last stanza reads:

> And may her bridegroom bring her to a house
> Where all's accustomed, ceremonious;
> For arrogance and hatred are the wares
> Peddled in the thoroughfares.
> How but in custom and in ceremony
> Are innocence and beauty born?
> Ceremony's a name for the rich horn,
> And custom for the spreading laurel tree.
> (*Variorum* 405-06)

Innocence is born of "custom and ceremony" which are other names for wealth ("the rich horn") and eminence ("the spreading laurel tree"), for what Yeats revered in the culture of the great houses. Indeed his own contribution to this culture may also be implied as the foliage of the laurel has long been an emblem of poetic distinction. On the other hand "arrogance and hatred" are "peddled in the thoroughfares" by political demagogues, those who "labour for hatred, and so for sterility in various kinds" (Notes to **"Meditations in Time of Civil War," *Variorum*** 827). In **"The Leaders of the Crowd"** Yeats describes these demagogues as slandering their opponents in order to "keep their certainty," which is compounded by a disastrous loss of confidence by those whose position has been systematically undermined by what Yeats calls "Whiggery," a "levelling, rancorous, rational sort of mind." The wanton destruction of the great houses, of "all / That comes of the best knit to the best," would never enable "mean roof-trees" to acquire "the gifts that govern men" (**"Upon a House Shaken by the Land Agitation"**). The house was Coole Park, the home of Lady Gregory, both house and owner embodiments of the Ascendancy, the Anglo-Irish tradition Yeats so revered and of which he considered his own family to have been a part. Denis Donoghue has suggested that by this time Yeats had given up thinking of "the Big House" as an emblem of intelligence in active relation to power: "He saw it now as an aesthetic image of defeat, the enslavement of the strong to the weak" (56). This provides a context for the anguished complaint which ends the first stanza:

> The best lack all conviction, while the worst
> Are full of passionate intensity,

a context in which "the best" and "the worst," words whose meanings are inevitably relative and subjective, echo the sense of the preceding imagery.

Yeats shared the Nietzschean, anti-libertarian view that Christianity had culminated in an egalitarian democracy which, disintegrating into "mere anarchy," could not control the violence, the "blood-dimmed tide," it had loosed on the world, signaling the approach of a new era: "All our scientific, democratic, fact-accumulating, heterogeneous civilisation belongs to the outward gyre and prepares not the continuance of itself but the revelation as in a lightning flash . . . of the civilisation that must slowly take its place" (***Variorum*** 825).

Such is the foundation on which he builds the symbolic structure of the second stanza. The revelation is indeed in the nature of a lightning flash and is both intensely personal and explicitly anti-millennarian, shattering the ostensible Christian conviction that anarchy and violence herald the Second Coming. "Hardly are those words out" before he catches his first glimpse of the monolithic sphinx, the "vast image" (originally "lost image") forgotten but surviving in Spiritus Mundi: "Antithetical revelation is an intellectual influx neither from beyond mankind nor born of a virgin, but begotten from our spirit and history" (*A Vision* 262). For Yeats a "very

ancient symbol" was more than a literary device; it was a part of the "dwelling house of symbols, of images that are living souls," and of the "great memory that renews the world and men's thoughts age after age," which he named Spiritus Mundi (***Essays and Introductions*** 79). He bought Thoor Ballylee not because it would make a comfortable home but because the tower, "important in Maeterlinck as in Shelley," was an ancient symbol he could actually live in. Indeed it fulfilled the requirements of a perfect symbol: it visibly existed and had a physical history (Gordon and Fletcher 26). These attributes are shared by the lion-bodied "shape," which, possessing a man's head, is clearly the male Egyptian sphinx, a royal portrait type through most of Egyptian history, symbolizing both the mighty strength and protective power of Egypt's ruler. All the Egyptian sphinxes are representations of Horus, the Egyptian God of Light, who was reborn each day as the rising sun, the symbol of renewed life, and who was also the Egyptian sky-god who took the form of a falcon, a bird whose figure represented his name and was thus sacred to him. There can be little doubt that Yeats would have been familiar with this mythology; he had even considered introducing the revelation which eventually emerges as sphinx and rough beast with the words, "Surely the great falcon must come." He had long been aware of the sphinx as an ancient symbol, and in the 1890s it had something of a vogue among those symbolist painters he most admired. Charles Ricketts, "my education in so many things" (*A Vision* 298), had designed Wilde's *Sphinx* (1894), which is "among the most perfect and wholly characteristic productions of the 1890s," while Moreau's *The Sphinx* appeared as an illustration in the 1897 volume of the *Pageant,* a magazine in whose production Ricketts had a large share and in which one of Yeats's stories appeared in 1896 (Gordon and Fletcher 96, 98). Moreover his "instructors" had impressed on Yeats the symbolic significance of the east that had affected European civilization—Asia Minor, Mesopotamia, Egypt: "The East in my symbolism . . . is always human power . . . stretched to its utmost" (*A Vision* 257).

The vast image "troubles" his sight, implying not so much fear as imperfect vision, like a medium's confused first contact with an unknown spirit. Indeed the shape, situated "somewhere in sands of the desert," manages to appear monumental and vague at the same time, while often in Yeats the desert symbolizes the aridity of attitudes he disliked, notably liberal-democratic individualism and Christian-Platonic idealism and other-worldliness (*Variorum* 828). Plato in separating "the Eternal Ideas from Nature . . . prepares the Christian desert and the Stoic suicide" (*A Vision* 271), and this contrast between "idealism" and "nature" or "reality"—possibly derived from, certainly confirmed by, his reading of Nietzsche—became a cardinal feature of his philosophy. The creature has a "lion body and the head of a man," a fusion of awesome humanity and potent beast, of intellect and myth; it has "put on his knowledge with his power" (**"Leda and the Swan"**). All the predominant associations so far (royal sphinx, bird of nobility, king of beasts) are those of majesty and power, and in his notes to the poem

Yeats allows his imaginary tribe to voice his own view of the revelation, which "will not come to the poor but to the great and learned and establish again for two thousand years prince and vizier" (*Variorum* 825).

Thus the sphinx's gaze is "blank and pitiless as the sun," reminiscent of "the lidless eye that loves the sun," the impassive look of the proud, stern, fearless mind of the Anglo-Irish aristocracy (**"Upon a House Shaken by the Land Agitation"**). The Christian or humanitarian is likely to find this pitiless gaze repugnant, but Yeats frequently repudiated humanitarian ideals. (He thought Synge necessary to the Irish dramatic movement partly because he was "incapable of a humanitarian purpose.") The debased "primary pity" of Christianity mocks the stoicism of a Swift, a Villon or indeed a Yeats, and contradicts the law of opposites; the Good Samaritan does not need his Lazarus, "they do not each die the other's life, live the other's death" (*A Vision* 275). Yeats was impressed by Nietzsche's claim that his attack on "die Mitleidigen," "the Pitying," a crucial element in his critique of Christianity, was in the tradition of Plato, Aristotle, the Stoics, Spinoza, La Rochefoucauld and Kant. Zarathustra, for example, warns his followers against pity: "All great love is above all its pity: for it seeketh—to create what is loved. . . . All creators, however, are hard" (*Thus Spake Zarathustra* 102). Thus there is growing tension between a conventional response, pitiless = cruel, for example, and the response Yeats is inviting.

After "twenty centuries of stony sleep" the creature has difficulty "moving its slow thighs," a powerful naturalistic touch applied to the enigma but which also has its function in the poem's symbolic structure: "Does not every new civilisation . . . imagine that it was born in revelation, or that it comes from dependence upon dark or unknown powers, that it can but open its eyes with difficulty after some long night's sleep or winter's hibernation?" (*Essays and Introductions* 472). Stallworthy suggests that "slow thighs" replaced the "slow feet" of an earlier version because the latter sounded too human (22). It is equally likely that Yeats rejected this borrowing from Ezra Pound's "The Return," which he quoted in full when dedicating *A Vision* to Pound and in which he found expressed his own excitement at the re-birth or re-discovery of an ancient tradition, of forgotten values, and at the same time a sense of awe at such a fearful experience. The descriptions in this poem anticipate those of **"The Second Coming"** as unidentified figures return "half-awakened," with "tentative / Movements, and . . . slow feet," reminiscent both of the sphinx's labored progress and of its recent arousal after lying dormant for two thousand years (*A Vision* 29).

The darkness again obscures the revelation but not before it has engendered his certain conviction

> That twenty centuries of stony sleep
> Were vexed to nightmare by a rocking cradle

implying a degree of understanding of the creature's frustration imprisoned in sleep in the Christian desert. Yeats

enjoyed the description of the Christian phenomenon as a "fabulous, formless darkness" which blotted out "every beautiful thing," and "the darkness drops again" because the antithetical phases "are but, at the best, phases of a momentary illumination like that of a lightning flash" (*A Vision* 278, 284). They may even be embodied in some great man; when Yeats and his friends talked of Parnell's pride and impassivity (shared by the sphinx symbol), "the proceeding epoch with its democratic bonhomie seemed to grin through a horse collar." Parnell was the symbol that "made apparent, or made possible . . . that epoch's contrary: contrary, not negation, not refutation. . . . I am Blake's disciple, not Hegel's; 'contraries are positive. A negation is not a contrary'" (*Variorum* 835). The dialectic of a perpetual conflict between "contraries" or "two principles" provided a historical symbolism which avoided the idea that civilization continually returns to the same point, which implied development while denying progress, and which allowed him to see the world as "an object of contemplation, not as something to be remade" (*A Vision* 300), freeing him from any hint of reforming zeal. Thus his preference for the coming era was vindicated by historical necessity.

We have still to account for the transformation of the sphinx into the "rough beast" and to justify the view that we are meant to respond to that seemingly loathsome symbol with a mixture of awe and admiration, fear and favor. Yeats himself identified it with his vision of "laughing, ecstatic destruction" (*Explorations* 393), recalling his description of the "true personality" of Bishop Berkeley as "solitary, talkative, ecstatic, destructive," and thus inviting our approval since Berkeley, because of his opposition to the "materialistic" philosophies of Locke and Newton, represented Yeats's ideal of Irish intellectual achievement (*Essays and Introductions* 397). Moreover, it is in the nature of the dialectic that one era must end, and the next begin, in violence and Yeats's attitude to violence in his later years is unquestionably ambiguous. In terms of individual suffering he abhorred it; as an intrinsic element of historical necessity he accepted it, at times even welcomed it. Assuming the mask of Michael Robartes and employing a bird symbolism that illuminates the "shadows of the indignant desert birds," he wrote: "Dear predatory birds, prepare for war. . . . Test art, morality, custom, thought, by Thermopylae. . . . Love war because of its horror, that belief may be changed, civilisation renewed" (*A Vision* 52-53). This reads like Nietzsche at his most provocative and raises the question of whether it should be interpreted literally or symbolically. Although in both Yeats and Nietzsche references to joyful or ecstatic destruction, or indeed to an apparent glorification of war, are deliberately ambiguous, they often suggest the destruction of outdated and outworn beliefs, a "transvaluation of values." Such references are legion in Nietzsche's work. A "definite *joy even in destruction*" [Nietzsche's italics] is one of the prime conditions of a "Dionysian life-task" and a prerequisite of creativity: "Change of values. . . . Always doth he destroy who hath to be a creator," including self-destruction: "Ready must thou be to burn thyself in thine own flame; how couldst thou become new if thou have not first become ashes!" (*Ecce Homo* 113. *Zarathustra* 74, 79). If anything, Yeats's invocation to love war because its horror can have a regenerative effect is even more provocative than Nietzsche's pronouncements, one of the more notorious of which reads: "Your enemy shall ye seek; your war shall ye wage, and for the sake of your thoughts! And if your thoughts succumb, your uprightness shall still shout triumph thereby! Ye shall love peace as a means to new wars—and the short peace more than the long" (*Zarathustra* 62). I think that in such an instance there is little doubt that what Nietzsche was alluding to was a philosophical "enemy" and a personal, intellectual "war." Yet this does indicate how a philosophy which purports to be inspirational can become imprisoned in its own logical systematization. Those like Yeats who advocate a transvaluation of values do not create new values but substitute opposites in place of those they wish to destroy and Nietzsche was certainly aware of this:

> The time has come when we have to pay for having been Christians for two thousand years: we are losing the centre of gravity by virtue of which we have lived; we are lost for a while. Abruptly we plunge into the opposite valuations, with all the energy that such an extreme overvaluation of man has generated in man (*Will to Power* 20, section 30).

Apart from the fact that this could be read as a gloss on **"The Second Coming,"** consider how Yeats categorized his own transvaluation of values:

> After an age of necessity, truth, goodness, mechanism, science, democracy, abstraction, peace, comes an age of freedom, fiction, evil, kindred, art, aristocracy, particularity, war (*A Vision* 52).

The substitutions are deliberate and great care has been taken in arranging the contrasting concepts. Compare this:

> A primary dispensation looking beyond itself towards a transcendent power is dogmatic, levelling, unifying, feminine, humane, peace its means and end; an antithetical dispensation obeys imminent power, is expressive, hierarchical, multiple, masculine, harsh, surgical (*A Vision* 263).

To Yeats these were statements of fact, but more significantly they were statements of preference. Accordingly we have these symbolic contraries: a rocking cradle and a monolithic sphinx, the Second Coming and the vast image with an impassive gaze, Bethlehem and beast, since the "new civilisation [was] about to be born from all that our age had rejected" (*Explorations* 393), and the rough beast is bound for Bethlehem because "each age unwinds the thread another age had wound" (*A Vision* 270).[5]

The predictable response to these contraries is likely to be disgust because the emotive impact of the language is determined by the values of the dying era, values nevertheless which Yeats frequently repudiated, sometimes, as in **"The Gyres,"** with "tragic joy":

When a civilisation ends . . . the whole turns bottom upwards, Nietzsche's "transvaluation of all values." . . . Yet we who have hated the age are joyous and happy. The new discipline wherever enforced or thought will recall forgotten beautiful faces. Whenever we or our forefathers have been most Christian—not the Christ of Byzantine mosaic but the soft, domesticated Christ of the painter's brush . . . we have been haunted by those faces dark with mystery, cast up by that other power that has ever more and more wrestled with ours, each living the other's death, dying the other's life (*Explorations* 433-34).

The poem is in some respects an attempt to achieve a poetic ideal, what Nietzsche called the "return of language to the nature of imagery" (*Ecce Homo* 106), and Yeats is using language in the same provocative way that Nietzsche did. His antithetical rhetoric creates tension between a conventional response to words with certain accepted moral overtones and the reaction he is inviting. Thus the massed imagery of the second stanza becomes increasingly disturbing, culminating in the rough beast slouching towards Bethlehem, a provocative device favored by Yeats, often involving the use of oxymoron or paradox, because belief is not something we desire but comes from shock (*Explorations* 426). There is the "terrible beauty" of **"Easter 1916;"** the "turbulent child of the Altar," another symbol for antithetical revelation and a further contrast to the rocking cradle (*A Vision* 204); his invitation to love war because of its horror and because belief will be changed and civilization renewed; the frightening paradox of the last line of **"A Bronze Head,"** where his extreme pessimism concerning contemporary civilization made him wonder "what was left for massacre to save." Above all there are the dichotomies between the dying and burgeoning eras, in which goodness, democracy and peace will give place to evil, aristocracy and war. To Yeats the reverential attitude to the Second Coming, the rocking cradle and Bethlehem indicated the superficiality of the Christian/Humanitarian viewpoint compared with the fearless acceptance of "reality." This is not to imply that the rough beast holds no terror but that the terror is fundamental to a proper understanding of reality:

> I think profound philosophy must come from terror. . . . Whether we will or no we must ask the ancient questions: Is there reality anywhere? Is there a God? Is there a Soul? We cry with the Indian Sacred Book: "They have put a golden stopper into the neck of the bottle; pull it! Let out reality!" (*Essays and Introductions* 502-03).

Or as Yeats expressed it elsewhere, assuming the mask of Ribh in the last of the **"Supernatural Songs:"**

> Civilisation is hooped together, brought
> Under a rule, under the semblance of peace
> By manifold illusion; but man's life is thought,
> And he, despite his terror, cannot cease
> Ravening through century after century,
> Ravening, raging, and uprooting that he may come
> Into the desolation of reality.
>
> (*Variorum* 563)

One of the memorable sensations of Yeats's childhood was seeing a lost design by Nettleship, *God Creating Evil,*[6] a vast, terrifying face, a woman and a tiger rising from the forehead, which seemed blasphemous but at the same time profound: "It was many years before I understood that we must not demand even the welfare of the human race, nor traffic with divinity in our prayers. It moves outside our antinomies, it may be our lot to worship in terror: 'Did He who made the lamb make thee?' ' (**Essays and Introductions** 425).

The rough beast symbol offers contradictions or contradictory meanings that can co-exist, this being in the nature of the complex form. Yet often in Yeats, as in Blake and Nietzsche, apparent contradictions are complementary aspects of some profound truth. To some extent Blake's lamb and tiger were the inspiration for Yeats's contraries of rocking cradle and rough beast, which do not reflect a clash between Christian values and imminent chaos or a new barbarism, but between the contemporary, orthodox view of Christ and a Christ who "was still the half-brother of Dionysus," a figure partly grounded in myth, a "legitimate deduction" from the creed of St. Patrick. Such a deity embodied that "Unity of Being Dante compared to a perfectly proportioned human body, Blake's 'Imagination,' what the Upanishads have named 'Self': nor is this unity distant and therefore intellectually understandable, but imminent, differing from man to man and age to age, taking upon itself pain and ugliness, 'eye of newt, and toe of frog'" (**Essays and Introductions** 518). This echoes Nietzsche's references to the Hellene's "longing for the ugly," the resolute will to pessimism, to tragic myth, "to a conception of all that is terrible, evil, mysterious, destructive, fatal, at the basis of existence." This was a manifestation of a transvaluation of aesthetic values and became essential to his own aesthetic of tragedy and the sublime (*Ecce Homo* 152, 68). Nietzsche admired those he identified as the first European artists with a "universal literary culture," particularly Wagner and the representatives of French romanticism, who were "great discoverers in the realm of the sublime as also of the loathsome and dreadful . . . hankering after the strange, the exotic and the monstrous, the crooked, and the self-contradictory" (*Beyond Good and Evil* 194-95).[7] Yeats was also impressed by such an aesthetic transvaluation; as artistic "synthesis" was being carried to, and beyond, its limits, as the new gyre began to stir, he was excited by the "discovery of hitherto ignored ugliness" (*A Vision* 300). Thus the rough beast can appear genuinely disgusting as it slouches along and yet even this is a facet of its "divinity." It is perhaps not too fanciful to suggest that Yeats may have had at least at the back of his mind the experience of an acquaintance who, "seeking for an image of the Absolute, saw one persistent image, a slug, as though it were suggested to him that Being which is beyond human comprehension is mirrored in the least organised forms of life" (*A Vision* 284).

Yeats was convinced that in two or three generations secular thought would have to accept that "mechanical theory" had no reality. Then it might be possible to recapture the sense that, in the words of the Syrian in *The Resurrection,* there is something human knowledge cannot explain, something of supreme importance that "lies outside knowledge, outside order"—the irrational, the supernatural, myth. Yeats's Christ is a living part of a great tapestry, much older than "the child born in the cavern"; it is the embodiment of his belief that "the supernatural and the natural are knit together." He was sure that this belief would become generally accepted and that it would regenerate European society: "To escape a dangerous fanaticism we must study a new science; at that moment Europeans may find something attractive in a Christ posed against a background not of Judaism but of Druidism, not shut off in dead history, but flowing, concrete, phenomenal. I was born into this faith, have lived in it, and shall die in it" (**Essays and Introductions** 518). This is not a plea for irrationality, but a desire to redress the balance between mechanical theory and myth, to reach an acceptance of reality of which myth, the supernatural, that something which "lies outside knowledge, outside order," are an integral part. Yeats's critique of Christianity and what he considered its ramifications—humanitarianism, democracy, scientific rationalism—was not an attempt to destroy an old tradition so much as an attempt to revive an even older one, to reassert a morality which Christianity had destroyed, or at least had stood on its head, to recapture a world-view which existed before "the umbilical cord which united Christianity to the ancient world" was cut, in which nobody can say where Christianity begins and Druidism ends.

Nietzsche conceived of Christianity as "hostile to life," an attempt to deny "the doubt and terror of reality." He thus invented a "fundamental counter-dogma," an anti-Christian counter-evaluation of life: "I baptized it, not without some impertinence—for who could be sure of the proper name of the Antichrist?—with the name of a Greek God: I called it Dionysian" (*Ecce Homo* 140, 156). In the Greek pantheon Dionysus, like Christ, was a God who died and was reborn; he was also a god of vegetation and animal life who took on different animal forms, one of which was the lion. (Cavendish 147).[8] We have already seen that the Egyptian sphinx—part man, part lion—was a physical manifestation of just such another God, Horus, also represented by the figure of the falcon and revered as the rising sun, born afresh daily, the symbol of renewed life. Such an intricate pattern of ideas, symbols and myths cannot be coincidental nor entirely unconscious. It is a part of that pattern of thought which seemed to the poet as "natural and logical" as his style, and which gives to the sphinx/rough beast symbol the "imaginative richness of suggestion" that Yeats intended it to have.

"The Second Coming" is emblematic of the astonishing effect Yeats claimed his philosophy was having on both the intellectual content and the style of his poetry, and of the "intricate passion" that was beginning to characterize his work at this time. More than any other poem it marks the change to a more idiomatic use of language, a terse complexity of thought and imagery, an energetic muscularity of rhythm, in a word the "masculinity" he sought to achieve. L. A. G. Strong in a letter to Yeats expressed admiration for his ability to conjure up "with one swift, wrought phrase, a landscape, a sky, a weather and a history" (qtd. in Henn 111), and I have discussed what might be called Yeats's rhetoric of history. The idea of historical recurrence provided him with a consistent, even deterministic, interpretation of past and present and more importantly a prediction for the future. It helped him to come to terms with the violence of the contemporary world as an integral, necessary, even positive manifestation of a period of historical crisis. It also freed him from any suggestion of a revolutionary, or even a reformist, intention since the dialectical movement of history was itself in the process of engendering a civilization of which he could approve. This would be the antithesis of the two-thousand-year Christian era which he believed had culminated politically in a movement founded on Hobbes and popularized by the Encyclopaedists and the French Revolution, and which, having exhausted itself, was useless for centuries to come. However, in his preface to *A Vision* Yeats anticipated the predictable question and so asked it of himself: did he actually believe in his system, that history fixed from "our central date," the first day of "our era" (the birth of Christ), can be divided into contrasting periods of equal length? His answer was that he regarded them as stylistic arrangements of experience comparable to the cubes in the drawings of Wyndham Lewis, or the ovoids in Brancusi's sculptures: "They have helped me to hold in a single thought reality and justice" (25). They were thus the building blocks of his mature aesthetic, one which produced in his late poetry what is probably the finest body of work of any poet writing in English in the twentieth century.

I have attempted to divest the language and imagery of **"The Second Coming"** of the preconceptions that have been grafted onto it, preconceptions that were not Yeats's, and to explore what he intended to be its suggestive complexity. The following quotation from Richard Ellmann may be taken as indicative of the interpretation of the poem which has gained widespread currency:

> In spite of his promise . . . that the next era would be subjective and preferable to the present, the god of that era, who rises from the desert sands . . . is no beneficent Dionysus but a monster. The poet's vision of horror surmounts his vision of the cycles. . . . Whatever the new dispensation can bring, it inspires only a sense of horrible helplessness to avert what no man can desire. . . . Yeats is not fond of Christianity . . . yet at the end of the poem he envisages something far worse. The final intimation that the new god will be born in Bethlehem, which Christianity associates with passive infancy and the tenderness of maternal love, makes its brutishness particularly frightful (164-65, 259-60).

While this recognizes that Yeats had little veneration for Christianity, it invests the poem's Christian allusions with a sense of reverence which not only did he not share, but towards which he was deeply antagonistic. Because of a

failure, or an unwillingness, to respond to Yeats's antithetical rhetoric in the way he intended, such an interpretation not only attributes to him value judgments he did not make, they are to all intents and purposes the opposite of those he did make. For Yeats, "all things are from antithesis" (*A Vision* 268) and his rhetorical juxtapositions produce a dialectical tension as in the text he confronts: the center with a centrifugal force it cannot control; a blood-dimmed tide and the ceremony of innocence; the best and the worst, a lack of conviction and a passionate intensity; a stony sleep vexed to nightmare and a rocking cradle; a slouching, rough beast and Bethlehem. These are reinforced elsewhere by terror and beauty, horror and renewal, love and war, massacre and salvation, an altar and a turbulent child. Compared with such dynamic antitheses, the idea of a "beneficent Dionysus" would have been to both Yeats and Nietzsche a simple, and meaningless, contradiction in terms.

For Nietzsche the dionysian attitude was a passionate affirmation of life, of all aspects of life, including tragedy and pessimism, the doubt and terror of reality, pain and suffering. It led him to what he believed was his supreme philosophical insight, Eternal Recurrence, which was not so much Yeats's cyclical view of history as the recognition that this life is our eternal life, the willingness to affirm and relive each of life's experiences, however painful, again and again throughout eternity—"amor fati," the apotheosis of the present moment. In a sense this was Nietzsche's attempt to reclaim and reaffirm his own life, one which he believed had been unusually filled with pain and suffering. Yeats's idea of historical recurrence was a fusion of the personal and the world-historical. On the one hand it justified his rejection of the values and beliefs of the age, an age he characterized as looking beyond humanity to a transcendent power, as democratic, leveling, egalitarian, anarchic, heterogeneous, feminine, humane—"tender" qualities symbolized here by a rocking cradle, Bethlehem and The Second Coming. On the other hand it made it possible for him to reclaim for a future age those values he cherished, a future that would obey imminent power, would be aristocratic, hierarchical, multiple, masculine, harsh and surgical—"hard, astringent" qualities symbolized by a monolithic sphinx and a rough beast.

Thus the confrontation between the Second Coming and the rough beast occurs in Yeats's work in numerous forms, many of them Nietzschean in tone. Also writing out of a profound contempt for his age and what he considered to be its predominant values, Nietzsche almost willfully invited his contemporaries to misunderstand his rhetoric, his "philosophizing with a hammer": "Caesar Borgia as Pope! Do you understand me?" (*Complete Works* 16: 228). Not surprisingly most of them didn't. Nevertheless, this is a provocative assertion of a consistent theme in Nietzsche's work, the clash throughout human history of "Renaissance" and "Reformation" values—the confrontation between a "higher" order of values that are "hard" and "noble," that "say yea to life," that "assured a future," and "the opposing values of degeneration," which he characterized as the morality of decadence: "Have you understood me? Dionysus versus Christ" (*Ecce Homo* 24, 136, 145). What he was doing in fact was inviting his readers to be daring enough to understand him, and the same challenging themes and idioms are to be found in Yeats. In *A Vision* there is the same confrontation between Christianity and paganism, and between Christian and Renaissance values, which Yeats, like Nietzsche, loved to embody in representative mythological or historical figures; for example, the tender passivity of a Saint Catherine of Genoa and the hardness, the astringency of a Donatello or a Michelangelo (291).

Ultimately, however, despite their often contemptuous rhetoric, neither completely rejected Christian values. Nietzsche did believe that European culture in the second half of the nineteenth century needed a transfusion of those "hard," "noble" qualities he admired, a radical injection of will:

> Nowadays the taste and virtue of the age weaken and attenuate the will; . . . consequently, in the ideal of the philosopher, strength of will, sternness and capacity for prolonged resolution, must specially be included in the conception of "greatness": with as good a right as the opposite doctrine, with its ideal of a silly, renouncing, humble, selfless humanity, was suited to an opposite age—such as the sixteenth century, which suffered from its accumulated energy of will, and from the wildest torrents and floods of selfishness (*Beyond Good and Evil* 137).

Nevertheless, this was not so much a complete transvaluation of values as a question of reorientation, of readjusting an internal balance of personality. He hoped for a Superman who would be not some future world-historical figure, but an individual ideal to be pursued by all strong, free spirits, "the Roman Caesar with Christ's soul" (*Will to Power* 380 section 983). While to some extent this was also true of Yeats (his concept of a Christ who was still the half-brother of Dionysus was almost certainly influenced by Nietzsche's slogan, "Dionysus versus Christ"), he thought more in terms of a historical dichotomy, of a dialectical "balance" provided by the alternating supremacy of opposing values, symbolized variously by the turning of the Great Wheel, by the whirl of interlocking gyres, or by the partial gyrations of the alternating rise and fall of the two ends of a seesaw. In *The Birth of Tragedy* Nietzsche also claimed that "all the celebrated figures of the Greek stage—Prometheus, Oedipus, etc.—are but masks of this original hero, Dionysus. There is godhead behind all these masks" (229). When dedicating *A Vision* to Pound, Yeats wrote:

> I would have him [Oedipus] balance Christ. . . . What if Christ and Oedipus or, to shift the names, Saint Catherine of Genoa and Michael Angelo, are the two scales of a balance, the two butt-ends of a seesaw? What if every two thousand and odd years something happens in the world to make one sacred, the other secular; one wise, the other foolish; one fair, the other foul; one divine, the other devilish? (27-29).

With such a culture change foul becomes fair, the devilish becomes divine. In **"The Second Coming"** this metamorphosis is taking place.

NOTES

[1] For other examples of critical responses referred to here see Davie 76-79; Ellman 257-60.

[2] See Bloom 317-25; Bohlmann 178-79 (although his interpretation of the poem is necessarily very brief in the context of his general thesis, in my view it comes closest to the meaning Yeats intended); Jeffares 238-44; Melchiori 35-42; Stallworthy 17-25; Weeks 281-92.

[3] For discussions of Nietzsche's influence on Yeats see Bohlmann; Thatcher 139-73.

[4] Yeats's philosophical system is set out in *A Vision.* For explanatory accounts see Bloom 210-91; Ellmann 146-64; Schricker 110-22; Stock 122-64.

[5] In the light of Yeats's consuming interest in *Thus Spake Zarathustra,* there is a remarkable similarity between Yeats's symbolism in "The Second Coming" and Nietzsche's in "The Three Metamorphoses": "But in the loneliest wilderness happeneth the second metamorphosis: here the spirit becometh a lion; freedom will it capture, and lordship in its own wilderness. Its last Lord it here seeketh: hostile will it be to him, and to its last God. . . . My brethren, wherefore is there need of the lion in the spirit? . . . To create itself freedom, and give a holy Nay even unto duty: for that, my brethren, there is need of the lion. To assume the right to new values—that is the most formidable assumption for a load-bearing and reverent spirit. Verily, unto such a spirit it is preying, and the work of a beast of prey" (43-44).

[6] Gordon and Fletcher suggest that the drawing known as *God with Eyes Turned upon His own Glory* was the work Yeats referred to (93).

[7] Zarathustra actively encourages his followers to embrace such an aesthetic: "Ye are ugly? Well then, my brethren, take the sublime about you, the mantle of the ugly" (63). Yeats suggested that Synge's tragic view of reality manifested itself as a "hunger for harsh facts, for ugly, surprising things" (*Essays and Introductions* 308), while according to Robert O'Driscoll, Yeats considered Synge to be "the living embodiment of the philosophical principles he was discovering in Nietzsche" (qtd. in Bohlmann 47).

[8] For other non-Nietzschean discussions of Dionysus see Gernet 48-70; Flaceliere 11-87. For discussions of Nietzsche's concept of Dionysus and the Dionysian see Bohlmann 40-47, 59-62; Kaufmann passim; Silk and Stern chapters 3-10.

WORKS CITED

Bloom, Harold. *Yeats.* New York: Oxford UP, 1970.

Bohlmann, Otto. *Yeats and Nietzsche.* New Jersey: Barnes, 1982.

Cavendish, Richard, ed. *Mythology.* London: Macdonald, 1987.

Davie, Donald. "Michael Robartes and the Dancer." *An Honoured Guest.* Ed. D. Donoghue and J. R. Mulryne. London: Arnold, 1965. 73-87.

Donoghue, Denis. "Yeats, Ancestral Houses, and Anglo-Ireland." *We Irish.* Berkeley: U of California P, 1986. 52-66.

Drake, Nicholas. *The Poetry of W. B. Yeats.* London: Penguin, 1991.

Ellman, Richard. *The Identity of Yeats.* 2nd ed. London: Macmillan, 1964.

Flaceliere, Robert. *Greek Oracles.* Trans. Douglas Gorman. London: Elek, 1965.

Gernet, Louis. *The Anthropology of Ancient Greece.* Trans. John Hamilton, and Blaise Nagy. London: Johns Hopkins UP, 1981.

Gordon, D.J., and Ian Fletcher. *Images of a Poet.* Manchester, Eng.: Exhibition Catalogue, 1961.

Henn, T. R. "The Rhetoric of Yeats." *In Excited Reverie.* Ed. A. Norman Jeffares and K. G. W. Cross. London: Macmillan, 1965. 102-22.

Jeffares, A. Norman. *A Commentary on the Collected Poems of W. B. Yeats.* London: Macmillan, 1968.

Kaufmann, Walter. *Nietzsche: Philosopher, Psychologist, Antichrist.* Princeton: Princeton UP, 1974.

Kinsella, Thomas. "W. B. Yeats, The British Empire, James Joyce and Mother Grogan." *P. N. Review 89* 19.3 (1993): 10-14.

Martin, Graham. "The Later Poetry of W. B. Yeats." *From James to Eliot.* London: Penguin, 1983. Vol. 7 of *The New Pelican Guide to English Literature.* Ed. Boris Ford. 9 vols. Rev. ed. 1983.

Melchiori, Giorgio. *The Whole Mystery of Art.* Westport: Greenwood, 1961.

Nietzsche, Friedrich. *The Complete Works of Friedrich Nietzsche.* Ed. Oscar Levy. 18 vols. New York: Macmillan, 1909-11. Reissued New York: Russell, 1964.

————.*The Birth of Tragedy.* Trans. Clifton P. Fadiman. *The Philosophy of Nietzsche.* New York: Random, n.d. 165-340.

————.*Ecce Homo.* Trans. Clifton P. Fadiman. *The Philosophy of Nietzsche.* New York: Random, n.d. 3-161.

————.*Beyond Good and Evil.* Trans. Helen Zimmern. *The Philosophy of Nietzsche.* New York: Random, n.d. 1-237.

————.*Thus Spake Zarathustra.* Trans. Thomas Common. *The Philosophy of Nietzsche.* New York: Random, n.d. 25-325.

————.*The Will to Power.* Ed. Walter Kaufmann. London: Weidenfeld, 1968.

Schricker, Gale C. *A New Species of Man.* Lewisburg: Bucknell UP, 1982.

Silk, M. S., and J. P. Stern. *Nietzsche on Tragedy.* Cambridge: Cambridge UP, 1981.

Stallworthy, Jon. *Between the Lines.* Oxford: Clarendon, 1965.

Stock, A. G. *W. B. Yeats: His Poetry and Thought.* Cambridge: Cambridge UP, 1961.

Thatcher, David S. *Nietzsche in England: 1890-1914.* Toronto: U of Toronto P, 1970.

Unterecker, John. *A Reader's Guide to William Butler Yeats.* London: Thames, 1959.

Weeks, D. "Image and Idea in Yeats's 'Second Coming'." *PMLA* 63.1 (1948): 281-92.

Yeats, W. B. *Autobiographies.* London: Macmillan, 1961.

————.*Essays and Introductions.* London: Macmillan, 1961.

————.*Explorations.* London: Macmillan, 1962.

————.*The Letters of W. B. Yeats.* Ed. A. Wade. London: Hart-Davis, 1954.

————.*The Variorum Edition of the Poems of W. B. Yeats.* Eds. P. Allt, and R. K. Alspach. New York: Macmillan, 1966.

————.*A Vision.* Rev. ed. London: Macmillan, 1962.

FURTHER READING

Criticism

Jeffares, A. Norman. "The Second Coming." In *A New Commentary on the Poems of W. B. Yeats,* pp. 201-07. Stanford, Calif.: Stanford University Press, 1984.

    Reprints Yeats's philosophical annotation to "The Second Coming" and glosses the text of the poem.

Mazzaro, Jerome L. "The Second Coming." *The Explicator* XVI, No. 1 (October 1957): item 6.

> Views the falcon in Yeats's poem as an "implicit symbol of the chaos described in subsequent lines and related genetically to the image of the sphinx."

Stallworthy, Jon. "The Second Coming." *Agenda* 9, No. 4 (Autumn 1971): 24-33.

> Examines historical references and developments in symbolism suggested by early manuscript versions of "The Second Coming." Stallworthy concludes his analysis by viewing the poem's relationship to Yeats's "A Prayer for My Daughter."

Van Doren, Mark. "The Second Coming." In *Introduction to Poetry*, pp. 80-85. New York: William Sloane Associates, Inc., 1951.

> Explication of "The Second Coming" that emphasizes the coming of change and the horror of the poem's second section.

The following sources published by Gale contain additional coverage of Yeats's life and career: *Concise Dictionary of British Literary Biography, 1890-1914*; *Contemporary Authors*, Vols. 104, 127; *Contemporary Authors New Revision Series*, Vol. 45; *Dictionary of Literary Biography*, Vols. 10, 19, 98, 156; *DISCovering Authors*; *Major 20th-Century Writers*, Vol. 1; *Poetry Criticism*, Vol. 20; and *World Literature Criticism*.

Twentieth-Century
Literary Criticism

Cumulative Indexes
Volumes 1-93

How to Use This Index

Literary Criticism Series
Cumulative Author Index

See also CA 9-12R; DLB 48; DLBY 97

Burr, Anne 1937- .... **CLC 6**
   See also CA 25-28R

Burroughs, Edgar Rice 1875-1950 **TCLC 2, 32;**
   DAM NOV
   See also AAYA 11; CA 104; 132; DLB 8; MTCW
   1, 2; SATA 41

Burroughs, William S(eward) 1914-1997**CLC 1,**
   2, 5, 15, 22, 42, 75, 109; DA; DAB; DAC;
   DAM MST, NOV, POP; WLC
   See also AITN 2; CA 9-12R; 160; CANR 20, 52;
   DLB 2, 8, 16, 152; DLBY 81, 97; MTCW 1, 2

Burton, Sir Richard F(rancis) 1821-1890 **NCLC**
   42
   See also DLB 55, 166, 184

Busch, Frederick 1941- .... **CLC 7, 10, 18, 47**
   See also CA 33-36R; CAAS 1; CANR 45, 73; DLB
   6

Bush, Ronald 1946- .... **CLC 34**
   See also CA 136

Bustos, F(rancisco)
   See Borges, Jorge Luis

Bustos Domecq, H(onorio)
   See Bioy Casares, Adolfo; Borges, Jorge Luis

Butler, Octavia E(stelle) 1947- ..... **CLC 38, 121;**
   BLCS; DAM MULT, POP
   See also AAYA 18; BW 2, 3; CA 73-76; CANR
   12, 24, 38, 73; DLB 33; MTCW 1, 2; SATA 84

Butler, Robert Olen (Jr.) 1945- .. **CLC 81; DAM**
   POP
   See also CA 112; CANR 66; DLB 173; INT 112;
   MTCW 1

Butler, Samuel 1612-1680 .... **LC 16, 43**
   See also DLB 101, 126

Butler, Samuel 1835-1902**TCLC 1, 33; DA; DAB;**
   DAC; DAM MST, NOV; WLC
   See also CA 143; CDBLB 1890-1914; DLB 18, 57,
   174

Butler, Walter C.
   See Faust, Frederick (Schiller)

Butor, Michel (Marie Francois) 1926- **CLC 1, 3,**
   8, 11, 15
   See also CA 9-12R; CANR 33, 66; DLB 83;
   MTCW 1, 2

Butts, Mary 1892(?)-1937 .... **TCLC 77**
   See also CA 148

Buzo, Alexander (John) 1944- .... **CLC 61**
   See also CA 97-100; CANR 17, 39, 69

Buzzati, Dino 1906-1972 .... **CLC 36**
   See also CA 160; 33-36R; DLB 177

Byars, Betsy (Cromer) 1928- .... **CLC 35**
   See also AAYA 19; CA 33-36R; CANR 18, 36, 57;
   CLR 1, 16; DLB 52; INT CANR-18; JRDA;
   MAICYA; MTCW 1; SAAS 1; SATA 4, 46,
   80; SATA-Essay 108

Byatt, A(ntonia) S(usan Drabble) 1936- **CLC 19,**
   65; DAM NOV, POP
   See also CA 13-16R; CANR 13, 33, 50, 75; DLB
   14, 194; MTCW 1, 2

Byrne, David 1952- .... **CLC 26**
   See also CA 127

Byrne, John Keyes 1926-
   See Leonard, Hugh
   See also CA 102; CANR 78; INT 102

Byron, George Gordon (Noel) 1788-1824**NCLC 2,**
   12; DA; DAB; DAC; DAM MST, POET; PC
   16; WLC
   See also CDBLB 1789-1832; DLB 96, 110

Byron, Robert 1905-1941 .... **TCLC 67**
   See also CA 160; DLB 195

C. 3. 3.
   See Wilde, Oscar

Caballero, Fernan 1796-1877 .... **NCLC 10**

Cabell, Branch
   See Cabell, James Branch

Cabell, James Branch 1879-1958 .... **TCLC 6**
   See also CA 105; 152; DLB 9, 78; MTCW 1

Cable, George Washington 1844-1925 **T C L C**
   4; SSC 4
   See also CA 104; 155; DLB 12, 74; DLBD 13

Cabral de Melo Neto, Joao 1920- **CLC 76; DAM**
   MULT
   See also CA 151

Cabrera Infante, G(uillermo) 1929-**CLC 5, 25, 45,**
   120; DAM MULT; HLC
   See also CA 85-88; CANR 29, 65; DLB 113; HW
   1, 2; MTCW 1, 2

Cade, Toni
   See Bambara, Toni Cade

Cadmus and Harmonia
   See Buchan, John

Caedmon fl. 658-680 .... **CMLC 7**
   See also DLB 146

Caeiro, Alberto
   See Pessoa, Fernando (Antonio Nogueira)

Cage, John (Milton, Jr.) 1912-1992 .... **CLC 41**
   See also CA 13-16R; 169; CANR 9, 78; DLB 193;
   INT CANR-9

Cahan, Abraham 1860-1951 .... **TCLC 71**
   See also CA 108; 154; DLB 9, 25, 28

Cain, G.
   See Cabrera Infante, G(uillermo)

Cain, Guillermo
   See Cabrera Infante, G(uillermo)

Cain, James M(allahan) 1892-1977**CLC 3, 11, 28**
   See also AITN 1; CA 17-20R; 73-76; CANR 8, 34,
   61; MTCW 1

Caine, Mark
   See Raphael, Frederic (Michael)

Calasso, Roberto 1941- .... **CLC 81**
   See also CA 143

Calderon de la Barca, Pedro 1600-1681 . **LC 23;**
   DC 3; HLCS 1

Caldwell, Erskine (Preston) 1903-1987**CLC 1, 8,**
   14, 50, 60; DAM NOV; SSC 19
   See also AITN 1; CA 1-4R; 121; CAAS 1; CANR
   2, 33; DLB 9, 86; MTCW 1, 2

Caldwell, (Janet Miriam) Taylor (Holland) 1900-
   1985 .... **CLC 2, 28, 39; DAM NOV, POP**
   See also CA 5-8R; 116; CANR 5; DLBD 17

Calhoun, John Caldwell 1782-1850 ..... **NCLC 15**
   See also DLB 3

Calisher, Hortense 1911- **CLC 2, 4, 8, 38; DAM**
   NOV; SSC 15
   See also CA 1-4R; CANR 1, 22, 67; DLB 2; INT
   CANR-22; MTCW 1, 2

Callaghan, Morley Edward 1903-1990**CLC 3, 14,**
   41, 65; DAC; DAM MST
   See also CA 9-12R; 132; CANR 33, 73; DLB 68;
   MTCW 1, 2

Callimachus c. 305B.C.-c. 240B.C. ..... **CMLC 18**
   See also DLB 176

Calvin, John 1509-1564 .... **LC 37**

Calvino, Italo 1923-1985**CLC 5, 8, 11, 22, 33, 39,**
   73; DAM NOV; SSC 3
   See also CA 85-88; 116; CANR 23, 61; DLB 196;
   MTCW 1, 2

Cameron, Carey 1952- .... **CLC 59**
   See also CA 135

Cameron, Peter 1959- .... **CLC 44**
   See also CA 125; CANR 50

Campana, Dino 1885-1932 .... **TCLC 20**
   See also CA 117; DLB 114

Campanella, Tommaso 1568-1639 .... **LC 32**

Campbell, John W(ood, Jr.) 1910-1971 . **CLC 32**
   See also CA 21-22; 29-32R; CANR 34; CAP 2;
   DLB 8; MTCW 1

Campbell, Joseph 1904-1987 .... **CLC 69**
   See also AAYA 3; BEST 89:2; CA 1-4R; 124;
   CANR 3, 28, 61; MTCW 1, 2

Campbell, Maria 1940- .... **CLC 85; DAC**
   See also CA 102; CANR 54; NNAL

Campbell, (John) Ramsey 1946-**CLC 42; SSC 19**
   See also CA 57-60; CANR 7; INT CANR-7

Campbell, (Ignatius) Roy (Dunnachie) 1901-
   1957 .... **TCLC 5**
   See also CA 104; 155; DLB 20; MTCW 2

Campbell, Thomas 1777-1844 .... **NCLC 19**
   See also DLB 93; 144

Campbell, Wilfred .... **TCLC 9**
   See also Campbell, William

Campbell, William 1858(?)-1918
   See Campbell, Wilfred
   See also CA 106; DLB 92

Campion, Jane .... **CLC 95**
   See also CA 138

Campos, Alvaro de
   See Pessoa, Fernando (Antonio Nogueira)

Camus, Albert 1913-1960 **CLC 1, 2, 4, 9, 11, 14,**
   32, 63, 69; DA; DAB; DAC; DAM DRAM,
   MST, NOV; DC 2; SSC 9; WLC
   See also CA 89-92; DLB 72; MTCW 1, 2

Canby, Vincent 1924- .... **CLC 13**
   See also CA 81-84

Cancale
   See Desnos, Robert

Canetti, Elias 1905-1994 .. **CLC 3, 14, 25, 75, 86**
   See also CA 21-24R; 146; CANR 23, 61, 79; DLB
   85, 124; MTCW 1, 2

Canfield, Dorothea F.
   See Fisher, Dorothy (Frances) Canfield

Canfield, Dorothea Frances
   See Fisher, Dorothy (Frances) Canfield

Canfield, Dorothy
   See Fisher, Dorothy (Frances) Canfield

Canin, Ethan 1960- .... **CLC 55**
   See also CA 131; 135

Cannon, Curt
   See Hunter, Evan

Cao, Lan 1961- .... **CLC 109**
   See also CA 165

Cape, Judith
   See Page, P(atricia) K(athleen)

Capek, Karel 1890-1938 **TCLC 6, 37; DA; DAB;**
   DAC; DAM DRAM, MST, NOV; DC 1; WLC
   See also CA 104; 140; MTCW 1

Capote, Truman 1924-1984**CLC 1, 3, 8, 13, 19, 34,**
   38, 58; DA; DAB; DAC; DAM MST, NOV,
   POP; SSC 2; WLC
   See also CA 5-8R; 113; CANR 18, 62; CDALB
   1941-1968; DLB 2, 185; DLBY 80, 84; MTCW
   1, 2; SATA 91

Capra, Frank 1897-1991 .... **CLC 16**
   See also CA 61-64; 135

Caputo, Philip 1941- .... **CLC 32**
   See also CA 73-76; CANR 40

Caragiale, Ion Luca 1852-1912 .... **TCLC 76**
   See also CA 157

Card, Orson Scott 1951- **CLC 44, 47, 50; DAM**
   POP
   See also AAYA 11; CA 102; CANR 27, 47, 73;
   INT CANR-27; MTCW 1, 2; SATA 83

Cardenal, Ernesto 1925- . **CLC 31; DAM MULT,**
   POET; HLC; PC 22
   See also CA 49-52; CANR 2, 32, 66; HW 1, 2;
   MTCW 1, 2

Cardozo, Benjamin N(athan) 1870-1938**TCLC 65**
   See also CA 117; 164

Carducci, Giosue (Alessandro Giuseppe) 1835-
   1907 .... **TCLC 32**
   See also CA 163

Carew, Thomas 1595(?)-1640 .... **LC 13**
   See also DLB 126

Carey, Ernestine Gilbreth 1908- .... **CLC 17**
   See also CA 5-8R; CANR 71; SATA 2

Carey, Peter 1943- .... **CLC 40, 55, 96**
   See also CA 123; 127; CANR 53, 76; INT 127;
   MTCW 1, 2; SATA 94

Carleton, William 1794-1869 .... **NCLC 3**
   See also DLB 159

Carlisle, Henry (Coffin) 1926- .... **CLC 33**

CDALB 1968-1988; DLB 2, 173, 185; DLBY 81, 86; MTCW 1, 2

Dietrich, Robert
See Hunt, E(verette) Howard, (Jr.)

Difusa, Pati
See Almodovar, Pedro

Dillard, Annie 1945-CLC 9, 60, 115; DAM NOV
See also AAYA 6; CA 49-52; CANR 3, 43, 62; DLBY 80; MTCW 1, 2; SATA 10

Dillard, R(ichard) H(enry) W(ilde) 1937- CLC 5
See also CA 21-24R; CAAS 7; CANR 10; DLB 5

Dillon, Eilis 1920-1994 .... **CLC 17**
See also CA 9-12R; 147; CAAS 3; CANR 4, 38, 78; CLR 26; MAICYA; SATA 2, 74; SATA-Essay 105; SATA-Obit 83

Dimont, Penelope
See Mortimer, Penelope (Ruth)

Dinesen, Isak .... CLC 10, 29, 95; SSC 7
See also Blixen, Karen (Christentze Dinesen)
See also MTCW 1

Ding Ling .... **CLC 68**
See also Chiang, Pin-chin

Diphusa, Patty
See Almodovar, Pedro

Disch, Thomas M(ichael) 1940- .... CLC 7, 36
See also AAYA 17; CA 21-24R; CAAS 4; CANR 17, 36, 54; CLR 18; DLB 8; MAICYA; MTCW 1, 2; SAAS 15; SATA 92

Disch, Tom
See Disch, Thomas M(ichael)

d'Isly, Georges
See Simenon, Georges (Jacques Christian)

Disraeli, Benjamin 1804-1881 . NCLC 2, 39, 79
See also DLB 21, 55

Ditcum, Steve
See Crumb, R(obert)

Dixon, Paige
See Corcoran, Barbara

Dixon, Stephen 1936- .... CLC 52; SSC 16
See also CA 89-92; CANR 17, 40, 54; DLB 130

Doak, Annie
See Dillard, Annie

Dobell, Sydney Thompson 1824-1874 .. NCLC 43
See also DLB 32

Doblin, Alfred .... TCLC 13
See also Doeblin, Alfred

Dobrolyubov, Nikolai Alexandrovich 1836-1861 NCLC 5

Dobson, Austin 1840-1921 .... TCLC 79
See also DLB 35; 144

Dobyns, Stephen 1941- .... CLC 37
See also CA 45-48; CANR 2, 18

Doctorow, E(dgar) L(aurence) 1931-. CLC 6, 11, 15, 18, 37, 44, 65, 113; DAM NOV, POP
See also AAYA 22; AITN 2; BEST 89:3; CA 45-48; CANR 2, 33, 51, 76; CDALB 1968-1988; DLB 2, 28, 173; DLBY 80; MTCW 1, 2

Dodgson, Charles Lutwidge 1832-1898
See Carroll, Lewis
See also CLR 2; DA; DAB; DAC; DAM MST, NOV, POET; MAICYA; SATA 100; YABC 2

Dodson, Owen (Vincent) 1914-1983CLC 79; BLC 1; DAM MULT
See also BW 1; CA 65-68; 110; CANR 24; DLB 76

Doeblin, Alfred 1878-1957 .... TCLC 13
See also Doblin, Alfred
See also CA 110; 141; DLB 66

Doerr, Harriet 1910- .... CLC 34
See also CA 117; 122; CANR 47; INT 122

Domecq, H(onorio Bustos)
See Bioy Casares, Adolfo

Domecq, H(onorio) Bustos
See Bioy Casares, Adolfo; Borges, Jorge Luis

Domini, Rey
See Lorde, Audre (Geraldine)

Dominique

See Proust, (Valentin-Louis-George-Eugene-) Marcel

Don, A
See Stephen, Sir Leslie

Donaldson, Stephen R. 1947-CLC 46; DAM POP
See also CA 89-92; CANR 13, 55; INT CANR-13

Donleavy, J(ames) P(atrick) 1926- . CLC 1, 4, 6, 10, 45
See also AITN 2; CA 9-12R; CANR 24, 49, 62, 80; DLB 6, 173; INT CANR-24; MTCW 1, 2

Donne, John 1572-1631 .... LC 10, 24; DA; DAB; DAC; DAM MST, POET; PC 1; WLC
See also CDBLB Before 1660; DLB 121, 151

Donnell, David 1939(?)- .... CLC 34

Donoghue, P. S.
See Hunt, E(verette) Howard, (Jr.)

Donoso (Yanez), Jose 1924-1996CLC 4, 8, 11, 32, 99; DAM MULT; HLC; SSC 34
See also CA 81-84; 155; CANR 32, 73; DLB 113; HW 1, 2; MTCW 1, 2

Donovan, John 1928-1992 .... CLC 35
See also AAYA 20; CA 97-100; 137; CLR 3; MAICYA; SATA 72; SATA-Brief 29

Don Roberto
See Cunninghame Graham, R(obert) B(ontine)

Doolittle, Hilda 1886-1961CLC 3, 8, 14, 31, 34, 73; DA; DAC; DAM MST, POET; PC 5; WLC
See also H. D.
See also CA 97-100; CANR 35; DLB 4, 45; MTCW 1, 2

Dorfman, Ariel 1942- CLC 48, 77; DAM MULT; HLC
See also CA 124; 130; CANR 67, 70; HW 1, 2; INT 130

Dorn, Edward (Merton) 1929- .... CLC 10, 18
See also CA 93-96; CANR 42, 79; DLB 5; INT 93-96

Dorris, Michael (Anthony) 1945-1997 CLC 109; DAM MULT, NOV
See also AAYA 20; BEST 90:1; CA 102; 157; CANR 19, 46, 75; CLR 58; DLB 175; MTCW 2; NNAL; SATA 75; SATA-Obit 94

Dorris, Michael A.
See Dorris, Michael (Anthony)

Dorsan, Luc
See Simenon, Georges (Jacques Christian)

Dorsange, Jean
See Simenon, Georges (Jacques Christian)

Dos Passos, John (Roderigo) 1896-1970CLC 1, 4, 8, 11, 15, 25, 34, 82; DA; DAB; DAC; DAM MST, NOV; WLC
See also CA 1-4R; 29-32R; CANR 3; CDALB 1929-1941; DLB 4, 9; DLBD 1, 15; DLBY 96; MTCW 1, 2

Dossage, Jean
See Simenon, Georges (Jacques Christian)

Dostoevsky, Fedor Mikhailovich 1821-1881NCLC 2, 7, 21, 33, 43; DA; DAB; DAC; DAM MST, NOV; SSC 2, 33; WLC

Doughty, Charles M(ontagu) 1843-1926TCLC 27
See also CA 115; DLB 19, 57, 174

Douglas, Ellen .... CLC 73
See also Haxton, Josephine Ayres; Williamson, Ellen Douglas

Douglas, Gavin 1475(?)-1522 .... LC 20
See also DLB 132

Douglas, George
See Brown, George Douglas

Douglas, Keith (Castellain) 1920-1944 TCLC 40
See also CA 160; DLB 27

Douglas, Leonard
See Bradbury, Ray (Douglas)

Douglas, Michael
See Crichton, (John) Michael

Douglas, (George) Norman 1868-1952 TCLC 68
See also CA 119; 157; DLB 34, 195

Douglas, William

See Brown, George Douglas

Douglass, Frederick 1817(?)-1895 .NCLC 7, 55; BLC 1; DA; DAC; DAM MST, MULT; WLC
See also CDALB 1640-1865; DLB 1, 43, 50, 79; SATA 29

Dourado, (Waldomiro Freitas) Autran 1926-CLC 23, 60
See also CA 25-28R; CANR 34, 81; DLB 145; HW 2

Dourado, Waldomiro Autran
See Dourado, (Waldomiro Freitas) Autran

Dove, Rita (Frances) 1952-. CLC 50, 81; BLCS; DAM MULT, POET; PC 6
See also BW 2; CA 109; CAAS 19; CANR 27, 42, 68, 76; CDALBS; DLB 120; MTCW 1

Doveglion
See Villa, Jose Garcia

Dowell, Coleman 1925-1985 .... CLC 60
See also CA 25-28R; 117; CANR 10; DLB 130

Dowson, Ernest (Christopher) 1867-1900TCLC 4
See also CA 105; 150; DLB 19, 135

Doyle, A. Conan
See Doyle, Arthur Conan

Doyle, Arthur Conan 1859-1930 .. TCLC 7; DA; DAB; DAC; DAM MST, NOV; SSC 12; WLC
See also AAYA 14; CA 104; 122; CDBLB 1890-1914; DLB 18, 70, 156, 178; MTCW 1, 2; SATA 24

Doyle, Conan
See Doyle, Arthur Conan

Doyle, John
See Graves, Robert (von Ranke)

Doyle, Roddy 1958(?)- .... CLC 81
See also AAYA 14; CA 143; CANR 73; DLB 194

Doyle, Sir A. Conan
See Doyle, Arthur Conan

Doyle, Sir Arthur Conan
See Doyle, Arthur Conan

Dr. A
See Asimov, Isaac; Silverstein, Alvin

Drabble, Margaret 1939- CLC 2, 3, 5, 8, 10, 22, 53; DAB; DAC; DAM MST, NOV, POP
See also CA 13-16R; CANR 18, 35, 63; CDBLB 1960 to Present; DLB 14, 155; MTCW 1, 2; SATA 48

Drapier, M. B.
See Swift, Jonathan

Drayham, James
See Mencken, H(enry) L(ouis)

Drayton, Michael 1563-1631 LC 8; DAM POET
See also DLB 121

Dreadstone, Carl
See Campbell, (John) Ramsey

Dreiser, Theodore (Herman Albert) 1871-1945 TCLC 10, 18, 35, 83; DA; DAC; DAM MST, NOV; SSC 30; WLC
See also CA 106; 132; CDALB 1865-1917; DLB 9, 12, 102, 137; DLBD 1; MTCW 1, 2

Drexler, Rosalyn 1926- ....CLC 2, 6
See also CA 81-84; CANR 68

Dreyer, Carl Theodor 1889-1968 .... CLC 16
See also CA 116

Drieu la Rochelle, Pierre(-Eugene) 1893-1945 TCLC 21
See also CA 117; DLB 72

Drinkwater, John 1882-1937 .... TCLC 57
See also CA 109; 149; DLB 10, 19, 149

Drop Shot
See Cable, George Washington

Droste-Hulshoff, Annette Freiin von 1797-1848 NCLC 3
See also DLB 133

Drummond, Walter
See Silverberg, Robert

Drummond, William Henry 1854-1907 TCLC 25
See also CA 160; DLB 92

See also CA 9-12R
Ehrenbourg, Ilya (Grigoryevich)
See Ehrenburg, Ilya (Grigoryevich)
Ehrenburg, Ilya (Grigoryevich) 1891-1967
CLC 18, 34, 62
See also CA 102; 25-28R
Ehrenburg, Ilyo (Grigoryevich)
See Ehrenburg, Ilya (Grigoryevich)
Ehrenreich, Barbara 1941- .... **CLC 110**
See also BEST 90:4; CA 73-76; CANR 16, 37, 62;
MTCW 1, 2
Eich, Guenter 1907-1972 .... **CLC 15**
See also CA 111; 93-96; DLB 69, 124
Eichendorff, Joseph Freiherr von 1788-1857
NCLC 8
See also DLB 90
Eigner, Larry .... **CLC 9**
See also Eigner, Laurence (Joel)
See also CAAS 23; DLB 5
Eigner, Laurence (Joel) 1927-1996
See Eigner, Larry
See also CA 9-12R; 151; CANR 6; DLB 193
Einstein, Albert 1879-1955 .... **TCLC 65**
See also CA 121; 133; MTCW 1, 2
Eiseley, Loren Corey 1907-1977 .... **CLC 7**
See also AAYA 5; CA 1-4R; 73-76; CANR 6;
DLBD 17
Eisenstadt, Jill 1963- .... **CLC 50**
See also CA 140
Eisenstein, Sergei (Mikhailovich) 1898-1948
TCLC 57
See also CA 114; 149
Eisner, Simon
See Kornbluth, C(yril) M.
Ekeloef, (Bengt) Gunnar 1907-1968 .... **CLC 27;**
DAM POET; PC 23
See also CA 123; 25-28R
Ekelof, (Bengt) Gunnar
See Ekeloef, (Bengt) Gunnar
Ekelund, Vilhelm 1880-1949 .... **TCLC 75**
Ekwensi, C. O. D.
See Ekwensi, Cyprian (Odiatu Duaka)
Ekwensi, Cyprian (Odiatu Duaka) 1921- **CLC 4;**
BLC 1; DAM MULT
See also BW 2, 3; CA 29-32R; CANR 18, 42, 74;
DLB 117; MTCW 1, 2; SATA 66
Elaine .... **TCLC 18**
See also Leverson, Ada
El Crummo
See Crumb, R(obert)
Elder, Lonne III 1931-1996 .... **DC 8**
See also BLC 1; BW 1, 3; CA 81-84; 152; CANR
25; DAM MULT; DLB 7, 38, 44
Elia
See Lamb, Charles
Eliade, Mircea 1907-1986 .... **CLC 19**
See also CA 65-68; 119; CANR 30, 62; MTCW 1
Eliot, A. D.
See Jewett, (Theodora) Sarah Orne
Eliot, Alice
See Jewett, (Theodora) Sarah Orne
Eliot, Dan
See Silverberg, Robert
Eliot, George 1819-1880 **NCLC 4, 13, 23, 41, 49;**
DA; DAB; DAC; DAM MST, NOV; PC 20;
WLC
See also CDBLB 1832-1890; DLB 21, 35, 55
Eliot, John 1604-1690 .... **LC 5**
See also DLB 24
Eliot, T(homas) S(tearns) 1888-1965 **CLC 1, 2, 3,**
6, 9, 10, 13, 15, 24, 34, 41, 55, 57, 113; DA;
DAB; DAC; DAM DRAM, MST, POET; PC
5; WLC
See also AAYA 28; CA 5-8R; 25-28R; CANR 41;
CDALB 1929-1941; DLB 7, 10, 45, 63; DLBY
88; MTCW 1, 2
Elizabeth 1866-1941 .... **TCLC 41**

Elkin, Stanley L(awrence) 1930-1995 **CLC 4,**
6, 9, 14, 27, 51, 91; DAM NOV, POP; SSC
12
See also CA 9-12R; 148; CANR 8, 46; DLB 2, 28;
DLBY 80; INT CANR-8; MTCW 1, 2
Elledge, Scott .... **CLC 34**
Elliot, Don
See Silverberg, Robert
Elliott, Don
See Silverberg, Robert
Elliott, George P(aul) 1918-1980 .... **CLC 2**
See also CA 1-4R; 97-100; CANR 2
Elliott, Janice 1931- .... **CLC 47**
See also CA 13-16R; CANR 8, 29; DLB 14
Elliott, Sumner Locke 1917-1991 .... **CLC 38**
See also CA 5-8R; 134; CANR 2, 21
Elliott, William
See Bradbury, Ray (Douglas)
Ellis, A. E. .... **CLC 7**
Ellis, Alice Thomas .... **CLC 40**
See also Haycraft, Anna
See also DLB 194; MTCW 1
Ellis, Bret Easton 1964- **CLC 39, 71, 117; DAM**
POP
See also AAYA 2; CA 118; 123; CANR 51, 74;
INT 123; MTCW 1
Ellis, (Henry) Havelock 1859-1939 ..... **TCLC 14**
See also CA 109; 169; DLB 190
Ellis, Landon
See Ellison, Harlan (Jay)
Ellis, Trey 1962- .... **CLC 55**
See also CA 146
Ellison, Harlan (Jay) 1934- **CLC 1, 13, 42; DAM**
POP; SSC 14
See also AAYA 29; CA 5-8R; CANR 5, 46; DLB
8; INT CANR-5; MTCW 1, 2
Ellison, Ralph (Waldo) 1914-1994 **CLC 1, 3, 11, 54,**
86, 114; BLC 1; DA; DAB; DAC; DAM MST,
MULT, NOV; SSC 26; WLC
See also AAYA 19; BW 1, 3; CA 9-12R; 145;
CANR 24, 53; CDALB 1941-1968; DLB 2, 76;
DLBY 94; MTCW 1, 2
Ellmann, Lucy (Elizabeth) 1956- .... **CLC 61**
See also CA 128
Ellmann, Richard (David) 1918-1987 ..... **CLC 50**
See also BEST 89:2; CA 1-4R; 122; CANR 2, 28,
61; DLB 103; DLBY 87; MTCW 1, 2
Elman, Richard (Martin) 1934-1997 ..... **CLC 19**
See also CA 17-20R; 163; CAAS 3; CANR 47
Elron
See Hubbard, L(afayette) Ron(ald)
Eluard, Paul .... **TCLC 7, 41**
See also Grindel, Eugene
Elyot, Sir Thomas 1490(?)-1546 .... **LC 11**
Elytis, Odysseus 1911-1996 .... **CLC 15, 49, 100;**
DAM POET; PC 21
See also CA 102; 151; MTCW 1, 2
Emecheta, (Florence Onye) Buchi 1944- **CLC 14,**
48; BLC 2; DAM MULT
See also BW 2, 3; CA 81-84; CANR 27, 81; DLB
117; MTCW 1, 2; SATA 66
Emerson, Mary Moody 1774-1863 .... **NCLC 66**
Emerson, Ralph Waldo 1803-1882 .**NCLC 1, 38;**
DA; DAB; DAC; DAM MST, POET; PC 18;
WLC
See also CDALB 1640-1865; DLB 1, 59, 73
Eminescu, Mihail 1850-1889 .... **NCLC 33**
Empson, William 1906-1984 **CLC 3, 8, 19, 33, 34**
See also CA 17-20R; 112; CANR 31, 61; DLB 20;
MTCW 1, 2
Enchi, Fumiko (Ueda) 1905-1986 .... **CLC 31**
See also CA 129; 121; DLB 182
Ende, Michael (Andreas Helmuth) 1929-1995
CLC 31
See also CA 118; 124; 149; CANR 36; CLR 14;
DLB 75; MAICYA; SATA 61; SATA-Brief 42;
SATA-Obit 86

Endo, Shusaku 1923-1996 **CLC 7, 14, 19, 54,**
99; DAM NOV
See also CA 29-32R; 153; CANR 21, 54; DLB 182;
MTCW 1, 2
Engel, Marian 1933-1985 .... **CLC 36**
See also CA 25-28R; CANR 12; DLB 53; INT
CANR-12
Engelhardt, Frederick
See Hubbard, L(afayette) Ron(ald)
Enright, D(ennis) J(oseph) 1920- ..**CLC 4, 8, 31**
See also CA 1-4R; CANR 1, 42; DLB 27; SATA
25
Enzensberger, Hans Magnus 1929- ...... **CLC 43**
See also CA 116; 119
Ephron, Nora 1941- .... **CLC 17, 31**
See also AITN 2; CA 65-68; CANR 12, 39
Epicurus 341B.C.-270B.C. .... **CMLC 21**
See also DLB 176
Epsilon
See Betjeman, John
Epstein, Daniel Mark 1948- .... **CLC 7**
See also CA 49-52; CANR 2, 53
Epstein, Jacob 1956- .... **CLC 19**
See also CA 114
Epstein, Jean 1897-1953 .... **TCLC 92**
Epstein, Joseph 1937- .... **CLC 39**
See also CA 112; 119; CANR 50, 65
Epstein, Leslie 1938- .... **CLC 27**
See also CA 73-76; CAAS 12; CANR 23, 69
Equiano, Olaudah 1745(?)-1797 ..**LC 16; BLC 2;**
DAM MULT
See also DLB 37, 50
ER .... **TCLC 33**
See also CA 160; DLB 85
Erasmus, Desiderius 1469(?)-1536 .... **LC 16**
Erdman, Paul E(mil) 1932- .... **CLC 25**
See also AITN 1; CA 61-64; CANR 13, 43
Erdrich, Louise 1954- .. **CLC 39, 54, 120; DAM**
MULT, NOV, POP
See also AAYA 10; BEST 89:1; CA 114; CANR
41, 62; CDALBS; DLB 152, 175, 206; MTCW
1; NNAL; SATA 94
Erenburg, Ilya (Grigoryevich)
See Ehrenburg, Ilya (Grigoryevich)
Erickson, Stephen Michael 1950-
See Erickson, Steve
See also CA 129
Erickson, Steve 1950- .... **CLC 64**
See also Erickson, Stephen Michael
See also CANR 60, 68
Ericson, Walter
See Fast, Howard (Melvin)
Eriksson, Buntel
See Bergman, (Ernst) Ingmar
Ernaux, Annie 1940- .... **CLC 88**
See also CA 147
Erskine, John 1879-1951 .... **TCLC 84**
See also CA 112; 159; DLB 9, 102
Eschenbach, Wolfram von
See Wolfram von Eschenbach
Eseki, Bruno
See Mphahlele, Ezekiel
Esenin, Sergei (Alexandrovich) 1895-1925 **TCLC**
4
See also CA 104
Eshleman, Clayton 1935- .... **CLC 7**
See also CA 33-36R; CAAS 6; DLB 5
Espriella, Don Manuel Alvarez
See Southey, Robert
Espriu, Salvador 1913-1985 .... **CLC 9**
See also CA 154; 115; DLB 134
Espronceda, Jose de 1808-1842 .... **NCLC 39**
Esse, James
See Stephens, James
Esterbrook, Tom
See Hubbard, L(afayette) Ron(ald)
Estleman, Loren D. 1952- .. **CLC 48; DAM NOV,**

See Kuttner, Henry

Gardons, S. S.
See Snodgrass, W(illiam) D(e Witt)

Garfield, Leon 1921-1996 .... **CLC 12**
See also AAYA 8; CA 17-20R; 152; CANR 38, 41, 78; CLR 21; DLB 161; JRDA; MAICYA; SATA 1, 32, 76; SATA-Obit 90

Garland, (Hannibal) Hamlin 1860-1940 **TCLC 3; SSC 18**
See also CA 104; DLB 12, 71, 78, 186

Garneau, (Hector de) Saint-Denys 1912-1943 **TCLC 13**
See also CA 111; DLB 88

Garner, Alan 1934- .. **CLC 17; DAB; DAM POP**
See also AAYA 18; CA 73-76; CANR 15, 64; CLR 20; DLB 161; MAICYA; MTCW 1, 2; SATA 18, 69; SATA-Essay 108

Garner, Hugh 1913-1979 .... **CLC 13**
See also CA 69-72; CANR 31; DLB 68

Garnett, David 1892-1981 .... **CLC 3**
See also CA 5-8R; 103; CANR 17, 79; DLB 34; MTCW 2

Garos, Stephanie
See Katz, Steve

Garrett, George (Palmer) 1929- **CLC 3, 11, 51; SSC 30**
See also CA 1-4R; CAAS 5; CANR 1, 42, 67; DLB 2, 5, 130, 152; DLBY 83

Garrick, David 1717-1779 . **LC 15; DAM DRAM**
See also DLB 84

Garrigue, Jean 1914-1972 .... **CLC 2, 8**
See also CA 5-8R; 37-40R; CANR 20

Garrison, Frederick
See Sinclair, Upton (Beall)

Garth, Will
See Hamilton, Edmond; Kuttner, Henry

Garvey, Marcus (Moziah, Jr.) 1887-1940 . **TCLC 41; BLC 2; DAM MULT**
See also BW 1; CA 120; 124; CANR 79

Gary, Romain .... **CLC 25**
See also Kacew, Romain
See also DLB 83

Gascar, Pierre .... **CLC 11**
See also Fournier, Pierre

Gascoyne, David (Emery) 1916- .... **CLC 45**
See also CA 65-68; CANR 10, 28, 54; DLB 20; MTCW 1

Gaskell, Elizabeth Cleghorn 1810-1865 **NCLC 70; DAB; DAM MST; SSC 25**
See also CDBLB 1832-1890; DLB 21, 144, 159

Gass, William H(oward) 1924- **CLC 1, 2, 8, 11, 15, 39; SSC 12**
See also CA 17-20R; CANR 30, 71; DLB 2; MTCW 1, 2

Gasset, Jose Ortega y
See Ortega y Gasset, Jose

Gates, Henry Louis, Jr. 1950- .. **CLC 65; BLCS; DAM MULT**
See also BW 2, 3; CA 109; CANR 25, 53, 75; DLB 67; MTCW 1

Gautier, Theophile 1811-1872 **NCLC 1, 59; DAM POET; PC 18; SSC 20**
See also DLB 119

Gawsworth, John
See Bates, H(erbert) E(rnest)

Gay, John 1685-1732 .... **LC 49; DAM DRAM**
See also DLB 84, 95

Gay, Oliver
See Gogarty, Oliver St. John

Gaye, Marvin (Penze) 1939-1984 .... **CLC 26**
See also CA 112

Gebler, Carlo (Ernest) 1954- .... **CLC 39**
See also CA 119; 133

Gee, Maggie (Mary) 1948- .... **CLC 57**
See also CA 130; DLB 207

Gee, Maurice (Gough) 1931- .... **CLC 29**
See also CA 97-100; CANR 67; CLR 56; SATA 46, 101

Gelbart, Larry (Simon) 1923- .... **CLC 21, 61**
See also CA 73-76; CANR 45

Gelber, Jack 1932- .... **CLC 1, 6, 14, 79**
See also CA 1-4R; CANR 2; DLB 7

Gellhorn, Martha (Ellis) 1908-1998 **CLC 14, 60**
See also CA 77-80; 164; CANR 44; DLBY 82, 98

Genet, Jean 1910-1986 **CLC 1, 2, 5, 10, 14, 44, 46; DAM DRAM**
See also CA 13-16R; CANR 18; DLB 72; DLBY 86; MTCW 1, 2

Gent, Peter 1942- .... **CLC 29**
See also AITN 1; CA 89-92; DLBY 82

Gentlewoman in New England, A
See Bradstreet, Anne

Gentlewoman in Those Parts, A
See Bradstreet, Anne

George, Jean Craighead 1919- .... **CLC 35**
See also AAYA 8; CA 5-8R; CANR 25; CLR 1; DLB 52; JRDA; MAICYA; SATA 2, 68

George, Stefan (Anton) 1868-1933 .. **TCLC 2, 14**
See also CA 104

Georges, Georges Martin
See Simenon, Georges (Jacques Christian)

Gerhardi, William Alexander
See Gerhardie, William Alexander

Gerhardie, William Alexander 1895-1977 **CLC 5**
See also CA 25-28R; 73-76; CANR 18; DLB 36

Gerstler, Amy 1956- .... **CLC 70**
See also CA 146

Gertler, T. .... **CLC 34**
See also CA 116; 121; INT 121

Ghalib .... **NCLC 39, 78**
See also Ghalib, Hsadullah Khan

Ghalib, Hsadullah Khan 1797-1869
See Ghalib
See also DAM POET

Ghelderode, Michel de 1898-1962 **CLC 6, 11; DAM DRAM**
See also CA 85-88; CANR 40, 77

Ghiselin, Brewster 1903- .... **CLC 23**
See also CA 13-16R; CAAS 10; CANR 13

Ghose, Aurabinda 1872-1950 .... **TCLC 63**
See also CA 163

Ghose, Zulfikar 1935- .... **CLC 42**
See also CA 65-68; CANR 67

Ghosh, Amitav 1956- .... **CLC 44**
See also CA 147; CANR 80

Giacosa, Giuseppe 1847-1906 .... **TCLC 7**
See also CA 104

Gibb, Lee
See Waterhouse, Keith (Spencer)

Gibbon, Lewis Grassic .... **TCLC 4**
See also Mitchell, James Leslie

Gibbons, Kaye 1960- ..... **CLC 50, 88; DAM POP**
See also CA 151; CANR 75; MTCW 1

Gibran, Kahlil 1883-1931 **TCLC 1, 9; DAM POET, POP; PC 9**
See also CA 104; 150; MTCW 2

Gibran, Khalil
See Gibran, Kahlil

Gibson, William 1914- **CLC 23; DA; DAB; DAC; DAM DRAM, MST**
See also CA 9-12R; CANR 9, 42, 75; DLB 7; MTCW 1; SATA 66

Gibson, William (Ford) 1948- **CLC 39, 63; DAM POP**
See also AAYA 12; CA 126; 133; CANR 52; MTCW 1

Gide, Andre (Paul Guillaume) 1869-1951 **TCLC 5, 12, 36; DA; DAB; DAC; DAM MST, NOV; SSC 13; WLC**
See also CA 104; 124; DLB 65; MTCW 1, 2

Gifford, Barry (Colby) 1946- .... **CLC 34**
See also CA 65-68; CANR 9, 30, 40

Gilbert, Frank

See De Voto, Bernard (Augustine)

Gilbert, W(illiam) S(chwenck) 1836-1911 **TCLC 3; DAM DRAM, POET**
See also CA 104; 173; SATA 36

Gilbreth, Frank B., Jr. 1911- .... **CLC 17**
See also CA 9-12R; SATA 2

Gilchrist, Ellen 1935- . **CLC 34, 48; DAM POP; SSC 14**
See also CA 113; 116; CANR 41, 61; DLB 130; MTCW 1, 2

Giles, Molly 1942- .... **CLC 39**
See also CA 126

Gill, Eric 1882-1940 .... **TCLC 85**

Gill, Patrick
See Creasey, John

Gilliam, Terry (Vance) 1940- .... **CLC 21**
See also Monty Python
See also AAYA 19; CA 108; 113; CANR 35; INT 113

Gillian, Jerry
See Gilliam, Terry (Vance)

Gilliatt, Penelope (Ann Douglass) 1932-1993 **CLC 2, 10, 13, 53**
See also AITN 2; CA 13-16R; 141; CANR 49; DLB 14

Gilman, Charlotte (Anna) Perkins (Stetson) 1860-1935 .... **TCLC 9, 37; SSC 13**
See also CA 106; 150; MTCW 1

Gilmour, David 1949- .... **CLC 35**
See also CA 138, 147

Gilpin, William 1724-1804 .... **NCLC 30**

Gilray, J. D.
See Mencken, H(enry) L(ouis)

Gilroy, Frank D(aniel) 1925- .... **CLC 2**
See also CA 81-84; CANR 32, 64; DLB 7

Gilstrap, John 1957(?)- .... **CLC 99**
See also CA 160

Ginsberg, Allen 1926-1997 **CLC 1, 2, 3, 4, 6, 13, 36, 69, 109; DA; DAB; DAC; DAM MST, POET; PC 4; WLC**
See also AITN 1; CA 1-4R; 157; CANR 2, 41, 63; CDALB 1941-1968; DLB 5, 16, 169; MTCW 1, 2

Ginzburg, Natalia 1916-1991 . **CLC 5, 11, 54, 70**
See also CA 85-88; 135; CANR 33; DLB 177; MTCW 1, 2

Giono, Jean 1895-1970 .... **CLC 4, 11**
See also CA 45-48; 29-32R; CANR 2, 35; DLB 72; MTCW 1

Giovanni, Nikki 1943- **CLC 2, 4, 19, 64, 117; BLC 2; DA; DAB; DAC; DAM MST, MULT, POET; PC 19; WLCS**
See also AAYA 22; AITN 1; BW 2, 3; CA 29-32R; CAAS 6; CANR 18, 41, 60; CDALBS; CLR 6; DLB 5, 41; INT CANR-18; MAICYA; MTCW 1, 2; SATA 24, 107

Giovene, Andrea 1904- .... **CLC 7**
See also CA 85-88

Gippius, Zinaida (Nikolayevna) 1869-1945
See Hippius, Zinaida
See also CA 106

Giraudoux, (Hippolyte) Jean 1882-1944 **TCLC 2, 7; DAM DRAM**
See also CA 104; DLB 65

Gironella, Jose Maria 1917- .... **CLC 11**
See also CA 101

Gissing, George (Robert) 1857-1903 **TCLC 3, 24, 47**
See also CA 105; 167; DLB 18, 135, 184

Giurlani, Aldo
See Palazzeschi, Aldo

Gladkov, Fyodor (Vasilyevich) 1883-1958 **TCLC 27**
See also CA 170

Glanville, Brian (Lester) 1931- .... **CLC 6**
See also CA 5-8R; CAAS 9; CANR 3, 70; DLB 15, 139; SATA 42

Glasgow, Ellen (Anderson Gholson) 1873-1945

See also CA 5-8R; CANR 6; CLR 47; DLB 88;
JRDA; MAICYA; SAAS 10; SATA 6, 74
Harris, Frank 1856-1931 .... **TCLC 24**
See also CA 109; 150; CANR 80; DLB 156, 197
Harris, George Washington 1814-1869**NCLC 23**
See also DLB 3, 11
Harris, Joel Chandler 1848-1908**TCLC 2; SSC 19**
See also CA 104; 137; CANR 80; CLR 49; DLB
11, 23, 42, 78, 91; MAICYA; SATA 100;
YABC 1
Harris, John (Wyndham Parkes Lucas) Beynon
1903-1969
See Wyndham, John
See also CA 102; 89-92
Harris, MacDonald .... **CLC 9**
See also Heiney, Donald (William)
Harris, Mark 1922- .... **CLC 19**
See also CA 5-8R; CAAS 3; CANR 2, 55; DLB 2;
DLBY 80
Harris, (Theodore) Wilson 1921- .... **CLC 25**
See also BW 2, 3; CA 65-68; CAAS 16; CANR
11, 27, 69; DLB 117; MTCW 1
Harrison, Elizabeth Cavanna 1909-
See Cavanna, Betty
See also CA 9-12R; CANR 6, 27
Harrison, Harry (Max) 1925- .... **CLC 42**
See also CA 1-4R; CANR 5, 21; DLB 8; SATA 4
Harrison, James (Thomas) 1937-**CLC 6, 14, 33,
66; SSC 19**
See also CA 13-16R; CANR 8, 51, 79; DLBY 82;
INT CANR-8
Harrison, Jim
See Harrison, James (Thomas)
Harrison, Kathryn 1961- .... **CLC 70**
See also CA 144; CANR 68
Harrison, Tony 1937- .... **CLC 43**
See also CA 65-68; CANR 44; DLB 40; MTCW 1
Harriss, Will(ard Irvin) 1922- .... **CLC 34**
See also CA 111
Harson, Sley
See Ellison, Harlan (Jay)
Hart, Ellis
See Ellison, Harlan (Jay)
Hart, Josephine 1942(?)- .... **CLC 70; DAM POP**
See also CA 138; CANR 70
Hart, Moss 1904-1961 ..... **CLC 66; DAM DRAM**
See also CA 109; 89-92; DLB 7
Harte, (Francis) Bret(t) 1836(?)-1902**TCLC 1, 25;
DA; DAC; DAM MST; SSC 8; WLC**
See also CA 104; 140; CANR 80; CDALB 1865-
1917; DLB 12, 64, 74, 79, 186; SATA 26
Hartley, L(eslie) P(oles) 1895-1972 ... **CLC 2, 22**
See also CA 45-48; 37-40R; CANR 33; DLB 15,
139; MTCW 1, 2
Hartman, Geoffrey H. 1929- .... **CLC 27**
See also CA 117; 125; CANR 79; DLB 67
Hartmann, Sadakichi 1867-1944 .... **TCLC 73**
See also CA 157; DLB 54
Hartmann von Aue c. 1160-c. 1205 ..... **CMLC 15**
See also DLB 138
Hartmann von Aue 1170-1210 .... **CMLC 15**
Haruf, Kent 1943- .... **CLC 34**
See also CA 149
Harwood, Ronald 1934- .. **CLC 32; DAM DRAM,
MST**
See also CA 1-4R; CANR 4, 55; DLB 13
Hasegawa Tatsunosuke
See Futabatei, Shimei
Hasek, Jaroslav (Matej Frantisek) 1883-1923
TCLC 4
See also CA 104; 129; MTCW 1, 2
Hass, Robert 1941- .... **CLC 18, 39, 99; PC 16**
See also CA 111; CANR 30, 50, 71; DLB 105, 206;
SATA 94
Hastings, Hudson
See Kuttner, Henry
Hastings, Selina .... **CLC 44**

Hathorne, John 1641-1717 .... **LC 38**
Hatteras, Amelia
See Mencken, H(enry) L(ouis)
Hatteras, Owen .... **TCLC 18**
See also Mencken, H(enry) L(ouis); Nathan,
George Jean
Hauptmann, Gerhart (Johann Robert) 1862-1946
TCLC 4; DAM DRAM
See also CA 104; 153; DLB 66, 118
Havel, Vaclav 1936-**CLC 25, 58, 65; DAM DRAM;
DC 6**
See also CA 104; CANR 36, 63; MTCW 1, 2
Haviaras, Stratis .... **CLC 33**
See also Chaviaras, Strates
Hawes, Stephen 1475(?)-1523(?) .... **LC 17**
See also DLB 132
Hawkes, John (Clendennin Burne, Jr.) 1925-1998
CLC 1, 2, 3, 4, 7, 9, 14, 15, 27, 49
See also CA 1-4R; 167; CANR 2, 47, 64; DLB 2, 7;
DLBY 80, 98; MTCW 1, 2
Hawking, S. W.
See Hawking, Stephen W(illiam)
Hawking, Stephen W(illiam) 1942-**CLC 63, 105**
See also AAYA 13; BEST 89:1; CA 126; 129;
CANR 48; MTCW 2
Hawkins, Anthony Hope
See Hope, Anthony
Hawthorne, Julian 1846-1934 .... **TCLC 25**
See also CA 165
Hawthorne, Nathaniel 1804-1864 **NCLC 39; DA;
DAB; DAC; DAM MST, NOV; SSC 3, 29;
WLC**
See also AAYA 18; CDALB 1640-1865; DLB 1,
74; YABC 2
Haxton, Josephine Ayres 1921-
See Douglas, Ellen
See also CA 115; CANR 41
Hayaseca y Eizaguirre, Jorge
See Echegaray (y Eizaguirre), Jose (Maria
Waldo)
Hayashi, Fumiko 1904-1951 .... **TCLC 27**
See also CA 161; DLB 180
Haycraft, Anna
See Ellis, Alice Thomas
See also CA 122; MTCW 2
Hayden, Robert E(arl) 1913-1980**CLC 5, 9, 14, 37;
BLC 2; DA; DAC; DAM MST, MULT, POET;
PC 6**
See also BW 1, 3; CA 69-72; 97-100; CABS 2;
CANR 24, 75; CDALB 1941-1968; DLB 5, 76;
MTCW 1, 2; SATA 19; SATA-Obit 26
Hayford, J(oseph) E(phraim) Casely
See Casely-Hayford, J(oseph) E(phraim)
Hayman, Ronald 1932- .... **CLC 44**
See also CA 25-28R; CANR 18, 50; DLB 155
Haywood, Eliza (Fowler) 1693(?)-1756 . **LC 1, 44**
See also DLB 39
Hazlitt, William 1778-1830 .... **NCLC 29**
See also DLB 110, 158
Hazzard, Shirley 1931- .... **CLC 18**
See also CA 9-12R; CANR 4, 70; DLBY 82;
MTCW 1
Head, Bessie 1937-1986**CLC 25, 67; BLC 2; DAM
MULT**
See also BW 2, 3; CA 29-32R; 119; CANR 25;
DLB 117; MTCW 1, 2
Headon, (Nicky) Topper 1956(?)- .... **CLC 30**
Heaney, Seamus (Justin) 1939-**CLC 5, 7, 14, 25,
37, 74, 91; DAB; DAM POET; PC 18; WLCS**
See also CA 85-88; CANR 25, 48, 75; CDBLB
1960 to Present; DLB 40; DLBY 95; MTCW 1,
2
Hearn, (Patricio) Lafcadio (Tessima Carlos) 1850-
1904 .... **TCLC 9**
See also CA 105; 166; DLB 12, 78, 189
Hearne, Vicki 1946- .... **CLC 56**
See also CA 139

Hearon, Shelby 1931- .... **CLC 63**
See also AITN 2; CA 25-28R; CANR 18, 48
Heat-Moon, William Least .... **CLC 29**
See also Trogdon, William (Lewis)
See also AAYA 9
Hebbel, Friedrich 1813-1863 .... **NCLC 43; DAM
DRAM**
See also DLB 129
Hebert, Anne 1916-**CLC 4, 13, 29; DAC; DAM
MST, POET**
See also CA 85-88; CANR 69; DLB 68; MTCW 1,
2
Hecht, Anthony (Evan) 1923-**CLC 8, 13, 19; DAM
POET**
See also CA 9-12R; CANR 6; DLB 5, 169
Hecht, Ben 1894-1964 .... **CLC 8**
See also CA 85-88; DLB 7, 9, 25, 26, 28, 86
Hedayat, Sadeq 1903-1951 .... **TCLC 21**
See also CA 120
Hegel, Georg Wilhelm Friedrich 1770-1831
NCLC 46
See also DLB 90
Heidegger, Martin 1889-1976 .... **CLC 24**
See also CA 81-84; 65-68; CANR 34; MTCW 1, 2
Heidenstam, (Carl Gustaf) Verner von 1859-1940
TCLC 5
See also CA 104
Heifner, Jack 1946- .... **CLC 11**
See also CA 105; CANR 47
Heijermans, Herman 1864-1924 .... **TCLC 24**
See also CA 123
Heilbrun, Carolyn G(old) 1926- .... **CLC 25**
See also CA 45-48; CANR 1, 28, 58
Heine, Heinrich 1797-1856 . **NCLC 4, 54; PC 25**
See also DLB 90
Heinemann, Larry (Curtiss) 1944- .... **CLC 50**
See also CA 110; CAAS 21; CANR 31, 81; DLBD
9; INT CANR-31
Heiney, Donald (William) 1921-1993
See Harris, MacDonald
See also CA 1-4R; 142; CANR 3, 58
Heinlein, Robert A(nson) 1907-1988**CLC 1, 3, 8,
14, 26, 55; DAM POP**
See also AAYA 17; CA 1-4R; 125; CANR 1, 20,
53; DLB 8; JRDA; MAICYA; MTCW 1, 2;
SATA 9, 69; SATA-Obit 56
Helforth, John
See Doolittle, Hilda
Hellenhofferu, Vojtech Kapristian z
See Hasek, Jaroslav (Matej Frantisek)
Heller, Joseph 1923- **CLC 1, 3, 5, 8, 11, 36, 63;
DA; DAB; DAC; DAM MST, NOV, POP;
WLC**
See also AAYA 24; AITN 1; CA 5-8R; CABS 1;
CANR 8, 42, 66; DLB 2, 28; DLBY 80; INT
CANR-8; MTCW 1, 2
Hellman, Lillian (Florence) 1906-1984**CLC 2, 4,
8, 14, 18, 34, 44, 52; DAM DRAM; DC 1**
See also AITN 1, 2; CA 13-16R; 112; CANR 33;
DLB 7; DLBY 84; MTCW 1, 2
Helprin, Mark 1947- .. **CLC 7, 10, 22, 32; DAM
NOV, POP**
See also CA 81-84; CANR 47, 64; CDALBS;
DLBY 85; MTCW 1, 2
Helvetius, Claude-Adrien 1715-1771 .... **LC 26**
Helyar, Jane Penelope Josephine 1933-
See Poole, Josephine
See also CA 21-24R; CANR 10, 26; SATA 82
Hemans, Felicia 1793-1835 .... **NCLC 71**
See also DLB 96
Hemingway, Ernest (Miller) 1899-1961**CLC 1, 3,
6, 8, 10, 13, 19, 30, 34, 39, 41, 44, 50, 61, 80;
DA; DAB; DAC; DAM MST, NOV; SSC 1,
25; WLC**
See also AAYA 19; CA 77-80; CANR 34; CDALB
1917-1929; DLB 4, 9, 102, 210; DLBD 1, 15, 16;
DLBY 81, 87, 96, 98; MTCW 1, 2

Author Index

See also DLB 24, 200

Knister, Raymond 1899-1932 .... **TCLC 56**
See also DLB 68

Knowles, John 1926-CLC **1, 4, 10, 26; DA; DAC; DAM MST, NOV**
See also AAYA 10; CA 17-20R; CANR 40, 74, 76; CDALB 1968-1988; DLB 6; MTCW 1, 2; SATA 8, 89

Knox, Calvin M.
See Silverberg, Robert

Knox, John c. 1505-1572 .... **LC 37**
See also DLB 132

Knye, Cassandra
See Disch, Thomas M(ichael)

Koch, C(hristopher) J(ohn) 1932- .... **CLC 42**
See also CA 127

Koch, Christopher
See Koch, C(hristopher) J(ohn)

Koch, Kenneth 1925- **CLC 5, 8, 44; DAM POET**
See also CA 1-4R; CANR 6, 36, 57; DLB 5; INT CANR-36; MTCW 2; SATA 65

Kochanowski, Jan 1530-1584 .... **LC 10**

Kock, Charles Paul de 1794-1871 .... **NCLC 16**

Koda Shigeyuki 1867-1947
See Rohan, Koda
See also CA 121

Koestler, Arthur 1905-1983CLC **1, 3, 6, 8, 15, 33**
See also CA 1-4R; 109; CANR 1, 33; CDBLB 1945-1960; DLBY 83; MTCW 1, 2

Kogawa, Joy Nozomi 1935- **CLC 78; DAC; DAM MST, MULT**
See also CA 101; CANR 19, 62; MTCW 2; SATA 99

Kohout, Pavel 1928- .... **CLC 13**
See also CA 45-48; CANR 3

Koizumi, Yakumo
See Hearn, (Patricio) Lafcadio (Tessima Carlos)

Kolmar, Gertrud 1894-1943 .... **TCLC 40**
See also CA 167

Komunyakaa, Yusef 1947- ... **CLC 86, 94; BLCS**
See also CA 147; DLB 120

Konrad, George
See Konrad, Gyoergy

Konrad, Gyoergy 1933- .... **CLC 4, 10, 73**
See also CA 85-88

Konwicki, Tadeusz 1926- .... **CLC 8, 28, 54, 117**
See also CA 101; CAAS 9; CANR 39, 59; MTCW 1

Koontz, Dean R(ay) 1945- .. **CLC 78; DAM NOV, POP**
See also AAYA 9; BEST 89:3, 90:2; CA 108; CANR 19, 36, 52; MTCW 1; SATA 92

Kopernik, Mikolaj
See Copernicus, Nicolaus

Kopit, Arthur (Lee) 1937- **CLC 1, 18, 33; DAM DRAM**
See also AITN 1; CA 81-84; CABS 3; DLB 7; MTCW 1

Kops, Bernard 1926- .... **CLC 4**
See also CA 5-8R; DLB 13

Kornbluth, C(yril) M. 1923-1958 .... **TCLC 8**
See also CA 105; 160; DLB 8

Korolenko, V. G.
See Korolenko, Vladimir Galaktionovich

Korolenko, Vladimir
See Korolenko, Vladimir Galaktionovich

Korolenko, Vladimir G.
See Korolenko, Vladimir Galaktionovich

Korolenko, Vladimir Galaktionovich 1853-1921 **TCLC 22**
See also CA 121

Korzybski, Alfred (Habdank Skarbek) 1879-1950 **TCLC 61**
See also CA 123; 160

Kosinski, Jerzy (Nikodem) 1933-1991 **CLC 1, 2, 3, 6, 10, 15, 53, 70; DAM NOV**
See also CA 17-20R; 134; CANR 9, 46; DLB 2;

DLBY 82; MTCW 1, 2

Kostelanetz, Richard (Cory) 1940- .... **CLC 28**
See also CA 13-16R; CAAS 8; CANR 38, 77

Kostrowitzki, Wilhelm Apollinaris de 1880-1918
See Apollinaire, Guillaume
See also CA 104

Kotlowitz, Robert 1924- .... **CLC 4**
See also CA 33-36R; CANR 36

Kotzebue, August (Friedrich Ferdinand) von 1761-1819 .... **NCLC 25**
See also DLB 94

Kotzwinkle, William 1938- .... **CLC 5, 14, 35**
See also CA 45-48; CANR 3, 44; CLR 6; DLB 173; MAICYA; SATA 24, 70

Kowna, Stancy
See Szymborska, Wislawa

Kozol, Jonathan 1936- .... **CLC 17**
See also CA 61-64; CANR 16, 45

Kozoll, Michael 1940(?)- .... **CLC 35**

Kramer, Kathryn 19(?)- .... **CLC 34**

Kramer, Larry 1935- **CLC 42; DAM POP; DC 8**
See also CA 124; 126; CANR 60

Krasicki, Ignacy 1735-1801 .... **NCLC 8**

Krasinski, Zygmunt 1812-1859 .... **NCLC 4**

Kraus, Karl 1874-1936 .... **TCLC 5**
See also CA 104; DLB 118

Kreve (Mickevicius), Vincas 1882-1954TCLC **27**
See also CA 170

Kristeva, Julia 1941- .... **CLC 77**
See also CA 154

Kristofferson, Kris 1936- .... **CLC 26**
See also CA 104

Krizanc, John 1956- .... **CLC 57**

Krleza, Miroslav 1893-1981 .... **CLC 8, 114**
See also CA 97-100; 105; DLB 147

Kroetsch, Robert 1927-**CLC 5, 23, 57; DAC; DAM POET**
See also CA 17-20R; CANR 8, 38; DLB 53; MTCW 1

Kroetz, Franz
See Kroetz, Franz Xaver

Kroetz, Franz Xaver 1946- .... **CLC 41**
See also CA 130

Kroker, Arthur (W.) 1945- .... **CLC 77**
See also CA 161

Kropotkin, Peter (Aleksieevich) 1842-1921TCLC **36**
See also CA 119

Krotkov, Yuri 1917- .... **CLC 19**
See also CA 102

Krumb
See Crumb, R(obert)

Krumgold, Joseph (Quincy) 1908-1980 **CLC 12**
See also CA 9-12R; 101; CANR 7; MAICYA; SATA 1, 48; SATA-Obit 23

Krumwitz
See Crumb, R(obert)

Krutch, Joseph Wood 1893-1970 .... **CLC 24**
See also CA 1-4R; 25-28R; CANR 4; DLB 63, 206

Krutzch, Gus
See Eliot, T(homas) S(tearns)

Krylov, Ivan Andreevich 1768(?)-1844 .. **NCLC 1**
See also DLB 150

Kubin, Alfred (Leopold Isidor) 1877-1959 **TCLC 23**
See also CA 112; 149; DLB 81

Kubrick, Stanley 1928-1999 .... **CLC 16**
See also AAYA 30; CA 81-84; 177; CANR 33; DLB 26

Kumin, Maxine (Winokur) 1925-**CLC 5, 13, 28; DAM POET; PC 15**
See also AITN 2; CA 1-4R; CAAS 8; CANR 1, 21, 69; DLB 5; MTCW 1, 2; SATA 12

Kundera, Milan 1929-**CLC 4, 9, 19, 32, 68, 115; DAM NOV; SSC 24**
See also AAYA 2; CA 85-88; CANR 19, 52, 74; MTCW 1, 2

Kunene, Mazisi (Raymond) 1930- .... **CLC 85**
See also BW 1, 3; CA 125; CANR 81; DLB 117

Kunitz, Stanley (Jasspon) 1905-CLC **6, 11, 14; PC 19**
See also CA 41-44R; CANR 26, 57; DLB 48; INT CANR-26; MTCW 1, 2

Kunze, Reiner 1933- .... **CLC 10**
See also CA 93-96; DLB 75

Kuprin, Aleksandr Ivanovich 1870-1938TCLC **5**
See also CA 104

Kureishi, Hanif 1954(?)- .... **CLC 64**
See also CA 139; DLB 194

Kurosawa, Akira 1910-1998 **CLC 16, 119; DAM MULT**
See also AAYA 11; CA 101; 170; CANR 46

Kushner, Tony 1957(?)-CLC **81; DAM DRAM; DC 10**
See also CA 144; CANR 74; MTCW 2

Kuttner, Henry 1915-1958 .... **TCLC 10**
See also Vance, Jack
See also CA 107; 157; DLB 8

Kuzma, Greg 1944- .... **CLC 7**
See also CA 33-36R; CANR 70

Kuzmin, Mikhail 1872(?)-1936 .... **TCLC 40**
See also CA 170

Kyd, Thomas 1558-1594LC **22; DAM DRAM; DC 3**
See also DLB 62

Kyprianos, Iossif
See Samarakis, Antonis

La Bruyere, Jean de 1645-1696 .... **LC 17**

Lacan, Jacques (Marie Emile) 1901-1981CLC **75**
See also CA 121; 104

Laclos, Pierre Ambroise Francois Choderlos de 1741-1803 .... **NCLC 4**

La Colere, Francois
See Aragon, Louis

Lacolere, Francois
See Aragon, Louis

La Deshabilleuse
See Simenon, Georges (Jacques Christian)

Lady Gregory
See Gregory, Isabella Augusta (Persse)

Lady of Quality, A
See Bagnold, Enid

La Fayette, Marie (Madelaine Pioche de la Vergne Comtes 1634-1693 .... **LC 2**

Lafayette, Rene
See Hubbard, L(afayette) Ron(ald)

Laforgue, Jules 1860-1887 **NCLC 5, 53; PC 14; SSC 20**

Lagerkvist, Paer (Fabian) 1891-1974 **CLC 7, 10, 13, 54; DAM DRAM, NOV**
See also Lagerkvist, Par
See also CA 85-88; 49-52; MTCW 1, 2

Lagerkvist, Par .... **SSC 12**
See also Lagerkvist, Paer (Fabian)
See also MTCW 2

Lagerloef, Selma (Ottiliana Lovisa) 1858-1940 **TCLC 4, 36**
See also Lagerlof, Selma (Ottiliana Lovisa)
See also CA 108; MTCW 2; SATA 15

Lagerlof, Selma (Ottiliana Lovisa)
See Lagerloef, Selma (Ottiliana Lovisa)
See also CLR 7; SATA 15

La Guma, (Justin) Alex(ander) 1925-1985 .. **C L C 19; BLCS; DAM NOV**
See also BW 1, 3; CA 49-52; 118; CANR 25, 81; DLB 117; MTCW 1, 2

Laidlaw, A. K.
See Grieve, C(hristopher) M(urray)

Lainez, Manuel Mujica
See Mujica Lainez, Manuel
See also HW 1

Laing, R(onald) D(avid) 1927-1989 .... **CLC 95**
See also CA 107; 129; CANR 34; MTCW 1

Lamartine, Alphonse (Marie Louis Prat) de 1790-1869 **NCLC 11; DAM POET; PC 16**

Lamb, Charles 1775-1834 ..... **NCLC 10; DA; DAB; DAC; DAM MST; WLC**
See also CDBLB 1789-1832; DLB 93, 107, 163; SATA 17

Lamb, Lady Caroline 1785-1828 .... **NCLC 38**
See also DLB 116

Lamming, George (William) 1927- **CLC 2, 4, 66; BLC 2; DAM MULT**
See also BW 2, 3; CA 85-88; CANR 26, 76; DLB 125; MTCW 1, 2

L'Amour, Louis (Dearborn) 1908-1988 **CLC 25, 55; DAM NOV, POP**
See also AAYA 16; AITN 2; BEST 89:2; CA 1-4R; 125; CANR 3, 25, 40; DLB 206; DLBY 80; MTCW 1, 2

Lampedusa, Giuseppe (Tomasi) di 1896-1957 **TCLC 13**
See also Tomasi di Lampedusa, Giuseppe
See also CA 164; DLB 177; MTCW 2

Lampman, Archibald 1861-1899 .... **NCLC 25**
See also DLB 92

Lancaster, Bruce 1896-1963 .... **CLC 36**
See also CA 9-10; CANR 70; CAP 1; SATA 9

Lanchester, John .... **CLC 99**

Landau, Mark Alexandrovich
See Aldanov, Mark (Alexandrovich)

Landau-Aldanov, Mark Alexandrovich
See Aldanov, Mark (Alexandrovich)

Landis, Jerry
See Simon, Paul (Frederick)

Landis, John 1950- .... **CLC 26**
See also CA 112; 122

Landolfi, Tommaso 1908-1979 .... **CLC 11, 49**
See also CA 127; 117; DLB 177

Landon, Letitia Elizabeth 1802-1838 ... **NCLC 15**
See also DLB 96

Landor, Walter Savage 1775-1864 ...... **NCLC 14**
See also DLB 93, 107

Landwirth, Heinz 1927-
See Lind, Jakov
See also CA 9-12R; CANR 7

Lane, Patrick 1939- .... **CLC 25; DAM POET**
See also CA 97-100; CANR 54; DLB 53; INT 97-100

Lang, Andrew 1844-1912 .... **TCLC 16**
See also CA 114; 137; DLB 98, 141, 184; MAICYA; SATA 16

Lang, Fritz 1890-1976 .... **CLC 20, 103**
See also CA 77-80; 69-72; CANR 30

Lange, John
See Crichton, (John) Michael

Langer, Elinor 1939- .... **CLC 34**
See also CA 121

Langland, William 1330(?)-1400(?) **LC 19; DA; DAB; DAC; DAM MST, POET**
See also DLB 146

Langstaff, Launcelot
See Irving, Washington

Lanier, Sidney 1842-1881 **NCLC 6; DAM POET**
See also DLB 64; DLBD 13; MAICYA; SATA 18

Lanyer, Aemilia 1569-1645 .... **LC 10, 30**
See also DLB 121

Lao-Tzu
See Lao Tzu

Lao Tzu fl. 6th cent. B.C.- .... **CMLC 7**

Lapine, James (Elliot) 1949- .... **CLC 39**
See also CA 123; 130; CANR 54; INT 130

Larbaud, Valery (Nicolas) 1881-1957 .... **TCLC 9**
See also CA 106; 152

Lardner, Ring
See Lardner, Ring(gold) W(ilmer)

Lardner, Ring W., Jr.
See Lardner, Ring(gold) W(ilmer)

Lardner, Ring(gold) W(ilmer) 1885-1933 **TCLC 2, 14; SSC 32**

See also CA 104; 131; CDALB 1917-1929; DLB 11, 25, 86; DLBD 16; MTCW 1, 2

Laredo, Betty
See Codrescu, Andrei

Larkin, Maia
See Wojciechowska, Maia (Teresa)

Larkin, Philip (Arthur) 1922-1985 **CLC 3, 5, 8, 9, 13, 18, 33, 39, 64; DAB; DAM MST, POET; PC 21**
See also CA 5-8R; 117; CANR 24, 62; CDBLB 1960 to Present; DLB 27; MTCW 1, 2

Larra (y Sanchez de Castro), Mariano Jose de 1809-1837 .... **NCLC 17**

Larsen, Eric 1941- .... **CLC 55**
See also CA 132

Larsen, Nella 1891-1964 **CLC 37; BLC 2; DAM MULT**
See also BW 1; CA 125; DLB 51

Larson, Charles R(aymond) 1938- .... **CLC 31**
See also CA 53-56; CANR 4

Larson, Jonathan 1961-1996 .... **CLC 99**
See also AAYA 28; CA 156

Las Casas, Bartolome de 1474-1566 .... **LC 31**

Lasch, Christopher 1932-1994 .... **CLC 102**
See also CA 73-76; 144; CANR 25; MTCW 1, 2

Lasker-Schueler, Else 1869-1945 .... **TCLC 57**
See also DLB 66, 124

Laski, Harold 1893-1950 .... **TCLC 79**

Latham, Jean Lee 1902-1995 .... **CLC 12**
See also AITN 1; CA 5-8R; CANR 7; CLR 50; MAICYA; SATA 2, 68

Latham, Mavis
See Clark, Mavis Thorpe

Lathen, Emma .... **CLC 2**
See also Hennissart, Martha; Latsis, Mary J(ane)

Lathrop, Francis
See Leiber, Fritz (Reuter, Jr.)

Latsis, Mary J(ane) 1927(?)-1997
See Lathen, Emma
See also CA 85-88; 162

Lattimore, Richmond (Alexander) 1906-1984 **CLC 3**
See also CA 1-4R; 112; CANR 1

Laughlin, James 1914-1997 .... **CLC 49**
See also CA 21-24R; 162; CAAS 22; CANR 9, 47; DLB 48; DLBY 96, 97

Laurence, (Jean) Margaret (Wemyss) 1926-1987 **CLC 3, 6, 13, 50, 62; DAC; DAM MST; SSC 7**
See also CA 5-8R; 121; CANR 33; DLB 53; MTCW 1, 2; SATA-Obit 50

Laurent, Antoine 1952- .... **CLC 50**

Lauscher, Hermann
See Hesse, Hermann

Lautreamont, Comte de 1846-1870 **NCLC 12; SSC 14**

Laverty, Donald
See Blish, James (Benjamin)

Lavin, Mary 1912-1996 .... **CLC 4, 18, 99; SSC 4**
See also CA 9-12R; 151; CANR 33; DLB 15; MTCW 1

Lavond, Paul Dennis
See Kornbluth, C(yril) M.; Pohl, Frederik

Lawler, Raymond Evenor 1922- .... **CLC 58**
See also CA 103

Lawrence, D(avid) H(erbert Richards) 1885-1930 **TCLC 2, 9, 16, 33, 48, 61, 93; DA; DAB; DAC; DAM MST, NOV, POET; SSC 4, 19; WLC**
See also CA 104; 121; CDBLB 1914-1945; DLB 10, 19, 36, 98, 162, 195; MTCW 1, 2

Lawrence, T(homas) E(dward) 1888-1935 **TCLC 18**
See also Dale, Colin
See also CA 115; 167; DLB 195

Lawrence of Arabia
See Lawrence, T(homas) E(dward)

Lawson, Henry (Archibald Hertzberg) 1867-1922 .... **TCLC 27; SSC 18**
See also CA 120

Lawton, Dennis
See Faust, Frederick (Schiller)

Laxness, Halldor .... **CLC 25**
See also Gudjonsson, Halldor Kiljan

Layamon fl. c. 1200- .... **CMLC 10**
See also DLB 146

Laye, Camara 1928-1980 **CLC 4, 38; BLC 2; DAM MULT**
See also BW 1; CA 85-88; 97-100; CANR 25; MTCW 1, 2

Layton, Irving (Peter) 1912- .. **CLC 2, 15; DAC; DAM MST, POET**
See also CA 1-4R; CANR 2, 33, 43, 66; DLB 88; MTCW 1, 2

Lazarus, Emma 1849-1887 .... **NCLC 8**

Lazarus, Felix
See Cable, George Washington

Lazarus, Henry
See Slavitt, David R(ytman)

Lea, Joan
See Neufeld, John (Arthur)

Leacock, Stephen (Butler) 1869-1944 . **TCLC 2; DAC; DAM MST**
See also CA 104; 141; CANR 80; DLB 92; MTCW 2

Lear, Edward 1812-1888 .... **NCLC 3**
See also CLR 1; DLB 32, 163, 166; MAICYA; SATA 18, 100

Lear, Norman (Milton) 1922- .... **CLC 12**
See also CA 73-76

Leautaud, Paul 1872-1956 .... **TCLC 83**
See also DLB 65

Leavis, F(rank) R(aymond) 1895-1978 .. **CLC 24**
See also CA 21-24R; 77-80; CANR 44; MTCW 1, 2

Leavitt, David 1961- .... **CLC 34; DAM POP**
See also CA 116; 122; CANR 50, 62; DLB 130; INT 122; MTCW 2

Leblanc, Maurice (Marie Emile) 1864-1941 **TCLC 49**
See also CA 110

Lebowitz, Fran(ces Ann) 1951(?)- .... **CLC 11, 36**
See also CA 81-84; CANR 14, 60, 70; INT CANR-14; MTCW 1

Lebrecht, Peter
See Tieck, (Johann) Ludwig

le Carre, John .... **CLC 3, 5, 9, 15, 28**
See also Cornwell, David (John Moore)
See also BEST 89:4; CDBLB 1960 to Present; DLB 87; MTCW 2

Le Clezio, J(ean) M(arie) G(ustave) 1940- . **CLC 31**
See also CA 116; 128; DLB 83

Leconte de Lisle, Charles-Marie-Rene 1818-1894 **NCLC 29**

Le Coq, Monsieur
See Simenon, Georges (Jacques Christian)

Leduc, Violette 1907-1972 .... **CLC 22**
See also CA 13-14; 33-36R; CANR 69; CAP 1

Ledwidge, Francis 1887(?)-1917 .... **TCLC 23**
See also CA 123; DLB 20

Lee, Andrea 1953- **CLC 36; BLC 2; DAM MULT**
See also BW 1, 3; CA 125

Lee, Andrew
See Auchincloss, Louis (Stanton)

Lee, Chang-rae 1965- .... **CLC 91**
See also CA 148

Lee, Don L. .... **CLC 2**
See also Madhubuti, Haki R.

Lee, George W(ashington) 1894-1976 . **CLC 52; BLC 2; DAM MULT**
See also BW 1; CA 125; DLB 51

Lee, (Nelle) Harper 1926- **CLC 12, 60; DA; DAB; DAC; DAM MST, NOV; WLC**

See also AAYA 13; CA 13-16R; CANR 51; CDALB 1941-1968; DLB 6; MTCW 1, 2; SATA 11

Lee, Helen Elaine 1959(?)- .... **CLC 86**
See also CA 148

Lee, Julian
See Latham, Jean Lee

Lee, Larry
See Lee, Lawrence

Lee, Laurie 1914-1997**CLC 90; DAB; DAM POP**
See also CA 77-80; 158; CANR 33, 73; DLB 27; MTCW 1

Lee, Lawrence 1941-1990 .... **CLC 34**
See also CA 131; CANR 43

Lee, Li-Young 1957- .... **PC 24**
See also CA 153; DLB 165

Lee, Manfred B(ennington) 1905-1971 .. **CLC 11**
See also Queen, Ellery
See also CA 1-4R; 29-32R; CANR 2; DLB 137

Lee, Shelton Jackson 1957(?)-**CLC 105; BLCS; DAM MULT**
See also Lee, Spike
See also BW 2, 3; CA 125; CANR 42

Lee, Spike
See Lee, Shelton Jackson
See also AAYA 4, 29

Lee, Stan 1922- .... **CLC 17**
See also AAYA 5; CA 108; 111; INT 111

Lee, Tanith 1947- .... **CLC 46**
See also AAYA 15; CA 37-40R; CANR 53; SATA 8, 88

Lee, Vernon .... **TCLC 5; SSC 33**
See also Paget, Violet
See also DLB 57, 153, 156, 174, 178

Lee, William
See Burroughs, William S(eward)

Lee, Willy
See Burroughs, William S(eward)

Lee-Hamilton, Eugene (Jacob) 1845-1907 **TCLC 22**
See also CA 117

Leet, Judith 1935- .... **CLC 11**

Le Fanu, Joseph Sheridan 1814-1873**NCLC 9, 58; DAM POP; SSC 14**
See also DLB 21, 70, 159, 178

Leffland, Ella 1931- .... **CLC 19**
See also CA 29-32R; CANR 35, 78; DLBY 84; INT CANR-35; SATA 65

Leger, Alexis
See Leger, (Marie-Rene Auguste) Alexis Saint-Leger

Leger, (Marie-Rene Auguste) Alexis Saint-Leger 1887-1975**CLC 4, 11, 46; DAM POET; PC 23**
See also CA 13-16R; 61-64; CANR 43; MTCW 1

Leger, Saintleger
See Leger, (Marie-Rene Auguste) Alexis Saint-Leger

Le Guin, Ursula K(roeber) 1929- **CLC 8, 13, 22, 45, 71; DAB; DAC; DAM MST, POP; SSC 12**
See also AAYA 9, 27; AITN 1; CA 21-24R; CANR 9, 32, 52, 74; CDALB 1968-1988; CLR 3, 28; DLB 8, 52; INT CANR-32; JRDA; MAICYA; MTCW 1, 2; SATA 4, 52, 99

Lehmann, Rosamond (Nina) 1901-1990 .. **CLC 5**
See also CA 77-80; 131; CANR 8, 73; DLB 15; MTCW 2

Leiber, Fritz (Reuter, Jr.) 1910-1992 .... **CLC 25**
See also CA 45-48; 139; CANR 2, 40; DLB 8; MTCW 1, 2; SATA 45; SATA-Obit 73

Leibniz, Gottfried Wilhelm von 1646-1716**LC 35**
See also DLB 168

Leimbach, Martha 1963-
See Leimbach, Marti
See also CA 130

Leimbach, Marti .... **CLC 65**
See also Leimbach, Martha

Leino, Eino .... **TCLC 24**
See also Loennbohm, Armas Eino Leopold

Leiris, Michel (Julien) 1901-1990 .... **CLC 61**
See also CA 119; 128; 132

Leithauser, Brad 1953- .... **CLC 27**
See also CA 107; CANR 27, 81; DLB 120

Lelchuk, Alan 1938- .... **CLC 5**
See also CA 45-48; CAAS 20; CANR 1, 70

Lem, Stanislaw 1921- .... **CLC 8, 15, 40**
See also CA 105; CAAS 1; CANR 32; MTCW 1

Lemann, Nancy 1956- .... **CLC 39**
See also CA 118; 136

Lemonnier, (Antoine Louis) Camille 1844-1913 **TCLC 22**
See also CA 121

Lenau, Nikolaus 1802-1850 .... **NCLC 16**

L'Engle, Madeleine (Camp Franklin) 1918- **C L C 12; DAM POP**
See also AAYA 28; AITN 2; CA 1-4R; CANR 3, 21, 39, 66; CLR 1, 14, 57; DLB 52; JRDA; MAICYA; MTCW 1, 2; SAAS 15; SATA 1, 27, 75

Lengyel, Jozsef 1896-1975 .... **CLC 7**
See also CA 85-88; 57-60; CANR 71

Lenin 1870-1924
See Lenin, V. I.
See also CA 121; 168

Lenin, V. I. .... **TCLC 67**
See also Lenin

Lennon, John (Ono) 1940-1980 .... **CLC 12, 35**
See also CA 102

Lennox, Charlotte Ramsay 1729(?)-1804**NCLC 23**
See also DLB 39

Lentricchia, Frank (Jr.) 1940- .... **CLC 34**
See also CA 25-28R; CANR 19

Lenz, Siegfried 1926- .... **CLC 27; SSC 33**
See also CA 89-92; CANR 80; DLB 75

Leonard, Elmore (John, Jr.) 1925- . **CLC 28, 34, 71, 120; DAM POP**
See also AAYA 22; AITN 1; BEST 89:1, 90:4; CA 81-84; CANR 12, 28, 53, 76; DLB 173; INT CANR-28; MTCW 1, 2

Leonard, Hugh .... **CLC 19**
See also Byrne, John Keyes
See also DLB 13

Leonov, Leonid (Maximovich) 1899-1994**CLC 92; DAM NOV**
See also CA 129; CANR 74, 76; MTCW 1, 2

Leopardi, (Conte) Giacomo 1798-1837 **NCLC 22**

Le Reveler
See Artaud, Antonin (Marie Joseph)

Lerman, Eleanor 1952- .... **CLC 9**
See also CA 85-88; CANR 69

Lerman, Rhoda 1936- .... **CLC 56**
See also CA 49-52; CANR 70

Lermontov, Mikhail Yuryevich 1814-1841 **N C L C 47; PC 18**
See also DLB 205

Leroux, Gaston 1868-1927 .... **TCLC 25**
See also CA 108; 136; CANR 69; SATA 65

Lesage, Alain-Rene 1668-1747 .... **LC 2, 28**

Leskov, Nikolai (Semyonovich) 1831-1895**N C L C 25; SSC 34**

Lessing, Doris (May) 1919-**CLC 1, 2, 3, 6, 10, 15, 22, 40, 94; DA; DAB; DAC; DAM MST, NOV; SSC 6; WLCS**
See also CA 9-12R; CAAS 14; CANR 33, 54, 76; CDBLB 1960 to Present; DLB 15, 139; DLBY 85; MTCW 1, 2

Lessing, Gotthold Ephraim 1729-1781 .... **LC 8**
See also DLB 97

Lester, Richard 1932- .... **CLC 20**

Lever, Charles (James) 1806-1872 ...... **NCLC 23**
See also DLB 21

Leverson, Ada 1865(?)-1936(?) .... **TCLC 18**
See also Elaine
See also CA 117; DLB 153

Levertov, Denise 1923-1997**CLC 1, 2, 3, 5, 8, 15, 28, 66; DAM POET; PC 11**
See also CA 1-4R; 163; CAAS 19; CANR 3, 29, 50; CDALBS; DLB 5, 165; INT CANR-29; MTCW 1, 2

Levi, Jonathan .... **CLC 76**

Levi, Peter (Chad Tigar) 1931- .... **CLC 41**
See also CA 5-8R; CANR 34, 80; DLB 40

Levi, Primo 1919-1987 ...... **CLC 37, 50; SSC 12**
See also CA 13-16R; 122; CANR 12, 33, 61, 70; DLB 177; MTCW 1, 2

Levin, Ira 1929- .... **CLC 3, 6; DAM POP**
See also CA 21-24R; CANR 17, 44, 74; MTCW 1, 2; SATA 66

Levin, Meyer 1905-1981 .... **CLC 7; DAM POP**
See also AITN 1; CA 9-12R; 104; CANR 15; DLB 9, 28; DLBY 81; SATA 21; SATA-Obit 27

Levine, Norman 1924- .... **CLC 54**
See also CA 73-76; CAAS 23; CANR 14, 70; DLB 88

Levine, Philip 1928- **CLC 2, 4, 5, 9, 14, 33, 118; DAM POET; PC 22**
See also CA 9-12R; CANR 9, 37, 52; DLB 5

Levinson, Deirdre 1931- .... **CLC 49**
See also CA 73-76; CANR 70

Levi-Strauss, Claude 1908- .... **CLC 38**
See also CA 1-4R; CANR 6, 32, 57; MTCW 1, 2

Levitin, Sonia (Wolff) 1934- .... **CLC 17**
See also AAYA 13; CA 29-32R; CANR 14, 32, 79; CLR 53; JRDA; MAICYA; SAAS 2; SATA 4, 68

Levon, O. U.
See Kesey, Ken (Elton)

Levy, Amy 1861-1889 .... **NCLC 59**
See also DLB 156

Lewes, George Henry 1817-1878 .... **NCLC 25**
See also DLB 55, 144

Lewis, Alun 1915-1944 .... **TCLC 3**
See also CA 104; DLB 20, 162

Lewis, C. Day
See Day Lewis, C(ecil)

Lewis, C(live) S(taples) 1898-1963**CLC 1, 3, 6, 14, 27; DA; DAB; DAC; DAM MST, NOV, POP; WLC**
See also AAYA 3; CA 81-84; CANR 33, 71; CDBLB 1945-1960; CLR 3, 27; DLB 15, 100, 160; JRDA; MAICYA; MTCW 1, 2; SATA 13, 100

Lewis, Janet 1899-1998 .... **CLC 41**
See also Winters, Janet Lewis
See also CA 9-12R; 172; CANR 29, 63; CAP 1; DLBY 87

Lewis, Matthew Gregory 1775-1818**NCLC 11, 62**
See also DLB 39, 158, 178

Lewis, (Harry) Sinclair 1885-1951 **TCLC 4, 13, 23, 39; DA; DAB; DAC; DAM MST, NOV; WLC**
See also CA 104; 133; CDALB 1917-1929; DLB 9, 102; DLBD 1; MTCW 1, 2

Lewis, (Percy) Wyndham 1882(?)-1957**TCLC 2, 9; SSC 34**
See also CA 104; 157; DLB 15; MTCW 2

Lewisohn, Ludwig 1883-1955 .... **TCLC 19**
See also CA 107; DLB 4, 9, 28, 102

Lewton, Val 1904-1951 .... **TCLC 76**

Leyner, Mark 1956- .... **CLC 92**
See also CA 110; CANR 28, 53; MTCW 2

Lezama Lima, Jose 1910-1976 . **CLC 4, 10, 101; DAM MULT; HLCS 2**
See also CA 77-80; CANR 71; DLB 113; HW 1, 2

L'Heureux, John (Clarke) 1934- .... **CLC 52**
See also CA 13-16R; CANR 23, 45

Liddell, C. H.
See Kuttner, Henry

Lie, Jonas (Lauritz Idemil) 1833-1908(?)**TCLC 5**
See also CA 115

Lieber, Joel 1937-1971 .... **CLC 6**

Loxsmith, John
See Brunner, John (Kilian Houston)
Loy, Mina .... **CLC 28; DAM POET; PC 16**
See also Lowry, Mina Gertrude
See also DLB 4, 54
Loyson-Bridet
See Schwob, Marcel (Mayer Andre)
Lucan 39-65 .... **CMLC 33**
See also DLB 211
Lucas, Craig 1951- .... **CLC 64**
See also CA 137; CANR 71
Lucas, E(dward) V(errall) 1868-1938 **T C L C 73**
See also CA 176; DLB 98, 149, 153; SATA 20
Lucas, George 1944- .... **CLC 16**
See also AAYA 1, 23; CA 77-80; CANR 30; SATA 56
Lucas, Hans
See Godard, Jean-Luc
Lucas, Victoria
See Plath, Sylvia
Lucian c. 120-c. 180 .... **CMLC 32**
See also DLB 176
Ludlam, Charles 1943-1987 .... **CLC 46, 50**
See also CA 85-88; 122; CANR 72
Ludlum, Robert 1927- . **CLC 22, 43; DAM NOV, POP**
See also AAYA 10; BEST 89:1, 90:3; CA 33-36R; CANR 25, 41, 68; DLBY 82; MTCW 1, 2
Ludwig, Ken .... **CLC 60**
Ludwig, Otto 1813-1865 .... **NCLC 4**
See also DLB 129
Lugones, Leopoldo 1874-1938 **TCLC 15; HLCS 2**
See also CA 116; 131; HW 1
Lu Hsun 1881-1936 .... **TCLC 3; SSC 20**
See also Shu-Jen, Chou
Lukacs, George .... **CLC 24**
See also Lukacs, Gyorgy (Szegeny von)
Lukacs, Gyorgy (Szegeny von) 1885-1971
See Lukacs, George
See also CA 101; 29-32R; CANR 62; MTCW 2
Luke, Peter (Ambrose Cyprian) 1919-1995 **C L C 38**
See also CA 81-84; 147; CANR 72; DLB 13
Lunar, Dennis
See Mungo, Raymond
Lurie, Alison 1926- .... **CLC 4, 5, 18, 39**
See also CA 1-4R; CANR 2, 17, 50; DLB 2; MTCW 1; SATA 46
Lustig, Arnost 1926- .... **CLC 56**
See also AAYA 3; CA 69-72; CANR 47; SATA 56
Luther, Martin 1483-1546 .... **LC 9, 37**
See also DLB 179
Luxemburg, Rosa 1870(?)-1919 .... **TCLC 63**
See also CA 118
Luzi, Mario 1914- .... **CLC 13**
See also CA 61-64; CANR 9, 70; DLB 128
Lyly, John 1554(?)-1606 **LC 41; DAM DRAM; DC 7**
See also DLB 62, 167
L'Ymagier
See Gourmont, Remy (-Marie-Charles) de
Lynch, B. Suarez
See Bioy Casares, Adolfo; Borges, Jorge Luis
Lynch, B. Suarez
See Bioy Casares, Adolfo
Lynch, David (K.) 1946- .... **CLC 66**
See also CA 124; 129
Lynch, James
See Andreyev, Leonid (Nikolaevich)
Lynch Davis, B.
See Bioy Casares, Adolfo; Borges, Jorge Luis
Lyndsay, Sir David 1490-1555 .... **LC 20**
Lynn, Kenneth S(chuyler) 1923- .... **CLC 50**
See also CA 1-4R; CANR 3, 27, 65
Lynx
See West, Rebecca

Lyons, Marcus
See Blish, James (Benjamin)
Lyre, Pinchbeck
See Sassoon, Siegfried (Lorraine)
Lytle, Andrew (Nelson) 1902-1995 .... **CLC 22**
See also CA 9-12R; 150; CANR 70; DLB 6; DLBY 95
Lyttelton, George 1709-1773 .... **LC 10**
Maas, Peter 1929- .... **CLC 29**
See also CA 93-96; INT 93-96; MTCW 2
Macaulay, Rose 1881-1958 .... **TCLC 7, 44**
See also CA 104; DLB 36
Macaulay, Thomas Babington 1800-1859 **NCLC 42**
See also CDBLB 1832-1890; DLB 32, 55
MacBeth, George (Mann) 1932-1992 **CLC 2, 5, 9**
See also CA 25-28R; 136; CANR 61, 66; DLB 40; MTCW 1; SATA 4; SATA-Obit 70
MacCaig, Norman (Alexander) 1910- . **CLC 36; DAB; DAM POET**
See also CA 9-12R; CANR 3, 34; DLB 27
MacCarthy, Sir (Charles Otto) Desmond 1877-1952 **TCLC 36**
See also CA 167
MacDiarmid, Hugh .. **CLC 2, 4, 11, 19, 63; PC 9**
See also Grieve, C(hristopher) M(urray)
See also CDBLB 1945-1960; DLB 20
MacDonald, Anson
See Heinlein, Robert A(nson)
Macdonald, Cynthia 1928- .... **CLC 13, 19**
See also CA 49-52; CANR 4, 44; DLB 105
MacDonald, George 1824-1905 .... **TCLC 9**
See also CA 106; 137; CANR 80; DLB 18, 163, 178; MAICYA; SATA 33, 100
Macdonald, John
See Millar, Kenneth
MacDonald, John D(ann) 1916-1986 . **CLC 3, 27, 44; DAM NOV, POP**
See also CA 1-4R; 121; CANR 1, 19, 60; DLB 8; DLBY 86; MTCW 1, 2
Macdonald, John Ross
See Millar, Kenneth
Macdonald, Ross .... **CLC 1, 2, 3, 14, 34, 41**
See also Millar, Kenneth
See also DLBD 6
MacDougal, John
See Blish, James (Benjamin)
MacEwen, Gwendolyn (Margaret) 1941-1987 **CLC 13, 55**
See also CA 9-12R; 124; CANR 7, 22; DLB 53; SATA 50; SATA-Obit 55
Macha, Karel Hynek 1810-1846 .... **NCLC 46**
Machado (y Ruiz), Antonio 1875-1939 .. **TCLC 3**
See also CA 104; 174; DLB 108; HW 2
Machado de Assis, Joaquim Maria 1839-1908 **TCLC 10; BLC 2; HLCS 2; SSC 24**
See also CA 107; 153
Machen, Arthur .... **TCLC 4; SSC 20**
See also Jones, Arthur Llewellyn
See also DLB 36, 156, 178
Machiavelli, Niccolo 1469-1527 .. **LC 8, 36; DA; DAB; DAC; DAM MST; WLCS**
MacInnes, Colin 1914-1976 .... **CLC 4, 23**
See also CA 69-72; 65-68; CANR 21; DLB 14; MTCW 1, 2
MacInnes, Helen (Clark) 1907-1985 **CLC 27, 39; DAM POP**
See also CA 1-4R; 117; CANR 1, 28, 58; DLB 87; MTCW 1, 2; SATA 22; SATA-Obit 44
Mackenzie, Compton (Edward Montague) 1883-1972 .... **CLC 18**
See also CA 21-22; 37-40R; CAP 2; DLB 34, 100
Mackenzie, Henry 1745-1831 .... **NCLC 41**
See also DLB 39
Mackintosh, Elizabeth 1896(?)-1952
See Tey, Josephine
See also CA 110

MacLaren, James
See Grieve, C(hristopher) M(urray)
Mac Laverty, Bernard 1942- .... **CLC 31**
See also CA 116; 118; CANR 43; INT 118
MacLean, Alistair (Stuart) 1922(?)-1987 **CLC 3, 13, 50, 63; DAM POP**
See also CA 57-60; 121; CANR 28, 61; MTCW 1; SATA 23; SATA-Obit 50
Maclean, Norman (Fitzroy) 1902-1990 . **CLC 78; DAM POP; SSC 13**
See also CA 102; 132; CANR 49; DLB 206
MacLeish, Archibald 1892-1982 **CLC 3, 8, 14, 68; DAM POET**
See also CA 9-12R; 106; CANR 33, 63; CDALBS; DLB 4, 7, 45; DLBY 82; MTCW 1, 2
MacLennan, (John) Hugh 1907-1990 **CLC 2, 14, 92; DAC; DAM MST**
See also CA 5-8R; 142; CANR 33; DLB 68; MTCW 1, 2
MacLeod, Alistair 1936- .. **CLC 56; DAC; DAM MST**
See also CA 123; DLB 60; MTCW 2
Macleod, Fiona
See Sharp, William
MacNeice, (Frederick) Louis 1907-1963 **CLC 1, 4, 10, 53; DAB; DAM POET**
See also CA 85-88; CANR 61; DLB 10, 20; MTCW 1, 2
MacNeill, Dand
See Fraser, George MacDonald
Macpherson, James 1736-1796 .... **LC 29**
See also Ossian
See also DLB 109
Macpherson, (Jean) Jay 1931- .... **CLC 14**
See also CA 5-8R; DLB 53
MacShane, Frank 1927- .... **CLC 39**
See also CA 9-12R; CANR 3, 33; DLB 111
Macumber, Mari
See Sandoz, Mari(e Susette)
Madach, Imre 1823-1864 .... **NCLC 19**
Madden, (Jerry) David 1933- .... **CLC 5, 15**
See also CA 1-4R; CAAS 3; CANR 4, 45; DLB 6; MTCW 1
Maddern, Al(an)
See Ellison, Harlan (Jay)
Madhubuti, Haki R. 1942- ... **CLC 6, 73; BLC 2; DAM MULT, POET; PC 5**
See also Lee, Don L.
See also BW 2, 3; CA 73-76; CANR 24, 51, 73; DLB 5, 41; DLBD 8; MTCW 2
Maepenn, Hugh
See Kuttner, Henry
Maepenn, K. H.
See Kuttner, Henry
Maeterlinck, Maurice 1862-1949 **TCLC 3; DAM DRAM**
See also CA 104; 136; CANR 80; DLB 192; SATA 66
Maginn, William 1794-1842 .... **NCLC 8**
See also DLB 110, 159
Mahapatra, Jayanta 1928- **CLC 33; DAM MULT**
See also CA 73-76; CAAS 9; CANR 15, 33, 66
Mahfouz, Naguib (Abdel Aziz Al-Sabilgi) 1911(?)-
See Mahfuz, Najib
See also BEST 89:2; CA 128; CANR 55; DAM NOV; MTCW 1, 2
Mahfuz, Najib .... **CLC 52, 55**
See also Mahfouz, Naguib (Abdel Aziz Al-Sabilgi)
See also DLBY 88
Mahon, Derek 1941- .... **CLC 27**
See also CA 113; 128; DLB 40
Mailer, Norman 1923- **CLC 1, 2, 3, 4, 5, 8, 11, 14, 28, 39, 74, 111; DA; DAB; DAC; DAM MST, NOV, POP**
See also AITN 2; CA 9-12R; CABS 1; CANR 28,

74, 77; CDALB 1968-1988; DLB 2, 16, 28, 185; DLBD 3; DLBY 80, 83; MTCW 1, 2

Maillet, Antonine 1929- ...... **CLC 54, 118; DAC**
See also CA 115; 120; CANR 46, 74, 77; DLB 60; INT 120; MTCW 2

Mais, Roger 1905-1955 .... **TCLC 8**
See also BW 1, 3; CA 105; 124; DLB 125; MTCW 1

Maistre, Joseph de 1753-1821 .... **NCLC 37**

Maitland, Frederic 1850-1906 .... **TCLC 65**

Maitland, Sara (Louise) 1950- .... **CLC 49**
See also CA 69-72; CANR 13, 59

Major, Clarence 1936- .. **CLC 3, 19, 48; BLC 2; DAM MULT**
See also BW 2, 3; CA 21-24R; CAAS 6; CANR 13, 25, 53; DLB 33

Major, Kevin (Gerald) 1949- .... **CLC 26; DAC**
See also AAYA 16; CA 97-100; CANR 21, 38; CLR 11; DLB 60; INT CANR-21; JRDA; MAICYA; SATA 32, 82

Maki, James
See Ozu, Yasujiro

Malabaila, Damiano
See Levi, Primo

Malamud, Bernard 1914-1986 **CLC 1, 2, 3, 5, 8, 9, 11, 18, 27, 44, 78, 85; DA; DAB; DAC; DAM MST, NOV, POP; SSC 15; WLC**
See also AAYA 16; CA 5-8R; 118; CABS 1; CANR 28, 62; CDALB 1941-1968; DLB 2, 28, 152; DLBY 80, 86; MTCW 1, 2

Malan, Herman
See Bosman, Herman Charles; Bosman, Herman Charles

Malaparte, Curzio 1898-1957 .... **TCLC 52**

Malcolm, Dan
See Silverberg, Robert

Malcolm X .... **CLC 82, 117; BLC 2; WLCS**
See also Little, Malcolm

Malherbe, Francois de 1555-1628 .... **LC 5**

Mallarme, Stephane 1842-1898 **NCLC 4, 41; DAM POET; PC 4**

Mallet-Joris, Francoise 1930- .... **CLC 11**
See also CA 65-68; CANR 17; DLB 83

Malley, Ern
See McAuley, James Phillip

Mallowan, Agatha Christie
See Christie, Agatha (Mary Clarissa)

Maloff, Saul 1922- .... **CLC 5**
See also CA 33-36R

Malone, Louis
See MacNeice, (Frederick) Louis

Malone, Michael (Christopher) 1942- .. **CLC 43**
See also CA 77-80; CANR 14, 32, 57

Malory, (Sir) Thomas 1410(?)-1471(?) **LC 11; DA; DAB; DAC; DAM MST; WLCS**
See also CDBLB Before 1660; DLB 146; SATA 59; SATA-Brief 33

Malouf, (George Joseph) David 1934- **CLC 28, 86**
See also CA 124; CANR 50, 76; MTCW 2

Malraux, (Georges-)Andre 1901-1976 **CLC 1, 4, 9, 13, 15, 57; DAM NOV**
See also CA 21-22; 69-72; CANR 34, 58; CAP 2; DLB 72; MTCW 1, 2

Malzberg, Barry N(athaniel) 1939- .... **CLC 7**
See also CA 61-64; CAAS 4; CANR 16; DLB 8

Mamet, David (Alan) 1947- **CLC 9, 15, 34, 46, 91; DAM DRAM; DC 4**
See also AAYA 3; CA 81-84; CABS 3; CANR 15, 41, 67, 72; DLB 7; MTCW 1, 2

Mamoulian, Rouben (Zachary) 1897-1987 **CLC 16**
See also CA 25-28R; 124

Mandelstam, Osip (Emilievich) 1891(?)-1938(?) **TCLC 2, 6; PC 14**
See also CA 104; 150; MTCW 2

Mander, (Mary) Jane 1877-1949 .... **TCLC 31**
See also CA 162

Mandeville, John fl. 1350- .... **CMLC 19**

See also DLB 146

Mandiargues, Andre Pieyre de .... **CLC 41**
See also Pieyre de Mandiargues, Andre
See also DLB 83

Mandrake, Ethel Belle
See Thurman, Wallace (Henry)

Mangan, James Clarence 1803-1849 .. **NCLC 27**

Maniere, J.-E.
See Giraudoux, (Hippolyte) Jean

Mankiewicz, Herman (Jacob) 1897-1953 **TCLC 85**
See also CA 120; 169; DLB 26

Manley, (Mary) Delariviere 1672(?)-1724 **LC 1, 42**
See also DLB 39, 80

Mann, Abel
See Creasey, John

Mann, Emily 1952- .... **DC 7**
See also CA 130; CANR 55

Mann, (Luiz) Heinrich 1871-1950 .... **TCLC 9**
See also CA 106; 164; DLB 66, 118

Mann, (Paul) Thomas 1875-1955 **TCLC 2, 8, 14, 21, 35, 44, 60; DA; DAB; DAC; DAM MST, NOV; SSC 5; WLC**
See also CA 104; 128; DLB 66; MTCW 1, 2

Mannheim, Karl 1893-1947 .... **TCLC 65**

Manning, David
See Faust, Frederick (Schiller)

Manning, Frederic 1887(?)-1935 .... **TCLC 25**
See also CA 124

Manning, Olivia 1915-1980 .... **CLC 5, 19**
See also CA 5-8R; 101; CANR 29; MTCW 1

Mano, D. Keith 1942- .... **CLC 2, 10**
See also CA 25-28R; CAAS 6; CANR 26, 57; DLB 6

Mansfield, Katherine **TCLC 2, 8, 39; DAB; SSC 9, 23; WLC**
See also Beauchamp, Kathleen Mansfield
See also DLB 162

Manso, Peter 1940- .... **CLC 39**
See also CA 29-32R; CANR 44

Mantecon, Juan Jimenez
See Jimenez (Mantecon), Juan Ramon

Manton, Peter
See Creasey, John

Man Without a Spleen, A
See Chekhov, Anton (Pavlovich)

Manzoni, Alessandro 1785-1873 .... **NCLC 29**

Map, Walter 1140-1209 .... **CMLC 32**

Mapu, Abraham (ben Jekutiel) 1808-1867 **NCLC 18**

Mara, Sally
See Queneau, Raymond

Marat, Jean Paul 1743-1793 .... **LC 10**

Marcel, Gabriel Honore 1889-1973 .... **CLC 15**
See also CA 102; 45-48; MTCW 1, 2

Marchbanks, Samuel
See Davies, (William) Robertson

Marchi, Giacomo
See Bassani, Giorgio

Margulies, Donald .... **CLC 76**

Marie de France c. 12th cent. - **CMLC 8; PC 22**
See also DLB 208

Marie de l'Incarnation 1599-1672 .... **LC 10**

Marier, Captain Victor
See Griffith, D(avid Lewelyn) W(ark)

Mariner, Scott
See Pohl, Frederik

Marinetti, Filippo Tommaso 1876-1944 **TCLC 10**
See also CA 107; DLB 114

Marivaux, Pierre Carlet de Chamblain de 1688-1763 .... **LC 4; DC 7**

Markandaya, Kamala .... **CLC 8, 38**
See also Taylor, Kamala (Purnaiya)

Markfield, Wallace 1926- .... **CLC 8**
See also CA 69-72; CAAS 3; DLB 2, 28

Markham, Edwin 1852-1940 .... **TCLC 47**
See also CA 160; DLB 54, 186

Markham, Robert

See Amis, Kingsley (William)

Marks, J
See Highwater, Jamake (Mamake)

Marks-Highwater, J
See Highwater, Jamake (Mamake)

Markson, David M(errill) 1927- .... **CLC 67**
See also CA 49-52; CANR 1

Marley, Bob .... **CLC 17**
See also Marley, Robert Nesta

Marley, Robert Nesta 1945-1981
See Marley, Bob
See also CA 107; 103

Marlowe, Christopher 1564-1593 **LC 22, 47; DA; DAB; DAC; DAM DRAM, MST; DC 1; WLC**
See also CDBLB Before 1660; DLB 62

Marlowe, Stephen 1928-
See Queen, Ellery
See also CA 13-16R; CANR 6, 55

Marmontel, Jean-Francois 1723-1799 .... **LC 2**

Marquand, John P(hillips) 1893-1960 **CLC 2, 10**
See also CA 85-88; CANR 73; DLB 9, 102; MTCW 2

Marques, Rene 1919-1979 **CLC 96; DAM MULT; HLC**
See also CA 97-100; 85-88; CANR 78; DLB 113; HW 1, 2

Marquez, Gabriel (Jose) Garcia
See Garcia Marquez, Gabriel (Jose)

Marquis, Don(ald Robert Perry) 1878-1937 **TCLC 7**
See also CA 104; 166; DLB 11, 25

Marric, J. J.
See Creasey, John

Marryat, Frederick 1792-1848 .... **NCLC 3**
See also DLB 21, 163

Marsden, James
See Creasey, John

Marsh, (Edith) Ngaio 1899-1982 **CLC 7, 53; DAM POP**
See also CA 9-12R; CANR 6, 58; DLB 77; MTCW 1, 2

Marshall, Garry 1934- .... **CLC 17**
See also AAYA 3; CA 111; SATA 60

Marshall, Paule 1929- **CLC 27, 72; BLC 3; DAM MULT; SSC 3**
See also BW 2, 3; CA 77-80; CANR 25, 73; DLB 157; MTCW 1, 2

Marshallik
See Zangwill, Israel

Marsten, Richard
See Hunter, Evan

Marston, John 1576-1634 .. **LC 33; DAM DRAM**
See also DLB 58, 172

Martha, Henry
See Harris, Mark

Marti (y Perez), Jose (Julian) 1853-1895 **NCLC 63; DAM MULT; HLC**
See also HW 2

Martial c. 40-c. 104 .... **PC 10**
See also DLB 211

Martin, Ken
See Hubbard, L(afayette) Ron(ald)

Martin, Richard
See Creasey, John

Martin, Steve 1945- .... **CLC 30**
See also CA 97-100; CANR 30; MTCW 1

Martin, Valerie 1948- .... **CLC 89**
See also BEST 90:2; CA 85-88; CANR 49

Martin, Violet Florence 1862-1915 ..... **TCLC 51**

Martin, Webber
See Silverberg, Robert

Martindale, Patrick Victor
See White, Patrick (Victor Martindale)

Martin du Gard, Roger 1881-1958 ...... **TCLC 24**
See also CA 118; DLB 65

Martineau, Harriet 1802-1876 .... **NCLC 26**
See also DLB 21, 55, 159, 163, 166, 190; YABC 2

WLCS

See also CA 104; 130; CDALB 1917-1929; DLB 45; MTCW 1, 2

Miller, Arthur 1915-CLC **1, 2, 6, 10, 15, 26, 47, 78; DA; DAB; DAC; DAM DRAM, MST; DC 1; WLC**

See also AAYA 15; AITN 1; CA 1-4R; CABS 3; CANR 2, 30, 54, 76; CDALB 1941-1968; DLB 7; MTCW 1, 2

Miller, Henry (Valentine) 1891-1980CLC **1, 2, 4, 9, 14, 43, 84; DA; DAB; DAC; DAM MST, NOV; WLC**

See also CA 9-12R; 97-100; CANR 33, 64; CDALB 1929-1941; DLB 4, 9; DLBY 80; MTCW 1, 2

Miller, Jason 1939(?)- .... CLC **2**

See also AITN 1; CA 73-76; DLB 7

Miller, Sue 1943- .... CLC **44; DAM POP**

See also BEST 90:3; CA 139; CANR 59; DLB 143

Miller, Walter M(ichael, Jr.) 1923-CLC **4, 30**

See also CA 85-88; DLB 8

Millett, Kate 1934- .... CLC **67**

See also AITN 1; CA 73-76; CANR 32, 53, 76; MTCW 1, 2

Millhauser, Steven (Lewis) 1943-CLC **21, 54, 109**

See also CA 110; 111; CANR 63; DLB 2; INT 111; MTCW 2

Millin, Sarah Gertrude 1889-1968 .... CLC **49**

See also CA 102; 93-96

Milne, A(lan) A(lexander) 1882-1956TCLC **6, 88; DAB; DAC; DAM MST**

See also CA 104; 133; CLR 1, 26; DLB 10, 77, 100, 160; MAICYA; MTCW 1, 2; SATA 100; YABC 1

Milner, Ron(ald) 1938- .. CLC **56; BLC 3; DAM MULT**

See also AITN 1; BW 1; CA 73-76; CANR 24, 81; DLB 38; MTCW 1

Milnes, Richard Monckton 1809-1885 NCLC **61**

See also DLB 32, 184

Milosz, Czeslaw 1911-CLC **5, 11, 22, 31, 56, 82; DAM MST, POET; PC 8; WLCS**

See also CA 81-84; CANR 23, 51; MTCW 1, 2

Milton, John 1608-1674LC **9, 43; DA; DAB; DAC; DAM MST, POET; PC 19; WLC**

See also CDBLB 1660-1789; DLB 131, 151

Min, Anchee 1957- .... CLC **86**

See also CA 146

Minehaha, Cornelius

See Wedekind, (Benjamin) Frank(lin)

Miner, Valerie 1947- .... CLC **40**

See also CA 97-100; CANR 59

Minimo, Duca

See D'Annunzio, Gabriele

Minot, Susan 1956- .... CLC **44**

See also CA 134

Minus, Ed 1938- .... CLC **39**

Miranda, Javier

See Bioy Casares, Adolfo

Miranda, Javier

See Bioy Casares, Adolfo

Mirbeau, Octave 1848-1917 .... TCLC **55**

See also DLB 123, 192

Miro (Ferrer), Gabriel (Francisco Victor) 1879-1930 .... TCLC **5**

See also CA 104

Mishima, Yukio 1925-1970CLC **2, 4, 6, 9, 27; DC 1; SSC 4**

See Hiraoka, Kimitake

See also DLB 182; MTCW 2

Mistral, Frederic 1830-1914 .... TCLC **51**

See also CA 122

Mistral, Gabriela .... TCLC **2; HLC**

See Godoy Alcayaga, Lucila

See also MTCW 2

Mistry, Rohinton 1952- .... CLC **71; DAC**

See also CA 141

Mitchell, Clyde

See Ellison, Harlan (Jay); Silverberg, Robert

Mitchell, James Leslie 1901-1935

See Gibbon, Lewis Grassic

See also CA 104; DLB 15

Mitchell, Joni 1943- .... CLC **12**

See also CA 112

Mitchell, Joseph (Quincy) 1908-1996 ... CLC **98**

See also CA 77-80; 152; CANR 69; DLB 185; DLBY 96

Mitchell, Margaret (Munnerlyn) 1900-1949 TCLC **11; DAM NOV, POP**

See also AAYA 23; CA 109; 125; CANR 55; CDALBS; DLB 9; MTCW 1, 2

Mitchell, Peggy

See Mitchell, Margaret (Munnerlyn)

Mitchell, S(ilas) Weir 1829-1914 ... TCLC **36**

See also CA 165; DLB 202

Mitchell, W(illiam) O(rmond) 1914-1998CLC **25; DAC; DAM MST**

See also CA 77-80; 165; CANR 15, 43; DLB 88

Mitchell, William 1879-1936 .... TCLC **81**

Mitford, Mary Russell 1787-1855 .... NCLC **4**

See also DLB 110, 116

Mitford, Nancy 1904-1973 .... CLC **44**

See also CA 9-12R; DLB 191

Miyamoto, (Chujo) Yuriko 1899-1951 . TCLC **37**

See also CA 170, 174; DLB 180

Miyazawa, Kenji 1896-1933 .... TCLC **76**

See also CA 157

Mizoguchi, Kenji 1898-1956 .... TCLC **72**

See also CA 167

Mo, Timothy (Peter) 1950(?)- .... CLC **46**

See also CA 117; DLB 194; MTCW 1

Modarressi, Taghi (M.) 1931- .... CLC **44**

See also CA 121; 134; INT 134

Modiano, Patrick (Jean) 1945- .... CLC **18**

See also CA 85-88; CANR 17, 40; DLB 83

Moerck, Paal

See Roelvaag, O(le) E(dvart)

Mofolo, Thomas (Mokopu) 1875(?)-1948TCLC **22; BLC 3; DAM MULT**

See also CA 121; 153; MTCW 2

Mohr, Nicholasa 1938-CLC **12; DAM MULT; HLC**

See also AAYA 8; CA 49-52; CANR 1, 32, 64; CLR 22; DLB 145; HW 1, 2; JRDA; SAAS 8; SATA 8, 97

Mojtabai, A(nn) G(race) 1938- CLC **5, 9, 15, 29**

See also CA 85-88

Moliere 1622-1673 LC **10, 28; DA; DAB; DAC; DAM DRAM, MST; WLC**

Molin, Charles

See Mayne, William (James Carter)

Molnar, Ferenc 1878-1952TCLC **20; DAM DRAM**

See also CA 109; 153

Momaday, N(avarre) Scott 1934- CLC **2, 19, 85, 95; DA; DAB; DAC; DAM MST, MULT, NOV, POP; PC 25; WLCS**

See also AAYA 11; CA 25-28R; CANR 14, 34, 68; CDALBS; DLB 143, 175; INT CANR-14; MTCW 1, 2; NNAL; SATA 48; SATA-Brief 30

Monette, Paul 1945-1995 .... CLC **82**

See also CA 139; 147

Monroe, Harriet 1860-1936 .... TCLC **12**

See also CA 109; DLB 54, 91

Monroe, Lyle

See Heinlein, Robert A(nson)

Montagu, Elizabeth 1720-1800 .... NCLC **7**

Montagu, Mary (Pierrepont) Wortley 1689-1762 LC **9; PC 16**

See also DLB 95, 101

Montagu, W. H.

See Coleridge, Samuel Taylor

Montague, John (Patrick) 1929- ..... CLC **13, 46**

See also CA 9-12R; CANR 9, 69; DLB 40; MTCW 1

Montaigne, Michel (Eyquem) de 1533-1592LC **8;**

DA; DAB; DAC; DAM MST; WLC

Montale, Eugenio 1896-1981CLC **7, 9, 18; PC 13**

See also CA 17-20R; 104; CANR 30; DLB 114; MTCW 1

Montesquieu, Charles-Louis de Secondat 1689-1755 .... LC **7**

Montgomery, (Robert) Bruce 1921-1978

See Crispin, Edmund

See also CA 104

Montgomery, L(ucy) M(aud) 1874-1942TCLC **51; DAC; DAM MST**

See also AAYA 12; CA 108; 137; CLR 8; DLB 92; DLBD 14; JRDA; MAICYA; MTCW 2; SATA 100; YABC 1

Montgomery, Marion H., Jr. 1925- .... CLC **7**

See also AITN 1; CA 1-4R; CANR 3, 48; DLB 6

Montgomery, Max

See Davenport, Guy (Mattison, Jr.)

Montherlant, Henry (Milon) de 1896-1972CLC **8, 19; DAM DRAM**

See also CA 85-88; 37-40R; DLB 72; MTCW 1

Monty Python

See Chapman, Graham; Cleese, John (Marwood); Gilliam, Terry (Vance); Idle, Eric; Jones, Terence Graham Parry; Palin, Michael (Edward)

See also AAYA 7

Moodie, Susanna (Strickland) 1803-1885 NCLC **14**

See also DLB 99

Mooney, Edward 1951-

See Mooney, Ted

See also CA 130

Mooney, Ted .... CLC **25**

See also Mooney, Edward

Moorcock, Michael (John) 1939- CLC **5, 27, 58**

See also Bradbury, Edward P.

See also AAYA 26; CA 45-48; CAAS 5; CANR 2, 17, 38, 64; DLB 14; MTCW 1, 2; SATA 93

Moore, Brian 1921-1999CLC **1, 3, 5, 7, 8, 19, 32, 90; DAB; DAC; DAM MST**

See also CA 1-4R; 174; CANR 1, 25, 42, 63; MTCW 1, 2

Moore, Edward

See Muir, Edwin

Moore, G. E. 1873-1958 .... TCLC **89**

Moore, George Augustus 1852-1933TCLC **7; SSC 19**

See also CA 104; 177; DLB 10, 18, 57, 135

Moore, Lorrie .... CLC **39, 45, 68**

See also Moore, Marie Lorena

Moore, Marianne (Craig) 1887-1972CLC **1, 2, 4, 8, 10, 13, 19, 47; DA; DAB; DAC; DAM MST, POET; PC 4; WLCS**

See also CA 1-4R; 33-36R; CANR 3, 61; CDALB 1929-1941; DLB 45; DLBD 7; MTCW 1, 2; SATA 20

Moore, Marie Lorena 1957-

See Moore, Lorrie

See also CA 116; CANR 39

Moore, Thomas 1779-1852 .... NCLC **6**

See also DLB 96, 144

Morand, Paul 1888-1976 .... CLC **41; SSC 22**

See also CA 69-72; DLB 65

Morante, Elsa 1918-1985 .... CLC **8, 47**

See also CA 85-88; 117; CANR 35; DLB 177; MTCW 1, 2

Moravia, Alberto 1907-1990CLC **2, 7, 11, 27, 46; SSC 26**

See also Pincherle, Alberto

See also DLB 177; MTCW 2

More, Hannah 1745-1833 .... NCLC **27**

See also DLB 107, 109, 116, 158

More, Henry 1614-1687 .... LC **9**

See also DLB 126

More, Sir Thomas 1478-1535 .... LC **10, 32**

Moreas, Jean .... TCLC **18**

See also CA 140

Ouida .... TCLC 43
See also De La Ramee, (Marie) Louise
See also DLB 18, 156

Ousmane, Sembene 1923- .... CLC 66; BLC 3
See also BW 1, 3; CA 117; 125; CANR 81; MTCW
1

Ovid 43B.C.-17 ...... CMLC 7; DAM POET; PC 2
See also DLB 211

Owen, Hugh
See Faust, Frederick (Schiller)

Owen, Wilfred (Edward Salter) 1893-1918 TCLC
5, 27; DA; DAB; DAC; DAM MST, POET;
PC 19; WLC
See also CA 104; 141; CDBLB 1914-1945; DLB
20; MTCW 2

Owens, Rochelle 1936- .... CLC 8
See also CA 17-20R; CAAS 2; CANR 39

Oz, Amos 1939-CLC 5, 8, 11, 27, 33, 54; DAM
NOV
See also CA 53-56; CANR 27, 47, 65; MTCW 1, 2

Ozick, Cynthia 1928-CLC 3, 7, 28, 62; DAM NOV,
POP; SSC 15
See also BEST 90:1; CA 17-20R; CANR 23, 58;
DLB 28, 152; DLBY 82; INT CANR-23; MTCW
1, 2

Ozu, Yasujiro 1903-1963 .... CLC 16
See also CA 112

Pacheco, C.
See Pessoa, Fernando (Antonio Nogueira)

P'a Chin .... CLC 18
See also Li Fei-kan

Pack, Robert 1929- .... CLC 13
See also CA 1-4R; CANR 3, 44; DLB 5

Padgett, Lewis
See Kuttner, Henry

Padilla (Lorenzo), Heberto 1932- .... CLC 38
See also AITN 1; CA 123; 131; HW 1

Page, Jimmy 1944- .... CLC 12

Page, Louise 1955- .... CLC 40
See also CA 140; CANR 76

Page, P(atricia) K(athleen) 1916- .... CLC 7, 18;
DAC; DAM MST; PC 12
See also CA 53-56; CANR 4, 22, 65; DLB 68;
MTCW 1

Page, Thomas Nelson 1853-1922 .... SSC 23
See also CA 118; 177; DLB 12, 78; DLBD 13

Pagels, Elaine Hiesey 1943- .... CLC 104
See also CA 45-48; CANR 2, 24, 51

Paget, Violet 1856-1935
See Lee, Vernon
See also CA 104; 166

Paget-Lowe, Henry
See Lovecraft, H(oward) P(hillips)

Paglia, Camille (Anna) 1947- .... CLC 68
See also CA 140; CANR 72; MTCW 2

Paige, Richard
See Koontz, Dean R(ay)

Paine, Thomas 1737-1809 .... NCLC 62
See also CDALB 1640-1865; DLB 31, 43, 73, 158

Pakenham, Antonia
See Fraser, (Lady) Antonia (Pakenham)

Palamas, Kostes 1859-1943 .... TCLC 5
See also CA 105

Palazzeschi, Aldo 1885-1974 .... CLC 11
See also CA 89-92; 53-56; DLB 114

Paley, Grace 1922-CLC 4, 6, 37; DAM POP; SSC
8
See also CA 25-28R; CANR 13, 46, 74; DLB 28;
INT CANR-13; MTCW 1, 2

Palin, Michael (Edward) 1943- .... CLC 21
See also Monty Python
See also CA 107; CANR 35; SATA 67

Palliser, Charles 1947- .... CLC 65
See also CA 136; CANR 76

Palma, Ricardo 1833-1919 .... TCLC 29
See also CA 168

Pancake, Breece Dexter 1952-1979
See Pancake, Breece D'J
See also CA 123; 109

Pancake, Breece D'J .... CLC 29
See also Pancake, Breece Dexter
See also DLB 130

Panko, Rudy
See Gogol, Nikolai (Vasilyevich)

Papadiamantis, Alexandros 1851-1911 TCLC 29
See also CA 168

Papadiamantopoulos, Johannes 1856-1910
See Moreas, Jean
See also CA 117

Papini, Giovanni 1881-1956 .... TCLC 22
See also CA 121

Paracelsus 1493-1541 .... LC 14
See also DLB 179

Parasol, Peter
See Stevens, Wallace

Pardo Bazan, Emilia 1851-1921 .... SSC 30

Pareto, Vilfredo 1848-1923 .... TCLC 69
See also CA 175

Parfenie, Maria
See Codrescu, Andrei

Parini, Jay (Lee) 1948- .... CLC 54
See also CA 97-100; CAAS 16; CANR 32

Park, Jordan
See Kornbluth, C(yril) M.; Pohl, Frederik

Park, Robert E(zra) 1864-1944 .... TCLC 73
See also CA 122; 165

Parker, Bert
See Ellison, Harlan (Jay)

Parker, Dorothy (Rothschild) 1893-1967 CLC 15,
68; DAM POET; SSC 2
See also CA 19-20; 25-28R; CAP 2; DLB 11, 45,
86; MTCW 1, 2

Parker, Robert B(rown) 1932- .... CLC 27; DAM
NOV, POP
See also AAYA 28; BEST 89:4; CA 49-52; CANR
1, 26, 52; INT CANR-26; MTCW 1

Parkin, Frank 1940- .... CLC 43
See also CA 147

Parkman, Francis, Jr. 1823-1893 .... NCLC 12
See also DLB 1, 30, 186

Parks, Gordon (Alexander Buchanan) 1912-CLC
1, 16; BLC 3; DAM MULT
See also AITN 2; BW 2, 3; CA 41-44R; CANR 26,
66; DLB 33; MTCW 2; SATA 8, 108

Parmenides c. 515B.C.-c. 450B.C. ...... CMLC 22
See also DLB 176

Parnell, Thomas 1679-1718 .... LC 3
See also DLB 94

Parra, Nicanor 1914- CLC 2, 102; DAM MULT;
HLC
See also CA 85-88; CANR 32; HW 1; MTCW 1

Parrish, Mary Frances
See Fisher, M(ary) F(rances) K(ennedy)

Parson
See Coleridge, Samuel Taylor

Parson Lot
See Kingsley, Charles

Partridge, Anthony
See Oppenheim, E(dward) Phillips

Pascal, Blaise 1623-1662 .... LC 35

Pascoli, Giovanni 1855-1912 .... TCLC 45
See also CA 170

Pasolini, Pier Paolo 1922-1975 CLC 20, 37, 106;
PC 17
See also CA 93-96; 61-64; CANR 63; DLB 128,
177; MTCW 1

Pasquini
See Silone, Ignazio

Pastan, Linda (Olenik) 1932- ..... CLC 27; DAM
POET
See also CA 61-64; CANR 18, 40, 61; DLB 5

Pasternak, Boris (Leonidovich) 1890-1960 C L C
7, 10, 18, 63; DA; DAB; DAC; DAM MST,
NOV, POET; PC 6; SSC 31; WLC
See also CA 127; 116; MTCW 1, 2

Patchen, Kenneth 1911-1972 CLC 1, 2, 18; DAM
POET
See also CA 1-4R; 33-36R; CANR 3, 35; DLB 16,
48; MTCW 1

Pater, Walter (Horatio) 1839-1894 .... NCLC 7
See also CDBLB 1832-1890; DLB 57, 156

Paterson, A(ndrew) B(arton) 1864-1941 TCLC 32
See also CA 155; SATA 97

Paterson, Katherine (Womeldorf) 1932-CLC 12,
30
See also AAYA 1; CA 21-24R; CANR 28, 59; CLR
7, 50; DLB 52; JRDA; MAICYA; MTCW 1;
SATA 13, 53, 92

Patmore, Coventry Kersey Dighton 1823-1896
NCLC 9
See also DLB 35, 98

Paton, Alan (Stewart) 1903-1988 CLC 4, 10,
25, 55, 106; DA; DAB; DAC; DAM MST,
NOV; WLC
See also AAYA 26; CA 13-16; 125; CANR 22;
CAP 1; DLBD 17; MTCW 1, 2; SATA 11;
SATA-Obit 56

Paton Walsh, Gillian 1937-
See Walsh, Jill Paton
See also CANR 38; JRDA; MAICYA; SAAS 3;
SATA 4, 72, 109

Patton, George S. 1885-1945 .... TCLC 79

Paulding, James Kirke 1778-1860 .... NCLC 2
See also DLB 3, 59, 74

Paulin, Thomas Neilson 1949-
See Paulin, Tom
See also CA 123; 128

Paulin, Tom .... CLC 37
See also Paulin, Thomas Neilson
See also DLB 40

Paustovsky, Konstantin (Georgievich) 1892-1968
CLC 40
See also CA 93-96; 25-28R

Pavese, Cesare 1908-1950 TCLC 3; PC 13; SSC 19
See also CA 104; 169; DLB 128, 177

Pavic, Milorad 1929- .... CLC 60
See also CA 136; DLB 181

Pavlov, Ivan Petrovich 1849-1936 .... TCLC 91
See also CA 118

Payne, Alan
See Jakes, John (William)

Paz, Gil
See Lugones, Leopoldo

Paz, Octavio 1914-1998 CLC 3, 4, 6, 10, 19, 51, 65,
119; DA; DAB; DAC; DAM MST, MULT,
POET; HLC; PC 1; WLC
See also CA 73-76; 165; CANR 32, 65; DLBY 90,
98; HW 1, 2; MTCW 1, 2

p'Bitek, Okot 1931-1982 CLC 96; BLC 3; DAM
MULT
See also BW 2, 3; CA 124; 107; DLB 125; MTCW
1, 2

Peacock, Molly 1947- .... CLC 60
See also CA 103; CAAS 21; CANR 52; DLB 120

Peacock, Thomas Love 1785-1866 ...... NCLC 22
See also DLB 96, 116

Peake, Mervyn 1911-1968 .... CLC 7, 54
See also CA 5-8R; 25-28R; CANR 3; DLB 15, 160;
MTCW 1; SATA 23

Pearce, Philippa .... CLC 21
See also Christie, (Ann) Philippa
See also CLR 9; DLB 161; MAICYA; SATA 1, 67

Pearl, Eric
See Elman, Richard (Martin)

Pearson, T(homas) R(eid) 1956- .... CLC 39
See also CA 120; 130; INT 130

Peck, Dale 1967- .... CLC 81
See also CA 146; CANR 72

Peck, John 1941- .... CLC 3
See also CA 49-52; CANR 3

Peck, Richard (Wayne) 1934- .... **CLC 21**
See also AAYA 1, 24; CA 85-88; CANR 19, 38; CLR 15; INT CANR-19; JRDA; MAICYA; SAAS 2; SATA 18, 55, 97
Peck, Robert Newton 1928- **CLC 17; DA; DAC; DAM MST**
See also AAYA 3; CA 81-84; CANR 31, 63; CLR 45; JRDA; MAICYA; SAAS 1; SATA 21, 62; SATA-Essay 108
Peckinpah, (David) Sam(uel) 1925-1984 **CLC 20**
See also CA 109; 114
Pedersen, Knut 1859-1952
See Hamsun, Knut
See also CA 104; 119; CANR 63; MTCW 1, 2
Peeslake, Gaffer
See Durrell, Lawrence (George)
Peguy, Charles Pierre 1873-1914 .... **TCLC 10**
See also CA 107
Peirce, Charles Sanders 1839-1914 **TCLC 81**
Pena, Ramon del Valle y
See Valle-Inclan, Ramon (Maria) del
Pendennis, Arthur Esquir
See Thackeray, William Makepeace
Penn, William 1644-1718 .... **LC 25**
See also DLB 24
Pepece
See Prado (Calvo), Pedro
Pepys, Samuel 1633-1703 **LC 11; DA; DAB; DAC; DAM MST; WLC**
See also CDBLB 1660-1789; DLB 101
Percy, Walker 1916-1990 **CLC 2, 3, 6, 8, 14, 18, 47, 65; DAM NOV, POP**
See also CA 1-4R; 131; CANR 1, 23, 64; DLB 2; DLBY 80, 90; MTCW 1, 2
Percy, William Alexander 1885-1942 . **TCLC 84**
See also CA 163; MTCW 2
Perec, Georges 1936-1982 .... **CLC 56, 116**
See also CA 141; DLB 83
Pereda (y Sanchez de Porrua), Jose Maria de 1833-1906 .... **TCLC 16**
See also CA 117
Pereda y Porrua, Jose Maria de
See Pereda (y Sanchez de Porrua), Jose Maria de
Peregoy, George Weems
See Mencken, H(enry) L(ouis)
Perelman, S(idney) J(oseph) 1904-1979 **CLC 3, 5, 9, 15, 23, 44, 49; DAM DRAM; SSC 32**
See also AITN 1, 2; CA 73-76; 89-92; CANR 18; DLB 11, 44; MTCW 1, 2
Peret, Benjamin 1899-1959 .... **TCLC 20**
See also CA 117
Peretz, Isaac Loeb 1851(?)-1915 **TCLC 16; SSC 26**
See also CA 109
Peretz, Yitzhok Leibush
See Peretz, Isaac Loeb
Perez Galdos, Benito 1843-1920 **TCLC 27; HLCS 2**
See also CA 125; 153; HW 1
Perrault, Charles 1628-1703 .... **LC 2**
See also MAICYA; SATA 25
Perry, Brighton
See Sherwood, Robert E(mmet)
Perse, St.-John
See Leger, (Marie-Rene Auguste) Alexis Saint-Leger
Perutz, Leo(pold) 1882-1957 .... **TCLC 60**
See also CA 147; DLB 81
Peseenz, Tulio F.
See Lopez y Fuentes, Gregorio
Pesetsky, Bette 1932- .... **CLC 28**
See also CA 133; DLB 130
Peshkov, Alexei Maximovich 1868-1936
See Gorky, Maxim
See also CA 105; 141; DA; DAC; DAM DRAM, MST, NOV; MTCW 2
Pessoa, Fernando (Antonio Nogueira) 1888-1935 **TCLC 27; DAM MULT; HLC; PC 20**

See also CA 125
Peterkin, Julia Mood 1880-1961 .... **CLC 31**
See also CA 102; DLB 9
Peters, Joan K(aren) 1945- .... **CLC 39**
See also CA 158
Peters, Robert L(ouis) 1924- .... **CLC 7**
See also CA 13-16R; CAAS 8; DLB 105
Petofi, Sandor 1823-1849 .... **NCLC 21**
Petrakis, Harry Mark 1923- .... **CLC 3**
See also CA 9-12R; CANR 4, 30
Petrarch 1304-1374 **CMLC 20; DAM POET; PC 8**
Petrov, Evgeny .... **TCLC 21**
See also Kataev, Evgeny Petrovich
Petry, Ann (Lane) 1908-1997 .... **CLC 1, 7, 18**
See also BW 1, 3; CA 5-8R; 157; CAAS 6; CANR 4, 46; CLR 12; DLB 76; JRDA; MAICYA; MTCW 1; SATA 5; SATA-Obit 94
Petursson, Halligrimur 1614-1674 .... **LC 8**
Peychinovich
See Vazov, Ivan (Minchov)
Phaedrus c. 18B.C.-c. 50 .... **CMLC 25**
See also DLB 211
Philips, Katherine 1632-1664 .... **LC 30**
See also DLB 131
Philipson, Morris H. 1926- .... **CLC 53**
See also CA 1-4R; CANR 4
Phillips, Caryl 1958- **CLC 96; BLCS; DAM MULT**
See also BW 2; CA 141; CANR 63; DLB 157; MTCW 2
Phillips, David Graham 1867-1911 ...... **TCLC 44**
See also CA 108; 176; DLB 9, 12
Phillips, Jack
See Sandburg, Carl (August)
Phillips, Jayne Anne 1952- **CLC 15, 33; SSC 16**
See also CA 101; CANR 24, 50; DLBY 80; INT CANR-24; MTCW 1, 2
Phillips, Richard
See Dick, Philip K(indred)
Phillips, Robert (Schaeffer) 1938- .... **CLC 28**
See also CA 17-20R; CAAS 13; CANR 8; DLB 105
Phillips, Ward
See Lovecraft, H(oward) P(hillips)
Piccolo, Lucio 1901-1969 .... **CLC 13**
See also CA 97-100; DLB 114
Pickthall, Marjorie L(owry) C(hristie) 1883-1922 **TCLC 21**
See also CA 107; DLB 92
Pico della Mirandola, Giovanni 1463-1494 **LC 15**
Piercy, Marge 1936- .... **CLC 3, 6, 14, 18, 27, 62**
See also CA 21-24R; CAAS 1; CANR 13, 43, 66; DLB 120; MTCW 1, 2
Piers, Robert
See Anthony, Piers
Pieyre de Mandiargues, Andre 1909-1991
See Mandiargues, Andre Pieyre de
See also CA 103; 136; CANR 22
Pilnyak, Boris .... **TCLC 23**
See also Vogau, Boris Andreyevich
Pincherle, Alberto 1907-1990 **CLC 11, 18; DAM NOV**
See also Moravia, Alberto
See also CA 25-28R; 132; CANR 33, 63; MTCW 1
Pinckney, Darryl 1953- .... **CLC 76**
See also BW 2, 3; CA 143; CANR 79
Pindar 518B.C.-446B.C. .... **CMLC 12; PC 19**
See also DLB 176
Pineda, Cecile 1942- .... **CLC 39**
See also CA 118
Pinero, Arthur Wing 1855-1934 **TCLC 32; DAM DRAM**
See also CA 110; 153; DLB 10
Pinero, Miguel (Antonio Gomez) 1946-1988 **CLC 4, 55**
See also CA 61-64; 125; CANR 29; HW 1
Pinget, Robert 1919-1997 .... **CLC 7, 13, 37**

See also CA 85-88; 160; DLB 83
Pink Floyd
See Barrett, (Roger) Syd; Gilmour, David; Mason, Nick; Waters, Roger; Wright, Rick
Pinkney, Edward 1802-1828 .... **NCLC 31**
Pinkwater, Daniel Manus 1941- .... **CLC 35**
See also Pinkwater, Manus
See also AAYA 1; CA 29-32R; CANR 12, 38; CLR 4; JRDA; MAICYA; SAAS 3; SATA 46, 76
Pinkwater, Manus
See Pinkwater, Daniel Manus
See also SATA 8
Pinsky, Robert 1940- **CLC 9, 19, 38, 94, 121; DAM POET**
See also CA 29-32R; CAAS 4; CANR 58; DLBY 82, 98; MTCW 2
Pinta, Harold
See Pinter, Harold
Pinter, Harold 1930- **CLC 1, 3, 6, 9, 11, 15, 27, 58, 73; DA; DAB; DAC; DAM DRAM, MST; WLC**
See also CA 5-8R; CANR 33, 65; CDBLB 1960 to Present; DLB 13; MTCW 1, 2
Piozzi, Hester Lynch (Thrale) 1741-1821 **NCLC 57**
See also DLB 104, 142
Pirandello, Luigi 1867-1936 ... **TCLC 4, 29; DA; DAB; DAC; DAM DRAM, MST; DC 5; SSC 22; WLC**
See also CA 104; 153; MTCW 2
Pirsig, Robert M(aynard) 1928- .. **CLC 4, 6, 73; DAM POP**
See also CA 53-56; CANR 42, 74; MTCW 1, 2; SATA 39
Pisarev, Dmitry Ivanovich 1840-1868 .. **NCLC 25**
Pix, Mary (Griffith) 1666-1709 .... **LC 8**
See also DLB 80
Pixerecourt, (Rene Charles) Guilbert de 1773-1844 **NCLC 39**
See also DLB 192
Plaatje, Sol(omon) T(shekisho) 1876-1932 **TCLC 73; BLCS**
See also BW 2, 3; CA 141; CANR 79
Plaidy, Jean
See Hibbert, Eleanor Alice Burford
Planche, James Robinson 1796-1880 .. **NCLC 42**
Plant, Robert 1948- .... **CLC 12**
Plante, David (Robert) 1940- **CLC 7, 23, 38; DAM NOV**
See also CA 37-40R; CANR 12, 36, 58; DLBY 83; INT CANR-12; MTCW 1
Plath, Sylvia 1932-1963 **CLC 1, 2, 3, 5, 9, 11, 14, 17, 50, 51, 62, 111; DA; DAB; DAC; DAM MST, POET; PC 1; WLC**
See also AAYA 13; CA 19-20; CANR 34; CAP 2; CDALB 1941-1968; DLB 5, 6, 152; MTCW 1, 2; SATA 96
Plato 428(?)B.C.-348(?)B.C. **CMLC 8; DA; DAB; DAC; DAM MST; WLCS**
See also DLB 176
Platonov, Andrei .... **TCLC 14**
See also Klimentov, Andrei Platonovich
Platt, Kin 1911- .... **CLC 26**
See also AAYA 11; CA 17-20R; CANR 11; JRDA; SAAS 17; SATA 21, 86
Plautus c. 251B.C.-184B.C. ...... **CMLC 24; DC 6**
See also DLB 211
Plick et Plock
See Simenon, Georges (Jacques Christian)
Plimpton, George (Ames) 1927- .... **CLC 36**
See also AITN 1; CA 21-24R; CANR 32, 70; DLB 185; MTCW 1, 2; SATA 10
Pliny the Elder c. 23-79 .... **CMLC 23**
See also DLB 211
Plomer, William Charles Franklin 1903-1973 **CLC 4, 8**
See also CA 21-22; CANR 34; CAP 2; DLB 20,

Putnam, Arthur Lee
  See Alger, Horatio, Jr.
Puzo, Mario 1920-1999**CLC 1, 2, 6, 36, 107; DAM NOV, POP**
  See also CA 65-68; CANR 4, 42, 65; DLB 6; MTCW 1, 2
Pygge, Edward
  See Barnes, Julian (Patrick)
Pyle, Ernest Taylor 1900-1945
  See Pyle, Ernie
  See also CA 115; 160
Pyle, Ernie 1900-1945 .... **TCLC 75**
  See also Pyle, Ernest Taylor
  See also DLB 29; MTCW 2
Pyle, Howard 1853-1911 .... **TCLC 81**
  See also CA 109; 137; CLR 22; DLB 42, 188; DLBD 13; MAICYA; SATA 16, 100
Pym, Barbara (Mary Crampton) 1913-1980 **C L C 13, 19, 37, 111**
  See also CA 13-14; 97-100; CANR 13, 34; CAP 1; DLB 14, 207; DLBY 87; MTCW 1, 2
Pynchon, Thomas (Ruggles, Jr.) 1937-**CLC 2, 3, 6, 9, 11, 18, 33, 62, 72; DA; DAB; DAC; DAM MST, NOV, POP; SSC 14; WLC**
  See also BEST 90:2; CA 17-20R; CANR 22, 46; 73; DLB 2, 173; MTCW 1, 2
Pythagoras c. 570B.C.-c. 500B.C. .... **CMLC 22**
  See also DLB 176
Q
  See Quiller-Couch, SirArthur (Thomas)
Qian Zhongshu
  See Ch'ien Chung-shu
Qroll
  See Dagerman, Stig (Halvard)
Quarrington, Paul (Lewis) 1953- .... **CLC 65**
  See also CA 129; CANR 62
Quasimodo, Salvatore 1901-1968 .... **CLC 10**
  See also CA 13-16; 25-28R; CAP 1; DLB 114; MTCW 1
Quay, Stephen 1947- .... **CLC 95**
Quay, Timothy 1947- .... **CLC 95**
Queen, Ellery .... **CLC 3, 11**
  See also Dannay, Frederic; Davidson, Avram (James); Lee, Manfred B(ennington); Marlowe, Stephen; Sturgeon, Theodore (Hamilton); Vance, John Holbrook
Queen, Ellery, Jr.
  See Dannay, Frederic; Lee, Manfred B(ennington)
Queneau, Raymond 1903-1976 **CLC 2, 5, 10, 42**
  See also CA 77-80; 69-72; CANR 32; DLB 72; MTCW 1, 2
Quevedo, Francisco de 1580-1645 .... **LC 23**
Quiller-Couch, SirArthur (Thomas) 1863-1944 **TCLC 53**
  See also CA 118; 166; DLB 135, 153, 190
Quin, Ann (Marie) 1936-1973 .... **CLC 6**
  See also CA 9-12R; 45-48; DLB 14
Quinn, Martin
  See Smith, Martin Cruz
Quinn, Peter 1947- .... **CLC 91**
Quinn, Simon
  See Smith, Martin Cruz
Quiroga, Horacio (Sylvestre) 1878-1937 . **T C L C 20; DAM MULT; HLC**
  See also CA 117; 131; HW 1; MTCW 1
Quoirez, Francoise 1935- .... **CLC 9**
  See also Sagan, Francoise
  See also CA 49-52; CANR 6, 39, 73; MTCW 1, 2
Raabe, Wilhelm (Karl) 1831-1910 ...... **TCLC 45**
  See also CA 167; DLB 129
Rabe, David (William) 1940-**CLC 4, 8, 33; DAM DRAM**
  See also CA 85-88; CABS 3; CANR 59; DLB 7
Rabelais, Francois 1483-1553 . **LC 5; DA; DAB; DAC; DAM MST; WLC**
Rabinovitch, Sholem 1859-1916

  See Aleichem, Sholom
  See also CA 104
Rabinyan, Dorit 1972- .... **CLC 119**
  See also CA 170
Rachilde 1860-1953 .... **TCLC 67**
  See also DLB 123, 192
Racine, Jean 1639-1699**LC 28; DAB; DAM MST**
Radcliffe, Ann (Ward) 1764-1823 .... **NCLC 6, 55**
  See also DLB 39, 178
Radiguet, Raymond 1903-1923 .... **TCLC 29**
  See also CA 162; DLB 65
Radnoti, Miklos 1909-1944 .... **TCLC 16**
  See also CA 118
Rado, James 1939- .... **CLC 17**
  See also CA 105
Radvanyi, Netty 1900-1983
  See Seghers, Anna
  See also CA 85-88; 110
Rae, Ben
  See Griffiths, Trevor
Raeburn, John (Hay) 1941- .... **CLC 34**
  See also CA 57-60
Ragni, Gerome 1942-1991 .... **CLC 17**
  See also CA 105; 134
Rahv, Philip 1908-1973 .... **CLC 24**
  See also Greenberg, Ivan
  See also DLB 137
Raimund, Ferdinand Jakob 1790-1836 **NCLC 69**
  See also DLB 90
Raine, Craig 1944- .... **CLC 32, 103**
  See also CA 108; CANR 29, 51; DLB 40
Raine, Kathleen (Jessie) 1908- .... **CLC 7, 45**
  See also CA 85-88; CANR 46; DLB 20; MTCW 1
Rainis, Janis 1865-1929 .... **TCLC 29**
  See also CA 170
Rakosi, Carl 1903- .... **CLC 47**
  See also Rawley, Callman
  See also CAAS 5; DLB 193
Raleigh, Richard
  See Lovecraft, H(oward) P(hillips)
Raleigh, Sir Walter 1554(?)-1618 ...... **LC 31, 39**
  See also CDBLB Before 1660; DLB 172
Rallentando, H. P.
  See Sayers, Dorothy L(eigh)
Ramal, Walter
  See de la Mare, Walter (John)
Ramana Maharshi 1879-1950 .... **TCLC 84**
Ramoacn y Cajal, Santiago 1852-1934 **TCLC 93**
Ramon, Juan
  See Jimenez (Mantecon), Juan Ramon
Ramos, Graciliano 1892-1953 .... **TCLC 32**
  See also CA 167; HW 2
Rampersad, Arnold 1941- .... **CLC 44**
  See also BW 2, 3; CA 127; 133; CANR 81; DLB 111; INT 133
Rampling, Anne
  See Rice, Anne
Ramsay, Allan 1684(?)-1758 .... **LC 29**
  See also DLB 95
Ramuz, Charles-Ferdinand 1878-1947 **TCLC 33**
  See also CA 165
Rand, Ayn 1905-1982**CLC 3, 30, 44, 79; DA; DAC; DAM MST, NOV, POP; WLC**
  See also AAYA 10; CA 13-16R; 105; CANR 27, 73; CDALBS; MTCW 1, 2
Randall, Dudley (Felker) 1914- **CLC 1; BLC 3; DAMMULT**
  See also BW 1, 3; CA 25-28R; CANR 23; DLB 41
Randall, Robert
  See Silverberg, Robert
Ranger, Ken
  See Creasey, John
Ransom, John Crowe 1888-1974 **CLC 2, 4, 5, 11, 24; DAM POET**
  See also CA 5-8R; 49-52; CANR 6, 34; CDALBS; DLB 45, 63; MTCW 1, 2
Rao, Raja 1909- .... **CLC 25, 56; DAM NOV**

  See also CA 73-76; CANR 51; MTCW 1, 2
Raphael, Frederic (Michael) 1931- ... **CLC 2, 14**
  See also CA 1-4R; CANR 1; DLB 14
Ratcliffe, James P.
  See Mencken, H(enry) L(ouis)
Rathbone, Julian 1935- .... **CLC 41**
  See also CA 101; CANR 34, 73
Rattigan, Terence (Mervyn) 1911-1977 .. **CLC 7; DAMDRAM**
  See also CA 85-88; 73-76; CDBLB 1945-1960; DLB 13; MTCW 1, 2
Ratushinskaya, Irina 1954- .... **CLC 54**
  See also CA 129; CANR 68
Raven, Simon (Arthur Noel) 1927- .... **CLC 14**
  See also CA 81-84
Ravenna, Michael
  See Welty, Eudora
Rawley, Callman 1903-
  See Rakosi, Carl
  See also CA 21-24R; CANR 12, 32
Rawlings, Marjorie Kinnan 1896-1953**T C L C 4**
  See also AAYA 20; CA 104; 137; CANR 74; DLB 9, 22, 102; DLBD 17; JRDA; MAICYA; MTCW 2; SATA 100; YABC 1
Ray, Satyajit 1921-1992**CLC 16, 76; DAM MULT**
  See also CA 114; 137
Read, Herbert Edward 1893-1968 .... **CLC 4**
  See also CA 85-88; 25-28R; DLB 20, 149
Read, Piers Paul 1941- .... **CLC 4, 10, 25**
  See also CA 21-24R; CANR 38; DLB 14; SATA 21
Reade, Charles 1814-1884 .... **NCLC 2, 74**
  See also DLB 21
Reade, Hamish
  See Gray, Simon (James Holliday)
Reading, Peter 1946- .... **CLC 47**
  See also CA 103; CANR 46; DLB 40
Reaney, James 1926- **CLC 13; DAC; DAM MST**
  See also CA 41-44R; CAAS 15; CANR 42; DLB 68; SATA 43
Rebreanu, Liviu 1885-1944 .... **TCLC 28**
  See also CA 165
Rechy, John (Francisco) 1934- **CLC 1, 7, 14, 18, 107; DAM MULT; HLC**
  See also CA 5-8R; CAAS 4; CANR 6, 32, 64; DLB 122; DLBY 82; HW 1, 2; INT CANR-6
Redcam, Tom 1870-1933 .... **TCLC 25**
Reddin, Keith .... **CLC 67**
Redgrove, Peter (William) 1932- ...... **CLC 6, 41**
  See also CA 1-4R; CANR 3, 39, 77; DLB 40
Redmon, Anne .... **CLC 22**
  See also Nightingale, Anne Redmon
  See also DLBY 86
Reed, Eliot
  See Ambler, Eric
Reed, Ishmael 1938- . **CLC 2, 3, 5, 6, 13, 32, 60; BLC 3; DAM MULT**
  See also BW 2, 3; CA 21-24R; CANR 25, 48, 74; DLB 2, 5, 33, 169; DLBD 8; MTCW 1, 2
Reed, John (Silas) 1887-1920 .... **TCLC 9**
  See also CA 106
Reed, Lou .... **CLC 21**
  See also Firbank, Louis
Reeve, Clara 1729-1807 .... **NCLC 19**
  See also DLB 39
Reich, Wilhelm 1897-1957 .... **TCLC 57**
Reid, Christopher (John) 1949- .... **CLC 33**
  See also CA 140; DLB 40
Reid, Desmond
  See Moorcock, Michael (John)
Reid Banks, Lynne 1929-
  See Banks, Lynne Reid
  See also CA 1-4R; CANR 6, 22, 38; CLR 24; JRDA; MAICYA; SATA 22, 75
Reilly, William K.
  See Creasey, John

Reiner, Max
   See Caldwell, (Janet Miriam) Taylor (Holland)
Reis, Ricardo
   See Pessoa, Fernando (Antonio Nogueira)
Remarque, Erich Maria 1898-1970 CLC 21; DA;
      DAB; DAC; DAM MST, NOV
   See also AAYA 27; CA 77-80; 29-32R; DLB 56;
      MTCW 1, 2
Remington, Frederic 1861-1909 .... TCLC 89
   See also CA 108; 169; DLB 12, 186, 188; SATA 41
Remizov, A.
   See Remizov, Aleksei (Mikhailovich)
Remizov, A. M.
   See Remizov, Aleksei (Mikhailovich)
Remizov, Aleksei (Mikhailovich) 1877-1957
      TCLC 27
   See also CA 125; 133
Renan, Joseph Ernest 1823-1892 .... NCLC 26
Renard, Jules 1864-1910 .... TCLC 17
   See also CA 117
Renault, Mary .... CLC 3, 11, 17
   See also Challans, Mary
   See also DLBY 83; MTCW 2
Rendell, Ruth (Barbara) 1930- CLC 28, 48; DAM
      POP
   See also Vine, Barbara
   See also CA 109; CANR 32, 52, 74; DLB 87; INT
      CANR-32; MTCW 1, 2
Renoir, Jean 1894-1979 .... CLC 20
   See also CA 129; 85-88
Resnais, Alain 1922- .... CLC 16
Reverdy, Pierre 1889-1960 .... CLC 53
   See also CA 97-100; 89-92
Rexroth, Kenneth 1905-1982 CLC 1, 2, 6, 11, 22,
      49, 112; DAM POET; PC 20
   See also CA 5-8R; 107; CANR 14, 34, 63; CDALB
      1941-1968; DLB 16, 48, 165, 212; DLBY 82; INT
      CANR-14; MTCW 1, 2
Reyes, Alfonso 1889-1959 ... TCLC 33; HLCS 2
   See also CA 131; HW 1
Reyes y Basoalto, Ricardo Eliecer Neftali
   See Neruda, Pablo
Reymont, Wladyslaw (Stanislaw) 1868(?)-1925
      TCLC 5
   See also CA 104
Reynolds, Jonathan 1942- .... CLC 6, 38
   See also CA 65-68; CANR 28
Reynolds, Joshua 1723-1792 .... LC 15
   See also DLB 104
Reynolds, Michael Shane 1937- .... CLC 44
   See also CA 65-68; CANR 9
Reznikoff, Charles 1894-1976 .... CLC 9
   See also CA 33-36; 61-64; CAP 2; DLB 28, 45
Rezzori (d'Arezzo), Gregor von 1914-1998 C L C
      25
   See also CA 122; 136; 167
Rhine, Richard
   See Silverstein, Alvin
Rhodes, Eugene Manlove 1869-1934 ... TCLC 53
Rhodius, Apollonius c. 3rd cent. B.C.- CMLC 28
   See also DLB 176
R'hoone
   See Balzac, Honore de
Rhys, Jean 1890(?)-1979 CLC 2, 4, 6, 14, 19, 51;
      DAM NOV; SSC 21
   See also CA 25-28R; 85-88; CANR 35, 62; CDBLB
      1945-1960; DLB 36, 117, 162; MTCW 1, 2
Ribeiro, Darcy 1922-1997 .... CLC 34
   See also CA 33-36R; 156
Ribeiro, Joao Ubaldo (Osorio Pimentel) 1941-
      CLC 10, 67
   See also CA 81-84
Ribman, Ronald (Burt) 1932- .... CLC 7
   See also CA 21-24R; CANR 46, 80
Ricci, Nino 1959- .... CLC 70
   See also CA 137
Rice, Anne 1941- .... CLC 41; DAM POP
   See also AAYA 9; BEST 89:2; CA 65-68; CANR
      12, 36, 53, 74; MTCW 2
Rice, Elmer (Leopold) 1892-1967 CLC 7, 49; DAM
      DRAM
   See also CA 21-22; 25-28R; CAP 2; DLB 4, 7;
      MTCW 1, 2
Rice, Tim(othy Miles Bindon) 1944- .... CLC 21
   See also CA 103; CANR 46
Rich, Adrienne (Cecile) 1929- CLC 3, 6, 7, 11, 18,
      36, 73, 76; DAM POET; PC 5
   See also CA 9-12R; CANR 20, 53, 74; CDALBS;
      DLB 5, 67; MTCW 1, 2
Rich, Barbara
   See Graves, Robert (von Ranke)
Rich, Robert
   See Trumbo, Dalton
Richard, Keith .... CLC 17
   See also Richards, Keith
Richards, David Adams 1950- ..... CLC 59; DAC
   See also CA 93-96; CANR 60; DLB 53
Richards, I(vor) A(rmstrong) 1893-1979 C L C
      14, 24
   See also CA 41-44R; 89-92; CANR 34, 74; DLB
      27; MTCW 2
Richards, Keith 1943-
   See Richard, Keith
   See also CA 107; CANR 77
Richardson, Anne
   See Roiphe, Anne (Richardson)
Richardson, Dorothy Miller 1873-1957 TCLC 3
   See also CA 104; DLB 36
Richardson, Ethel Florence (Lindesay) 1870-1946
   See Richardson, Henry Handel
   See also CA 105
Richardson, Henry Handel .... TCLC 4
   See also Richardson, Ethel Florence (Lindesay)
   See also DLB 197
Richardson, John 1796-1852 .... NCLC 55; DAC
   See also DLB 99
Richardson, Samuel 1689-1761 ... LC 1, 44; DA;
      DAB; DAC; DAM MST, NOV; WLC
   See also CDBLB 1660-1789; DLB 39
Richler, Mordecai 1931- CLC 3, 5, 9, 13, 18, 46,
      70; DAC; DAM MST, NOV
   See also AITN 1; CA 65-68; CANR 31, 62; CLR
      17; DLB 53; MAICYA; MTCW 1, 2; SATA 44,
      98; SATA-Brief 27
Richter, Conrad (Michael) 1890-1968 ... CLC 30
   See also AAYA 21; CA 5-8R; 25-28R; CANR 23;
      DLB 9, 212; MTCW 1, 2; SATA 3
Ricostranza, Tom
   See Ellis, Trey
Riddell, Charlotte 1832-1906 .... TCLC 40
   See also CA 165; DLB 156
Ridgway, Keith 1965- .... CLC 119
   See also CA 172
Riding, Laura .... CLC 3, 7
   See also Jackson, Laura (Riding)
Riefenstahl, Berta Helene Amalia 1902-
   See Riefenstahl, Leni
   See also CA 108
Riefenstahl, Leni .... CLC 16
   See also Riefenstahl, Berta Helene Amalia
Riffe, Ernest
   See Bergman, (Ernst) Ingmar
Riggs, (Rolla) Lynn 1899-1954 . TCLC 56; DAM
      MULT
   See also CA 144; DLB 175; NNAL
Riis, Jacob A(ugust) 1849-1914 .... TCLC 80
   See also CA 113; 168; DLB 23
Riley, James Whitcomb 1849-1916 .... TCLC 51;
      DAM POET
   See also CA 118; 137; MAICYA; SATA 17
Riley, Tex
   See Creasey, John
Rilke, Rainer Maria 1875-1926 . TCLC 1, 6, 19;
      DAM POET; PC 2
   See also CA 104; 132; CANR 62; DLB 81;
      MTCW 1, 2
Rimbaud, (Jean Nicolas) Arthur 1854-1891
      NCLC 4, 35; DA; DAB; DAC; DAM MST,
      POET; PC 3; WLC
Rinehart, Mary Roberts 1876-1958 .... TCLC 52
   See also CA 108; 166
Ringmaster, The
   See Mencken, H(enry) L(ouis)
Ringwood, Gwen(dolyn Margaret) Pharis 1910-1984
      CLC 48
   See also CA 148; 112; DLB 88
Rio, Michel 19(?)- .... CLC 43
Ritsos, Giannes
   See Ritsos, Yannis
Ritsos, Yannis 1909-1990 .... CLC 6, 13, 31
   See also CA 77-80; 133; CANR 39, 61; MTCW 1
Ritter, Erika 1948(?)- .... CLC 52
Rivera, Jose Eustasio 1889-1928 .... TCLC 35
   See also CA 162; HW 1, 2
Rivers, Conrad Kent 1933-1968 .... CLC 1
   See also BW 1; CA 85-88; DLB 41
Rivers, Elfrida
   See Bradley, Marion Zimmer
Riverside, John
   See Heinlein, Robert A(nson)
Rizal, Jose 1861-1896 .... NCLC 27
Roa Bastos, Augusto (Antonio) 1917- . CLC 45;
      DAM MULT; HLC
   See also CA 131; DLB 113; HW 1
Robbe-Grillet, Alain 1922- CLC 1, 2, 4, 6, 8, 10,
      14, 43
   See also CA 9-12R; CANR 33, 65; DLB 83;
      MTCW 1, 2
Robbins, Harold 1916-1997 .. CLC 5; DAM NOV
   See also CA 73-76; 162; CANR 26, 54; MTCW 1,
      2
Robbins, Thomas Eugene 1936-
   See Robbins, Tom
   See also CA 81-84; CANR 29, 59; DAM NOV,
      POP; MTCW 1, 2
Robbins, Tom .... CLC 9, 32, 64
   See also Robbins, Thomas Eugene
   See also BEST 90:3; DLBY 80; MTCW 2
Robbins, Trina 1938- .... CLC 21
   See also CA 128
Roberts, Charles G(eorge) D(ouglas) 1860-1943
      TCLC 8
   See also CA 105; CLR 33; DLB 92; SATA 88;
      SATA-Brief 29
Roberts, Elizabeth Madox 1886-1941 .. TCLC 68
   See also CA 111; 166; DLB 9, 54, 102; SATA 33;
      SATA-Brief 27
Roberts, Kate 1891-1985 .... CLC 15
   See also CA 107; 116
Roberts, Keith (John Kingston) 1935- . CLC 14
   See also CA 25-28R; CANR 46
Roberts, Kenneth (Lewis) 1885-1957 .. TCLC 23
   See also CA 109; DLB 9
Roberts, Michele (B.) 1949- .... CLC 48
   See also CA 115; CANR 58
Robertson, Ellis
   See Ellison, Harlan (Jay); Silverberg, Robert
Robertson, Thomas William 1829-1871 NCLC 35;
      DAM DRAM
Robeson, Kenneth
   See Dent, Lester
Robinson, Edwin Arlington 1869-1935 . TCLC 5;
      DA; DAC; DAM MST, POET; PC 1
   See also CA 104; 133; CDALB 1865-1917; DLB
      54; MTCW 1, 2
Robinson, Henry Crabb 1775-1867 ..... NCLC 15
   See also DLB 107
Robinson, Jill 1936- .... CLC 10
   See also CA 102; INT 102
Robinson, Kim Stanley 1952- .... CLC 34
   See also AAYA 26; CA 126; SATA 109

POET

Russell, (Henry) Ken(neth Alfred) 1927-**CLC 16**
See also CA 105

Russell, William Martin 1947- .... **CLC 60**
See also CA 164

Rutherford, Mark .... **TCLC 25**
See also White, William Hale
See also DLB 18

Ruyslinck, Ward 1929- .... **CLC 14**
See also Belser, Reimond Karel Maria de

Ryan, Cornelius (John) 1920-1974 .... **CLC 7**
See also CA 69-72; 53-56; CANR 38

Ryan, Michael 1946- .... **CLC 65**
See also CA 49-52; DLBY 82

Ryan, Tim
See Dent, Lester

Rybakov, Anatoli (Naumovich) 1911-1998**CLC 23, 53**
See also CA 126; 135; 172; SATA 79; SATA-Obit 108

Ryder, Jonathan
See Ludlum, Robert

Ryga, George 1932-1987 .. **CLC 14; DAC; DAM MST**
See also CA 101; 124; CANR 43; DLB 60

S. H.
See Hartmann, Sadakichi

S. S.
See Sassoon, Siegfried (Lorraine)

Saba, Umberto 1883-1957 .... **TCLC 33**
See also CA 144; CANR 79; DLB 114

Sabatini, Rafael 1875-1950 .... **TCLC 47**
See also CA 162

Sabato, Ernesto (R.) 1911- ... **CLC 10, 23; DAM MULT; HLC**
See also CA 97-100; CANR 32, 65; DLB 145; HW 1, 2; MTCW 1, 2

Sa-Carniero, Mario de 1890-1916 .... **TCLC 83**

Sacastru, Martin
See Bioy Casares, Adolfo

Sacastru, Martin
See Bioy Casares, Adolfo

Sacher-Masoch, Leopold von 1836(?)-1895**NCLC 31**

Sachs, Marilyn (Stickle) 1927- .... **CLC 35**
See also AAYA 2; CA 17-20R; CANR 13, 47; CLR 2; JRDA; MAICYA; SAAS 2; SATA 3, 68

Sachs, Nelly 1891-1970 .... **CLC 14, 98**
See also CA 17-18; 25-28R; CAP 2; MTCW 2

Sackler, Howard (Oliver) 1929-1982 ..... **CLC 14**
See also CA 61-64; 108; CANR 30; DLB 7

Sacks, Oliver (Wolf) 1933- .... **CLC 67**
See also CA 53-56; CANR 28, 50, 76; INT CANR-28; MTCW 1, 2

Sadakichi
See Hartmann, Sadakichi

Sade, Donatien Alphonse Francois, Comte de 1740-1814 .... **NCLC 47**

Sadoff, Ira 1945- .... **CLC 9**
See also CA 53-56; CANR 5, 21; DLB 120

Saetone
See Camus, Albert

Safire, William 1929- .... **CLC 10**
See also CA 17-20R; CANR 31, 54

Sagan, Carl (Edward) 1934-1996 .... **CLC 30, 112**
See also AAYA 2; CA 25-28R; 155; CANR 11, 36, 74; MTCW 1, 2; SATA 58; SATA-Obit 94

Sagan, Francoise .... **CLC 3, 6, 9, 17, 36**
See also Quoirez, Francoise
See also DLB 83; MTCW 2

Sahgal, Nayantara (Pandit) 1927- .... **CLC 41**
See also CA 9-12R; CANR 11

Saint, H(arry) F. 1941- .... **CLC 50**
See also CA 127

St. Aubin de Teran, Lisa 1953-
See Teran, Lisa St. Aubin de
See also CA 118; 126; INT 126

Saint Birgitta of Sweden c. 1303-1373**C M L C 24**

Sainte-Beuve, Charles Augustin 1804-1869 **NCLC 5**

Saint-Exupery, Antoine (Jean Baptiste Marie Roger) de 1900-1944**TCLC 2, 56; DAM NOV; WLC**
See also CA 108; 132; CLR 10; DLB 72; MAICYA; MTCW 1, 2; SATA 20

St. John, David
See Hunt, E(verette) Howard, (Jr.)

Saint-John Perse
See Leger, (Marie-Rene Auguste) Alexis Saint-Leger

Saintsbury, George (Edward Bateman) 1845-1933 **TCLC 31**
See also CA 160; DLB 57, 149

Sait Faik .... **TCLC 23**
See also Abasiyanik, Sait Faik

Saki .... **TCLC 3; SSC 12**
See Munro, H(ector) H(ugh)
See also MTCW 2

Sala, George Augustus .... **NCLC 46**

Salama, Hannu 1936- .... **CLC 18**

Salamanca, J(ack) R(ichard) 1922-**CLC 4, 15**
See also CA 25-28R

Sale, J. Kirkpatrick
See Sale, Kirkpatrick

Sale, Kirkpatrick 1937- .... **CLC 68**
See also CA 13-16R; CANR 10

Salinas, Luis Omar 1937-**CLC 90; DAM MULT; HLC**
See also CA 131; CANR 81; DLB 82; HW 1, 2

Salinas (y Serrano), Pedro 1891(?)-1951**TCLC 17**
See also CA 117; DLB 134

Salinger, J(erome) D(avid) 1919-**CLC 1, 3, 8, 12, 55, 56; DA; DAB; DAC; DAM MST, NOV, POP; SSC 2, 28; WLC**
See also AAYA 2; CA 5-8R; CANR 39; CDALB 1941-1968; CLR 18; DLB 2, 102, 173; MAICYA; MTCW 1, 2; SATA 67

Salisbury, John
See Caute, (John) David

Salter, James 1925- .... **CLC 7, 52, 59**
See also CA 73-76; DLB 130

Saltus, Edgar (Everton) 1855-1921 .... **TCLC 8**
See also CA 105; DLB 202

Saltykov, Mikhail Evgrafovich 1826-1889 **N C L C 16**

Samarakis, Antonis 1919- .... **CLC 5**
See also CA 25-28R; CAAS 16; CANR 36

Sanchez, Florencio 1875-1910 .... **TCLC 37**
See also CA 153; HW 1

Sanchez, Luis Rafael 1936- .... **CLC 23**
See also CA 128; DLB 145; HW 1

Sanchez, Sonia 1934-**CLC 5, 116; BLC 3; DAM MULT; PC 9**
See also BW 2, 3; CA 33-36R; CANR 24, 49, 74; CLR 18; DLB 41; DLBD 8; MAICYA; MTCW 1, 2; SATA 22

Sand, George 1804-1876 ... **NCLC 2, 42, 57; DA; DAB; DAC; DAM MST, NOV; WLC**
See also DLB 119, 192

Sandburg, Carl (August) 1878-1967**CLC 1, 4, 10, 15, 35; DA; DAB; DAC; DAM MST, POET; PC 2; WLC**
See also AAYA 24; CA 5-8R; 25-28R; CANR 35; CDALB 1865-1917; DLB 17, 54; MAICYA; MTCW 1, 2; SATA 8

Sandburg, Charles
See Sandburg, Carl (August)

Sandburg, Charles A.
See Sandburg, Carl (August)

Sanders, (James) Ed(ward) 1939- **CLC 53; DAM POET**
See also CA 13-16R; CAAS 21; CANR 13, 44, 78; DLB 16

Sanders, Lawrence 1920-1998**CLC 41; DAM POP**
See also BEST 89:4; CA 81-84; 165; CANR 33, 62; MTCW 1

Sanders, Noah
See Blount, Roy (Alton), Jr.

Sanders, Winston P.
See Anderson, Poul (William)

Sandoz, Mari(e Susette) 1896-1966 ...... **CLC 28**
See also CA 1-4R; 25-28R; CANR 17, 64; DLB 9, 212; MTCW 1, 2; SATA 5

Saner, Reg(inald Anthony) 1931- .... **CLC 9**
See also CA 65-68

Sankara 788-820 .... **CMLC 32**

Sannazaro, Jacopo 1456(?)-1530 .... **LC 8**

Sansom, William 1912-1976**CLC 2, 6; DAM NOV; SSC 21**
See also CA 5-8R; 65-68; CANR 42; DLB 139; MTCW 1

Santayana, George 1863-1952 .... **TCLC 40**
See also CA 115; DLB 54, 71; DLBD 13

Santiago, Danny .... **CLC 33**
See also James, Daniel (Lewis)
See also DLB 122

Santmyer, Helen Hoover 1895-1986 ...... **CLC 33**
See also CA 1-4R; 118; CANR 15, 33; DLBY 84; MTCW 1

Santoka, Taneda 1882-1940 .... **TCLC 72**

Santos, Bienvenido N(uqui) 1911-1996 **CLC 22; DAM MULT**
See also CA 101; 151; CANR 19, 46

Sapper .... **TCLC 44**
See also McNeile, Herman Cyril

Sapphire
See Sapphire, Brenda

Sapphire, Brenda 1950- .... **CLC 99**

Sappho fl. 6th cent. B.C.- **CMLC 3; DAM POET; PC 5**
See also DLB 176

Saramago, Jose 1922- .... **CLC 119; HLCS 1**
See also CA 153

Sarduy, Severo 1937-1993 .. **CLC 6, 97; HLCS 1**
See also CA 89-92; 142; CANR 58, 81; DLB 113; HW 1, 2

Sargeson, Frank 1903-1982 .... **CLC 31**
See also CA 25-28R; 106; CANR 38, 79

Sarmiento, Felix Ruben Garcia
See Dario, Ruben

Saro-Wiwa, Ken(ule Beeson) 1941-1995**CLC 114**
See also BW 2; CA 142; 150; CANR 60; DLB 157

Saroyan, William 1908-1981**CLC 1, 8, 10, 29, 34, 56; DA; DAB; DAC; DAM DRAM, MST, NOV; SSC 21; WLC**
See also CA 5-8R; 103; CANR 30; CDALBS; DLB 7, 9, 86; DLBY 81; MTCW 1, 2; SATA 23; SATA-Obit 24

Sarraute, Nathalie 1900-**CLC 1, 2, 4, 8, 10, 31, 80**
See also CA 9-12R; CANR 23, 66; DLB 83; MTCW 1, 2

Sarton, (Eleanor) May 1912-1995 **CLC 4, 14, 49, 91; DAM POET**
See also CA 1-4R; 149; CANR 1, 34, 55; DLB 48; DLBY 81; INT CANR-34; MTCW 1, 2; SATA 36; SATA-Obit 86

Sartre, Jean-Paul 1905-1980 . **CLC 1, 4, 7, 9, 13, 18, 24, 44, 50, 52; DA; DAB; DAC; DAM DRAM, MST, NOV; DC 3; SSC 32; WLC**
See also CA 9-12R; 97-100; CANR 21; DLB 72; MTCW 1, 2

Sassoon, Siegfried (Lorraine) 1886-1967 .. **C L C 36; DAB; DAM MST, NOV, POET; PC 12**
See also CA 104; 25-28R; CANR 36; DLB 20, 191; DLBD 18; MTCW 1, 2

Satterfield, Charles
See Pohl, Frederik

Saul, John (W. III) 1942- ... **CLC 46; DAM NOV, POP**

See also AAYA 10; BEST 90:4; CA 81-84;
CANR 16, 40, 81; SATA 98
Saunders, Caleb
See Heinlein, Robert A(nson)
Saura (Atares), Carlos 1932- .... **CLC 20**
See also CA 114; 131; CANR 79; HW 1
Sauser-Hall, Frederic 1887-1961 .... **CLC 18**
See also Cendrars, Blaise
See also CA 102; 93-96; CANR 36, 62; MTCW 1
Saussure, Ferdinand de 1857-1913 ..... **TCLC 49**
Savage, Catharine
See Brosman, Catharine Savage
Savage, Thomas 1915- .... **CLC 40**
See also CA 126; 132; CAAS 15; INT 132
Savan, Glenn 19(?)- .... **CLC 50**
Sayers, Dorothy L(eigh) 1893-1957 **TCLC 2, 15;
DAM POP**
See also CA 104; 119; CANR 60; CDBLB 1914-
1945; DLB 10, 36, 77, 100; MTCW 1, 2
Sayers, Valerie 1952- .... **CLC 50**
See also CA 134; CANR 61
Sayles, John (Thomas) 1950- ...... **CLC 7, 10, 14**
See also CA 57-60; CANR 41; DLB 44
Scammell, Michael 1935- .... **CLC 34**
See also CA 156
Scannell, Vernon 1922- .... **CLC 49**
See also CA 5-8R; CANR 8, 24, 57; DLB 27; SATA
59
Scarlett, Susan
See Streatfeild, (Mary) Noel
Scarron
See Mikszath, Kalman
Schaeffer, Susan Fromberg 1941- **CLC 6, 11, 22**
See also CA 49-52; CANR 18, 65; DLB 28;
MTCW 1, 2; SATA 22
Schary, Jill
See Robinson, Jill
Schell, Jonathan 1943- .... **CLC 35**
See also CA 73-76; CANR 12
Schelling, Friedrich Wilhelm Joseph von 1775-
1854 .... **NCLC 30**
See also DLB 90
Schendel, Arthur van 1874-1946 .... **TCLC 56**
Scherer, Jean-Marie Maurice 1920-
See Rohmer, Eric
See also CA 110
Schevill, James (Erwin) 1920- .... **CLC 7**
See also CA 5-8R; CAAS 12
Schiller, Friedrich 1759-1805 **NCLC 39, 69; DAM
DRAM**
See also DLB 94
Schisgal, Murray (Joseph) 1926- .... **CLC 6**
See also CA 21-24R; CANR 48
Schlee, Ann 1934- .... **CLC 35**
See also CA 101; CANR 29; SATA 44; SATA-
Brief 36
Schlegel, August Wilhelm von 1767-1845 **NCLC
15**
See also DLB 94
Schlegel, Friedrich 1772-1829 .... **NCLC 45**
See also DLB 90
Schlegel, Johann Elias (von) 1719(?)-1749 **LC 5**
Schlesinger, Arthur M(eier), Jr. 1917- **CLC 84**
See also AITN 1; CA 1-4R; CANR 1, 28, 58; DLB
17; INT CANR-28; MTCW 1, 2; SATA 61
Schmidt, Arno (Otto) 1914-1979 .... **CLC 56**
See also CA 128; 109; DLB 69
Schmitz, Aron Hector 1861-1928
See Svevo, Italo
See also CA 104; 122; MTCW 1
Schnackenberg, Gjertrud 1953- .... **CLC 40**
See also CA 116; DLB 120
Schneider, Leonard Alfred 1925-1966
See Bruce, Lenny
See also CA 89-92
Schnitzler, Arthur 1862-1931 **TCLC 4; SSC 15**
See also CA 104; DLB 81, 118

Schoenberg, Arnold 1874-1951 ...... **TCLC 75**
See also CA 109
Schonberg, Arnold
See Schoenberg, Arnold
Schopenhauer, Arthur 1788-1860 .... **NCLC 51**
See also DLB 90
Schor, Sandra (M.) 1932(?)-1990 .... **CLC 65**
See also CA 132
Schorer, Mark 1908-1977 .... **CLC 9**
See also CA 5-8R; 73-76; CANR 7; DLB 103
Schrader, Paul (Joseph) 1946- .... **CLC 26**
See also CA 37-40R; CANR 41; DLB 44
Schreiner, Olive (Emilie Albertina) 1855-1920
TCLC 9
See also CA 105; 154; DLB 18, 156, 190
Schulberg, Budd (Wilson) 1914- ...... **CLC 7, 48**
See also CA 25-28R; CANR 19; DLB 6, 26, 28;
DLBY 81
Schulz, Bruno 1892-1942 . **TCLC 5, 51; SSC 13**
See also CA 115; 123; MTCW 2
Schulz, Charles M(onroe) 1922- .... **CLC 12**
See also CA 9-12R; CANR 6; INT CANR-6;
SATA 10
Schumacher, E(rnst) F(riedrich) 1911-1977
CLC 80
See also CA 81-84; 73-76; CANR 34
Schuyler, James Marcus 1923-1991 **CLC 5, 23;
DAM POET**
See also CA 101; 134; DLB 5, 169; INT 101
Schwartz, Delmore (David) 1913-1966 **CLC 2, 4,
10, 45, 87; PC 8**
See also CA 17-18; 25-28R; CANR 35; CAP 2;
DLB 28, 48; MTCW 1, 2
Schwartz, Ernst
See Ozu, Yasujiro
Schwartz, John Burnham 1965- .... **CLC 59**
See also CA 132
Schwartz, Lynne Sharon 1939- .... **CLC 31**
See also CA 103; CANR 44; MTCW 2
Schwartz, Muriel A.
See Eliot, T(homas) S(tearns)
Schwarz-Bart, Andre 1928- .... **CLC 2, 4**
See also CA 89-92
Schwarz-Bart, Simone 1938- ...... **CLC 7; BLCS**
See also BW 2; CA 97-100
Schwitters, Kurt (Hermann Edward Karl Julius)
1887-1948 .... **TCLC 95**
See also CA 158
Schwob, Marcel (Mayer Andre) 1867-1905 **TCLC
20**
See also CA 117; 168; DLB 123
Sciascia, Leonardo 1921-1989 .... **CLC 8, 9, 41**
See also CA 85-88; 130; CANR 35; DLB 177;
MTCW 1
Scoppettone, Sandra 1936- .... **CLC 26**
See also AAYA 11; CA 5-8R; CANR 41, 73; SATA
9, 92
Scorsese, Martin 1942- .... **CLC 20, 89**
See also CA 110; 114; CANR 46
Scotland, Jay
See Jakes, John (William)
Scott, Duncan Campbell 1862-1947 **TCLC 6; DAC**
See also CA 104; 153; DLB 92
Scott, Evelyn 1893-1963 .... **CLC 43**
See also CA 104; 112; CANR 64; DLB 9, 48
Scott, F(rancis) R(eginald) 1899-1985 .. **CLC 22**
See also CA 101; 114; DLB 88; INT 101
Scott, Frank
See Scott, F(rancis) R(eginald)
Scott, Joanna 1960- .... **CLC 50**
See also CA 126; CANR 53
Scott, Paul (Mark) 1920-1978 .... **CLC 9, 60**
See also CA 81-84; 77-80; CANR 33; DLB 14,
207; MTCW 1
Scott, Sarah 1723-1795 .... **LC 44**
See also DLB 39
Scott, Walter 1771-1832 **NCLC 15, 69; DA; DAB;**

DAC; DAM MST, NOV, POET; PC 13;
SSC 32; WLC
See also AAYA 22; CDBLB 1789-1832; DLB 93,
107, 116, 144, 159; YABC 2
Scribe, (Augustin) Eugene 1791-1861 **NCLC 16;
DAM DRAM; DC 5**
See also DLB 192
Scrum, R.
See Crumb, R(obert)
Scudery, Madeleine de 1607-1701 .... **LC 2**
Scum
See Crumb, R(obert)
Scumbag, Little Bobby
See Crumb, R(obert)
Seabrook, John
See Hubbard, L(afayette) Ron(ald)
Sealy, I. Allan 1951- .... **CLC 55**
Search, Alexander
See Pessoa, Fernando (Antonio Nogueira)
Sebastian, Lee
See Silverberg, Robert
Sebastian Owl
See Thompson, Hunter S(tockton)
Sebestyen, Ouida 1924- .... **CLC 30**
See also AAYA 8; CA 107; CANR 40; CLR 17;
JRDA; MAICYA; SAAS 10; SATA 39
Secundus, H. Scriblerus
See Fielding, Henry
Sedges, John
See Buck, Pearl S(ydenstricker)
Sedgwick, Catharine Maria 1789-1867 **NCLC 19**
See also DLB 1, 74
Seelye, John (Douglas) 1931- .... **CLC 7**
See also CA 97-100; CANR 70; INT 97-100
Seferiades, Giorgos Stylianou 1900-1971
See Seferis, George
See also CA 5-8R; 33-36R; CANR 5, 36; MTCW
1
Seferis, George .... **CLC 5, 11**
See also Seferiades, Giorgos Stylianou
Segal, Erich (Wolf) 1937- **CLC 3, 10; DAM POP**
See also BEST 89:1; CA 25-28R; CANR 20, 36,
65; DLBY 86; INT CANR-20; MTCW 1
Seger, Bob 1945- .... **CLC 35**
Seghers, Anna .... **CLC 7**
See also Radvanyi, Netty
See also DLB 69
Seidel, Frederick (Lewis) 1936- .... **CLC 18**
See also CA 13-16R; CANR 8; DLBY 84
Seifert, Jaroslav 1901-1986 .... **CLC 34, 44, 93**
See also CA 127; MTCW 1, 2
Sei Shonagon c. 966-1017(?) .... **CMLC 6**
Séjour, Victor 1817-1874 .... **DC 10**
See also DLB 50
Sejour Marcou et Ferrand, Juan Victor
See Séjour, Victor
Selby, Hubert, Jr. 1928- **CLC 1, 2, 4, 8; SSC 20**
See also CA 13-16R; CANR 33; DLB 2
Selzer, Richard 1928- .... **CLC 74**
See also CA 65-68; CANR 14
Sembene, Ousmane
See Ousmane, Sembene
Senancour, Etienne Pivert de 1770-1846 **NCLC 16**
See also DLB 119
Sender, Ramon (Jose) 1902-1982 .. **CLC 8; DAM
MULT; HLC**
See also CA 5-8R; 105; CANR 8; HW 1; MTCW
1
Seneca, Lucius Annaeus c. 1-c. 65 **CMLC 6; DAM
DRAM; DC 5**
See also DLB 211
Senghor, Leopold Sedar 1906- **CLC 54; BLC 3;
DAM MULT, POET; PC 25**
See also BW 2, 3; CA 116; 125; CANR 47, 74;
MTCW 1, 2
Senna, Danzy 1970- .... **CLC 119**
See also CA 169

Silkin, Jon 1930- .... **CLC 2, 6, 43**
See also CA 5-8R; CAAS 5; DLB 27
Silko, Leslie (Marmon) 1948- **CLC 23, 74, 114;**
DA; DAC; DAM MST, MULT, POP; WLCS
See also AAYA 14; CA 115; 122; CANR 45, 65;
DLB 143, 175; MTCW 2; NNAL
Sillanpaa, Frans Eemil 1888-1964 .... **CLC 19**
See also CA 129; 93-96; MTCW 1
Sillitoe, Alan 1928- .... **CLC 1, 3, 6, 10, 19, 57**
See also AITN 1; CA 9-12R; CAAS 2; CANR 8,
26, 55; CDBLB 1960 to Present; DLB 14, 139;
MTCW 1, 2; SATA 61
Silone, Ignazio 1900-1978 .... **CLC 4**
See also CA 25-28; 81-84; CANR 34; CAP 2;
MTCW 1
Silver, Joan Micklin 1935- .... **CLC 20**
See also CA 114; 121; INT 121
Silver, Nicholas
See Faust, Frederick (Schiller)
Silverberg, Robert 1935- ...... **CLC 7; DAM POP**
See also AAYA 24; CA 1-4R; CAAS 3; CANR 1,
20, 36; CLR 59; DLB 8; INT CANR-20;
MAICYA; MTCW 1, 2; SATA 13, 91; SATA-
Essay 104
Silverstein, Alvin 1933- .... **CLC 17**
See also CA 49-52; CANR 2; CLR 25; JRDA;
MAICYA; SATA 8, 69
Silverstein, Virginia B(arbara Opshelor) 1937-
CLC 17
See also CA 49-52; CANR 2; CLR 25; JRDA;
MAICYA; SATA 8, 69
Sim, Georges
See Simenon, Georges (Jacques Christian)
Simak, Clifford D(onald) 1904-1988 . **CLC 1, 55**
See also CA 1-4R; 125; CANR 1, 35; DLB 8;
MTCW 1; SATA-Obit 56
Simenon, Georges (Jacques Christian) 1903-1989
CLC 1, 2, 3, 8, 18, 47; DAM POP
See also CA 85-88; 129; CANR 35; DLB 72; DLBY
89; MTCW 1, 2
Simic, Charles 1938-**CLC 6, 9, 22, 49, 68; DAM**
POET
See also CA 29-32R; CAAS 4; CANR 12, 33, 52,
61; DLB 105; MTCW 2
Simmel, Georg 1858-1918 .... **TCLC 64**
See also CA 157
Simmons, Charles (Paul) 1924- .... **CLC 57**
See also CA 89-92; INT 89-92
Simmons, Dan 1948- .... **CLC 44; DAM POP**
See also AAYA 16; CA 138; CANR 53, 81
Simmons, James (Stewart Alexander) 1933-**CLC**
43
See also CA 105; CAAS 21; DLB 40
Simms, William Gilmore 1806-1870 .... **NCLC 3**
See also DLB 3, 30, 59, 73
Simon, Carly 1945- .... **CLC 26**
See also CA 105
Simon, Claude 1913-1984**CLC 4, 9, 15, 39; DAM**
NOV
See also CA 89-92; CANR 33; DLB 83; MTCW 1
Simon, (Marvin) Neil 1927-**CLC 6, 11, 31, 39, 70;**
DAM DRAM
See also AITN 1; CA 21-24R; CANR 26, 54; DLB
7; MTCW 1, 2
Simon, Paul (Frederick) 1941(?)- .... **CLC 17**
See also CA 116; 153
Simonon, Paul 1956(?)- .... **CLC 30**
Simpson, Harriette
See Arnow, Harriette (Louisa) Simpson
Simpson, Louis (Aston Marantz) 1923-**CLC 4, 7,**
9, 32; DAM POET
See also CA 1-4R; CAAS 4; CANR 1, 61; DLB 5;
MTCW 1
Simpson, Mona (Elizabeth) 1957- .... **CLC 44**
See also CA 122; 135; CANR 68
Simpson, N(orman) F(rederick) 1919- . **CLC 29**
See also CA 13-16R; DLB 13

Sinclair, Andrew (Annandale) 1935-. **CLC 2,**
14
See also CA 9-12R; CAAS 5; CANR 14, 38;
DLB 14; MTCW 1
Sinclair, Emil
See Hesse, Hermann
Sinclair, Iain 1943-............................... **CLC 76**
See also CA 132; CANR 81
Sinclair, Iain MacGregor
See Sinclair, Iain
Sinclair, Irene
See Griffith, D(avid Lewelyn) W(ark)
Sinclair, Mary Amelia St. Clair 1865(?)-1946
See Sinclair, May
See also CA 104
Sinclair, May 1863-1946 .... **TCLC 3, 11**
See also Sinclair, Mary Amelia St. Clair
See also CA 166; DLB 36, 135
Sinclair, Roy
See Griffith, D(avid Lewelyn) W(ark)
Sinclair, Upton (Beall) 1878-1968**CLC 1, 11, 15,**
63; DA; DAB; DAC; DAM MST, NOV; WLC
See also CA 5-8R; 25-28R; CANR 7; CDALB 1929-
1941; DLB 9; INT CANR-7; MTCW 1, 2;
SATA 9
Singer, Isaac
See Singer, Isaac Bashevis
Singer, Isaac Bashevis 1904-1991**CLC 1, 3, 6, 9,**
11, 15, 23, 38, 69, 111; DA; DAB; DAC; DAM
MST, NOV; SSC 3; WLC
See also AITN 1, 2; CA 1-4R; 134; CANR 1, 39;
CDALB 1941-1968; CLR 1; DLB 6, 28, 52;
DLBY 91; JRDA; MAICYA; MTCW 1, 2;
SATA 3, 27; SATA-Obit 68
Singer, Israel Joshua 1893-1944 .... **TCLC 33**
See also CA 169
Singh, Khushwant 1915- .... **CLC 11**
See also CA 9-12R; CAAS 9; CANR 6
Singleton, Ann
See Benedict, Ruth (Fulton)
Sinjohn, John
See Galsworthy, John
Sinyavsky, Andrei (Donatevich) 1925-1997**CLC 8**
See also CA 85-88; 159
Sirin, V.
See Nabokov, Vladimir (Vladimirovich)
Sissman, L(ouis) E(dward) 1928-1976 **CLC 9, 18**
See also CA 21-24R; 65-68; CANR 13; DLB 5
Sisson, C(harles) H(ubert) 1914- .... **CLC 8**
See also CA 1-4R; CAAS 3; CANR 3, 48; DLB 27
Sitwell, Dame Edith 1887-1964**CLC 2, 9, 67; DAM**
POET; PC 3
See also CA 9-12R; CANR 35; CDBLB 1945-1960;
DLB 20; MTCW 1, 2
Siwaarmill, H. P.
See Sharp, William
Sjoewall, Maj 1935- .... **CLC 7**
See also CA 65-68; CANR 73
Sjowall, Maj
See Sjoewall, Maj
Skelton, John 1463-1529 .... **PC 25**
Skelton, Robin 1925-1997 .... **CLC 13**
See also AITN 2; CA 5-8R; 160; CAAS 5; CANR
28; DLB 27, 53
Skolimowski, Jerzy 1938- .... **CLC 20**
See also CA 128
Skram, Amalie (Bertha) 1847-1905 .... **TCLC 25**
See also CA 165
Skvorecky, Josef (Vaclav) 1924-**CLC 15, 39, 69;**
DAC; DAM NOV
See also CA 61-64; CAAS 1; CANR 10, 34, 63;
MTCW 1, 2
Slade, Bernard .... **CLC 11, 46**
See also Newbound, Bernard Slade
See also CAAS 9; DLB 53
Slaughter, Carolyn 1946- .... **CLC 56**
See also CA 85-88

Slaughter, Frank G(ill) 1908- .... **CLC 29**
See also AITN 2; CA 5-8R; CANR 5; INT
CANR-5
Slavitt, David R(ytman) 1935- .... **CLC 5, 14**
See also CA 21-24R; CAAS 3; CANR 41; DLB 5,
6
Slesinger, Tess 1905-1945 .... **TCLC 10**
See also CA 107; DLB 102
Slessor, Kenneth 1901-1971 .... **CLC 14**
See also CA 102; 89-92
Slowacki, Juliusz 1809-1849 .... **NCLC 15**
Smart, Christopher 1722-1771**LC 3; DAM POET;**
PC 13
See also DLB 109
Smart, Elizabeth 1913-1986 .... **CLC 54**
See also CA 81-84; 118; DLB 88
Smiley, Jane (Graves) 1949- **CLC 53, 76; DAM**
POP
See also CA 104; CANR 30, 50, 74; INT CANR-
30
Smith, A(rthur) J(ames) M(arshall) 1902-1980
CLC 15; DAC
See also CA 1-4R; 102; CANR 4; DLB 88
Smith, Adam 1723-1790 .... **LC 36**
See also DLB 104
Smith, Alexander 1829-1867 .... **NCLC 59**
See also DLB 32, 55
Smith, Anna Deavere 1950- .... **CLC 86**
See also CA 133
Smith, Betty (Wehner) 1896-1972 .... **CLC 19**
See also CA 5-8R; 33-36R; DLBY 82; SATA 6
Smith, Charlotte (Turner) 1749-1806 . **NCLC 23**
See also DLB 39, 109
Smith, Clark Ashton 1893-1961 .... **CLC 43**
See also CA 143; CANR 81; MTCW 2
Smith, Dave .... **CLC 22, 42**
See also Smith, David (Jeddie)
See also CAAS 7; DLB 5
Smith, David (Jeddie) 1942-
See Smith, Dave
See also CA 49-52; CANR 1, 59; DAM POET
Smith, Florence Margaret 1902-1971
See Smith, Stevie
See also CA 17-18; 29-32R; CANR 35; CAP 2;
DAM POET; MTCW 1, 2
Smith, Iain Crichton 1928-1998 .... **CLC 64**
See also CA 21-24R; 171; DLB 40, 139
Smith, John 1580(?)-1631 .... **LC 9**
See also DLB 24, 30
Smith, Johnston
See Crane, Stephen (Townley)
Smith, Joseph, Jr. 1805-1844 .... **NCLC 53**
Smith, Lee 1944- .... **CLC 25, 73**
See also CA 114; 119; CANR 46; DLB 143; DLBY
83; INT 119
Smith, Martin
See Smith, Martin Cruz
Smith, Martin Cruz 1942-**CLC 25; DAM MULT,**
POP
See also BEST 89:4; CA 85-88; CANR 6, 23, 43,
65; INT CANR-23; MTCW 2; NNAL
Smith, Mary-Ann Tirone 1944- .... **CLC 39**
See also CA 118; 136
Smith, Patti 1946- .... **CLC 12**
See also CA 93-96; CANR 63
Smith, Pauline (Urmson) 1882-1959 ... **TCLC 25**
Smith, Rosamond
See Oates, Joyce Carol
Smith, Sheila Kaye
See Kaye-Smith, Sheila
Smith, Stevie .... **CLC 3, 8, 25, 44; PC 12**
See also Smith, Florence Margaret
See also DLB 20; MTCW 2
Smith, Wilbur (Addison) 1933- ...., **CLC 33**
See also CA 13-16R; CANR 7, 46, 66; MTCW 1, 2
Smith, William Jay 1918- .... **CLC 6**
See also CA 5-8R; CANR 44; DLB 5; MAICYA;

173; DLBY 81
Suknaski, Andrew 1942- .... **CLC 19**
　See also CA 101; DLB 53
Sullivan, Vernon
　See Vian, Boris
Sully Prudhomme 1839-1907 .... **TCLC 31**
Su Man-shu .... **TCLC 24**
　See also Su, Chien
Summerforest, Ivy B.
　See Kirkup, James
Summers, Andrew James 1942- .... **CLC 26**
Summers, Andy
　See Summers, Andrew James
Summers, Hollis (Spurgeon, Jr.) 1916- **CLC 10**
　See also CA 5-8R; CANR 3; DLB 6
Summers, (Alphonsus Joseph-Mary Augustus)
　Montague 1880-1948 .... **TCLC 16**
　See also CA 118; 163
Sumner, Gordon Matthew .... **CLC 26**
　See also Sting
Surtees, Robert Smith 1803-1864 .... **NCLC 14**
　See also DLB 21
Susann, Jacqueline 1921-1974 .... **CLC 3**
　See also AITN 1; CA 65-68; 53-56; MTCW 1, 2
Su Shih 1036-1101 .... **CMLC 15**
Suskind, Patrick
　See Sueskind, Patrick
　See also CA 145
Sutcliff, Rosemary 1920-1992 .... **CLC 26; DAB;**
　DAC; DAM MST, POP
　See also AAYA 10; CA 5-8R; 139; CANR 37;
　CLR 1, 37; JRDA; MAICYA; SATA 6, 44, 78;
　SATA-Obit 73
Sutro, Alfred 1863-1933 .... **TCLC 6**
　See also CA 105; DLB 10
Sutton, Henry
　See Slavitt, David R(ytman)
Svevo, Italo 1861-1928 .... **TCLC 2, 35; SSC 25**
　See also Schmitz, Aron Hector
Swados, Elizabeth (A.) 1951- .... **CLC 12**
　See also CA 97-100; CANR 49; INT 97-100
Swados, Harvey 1920-1972 .... **CLC 5**
　See also CA 5-8R; 37-40R; CANR 6; DLB 2
Swan, Gladys 1934- .... **CLC 69**
　See also CA 101; CANR 17, 39
Swarthout, Glendon (Fred) 1918-1992 .. **CLC 35**
　See also CA 1-4R; 139; CANR 1, 47; SATA 26
Sweet, Sarah C.
　See Jewett, (Theodora) Sarah Orne
Swenson, May 1919-1989 **CLC 4, 14, 61, 106; DA;**
　DAB; DAC; DAM MST, POET; PC 14
　See also CA 5-8R; 130; CANR 36, 61; DLB 5;
　MTCW 1, 2; SATA 15
Swift, Augustus
　See Lovecraft, H(oward) P(hillips)
Swift, Graham (Colin) 1949- .... **CLC 41, 88**
　See also CA 117; 122; CANR 46, 71; DLB 194;
　MTCW 2
Swift, Jonathan 1667-1745 **LC 1, 42; DA; DAB;**
　DAC; DAM MST, NOV, POET; PC 9; WLC
　See also CDBLB 1660-1789; CLR 53; DLB 39, 95,
　101; SATA 19
Swinburne, Algernon Charles 1837-1909 **TCLC**
　8, 36; DA; DAB; DAC; DAM MST, POET;
　PC 24; WLC
　See also CA 105; 140; CDBLB 1832-1890; DLB
　35, 57
Swinfen, Ann .... **CLC 34**
Swinnerton, Frank Arthur 1884-1982 .. **CLC 31**
　See also CA 108; DLB 34
Swithen, John
　See King, Stephen (Edwin)
Sylvia
　See Ashton-Warner, Sylvia (Constance)
Symmes, Robert Edward
　See Duncan, Robert (Edward)
Symonds, John Addington 1840-1893 . **NCLC 34**

See also DLB 57, 144
Symons, Arthur 1865-1945 .... **TCLC 11**
　See also CA 107; DLB 19, 57, 149
Symons, Julian (Gustave) 1912-1994 **CLC 2, 14,**
　32
　See also CA 49-52; 147; CAAS 3; CANR 3, 33,
　59; DLB 87, 155; DLBY 92; MTCW 1
Synge, (Edmund) J(ohn) M(illington) 1871-1909
　TCLC 6, 37; DAM DRAM; DC 2
　See also CA 104; 141; CDBLB 1890-1914; DLB
　10, 19
Syruc, J.
　See Milosz, Czeslaw
Szirtes, George 1948- .... **CLC 46**
　See also CA 109; CANR 27, 61
Szymborska, Wislawa 1923- .... **CLC 99**
　See also CA 154; DLBY 96; MTCW 2
T. O., Nik
　See Annensky, Innokenty (Fyodorovich)
Tabori, George 1914- .... **CLC 19**
　See also CA 49-52; CANR 4, 69
Tagore, Rabindranath 1861-1941 ... **TCLC 3, 53;**
　DAM DRAM, POET; PC 8
　See also CA 104; 120; MTCW 1, 2
Taine, Hippolyte Adolphe 1828-1893 ... **NCLC 15**
Talese, Gay 1932- .... **CLC 37**
　See also AITN 1; CA 1-4R; CANR 9, 58; DLB
　185; INT CANR-9; MTCW 1, 2
Tallent, Elizabeth (Ann) 1954- .... **CLC 45**
　See also CA 117; CANR 72; DLB 130
Tally, Ted 1952- .... **CLC 42**
　See also CA 120; 124; INT 124
Talvik, Heiti 1904-1947 .... **TCLC 87**
Tamayo y Baus, Manuel 1829-1898 .... **NCLC 1**
Tammsaare, A(nton) H(ansen) 1878-1940 **TCLC**
　27
　See also CA 164
Tam'si, Tchicaya U
　See Tchicaya, Gerald Felix
Tan, Amy (Ruth) 1952- **CLC 59, 120; DAM MULT,**
　NOV, POP
　See also AAYA 9; BEST 89:3; CA 136; CANR
　54; CDALBS; DLB 173; MTCW 2; SATA 75
Tandem, Felix
　See Spitteler, Carl (Friedrich Georg)
Tanizaki, Jun'ichiro 1886-1965 . **CLC 8, 14, 28;**
　SSC 21
　See also CA 93-96; 25-28R; DLB 180; MTCW 2
Tanner, William
　See Amis, Kingsley (William)
Tao Lao
　See Storni, Alfonsina
Tarassoff, Lev
　See Troyat, Henri
Tarbell, Ida M(inerva) 1857-1944 .... **TCLC 40**
　See also CA 122; DLB 47
Tarkington, (Newton) Booth 1869-1946 **TCLC 9**
　See also CA 110; 143; DLB 9, 102; MTCW 2;
　SATA 17
Tarkovsky, Andrei (Arsenyevich) 1932-1986 **CLC**
　75
　See also CA 127
Tartt, Donna 1964(?)- .... **CLC 76**
　See also CA 142
Tasso, Torquato 1544-1595 .... **LC 5**
Tate, (John Orley) Allen 1899-1979 **CLC 2, 4, 6, 9,**
　11, 14, 24
　See also CA 5-8R; 85-88; CANR 32; DLB 4, 45,
　63; DLBD 17; MTCW 1, 2
Tate, Ellalice
　See Hibbert, Eleanor Alice Burford
Tate, James (Vincent) 1943- .... **CLC 2, 6, 25**
　See also CA 21-24R; CANR 29, 57; DLB 5, 169
Tavel, Ronald 1940- .... **CLC 6**
　See also CA 21-24R; CANR 33
Taylor, C(ecil) P(hilip) 1929-1981 .... **CLC 27**
　See also CA 25-28R; 105; CANR 47

Taylor, Edward 1642(?)-1729 ..... **LC 11; DA;**
　DAB; DAC; DAM MST, POET
　See also DLB 24
Taylor, Eleanor Ross 1920- .... **CLC 5**
　See also CA 81-84; CANR 70
Taylor, Elizabeth 1912-1975 .... **CLC 2, 4, 29**
　See also CA 13-16R; CANR 9, 70; DLB 139;
　MTCW 1; SATA 13
Taylor, Frederick Winslow 1856-1915 **TCLC 76**
Taylor, Henry (Splawn) 1942- .... **CLC 44**
　See also CA 33-36R; CAAS 7; CANR 31; DLB 5
Taylor, Kamala (Purnaiya) 1924-
　See Markandaya, Kamala
　See also CA 77-80
Taylor, Mildred D. .... **CLC 21**
　See also AAYA 10; BW 1; CA 85-88; CANR 25;
　CLR 9, 59; DLB 52; JRDA; MAICYA; SAAS
　5; SATA 15, 70
Taylor, Peter (Hillsman) 1917-1994 **CLC 1, 4, 18,**
　37, 44, 50, 71; SSC 10
　See also CA 13-16R; 147; CANR 9, 50; DLBY 81;
　94; INT CANR-9; MTCW 1, 2
Taylor, Robert Lewis 1912-1998 .... **CLC 14**
　See also CA 1-4R; 170; CANR 3, 64; SATA 10
Tchekhov, Anton
　See Chekhov, Anton (Pavlovich)
Tchicaya, Gerald Felix 1931-1988 .. **CLC 101**
　See also CA 129; 125; CANR 81
Tchicaya U Tam'si
　See Tchicaya, Gerald Felix
Teasdale, Sara 1884-1933 .... **TCLC 4**
　See also CA 104; 163; DLB 45; SATA 32
Tegner, Esaias 1782-1846 .... **NCLC 2**
Teilhard de Chardin, (Marie Joseph) Pierre 1881-
　1955 .... **TCLC 9**
　See also CA 105
Temple, Ann
　See Mortimer, Penelope (Ruth)
Tennant, Emma (Christina) 1937- .. **CLC 13, 52**
　See also CA 65-68; CAAS 9; CANR 10, 38, 59;
　DLB 14
Tenneshaw, S. M.
　See Silverberg, Robert
Tennyson, Alfred 1809-1892 . **NCLC 30, 65; DA;**
　DAB; DAC; DAM MST, POET; PC 6; WLC
　See also CDBLB 1832-1890; DLB 32
Teran, Lisa St. Aubin de .... **CLC 36**
　See also St. Aubin de Teran, Lisa
Terence c. 184B.C.-c. 159B.C. . **CMLC 14; DC 7**
　See also DLB 211
Teresa de Jesus, St. 1515-1582 .... **LC 18**
Terkel, Louis 1912-
　See Terkel, Studs
　See also CA 57-60; CANR 18, 45, 67; MTCW 1, 2
Terkel, Studs .... **CLC 38**
　See also Terkel, Louis
　See also AITN 1; MTCW 2
Terry, C. V.
　See Slaughter, Frank G(ill)
Terry, Megan 1932- .... **CLC 19**
　See also CA 77-80; CABS 3; CANR 43; DLB 7
Tertullian c. 155-c. 245 .... **CMLC 29**
Tertz, Abram
　See Sinyavsky, Andrei (Donatevich)
Tesich, Steve 1943(?)-1996 .... **CLC 40, 69**
　See also CA 105; 152; DLBY 83
Tesla, Nikola 1856-1943 .... **TCLC 88**
Teternikov, Fyodor Kuzmich 1863-1927
　See Sologub, Fyodor
　See also CA 104
Tevis, Walter 1928-1984 .... **CLC 42**
　See also CA 113
Tey, Josephine .... **TCLC 14**
　See also Mackintosh, Elizabeth
　See also DLB 77
Thackeray, William Makepeace 1811-1863 **NCLC**
　5, 14, 22, 43; DA; DAB; DAC; DAM MST,

NOV; WLC
See also CDBLB 1832-1890; DLB 21, 55, 159, 163; SATA 23

Thakura, Ravindranatha
See Tagore, Rabindranath

Tharoor, Shashi 1956- .... **CLC 70**
See also CA 141

Thelwell, Michael Miles 1939- .... **CLC 22**
See also BW 2; CA 101

Theobald, Lewis, Jr.
See Lovecraft, H(oward) P(hillips)

Theodorescu, Ion N. 1880-1967
See Arghezi, Tudor
See also CA 116

Theriault, Yves 1915-1983 **CLC 79; DAC; DAM MST**
See also CA 102; DLB 88

Theroux, Alexander (Louis) 1939- .... **CLC 2, 25**
See also CA 85-88; CANR 20, 63

Theroux, Paul (Edward) 1941- **CLC 5, 8, 11, 15, 28, 46; DAM POP**
See also AAYA 28; BEST 89:4; CA 33-36R; CANR 20, 45, 74; CDALBS; DLB 2; MTCW 1, 2; SATA 44, 109

Thesen, Sharon 1946- .... **CLC 56**
See also CA 163

Thevenin, Denis
See Duhamel, Georges

Thibault, Jacques Anatole Francois 1844-1924
See France, Anatole
See also CA 106; 127; DAM NOV; MTCW 1, 2

Thiele, Colin (Milton) 1920- .... **CLC 17**
See also CA 29-32R; CANR 12, 28, 53; CLR 27; MAICYA; SAAS 2; SATA 14, 72

Thomas, Audrey (Callahan) 1935-**CLC 7, 13, 37, 107; SSC 20**
See also AITN 2; CA 21-24R; CAAS 19; CANR 36, 58; DLB 60; MTCW 1

Thomas, D(onald) M(ichael) 1935-**CLC 13, 22, 31**
See also CA 61-64; CAAS 11; CANR 17, 45, 75; CDBLB 1960 to Present; DLB 40, 207; INT CANR-17; MTCW 1, 2

Thomas, Dylan (Marlais) 1914-1953 **TCLC 1, 8, 45; DA; DAB; DAC; DAM DRAM, MST, POET; PC 2; SSC 3; WLC**
See also CA 104; 120; CANR 65; CDBLB 1945-1960; DLB 13, 20, 139; MTCW 1, 2; SATA 60

Thomas, (Philip) Edward 1878-1917 ... **TCLC 10; DAM POET**
See also CA 106; 153; DLB 98

Thomas, Joyce Carol 1938- .... **CLC 35**
See also AAYA 12; BW 2, 3; CA 113; 116; CANR 48; CLR 19; DLB 33; INT 116; JRDA; MAICYA; MTCW 1, 2; SAAS 7; SATA 40, 78

Thomas, Lewis 1913-1993 .... **CLC 35**
See also CA 85-88; 143; CANR 38, 60; MTCW 1, 2

Thomas, M. Carey 1857-1935 .... **TCLC 89**

Thomas, Paul
See Mann, (Paul) Thomas

Thomas, Piri 1928- .... **CLC 17; HLCS 2**
See also CA 73-76; HW 1

Thomas, R(onald) S(tuart) 1913- **CLC 6, 13, 48; DAB; DAM POET**
See also CA 89-92; CAAS 4; CANR 30; CDBLB 1960 to Present; DLB 27; MTCW 1

Thomas, Ross (Elmore) 1926-1995 .... **CLC 39**
See also CA 33-36R; 150; CANR 22, 63

Thompson, Francis Clegg
See Mencken, H(enry) L(ouis)

Thompson, Francis Joseph 1859-1907 .. **TCLC 4**
See also CA 104; CDBLB 1890-1914; DLB 19

Thompson, Hunter S(tockton) 1939- **CLC 9, 17, 40, 104; DAM POP**
See also BEST 89:1; CA 17-20R; CANR 23, 46, 74, 77; DLB 185; MTCW 1, 2

Thompson, James Myers

See Thompson, Jim (Myers)

Thompson, Jim (Myers) 1906-1977(?) .. **CLC 69**
See also CA 140

Thompson, Judith .... **CLC 39**

Thomson, James 1700-1748**LC 16, 29, 40; DAM POET**
See also DLB 95

Thomson, James 1834-1882**NCLC 18; DAM POET**
See also DLB 35

Thoreau, Henry David 1817-1862**NCLC 7, 21, 61; DA; DAB; DAC; DAM MST; WLC**
See also CDALB 1640-1865; DLB 1

Thornton, Hall
See Silverberg, Robert

Thucydides c. 455B.C.-399B.C. .... **CMLC 17**
See also DLB 176

Thurber, James (Grover) 1894-1961 . **CLC 5, 11, 25; DA; DAB; DAC; DAM DRAM, MST, NOV; SSC 1**
See also CA 73-76; CANR 17, 39; CDALB 1929-1941; DLB 4, 11, 22, 102; MAICYA; MTCW 1, 2; SATA 13

Thurman, Wallace (Henry) 1902-1934 . **TCLC 6; BLC 3; DAM MULT**
See also BW 1, 3; CA 104; 124; CANR 81; DLB 51

Ticheburn, Cheviot
See Ainsworth, William Harrison

Tieck, (Johann) Ludwig 1773-1853 **NCLC 5, 46; SSC 31**
See also DLB 90

Tiger, Derry
See Ellison, Harlan (Jay)

Tilghman, Christopher 1948(?)- .... **CLC 65**
See also CA 159

Tillinghast, Richard (Williford) 1940- **CLC 29**
See also CA 29-32R; CAAS 23; CANR 26, 51

Timrod, Henry 1828-1867 .... **NCLC 25**
See also DLB 3

Tindall, Gillian (Elizabeth) 1938- ..:........ **CLC 7**
See also CA 21-24R; CANR 11, 65

Tiptree, James, Jr. .... **CLC 48, 50**
See also Sheldon, Alice Hastings Bradley
See also DLB 8

Titmarsh, Michael Angelo
See Thackeray, William Makepeace

Tocqueville, Alexis (Charles Henri Maurice Clerel, Comte) de 1805-1859 .... **NCLC 7, 63**

Tolkien, J(ohn) R(onald) R(euel) 1892-1973 **C L C 1, 2, 3, 8, 12, 38; DA; DAB; DAC; DAM MST, NOV, POP; WLC**
See also AAYA 10; AITN 1; CA 17-18; 45-48; CANR 36; CAP 2; CDBLB 1914-1945; CLR 56; DLB 15, 160; JRDA; MAICYA; MTCW 1, 2; SATA 2, 32, 100; SATA-Obit 24

Toller, Ernst 1893-1939 .... **TCLC 10**
See also CA 107; DLB 124

Tolson, M. B.
See Tolson, Melvin B(eaunorus)

Tolson, Melvin B(eaunorus) 1898(?)-1966 .. **C L C 36, 105; BLC 3; DAM MULT, POET**
See also BW 1, 3; CA 124; 89-92; CANR 80; DLB 48, 76

Tolstoi, Aleksei Nikolaevich
See Tolstoy, Alexey Nikolaevich

Tolstoy, Alexey Nikolaevich 1882-1945**TCLC 18**
See also CA 107; 158

Tolstoy, Count Leo
See Tolstoy, Leo (Nikolaevich)

Tolstoy, Leo (Nikolaevich) 1828-1910**TCLC 4, 11, 17, 28, 44, 79; DA; DAB; DAC; DAM MST, NOV; SSC 9, 30; WLC**
See also CA 104; 123; SATA 26

Tomasi di Lampedusa, Giuseppe 1896-1957
See Lampedusa, Giuseppe (Tomasi) di
See also CA 111

Tomlin, Lily .... **CLC 17**

See also Tomlin, Mary Jean

Tomlin, Mary Jean 1939(?)-
See Tomlin, Lily
See also CA 117

Tomlinson, (Alfred) Charles 1927- **CLC 2, 4, 6, 13, 45; DAM POET; PC 17**
See also CA 5-8R; CANR 33; DLB 40

Tomlinson, H(enry) M(ajor) 1873-1958 **TCLC 71**
See also CA 118; 161; DLB 36, 100, 195

Tonson, Jacob
See Bennett, (Enoch) Arnold

Toole, John Kennedy 1937-1969 ...... **CLC 19, 64**
See also CA 104; DLBY 81; MTCW 2

Toomer, Jean 1894-1967**CLC 1, 4, 13, 22; BLC 3; DAM MULT; PC 7; SSC 1; WLCS**
See also BW 1; CA 85-88; CDALB 1917-1929; DLB 45, 51; MTCW 1, 2

Torley, Luke
See Blish, James (Benjamin)

Tornimparte, Alessandra
See Ginzburg, Natalia

Torre, Raoul della
See Mencken, H(enry) L(ouis)

Torrey, E(dwin) Fuller 1937- .... **CLC 34**
See also CA 119; CANR 71

Torsvan, Ben Traven
See Traven, B.

Torsvan, Benno Traven
See Traven, B.

Torsvan, Berick Traven
See Traven, B.

Torsvan, Berwick Traven
See Traven, B.

Torsvan, Bruno Traven
See Traven, B.

Torsvan, Traven
See Traven, B.

Tournier, Michel (Edouard) 1924-**CLC 6, 23, 36, 95**
See also CA 49-52; CANR 3, 36, 74; DLB 83; MTCW 1, 2; SATA 23

Tournimparte, Alessandra
See Ginzburg, Natalia

Towers, Ivar
See Kornbluth, C(yril) M.

Towne, Robert (Burton) 1936(?)- .... **CLC 87**
See also CA 108; DLB 44

Townsend, Sue .... **CLC 61**
See also Townsend, Susan Elaine
See also AAYA 28; SATA 55, 93; SATA-Brief 48

Townsend, Susan Elaine 1946-
See Townsend, Sue
See also CA 119; 127; CANR 65; DAB; DAC; DAM MST

Townshend, Peter (Dennis Blandford) 1945-**CLC 17, 42**
See also CA 107

Tozzi, Federigo 1883-1920 .... **TCLC 31**
See also CA 160

Traill, Catharine Parr 1802-1899 .... **NCLC 31**
See also DLB 99

Trakl, Georg 1887-1914 .... **TCLC 5; PC 20**
See also CA 104; 165; MTCW 2

Transtroemer, Tomas (Goesta) 1931-**CLC 52, 65; DAM POET**
See also CA 117; 129; CAAS 17

Transtromer, Tomas Gosta
See Transtroemer, Tomas (Goesta)

Traven, B. (?)-1969 .... **CLC 8, 11**
See also CA 19-20; 25-28R; CAP 2; DLB 9, 56; MTCW 1

Treitel, Jonathan 1959- .... **CLC 70**

Tremain, Rose 1943- .... **CLC 42**
See also CA 97-100; CANR 44; DLB 14

Tremblay, Michel 1942-**CLC 29, 102; DAC; DAM MST**
See also CA 116; 128; DLB 60; MTCW 1, 2

Waldo, Edward Hamilton
  See Sturgeon, Theodore (Hamilton)
Walker, Alice (Malsenior) 1944-**CLC 5, 6, 9, 19, 27, 46, 58, 103; BLC 3; DA; DAB; DAC; DAM MST, MULT, NOV, POET, POP; SSC 5; WLCS**
  See also AAYA 3; BEST 89:4; BW 2, 3; CA 37-40R; CANR 9, 27, 49, 66; CDALB 1968-1988; DLB 6, 33, 143; INT CANR-27; MTCW 1, 2; SATA 31
Walker, David Harry 1911-1992 .... **CLC 14**
  See also CA 1-4R; 137; CANR 1; SATA 8; SATA-Obit 71
Walker, Edward Joseph 1934-
  See Walker, Ted
  See also CA 21-24R; CANR 12, 28, 53
Walker, George F. 1947-**CLC 44, 61; DAB; DAC; DAM MST**
  See also CA 103; CANR 21, 43, 59; DLB 60
Walker, Joseph A. 1935- **CLC 19; DAM DRAM, MST**
  See also BW 1, 3; CA 89-92; CANR 26; DLB 38
Walker, Margaret (Abigail) 1915-1998**CLC 1, 6; BLC; DAM MULT; PC 20**
  See also BW 2, 3; CA 73-76; 172; CANR 26, 54, 76; DLB 76, 152; MTCW 1, 2
Walker, Ted .... **CLC 13**
  See also Walker, Edward Joseph
  See also DLB 40
Wallace, David Foster 1962- .... **CLC 50, 114**
  See also CA 132; CANR 59; MTCW 2
Wallace, Dexter
  See Masters, Edgar Lee
Wallace, (Richard Horatio) Edgar 1875-1932 **TCLC 57**
  See also CA 115; DLB 70
Wallace, Irving 1916-1990**CLC 7, 13; DAM NOV, POP**
  See also AITN 1; CA 1-4R; 132; CAAS 1; CANR 1, 27; INT CANR-27; MTCW 1, 2
Wallant, Edward Lewis 1926-1962 .... **CLC 5, 10**
  See also CA 1-4R; CANR 22; DLB 2, 28, 143; MTCW 1, 2
Wallas, Graham 1858-1932 .... **TCLC 91**
Walley, Byron
  See Card, Orson Scott
Walpole, Horace 1717-1797 .... **LC 49**
  See also DLB 39, 104
Walpole, Hugh (Seymour) 1884-1941 ... **TCLC 5**
  See also CA 104; 165; DLB 34; MTCW 2
Walser, Martin 1927- .... **CLC 27**
  See also CA 57-60; CANR 8, 46; DLB 75, 124
Walser, Robert 1878-1956 .... **TCLC 18; SSC 20**
  See also CA 118; 165; DLB 66
Walsh, Jill Paton .... **CLC 35**
  See also Paton Walsh, Gillian
  See also AAYA 11; CLR 2; DLB 161; SAAS 3
Walter, Villiam Christian
  See Andersen, Hans Christian
Wambaugh, Joseph (Aloysius, Jr.) 1937-**CLC 3, 18; DAM NOV, POP**
  See also AITN 1; BEST 89:3; CA 33-36R; CANR 42, 65; DLB 6; DLBY 83; MTCW 1, 2
Wang Wei 699(?)-761(?) .... **PC 18**
Ward, Arthur Henry Sarsfield 1883-1959
  See Rohmer, Sax
  See also CA 108; 173
Ward, Douglas Turner 1930- .... **CLC 19**
  See also BW 1; CA 81-84; CANR 27; DLB 7, 38
Ward, E. D.
  See Lucas, E(dward) V(errall)
Ward, Mary Augusta
  See Ward, Mrs. Humphry
Ward, Mrs. Humphry 1851-1920 .... **TCLC 55**
  See also DLB 18
Ward, Peter
  See Faust, Frederick (Schiller)

Warhol, Andy 1928(?)-1987 .... **CLC 20**
  See also AAYA 12; BEST 89:4; CA 89-92; 121; CANR 34
Warner, Francis (Robert le Plastrier) 1937-**CLC 14**
  See also CA 53-56; CANR 11
Warner, Marina 1946- .... **CLC 59**
  See also CA 65-68; CANR 21, 55; DLB 194
Warner, Rex (Ernest) 1905-1986 .... **CLC 45**
  See also CA 89-92; 119; DLB 15
Warner, Susan (Bogert) 1819-1885 ....**NCLC 31**
  See also DLB 3, 42
Warner, Sylvia (Constance) Ashton
  See Ashton-Warner, Sylvia (Constance)
Warner, Sylvia Townsend 1893-1978 **CLC 7, 19; SSC 23**
  See also CA 61-64; 77-80; CANR 16, 60; DLB 34, 139; MTCW 1, 2
Warren, Mercy Otis 1728-1814 ....**NCLC 13**
  See also DLB 31, 200
Warren, Robert Penn 1905-1989 . **CLC 1, 4, 6, 8, 10, 13, 18, 39, 53, 59; DA; DAB; DAC; DAM MST, NOV, POET; SSC 4; WLC**
  See also AITN 1; CA 13-16R; 129; CANR 10, 47; CDALB 1968-1988; DLB 2, 48, 152; DLBY 80, 89; INT CANR-10; MTCW 1, 2; SATA 46; SATA-Obit 63
Warshofsky, Isaac
  See Singer, Isaac Bashevis
Warton, Thomas 1728-1790 **LC 15; DAM POET**
  See also DLB 104, 109
Waruk, Kona
  See Harris, (Theodore) Wilson
Warung, Price 1855-1911 .... **TCLC 45**
Warwick, Jarvis
  See Garner, Hugh
Washington, Alex
  See Harris, Mark
Washington, Booker T(aliaferro) 1856-1915 **TCLC 10; BLC 3; DAM MULT**
  See also BW 1; CA 114; 125; SATA 28
Washington, George 1732-1799 .... **LC 25**
  See also DLB 31
Wassermann, (Karl) Jakob 1873-1934 . **TCLC 6**
  See also CA 104; 163; DLB 66
Wasserstein, Wendy 1950-**CLC 32, 59, 90; DAM DRAM; DC 4**
  See also CA 121; 129; CABS 3; CANR 53, 75; INT 129; MTCW 2; SATA 94
Waterhouse, Keith (Spencer) 1929- ..... **CLC 47**
  See also CA 5-8R; CANR 38, 67; DLB 13, 15; MTCW 1, 2
Waters, Frank (Joseph) 1902-1995 .... **CLC 88**
  See also CA 5-8R; 149; CAAS 13; CANR 3, 18, 63; DLB 212; DLBY 86
Waters, Roger 1944- .... **CLC 35**
Watkins, Frances Ellen
  See Harper, Frances Ellen Watkins
Watkins, Gerrold
  See Malzberg, Barry N(athaniel)
Watkins, Gloria 1955(?)-
  See hooks, bell
  See also BW 2; CA 143; MTCW 2
Watkins, Paul 1964- .... **CLC 55**
  See also CA 132; CANR 62
Watkins, Vernon Phillips 1906-1967 .... **CLC 43**
  See also CA 9-10; 25-28R; CAP 1; DLB 20
Watson, Irving S.
  See Mencken, H(enry) L(ouis)
Watson, John H.
  See Farmer, Philip Jose
Watson, Richard F.
  See Silverberg, Robert
Waugh, Auberon (Alexander) 1939- .... **CLC 7**
  See also CA 45-48; CANR 6, 22; DLB 14, 194
Waugh, Evelyn (Arthur St. John) 1903-1966**CLC 1, 3, 8, 13, 19, 27, 44, 107; DA; DAB; DAC;**

DAM MST, NOV, POP; WLC
  See also CA 85-88; 25-28R; CANR 22; CDBLB 1914-1945; DLB 15, 162, 195; MTCW 1, 2
Waugh, Harriet 1944- .... **CLC 6**
  See also CA 85-88; CANR 22
Ways, C. R.
  See Blount, Roy (Alton), Jr.
Waystaff, Simon
  See Swift, Jonathan
Webb, (Martha) Beatrice (Potter) 1858-1943 **TCLC 22**
  See also Potter, (Helen) Beatrix
  See also CA 117; DLB 190
Webb, Charles (Richard) 1939- .... **CLC 7**
  See also CA 25-28R
Webb, James H(enry), Jr. 1946- .... **CLC 22**
  See also CA 81-84
Webb, Mary (Gladys Meredith) 1881-1927 **TCLC 24**
  See also CA 123; DLB 34
Webb, Mrs. Sidney
  See Webb, (Martha) Beatrice (Potter)
Webb, Phyllis 1927- .... **CLC 18**
  See also CA 104; CANR 23; DLB 53
Webb, Sidney (James) 1859-1947 .... **TCLC 22**
  See also CA 117; 163; DLB 190
Webber, Andrew Lloyd .... **CLC 21**
  See also Lloyd Webber, Andrew
Weber, Lenora Mattingly 1895-1971 ..... **CLC 12**
  See also CA 19-20; 29-32R; CAP 1; SATA 2; SATA-Obit 26
Weber, Max 1864-1920 .... **TCLC 69**
  See also CA 109
Webster, John 1579(?)-1634(?)**LC 33; DA; DAB; DAC; DAM DRAM, MST; DC 2; WLC**
  See also CDBLB Before 1660; DLB 58
Webster, Noah 1758-1843 ....**NCLC 30**
  See also DLB 1, 37, 42, 43, 73
Wedekind, (Benjamin) Frank(lin) 1864-1918 **TCLC 7; DAM DRAM**
  See also CA 104; 153; DLB 118
Weidman, Jerome 1913-1998 .... **CLC 7**
  See also AITN 2; CA 1-4R; 171; CANR 1; DLB 28
Weil, Simone (Adolphine) 1909-1943 .. **TCLC 23**
  See also CA 117; 159; MTCW 2
Weininger, Otto 1880-1903 .... **TCLC 84**
Weinstein, Nathan
  See West, Nathanael
Weinstein, Nathan von Wallenstein
  See West, Nathanael
Weir, Peter (Lindsay) 1944- .... **CLC 20**
  See also CA 113; 123
Weiss, Peter (Ulrich) 1916-1982 **CLC 3, 15, 51; DAM DRAM**
  See also CA 45-48; 106; CANR 3; DLB 69, 124
Weiss, Theodore (Russell) 1916- ..**CLC 3, 8, 14**
  See also CA 9-12R; CAAS 2; CANR 46; DLB 5
Welch, (Maurice) Denton 1915-1948 .. **TCLC 22**
  See also CA 121; 148
Welch, James 1940-**CLC 6, 14, 52; DAM MULT, POP**
  See also CA 85-88; CANR 42, 66; DLB 175; NNAL
Weldon, Fay 1931-**CLC 6, 9, 11, 19, 36, 59; DAM POP**
  See also CA 21-24R; CANR 16, 46, 63; CDBLB 1960 to Present; DLB 14, 194; INT CANR-16; MTCW 1, 2
Wellek, Rene 1903-1995 .... **CLC 28**
  See also CA 5-8R; 150; CAAS 7; CANR 8; DLB 63; INT CANR-8
Weller, Michael 1942- .... **CLC 10, 53**
  See also CA 85-88
Weller, Paul 1958- .... **CLC 26**
Wellershoff, Dieter 1925- .... **CLC 46**
  See also CA 89-92; CANR 16, 37

Author Index

Wordsworth, William 1770-1850 .. NCLC 12,
38; DA; DAB; DAC; DAM MST, POET;
PC 4; WLC
See also CDBLB 1789-1832; DLB 93, 107
Wouk, Herman 1915- CLC 1, 9, 38; DAM NOV,
POP
See also CA 5-8R; CANR 6, 33, 67; CDALBS;
DLBY 82; INT CANR-6; MTCW 1, 2
Wright, Charles (Penzel, Jr.) 1935- CLC 6, 13,
28, 119
See also CA 29-32R; CAAS 7; CANR 23, 36, 62;
DLB 165; DLBY 82; MTCW 1, 2
Wright, Charles Stevenson 1932- CLC 49; BLC
3; DAM MULT, POET
See also BW 1; CA 9-12R; CANR 26; DLB 33
Wright, Frances 1795-1852 .... NCLC 74
See also DLB 73
Wright, Frank Lloyd 1867-1959 .... TCLC 95
See also CA 174
Wright, Jack R.
See Harris, Mark
Wright, James (Arlington) 1927-1980 CLC 3, 5,
10, 28; DAM POET
See also AITN 2; CA 49-52; 97-100; CANR 4, 34,
64; CDALBS; DLB 5, 169; MTCW 1, 2
Wright, Judith (Arandell) 1915- CLC 11, 53; PC
14
See also CA 13-16R; CANR 31, 76; MTCW 1,
2; SATA 14
Wright, L(aurali) R. 1939- .... CLC 44
See also CA 138
Wright, Richard (Nathaniel) 1908-1960 CLC 1, 3,
4, 9, 14, 21, 48, 74; BLC 3; DA; DAB; DAC;
DAM MST, MULT, NOV; SSC 2; WLC
See also AAYA 5; BW 1; CA 108; CANR 64;
CDALB 1929-1941; DLB 76, 102; DLBD 2;
MTCW 1, 2
Wright, Richard B(ruce) 1937- .... CLC 6
See also CA 85-88; DLB 53
Wright, Rick 1945- .... CLC 35
Wright, Rowland
See Wells, Carolyn
Wright, Stephen 1946- .... CLC 33
Wright, Willard Huntington 1888-1939
See Van Dine, S. S.
See also CA 115; DLBD 16
Wright, William 1930- .... CLC 44
See also CA 53-56; CANR 7, 23
Wroth, Lady Mary 1587-1653(?) .... LC 30
See also DLB 121
Wu Ch'eng-en 1500(?)-1582(?) .... LC 7
Wu Ching-tzu 1701-1754 .... LC 2
Wurlitzer, Rudolph 1938(?)- .... CLC 2, 4, 15
See also CA 85-88; DLB 173
Wycherley, William 1641-1715. LC 8, 21; DAM
DRAM
See also CDBLB 1660-1789; DLB 80
Wylie, Elinor (Morton Hoyt) 1885-1928 TCLC 8;
PC 23
See also CA 105; 162; DLB 9, 45
Wylie, Philip (Gordon) 1902-1971 .... CLC 43
See also CA 21-22; 33-36R; CAP 2; DLB 9
Wyndham, John .... CLC 19
See also Harris, John (Wyndham Parkes Lucas)
Beynon
Wyss, Johann David Von 1743-1818 ... NCLC 10
See also JRDA; MAICYA; SATA 29; SATA-Brief
27
Xenophon c. 430B.C.-c. 354B.C. .... CMLC 17
See also DLB 176
Yakumo Koizumi
See Hearn, (Patricio) Lafcadio (Tessima Carlos)
Yamamoto, Hisaye 1921- .. SSC 34; DAM MULT
Yanez, Jose Donoso
See Donoso (Yanez), Jose
Yanovsky, Basile S.
See Yanovsky, V(assily) S(emenovich)

Yanovsky, V(assily) S(emenovich) 1906-1989
CLC 2, 18
See also CA 97-100; 129
Yates, Richard 1926-1992 .... CLC 7, 8, 23
See also CA 5-8R; 139; CANR 10, 43; DLB 2;
DLBY 81, 92; INT CANR-10
Yeats, W. B.
See Yeats, William Butler
Yeats, William Butler 1865-1939 TCLC 1, 11, 18,
31, 93; DA; DAB; DAC; DAM DRAM, MST,
POET; PC 20; WLC
See also CA 104; 127; CANR 45; CDBLB 1890-
1914; DLB 10, 19, 98, 156; MTCW 1, 2
Yehoshua, A(braham) B. 1936- .... CLC 13, 31
See also CA 33-36R; CANR 43
Yep, Laurence Michael 1948- .... CLC 35
See also AAYA 5; CA 49-52; CANR 1, 46; CLR 3,
17, 54; DLB 52; JRDA; MAICYA; SATA 7, 69
Yerby, Frank G(arvin) 1916-1991 . CLC 1, 7, 22;
BLC 3; DAM MULT
See also BW 1, 3; CA 9-12R; 136; CANR 16, 52;
DLB 76; INT CANR-16; MTCW 1
Yesenin, Sergei Alexandrovich
See Esenin, Sergei (Alexandrovich)
Yevtushenko, Yevgeny (Alexandrovich) 1933-
CLC 1, 3, 13, 26, 51; DAM POET
See also CA 81-84; CANR 33, 54; MTCW 1
Yezierska, Anzia 1885(?)-1970 .... CLC 46
See also CA 126; 89-92; DLB 28; MTCW 1
Yglesias, Helen 1915- .... CLC 7, 22
See also CA 37-40R; CAAS 20; CANR 15, 65;
INT CANR-15; MTCW 1
Yokomitsu Riichi 1898-1947 .... TCLC 47
See also CA 170
Yonge, Charlotte (Mary) 1823-1901 .... TCLC 48
See also CA 109; 163; DLB 18, 163; SATA 17
York, Jeremy
See Creasey, John
York, Simon
See Heinlein, Robert A(nson)
Yorke, Henry Vincent 1905-1974 .... CLC 13
See also Green, Henry
See also CA 85-88; 49-52
Yosano Akiko 1878-1942 .... TCLC 59; PC 11
See also CA 161
Yoshimoto, Banana .... CLC 84
See also Yoshimoto, Mahoko
Yoshimoto, Mahoko 1964-
See Yoshimoto, Banana
See also CA 144
Young, Al(bert James) 1939- .. CLC 19; BLC 3;
DAM MULT
See also BW 2, 3; CA 29-32R; CANR 26, 65; DLB
33
Young, Andrew (John) 1885-1971 .... CLC 5
See also CA 5-8R; CANR 7, 29
Young, Collier
See Bloch, Robert (Albert)
Young, Edward 1683-1765 .... LC 3, 40
See also DLB 95
Young, Marguerite (Vivian) 1909-1995 . CLC 82
See also CA 13-16; 150; CAP 1
Young, Neil 1945- .... CLC 17
See also CA 110
Young Bear, Ray A. 1950- CLC 94; DAM MULT
See also CA 146; DLB 175; NNAL
Yourcenar, Marguerite 1903-1987 CLC 19, 38, 50,
87; DAM NOV
See also CA 69-72; CANR 23, 60; DLB 72; DLBY
88; MTCW 1, 2
Yurick, Sol 1925- .... CLC 6
See also CA 13-16R; CANR 25
Zabolotsky, Nikolai Alekseevich 1903-1958
TCLC 52
See also CA 116; 164
Zamiatin, Yevgenii
See Zamyatin, Evgeny Ivanovich

Zamora, Bernice (B. Ortiz) 1938- .. CLC 89;
DAM MULT; HLC
See also CA 151; CANR 80; DLB 82; HW 1, 2
Zamyatin, Evgeny Ivanovich 1884-1937 TCLC 8, 37
See also CA 105; 166
Zangwill, Israel 1864-1926 .... TCLC 16
See also CA 109; 167; DLB 10, 135, 197
Zappa, Francis Vincent, Jr. 1940-1993
See Zappa, Frank
See also CA 108; 143; CANR 57
Zappa, Frank .... CLC 17
See also Zappa, Francis Vincent, Jr.
Zaturenska, Marya 1902-1982 .... CLC 6, 11
See also CA 13-16R; 105; CANR 22
Zeami 1363-1443 .... DC 7
Zelazny, Roger (Joseph) 1937-1995 ...... CLC 21
See also AAYA 7; CA 21-24R; 148; CANR 26,
60; DLB 8; MTCW 1, 2; SATA 57; SATA-Brief
39
Zhdanov, Andrei Alexandrovich 1896-1948 TCLC
18
See also CA 117; 167
Zhukovsky, Vasily (Andreevich) 1783-1852 NCLC
35
See also DLB 205
Ziegenhagen, Eric .... CLC 55
Zimmer, Jill Schary
See Robinson, Jill
Zimmerman, Robert
See Dylan, Bob
Zindel, Paul 1936- CLC 6, 26; DA; DAB; DAC;
DAM DRAM, MST, NOV; DC 5
See also AAYA 2; CA 73-76; CANR 31, 65;
CDALBS; CLR 3, 45; DLB 7, 52; JRDA;
MAICYA; MTCW 1, 2; SATA 16, 58, 102
Zinov'Ev, A. A.
See Zinoviev, Alexander (Aleksandrovich)
Zinoviev, Alexander (Aleksandrovich) 1922- CLC
19
See also CA 116; 133; CAAS 10
Zoilus
See Lovecraft, H(oward) P(hillips)
Zola, Emile (Edouard Charles Antoine) 1840-1902
TCLC 1, 6, 21, 41; DA; DAB; DAC; DAM
MST, NOV; WLC
See also CA 104; 138; DLB 123
Zoline, Pamela 1941- .... CLC 62
See also CA 161
Zorrilla y Moral, Jose 1817-1893 .... NCLC 6
Zoshchenko, Mikhail (Mikhailovich) 1895-1958
TCLC 15; SSC 15
See also CA 115; 160
Zuckmayer, Carl 1896-1977 .... CLC 18
See also CA 69-72; DLB 56, 124
Zuk, Georges
See Skelton, Robin
Zukofsky, Louis 1904-1978 CLC 1, 2, 4, 7, 11, 18;
DAM POET; PC 11
See also CA 9-12R; 77-80; CANR 39; DLB 5, 165;
MTCW 1
Zweig, Paul 1935-1984 ....,............. CLC 34, 42
See also CA 85-88; 113
Zweig, Stefan 1881-1942 .... TCLC 17
See also CA 112; 170; DLB 81, 118
Zwingli, Huldreich 1484-1531 .... LC 37
See also DLB 179

Literary Criticism Series
Cumulative Topic Index

This index lists all topic entries in Gale's *Classical and Medieval Literature Criticism, Contemporary Literary Criticism, Literature Criticism from 1400 to 1800, Nineteenth-Century Literature Criticism,* and *Twentieth-Century Literary Criticism.*

Age of Johnson LC 15: 1-87
Johnson's London, 3-15
aesthetics of neoclassicism, 15-36
"age of prose and reason," 36-45
clubmen and bluestockings, 45-56
printing technology, 56-62
periodicals: "a map of busy life," 62-74
transition, 74-86

Age of Spenser LC 39: 1-70
Overviews, 2-21
Literary Style, 22-34
Poets and the Crown, 34-70

AIDS in Literature CLC 81: 365-416

Alcohol and Literature TCLC 70: 1-58 .
overview, 2-8
fiction, 8-48
poetry and drama, 48-58

American Abolitionism NCLC 44: 1-73
overviews, 2-26
abolitionist ideals, 26-46
the literature of abolitionism, 46-72

American Autobiography TCLC 86: 1-115
overviews, 3-36
American authors and autobiography, 36-82
African-American autobiography, 82-114

American Black Humor Fiction TCLC 54: 1-85
characteristics of black humor, 2-13
origins and development, 13-38
black humor distinguished from related literary trends, 38-60
black humor and society, 60-75
black humor reconsidered, 75-83

American Civil War in Literature NCLC 32: 1-109
overviews, 2-20
regional perspectives, 20-54
fiction popular during the war, 54-79
the historical novel, 79-108

American Frontier in Literature NCLC 28: 1-103
definitions, 2-12
development, 12-17
nonfiction writing about the frontier, 17-30
frontier fiction, 30-45
frontier protagonists, 45-66
portrayals of Native Americans, 66-86
feminist readings, 86-98
twentieth-century reaction against frontier literature, 98-100

American Humor Writing NCLC 52: 1-59
overviews, 2-12
the Old Southwest, 12-42
broader impacts, 42-5
women humorists, 45-58

American Mercury, **The** TCLC 74: 1-80

American Popular Song, Golden Age of TCLC 42: 1-49
background and major figures, 2-34
the lyrics of popular songs, 34-47

American Proletarian Literature TCLC 54: 86-175
overviews, 87-95
American proletarian literature and the American Communist Party, 95-111
ideology and literary merit, 111-7
novels, 117-39
Gastonia, 136-48
drama, 148-54
journalism, 154-9
proletarian literature in the United States, 159-74

American Romanticism NCLC 44: 74-138
overviews, 74-84
sociopolitical influences, 84-104
Romanticism and the American frontier, 104-15
thematic concerns, 115-37

American Western Literature TCLC 46: 1-100
definition and development of American Western literature, 2-7
characteristics of the Western novel, 8-23
Westerns as history and fiction, 23-34
critical reception of American Western literature, 34-41
the Western hero, 41-73
women in Western fiction, 73-91
later Western fiction, 91-9

Art and Literature TCLC 54: 176-248
overviews, 176-93
definitions, 193-219
influence of visual arts on literature, 219-31
spatial form in literature, 231-47

Arthurian Literature CMLC 10: 1-127
historical context and literary beginnings, 2-27
development of the legend through Malory, 27-64
development of the legend from Malory to the Victorian Age, 65-81
themes and motifs, 81-95
principal characters, 95-125

Arthurian Revival NCLC 36: 1-77
overviews, 2-12
Tennyson and his influence, 12-43
other leading figures, 43-73
the Arthurian legend in the visual arts, 73-6

Australian Literature TCLC 50: 1-94
origins and development, 2-21
characteristics of Australian literature, 21-33
historical and critical perspectives, 33-41
poetry, 41-58
fiction, 58-76
drama, 76-82
Aboriginal literature, 82-91

Beat Generation, Literature of the TCLC 42: 50-102
overviews, 51-9
the Beat generation as a social phenomenon, 59-62
development, 62-5
Beat literature, 66-96
influence, 97-100

The Bell Curve Controversy CLC 91: 281-330

Bildungsroman **in Nineteenth-Century Literature** NCLC 20: 92-168
surveys, 93-113
in Germany, 113-40
in England, 140-56
female *Bildungsroman,* 156-67

Topic Index

Topic Index

Topic Index

Topic Index

Twentieth-Century Literary Criticism
Cumulative Nationality Index

Nationality Index

TCLC-93 Title Index

Title Index

ISBN 0-7876-2750-X

90000